MW01108489

Psychology Applied to Modern Life: Adjustment in the 21st Century

Personal Applications Edition

Wayne Weiten
University of Nevada, Las Vegas

Margaret A. Lloyd
Georgia Southern University

John Pulver
Community College of Southern Nevada

THOMSON
━━━━━✦━━━━━ ™
WADSWORTH

Australia · Canada · Mexico · Singapore · Spain · United Kingdom · United States

THOMSON
—————★—————™
WADSWORTH

Psychology Applied to Modern Life: Adjustment in the 21st Century
Weiten/Lloyd/Pulver

Custom Editor:
Lisa Capozzolo

Project Development Editor:
Laura Hoevenaar

Marketing Coordinator:
Sara Mercurio

Production/Manufacturing Supervisor:
Donna M. Brown

Project Coordinator:
Terri Daley

Pre-Media Services Supervisor:
Dan Plofchan

Rights and Permissions Specialist:
Bahman Naraghi

Senior Prepress Specialist:
Joel Brennecke

Cover Design:
Krista Pierson

Cover Image:
© Getty Images

Printer:
BR Corporation

The Adaptable Courseware Program consists of products and additions to
existing Wadsworth products that are produced from camera-ready copy.
Peer review, class testing, and accuracy are primarily the responsibility of
the author(s).

Student Edition: ISBN 0-495-15836-4

Thomson Custom Solutions
5191 Natorp Boulevard
Mason, OH 45040
www.thomsoncustom.com

Thomson Higher Education
10 Davis Drive
Belmont, CA 94002-3098
USA

Asia (Including India):
Thomson Learning
60 Albert Street, #15-01
Albert Complex
Singapore 189969
Tel 65 336-6411
Fax 65 336-7411

Australia/New Zealand:
Thomson Learning Australia
102 Dodds Street
Southbank, Victoria 3006
Australia

Latin America:
Thomson Learning
Seneca 53
Colonia Polano
11560 Mexico, D.F., Mexico
Tel (525) 281-2906
Fax (525) 281-2656

Canada:
Thomson Nelson
1120 Birchmount Road
Toronto, Ontario
Canada M1K 5G4
Tel (416) 752-9100
Fax (416) 752-8102

UK/Europe/Middle East/Africa:
Thomson Learning
High Holborn House
50-51 Bedford Row
London, WC1R 4L$
United Kingdom
Tel 44 (020) 7067-2500
Fax 44 (020) 7067-2600

Spain (Includes Portugal):
Thomson Paraninfo
Calle Magallanes 25
28015 Madrid
España
Tel 34 (0)91 446-3350
Fax 34 (0)91 445-6218

To the Instructor

Many students enter adjustment courses with great expectations. They've ambled through their local bookstores, and in the "Psychology" section they've seen numerous self-help books that offer highly touted recipes for achieving happiness for a mere $12.95. After paying far more money to enroll in a college course that deals with the same issues as the self-help books, many students expect a revelatory experience. However, the majority of us with professional training in psychology or counseling take a rather dim view of self-help books and the pop psychology they represent. Psychologists tend to see this literature as oversimplified, intellectually dishonest, and opportunistic and often summarily dismiss the pop psychology that so many students have embraced. Instructors try to supplant pop psychology with more sophisticated academic psychology, which is more complex and less accessible.

In this textbook, we have tried to come to grips with this problem of differing expectations between student and teacher. Our goal has been to produce a comprehensive, serious, research-oriented treatment of the topic of adjustment that also acknowledges the existence of popular psychology and looks critically at its contributions. Our approach involves the following:

■ In Chapter 1 we confront the phenomenon of popular self-help books. We try to take the student beneath the seductive surface of such books and analyze some of their typical flaws. Our goal is to make the student a more critical consumer of this type of literature.

■ While encouraging a more critical attitude toward self-help books, we do not suggest that they should all be dismissed. Instead, we acknowledge that some of them offer authentic insights. With this in mind, we highlight some of the better books in Recommended Reading boxes sprinkled throughout the text. These recommended books tie in with the adjacent topical coverage and show the student the interface between academic and popular psychology.

■ We try to provide the student with a better appreciation of the merits of the empirical approach. This effort to clarify the role of research, which is rare for an adjustment text, appears in the first chapter.

■ Recognizing that adjustment students want to leave the course with concrete, personally useful information, we end each chapter with an application section. The Applications are "how to" discussions that address everyday problems. While they focus on issues that are relevant to the content of the particular chapter, they contain more explicit advice than the text proper.

In summary, we have tried to make this book both rigorous and applied. We hope that our approach will help students to better appreciate the value of scientific psychology.

Philosophy

A certain philosophy is inherent in any systematic treatment of the topic of adjustment. Our philosophy can be summarized as follows:

■ We believe that an adjustment text should be a resource book for students. We have tried to design this book so that it encourages and facilitates the pursuit of additional information on adjustment-related topics. It should serve as a point of departure for more learning.

■ We believe in theoretical eclecticism. This book will not indoctrinate your students along the lines of any single theoretical orientation. The psychodynamic, behavioral, and humanistic schools of thought are all treated with respect, as are cognitive, biological, evolutionary, and other perspectives.

■ We believe that effective adjustment requires taking charge of one's own life. Throughout the book we try to promote the notion that active coping efforts are generally superior to passivity and complacency.

Changes in the Eighth Edition

One of the exciting things about psychology is that it is not a stagnant discipline. It continues to progress at what seems a faster and faster pace. A good textbook must evolve with the discipline. Although the professors and students who used the earlier editions of this book did not clamor for change, we've made some significant alterations.

For example, we have implemented an entirely new design that is intended to be more open and friendly looking. All of the figures in the book have been redrawn. This process has allowed us to achieve greater consistency in style, make the graphics more attractive and modern looking, and enhance the pedagogical clarity of many figures. Color has been added to the integrated running glossary to make this pedagogical feature more prominent, and the look of the Applications has been changed so that students will no longer wonder whether these elements are an integral part of the chapters. And, of course, we have made countless content changes to keep up with new developments in psychology—adding and deleting some topics, condensing and reorganizing others, and updating everything (there are 1198 new references).

The principal other change is the addition of boxes called "Living in Today's World." These features were originally developed in the previous edition to address issues that surfaced in the aftermath of the 9/11 terrorist attacks in the United States (they were called Sidebars on Current Events). Continuing in this vein, many of the boxes in this edition deal with concerns raised by the ongoing specter of terrorism in today's world. For example, we discuss how people tend to be affected by traumatic events, how people can cope more effectively with personal trauma, and how people can think more rationally about the threat of terrorism. However, in this edition we have broadened the scope of coverage in this series of boxes to include additional adjustment issues that are especially pertinent in light of current events, such as the controversy over whether the government should promote marriage and problems associated with living up to today's unrealistic ideals of physical attractiveness.

Writing Style

This book has been written with the student reader in mind. We have tried to integrate the technical jargon of our discipline into a relatively informal and down-to-earth writing style. We use concrete examples extensively to clarify complex concepts and to help maintain student interest.

Features

This text contains a number of features intended to stimulate interest and enhance students' learning. These special features include Applications, Recommended Reading boxes, Internet-related features, Practice Tests, a didactic illustration program, and cartoons.

Applications
The Applications should be of special interest to most students. They are tied to chapter content in a way that should show students how practical applications emerge out of theory and research. Although some of the material covered in these sections shows up frequently in adjustment texts, much of it is unique. Some of the Applications include the following:

- Understanding Intimate Violence
- Monitoring Your Stress
- Understanding Eating Disorders
- Getting Ahead in the Job Game
- Building Self-Esteem
- Enhancing Sexual Relationships
- Bridging the Gender Gap in Communication

Recommended Reading Boxes
Recognizing students' interest in self-help books, we have sifted through hundreds of them to identify some that may be especially useful. These books are featured in boxes that briefly review some of the higher-quality books.

These Recommended Reading boxes are placed where they are germane to the material being covered in the text. Some of the recommended books are well known, while others are obscure. Although we make it clear that we don't endorse every idea in every book, we think they all have something worthwhile to offer. This feature replaces the conventional suggested readings lists that usually appear at the ends of chapters, where they are almost universally ignored by students.

Internet-Related Features
The Internet is rapidly altering the landscape of modern life, and students clearly need help dealing with the information explosion in cyberspace. To assist them, we have included two features. First, we recruited web expert Vincent Hevern to write a concise essay that explains the essentials of the Internet to the uninitiated. This essay, which appears in the front of the book, briefly explains URLs, domain names, hyperlinks, search engines, and so forth. It also provides students with realistic warnings about the instability of URLs and the questionable validity of much of the information available on the web. Second, we also asked Professor Hevern to evaluate hundreds of psychology- and adjustment-related sites on the web and come up with some recommended sites that appear to provide reasonably accurate, balanced, and empirically sound information. Short descriptions of these recommended websites are dispersed throughout the chapters, adjacent to related topical coverage. Because URLs change frequently, we have not included the URLs for the Web Links in the book. Insofar as students are interested in visiting these sites, we recommend that they do so through the *Psychology Applied to Modern Life* home page at the Wadsworth Psychology Website (http://psychology.wadsworth. com/weiten_lloyd8e). Links to all the recommended websites are maintained there, and the Wadsworth webmaster will periodically update the URLs. Of course, students can also use search engines such as Google to locate the recommended websites.

Practice Tests
Each chapter ends with a ten-item multiple-choice Practice Test that should give students a fairly realistic assessment of their mastery of that chapter and valuable practice in taking the type of test that many of them will face in the classroom (if the instructor uses the Test Bank). This feature grew out of some research on students' use of textbook pedagogical devices (see Weiten, Guadagno, & Beck, 1996). This research indicated that students pay scant attention to some standard pedagogical devices. When students were grilled to gain a better understanding of this perplexing finding, it quickly became apparent that students are pragmatic about pedagogy. Essentially, their refrain was, "We want study aids that will help us pass the next test." With this mandate in mind, we added the Practice Tests. They should be very realistic, as many of the items came from the Test Bank for previous editions (these items do not appear in the Test Bank for the current edition).

Didactic Illustration Program

The illustration program is once again in full color, and many new figures have been added along with the redrawing of all the graphics. Although the illustrations are intended to make the book attractive and to help maintain student interest, they are not merely decorative: They have been carefully selected and crafted for their didactic value to enhance the educational goals of the text.

Cartoons

A little comic relief usually helps keep a student interested, so we've sprinkled numerous cartoons throughout the book. Like the figures, most of these have been chosen to reinforce ideas in the text.

Learning Aids

Because this book is rigorous, substantive, and sizable, a number of learning aids have been incorporated into the text to help the reader digest the wealth of material:

- The *outline* at the beginning of each chapter provides the student with a preview and overview of what will be covered.
- *Headings* are used extensively to keep material well organized.
- To help alert your students to key points, *learning objectives* are distributed throughout the chapters, after the level-1 headings.
- *Key terms* are identified with **blue italicized boldface** type to indicate that these are important vocabulary items that are part of psychology's technical language.
- An *integrated running glossary* provides an on-the-spot definition of each key term as it is introduced in the text. These formal definitions are printed in **blue boldface** type.
- An *alphabetical glossary* is found in the back of the book, as key terms are usually defined in the integrated running glossary only when they are first introduced.
- *Italics* are used liberally throughout the text to emphasize important points.
- A *chapter review* is found at the end of each chapter. Each review includes a concise but thorough summary of the chapter's key ideas, a list of the key terms that were introduced in the chapter, and a list of important theorists and researchers who were discussed in the chapter.

Supplementary Materials

A complete teaching/learning package has been developed to supplement *Psychology Applied to Modern Life.* These supplementary materials have been carefully coordinated to provide effective support for the text. (Available to qualified adopters. Please consult your local sales representative for details.)

Instructor's Manual (0-495-03031-7)

The *Instructor's Manual,* written by Lenore Frigo of Shasta College, is available as a convenient aid for your educational endeavors. It provides a thorough overview of each chapter, along with a list of relevant films and InfoTrac College Edition® integration. It also includes a wealth of suggestions for lecture topics, class demonstrations, exercises, and discussion questions, organized around the content of each chapter in the text.

Test Bank (0-495-03029-5)

The *Test Bank,* written by Mary Ann Valentino of Fresno City College and David Ward of Arkansas Tech University, contains an extensive collection of multiple-choice questions for objective tests, all closely tied to the learning objectives found in the text chapters. We're confident that you will find this to be a dependable and usable test bank.

ExamView® Computerized Testing (0-495-00418-9)

Windows®/Macintosh® CD-ROM
Preloaded with all of the questions in the *Test Bank,* ExamView allows you to create, deliver, and customize tests and study guides (both print and online) in minutes. ExamView offers both a Quick Test Wizard and an Online Test Wizard that guides you step by step through the process of creating tests, while its unique "what you see is what you get" capability allows you to see the test you are creating onscreen exactly as it will print or display online. You can build tests of up to 250 questions using up to 12 question types. Using ExamView's complete word-processing capabilities, you can enter an unlimited number of new questions or edit existing questions.

Multimedia Manager Instructor's Resource CD-ROM (0-534-24863-2)

This one-stop lecture and class preparation tool makes it easy for you to assemble, edit, publish, and present custom lectures for your course, using Microsoft® PowerPoint®. The Multimedia Manager lets you bring together text-specific lecture outlines, written by Lisa Garner of Tallahassee Community College, and art from the text, along with video and animations from the web or your own materials—culminating in a powerful, personalized, media-enhanced presentation. The CD-ROM also contains the full Instructor's Manual, Test Bank, and other instructor resources.

Transparency Acetates Set (0-495-03028-7)

There are 50 acetates in this package, compiled by Susan Shapiro of Indiana University East, along with general comments on using these acetates.

Study Guide (0-495-03032-5)

The *Study Guide,* written by William Addison of Eastern Illinois University, is designed to help students master the information contained in the text. It contains a programmed review of learning objectives, quiz boxes, and a self-test for each chapter. Your students should find it helpful in their study efforts.

Critical Thinking with Psychology: Separating Sense from Nonsense, Second Edition (0-534-53659-X)

Students may have a difficult time distinguishing between the true science of human thought and behavior and pop psychology. This small paperback, written by John Ruscio, provides a tangible and compelling framework for making that distinction, teaching the fundamentals of scientific reasoning.

InfoTrac® College Edition . . . now with InfoMarks®!

NOT SOLD SEPARATELY. Available for packaging with the text! Now FREE four-month access to InfoTrac College Edition's online database of more than 18 million reliable, full-length articles from 5000 academic journals and periodicals includes access to InfoMarks—stable URLs that can be linked to articles, journals, and searches. InfoMarks allow you to use a simple copy and paste technique to create instant and continually updated online readers, content services, bibliographies, electronic "reserve" readings, and current topic sites. And to help students use the research they gather, their free four-month subscription to InfoTrac College Edition includes access to InfoWrite, a complete set of online critical thinking and paper-writing tools. To take a quick tour of InfoTrac College Edition, visit http://www.infotrac-college.com/ and select the User Demo. *(Journals subject to change. Certain restrictions may apply. For additional information, please consult your local Thomson representative.)*

Culture and Modern Life (0-534-49688-1)

Culture and Modern Life is a small paperback intended to help your students appreciate how cultural factors moderate psychological processes and how the viewpoint of one's own culture can distort one's interpretation of the behavior of people from other cultures. Written by David Matsumoto, a leading authority on cross-cultural psychology, this supplementary book should greatly enhance your students' understanding of how culture can influence adjustment. *Culture and Modern Life* can be ordered shrinkwrapped with the text.

Personal Explorations Workbook (0-495-03035-X)

The *Personal Explorations Workbook* is a small booklet assembled by John Pulver of the Community College of Southern Nevada and Wayne Weiten. It contains experiential exercises for each text chapter, designed to help your students achieve personal insights. The questionnaires are psychological tests or scales that your students can administer and score for themselves. The "Personal Probes" consist of questions intended to help students think about themselves in relation to issues raised in the text. In addition to generating student interest, these exercises can be fruitful in stimulating class discussion. The *Personal Explorations Workbook* can be ordered shrinkwrapped with the text.

Critical Thinking Exercises

We have developed a set of critical thinking exercises that will be posted on the Internet at the Wadsworth Psychology Website (http://psychology.wadsworth.com/weiten_lloyd8e). Written by Jeffry Ricker, these exercises are intended to introduce students to specific critical thinking skills, such as recognizing extraneous variables, sampling bias, and fallacies in reasoning. The exercises also challenge students to apply these skills to adjustment-related topics on a chapter-by-chapter basis.

Book Companion Website: http://psychology.wadsworth.com/ weiten_lloyd8e

This comprehensive website includes learning objectives, a full glossary, flashcards, crossword puzzles, InfoTrac College Edition articles with questions, web links, and tutorial quizzes.

WebTutor™ ToolBox for WebCT®
WebTutor™ ToolBox for Blackboard®

Preloaded with content and available via a free access code when packaged with this text, WebTutor ToolBox pairs all the content of this text's rich Book Companion Website with sophisticated course management functionality. You can assign materials (including online quizzes) and have the results flow automatically to your grade book. WebTutor ToolBox is ready to use as soon as you log on—or you can customize its preloaded content by uploading images and other resources, adding web links, or creating your own practice materials.

Acknowledgments

This book has been an enormous undertaking, and we want to express our gratitude to the innumerable people who have influenced its evolution. To begin with, we must cite the contribution of our students who have taken the adjustment course. It is trite to say that they have been a continuing inspiration—but they have.

We also want to express our appreciation for the time and effort invested by the authors of our Internet essay and various ancillary books and materials: Vinny Hevern (LeMoyne College), Bill Addison (Eastern Illinois University), Jeffry Ricker (Scottsdale Community College), John Pulver (Community College of Southern Nevada), David Matsumoto (San Francisco State University), Lenore Frigo (Shasta College), Lisa Garner (Tallahassee Community College), Susan Shapiro (Indiana University East), Mary Ann Valentino (Fresno City College), and David Ward (Arkansas Tech University). In spite of tight schedules, they all did commendable work.

The quality of a textbook depends greatly on the quality of the prepublication reviews by psychology professors around the country. The reviewers listed on page x have contributed to the development of this book by providing constructive reviews of various portions of the manuscript in this or earlier editions. We are grateful to all of them.

We would also like to thank Michele Sordi, who has served as editor of this edition. She has done a wonderful job following in the footsteps of Claire Verduin, Eileen Murphy, and Edith Beard Brady, to whom we remain indebted. We are also grateful to Jackie Estrada, for an excellent job of copy editing and indexing; Tom Dorsaneo, who performed superbly as our production editor; Linda Beaupre, who created the colorful, inviting new design; Linda Rill, who provided outstanding photo and permissions research; Carol Zuber-Mallison, who created the new graphics; Alma Bell of Thompson Type who oversaw the composition; and Fiorella Ljunggren, who shepherded previous editions into existence. Others who have made significant contributions to this project include Jennie Redwitz (project manager), Jennifer Wilkinson (development editor), Jennifer Keever (ancillaries editor), Dory Schaefer and Marlene Veach (marketing), Jessica Kim (editorial assistant), and Vernon Boes (art director).

In addition, Wayne Weiten would like to thank his wife, Beth Traylor, who has been a steady source of emotional support despite the demands of her medical career, and his twelve-year-old son, T. J., who adds a wealth of laughter to his dad's life. He is also grateful to his former colleagues at the College of DuPage and at Santa Clara University, for their counsel and assistance, and to Mike Beede for his assistance with the references. Marky Lloyd would like to thank graduate student Gizelle George for preparing much of the reference list. She is also grateful to Janis Bohan and Glenda Russell for their suggestions for resources on gay and lesbian issues. She also wishes to thank Judith A. Holleman for her assistance and support.

Wayne Weiten
Margaret A. Lloyd

Reviewers

Bette Ackerman
Rhodes College

Jeff Banks
Pepperdine University

Marsha K. Beauchamp
Mt. San Antonio College

John R. Blakemore
Monterey Peninsula College

Barbara A. Boccaccio
Tunxis Community College

Paul Bowers
Grayson County College

Tamara L. Brown
University of Kentucky

George Bryant
East Texas State University

James F. Calhoun
University of Georgia

Robert Cameron
Fairmont State College

M. K. Clampit
Bentley College

Meg Clark
*California State Polytechnic
University–Pomona*

Stephen S. Coccia
Orange County Community College

Dennis Coon
Santa Barbara City College

Katherine A. Couch
Eastern Oklahoma State College

Tori Crews
American River College

Salvatore Cullari
Lebanon Valley College

Kenneth S. Davidson
Wayne State University

Richard Fuhrer
University of Wisconsin–Eau Claire

R. Kirkland Gable
California Lutheran University

Lee Gills
Georgia College

Lawrence Grebstein
University of Rhode Island

Bryan Gros
Louisiana State University

Barbara Hansen Lemme
College of DuPage

Robert Helm
Oklahoma State University

Barbara Hermann
Gainesville College

Jeanne L. Higbee
University of Minnesota

Robert Higgins
Central Missouri State University

Clara E. Hill
University of Maryland

Michael Hirt
Kent State University

Fred J. Hitti
Monroe Community College

William M. Hooper
Clayton College and State University

Joseph Horvat
Weber State University

Kathy Howard
Harding University

Teresa A. Hutchens
University of Tennessee–Knoxville

Jerry Jensen
*Minneapolis Community &
Technical College*

Walter Jones
College of DuPage

Wayne Joose
Calvin College

Bradley Karlin
Texas A&M University

Margaret Karolyi
University of Akron

Lambros Karris
Husson College

Martha Kuehn
Central Lakes College

Susan Kupisch
Austin Peay State University

Robert Lawyer
Delgado Community College

Jimi Leopold
Tarleton State University

Harold List
Massachusetts Bay Community College

Corliss A. Littlefield
Morgan Community College

Louis A. Martone
Miami Dade Community College

Richard Maslow
San Joaquin Delta College

Sherri McCarthy
Northern Arizona University

William T. McReynolds
University of Tampa

Fred Medway
*University of South Carolina–
Columbia*

Frederick Meeker
*California State Polytechnic
University–Pomona*

Mitchell Metzger
*Pennsylvania State University—
Shenago Campus*

John Moritsugu
Pacific Lutheran University

Jeanne O'Kon
Tallahassee Community College

Gary Oliver
College of DuPage

William Penrod
Middle Tennessee State University

Joseph Philbrick
*California State Polytechnic
University–Pomona*

Barbara M. Powell
Eastern Illinois University

James Prochaska
University of Rhode Island

Katherine Elaine Royal
Middle Tennessee State University

Joan Royce
Riverside Community College

Joan Rykiel
Ocean County College

John Sample
Slippery Rock University

Thomas K. Savill
Metropolitan State College of Denver

Patricia Sawyer
Middlesex Community College

Carol Schachat
De Anza College

Norman R. Schultz
Clemson University

Dale Simmons
Oregon State University

Sangeeta Singg
Angelo State University

Valerie Smead
Western Illinois University

Dolores K. Sutter
Tarrant County College–Northeast

Karl Swain
Community College of Southern Nevada

Kenneth L. Thompson
Central Missouri State University

David L. Watson
University of Hawaii

Deborah S. Weber
University of Akron

Clair Wiederholt
Madison Area Technical College

J. Oscar Williams
Diablo Valley College

Raymond Wolf
Moraine Park Technical College

Raymond Wolfe
State University of New York at Geneseo

Michael Wolff
Southwestern Oklahoma State University

Madeleine E. Wright
Houston Community College

Norbert Yager
Henry Ford Community College

Brief Contents

Contents

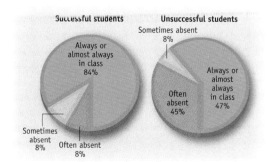

CHAPTER 2

Theories of Personality   32

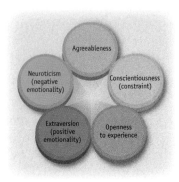

© Laura Dwight/PhotoEdit

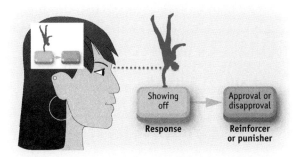

CHAPTER 3

Stress and Its Effects   70

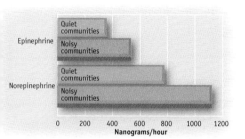

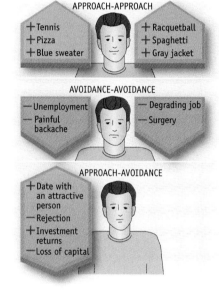

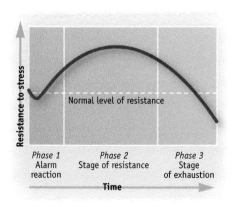

CHAPTER 4

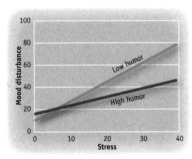

Coping Processes   104

© Paul Thomas/The Image Bank/Getty Images

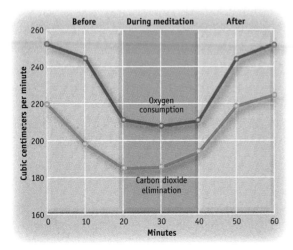

CHAPTER 5

The Self   138

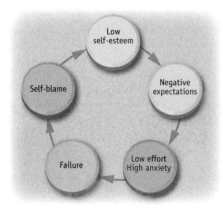

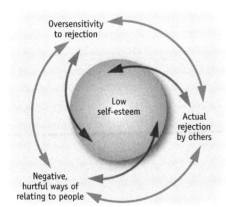

CHAPTER 6

Social Thinking and Social Influence   170

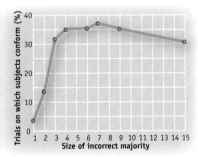

© RNT Productions/Corbis

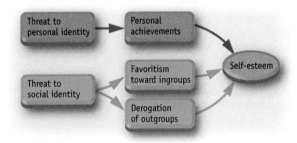

CHAPTER 7

Interpersonal Communication   200

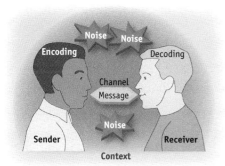

© Eric K. K. Yu/Corbis

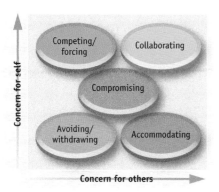

CHAPTER 8

Friendship and Love   234

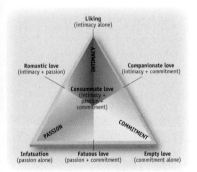

© 2004 AP/Wide World Photos

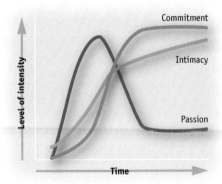

CHAPTER 9

Marriage and Intimate Relationships   268

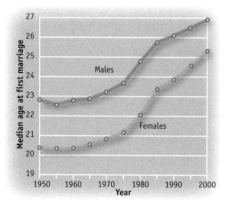

© Matthew McVay/Corbis Saba

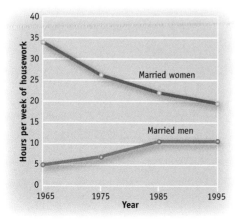

PART THREE Developmental Transitions

CHAPTER 10

Gender and Behavior   302

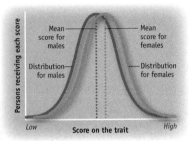

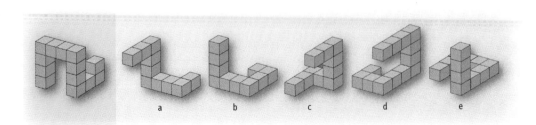

CHAPTER 11

Development in Adolescence and Adulthood   336

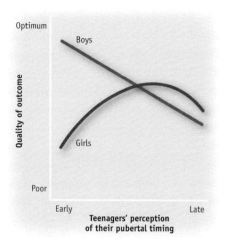

Optimum

Boys

Girls

Poor

Quality of outcome

Early   Late

Teenagers' perception
of their pubertal timing

© David Young-Wolff/Stone/Getty Images

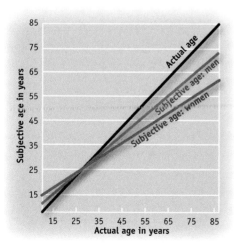

Subjective age in years

Actual age

Subjective age: men

Subjective age: women

85
75
65
55
45
35
25
15

15   25   35   45   55   65   75   85
Actual age in years

CHAPTER 12

Careers and Work 372

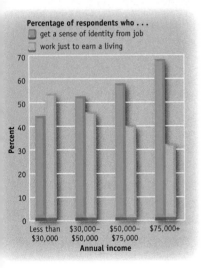

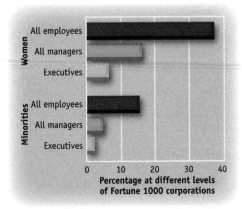

CHAPTER 13

Development and Expression of Sexuality   406

© Paul Wright/Masterfile

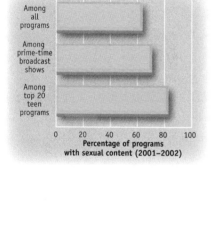

© Mark Romanelli/The Image Bank/Getty Images

PART FOUR Mental and Physical Health

CHAPTER 14

Psychology and Physical Health   442

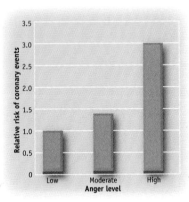

© Jim Cummings/Taxi/Getty Images

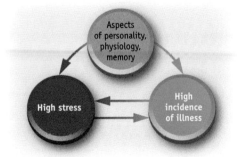

CHAPTER 15

Psychological Disorders 480

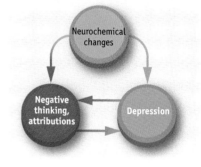

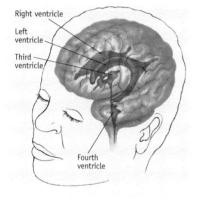

CHAPTER 16

Psychotherapy 516

National Library of Medicine

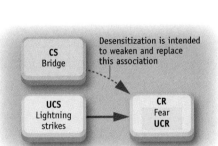

To the Student

In most college courses students spend more time with their textbooks than with their professors. Given this reality, it helps if you like your textbook. Making textbooks likable, however, is a tricky proposition. By its very nature, a textbook must introduce a great many new concepts, ideas, and theories. If it doesn't, it isn't much of a textbook, and instructors won't choose to use it—so you'll never see it anyway. Consequently, we have tried to make this book as likable as possible without compromising the academic content that your instructor demands. Thus, we have tried to make the book lively, informal, engaging, well organized, easy to read, practical, and occasionally humorous. Before you plunge into Chapter 1, let us explain some of the key features that can help you get the most out of the book.

Learning Aids

Mastering the content of this text involves digesting a great deal of information. To facilitate this learning process, we've incorporated a number of instructional aids into the book.

■ *Outlines* at the beginning of each chapter provide you with both a preview and an overview of what will be covered.

■ *Headings* are used extensively to keep material well organized.

■ To help alert you to key points, *learning objectives* are found throughout the chapters, immediately after the level-1 headings.

■ *Key terms* are identified with **blue italicized boldface** type to indicate that these are important vocabulary items that are part of psychology's technical language.

■ An *integrated running glossary* provides an on-the-spot definition of each key term as it's introduced in the text. These formal definitions are printed in **blue boldface** type. It is often difficult for students to adapt to the jargon used by scientific disciplines. However, learning this terminology is an essential part of your educational experience. The integrated running glossary is meant to make this learning process as painless as possible.

■ An *alphabetical glossary* is provided in the back of the book, as key terms are usually defined in the running glossary only when they are first introduced. If you run into a technical term that was introduced in an earlier chapter and you can't remember its meaning, you can look it up in the alphabetical glossary instead of backtracking to find the place where it first appeared.

■ *Italics* are used liberally throughout the book to emphasize important points.

■ A *chapter review* near the end of each chapter includes a thorough summary of the chapter, and lists key terms and important theorists, with page references. Reading over these review materials can help ensure that you've digested the key points in the chapter.

■ Each chapter ends with a ten-item *practice test* that should give you a realistic assessment of your mastery of that chapter and valuable practice taking multiple-choice tests that will probably be representative of what you will see in class (if your instructor uses the test bank designed for this book).

Recommended Reading Boxes

This text should function as a resource book. To facilitate this goal, particularly interesting self-help books on various topics are highlighted in boxes within the chapters. Each box provides a brief description of the book. We do not agree with everything in these recommended books, but all of them are potentially useful or intriguing. The main purpose of this feature is to introduce you to some of the better self-help books that are available.

Living in Today's World Boxes

These boxes were originally developed to address issues that surfaced in the aftermath of the 9/11 terrorist attacks in the United States. Continuing in this vein, many of the boxes in this edition deal with concerns raised by the threat of terrorism in today's world. For example, we discuss how people tend to be affected by traumatic events, how people can cope more effectively with personal trauma, and how people can think more rationally about the threat of terrorism. However, in this edition we have broadened the scope of coverage in these boxes to include additional adjustment issues that are especially pertinent in light of current events, such as the controversy over whether the government should promote marriage and problems associated with living up to today's unrealistic ideals of physical attractiveness. We hope these digressions on pressing, contemporary issues prove helpful.

Web Links (by Vincent Hevern)

To help make this book a rich resource guide, we have included Web Links, which are recommended websites that can provide you with additional information on adjustment-related topics. The recommended sites were selected by Vincent Hevern, the Internet editor for the Society for the Teaching of Psychology. Professor Hevern sought out sites that are interesting, that are relevant to adjustment, and that provide accurate, empirically sound information. As with the Recommended Reading boxes, we cannot say that we agree with everything posted on these web pages, but we think they have some real value. The Web Links are dispersed throughout the chapters, adjacent to related topical coverage. Because URLs change frequently, we have not included the URLs for the Web Links in the book. If you are interested in visiting these sites, we recommend that you do so through the *Psychology Applied to Modern Life* home page at the Wadsworth Psychology Website (http://psychology.wadsworth.com/weiten_lloyd8e). Links to all the recommended websites will be maintained there, and the Wadsworth webmaster will periodically update the URLs. Of course, you can also use a search engine, such as Google, to locate the recommended websites. By the way, if you are not particularly sophisticated about the Internet, we strongly suggest that you read Professor Hevern's essay on the Internet, which follows this preface.

Study Guide (0-495-03032-5)

The study guide that accompanies this text, written by William Addison of Eastern Illinois University, is an excellent resource designed to assist you in mastering the information contained in the book. It includes a wealth of review exercises to help you organize information and a self-test for assessing your mastery. You should be able to purchase it at your college bookstore.

InfoTrac® College Edition . . . now with InfoMarks®!

NOT SOLD SEPARATELY. Available for packaging with the text! Now FREE four-month access to InfoTrac College Edition's online database of more than 18 million reliable, full-length articles from 5000 academic journals and periodicals includes access to InfoMarks—stable URLs that can be linked to articles, journals, and searches. InfoMarks allow you to use a simple copy and paste technique to create instant and continually updated online

readers, content services, bibliographies, electronic "reserve" readings, and current topic sites. And to help you use the research you gather, your free four-month subsciption to InfoTrac College Edition includes access to InfoWrite, a complete set of online critical thinking and paper-writing tools. To take a quick tour of InfoTrac College Edition, visit http://www.infotrac-college.com/ and select the User Demo.

Personal Explorations Workbook (0-495-03035-X)

The *Personal Explorations Workbook* is a small booklet that contains interesting, thought-provoking experiential exercises for each text chapter. These exercises are designed to help you achieve personal insights. The Questionnaires are psychological tests or scales that you can administer, so you can see how you score on various traits discussed in the text. The Personal Probes consist of questions intended to help you think about issues in your personal life in relation to concepts and ideas discussed in the text. Many students find these exercises to be quite interesting, even fun. Hence, we encourage you to use the *Personal Explorations Workbook*. The exercises related to each chapter are listed at the end of each chapter on the same page as the Practice Test.

A Concluding Note

We sincerely hope that you find this book enjoyable. If you have any comments or advice that might help us improve the next edition, please write to us in care of the publisher, Wadsworth Publishing Company, 10 Davis Drive, Belmont, California 94002. There is a form in the back of the book that you can use to provide us with feedback. Finally, let us wish you good luck. We hope you enjoy your course and learn a great deal.

Wayne Weiten
Margaret A. Lloyd

Applied Psychology and the Internet: What Should a Student Know?

by Vincent W. Hevern, Le Moyne College

Imagine walking into a huge bookstore at a mall to look for a good book in "applied psychology." Your first reaction is confusion. The store is gigantic and you're unsure even where to begin your search. No one seems to be around to tell you where to look. Eventually you discover that some titles of interest are shelved in a "Psychology" section but a lot of others are found in a separate "Self-Help" section. What's the difference, you wonder? After a careful look at the books, you begin to notice that many (not all) of the *psychology* books contain research references to support their conclusions. But, many (not all) of the *self-help* books don't have any references. Indeed, many self-help books have catchy titles, flashy covers, and bold claims, but little scientific support for the claims they make.

The World Wide Web (WWW or "the web") on the Internet ("the Net") is much like one of those huge bookstores. The selection is enormous, and it's sometimes difficult to find what you're looking for. For many users, the Net can seem intimidating, and students may feel they don't know how the Net works. On top of that, much of the web is filled with weak or poor resources of dubious validity. So what can you do?

Wayne Weiten and Marky Lloyd, the authors of this textbook, asked me to put together some advice and guidelines for students like yourself who may turn to the Net for help. They know that I've been using the Net intensively for years in teaching and research with undergraduates. So I'm going to share with you what I believe to be the really important stuff about the Internet—information that should make your life as a student easier and, in the end, help you to learn even more about the fascinating world of applied psychology.

General Comments About the Internet

We now know that something of a fundamental change in the way people exchange ideas and information took place around the time many of you were attending elementary school. For over twenty years, the Internet had been the tool of a relatively small group of lab scientists communicating mostly with each other. Suddenly, in the mid-1990s, the Net began to expand rapidly beyond the research laboratory. It first reached tens and then hundreds of millions of people as vast numbers of computers, large and small, were interconnected to form what is often called *cyberspace*. Thus, in the 21st century learning to navigate the Internet is as crucial as learning to read or to write—most of us will probably use the Net in some form at work or at home for the rest of our lives.

So, what are some basic notions to understand the Internet and how it works? Let me propose briefly eight crucial ideas.

1. *The goal of the Internet is communication—the rapid exchange of information—between people separated from each other.* Electronic mail (e-mail) and the World Wide Web (WWW, of just "the web") are currently the two most important ways of communicating in cyberspace even though the Net also uses other formats to do so.

2. *Every piece of information on the Net—every web page, every graphic, every movie or sound, every e-mail box—has a unique, short, and structured address called a URL (or uniform resource locator).* Take, for example, the URL for materials related to psychology maintained by the publisher of this book:

http://psychology.wadsworth.com/

This example shows all three elements of a URL: (a) to the left of the double forward slashes (//) is the protocol that tells the Net how to transfer the information. Here it is *http:* which means "use hypertext transfer protocol"—the most frequent protocol on the Net; (b) to the right of the double slashes up to the first forward slash (/) is the *domain name* that indicates which computer on the Net from which to get the information. Here the name of the computer is "www.wadsworth.com". (c) finally, everything after the first forward slash is called the *pathway*, which indicates where the information is located within that particular computer. Here the pathway consists of the location "psychology_d/".

3. *The foundation of the web rests on hypertext links ("hyperlinks") that are contained within documents (or web pages) displayed online.* A hyperlink is a highlighted word, phrase, or graphic image within an onscreen document that refers to some other document or web page elsewhere. Part of every hyperlink on a computer screen includes the URL of the document which is hidden from view on the screen but stored within the computer displaying the document. Users can easily move from one document to another on screen because of hypertext links and their URLs.

4. *The last element of the domain name (the "domain" itself) indicates what type of organization sponsors the link.* Four important domains are *.com* (commercial

businesses), *.edu* (colleges and universities), *.gov* (governmental agencies), and *.org* (non-profit organizations).

5. *The Internet is too large for any one individual to know all the important resources that can be found there.* Users, even experienced ones, often need help to find what they're looking for. In the chapters ahead, you will find many recommended websites that I have carefully selected based on their quality and their suitability for undergraduates. In making these selections, I emphasized quality over quantity and strived to send you to excellent gateway sites that are rich in links to related sites. I hope these links help you to begin to explore the field of psychology on the Internet.

6. *URLs are relatively unstable.* Many websites are moved or changed each year, as new computer systems are installed to replace older ones. Thus, links or URLs that are good one day may be useless the next. That is why we have not included the URLs for our recommended websites in the book. If you want to check out a recommended website, we suggest that you do so through the *Psychology Applied to Modern Life* home page at the Wadsworth Psychology Website (http://psychology.wadsworth.com/weiten_lloyd8e). Links to all the recommended websites will be maintained there, and the Wadsworth webmaster will periodically update the URLs. Of course, you can also use a search engine, such as Google, to locate the recommended websites.

7. *The web is a world-wide democracy on which anyone can post materials. Hence, the quality of information found online varies tremendously.* Some material is first rate, up to date, and backed up by good research and professional judgment. But a great deal of information online is junk—second rate, based on poor or invalid research, and filled with many errors. Frankly, some sites are downright wacky, and others are run by hucksters and hate-mongers. Thus, users need to learn to tell the difference between reputable and disreputable web resources.

8. *Knowledge has a monetary value.* Although the Internet started out as a noncommercial enterprise where almost everything was free, things have changed swiftly. Owners of knowledge (the holders of commercial "copyrights") usually expect to be paid for sharing what they own over the Net. Thus, many commercial businesses, such as the publishers of academic journals or books, either do not make journal articles available on line for free or expect users to pay some type of fee for accessing their materials. Cognizant of this problem, the publisher of this text has entered into an agreement with a major online resource for magazine and journal articles and other types of information called InfoTrac College Edition. Your text may have come bundled with a free four-month subscription to InfoTrac College Edition, which provides easy access to full-text versions of thousands of periodicals. If you received an InfoTrac College Edition subscription with this book, it would be wise to take advantage of this valuable resource.

Some Suggestions for Action

In light of these ideas, how might students approach the Internet? What should you do to make the most of your time online? Let's review some general suggestions for exploring the Internet.

1. *Learn to navigate the Net before you get an assignment requiring you to do so.* If you've never used the Net before, start now to get a feel for it. Consider doing what lots of students do: Ask a friend who knows the Net to work with you directly so you can quickly get personal experience in cyberspace. What if you "hate" computers or they make you uncomfortable? Recent research has shown that students' fears of using computers tend to diminish once they get some practical experience during the course of a single semester.

2. *Learn how the software browser on your computer works.* Every popular web browser, such as Microsoft Internet Explorer, Mozilla Firefox, or Safari (for Mac users), is filled with many simple tricks and helpful shortcuts. Ask your friends or the computer consultants at school. Learning the tricks makes Net-based research much easier. (Hint: Find out what happens when you hold down the right-hand mouse button on a PC or the whole button on a Mac once you have the cursor on top of a hyperlink.)

3. *Get to know the different types of online help to find resources on the web.* These resources currently fall into three general categories: (a) *General guides or directories* such as Yahoo! (www.yahoo.com) are similar to the Yellow Pages for telephones. You ask the online guide to show you what's listed in its directory under a category heading you supply. (b) *Search engines* such as Google (www.google.com), Scirus (www.scirus.com), AllTheWeb (www.alltheweb.com), and Teoma (www.teoma.com) are huge databases that generally collect the names and URLs of millions of pages on the Net along with many lines of text from these pages. They can be searched by either keywords or phrases and provide ranked listings of web pages that contain the search target words or phrases. (c) *Expert subject guides* such as Russ Dewey's *PsychWeb* (www.psychwww.com) or Scott Plous' *Social Psychology Network* (www.socialpsychology.org) provide links to online resources in more narrow or specific fields. Volunteer specialists who claim to be experts on the topic select the links. Recent innovative features of websites include the vast graphic image database at Google, the "between the covers" text search capability of many books at Amazon.com, and the Wayback Machine's post-1995 archive of more than 30 billion pages of the web itself (www.archive.org).

4. *Carefully check everything you type online because even the slightest error in spelling a URL or an e-mail address will cause a failure to retrieve the web page or to deliver the e-mail message.* Remember that computers are stupid and will do exactly and only what you tell them to do. They don't read minds.

Using the Internet in Psychology

Are there specific suggestions for students of psychology about using the Net? Here are five that I think are very important.

1. *Plan what to look for before going online.* Too many psychology students jump right to the web when they're given a research task, before giving careful thought to what they're looking for. They get frustrated easily because the web doesn't seem to have anything about the topic. It would be better (a) to think about the subject you are researching and what specifically you want to learn about that topic, (b) to recall what you already know that relates to the topic, especially psychological concepts and vocabulary words associated with the topic, and (c) to devise a strategy for getting the information you desire. Consult your school's reference library staff or your teachers for suggestions.

2. *Do not rely on the Internet as your principal or only source of data or references in a research project* (especially if you want a good grade). The Net may be easy to use, but your teachers will expect you to cite journal articles, books, and other printed sources more than you cite Internet materials in research. Developing your library skills is essential.

3. *As noted before, don't expect to find many full-text journal articles or other copyrighted commercial materials online for free.* Consult your school's reference librarians about online access to such materials. Many schools now subscribe to online full-text databases that allow you to research articles and other information sources with your own computer. On the web itself, you are more likely to uncover government reports, specialized technical materials from nonprofit organizations, current news and opinion, and general sorts of information rather than findings of specific research studies (though, if they were recently in the news, you may find some of these, too.)

4. *Learn to recognize the characteristics of a good online resource site.* Good sites have webmasters or editors personally identified by name and affiliation. Such persons may be professionals or staff members at a reputable institution such as a hospital or university. These sites seem to provide a broad set of resources, are balanced and reasonably objective in their content, and avoid sensational or one-sided viewpoints. Reputable sites tend not to promote specific products or services for money or, if they do, acknowledge there are other resources that browsers may consider.

5. *If you contact anyone online for help, be courteous.* Introduce yourself as you would if you were standing in a faculty member's office. Give your name, your school, and a full statement of what help you are asking for and what you've tried to do that hasn't worked. Don't demand that someone help you. Be sure you've done adequate research on your own before contacting an expert on the web. And don't be surprised if your request for help is turned down by a webmaster or editor. Frankly, he or she has already done a lot of volunteer work by editing the site online.

I hope some of these ideas and suggestions help. The Internet offers an awesome array of learning resources related to psychology. Welcome to an exciting new world of discovery.

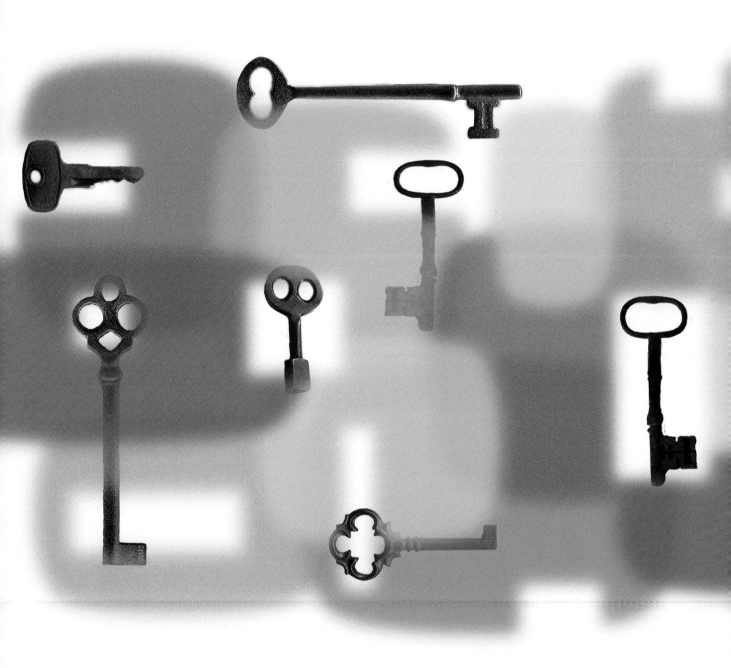

EIGHTH EDITION

Psychology Applied to Modern Life

ADJUSTMENT IN THE 21ST CENTURY

Adjusting to Modern Life

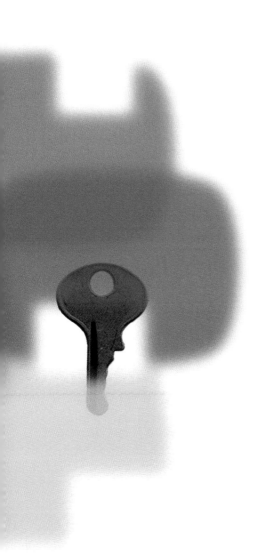

The immense Boeing 747 lumbers into position to accept its human cargo. The eager passengers-to-be scurry on board. In a tower a few hundred yards away, air traffic controllers diligently monitor radar screens, radio transmissions, and digital readouts of weather information. At the reservation desks in the airport terminal, clerks punch up the appropriate ticket information on their computer terminals and quickly process the steady stream of passengers. Mounted on the wall are video terminals displaying up-to-the-minute information on flight arrivals, departures, and delays. Back in the cockpit of the plane, the flight crew calmly scans the complex array of dials, meters, and lights to assess the aircraft's readiness for flight. In a few minutes, the airplane will slice into the cloudy, snow-laden skies above Chicago. In a mere three hours its passengers will be transported from the piercing cold of a Chicago winter to the balmy beaches of the Bahamas. Another everyday triumph for technology will have taken place.

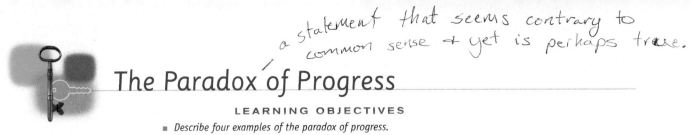

a statement that seems contrary to common sense + yet is perhaps true.

The Paradox of Progress

LEARNING OBJECTIVES

- Describe four examples of the paradox of progress.
- Explain what is meant by the paradox of progress and how theorists have explained it.

We are the children of technology. We take for granted such impressive feats as transporting 300 people over 1500 miles in a matter of hours. After all, we live in a time of unparalleled progress. Our modern Western society has made extraordinary strides in transportation, energy, communication, agriculture, and medicine. Yet despite our technological progress, social problems and personal difficulties seem more prevalent and more prominent than ever before. This paradox is evident in many aspects of contemporary life, as seen in the following examples.

Point. Modern technology has provided us with countless time-saving devices—automobiles, telephones, vacuum cleaners, dishwashers, photocopiers, fax machines. Today, cell phones allow people to talk to friends or colleagues and battle rush hour at the same time. In a matter of seconds a personal computer can perform calculations that would take months if done by hand.

Counterpoint. Nonetheless, most of us complain about not having enough time. Our schedule books are overflowing with appointments, commitments, and plans. Surveys suggest that most of us spend more and more time working and have less and less time for ourselves (Schor, 1991). Time has become such a precious commodity, one national survey found that 51 percent of the adult respondents would rather have more time than more money (Weil & Rosen, 1997). As social critic Jeremy Rifkin (1989) notes, "It is ironic in a culture so committed to saving time that we feel increasingly deprived of the very thing we value" (p. 19). Where has all our free time gone? Recent research suggests that virtually all the additional leisure time gained over the last 30 years has been absorbed by one of technology's most seductive inventions—television (Robinson & Godbey, 1997).

Point. Thanks in large part to technological advances, we live in extraordinary affluence. Undeniably, there are pockets of genuine poverty, but social critics Paul Wachtel (1989), David Myers (2000), and Gregg Easterbrook (2003) argue convincingly that in North America and Europe the middle and upper classes are larger and wealthier than ever before. Most of us take for granted things that were once considered luxuries, such as color television and air conditioning. People spend vast amounts of money on expensive automobiles, audio systems, computers, projection TVs, clothing, and vacations. In the late 1990s, the amount of money spent on luxury goods increased four times faster than overall spending (Frank, 1999). Wachtel quotes a New York museum director who asserts that "shopping is the chief cultural activity in the United States" (p. 23).

Counterpoint. In spite of this economic abundance, research suggests that most people do not feel very good about their financial well-being. For example, when one survey inquired about Americans' satisfaction with 13 aspects of their lives, the results showed that people were least satisfied with their finances (Myers, 2000). In his book titled *The High Price of Materialism,* Tim Kasser (2002) summarizes research showing that people who are especially concerned with money and possessions tend to report lower levels of happiness than others. Why are people so dissatisfied with their economic well-being? One problem is that advertising helps foster an insatiable thirst for consumption and the belief that material goods are the key to happiness (Kanner & Soule, 2004; Kasser et al., 2004). Hence, studies find that the gap between what people have and what they desire is greater in the material domain than in other areas of life (Solberg, Diener, & Robinson, 2004).

Point. The range of life choices available to people in modern societies has increased exponentially in recent decades. For example, Barry Schwartz (2004) describes how a simple visit to a local supermarket can require a consumer to choose from 285 varieties of cookies, 61 suntan lotions, 150 lipsticks, and 175 salad dressings. Although increased choice is most tangible in the realm of consumer goods and services, Schwartz argues that it also extends into more significant domains of life. Today, people tend to have unprecedented opportunities to make choices about how they will be educated (e.g., vastly more flexible college curricula are available), how and where they will work (e.g., telecommuting presents employees with all sorts of new choices about how to accomplish their work), how their intimate relationships will unfold (e.g., people have increased freedom to delay marriage, cohabit, not have children, and so forth), and even how they will look (advances in plastic surgery have made personal appearance a matter of choice).

Counterpoint. Although increased freedom of choice sounds attractive, Schwartz (2004) argues that the overabundance of choices in modern life has unexpected

LIVING IN TODAY'S WORLD

Life May Never Be the Same Again: Implications for Adjustment

The citizens of the United States received a gigantic wake-up call on September 11, 2001, in the form of the horrific, tragic terrorist attacks on the World Trade Center and the Pentagon. Life in the United States and much of the Western world may never be quite the same again. The specter of terrorism has psychological repercussions for virtually everyone in the United States (Danieli, Engdahl, & Schlenger, 2004). People are upset about the many things that they used to take for granted but have lost, such as being able to fly to a business meeting without a second thought, to pick up mail without worrying about contamination, to walk into a tall building without being searched, and to interact with strangers without being suspicious. They are angry about the injustice of it all, disgusted by the senseless violence, and anxious about what future terrorist attacks might bring. Above all else, Americans have lost their sense of invulnerability.

In light of the fundamental ways in which our lives have been changed, you might wonder whether the principal premise of this book—that the basic challenge of modern life is the quest for meaning and direction— might suddenly seem irrelevant. In reality, the situation is quite the opposite. Perhaps more than before, because of the threat of terrorism, people are questioning the meaning of their lives. Americans are wondering whether what they do matters, whether what they cherish is important, and whether what they have worked for has been worth it. The terrorist-induced jolt to our collective psyche has made the search for a sense of direction even more relevant to contemporary life.

That said, the threat of terrorism raises some important issues that an adjustment textbook should attempt to address. Fortunately, the field of psychology has much to contribute to the battle against terrorism (Marsella, 2004). After all, terrorism is *psychological* warfare (Lev-

© AP/Wide World Photos

ant, Barbanel, & DeLeon, 2004). The goal of terrorism is to provoke psychological vulnerability and agitation in a population. The death, destruction, and havoc wreaked by terrorists is not an end in itself, but a means to an end—the creation of widespread anxiety, alarm, and panic.

In each chapter you will find boxes labeled "Living in Today's World," which address some of the adjustment issues raised by the threat of terrorism itself, related problems spawned by terrorism, and a variety of other challenges unique to our modern world. These boxes discuss such topics as how people tend to react to traumatic events, how people can cope more effectively with personal trauma, whether the government should promote marriage, how resilience can be enhanced in children, how workers can cope with unemployment, and other contemporary issues. We sincerely hope that this feature proves helpful.

costs. He argues that people routinely make errors even when choosing among a handful of alternatives and that errors become much more likely when decisions become vastly more complex. And he explains how having more alternatives increases the potential for rumination, postdecision regret, and anticipated regret. Ultimately, he argues, the malaise associated with choice overload undermines individuals' happiness and con-

tributes to depression. Consistent with this analysis, studies have found that the incidence of depressive disorders has increased dramatically—perhaps tenfold— over the last 50 years (Diener & Seligman, 2004). Average anxiety levels have also gone up substantially in recent decades (Twenge, 2000). It is hard to say whether choice overload is the chief culprit underlying these trends, but it is clear that increased freedom of choice

Barry Schwartz argues that people in modern societies suffer from choice overload. He maintains that the endless choices people are presented with lead them to waste countless hours weighing trivial decisions and ruminating about whether their decisions were optimal.

© Randy Faris/Corbis

has not resulted in enhanced tranquillity or improved mental health.

Point. Modern technology has gradually provided us with unprecedented control over the world around us. Advances in agriculture have dramatically increased food production, and biotechnology advocates claim that genetically modified crops will make our food supply more reliable that ever before. Elaborate water supply systems, made up of hundreds of miles of canals, tunnels, and pipelines, along with dams, reservoirs, and pumping stations, permit massive metropolitan areas to grow in inhospitable deserts. Thanks to progress in medicine, doctors can reattach severed limbs, use lasers to correct microscopic defects in the eye, and even replace the human heart.

Counterpoint. Unfortunately, modern technology has also had a devastating negative impact on the world around us, leading to environmental problems such as global warming, destruction of the ozone layer, deforestation, exhaustion of much of the world's fisheries, widespread air and water pollution, and extensive exposure of plants and animals to toxic chemicals (Oskamp, 2000). Many experts worry that in a few generations the earth's resources will be too depleted to sustain an adequate quality of life (Winter, 2004). To most people, these crises sound like technical problems that call for technological answers, but they are also behavioral problems in that they are fueled by overpopulation and overconsumption (Howard, 2000). In North America, the crucial problem is excessive consumption of the world's natural resources. For example, the United States houses 5 percent of the world's population but guzzles 25 percent of its commercial energy (Flavin & Dunn, 1999).

All these apparent contradictions reflect the same theme: *The technological advances of the past century, impressive though they may be, have not led to perceptible improvement in our collective health and happiness.* Indeed, many social critics argue that the quality of our lives and our sense of personal fulfillment have declined rather than increased. This is the paradox of progress.

What is the cause of this paradox? Many explanations have been offered. Erich Fromm (1963, 1981) has argued that the progress we value so much has scrambled our value systems and undermined our traditional sources of emotional security, such as family, community, and religion. Alvin Toffler (1970, 1980) attributes our collective alienation and distress to our being overwhelmed by rapidly accelerating cultural change. Robert Kegan (1994) maintains that the mental demands of modern life have become so complex, confusing, and contradictory that most of us are "in over our heads." Tim Kasser (2002) speculates that excessive materialism weakens the social ties that bind us, stokes the fires of insecurity, and undermines our collective sense of well-being. Whatever the explanation, many theorists agree that *the basic challenge of modern life has become the search for meaning or a sense of direction* (Naylor, Willimon, & Naylor, 1994). This search involves struggling with such problems as forming a solid sense of identity, arriving at a coherent philosophy of life, and developing a clear vision of a future that realistically promises fulfillment. Centuries ago, problems of this kind were probably much simpler. As we'll see in the next section, today it appears that many of us are floundering in a sea of confusion.

The Search for Direction

- *Provide some examples of people's search for direction.*
- *Describe three problems that are common to popular self-help books.*
- *Summarize advice about what to look for in quality self-help books.*
- *Summarize the philosophy underlying this textbook.*

We live in a time of unparalleled social and technological mutation. According to a host of social critics, the kaleidoscope of change that we see around us creates feelings of anxiety and uncertainty, which we try to alleviate by searching for a sense of direction. This search, which sometimes goes awry, manifests itself in many ways.

■ For example, we could discuss how hundreds of thousands of Americans have invested large sums of money to enroll in "self-realization" programs such as est training, Scientology, and Silva Mind Control. These programs typically promise to provide profound enlightenment and quickly turn one's life around. Many participants claim that the programs have revolutionized their lives. However, most experts characterize such programs as intellectually bankrupt, and magazine exposés reveal that they are simply lucrative money-making schemes (Behar, 1991; Pressman, 1993). More than anything else, the success of these programs demonstrates just how desperate some people are for a sense of direction and purpose in their lives.

■ We could also discuss how a host of unorthodox religious groups—commonly called *cults*—have attracted hundreds of thousands of converts who voluntarily embrace a life of regimentation, obedience, and zealous ideology. Most of these cults flourish in obscurity, unless bizarre incidents—such as the mass suicide of the Heaven's Gate cult—attract public attention. It is widely believed that cults use brainwashing and mind control to seduce lonely outsiders, but in reality converts are a diverse array of normal people who are swayed by remarkably ordinary social influence strategies (Baron, 2000; Deikman, 1990). According to Philip Zimbardo (1992), people join cults because these groups appear to provide simple solutions to complex problems, a sense of purpose, and a structured lifestyle that reduces feelings of uncertainty.

■ And, if you would like a mundane, everyday example of people's search for direction, you need look no farther than your radio, where you will find that the hottest nationally syndicated personality is "Dr. Laura," who doles out advice to more than 15 million listeners a week over a network of nearly 300 stations (Bendis,

There are many manifestations of our search for a sense of direction, including the emergence of cults, such as the Raelian UFO cult, and the astonishing popularity of "Dr. Laura."

1997). Although only seven or eight people get through to her during each show, an astonishing 75,000 people call each day to seek her unique brand of blunt, outspoken, judgmental advice. Dr. Laura, who is not a psychologist or psychiatrist (her doctorate is in physiology), analyzes callers' problems in more of a moral than psychological framework. Unlike most therapists, she unabashedly preaches to her audience about how they ought to lead their lives. In many instances she is insulting and abusive to her callers, models remarkable intolerance, and provides terrible advice (Epstein, 2001). In an editorial in *Psychology Today,* Robert Epstein (2001) concludes that "no legitimate mental health professional would ever give the kind of hateful, divisive advice that Schlessinger doles out daily" (p. 5). Yet, the remarkable popularity of her highly prescriptive advice demonstrates once again that many people are eager for guidance and direction.

Although we might choose to examine any of these examples of people's search for a sense of direction, we will reserve our in-depth analysis for a manifestation of this search that is even more germane to our focus on everyday adjustment: the spectacular success of best-selling "self-help" books.

Self-Help Books

In the year 2000, Americans spent $563 million on "self-help books" that offer do-it-yourself treatments for common personal problems (Paul, 2001). Their fascination with self-improvement is nothing new. For decades American readers have displayed a voracious appetite for self-help books such as *I'm OK—You're OK* (Harris, 1967), *Your Erroneous Zones* (Dyer, 1976), *How to Be Awake and Alive* (Newman & Berkowitz, 1976), *Living, Loving & Learning* (Buscaglia, 1982), *Men Are from Mars, Women Are from Venus* (Gray, 1992), *Ageless Body, Timeless Mind* (Chopra, 1993), *Don't Sweat the Small Stuff . . . and It's All Small Stuff* (Carlson, 1997), *Life Strategies* (McGraw, 1999), *Making Peace with Your Past* (Bloomfield, 2000), *Self-Nurture* (Domar & Dreher, 2000), and *Happiness Is Free* (Dwoskin & Levenson, 2002). With their simple recipes for achieving happiness, these books have generally not been timid about promising to change the quality of the reader's life. Consider the following excerpt from

---

WEB LINK 1.1

Psychological Self-Help
Clinical psychologist and professor Clayton E. Tucker-Ladd has spent some 25 years exploring how individuals may help themselves deal with personal issues and problems from a psychological perspective. Here he has assembled an online 15-chapter book, grounded in up-to-date research, that complements this textbook extremely well. **Note: The URLs (addresses) for the Web Links can be found on the website for this text (http://www.psychology. wadsworth.com/weiten_lloyd8e), or you can find them using a search engine such as Google.**

the back cover of a self-help book titled *Self Creation* (Weinberg, 1979):

More than any book ever written, Self Creation *shows you who you are and reveals the secret to controlling your own life. It contains an action blueprint built around a clear-cut principle as basic and revolutionary as the law of gravity. With it you will discover how to conquer bad habits, solve sexual problems, overcome depression and shyness, deal with infuriating people, be decisive, enhance your career, increase creativity. And it will show you how to love and be loved. You created you. Now you can start to reap the boundless benefits of self-confidence, self-reliance, self-determination with* Self Creation.

If only it were that easy! If only someone could hand you a book that would solve all your problems! Unfortunately, it is not that simple. Merely reading a book is not likely to turn your life around. If the consumption of these literary narcotics were even remotely as helpful as their publishers claim, we would be a nation of serene, happy, well-adjusted people. It is clear, however, that serenity is not the dominant national mood. Quite the contrary, as already noted, in recent decades Americans' average anxiety level has moved upward (Twenge, 2000) and the prevalence of depression has increased dramatically (Ingram, Scott, & Siegle, 1999). The multitude of self-help books that crowd bookstore shelves represent just one more symptom of our collective distress and our search for the elusive secret of happiness.

The Value of Self-Help Books

It is somewhat unfair to lump all self-help books together for a critique, because they vary widely in quality (Fried & Schultis, 1995; Norcross et al., 2003). Surveys exploring psychotherapists' opinions of self-help books suggest that there are some excellent books that offer authentic insights and sound advice (Starker, 1990, 1992). Many therapists encourage their patients to read selected self-help books (Campbell & Smith, 2003), and some books that have been tested in clinical trials have proven helpful (Floyd, 2003; Gregory et al., 2004).

Thus, it would be foolish to dismiss all these books as shallow drivel. In fact, some of the better self-help books are highlighted in the Recommended Reading boxes that appear throughout this text. Unfortunately, however, the gems are easily lost in the mountains of rubbish. A great many self-help books offer little of real value to the reader. Generally, they suffer from three fundamental shortcomings.

A glance at bookstore shelves verifies that the boom in self-help books continues unabated, fueled by people's ongoing need for guidance and direction in their personal lives.

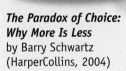

**The Paradox of Choice:
Why More Is Less**
by Barry Schwartz
(HarperCollins, 2004)

In *The Paradox of Choice,* Barry Schwartz argues that people in modern, affluent societies suffer a variety of negative consequences because they face an overabundance of choices in their personal lives (see p. 2). Schwartz recognizes that his argument seems counterintuitive, as most people cherish their freedom of choice. But he maintains that "the fact that *some* choice is good doesn't necessarily mean that *more* choice is better" (p. 3). In perhaps the most interesting part of the book, Schwartz outlines the differences between *maximizers* and *satisficers.* Maximizers need to feel confident that virtually every decision has yielded the best possible outcome. In contrast, satisficers are frequently willing to settle for outcomes that are good enough. He emphasizes that satisficers try to meet certain standards—sometimes very high standards—in making their decisions, but they do not feel compelled to select the *best* possible printer, mattress, vacation, and so forth. Although maximizing sounds like an admirable goal, Schwartz reports that high maximization scores are associated with reduced optimism and happiness and increased depression—and he raises doubts about whether maximizing tends to lead to better decisions.

Does Schwartz have a solution for the problem of excessive choice? Yes, his final chapter offers advice for making the overabundance of choices in our modern world less painful. Among other things, he suggests that people should (1) decide which choices really matter, (2) satisfice more and maximize less, (3) avoid rumination about decisions, (4) let go of decision regrets, and (5) recognize that constraints on choice can sometimes be liberating. Schwartz's writing is clear, concise, and engaging. The book is loaded with charming anecdotes that provide real-life examples of the issues discussed, but Schwartz's conclusions are based on research rather than anecdotal evidence. In the final analysis, *The Paradox of Choice* delivers an enticing two-for-one bargain: it is a thought-provoking essay in social criticism and a sound, realistic self-help book.

First, they are dominated by "psychobabble." The term *psychobabble,* coined by R. D. Rosen (1977), seems appropriate to describe the "hip" but hopelessly vague language used in many of these books. Statements such as "It's beautiful if you're unhappy," "You've got to get in touch with yourself," "You have to be up front," "You

gotta be you 'cause you're you," and "You need a real high-energy experience" are typical examples of this language. At best, such terminology is ill-defined; at worst, it is meaningless. Consider the following example, taken from a question/answer booklet promoting *est* training:

The EST training doesn't change the content of anyone's life, nor does it change what anyone knows. It deals with the context or the way we hold the content. . . . Transformation occurs as a recontextualization. . . . "Getting it" means being able to discover when you have been maintaining (or are stuck with) a position which costs you more in aliveness than it is worth, realizing that you are the source of that position, and being able to choose to give up that position or hold it in a way that expands the quality of your life.

What exactly does this paragraph say? Who knows? The statements are so ambiguous and enigmatic that you can read virtually any meaning into them. Therein lies the problem with psychobabble; it is often so obscure as to be unintelligible. Clarity is sacrificed in favor of a hip jargon that prevents, rather than enhances, effective communication.

A second problem is that self-help books tend to place more emphasis on sales than on scientific soundness. The advice offered in these books is far too rarely based on solid, scientific research (Ellis, 1993; Paul, 2001; Rosen, 1987). Instead, the ideas are frequently based on the authors' intuitive analyses, which may be highly speculative. Moreover, even when responsible authors provide scientifically valid advice and are careful not to mislead their readers, sales-hungry publishers often slap outrageous, irresponsible promises on the books' covers (much to the dismay of some authors).

The third shortcoming is that self-help books don't usually provide explicit directions about how to change your behavior. These books tend to be smoothly written and "touchingly human" in tone. They often strike responsive chords in the reader by aptly describing a common problem that many of us experience. The reader says, "Yes, that's me!" Unfortunately, when the book focuses on how to deal with the problem, it usu-

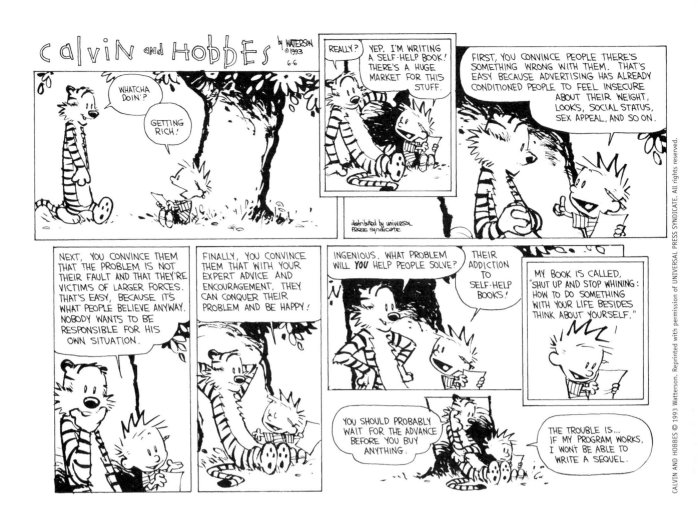

ally provides only a vague distillation of simple common sense, which could be covered in 2 rather than 200 pages. These books often fall back on inspirational cheerleading in the absence of sound, explicit advice.

What to Look for in Self-Help Books
Because self-help books vary so widely in quality, it seems a good idea to provide you with some guidelines about what to look for in seeking genuinely helpful books. The following thoughts give you some criteria for judging books of this type.

1. Clarity in communication is essential. Advice won't do you much good if you can't understand it. Try to avoid drowning in the murky depths of psychobabble.

2. This may sound backward, but look for books that do not promise too much in the way of immediate change. The truly useful books tend to be appropriately cautious in their promises and realistic about the challenge of altering your behavior.

3. Try to select books that mention, at least briefly, the theoretical or research basis for the program they advocate. It is understandable that you may not be interested in a detailed summary of research that supports a particular piece of advice. However, you should be interested in whether the advice is based on published research, widely accepted theory, anecdotal evidence, clinical interactions with patients, or pure speculation by the author. Books that are based on more than personal anecdotes and speculation should have a list of references in the back (or at the end of each chapter).

4. Look for books that provide detailed, explicit directions about how to alter your behavior. Generally, these directions represent the crucial core of the book. If they are inadequate in detail, you have been shortchanged.

5. More often than not, books that focus on a particular kind of problem, such as overeating, loneliness, or marital difficulties, deliver more than those that promise to cure all of life's problems with a few simple ideas. Books that cover everything are usually superficial and disappointing. Books that devote a great deal of thought to a particular topic tend to be written by authors with genuine expertise on that topic. Such books are more likely to pay off for you.

The Approach of This Textbook

Clearly, in spite of our impressive technological progress, we are a people beset by a great variety of personal problems. Living in our complex, modern society is a formidable challenge. This book is about that challenge. It is about you. It is about life. Specifically, it summarizes for you the scientific research on human behavior that appears relevant to the challenge of living effectively in contemporary society. It draws primarily, but not exclusively, from the science we call psychology.

This text deals with the same kinds of problems addressed by self-help books, self-realization programs, and Dr. Laura: anxiety, stress, interpersonal relationships, frustration, loneliness, depression, self-control. However, it makes no boldly seductive promises about solving your personal problems, turning your life around, or helping you achieve tranquility. Such promises simply aren't realistic. Psychologists have long rec-

ognized that changing a person's behavior is a difficult challenge, fraught with frustration and failure (Seligman, 1994). Troubled individuals sometimes spend years in therapy without resolving their problems.

This reality does not mean that you should be pessimistic about your potential for personal growth. You most certainly can change your behavior. Moreover, you can often change it on your own without consulting a professional psychologist. We would not be writing this text if we did not believe that some of our readers could derive some personal benefit from this encounter. But it is important that you have realistic expectations. Reading this book will not be a revelatory experience. No mysterious secrets are about to be unveiled. All this book can do is give you some potentially useful information and point you in some potentially beneficial directions. The rest is up to you.

In view of our criticisms of self-realization programs and self-help books, it seems essential that we explicitly lay out the philosophy that underlies the writing of this text. The following statements summarize the assumptions and goals of this book.

1. *This text is based on the premise that accurate knowledge about the principles of psychology can be of value to you in everyday life.* It has been said that knowledge is power. Greater awareness of why people behave as they do should help you in interacting with others as well as in trying to understand yourself.

2. *This text attempts to foster a critical attitude about psychological issues and to enhance your critical thinking skills.* Information is important, but people also need to develop effective strategies for evaluating information. Critical thinking involves subjecting ideas to systematic, skeptical scrutiny. Critical thinkers ask tough questions, such as: What exactly is being asserted? What assumptions underlie this assertion? What evidence or reasoning supports this assertion? Are there alternative explanations? Some general guidelines for thinking critically are outlined in Figure 1.1. We have already attempted to illustrate the importance of a critical attitude in our evaluation of self-help books, and we'll continue to model critical thinking strategies throughout the text.

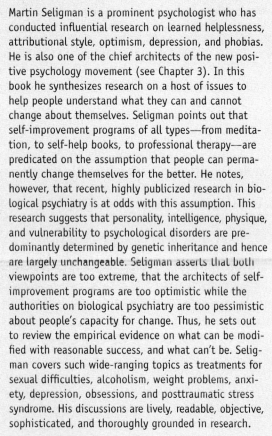

RECOMMENDED READING

What You Can Change and What You Can't
by Martin E. P. Seligman
(Knopf, 1994)

Martin Seligman is a prominent psychologist who has conducted influential research on learned helplessness, attributional style, optimism, depression, and phobias. He is also one of the chief architects of the new positive psychology movement (see Chapter 3). In this book he synthesizes research on a host of issues to help people understand what they can and cannot change about themselves. Seligman points out that self-improvement programs of all types—from meditation, to self-help books, to professional therapy—are predicated on the assumption that people can permanently change themselves for the better. He notes, however, that recent, highly publicized research in biological psychiatry is at odds with this assumption. This research suggests that personality, intelligence, physique, and vulnerability to psychological disorders are predominantly determined by genetic inheritance and hence are largely unchangeable. Seligman asserts that both viewpoints are too extreme, that the architects of self-improvement programs are too optimistic while the authorities on biological psychiatry are too pessimistic about people's capacity for change. Thus, he sets out to review the empirical evidence on what can be modified with reasonable success, and what can't be. Seligman covers such wide-ranging topics as treatments for sexual difficulties, alcoholism, weight problems, anxiety, depression, obsessions, and posttraumatic stress syndrome. His discussions are lively, readable, objective, sophisticated, and thoroughly grounded in research.

Cover copyright © 1994 Alfred A. Knopf, Inc. Reprinted by permission.

WEB LINK 1.3

Foundation for Critical Thinking
How can students best develop those skills that go beyond merely acquiring information to actively weighing and judging information? The many resources of the Foundation for Critical Thinking at Sonoma State University are directed primarily toward teachers at every level to help them develop their students' critical thinking abilities.

● FIGURE 1.1

Guidelines for Thinking Critically

1 Ask questions; be willing to wonder. To think critically you must be willing to think creatively—that is, to be curious about the puzzles of human behavior, to wonder why people act the way they do, and to question received explanations and examine new ones.

2 Define the problem. Identify the issues involved in clear and concrete terms, rather than vague generalities such as "happiness," "potential," or "meaningfulness." What does meaningfulness mean, exactly?

3 Examine the evidence. Consider the nature of the evidence that supports all aspects of the problem under examination. Is it reliable? Valid? Is it someone's personal assertion or speculation? Does the evidence come from one or two narrow studies, or from repeated research?

4 Analyze biases and assumptions—your own and those of others. What prejudices, deeply held values, and other personal biases do you bring to your evaluation of a problem? Are you willing to consider evidence that contradicts your beliefs? Be sure you can identify the bias of others, in order to evaluate their arguments as well.

5 Avoid emotional reasoning ("If I feel this way, it must be true"). Remember that everyone holds convictions and ideas about how the world should operate and that your opponents are as serious about their convictions as you are about yours. Feelings are important, but they should not substitute for careful appraisal of arguments and evidence.

6 Don't oversimplify. Look beyond the obvious. Reject simplistic, either-or thinking. Look for logical contradictions in arguments. Be wary of "arguments by anecdote."

7 Consider other interpretations. Before you leap to conclusions, think about other explanations. Be especially careful about assertions of cause and effect.

8 Tolerate uncertainty. This may be the hardest step in becoming a critical thinker, for it requires the ability to accept some guiding ideas and beliefs—yet the willingness to give them up when evidence and experience contradict them.

Guidelines for thinking critically. Critical thinking should not be equated with negative thinking; it's not a matter of learning how to tear down others' ideas. Rather, critical thinkers carefully subject others' ideas—and their own—to careful, systematic, objective evaluation. The guidelines shown here, taken from Wade and Tavris (1990), provide a succinct overview of what it means to think critically.

From Wade, C., & Tavris, C. (1990). *Learning to Think Critically: A Handbook to Accompany Psychology.* New York: Harper & Row. Copyright © 1990 by Harper & Row Publishers, Inc. Reprinted by permission of Pearson Education, Inc.

3. *This text should open doors.* The coverage in this book is broad; we tackle many topics. Therefore, in some places it may lack the depth or detail that you would like. However, you should think of it as a resource book that can introduce you to other books or techniques or therapies, which you can then pursue on your own.

4. *This text assumes that the key to effective adjustment is to take charge of your own life.* If you are dissatis-fied with some aspect of your life, it does no good to sit around and mope about it. You have to take an active role in attempting to improve the quality of your life. Doing so may involve learning a new skill or pursuing a particular kind of help. In any case, it is generally best to meet problems head-on rather than trying to avoid them.

The Psychology of Adjustment

LEARNING OBJECTIVES

■ *Describe the two key facets of psychology.*
■ *Explain the concept of adjustment.*

Now that we have spelled out our approach in writing this text, it is time to turn to the task of introducing you to some basic concepts. In this section, we'll discuss the nature of psychology and the concept of adjustment.

What Is Psychology?

Psychology **is the science that studies behavior and the physiological and mental processes that underlie it, and it is the profession that applies the accumulated knowledge of this science to practical problems.** Psychology leads a complex dual existence as both a *science*

and a *profession.* Let's examine the science first. Psychology is an area of scientific study, much like biology or physics. Whereas biology focuses on life processes and physics focuses on matter and energy, psychology focuses on *behavior* and *related mental and physiological processes.*

Psychology looks at behavior. ***Behavior* is any overt (observable) response or activity by an organism.** Psychology does *not* confine itself to the study of human behavior. Many psychologists believe that the principles of behavior are much the same for all animals, including humans. As a result, these psychologists often prefer to study animals—mainly because they can exert more control over the factors influencing the animals' behavior.

Psychology is also interested in the mental processes—the thoughts, feelings, and wishes—that accompany behavior. Mental processes are more difficult to study than behavior because they are private and not directly observable. However, they exert critical influence over human behavior, so psychologists have strived to improve their ability to "look inside the mind."

Finally, psychology includes the study of the physiological processes that underlie behavior. Thus, some psychologists try to figure out how bodily processes such as neural impulses, hormonal secretions, and genetic coding regulate behavior.

Practically speaking, all this means that psychologists study a great variety of phenomena. Psychologists are interested in maze running in rats, salivation in dogs, and brain functioning in cats, as well as visual perception in humans, play in children, and social interaction in adults.

As you probably know, psychology is not all pure science. It has a highly practical side, represented by the many psychologists who provide a variety of professional services to the public. Although the profession of psychology is quite prominent today, this aspect of psychology was actually slow to develop. Until the 1950s psychologists were found almost exclusively in the halls of academia, teaching and doing research. However, the demands of World War II in the 1940s stimulated rapid growth in psychology's first professional specialty—clinical psychology. *Clinical psychology* **is the branch of psychology concerned with the diagnosis and treatment of psychological problems and disorders.** During World War II, a multitude of academic psychologists were pressed into service as clinicians to screen military recruits and treat soldiers suffering from trauma. Many found their clinical work interesting and returned from the war to set up training programs to meet the continued high demand for clinical services. Soon, about half of the new Ph.D.'s in psychology were specializing in clinical work. Psychology had come of age as a profession.

What Is Adjustment?

We have used the term *adjustment* several times without clarifying its exact meaning. The concept of adjustment was originally borrowed from biology. It was modeled after the biological term *adaptation,* which refers to efforts by a species to adjust to changes in its environment. Just as a field mouse has to adapt to an unusually brutal winter, a person has to adjust to changes in circumstances such as a new job, a financial setback, or the loss of a loved one. Thus, *adjustment* **refers to the psychological processes through which people manage or cope with the demands and challenges of everyday life.**

The demands of everyday life are diverse, so in studying the process of adjustment we will encounter a broad variety of topics. In the first section of this book, "The Dynamics of Adjustment," we discuss general issues, such as how personality affects people's patterns of adjustment, how individuals are affected by stress, and how they use coping strategies to deal with stress. In the second section, "The Interpersonal Realm," we examine the adjustments that people make in their social relationships, exploring such topics as individuals' perceptions of others, interpersonal communication, behavior in groups, friendship, and intimate relationships. In the third section, "Developmental Transitions," we look at how individuals adjust to changing demands as they grow older. We discuss such topics as the development of gender roles, the emergence of sexuality, phases of adult development, and transitions in the world of work. Finally, in the fourth section, "Mental and Physical Health," we discuss how the process of adjustment influences a person's psychological and physical wellness.

As you can see, the study of adjustment delves into nearly every corner of people's lives, and we'll be discussing a diverse array of issues and topics. Before we begin considering these topics in earnest, however, we need to take a closer look at psychology's approach to investigating behavior—the scientific method.

The Scientific Approach to Behavior

LEARNING OBJECTIVES

- *Explain the nature of empiricism.*
- *Explain two advantages of the scientific approach to understanding behavior.*
- *Describe the experimental method, distinguishing between independent and dependent variables and between experimental and control groups.*

- *Distinguish between positive and negative correlation and explain what the size of a correlation coefficient means.*
- *Describe three correlational research methods.*
- *Compare the advantages and disadvantages of experimental versus correlational research.*

We all expend a great deal of effort in trying to understand our own behavior as well as the behavior of others. We wonder about any number of behavioral questions: Why am I so anxious when I interact with new people? Why is Sam always trying to be the center of attention at the office? Why does Joanna cheat on her wonderful husband? Are extraverts happier than introverts? Is depression more common during the Christmas holidays? Given that psychologists' principal goal is to explain behavior, how are their efforts different from everyone else's? The key difference is that psychology is a *science,* committed to *empiricism.*

The Commitment to Empiricism

Empiricism is the premise that knowledge should be acquired through observation. When we say that scientific psychology is empirical, we mean that its conclusions are based on systematic observation rather than on reasoning, speculation, traditional beliefs, or common sense. Scientists are not content with having ideas that sound plausible; they must conduct research to *test* their ideas. Whereas our everyday speculations are informal, unsystematic, and highly subjective, scientists' investigations are formal, systematic, and objective.

In these investigations, scientists formulate testable hypotheses, gather data (make observations) relevant to their hypotheses, use statistics to analyze these data, and report their results to the public and other scientists, typically by publishing their findings in a technical journal. The process of publishing scientific studies allows other experts to evaluate and critique new research findings.

Advantages of the Scientific Approach

Science is certainly not the only method that can be used to draw conclusions about behavior. We can also turn to logic, casual observation, and good old-fashioned common sense. Because the scientific method often requires painstaking effort, it seems reasonable to ask: What exactly are the advantages of the empirical approach?

The scientific approach offers two major advantages. The first is its clarity and precision. Common-sense notions about behavior tend to be vague and ambiguous. Consider the old truism "Spare the rod and spoil the child." What does this generalization about child-rearing amount to? How severely should children be punished if parents are not to "spare the rod"? How do parents assess whether a child qualifies as "spoiled"? Such statements can have different meanings to different people. When people disagree about this assertion, it may be because they are talking about entirely different things. In contrast, the empirical approach requires that scientists specify *exactly* what they are talking about when they formulate hypotheses. This clarity and precision enhance communication about important ideas.

The second advantage offered by the scientific approach is its relative intolerance of error. Scientists subject their ideas to empirical tests. They also scrutinize one another's findings with a critical eye. They demand objective data and thorough documentation before they accept ideas. When the findings of two studies conflict, they try to figure out why the studies reached different conclusions, usually by conducting additional research. In contrast, common sense and casual observation often tolerate contradictory generalizations, such as "Opposites attract" and "Birds of a feather flock together." Furthermore, commonsense analyses involve little effort to verify ideas or detect errors, so that many myths about behavior come to be widely believed.

All this is not to say that science has a copyright on truth. However, the scientific approach does tend to yield more accurate and dependable information than casual analyses and armchair speculation. Knowledge of empirical data can thus provide a useful benchmark against which to judge claims and information from other kinds of sources.

Now that we have an overview of how the scientific enterprise works, we can look at some of the specific research methods that psychologists depend on most. The two main types of research methods in psychology are *experimental* and *correlational.* We discuss them separately because there is an important distinction between them.

Experimental Research: Looking for Causes

Does misery love company? This question intrigued social psychologist Stanley Schachter. How does anxiety affect people's desire to be with others? When they feel anxious, do they want to be left alone, or do they prefer to have others around? Schachter's hypothesis was that increases in anxiety would cause increases in the desire to be with others, which psychologists call the *need for affiliation.* To test this hypothesis, Schachter (1959) designed a clever experiment. **The *experiment* is a research method in which the investigator manipulates one (independent) variable under carefully controlled conditions and observes whether any changes occur in a second (dependent) variable as a result.** Psychologists depend on this method more than any other.

Independent and Dependent Variables
An experiment is designed to find out whether changes in one variable (let's call it *x*) cause changes in another variable (let's call it *y*). To put it more concisely, we want to know how *x* affects *y*. In this formulation, we refer

to *x* as the independent variable, and we call *y* the dependent variable. **An *independent variable* is a condition or event that an experimenter varies in order to see its impact on another variable.** The independent variable is the variable that the experimenter controls or manipulates. It is hypothesized to have some effect on the dependent variable. The experiment is conducted to verify this effect. **The *dependent variable* is the variable that is thought to be affected by the manipulations of the independent variable.** In psychology studies, the dependent variable usually is a measurement of some aspect of the subjects' behavior.

In Schachter's experiment, *the independent variable was the participants' anxiety level,* which he manipulated in the following way. Subjects assembled in his laboratory were told by a Dr. Zilstein that they would be participating in a study on the physiological effects of electric shock and that they would receive a series of electric shocks. Half of the participants were warned that the shocks would be very painful. They made up the *high-anxiety* group. The other half of the participants, assigned to the *low-anxiety* group, were told that the shocks would be mild and painless. These procedures were simply intended to evoke different levels of anxiety. In reality, no one was actually shocked at any time. Instead, the experimenter indicated that there would be a delay while he prepared the shock apparatus for use. The participants were asked whether they would prefer to wait alone or in the company of others. *This measure of the subjects' desire to affiliate with others was the dependent variable.*

Experimental and Control Groups

To conduct an experiment, an investigator typically assembles two groups of participants who are treated differently in regard to the independent variable. We call these groups the experimental and control groups. **The *experimental group* consists of the subjects who receive some special treatment in regard to the independent variable. The *control group* consists of similar subjects who do not receive the special treatment given to the experimental group.**

Let's return to the Schachter study to illustrate. In this study, the participants in the high-anxiety condition were the experimental group. They received a special treatment designed to create an unusually high level of anxiety. The participants in the low-anxiety condition were the control group.

It is crucial that the experimental and control groups be similar except for the different treatment they receive in regard to the independent variable. This stipulation brings us to the logic that underlies the experimental method. If the two groups are alike in all respects *except for the variation created by the manipulation of the independent variable,* then any differences

WEB LINK 1.4

Research Methods Tutorials
Bill Trochim's classes in research and program design at Cornell University have assembled tutorial guides for undergraduate and graduate students for more than 50 topics at this subpage of the Web Center for Social Research Methods. Students new to research design may find these tutorials particularly helpful.

between the two groups on the dependent variable *must be due to this manipulation of the independent variable.* In this way researchers isolate the effect of the independent variable on the dependent variable. In his experiment, Schachter isolated the impact of anxiety on need for affiliation. What did he find? As predicted, he found that increased anxiety led to increased affiliation. The percentage of people who wanted to wait with others was nearly twice as high in the high-anxiety group as in the low-anxiety group.

The logic of the experimental method rests heavily on the assumption that the experimental and control groups are alike in all important matters except for their different treatment with regard to the independent variable. Any other differences between the two groups cloud the situation and make it difficult to draw solid conclusions about the relationship between the independent variable and the dependent variable. To summarize our discussion of the experimental method, Figure 1.2 provides an overview of the various elements in an experiment, using Schachter's study as an example.

Advantages and Disadvantages

The experiment is a powerful research method. Its principal advantage is that it allows scientists to draw conclusions about cause-and-effect relationships between variables. Researchers can draw these conclusions about causation because the precise control available in the experiment permits them to isolate the relationship between the independent variable and the dependent variable. No other research method can duplicate this advantage.

For all its power, however, the experimental method has its limitations. One disadvantage is that researchers are often interested in the effects of variables that cannot be manipulated (as independent variables) because of ethical concerns or practical realities. For example, you might want to know whether being brought up in an urban area as opposed to a rural area affects people's values. A true experiment would require you to assign similar families to live in urban and rural areas, which obviously is impossible to do. To explore this question, you would have to use correlational research methods, which we turn to next.

Correlational Research: Looking for Links

As we just noted, in some situations psychologists cannot exert experimental control over the variables they want to study. In such situations, all a researcher can do is make systematic observations to see whether a link or association exists between the variables of interest. Such an association is called a correlation. **A *correla-*** *tion* exists when two variables are related to each other. The definitive aspect of correlational studies is that the researchers cannot control the variables under study.

Measuring Correlation

The results of correlational research are often summarized with a statistic called the *correlation coefficient*. We'll be refering to this widely used statistic frequently as we discuss studies throughout the remainder of this text. **A *correlation coefficient* is a numerical index of the degree of relationship that exists between two variables.** A correlation coefficient indicates (1) how strongly related two variables are and (2) the direction (positive or negative) of the relationship.

Two *kinds* of relationships can be described by a correlation. A *positive* correlation indicates that two variables covary in the same direction. This means that high scores on variable *x* are associated with high scores on variable *y* and that low scores on variable *x* are associated with low scores on variable *y.* For example, there is a positive correlation between high school grade point average (GPA) and subsequent college GPA. That is, people who do well in high school tend to do well in college, and those who perform poorly in high school tend to perform poorly in college (see Figure 1.3 on the next page).

In contrast, a *negative* correlation indicates that two variables covary in the opposite direction. This means that people who score high on variable *x* tend to score low on variable *y*, whereas those who score low on *x* tend to score high on *y*. For example, in most college courses, there is a negative correlation between how frequently a student is absent and how well the student performs on exams. Students who have a high number of absences tend to earn low exam scores, while students who have a low number of absences tend to get higher exam scores (see Figure 1.3).

While the positive or negative sign indicates whether an association is direct or inverse, the *size* of the coefficient indicates the *strength* of the association between two variables. A correlation coefficient can vary between 0 and +1.00 (if positive) or between 0 and −1.00 (if negative). A coefficient near zero tells us there is no relationship between the variables. The closer the correlation to either −1.00 or +1.00, the stronger the relationship. Thus, a correla-

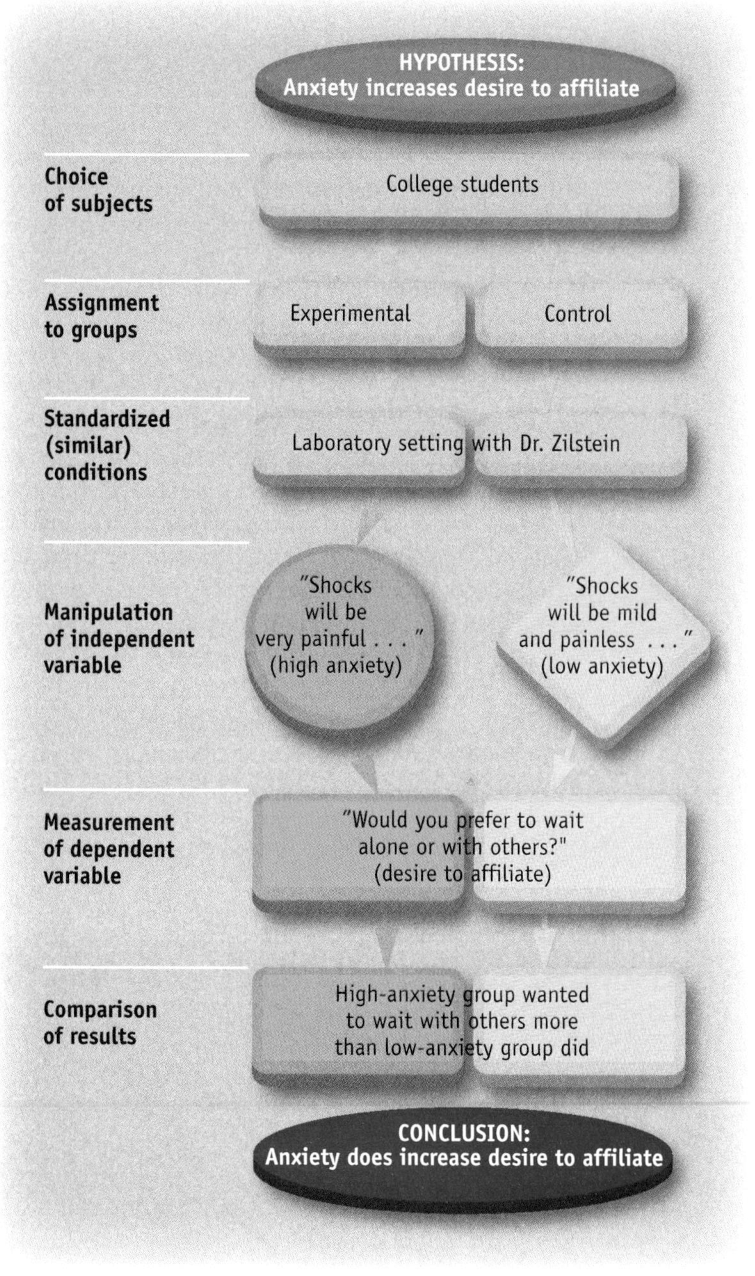

● FIGURE 1.2

The basic elements of an experiment. This diagram provides an overview of the key features of the experimental method, as illustrated by Schachter's study of anxiety and affiliation. The logic of the experiment rests on treating the experimental and control groups alike except for the manipulation of the independent variable.

Positive and negative correlations. Variables are positively correlated if they tend to increase and decrease together and are negatively correlated if one variable tends to increase when the other decreases. Hence, the terms *positive correlation* and *negative correlation* refer to the *direction* of the relationship between two variables.

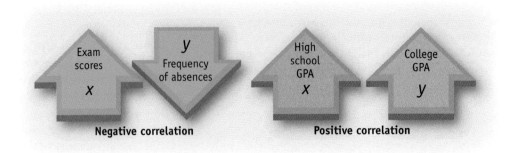

tion of +.90 represents a stronger tendency for variables to be associated than a correlation of −.40 does (see Figure 1.4). Likewise, a correlation of −.75 represents a stronger relationship than a correlation of −.45. Keep in mind that the *strength* of a correlation depends only on the size of the coefficient. The positive or negative sign simply shows whether the correlation is direct or inverse. Therefore, a correlation of −.60 reflects a stronger relationship than a correlation of +.30.

Correlational research methods comprise a number of approaches, including naturalistic observation, case studies, and surveys. Let's examine each of these to see how researchers use them to detect associations between variables.

Naturalistic Observation

In *naturalistic observation* a researcher engages in careful observation of behavior without intervening directly with the subjects. This type of research is called

naturalistic because behavior is allowed to unfold naturally (without interference) in its natural environment—that is, the setting in which it would normally occur.

As an example, consider a study by Stoffer, Davis, and Brown (1977), which sought to determine whether it is a good idea for students to reconsider and change answers on multiple-choice tests. The conventional wisdom is that "your first hunch is your best hunch," and it is widely believed that students should not go back and change their answers. To put this idea to an empirical test, Stoffer and his colleagues studied the answer changes made by college students on their regular exams in a psychology course. They simply examined students' answer sheets for evidence of response changes, such as erasures or crossing out of responses. As Figure 1.5 shows, they found that changes that went from a wrong answer to a right answer outnumbered changes that went from a right answer to a wrong answer by a mar-

Interpreting correlation coefficients. The magnitude of a correlation coefficient indicates the strength of the relationship between two variables. The closer a correlation is to either +1.00 or −1.00, the stronger the relationship between the variables. The square of a correlation, which is called the coefficient of determination, is an index of a correlation's strength and predictive power.

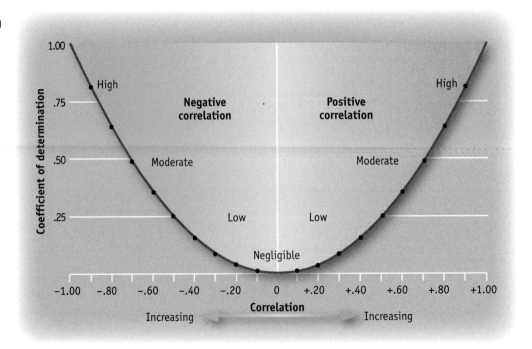

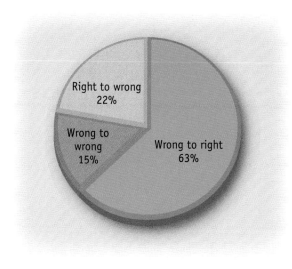

● FIGURE 1.5

The effects of answer changing on multiple-choice exams.
In a study of answer changes, Stoffer et al. (1977) found that wrong-to-right changes outnumbered right-to-wrong changes by a sizable margin. These results are similar to those of other studies on this issue.

gin of nearly 3 to 1! The correlation between the number of changes students made and their net gain from answer changing was +.49, indicating that the more answer changing students engaged in, the more they improved their scores. These results, which have been replicated in a number of other studies (Benjamin, Cavell, & Shallenberger, 1984), show that popular beliefs about the harmful effects of answer changing are inaccurate.

Case Studies

A *case study* is an in-depth investigation of an individual participant. Psychologists typically assemble case studies in clinical settings where an effort is being made to diagnose and treat some psychological problem. To achieve an understanding of an individual, a clinician may use a variety of procedures, including interviewing the person, interviewing others who know the individual, direct observation, examination of records, and psychological testing. Usually, a single case study does not provide much basis for deriving general laws of behavior. If researchers have a number of case studies available, however, they can look for threads of consistency among them, and they may be able to draw some general conclusions.

This was the strategy used by a research team (Farina et al., 1986) that studied psychiatric patients' readjustment to their community after their release from a mental hospital. The researchers wanted to know whether the patients' physical attractiveness was related to their success in readjustment. As we'll discuss in upcoming chapters, good-looking people tend to be treated more nicely by others than homely people are, suggesting that attractive patients may have an easier time adjusting to life outside the hospital. To find out, the research team compiled case history data (and ratings of physical attractiveness) for patients just before their discharge from a mental hospital and six months later. A modest positive correlation (.38) was found between patients' attractiveness and their postdischarge social adjustment. Thus, the better-looking patients were better off, suggesting that physical attractiveness plays a role in psychiatric patients' readjustment to community living.

Surveys

Surveys are structured questionnaires designed to solicit information about specific aspects of participants' behavior. They are sometimes used to measure dependent variables in experiments, but they are mainly used in correlational research. Surveys are commonly used to gather data on people's attitudes and on aspects of behavior that are difficult to observe directly (marital interactions, for instance). As an example, consider a study by Alvin Cooper and his colleagues (1999) which examined people's Internet sexual pursuits. Cooper and his associates gathered data from an online questionnaire that was posted for seven weeks at the MSNBC website. The final sample consisted of 9,177 anonymous volunteers. The self-selected sample clearly was not representative of the general adult population in the United States, but the participants' demographic data suggested that they *were* reasonably representative of that portion of the population that visits sexually explicit websites.

What did the survey reveal? Male respondents outnumbered female respondents by about 6 to 1. Men reported mostly going to sites that featured visual erotica, whereas women were more likely to visit sexually themed chat rooms. Only 8–9 percent of the respondents reported spending more than 10 hours per week in online sexual pursuits (see Figure 1.6 on the next page). Although 87 percent of the subjects indicated that they never felt guilty about their behavior, 70 percent admitted keeping the extent of their online sexual activities secret from others. Among "heavy users" of Internet sex sites (more than 10 hours per week), about

WEB LINK 1.5

American Psychological Association (APA)
As the largest professional organization of psychologists, the APA continually publicizes the latest research findings for most topics discussed in this textbook. Students should consider using the excellent search engines at the APA's online site when looking for leads to new scientific research on adjustment issues.

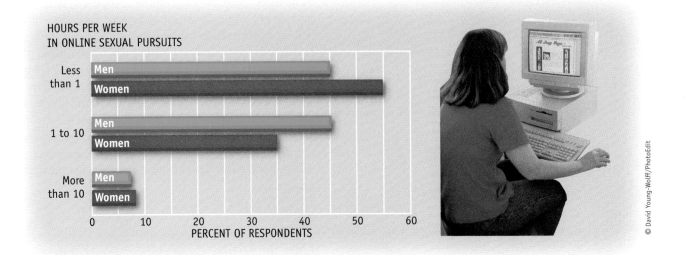

HOURS PER WEEK
IN ONLINE SEXUAL PURSUITS

● FIGURE 1.6

Time devoted to Internet sexual pursuits. In the online survey conducted by Cooper and his colleagues (1999), over 9,000 respondents provided information on how much time they spend weekly visiting sexually oriented websites. As you can see, the vast majority of participants reported that they spend 10 hours or less each week in online sexual pursuits. (Based on Cooper et al., 1999)

one-half admitted that their online activities were interfering with their lives. The authors conclude that "the vast majority of online users generally seem to use Internet sexual venues in casual ways that may not be problematic," but they emphasize that heavy users may be at risk for psychological difficulties.

Advantages and Disadvantages

Correlational research methods give psychologists a way to explore questions that they could not examine with experimental procedures. Consider the study of the association between attractiveness and adjustment in psychiatric patients. Obviously, Farina et al. (1986) could not manipulate the physical attractiveness of their subjects. But correlational methods allowed them to gather useful information on whether a link exists between attractiveness and adjustment. Thus, *correlational research broadens the scope of phenomena that psychologists can study.*

Unfortunately, correlational methods have one major disadvantage. The investigator does not have the opportunity to control events in a way to isolate cause and effect. *Consequently, correlational research cannot demonstrate conclusively that two variables are causally related.* The crux of the problem is that correlation is no assurance of causation.

When we find that variables x and y are correlated, we can safely conclude only that x and y are related. We do not know *how* x and y are related. We do not know whether x causes y, whether y causes x, or whether both are caused by a third variable. For example, survey studies show a positive correlation between marital satisfaction and sexual satisfaction (Hunt, 1974; Christopher & Sprecher, 2000). Although it's clear that good sex and

● FIGURE 1.7

Possible causal relations between correlated variables. When two variables are correlated, there are several possible explanations. It could be that x causes y, that y causes x, or that a third variable, z, causes changes in both x and y. As the correlation between marital satisfaction and sexual satisfaction illustrates, the correlation itself does not provide the answer.

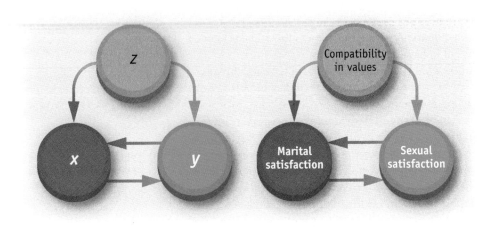

a healthy marriage go hand in hand, it's hard to tell what's causing what. We don't know whether healthy marriages promote good sex or whether good sex promotes healthy marriages. Moreover, we can't rule out the possibility that both are caused by a third variable. Perhaps sexual satisfaction and marital satisfaction are both caused by compatibility in values. The plausible

causal relationships in this case are diagrammed for you in Figure 1.7, which illustrates the "third-variable problem" in interpreting correlations. This problem occurs frequently in correlational research. Indeed, it will surface in the next section, where we review the empirical research on the determinants of happiness.

The Roots of Happiness: An Empirical Analysis

LEARNING OBJECTIVES

- Discuss the prevalence of reported happiness in modern society.
- List the various factors that are surprisingly unrelated to happiness.
- Explain how health, social activity, and religion are related to happiness.

- Discuss how love, work, and personality are related to happiness.
- Summarize the conclusions drawn about the determinants of happiness.

What exactly makes a person happy? This question has been the subject of much speculation. Commonsense hypotheses about the roots of happiness abound. For example, you have no doubt heard that money cannot buy happiness. But do you believe it? A television commercial says, "If you've got your health, you've got just about everything." Is health indeed the key? What if you're healthy but poor, unemployed, and lonely? We often hear about the joys of parenthood, the joys of youth, and the joys of the simple, rural life. Are these the factors that promote happiness?

In recent years, social scientists have begun putting these and other hypotheses to empirical test. Quite a number of survey studies have been conducted to explore the determinants of **subjective well-being—individuals' personal assessments of their overall happiness or life satisfaction.** The findings of these studies are quite interesting. We review this research because it is central to the topic of adjustment and because it illustrates the value of collecting data and putting ideas to an empirical test. As you will see, many commonsense notions about happiness appear to be inaccurate.

The first of these is the apparently widespread assumption that most people are relatively unhappy. Writers, social scientists, and the general public seem to believe that people around the world are predominantly dissatisfied, yet empirical surveys consistently find that the vast majority of respondents—even those who are poor or disabled—characterize themselves as fairly happy (Diener & Diener, 1996). When people are asked to rate their happiness, only a small minority place

themselves below the neutral point on the various scales used (see Figure 1.8). When the average subjective well-being of entire nations is computed, based on almost 1000 surveys, the means cluster toward the positive end of the scale, as shown in Figure 1.9 on the next page (Veenhoven, 1993). That's not to say that everyone is equally happy. Researchers have found substantial and

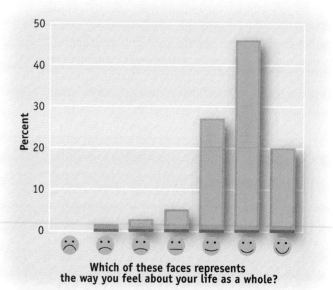

(● FIGURE 1.8)

Measuring happiness with a nonverbal scale. Researchers have used a variety of methods to estimate the distribution of happiness. For example, in one study in the United States, respondents were asked to examine the seven facial expressions shown and to select the one that "comes closest to expressing how you feel about your life as a whole." As you can see, the vast majority of participants chose happy faces. (Data adapted from Myers, 1992)

thought-provoking disparities among people in subjective well-being, which we will analyze momentarily. But the overall picture seems rosier than anticipated.

What Isn't Very Important?

Let us begin our discussion of individual differences in happiness by highlighting those things that turn out to be relatively unimportant determinants of subjective well-being. Quite a number of factors that one might expect to be influential appear to bear little or no relationship to general happiness.

Money. There *is* a positive correlation between income and subjective feelings of happiness, but the association is surprisingly weak (Diener & Seligman, 2004). For example, one study found a correlation of just .13 between income and happiness in the United States (Diener et al., 1993). Admittedly, being very poor can make people unhappy, but once people ascend above the poverty level, there is little relation between income and happiness. On the average, even wealthy people are only marginally happier than those in the middle classes. The problem with money is that in this era of voracious consumption, rising income contributes to escalating material desires (Frey & Stutzer, 2002). When these growing material desires outstrip what people can afford, dissatisfaction is likely (Solberg et al., 2002). Thus, complaints about not having enough money are routine even among people who earn hefty six-figure incomes. Interestingly, there is some evidence that people who place an especially strong emphasis on the pursuit of wealth and materialistic goals tend to be somewhat less happy than others (Ryan & Deci, 2001). Perhaps they are so focused on financial success that they don't derive much satisfaction from their family life (Nickerson et al, 2003).

Age. Age and happiness are consistently found to be unrelated. Age accounts for less than 1 percent of the variation in people's happiness (Inglehart, 1990; Myers & Diener, 1997). The key factors influencing subjective well-being may shift some as people grow older—work becomes less important, health more so—but people's average level of happiness tends to remain remarkably stable over the life span.

Gender. Women are treated for depressive disorders about twice as often as men, so one might expect that women are less happy on the average. However, like age, gender accounts for less than 1 percent of the variation in people's subjective well-being (Myers, 1992).

Parenthood. Children can be a tremendous source of joy and fulfillment, but they can also be a tremendous

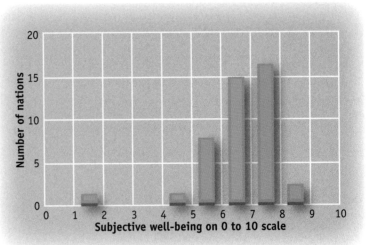

● FIGURE 1.9

The subjective well-being of nations. Veenhoven (1993) combined the results of almost 1000 surveys to calculate the average subjective well-being reported by representative samples from 43 nations. The mean happiness scores clearly pile up at the positive end of the distribution, with only two scores falling below the neutral point of 5. (Data adapted from Diener and Diener, 1996)

source of headaches and hassles. Compared to childless couples, parents worry more and experience more marital problems (Argyle, 1987). Apparently, the good and bad aspects of parenthood balance each other out, because the evidence indicates that people who have children are neither more nor less happy than people without children (Argyle, 2001).

Intelligence. Intelligence is a highly valued trait in modern society, but researchers have not found an association between IQ scores and happiness (Diener, 1984). Educational attainment also appears to be unrelated to life satisfaction (Ross & Van Willigen, 1997).

Physical attractiveness. Good-looking people enjoy a variety of advantages in comparison to unattractive people. Given that physical attractiveness is an important resource in Western society, we might expect attractive people to be happier than others, but the available data indicate that the correlation between attractiveness and happiness is negligible (Diener, Wolsic, & Fujita, 1995).

What Is Somewhat Important?

Research has identified three facets of life that appear to have a moderate impact on subjective well-being: health, social activity, and religious belief.

Health. Good physical health would seem to be an essential requirement for happiness, but people adapt to health problems. Research reveals that individuals who develop serious, disabling health conditions aren't as unhappy as one might guess (Myers, 1992). Good health may not, by itself, produce happiness, because people tend to take good health for granted. Such considerations may help explain why researchers find only a moderate positive correlation (average = .32) between health status and subjective well-being (Argyle, 1999).

Social activity.   Humans are social animals, and people's interpersonal relations *do* appear to contribute to their happiness. People who are satisfied with their friendship networks and who are socially active report above-average levels of happiness (Diener & Seligman, 2004; Myers, 1999). And people who are exceptionally happy tend to report greater satisfaction with their social relations than others (Diener & Seligman, 2002).

Religion.   The link between religiosity and subjective well-being is modest, but a number of surveys suggest that people with heartfelt religious convictions are more likely to be happy than people who characterize themselves as nonreligious (Argyle, 1999; Ferris, 2002). Researchers aren't sure how religious faith fosters happiness, but Myers (1992) offers some interesting conjectures. Among other things, he discusses how religion can give people a sense of purpose and meaning in their lives, help them accept their setbacks gracefully, connect them to a caring, supportive community, and comfort them by putting their ultimate mortality in perspective.

What Is Very Important?

The list of factors that turn out to be very important ingredients of happiness is surprisingly short. Only a few variables are strongly related to overall happiness.

Love and marriage.   Romantic relationships can be stressful, but people consistently rate being in love as one of the most critical ingredients of happiness (Myers, 1999). Furthermore, although people complain a lot about their marriages, the evidence indicates that marital status is a key correlate of happiness. Among both men and women, married people are happier than people who are single or divorced (see Figure 1.10 on the next page; Myers & Diener, 1995) and this relationship holds around the world in widely different cultures (Diener et al., 2000). However, the causal relations underlying this correlation are unclear. It may be that happiness causes marital satisfaction more than marital satisfaction promotes happiness. Perhaps people who are happy tend to have better intimate relationships and more stable marriages, while people who are unhappy have greater difficulty finding and keeping mates.

Work.   Given the way people often complain about their jobs, we might not expect work to be a key source of happiness, but it is. Although less critical than love and marriage, job satisfaction is strongly associated with general happiness (Warr, 1999). Studies also show that unemployment has very negative effects on subjective well-being (Lucas et al., 2004). It is difficult to sort out whether job satisfaction causes happiness or vice versa, but evidence suggests that causation flows both ways (Argyle, 2001).

Personality.   The best predictor of individuals' future happiness is their past happiness (Diener & Lucas, 1999). Some people seem destined to be happy and others unhappy, regardless of their triumphs or setbacks. The limited influence of life events was apparent in a stunning study that found only marginal differences

● FIGURE 1.10

Happiness and marital status. This graph shows the percentage of adults characterizing themselves as "Very happy" as a function of marital status. Among both women and men, happiness shows up more in those who are married, as opposed to those who are separated, who are divorced, or who have never married. These data and many other findings suggest that marital satisfaction is a key ingredient of happiness.

Adapted from Myers, D. G. (1999). Close relationships and quality of life. In D. Kahneman, E. Diener, & N. Schwarz (Eds.), *Well-being: The foundations of hedonic psychology.* New York: Russell Sage Foundation. Copyright © 1999. Reprinted by permission of the Russell Sage Foundation.

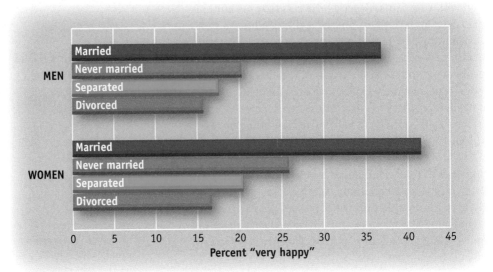

in overall happiness between recent lottery winners and recent accident victims who became quadriplegics (Brickman, Coates, & Janoff-Bulman, 1978). Investigators were amazed that extremely fortuitous and horrible events like these didn't have a dramatic impact on happiness. Actually, *several* lines of evidence suggest that happiness does not depend on external circumstances—buying a nice house, getting promoted—as much as on internal factors, such as one's outlook on life (Lykken & Tellegen, 1996). With this reality in mind, researchers have begun to look for links between personality and subjective well-being, and they have found some rela-

tively strong correlations. For example, *extraversion* (sometimes referred to as *positive emotionality*) is one of the better predictors of happiness. People who are outgoing, upbeat, and sociable tend to be happier than others (Fleeson, Malanos, & Achille, 2002). Additional personality correlates of happiness include self-esteem and optimism (Lucas, Diener, & Suh, 1996).

Conclusions

We must be cautious in drawing inferences about the causes of happiness, because most of the available data are correlational data (see Figure 1.11). Nonetheless, the empirical evidence suggests that many popular beliefs about the sources of happiness are unfounded. The data also demonstrate that happiness is shaped by a complex constellation of variables. Despite this complexity, however, a number of worthwhile insights about human adjustment can be gleaned from research on the correlates of subjective well-being.

First, research on happiness demonstrates that the determinants of subjective well-being are precisely that: subjective. *Objective realities are not as important as subjective feelings.* In other words, your health, your wealth, your job, and your age are not as influential as how you feel about your health, wealth, job, and age (Schwarz & Strack, 1999).

Second, *when it comes to happiness everything is relative* (Argyle, 1999; Hagerty, 2000). In other words, you evaluate what you have relative to what the people around you have. Thus, people who are wealthy assess what they have by comparing themselves with their wealthy friends and neighbors. This is one reason for the low correlation between wealth and happiness. You

Research shows that happiness does not depend on people's positive and negative experiences as much as one would expect. Some people, presumably because of their personality, seem destined to be happy in spite of major setbacks, and others seem destined to cling to unhappiness even though their lives seem reasonably pleasant.

Research on the correlates of happiness suggests that two key ingredients of happiness are a rewarding work life and satisfaction in intimate relationships.

might have a lovely home, but if it sits next to a neighbor's palatial mansion, it might be a source of more dissatisfaction than happiness. People's evaluations are also made relative to their *expectations*. Research suggests that bad outcomes feel worse when unexpected, than when expected, while good outcomes feel better when unexpected than when expected (Shepperd & McNulty, 2002). Thus, the same objective event, such as a pay raise of $2000 annually, may generate positive feelings in someone who wasn't expecting a raise and negative feelings in someone expecting a much larger increase in salary.

Third, *research on subjective well-being indicates that people often adapt to their circumstances*. This adaptation effect is one reason that an increase in income doesn't necessarily bring an increase in happiness. Thus, *hedonic adaptation* occurs when the mental scale that people use to judge the pleasantness-unpleasantness of their experiences shifts so that their neutral point, or baseline for comparison, is changed. Unfortunately, when people's experiences improve, hedonic adaptation may *sometimes* put them on a *hedonic treadmill*—their neutral point moves upward, so that the improvements yield no real benefits (Kahneman, 1999). However, when people have to grapple with major setbacks, hedonic adaptation probably helps protect their mental and physical health. For example, people who are sent to prison and people who develop debilitating diseases are not as unhappy as one might assume because they adapt to their changed situations and evaluate events from a new perspective (Frederick & Loewenstein, 1999). That's not to say that hedonic adaptation in the face of life's difficulties is inevitable or complete (Lucas et al., 2003). People who suffer major setbacks, such as the death of a spouse or serious illness, often are not as happy as they were before the setback, but generally they are not nearly as unhappy as they or others would have predicted.

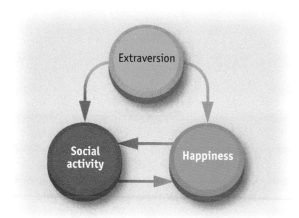

● FIGURE 1.11

Possible causal relations among the correlates of happiness. Although we have considerable data on the correlates of happiness, it is difficult to untangle the possible causal relationships. For example, we know that a moderate positive correlation exists between social activity and happiness, but we can't say for sure whether high social activity causes happiness or whether happiness causes people to be more socially active. Moreover, in light of the finding that a third variable—extraversion—correlates with both variables, we have to consider the possibility that extraversion causes both greater social activity and greater happiness.

Improving Academic Performance

LEARNING OBJECTIVES

- List three steps for developing sound study habits.
- Describe the SQ3R method of effective reading.
- Summarize advice on how to get more out of lectures.
- Summarize how memory is influenced by practice, interference, depth of processing, and organization.
- Describe several verbal and visual mnemonic devices.

Answer the following "true" or "false."

__F__ **1.** If you have a professor who delivers chaotic, hard-to-follow lectures, there is little point in attending class.

__F__ **2.** Cramming the night before an exam is an efficient way to study.

__F__ **3.** In taking lecture notes, you should try to be a "human tape recorder" (that is, take down everything exactly as said by your professor).

__F__ **4.** Outlining reading assignments is a waste of time.

As you will soon learn, all of these statements are false. If you answered them all correctly, you may already have acquired the kinds of skills and habits that lead to academic success. If so, however, you are not typical. Today, a huge number of students enter college with remarkably poor study skills and habits—and it's not entirely their fault. The U.S. educational system generally does not provide much in the way of formal instruction on good study techniques. In this first Application, we will try to remedy this deficiency to some extent by sharing some insights that psychology can provide on how to improve your academic performance. We will discuss how to promote better study habits, how to enhance reading efforts, how to get more out of lectures, and how to make your memory more effective.

Developing Sound Study Habits

Effective study is crucial to success in college. You may run into a few classmates who boast about getting good grades without studying, but you can be sure that if they perform well on exams, they study. Students who claim otherwise simply want to be viewed as extremely bright rather than as studious.

Learning can be immensely gratifying, but studying usually involves hard work. The first step toward effective study habits is to face this reality. You don't have to feel guilty if you don't look forward to studying. Most students don't. Once you accept the premise that studying doesn't come naturally, it should be clear that you need to set up an organized program to promote adequate study. Such a program should include the following three considerations (Siebert, 1995).

Set up a schedule for studying. If you wait until the urge to study hits you, you may still be waiting when the exam rolls around. Thus, it is important to allocate definite times to studying. Review your time obligations (work, housekeeping, and so on) and figure out in advance when you can study. In allotting certain times to studying, keep in mind that you need to be wide awake and alert. Be realistic, too, about how long you can study at one time before you wear down from fatigue. Allow time for study breaks; they can revive sagging concentration.

It's important to write down your study schedule. Doing so serves as a reminder and increases your commitment to the schedule. As shown in Figure 1.12, you should begin by setting up a general schedule for the quarter or semester. Then, at the beginning of each week, plan the specific assignments that you intend to work on during each study session. This approach should help you to avoid cramming for exams at the last minute.

In planning your weekly schedule, try to avoid the tendency to put off working on major tasks such as term papers and reports. Time management experts such as Alan Lakein (1996) point out that many of us tend to tackle simple, routine tasks first, saving larger tasks for later, when we supposedly will have more time. This common tendency leads many of us to delay working on major assignments until it's too late to do a good job. You can avoid this trap by breaking major assignments into smaller component tasks that you schedule individually.

Find a place to study where you can concentrate. Where you study is also important. The key is to find a place where distractions are likely to be minimal. Most people cannot study effectively while watching TV, listening to loud music, or overhearing conversations.

Don't depend on willpower to carry you through these distractions. It's much easier to plan ahead and avoid the distractions altogether.

Reward your studying. One of the reasons it is so difficult to motivate oneself to study regularly is that the payoffs for studying often lie in the distant future. The ultimate reward, a degree, may be years away. Even shorter-term rewards, such as an A in the course, may be weeks or months off. To combat this problem, it helps to give yourself immediate rewards for studying. It is easier to motivate yourself to study if you reward yourself with a tangible payoff, such as a snack, TV show, or phone call to a friend, when you finish. Thus, you should set realistic study goals and then reward yourself when you meet them. This systematic manipulation of rewards involves harnessing the principles of *behavior modification,* which are described in some detail in the Chapter 4 Application.

Improving Your Reading

Much of your study time is spent reading and absorbing information. *These efforts must be active.* If you engage in passive reading, the information will pass right through you. Many students deceive themselves into thinking that they are studying if they run a marker through a few sentences here and there in their text. If such highlighting isn't done with thoughtful selectivity, the student is simply turning a textbook into a coloring book. Research suggests that highlighting selected textbook material *is* a useful strategy—if students are reasonably effective in identifying the main ideas in the material and if they subsequently review the main ideas they have highlighted (Caverly, Orlando, & Mullen, 2000).

You can choose from a number of methods for actively attacking your reading assignments. One of the more worthwhile strategies is Robinson's (1970) SQ3R method. **SQ3R is a study system designed to promote effective reading that includes five steps: survey, question, read, recite, and review.** Its name is an abbreviation for the five steps in the procedure:

Step 1: Survey
Before you plunge into the actual reading, glance over the topic headings in the chapter and try to get an overview of the material. Try to understand how the various chapter segments are related. If there is a chapter outline or summary, consult it to get a feel for the chapter. If you know where the chapter is

going, you can better appreciate and organize the information you are about to read.

Step 2: Question
Once you have an overview of your reading assignment, proceed through it one section at a time. Take a look at the heading of the first section and convert it into a question. This is usually quite simple. If the heading is "prenatal risk factors," your question should be "what are sources of risk during prenatal development?" If the heading is "stereotyping," your question should be "what is stereotyping?" Asking these questions gets you actively involved in your reading and helps you identify the main ideas.

Step 3: Read
Only now, in the third step, are you ready to sink your teeth into the reading. Read only the specific section that you have decided to tackle. Read it with an eye toward

● FIGURE 1.12

Example of an activity schedule. One student's general activity schedule for a semester is shown here. Each week the student fills in the specific assignments to work on during the upcoming study sessions.

	Mon	Tues	Wed	Thurs	Fri	Sat	Sun
8 A.M.						Work	
9 A.M.	History	Study	History	Study	History	Work	
10 A.M.	Psych		Psych		Psych	Work	
11 A.M.	Study	French	Study	French	Study	Work	
Noon	Math	Study	Math	Study	Math	Work	Study
1 P.M.							Study
2 P.M.	Study		Study		Study		Study
3 P.M.	Study	English	Study	English	Study		Study
4 P.M.							
5 P.M.							
6 P.M.	Work	Study	Work				Study
7 P.M.	Work	Study	Work				Study
8 P.M.	Work	Study	Work				Study
9 P.M.	Work	Study	Work				Study
10 P.M.	Work		Work				

Although some students downplay the importance of study efforts, the reality is that effective study habits are crucial to academic success.

answering the question that you just formulated. If necessary, reread the section until you can answer that question. Decide whether the segment addresses any other important questions and answer them as well.

Step 4: Recite

Now that you can answer the key question for the section, recite it out loud to yourself. Use your own words for the answer, because that requires understanding instead of simple memorization. Don't move on to the next section until you understand the main idea(s) of the current section. You may want to write down these ideas for review later. When you have fully digested the first section, go on to the next. Repeat steps 2 through 4 with the next section. Once you have mastered the crucial points there, you can continue. Keep repeating steps 2 through 4, section by section, until you finish the chapter.

Step 5: Review

When you have read the chapter, test and refresh your memory by going back over the key points. Repeat your

questions and try to answer them without consulting your book or notes. This review should fortify your retention of the main ideas and alert you to any key ideas that you haven't mastered. It should also help you to see the relationships between the main ideas.

The SQ3R method does not have to be applied rigidly. For example, it is often wise to break your reading assignment into smaller segments than those separated by section headings. In fact, you should probably apply SQ3R to many texts on a paragraph by paragraph basis. Obviously, doing so will require you to formulate some questions without the benefit of topic headings. However, the headings are not absolutely necessary to use this technique. If you don't have enough headings, you can simply reverse the order of steps 2 and 3. Read the paragraph first and then formulate a question that addresses the basic idea of the paragraph. The point is that you can be flexible in your use of the SQ3R technique.

Using the SQ3R method does not automatically lead to improved mastery of textbook reading assignments. It won't be effective unless it is applied diligently and skillfully and it tends to be more helpful to students with low to medium reading ability (Caverly, Orlando, & Mullen, 2000). Any strategy that facilitates active processing of text material, the identification of key ideas, and effective review of these ideas should enhance your reading.

Getting More Out of Lectures

Although lectures are sometimes boring and tedious, it is a simple fact that poor class attendance is associated with poor grades. For example, in one study, Lindgren (1969) found that absences from class were much more common among "unsuccessful" students (grade average of C− or below) than among "successful" students (grade average of B or above), as is shown in Figure 1.13. Even when you have an instructor who delivers hard-to-follow lectures from which you learn virtually nothing, it is still important to go to class. If nothing else, you'll get a feel for how the instructor thinks. Doing so can help you anticipate the content of exams and respond in the manner your professor expects.

Fortunately, most lectures are reasonably coherent. Studies indicate that attentive note taking *is* associated with enhanced learning and performance in college classes (Cohn, Cohn, & Bradley, 1995; O'Donnell & Dansereau, 1993). However, research also shows that many students' lecture notes are surprisingly incomplete, with the average student often recording less than 40 percent of the crucial ideas in a lecture (Armbruster, 2000). Thus, the key to getting more out of lectures is to stay motivated, stay attentive, and expend

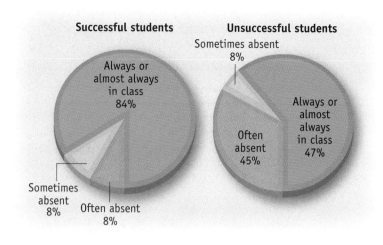

Successful students

Always or almost always in class 84%

Sometimes absent 8%

Often absent 8%

Unsuccessful students

Sometimes absent 8%

Always or almost always in class 47%

Often absent 45%

● FIGURE 1.13

Successful and unsuccessful students' class attendance. Lindgren (1969) found that attendance was much better among successful students than unsuccessful students. (Data from Lindgren, 1969.)

the effort to make your notes as complete as possible. Books on study skills (Longman & Atkinson, 2002; Sotiriou, 2002) offer a number of suggestions on how to take good-quality lecture notes. These suggestions include:

■ Use *active listening procedures*. With active listening, you focus full attention on the speaker. Try to anticipate what's coming and search for deeper meanings. Pay attention to nonverbal signals that may serve to further clarify the lecturer's intent or meaning.

■ When course material is especially complex and difficult, it is a good idea to prepare for the lecture by reading ahead on the scheduled subject in your text. Then you have less information to digest that is brand new.

■ Don't try to be a human tape recorder. Instead, try to write down the lecturer's thoughts in your own words. Doing so forces you to organize the ideas in a way that makes sense to you. In taking notes, look for subtle and not-so-subtle clues about what the instructor considers to be important. These clues may range from simply repeating main points to saying things like "You'll run into this again."

■ Ask questions during lectures. Doing so keeps you actively involved and allows you to clarify points you may have misunderstood. Many students are more bashful about asking questions than they should be. They don't realize that most professors welcome questions.

Applying Memory Principles

Scientific investigation of memory processes dates back to 1885, when Hermann Ebbinghaus published a se-

ries of insightful studies. Since then, psychologists have discovered a number of principles about memory that are relevant to helping you improve your study skills.

Engage in Adequate Practice

Practice makes perfect, or so you've heard. In reality, practice is not likely to guarantee perfection, but repeatedly reviewing information usually leads to improved retention. Studies show that retention improves with increased rehearsal (Greene, 1992). Continued rehearsal may also pay off by improving your *understanding* of assigned material (Bromage & Mayer, 1986). As you go over information again and again, your increased familiarity with the material may permit you to focus selectively on the most important points, thus enhancing your understanding.

Evidence suggests that it even pays to overlearn material (Driskell, Wilis, & Copper, 1992). **Overlearning is continued rehearsal of material after you have first appeared to master it.** In one study, after participants mastered a list of nouns (they recited the list without error), Krueger (1929) required them to continue rehearsing for 50 percent or 100 percent more trials. Measuring retention at intervals of up to 28 days, Kreuger found that overlearning led to better recall of the list. The implication of this finding is simple: You should not quit rehearsing material just because you appear to have mastered it.

Use Distributed Practice

Let's assume that you are going to study 9 hours for an exam. Is it better to "cram" all of your study into one 9-hour period (massed practice) or distribute it among, say, three 3-hour periods on successive days (distributed practice)? The evidence indicates that retention tends to be greater after distributed practice than massed practice (Glenberg, 1992; Payne & Wenger, 1996). This advantage is especially apparent if the intervals between practice periods are fairly long, such as 24 hours (Zechmeister & Nyberg, 1982). The inefficiency of massed practice means that cramming is an ill-advised study strategy for most students (Dempster, 1996). Cramming will strain your memorization capabilities and tax your energy level. It may also stoke the fires of test anxiety.

Minimize Interference

Interference occurs when people forget information because of competition from other learned material. Research suggests that interference is a major cause of forgetting, so you'll probably want to think about how you can minimize interference. Doing so is especially important for students, because memorizing information for one course can interfere with retaining information in another course. It may help to allocate study for specific courses to specific days. Thorndyke and Hayes-Roth (1979) found that similar material produced less interference when it was learned on different days. Thus, the day before an exam in a course, it is probably best to study for that course only. If demands in other courses make that impossible, study the test material last. Of course, studying for other classes is not the only source of interference in a student's life. Other normal waking activities also produce interference. Therefore, it is a good idea to conduct one last, thorough review of material as close to exam time as possible (Anderson, 1980).

Organize Information

Retention tends to be greater when information is well organized. Hierarchical organization is particularly helpful when it is applicable (Tigner, 1999). Thus, it may be a good idea to *outline* reading assignments for school. Consistent with this reasoning, there is some empirical evidence that outlining material from textbooks can enhance retention of the material (McDaniel, Waddill, & Shakesby, 1996).

Emphasize Deep Processing

Research suggests that how *often* you go over material is less critical than the *depth* of processing that you engage in (Craik & Tulving, 1975). Thus, if you expect to remember what you read, you have to wrestle fully with its meaning. Many students could probably benefit if they spent less time on rote repetition and devoted more effort to actually paying attention to and analyzing the meaning of their reading assignments. In particular, it is useful to make material *personally* meaningful. When you read your textbooks, try to relate information to your own life and experience. For example, if you're reading in your psychology text about the personality trait of assertiveness, you can think about which people you know who are particularly assertive and why you would characterize them as being that way.

Use Verbal Mnemonics

Of course, it's not always easy to make something personally meaningful. When you study chemistry, you may have a hard time relating to polymers at a personal level. This problem has led to the development of many *mnemonic devices,* **or strategies for enhancing memory,** that are designed to make abstract material more meaningful.

Acrostics and acronyms. *Acrostics* are phrases (or poems) in which the first letter of each word (or line) functions as a cue to help you recall the abstract words that begin with the same letter. For instance, you may remember the order of musical notes with the saying "Every good boy does fine" (or "deserves favor"). A variation on acrostics is the *acronym*—a word formed out of the first letters of a series of words. Students memorizing the order of colors in the light spectrum often store the name "Roy G. Biv" to remember red, orange, yellow, green, blue, indigo, and violet.

Narrative methods. Another useful way to remember a list of words is to create a story that includes each of the words in the right order. The narrative increases the meaningfulness of the words and links them in a specific order. Examples of this technique can be seen in Figure 1.14. Bower and Clark (1969) found that this procedure enhanced subjects' recall of lists of unrelated words.

Rhymes. Another verbal mnemonic that people often rely on is rhyming. You've probably repeated, "I before E except after C" thousands of times. Perhaps you also remember the number of days in each month with the old standby, "Thirty days hath September . . ." Rhyming something to remember it is an old and useful trick.

Word Lists to Be Memorized and Stories Constructed from Them

Word lists		Stories
Bird	Nurse	A man dressed in a *Bird Costume* and wearing a *Mailbox* on his *Head* was seen leaping into the *River*. A *Nurse* ran out of a nearby *Theater* and applied *Wax* to his *Eyelids,* but her efforts were in vain. He died and was tossed into the *Furnace*.
Costume	Theater	
Mailbox	Wax	
Head	Eyelid	
River	Furnace	
Rustler	Fuzz	A *Rustler* lived in a *Penthouse* on top of a *Mountain*. His specialty was the three-toed *Sloth*. He would take his captive animals to a *Tavern* where he would remove *Fuzz* from their *Glands*. Unfortunately, all this exposure to sloth fuzz caused him to grow *Antlers*. So he gave up his profession and went to work in a *Pencil* factory. As a precaution he also took a lot of *Vitamin* E.
Penthouse	Gland	
Mountain	Antler	
Sloth	Pencil	
Tavern	Vitamin	

● **FIGURE 1.14**

The narrative method. Two examples of the narrative method for memorizing lists are shown here (Bower & Clark, 1969). The words to be memorized are listed on the left, and the stories constructed to remember them are shown on the right.

Adapted from Bower, G. H., & Clark, M. C. (1969). Narrative stories as mediators of serial learning. *Psychonomic Science, 14,* 181–182. Copyright © 1969 by the Psychonomic Society. Adapted by permission of the Psychonomic Society and the author.

Use Visual Mnemonics

Memory can be improved through the use of visual imagery. One influential theory (Paivio, 1986) proposes that visual images create a second memory code and that two codes are better than one. Many popular mnemonic devices depend on visual imagery, including the link method and the method of loci.

Link method. The *link method* involves forming a mental image of items to be remembered in a way that links them together. For instance, suppose that you are going to stop at the drugstore on the way home and you need to remember to pick up a news magazine, shaving cream, film, and pens. To remember these items, you might visualize a public figure likely to be in the magazine shaving with a pen while being photographed. Some researchers suggest that bizarre images may be remembered better (Iaccino, 1996; Worthen, 1997).

Method of loci. The *method of loci* involves taking an imaginary walk along a familiar path where you have associated images of items you want to remember with certain locations. The first step is to commit to memory a series of loci, or places along a path. Usually these loci are specific locations in your home or neighborhood. Then envision each thing you want to remember in one of these locations. Try to form distinctive, vivid images. When you need to remember the items, imagine yourself walking along the path. The various loci on your path should serve as retrieval cues for the images that you formed (see Figure 1.15). The method of loci assures that items are remembered in their correct order because the order is determined by the sequence of locations along the pathway. Empirical studies have supported the value of this method for memorizing lists (Crovitz, 1971; De Beni, Mo, & Cornoldi, 1997).

● **FIGURE 1.15**

The method of loci. In this example from Bower (1970), a person about to go shopping pairs items to be remembered with familiar places (loci) arranged in a natural sequence: (1) hot dogs/driveway; (2) cat food/garage; (3) tomatoes/front door; (4) bananas/coat closet; (5) whiskey/kitchen sink. As the last panel shows, the shopper recalls the items by mentally touring the loci associated with them.

Adapted from Bower, G. H. (1970). Analysis of a mnemonic device. *American Scientist, 58,* 496–499. Copyright © 1970 by Scientific Research Society. Reprinted by permission of the publisher and author.

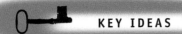

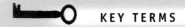

KEY IDEAS

The Paradox of Progress

■ Although our modern era has seen great technological progress, personal problems have not diminished. In spite of many time-saving devices, people tend to have less free time. Although affluence is widespread, most people worry about economic decline.

■ The life choices available to people have increased greatly, but Schwartz argues that choice overload undermines individuals' happiness. Although we have unprecedented control over the world around us, we seem to create as many problems as we solve. Thus, many theorists argue that technological progress has brought new, and possibly more difficult, adjustment problems.

The Search for Direction

■ According to many theorists, the basic challenge of modern life has become the search for a sense of direction and meaning. This search has many manifestations, including the appeal of self-realization programs, religious cults, and media "therapists" such as Dr. Laura.

■ The enormous popularity of self-help books is an interesting manifestation of people's struggle to find a sense of direction. Some self-help books offer worthwhile advice, but most are dominated by psychobabble and are not based on scientific research. Many also lack explicit advice on how to change behavior.

■ Although this text deals with many of the same issues as self-realization programs, self-help books, and other types of pop psychology, its philosophy and approach are quite different.

The Psychology of Adjustment

■ Psychology is both a science and a profession that focuses on behavior and related mental and physiological processes.

■ Adjustment is a broad area of study in psychology concerned with how people adapt effectively or ineffectively to the demands and pressures of everyday life.

The Scientific Approach to Behavior

■ The scientific approach to understanding behavior is empirical. Psychologists base their conclusions on formal, systematic, objective tests of their hypotheses, rather than reasoning, speculation, or common sense. The scientific approach is advantageous in that it puts a premium on clarity and has little tolerance for error.

■ Experimental research involves manipulating an independent variable to discover its effects on a dependent variable. The experimenter usually does so by comparing experimental and control groups, which must be alike except for the variation created by the manipulation of the independent variable. Experiments permit conclusions about cause-effect relationships between variables, but this method isn't usable for the study of many questions.

■ Psychologists conduct correlational research when they are unable to exert control over the variables they want to study. The correlation coefficient is a numerical index of the degree of relationship between two variables. Correlational research methods include naturalistic observation, case studies, and surveys. Correlational research facilitates the investigation of many issues that are not open to experimental study, but it cannot demonstrate that two variables are causally related.

The Roots of Happiness: An Empirical Analysis

■ A scientific analysis of happiness reveals that many commonsense notions about the roots of happiness appear to be incorrect, including the notion that most people are unhappy. Factors such as money, age, gender, parenthood, intelligence, and attractiveness are not correlated with subjective well-being.

■ Physical health, social relationships, and religious faith appear to have a modest impact on feelings of happiness. The only factors that are clearly and strongly related to happiness are love and marriage, work satisfaction, and personality.

■ There are no simple recipes for achieving happiness, but it helps to understand that happiness is a relative concept mediated by people's highly subjective assessments of their lives.

Application: Improving Academic Performance

■ To foster sound study habits, you should devise a written study schedule and reward yourself for following it. You should also try to find places for studying that are relatively free of distractions.

■ You should use active reading techniques, such as SQ3R, to select the most important ideas from the material you read. Good note taking can help you get more out of lectures. It's important to use active listening techniques and to record lecturers' ideas in your own words.

■ Rehearsal, even when it involves overlearning, facilitates retention. Distributed practice and deeper processing tend to improve memory. It is wise to plan study sessions so as to minimize interference. Evidence also suggests that organization facilitates retention, so outlining reading assignments can be valuable.

■ Meaningfulness can be enhanced through the use of verbal mnemonics such as acrostics, acronyms, and narrative methods. The link method and the method of loci are mnemonic devices that depend on the value of visual imagery.

KEY TERMS

Adjustment   p. 12
Behavior   p. 11
Case study   p. 17
Clinical psychology   p. 12
Control group   p. 14
Correlation   p. 15
Correlation coefficient   p. 15
Dependent variable   p. 14
Empiricism   p. 13
Experiment   p. 13
Experimental group   p. 14

Hedonic adaptation   p. 23
Independent variable   p. 14
Interference   p. 27
Mnemonic devices   p. 28
Naturalistic observation   p. 16
Overlearning   p. 27
Psychology   p. 11
SQ3R   p. 25
Subjective well-being   p. 19
Surveys   p. 17

KEY PEOPLE

David Myers   p. 2
Barry Schwartz   pp. 2–3

Martin Seligman   p. 2

PRACTICE TEST

1. Technological advances have not led to perceptible improvement in our collective health and happiness. This statement defines
   a. escape from freedom.
   b. the point/counterpoint phenomenon.
   c. modern society.
   d. the paradox of progress.

2. Kasser argues that the correlation between happiness and materialism (a strong focus on money and possessions) is
   a. positive.
   b. negative.
   c. zero.
   d. about +1.24.

3. Which of the following is *not* offered in the text as a criticism of self-help books?
   a. They are infrequently based on solid research.
   b. Most don't provide explicit directions for changing behavior.
   c. The topics they cover are often quite narrow.
   d. Many are dominated by psychobabble.

4. The adaptation of animals when environments change is similar to _____ in humans.
   a. orientation
   b. assimilation
   c. evolution
   d. adjustment

5. An experiment is a research method in which the investigator manipulates the _____ variable and observes whether changes occur in a (an) _____ variable as a result.
   a. independent; dependent
   b. control; experimental
   c. experimental; control
   d. dependent; independent

6. A researcher wants to determine whether a certain diet causes children to learn better in school. In the study, the independent variable is
   a. the type of diet.
   b. a measure of learning performance.
   c. the age or grade level of the children.
   d. the intelligence level of the children.

7. A psychologist collected background information about a psychopathic killer, talked to him and people who knew him, and gave him psychological tests. Which research method was she using?
   a. Case study
   b. Naturalistic observation
   c. Survey
   d. Experiment

8. The principal advantage of experimental research is that
   a. it has a scientific basis and is therefore convincing to people.
   b. experiments replicate real-life situations.
   c. an experiment can be designed for any research problem.
   d. it allows the researcher to draw cause-and-effect conclusions.

9. Research has shown that which of the following is moderately correlated with happiness?
   a. Income   *Isn't very Important*
   b. Intelligence   *"   "   "*
   c. Parenthood   *"   "   "*
   d. Social activity

10. A good reason for taking notes in your own words, rather than verbatim, is that
    a. most lecturers are quite wordy.
    b. "translating" on the spot is good mental exercise.
    c. it reduces the likelihood that you'll later engage in plagiarism.
    d. it forces you to assimilate the information in a way that makes sense to you.

Book Companion Website

Visit the Book Companion Website at **http://psychology.wadsworth.com/weiten_lloyd8e**, where you will find tutorial quizzes, flashcards, and weblinks for every chapter, a final exam, and more! You can also link to the Thomson Wadsworth Psychology Resource Center (accessible directly at **http://psychology.wadsworth.com**) for a range of psychology-related resources.

Personal Explorations Workbook

The following exercises in your *Personal Explorations Workbook* may enhance your self-understanding in relation to issues raised in this chapter. **Questionnaire 1.1:** Testwiseness Scale. **Personal Probe 1.1:** What Are Your Study Habits Like? **Personal Probe 1.2:** What Factors Affect Your Current Adjustment in Life?

ANSWERS

1. d Page 4
2. b Page 2
3. c Pages 8–9
4. d Page 12
5. a Pages 13–14
6. a Page 14
7. a Page 17
8. d Page 14
9. d Pages 20–21
10. d Page 27

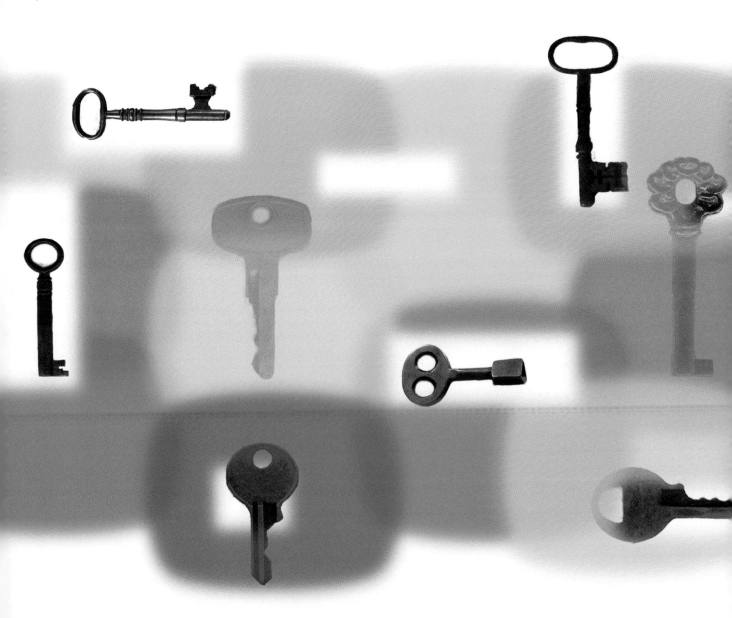

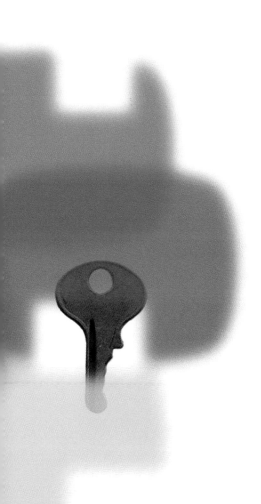

Theories of Personality

Imagine that you are hurtling upward in an elevator with three other persons when suddenly a power blackout brings the elevator to a halt 45 stories above the ground. Your three companions might adjust to this predicament differently. One might crack jokes to relieve tension. Another might make ominous predictions that "we'll never get out of here." The third might calmly think about how to escape from the elevator. These varied ways of coping with the same stressful situation occur because each person has a different personality. Personality differences significantly influence people's patterns of adjustment. Thus, theories intended to explain personality can contribute to our effort to understand adjustment processes.

In this chapter, we will introduce you to various theories that attempt to explain the structure and development of personality. Our review of personality theory will also serve to acquaint you with four major theoretical perspectives in psychology: the psychodynamic, behavioral, humanistic, and biological perspectives. These theoretical approaches are conceptual models that help explain behavior. Familiarity with them will help you understand many of the ideas that you will encounter in this book, as well as in other books about psychology.

The Nature of Personality

To discuss theories of personality effectively, we need to digress momentarily to come up with a definition of personality and to discuss the concept of personality traits.

What Is Personality?

What does it mean if you say that a friend has an optimistic personality? Your statement suggests that the person has a fairly *consistent tendency* to behave in a cheerful, hopeful, enthusiastic way, looking at the bright side of things, across a wide variety of situations. In a similar vein, if you note that a friend has an "outgoing" personality, you mean that she or he consistently behaves in a friendly, open, and extraverted manner in a variety of circumstances. Although no one is entirely consistent in his or her behavior, this quality of *consistency across situations* lies at the core of the concept of personality.

Distinctiveness is also central to the concept of personality. Everyone has traits seen in other people, but each individual has her or his own distinctive *set* of personality traits. Each person is unique. Thus, as illustrated by our elevator scenario, the concept of personality helps explain why people don't all act alike in the same situation.

In summary, we use the idea of personality to explain (1) the stability in a person's behavior over time and across situations (consistency) and (2) the behavioral differences among people reacting to the same situation (distinctiveness). We can combine these ideas into the following definition: **personality refers to an individual's unique constellation of consistent behavioral traits.** Let's look more closely at the concept of traits.

What Are Personality Traits?

We all make remarks like "Melanie is very *shrewd*" or "Doug is too *timid* to succeed in that job" or "I wish I could be as *self-assured* as Antonio." When we attempt to describe an individual's personality, we usually do so in terms of specific aspects of personality, called traits. **A *personality trait* is a durable disposition to behave in a particular way in a variety of situations.** Adjectives such as *honest, dependable, moody, impulsive, suspicious, anxious, excitable, domineering,* and *friendly* describe dispositions that represent personality traits.

Most trait theories of personality, such as those of Gordon Allport (1937, 1961) and Raymond Cattell

(1950, 1966) assume that some traits are more basic than others. According to this notion, a small number of fundamental traits determine other, more superficial traits. For example, a person's tendency to be impulsive, restless, irritable, boisterous, and impatient might all derive from a more basic tendency to be excitable.

In recent years, Robert McCrae and Paul Costa (1987, 1997, 1999) have stimulated a lively debate among psychologists by arguing that the vast majority of personality traits derive from just five higher-order traits that have come to be known as the "Big Five": extraversion, neuroticism, openness to experience, agreeableness, and conscientiousness (see Figure 2.1). Let's take a closer look at these traits:

1. *Extraversion.* People who score high in extraversion are characterized as outgoing, sociable, upbeat, friendly, assertive, and gregarious. Referred to as *positive emotionality* in some trait models, extraversion has been studied extensively in research for many decades (Watson & Clark, 1997).

2. *Neuroticism.* People who score high in neuroticism tend to be anxious, hostile, self-conscious, inse-

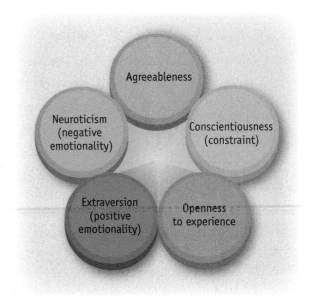

● FIGURE 2.1

The five-factor model of personality. Trait models attempt to break down personality into its basic dimensions. McCrae and Costa (1987, 1997) maintain that personality can be described adequately with the five higher-order traits identified here, widely known as the Big Five traits.

cure, and vulnerable. Like extraversion, this trait has been the subject of thousands of studies. In some trait models it is called *negative emotionality* (Church, 1994).

3. *Openness to experience.* Openness is associated with curiosity, flexibility, vivid fantasy, imaginativeness, artistic sensitivity, and unconventional attitudes. McCrae (1996) maintains that its importance has been underestimated. Citing evidence that openness fosters liberalism, he argues that this trait is the key determinant of people's political attitudes and ideology.

4. *Agreeableness.* Those who score high in agreeableness tend to be sympathetic, trusting, cooperative, modest, and straightforward. People who score at the opposite end of this personality dimension are characterized as suspicious, antagonistic, and aggressive. Agreeableness may have its roots in childhood temperament and appears to promote altruistic (helping) behavior in social interactions (Graziano & Eisenberg, 1997).

5. *Conscientiousness.* Conscientious people tend to be diligent, disciplined, well organized, punctual, and dependable. Referred to as *constraint* in some trait models, conscientiousness is associated with higher productivity in a variety of occupational areas (Hogan & Ones, 1997).

McCrae and Costa maintain that personality can be described adequately by measuring the five basic traits that they've identified. Their bold claim has been supported in many studies by other researchers, and the five-factor model has become the dominant conception of personality structure in contemporary psychology (John & Srivastava, 1999; Wiggins & Trapnell, 1997). These traits have been characterized as the "latitude and longitude" along which personality should be mapped (Ozer & Reise, 1994, p. 361). Thousands of studies have been conducted exploring correlations between the Big Five traits and such other characteristics as self-esteem (Watson, Suls, & Haig, 2002), transformational leadership (Judge & Bono, 2000), social status (Anderson et al., 2001), and well-being at midlife (Siegler & Brummett, 2000).

However, some theorists maintain that more than five traits are necessary to account for most of the variation seen in human personality (Benet & Waller, 1995; Ashton et al., 2004). Ironically, other theorists have argued for three- or four-factor models of personality (Church & Burke, 1994; Eysenck, 1992).

The debate about how many dimensions are necessary to describe personality is likely to continue for many years to come. As you'll see throughout the chapter, the study of personality is an area in psychology that has a long history of "dueling theories." We'll begin our tour of these theories by examining the influential work of Sigmund Freud and his followers.

Psychodynamic Perspectives

LEARNING OBJECTIVES

- Describe Freud's three components of personality and how they are distributed across levels of awareness.
- Explain the importance of sexual and aggressive conflicts in Freud's theory.
- Describe seven defense mechanisms identified by Freud.
- Outline Freud's stages of psychosexual development and their theorized relations to adult personality.

- Summarize Jung's views on the unconscious.
- Summarize Adler's views on key issues relating to personality.
- Evaluate the strengths and weaknesses of psychodynamic theories of personality.

Psychodynamic theories **include all the diverse theories descended from the work of Sigmund Freud that focus on unconscious mental forces.** Freud inspired many brilliant scholars who followed in his intellectual footsteps. Some of these followers simply refined and updated Freud's theory. Others veered off in new directions and established independent, albeit related, schools of thought. Today, the psychodynamic umbrella covers a large collection of related theories. In this section, we'll examine Freud's ideas in some detail and then take a brief look at the work of two of his most significant followers, Carl Jung and Alfred Adler. Another psychodynamic theorist, Erik Erikson, is covered in a later chapter on adolescent and adult development (see Chapter 11).

Freud's Psychoanalytic Theory

Born in 1856, Sigmund Freud grew up in a middle-class Jewish home in Vienna, Austria. He showed an early interest in intellectual pursuits and became an intense, hardworking young man. He dreamed of achieving fame by making an important discovery. His determination was such that in medical school he dissected 400 male eels to prove for the first time that they had testes. His work with eels did not make him famous. However, his later work with people made him one of

Sigmund Freud

National Library of Medicine

the most influential and controversial figures of modern times.

Freud was a physician specializing in neurology when he began his medical practice in Vienna near the end of the 19th century. Like other neurologists in his era, he often treated people troubled by nervous problems such as irrational fears, obsessions, and anxieties. Eventually he devoted himself to the treatment of mental disorders using an innovative procedure he developed, called *psychoanalysis*, which required lengthy verbal interactions in which Freud probed deeply into patients' lives. Decades of experience with his patients provided much of the inspiration for Freud's theory of personality.

Although Freud's theory gradually gained prominence, most of Freud's contemporaries were uncomfortable with the theory, for at least three reasons. First, he argued that unconscious forces govern human behavior. This idea was disturbing because it suggested that people are not masters of their own minds. Second, he claimed that childhood experiences strongly determine adult personality. This notion distressed many, because it suggested that people are not masters of their own destinies. Third, he said that individuals' personalities are shaped by how they cope with their sexual urges. This assertion offended the conservative, Victorian values of his time. Thus, Freud endured a great deal of criticism, condemnation, and outright ridicule, even after his work began to attract more favorable attention. What were these ideas that generated so much controversy?

Freud's psychoanalytic theory was based on decades of clinical work. He treated a great many patients in the consulting room pictured here. The room contains numerous artifacts from other cultures—and the original psychoanalytic couch.

Structure of Personality

Freud (1901, 1920) divided personality structure into three components: the id, the ego, and the superego. He saw a person's behavior as the outcome of interactions among these three components.

The *id* is the primitive, instinctive component of personality that operates according to the pleasure principle. Freud referred to the id as the reservoir of psychic energy. By this he meant that the id houses the raw biological urges (to eat, sleep, defecate, copulate, and so on) that energize human behavior. The id operates according to the *pleasure principle*, which demands immediate gratification of its urges. The id engages in *primary process thinking*, which is primitive, illogical, irrational, and fantasy oriented.

The *ego* is the decision-making component of personality that operates according to the reality principle. The ego mediates between the id, with its forceful desires for immediate satisfaction, and the external social world, with its expectations and norms regarding suitable behavior. The ego considers social realities—society's norms, etiquette, rules, and customs—in deciding how to behave. The ego is guided by the *reality principle,* which seeks to delay gratification of the id's urges until appropriate outlets and situations can be found. In short, to stay out of trouble, the ego often works to tame the unbridled desires of the id. As Freud put it, the ego is "like a man on horseback, who has to hold in check the superior strength of the horse" (Freud, 1923, p. 15).

In the long run, the ego wants to maximize gratification, just like the id. However, the ego engages in *secondary process thinking,* which is relatively rational, realistic, and oriented toward problem solving. Thus, the ego strives to avoid negative consequences from society and its representatives (for example, punishment by parents or teachers) by behaving "properly." It also attempts to achieve long-range goals that sometimes require putting off gratification.

While the ego concerns itself with practical realities, **the *superego* is the moral component of personality that incorporates social standards about what represents right and wrong.** Throughout their lives, but especially during childhood, individuals receive training about what is good and bad behavior. Eventually they internalize many of these social norms, meaning that they truly *accept* certain moral principles, then *they* put pressure on *themselves* to live up to these standards. The superego emerges out of the ego at around 3 to 5 years of age. In some people, the superego can become irrationally demanding in its striving for moral perfection. Such people are plagued by excessive guilt.

According to Freud, the id, ego, and superego are distributed across three levels of awareness. He contrasted the unconscious with the conscious and preconscious (see Figure 2.2). **The *conscious* consists of whatever one is aware of at a particular point in time.** For

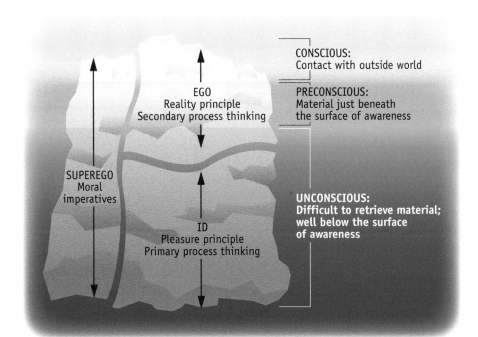

Freud's model of personality structure. Freud theorized that people have three levels of awareness: the conscious, the preconscious, and the unconscious. To dramatize the size of the unconscious, he compared it to the portion of an iceberg that lies beneath the water's surface. Freud also divided personality structure into three components—id, ego, and superego—that operate according to different principles and exhibit different modes of thinking. In Freud's model, the id is entirely unconscious, but the ego and superego operate at all three levels of awareness.

example, at this moment your conscious may include the current train of thought in this text and a dim awareness in the back of your mind that your eyes are getting tired and you're beginning to get hungry. **The *preconscious* contains material just beneath the surface of awareness that can be easily retrieved.** Examples might include your middle name, what you had for supper last night, or an argument you had with a friend yesterday. **The *unconscious* contains thoughts, memories, and desires that are well below the surface of conscious awareness but that nonetheless exert great influence on one's behavior.** Examples of material that might be found in your unconscious would include a forgotten trauma from childhood or hidden feelings of hostility toward a parent.

Conflict and Defense Mechanisms

Freud assumed that behavior is the outcome of an ongoing series of internal conflicts. Internal battles among the id, ego, and superego are routine. Why? Because the id wants to gratify its urges immediately, but the norms of civilized society frequently dictate otherwise. For example, your id might feel an urge to clobber a co-worker

who constantly irritates you. However, society frowns on such behavior, so your ego would try to hold this urge in check, and you would find yourself in a conflict. You may be experiencing conflict at this very moment. In Freudian terms, your id may be secretly urging you to abandon reading this chapter so you can watch television or go online. Your ego may be weighing this appealing option against your society-induced need to excel in school.

Freud believed that conflicts dominate people's lives. He asserted that individuals career from one conflict to another. The following scenario provides a fanciful illustration of how the three components of personality interact to create constant conflicts.

Imagine your alarm clock ringing obnoxiously as you lurch across the bed to shut it off. It's 7 a.m. and time to get up for your history class. However, your id (operating according to the pleasure principle) urges you to return to the immediate gratification of additional sleep. Your ego (operating according to the reality principle) points out that you really must go to class since you haven't been able to decipher the stupid textbook on your own. Your id (in its typical unrealistic fashion) smugly assures you that you will get the A that you need. It suggests lying back to dream about how impressed your roommate will be. Just as you're relaxing, your superego jumps into the fray. It tries to make you feel guilty about the tuition your parents paid for the class that you're about to skip. You haven't even gotten out of bed yet—and there is already a pitched battle in your psyche.

Let's say your ego wins the battle. You pull yourself out of bed and head for class. On the way, you pass a donut shop and your id clamors for cinnamon rolls. Your

WEB LINK 2.1

Sigmund Freud Museum, Vienna, Austria
This online museum, in both English and German versions, offers a detailed chronology of Freud's life and explanations of the most important concepts of psychoanalysis. The highlights, though, are the rich audiovisual resources, including online photos, amateur movie clips, and voice recordings of Freud.

ego reminds you that you're gaining weight and that you are supposed to be on a diet. Your id wins this time. After you've attended your history lecture, your ego reminds you that you need to do some library research for a paper in philosophy. However, your id insists on returning to your apartment to watch some sitcom reruns. It's only midmorning—and already you have been through a series of internal conflicts.

Freud believed that conflicts centering on sexual and aggressive impulses are especially likely to have far-reaching consequences. Why did he emphasize sex and aggression? Two reasons were prominent in his thinking. First, Freud thought that sex and aggression are subject to more complex and ambiguous social controls than other basic motives. The norms governing sexual and aggressive behavior are subtle, and people often get mixed messages about what is appropriate. Thus, he believed that these two drives are the source of much confusion.

Second, Freud noted that the sexual and aggressive drives are thwarted more regularly than other basic biological urges. Think about it: If you get hungry or thirsty, you can simply head for a nearby vending machine or a drinking fountain. But if a department store clerk infuriates you, you aren't likely to slug the clerk, because that isn't socially acceptable. Likewise, when you see an attractive person who inspires lustful urges, you don't normally walk up and propose a tryst in a nearby broom closet. There is nothing comparable to vending machines or drinking fountains for the satisfaction of sexual and aggressive urges. Thus, Freud gave great importance to these needs because social norms dictate that they are routinely frustrated.

Most psychic conflicts are trivial and are quickly resolved one way or the other. Occasionally, however, a conflict will linger for days, months, and even years,

"ALL I WANT FROM THEM IS A SIMPLE MAJORITY ON THINGS."

Cartoon © 1999 by Sidney Harris

creating internal tension. Indeed, Freud believed that lingering conflicts rooted in childhood experiences cause most personality disturbances. More often than not, these prolonged and troublesome conflicts involve sexual and aggressive impulses that society wants to tame. These conflicts are often played out entirely in the unconscious. Although you may not be aware of these unconscious battles, they can produce *anxiety* that slips to the surface of conscious awareness. This anxiety is attributable to your ego worrying about the id getting out of control and doing something terrible.

The arousal of anxiety is a crucial event in Freud's theory of personality functioning (see Figure 2.3). Anxiety is distressing, so people try to rid themselves of this unpleasant emotion any way they can. This effort to ward off anxiety often involves the use of defense mechanisms. **Defense mechanisms are largely unconscious reactions that protect a person from painful emotions such as anxiety and guilt.** Typically, they are mental

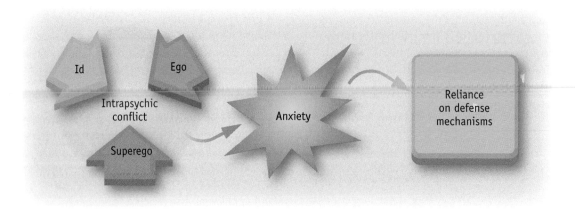

● FIGURE 2.3

Freud's model of personality dynamics. According to Freud, unconscious conflicts between the id, ego, and superego sometimes lead to anxiety. This discomfort may lead to the use of defense mechanisms, which may temporarily relieve anxiety.

maneuvers that work through self-deception. A common example is *rationalization,* **which involves creating false but plausible excuses to justify unacceptable behavior.** You would be rationalizing if, after cheating someone in a business transaction, you tried to reduce your guilt by explaining that "everyone does it."

Characterized as "the flagship in the psychoanalytic fleet of defense mechanisms" (Paulhus, Fridhandler, & Hayes, 1997, p. 545), repression is the most basic and widely used defense mechanism. *Repression* **involves keeping distressing thoughts and feelings buried in the unconscious.** People tend to repress desires that make them feel guilty, conflicts that make them anxious, and memories that are painful. Repression is "motivated forgetting." If you forget a dental appointment or the name of someone you don't like, repression may be at work.

Self-deception can also be seen in the mechanisms of projection and displacement. *Projection* **involves attributing one's own thoughts, feelings, or motives to another.** For example, if your lust for a co-worker makes you feel guilty, you might attribute any latent sexual tension between the two of you to the *other person's* desire to seduce you. *Displacement* **involves diverting emotional feelings (usually anger) from their original source to a substitute target.** If your boss gives you a hard time at work and you come home and slam the door, kick the dog, and scream at your spouse, you are displacing your anger onto irrelevant targets. Unfortunately, social constraints often force people to hold back their anger until they end up lashing out at the people they love the most.

Other prominent defense mechanisms include reaction formation, regression, and identification. *Reaction formation* **involves behaving in a way that is exactly the opposite of one's true feelings.** Guilt about sexual desires often leads to reaction formation. Freud theorized that many males who ridicule homosexuals are defending against their own latent homosexual impulses. The telltale sign of reaction formation is the exaggerated quality of the opposite behavior.

Regression **involves a reversion to immature patterns of behavior.** When anxious about their self-worth, some adults respond with childish boasting and bragging (as opposed to subtle efforts to impress others). For example, a fired executive having difficulty finding a new job might start making ridiculous statements about his incomparable talents and achievements. Such bragging is regressive when it is marked by massive exaggerations that anyone can see through.

Identification **involves bolstering self-esteem by forming an imaginary or real alliance with some person or group.** For example, youngsters often shore up precarious feelings of self-worth by identifying with rock stars, movie stars, or famous athletes. Adults may join exclusive country clubs or civic organizations with which they identify.

Additional examples of the defense mechanisms we've described can be found in Figure 2.4. If you see defensive maneuvers that you have used, you shouldn't be surprised. According to Freud, everyone uses defense mechanisms to some extent. They become problematic only when a person depends on them excessively. The seeds for psychological disorders are sown when defenses lead to wholesale distortion of reality.

Development: Psychosexual Stages

Freud made the startling assertion that the foundation of an individual's personality is laid down by the ten-

Defense Mechanisms, with Examples

Definition	Example
Repression involves keeping distressing thoughts and feelings buried in the unconscious.	A traumatized soldier has no recollection of the details of a close brush with death.
Projection involves attributing one's own thoughts, feelings, or motives to another person.	A woman who dislikes her boss thinks she likes her boss but feels that the boss doesn't like her.
Displacement involves diverting emotional feelings (usually anger) from their original source to a substitute target.	After a parental scolding, a young girl takes her anger out on her little brother.
Reaction formation involves behaving in a way that is exactly the opposite of one's true feelings.	A parent who unconsciously resents a child spoils the child with outlandish gifts.
Regression involves a reversion to immature patterns of behavior.	An adult has a temper tantrum when he doesn't get his way.
Rationalization involves the creation of false but plausible excuses to justify unacceptable behavior.	A student watches TV instead of studying, saying that "additional study wouldn't do any good anyway."
Identification involves bolstering self-esteem by forming an imaginary or real alliance with some person or group.	An insecure young man joins a fraternity to boost his self-esteem.

● FIGURE 2.4

Defense mechanisms. According to Freud, people use a variety of defense mechanisms to protect themselves from painful emotions. Definitions of seven commonly used defense mechanisms are shown on the left, along with examples of each on the right. This list is not exhaustive; additional defense mechanisms are discussed in Chapter 4.

der age of 5! To shed light on these crucial early years, Freud formulated a stage theory of development. He emphasized how young children deal with their immature, but powerful, sexual urges (he used the term "sexual" in a general way to refer to many urges for physical pleasure, not just the urge to copulate). According to Freud, these sexual urges shift in focus as children progress from one stage to another. Indeed, the names for the stages (oral, anal, genital, and so on) are based on where children are focusing their erotic energy at the time. Thus, *psychosexual stages* **are developmental periods with a characteristic sexual focus that leave their mark on adult personality.**

Freud theorized that each psychosexual stage has its own unique developmental challenges or tasks, as outlined in Figure 2.5. The way these challenges are handled supposedly shapes personality. The notion of *fixation* plays an important role in this process. *Fixation* **is a failure to move forward from one stage to another as expected.** Essentially, the child's development stalls for awhile. Fixation is caused by *excessive gratification* of needs at a particular stage or by *excessive frustration* of those needs. Either way, fixations left over from childhood affect adult personality. Generally, fixation leads to an overemphasis on the psychosexual needs that were prominent during the fixated stage.

Freud described a series of five psychosexual stages. Let's examine some of the major features of each stage.

Oral stage. This stage usually encompasses the first year of life. During this stage the main source of erotic stimulation is the mouth (in biting, sucking, chewing, and so on). How caretakers handle the child's feeding experiences is supposed to be crucial to subsequent development. Freud attributed considerable importance to the manner in which the child is weaned from the breast or the bottle. According to Freud, fixation at the oral stage could form the basis for obsessive eating or smoking later in life (among many other things).

Anal stage. In their second year, children supposedly get their erotic pleasure from their bowel movements, through either the expulsion or retention of the feces. The crucial event at this time involves toilet training, which represents society's first systematic effort to regulate the child's biological urges. Severely punitive toilet training is thought to lead to a variety of possible outcomes. For example, excessive punishment might produce a latent feeling of hostility toward the "trainer," who usually is the mother. This hostility might generalize to women in general. Another possibility is that heavy reliance on punitive measures might lead to an association between genital concerns and the anxiety that the punishment arouses. This genital anxiety derived from severe toilet training could evolve into anxiety about sexual activities later in life.

Phallic stage. Around age 4, the genitals become the focus for the child's erotic energy, largely through self-stimulation. During this pivotal stage, the *Oedipal complex* emerges. Little boys develop an erotically tinged preference for their mother. They also feel hostility toward their father, whom they view as a competitor for mom's affection. Little girls develop a special attachment to their father. At about the same time, they learn that their genitals are very different from those of little boys, and they supposedly develop *penis envy*. According to Freud, girls feel hostile toward their mother because they blame her for their anatomical "deficiency."

To summarize, in **the *Oedipal complex* children manifest erotically tinged desires for their other-gender parent, accompanied by feelings of hostility toward their same-gender parent.** The name for this syndrome was taken from the Greek myth of Oedipus, who was separated from his parents at birth. Not knowing the identity of his real parents, he inadvertently killed his father and married his mother.

According to Freud, the way parents and children deal with the sexual and aggressive conflicts inherent in

FIGURE 2.5

Freud's stages of psychosexual development. Freud theorized that people evolve through the series of psychosexual stages summarized here. The manner in which certain key tasks and experiences are handled during each stage is thought to leave a lasting imprint on one's adult personality.

Freud's Stages of Psychosexual Development

Stage	Approximate ages	Erotic focus	Key tasks and experiences
Oral	0–1	Mouth (sucking, biting)	Weaning (from breast or bottle)
Anal	2–3	Anus (expelling or retaining feces)	Toilet training
Phallic	4–5	Genitals (masturbating)	Identifying with adult role models; coping with Oedipal crisis
Latency	6–12	None (sexually repressed)	Expanding social contacts
Genital	Puberty onward	Genitals (being sexually intimate)	Establishing intimate relationships; contributing to society through working

According to Freudian theory, a child's feeding experiences are crucial to later development. Fixation at the oral stage could lead to an overemphasis on, for example, smoking or eating in adulthood.

© Michael Newman/PhotoEdit

the Oedipal complex is of paramount importance. The child has to resolve the dilemma by giving up the sexual longings for the other-sex parent and the hostility toward the same-sex parent. Healthy psychosexual development is supposed to hinge on the resolution of the Oedipal conflict. Why? Because continued hostile relations with the same-sex parent may prevent the child from identifying adequately with that parent. Without such identification, Freudian theory predicts that many aspects of the child's development won't progress as they should.

Latency and genital stages. Freud believed that from age 6 through puberty, the child's sexuality is suppressed—it becomes "latent." Important events during this *latency stage* center on expanding social contacts beyond the family. With the advent of puberty, the child evolves into the *genital stage*. Sexual urges reappear and focus on the genitals once again. At this point the sexual energy is normally channeled toward peers of the other sex, rather than toward oneself, as in the phallic stage.

In arguing that the early years shape personality, Freud did not mean that personality development comes to an abrupt halt in middle childhood. However, he did believe that the foundation for one's adult personality is solidly entrenched by this time. He maintained that future developments are rooted in early, formative experiences and that significant conflicts in later years are replays of crises from childhood.

In fact, Freud believed that unconscious sexual conflicts rooted in childhood experiences cause most personality disturbances. His steadfast belief in the psychosexual origins of psychological disorders eventually led to bitter theoretical disputes with two of his most brilliant colleagues: Carl Jung and Alfred Adler. Jung and Adler both argued that Freud overemphasized sexuality. Freud summarily rejected their ideas, and the other two theorists felt compelled to go their own way, developing their own psychodynamic theories of personality.

Jung's Analytical Psychology

Swiss psychiatrist Carl Jung called his new approach *analytical psychology* to differentiate it from Freud's psychoanalytic theory. Like Freud, Jung (1921, 1933) emphasized the unconscious determinants of personality. However, he proposed that the unconscious consists of two layers. The first layer, called the *personal unconscious,* is essentially the same as Freud's version of the unconscious. The personal unconscious houses material that is not within one's conscious awareness because it has been repressed or forgotten. In addition, Jung theorized the existence of a deeper layer he called the collective unconscious. **The *collective unconscious* is a storehouse of latent memory traces inherited from people's ancestral past that is shared with the entire human race.** Jung called these ancestral memories *archetypes*. They are not memories of actual, personal experiences. Instead, *archetypes* **are emotionally charged images and thought forms that**

Carl Jung

© Bettmann/Corbis

WEB LINK 2.2

C. G. Jung, Analytical Psychology and Culture
Synchronicity, archetypes, collective unconscious, introversion, extraversion—these and many other important concepts arising from analytical psychology and Jung's tremendously influential theorizing are examined at this comprehensive site.

have universal meaning. These archetypal images and ideas show up frequently in dreams and are often manifested in a culture's use of symbols in art, literature, and religion. Jung felt that an understanding of archetypal symbols helped him make sense of his patients' dreams. Doing so was of great concern to him because he depended extensively on dream analysis in his treatment of patients.

Jung's unusual ideas about the collective unconscious had little impact on the mainstream of thinking in psychology. Their influence was felt more in other fields, such as anthropology, philosophy, art, and religious studies. However, many of Jung's other ideas *have* been incorporated into the mainstream of psychology. For instance, Jung was the first to describe the introverted (inner-directed) and extraverted (outer-directed) personality types. *Introverts* tend to be preoccupied with the internal world of their own thoughts, feelings, and experiences. They generally are contemplative and aloof. In contrast, *extraverts* tend to be interested in the external world of people and things. They're more likely to be outgoing, talkative, and friendly, instead of reclusive.

Adler's Individual Psychology

Alfred Adler was a charter member of Freud's inner circle—the Vienna Psychoanalytic Society. However, he soon began to develop his own theory of personality, which he christened *individual psychology.* Adler (1917, 1927) argued that the foremost human drive is not sexuality, but a *striving for superiority.* Adler viewed striving for superiority as a universal drive to adapt, improve oneself, and master life's challenges. He noted that young children understandably feel weak and helpless in comparison to more competent older children and adults. These early inferiority feelings supposedly motivate individuals to acquire new skills and develop new talents.

Adler asserted that everyone has to work to overcome some feelings of inferiority. *Compensation* **involves efforts to overcome imagined or real inferiorities by developing one's abilities.** Adler believed that

Alfred Adler

compensation is entirely normal. However, in some people inferiority feelings can become excessive, resulting in what is widely known today as an *inferiority complex*—exaggerated feelings of weakness and inadequacy. Adler thought that either parental pampering or parental neglect (or actual physical handicaps) could cause an inferiority problem. Thus, he agreed with Freud on the importance of early childhood, although he focused on different aspects of parent-child relations.

Adler explained personality disturbances by noting that an inferiority complex can distort the normal process of striving for superiority (see Figure 2.6). He maintained that some people engage in *overcompensation* in order to conceal, even from themselves, their feelings of inferiority. Instead of working to master life's challenges, people with an inferiority complex work to achieve status, gain power over others, and acquire the trappings of success (fancy clothes, impressive cars, or whatever looks important to them). They tend to flaunt their success in an effort to cover up their underlying inferiority complex. The problem is that such people engage in unconscious self-deception, worrying more about *appearances* than *reality.*

Adler's theory stressed the social context of personality development (Hoffman, 1994). For instance, it was Adler who first focused attention on the possible importance of *birth order* as a factor governing personality. He noted that firstborns, second children, and later-born children enter varied home environments and are treated differently by parents and that these experiences are likely to affect their personality. For example, he hypothesized that only children are often spoiled by excessive attention from parents and that firstborns are often problem children because they become upset when they're "dethroned" by a second child. Adler's theory stimulated hundreds of studies on the effects of birth order, but these studies generally failed to support his hypotheses and did not uncover any reliable correlations between birth order and personality (Ernst & Angst, 1983; Harris, 2000).

In recent years, however, Frank Sulloway (1995, 1996) has argued persuasively that birth order *does* have an impact on personality. Sulloway's reformulated hypotheses focus on how the Big Five traits are shaped by competition among siblings as they struggle to find a "niche" in their family environments. For example, he hypothesizes that firstborns should be more conscientious but less agreeable and open to experience than later-borns. In light of these personality patterns, he further speculates that firstborns tend to be conventional and achievement oriented, whereas later-borns tend to be liberal and rebellious. To evaluate his hypotheses, Sulloway reexamined decades of research on birth order. After eliminating many studies that failed to control for important confounding variables, such as social class and family size, he concluded that the re-

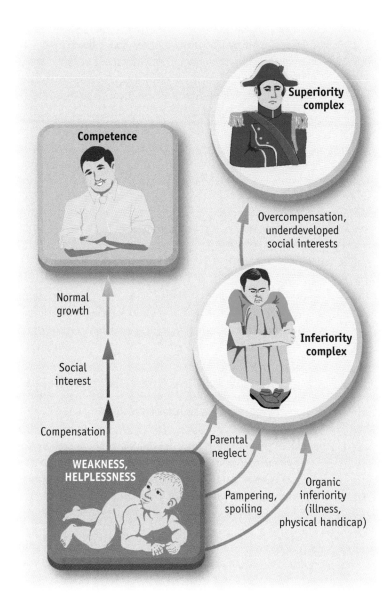

● FIGURE 2.6

Adler's view of personality development. Like Freud, Adler believed that early childhood experiences exert momentous influence over adult personality. However, he focused on children's social interactions rather than on their grappling with their sexuality. According to Adler, the roots of personality disturbances typically lie in excessive parental neglect or pampering, which can lead to overcompensation.

sults of the remaining, well-controlled studies provided impressive evidence in favor of his hypotheses. Some subsequent studies have provided additional support for Sulloway's analyses (Paulhus, Trapnell, & Chen, 1999), but others have not (Freese, Powell, & Steelman, 1999; Harris, 2000). More studies will be needed, as research on birth order is enjoying a bit of a renaissance.

Evaluating Psychodynamic Perspectives

The psychodynamic approach has given us a number of far-reaching theories of personality. These theories yielded some bold new insights for their time. Psychodynamic theory and research have demonstrated that (1) unconscious forces can influence behavior, (2) internal conflict often plays a key role in generating psychological distress, (3) early childhood experiences can exert considerable influence over adult personality, and (4) people do rely on defense mechanisms to reduce their experience of unpleasant emotions (Westen, 1998; Westen & Gabbard, 1999).

In a more negative vein, psychodynamic formulations have been criticized on several grounds, including the following (Fine, 1990; Macmillan, 1991; Torrey, 1992):

1. *Poor testability.* Scientific investigations require testable hypotheses. Psychodynamic ideas have often been too vague to permit a clear scientific test. Concepts such as the superego, the preconscious, and collective unconscious are difficult to measure.

2. *Inadequate evidence.* The empirical evidence on psychodynamic theories has often been characterized as inadequate. The approach depends too much on case studies, in which it is easy for clinicians to see what they expect to see based on their theory. Recent reexaminations of Freud's own clinical work suggest that he sometimes distorted his patients' case histories to mesh with his theory (Esterson, 1993; Sulloway, 1991) and that a substantial disparity existed between Freud's writings and his actual therapeutic methods (Lynn & Vaillant, 1998). Insofar as researchers have accumulated evidence on psychodynamic theories, it has provided only modest support for the central hypotheses (Fisher & Greenberg, 1985, 1996; Westen & Gabbard, 1999).

3. *Sexism.* Many critics have argued that psychodynamic theories harbor a bias against women. Freud believed that females' penis envy made them feel inferior to males. He also thought that females tended to develop weaker superegos and to be more prone to neurosis than males. He dismissed female patients' reports of sexual molestation during childhood as mere fantasies. Admittedly, sexism isn't unique to Freudian theories, and the sex bias in modern psychodynamic theories has been reduced to some degree. But the psychodynamic approach has generally provided a rather male-centered viewpoint (Lerman, 1986; Person, 1990).

It's easy to ridicule Freud for concepts such as penis envy and to point to ideas that have turned out to be wrong. Remember, though, that Freud, Jung, and Adler began to fashion their theories over a century ago. It is not entirely fair to compare these theories to other models that are only a decade old. That's like asking the Wright brothers to race a supersonic jet. Freud and his psychodynamic colleagues deserve great credit for breaking new ground. Standing at a distance a century later, we have to be impressed by the extraordinary impact that psychodynamic theory has had on modern thought. No other theoretical perspective in psychology has been as influential, except for the one we turn to next—behaviorism.

Behavioral Perspectives

LEARNING OBJECTIVES

- Describe Pavlov's classical conditioning and its contribution to understanding personality.
- Discuss how Skinner's principles of operant conditioning can be applied to personality development.
- Describe Bandura's social cognitive theory and his concept of self-efficacy.
- Evaluate the strengths and weaknesses of behavioral theories of personality.

Behaviorism is a theoretical orientation based on the premise that scientific psychology should study observable behavior. Behaviorism has been a major school of thought in psychology since 1913, when John B. Watson published an influential article. Watson argued that psychology should abandon its earlier focus on the mind and mental processes and focus exclusively on overt behavior. He contended that psychology could not study mental processes in a scientific manner because they are private and not accessible to outside observation.

In completely rejecting mental processes as a suitable subject for scientific study, Watson took an extreme position that is no longer dominant among modern behaviorists. Nonetheless, his influence was enormous, as psychology did shift its primary focus from the study of the mind to the study of behavior.

The behaviorists have shown little interest in internal personality structures such as Freud's id, ego, and superego, because such structures can't be observed. They prefer to think in terms of "response tendencies," which can be observed. Thus, most behaviorists view

an individual's personality as a *collection of response tendencies that are tied to various stimulus situations*. A specific situation may be associated with a number of response tendencies that vary in strength, depending on an individual's past experience (see Figure 2.7).

Although behaviorists have shown relatively little interest in personality structure, they have focused extensively on personality *development*. They explain development the same way they explain everything else—through learning. Specifically, they focus on how children's response tendencies are shaped through classical conditioning, operant conditioning, and observational learning. Let's look at these processes.

Pavlov's Classical Conditioning

Do you go weak in the knees when you get a note at work that tells you to go see your boss? Do you get anxious when you're around important people? When you're driving, does your heart skip a beat at the sight of a police car—even when you're driving under the speed limit? If so, you probably acquired these common re-

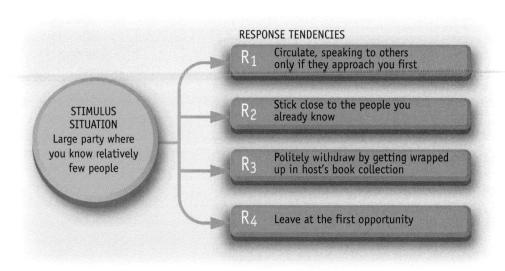

● FIGURE 2.7

A behavioral view of personality. Behaviorists devote little attention to the structure of personality because it is unobservable, but they implicitly view personality as an individual's collection of response tendencies. A possible hierarchy of response tendencies for a specific stimulus situation is shown here.

STIMULUS SITUATION
Large party where you know relatively few people

RESPONSE TENDENCIES

R₁ Circulate, speaking to others only if they approach you first

R₂ Stick close to the people you already know

R₃ Politely withdraw by getting wrapped up in host's book collection

R₄ Leave at the first opportunity

sponses through classical conditioning. ***Classical conditioning* is a type of learning in which a neutral stimulus acquires the capacity to evoke a response that was originally evoked by another stimulus.** This process was first described back in 1903 by Ivan Pavlov.

Ivan Pavlov

Pavlov was a prominent Russian physiologist who did Nobel Prize–winning research on digestion. He was a dedicated scientist who was obsessed with his research. Legend has it that Pavlov severely reprimanded an assistant who was late for an experiment because he was trying to avoid street fighting in the midst of the Russian Revolution. The assistant defended his tardiness, saying, "But Professor, there's a revolution going on, with shooting in the streets!" Pavlov supposedly replied, "Next time there's a revolution, get up earlier!" (Fancher, 1979; Gantt, 1975).

The Conditioned Reflex

Pavlov (1906) was studying digestive processes in dogs when he discovered that the dogs could be trained to salivate in response to the sound of a tone. What was so significant about a dog salivating when a tone was rung? The key was that the tone started out as a *neutral* stimulus; that is, originally it did not produce the response of salivation (after all, why should it?). However, Pavlov managed to change that by pairing the tone with a stimulus (meat powder) that did produce the salivation response. Through this process, the tone acquired the capacity to trigger the response of salivation. What Pavlov had demonstrated was *how learned reflexes are acquired.*

At this point we need to introduce the special vocabulary of classical conditioning (see Figure 2.8). In Pavlov's experiment the bond between the meat powder and salivation was a natural association that was not created through conditioning. In unconditioned bonds, **the *unconditioned stimulus (UCS)* is a stimulus that evokes an unconditioned response without previous conditioning. The *unconditioned response (UCR)* is an unlearned reaction to an unconditioned stimulus that occurs without previous conditioning.**

In contrast, the link between the tone and salivation was established through conditioning. In conditioned bonds, **the *conditioned stimulus (CS)* is a previously neutral stimulus that has acquired the capacity to evoke a conditioned response through conditioning. The *conditioned response (CR)* is a learned reaction to a conditioned stimulus that occurs because of previous conditioning.** Note that the unconditioned response and conditioned response often involve the same behavior (although there may be subtle differences). In Pavlov's initial demonstration, salivation

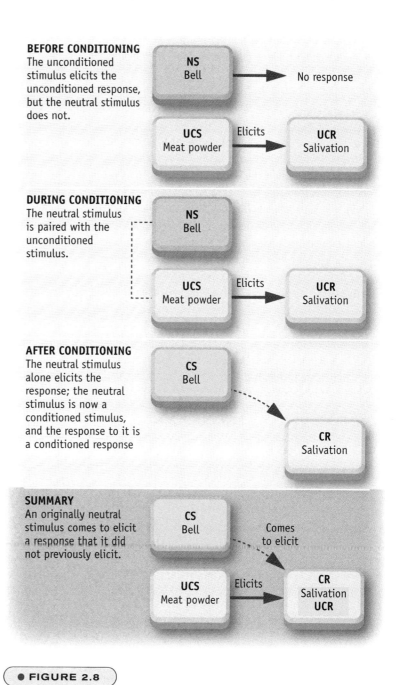

● **FIGURE 2.8**

The process of classical conditioning. The sequence of events in classical conditioning is outlined here. As we encounter new examples of classical conditioning throughout the book, you will see diagrams like that shown in the fourth panel, which summarizes the process.

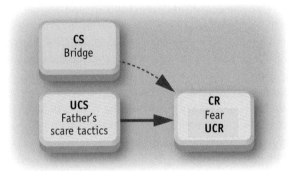

● FIGURE 2.9

Classical conditioning of a phobia. Many emotional responses that would otherwise be puzzling can be explained as a result of classical conditioning. In the case of one woman's bridge phobia, the fear originally elicited by her father's scare tactics became a conditioned response to the stimulus of bridges.

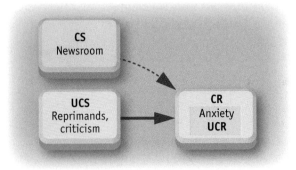

● FIGURE 2.10

Classical conditioning of anxiety. A stimulus (in this case, a newsroom) that is frequently paired with anxiety-arousing events (reprimands and criticism) may come to elicit anxiety by itself, through classical conditioning.

was an unconditioned response when evoked by the UCS (meat powder) and a conditioned response when evoked by the CS (the tone). The procedures involved in classical conditioning are outlined in Figure 2.8.

Pavlov's discovery came to be called the *conditioned reflex*. Classically conditioned responses are viewed as reflexes because most of them are relatively involuntary. Responses that are a product of classical conditioning are said to be *elicited*. This word is meant to convey the idea that these responses are triggered automatically.

Classical Conditioning in Everyday Life

What is the role of classical conditioning in shaping personality in everyday life? Among other things, it contributes to the acquisition of emotional responses, such as anxieties, fears, and phobias (Ayres, 1998; McAllister & McAllister, 1995). This is a relatively small but important class of responses, as maladaptive emotional reactions underlie many adjustment problems. For example, one middle-aged woman reported being troubled by a bridge phobia so severe that she couldn't drive on interstate highways because of all the viaducts she would have to cross. She was able to pinpoint the source of her phobia. Many years before, when her family would drive to visit her grandmother, they had to cross a little used, rickety, dilapidated bridge out in the countryside. Her father, in a misguided attempt at humor, made a major production out of these crossings. He would stop

WEB LINK 2.3

Behavior Analysis and Learning
A multitude of annotated links, all focusing on learning through conditioning, have been compiled at the excellent Psychology Centre site at Athabasca University (Alberta, Canada).

short of the bridge and carry on about the enormous danger of the crossing. Obviously, he thought the bridge was safe or he wouldn't have driven across it. However, the naive young girl was terrified by her father's scare tactics, and the bridge became a conditioned stimulus eliciting great fear (see Figure 2.9). Unfortunately, the fear spilled over to all bridges, and 40 years later she was still carrying the burden of this phobia. Although a number of processes can cause phobias, it is clear that classical conditioning is responsible for many of our irrational fears.

Classical conditioning also appears to account for more realistic and moderate anxiety responses. For example, imagine a news reporter in a high-pressure job where he consistently gets negative feedback about his work from his bosses. The negative comments from his supervisors function as a UCS eliciting anxiety. These reprimands are paired with the noise and sight of the newsroom, so that the newsroom becomes a CS triggering anxiety, even when his supervisors are absent (see Figure 2.10). Our poor reporter might even reach a point at which the mere *thought* of the newsroom elicits anxiety when he is elsewhere.

Fortunately, not every frightening experience leaves a conditioned fear in its wake. A variety of factors influence whether a conditioned response is acquired in a particular situation. Furthermore, a newly formed stimulus-response bond does not necessarily last indefinitely. The right circumstances can lead to **extinction—the gradual weakening and disappearance of a conditioned response tendency.** What leads to extinction in classical conditioning? It is the consistent presentation of the CS *alone*, without the UCS. For example, when Pavlov consistently presented *only* the tone to a previously conditioned dog, the tone gradually stopped eliciting the response of salivation. How long it takes to extinguish a conditioned response depends on many factors. Foremost among them is the strength of the conditioned bond when extinction begins. Some conditioned responses extinguish quickly, while others are difficult to weaken.

Skinner's Operant Conditioning

Even Pavlov recognized that classical conditioning is not the only form of conditioning. Classical conditioning best explains reflexive responding controlled by stimuli that *precede* the response. However, both animals and humans make many responses that don't fit this description. Consider the response you are engaging in right now—studying. It is definitely not a reflex (life might be easier if it were). The stimuli that govern it (exams and grades) do not precede it. Instead, your studying response is mainly influenced by events that follow it—specifically, its *consequences*.

This kind of learning is called *operant conditioning*. **Operant conditioning is a form of learning in which voluntary responses come to be controlled by their consequences.** Operant conditioning probably governs a larger share of human behavior than classical conditioning, since most human responses are voluntary rather than reflexive. Because they are voluntary, operant responses are said to be *emitted* rather than *elicited*.

The study of operant conditioning was led by B. F. Skinner (1953, 1974, 1990), a Harvard University psychologist who spent most of his career studying simple responses made by laboratory rats and pigeons. The fundamental principle of operant conditioning is uncommonly simple. Skinner demonstrated that *organisms tend to repeat those responses that are followed by favorable consequences, and they tend not to repeat those responses that are followed by neutral or unfavorable consequences.* In Skinner's scheme, favorable, neutral, and unfavorable consequences involve reinforcement, extinction, and punishment, respectively. We'll look at each of these concepts in turn.

Courtesy of B. F. Skinner

B. F. Skinner

The Power of Reinforcement

According to Skinner, reinforcement can occur in two ways, which he called *positive reinforcement* and *negative reinforcement*. **Positive reinforcement occurs when a response is strengthened (increases in frequency) because it is followed by the arrival of a (presumably) pleasant stimulus.** Positive reinforcement is roughly synonymous with the concept of reward. Notice, however, that reinforcement is defined *after the fact*, in terms of its effect on behavior. Why? Because reinforcement is subjective. Something that serves as a reinforcer for one person may not function as a reinforcer for an-

other. For example, peer approval is a potent reinforcer for most people, but not all.

Positive reinforcement motivates much of everyday behavior. You study hard because good grades are likely to follow as a result. You go to work because this behavior produces paychecks. Perhaps you work extra hard in the hopes of winning a promotion or a pay raise. In each of these examples, certain responses occur because they have led to positive outcomes in the past.

Positive reinforcement influences personality development in a straightforward way. Responses followed by pleasant outcomes are strengthened and tend to become habitual patterns of behavior. For example, a youngster might clown around in class and gain appreciative comments and smiles from schoolmates. This social approval will probably reinforce clowning-around behavior (see Figure 2.11). If such behavior is reinforced with some regularity, it will gradually become an integral element of the youth's personality. Similarly, whether or not a youngster develops traits such as independence, assertiveness, or selfishness depends on whether the child is reinforced for such behaviors by parents and by other influential persons.

Negative reinforcement **occurs when a response is strengthened (increases in frequency) because it is followed by the removal of a (presumably) unpleasant stimulus.** Don't let the word *negative* here confuse you. Negative reinforcement *is* reinforcement. Like positive reinforcement, it strengthens a response. How-

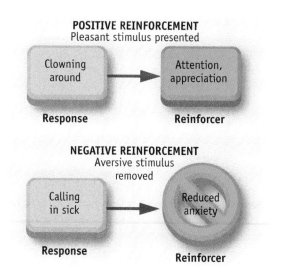

POSITIVE REINFORCEMENT
Pleasant stimulus presented

Clowning around → Attention, appreciation

Response   **Reinforcer**

NEGATIVE REINFORCEMENT
Aversive stimulus removed

Calling in sick → Reduced anxiety

Response   **Reinforcer**

● FIGURE 2.11

Positive and negative reinforcement in operant conditioning. Positive reinforcement occurs when a response is followed by a favorable outcome, so that the response is strengthened. In negative reinforcement, the removal (symbolized here by the "No" sign) of an aversive stimulus serves as a reinforcer. Negative reinforcement produces the same result as positive reinforcement: The person's tendency to emit the reinforced response is strengthened (the response becomes more frequent).

ever, this strengthening occurs because the response gets rid of an aversive stimulus. Consider a few examples: You rush home in the winter to get out of the cold. You clean your house to get rid of a mess. Parents give in to their child's begging to halt his whining.

Negative reinforcement plays a major role in the development of avoidance tendencies. As you may have noticed, many people tend to avoid facing up to awkward situations and sticky personal problems. This personality trait typically develops because avoidance behavior gets rid of anxiety and is therefore negatively reinforced. Recall our imaginary newspaper reporter, whose work environment (the newsroom) elicits anxiety (as a result of classical conditioning). He might notice that on days when he calls in sick, his anxiety evaporates, so that this response is gradually strengthened—through negative reinforcement (shown in Figure 2.11). If his avoidance behavior continues to be successful in reducing his anxiety, it might carry over into other areas of his life and become a central aspect of his personality.

Extinction and Punishment

Like the effects of classical conditioning, the effects of operant conditioning may not last forever. In both types of conditioning, *extinction* refers to the gradual weakening and disappearance of a response. In operant conditioning, extinction begins when a previously reinforced response stops producing positive consequences. As extinction progresses, the response typically becomes less and less frequent and eventually disappears.

Thus, the response tendencies that make up one's personality are not necessarily permanent. For example, the youngster who found that his classmates reinforced clowning around in grade school might find that his attempts at comedy earn nothing but indifferent stares in high school. This termination of reinforcement would probably lead to the gradual extinction of the clowning-around behavior. How quickly an operant response extinguishes depends on many factors in the person's earlier reinforcement history.

Some responses may be weakened by punishment. In Skinner's scheme, **punishment occurs when a response is weakened (decreases in frequency) because it is followed by the arrival of a (presumably) unpleasant stimulus.** The concept of punishment in operant conditioning confuses many students on two counts. First, it is often mixed up with negative reinforcement because both involve aversive (unpleasant) stimuli. Please note, however, that they are altogether different events with opposite outcomes! In negative reinforcement, a response leads to the removal of something aversive, and this response is strengthened.

In punishment, a response leads to the arrival of something aversive, and this response tends to be weakened.

The second source of confusion involves assuming that punishment as only a disciplinary procedure used by parents, teachers, and other authority figures. In the operant model, punishment occurs whenever a response leads to negative consequences. Defined in this way, the concept goes far beyond actions such as parents spanking children or teachers handing out detentions. For example, if you wear a new outfit and your friends make fun of it and hurt your feelings, your behavior has been punished, and your tendency to wear this clothing will decline. Similarly, if you go to a restaurant and have a horrible meal, in Skinner's terminology your response has led to punishment.

The impact of punishment on personality development is just the opposite of reinforcement. Generally speaking, those patterns of behavior that lead to punishing (that is, negative) consequences tend to be weakened. For instance, if your impulsive decisions always backfire, your tendency to be impulsive should decline.

According to Skinner (1987), conditioning in humans operates much as it does in the rats and pigeons that he has studied in his laboratory. Hence, he assumes that conditioning strengthens and weakens people's response tendencies "mechanically"—that is, without their conscious participation. Like John Watson (1913) before him, Skinner asserted that we can explain behavior without being concerned about individuals' mental processes.

Skinner's ideas continue to be influential, but his mechanical view of conditioning has not gone unchallenged by other behaviorists. Theorists such as Albert

The behavioral approach to personality centers around the principle of reinforcement—behaviors that are followed by favorable outcomes, such as attention, laughter, approval, and appreciation, tend to be strengthened and become more frequent.

Bandura have developed somewhat different behavioral models in which cognition plays a role. *Cognition* is another name for the thought processes that behaviorists have traditionally shown little interest in.

Bandura's Social Cognitive Theory

Albert Bandura

Courtesy, Albert Bandura

Albert Bandura is one of several theorists who have added a cognitive flavor to behaviorism since the 1960s. Bandura (1977), Walter Mischel (1973), and Julian Rotter (1982) take issue with Skinner's view. They point out that humans obviously are conscious, thinking, feeling beings. Moreover, these theorists argue that in neglecting cognitive processes, Skinner ignores the most distinctive and important feature of human behavior. Bandura and like-minded theorists originally called their modified brand of behaviorism *social learning theory*. Today, Bandura refers to his model as *social cognitive theory*.

Bandura (1986, 1999) agrees with the basic thrust of behaviorism in that he believes that personality is largely shaped through learning. However, he contends that conditioning is not a mechanical process in which people are passive participants. Instead, he maintains that individuals actively seek out and process information about their environment in order to maximize their favorable outcomes.

Observational Learning

Bandura's foremost theoretical contribution has been his description of observational learning. ***Observational learning* occurs when an organism's responding is influenced by the observation of others, who are called models.** Bandura does not view observational learning as entirely separate from classical and operant conditioning. Instead, he asserts that both classical and operant conditioning can take place indirectly when one person observes another's conditioning (see Figure 2.12).

To illustrate, suppose you observe a friend behaving assertively with a car salesman. Let's say that her assertiveness is reinforced by the exceptionally good buy she gets on the car. Your own tendency to behave assertively with salespeople might well be strengthened as a result. Notice that the favorable consequence is experienced by your friend, not you. Your friend's tendency to bargain assertively should be reinforced directly. But your tendency to bargain assertively may also be reinforced indirectly.

The theories of Skinner and Pavlov make no allowance for this type of indirect learning. After all, this observational learning requires that you pay *attention* to your friend's behavior, that you *understand* its consequences, and that you store this *information* in *memory*. Obviously, attention, understanding, information, and memory involve cognition, which behaviorists used to ignore.

As social cognitive theory has been refined, some models have become more influential than others (Bandura, 1986). Both children and adults tend to imitate people they like or respect more so than people they don't. People are also especially prone to imitate the behavior of those they consider attractive or powerful (such as celebrities). In addition, imitation is more likely when individuals see similarity between the model and themselves. Thus, children imitate same-sex role models somewhat more than other-sex models. Finally, as noted before, people are more likely to copy a model if they see the model's behavior leading to positive outcomes.

According to social cognitive theory, models have a great impact on personality development. Children learn to be assertive, conscientious, self-sufficient, dependable, easygoing, and so forth by observing others behaving in these ways. Parents, teachers, relatives, siblings, and peers serve as models for young children. Bandura and his colleagues have done extensive research showing how models influence the development of aggressiveness, gender roles, and moral standards in children (Bandura, 1973; Bussey & Bandura, 1984; Mischel & Mischel, 1976). Their research on modeling and aggression has been particularly influential.

Self-Efficacy

Bandura (1993, 1997) believes that *self-efficacy* is a crucial element of personality. ***Self-efficacy* is one's belief**

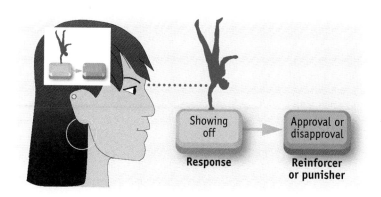

● FIGURE 2.12

Observational learning. In observational learning, an observer attends to and stores a mental representation of a model's behavior (for example, showing off) and its consequences (such as approval or disapproval from others). According to social cognitive theory, many of our characteristic responses are acquired through observation of others' behavior.

about one's ability to perform behaviors that should lead to expected outcomes. When a person's self-efficacy is high, he or she feels confident in executing the responses necessary to earn reinforcers. When self-efficacy is low, the individual worries that the necessary responses may be beyond her or his abilities. Perceptions of self-efficacy are subjective and specific to different kinds of tasks. For instance, you might feel extremely confident about your ability to handle difficult social situations but doubtful about your ability to handle academic challenges. Although specific perceptions of self-efficacy predict behavior best, these perceptions are influenced by general feelings of self-efficacy, which can be measured with the scale shown in Figure 2.13 (Sherer et al., 1982).

Perceptions of self-efficacy can influence which challenges people tackle and how well they perform. Studies have found that feelings of greater self-efficacy are associated with greater success in giving up smoking (Boudreaux et al., 1998); greater adherence to an exercise regimen (Rimal, 2001); better outcomes in substance abuse treatment (Bandura, 1999); more success in coping with medical rehabilitation (Waldrop et al., 2001); better self-care among diabetics (Williams & Bond, 2002); greater persistence and effort in academic pursuits (Zimmerman, 1995); higher levels of academic performance (Chemers, Hu, & Garcia, 2001); reduced vulnerability to anxiety and depression in childhood (Muris, 2002); enhanced performance in athletic competition (Kane et al., 1996); greater receptiveness to technological training (Christoph, Schoenfeld, & Tan-

sky, 1998); higher work-related performance (Stajkovic & Luthans, 1998); and greater resistance to stress (Jex et al., 2001), among many other things.

Evaluating Behavioral Perspectives

Behavioral theories are firmly rooted in empirical research rather than clinical intuition. Pavlov's model has shed light on how conditioning can account for people's sometimes troublesome emotional responses. Skinner's work has demonstrated how personality is shaped by the consequences of behavior. Bandura's social cognitive theory has shown how people's observations mold their characteristic behavior.

Behaviorists, in particular Walter Mischel (1973, 1990), have also provided the most thorough account of why people are only moderately consistent in their behavior. For example, a person who is shy in one context might be quite outgoing in another. Other models of personality largely ignore this inconsistency. The behaviorists have shown that this inconsistency occurs because people behave in ways they think will lead to reinforcement in the situation at hand. In other words, situational factors play a significant role in controlling behavior.

Of course, each theoretical approach has its shortcomings, and the behavioral approach is no exception. Major lines of criticism include the following (Liebert & Liebert, 1998; Maddi, 1989):

1. *Dilution of the behavioral approach.* The behaviorists used to be criticized because they neglected cog-

---

● FIGURE 2.13

Sample items from the Self-Efficacy Scale. The eight items shown here are taken from the Self-Efficacy Scale, developed by Sherer et al. (1982), a 23-item measure of general expectations of self-efficacy that are not tied to specific situations. The more items you agree with, the stronger your self-efficacy. High scores on the complete scale are predictive of vocational and educational success.

Adapted from Sherer, M., Maddox, J. E., Mercandante, B., Prentice-Dunn, S., Jacobs, B., & Rogers, R. W. (1982). The Self-Efficacy Scale: Construction and validation. *Psychological Reports, 51,* 663–671. Copyright © Psychological Reports 1982. Reproduced with permission of the authors and publisher.

The Self-Efficacy Scale

Instructions: This questionnaire is a series of statements about your personal attitudes and traits. Each statement represents a commonly held belief. Read each statement and decide to what extent it describes you. There are no right or wrong answers. You will probably agree with some statements and disagree with others. Please indicate your own personal feelings about each statement below by marking the letter that describes your attitude or feeling. Please be very truthful and describe yourself as you really are, not as you would like to be.

A = Disagree strongly   D = Agree moderately
B = Disagree moderately   E = Agree strongly
C = Neither agree nor disagree

1. _____ When I make plans I am certain I can make them work.

2. _____ If I can't do a job the first time, I keep trying until I can.

3. _____ If I see someone I would like to meet, I go to that person instead of waiting for him or her to come to me.

4. _____ When I have something unpleasant to do, I stick to it until I finish it.

5. _____ When I decide to do something, I go right to work on it.

6. _____ When I'm trying to become friends with someone who seems uninterested at first, I don't give up very easily.

7. _____ Failure just makes me try harder.

8. _____ I am a self-reliant person.

nitive processes, which clearly are important factors in human behavior. The rise of social cognitive theory blunted this criticism. However, social cognitive theory undermines the foundation on which behaviorism was built—the idea that psychologists should study only observable behavior. Thus, some critics complain that behavioral theories aren't very behavioral anymore.

2. *Overdependence on animal research.* Many principles in behavioral theories were discovered through research on animals. Some critics, especially humanistic theorists, argue that behaviorists depend too much on animal research and that they indiscriminately generalize from the behavior of animals to the behavior of humans.

Humanistic Perspectives

LEARNING OBJECTIVES

- Discuss humanism as a school of thought in psychology.
- Explain Rogers's views on self-concept, development, and defensive behavior.

- Describe Maslow's hierarchy of needs, and summarize his findings on self-actualizing persons.
- Evaluate the strengths and weaknesses of humanistic theories of personality.

Humanistic theory emerged in the 1950s as something of a backlash against the behavioral and psychodynamic theories (Cassel, 2000; DeCarvalho, 1991). The principal charge hurled at these two models was that they were dehumanizing. Freudian theory was criticized for its belief that primitive, animalistic drives dominate behavior. Behaviorism was criticized for its preoccupation with animal research. Critics argued that both schools view people as helpless pawns controlled by their environment and their past, with little capacity for self-direction. Many of these critics blended into a loose alliance that came to be known as humanism because of its exclusive interest in human behavior. *Hu-manism* **is a theoretical orientation that emphasizes the unique qualities of humans, especially their free will and their potential for personal growth.** Humanistic psychologists do not believe that we can learn anything of significance about the human condition from animal research.

Humanistic theorists take an optimistic view of human nature. In contrast to most psychodynamic and behavioral theorists, humanistic theorists believe that (1) human nature includes an innate drive toward personal growth, (2) individuals have the freedom to chart their courses of action and are not pawns of their environment, and (3) humans are largely conscious

and rational beings who are not dominated by unconscious, irrational needs and conflicts. Humanistic theorists also maintain that one's subjective view of the world is more important than objective reality. According to this notion, if you *think* you are homely, or bright, or sociable, these beliefs will influence your behavior more than the actual realities of how homely, bright, or sociable you are.

The humanistic approach clearly provides a different perspective on personality than either the psychodynamic or behavioral approach. In this section we'll review the ideas of the two most influential humanistic theorists, Carl Rogers and Abraham Maslow.

Rogers's Person-Centered Theory

Carl Rogers (1951, 1961, 1980) was one of the founders of the human potential movement, which emphasizes personal growth through sensitivity training, encounter groups, and other exercises intended to help people get in touch with their true selves. Working at the University of Chicago in the 1940s, Rogers devised a major new approach to psychotherapy. Like Freud, Rogers based his personality theory on his extensive therapeutic interactions with many clients. Because of his emphasis on a person's subjective point of view, Rogers called his approach a *person-centered theory.*

Carl Rogers

The Self and Its Development
Rogers viewed personality structure in terms of just one construct. He called this construct the *self,* although it is more widely known today as the *self-concept.* **A *self-concept* is a collection of beliefs about one's own**

WEB LINK 2.4

Personality Theories
C. George Boeree, who teaches personality theory at Shippensburg University, has assembled an online textbook that discusses more than 20 important personality theorists in depth. All of the important figures cited in this chapter (except for the behaviorists such as Skinner and Pavlov) receive attention at this valuable site.

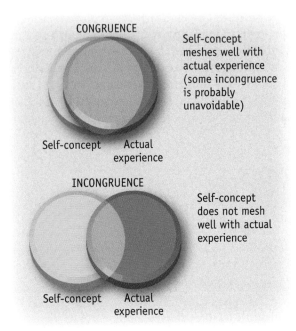
CONGRUENCE

Self-concept meshes well with actual experience (some incongruence is probably unavoidable)

Self-concept   Actual experience

INCONGRUENCE

Self-concept does not mesh well with actual experience

Self-concept   Actual experience

● **FIGURE 2.14**

Rogers's view of personality structure. In Rogers's model, the self-concept is the only important structural construct. However, Rogers acknowledged that one's self-concept may not jell with the realities of one's actual experience—a condition called incongruence. Different people have varied amounts of incongruence between their self-concept and reality.

nature, unique qualities, and typical behavior. Your self-concept is your mental picture of yourself. It is a collection of self-perceptions. For example, a self-concept might include such beliefs as "I am easygoing" or "I am pretty" or "I am hardworking."

Rogers stressed the subjective nature of the self-concept. Your self-concept may not be entirely consistent with your actual experiences. To put it more bluntly, your self-concept may be inaccurate. Most people are prone to distort their experiences to some extent to promote a relatively favorable self-concept. For example, you may believe that you are quite bright academically, but your grade transcript might suggest otherwise. Rogers used the term *incongruence* **to refer to the disparity between one's self-concept and one's actual experience.** In contrast, if a person's self-concept is reasonably accurate, it is said to be *congruent* with reality. Everyone experiences *some* incongruence; the crucial issue is how much (see Figure 2.14). Rogers maintained that a great deal of incongruence undermines a person's psychological well-being.

In terms of personality development, Rogers was concerned with how childhood experiences promote congruence or incongruence. According to Rogers, everyone has a strong need for affection, love, and accep-

tance from others. Early in life, parents provide most of this affection. Rogers maintained that some parents make their affection *conditional*. That is, they make it depend on the child's behaving well and living up to expectations. When parental love seems conditional, children often distort and block out of their self-concept those experiences that make them feel unworthy of love. At the other end of the spectrum, Rogers asserted that some parents make their affection *unconditional*. Their children have less need to block out unworthy experiences because they have been assured that they are worthy of affection no matter what they do.

Rogers believed that unconditional love from parents fosters congruence and that conditional love fosters incongruence. He further theorized that individuals who grow up believing that affection from others (besides their parents) is conditional go on to distort more and more of their experiences to feel worthy of acceptance from a wider and wider array of people, making the incongruence grow.

Anxiety and Defense

According to Rogers, experiences that threaten people's personal views of themselves are the principal cause of troublesome anxiety. The more inaccurate your self-concept, the more likely you are to have experiences that clash with your self-perceptions. Thus, people with highly incongruent self-concepts are espe-

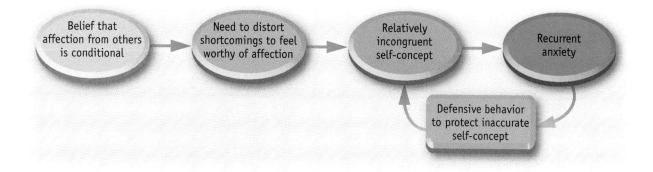

Rogers's view of personality development and dynamics. Rogers's theory of development posits that conditional love leads to a need to distort experiences, which fosters an incongruent self-concept. Incongruence makes one prone to recurrent anxiety, which triggers defensive behavior, which fuels more incongruence.

cially likely to be plagued by recurrent anxiety (see Figure 2.15).

To ward off this anxiety, such people often behave defensively. Thus, they ignore, deny, and twist reality to protect their self-concept. Consider a young woman who, like most of us, considers herself a "nice person." Let us suppose that in reality she is rather conceited and selfish, and she gets feedback from both boyfriends and girlfriends that she is a "self-centered, snotty brat." How might she react in order to protect her self-concept? She might ignore or block out those occasions when she behaves selfishly and then deny the accusations by her friends that she is self-centered. She might also attribute her girlfriends' negative comments to their jealousy of her good looks and blame the boyfriends' negative remarks on their disappointment because she won't get more serious with them. Meanwhile, she might start doing some kind of charity work to show everyone (including herself) that she really is a nice person. As you can see, people often go to great lengths to defend their self-concept.

Rogers's theory can explain defensive behavior and personality disturbances, but he also emphasized the importance of psychological health. Rogers held that psychological health is rooted in a congruent self-concept. In turn, congruence is rooted in a sense of personal worth, which stems from a childhood saturated with unconditional affection from parents and others. These themes are similar to those emphasized by the other major humanistic theorist, Abraham Maslow.

Maslow's Theory of Self-Actualization

Abraham Maslow grew up in Brooklyn and spent much of his career at Brandeis University, where he provided crucial leadership for the fledgling humanistic move-

Abraham Maslow

ment. Like Rogers, Maslow (1968, 1970) argued that psychology should take a greater interest in the nature of the healthy personality, instead of dwelling on the causes of disorders. "To oversimplify the matter somewhat," he said, "it is as if Freud supplied to us the sick half of psychology and we must now fill it out with the healthy half" (Maslow, 1968, p. 5). Maslow's key contributions were his analysis of how motives are organized hierarchically and his description of the healthy personality.

Hierarchy of Needs

Maslow proposed that human motives are organized into a *hierarchy of needs*—a systematic arrangement of needs, according to priority, in which basic needs must be met before less basic needs are aroused. This hierarchical arrangement is usually portrayed as a pyramid (see Figure 2.16 on the next page). The needs toward the bottom of the pyramid, such as physiological or security needs, are the most basic. Higher levels in the pyramid consist of progressively less basic needs. When a person manages to satisfy a level of needs reasonably well (complete satisfaction is not necessary), *this satisfaction activates needs at the next level.*

Like Rogers, Maslow argued that humans have an innate drive toward personal growth—that is, evolution toward a higher state of being. Thus, he described the needs in the uppermost reaches of his hierarchy as *growth needs.* These include the needs for knowledge, understanding, order, and aesthetic beauty. Foremost among the growth needs is the *need for self-actualization,* which is the need to fulfill one's potential; it is the highest need in Maslow's motivational hi-

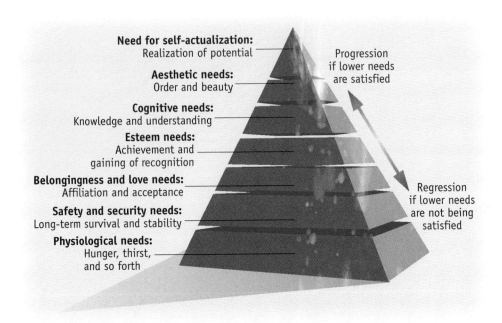

According to Maslow, human needs are arranged in a hierarchy, and individuals must satisfy their basic needs first, before they progress to higher needs. In the diagram, higher levels in the pyramid represent progressively less basic needs. People progress upward in the hierarchy when lower needs are satisfied reasonably well, but they may regress back to lower levels if basic needs cease to be satisfied.

erarchy. Maslow summarized this concept with a simple statement: "What a man *can* be, he *must* be." According to Maslow, people will be frustrated if they are unable to fully utilize their talents or pursue their true interests. For example, if you have great musical talent but must work as an accountant, or if you have scholarly interests but must work as a sales clerk, your need for self-actualization will be thwarted.

The Healthy Personality

Because of his interest in self-actualization, Maslow set out to discover the nature of the healthy personality. He tried to identify people of exceptional mental health so that he could investigate their characteristics. In one case, he used psychological tests and interviews to sort out the healthiest 1 percent of a sizable population of college students. He also studied admired historical figures (such as Thomas Jefferson and psychologist-philosopher William James) and personal acquaintances characterized by superior adjustment. Over a period of years, he accumulated his case histories and gradually sketched, in broad strokes, a picture of ideal psychological health.

Maslow called people with exceptionally healthy personalities *self-actualizing persons* because of their commitment to continued personal growth. He identified various traits characteristic of self-actualizing people, which are listed in Figure 2.17. In brief, Maslow found that self-actualizers are accurately tuned in to reality and are at peace with themselves. He found that they are open and spontaneous and that they retain a fresh appreciation of the world around them. Socially, they are sensitive to others' needs and enjoy rewarding interpersonal relations. However, they are not dependent on others for approval, nor are they uncomfort-

able with solitude. They thrive on their work, and they enjoy their sense of humor. Maslow also noted that they have "peak experiences" (profound emotional highs) more often than others. Finally, he found that they strike a nice balance between many polarities in personality, so that they can be both childlike and mature, rational and intuitive, conforming and rebellious.

Characteristics of Self-Actualizing People

- Clear, efficient perception of reality and comfortable relations with it
- Spontaneity, simplicity, and naturalness
- Problem centering (having something outside themselves they "must" do as a mission)
- Detachment and need for privacy
- Autonomy, independence of culture and environment
- Continued freshness of appreciation
- Mystical and peak experiences
- Feelings of kinship and identification with the human race
- Strong friendships, but limited in number
- Democratic character structure
- Ethical discrimination between means and ends, between good and evil
- Philosophical, unhostile sense of humor
- Balance between polarities in personality

● FIGURE 2.17

Characteristics of self-actualizing people. Humanistic theorists emphasize psychological health instead of maladjustment. Maslow's sketch of the self-actualizing person provides a provocative picture of the healthy personality.

PEANUTS reprinted by permission of United Feature Syndicate, Inc.

Evaluating Humanistic Perspectives

The humanists added a refreshing perspective to the study of personality. Their argument that a person's subjective views may be more important than objective reality has proven compelling. Today, even behavioral theorists have begun to consider subjective personal factors such as beliefs and expectations. The humanistic approach also deserves credit for making the self-concept an important construct in psychology. Finally, one could argue that the humanists' optimistic, growth, and health-oriented approach laid the foundation for the emergence of the positive psychology movement that is increasingly influential in contemporary psychology (Sheldon & Kasser, 2001b; Taylor, 2001).

Of course, there is a negative side to the balance sheet as well. Critics have identified some weaknesses in the humanistic approach to personality, including the following (Burger, 2000):

1. *Poor testability.* Like psychodynamic theorists, the humanists have been criticized for proposing hypotheses that are difficult to put to a scientific test. Humanistic concepts such as personal growth and self-actualization are difficult to define and measure.

2. *Unrealistic view of human nature.* Critics also charge that the humanists have been overly optimistic in their assumptions about human nature and unrealistic in their descriptions of the healthy personality.

WEB LINK 2.5

Great Ideas in Personality
At this site, personality psychologist G. Scott Acton demonstrates that scientific research programs in personality generate broad and compelling ideas about what it is to be a human being. He charts the contours of 12 research perspectives, including behaviorism, behavioral genetics, and sociobiology, and supports them with extensive links to published and online resources associated with each perspective.

For instance, Maslow's self-actualizing people sound *perfect*. In reality, Maslow had a hard time finding self-actualizing persons. When he searched among the living, the results were so disappointing that he turned to the study of historical figures. Thus, humanistic portraits of psychological health are perhaps a bit unrealistic.

3. *Inadequate evidence.* Humanistic theories are based primarily on discerning but uncontrolled observations in clinical settings. Case studies can be valuable in generating ideas, but they are ill-suited for building a solid database. More experimental research is needed to catch up with the theorizing in the humanistic camp. This situation is precisely the opposite of the one you'll encounter in the next section, on biological perspectives, where more theorizing is needed to catch up with the research.

Biological Perspectives

LEARNING OBJECTIVES

- *Describe Eysenck's views on personality structure and development.*
- *Summarize recent twin studies that support the idea that personality is largely inherited.*
- *Summarize evolutionary analyses of why certain personality traits appear to be important.*
- *Evaluate the strengths and weaknesses of biological theories of personality.*

Like many identical twins reared apart, Jim Lewis and Jim Springer found they had been leading eerily similar lives. Separated four weeks after birth in 1940, the Jim twins grew up 45 miles apart in Ohio and were reunited in 1979. Eventually, they discovered that both drove the

same model blue Chevrolet, chain-smoked Salems, chewed their fingernails, and owned dogs named Toy. Each had spent a good deal of time vacationing at the same three-block strip of beach in Florida. More important, when tested for such personality traits as flexibility, self-control,

The striking parallels in the lives of Jim Lewis and Jim Springer, identical twins separated soon after birth and reunited as adults, suggest that heredity may have a powerful impact on personality.

and sociability, the twins responded almost exactly alike. (Leo, 1987, p. 63)

So began a *Time* magazine summary of a major twin study conducted at the University of Minnesota, where investigators have been exploring the hereditary roots of personality. The research team has managed to locate and complete testing on 44 rare pairs of identical twins separated early in life. Not all the twin pairs have been as similar as Jim Lewis and Jim Springer, but many of the parallels have been uncanny (Lykken et al., 1992). Identical twins Oskar Stohr and Jack Yufe were separated soon after birth. Oskar was sent to a Nazi-run school in Czechoslovakia, while Jack was raised in a Jewish home on a Caribbean island. When they were reunited for the first time during middle age, they both showed up wearing similar mustaches, haircuts, shirts, and wire-rimmed glasses. A pair of previously separated female twins both arrived at the Minneapolis airport wearing seven rings on their fingers. One had a son named Richard Andrew, and the other had a son named Andrew Richard!

Could personality be largely inherited? These anecdotal reports of striking resemblances between identical twins reared apart certainly raise this possibility. In this section we'll discuss Hans Eysenck's theory, which emphasizes the influence of heredity, and look at behavioral genetics and evolutionary perspectives on personality.

Eysenck's Theory

Hans Eysenck was born in Germany but fled to London during the era of Nazi rule. He went on to become one

Hans Eysenck

of Britain's most prominent psychologists. According to Eysenck (1967), "Personality is determined to a large extent by a person's genes" (p. 20). How is heredity linked to personality in Eysenck's model? In part, through conditioning concepts borrowed from behavioral theory. Eysenck (1967, 1982, 1991) theorizes that some people can be conditioned more readily than others because of inherited differences in their physiological functioning (specifically, their level of arousal). These variations in "conditionability" are assumed to influence the personality traits that people acquire through conditioning.

Eysenck views personality structure as a hierarchy of traits. Numerous superficial traits are derived from a smaller number of more basic traits, which are derived from a handful of fundamental higher-order traits, as shown in Figure 2.18. Eysenck has shown a special interest in explaining variations in *extraversion-introversion*, the trait dimension first described years earlier by Carl Jung. He has proposed that introverts tend to have higher levels of physiological arousal than extraverts. This higher arousal purportedly motivates them to avoid social situations that will further elevate their arousal and makes them more easily conditioned than extraverts. According to Eysenck, people who condition easily acquire more conditioned inhibitions than others. These inhibitions, coupled with their relatively high arousal, make them more bashful, tentative, and uneasy in social situations. This social discomfort leads them to turn inward. Hence, they become introverted.

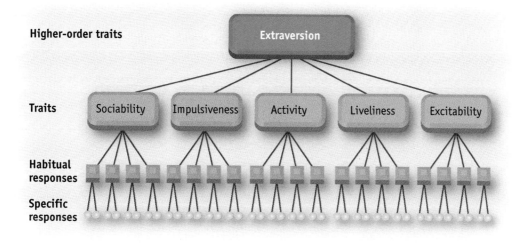

Higher-order traits

Extraversion

Traits

Sociability · Impulsiveness · Activity · Liveliness · Excitability

Habitual responses

Specific responses

● **FIGURE 2.18**

Eysenck's model of personality structure. Eysenck describes personality structure as a hierarchy of traits. In this scheme, a few higher-order traits (such as extraversion) determine a host of lower-order traits (such as sociability), which determine one's habitual responses (such as going to lots of parties).

From Eysenck, H. J. (1967). *The biological basis of personality*, p. 36. Springfield, IL: Charles C. Thomas. Courtesy of Charles C. Thomas.

Recent Research in Behavioral Genetics

Recent twin studies have provided impressive support for Eysenck's hypothesis that personality is largely inherited. In *twin studies* researchers assess hereditary influence by comparing the resemblance of identical twins and fraternal twins on a trait. The logic underlying this comparison is as follows. *Identical twins* emerge from one egg that splits, so that their genetic makeup is exactly the same (100 percent overlap). *Fraternal twins* result when two eggs are fertilized simultaneously; their genetic overlap is only 50 percent. Both types of twins *usually* grow up in the same home, at the same time, exposed to the same relatives, neighbors, peers, teachers, events, and so forth. Thus, both kinds of twins normally develop under similar environmental conditions, but identical twins share more genetic kinship. Hence, if sets of identical twins exhibit more personality resemblance than sets of fraternal twins, this greater similarity is probably attributable to heredity rather than to environment. The results of twin studies can be used to estimate the heritability of personality traits and other characteristics. **A *heritability ratio* is an estimate of the proportion of trait variability in a population that is determined by variations in genetic inheritance.** Heritability can be estimated for any trait. For example, the heritability of height is estimated to be around 90 percent (Plomin, 1994), whereas the heritability of intelligence appears to be about 50–70 percent (Bouchard et al., 1990).

The accumulating evidence from twin studies suggests that heredity exerts considerable influence over many personality traits (Rowe, 1997, 1999). For instance,

in research on the Big Five personality traits, identical twins have been found to be much more similar than fraternal twins on all five traits (Loehlin, 1992). Some skeptics still wonder whether identical twins might exhibit more personality resemblance than fraternal twins because they are raised more similarly. In other words, they wonder whether environmental factors (rather than heredity) could be responsible for identical twins' greater similarity. This nagging question can be answered only by studying identical twins who have been reared apart. Which is why the twin study at the University of Minnesota was so important.

The Minnesota study (Tellegen et al., 1988) was the first to administer the same personality test to identical and fraternal twins reared together as well as apart. Most of the twins reared apart were separated quite early in life (median age of 2.5 months) and remained separated for a long time (median period of almost 34 years). Nonetheless, on all three of the higher-order traits examined, the identical twins reared apart displayed more personality resemblance than fraternal twins reared together. Based on the pattern of correlations observed, the researchers estimated that the heritability of personality is around 50 percent. Another large-scale twin study of the Big Five traits conducted in Germany and Poland yielded similar conclusions (Riemann, Angleitner, & Strelau, 1997). The heritability estimates based on the data from this study, which are shown in Figure 2.19 on the next page, are in the same range as the estimates from the Minnesota study.

Research on the genetic bases of personality has inadvertently turned up another interesting finding that is apparent in the data shown in Figure 2.19. A num-

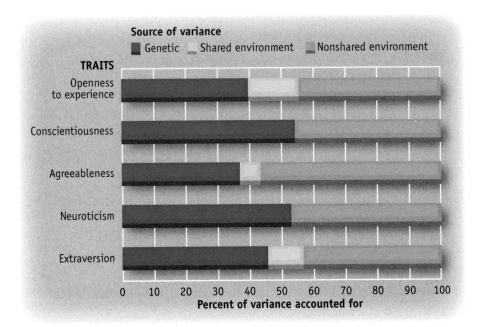

● FIGURE 2.19

Heritability and environmental variance for the Big Five traits.
Based on the twin study data of Riemann et al. (1997), Plomin and Caspi (1999) estimated the heritability of each of the Big Five traits. The data also allowed them to estimate the amount of variance on each trait attributable to shared environment and nonshared environment. As you can see, the heritability estimates hovered in the vicinity of 40 percent, with two exceeding 50 percent. As in other studies, the influence of shared environment was very modest.

Based on Plomin, R., & Caspi, A. (1999). Behavioral genetics and personality. In L. A. Pervin & O. P. John (Eds.), *Handbook of Personality: Theory and Research*. New York: The Guilford Press. Adapted by permission.

ber of recent studies have found that shared family environment has surprisingly little impact on personality (Beer, Arnold, & Loehlin, 1998; Plomin & Caspi, 1999). This finding is surprising in that social scientists have long assumed that the family environment shared by children growing up together led to some personality resemblance among them. *These findings have led some theorists to conclude that parents don't matter—that they wield very little influence over how their children develop* (Cohen, 1999; Harris, 1998; Rowe, 1994).

Critics of this conclusion have argued that the methods used in behavioral genetics studies have probably underestimated the impact of shared environment on personality (Collins et al., 2000; Stoolmiller, 1999). They also note that shared experiences—such as being raised with authoritarian discipline—may often have different effects on two siblings, which obscures the impact of environment but is not the same result as having no effect (Turkheimer & Waldron, 2000). Furthermore, the critics argue, decades of research in developmental psychology have clearly demonstrated that parents have significant influence on their children (Maccoby, 2000).

Although the assertion that "parents don't matter" seems premature and overstated, the perplexing findings in behavioral genetics studies of personality have led researchers to investigate why children from the same family are often so different. Thus far, the evidence suggests that children in the same family experience home environments that are not nearly as homogeneous as previously assumed (Hetherington, Reiss, & Plomin, 1994; Pike et al., 2000). Children in the same home may be treated quite differently, because gender and birth order can influence parents' approaches to child-rearing. Temperamental differences between children may also evoke differences in parenting. Focusing on how environmental factors vary *within* families represents a promising new way to explore the determinants of personality.

The Evolutionary Approach to Personality

In the realm of biological approaches to personality, the most recent development has been the emergence of an evolutionary perspective. Evolutionary psychologists assert that the patterns of behavior seen in a species are products of evolution in the same way that anatomical characteristics are. ***Evolutionary psychology* examines behavioral processes in terms of their adaptive value for members of a species over the course of many generations.** The basic premise of evolutionary psychology is that natural selection favors behaviors that enhance organisms' reproductive success—that is, passing on genes to the next generation. Thus, evolutionary analyses of personality focus on how various traits—and the ability to recognize these traits in others—may have contributed to reproductive fitness in ancestral human populations.

For example, David Buss (1991, 1995, 1997) has argued that the Big Five personality traits stand out as important dimensions of personality across a variety of cultures because those traits have had significant adaptive implications. Buss points out that humans have historically depended heavily on groups, which afford protection from predators or enemies, opportunities for sharing food, and a diverse array of other benefits. In the context of these group interactions, people have had to make difficult but crucial judgments about the characteristics of others, asking such questions as: Who will make a good member of my coalition? Who can I depend on when in need? Who will share their resources? Thus, Buss (1995) argues, "Those individuals able to accurately discern and act upon these individual differences likely enjoyed a considerable reproductive advantage" (p. 22). According to Buss, the Big Five emerge as fundamental dimensions of personality because humans have evolved special sensitivity to variations in the ability to bond with others (extraversion), the willingness to cooperate and collaborate (agreeableness), the tendency to be reliable and ethical (conscientiousness), the capacity to be an innovative problem solver (openness to experience), and the ability to handle stress (low neuroticism). In a nutshell, the Big Five supposedly reflect the most salient personality features in ancestral humans' adaptive landscape.

Evaluating Biological Perspectives

Although evolutionary analyses of personality are pretty speculative, recent research in behavioral genetics has provided convincing evidence that biological factors help shape personality. Nonetheless, we must take note of some weaknesses in biological approaches to personality:

1. *Problems with estimates of hereditary influence.* Efforts to carve personality into genetic and environmental components with statistics are ultimately artificial. The effects of heredity and environment are twisted together in complicated interactions that can't be separated cleanly (Brody & Crowley, 1995; Funder, 2001). Although heritability ratios sound precise, they are estimates based on a complicated chain of inferences that are subject to debate.

2. *Lack of adequate theory.* At present there is no comprehensive biological theory of personality. Eysenck's model does not provide a systematic overview of how biological factors govern personality development (and it was never intended to). Evolutionary analyses of personality are even more limited in scope. Additional theoretical work is needed to catch up with recent empirical findings on the biological basis for personality.

A Contemporary Empirical Approach: Terror Management Theory

LEARNING OBJECTIVES
- *Explain the chief concepts and hypotheses of terror management theory.*
- *Describe how reminders of death influence people's behavior.*

So far, our coverage has been largely devoted to grand, panoramic theories of personality. In this section we'll examine a new approach to understanding personality functioning that has a narrower focus than the classic theories of personality. *Terror management theory* emerged as an influential perspective in the 1990s. Although the theory borrows from Freudian and evolutionary formulations, it provides its own unique analysis of the human condition. This fresh perspective is currently generating a huge volume of research, and it seems especially relevant to contemporary adjustment issues.

Essentials of Terror Management Theory

One of the chief goals of terror management theory is to explain why people need self-esteem (Solomon, Greenberg, & Pyszczynski, 1991). The theory begins with the assumption that humans share an evolutionary heritage with other animals that includes an instinctive drive for self-preservation. However, unlike other animals, humans have evolved complex cognitive abilities that permit self-awareness and contemplation of the future. These cognitive capacities make humans keenly aware of the inevitability of death—they appreciate that life can be snuffed out unpredictably at any time. The collision between humans' self-preservation instinct and their awareness of the inevitability of death creates the potential for experiencing anxiety, alarm, and terror when people think about their mortality (see Figure 2.20).

How do humans deal with this potential for terror? According to terror management theory, "What saves us is culture. Cultures provide ways to view the world—worldviews—that 'solve' the existential crisis engendered by the awareness of death" (Pyszczynski, Solomon, & Greenberg, 2004, p. 16). Cultural worldviews diminish anxiety by providing answers to universal questions such as Why am I here? and What is the meaning of life? Cultures create stories, traditions, and institutions that give their members a sense of being part of an enduring legacy through their contributions to their families, tribes, schools, churches, professions, and so forth. Thus, faith in a cultural worldview can give people a sense of order, meaning, and context that can soothe their fear of death.

Where does self-esteem fit into the picture? Self-esteem is viewed as a sense of personal worth that depends on one's confidence in the validity of one's cultural worldview and the belief that one is living up to the standards prescribed by that worldview. "It is the feeling that one is a valuable contributor to a meaningful universe" (Pyszczynski et al., 2004, p. 437). Hence, self-esteem buffers people from the profound anxiety associated with the awareness that they are transient animals destined to die. In other words, self-esteem serves a *terror management* function (refer to Figure 2.20).

The notion that self-esteem functions as an *anxiety buffer* has been supported by numerous studies (Pyszczynski et al., 2004). In many of these experiments, researchers have manipulated what they call *mortality salience* by asking subjects to briefly think about their own death. Consistent with the anxiety buffer hypothesis, reminding people of their mortality leads subjects to engage in a variety of behaviors that are likely to bolster their self-esteem, thus reducing anxiety (see Chapter 5 for more on the terror management function of self-esteem).

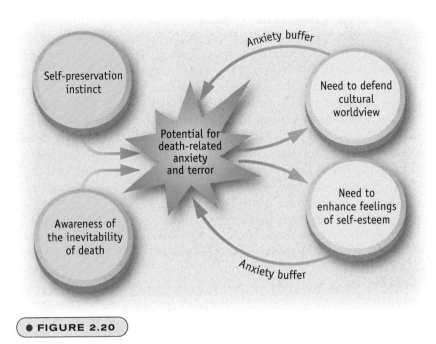

● FIGURE 2.20

Overview of terror management theory. This graphic maps out the relations among the key concepts proposed by terror management theory. The theory asserts that humans' unique awareness of the inevitability of death fosters a need to defend one's cultural worldview and one's self-esteem, which serve to protect one from mortality-related anxiety.

Applications of Terror Management Theory

Increasing mortality salience also leads people to work harder at defending their cultural worldview. For instance, after briefly pondering their mortality, research participants (1) hand out harsher penalties to moral transgressors, (2) respond more negatively to people who criticize their country, (3) give larger rewards to people who uphold cultural standards, and (4) show more respect for cultural icons, such as a flag (Greenberg et al., 1990; Rosenblatt et al., 1989). This need to defend one's cultural worldview may even fuel prejudice and aggression. Reminding subjects of their mortality leads to (1) more negative evaluations of people from different religious or ethnic backgrounds, (2) more stereotypic thinking about minority group members, and (3) more aggressive behavior toward people with opposing political views (McGregor et al., 1998; Schimel et al., 1999).

Terror management theory asserts that much of our behavior is motivated by the overlapping needs to defend our cultural worldview and to preserve our self-esteem. This perspective yields novel hypotheses regarding many phenomena. For instance, Solomon, Greenberg, and Pyszczynski (2004) explain excessive materialism in terms of the anxiety-buffering function of self-esteem. Specifically, they argue that "conspicuous possession and consumption are thinly veiled efforts to assert that one is special and therefore more than just an animal fated to die and decay" (p. 134). In another thought-provoking analysis, the architects of terror management theory argue that people high in neuroticism tend to be especially uptight about sex because sexuality lies at the core of humans' animal nature and hence their ultimate mortality (Goldenberg et al., 1999). Terror management theory has also been used to explain depressive disorders. According to Arndt et al. (2000), depression occurs when individuals' anxiety buffer fails and they lose faith in the cultural worldview that gave their life meaning. One recent study even applied terror management theory to the political process. Cohen et al. (2004) found that mortality salience increases subjects' preference for "charismatic" candidates who articulate a grand vision that makes people feel like they are part of an important movement of lasting significance.

Understanding Reactions to 9/11

Although its name might suggest otherwise, terror management theory was not developed to deal with the phenomenon of terrorism in the aftermath of 9/11. Terror management theory has been around since the mid-1980s, and as the text explains, it is a wide-ranging theory that analyzes the many ramifications of humans' existential struggle with the inevitability of death (see pp. 59–60, 62). Nonetheless, given its central focus on the effects of reminding people of their mortality, the theory can help us understand the psychological impact of the 9/11 terrorist attacks in the United States.

In their book *In the Wake of 9/11*, Tom Pyszczynski, Sheldon Solomon, and Jeff Greenberg (2003) point out that the tragic events of 9/11 produced a powerful, nationwide manipulation of mortality salience. The televised images of death and destruction seen that day made most Americans feel extremely vulnerable. Moreover, the terrorists dealt Americans a double blow in that the destruction was inflicted on two respected icons of American culture: the Pentagon and the World Trade Center. Thus, the 9/11 terrorist strikes were attacks on Americans' cultural worldview, which terror management theory asserts is humanity's main defense against death anxiety.

According to the architects of terror management theory, many of the reactions seen across the country after 9/11 were exactly what one would expect based on their theory. Included among these reactions were the following.

Reaffirmation of cultural worldviews. When mortality salience is elevated, terror management theory predicts that people will embrace their cultural worldviews even more strongly than before. Consistent with this prediction, in the months following 9/11, church attendance and the sale of bibles both increased dramatically. Thus, people reaffirmed their faith in organized religion, which represents the foundation of many individuals' cultural worldview. People also became much more overtly patriotic. Flags flew everywhere, patriotic songs were all over the radio, and corporate logos were redesigned in red, white, and blue. Thus, people proudly proclaimed their faith in the American way.

Reduced tolerance. Research on terror management processes has shown that when death anxiety is heightened, people become less tolerant of opposing views and more prejudiced against those who are different. Consistent with this analysis, in the aftermath of 9/11, individuals who questioned government policies met more hostility than usual. Increased prejudice and bigotry toward Arab Americans and people of Middle Eastern descent was also readily apparent.

Increased altruism. Altruism, which consists of unselfish concern for the welfare of others, is a highly respected virtue in most cultures. Behaving in an altruistic manner makes people feel like they are good citizens, thus reaffirming their commitment to their cultural worldview and enhancing their self-esteem. Hence, terror management theory would anticipate that increased mortality salience would stimulate increased altruism, which clearly was seen in the months after the terrorist assaults. Many people traveled to New York or Washington to help in whatever way they could after the attacks. Blood donations reached unprecedented levels, and charitable giving skyrocketed.

Intensified need for heroes. Research indicates that reminders of mortality increase the tendency to admire those who uphold cultural standards. More than ever, people need heroes who personify cultural values. This need was apparent in the aftermath of 9/11 in the way the media made firefighters into larger-than-life heroes. This analysis is not meant to suggest that firefighters did not deserve to be characterized as heroic. Rather, the point is that firefighters had a long history of heroic behavior that largely went unrecognized until a massive increase in mortality salience created an urgent need for uplifting heroes.

Admittedly, some of the reactions to 9/11 predicted by terror management theory could also be explained by other theoretical perspectives. Nonetheless, terror management theory seems to provide a perspective that is uniquely well suited to understanding some of the effects of terrorism on our collective psyche.

Terror management theory has been applied to a remarkably diverse array of phenomena. For example, it has been used to explain conspicuous consumption and to predict people's voting preferences.

Although terror management theory is narrower in scope than psychoanalytic, behavioral, and humanistic theories, it has wide-ranging implications and is being applied to more and more aspects of human behavior. In particular, given its focus on death anxiety, it has much to say about people's reactions to terrorism (see the Living in Today's World box on page 61).

At first glance, a theory that explains everything from prejudice to compulsive shopping in terms of death anxiety may seem highly implausible. After all, most people do not appear to walk around all day obsessing about the possibility of their death. The architects of terror management theory are well aware of this reality. They explain that the defensive reactions uncovered in their research generally occur when death anx-

iety surfaces on the fringes of conscious awareness and that these reactions are automatic and subconscious (Pyszczynski, Greenberg, & Solomon, 1999). They also assert that people experience far more reminders of their mortality than most of us appreciate. They point out that people may be reminded of their mortality by a host of everyday events, such as driving by a cemetery or funeral home, reading about an auto accident, visiting a doctor's office, hearing about a celebrity's heart attack, learning about alarming medical research, skipping over the obituaries in the newspaper, and so forth. Thus, the processes discussed by terror management theory may be more commonplace that one might guess.

An Epilogue on Theoretical Diversity

LEARNING OBJECTIVES

- Discuss why the subject of personality has generated so much theoretical diversity.
- Compare and contrast the personality theories of Freud, Skinner, Rogers, and Eysenck.

Figure 2.21 provides a comparative overview of the ideas of Freud, Skinner, Rogers, and Eysenck, as representatives of the psychodynamic, behavioral, humanistic, and biological approaches to personality. Most of this information was covered in the chapter, but the figure organizes it so that the similarities and differences between the theories become more apparent. As you can see, there are many fundamental points of disagreement. Our review of perspectives on personality should have made one thing abundantly clear: Psychology is marked by theoretical diversity.

Why do we have so many competing points of view? One reason is that no single theory can adequately explain everything that we know about personality. Sometimes different theories focus on different aspects of behavior. Sometimes there is simply more than one way to look at something. Is the glass half empty or half full? Obviously, it is both. To take an example from another science, physicists wrestled for years with the nature of light. Is it a wave, or is it a particle? In the end, it proved useful to think of light sometimes as a wave, and sometimes as a particle. Similarly, if a business executive

Overview of Four Approaches to Personality

	Sigmund Freud: A psychodynamic view	B. F. Skinner: A behavioral view	Carl Rogers: A humanistic view	Hans Eysenck: A biological view
Source of data and observations	Case studies from clinical practice of psychoanalysis	Laboratory experiments primarily with animals	Case studies from clinical practice of client-centered therapy	Twin, family, and adoption studies of hereditary influence; factor analysis studies of personality structure
Key motivational forces	Sex and aggression; need to reduce tension produced by internal conflicts	Pursuit of primary (unlearned) and secondary (learned) reinforcers; priorities depend on personal history	Actualizing tendency (need for personal growth) and self-actualizing tendency (need to maintain self-concept)	No specific motivational forces singled out
Model of personality structure	Three interacting components (id, ego, super-ego) operating at three levels of consciousness	Collection of response tendencies tied to specific stimulus situations	Self-concept, which may or may not be congruent with actual experience	Hierarchy of traits, with specific traits derived from more fundamental, general traits
View of personality development	Emphasis on fixation or progress through psychosexual stages; experiences in early childhood leave lasting mark on adult personality	Personality evolves gradually over the life span (not in stages); responses followed by reinforcement become more frequent	Children who receive unconditional love have less need to be defensive; they develop more accurate, congruent self-concepts; conditional love fosters incongruence	Emphasis on unfolding of genetic blueprint with maturation; inherited predispositions interact with learning experiences
Roots of disorders	Unconscious fixations and unresolved conflicts from childhood, usually centered on sex and aggression	Maladaptive behavior due to faulty learning; the "symptom" is the problem, not a sign of underlying disease	Incongruence between self-concept and actual experience; overdependence on others for approval and sense of worth	Genetic vulnerability activated in part by environmental factors
Importance of nature (biology, heredity) vs. nurture (environment, experience)	Nature: emphasis on biological basis of instinctual drives	Nurture: strong emphasis on learning, conditioning, role of experience	Nurture: interested in innate potentials, but humanists believe we can rise above our biological heritage	Nature: strong emphasis on how hereditary predispositions shape personality
Importance of person factors vs. situation factors	Person: main interest is in internal factors (id, ego, conflicts, defenses, etc.)	Situation: strong emphasis on how one responds to specific stimulus situations	Person: focus on self-concept, which is stable	Person: interested in stable traits molded by heredity

● FIGURE 2.21

Comparison of four theoretical perspectives on personality. This chart compares the theories of Freud, Skinner, Rogers, and Eysenck to highlight the similarities and differences between the psychodynamic, behavioral, humanistic, and biological approaches to personality.

lashes out at her employees with stinging criticism, is she releasing pent-up aggressive urges (a psychoanalytic view)? Is she making a habitual response to the stimulus of incompetent work (a behavioral view)? Is she trying to act like a tough boss because that's a key aspect of her self-concept (a humanistic view)? Or is she exhibiting an inherited tendency to be aggressive (a biological view)? In some cases, all four of these explanations might have some validity.

In short, it is an oversimplification to expect that one view has to be right while all others are wrong. Life is rarely that simple. In view of the complexity of per-

sonality, it would be surprising if there were *not* a number of different theories. It's probably best to think of the various theoretical orientations in psychology as complementary viewpoints, each with its own advantages and limitations. Indeed, modern psychologists increasingly recognize that theoretical diversity is a strength rather than a weakness (Hilgard, 1987; Kleinginna & Kleinginna, 1988). As we proceed through this text, you will see how differing theoretical perspectives often inspire fruitful research and how they sometimes converge on a more complete understanding of behavior than could be achieved by any one perspective alone.

APPLICATION

Assessing Your Personality

LEARNING OBJECTIVES

- Explain the concepts of standardization, test norms, reliability, and validity.
- Discuss the value and the limitations of self-report inventories.
- Discuss the value and limitations of projective tests.

Answer the following "true" or "false."

___ **1.** Responses to personality tests are subject to unconscious distortion.

___ **2.** The results of personality tests are often misunderstood.

___ **3.** Personality test scores should be interpreted with caution.

___ **4.** Personality tests may be quite useful in helping people to learn more about themselves.

If you answered "true" to all four questions, you earned a perfect score. Yes, personality tests are subject to distortion. Admittedly, test results are often misunderstood, and they should be interpreted cautiously. In spite of these problems, however, psychological tests can be very useful.

We all engage in efforts to size up our own personality as well as that of others. When you think to yourself that "this salesman is untrustworthy," or when you remark to a friend that "Howard is too timid and submissive," you are making personality assessments. In a sense, then, personality assessment is part of daily life. However, psychological tests provide much more systematic assessments than casual observations do.

The value of psychological tests lies in their ability to help people form a realistic picture of their personal qualities. In light of this value, we have included a variety of personality tests in the *Personal Explorations Workbook* that is available to accompany this text, and we have sprinkled a number of short tests throughout the text itself. Most of these questionnaires are widely used personality tests. We hope that you may gain some insights by responding to these scales. But it's important to understand the logic and limitations of such tests. To facilitate your use of these and other tests, this Application discusses some of the basics of psychological testing.

Key Concepts in Psychological Testing

A *psychological test* is a standardized measure of a sample of a person's behavior. Psychological tests are measurement instruments. They are used to measure abilities, aptitudes, and personality traits.

Note that your responses to a psychological test represent a *sample* of your behavior. This fact should alert you to one of the key limitations of psychological tests: It's always possible that a particular behavior sample is not representative of your characteristic behavior. We all have our bad days. A stomachache, a fight with a friend, a problem with your car—all might affect your responses to a particular test on a particular day. Because of the limitations of the sampling process, test scores should always be interpreted *cautiously.* Most psychological tests are sound measurement devices, but test results should not be viewed as the "final word" on one's personality and abilities because of the ever-present sampling problem.

Most psychological tests can be placed in one of two broad categories: (1) mental ability tests, and (2) personality tests. *Mental ability tests,* such as intelligence tests, aptitude tests, and achievement tests, often serve as gateways to schooling, training programs, and jobs. *Personality* tests measure various aspects of personality, including motives, interests, values, and attitudes. Many psychologists prefer to call these tests personality *scales,* since the questions do not have right and wrong answers as do those on tests of mental abilities.

Standardization and Norms

Both personality scales and tests of mental abilities are standardized measures of behavior. *Standardization refers to the uniform procedures used to administer and score a test.* All subjects get the same instructions, the same questions, the same time limits, and so on, so that their scores can be compared meaningfully.

The standardization of a test's scoring system includes the development of test norms. *Test norms provide information about where a score on a psychological test ranks in relation to other scores on that test.* Why do we need test norms? Because in psychological testing, everything is relative. Psychological tests tell you how you score *relative to other people.* They tell you, for instance, that you are average in impulsiveness, or slightly above average in assertiveness, or far below average in anxiety. These interpretations are derived from the test norms.

Reliability and Validity

Any kind of measuring device, whether it's a tire gauge, a stopwatch, or a psychological test, should be reasonably consistent. That is, repeated measurements should yield reasonably similar results. To appreciate the importance of reliability, think about how you would react if a tire pressure gauge gave you several different readings for the same tire. You would probably conclude that the gauge was broken and toss it into the garbage, because you know that consistency in measurement is essential to accuracy.

Reliability refers to the measurement consistency of a test. A reliable test is one that yields similar results upon repetition of the test (see Figure 2.22). Like most other types of measuring devices, psychological tests are not perfectly reliable. They usually do not yield the exact same score when repeated. A certain amount of inconsistency is unavoidable because human behavior is variable. Personality tests tend to have lower reliability than mental ability tests because daily fluctuations in mood influence how people respond to such tests.

Even if a test is quite reliable, we still need to be concerned about its validity. *Validity* refers to the ability of a test to measure what it was designed to measure. If we develop a new test of assertiveness, we have to provide some evidence that it really measures assertiveness. Validity can be demonstrated in a variety of ways. Most of them involve correlating scores on a test with other measures of the same trait, or with related traits.

Self-Report Inventories

The vast majority of personality tests are self-report inventories. *Self-report inventories* are personality scales that ask individuals to answer a series of questions about their characteristic behavior. When you respond to a self-report personality scale, you endorse statements as true or false as applied to you, you indicate how often you behave in a particular way, or you rate yourself with respect to certain qualities. For example, on the Minnesota Multiphasic Personality Inventory, people respond "true," "false," or "cannot say" to 567 statements such as the following:

I get a fair deal from most people.
I have the time of my life at parties.
I am glad that I am alive.
Several people are following me everywhere.

The logic underlying this approach is simple: Who knows you better than you do? Who has known you longer? Who has more access to your private feelings?

The entire range of personality traits can be measured with self-report inventories. Some scales measure just one trait dimension, such as the Self-Efficacy Scale discussed earlier or the measure of sensation seeking shown in Figure 2.23 on the next page. Others simultaneously assess a multitude of traits. The Sixteen Personality Factor Questionnaire (16PF), developed by Raymond Cattell and his colleagues (Cattell, Eber, & Tatsuoka, 1970), is a representative example of a multitrait inventory. The 16PF is a 187-item scale that measures 16 basic dimensions of personality, called source traits, which are shown in Figure 2.24 on p. 67.

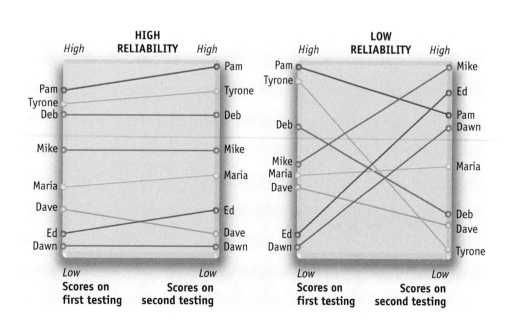

● FIGURE 2.22

Test reliability. Subjects' scores on the first administration of an assertiveness test are represented on the left, and their scores on a second administration (a few weeks later) are represented on the right. If subjects obtain similar scores on both administrations, the test measures assertiveness consistently and is said to have high reliability. If subjects get very different scores when they take the assertiveness test a second time, the test is said to have low reliability.

A brief scale to assess sensation seeking as a trait. First described by Marvin Zuckerman (1979, 1995), *sensation seeking* is a personality trait characterized by a generalized preference for high or low levels of sensory stimulation. People who are high in sensation seeking need a high level of stimulation. They are easily bored and they like activities that may involve some physical risk. They may satisfy their appetite for stimulation by experimenting with drugs, numerous sexual partners, and novel experiences. Follow the instructions for this version of the Sensation Seeking Scale to obtain a rough estimate of your sensation seeking tendencies. (Adapted from Grasha & Kirschenbaum, 1986)

Measuring Sensation Seeking

Answer true or false to each of the items listed below. A "T" means that the item expresses your preference most of the time. An "F" means that you do not agree that the item is generally true for you. After completing the test, score your responses according to the instructions that follow the test items.

T F **1.** I would really enjoy skydiving.

T F **2.** I can imagine myself driving a sports car in a race and loving it.

T F **3.** My life is very secure and comfortable—the way I like it.

T F **4.** I usually like emotionally expressive or artistic people, even if they are sort of wild.

T F **5.** I like the idea of seeing many of the same warm, supportive faces in my everyday life.

T F **6.** I like doing adventurous things and would have enjoyed being a pioneer in the early days of this country.

T F **7.** A good photograph should express peacefulness creatively.

T F **8.** The most important thing in living is fully experiencing all emotions.

T F **9.** I like creature comforts when I go on a trip or vacation.

T F **10.** Doing the same things each day really gets to me.

T F **11.** I love snuggling in front of a fire on a wintry day.

T F **12.** I would like to try several types of drugs as long as they didn't harm me permanently.

T F **13.** Drinking and being rowdy really appeals to me on the weekend.

T F **14.** Rational people try to avoid dangerous situations.

T F **15.** I prefer Figure A to Figure B.

A

B

Give yourself 1 point for answering "T" to the following items: 1, 2, 4, 6, 8, 10, 12, and 13. Also give yourself 1 point for answering "F" to the following items: 3, 5, 7, 9, 11, 14, and 15. Add up your points, and compare your total to the following norms: 11–15, high sensation seeker; 6–10, moderate sensation seeker; 0–5, low sensation seeker. Bear in mind that this is a shortened version of the Sensation Seeking Scale and that it provides only a rough approximation of your status on this personality trait.

As we noted earlier, some theorists believe that only five trait dimensions are required to provide a full description of personality. This view led to the creation of the NEO Personality Inventory. Developed by Paul Costa and Robert McCrae (1985, 1992), the NEO Inventory is designed to measure the Big Five traits: neuroticism, extraversion, openness to experience, agreeableness, and conscientiousness. The NEO Inventory is widely used in research and clinical work.

To appreciate the strengths of self-report inventories, consider how else you might assess your personality. For instance, how assertive are you? You probably have some vague idea, but can you accurately estimate how your assertiveness compares to others'? To do that, you need a great deal of comparative information about others' usual behavior—information that all of us lack. In contrast, a self-report inventory inquires about your typical behavior in a wide variety of circumstances requiring assertiveness and generates an exact comparison with the typical behavior reported by many other respondents for the same circumstances. Thus, self-report inventories are much more thorough and precise than casual observations are.

However, these tests are only as accurate as the information that the test-takers provide. Deliberate deception can be a problem with these tests, and some people are unconsciously influenced by the social desirability or acceptability of the statements (Kline, 1995; Paulhus, 1991). Without realizing it, they endorse only those statements that make them look good. This problem provides another reason why personality test results should always be regarded as suggestive rather than definitive.

Projective Tests

Projective tests, which all take a rather indirect approach to the assessment of personality, are used extensively in clinical work. **Projective tests ask people to respond to vague, ambiguous stimuli in ways that may reveal the respondents' needs, feelings, and personality traits.**

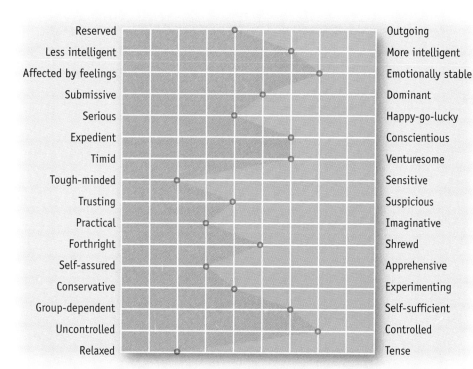

● FIGURE 2.24

The Sixteen Personality Factor Questionnaire (16PF). Cattell's 16PF is designed to assess 16 basic dimensions of personality. The pairs of traits listed across from each other in the figure define the 16 factors measured by this self-report inventory. The profile shown is the average profile seen among a group of airline pilots who took the test.

Adapted from Cattell, R. B. (1973, July). Personality pinned down. *Psychology Today*, 40–46. Reprinted by permission of Psychology Today Magazine. Copyright © 1973 Sussex Publishers, Inc.

The Rorschach test, for instance, consists of a series of ten inkblots. Respondents are asked to describe what they see in the blots (see the adjacent photo). In the Thematic Apperception Test (TAT), a series of pictures of simple scenes is presented to subjects who are asked to tell stories about what is happening in the scenes and what the characters are feeling. For instance, one TAT card shows a young boy contemplating a violin resting on a table in front of him.

The assumption underlying projective testing is that ambiguous materials can serve as a blank screen onto which people project their characteristic concerns, conflicts, and desires. Thus, a competitive person who is shown the TAT card of the boy at the table with the violin might concoct a story about how the boy is contemplating an upcoming musical competition at which he hopes to excel. The same card shown to a person high in impulsiveness might elicit a story about how the boy is planning to sneak out the door to go dirt-bike riding with friends.

Proponents of projective tests assert that the tests have two unique strengths. First, they are not transparent to subjects. That is, the subject doesn't know how the test provides information to the tester. Hence, it's difficult for people to engage in intentional deception. Second, the indirect approach used in these tests may make them especially sensitive to unconscious features of personality.

Unfortunately, these alleged strengths are based on mere speculation. Moreover, there is inadequate evidence for the reliability and validity of projective measures (Lanyon & Goodstein, 1997; Lilienfeld, Wood, & Garb, 2000). In particular, serious doubts have been raised about the research evidence on the Rorschach test (Garb, Florio, & Grove, 1998; Hunsley, Lee, & Wood, 2003). In spite of these problems, projective tests continue to be widely used by clinicians (Watkins et al., 1995). About 40 years ago, a reviewer characterized the critics of projective tests as "doubting statisticians" and the users of projective tests as "enthusiastic clinicians" (Adcock, 1965). Decades of research notwithstanding, little has changed since then.

In projective tests, such as the Rorschach, stimuli are deliberately vague and ambiguous to serve as a blank screen onto which subjects can project their concerns, conflicts, and desires.

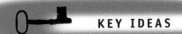

KEY IDEAS

The Nature of Personality

■ The concept of personality explains the consistency in individuals' behavior over time and situations while also explaining their distinctiveness. Personality traits are dispositions to behave in certain ways. Some theorists suggest that the complexity of personality can be reduced to just five basic traits: extraversion, neuroticism, openness to experience, agreeableness, and conscientiousness.

Psychodynamic Perspectives

■ Freud's psychoanalytic theory emphasizes the importance of the unconscious. Freud described personality structure in terms of three components (id, ego, and superego) that are involved in internal conflicts, which generate anxiety.

■ According to Freud, people often ward off anxiety and other unpleasant emotions with defense mechanisms, which work through self-deception. Freud believed that the first five years of life are extremely influential in shaping adult personality. He describes five psychosexual stages that children undergo in their personality development.

■ Jung's analytical psychology stresses the importance of the collective unconscious. Adler's individual psychology emphasizes how people strive for superiority to compensate for feelings of inferiority.

Behavioral Perspectives

■ Behavioral theories view personality as a collection of response tendencies shaped through learning. Pavlov's classical conditioning can explain how people acquire emotional responses.

■ Skinner's model of operant conditioning shows how consequences such as reinforcement, extinction, and punishment shape behavior. Bandura's social cognitive theory shows how people can be conditioned indirectly through observation. He views self-efficacy as an especially important personality trait.

Humanistic Perspectives

■ Humanistic theories take an optimistic view of people's conscious, rational ability to chart their own courses of action. Rogers focused on the self-concept as the critical aspect of personality. He maintained that incongruence between one's self-concept and reality creates anxiety and leads to defensive behavior.

■ Maslow theorized that needs are arranged hierarchically. He asserted that psychological health depends on fulfilling the need for self-actualization.

Biological Perspectives

■ Eysenck believes that inherited individual differences in physiological functioning affect conditioning and thus influence personality. Recent twin studies have provided impressive evidence that genetic factors shape personality. Behavioral genetics research also suggests that the family has surprisingly little influence over personality. Evolutionary psychologists maintain that natural selection has favored the emergence of the Big Five traits as crucial dimensions of personality.

A Contemporary Empirical Approach: Terror Management Theory

■ Terror management theory proposes that self-esteem and faith in a cultural worldview shield people from the profound anxiety associated with their mortality. Consistent with this analysis, increasing mortality salience leads people to make efforts to bolster their self-esteem and defend their worldviews. These defensive reactions are automatic and subconscious.

An Epilogue on Theoretical Diversity

■ The study of personality illustrates how great the theoretical diversity in psychology is. This diversity is a strength in that it fuels research that helps psychology move toward a more complete understanding of behavior.

Application: Assessing Your Personality

■ Psychological tests are standardized measures of behavior—usually mental abilities or aspects of personality. Test norms indicate what represents a high or low score. Psychological tests should produce consistent results upon retesting, a quality called reliability. Validity refers to the degree to which a test measures what it was designed to measure.

■ Self-report inventories, such as the 16PF and NEO Personality Inventory, ask respondents to describe themselves. Self-report inventories can provide a better snapshot of personality than casual observations can, but they are vulnerable to deception and social desirability bias.

■ Projective tests, such as the Rorschach and TAT, assume that people's responses to ambiguous stimuli reveal something about their personality. Projective tests' reliability and validity appear to be disturbingly low.

KEY TERMS

Archetypes pp. 41–42
Behaviorism p. 44
Classical conditioning p. 45
Collective unconscious p. 41
Compensation p. 42
Conditioned response (CR) p. 45
Conditioned stimulus (CS) p. 45
Conscious p. 36
Defense mechanisms p. 38
Displacement p. 39
Ego p. 36
Evolutionary psychology p. 58
Extinction p. 46
Fixation p. 40
Heritability ratio p. 57
Hierarchy of needs p. 53
Humanism p. 51
Id p. 36
Identification p. 39
Incongruence p. 52
Need for self-actualization p. 13
Negative reinforcement p. 47
Observational learning p. 49
Oedipal complex p. 40
Operant conditioning p. 47

Personality p. 34
Personality trait p. 34
Positive reinforcement p. 47
Preconscious p. 37
Projection p. 39
Projective tests p. 66
Psychodynamic theories p. 34
Psychological test p. 64
Psychosexual stages p. 40
Punishment p. 47
Rationalization p. 39
Reaction formation p. 39
Regression p. 35
Reliability p. 65
Repression p. 39
Self-concept pp. 51–52
Self-efficacy pp. 49–50
Self-report inventories p. 65
Standardization p. 64
Superego p. 36
Test norms p. 64
Unconditioned response (UCR) p. 45
Unconditioned stimulus (UCS) p. 45
Unconscious p. 37
Validity p. 65

KEY PEOPLE

Alfred Adler pp. 42–43
Albert Bandura pp. 49–50
Hans Eysenck pp. 56–58
Sigmund Freud pp. 35–41
Carl Jung pp. 41–42

Abraham Maslow pp. 53–54
Ivan Pavlov pp. 44–46
Carl Rogers pp. 51–53
B. F. Skinner pp. 47–48

Key People

David Myers

Berry Schwartz

Martin Seligman

Sigmund Freud - Psychoanalytic Theory

unconscious

1. id, ego + superego
2. 7 Defense Mechanisms
3. 5 Psychosexual Stages

2 *unconscious* Carl Jung - Analytical Psychology

Personal
+ Collective - ancestral memories called archetypes
Introvert + Extravert

Alfred Adler - Individual Psychology

Birth order

1 *Behavioral* John B. Watson - Behavioral
study of Behavior

Ivan Pavlow - Classical Conditioning

B. F. Skinner - Operant Conditioning
is a form of learning in which voluntary
responses come to be controlled by their consequences

Page 2

Albert Bandura – Cognitive Theory
- Observable Learning
- Self-Efficacy

Humanistic Theory

Carl Rogers – Self-Concept

Abraham Maslow – Hierarchy of Needs *according to priority*
- Self-Actualization

1. Which of the following is *not* included in McCrae and Costa's five-factor model of personality?
   a. Neuroticism
   b. Extraversion
   c. Conscientiousness
   d. Authoritarianism

2. You're feeling guilty after your third bowl of ice cream. You tell yourself it's all right because yesterday you skipped lunch. Which defense mechanism is at work?
   a. Conceptualization
   b. Displacement
   c. Rationalization
   d. Identification

3. According to Adler, _____ is a universal drive to adapt, improve oneself, and master life's challenges.
   a. compensation
   b. striving for superiority
   c. avoiding inferiority
   d. social interest

4. The strengthening of a response tendency by virtue of the fact that the response leads to the removal of an unpleasant stimulus is
   a. positive reinforcement.
   b. negative reinforcement.
   c. primary reinforcement.
   d. punishment.

5. Self-efficacy is
   a. the ability to fulfill one's potential.
   b. one's belief about one's ability to perform behaviors that should lead to expected outcomes.
   c. a durable disposition to behave in a particular way in a variety of situations.
   d. a collection of beliefs about one's nature, unique qualities, and typical behavior.

6. According to Rogers, disparity between one's self-concept and actual experience is referred to as
   a. a delusional system.
   b. dissonance.
   c. conflict.
   d. incongruence.

7. According to Maslow, which of the following is *not* characteristic of self-actualizing persons?
   a. Accurate perception of reality
   b. Being open and spontaneous
   c. Being uncomfortable with solitude
   d. Sensitivity to others' needs

8. If identical twins exhibit more personality resemblance than fraternal twins, it's probably due mostly to
   a. similar treatment from parents.
   b. their greater genetic overlap.
   c. their strong identification with each other.
   d. others' expectations that they should be similar.

9. Research on terror management theory has shown that increased mortality salience leads to all of the following except:
   a. increased striving for self-esteem.
   b. more stereotypic thinking about minorities.
   c. more aggressive behavior toward people with opposing views.
   d. reduced respect for cultural icons.

10. In psychological testing, consistency of results over repeated measurements refers to
    a. standardization.
    b. validity.
    c. statistical significance.
    d. reliability.

Book Companion Website

Visit the Book Companion Website at **http://psychology. wadsworth.com/weiten_lloyd8e**, where you will find tutorial quizzes, flashcards, and weblinks for every chapter, a final exam, and more! You can also link to the Thomson Wadsworth Psychology Resource Center (accessible directly at **http://psychology.wadsworth.com**) for a range of psychology-related resources.

Personal Explorations Workbook

The following exercises in your *Personal Explorations Workbook* may enhance your self-understanding in relation to issues raised in this chapter. **Questionnaire 2.1:** Desirability of Control Scale. **Personal Probe 2.1:** Who Are You? **Personal Probe 2.2:** How You See Personality.

ANSWERS

1. d Pages 34–35
2. c Page 39
3. b Page 42
4. b Pages 47–48
5. b Pages 49–50
6. d Page 52
7. c Page 54
8. b Pages 57–58
9. d Pages 59–62
10. d Page 65

Stress and Its Effects

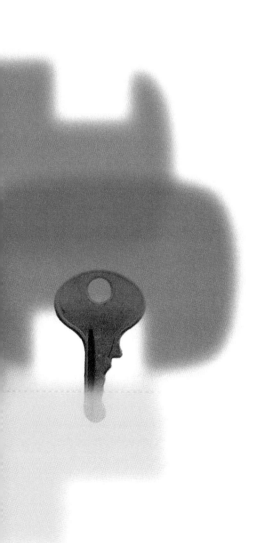

You're in your car headed home from school with a classmate. Traffic is barely moving. A radio report indicates that the traffic jam is only going to get worse. You groan as you fiddle impatiently with the radio. Another motorist nearly takes your fender off trying to cut into your lane. Your pulse quickens as you shout insults at the driver, who cannot even hear you. You think about the term paper that you have to work on tonight. Your stomach knots up as you recall all the crumpled drafts you tossed into the wastebasket last night. If you don't finish the paper soon, you won't be able to find any time to study for your math test, not to mention your biology quiz. Suddenly you remember that you promised the person you're dating that the two of you would get together tonight. There's no way. Another fight looms on the horizon. Your classmate asks how you feel about the tuition increase the college announced yesterday. You've been trying not to think about it. You're already in debt up to your ears. Your parents are bugging you about changing schools, but you don't want to leave your friends. Your heartbeat quickens as you contemplate the debate you'll have to wage with your parents. You feel wired with tension as you realize that the stress in your life never seems to let up.

Many circumstances can create stress in people's lives. Stress comes in all sorts of packages: large and small, pretty and ugly, simple and complex. All too often, the package is a surprise. In this chapter, we try to sort out these packages. We analyze the nature of stress, outline the major types of stress, and discuss how people respond to stressful events at several levels.

In a sense, stress is what a course on adjustment is all about. Recall from Chapter 1 that adjustment essentially deals with how people manage to cope with various demands and pressures. These demands or pressures represent the core of stressful experience. Thus, the central theme in a course such as this is: How do people adjust to stress, and how might they adjust more effectively?

The Nature of Stress

LEARNING OBJECTIVES

- Describe the nature of stress and discuss how common it is.
- Distinguish between primary and secondary appraisal of stress.
- Summarize the evidence on ambient stress.
- Explain how culture and ethnicity are related to stress.

Over the years, the term *stress* has been used in different ways by different theorists. Some have viewed stress as a *stimulus* event that presents difficult demands (a divorce, for instance), while others have viewed stress as the *response* of physiological arousal elicited by a troublesome event (Cooper & Dewe, 2004). However, the emerging consensus among contemporary researchers is that stress is neither a stimulus nor a response but a special stimulus-response transaction in which one feels threatened (McEwen, 2000). Hence, we will define *stress* **as any circumstances that threaten or are perceived to threaten one's well-being and thereby tax one's coping abilities.** The threat may be to one's immediate physical safety, long-range security, self-esteem, reputation, or peace of mind. Stress is a complex concept—so let's dig a little deeper.

Stress Is an Everyday Event

The term *stress* tends to spark images of overwhelming, traumatic crises. People think of hijackings, hurricanes, military combat, and nuclear accidents. Undeniably, these are extremely stressful events. Studies conducted in the aftermath of tornadoes, floods, earthquakes, and the like typically find elevated rates of psychological problems and physical illness in the communities affected by these disasters (Brende, 2000; Raphael & Dobson, 2000). However, these unusual and infrequent events represent the tip of the iceberg. Many everyday events, such as waiting in line, having car trouble, shopping for Christmas presents, misplacing your checkbook, and staring at bills you can't pay, are also stressful. Of course, major and minor stressors are not entirely independent. A major stressful event, such as going through a divorce, can trigger a cascade of minor stressors, such as looking for an attorney, taking on new household responsibilities, and so forth (Pillow, Zautra, & Sandler, 1996).

You might guess that minor stressors would produce minor effects, but that isn't necessarily true. Research shows that routine hassles may have significant negative effects on a person's mental and physical health (Delongis, Folkman, & Lazarus, 1988). Richard Lazarus and his colleagues have devised a scale to measure stress in the form of daily hassles. Their scale lists 117 everyday problems, such as misplacing things, struggling

Courtesy of Richard Lazarus

Richard Lazarus

with rising prices, dealing with delays, and so forth. When they compared their hassles scale against another scale that assessed stress in the form of major life events, they found that scores on their hassles scale were more strongly related to subjects' mental health than the scores on the other scale were (Kanner et al., 1981). Other investigators, working with different types of samples and different measures of hassles, have also found that everyday hassles are predictive of mental and physical health (Chang & Sanna, 2003; Sher, 2003).

Why would minor hassles be more strongly related to mental health than major stressful events? The answer isn't entirely clear yet, but many theorists believe that stressful events can have a *cumulative* or *additive* impact (Seta, Seta, & McElroy, 2002). In other words, stress can add up. Routine stresses at home, at school, and at work might be fairly benign individually, but collectively they could create great strain.

Stress Lies in the Eye of the Beholder

The experience of feeling threatened depends on what events you notice and how you choose to appraise or interpret them (Monroe & Kelley, 1995). Events that are stressful for one person may be "ho-hum" routine for another. For example, many people find flying in an airplane somewhat stressful, but frequent fliers may not even raise an eyebrow. Some people enjoy the excitement of going out on a date with someone new; others find the uncertainty terrifying.

In discussing appraisals of stress, Lazarus and Folkman (1984) distinguish between primary and secondary appraisal (see Figure 3.1). *Primary appraisal* **is an initial evaluation of whether an event is (1) irrelevant to you, (2) relevant, but not threatening, or (3) stressful.** When you view an event as stressful, you are likely to make a *secondary appraisal,* **which is an evaluation of your coping resources and options for dealing with the stress.** Thus, your primary appraisal would determine whether you saw an upcoming job interview as stressful. Your secondary appraisal would

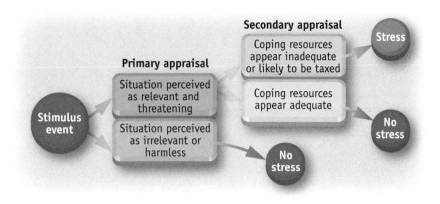

● FIGURE 3.1

Primary and secondary appraisal of stress. *Primary appraisal* is an initial evaluation of whether an event is (1) irrelevant to you, (2) relevant, but not threatening, or (3) stressful. When you view an event as stressful, you are likely to make a *secondary appraisal,* which is an evaluation of your coping resources and options for dealing with the stress. Thus, your primary appraisal would determine whether you saw an upcoming job interview as stressful. Your secondary appraisal would determine how stressful the interview appeared in light of your assessment of your ability to deal with the event. (Based on Lazarus & Folkman, 1994)

determine how stressful the interview appeared, in light of your assessment of your ability to deal with the event.

Often, people are not very objective in their appraisals of potentially stressful events. A study of hospitalized patients awaiting surgery showed only a slight correlation between the objective seriousness of a person's upcoming surgery and the amount of fear the person experienced (Janis, 1958). Clearly, some people are more prone to feel threatened by life's difficulties than others. A number of studies have shown that anxious, neurotic people report more stress than others (Cooper & Bright, 2001; Watson, David, & Suls, 1999), as do people who are relatively unhappy (Seidlitz & Diener, 1993). Thus, stress lies in the eye (actually, the mind) of the beholder, and people's appraisals of stressful events are highly subjective.

Stress May Be Embedded in the Environment

Although the perception of stress is a highly personal matter, many kinds of stress come from the environmental circumstances that individuals share with others. *Ambient stress* consists of chronic environmental conditions that, although not urgent, are negatively valued and that place adaptive de-

mands on people. Features of the environment such as excessive noise, heat, and pollution can threaten well-being and leave their mark on mental and physical health.

For example, investigators have found an association between chronic exposure to high levels of noise and elevated blood pressure among children attending school near Los Angeles International Airport (Cohen et al., 1980). Similarly, studies of children living near Munich International Airport (Evans, Hygge, & Bullinger, 1995; Hygge, Evans, & Bullinger, 2002) have found elevated stress hormones, reading and memory deficits, and poor task persistence in samples of schoolchildren (see Figure 3.2).

Crowding is another source of environmental stress. Temporary experiences of crowding, such as being packed into a rock concert venue with thousands of other fans, can be stressful. However, most of the research on crowding has focused on the effects of residential density. Generally, studies find an association between high density and increased physiological arousal, psychological distress, and social withdrawal (Evans, 2001; Evans, LePore, & Schroeder, 1996). Psychologists have also explored the repercussions of living in areas that are at risk for disaster. For instance, studies suggest that people who live near a nuclear power plant or in an area prone to earthquakes or hurricanes may experience increased stress (Carr, 2000; Dougall & Baum, 2000).

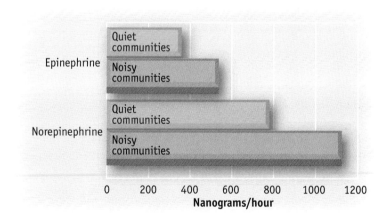

● FIGURE 3.2

Excessive noise and stress hormones. Evans, Hygge, and Bullinger (1995) compared children from noisy areas near Munich International Airport with similar children from quiet neighborhoods in Munich. They found elevated levels of two hormones associated with stress reactions in the children exposed to the high noise of the airport.

Adapted from Evans, G. W., Hygge, S., & Bullinger, M. (1995). Chronic noise and psychological stress. *Psychological Science, 6,* 333–338. Copyright © 1995 Blackwell Publishers. Adapted by permission.

Stress can be caused by environmental circumstances such as pollution, excessive noise and crowding, traffic jams, and urban decay.

Recently, investigators have examined urban poverty and violence as a source of environmental stress. Ewart and Suchday (2002) developed a scale called the City Stress Index to measure participants' exposure to street crime, gang activity, drug dealing, neighborhood decay, and unruly behavior. They found that scores on the City Stress Index correlated (modestly) with measures of subjects' depressive symptoms, hostility, and irritability. In retrospect, it should come as no surprise that urban decay and violence produce ambient stress. It is hoped that the creation of the City Stress Index will facilitate more research on the long-term repercussions of this type of stress.

Stress May Be Self-Imposed

We tend to think of stress as something imposed on us from without. However, a study of college students' stress found that stress is self-imposed surprisingly often (Epstein & Katz, 1992). For example, you might sign up for extra classes to get through school quickly. Or you might actively seek additional responsibilities at work to impress your boss. People frequently put pressure on themselves to get good grades or to climb the corporate ladder rapidly. Many people create stress by embracing unrealistic expectations for themselves. In short, people have more control over their stress than they probably realize.

Stress Is Influenced by Culture

Although certain types of events (such as the loss of a loved one) are probably viewed as stressful in virtually all human societies, cultures vary greatly in the predominant forms of stress their people experience. Obviously, the challenges of daily living encountered in modern, Western cities like Montreal or Philadelphia are quite different from the day-to-day difficulties experienced in indigenous societies in Africa or South America. The potential importance of culture is illustrated by the substantial body of evidence that cultural change—such as increased modernization and urbanization and shifting values and customs—has been a major source of stress in many societies around the world (Dessler, 2000). In some cases, a specific cultural group may be exposed to pervasive stress that is unique to that group (Berry & Ataca, 2000). For example, the devastating drought and famine in Sudan in 1985 and the ethnic cleansing of Albanians in Kosovo in 1999 were extraordinary forms of stress distinctive to these societies. Our discussion of stress will largely focus on the types of stressors confronted in everyday life in contemporary, Western society, but you should be aware that life in our society is not necessarily representative of life around the world.

Moreover, even within the modern, Western world, disparities can be found in the constellation of stressors experienced by specific cultural groups (Mino, Profit, & Pierce, 2000). In recent years, researchers have shown a new interest in the effects of ethnicity-related sources

WEB LINK 3.1

Centre for Stress Management
This British website houses a diverse collection of brief online articles concerned with many aspects of the stress process. It also features links to many other sites around the world that provide information on stress.

of stress experienced by African Americans, Hispanic Americans, and other minority groups (Contrada et al., 2000). Social scientists interested in ethnicity have traditionally focused their attention on the causes of institutional racism, such as discrimination in hiring and in access to health care. But their focus has been shifting to the effects of subtle discrimination in day-to-day living. Although overt racial discrimination in America clearly has declined in recent decades, covert expressions of ethnic prejudice continue to be commonplace (Dovidio & Gaertner, 1999). For example, in one study of 520 African Americans, 96 percent of the respondents reported experiencing some type of racist discrimination in the most recent year—and 95 percent of these subjects indicated that they found this discrimination to be stressful (Klonoff & Landrine, 1999).

Everyday discrimination can take many forms, including verbal insults (ethnic slurs), negative evaluations, avoidance, denial of equal treatment, and threats of aggression. Feldman-Barrett and Swim (1998) emphasize that these acts of discrimination are often ambiguous (examples: "the clerk seemed to be ignoring me," "the teacher seemed disdainful of me"). Hence, theorists assert that minority group members may experience stress not only from explicit discrimination but also from the subjective perception of discrimination in ambiguous situations and even from the anticipation of the possibility of discrimination at upcoming events (example: "I'm worried that no one will talk to me at the get-together for new employees").

In addition to discrimination, members of ethnic minorities experience stress because they are keenly aware of negative racial stereotypes and often worry that others will interpret their behavior in ways that confirm these derogatory stereotypes (Steele, 1997). So the threat of *stereotype confirmation* can become a source of chronic apprehension. At the other extreme, individuals are often chastised by members of their own group for "acting white" or abandoning their cultural heritage

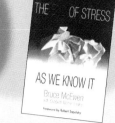

(Contrada et al., 2000). Thus, ethnic minorities may be under constant pressure to conform to the expectations and values of their own group. It seems likely that the extra layer of stress experienced by minority group members takes its toll on them, but scientists have just begun to investigate the degree to which ethnicity-related stress may have detrimental effects on individuals' mental and physical health (Clark et al., 1999).

Major Types of Stress

LEARNING OBJECTIVES

- Distinguish between acute and chronic stressors.
- Describe frustration as a form of stress.
- Outline the three types of conflict, and discuss typical reactions to conflicts.
- Summarize evidence on life change as a form of stress.
- Discuss evidence on pressure as a form of stress.

An enormous variety of events can be stressful for one person or another. To achieve a better understanding of stress, theorists have tried to analyze the nature of stressful events and divide them into subtypes. One sensible distinction involves differentiating between *acute stressors and chronic stressors* (Dougall & Baum, 2001). **Acute**

stressors are threatening events that have a relatively short duration and a clear endpoint. Examples would include having a difficult encounter with a belligerent drunk, waiting for the results of a medical test, or having your home threatened by severe flooding. **Chronic stressors are threatening events that have a relatively**

long duration and no readily apparent time limit. Examples would include persistent financial strains produced by huge credit card debts, ongoing pressures from a hostile boss at work, or the demands of caring for a sick family member over a period of years. Of course, this distinction is far from perfect. It is hard to decide where to draw the line between a short-lived versus lengthy stressor, and even brief stressors can have long-lasting effects.

None of the proposed schemes for classifying stressful events has turned out to be altogether satisfactory. Classifying stressful events into nonintersecting categories is virtually impossible. Although this problem presents conceptual headaches for researchers, it need not prevent us from describing four major types of stress: frustration, conflict, change, and pressure. As you read about each of them, you'll surely recognize some familiar situations.

Frustration

"It has been very frustrating to watch the rapid deterioration of my parents' relationship. Over the last year or two they have argued constantly and have refused to seek any professional help. I have tried to talk to them, but they kind of shut me and my brother out of their problem. I feel very helpless and sometimes even very angry, not at them, but at the whole situation."

This scenario illustrates frustration. As psychologists use the term, **frustration occurs in any situation in which the pursuit of some goal is thwarted.** In essence, you experience frustration when you want something and you can't have it. Everyone has to deal with frustration virtually every day. Traffic jams, difficult daily commutes, and annoying drivers, for instance, are a routine source of frustration that can elicit anger and aggression (Hennessy & Wiesenthal, 1999; Rasmussen, Knapp, & Garner, 2000). Fortunately, most frustrations are brief and insignificant. You may be quite upset when you go to the auto shop to pick up your car and find that it hasn't been fixed as promised. However, a few days later you'll probably have your precious car back, and all will be forgotten.

Of course, some frustrations can be sources of significant stress. *Failures* and *losses* are two common kinds of frustration that are often very stressful. All people fail in at least some of their endeavors. Some make failure almost inevitable by setting unrealistic goals for themselves. People tend to forget that for every newly appointed vice-president in the business world, there are dozens of middle-level executives who don't get promoted. Losses may be especially frustrating when people are deprived of something they are accustomed to having. For example, there are few things that are

more frustrating than losing a dearly loved friend or family member.

More often than not, frustration appears to be the culprit at work when people feel troubled by environmental stress (Graig, 1993). Excessive noise, heat, pollution, and crowding are most likely stressful because they frustrate the desire for quiet, a comfortable body temperature, clean air, and adequate privacy.

Conflict

"Should I or shouldn't I? I became engaged at Christmas. My fiancé surprised me with a ring. I knew if I refused the ring he would be terribly hurt and our relationship would suffer. However, I don't really know whether or not I want to marry him. On the other hand, I don't want to lose him either."

Like frustration, conflict is an unavoidable feature of everyday life. That perplexing question "Should I or shouldn't I?" comes up countless times on a daily basis. **Conflict occurs when two or more incompatible motivations or behavioral impulses compete for expression.** As we discussed in Chapter 2, Sigmund Freud proposed over a century ago that internal conflicts generate considerable psychological distress. This link between conflict and distress was measured with precision in studies by Laura King and Robert Emmons (1990, 1991). They used an elaborate questionnaire to assess the overall amount of internal conflict experienced by subjects. They found higher levels of conflict to be associated with higher levels of psychological distress.

Conflicts come in three types, which were originally described by Kurt Lewin (1935) and investigated extensively by Neal Miller (1944, 1959). These types—approach-approach, avoidance-avoidance, and approach-avoidance—are diagrammed in Figure 3.3.

Courtesy, Neal Miller

Neal Miller

In an **approach-approach conflict a choice must be made between two attractive goals.** The problem, of course, is that you can choose just one of the two goals. For example, you have a free afternoon;

WEB LINK 3.2

Stress, Trauma, Anxiety, Fears, and Psychosomatic Disorders
This resource, which constitutes Chapter 5 of Clayton E. Tucker-Ladd's online text, *Psychological Self-Help*, provides a particularly fine discussion of the nature of stress and its relationship to psychological and physical disorders.

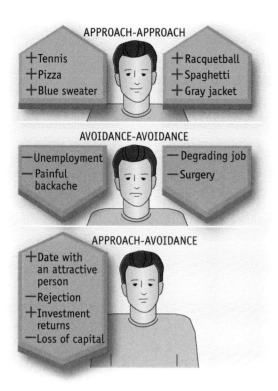

● FIGURE 3.3

Types of conflict. Psychologists have identified three basic types of conflict. In approach-approach and avoidance-avoidance conflicts, the person is torn between two goals. In an approach-avoidance conflict only one goal is under consideration, but it has both positive and negative aspects.

should you play tennis or go to the movies? You're out for a meal; do you want to order the pizza or the spaghetti? You can't afford both; should you buy the blue sweater or the gray jacket? Among the three kinds of conflict, the approach-approach type tends to be the least stressful. People usually don't stagger out of restaurants, exhausted by the stress of choosing which of several appealing entrees to eat. In approach-approach conflicts you typically have a reasonably happy ending, whichever way you decide to go. Nonetheless, approach-approach conflicts centering on important issues may

sometimes be troublesome. If you are torn between two appealing college majors or two attractive boy-friends, you may find the decision-making process quite stressful.

In an *avoidance-avoidance conflict* a choice must be made between two unattractive goals. Forced to choose between two repelling alternatives, you are, as they say, "caught between a rock and a hard place." For example, let's say you have painful backaches. Should you submit to surgery that you dread, or should you continue to live with the pain? Obviously, avoidance-avoidance conflicts are most unpleasant and highly stressful. Typically, people keep delaying their decision as long as possible, hoping that they will somehow be able to escape the conflict situation. For example, you might delay surgery in the hope that your backaches will disappear on their own.

In an *approach-avoidance conflict* a choice must be made about whether to pursue a single goal that has both attractive and unattractive aspects. For instance, imagine that you're offered a career promotion that will mean a large increase in pay. The catch is that you will have to move to a city that you hate. Approach-avoidance conflicts are common, and they can be highly stressful. Any time you have to take a risk to pursue some desirable outcome, you are likely to find yourself in an approach-avoidance conflict. Should you risk rejection by asking out that attractive person in class? Should you risk your savings by investing in a new business that could fail?

Approach-avoidance conflicts often produce *vacillation.* That is, people go back and forth, beset by indecision. They decide to go ahead, then not to, then to go ahead again. Humans are not unique in this respect. Many years ago, Neal Miller (1944) observed the same vacillation in his groundbreaking research with rats. He created approach-avoidance conflicts in hungry rats by alternately feeding and shocking them at one end of a runway apparatus. Eventually, these rats tended to hover near the center of the runway. They would alternately approach and retreat from the goal box at the end of the alley.

BLONDIE © 2001. Reprinted with special permission of King Features Syndicate.

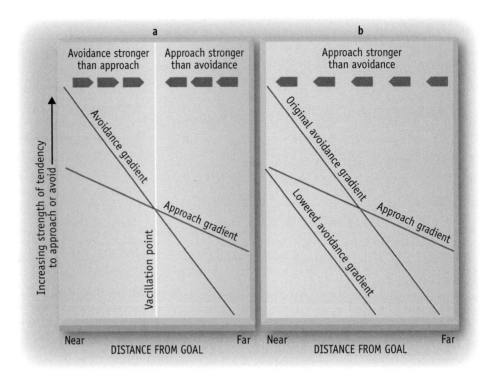

● **FIGURE 3.4**

Approach-avoidance conflict.
(a) According to Neal Miller (1959), as you near a goal that has positive and negative features, avoidance motivation tends to rise faster than approach motivation (that's why the avoidance gradient has a steeper slope than the approach gradient), sending you into retreat. However, if you retreat far enough, you'll eventually reach a point where approach motivation is stronger than avoidance motivation, and you may decide to go ahead once again. The ebb and flow of this process leads to vacillation around the point where the two gradients intersect. **(b)** As the avoidance gradient is lowered, the person comes closer and closer to the goal. If the avoidance gradient can be lowered far enough, the person should be able to resolve the conflict and reach the goal.

In a series of studies, Miller (1959) plotted out how an organism's tendency to approach a goal (the approach gradient in Figure 3.4a) and to retreat from a goal (the avoidance gradient in Figure 3.4a) increase as the organism nears the goal. He found that avoidance motivation increases more rapidly than approach motivation (as reflected by the avoidance gradient's steeper slope in Figure 3.4a). Based on this principle, Miller concluded that *in trying to resolve an approach-avoidance conflict, we should focus more on decreasing avoidance motivation than on increasing approach motivation.*

How would this insight apply to complex human dilemmas? Imagine that you are counseling a friend who is vacillating over whether to ask someone out on a date. Miller would assert that you should attempt to downplay the negative aspects of possible rejection (thus lowering the avoidance gradient) rather than dwelling on how much fun the date could be (thus raising the approach gradient). Figure 3.4b shows the effects of lowering the avoidance gradient. If it is lowered far enough, the person should reach the goal (make a decision and take action).

Change

"After my divorce, I lived alone for four years. Six months ago, I married a wonderful woman who has two children from her previous marriage. My biggest stress is suddenly having to adapt to living with three people instead of by myself. I was pretty set in my ways. I had certain routines. Now everything is chaos. I love my wife and I'm fond of the kids, and they're not really doing anything wrong, but

my house and my life just aren't the same and I am having trouble dealing with it all."

Life changes may represent a key type of stress. **Life changes are any noticeable alterations in one's living circumstances that require readjustment.** Research on life change began when Thomas Holmes, Richard Rahe, and their colleagues set out to explore the relation between stressful life events and physical illness (Holmes & Rahe, 1967; Rahe & Arthur, 1978). They interviewed thousands of tuberculosis patients to find out what kinds of events preceded the onset of their disease. Surprisingly, the frequently cited events were not uniformly negative. The list included plenty of aversive events, as expected, but patients also mentioned many seemingly positive events, such as getting married, having a baby, or getting promoted.

Why would positive events, such as moving to a nicer home, produce stress? According to Holmes and Rahe, it is because they produce *change*. Their thesis is that disruptions of daily routines are stressful. According to their theory, changes in personal relationships, changes at work, changes in finances, and so forth can be stressful even when the changes are welcomed.

Based on this analysis, Holmes and Rahe (1967) developed the Social Readjustment Rating Scale (SRRS) to measure life change as a form of stress. The scale assigns numerical values to 43 major life events that are supposed to reflect the magnitude of the readjustment required by each change (see Figure 3.5). In responding to the scale, respondents are asked to indicate how often they experienced any of these 43 events during a cer-

Social Readjustment Rating Scale

Life event	Mean value	Life event	Mean value
Death of a spouse	100	Son or daughter leaving home	29
Divorce	73	Trouble with in-laws	29
Marital separation	65	Outstanding personal achievement	28
Jail term	63	Spouse begins or stops work	26
Death of close family member	63	Begin or end school	26
Personal injury or illness	53	Change in living conditions	25
Marriage	50	Revision of personal habits	24
Fired at work	47	Trouble with boss	23
Marital reconciliation	45	Change in work hours or conditions	20
Retirement	45	Change in residence	20
Change in health of family member	44	Change in school	20
Pregnancy	40	Change in recreation	19
Sex difficulties	39	Change in church activities	19
Gain of a new family member	39	Change in social activities	18
Business readjustment	39	Loan for lesser purchase (car, TV, etc.)	17
Change in financial state	38	Change in sleeping habits	16
Death of a close friend	37	Change in number of family get-togethers	15
Change to a different line of work	36	Change in eating habits	15
Change in number of arguments with spouse	35	Vacation	13
Mortgage or loan for major purchase	31	Christmas	12
Foreclosure of mortgage or loan	30	Minor violations of the law	11
Change in responsibilities at work	29		

● FIGURE 3.5

Social Readjustment Rating Scale (SRRS). Devised by Holmes and Rahe (1967), this scale is designed to measure the change-related stress in one's life. The numbers on the right are supposed to reflect the average amount of stress (readjustment) produced by each event. Respondents check off the events that have occurred to them recently and add up the associated numbers to arrive at their stress scores. See the Application for a detailed critique of the SRRS.

Adapted from Holmes, T. H., & Rahe, R. (1967). The Social Readjustment Rating Scale. *Journal of Psychosomatic Research, 11*, 213–218. Copyright © 1967 by Elsevier Science Publishing Co. Reprinted by permission.

tain time period (typically, the past year). The person then adds up the numbers associated with each event checked. This sum is an index of the amount of change-related stress the person has recently experienced.

The SRRS and similar scales have been used in thousands of studies by researchers all over the world. Overall, these studies have shown that people with higher scores on the SRRS tend to be more vulnerable to many kinds of physical illness—and many types of psychological problems as well (Derogatis & Coons, 1993; Rahe et al., 2000; Scully, Tosi, & Banning, 2000). These results have attracted a great deal of attention, and the SRRS has been reprinted in many newspapers and popular magazines. The attendant publicity has led to the widespread conclusion that life change is inherently stressful.

More recently, however, experts have criticized this research, citing problems with the methods used and

raising questions about the meaning of the findings (Hobson & Delunas, 2001; Jones & Kinman, 2001; Monroe & McQuaid, 1994). At this point, it is a key interpretive issue that concerns us. Many critics have argued that the SRRS does not measure *change* exclusively. The list of life changes on the SRRS is dominated by events that are clearly negative or undesirable (death of a spouse, fired at work, and so on). These negative events probably generate great frustration. So even though the scale contains some positive events, it could be that frustration (generated by negative events), rather than change, creates most of the stress assessed by the scale.

To investigate this possibility, researchers came up with ways to take into account the desirability and undesirability of subjects' life changes. Participants were asked to indicate the desirability of the events that they checked off on the SRRS and similar scales. The findings in these

Pressure comes in two varieties: pressure to perform and pressure to conform. For example, workers on assembly lines are often expected to maintain high productivity with few mistakes (performance pressure) and suburban homeowners are typically expected to maintain well-groomed exteriors (conformity pressure).

studies clearly indicated that life change is *not* the crucial dimension measured by the SRRS. Undesirable or negative life events cause most of the stress tapped by the SRRS (McLean & Link, 1994; Turner & Wheaton, 1995).

Should we discard the notion that change is stressful? Not entirely. Other lines of research, independent of work with the SRRS, support the hypothesis that change is an important form of stress. For instance, researchers have found associations between geographic mobility and impaired mental and physical health that presumably reflect the impact of change (Brett, 1980; Shuval, 1993). A study by Brown and McGill (1989) suggests that desirable life changes may be stressful for some people but not for others. More research is needed, but it is quite plausible that change constitutes a major type of stress in people's lives. However, we have little reason to believe that change is *inherently* or *inevitably* stressful. Some life changes may be quite challenging, while others may be quite benign.

Pressure

"My father questioned me at dinner about some things I did not want to talk about. I know he doesn't want to hear my answers, at least not the truth. My father told me when I was little that I was his favorite because I was 'pretty near perfect' and I've spent my life trying to keep that up, even though it's obviously not true. Recently, he has begun to realize this and it's made our relationship very strained and painful."

At one time or another, most of us have probably remarked that we were "under pressure." What does that expression mean? **Pressure involves expectations or demands that one behave in a certain way.** Pressure can be divided into two subtypes: the pressure to *perform* and the pressure to *conform*. You are under pressure to perform when you are expected to execute tasks and responsibilities quickly, efficiently, and successfully. For example, salespeople are usually under pressure to move lots of merchandise. Professors at research institutions are often under pressure to publish in prestigious journals. Comedians are under pressure to be amusing. Secretaries are often under pressure to complete lots of clerical work in very little time. Pressures to conform to others' expectations are also common.

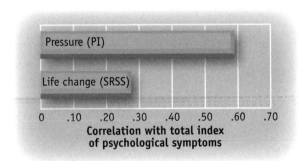

● **FIGURE 3.6**

Pressure and psychological symptoms. A comparison of pressure and life change as sources of stress suggests that pressure may be more strongly related to mental health than change is. In one study, Weiten (1988) found a correlation of .59 between scores on the Pressure Inventory (PI) and symptoms of psychological distress. In the same sample, the correlation between SRRS scores and psychological symptoms was only .28.

Businessmen are expected to wear suits and ties. Suburban homeowners are expected to keep their lawns manicured. Teenagers are expected to adhere to their parents' values and rules. Young adults are expected to get themselves married by the time they're 30.

Although widely discussed by the general public, the concept of pressure has received scant attention from researchers. However, one scale has been developed to measure pressure as a form of life stress (Weiten,

1988). Studies with this scale have found a strong relationship between pressure and a variety of psychological symptoms and problems (Weiten, 1988, 1998). In fact, pressure has turned out to be more strongly related to measures of mental health than are the SRRS and other established measures of stress (see Figure 3.6). These findings suggest that pressure may be an important form of stress that merits more attention from researchers.

Responding to Stress

LEARNING OBJECTIVES

- List three categories of negative emotions commonly elicited by stress.
- Discuss the role of positive emotions in the stress process.
- Explain the effects of emotional arousal on coping efforts, and describe the inverted-U hypothesis.

- Describe the fight-or-flight response and the three stages of the general adaptation syndrome.
- Distinguish between the two major pathways along which the brain sends signals to the endocrine system in response to stress.
- Explain the concept of coping.

The human response to stress is complex and multidimensional. Stress affects people at several levels. Consider again the chapter's opening scenario, in which you're driving home in heavy traffic, thinking about overdue papers, tuition increases, and parental pressures. Let's look at some of the reactions we mentioned. When you groan in reaction to the traffic report, you're experiencing an *emotional response* to stress—in this case, annoyance and anger. When your pulse quickens and your stomach knots up, you're exhibiting *physiological responses* to stress. When you shout insults at another driver, your verbal aggression is a *behavioral*

response to the stress at hand. Thus, we can analyze people's reactions to stress at three levels: (1) their emotional responses, (2) their physiological responses, and (3) their behavioral responses. Figure 3.7 depicts these three levels of response.

Emotional Responses

Emotion is an elusive concept. Psychologists debate about how to define emotion, and many conflicting theories purport to explain emotion. However, everybody has had extensive personal experience with emotions.

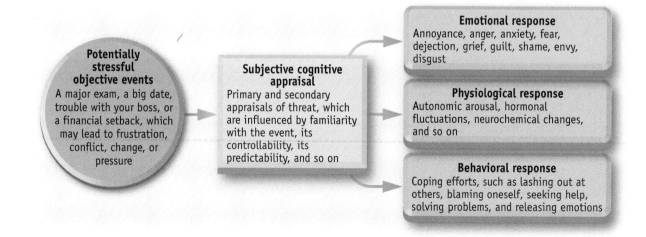

● FIGURE 3.7

The multidimensional response to stress. A potentially stressful event, such as a major exam, will elicit a subjective, cognitive appraisal of how threatening the event is. If the event is viewed with alarm, the stress may trigger emotional, physiological, and behavioral reactions. The human response to stress is multidimensional.

Everyone has a good idea of what it means to be anxious, elated, gloomy, jealous, disgusted, excited, guilty, or nervous. So rather than pursue the technical debates about emotion, we'll rely on your familiarity with the concept and simply note that *emotions* **are powerful, largely uncontrollable feelings, accompanied by physiological changes.** When people are under stress, they often react emotionally. More often than not, stress tends to elicit unpleasant emotions (Lazarus, 1993).

Negative Emotions

There are no simple one-to-one connections between certain types of stressful events and particular emotions, but researchers *have* begun to uncover some strong links between specific *cognitive reactions to stress (appraisals)* and specific emotions (Smith & Lazarus, 1993). For example, self-blame tends to lead to guilt, helplessness to sadness, and so forth. Although stressful events can evoke many negative emotions, some are certainly more

LIVING IN TODAY'S WORLD

Common Reactions to Traumatic Events

In this post-9/11 world, social scientists and the lay public are increasingly interested in understanding people's reactions to traumatic events. The 2001 terrorist attacks on the World Trade Center and the Pentagon exposed millions of television viewers to death and destruction of unprecedented magnitude in real time, and virtually everyone saw the horrific events replayed again and again in the ensuing weeks. Moreover, the threat of additional terrorist attacks, which could have even more far-reaching consequences, lingers. In light of these unpleasant realities, what can psychological research tell us about how people respond to traumatic events? There is a rich research literature on reactions to major disasters (such as earthquakes and hurricanes) and to personal trauma (such as automobile accidents and armed robberies). Based on this research, common reactions to traumatic events include the following (Danieli, Engdahl, & Schlenger, 2004; Flannery, 1999; Foa et al., 2001):

Fear and anxiety. Anxiety is a normal response to threatening events. Many people find that certain cues associated with a traumatic event repeatedly trigger their anxiety.

Reexperiencing the trauma. Many people are troubled by unwanted thoughts of the traumatic event that they are unable to control. Some experience flashbacks in which they vividly relive the traumatic moments. Nightmares about traumatic experiences are also common.

Increased arousal. In the aftermath of traumatic events people tend to feel jumpy, jittery, and physically on edge. This physiological arousal may make sleep difficult.

Avoidance. Many people try to avoid situations or cues that remind them of their trauma. People also tend to suppress painful thoughts and feelings. This coping strategy sometimes results in feelings of psychological numbness.

Anger and irritability. Anger is a normal response to the perceived injustice of disastrous events. Coupled with increased arousal, this anger makes many people highly irritable. Ironically, some people get angry with themselves about their irritability.

Grief and depression. In the wake of traumatic events, people often experience sadness, despair, and hopelessness. Future plans that once were important seem trivial. Activities that were once enjoyable seem empty. People understandably grieve for what they have lost.

Increased sense of vulnerability. Traumatic events often lead to negative changes in one's view of the world. People come to believe that the world is a dangerous place and that others cannot be trusted. One's sense of self-efficacy may be undermined by feelings of helplessness, vulnerability, and the perception that events are uncontrollable.

These reactions are normal short-term responses to traumatic events. Experiencing such reactions does not mean that you are weak or that you are "losing it." For most people these reactions usually dissipate within three months, although others may recover more slowly. If reactions such as these persist indefinitely and interfere with one's social, occupational, or family functioning, a diagnosis of *posttraumatic stress disorder* may be applicable (see pages 90–91 and Chapter 15). If your reactions to a traumatic event are especially severe, persistent, and disabling, it may be wise to seek professional help (see Chapter 16).

likely than others. Common negative emotional responses to stress include (Lazarus, 1993):

■ *Annoyance, anger, and rage.* Stress often produces feelings of anger ranging in intensity from mild annoyance to uncontrollable rage. Frustration is particularly likely to generate anger.

■ *Apprehension, anxiety, and fear.* Stress probably evokes anxiety and fear more frequently than any other emotions. As we saw in Chapter 2, Freudian theory has long recognized the link between conflict and anxiety. However, anxiety can also be elicited by the pressure to perform, the threat of impending frustration, or the uncertainty associated with change.

■ *Dejection, sadness, and grief.* Sometimes stress—especially frustration—simply brings one down. Routine setbacks, such as traffic tickets and poor grades, often produce feelings of dejection. More profound setbacks, such as deaths and divorces, typically leave one grief-stricken.

Of course, the above list is not exhaustive. In his insightful analyses of stress-emotion relations, Richard Lazarus (1991, 1993) mentions five other negative emotions that often figure prominently in reactions to stress: guilt, shame, envy, jealousy, and disgust.

Positive Emotions

Although investigators have tended to focus heavily on the connection between stress and negative emotions, research shows that positive emotions also occur during periods of stress (Folkman, 1997). Although this finding seems counterintuitive, researchers have found that people experience a diverse array of pleasant emotions even while enduring the most dire of circumstances. Consider, for example, the results of a five-year study of coping patterns in 253 caregiving partners of men with AIDS (Folkman et al., 1997). Surprisingly, over the course of the study, the caregivers reported experiencing positive emotions about as often as they experienced negative emotions—except during the time immediately surrounding the death of their partners.

Similar findings have been observed in some other studies of serious stress that made an effort to look for positive emotions. The most interesting was a recent study that examined subjects' emotional functioning early in 2001 and then again in the weeks following the 9/11 terrorist attacks in the United States (Fredrickson et al., 2003). Like most U.S. citizens, these subjects reported many negative emotions in the aftermath of 9/11, including anger, sadness, and fear. However, within this "dense cloud of anguish" positive emotions also emerged. For example, people felt gratitude for the safety of their loved ones; many took stock and counted their blessings; and quite a few reported renewed love for their friends and family. Fredrickson et al. (2003) also

WEB LINK 3.3

Stress Management
From the University of Nebraska's (Lincoln) Department of Health and Human Performance, Wesley Sime provides both a general overview and an educational tutorial for issues involved in human stress management.

found that the frequency of pleasant emotions correlated positively with a measure of subjects' resilience, whereas unpleasant emotions correlated negatively with resilience (see Figure 3.8). Based on their analyses, the researchers concluded that "positive emotions in the aftermath of crises buffer resilient people against depression and fuel thriving" (p. 365). Thus, contrary to common sense, positive emotions do *not* vanish during times of severe stress. Moreover, these positive emotions appear to play a key role in helping people bounce back from the negative emotions associated with stress (Tugade & Fredrickson, 2004).

How do positive emotions promote resilience in the face of stress? Susan Folkman and Judith Moskowitz (2000) argue that positive emotions experienced while under duress can promote creativity and flexibility in problem solving, facilitate the processing of important

Correlation Between Resilience and the Frequency of Selected Emotions in the Aftermath of 9/11

Specific emotions	Correlation with resilience
Negative emotions	
Angry/irritated/annoyed	−.44*
Sad/downhearted/unhappy	−.29*
Scared/fearful/afraid	−.19
Disgust/distaste/revulsion	−.09
Positive emotions	
Grateful/appreciative/thankful	.13
Glad/happy/joyful	.52*
Hopeful/optimistic/encouraged	.40*
Content/serene/peaceful	.47*

*Statistically significant

● FIGURE 3.8

Positive and negative emotions as correlates of resilience. In their study of emotional responses to the 9/11 terrorist attacks, Fredrickson et al. (2003) asked subjects to rate the frequency with which they experienced 20 different emotions in the aftermath of 9/11. The frequency ratings for specific emotions were then correlated with a measure of participants' resiliency. Representative results (for 8 of the 20 emotions studied) are shown here. As you can see, the frequency of pleasant emotions correlated positively with resiliency, whereas the opposite was true for negative emotions. (Adapted from Fredrickson et al., 2003)

information about oneself, and reduce the adverse physiological effects of stress. Positive emotions can also enhance immune system functioning, increase valuable social support available from friends and family, and promote proactive coping efforts (Salovey et al., 2000). In sum, positive emotions can contribute to building social, intellectual, and physical resources that can be helpful in dealing with stress (Fredrickson, 1998, 2001). Research on the interface between stress and positive emotions is in its infancy, and much remains to be learned.

Susan Folkman

Effects of Emotional Arousal

Emotional responses are a natural and normal part of life. Even unpleasant emotions serve important purposes. Like physical pain, painful emotions can serve as warnings that one needs to take action. However, strong emotional arousal can also hamper efforts to cope with stress. For example, research has found that high emotional arousal can sometimes interfere with attention and memory retrieval and can impair judgment and decision making (Janis, 1993; Mandler, 1993).

The well-known problem of *test anxiety* illustrates how emotional arousal can hurt performance. Often students who score poorly on an exam will nonetheless insist that they know the material. Many of them are probably telling the truth. Several researchers have found a negative correlation between test-related anxiety and exam performance. That is, students who display high test anxiety tend to score low on exams (Hancock, 2001; Naveh-Benjamin et al., 1997). Test anxiety can interfere with test taking in several ways, but one critical consideration appears to be the disruption of attention to the test (Keough et al., 2004). Many test-anxious students waste too much time worrying about how they're doing and wondering whether others are having similar problems. In other words, their minds wander too much from the task of taking the test.

Although emotional arousal may hurt coping efforts, this isn't *necessarily* the case. The *inverted-U hypothesis* predicts that task performance should improve with increased emotional arousal—up to a point, after which further increases in arousal become disruptive and performance deteriorates (Anderson, 1990; Mandler, 1993). This idea is referred to as the inverted-U hypothesis because plotting performance as a function of arousal results in graphs that approximate an upside-down U (see Figure 3.9). In these graphs, the level of arousal at which performance peaks is characterized as the *optimal level of arousal* for a task.

This optimal level of arousal appears to depend in part on the complexity of the task at hand. The conventional wisdom is that *as tasks become more complex, the optimal level of arousal (for peak performance) tends to decrease.* This relationship is depicted in Figure 3.9. As you can see, a fairly high level of arousal should be optimal on simple tasks (such as driving eight hours to help a friend in a crisis). However, performance should

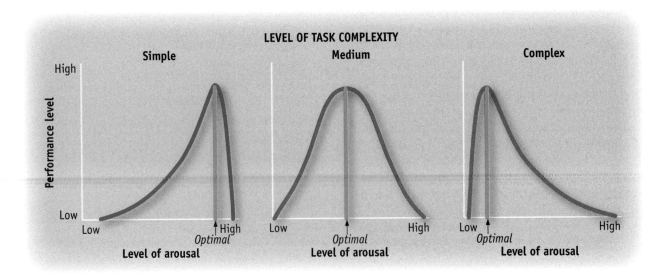

Courtesy, Susan Folkman

(● **FIGURE 3.9**)

Arousal and performance. Graphs of the relationship between emotional arousal and task performance tend to resemble an inverted U, as increased arousal is associated with improved performance up to a point, after which higher arousal leads to poorer performance. The optimal level of arousal for a task depends on the complexity of the task. On complex tasks, a relatively low level of arousal tends to be optimal. On simple tasks, however, performance may peak at a much higher level of arousal.

peak at a lower level of arousal on complex tasks (such as making a major decision in which you have to weigh many factors).

The research evidence on the inverted-U hypothesis is inconsistent and subject to varied interpretations (Neiss, 1988, 1990). Hence, it may be risky to generalize this principle to the complexities of everyday coping efforts. Nonetheless, the inverted-U hypothesis provides a plausible model of how emotional arousal could have either beneficial or disruptive effects on coping, depending on the nature of the stressful demands.

Physiological Responses

As we have seen, stress frequently elicits strong emotional responses. These responses bring about important physiological changes. Even in cases of moderate stress, you may notice that your heart has started beating faster, you have begun to breathe harder, and you are perspiring more than usual. How does all this (and much more) happen? Let's see.

The "Fight-or-Flight" Response

The *fight-or-flight response* is a physiological reaction to threat that mobilizes an organism for attacking (fight) or fleeing (flight) an enemy. First described by Walter Cannon (1932), the fight-or-flight response occurs in the body's autonomic nervous system. **The autonomic nervous system (ANS) is made up of the nerves that connect to the heart, blood vessels, smooth muscles, and glands.** As its name hints, the autonomic nervous system is somewhat *autonomous*. That is, it controls involuntary, visceral functions that people don't normally think about, such as heart rate, digestion, and perspiration.

The autonomic nervous system can be broken into two divisions (see Figure 3.10). The *parasympathetic division* of the ANS generally conserves bodily resources. For instance, it slows heart rate and promotes digestion to help the body save and store energy. The fight-or-flight response is mediated by the *sympathetic division* of the autonomic nervous system, which mobilizes bodily resources for emergencies. In one experiment, Cannon studied the fight-or-flight response in cats by confronting them with dogs. Among other things, he noticed an immediate acceleration in breathing and heart rate and a reduction in digestive processes.

Shelley Taylor and her colleagues (2000) have questioned whether the fight-or-flight model applies equally well to both males and females. They note that in most species females have more responsibility for the care of young offspring than males do. Using an evolutionary perspective, they argue that this disparity may make fighting and fleeing less adaptive for females, as both responses may endanger offspring and thus reduce the likelihood of an animal passing on its genes. Taylor and colleagues maintain that evolutionary processes have fostered more of a "tend and befriend" response

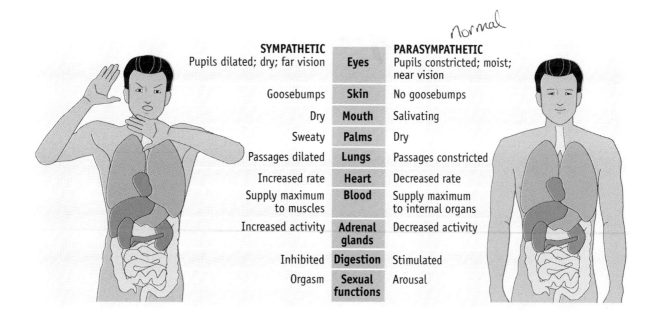

SYMPATHETIC		PARASYMPATHETIC
Pupils dilated; dry; far vision	**Eyes**	Pupils constricted; moist; near vision
Goosebumps	**Skin**	No goosebumps
Dry	**Mouth**	Salivating
Sweaty	**Palms**	Dry
Passages dilated	**Lungs**	Passages constricted
Increased rate	**Heart**	Decreased rate
Supply maximum to muscles	**Blood**	Supply maximum to internal organs
Increased activity	**Adrenal glands**	Decreased activity
Inhibited	**Digestion**	Stimulated
Orgasm	**Sexual functions**	Arousal

● FIGURE 3.10

The autonomic nervous system (ANS). The ANS is composed of the nerves that connect to the heart, blood vessels, smooth muscles, and glands. The ANS is subdivided into the *sympathetic division,* which mobilizes bodily resources in times of need, and the *parasympathetic division,* which conserves bodily resources. Some of the key functions controlled by each division of the ANS are summarized in the center of the diagram.

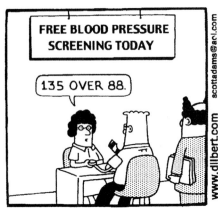

to stress in females. According to this analysis, in reacting to stress, females allocate more effort to the care of offspring and to seeking help and support. More research is needed to evaluate this provocative analysis. Although there may be sex differences in behavioral responses to stress, as hypothesized by Taylor and her colleagues, they are quick to note that the "basic neuroendocrine core of stress responses" is largely the same for males and females.

The fight-or-flight response is not limited to the animal kingdom. Elements of the fight-or-flight response are also seen in humans. Imagine your reaction if your car were to spin out of control on the highway. Your heart would race, and your blood pressure would surge. You might get "goosebumps" and experience a "knot in your stomach." These reflex responses are part of the fight-or-flight syndrome seen in many species.

In a sense, this automatic reaction is a leftover from our evolutionary past. It is clearly an adaptive response for many animals, as the threat of predators often requires a swift response of fighting or fleeing. Likewise, the fight-or-flight response probably was adaptive among ancestral humans who routinely had to deal with acute stressors involving threats to their physical safety. But in our modern world, the fight-or-flight response may be less adaptive for human functioning than it was thousands of generations ago (Neese & Young, 2000). Most modern stressors cannot be handled simply through fight or flight. Work pressures, marital problems, and financial difficulties require far more

complex responses. Moreover, these chronic stressors often continue for lengthy periods of time, so that the fight-or-flight response leaves one in a state of enduring physiological arousal. Concern about the effects of prolonged physical arousal was first voiced by Hans Selye, a Canadian scientist who conducted extensive research on stress.

The General Adaptation Syndrome

The concept of stress was popularized in both scientific and lay circles by Hans Selye (1936, 1956, 1982). Although born in Vienna, Selye spent his entire professional career at McGill University in Montreal. Beginning in the 1930s, Selye exposed laboratory animals to a diverse array of both physical and psychological stressors (heat, cold, pain, mild shock, restraint, and so

Hans Selye

on). The patterns of physiological arousal he observed in the animals were largely the same, regardless of the type of stress. Thus, Selye concluded that stress reactions are *nonspecific*. In other words, they do not vary according to the specific type of stress encountered. Initially, Selye wasn't sure what to call this nonspecific response to a variety of noxious agents. In the 1940s, he decided to call it *stress*, and his influential writings gradually helped make the word part of our everyday vocabulary (Cooper & Dewe, 2004).

Selye (1956, 1974) formulated a seminal theory of stress reactions called the general adaptation syndrome (see Figure 3.11). **The *general adaptation syndrome* is a model of the body's stress response, consisting of three stages: alarm, resistance, and exhaustion.** In the first stage of the general adaptation syndrome, an *alarm reaction* occurs when an organism recognizes the existence of a threat. Physiological arousal increases as the body musters its resources to combat the challenge. Selye's alarm reaction is essentially the fight-or-flight response originally described by Cannon.

WEB LINK 3.4

The American Institute of Stress
The American Institute of Stress is a nonprofit organization established in 1978 at the request of stress pioneer Hans Selye. Its Board of Trustees reads like a who's who of stress research. The resources available online are a bit limited, as one has to send for the information packets published by the institute. But the site contains an interesting tribute to Selye.

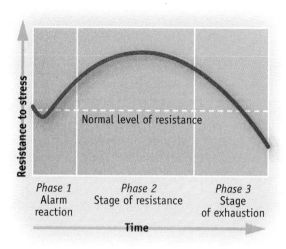

● FIGURE 3.11

The general adaptation syndrome. According to Selye, the physiological response to stress can be broken into three phases. During the first phase, the body mobilizes its resources for resistance after a brief initial shock. In the second phase, resistance levels off and eventually begins to decline. If the third phase of the general adaptation syndrome is reached, resistance is depleted, leading to health problems and exhaustion.

However, Selye took his investigation of stress a couple of steps further by exposing laboratory animals to *prolonged stress,* similar to the chronic stress often endured by humans. If stress continues, the organism may progress to the second phase of the general adaptation syndrome, called the *stage of resistance.* During this phase, physiological changes stabilize as coping efforts get under way. Typically, physiological arousal continues to be higher than normal, although it may level off somewhat as the organism becomes accustomed to the threat.

If the stress continues over a substantial period of time, the organism may enter the third stage, called the *stage of exhaustion.* According to Selye, the body's resources for fighting stress are limited. If the stress cannot be overcome, the body's resources may be depleted, and physiological arousal will decrease. Eventually, the individual may collapse from exhaustion. During this phase, the organism's resistance declines. This reduced resistance may lead to what Selye called "diseases of adaptation," such as ulcers or high blood pressure.

Selye's theory and research forged a link between stress and physical illness. He showed how prolonged physiological arousal that is meant to be adaptive could lead to diseases. His theory has been criticized because it ignores individual differences in the appraisal of stress (Lazarus & Folkman, 1984), and his belief that stress reactions are nonspecific remains the subject of debate (Kemeny, 2003; McCarty & Pacak, 2000). However, his

model provided guidance for generations of researchers who worked out the details of how stress reverberates throughout the body. Let's look at some of those details.

Brain-Body Pathways

When you experience stress, your brain sends signals to the endocrine system along two major pathways (Clow, 2001; Dallman, Bhatnagar, & Viau, 2000; Felker & Hubbard, 1998). **The *endocrine system* consists of glands that secrete chemicals called hormones into the bloodstream.** The major endocrine glands, such as the pituitary, pineal, thyroid, and adrenal glands, are shown in Figure 3.12.

The hypothalamus, a small structure near the base of the brain, appears to initiate action along both pathways. The first pathway (shown on the right in Figure 3.13 on the next page) is routed through the autonomic nervous system. The hypothalamus activates the sympathetic division of the ANS. A key part of this acti-

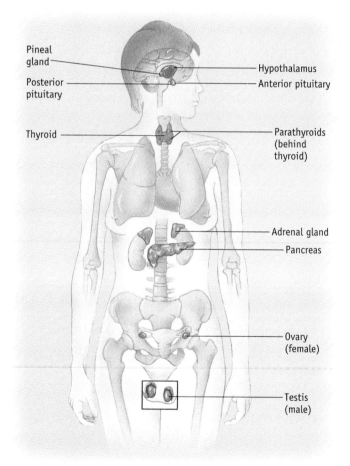

● FIGURE 3.12

The endocrine system. The endocrine glands secrete hormones into the bloodstream. The locations of the principal endocrine glands are shown here. The hormones released by these glands regulate a variety of physical functions and play a key role in the physiological response to stress.

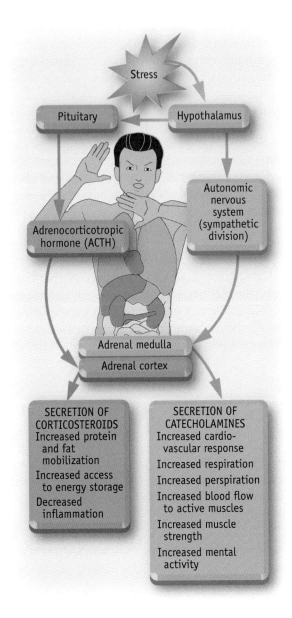

tating alertness. Digestive processes are inhibited to conserve your energy. The pupils of your eyes dilate, increasing visual sensitivity.

The second pathway (shown on the left in Figure 3.13) involves more direct communication between the brain and the endocrine system. The hypothalamus sends signals to the so-called master gland of the endocrine system, the pituitary gland. The pituitary secretes a hormone (ACTH) that stimulates the outer part of the adrenal glands (the adrenal cortex) to release another important set of hormones—*corticosteroids*. These hormones stimulate the release of chemicals that help increase your energy and help inhibit tissue inflammation in case of injury (Munck, 2000).

Stress can also produce other physiological changes that we are just beginning to understand. The most critical changes occur in the immune system. Your immune system provides you with resistance to infections. However, evidence indicates that stress can suppress certain aspects of the multifaceted immune response, reducing its overall effectiveness in repelling invasions by infectious agents (Chiappelli & Hodgson, 2000). In a thorough review of 30 years of research on stress and immunity, Segerstrom and Miller (2004) conclude that chronic stress can reduce both *cellular immune responses* (which attack intracellular pathogens, such as viruses) and *humoral immune responses* (which attack extracellular pathogens, such as bacteria). They also report that the *duration* of a stressful event is a key factor determining its impact on immune function. Long-lasting stressors, such as caring for a seriously ill spouse or enduring unemployment for months, are associated with greater immune suppression than relatively brief stressors.

The exact mechanisms underlying immune suppression are complicated, but it appears likely that both sets of stress hormones (catecholamines and corticosteroids) contribute (Dantzer & Mormede, 1995). In any case, it is becoming clear that physiological responses to stress extend into every corner of the body. Moreover, some of these responses may persist long after a stressful event has ended (Esterling et al., 1994). As you will see, these physiological reactions can have an impact on both mental and physical health.

Behavioral Responses

Although people respond to stress at several levels, their behavior is the crucial dimension of these reactions. Emotional and physiological responses to stress—which are often undesirable—tend to be largely automatic. However, dealing effectively with stress at the behavioral level may shut down these potentially harmful emotional and physiological reactions.

Most behavioral responses to stress involve coping. *Coping* **refers to active efforts to master, reduce,**

● FIGURE 3.13

Brain-body pathways in stress. In times of stress, the brain sends signals along two pathways. The pathway through the autonomic nervous system (shown in blue on the right) controls the release of catecholamine hormones that help mobilize the body for action. The pathway through the pituitary gland and the endocrine system (shown in brown on the left) controls the release of corticosteroid hormones that increase energy and ward off tissue inflammation.

vation involves stimulating the central part of the adrenal glands (the adrenal medulla) to release large amounts of *catecholamines* into the bloodstream. These hormones radiate throughout your body, producing many important physiological changes. The net result of catecholamine elevation is that your body is mobilized for action (Lundberg, 2000). Heart rate and blood flow increase, pumping more blood to your brain and muscles. Respiration and oxygen consumption speed up, facili-

or tolerate the demands created by stress. Notice that this definition is neutral as to whether coping efforts are healthy or maladaptive. The popular use of the term often implies that coping is inherently healthy. When we say that someone "coped with her problems," we imply that she handled them effectively.

In reality, coping responses may be either healthy or unhealthy (Moos & Schaefer, 1993). For example, if you were flunking a history course at midterm, you might cope with this stress by (1) increasing your study efforts, (2) seeking help from a tutor, (3) blaming your professor for your poor grade, or (4) giving up on the class. Clearly, the first two coping responses would be healthier than the second two.

People cope with stress in an endless variety of ways. Because of the complexity and importance of coping processes, we'll devote all of the next chapter to ways of coping. At this point, it is sufficient to note that coping strategies help determine whether stress has any positive or negative effects on an individual. In the next section, we'll see what some of those effects can be as we discuss the possible outcomes of people's struggles with stress.

The Potential Effects of Stress

LEARNING OBJECTIVES

- *Explain the phenomenon of choking under pressure.*
- *Summarize evidence on how stress can affect cognitive functioning.*
- *Describe the symptoms and causes of burnout.*
- *Discuss the prevalence, symptoms, and causes of posttraumatic stress disorder.*
- *Discuss the potential impact of stress on mental and physical health.*
- *Describe positive psychology and three ways in which stress might lead to beneficial effects.*

People struggle with many stressors every day, most of which come and go without leaving any enduring imprint. However, when stress is severe or when demands pile up, stress may have long-lasting effects. These effects, often called "adaptational outcomes," are relatively durable (though not necessarily permanent) consequences of exposure to stress. Although stress can have beneficial effects, research has focused mainly on possible negative outcomes, so you'll find our coverage slanted in that direction.

Impaired Task Performance

Frequently, stress takes its toll on the ability to perform effectively on a task at hand. For instance, Roy Baumeister (1984) theorized that pressure to perform often makes people self-conscious and that this elevated self-consciousness disrupts their attention, thereby interfering with performance. He theorizes that attention may be distorted in two ways. First, elevated self-consciousness may divert attention from the demands of the task, creating distractions. Second, on well-learned tasks that should be executed almost automatically, the self-conscious person may focus *too* much attention on the task. Thus, the person thinks too much about what he or she is doing.

Baumeister (1984) found support for his theory in a series of laboratory experiments in which he manipulated the pressure to perform well on a simple perceptual-motor task. His theory also garnered some support in a pair of studies of the past performance of professional sports teams in championship contests (Baumeister, 1995; Baumeister & Steinhilber, 1984). These findings were particularly impressive in that gifted professional athletes are probably less likely to choke under pressure than virtually any other sample one might assemble. Laboratory research on "normal" subjects is more pertinent to the issue, and it suggests that choking under pressure is fairly common (Butler & Baumeister, 1998; Lewis & Linder, 1997).

Disruption of Cognitive Functioning

An interesting experimental study suggests that Baumeister is on the right track in looking to *attention* to explain how stress impairs task performance. In a study of stress and decision making, Keinan (1987) was able to measure three specific aspects of subjects' attention under stressful and nonstressful conditions. Keinan found that stress disrupted two out of the three aspects of attention measured in the study. Stress increased subjects' tendency (1) to jump to a conclusion too quickly without considering all their options and (2) to do an unsystematic, poorly organized review of their available options. The results of some studies also suggest that stress can have detrimental effects on certain aspects of memory functioning (Kellogg, Hopko, & Ashcraft, 1999; Shors, 2004).

Severe stress may leave people dazed and confused, in a state of shock (Valent, 2000; Weisaeth, 1993). In these states, people report feeling emotionally numb, and they respond in a flat, apathetic fashion to events around them. They often stare off into space and have difficulty maintaining a coherent train of thought. Their behavior frequently has an automatic, rigid, stereotyped quality. Fortunately, this disorientation usually occurs only in extreme situations involving overwhelming stress, such as surviving a fire, a flood, or a tornado.

Burnout

Burnout is an overused buzzword that means different things to different people. Nonetheless, a few researchers have described burnout in a systematic way that has facilitated scientific study of the syndrome (Maslach & Leiter, 1997; Pines, 1993). *Burnout involves physical and emotional exhaustion, cynicism, and a lowered sense of self-efficacy that is attributable to work-related stress.* Exhaustion, which is central to burnout, includes chronic fatigue, weakness, and low energy. Cynicism is manifested in highly negative attitudes toward oneself, one's work, and life in general. Reduced self-efficacy involves declining feelings of competence at work that give way to feelings of hopelessness and helplessness.

What causes burnout? According to Leiter and Maslach (2001), "burnout is a cumulative stress reaction to ongoing occupational stressors" (p. 418). The conventional wisdom is that burnout occurs because of some flaw or weakness within the person, but Christina Maslach (2003) asserts that "the research case is much stronger for the contrasting argument that burnout is more a function of the situation than of the person" (p. 191). Factors in the workplace that appear to promote burnout include work overload, interpersonal conflicts at work, lack of control over work responsibilities and outcomes, and inadequate recognition for one's work (see Figure 3.14). As you might expect, burnout is associated with increased absenteeism and reduced productivity at work, as well as increased vulnerability to a variety of health problems (Maslach & Leiter, 2000).

Posttraumatic Stress Disorders

Extremely stressful, traumatic incidents can leave a lasting imprint on victims' psychological functioning. *Posttraumatic stress disorder (PTSD) involves enduring psychological disurbance attributed to the experience of a major traumatic event.* Researchers began to appreciate the frequency and severity of posttraumatic stress disorders after the Vietnam war ended in 1975 and a great many psychologically scarred veterans returned home. These veterans displayed a diverse array of psychological problems and symptoms that in many cases lingered much longer than expected. Studies suggest that nearly a half million Vietnam veterans were

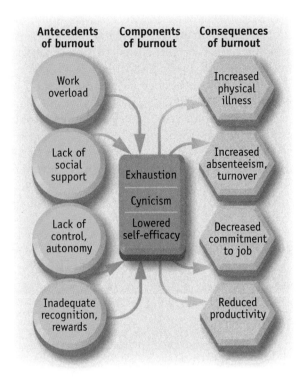

● **FIGURE 3.14**

The antecedents, components, and consequences of burnout. Christina Maslach and Michael Leiter have developed a systematic model of burnout that specifies its antecedents, components, and consequences. The antecedents on the left in the diagram are the stressful features of the work environment that cause burnout. The burnout syndrome itself consists of the three components shown in the center of the diagram. Some of the unfortunate results of burnout are listed on the right. (Based on Leiter & Maslach, 2001)

still suffering from PTSD over a decade after the end of the war (Schlenger et al., 1992).

Although posttraumatic stress disorders are widely associated with the experiences of Vietnam veterans, they are seen in response to other cases of traumatic stress as well, and they appear to be much more common than originally believed. Research suggests that 7–8 percent of people have suffered from PTSD at some point in their lives, with prevalence higher among women (10 percent) than men (5 percent) (Ozer et al.,

2003). PTSD is seen in children as well as adults (La Greca, 2000). In some instances, PTSD does not surface until many months or years after a person's exposure to severe stress (Holen, 2000).

What types of stress besides combat are severe enough to produce PTSD? The syndrome is frequently seen after a rape, a serious automobile accident, a robbery or assault, or the witnessing of someone's death (Koren, Arnon, & Klein, 1999; Stein et al., 1997b). Studies indicate that PTSD is also common in the wake of major disasters, such as floods, hurricanes, earthquakes, fires, and so forth (Koopman, Classen, & Spiegel, 1994; Vernberg et al., 1996). Vulnerability to PTSD is not limited to victims, survivors, and witnesses of traumatic events. Rescue workers and cleanup crews who have to grapple with the gruesome carnage of major disasters, dangerous working conditions, and tremendous fatigue also have an elevated risk for PTSD and often are "forgotten victims" of disasters (Ursano et al., 1999). Unfortunately, research by Stein et al. (1997b) suggests that the various types of traumatic events that can cause PTSD are more common than most people realize (see Figure 3.15).

What are the symptoms of posttraumatic stress disorders? Common symptoms include reexperiencing the traumatic event in the form of nightmares and flashbacks, emotional numbing, alienation, problems in social relations, and elevated arousal, anxiety, and guilt (Flannery, 1999; Shalev, 2001). PTSD is also associated with an elevated risk for substance abuse, depression, and anxiety disorders, as well as a great variety of physical health problems (Fairbank, Ebert, & Caddell, 2001). The frequency and severity of post-

WEB LINK 3.6

David Baldwin's Trauma Information Pages
This site has long been recognized as the premier repository for web-based and other resources relating to emotional trauma, traumatic stress, and posttraumatic stress disorder. David Baldwin has assembled more than 1000 links to information about these issues.

traumatic symptoms usually decline gradually over time, but in many cases the symptoms never completely disappear.

Although PTSD is fairly common in the wake of traumatic events, the vast majority of people who experience such events do *not* develop PTSD (Ozer & Weiss, 2004). Hence, a current focus of research is to determine what factors make certain people more susceptible than others to the ravages of severe stress. According to McKeever and Huff (2003), this vulnerability probably depends on complex interactions among a host of biological and environmental factors. One key predictor that emerged in a recent review of the relevant research is the *intensity of one's reaction at the time of the traumatic event* (Ozer et al., 2003). Individuals who have especially intense emotional reactions during or immediately after the traumatic event go on to show elevated vulnerability to PTSD. Vulnerability seems to be greatest among people whose reactions are so intense that they report dissociative experiences (a sense that things are not real, that time is stretching out, that one is watching oneself in a movie). You can consult Chapter 15 for a fuller discussion of PTSD risk factors.

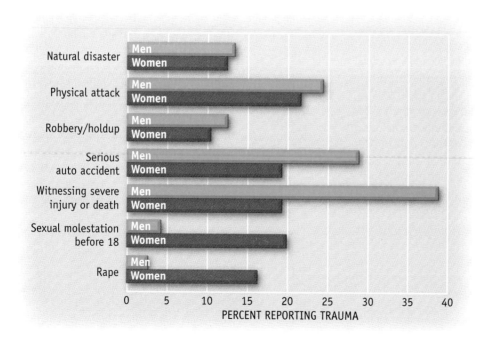

● FIGURE 3.15

The prevalence of traumatic events. We tend to think that traumatic events are relatively unusual and infrequent, but research by Stein et al. (1997b) suggests otherwise. When they interviewed over 1000 people in Winnipeg, they found that 74.2 percent of the women and 81.3 percent of the men reported having experienced at least one highly traumatic event. The percentage of respondents reporting specific types of traumatic events are summarized in this graph.

Major disasters, such as the December 2004 tsunami that devastated vast regions of Southeast Asia, are just one of about a half-dozen types of calamitous events that frequently lead to posttraumatic stress disorders.

© Kim Kyung-Hoon/Reuters/Corbis

Psychological Problems and Disorders

Posttraumatic stress disorders are caused by an acute episode of extreme stress. Of greater relevance to most of us are the effects of chronic, prolonged, everyday stress. On the basis of clinical impressions, psychologists have long suspected that chronic stress might contribute to many types of psychological problems and mental disorders. Since the late 1960s, advances in the measurement of stress have allowed researchers to verify these suspicions in empirical studies. In the domain of common psychological problems, studies indicate that stress may contribute to poor academic performance (Akgun & Ciarrochi, 2003), insomnia and other sleep disturbances (Vgontzas, Bixler, & Kales, 2000), sexual difficulties (Lemack, Uzzo, & Poppas, 1998), alcohol abuse (Colder, 2001), and drug abuse (Goeders, 2004).

Above and beyond these everyday problems, research reveals that stress often contributes to the onset of full-fledged psychological disorders, including depression (Rehm, Wagner, & Ivens-Tyndal, 2001), schizophrenia (McGlashan & Hoffman, 2000), anxiety disorders (Falsetti & Ballenger, 1998), and eating disorders (Cooper, 1995). We'll discuss the complex relations between stress and mental disorders in detail in Chapter 15.

Physical Illness

Stress can also have an impact on one's physical health. The idea that stress can contribute to physical ailments is not entirely new. Evidence that stress can cause phys-

ical illness began to accumulate back in the 1930s. By the 1950s, the concept of psychosomatic disease was widely accepted. *Psychosomatic diseases* **were defined as genuine physical ailments thought to be caused in part by stress and other psychological factors.** The classic psychosomatic illnesses were high blood pressure, peptic ulcers, asthma, skin disorders such as eczema and hives, and migraine and tension headaches (Kaplan, 1989; Rogers, Fricchione, & Reich, 1999). Please note, these diseases were not regarded as *imagined* physical ailments. The term *psychosomatic* has often been misused to refer to physical ailments that are "all in one's head," but that is an entirely different syndrome (see Chapter 15). Rather, psychosomatic diseases were viewed as authentic organic maladies that were heavily stress related.

Since the 1970s, the concept of psychosomatic disease has gradually fallen into disuse because research has shown that stress can contribute to the development of a diverse array of other diseases previously believed to be purely physiological in origin. Although there is room for debate on some specific diseases, stress may influence the onset and course of heart disease, stroke, tuberculosis, multiple sclerosis, arthritis, diabetes, leukemia, cancer, various types of infectious disease, and probably many other types of illnesses (Critelli & Ee, 1996; Dougall & Baum, 2001; Hubbard & Workman, 1998). Thus, it has become apparent that there is nothing unique about the psychosomatic diseases that requires a special category. Modern evidence continues to demonstrate that the classic psychosomatic diseases are influenced by stress, but so are numerous other diseases (Levenson et al., 1999). Of course, stress is only one of many factors that may contribute to the development of physical illness. Nonetheless, it is sobering to realize that stress can have an impact on one's physical health.

Positive Effects

The effects of stress are not entirely negative. Recent years have brought increased interest in positive aspects of the stress process, including favorable outcomes that follow in the wake of stress (Folkman & Moskowitz, 2000). To some extent, the new focus on the possible benefits of stress reflects a new emphasis on "positive psychology." Some influential theorists have argued that the field of psychology has historically devoted too much attention to pathology, weakness, and damage and how to heal suffering (Seligman, 2003). This approach has yielded valuable insights and progress, but it has also resulted in an unfortunate neglect of the forces that make life worth living. The positive psychology movement seeks to shift the field's focus away from negative experiences. As Martin Seligman and Mihaly Csikszentmihalyi (2000) put it, "The aim of positive psychology is to begin to catalyze a change in the focus of psychology from preoccupation with only repairing the worst things in life to also building positive qualities" (p. 5). The advocates of positive psychology argue for increased research on well-being, contentment, hope, courage, perseverance, nurturance, tolerance, and other human strengths and virtues (Aspinwall & Staudinger, 2003; Peterson & Seligman, 2004). One of these strengths is resilience in the face of stress, which promises to be a burgeoning area of research in the years to come.

The beneficial effects of stress may prove more difficult to pinpoint than the harmful effects because they may be more subtle. Although research data are sparse, there appear to be at least three ways in which stress can have positive effects.

First, stressful events help satisfy the need for stimulation and challenge. Studies suggest that most people prefer an intermediate level of stimulation and challenge in their lives (Sutherland, 2000). Although we think of stress in terms of stimulus overload, underload can be stressful as well (Goldberger, 1993). Thus, most people would experience a suffocating level of boredom if they lived a stress-free existence. In a sense, then, stress fulfills a basic need of the human organism.

Second, stress can promote personal growth or self-improvement (Tedeschi, Park, & Calhoun, 1998). For example, studies of people grappling with major health problems show that the majority report having derived benefits from their adversity (Tennen & Affleck, 1999). Stressful events sometimes force people to develop new skills, reevaluate priorities, learn new insights, and acquire new strengths. In other words, the adaptation process initiated by stress may lead to personal changes that are changes for the better. Confronting and con-

quering a stressful challenge may lead to improvements in specific coping abilities and to an enhanced self-concept. For example, a breakup with a boyfriend or a girlfriend may lead individuals to change aspects of their behavior that they find unsatisfactory. Moreover, even if people do not conquer stressors, they may be able to learn from their mistakes. Thus, researchers have begun to explore the growth potential of stressful events (Calhoun & Tedeschi, 2001; Park & Fenster, 2004).

Third, today's stress can inoculate individuals so that they are less affected by tomorrow's stress. Some studies suggest that exposure to stress can increase stress tolerance—as long as the stress isn't overwhelming (Meichenbaum, 1993). Thus, a woman who has previously endured business setbacks may be much better prepared than most people to deal with a bank foreclosure on her home. In light of the negative effects that stress can have, improved stress tolerance is a desirable goal. We'll look next at the factors that influence the ability to tolerate stress.

Factors Influencing Stress Tolerance

LEARNING OBJECTIVES

- *Explain how social support moderates the impact of stress.*
- *Describe the hardiness syndrome and how it influences stress tolerance.*
- *Discuss how optimism is related to stress tolerance.*

Some people seem to be able to withstand the ravages of stress better than others (Holahan & Moos, 1990, 1994). Why? Because a number of *moderator variables* can soften the impact of stress on physical and mental health. To shed light on differences in how well people tolerate stress, we'll look at a number of key moderator variables, including social support, hardiness, and optimism. As you'll see, these factors influence people's emotional, physical, and behavioral responses to stress. These complexities are diagrammed in Figure 3.16, which builds on Figure 3.7 to provide a more complete overview of the factors involved in individual reactions to stress.

Social Support

Friends may be good for your health! This startling conclusion emerges from studies on social support as a moderator of stress. *Social support refers to various types of aid and succor provided by members of one's social networks.* For example, Jemmott and Magloire (1988) examined the effect of social support on

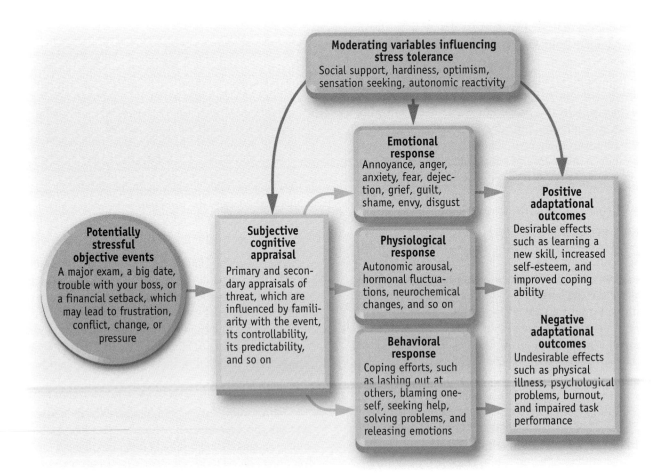

● **FIGURE 3.16**

Overview of the stress process. This diagram builds on Figure 3.7 (the multidimensional response to stress) to provide a more complete overview of the factors involved in stress. This diagram adds the potential effects of stress (seen on the far right) by listing some of the positive and negative adaptational outcomes that may result from stress. It also completes the picture by showing that moderating variables (seen at the top) can intervene to influence the effects of stress.

immune response in a group of students going through the stress of final exams. They found that students who reported stronger social support had higher levels of an antibody that plays a key role in warding off respiratory infections. Positive correlations between high social support and greater immunal functioning have been observed in quite a number of studies with diverse samples (Uchino, Cacioppo, & Kiecolt-Glaser, 1996).

Over the last two decades, a vast body of studies have found evidence that social support is favorably related to physical health (Wills & Fegan, 2001). Social support seems to be good medicine for the mind as well as the body, as most studies also find an association between social support and mental health (Davis, Morris, & Kraus, 1998; Sarason, Pierce, & Sarason, 1994). It appears that social support serves as a protective buffer during times of high stress, reducing the negative impact of stressful events—and that social support has its own positive effects on health, which may be apparent even when people aren't under great stress (Peirce et al., 1996; Wills & Fegan, 2001). The stress-buffering effects of social support were apparent in a study that found strong social support to be a key factor reducing the likelihood of posttraumatic stress disorders among Vietnam veterans (King et al., 1998).

The mechanisms underlying the connection between social support and wellness have been the subject of considerable debate (Hobfoll & Vaux, 1993). A variety of mechanisms may be at work. Among other things, social support could promote wellness by: making appraisals of stressful events more benign, dampening the intensity of physiological reactions to stress, reducing health-impairing behaviors such as smoking and drinking, encouraging preventive behaviors such as regular exercise and medical checkups, and fostering more constructive coping efforts (Wills & Fegan, 2001).

Interestingly, a recent study suggests that *providing* social support to others can also be beneficial (Brown et al., 2003). Another study found that the personality trait of *sociability* (being friendly and agreeable), which certainly helps people to build supportive social networks, is independently associated with reduced susceptibility to infectious disease (Cohen et al., 2003). Yet another study has demonstrated that pet owners view their pets as sources of support in their lives, with resultant health benefits (Allen, Blascovich, & Mendes, 2002). Thus, it appears that social support is not the only feature of our social relations that has some bearing on our wellness.

The availability of social support is a key factor influencing stress tolerance. Decades of research have shown that social support reduces the negative effects of stress and has positive effects of its own.

Hardiness

Another line of research indicates that a syndrome called *hardiness* may moderate the impact of stressful events. Suzanne (Kobasa) Ouellette reasoned that if stress affects some people less than others, then some people must be *hardier* than others. Hence, she set out to determine what factors might be the key to these differences in hardiness.

Suzanne Ouellette

Kobasa (1979) used a modified version of the Holmes and Rahe (1967) stress scale (SRRS) to measure the amount of stress experienced by a group of executives. As in most other studies, she found a modest correlation between stress and the incidence of physical illness. However, she carried her investigation one step further than previous studies. She compared the high-stress executives who exhibited the expected high incidence of illness against the high-stress executives who stayed healthy. She administered a battery of psychological tests and found that the hardier executives "were more committed, felt more in control, and had bigger appetites for challenge" (Kobasa, 1984, p. 70). These traits have also shown up in many other studies of hardiness (Maddi, 1999, 2002; Ouellette, 1993).

Thus, **hardiness is a syndrome marked by commitment, challenge, and control that is purportedly associated with strong stress resistance.** Hardiness may reduce the effects of stress by altering stress appraisals or fostering more active coping (Crowley, Hayslip, & Hobdy, 2003; Maddi & Hightower, 1999). The benefits of hardiness showed up in a study of Vietnam

CALVIN AND HOBBES © Watterson. Reprinted with permission of UNIVERSAL PRESS SYNDICATE. All rights reserved.

veterans, which found that higher hardiness was related to a lower likelihood of developing posttraumatic stress disorders (King et al., 1998). Although the research on hardiness is promising, there is extensive debate about how to measure hardiness and about its key elements (Klag & Bradley, 2004; Oullette & DiPlacido, 2001; Younkin & Betz, 1996).

Optimism

Defining *optimism* **as a general tendency to expect good outcomes,** Michael Scheier and Charles Carver (1985) found a correlation between optimism as measured by the Life Orientation Test (see Figure 3.17) and relatively good physical health in a sample of college students. In another study that focused on surgical patients, optimism was found to be associated with a faster recovery and a quicker return to normal activities after coronary artery bypass surgery (Scheier et al., 1989). Yet another study found optimism to be associated with more effective immune functioning (Segerstrom et al., 1998). Twenty years of research with the Life Orientation Test has consistently shown that optimism is associated with better mental and physical health (Scheier, Carver, & Bridges, 2001).

In a related line of research, Christopher Peterson and Martin Seligman have studied how people explain bad events (personal setbacks, mishaps, disappointments, and such). They identified a *pessimistic explanatory style,* in which people tend to blame setbacks on

their own personal shortcomings, versus an *optimistic explanatory style,* which leads people to attribute setbacks to temporary situational factors. In two retrospective studies of people born many decades ago, they found an association between this optimistic explanatory style and relatively good health (Peterson, Seligman, & Vaillant, 1988) and increased longevity (Peter-

● **FIGURE 3.17**

The Life Orientation Test (LOT). The personality trait of optimism, which appears to foster resilience in the face of stress, can be measured by the Life Orientation Test (LOT) developed by Scheier and Carver (1985). Follow the instructions for this scale to obtain an estimate of your own optimism. High and low scores are based on scoring three-fifths of a standard deviation above or below the mean.

Adapted from Scheier, M. F., & Carver, C. S. (1985). Optimism, coping, and health: Assessment and implications of generalized outcome expectancies. *Health Psychology, 4,* 219–247. Copyright © 1985 Lawrence Erlbaum & Associates. Adapted by permission of the publisher and authors.

Measuring Optimism

In the following spaces, mark how much you agree with each of the items, using the following scale:

4 = strongly agree
3 = agree
2 = neutral
1 = disagree
0 = strongly disagree

_____ 1. In uncertain times, I usually expect the best.
_____ 2. It's easy for me to relax.
_____ 3. If something can go wrong for me, it will.
_____ 4. I always look on the bright side of things.
_____ 5. I'm always optimistic about my future.
_____ 6. I enjoy my friends a lot.
_____ 7. It's important for me to keep busy.
_____ 8. I hardly ever expect things to go my way.
_____ 9. Things never work out the way I want them to.
_____ 10. I don't get upset too easily.
_____ 11. I'm a believer in the idea that "every cloud has a silver lining."
_____ 12. I rarely count on good things happening to me.

Scoring
Cross out and ignore the responses you entered for items 2, 6, 7, and 10, which are "filler" items. For items 3, 8, 9, and 12, you need to reverse the numbers you entered. If you entered a 4, change it to 0. If you entered a 3, change it to 1. If you entered a 2, leave it unchanged. If you entered a 1, change it to 3. If you entered a 0, change it to 4. Now add up the numbers for items 1, 3, 4, 5, 8, 9, 11, 12, using the new numbers for the reversed items. This sum is your score on the Life Orientation Test. For college students, approximate norms are as follows: High score (25–32), intermediate score (18–24), low score (0–17).

son et al., 1998). Many other studies have linked the optimistic explanatory style to superior physical health (Peterson & Bossio, 2001), as well as higher academic achievement, increased job productivity, enhanced athletic performance, and higher marital satisfaction (Gillham et al., 2001).

Why does optimism promote a host of desirable outcomes? Above all else, research suggests that opti-mists cope with stress in more adaptive ways than pessimists (Aspinwall, Richter, & Hoffman, 2001; Carver & Scheier, 2002; Chang, 1996). Optimists are more likely to engage in action-oriented, problem-focused, carefully planned coping and are more willing than pessimists to seek social support. In comparison, pessimists are more likely to deal with stress by avoiding it, giving up, or engaging in denial.

APPLICATION

Monitoring Your Stress

LEARNING OBJECTIVES

- List five problems with the SRRS.
- Summarize how the LES corrects some of the problems that are characteristic of the SRRS.
- Explain why one should be cautious in interpreting scores on stress scales.

Rank the following five events in terms of how stressful they would be for you (1 = most stressful, 5 = least stressful):

____ **1.** Change in residence
____ **2.** Fired at work
____ **3.** Death of a close family member
____ **4.** Pregnancy
____ **5.** Personal injury or illness

All five events appear on the Social Readjustment Rating Scale (SRRS), developed by Holmes and Rahe (1967), which we described earlier (see Figure 3.5). If you ranked them in the same order as Holmes and Rahe's subjects, the rankings would be 5, 3, 1, 4, and 2. If you didn't rank them in that order, don't worry about it. That merely shows that the perception of stress is personal and subjective. Unfortunately, the SRRS fails to take this subjectivity into account. That is just one of a number of basic problems with the SRRS.

The SRRS and the research associated with it have received a great deal of publicity. The scale has been reprinted in many popular newspapers and magazines. In these articles, readers have been encouraged to attribute great significance to their scores. They have sometimes been told that they should reduce or minimize change in their lives if their scores are high (Cohen, 1979). Such bold advice could be counterproductive and needs to be qualified carefully. Therefore, in this application section we'll elaborate on some of the problems with the SRRS as a measurement scale, introduce you to an improved scale for measuring stress, and explain why scores on any stress scale should be interpreted with caution.

Problems with the SRRS

As you learned earlier in this chapter, the SRRS was developed in the early 1960s by Thomas Holmes and Richard Rahe (1967). They designed the scale to measure the amount of change-related stress that people experience. In a host of studies, these scores have been found to be related to the likelihood of developing an intimidating array of physical illnesses and psychological problems (Derogatis & Coons, 1993; Dougall & Baum, 2001; Turner & Wheaton, 1995).

Thomas Holmes

Before we discuss the shortcomings of the SRRS, we should emphasize that Holmes and Rahe deserve enormous credit for recognizing the potential importance of stress and for developing a scale that would permit its measurement. They pioneered a new area of research that has turned out to be extremely productive. However, their groundbreaking foray into the assessment of stress was not without its flaws, and their scale has been improved on. So, borrowing from the analyses of a number of critics (Derogatis, 1982; Rabkin, 1993; Schroeder & Costa, 1984), let's look at some of the major problems with the SRRS. Although our list is not exhaustive, we highlight the key problems.

First, as already discussed, the assumption that the SRRS measures change exclusively has been shown to be inaccurate. We now have ample evidence that the desirability of events affects adaptational outcomes more than the amount of change that they require (Turner & Wheaton, 1995). Thus, it seems prudent to view the SRRS as a measure of diverse forms of stress, rather than as a measure of change-related stress (McLean & Link, 1994).

Second, the SRRS fails to take into account differences among people in their subjective perception of how stressful an event is. For instance, while divorce may deserve a stress value of 73 for *most* people, a particular person's divorce might generate much less stress and merit a value of only 25.

Third, many of the events listed on the SRRS and similar scales are highly ambiguous, leading people to be inconsistent as to which events they report experiencing (Monroe & McQuaid, 1994). For instance, what qualifies as "trouble with boss"? Should you check that because you're sick and tired of your supervisor? What constitutes a "change in living conditions"? Does your purchase of a great new sound system qualify? As you can see, the SRRS includes many "events" that are described inadequately, producing considerable ambiguity about the meaning of one's response. Problems in recalling events over a period of a year also lead to inconsistent responding on stress scales, thus lowering their reliability (Klein & Rubovits, 1987).

Fourth, the SRRS does not sample from the domain of stressful events very thoroughly. Do the 43 events listed on the SRRS exhaust all the major stresses that people typically experience? Studies designed to explore that question have found many significant omissions (Dohrenwend et al, 1993; Wheaton, 1994).

Fifth, the correlation between SRRS scores and health outcomes may be inflated because subjects' neuroticism affects both their responses to stress scales and their self-reports of health problems. Neurotic individuals have a tendency to recall more stress than others and to recall more symptoms of illness than others (Watson, David, & Suls, 1999). These tendencies mean that some of the correlation between high stress and high illness may simply reflect the effects of subjects' neuroticism (Critelli & Ee, 1996). This is another case of the third variable problem in correlation that we introduced in Chapter 1 (see Figure 3.18). The possible contaminating effects of neuroticism obscure the meaning of scores on the SRRS and similar measures of stress.

The Life Experiences Survey

In light of these problems, a number of researchers have attempted to develop improved versions of the SRRS. For example, the Life Experiences Survey (LES), assembled by Irwin Sarason and colleagues (1978), has become a widely used measure of stress in contemporary research (for examples see Ames et al., 2001; Denisoff & Endler, 2000; Malefo, 2000). The LES revises and builds on the SRRS in a variety of ways that correct, at

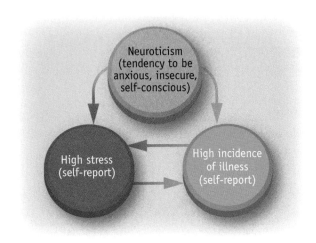

● FIGURE 3.18

Neuroticism as a possible factor underlying the stress-illness correlation. Many studies have found a correlation between subjects' scores on self-report stress scales, such as the SRRS, and their reports of how much illness they have experienced. However, neurotic subjects, who are anxious, insecure, and self-conscious, tend to recall more stress *and* more illness than others. Although there is a great deal of evidence that stress contributes to the causation of illness, some of the stress-illness correlation may be due to neuroticism causing high recall of both stress and illness.

least in part, most of the problems just discussed (see Hobson & Delunas, 2001 and Rahe et al., 2000 for other modernized versions of the SRRS).

Specifically, the LES recognizes that stress involves more than mere change and asks respondents to indicate whether events had a positive or negative impact on them. This strategy permits the computation of positive change, negative change, and total change scores, which helps researchers gain much more insight into which facets of stress are most crucial.

The LES also takes into consideration differences among people in their appraisal of stress, by dropping the normative weights and replacing them with personally assigned weightings of the impact of relevant events. Ambiguity in items is decreased by providing more elaborate descriptions of many items to clarify their meaning. The scale still contains some ambiguity, but there is no complete solution for this problem.

The LES deals with the failure of the SRRS to sample the full domain of stressful events in several ways. First, some significant omissions from the SRRS have been added to the LES. Second, the LES allows the respondent to write in personally important events that are not included on the scale. Third, the LES reprinted here (in Figure 3.19) has an extra section just for students. Sarason et al. (1978) suggest that special, tailored sections of this sort be added for specific populations whenever it is useful.

Arriving at your scores on the LES is very simple. Respond to the items in Figure 3.19 and add up all the positive impact ratings on the right side. The total is

The Life Experiences Survey (LES). Like the SRRS, the LES is designed to measure change-related stress. However, Sarason, Johnson, and Siegel (1978) corrected many of the problems apparent in the SRRS. Follow the instructions in the text to determine your positive, negative, and total change scores.

Instructions. Listed below are a number of events that sometimes bring about change in the lives of those who experience them and that necessitate social readjustment. Examine each event on the list and if that event has occurred in your life during the past year please indicate the extent to which you viewed the event as having either a positive or negative impact on your life at the time the event occurred. That is, circle a number on the appropriate line to indicate the type and extent of impact that the event had. A rating of –3 would indicate an extremely negative impact. A rating of 0 suggests no impact, either positive or negative. A rating of +3 would indicate an extremely positive impact.

The Life Experiences Survey (LES)

	Extremely negative	Moderately negative	Somewhat negative	No impact	Slightly positive	Moderately positive	Extremely positive
Section 1							
1. Marriage	–3	–2	–1	0	+1	+2	+3
2. Detention in jail or comparable institution	–3	–2	–1	0	+1	+2	+3
3. Death of spouse	–3	–2	–1	0	+1	+2	+3
4. Major change in sleeping habits	–3	–2	–1	0	+1	+2	+3
5. Death of a close family member	–3	–2	–1	0	+1	+2	+3
a. Mother	–3	–2	–1	0	+1	+2	+3
b. Father	–3	–2	–1	0	+1	+2	+3
c. Brother	–3	–2	–1	0	+1	+2	+3
d. Sister	–3	–2	–1	0	+1	+2	+3
e. Grandmother	–3	–2	–1	0	+1	+2	+3
f. Grandfather	–3	–2	–1	0	+1	+2	+3
g. Other (specify)	–3	–2	–1	0	+1	+2	+3
6. Major change in eating habits (much more or much less food intake)	–3	–2	–1	0	+1	+2	+3
7. Foreclosure on mortgage or loan	–3	–2	–1	0	+1	+2	+3
8. Death of a close friend	–3	–2	–1	0	+1	+2	+3
9. Outstanding personal achievement	–3	–2	–1	0	+1	+2	+3
10. Minor law violations	–3	–2	–1	0	+1	+2	+3
11. Male: Wife/girlfriend's pregnancy	–3	–2	–1	0	+1	+2	+3
12. Female: Pregnancy	–3	–2	–1	0	+1	+2	+3
13. Changed work situation (different work responsibility, major change in working conditions, working hours, etc.)	–3	–2	–1	0	+1	+2	+3
14. New job	–3	–2	–1	0	+1	+2	+3
15. Serious illness or injury of close family member:							
a. Mother	–3	–2	–1	0	+1	+2	+3
b. Father	–3	–2	–1	0	+1	+2	+3
c. Brother	–3	–2	–1	0	+1	+2	+3
d. Sister	–3	–2	–1	0	+1	+2	+3
e. Grandmother	–3	–2	–1	0	+1	+2	+3
f. Grandfather	–3	–2	–1	0	+1	+2	+3
g. Spouse	–3	–2	–1	0	+1	+2	+3
h. Other (specify)	–3	–2	–1	0	+1	+2	+3
16. Sexual difficulties	–3	–2	–1	0	+1	+2	+3
17. Trouble with employer (in danger of losing job, being suspended, being demoted, etc.)	–3	–2	–1	0	+1	+2	+3
18. Trouble with in-laws	–3	–2	–1	0	+1	+2	+3
19. Major change in financial status (a lot better off or a lot worse off)	–3	–2	–1	0	+1	+2	+3

(continued)

Adapted from Sarason, I. G., Johnson, J. H., & Siegel, J. M. (1978). Assessing the impact of life changes. *Journal of Consulting and Clinical Psychology, 46,* 932–946. Copyright © 1978 by the American Psychological Association. Reprinted by permission of the authors.

The Life Experiences Survey (LES) *(continued)*

	Extremely negative	Moderately negative	Somewhat negative	No impact	Slightly positive	Moderately positive	Extremely positive
20. Major change in closeness of family members (increased or decreased closeness)	−3	−2	−1	0	+1	+2	+3
21. Gaining a new family member (through birth, adoption, family member moving in, etc.)	−3	−2	−1	0	+1	+2	+3
22. Change in residence	−3	−2	−1	0	+1	+2	+3
23. Marital separation from mate (due to conflict)	−3	−2	−1	0	+1	+2	+3
24. Major change in church activities (increased or decreased attendance)	−3	−2	−1	0	+1	+2	+3
25. Marital reconciliation with mate							
26. Major change in number of arguments with spouse (a lot more or a lot fewer)	−3	−2	−1	0	+1	+2	+3
27. Married male: Change in wife's work outside the home (beginning work, ceasing work, changing to a new job, etc.)	−3	−2	−1	0	+1	+2	+3
28. Married female: Change in husband's work (loss of job, beginning new job, retirement, etc.)	−3	−2	−1	0	+1	+2	+3
29. Major change in usual type and/or amount of recreation	−3	−2	−1	0	+1	+2	+3
30. Borrowing for a major purchase (buying a home, business, etc.)	−3	−2	−1	0	+1	+2	+3
31. Borrowing for a smaller purchase (buying a car or TV, getting school loan, etc.)	−3	−2	−1	0	+1	+2	+3
32. Being fired from job	−3	−2	−1	0	+1	+2	+3
33. Male: Wife/girlfriend having abortion							
34. Female: Having abortion	−3	−2	−1	0	+1	+2	+3
35. Major personal illness or injury	−3	−2	−1	0	+1	+2	+3
36. Major change in social activities, e.g., parties, movies, visiting (increased or decreased participation)	−3	−2	−1	0	+1	+2	+3
37. Major change in living conditions of family (building new home, remodeling, deterioration of home or neighborhood, etc.)	−3	−2	−1	0	+1	+2	+3

(continued)

your positive change score. Your negative change score is the sum of all of the negative impact ratings that you made on the left. Adding these two values yields your total change score. Approximate norms for all three of these scores are listed in Figure 3.20 so that you can get some idea of what your score means.

Research to date suggests that the negative change score is the crucial one; positive change has not been found to be a good predictor of adaptational outcomes. Thus far, research has shown that negative change scores are related to a variety of negative adaptational outcomes.

● FIGURE 3.20

Norms for the Life Experiences Survey (LES). Approximate norms for college students taking the LES are shown for negative, positive, and total change scores. These norms are based on 345 undergraduates studied by Sarason, Johnson, and Siegel (1978). Data for males and females were combined, as gender differences were negligible. Negative change scores are the best predictor of adaptational outcomes.

Adapted from Sarason, I. G., Johnson, J. H., & Siegel, J. M. (1978). Assessing the impact of life changes. *Journal of Consulting and Clinical Psychology, 46*, 932–946. Copyright © 1978 by the American Psychological Association. Reprinted by permission of the authors.

Norms for LES

Score category	Negative change	Positive change	Total change
High	14 and above	16 and above	28 and above
Medium	4–13	7–15	12–27
Low	0–3	0–6	0–11

The Life Experiences Survey (LES) *(continued)*

	Extremely negative	Moderately negative	Somewhat negative	No impact	Slightly positive	Moderately positive	Extremely positive
38. Divorce	−3	−2	−1	0	+1	+2	+3
39. Serious injury or illness of close friend	−3	−2	−1	0	+1	+2	+3
40. Retirement from work	−3	−2	−1	0	+1	+2	+3
41. Son or daughter leaving home (due to marriage, college, etc.)	−3	−2	−1	0	+1	+2	+3
42. End of formal schooling	−3	−2	−1	0	+1	+2	+3
43. Separation from spouse (due to work, travel, etc.)	−3	−2	−1	0	+1	+2	+3
44. Engagement	−3	−2	−1	0	+1	+2	+3
45. Breaking up with boyfriend/girlfriend	−3	−2	−1	0	+1	+2	+3
46. Leaving home for the first time	−3	−2	−1	0	+1	+2	+3
47. Reconciliation with boyfriend/girlfriend	−3	−2	−1	0	+1	+2	+3
Other recent experiences that have had an impact on your life. List and rate.							
48. _____	−3	−2	−1	0	+1	+2	+3
49. _____	−3	−2	−1	0	+1	+2	+3
50. _____	−3	−2	−1	0	+1	+2	+3
Section 2. Students only							
51. Beginning a new school experience at a higher academic level (college, graduate school, professional school)	−3	−2	−1	0	+1	+2	+3
52. Changing to a new school at the same academic level (undergraduate, graduate, etc.)	−3	−2	−1	0	+1	+2	+3
53. Academic probation	−3	−2	−1	0	+1	+2	+3
54. Being dismissed from dormitory or other residence	−3	−2	−1	0	+1	+2	+3
55. Failing an important exam	−3	−2	−1	0	+1	+2	+3
56. Changing a major	−3	−2	−1	0	+1	+2	+3
57. Failing a course	−3	−2	−1	0	+1	+2	+3
58. Dropping a course	−3	−2	−1	0	+1	+2	+3
59. Joining a fraternity/sorority	−3	−2	−1	0	+1	+2	+3
60. Financial problems concerning school (in danger of not having sufficient money to continue)	−3	−2	−1	0	+1	+2	+3

A Cautionary Note

There is merit in getting an estimate of how much stress you have experienced lately, but scores on the LES or any measure of stress should be interpreted with caution. You need not panic if you add up your negative change score and find that it falls in the "high" category. Although it is clear that a connection exists between stress and a variety of undesirable adaptational outcomes, a high score shouldn't cause undue concern.

For one thing, the strength of the association between stress and adaptational problems is modest. Most of the correlations observed between stress scores and illness have been low to moderate in magnitude, often less than .30 (Monroe & McQuaid, 1994). For researchers and theorists, it is interesting to find any relationship at all. However, the link between stress and adaptational problems is too weak to permit us to make confident predictions about individuals. Many people endure high levels of stress without developing significant problems.

Second, stress is only one of a multitude of variables that affect susceptibility to various maladies. Stress interacts with many other factors, such as lifestyle, coping skills, social support, hardiness, and genetic inheritance, in influencing one's mental and physical health.

It's important to remember that stress is only one actor on a crowded stage. In light of these considerations, you should evaluate the potential meaning of SRRS or LES scores with caution. A high score should be food for thought, but not reason for alarm.

KEY IDEAS

The Nature of Stress

■ Stress involves transactions with the environment that are perceived to be threatening. Stress is a common, everyday event, and even routine hassles can be problematic. To a large degree, stress lies in the eye of the beholder. According to Lazarus and Folkman, primary appraisal determines whether events appear threatening, and secondary appraisal assesses whether one has the resources to cope with challenges.

■ Some of the stress that people experience comes from their environment. Examples of environmental stimuli that can be stressful include excessive noise, crowding, and urban decay. Much everyday stress is self-imposed. Stress can vary with culture. Within Western culture, ethnicity can be a source of stress in a variety of ways.

Major Types of Stress

■ Major types of stress include frustration, conflict, change, and pressure. Frustration occurs when an obstacle prevents one from attaining some goal. There are three principal types of conflict: approach-approach, avoidance-avoidance, and approach-avoidance. The latter is especially stressful. Vacillation is a common response to approach-avoidance conflict.

■ A large number of studies with the SRRS suggest that change is stressful. Although that may be true, it is now clear that the SRRS is a measure of general stress rather than just change-related stress. Two kinds of pressure (to perform and to conform) also appear to be stressful.

Responding to Stress

■ Emotional reactions to stress typically involve anger, fear, or sadness. However, people also experience positive emotions while under stress and these positive emotions may promote resilience. Emotional arousal may interfere with coping. As tasks get more complex, the optimal level of arousal declines.

■ Physiological arousal in response to stress was originally called the fight-or-flight response by Cannon. Selye's general adaptation syndrome describes three stages in the physiological reaction to stress: alarm, resistance, and exhaustion. Diseases of adaptation may appear during the stage of exhaustion.

■ In response to stress, the brain sends signals along two major pathways to the endocrine system. Actions along these paths release two sets of hormones into the bloodstream, catecholamines and corticosteroids. Stress can also lead to suppression of the immune response, especially when the stress is chronic and long-lasting. Behavioral responses to stress involve coping, which may be healthy or maladaptive. If people cope effectively with stress, they can short-circuit potentially harmful emotional and physical responses.

The Potential Effects of Stress

■ Common negative effects of stress include impaired task performance, disruption of attention and other cognitive processes, pervasive emotional exhaustion known as burnout, posttraumatic stress disorders, a host of everyday psychological problems, full-fledged psychological disorders, and varied types of damage to physical health.

■ However, stress can also have positive effects. Stress fulfills a basic human need for challenge and can lead to personal growth and self-improvement.

Factors Influencing Stress Tolerance

■ People differ in how much stress they can tolerate without experiencing ill effects. A person's social support can be a key consideration in buffering the effects of stress. The personality factors associated with hardiness—commitment, challenge, and control—may increase stress tolerance. People high in optimism also have advantages in coping with stress.

Application: Monitoring Your Stress

■ It can be useful to attempt to measure the amount of stress in one's life, but the much-used SRRS is marred by a variety of shortcomings. It does not really measure change exclusively, and it fails to account for the subjective nature of stress. Some of the items on the SRRS are ambiguous, and the scale does not sample the domain of stress thoroughly.

■ In contrast, the LES is an improved measure of stress that recognizes the subjectivity of stress and the importance of the desirability of life events. The LES also samples the domain of stressful events a little more thoroughly and has less ambiguity than the SRRS. Negative change scores on the LES have been found to be predictive of a variety of adaptational outcomes.

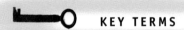

KEY TERMS

Acute stressors   p. 75
Ambient stress   p. 73
Approach-approach conflict
   p. 76
Approach-avoidance conflict
   p. 77
Autonomic nervous system
   (ANS)   p. 85
Avoidance-avoidance conflict
   p. 77
Burnout   p. 90
Chronic stressors   pp. 75–76
Conflict   p. 76
Coping   pp. 88–89
Emotions   p. 82
Endocrine system   p. 86
Fight-or-flight response
   p. 85

Frustration   p. 76
General adaptation syndrome
   p. 86
Hardiness   p. 95
Life changes   p. 78
Optimism   p. 96
Posttraumatic stress disorder
   (PTSD)   p. 90
Pressure   p. 80
Primary appraisal   p. 72
Psychosomatic diseases
   p. 92
Secondary appraisal   p. 72
Social support   p. 94
Stress   p. 72

KEY PEOPLE

Susan Folkman   pp. 83–84
Thomas Holmes and Richard
   Rahe   pp. 68–70
Suzanne (Kobasa) Ouellette
   pp. 95–96

Richard Lazarus   p. 72
Neal Miller   pp. 76–78
Hans Selye   pp. 86–87
Shelley Taylor   pp. 85–86

1. Concerning the nature of stress, which statement is *not* accurate?
   a. Stress is an everyday event.
   b. Stress lies in the eye of the beholder.
   c. Stress may be embedded in the environment.
   d. Stress is always imposed on us by others.

2. Secondary appraisal refers to:
   a. second thoughts about what to do in a stressful situation.
   b. second thoughts about whether an event is genuinely threatening.
   c. initial evaluation of an event's relevance, threat, and stressfulness.
   d. evaluation of coping resources and options for dealing with a stressful event.

3. An approach-avoidance conflict may best be resolved by _____ the avoidance motivation rather than _____ the approach motivation.
   a. decreasing, decreasing
   b. decreasing, increasing
   c. increasing, decreasing
   d. increasing, increasing

4. José just completed writing an 8-page term paper. When he went to save it, the computer crashed and he lost all his work. What type of stress is José experiencing?
   a. Frustration   c. Life change
   b. Conflict   d. Pressure

5. The optimal level of arousal for a task appears to depend in part on:
   a. one's position on the optimism/pessimism scale.
   b. how much physiological change an event stimulates.
   c. the complexity of the task at hand.
   d. how imminent a stressful event is.

6. The fight-or-flight response is mediated by the:
   a. sympathetic division of the autonomic nervous system.
   b. sympathetic division of the endocrine system.
   c. visceral division of the peripheral nervous system.
   d. parasympathetic division of the autonomic nervous system.

7. Selye exposed lab animals to various stressors and found that:
   a. each type of stress caused a particular physiological response.
   b. each type of animal responded to stress differently.
   c. patterns of physiological arousal were similar, regardless of the type of stress.
   d. patterns of physiological arousal were different, even when stressors were similar.

8. Stress can _____ the functioning of the immune system.
   a. stimulate   c. suppress
   b. destroy   d. enhance

9. Salvador works as a security guard at a shopping center. His boss overloads him with responsibility but never gives him any credit for all his hard work. He feels worn down, disillusioned, and helpless at work. Salvador is probably experiencing:
   a. an alarm reaction.
   b. burnout.
   c. posttraumatic stress disorder.
   d. a psychosomatic disorder.

10. A personality syndrome marked by commitment, challenge, and control and that appears to be related to stress resistance is called:
    a. hardiness.   c. courage.
    b. optimism.   d. conscientiousness.

Book Companion Website

Visit the Book Companion Website at **http://psychology. wadsworth.com/weiten_lloyd8e,** where you will find tutorial quizzes, flashcards, and weblinks for every chapter, a final exam, and more! You can also link to the Thomson Wadsworth Psychology Resource Center (accessible directly at **http://psychology.wadsworth.com**) for a range of psychology-related resources.

Personal Explorations Workbook

The following exercises in your *Personal Explorations Workbook* may enhance your self-understanding in relation to issues raised in this chapter. **Questionnaire 3.1:** Sensation-Seeking Scale. **Personal Probe 3.1:** Where's the Stress in Your Life? **Personal Probe 3.2:** Stress—How Do You Control It? **Personal Probe 3.3:** Working Through and Assessing the Impact of a Stressful Event.

ANSWERS

1. d Pages 72–73
2. d Pages 72–73
3. b Pages 77–78
4. a Page 76
5. c Pages 77–78
6. a Pages 85–86
7. c Pages 86–87
8. c Page 88
9. b Page 90
10. a Pages 95–96

Coping Processes

"I have begun to believe that I have intellectually and emotionally out-grown my husband. However, I'm not really sure what this means or what I should do. Maybe this feeling is normal and I should ignore it and con-tinue my present relationship. This seems to be the safest route. Maybe I should seek a lover while continuing with my husband. Then again, maybe I should start anew and hope for a beautiful ending with or without a better mate."

The woman quoted above is in the throes of a thorny conflict. Although it is hard to tell just how much emotional turmoil she is experiencing, it's clear that she is under substantial stress. What should she do? Is it psychologi-cally healthy to remain in an emotionally hollow marriage? Is seeking a se-cret lover a reasonable way to cope with this unfortunate situation? Should she just strike out on her own and let the chips fall where they may? These questions have no simple answers. As you'll soon see, decisions about how to cope with life's difficulties can be terribly complex.

In the previous chapter we discussed the nature of stress and its effects. We learned that stress can be a challenging, exciting stimulus to personal growth. However, we also saw that stress can prove damaging to people's psychological and physical health because it often triggers physiological re-sponses that may be harmful. These responses to stress tend to be largely automatic. Controlling them depends on the coping responses people make to stressful situations. Thus, a person's mental and physical health depends, in part, on his or her ability to cope effectively with stress.

This chapter focuses on how people cope with stress. We begin with a general discussion of the concept of coping. Then we review some common coping patterns that tend to have relatively little value. After discussing these ill-advised coping techniques, we offer an overview of what it means to engage in healthier, "constructive" coping. The remainder of the chapter expands on the specifics of constructive coping. We hope our discussion provides you with some new ideas about how to deal with the stresses of modern life.

The Concept of Coping

LEARNING OBJECTIVES

- *Describe the variety of coping strategies that people use.*
- *Discuss whether individuals display distinctive styles of coping.*

In Chapter 3, you learned that *coping* **refers to efforts to master, reduce, or tolerate the demands created by stress.** Let's take a closer look at this concept and discuss some general points about coping.

People cope with stress in many ways. A number of researchers have attempted to identify and classify the various coping techniques that people use in dealing with stress. Their work reveals quite a variety of coping strategies. For instance, in a study of how 255 adult subjects dealt with stress, McCrae (1984) identified 28 coping techniques. In another study, Carver, Scheier, and Weintraub (1989) found that they could sort their participants' coping tactics into 14 categories, which are listed in Figure 4.1. Thus, in grappling with stress, people select their coping tactics from a large and varied menu of options.

Individuals have their own styles of coping. Even with a large menu of coping tactics to choose from, most people come to rely on some strategies more than others (Carver & Scheier, 1994; Heszen-Niejodek, 1997). Of course, an individual's coping strategies are also influenced by situational demands, and Cheng (2001) has argued that *flexibility* in coping is more desirable than consistently relying on the same strategy. The need for flexibility may explain why people's coping strategies show only moderate stability across varied situations (Schwartz et al., 1999). Nonetheless, to some extent, each person has an individual style of coping with life's difficulties. As we progress through this chapter, it may be fruitful for you to analyze your own style of coping.

Coping strategies vary in their adaptive value. In everyday terms, when we say that someone "coped with her problems," we imply that she handled them effectively. In reality, however, coping processes range from the helpful to the counterproductive (Carver et al., 1989; Vaillant, 2000). For example, coping with the disappointment of not getting a promotion by plotting to

From Carver, C. S., Scheier, M. F., & Weintraub, J. K. (1989). Assessing coping strategies: A theoretically based approach. *Journal of Personality and Social Psychology, 56(2),* 267–283. Copyright 1989 by the American Psychological Association. Reprinted by permission of the authors.

● FIGURE 4.1

Classifying coping strategies. Carver, Scheier, and Weintraub (1989) sorted their subjects' coping responses into 14 categories. The categories are listed here (column 1) with a representative example from each category (column 2). As you can see, people use quite a variety of coping strategies.

Types of Coping Strategies

Coping strategy	Example
Active coping	I take additional action to try to get rid of the problem.
Planning	I come up with a strategy about what to do.
Suppression of competing activities	I put aside other activities in order to concentrate on this.
Restraint coping	I force myself to wait for the right time to do something.
Seeking social support for instrumental reasons	I ask people who have had similar experiences what they did.
Seeking social support for emotional reasons	I talk to someone about how I feel.
Positive reinterpretation and growth	I look for the good in what is happening.
Acceptance	I learn to live with it.
Turning to religion	I seek God's help.
Focus on and venting of emotions	I get upset and let my emotions out.
Denial	I refuse to believe that it has happened.
Behavioral disengagement	I give up the attempt to get what I want.
Mental disengagement	I turn to work or other substitute activities to take my mind off things.
Alcohol-drug disengagement	I drink alcohol or take drugs in order to think about it less.

sabotage your company's computer system would be a negative way of coping. Hence, we will distinguish between coping patterns that tend to be helpful and those that tend to be maladaptive. Bear in mind, however, that our generalizations about the adaptive value of various coping strategies are based on trends or tendencies.

No coping strategy can guarantee a successful outcome. Furthermore, the adaptive value of a coping technique depends on the exact nature of the situation. As you'll see in the next section, even ill-advised coping strategies may have adaptive value in some instances.

Common Coping Patterns of Limited Value

LEARNING OBJECTIVES

- Analyze the adaptive value of giving up as a response to stress.
- Describe the adaptive value of aggression as a response to stress.
- Evaluate the adaptive value of indulging yourself as a response to stress.
- Discuss the adaptive value of negative self-talk as a response to stress.
- Explain how defense mechanisms work.
- Evaluate the adaptive value of defense mechanisms, including recent work on healthy illusions.

"Recently, after an engagement of 22 months, my fiancée told me that she was in love with someone else, and that we were through. I've been a wreck ever since. I can't study because I keep thinking about her. I think constantly about what I did wrong in the relationship and why I wasn't good enough for her. Getting drunk is the only way I can get her off my mind. Lately, I've been getting plastered about five or six nights a week. My grades are really hurting, but I'm not sure that I care."

This young man is going through a difficult time and does not appear to be handling it very well. He's blaming himself for the breakup with his fiancée. He's turning to alcohol to dull the pain that he feels, and it sounds like he may be giving up on school. These coping responses aren't particularly unusual in such situations, but they're only going to make his problems worse.

In this section, we'll examine some relatively common coping patterns that tend to be less than optimal. Specifically, we'll discuss giving up, aggression, self-indulgence, blaming yourself, and defense mechanisms. Some of these coping tactics may be helpful in certain circumstances, but more often than not, they are counterproductive.

Giving Up

When confronted with stress, people sometimes simply give up and withdraw from the battle. This response of apathy and inaction tends to be associated with the emotional reactions of sadness and dejection. Martin Seligman (1974, 1992) has

Martin Seligman

developed a model of this giving-up syndrome that appears to shed light on its causes. In Seligman's original research, animals were subjected to electric shocks they could not escape. The animals were then given an opportunity to learn a response that would allow them to escape the shock. However, many of the animals became so apathetic and listless they didn't even try to learn the escape response. When researchers made similar manipulations with *human* subjects using inescapable noise (rather than shock) as the stressor, they observed parallel results (Hiroto & Seligman, 1975). This syndrome is referred to as learned helplessness. ***Learned helplessness is passive behavior produced by exposure to unavoidable aversive events.*** Unfortunately, this tendency to give up may be transferred to situations in which one is not really helpless. Hence, some people routinely respond to stress with fatalism and resignation, passively accepting setbacks that might be dealt with effectively. Interestingly, Evans and Stecker (2004) argue that environmental stressors, such as excessive noise, crowding, and traffic (see Chapter 3), often produce a syndrome that resembles learned helplessness.

Seligman originally viewed learned helplessness as a product of conditioning. However, research with human participants has led Seligman and his colleagues to revise their theory. Their current model proposes that people's *cognitive interpretation* of aversive events determines whether they develop learned helplessness. Specifically, helplessness seems to occur when individuals come to believe that events are beyond their control. This belief is particularly likely to emerge in people who exhibit a pessimistic explanatory style. Among other things, such people tend to attribute setbacks to personal inadequacies instead of situational factors

(Abramson, Seligman, & Teasdale, 1978; Seligman, 1990).

As you might guess, giving up is not a highly regarded method of coping. Carver and his colleagues (1989, 1993) have studied this coping strategy, which they refer to as *behavioral disengagement,* and found that it is associated with increased rather than decreased distress. Furthermore, many studies suggest that learned helplessness can contribute to depression (Seligman & Isaacowitz, 2000). However, giving up could be adaptive in some instances. For example, if you were thrown into a job that you were not equipped to handle, it might be better to quit rather than face constant pressure and diminishing self-esteem. There is something to be said for recognizing one's limitations and unrealistic goals.

Striking Out at Others

A young man, aged 17, cautiously edged his car into traffic on the Corona Expressway in Los Angeles. His slow speed apparently irritated the men in a pickup truck behind him. Unfortunately, he angered the wrong men—they shot him to death. During that same weekend there were six other roadside shootings in the Los Angeles area. All of them were triggered by minor incidents or "fender benders." Frustrated motorists are attacking each other more and more frequently, especially on the overburdened highways of Los Angeles.

These tragic incidents of highway violence—so-called "road rage"—vividly illustrate that people often respond to stressful events by striking out at others with aggressive behavior. *Aggression* **is any behavior intended to hurt someone, either physically or verbally.** Snarls, curses, and insults are much more common than shootings or fistfights, but aggression of any kind can be problematic. Many years ago, a team of psychologists (Dollard et al., 1939) proposed the frustration-aggression hypothesis, which held that aggression is always due to frustration. Decades of research eventually showed that there isn't an inevitable link between frustration and aggression, but this research also supported the basic idea that frustration frequently elicits aggression (Berkowitz, 1989).

People often lash out aggressively at others who had nothing to do with their frustration, especially when they can't vent their anger at the real source of their frustration. Thus, you'll probably suppress your anger rather

Lashing out at others with verbal aggression tends to be an ineffective coping tactic that often backfires, creating additional stress.

RECOMMENDED READING

Anger: The Misunderstood Emotion
by Carol Tavris (Simon & Schuster, 1989)

With the possible exception of anxiety, anger is the emotion elicited by stress more than any other. It's a powerful emotion that can be harnessed to achieve admirable goals. The work of some of the world's great reformers and leaders has been fueled by moral outrage. However, anger also lies at the center of many human woes—wrecked friendships, destroyed marriages, murders, and wars. Hence, anger is a profoundly important emotion. Carol Tavris analyzes virtually every facet of anger in her book. She carefully scrutinizes common beliefs about anger and concludes that many of them are inaccurate. For instance, she argues convincingly against the idea that aggression can drain off anger through catharsis and the idea that anger and aggression are overpowering, instinctual responses. Tavris's book is a delight to read. It's witty, lively, practical, thought provoking, and frequently eloquent.

than lash out verbally at a police officer who gives you a speeding ticket. Twenty minutes later, however, you might be downright brutal in rebuking a waiter who is slow in serving your lunch. As we discussed in Chapter 2, this diversion of anger to a substitute target was noticed long ago by Sigmund Freud, who called it *displacement.* Unfortunately, research suggests that when people are provoked, displaced aggression is a common response (Marcus-Newhall et al., 2000).

Freud theorized that behaving aggressively could get pent-up emotion out of one's system and thus be adaptive. He coined the term **catharsis to refer to this release of emotional tension.** The Freudian notion that it is a good idea to vent anger has become widely disseminated and accepted in modern society. Books, magazines, and self-appointed experts routinely advise that it is healthy to "blow off steam" and thereby release and reduce anger.

However, experimental research generally has *not* supported the catharsis hypothesis. Indeed, *most studies find just the opposite: behaving in an aggressive manner tends to fuel more anger and aggression* (Bushman, 2002; Bushman, Baumeister, & Stack, 1999). Moreover, Carol Tavris (1982, 1989) points out that aggressive behavior frequently backfires because it elicits aggressive responses from others that generate more anger. She asserts, "Aggressive catharses are almost impossible to find in continuing relationships because parents, children, spouses and bosses usually feel obliged to aggress back at you" (1982, p. 131). Thus, the adaptive value of aggressive behavior tends to be minimal. Hurting someone, especially an irrelevant someone, is not likely to alleviate frustration. Moreover, the interpersonal conflicts that often emerge from aggressive behavior may produce additional stress. If you pick a fight with your spouse after a terrible day at work, you may create new stress and lose valuable empathy and social support as well.

Indulging Yourself

Stress sometimes leads to reduced impulse control, or *self-indulgence* (Tice, Bratslavsky, & Baumeister, 2001).

Experts disagree about whether excessive Internet use should be characterized as an addiction, but inability to control online use appears to be an increasingly common syndrome.

For instance, after an exceptionally stressful day, some people head for their kitchen, a grocery store, or a restaurant in pursuit of something chocolate. In a similar vein, others cope with stress by making a beeline for the nearest shopping mall for a spending spree. Still others respond to stress by indulging in injudicious patterns of drinking, smoking, gambling, and drug use.

In their classification of coping responses, Moos and Billings (1982) list *developing alternative rewards* as a common response to stress. It makes sense that when things are going poorly in one area of your life, you may try to compensate by pursuing substitute forms of satisfaction. Thus, it is not surprising that there is evidence relating stress to increases in eating (Laitinen, Ek, & Sovio, 2002), smoking (Kassel, Stroud, & Paronis, 2003), and consumption of alcohol and drugs (Colder, 2001; Goeders, 2004).

A new manifestation of this coping strategy is the tendency to immerse oneself in the online world of the Internet. Kimberly Young (1998) has described a syndrome called *Internet addiction,* which consists of

spending an inordinate amount of time on the Internet and inability to control online use (see Figure 4.2). People who exhibit this syndrome tend to feel anxious, depressed, or empty when they are not online (Kandell, 1998). Their Internet use is so excessive, it begins to interfere with their functioning at work, at school, or at home, leading victims to start concealing the extent of their dependence on the Internet. Some people exhibit pathological Internet use for one particular purpose, such as online sex or online gambling, whereas others exhibit a general, global pattern of Internet addiction (Davis, 2001). It is difficult to estimate the prevalence of Internet addiction, but the syndrome does *not* appear to be rare (Greenfield, 1999; Morahan-Martin & Schumacher, 2000). Research suggests that Internet addiction is not limited to shy, male computer whizzes, as one might expect (Young, 1998). Although there is active debate about the wisdom of characterizing excessive Internet surfing as an *addiction* (Griffiths, 1999), it is clear that this new coping strategy is likely to become increasingly common.

There is nothing inherently maladaptive about indulging oneself as a way of coping with life's stresses. If a hot fudge sundae or some new clothes can calm your nerves after a major setback, who can argue? However, if a person consistently responds to stress with excessive self-indulgence, obvious problems are likely to develop. Excesses in eating may produce obesity. Excesses in drinking and drug use may endanger one's health and affect work quality. Excesses in spending may create

---

Internet Addiction Test

To assess your level of addiction, answer the following questions using this scale:

1 = Not at all	2 = Rarely	3 = Occasionally	4 = Often	5 = Always

	1	2	3	4	5
1. How often do you find that you stay online longer than you intended?	1	2	3	4	5
2. How often do you neglect household chores to spend more time online?	1	2	3	4	5
3. How often do you prefer the excitement of the Internet to intimacy with your partner?	1	2	3	4	5
4. How often do you form new relationships with fellow online users?	1	2	3	4	5
5. How often do others in your life complain to you about the amount of time you spend online?	1	2	3	4	5
6. How often do your grades or school work suffer because of the amount of time you spend online?	1	2	3	4	5
7. How often do you check your e-mail before something else that you need to do?	1	2	3	4	5
8. How often does your job performance or productivity suffer because of the Internet?	1	2	3	4	5
9. How often do you become defensive or secretive when anyone asks you what you do online?	1	2	3	4	5
10. How often do you block out disturbing thoughts about your life with soothing thoughts of the Internet?	1	2	3	4	5
11. How often do you find yourself anticipating when you will go online again?	1	2	3	4	5
12. How often do you fear that life without the Internet would be boring, empty, and joyless?	1	2	3	4	5
13. How often do you snap, yell, or act annoyed if someone bothers you while you are online?	1	2	3	4	5
14. How often do you lose sleep due to late-night log-ins?	1	2	3	4	5
15. How often do you feel preoccupied with the Internet when off-line, or fantasize about being online?	1	2	3	4	5
16. How often do you find yourself saying "just a few more minutes" when online?	1	2	3	4	5
17. How often do you try to cut down the amount of time you spend online and fail?	1	2	3	4	5
18. How often do you try to hide how long you've been online?	1	2	3	4	5
19. How often do you choose to spend more time online over going out with others?	1	2	3	4	5
20. How often do you feel depressed, moody, or nervous when you are off-line, which goes away once you are back online?	1	2	3	4	5

After you've answered all the questions, add the numbers you selected for each response to obtain a final score. The higher your score, the greater your level of addiction and the problems your Internet usage causes. Here's a general scale to help measure your score.

20–39 points: You are an average online user. You may surf the Web a bit too long at times, but you have control over your usage.

40–69 points: You are experiencing frequent problems because of the Internet. You should consider their full impact on your life.

70–100 points: Your Internet usage is causing significant problems in your life. You need to address them now.

(● **FIGURE 4.2**)

Measuring addiction to the Internet. The questions on Young's (1998) Internet Addiction Test highlight the traits that make up this syndrome. You can check to see whether you exhibit any signs of Internet addiction by responding to the items and computing your score.

From Young, K. S. (1998). *Caught in the Net: How to recognize the signs of Internet addiction—and a winning strategy for recovery.* New York: John Wiley. Copyright ©1998 John Wiley & Sons, Inc. This material is used by permission of John Wiley & Sons, Inc.

havoc in one's personal finances. Given the risks associated with self-indulgence, it has rather marginal adaptive value.

Blaming Yourself

In a postgame interview after a tough defeat, a prominent football coach was brutally critical of himself. He said that he had been outcoached, that he had made poor decisions, and that his game plan was faulty. He almost eagerly assumed all the blame for the loss himself. In reality, he had taken some reasonable chances that didn't go his way and had suffered the effects of poor execution by his players. Looking at it objectively, the loss was attributable to the collective failures of 50 or so players and coaches. However, the coach's unrealistically negative self-evaluation was a fairly typical response to frustration. When confronted by stress (especially frustration and pressure), people often become highly self-critical.

The tendency to engage in "negative self-talk" in response to stress has been noted by a number of influential theorists. As we will discuss in greater detail later in this chapter, Albert Ellis (1973, 1987) calls this phenomenon "catastrophic thinking" and focuses on how it is rooted in irrational assumptions. Aaron Beck (1976, 1987) analyzes negative self-talk into specific tendencies. Among other things, he asserts that people often (1) unreasonably attribute their failures to personal shortcomings, (2) focus on negative feedback from others while ignoring favorable feedback, and (3) make unduly pessimistic projections about the future. Thus, if you performed poorly on an exam, you might blame

it on your woeful stupidity, dismiss a classmate's comment that the test was unfair, and hysterically predict that you will flunk out of school.

Although recognizing one's weaknesses has value, Ellis and Beck agree that self-blame tends to be counterproductive. According to Ellis, catastrophic thinking causes, aggravates, and perpetuates emotional reactions to stress that are often problematic. Along even more serious lines, Beck marshals evidence that negative self-talk can contribute to the development of depressive disorders.

Using Defensive Coping

Defensive coping is a common response to stress. We noted in Chapter 2 that the concept of defense mechanisms was originally developed by Sigmund Freud. Though rooted in the psychoanalytic tradition, this concept has gained acceptance from psychologists of most persuasions (Cramer, 2000). Building on Freud's initial insights, modern psychologists have broadened the scope of the concept and added to Freud's list of defense mechanisms.

The Nature of Defense Mechanisms

Defense mechanisms **are largely unconscious reactions that protect a person from unpleasant emotions such as anxiety and guilt.** A number of strategies fit this definition. For example, Laughlin (1979) lists 49 different defenses. In our discussion of Freud's theory in Chapter 2, we described seven common defenses. Figure 4.3 introduces another five defenses that people use with some regularity. Although widely discussed in

Common Defense Mechanisms

Mechanism	Example
Denial of reality. Protecting oneself from unpleasant reality by refusing to perceive or face it.	A smoker concludes that the evidence linking cigarette use to health problems is scientifically worthless.
Fantasy. Gratifying frustrated desires by imaginary achievements.	A socially inept and inhibited young man imagines himself chosen by a group of women to provide them with sexual satisfaction.
Intellectualization (isolation). Cutting off emotion from hurtful situations or separating incompatible attitudes in logic-tight compartments.	A prisoner on death row awaiting execution resists appeal on his behalf and coldly insists that the letter of the law be followed.
Undoing. Atoning for or trying to magically dispel unacceptable desires or acts.	A teenager who feels guilty about masturbation ritually touches door knobs a prescribed number of times after each occurrence of the act.
Overcompensation. Covering up felt weaknesses by emphasizing some desirable characteristic, or making up for frustration in one area by overgratification in another.	A dangerously overweight woman goes on eating binges when she feels neglected by her husband.

● FIGURE 4.3

Additional defense mechanisms. Like the seven defense mechanisms described in our discussion of Freudian theory in Chapter 2 (see Figure 2.4), these five defenses are frequently used in our efforts to cope with stress.

Adapted from Carson, R. C., Butcher, J. N., & Coleman, J. C. (1988). *Abnormal psychology and modern life*. Glenview, IL: Scott, Foresman. Copyright © 1988 by Scott, Foresman and Company. Adapted by permission.

the popular press, defense mechanisms are often misunderstood. We will use a question-answer format to
elaborate on the nature of defense mechanisms in the
hopes of clearing up any misconceptions.

What do defense mechanisms defend against?
Above all else, defense mechanisms shield the individual from the *emotional discomfort* elicited by stress.
Their main purpose is to ward off unwelcome emotions
or to reduce their intensity. Foremost among the emotions guarded against is anxiety. People are especially
defensive when the anxiety is the result of some threat
to their self-esteem. They also use defenses to prevent
dangerous feelings of anger from exploding into acts
of aggression. Guilt and dejection are two other emotions that people often try to evade through defensive
maneuvers.

How do they work?
Defense mechanisms work
through *self-deception.* They accomplish their goals by
distorting reality so it does not appear so threatening.
Let's say you're doing poorly in school and are in danger of flunking out. Initially, you might use *denial* to
block awareness of the possibility that you could flunk
out. This tactic might temporarily fend off feelings of
anxiety. If it becomes difficult to deny the obvious, you
might resort to *fantasy,* daydreaming about how you will
salvage adequate grades by getting spectacular scores
on the upcoming final exams, when the objective fact
is that you are hopelessly behind in your studies. Thus,

defense mechanisms work their magic by bending reality in self-serving ways (Bowins, 2004).

Are they conscious or unconscious?
Mainstream
Freudian theory originally assumed that defenses operate entirely at an unconscious level. However, the
concept of defense mechanisms has been broadened to
include maneuvers that people may have some awareness of. Thus, defense mechanisms operate at varying
levels of awareness and can be conscious or unconscious
reactions (Erdelyi, 2001).

Are they normal?
Definitely. Everyone uses defense
mechanisms on a fairly regular basis. They are entirely
normal patterns of coping. The notion that only neurotic people use defense mechanisms is inaccurate.

Can Illusions Be Healthy?
The most critical question concerning defense mechanisms is: *Are they healthy?* This is a complicated question. More often than not, the answer is no. Generally,
defense mechanisms are poor ways of coping, for a number of reasons. First, defensive coping is an avoidance
strategy, and avoidance rarely provides a genuine solution to our problems. Holahan and Moos (1985, 1990)
have found that people who exhibit relatively high resistance to stress use avoidance strategies less than people who are frequently troubled by stress. Second, defenses such as denial, fantasy, and projection represent
"wishful thinking," which is likely to accomplish little.
In fact, in a study of how students coped with the stress
of taking the Medical College Admissions Test (MCAT),
Bolger (1990) found that students who engaged in a lot
of wishful thinking experienced greater increases in
anxiety than other students as the exam approached.
Third, a repressive coping style has been related to poor
health, in part because repression often leads people to
delay facing up to their problems (Weinberger, 1990).
For example, if you were to block out obvious warning
signs of cancer or diabetes and fail to obtain needed
medical care, your defensive behavior could be fatal.

Although defensive behavior tends to be relatively unhealthy, some defenses are healthier than others, and defense mechanisms can sometimes be adaptive (Cramer, 2002; Vaillant, 2000). For example, *overcompensation* for athletic failures could lead you to work extra hard in the classroom. And creative use of *fantasy* is sometimes the key to helping people deal effectively with a temporary period of frustration, such as a period of recovery in the hospital.

Most theorists used to regard accurate contact with reality as the hallmark of sound mental health (Jahoda, 1958; Jourard & Landsman, 1980). However, Shelley Taylor and Jonathon Brown (1988, 1994) have reviewed several lines of evidence suggesting that "illusions" may be adaptive for mental health and well-being. First, they note that "normal" people tend to have overly favorable self-images. In contrast, depressed subjects exhibit less favorable—but more realistic—self-concepts. Second, normal subjects overestimate the degree to which they control chance events. In comparison, depressed participants are less prone to this illusion of control. Third, normal individuals are more likely than depressed subjects to display unrealistic optimism in making projections about the future.

Courtesy, Shelley Taylor

Shelley Taylor

A variety of other studies have also provided support for the hypothesis that positive illusions promote well being. For example, studies of individuals diagnosed with AIDS show that those with unrealistically optimistic expectations of the likely course of their disease actually experience a less rapid course of illness (Reed et al., 1999). In a laboratory study, Taylor et al. (2003) found that subjects who tended to exhibit positive illusions showed lower cardiovascular responses to stress, quicker cardiovascular recovery from stress, and lower levels of a stress hormone.

As you might guess, critics have expressed considerable skepticism about the idea that illusions are adaptive. For example, Colvin and Block (1994) make an eloquent case for the traditional view that accuracy and realism are healthy. Moreover, they report data showing that overly favorable self-ratings are correlated with maladaptive personality traits (Colvin, Block, & Funder, 1995). One possible resolution to this debate is Roy Baumeister's (1989) theory that it's all a matter of degree and that there is an "optimal margin of illusion." According to Baumeister, extreme self-deception is maladaptive, but small illusions may often be beneficial.

The Nature of Constructive Coping

LEARNING OBJECTIVES

- Discuss whether constructive coping is related to intelligence.
- Describe the nature of constructive coping.

Our discussion thus far has focused on coping strategies that tend to be less than ideal. Of course, people also exhibit many healthful strategies for dealing with stress. We will use the term **constructive coping to refer to efforts to deal with stressful events that are judged to be relatively healthful.** No strategy of coping can guarantee a successful outcome. Even the healthiest coping responses may turn out to be ineffective in some cases. Thus, the concept of constructive coping is simply meant to convey a healthy, positive connotation, without promising success.

Constructive coping does not appear to depend particularly on one's intelligence—at least not the abstract, "academic" intelligence measured by conventional IQ tests. Seymour Epstein (1990) has shown an interest in "why smart people think dumb." His interest was stimulated in part by a course that he taught in which students kept daily records of their most positive and negative emotional experiences, for class discussion. Commenting on these discussions, Epstein noted,

"One cannot help but be impressed, when observing students in such a situation, with the degree to which some otherwise bright people lead their lives in a manifestly unintelligent and self-defeating manner" (Epstein & Meier, 1989, p. 333).

To investigate this matter more systematically, Epstein and Petra Meier (1989) devised an elaborate scale to assess the degree to which people engage in constructive coping and thinking. They found constructive thinking to be favorably related to mental and physical health and to measures of "success" in work, love, and social relationships. However, participants' IQ scores were only weakly related to their constructive coping scores and were largely unrelated to the measures of success in work, love, and social relationships.

What makes a coping strategy constructive? Frankly, in labeling certain coping responses constructive or healthy, psychologists are making value judgments. It's a gray area in which opinions will vary to some extent. Nonetheless, some consensus emerges from the bur-

geoning research on coping and stress management. Key themes in this literature include the following:

1. Constructive coping involves confronting problems directly. It is task-relevant and action oriented. It involves a conscious effort to rationally evaluate your options in an effort to solve your problems.

2. Constructive coping is based on reasonably realistic appraisals of your stress and coping resources. A little self-deception may sometimes be adaptive, but excessive self-deception and highly unrealistic negative thinking are not.

3. Constructive coping involves learning to recognize and manage potentially disruptive emotional reactions to stress.

4. Constructive coping involves learning to exert some control over potentially harmful or destructive habitual behaviors. It requires the acquisition of some behavioral self-control.

These points should give you a general idea of what we mean by constructive coping. They will guide our discourse in the remainder of this chapter as we discuss how to cope more effectively with stress. To organize our discussion, we will use a classification scheme proposed by Moos and Billings (1982) to divide constructive coping techniques into three broad categories: appraisal-focused coping, problem-focused coping, and emotion-focused coping (see Figure 4.4).

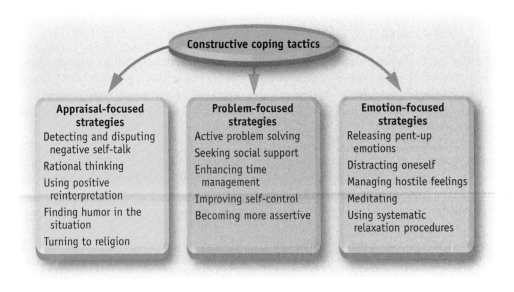

Overview of constructive coping tactics. Coping tactics can be organized in several ways, but we will use the classification scheme shown here, which consists of three categories: appraisal-focused, problem-focused, and emotion-focused. The list of coping tactics in each category is not exhaustive. We will discuss most, but not all, of the listed strategies in our coverage of constructive coping.

Appraisal-Focused Constructive Coping

LEARNING OBJECTIVES

■ *Explain Ellis's analysis of the causes of maladaptive emotions.*
■ *Describe some assumptions that contribute to catastrophic thinking.*
■ *Discuss the merits of positive reinterpretation and humor as coping strategies.*

People often underestimate the importance of the appraisal phase in the stress process. They fail to appreciate the highly subjective feelings that color the perception of threat to one's well-being. A useful way to deal with stress is to alter your appraisal of threatening events. In this section, we'll examine Albert Ellis's ideas about reappraisal and discuss the value of using humor and positive reinterpretation to cope with stress.

Ellis's Rational Thinking

Albert Ellis (1977, 1985, 1996, 2001) is a prominent theorist who believes that people can short-circuit their emotional reactions to stress by altering their appraisals of stressful events. Ellis's insights about stress appraisal are the foundation for his widely used system of therapy. **Rational-emotive behavior therapy is an approach to therapy that focuses on altering clients' patterns of irrational thinking to reduce maladaptive emotions and behavior.**

Ellis maintains that *you feel the way you think.* He argues that problematic emotional reactions are caused by negative self-talk, which, as we mentioned earlier, he calls catastrophic thinking. **Catastrophic thinking involves unrealistic appraisals of stress that exaggerate the magnitude of one's problems.** Ellis uses a simple A-B-C sequence to explain his ideas (see Figure 4.5).

Albert Ellis

Courtesy, Albert Ellis Institute

A. *Activating event.* The A in Ellis's system stands for the activating event that produces the stress. The activating event may be any potentially stressful transaction. Examples might include an automobile accident, the cancellation of a date, a delay while waiting in line at the bank, or a failure to get a promotion you were expecting.

B. *Belief system.* B stands for your belief about the event. This represents your appraisal of the stress. According to Ellis, people often view minor setbacks as disasters, engaging in catastrophic thinking: "How awful this is. I can't stand it! Things never turn out fairly for me. I'll be in this line forever. I'll never get promoted."

C. *Consequence.* C stands for the consequence of your negative thinking. When your appraisals of stressful events are highly negative, the consequence tends to be emotional distress. Thus, you feel angry, outraged, anxious, panic-stricken, disgusted, or dejected.

The commonsense view

A Activating event
Stress:
Someone stands you up on a date you looked forward to

→

C Consequence
Emotional turmoil:
You feel angry, anxious, agitated, dejected

Ellis's view

A Activating event
Stress:
Someone stands you up on a date you looked forward to

B Belief system
Irrational appraisal:
"This is terrible. I'll have a boring weekend. I'll never find anyone. I must be a worthless person."

Rational appraisal:
"This is unfortunate but I'll salvage the weekend. Someday I'll find someone who is mature and dependable."

C Consequence
Emotional turmoil:
You feel angry, anxious, agitated, dejected

Emotional calm:
You feel annoyed and subdued but remain hopeful

● FIGURE 4.5

Albert Ellis's A-B-C model of emotional reactions. Most people are prone to attribute their negative emotional reactions (C) directly to stressful events (A). However, Ellis argues that emotional reactions are really caused by the way individuals think about these events (B).

WEB LINK 4.2

The Albert Ellis Institute
Albert Ellis developed rational-emotive behavior therapy in the mid-1950s as an effective alternative to psychoanalytically inspired treatment approaches. This site demonstrates the growth of Ellis's approach over the subsequent decades.

Ellis asserts that most people do not understand the importance of phase B in this three-stage sequence. They unwittingly believe that the activating event (A) *causes* the consequent emotional turmoil (C). However, Ellis maintains that A does *not* cause C. It only appears to do so. Instead, Ellis asserts that B causes C. Emotional distress is actually caused by one's catastrophic thinking in appraising stressful events.

According to Ellis, it is common for people to turn inconvenience into disaster and make "mountains out of molehills." For instance, imagine that someone stands you up on a date that you were eagerly looking forward to. You might think, "Oh, this is terrible. I'm going to have another rotten, boring weekend. People always mistreat me. I'll never find anyone to fall in love with. I must be a crummy, worthless person." Ellis would argue that such thoughts are irrational. He would point out that it does not follow logically from being stood up that you (1) must have a lousy weekend, (2) will never fall in love, or (3) are a worthless person.

The Roots of Catastrophic Thinking

Ellis (1994, 1995) theorizes that unrealistic appraisals of stress are derived from the irrational assumptions that people hold. He maintains that if you scrutinize your catastrophic thinking, you will find that your reasoning is based on an unreasonable premise, such as "I must have approval from everyone" or "I must perform well in all endeavors." These faulty assumptions, which most people hold unconsciously, generate catastrophic thinking and emotional turmoil. To facilitate emotional self-control, it is important to learn to spot irrational assumptions and the unhealthy patterns of thought that they generate. Let's look at four particularly common irrational assumptions.

1. *I must have love and affection from certain people.* Everyone wants to be liked and loved. There is nothing wrong with that. However, many people foolishly believe that they should be liked by everyone they come into contact with. If you stop to think about it, that's clearly unrealistic. Once individuals fall in love, they tend to believe that their future happiness depends absolutely on the continuation of that one, special relationship. They believe that if their current love relationship were to end, they would never again be able to achieve a comparable one. This is an unrealistic view of the future. Such views make the person anxious during a relationship and severely depressed if it comes to an end.

2. *I must perform well in all endeavors.* We live in a highly competitive society. We are taught that victory brings happiness. Consequently, we feel that we must always win. For example, many sports enthusiasts are never satisfied unless they perform at their best level. However, by definition, their best level is not their typical level, and they set themselves up for inevitable frustration.

3. *Other people should always behave competently and be considerate of me.* People are often angered by others' stupidity and selfishness. For example, you may become outraged when a mechanic fails to fix your car properly or when a salesperson treats you rudely. It would be nice if others were always competent and considerate, but you know better—they are not! Yet many people go through life unrealistically expecting others' efficiency and kindness.

RECOMMENDED READING

How to Stubbornly Refuse to Make Yourself Miserable About Anything—Yes, Anything!
by Albert Ellis (Carol Communications, 1988)

This is one of the better "popular" books by Albert Ellis, the world-renowned architect of rational-emotive behavior therapy. At last count, Ellis had written around 50 books, about evenly divided between popular books intended for a general audience and technical books intended for mental health professionals. This book doesn't break any new ground for Ellis, but it does bring his ideas together in one succinct, readable summary, complete with exercises. Ellis is a bit prone to overstatement, asserting that his book "will help you achieve a profound philosophic change and a radically new outlook on life." Whether it does so or not, his ideas can clearly be helpful in coping with stress more effectively. If you tend to fall into the trap of overly negative thinking, this book is worth reading. Other recent self-help titles from Ellis that cover much of the same ground include *How to Make Yourself Happy and Remarkably Less Disturbable* (1999), *Feeling Better, Getting Better, Staying Better: Profound Self-Help Therapy for Your Emotions* (2001), and *Ask Albert Ellis: Straight Answers and Sound Advice from America's Best-Known Psychologist* (2003).

Cover image reprinted by permission of Carol Publishing Group.

4. *Events should always go the way I like.* Some people simply won't tolerate any kind of setback. They assume that things should always go their way. For example, some commuters become tense and angry each time they get stuck in a rush-hour traffic jam. They seem to believe that they are entitled to coast home easily every day, even though they know that rush hour rarely is a breeze. Such expectations are clearly unrealistic and doomed to be violated. Yet few people recognize the obvious irrationality of the assumption that underlies their anger unless it is pointed out to them.

Reducing Catastrophic Thinking

How can you reduce your unrealistic appraisals of stress? Ellis asserts that you must learn (1) how to detect catastrophic thinking and (2) how to dispute the irrational assumptions that cause it. Detection involves acquiring the ability to spot unrealistic pessimism and wild exaggeration in your thinking. Examine your self-talk closely. Ask yourself why you're getting upset. Force yourself to verbalize your concerns, covertly or out loud. Look for key words that often show up in catastrophic thinking, such as *should, ought, never,* and *must.*

Disputing your irrational assumptions requires subjecting your entire reasoning process to scrutiny. Try to root out the assumptions from which your conclusions are derived. Most of us are unaware of these assumptions. Once they are unearthed, their irrationality may be quite obvious. If your assumptions seem reasonable, ask yourself whether your conclusions follow logically. Try to replace your catastrophic thinking with more low-key, rational analyses. These strategies should help you to redefine stressful situations in ways that are less threatening. Strangely enough, another way to defuse such situations is to turn to humor.

Humor as a Stress Reducer

A number of years ago, the Chicago area experienced its worst flooding in about a century. Thousands of people saw their homes wrecked when two rivers spilled over their banks. As the waters receded, the flood victims returning to their homes were subjected to the inevitable TV interviews. A remarkable number of victims, surrounded by the ruins of their homes, *joked* about their misfortune. When the going gets tough, it may pay to laugh about it. In a study of coping styles, McCrae (1984) found that 40 percent of his subjects reported using humor to deal with stress.

Empirical evidence showing that humor moderates the impact of stress has been accumulating over the last 25 years (Lefcourt, 2001). For instance, in one influential study, Martin and Lefcourt (1983) found that a good sense of humor functioned as a buffer to lessen the negative impact of stress on mood. Some of their results are presented in Figure 4.6, which shows

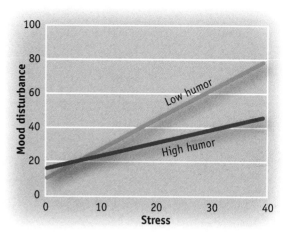

● **FIGURE 4.6**

Humor and coping. Martin and Lefcourt (1983) related stress to mood disturbance in subjects who were either high or low in their use of humor. Increased stress led to smaller increases in mood disturbance in the high-humor group, suggesting that humor has some value in efforts to cope with stress.

Adapted from Martin, R. A., & Lefcourt, H. M. (1983). Sense of humor as a moderator of the relation between stressors and moods. *Journal of Personality and Social Psychology, 45 (6),* 1313–1324. Copyright © 1983 by the American Psychological Association. Adapted by permission.

how mood disturbance increased as stress went up in two groups of participants—those who were high or low in their use of humor. Notice how higher stress leads to a smaller increase in mood disturbance in the high-humor group. Similar findings have been observed in other studies (Abel, 1998; Martin, 1996). Although there are some inconsistencies in the data, researchers have also found an association between humor and enhanced immune function, greater pain tolerance, and fewer symptoms of illness (Martin, 2001).

How does humor help to reduce the effects of stress and promote wellness? Several explanations have been proposed (see Figure 4.7 on the next page). One possibility is that humor affects appraisals of stressful events (Abel, 2002). Jokes can help people put a less-threatening spin on their trials and tribulations. Another possibility is that humor increases the experience of positive emotions (Martin, 2002). As we discussed in Chapter 3, positive emotions can help people bounce back from stressful events (Tugade & Fredrickson, 2004). Another hypothesis is that a good sense of humor facilitates positive social interactions, which promote social support, which is known to buffer the effects of stress (Martin, 2002). Finally, Lefcourt and colleagues (1995) argue that high-humor people may benefit from not taking themselves as seriously as low-humor people do. As they put it, "If persons do not regard themselves too seriously and do not have an inflated sense of self-importance, then defeats, embarrassments, and even tragedies should have less pervasive emotional consequences for them" (p. 375). Thus, humor is a rather versatile coping strategy that may have many benefits.

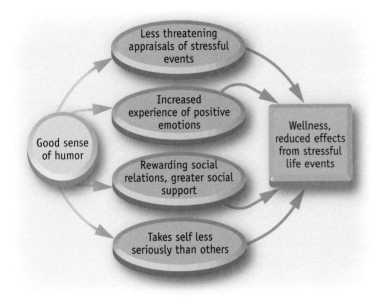

● FIGURE 4.7

Possible explanations for the link between humor and wellness. Research suggests that a good sense of humor buffers the effects of stress and promotes wellness. Four hypothesized explanations for the link between humor and wellness are outlined in the middle column of this diagram. As you can see, humor may have a variety of beneficial effects.

Positive Reinterpretation

When you are feeling overwhelmed by life's difficulties, you might try the commonsense strategy of recognizing that "things could be worse." No matter how terrible your problems seem, you probably know someone who has even bigger troubles. That is not to say that you should derive satisfaction from others' misfortune.

However, comparing your own plight with others' even tougher struggles can help you put your problems in perspective. Research suggests that this strategy of making positive comparisons with others is a common coping mechanism that can result in improved mood and self-esteem (Wills & Sandy, 2001). Moreover, this strategy does not depend on knowing others who are clearly worse off. You can simply imagine yourself in a similar situation with an even worse outcome (example: two broken legs after a horse-riding accident instead of just one). One healthy aspect of positive reinterpretation is that it can facilitate calming reappraisals of stress without the necessity of distorting reality.

Another way to engage in positive reinterpretation is to search for something good in a bad experience. Distressing though they may be, many setbacks have positive elements. After experiencing divorces, illnesses, firings, financial losses, and such, many people remark that "I came out of the experience better than I went in," or "I grew as a person." Studies of victims of natural disasters, heart attacks, and bereavement have found an association between this type of *benefit finding* under duress and relatively sound psychological and physical health (Tennen & Affleck, 2002). Of course, the positive aspects of a personal setback may be easy to see after the stressful event is behind you. The challenge is to recognize these positive aspects while you are still struggling with the setback, so that it becomes less stressful.

Problem-Focused Constructive Coping

LEARNING OBJECTIVES

- List and describe four steps in systematic problem solving.
- Discuss the adaptive value of seeking help as a coping strategy.
- Explain five common causes of wasted time.
- Describe evidence on the causes and consequences of procrastination.
- Summarize advice on managing time effectively.

Problem-focused coping includes efforts to remedy or conquer the stress-producing problem itself. In this category, we'll discuss systematic problem solving, the importance of seeking help, effective time management, and improvement of self-control.

Using Systematic Problem Solving

In dealing with life's problems, the most obvious course of action is to tackle the problems head-on. Obviously, people vary in their problem-solving skills. However,

evidence suggests that problem-solving skills can be enhanced through training (Heppner & Lee, 2002). With this thought in mind, we will sketch a general outline of how to engage in more systematic problem solving. The problem-solving plan described here is a synthesis of observations by various experts, especially Mahoney (1979), Miller (1978), and Chang and Kelly (1993).

Clarify the Problem

You can't tackle a problem if you're not sure what the problem is. Therefore, the first step in any systematic problem-solving effort is to clarify the nature of the problem. Sometimes the problem will be all too obvious. At other times the source of trouble may be quite difficult to pin down. In any case, you need to arrive at a specific concrete definition of your problem.

Two common tendencies typically hinder people's efforts to get a clear picture of their problems. First, they often describe their problems in vague generalities ("My life isn't going anywhere" or "I never have enough time"). Second, they tend to focus too much on negative feelings, thereby confusing the consequences of problems ("I'm so depressed all the time" or "I'm so nervous I can't concentrate") with the problems themselves.

Generate Alternative Courses of Action

The second step in systematic problem solving is to generate alternative courses of action. Notice that we did not call these alternative *solutions*. Many problems do not have a readily available solution that will completely resolve the problem. If you think in terms of searching for complete solutions, you may prevent yourself from considering many worthwhile courses of action. Instead, it is more realistic to search for alternatives that may produce some kind of improvement in your situation.

Besides avoiding the tendency to insist on solutions, you need to avoid the temptation to go with the first alternative that comes to mind. Many people are a little trigger-happy. They thoughtlessly try to follow through on the first response that occurs to them. Various lines of evidence suggest that it is wiser to engage in brainstorming about a problem. ***Brainstorming* is generating as many ideas as possible while withholding criticism and evaluation.** In other words, you generate alternatives without paying any attention to their apparent practicality. This approach facilitates creative expression of ideas.

Evaluate Your Alternatives and Select a Course of Action

Once you generate as many alternatives as you can, you need to start evaluating the possibilities. There are no simple criteria for judging the relative merits of your alternatives. However, you will probably want to address three general issues. First, ask yourself whether each alternative is realistic. In other words, what is the probability that you can successfully execute the intended course of action? Try to think of any obstacles you may have failed to anticipate. In making this assessment, it is important to try to avoid both foolish optimism and unnecessary pessimism.

Second, consider any costs or risks associated with each alternative. The "solution" to a problem is sometimes worse than the problem itself. Assuming you can successfully implement your intended course of action, what are the possible negative consequences? Finally, compare the desirability of the probable outcomes of each alternative. After eliminating the unrealistic possibilities, list the probable consequences (both good and bad) associated with each alternative. Then review and compare the desirability of these potential outcomes. In making your decision, you have to ask yourself "What is important to me? Which outcomes do I value the most?"

Take Action While Maintaining Flexibility

After you have chosen your course of action, you should follow through in implementing your plan. In so doing, try to maintain flexibility. Do not get locked into a particular course of action. Few choices are truly irreversible. You need to monitor results closely and be willing to revise your strategy.

In evaluating your course of action, try to avoid the simplistic success/failure dichotomy. You should simply look for improvement of any kind. If your plan doesn't work out too well, consider whether it was undermined by any circumstances that you could not have anticipated. Finally, remember that you can learn from your failures. Even if things did not work out, you may now have new information that will facilitate a new attack on the problem.

Seeking Help

In Chapter 3, we learned that social support can be a powerful force that helps buffer the deleterious effects of stress and that has positive effects of its own (Wills & Fegan, 2001). We discussed social support as if it were a stable, external resource available to different people in varying degrees. In reality, social supports fluctuate over time and evolve out of individuals' interactions with others (Newcomb, 1990). Some people have more support than others because they have personal characteristics that attract more support or because they make more effort to seek support.

In trying to tackle problems directly, it pays to keep in mind the value of seeking aid from friends, family, co-workers, and neighbors. Because of potential embarrassment, many people are reluctant to acknowledge their problems and look for help from others. What makes this reluctance so lamentable is that others can provide a great deal of help in many ways.

WEB LINK 4.3

Mind Tools
James Manktelow's site in England offers practical techniques to help people deal with the world more efficiently and effectively. The site houses useful information on several of the topics discussed in this chapter, including stress management, time management, and effective problem solving.

Thinking Rationally About the Threat of Terrorism

Acts of terrorism are intended to provoke psychological instability in a population. The death, destruction, and havoc wreaked by terrorists is not an end in itself, but a means to an end—the creation of widespread anxiety, fear, and alarm (Everly & Mitchell, 2001). Unfortunately, a normal feature of human mental processing makes it much too easy for terrorists to achieve their goal. However, being aware of this cognitive tendency can help people to be more rational about the threat of terrorist acts. To introduce you to this cognitive tendency, consider the following problem:

> *Various causes of death are paired up below. For each pairing, decide which is the more likely cause of death.*
> *Asthma or tornadoes?*
> *Syphilis or botulism (food poisoning)?*
> *Tuberculosis or floods?*

Would you believe that the first choice in each pair causes at least 18 times as many deaths as the second choice? If your guesses were wrong, don't feel bad. Most people tend to greatly overestimate the likelihood of dramatic, vivid—but infrequent—events that receive heavy media coverage. Thus, the number of fatalities caused by tornadoes, floods, and food poisonings is usually overestimated (Slovic, Fischhoff, & Lichtenstein, 1982), whereas fatalities caused by asthma and other run-of-the-mill diseases tend to be underestimated. This tendency to overestimate the improbable reflects the operation of the *availability heuristic,* which involves basing the estimated probability of an event on the ease with which relevant instances come to mind.

Relying on the availability heuristic is a normal cognitive tendency. However, to the extent that certain events occur infrequently but are easily available in memory, your estimates will be biased. Instances of floods, tornadoes, and other disasters are readily available in memory because these events receive a great deal of publicity. The same principle applies to terrorist acts. The round-the-clock news coverage of terrorist attacks means that they are constantly on people's minds and highly available in memory. The result is that people tend to greatly exaggerate the likelihood that they might be a victim of terrorism, and such overestimates fuel the anxiety and alarm that terrorists seek to create.

Admittedly, no one knows what the future might bring in the way of terrorist attacks. However, based on what has happened in recent years, your chances of being harmed by a terrorist are microscopic in comparison to your chances of perishing in an automobile accident (Myers, 2001). Since 9/11, many Americans have been reluctant to fly because the airplane hijackings that occurred on 9/11 remain salient in their minds. But think about: Even if you knew in advance that terrorists planned to blow up a commercial flight next week, your chances of choosing that specific flight would only be about 1 in 173,000.

In sum, it is wise to be mindful of the natural tendency to overestimate the likelihood that you might be harmed by terrorist attacks. Thinking more rationally about the probability of being victimized by terrorism can reduce people's collective sense of alarm and thwart the main objective of terrorism, which is the cultivation of fear.

Using Time More Effectively

Do you constantly feel that you have too much to do, and too little time to do it in? Do you feel overwhelmed by your responsibilities at work, at school, and at home? Do you feel like you're always rushing around, trying to meet an impossible schedule? If you answered yes to some of these questions, you're struggling with time pressure. You can estimate how well you manage time by responding to the brief questionnaire in Figure 4.8. If the results suggest that your time is out of your con-

trol, you may be able to make your life less stressful by learning sound time-management strategies.

R. Alec Mackenzie (1997), a prominent time-management researcher, points out that time is a non-renewable resource. It can't be stockpiled like money, food, or other precious resources. You can't turn back the clock. Furthermore, everyone, whether rich or poor, gets an equal share of time—24 hours per day, 7 days a week. Although time is our most equitably distributed resource, some people spend it much more wisely than others. Let's look at some of the ways in which people let time slip through their fingers without accomplishing much.

The Causes of Wasted Time

When people complain about "wasted time," they're usually upset because they haven't accomplished what they really wanted to do with their time. Wasted time is time devoted to unnecessary, unimportant, or unenjoyable activities. Why waste time on such activities? There are many reasons.

Inability to set or stick to priorities. Time consultant Alan Lakein (1996) emphasizes that it's often tempting to deal with routine, trivial tasks ahead of larger and more difficult tasks. Thus, students working on a major term paper often read their mail, do the dishes, fold the laundry, reorganize their desk, or dust the furniture instead of concentrating on the paper. Routine tasks are easy, and working on them allows people to rationalize their avoidance of more important tasks. Unfortunately, many of us spend too much time on trivial pursuits, leaving our more important tasks undone.

Inability to say no. Other people are constantly making demands on our time. They want us to exchange gossip in the hallway, go out to dinner on Friday night, cover their hours at work, help with a project, listen to their sales pitch on the phone, join a committee, or coach Little League. Clearly, we can't do everything that everyone wants us to. However, some people just can't say no to others' requests for their time. Such people end up fulfilling others' priorities instead of their own. Thus, McDougle (1987) concludes, "Perhaps the most successful way to prevent yourself from wasting time is by saying *no*" (p. 112).

Inability to delegate responsibility. Some tasks should be delegated to others—secretaries, subordinates, fellow committee members, assistant coaches, spouses, children, and so on. However, many people have difficulty delegating work to others. Barriers to delegation include unwillingness to give up any control, lack of confidence in subordinates, fear of being disliked, the need to feel needed, and the attitude that "I can do it better myself" (Mitchell, 1987). The problem, of course, is that people who can't delegate waste a lot of time on trivial work or others' work.

Inability to throw things away. Some people are pack rats who can't throw anything into the wastebasket. Their desks are cluttered with piles of mail, newspapers, magazines, reports, and books. Their filing cabinets overflow with old class notes or ancient memos.

How Well Do You Manage Your Time?

Listed below are ten statements that reflect generally accepted principles of good time management. Answer these items by circling the response most characteristic of how you perform your job. Please be honest. No one will know your answers except you.

1. Each day I set aside a small amount of time for planning and thinking about my job.
   0. Almost never 1. Sometimes 2. Often 3. Almost always

2. I set specific, written goals and put deadlines on them.
   0. Almost never 1. Sometimes 2. Often 3. Almost always

3. I make a daily "to do list," arrange items in order of importance, and try to get the important items done as soon as possible.
   0. Almost never 1. Sometimes 2. Often 3. Almost always

4. I am aware of the 80/20 rule and use it in doing my job. (The 80/20 rule states that 80 percent of your effectiveness will generally come from achieving only 20 percent of your goals.)
   0. Almost never 1. Sometimes 2. Often 3. Almost always

5. I keep a loose schedule to allow for crises and the unexpected.
   0. Almost never 1. Sometimes 2. Often 3. Almost always

6. I delegate everything I can to others.
   0. Almost never 1. Sometimes 2. Often 3. Almost always

7. I try to handle each piece of paper only once.
   0. Almost never 1. Sometimes 2. Often 3. Almost always

8. I eat a light lunch so I don't get sleepy in the afternoon.
   0. Almost never 1. Sometimes 2. Often 3. Almost always

9. I make an active effort to keep common interruptions (visitors, meetings, telephone calls) from continually disrupting my work day.
   0. Almost never 1. Sometimes 2. Often 3. Almost always

10. I am able to say no to others' requests for my time that would prevent my completing important tasks.
    0. Almost never 1. Sometimes 2. Often 3. Almost always

To get your score, give yourself

3 points for each "almost always"
2 points for each "often"
1 point for each "sometimes"
0 points for each "almost never"

Add up your points to get your total score.

If you scored

0–15	Better give some thought to managing your time.
15–20	You're doing OK, but there's room for improvement.
20–25	Very good.
25–30	You cheated!

● **FIGURE 4.8**

Assessing your time management. The brief questionnaire shown here is designed to evaluate the quality of one's time management. Although it is geared more for working adults than college students, it should allow you to get a rough handle on how well you manage your time.

From Le Boeuf, M. (1980, February). Managing time means managing yourself. *Business Horizons Magazine*, p. 45. Copyright © by the Foundation for the School of Business at Indiana University. Used with permission.

For many people, an inability to throw things away is a key factor promoting wasted time.

At home, their kitchen drawers bulge with rarely used utensils, their closets bulge with old clothes that are never worn, and their attics bulge with discarded junk. Pack rats waste time in at least two ways. First, they lose time looking for things that have disappeared among all the chaos. Second, they end up reshuffling the same paper, rereading the same mail, resorting the same reports, and so on. According to Mackenzie (1997), they would be better off if they made more use of their wastebaskets.

Inability to accept anything less than perfection. High standards are admirable, but some people have difficulty finishing projects because they expect them to be flawless. They can't let go. They dwell on minor problems and keep making microscopic changes in their papers, projects, and proposals. They are caught in what Emanuel (1987) calls the "paralysis of perfection." They end up spinning their wheels, redoing the same work over and over.

The Problem of Procrastination

Another time-related problem is *procrastination*—the tendency to delay tackling tasks until the last minute. Almost everyone procrastinates on occasion. For example, 70–90 percent of college students procrastinate before beginning academic assignments (Knaus, 2000). However, research suggests that about 20 percent of adults are chronic procrastinators (Ferrari, 2001). Procrastination is more likely when people have to work on aversive tasks or when they are worried about their performance being evaluated (Milgram, Marshevsky, & Sadeh, 1995; Senecal, Lavoie, & Koestner, 1997).

Although many people rationalize their delaying tactics by claiming that "I work best under pressure" (Ferrari, 1992; Lay, 1995), the empirical evidence suggests otherwise. Studies show that procrastination tends to have a negative impact on the quality of task performance (Ferrari, Johnson, & McCown, 1995; Tice & Baumeister, 1997). Why? Late starters may often underestimate how much time will be required to complete a task effectively, or they experience unforeseen delays and then run out of time because they didn't allow any "cushion." Another consideration is that waiting until the last minute may make a task more stressful—and as we saw in Chapter 3, performance often suffers under conditions of high stress. Moreover, performance may not be the only thing that suffers when people procrastinate. Studies indicate that as a deadline looms, procrastinators tend to experience elevated anxiety and increased health problems (Lay et al., 1989; Tice & Baumeister, 1997).

Why do people procrastinate? Personality factors that contribute to procrastination include low conscientiousness (Watson, 2001), low self-efficacy (Haycock, McCarthy, & Skay, 1998), and excessive perfectionism (Flett, Hewitt, & Martin, 1995). The type of irrational thinking described by Albert Ellis also seems to foster procrastination (Bridges & Roig, 1997), as does a strong fear of failure (Lay, 1992). Roy Baumeister (1997) argues that procrastination is one of many types of self-defeating behavior in which people choose courses of action that yield short-term gains despite their long-term costs. In the case of procrastination, the short-term payoff is the avoidance of an unpleasant task, whereas the long-term costs consist of impaired performance and increased stress.

Procrastination can also be a frequent problem in relation to health care. People who recognize that they need to alter their eating behavior or start an exercise regimen routinely put off these commitments, promising themselves that they will start tomorrow, or next week, or next month. In a similar vein, many people procrastinate about getting health checkups or even seeking medical treatment for existing maladies (Sirois, Melia-Gordon, & Pychyl, 2003). People who struggle with procrastination often impose deadlines and penalties on themselves. This practice can be helpful, but self-imposed deadlines are not as effective as externally imposed deadlines (Ariely & Wertenbroch, 2002).

Time-Management Techniques

What's the key to better time management? Most people assume that it's increased *efficiency*—that is, learning to perform tasks more quickly. Improved efficiency may help a little, but time-management experts maintain that efficiency is overrated. They emphasize that the key to better time management is increased *effectiveness*—that is, learning to allocate time to your most important tasks. This distinction is captured by a widely quoted slogan in the time-management literature: "Efficiency is doing the job right, while effectiveness is doing the right job." Let's look at the experts' suggestions about how to use time more effectively (based on Lakein, 1996; Mackenzie, 1997; Morgenstern, 2000):

1. *Monitor your use of time.* The first step toward better time management is to monitor your use of time to see where it all goes (Douglass & Douglass, 1993). Doing so requires keeping a written record of your activities, similar to that shown in Figure 4.9. At the end of each week, you should analyze how your time was allocated. Based on your personal roles and responsibilities, create categories of time use such as studying,

child care, housework, commuting, working at the office, working at home, going online, eating, and sleeping. For each day, add up the hours allocated to each category. Record this information on a summary sheet like that in Figure 4.10 (on the next page). Two weeks of record keeping should allow you to draw some conclusions about where your time goes. Your records will help you make informed decisions about reallocating your time. When you begin your time-management program, these records will also give you a baseline for comparison, so that you can see whether your program is working.

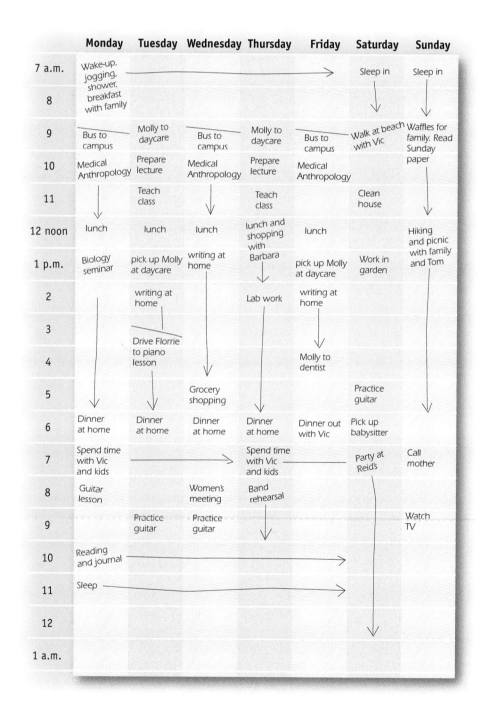

● FIGURE 4.9

Example of a time log. Experts recommend keeping a detailed record of how you use your time if you are to improve your time management. The example depicted here shows the kind of record keeping that should be done.

Time use summary. To analyze where your time goes, you need to review your time log and create a weekly time use summary, like the one shown here. The exact categories to be listed on the left depend on your circumstances and responsibilities.

Time Use Summary Form

Activity	Mon.	Tues.	Wed.	Thurs.	Fri.	Sat.	Sun.	Total	%
1. Sleeping	8	6	8	6	8	7	9	52	31
2. Eating	2	2	3	2	3	2	3	17	10
3. Commuting	2	2	2	2	2	0	0	10	6
4. Housework	0	1	0	3	0	0	2	6	4
5. In class	4	2	4	2	4	0	0	16	9
6. Part-time job	0	5	0	5	0	3	0	13	8
7. Studying	3	2	4	2	0	4	5	20	12
8. Relaxing	5	4	3	2	7	8	5	34	20
9.									
10.									

2. *Clarify your goals.* You can't wisely allocate your time unless you decide what you want to accomplish with your time. Lakein (1996) suggests that you ask yourself, "What are my lifetime goals?" Write down all the goals that you can think of, even relatively frivolous things like going deep-sea fishing or becoming a wine

RECOMMENDED READING

Time Management from the Inside Out: The Foolproof System for Taking Control of Your Schedule—and Your Life
by Julie Morgenstern (Henry Holt, 2000)

If you're locked in a perennial struggle with time—and if you're losing the battle—this book may be worth your time. Julie Morgenstern, whose first book dealt with improving personal organization, offers insightful analyses of why most of us never have enough time. She begins by describing a host of barriers to effective time use, such as unrealistic workloads, interruption-rich environments, unclear priorities, fear of failure, and perfectionism. She then discusses how to evaluate your use of time and how to prioritize your goals. She devotes quite a bit of attention to scheduling and planning and to modern devices intended to aid these processes (datebooks, computerized calendar programs, personal digital assistants, and so forth). This discussion is followed by a wealth of advice on how to be more efficient and make better choices in allocating your time. *Time Management from the Inside Out* is succinct, entertaining, and practical.

Cover image © 2000 by Henry Holt and Co. Reprinted by permission of Henry Holt & Co., LLC.

expert. Some of your goals will be in conflict. For instance, you can't become a vice-president at your company in Wichita and still move to the West Coast. Thus, the tough part comes next. You have to wrestle with your goal conflicts. Figure out which goals are most important to you, and order them in terms of priority. These priorities should guide you as you plan your activities on a daily, weekly, and monthly basis.

3. *Plan your activities using a schedule.* People resist planning because it takes time, but in the long run it saves time. Thorough planning is essential to effective time management (McGee-Cooper & Trammell, 1994). At the beginning of each week, you should make up a list of short-term goals. This list should be translated into daily "to do" lists of planned activities. To avoid the tendency to put off larger projects, break them into smaller, manageable components, and set deadlines for completing the components. Your planned activities should be allocated to various time slots on a written schedule. Schedule your most important activities into the time periods when you tend to be most energetic and productive.

4. *Protect your prime time.* The best-laid plans can quickly go awry because of interruptions. There isn't any foolproof way to eliminate interruptions, but you may be able to shift most of them into certain time slots while protecting your most productive time. The trick is to announce to your family, friends, and co-workers that you're blocking off certain periods of "quiet time" when visitors and phone calls will be turned away. Of course, you also have to block off periods of "available time" when you're ready to deal with everyone's problems.

5. *Increase your efficiency.* Although efficiency is not the key to better time management, it's not irrelevant. Time-management experts do offer some suggestions for improving efficiency, including the following (Klassen, 1987; Schilit, 1987):

- *Handle paper once.* When memos, letters, reports, and such arrive on your desk, they should not be stashed away to be read again and again before you deal with them. Most paperwork can and should be dealt with immediately.

- *Tackle one task at a time.* Jumping from one problem to another is inefficient. Insofar as possible, stick with a task until it's done. In scheduling your activities, try to allow enough time to complete tasks.

- *Group similar tasks together.* It's a good idea to bunch up small tasks that are similar. This strategy is useful when you're paying bills, replying to letters, returning phone calls, and so forth.

- *Make use of your downtime.* Most of us endure a lot of "downtime," waiting in doctors' offices, sitting in needless meetings, riding on buses and trains. In many of these situations, you may be able to get some of your easier work done—if you think ahead and bring it along.

Improving Self-Control

Self-discipline and self-control are the key to handling many of life's problems effectively. All four forms of stress described in Chapter 3 can create challenges to your self-control. Whether you're struggling with the *frustration* of poor grades in school, constant *conflicts* about your overeating, *pressure* to do well in sports, or downhill *changes* in finances that require readjustment, you will need reasonable self-control if you expect to make much progress.

For many people, however, satisfactory self-control is difficult to achieve. Fortunately, the last several decades have produced major advances in the technology of self-control. These advances have emerged from research on *behavior modification,* an approach to controlling behavior that utilizes the principles of learning and conditioning. Because of its importance, we'll devote the entire Application at the end of this chapter to improving self-control through behavior modification.

Emotion-Focused Constructive Coping

LEARNING OBJECTIVES

- *Describe the nature and value of emotional intelligence.*
- *Analyze the adaptive value of releasing pent-up emotions.*
- *Discuss the importance of managing hostility and forgiving others' transgressions.*
- *Summarize the evidence on the effects of meditation.*
- *Describe the requirements and procedure for Benson's relaxation response.*

Let's be realistic: There are going to be occasions when appraisal-focused coping and problem-focused coping are not successful in warding off emotional turmoil. Some problems are too serious to be whittled down much by reappraisal, and others simply can't be "solved." Moreover, even well-executed coping strategies may take time to work before emotional tensions begin to subside. Hence, it is helpful to be able to recognize and modulate one's emotions. In this section, we will discuss a variety of coping abilities and strategies that relate mainly to the regulation of one's emotions.

Enhancing Emotional Intelligence

According to some theorists, *emotional intelligence* is the key to being resilient in the face of stress (Slaski & Cartwright, 2003). The concept of emotional intelligence was originally formulated by Peter Salovey and John Mayer (1990). **Emotional intelligence consists of the ability to perceive and express emotion, assimilate emotion in thought, understand and reason with emotion, and regulate emotion.** Emotional intelligence includes four essential components (Salovey, Mayer, & Caruso, 2002). First, people need to be able

to accurately perceive emotions in themselves and others and have the ability to express their own emotions effectively. Second, people need to be aware of how their emotions shape their thinking, decision making, and coping with stress. Third, people need to be able to understand and analyze their emotions, which may often be complex and contradictory. Fourth, people need to be able to regulate their emotions so that they can dampen negative emotions and make effective use of positive emotions.

Several tests have been developed to measure the relatively new concept of emotional intelligence. The test that has the strongest empirical foundation is the Mayer-Salovey-Caruso Emotional Intelligence Test (2002). The authors have strived to make this test a performance-

WEB LINK 4.4

International Society for Traumatic Stress Studies
This site offers a vast storehouse of information relating to coping with traumatic events. The resources are divided into those for the general public, for professionals, and for the news media.

based measure of the ability to deal effectively with emotions rather than a measure of personality or temperament. Preliminary results suggest that they have made considerable progress toward this goal, as evidenced by the scale's ability to predict intelligent management of emotions in real-world situations (Ciarrochi, Dean, & Anderson, 2002; Lam & Kirby, 2002; Mayer et al., 2001). Illustrating the practical importance of emotional intelligence, scores on the scale also predict the quality of subjects' social interactions (Lopes et al., 2004).

Releasing Pent-Up Emotions *= better Health*

Try as you might to redefine situations as less stressful, you no doubt still go through times when you feel wired with stress-induced tension. When this happens, there's

RECOMMENDED READING

Emotional Intelligence: Why It Can Matter More Than IQ
by Daniel Goleman (Bantam Books, 1995)

It's great to see a book like this make the best-seller lists. It is a serious, scholarly, yet readable analysis of how emotional functioning is important in everyday life. Daniel Goleman is both a psychologist and a journalist who writes about the behavioral sciences for the *New York Times*. In this book, he synthesizes the research of many investigators as he argues that emotional intelligence may be more important to success than high IQ. The concept of emotional intelligence, as originally developed by Peter Salovey and John Mayer (1990), languished in relative obscurity until Goleman's book attracted attention. He views emotional intelligence more broadly than Salovey and Mayer, who focused primarily on people's ability to access, monitor, and express their own emotions and to interpret and understand others' emotions. Goleman includes all of their ingredients but adds social poise and skill, strong motivation and persistence, and some desirable personality traits, such as optimism and conscientiousness. One can argue that Goleman's concept of emotional intelligence is too much of a hodgepodge of traits to be measureable or meaningful, but his broad view yields a wide-ranging book that discusses innumerable examples of how social finesse and emotional sensitivity can foster career success, marital satisfaction, and physical and mental health. In the course of this analysis, Goleman discusses research on a diverse array of topics in an exceptionally lucid manner.

Cover image reprinted by permission of Bantam Books.

merit in the commonsense notion that you should try to release the emotions welling up inside. Why? Because the physiological arousal that accompanies emotions can become problematic. For example, research suggests that people who inhibit the expression of anger and other emotions are somewhat more likely than other people to have elevated blood pressure (Jorgensen et al., 1996). Moreover, research suggests that efforts to actively suppress emotions result in increased stress and autonomic arousal (Butler et al., 2003; Gross, 2001).

One interesting study looked at the repercussions of "psychological inhibition" in gay men who conceal their homosexual identity (Cole et al., 1996). Many gay individuals inhibit the public expression of their homosexuality to avoid stigmatization, discrimination, and even physical assault. Although hiding one's gay identity may be a sensible strategy, it entails vigilant inhibition of one's true feelings. To investigate the possible effects of this inhibition, Cole et al. (1996) tracked the incidence of cancer, pneumonia, bronchitis, sinusitis, and tuberculosis in a sample of 222 HIV-negative gay and bisexual men over a period of five years. As you can see in Figure 4.11, they found that the overall incidence of these diseases was noticeably higher among the men who concealed their homosexual identity. The investigators speculate that psychological inhibition may be detrimental to people's health.

If inhibition is bad, perhaps expression is good. James Pennebaker and his colleagues have shown that

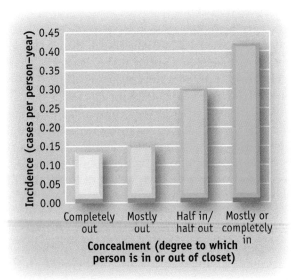

● FIGURE 4.11

Elevated health risk among gay men who conceal their homosexual identity. In a sample of gay and bisexual men, Cole et al. (1996) found that the more the men concealed their homosexual identity, the more likely they were to experience various diseases. The investigators speculate that the elevated incidence of disease may reflect the costs of inhibiting one's true feelings. (Data from Cole et al., 1996)

In times of stress, seeking support from one's friends is a very useful coping strategy. Releasing pent-up emotions by talking about one's difficulties appears to be a particularly beneficial coping mechanism.

talking or writing about traumatic events can have beneficial effects. For example, in one study of college students, half the subjects were asked to write three essays about their difficulties in adjusting to college. The other half wrote three essays about superficial topics. The participants who wrote about their personal problems and traumas enjoyed better health in the following months than the other subjects did (Pennebaker, Colder, & Sharp, 1990). A host of subsequent studies have replicated the finding that emotional disclosure, or "opening up," is associated with improved mood, more positive self-perceptions, fewer visits to physicians, and enhanced immune functioning (Hemenover, 2003; Smyth, 1998; Smyth & Pennebaker, 2001). Summarizing this research, Smyth and Pennebaker (1999) assert that "when people put their emotional upheavals into words, their physical and mental health seems to improve markedly." They conclude that "the act of disclosure itself is a powerful therapeutic agent" (p. 70).

The research on emotional disclosure indicates that both writing and talking about important personal issues can be beneficial (Smyth & Pennebaker, 2001). Thus, if you can find a good listener, it may be wise to let your secret fears, misgivings, and suspicions spill out in a candid conversation. Of course, confiding in others about one's problems can be awkward and difficult. Therein lies the beauty and appeal of the writing approach, which can be kept private. Figure 4.12 summarizes some guidelines for writing about personal issues and trauma that should make this coping strategy more effective.

Managing Hostility and Forgiving Others

Scientists have compiled quite a bit of evidence that hostility is related to increased risk for heart attacks and other types of illness (Williams, 2001; see Chapter 14). In light of this reality, many experts assert that people should strive to learn how to manage their feelings of hostility more effectively (Williams & Williams, 2001). The goal of hostility management is not merely to suppress the overt expression of hostility that may continue to seethe beneath the surface, but to actually reduce the frequency and intensity of one's hostile feelings. The first step toward this goal is to learn to quickly recognize one's anger. A variety of strategies can be used to decrease hostility, including reinterpretation of annoying events, distraction, and the kind of rational self-talk advocated by Ellis (Williams & Williams, 1993). Efforts to increase empathy and tolerance can also contribute to

Guidelines for Writing About Emotional Experiences

- Find a location where there will be no disturbances (from others, the phone, etc.)
- Set aside about 30 minutes each day: 20 minutes for writing, with a few minutes afterward to compose yourself if necessary.
- Write for three or four days, usually consecutively.
- Explore your deepest thoughts and feelings about any experiences or topics that are weighing heavily upon you.
- Explore how this topic is related to a variety of issues in your life: your childhood, your relationships, who you are, who you would like to be, and so forth.
- Write continuously, without regard for spelling or grammar.
- Remember that the writing is for you, not someone else.

● FIGURE 4.12

Using writing about emotional experiences as a coping strategy. Many studies have shown that writing about traumatic experiences and sensitive issues can have beneficial effects on mental and physical health. These guidelines can help you to use this coping strategy.

From Smyth, J. M. & Pennebaker, J. W. (1999). Sharing one's story. In C. R. Snyder (Ed.), *Coping: The psychology of what works.* Copyright © 1999 by Oxford University Press. Reprinted by permission.

hostility management, as can forgiveness, which has become the focus of a new line of research in psychology.

We tend to experience hostility and other negative emotions when we feel "wronged"—that is, when we believe that the actions of another person were harmful, immoral, or unjust. Our natural inclination is either to seek revenge or to avoid further contact with the offender (McCullough, 2001). *Forgiving* someone involves counteracting these natural tendencies and releasing the person from further liability for his or her transgression. Research suggests that forgiving is an effective emotion-focused coping strategy that is associated with better adjustment and well-being (McCullough & Witvliet, 2002; Worthington & Scherer, 2004). For example, in one study of divorced or permanently separated women reported by McCollough (2001), the extent to which the women had forgiven their former husbands was positively related to several measures of well-being and was inversely related to measures of anxiety and depression. In another study, when participants were instructed to actively think about a grudge they had nursed and to think about forgiving the grudge, forgiving thoughts were associated with more positive

emotions and reduced physiological arousal (Witvliet, Ludwig, & Vander Laan, 2001). Research also shows that vengefulness is correlated with more rumination and negative emotion and with lower life satisfaction (McCullough et al., 2001). Taken together, these findings suggest that it may be healthful for people to learn to forgive others more readily.

Meditating

Recent years have seen an explosion of interest in meditation as a method for relieving stress. **Meditation refers to a family of mental exercises in which a conscious attempt is made to focus attention in a nonanalytical way.** There are many approaches to meditation. In the United States, the most widely practiced approaches are those associated with yoga, Zen, and transcendental meditation (TM). However, meditation has been practiced throughout history as an element of all religious and spiritual traditions, including Judaism and Christianity. Moreover, the practice of meditation can be largely divorced from religious beliefs. In fact, most Americans who meditate have only vague ideas regarding its religious significance. Of interest to us is the possibility that meditation can calm inner emotional turmoil.

Most meditative techniques look deceptively simple. For example, in TM a person is supposed to sit in a comfortable position with eyes closed and silently focus attention on a *mantra,* a specially assigned Sanskrit word that creates a resonant sound. This exercise in mental self-discipline is to be practiced twice daily for 20 minutes. The technique has been described as "diving from the active surface of the mind to its quiet depths" (Bloomfield & Kory, 1976, p. 49).

Advocates of meditation claim that it can improve learning, energy level, work productivity, physical health, mental health, and general happiness while reducing tension and anxiety caused by stress (Alexander et al., 1990; Andresen, 2000). These are not exactly humble claims. Let's examine the scientific evidence on meditation.

What are the *physical effects* of going into the meditative state? Most studies find decreases in participants' heart rate, respiration rate, oxygen consumption, and carbon dioxide elimination (see Figure 4.13). Many researchers have also observed increases in skin resistance

In September 1994, Reg and Maggie Green were vacationing in Italy when their seven-year-old son Nicholas was shot and killed during a highway robbery. In an act of forgiveness that stunned Europe, the Greens chose to donate their son's organs, which went to seven Italians. The Greens, shown here five years after the incident, have weathered their horrific loss better than most, perhaps in part because of their willingness to forgive.

© Acey Harper/Time Line Pictures/Getty Images

WEB LINK 4.5

Stress Management and Emotional Wellness Links
This website functions as a gateway to a host of other sites that may be relevant to the subject of coping with stress. Included are links to sites that deal with humor, relaxation, meditation, increasing social support, crisis intervention, and stress management for college students.

and decreases in blood lactate—physiological indicators associated with relaxation. Taken together, these bodily changes suggest that meditation can lead to a potentially beneficial physiological state characterized by relaxation and suppression of arousal (Carrington, 1993; Fenwick, 1987; Travis, 2001).

To shed additional light on the physical effects of meditation, some researchers have begun to use new brain-imaging technologies in an effort to identify the neural circuits that are affected by meditation. For example, using a special type of brain scan to track blood flow in the brain, Andrew Newberg and his colleagues (2001) examined patterns of brain activity during meditation in a sample of eight experienced Tibetan Buddhist meditators. Among other things, they observed high activity in the prefrontal cortex, which is consistent with the focused attention that is central to meditation. They also found unusually low activity in an area in the parietal lobe that is known to process information on the body's location in space. This finding is interesting in that skilled meditators often report that their sense of individuality and separateness from others diminishes as they experience a sense of oneness with the world. Although the findings of Newberg and colleagues are preliminary, they suggest that it may be possible to pinpoint the neural bases of meditative experiences that previously seemed inexplicable.

What about the long-term psychological benefits that have been claimed for meditation? Research suggests that meditation may have some value in reducing the effects of stress (Anderson et al., 1999; Winzelberg & Luskin, 1999). In particular, regular meditation is associated with lower levels of some "stress hormones" (Infante et al., 2001). Research also suggests that meditation can improve mental health while reducing anxiety and drug abuse (Alexander et al., 1994). Other studies report that meditation may have beneficial effects on blood pressure (Barnes, Treiber, & Davis, 2001), self-esteem (Emavardhana & Tori, 1997), mood and one's sense of control (Easterlin & Cardena, 1999), happiness (Smith, Compton, & West, 1995), and overall physical health and well-being (Reibel et al., 2001).

At first glance these results are profoundly impressive, but they need to be viewed with some caution. At least some of these effects may be just as attainable through systematic relaxation or other mental focusing procedures (Shapiro, 1984; Smith, 1975). Critics also wonder whether placebo effects, sampling bias, and other methodological problems may contribute to some of the reported benefits of meditation (Bishop, 2002;

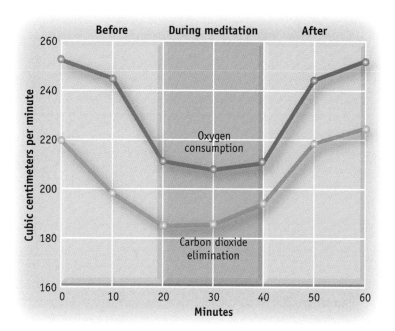

● FIGURE 4.13

Transcendental meditation (TM) and physiological arousal. The physiological changes shown on this graph (based on Wallace & Benson, 1972) indicate that meditation suppresses arousal, thus leading to a physical state that may have beneficial effects.

Adapted from Wallace, R. K., & Benson, H. (1972, February). The physiology of meditation. *Scientific American, 226,* 85–90. Graphic redrawn from illustration on p. 86 by Lorelle A. Raboni. Copyright © 1972 by Scientific American, Inc.

Shapiro, 1987). In a recent and relatively enthusiastic review of meditation research, Shapiro, Schwartz, & Santerre (2002) acknowledge that many meditation studies "do not use rigorous research design (including lack of randomization, lack of followup, and imprecise measurement of constructs) and sometimes are based on small samples" (p. 634).

Using Relaxation Procedures

Ample evidence suggests that systematic relaxation procedures can soothe emotional turmoil and reduce stress-induced physiological arousal (Lehrer & Woolfolk, 1984, 1993; Smyth et al., 2001). There are a number of worthwhile approaches to achieving beneficial relaxation. The most prominent systems are Jacobson's (1938) *progressive relaxation* (see McGuigan, 1993), Schultz and Luthe's (1969) *autogenic training* (see Linden, 1993), and Benson's (1975; Benson & Klipper, 1988) *relaxation response.* We'll discuss Benson's approach because it is a simple one that virtually anyone can learn to use.

After studying various approaches to meditation, Herbert Benson, a Harvard Medical School cardiologist, concluded that elaborate religious rituals and beliefs are not necessary for someone to profit from meditation. He also concluded that what makes meditation beneficial is the relaxation it induces. After "demystifying"

Benson's relaxation response.
The relaxation procedure advocated by Herbert Benson is a simple one that should be practiced daily.

From Benson, H., & Klipper, M. Z. (1975, 1988). *The relaxation response.* New York: Morrow. Copyright © 1975 by William Morrow & Co. Reprinted by permission of HarperCollins Publishers.

1 Sit quietly in a comfortable position.

2 Close your eyes.

3 Deeply relax all your muscles, beginning at your feet and progressing up to your face. Keep them relaxed.

4 Breathe through your nose. Become aware of your breathing. As you breathe out, say the word "one" silently to yourself. For example, breathe in . . . out "one"; in . . . out "one"; and so forth. Breathe easily and naturally.

5 Continue for 10 to 20 minutes. You may open your eyes to check the time, but do not use an alarm. When you finish, sit quietly for several minutes, at first with your eyes closed and later with your eyes opened. Do not stand up for a few minutes.

6 Do not worry about whether you are successful in achieving a deep level of relaxation. Maintain a passive attitude and permit relaxation to occur at its own pace. When distracting thoughts occur, try to ignore them by not dwelling on them, and return to repeating "one." With practice, the response should come with little effort. Practice the technique once or twice daily but not within two hours after any meal, since digestive processes seem to interfere with the elicitation of the relaxation response.

meditation, Benson (1975) set out to devise a simple, nonreligious procedure that could provide similar benefits. He calls his procedure the "relaxation response." According to Benson, four factors are critical to effective practice of the relaxation response:

1. *A quiet environment.* It is easiest to induce the relaxation response in a distraction-free environment. After you become skilled at the relaxation response, you may be able to accomplish it in a crowded subway. Initially, however, you should practice it in a quiet, calm place.

2. *A mental device.* To shift attention inward and keep it there, you need to focus it on a constant stimulus, such as a sound or word that you recite over and over. You may also choose to gaze fixedly at a bland object, such as a vase. Whatever the case, you need to focus your attention on something.

3. *A passive attitude.* It is important not to get upset when your attention strays to distracting thoughts. You must realize that such distractions are inevitable. Whenever your mind wanders from your attentional focus, calmly redirect attention to your mental device.

4. *A comfortable position.* Reasonable body comfort is essential to avoid a major source of potential distraction. Simply sitting up straight works well for most people. Some people can practice the relaxation response lying down, but for most people such a position is too conducive to sleep.

Benson's deceptively simple procedure for inducing the relaxation response is described in Figure 4.14. For full benefit, it should be practiced daily.

APPLICATION

Achieving Self-Control

LEARNING OBJECTIVES

- *Explain why traits cannot be target behaviors in self-modification programs.*
- *Describe the three kinds of information you should pursue in gathering your baseline data.*
- *Discuss how to use reinforcement to increase the strength of a response.*
- *Explain how to use reinforcement, control of antecedents, and punishment to decrease the strength of a response.*
- *Analyze issues related to fine-tuning and ending a self-modification program.*

Answer the following "yes" or "no."

yes **1.** Do you have a hard time passing up food, even when you're not hungry?

yes **2.** Do you wish you studied more often?

no **3.** Would you like to cut down on your smoking or drinking?

no **4.** Do you experience difficulty in getting yourself to exercise regularly?

yes **5.** Do you wish you had more willpower?

If you answered "yes" to any of these questions, you have struggled with the challenge of self-control. This Application discusses how you can use the techniques of behavior modification to improve your self-control. If you stop to think about it, self-control—or rather a lack of it—underlies many of the personal problems that people struggle with in everyday life.

Behavior modification is a systematic approach to changing behavior through the application of the principles of conditioning. Advocates of behavior modification assume that behavior is a product of learning, conditioning, and environmental control. They further assume that *what is learned can be unlearned.* Thus, they set out to "recondition" people to produce more desirable patterns of behavior.

The technology of behavior modification has been applied with great success in schools, businesses, hospitals, factories, child-care facilities, prisons, and mental health centers (Goodall, 1972; Kazdin, 1982, 2001; Rachman, 1992). Moreover, behavior modification techniques have proven particularly valuable in efforts to improve self-control. Our discussion will borrow liberally from an excellent book on self-modification by David Watson and Roland Tharp (2002). We will discuss five steps in the process of self-modification, which are outlined in Figure 4.15.

Specifying Your Target Behavior

The first step in a self-modification program is to specify the target behavior(s) that you want to change. Behavior modification can only be applied to a clearly defined, overt response, yet many people have difficulty pinpointing the behavior they hope to alter. They tend to describe their problems in terms of unobservable personality *traits* rather than overt behaviors. For example, asked what behavior he would like to change, a man might say, "I'm too irritable." That may be true, but it is of little help in designing a self-modification program. To use a behavioral approach, you need to translate vague statements about traits into precise descriptions of specific target behaviors.

To identify target responses, you need to ponder past behavior or closely observe future behavior and list specific *examples* of responses that lead to the trait de-

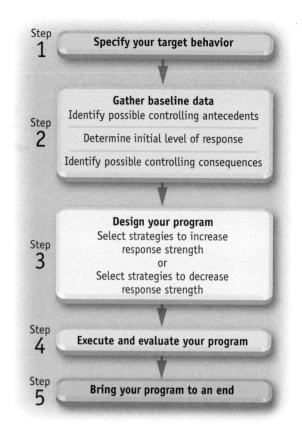

● FIGURE 4.15

Steps in a self-modification program. This flowchart provides an overview of the steps necessary to execute a self-modification program.

scription. For instance, the man who regards himself as "too irritable" might identify two overly frequent responses, such as arguing with his wife and snapping at his children. These are specific behaviors for which he could design a self-modification program.

Gathering Baseline Data

The second step in behavior modification is to gather baseline data. You need to systematically observe your target behavior for a period of time (usually a week or two) before you work out the details of your program. In gathering your baseline data, you need to monitor three things.

First, you need to determine the initial response level of your target behavior. After all, you can't tell whether your program is working effectively unless you have a baseline for comparison. In most cases, you would simply keep track of how often the target response occurs in a certain time interval. Thus, you might count the daily frequency of snapping at your children, smoking cigarettes, or biting your fingernails. If studying is your target behavior, you will probably monitor

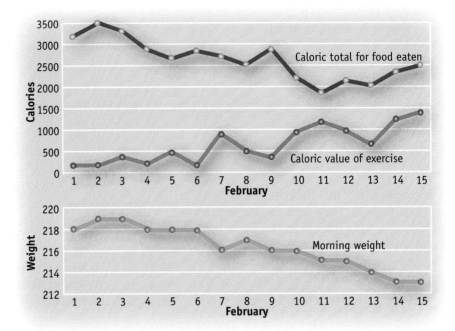

Example of record keeping in a self-modification program for losing weight. Graphic records are ideal for tracking progress in behavior modification efforts.

hours of study. If you want to modify your eating, you will probably keep track of how many calories you consume. Whatever the unit of measurement, *it is crucial to gather accurate data.* You should keep permanent written records, preferably in the form of some type of chart or graph (see Figure 4.16).

Second, you need to monitor the antecedents of your target behavior. ***Antecedents* are events that typically precede the target response.** Often these events play a major role in evoking your target behavior. For example, if your target is overeating, you might discover that the bulk of your overeating occurs late in the evening while you watch TV. If you can pinpoint this kind of antecedent-response connection, you may be able to design your program to circumvent or break the link.

Third, you need to monitor the typical consequences of your target behavior. Try to identify the reinforcers that are maintaining an undesirable target behavior or the unfavorable outcomes that are suppressing a desirable target behavior. In trying to identify reinforcers, remember that avoidance behavior is usually maintained by negative reinforcement (see Chapter 2). That is, the payoff for avoidance is usually the removal of something aversive, such as anxiety or a threat to self-esteem. You should also take into account the fact that a response may not be reinforced every time, as most behavior is maintained by intermittent reinforcement.

Designing Your Program

Once you have selected a target behavior and gathered adequate baseline data, it is time to plan your intervention program. Generally speaking, your program will be designed either to increase or to decrease the frequency of a target response.

Increasing Response Strength

Efforts to increase the frequency of a target response depend largely on the use of positive reinforcement. In other words, you reward yourself for behaving properly. Although the basic strategy is quite simple, doing it skillfully involves a number of considerations.

Selecting a reinforcer. To use positive reinforcement, you need to find a reward that will be effective for you. Reinforcement is subjective—what is reinforcing for one person may not be reinforcing for another. Figure 4.17 lists questions you can ask yourself to help you determine your personal reinforcers. Be sure to be realistic and choose a reinforcer that is really available to you.

You don't have to come up with spectacular new reinforcers that you've never experienced before. *You can use reinforcers that you are already getting.* However, you have to restructure the contingencies so that you get them only if you behave appropriately. For example, if you normally buy two compact discs per week, you might make these purchases contingent on studying a certain number of hours during the week. Making yourself earn rewards that you used to take for granted is often a useful strategy in a self-modification program.

Arranging the contingencies. Once you have chosen your reinforcer, you have to set up reinforcement contingencies. These contingencies will describe the exact behavioral goals that must be met and the rein-

What Are Your Reinforcers?

1. What will be the rewards of achieving your goal?
2. What kind of praise do you like to receive, from yourself and others?
3. What kinds of things do you like to have?
4. What are your major interests?
5. What are your hobbies?
6. What people do you like to be with?
7. What do you like to do with those people?
8. What do you do for fun?
9. What do you do to relax?
10. What do you do to get away from it all?
11. What makes you feel good?
12. What would be a nice present to receive?
13. What kinds of things are important to you?
14. What would you buy if you had an extra $20? $50? $100?
15. On what do you spend your money each week?
16. What behaviors do you perform every day? (Don't overlook the obvious or commonplace.)
17. Are there any behaviors you usually perform instead of the target behavior?
18. What would you hate to lose?
19. Of the things you do every day, which would you hate to give up?
20. What are your favorite daydreams and fantasies?
21. What are the most relaxing scenes you can imagine?

● FIGURE 4.17

Selecting a reinforcer. The questions listed here may help you to identify your personal reinforcers.

Adapted from Watson, D. L., & Tharp, R. G. (1997). *Self-directed behavior: Self-modification for personal adjustment.* Belmont, CA: Wadsworth. Reprinted by permission.

Responses Earning Tokens

Response	Amount	Number of Tokens
Jogging	1/2 mile	4
Jogging	1 mile	8
Jogging	2 miles	16
Tennis	1 hour	4
Tennis	2 hours	8
Sit-ups	25	1
Sit-ups	50	2

Redemption Value of Tokens

Reinforcer	Tokens required
Purchase one compact disc of your choice	30
Go to movie	50
Go to nice restaurant	100
Take special weekend trip	500

● FIGURE 4.18

Example of a token economy to reinforce exercise. This token economy was set up to strengthen three types of exercise behavior. The person can exchange tokens for four types of reinforcers.

forcement that may then be awarded. For example, in a program to increase exercise, you might make spending $40 on clothes (the reinforcer) contingent on having jogged 15 miles during the week (the target behavior).

Try to set behavioral goals that are both challenging and realistic. You want your goals to be challenging so that they lead to improvement in your behavior. However, setting unrealistically high goals—a common mistake in self-modification—often leads to unnecessary discouragement.

You also need to be concerned about doling out too much reinforcement. If reinforcement is too easy to get, you may become *satiated,* and the reinforcer may lose its motivational power. For example, if you were to reward yourself with virtually all the compact discs you wanted, this reinforcer would lose its incentive value.

One way to avoid the satiation problem is to put yourself on a token economy. **A *token economy* is a** system for doling out symbolic reinforcers that are exchanged later for a variety of genuine reinforcers. Thus, you might develop a point system for exercise behavior, accumulating points that can be spent on compact discs, movies, restaurant meals, and so forth. You can also use a token economy to reinforce a variety of related target behaviors, as opposed to a single, specific response. The token economy in Figure 4.18, for instance, is set up to strengthen three different, though related, responses (jogging, tennis, and sit-ups).

Shaping. In some cases, you may want to reinforce a target response that you are not currently capable of making, such as speaking in front of a large group or jogging ten miles a day. This situation calls for *shaping, which is accomplished by reinforcing closer and closer approximations of the desired response.* Thus, you might start jogging two miles a day and add a half-mile each week until you reach your goal. In shaping your behavior, you should set up a schedule spelling out how and when your target behaviors and reinforcement contingencies should change. Generally, it is a good idea to move forward gradually.

Decreasing Response Strength

Let's turn now to the challenge of reducing the frequency of an undesirable response. You can go about this task in a number of ways. Your principal options are reinforcement, control of antecedents, and punishment.

Reinforcement. Reinforcers can be used in an indirect way to decrease the frequency of a response. This may sound paradoxical, since you have learned that reinforcement strengthens a response. The trick lies in how you define the target behavior. For example, in the case of overeating you might define your target behavior as eating more than 1600 calories a day (a response that you want to decrease) or eating less than 1600 calories a day (a response that you want to increase). You can choose the latter definition and reinforce yourself whenever you eat less than 1600 calories in a day. Thus, you can reinforce yourself for not emitting a response, or for emitting it less, and thereby decrease a response through reinforcement.

Control of antecedents. A worthwhile strategy for decreasing the occurrence of an undesirable response may be to identify its antecedents and avoid exposure to them. This strategy is especially useful when you are trying to decrease the frequency of a consummatory response, such as smoking or eating. In the case of overeating, for instance, the easiest way to resist temptation is to avoid having to face it. Thus, you might stay away from enticing restaurants, minimize time spent in your kitchen, shop for groceries just after eating (when willpower is higher), and avoid purchasing favorite foods. Figure 4.19 lists a variety of suggestions for controlling antecedents to reduce overeating. Control of antecedents can also be helpful in a program to increase studying. The key often lies in *where* you study. You can reduce excessive socializing by studying somewhere devoid of people. Similarly, you can reduce loafing by studying someplace where there is no TV, stereo, or phone to distract you.

Punishment. The strategy of decreasing unwanted behavior by punishing yourself for that behavior is an obvious option that people tend to overuse. The biggest problem with punishment in a self-modification effort is the difficulty in following through and punishing oneself. Nonetheless, there may be situations in which your manipulations of reinforcers need to be bolstered by the threat of punishment. If you're going to use punishment, keep two guidelines in mind. First, do not use punishment alone. Use it in conjunction with positive reinforcement. If you set up a program in which you can earn only negative consequences, you probably won't stick to it. Second, use a relatively mild punishment so that you will actually be able to administer it to yourself. Nurnberger and Zimmerman (1970) developed a creative method of self-punishment. They had subjects write out a check to an organization they hated (for instance, the campaign of a political candidate whom they despised). The check was held by a third party who mailed it if subjects failed to meet their behavioral goals.

Controlling the Antecedents of Overeating

A. Shopping for food

1. Do not purchase problematic foods. These include
   a. very fattening, high-calorie foods
   b. your favorite foods, unless they have very low caloric values (you will be tempted to overconsume favorite foods)
   c. foods requiring little preparation (they make it too easy to eat)

2. To facilitate the above, you should
   a. use a shopping list from which you do not deviate
   b. shop just after eating (your willpower is reduced to jelly when you're hungry)
   c. carry only enough money to pay for items on your list

B. In your kitchen

1. Don't use your kitchen for anything other than food preparation and consumption.

2. Keep food stock stored out of sight.

3. If you have problematic foods in your kitchen (for other household members, of course), arrange cupboards and the refrigerator so that these foods are out of reach or in the rear.

4. Don't hover over cooking food. It will cook itself.

5. Prepare only enough food for immediate consumption.

C. While eating

1. Don't do anything besides eating. Watching TV or reading promotes mindless consumption.

2. Leave serving dishes on the kitchen counter or stove. Don't set them right in front of you.

3. Eat from a smaller dish. It will make a quantity of food appear greater.

4. Slow the pace of eating. Relax and enjoy your food.

D. After eating

1. Quickly put away or dispose of leftover foods.

2. Leave the kitchen as soon as you are through.

E. In regard to restaurants

1. Insofar as possible, do not patronize restaurants. Menus are written in a much too seductive style.

2. If social obligations require that you eat out, go to a restaurant that you don't particularly like.

3. When in restaurants, don't linger over the menu, and don't gawk at the food on other tables.

4. Avoid driving down streets and going to shopping centers that are loaded with alluring fast-food enterprises.

F. In general

1. Try to avoid boredom. Keep yourself busy.

2. Try to avoid excessive sleep loss and fatigue. Your self-control diminishes when you are tired.

3. Avoid excessive fasting. Skipping meals often leads to overeating later.

● FIGURE 4.19

Control of antecedents. Controlling antecedents that trigger overeating is often a crucial part of behavioral programs for weight loss. The tips listed here have proven useful to many people.

Such a punishment is relatively harmless, but it can serve as a strong source of motivation.

Executing and Evaluating Your Program

Once you have designed your program, the next step is to put it to work by enforcing the contingencies that you have carefully planned. During this period, you need to continue to accurately record the frequency of your target behavior so you can evaluate your progress. The success of your program depends on your not "cheating." The most common form of cheating is to reward yourself when you have not actually earned it.

You can do two things to increase the likelihood that you will comply with your program. One is to make up a *behavioral contract*—**a written agreement outlining a promise to adhere to the contingencies of a behavior modification program** (see Figure 4.20). The formality of signing such a contract in front of friends or family seems to make many people take their program more seriously. You can further reduce the likelihood of cheating by having someone other than yourself dole out the reinforcers and punishments.

Behavior modification programs often require some fine-tuning. So don't be surprised if you need to make a few adjustments. Several flaws are especially common in designing self-modification programs. Among those that you should look out for are (1) depending on a weak reinforcer, (2) permitting lengthy delays between appropriate behavior and delivery of reinforcers, and (3) trying to do too much too quickly by setting unrealistic goals. Often, a small revision or two can turn a failing program around and make it a success.

Ending Your Program

Generally, when you design your program you should spell out the conditions under which you will bring it to an end. Doing so involves setting terminal goals such as reaching a certain weight, studying with a certain regularity, or going without cigarettes for a certain length of time. Often, it is a good idea to phase out your program by planning a gradual reduction in the frequency or potency of your reinforcement for appropriate behavior.

If your program is successful, it may fade away without a conscious decision on your part. Often, new, improved patterns of behavior become self-maintaining. Responses such as eating right, exercising regularly, and studying diligently may become habitual. Whether you end your program intentionally or not, you should always be prepared to reinstitute the program if you find yourself slipping back to your old patterns of behavior.

I, _____, do hereby agree to initiate my self-change strategy as of (date) _____ and to continue it for a minimum period of _____ weeks—that is, until (date) _____.

My specific self-change strategy is to _____
_____
_____

I will do my best to execute this strategy to my utmost ability and to evaluate its effectiveness only after it has been honestly tried for the specified period of time.

Optional Self-Reward Clause: For every _____ day(s) that I successfully comply with my self-change contract, I will reward myself with _____
_____

In addition, at the end of my minimum period of personal experimentation, I will reward myself for having persisted in my self-change efforts. My reward at that time will be _____
_____

I hereby request that the witnesses who have signed below support me in my self-change efforts and encourage my compliance with the specifics of this contract. Their cooperation and encouragement throughout the project will be appreciated.

Signed _____

Date _____

Witness: _____

Witness: _____

● FIGURE 4.20

A behavioral contract. Behavior modification experts recommend the use of a formal, written contract similar to that shown here to increase commitment to one's self-modification program.

KEY IDEAS

The Concept of Coping

■ Coping involves behavioral efforts to master, reduce, or tolerate the demands created by stress. People cope with stress in many ways, but most have certain styles of coping. Coping strategies vary in their adaptive value.

Common Coping Patterns of Limited Value

■ Giving up, possibly best understood in terms of learned helplessness, is a common coping pattern that tends to be of limited value. Another is striking out at others with acts of aggression. Frequently caused by frustration, aggression tends to be counterproductive because it often creates new sources of stress.

■ Indulging oneself is a common coping strategy that is not inherently unhealthy, but it is frequently taken to excess and thus becomes maladaptive. Internet addiction is a new form of self-indulgence. Blaming yourself with negative self-talk is associated with depression.

■ Defensive coping is common and may involve any of a number of defense mechanisms. Although the adaptive value of defensive coping tends to be less than optimal, it depends on the situation. Taylor and Brown have argued that some illusions may be healthful, but their thesis has been controversial.

The Nature of Constructive Coping

■ Constructive coping, which includes efforts to deal with stress that are judged as relatively healthful, does not appear to depend on one's intelligence. Constructive coping is rational, realistic, and action oriented. It also involves managing emotions and learning self-control.

Appraisal-Focused Constructive Coping

■ Appraisal-focused constructive coping is facilitated by Ellis's suggestions on how to reduce catastrophic thinking by digging out the irrational assumptions that cause it. Other valuable strategies include using humor to deal with stress and looking for the positive aspects of setbacks and problems.

Problem-Focused Constructive Coping

■ Systematic problem solving can be facilitated by following a four-step process: (1) clarify the problem, (2) generate alternative courses of action, (3) evaluate your alternatives and select a course of action, and (4) take action while maintaining flexibility.

■ Other problem-focused coping tactics with potential value include seeking social support and acquiring strategies to improve self-control. Better time management can also aid problem-focused coping. Effective time management doesn't depend on increased efficiency so much as on setting priorities and allocating time wisely. It is also helpful to avoid the common tendency to procrastinate on aversive tasks.

Emotion-Focused Constructive Coping

■ Emotional intelligence may help people to be more resilient in the face of stress. Inhibition of emotions appears to be associated with increased health problems. Hence, it appears that releasing pent-up emotions is adaptive. Research shows that writing or talking about traumatic events or sensitive issues is associated with enhanced wellness.

■ Research suggests that it is wise for people to learn how to manage their feelings of hostility. New evidence also suggests that forgiving people for their offenses is healthier than nursing grudges.

■ Meditation can be helpful in soothing emotional turmoil. Meditation is associated with lower levels of stress hormones, improved mental health, and other indicators of wellness. Although less exotic, systematic relaxation procedures, such as Benson's relaxation response, can also be effective in reducing troublesome emotional arousal.

Application: Achieving Self-Control

■ In behavior modification, the principles of learning are used to change behavior directly. Behavior modification techniques can be used to increase one's self-control. The first step in self-modification is to specify the overt target behavior to be increased or decreased.

■ The second step is to gather baseline data about the initial rate of the target response and identify any typical antecedents and consequences associated with the behavior. The third step is to design a program. If you are trying to increase the strength of a response, you'll depend on positive reinforcement. The reinforcement contingencies should spell out exactly what you have to do to earn your reinforcer. A number of strategies can be used to decrease the strength of a response, including reinforcement, control of antecedents, and punishment.

■ The fourth step is to execute and evaluate the program. Self-modification programs often require some fine-tuning. The final step is to determine how and when you will phase out your program.

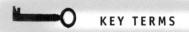

KEY TERMS

Aggression   p. 108
Antecedents   p. 132
Behavior modification   p. 131
Behavioral contract   p. 135
Brainstorming   p. 119
Catastrophic thinking   p. 115
Catharsis   p. 109
Constructive coping   p. 113
Coping   p. 106
Defense mechanisms   p. 111

Emotional intelligence   p. 125
Internet addiction   pp. 109–110
Learned helplessness   p. 107
Meditation   p. 128
Procrastination   p. 122
Rational-emotive therapy   p. 115
Shaping   p. 133
Token economy   p. 133

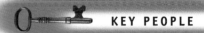

KEY PEOPLE

Herbert Benson   pp. 129–130
Albert Ellis   pp. 115–117
Sigmund Freud   pp. 111–112

Martin Seligman   pp. 107–108
Shelley Taylor   p. 113

PRACTICE TEST

1. The release of emotional tension as termed by Freud is called:
   a. flushing.
   b. catharsis.
   c. discharge.
   d. diversion.

2. Reggie works at a software firm. Today his boss unfairly blamed him for the fact that a new program is way behind schedule. The unjustified public criticism really had an impact on Reggie. Later that night at home, when Reggie couldn't find some tools that he misplaced, he lashed out at his wife in annoyance. Reggie's behavior illustrates:
   a. overcompensation.
   b. displaced aggression.
   c. self-indulgence.
   d. catastrophic thinking.

3. Bill feels sure that he failed his calculus exam and that he will have to retake the course. He is very upset. When he gets home, he orders himself a jumbo-size pizza and drinks two six-packs of beer. Bill's behavior illustrates which of the following coping strategies?
   a. Catastrophic thinking
   b. Defensive coping
   c. Self-indulgence
   d. Positive reinterpretation

4. Defense mechanisms involve the use of _____ to guard against negative _____.
   a. self-deception, behaviors
   b. self-deception, emotions
   c. self-denial, behaviors
   d. self-denial, emotions

5. Taylor and Brown found that normal people's self-images tend to be _____; depressed people's tend to be _____.
   a. accurate, inaccurate
   b. less favorable, more favorable
   c. overly favorable, more realistic
   d. more realistic, overly favorable

6. According to Albert Ellis, people's emotional reactions to life events result mainly from:
   a. their arousal level at the time.
   b. their beliefs about events.
   c. congruence between events and expectations.
   d. the consequences following events.

7. Which of the following is *not* listed in your text as a cause of wasted time?
   a. Inability to set priorities
   b. Inability to work diligently
   c. Inability to delegate responsibility
   d. Inability to throw things away

8. Research by James Pennebaker and his colleagues suggests that wellness is promoted by:
   a. depending on more mature defense mechanisms.
   b. strong self-criticism.
   c. writing about one's traumatic experiences.
   d. Iihibiting the expression of anger.

9. The first step in a self-modification program is:
   a. design your program.
   b. gather baseline data.
   c. specify your target behavior.
   d. any of the above; it doesn't matter.

10. A system providing for symbolic reinforcers is called a(n):
    a. extinction system.
    b. token economy.
    c. endocrine system.
    d. symbolic reinforcement system.

Book Companion Website

Visit the Book Companion Website at **http://psychology.wadsworth.com/weiten_lloyd8e,** where you will find tutorial quizzes, flashcards, and weblinks for every chapter, a final exam, and more! You can also link to the Thomson Wadsworth Psychology Resource Center (accessible directly at **http://psychology.wadsworth.com**) for a range of psychology-related resources.

Personal Explorations Workbook

The following exercises in your *Personal Explorations Workbook* may enhance your self-understanding in relation to issues raised in this chapter. **Questionnaire 4.1:** Barnes-Vulcano Rationality Test. **Personal Probe 4.1:** Can You Detect Your Irrational Thinking? **Personal Probe 4.2:** Analyzing Coping Strategies. **Personal Probe 4.3:** Recognizing Coping Tactics.

ANSWERS

1. b Page 109
2. b Pages 108–109
3. c Pages 109–110
4. b Page 112
5. c Page 113
6. b Pages 115–117
7. b Pages 121–122
8. c Pages 126–127
9. c Page 131
10. b Page 133

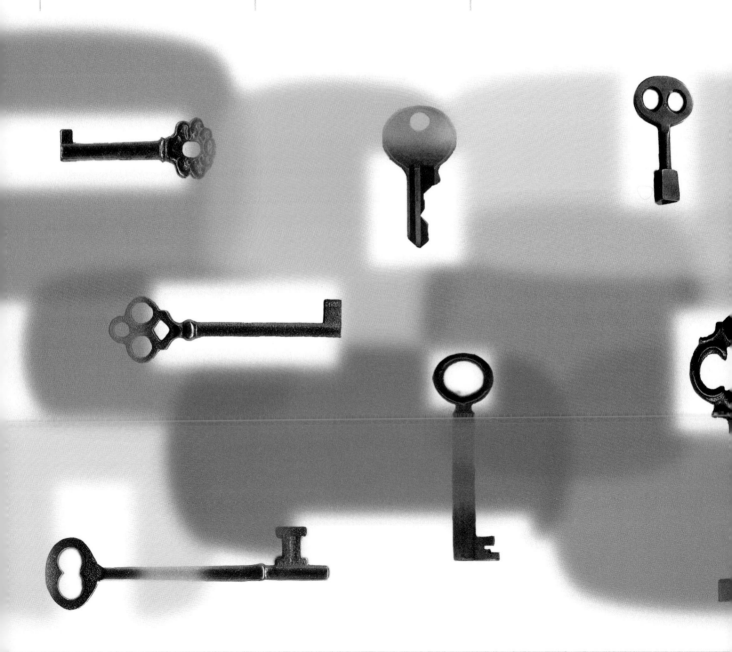

The Self

You've just taken your first exam in your first psychology course. Expecting a B, you're looking forward to getting your test back. Your instructor hands you your exam and you look at your grade: a C–. You're stunned! How could this be? You thought that you knew the material really well. As you sit there taking in this disappointing and disturbing turn of events, you anxiously search for possible explanations for your performance. "Did I read the chapters carefully? Do I need to revamp my study methods? Is this course a lot harder than I had thought? Am I really 'college material'?" As you leave the class, your mood has shifted from up to down. You're feeling dejected and already worrying about how you'll do on the next exam. This scenario illustrates the process of self-perception and the effect it can have on emotions, motivation, and goal setting. People engage in this process constantly to understand the causes of their own behavior.

In this chapter, we highlight the self and its role in adjustment. We start off by looking at two major components of the self: self-concept and self-esteem. Then we review some key principles of the self-perception process. Next, we turn to the important topic of self-regulation. Finally, we focus on how people present themselves to others. In the Application, we offer some suggestions for building self-esteem.

Self-Concept

LEARNING OBJECTIVES

- Describe some key aspects of the self-concept.
- Cite two types of self-discrepancies and describe their effects.
- Describe two ways of coping with self-discrepancies.
- Discuss important factors that help form the self-concept.
- Discuss how individualism and collectivism influence the self-concept.

If you were asked to describe yourself, what would you say? You'd probably start off with some physical attributes such as "I'm tall," "I'm of average weight," or "I'm blonde." Soon you'd move on to psychological characteristics: "I'm friendly," "I'm honest," "I'm reasonably intelligent," and so forth. How did you develop these beliefs about yourself? Have your self-views changed over time? Read on.

The Nature of the Self-Concept

Although we usually talk about the self-concept as a single entity, it is actually a multifaceted structure (Mischel & Morf, 2003). That is, the **self-concept is an organized collection of beliefs about the self.** These beliefs, also called *self-schemas,* are developed from past experience and are concerned with one's personality traits, abilities, physical features, values, goals, and social roles (Campbell, Assanand, & DiPaula, 2000). People have self-schemas on dimensions that are important to them, including both strengths and weaknesses. Figure 5.1 depicts the self-concepts of two hypothetical individuals.

Hazel Markus

Stanford University News Service, photo by L. A. Cicero

Each of these self-schemas is characterized by relatively distinct thoughts and feelings. For instance, you might have considerable information about your social skills and feel quite self-assured about them but have limited information and less confidence about your physical skills. Current thinking is that only a portion of the total self-concept operates at any one time. The self-concept that is accessible at any given moment has been termed the *working self-concept* by Hazel Markus, a leading researcher in this area (Markus & Wurf, 1987).

Self-schemas are dynamic and play a major role in processing self-relevant information. For example, when a particular self-schema is operating, its attendant thoughts and feelings strongly influence the way individuals process information about that aspect of the self. When you're in class, for example, the beliefs and emotions associated with your intellectual self-schema will influence how you process information

you receive in that setting. Similarly, when you're at a party (or thinking about a party when you're in class!), you tap into your social self-schema and the thoughts and feelings related to it.

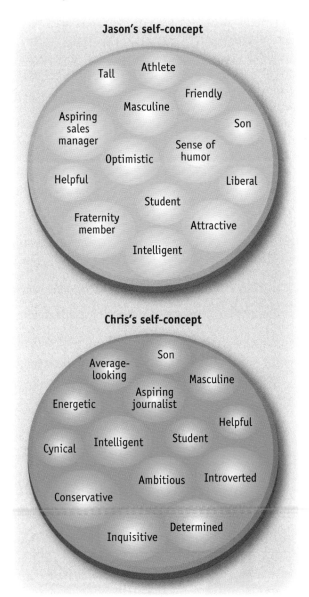

Jason's self-concept

Tall
Athlete
Friendly
Masculine
Aspiring sales manager
Son
Sense of humor
Optimistic
Helpful
Liberal
Student
Fraternity member
Attractive
Intelligent

Chris's self-concept

Son
Average-looking
Masculine
Aspiring journalist
Energetic
Helpful
Cynical
Intelligent
Student
Ambitious
Introverted
Conservative
Determined
Inquisitive

● **FIGURE 5.1**

The self-concept and self-schemas. The self-concept is composed of various self-schemas, or beliefs about the self. Jason and Chris have different self-concepts, in part, because they have different self-schemas.

Beliefs about the self influence not only current behavior but also future behavior. *Possible selves* **refer to one's conceptions about the kind of person one might become in the future** (Markus & Nurius, 1986). If you have narrowed your career choices to personnel manager and psychologist, these represent two possible selves in the career realm. Possible selves are developed from past experiences, current behavior, and future expectations. They make people attentive to goal-related information and role models and mindful of the need to practice goal-related skills. As such, they help individuals not only to envision desired future goals but also to achieve them (Cross & Markus, 1991). Interestingly, it has been found that, for individuals who have experienced traumatic events, psychological adjustment is best among those who are able to envision a variety of positive selves (Morgan & Janoff-Bulman, 1994). Sometimes, possible selves are negative and represent what you fear you might become—such as an alcoholic like Uncle George or an adult without an intimate relationship like your next-door neighbor. In this case, possible selves function as images to be avoided.

Individuals' beliefs about themselves are not set in concrete—but neither are they easily changed. People are strongly motivated to maintain a consistent view of the self across time and situations. Thus, once the self-concept is established, the individual has a tendency to preserve and defend it. In the context of this stability, however, self-beliefs do have a certain dynamic quality (Markus & Wurf, 1987). They seem to be most susceptible to change when people shift from an important and familiar social setting to an unfamiliar one—for example, when moving off to college or to a new city for one's first "real" job. This finding clearly underscores the social foundations of the self-concept.

Self-Discrepancies and Their Effects

According to Higgins, when people live up to their personal standards (ideal or ought selves), they experience high self-esteem; when they don't meet their own expectations, their self-esteem suffers (Moretti & Higgins, 1990). In addition, he says, certain types of self-discrepancies are associated with specific emotions (see Figure 5.2). One type of self-discrepancy occurs when the *actual* self is at odds with the *ideal* self. Such instances trigger *dejection-related* emotions (sadness, disappointment). As actual-ideal discrepancies outnumber actual-ideal congruencies, sadness increases and cheerfulness decreases (Higgins, Shah, & Friedman, 1997). Consider Tiffany's situation: She knows that she's attractive, but she is also overweight and would like to be thinner. Self-discrepancy theory predicts that she would feel dissatisfied and dejected. Interestingly, research has shown an association between discrepant actual/ideal views of body shape and eating disorders (Strauman et al., 1991).

A second type of discrepancy involves a mismatch between *actual* and *ought* selves. Let's say you don't stay in touch with your grandparents as often as you feel you should. According to Higgins, actual/ought self-

Self-Discrepancies

Some people perceive themselves pretty much the way they'd like to see themselves. Others experience a gap between what they actually see and what they'd like to see. For example, Nathan describes his actual self as "shy" but his ideal self as "outgoing." **Such mismatching of self-perceptions is termed** *self-discrepancy.* According to E. Tory Higgins (1987), individuals have several self-perceptions: an *actual self* (qualities you believe you *actually* possess), an *ideal self* (characteristics you would *like* to have), and an *ought self* (traits you believe you *should* possess). The ideal and ought selves serve as personal standards or self-guides that direct behavior.

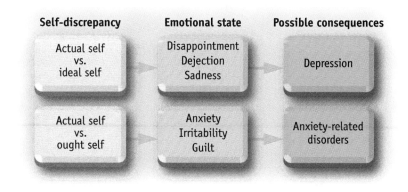

● FIGURE 5.2

Types of self-discrepancies, their effects on emotional states, and possible consequences. According to E. Tory Higgins (1989), discrepancies between actual and ideal selves produce disappointment and sadness, whereas discrepancies between actual and ought selves result in irritability and guilt. Such self-discrepancies can make individuals vulnerable to more serious psychological problems, such as depression and anxiety-related disorders.

discrepancies produce *agitation-related* emotions (irritability, anxiety, and guilt). As actual-ought discrepancies outnumber actual-ought congruencies, anxiety increases and calm emotions decrease (Higgins, Shah, & Friedman, 1997). Extreme discrepancies of this type can result in anxiety-related psychological disorders.

Everyone experiences self-discrepancies, yet most people manage to feel reasonably good about themselves. How is this possible? Three factors seem to be important: the amount of discrepancy you experience, your awareness of the discrepancy, and whether the discrepancy is actually important to you (Higgins, 1999). Thus, a pre-med major who gets a C in calculus will probably feel a lot worse than an English major who gets a C in the course.

Although people use both ideal and ought selves as personal standards, they usually rely on just one of these self-guides. These "preferences" are rooted in parent-child interactions and individual temperament (Higgins, 1987). If Kyle's parents typically communicate with him in terms of what they would *like* him to do, he will probably develop a strong *ideal* self-guide. If their communications usually take the form of what they think he *ought* to do, Kyle will probably develop a strong *ought* self-guide.

One study took a closer look at self-guide "preferences." The researchers first tested college students to determine their temperament and the self-guides (ideal or ought) students "preferred" (Manian, Strauman, & Denney, 1998). Then they asked participants to recall the parenting style their parents used. A preference for the ideal self-guide was strongly associated with a positive temperament and parental warmth, while a preference for the ought self-guide was strongly associated with a negative temperament and parental rejection. Of course, a retrospective study can't show that parenting style determines self-guide preferences, but the results are interesting. Other researchers report that "ideals" look for opportunities to advance their aspirations, while "oughts" keep an eye out for obstacles to their goals to avoid possible failures (Dweck, Higgins, & Grant-Pillow, 2003). Thus, self-guides can determine the types of goals you pursue and the way you pursue them.

Coping with Self-Discrepancies

Can individuals do anything to blunt the negative emotions and blows to self-esteem associated with self-discrepancies? Yes! For one thing, people can *change their behavior* to bring it more in line with their ideal or ought selves. For instance, if your ideal self is a person who gets above-average grades and your actual self just got a D on a test, you can study more effectively for the next

test to improve your grade. But what about the times you can't match your ideal standards? Perhaps you had your heart set on making the varsity tennis team, but didn't make the cut. Maybe you had planned to go to medical school, but barely managed to eek out C's in your science courses. One way to ease the discomfort associated with such discrepancies is to bring your ideal self a bit more in line with your actual abilities. Another option is to *blunt your self-awareness*. You can do so by avoiding situations that increase your self-awareness—you don't go to a party if you expect to spend a miserable evening talking to yourself.

Some people use alcohol to blunt self-awareness. In one study, college students were first put into either a high or a low self-awareness group based on test scores (Hull & Young, 1983). Then, both groups were given a brief version of an intelligence test as well as false feedback on their test performance. Half of the high self-awareness group were told that they had done quite well on the test and the other half were told that they had done quite poorly. Next, supposedly as part of a separate study, these participants were asked to taste and evaluate various wines for 15 minutes. The experimenters predicted that the high self-awareness participants who had been told that they had done poorly on the IQ test would drink more than the other groups, and this is precisely what the study found (see Figure 5.3). Those who couldn't escape negative information about themselves drank more alcohol to reduce their self-awareness. Similarly, in the real world, it has been found that alcoholics who have high self-awareness and who experience negative or painful life events relapse more quickly and completely (Hull, Young, & Jouriles, 1986).

Heightened self-awareness doesn't *always* make people focus on self-discrepancies and negative aspects of the self. If that were true, most people would feel a lot worse about themselves than they actually do. As

● FIGURE 5.3

Self-awareness and alcohol consumption. Individuals who were high in self-awareness drank significantly more wine in a 15-minute period if they believed that they had performed poorly on an IQ test than did any other group.

From Hull, J. G., & Young, R. D. (1983). Self-consciousness, self-esteem, and success-failure as determinants of alcohol consumption in male social drinkers. *Journal of Personality and Social Psychology, 44*, 1097–1109. Copyright © 1983 American Psychological Association. Reprinted by permission of the author.

When people don't live up to their personal standards, self-esteem suffers, and some turn to alcohol to blunt their awareness of the discrepancy.

you recall, self-concepts are made up of numerous self-beliefs—many of them positive, some negative. Because individuals have a need to feel good about themselves, they tend to focus on their positive features rather than their "warts" (Tesser, 2001).

Factors Shaping the Self-Concept

A variety of sources influence one's self-concept. Chief among them are one's own observations, feedback from others, and cultural values.

Your Own Observations

Your observations of your own behavior are obviously a major source of information about what you are like. Individuals begin observing their own behavior and drawing conclusions about themselves early in life. Children will make statements about who is the tallest, who can run fastest, or who can swing the highest. Leon Festinger's (1954) *social comparison theory* proposes that individuals compare themselves with others in order to assess their abilities and opinions. People compare themselves to others to determine how attractive they are, how they did on the history exam, how their social skills stack up, and so forth.

Although Festinger's original theory claimed that people engage in social comparison for the purpose of accurately assessing their abilities, research suggests that they also engage in social comparison to improve their skills and to maintain their self-image (Wood & Wilson, 2003). Furthermore, the reasons people engage in social comparison determine whom they choose for a point of comparison. A *reference group* is a set of people against whom individuals compare themselves. For example, if you want to know how you did on your first test in social psychology (ability appraisal), your reference group will be the entire class. On the other hand, if you want to improve your tennis game (skill development), your reference group will probably be limited to those of superior ability, because their skills give you something to strive for. And, if your self-esteem needs bolstering, you will probably compare yourself to those whom you perceive to be worse off than you so you can feel better about yourself.

The potential impact of such social comparisons was dramatically demonstrated in the classic "Mr. Clean/Mr. Dirty" study (Morse & Gergen, 1970). Subjects thought they were being interviewed for a job. Half the participants met another applicant who was neatly dressed and who appeared to be very competent. The other half encountered a competitor who was unkempt and disorganized. All subjects filled out measures of self-esteem both before and after the bogus job interviews. The results indicated that subjects who encountered the impressive competitor showed a decrease in self-esteem after the interview while those who met the unimpressive competitor showed increases in self-esteem. Thus, comparisons with others can have immediate effects on one's self-concept.

People's observations of their own behavior are not entirely objective. The general tendency is to distort reality in a positive direction (see Figure 5.4 on the next page). In other words, most people tend to evaluate themselves in a more positive light than they really merit (Taylor & Brown, 1988, 1994). The strength of this tendency was highlighted in a large survey of high school seniors conducted as part of the Scholastic Aptitude Test (SAT) (Myers, 1980). By definition, 50 percent of the students must be "above average" and 50 percent "below average" on specific questions. However, 100 percent of the

WEB LINK 5.2

Identity and Self
Professor Andy Lock at Massey University in New Zealand has posted the outline of a possible upper-level course that would explore contemporary psychological conceptions of the self and identity development, particularly from the social constructivist and cultural viewpoints. His site includes a full set of bibliographical and topical guides.

As she sees herself: Unchanged since age 22. Sociable, scintillating, sexy.

As the husband sees her: Older than her years. Someone more suited to suburban domesticity and PTA.

As he sees himself: Stylish haircut, rakish moustache, benevolent, generous, powerful. A smooth operator.

As the wife sees him: Somewhat of a slob, moody, not very decisive or strong.

Brooks/Cole Collection

● FIGURE 5.4

Distortions in self-images. How people see themselves may be different from how others see them. These pictures and text illustrate the subjective quality of self-concept and people's perception of others. Generally, self-images tend to be distorted in a positive direction.

respondents saw themselves as above average in "ability to get along with others." And 25 percent of the respondents thought that they belonged in the top 1 percent!

Although the general tendency is to distort reality in a positive direction, most people make both positive and negative distortions. For example, you might overrate your social skill, emotional stability, and intellectual ability while underrating your physical attractiveness. Also, a minority of people consistently evaluate themselves in an unrealistically negative way. Thus, the tendency to see oneself in an overly favorable light is strong but not universal.

Feedback from Others

Your self-concept is shaped significantly by the feedback you get from important people in your life. Early on, parents and other family members play a dominant role. Parents give their children a great deal of direct feedback, saying such things as "We're so proud of you" or "If you just tried harder, you could do a lot better in math." Most people, especially when young, take this sort of feedback to heart. Thus, it comes as no surprise that studies find a link between parents' views of a child and the child's self-concept (Berne & Savary, 1993; Burhans & Dweck, 1995). There is even stronger evidence for a relationship between children's *perceptions* of their parents' attitudes toward them and their own self-views (Felson, 1989, 1992).

Teachers, Little League coaches, Scout leaders, classmates, and friends also provide feedback during childhood. In later childhood and adolescence, parents and classmates are particularly important sources of feedback and support (Harter, 2003). Later in life, feedback from close friends and marriage partners assumes importance. In fact, there is evidence that a close partner's support and affirmation can bring the loved one's ac-

144   PART 2   The Interpersonal Realm

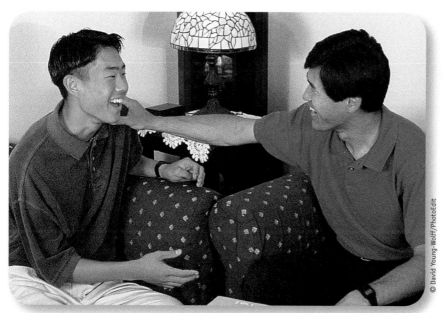

Whether positive or negative, feedback from others plays an important role in shaping a youngster's self-concept.

tual self-views and behavior more in line with his or her ideal self (Drigotas et al., 1999). For this situation to happen, the partner needs to hold views of the loved one that match the target person's ideal self and behave in ways to bring out the best in the person. If the target person's behavior can closely match the ideal self, then self-views can move nearer to the ideal self. Researchers have labeled this process the *Michelangelo phenomenon* to reflect the partner's role in "sculpting" into reality the ideal self of a loved one.

Keep in mind that people filter feedback from others through their existing self-perceptions. That is, individuals don't see themselves exactly as others see them, but rather as they *believe* others see them (Baumeister & Twenge, 2003; Tice & Wallace, 2003). Thus, feedback from others usually reinforces people's self-views.

Cultural Values

Your self-concept is also shaped by cultural values. Among other things, the society in which you are reared defines what is desirable and undesirable in personality and behavior. For example, American culture puts a high premium on individuality, competitive success, strength, and skill. When individuals meet cultural expectations, they feel good about themselves and experience increases in self-esteem and vice-versa (Cross & Gore, 2003).

Cross-cultural studies suggest that different cultures shape different conceptions of the self (Cross & Markus, 1999; Cross & Gore, 2003). One important way cultures differ is on the dimension of individualism versus collectivism (Hofstede, 1983; Triandis, 1989, 2001). *Individualism* involves putting personal goals ahead of group goals and defining one's identity in terms of personal attributes rather than group memberships. In contrast, *collectivism* involves putting group goals ahead of personal goals and defining one's identity in terms of the groups one belongs to (such as one's family, tribe, work group, social class, caste, and so on). Although it's tempting to think of these perspectives in either-or terms, it is more appropriate to view them as points along a continuum. Thus, it is more accurate to say that certain cultures are more or less individualistic (or collectivist) than others rather than seeing them as either individualistic or collectivist.

In comparison to individualistic cultures, collectivist cultures place a higher priority on shared values and resources, cooperation, and concern for how one's actions will affect other group members. Child-rearing patterns in collectivist cultures emphasize the importance of obedience, reliability, and proper behavior, whereas individualistic cultures stress the development of independence, self-esteem, and self-reliance.

A variety of factors influence societies' tendencies to cherish individualism or collectivism. Among other things, increases in a culture's affluence, education, urbanization, and social mobility tend to foster more individualism (Triandis, 1994). Many contemporary societies are in transition, but generally speaking North American and Western European cultures tend to be individualistic, whereas Asian, African, and Latin American cultures tend to be collectivist (Hofstede, 1980, 1983).

Individuals reared in individualistic cultures usually have an *independent* view of the self, perceiving themselves as unique, self-contained, and distinct from others. In contrast, individuals reared in collectivist cultures typically have an *interdependent* view of the self. They see themselves as inextricably connected to others and believe that harmonious relationships with others are of utmost importance. Thus, in describing herself, a person living in an individualistic culture might say, "I am kind," whereas someone in a collectivist culture might respond, "My family thinks I am kind" (Triandis, 2001). Figure 5.5 (on the next page) depicts the self-conceptions of individuals from these contrasting cultures.

Individuals with an independent view of the self are socialized to maintain their sense of self as a separate person—to "look out for number one," claim more than their share of credit for group successes, and disavow responsibility for group failure. Those with an

Independent and interdependent views of the self. (a) Individuals in cultures that support an independent view perceive the self as clearly separated from significant others. **(b)** Individuals in cultures that support an interdependent view perceive the self as inextricably connected to others.

Adapted from Markus, H. R., & Kitayama, S. (1991). Culture and the self: Implications for cognition, emotion, and motivation. *Psychological Review, 98*, 224–253.

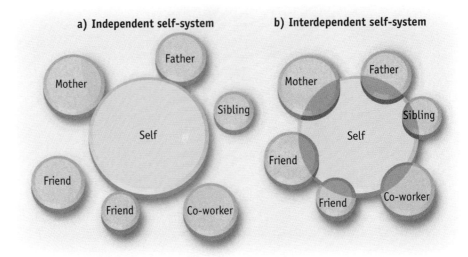

interdependent view of the self are taught to adjust themselves to the needs of the groups to which they belong and to maintain the interdependence among individuals. In this situation, social duties and obligations assume great importance and people are likely to see themselves as responsible for group failures (Cross & Gore, 2003).

Researchers have noted parallels between the self-views promoted by individualistic and collectivist cultures and the self-views of some groups. For example, women usually have more interdependent self-views than men (Cross & Madson, 1997). But don't take this to mean that men are less social than women; instead it means that men and women get their social needs met in different ways (Baumeister & Sommer, 1997). Thus

women are usually involved in close relationships involving intimate friends and family members (*relational* interdependence), while men interact in social groups such as clubs and sports teams (*collective* interdependence) (Gabriel & Gardner, 1999). These gender differences in self-views may explain other observed gender differences, such as women being more likely than men to share their feelings and thoughts with others. We'll take up such issues in subsequent chapters.

Cultural values are also responsible for various stereotypes that can mold people's self-perceptions and behavior. And stereotypes—about gender, ethnicity, class, sexual orientation, and religion—can influence self-conceptions.

Self-Esteem

LEARNING OBJECTIVES

- Describe the implications of self-concept confusion and self-esteem instability.
- Discuss how high and low self-esteem are related to adjustment.
- Distinguish between high self-esteem and narcissism, and discuss narcissism and aggression.

- Discuss some key influences in the development of self-esteem.
- Summarize the findings on ethnicity and gender regarding self-esteem.

One of the functions of the self-concept is to evaluate the self; the result of this self-evaluation is termed *self-esteem*. **Self-esteem refers to one's overall assessment of one's worth as a person.** Self-esteem is a global self-evaluation that blends many specific evaluations about one's adequacy as a student, an athlete, a worker, a spouse, a parent, or whatever is personally relevant. Figure 5.6 shows how specific elements of the self-concept may contribute to self-esteem. If you feel ba-

sically good about yourself, you probably have high self-esteem.

It has long been thought that individuals with low self-esteem hold strong negative views about themselves. In reality, it seems that the self-views of these individuals are not more negative, but more confused and tentative (Campbell, 1990; Campbell & Lavallee, 1993). In other words, their self-concepts seem to be less clear, less complete, more self-contradictory, and

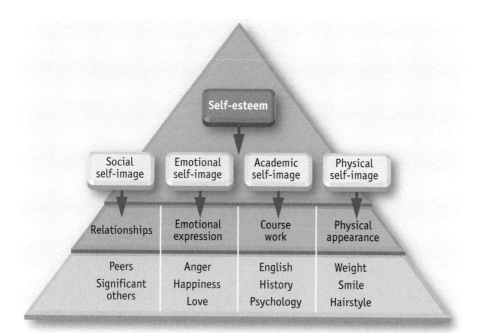

● FIGURE 5.6

The structure of self-esteem.
Self-esteem is a global evalua-tion that combines assessments of various aspects of one's self-concept, each of which is built up from many specific behaviors and experiences. (Adapted from Shavelson, Hubner, & Stanton, 1976)

more susceptible to short-term fluctuations than the self-views of high self-esteem individuals. According to Roy Baumeister (1998), an eminent researcher on the self, this "self-concept confusion" means that individuals with low self-esteem simply don't know themselves well enough to strongly endorse many personal attributes on self-esteem tests, which results in lower self-esteem scores.

Roy Baumeister

Studies generally show self-esteem to be quite stable over time, once past childhood (Trzesniewski, Donnellan, & Robins, 2003). In other words, if you have high self-esteem today, you are likely to have high self-esteem six months or two years from now. While it's true that baseline self-esteem is stable, it's also true that the ups and downs of daily life can produce short-term fluctuations in self-esteem. Recall your elation when that great-looking person at work asked you out and your distress when you saw that C– staring back at you on your last calculus exam. People vary in the stability of their self-esteem. Those whose self-esteem fluctuates in response to daily experiences are highly sensitive to interactions and events that have potential relevance to their self-worth, and they may even mistakenly view irrelevant events as having significance (Kernis & Goldman, 2003). Thus, in their eyes, their self-worth is always on the line. These tendencies have important implications for adjustment, as you'll see shortly.

Investigating self-esteem is challenging for several reasons. For one thing, it is difficult to obtain accurate measures of self-esteem. The problem is that researchers tend to rely on self-reports from subjects, which obviously may be biased. As you've seen, most individuals typically hold unrealistically positive views about themselves; moreover, some people may choose not to disclose their actual self-esteem on a questionnaire. Second, in probing self-esteem it is often quite difficult to separate cause from effect. Thousands of correlational studies report that high and low self-esteem are associated with various behavioral characteristics. For instance, you saw in Chapter 1 that self-esteem is a good predictor of happiness. However, it is hard to tell whether high self-esteem causes happiness or vice versa. You should keep this problem in pinpointing causation in mind as we zoom in on this fascinating topic.

The Importance of Self-Esteem

Popular wisdom holds that self-esteem is the key to practically all positive outcomes in life. In fact, its actual benefits are much fewer—but, we hasten to add, not unimportant. A recent comprehensive review of research looked at the purported and actual advantages of self-esteem (Baumeister et al., 2003). Let's look at the findings that relate to self-esteem and adjustment.

Self-Esteem and Adjustment

The clearest advantages of self-esteem are in the *emotional sphere.* Namely, self-esteem is strongly and consistently related to happiness. In fact, Baumeister and his colleagues are persuaded that high self-esteem actually leads to greater happiness, although they acknowledge that research has not clearly established the direction of causation. On the other side, low self-esteem is more likely than high self-esteem to lead to depression.

In the area of *achievement*, high self-esteem has not been shown to be a reliable cause of good academic performance. In fact, it may actually be the (weak) result of doing well in school. Baumeister and his colleagues speculate that other factors may underlie both self-esteem and academic performance. Regarding job performance, the results are mixed. Some studies find that high self-esteem is linked to better performance, but others find no difference. And it may be that occupational success leads to high self-esteem.

In the *interpersonal realm*, Baumeister and his colleagues report that people with high self-esteem claim to be more likable and attractive, to have better relationships, and to make better impressions on others than people with low self-esteem. Interestingly, these advantages seem to exist mainly in the minds of the beholders because objective data (ratings of peers) do not support these views. In fact, Mark Leary's *sociometer theory* suggests that self-esteem is actually a subjective measure of one's interpersonal popularity and success (Leary et al., 1995; Leary & Baumeister, 2000). Regarding romantic relationships, those with low self-esteem are more likely to distrust their partners' expressions of love and support and to worry about rejection compared to high self-esteem individuals. Still there is no evidence that self-esteem (high or low) is related to how quickly relationships end. When it comes to groups, high self-esteem people are more likely to speak up and to criticize the group's approach. And they are perceived as contributing more to groups.

What about self-esteem and *coping*, a key aspect of adjustment? Individuals with low self-esteem *and* a self-blaming attributional style are definitely at a disadvantage here. For one thing, they become more demoralized after a failure experience than those with high self-esteem do. For them, failure contributes to depression and undermines their motivation to do better the next time. By contrast, individuals with high self-esteem persist longer in the face of failure. Second, as can be seen in Figure 5.7, individuals with low self-esteem often have negative expectations about their performance (in a social situation, at a job interview, on a test). Because self-esteem affects expectations, it operates in a self-perpetuating fashion. As a result, they feel anxious and may not prepare for the challenge. Then, if they blame themselves when they do poorly, they feel depressed and deliver one more blow to their already battered self-esteem. Of course, this cycle also works (in the opposite way) for those with high self-esteem. In either case, the important point is that self-esteem can affect not only the present, but also the future.

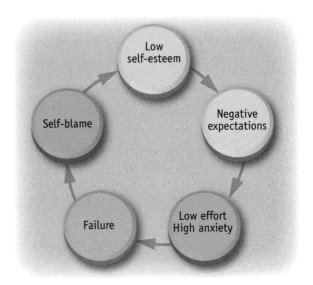

● **FIGURE 5.7**

The vicious circle of low self-esteem and poor performance. Low self-esteem is associated with low or negative expectations about performance. These low expectations often result in inadequate preparation and high anxiety, which heighten the likelihood of poor performance. Unsuccessful performance triggers self-blame, which feeds back to low self-esteem.

Adapted from Brehm, S. S., & Kassin, S. M. (1993). *Social Psychology*. Boston: Houghton Mifflin. Copyright © 1993 by Houghton Mifflin Company. Adapted with permission.

High Self-Esteem Versus Narcissism

Although feeling good about oneself is desirable, problems arise when people's self-views are inflated and unrealistic. **Narcissism is the tendency to regard oneself as grandiosely self-important.** Narcissistic individuals passionately want to think well of themselves and are highly sensitive to criticism (Twenge & Campbell, 2003). They are preoccupied with fantasies of success, believe that they deserve special treatment, and react aggressively when they experience threats to their self-views (ego threats). Those with fragile (unstable) self-esteem also respond in this manner (Kernis, 2003a, 2003b). On the other hand, individuals whose positive self-appraisals are secure or realistic are not so susceptible to ego threats and are less likely to resort to hostility and aggression in the face of them. Note that narcissists' aggression must be provoked; without provocation, they

WEB LINK 5.3

Self-Esteem vs. Narcissism: Implications for Teachers of Young Children
Self-esteem in early childhood can be undermined by well-intentioned, but ill-informed, teachers who misunderstand how self-esteem is developed. Lilian G. Katz explores durable foundations for a child's self-worth in this online book from ERIC, the Education Resources Information Center.

are no more likely to aggress than non-narcissists (Baumeister, Bushman, & Campbell, 2000; Twenge & Campbell, 2003).

Baumeister speculates that narcissists who experience ego threats are likely to engage in aggression such as partner abuse, rape, gang violence, individual and group hate crimes, and political terrorism (Baumeister, 1999; Baumeister, Smart, & Boden, 1996). Is there any evidence to support this idea? In a series of studies, researchers gave participants the opportunity to aggress against someone who had either insulted or praised an essay they had written (Bushman & Baumeister, 1998). The narcissistic participants reacted to their "insultors" with exceptionally high levels of aggression (see Figure 5.8). Another study compared male prisoners and college men on narcissism and self-esteem. Violent offenders scored significantly higher in narcissism, but their self-esteem scores were similar to those of the college men (Bushman & Baumeister, 2002).

These findings have important practical implications (Baumeister et al., 1996). Most rehabilitation programs for spousal abusers, delinquents, and criminals are based on the faulty belief that these individuals suffer from low self-esteem. In opposition to this view, current research suggests that efforts to boost (already inflated) self-esteem are misguided; a better approach is to help such individuals develop more self-control and more realistic views of themselves.

The Development of Self-Esteem

Because the foundations of self-esteem are laid early in life (Harter, 2003), psychologists have focused much of their attention on the role of parenting in self-esteem development. Indeed, there is ample evidence that parental involvement, acceptance, support, and exposure to clearly defined limits have marked influence on children's self-esteem (Felson, 1989; Harter, 1998). Two major dimensions underlie parenting behavior: acceptance and control (Maccoby & Martin, 1983). Diana Baumrind (1967, 1971, 1978) identified four distinct parenting styles as interactions between these two dimensions (see Figure 5.9). *Authoritative parenting* uses high emotional support and firm, but reasonable limits (high acceptance, high control). *Authoritarian parenting* entails low emotional support with rigid limits (low acceptance, high control). *Permissive parenting* uses high emotional support with few limits (high acceptance, low control), and *neglectful parenting* involves low emotional support and few limits (low acceptance, low control). Baumrind and others have found

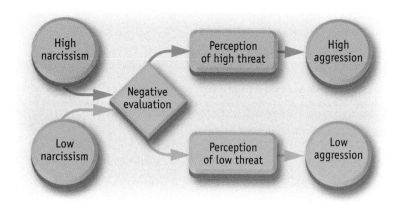

● FIGURE 5.8

The path from narcissism to aggression. Individuals who score high on narcissism perceive negative evaluations by others to be extremely threatening. This experience of ego threat triggers strong hostile feelings and aggressive behavior toward the evaluator in retaliation for the perceived criticism. Low scorers are less likely to perceive negative evaluations as threatening and, therefore, behave much less aggressively toward evaluators. (Adapted from Bushman & Baumeister, 1998).

correlations between parenting styles and children's traits and behaviors, including self-esteem (Furnham & Cheng, 2000; Maccoby & Martin, 1983). Authoritative parenting is associated with the highest self-esteem scores. Authoritarian parenting, permissive parenting, and neglectful parenting are second, third, and fourth in line. These studies were correlational, so they don't demonstrate that parenting style *causes* high or low self-esteem.

Of course, parents are not the only significant others in a person's life: teachers, classmates, and close friends also play important roles. As you would expect, children who perceive they have the most support from significant others have the highest self-esteem, whereas those who have the lowest perceived support

Parental acceptance

		Low	High
Parental control	High	**Authoritarian** (low acceptance, high control)	**Authoritative** (high acceptance, high control)
	Low	**Neglectful** (low acceptance, low control)	**Permissive** (high acceptance, low control)

● FIGURE 5.9

Baumrind's parenting styles. Four parenting styles result from the interactions of parental acceptance and parental control.

Adapted from Baumrind, D. (1971). Current patterns of parental authority [Monograph]. *Developmental Psychology, 4*(1, Part 2), 1–103. American Psychological Association. Adapted by permission of the author.

LIVING IN TODAY'S WORLD

Self-Esteem and Threats to Mortality

One consequence of living in a post–9-11 world is anxiety about subsequent terrorist attacks in the United States, as well as elsewhere. As explained in Chapter 2, *terror management theory (TMT)* (Greenberg, Solomon, & Pyszczynski, 1997) is an influential new theoretical perspective asserting that self-esteem plays a pivotal role in people's efforts to deal with the threats to mortality posed by modern terrorism. As you may recall, terror management theory notes that human beings are the only creatures who live with the knowledge that they will die. According to TMT, the instinctive desire to live is juxtaposed against the inevitability of death, which produces the potential for paralyzing terror (Pyszczynski, Greenberg, & Goldenberg, 2003). To diminish the existential terror resulting from the awareness of their mortality, people are thought to rely on two defenses: the first involves efforts aimed at validating one's cultural worldview, while the second bolsters self-esteem.

First, belonging to a culture supposedly reduces the fear of death because it provides a sense of meaning beyond oneself and a sense of belonging to a larger entity that will live beyond one's own lifetime. This idea has considerable support. Compared to participants who are not reminded about their own death, those for whom death is made salient are more likely to endorse negative evaluations of outgroup members (Schimel et al., 1999) and to endorse harsh punishments for those who violate cultural values (Greenberg et al., 1990).

More relevant to the current discussion is the second terror management mechanism, which ascribes great importance to self-esteem. Terror management theory proposes that the principal function of self-esteem is to serve as a buffer against death-related anxiety. The idea

is that people can reduce or ward off their fear of death by focusing on thoughts and experiences that help them feel good about themselves. This idea was supported in a series of experiments in which people were shown graphic scenes of death aimed at building anxiety about their own mortality (Greenberg et al., 1992). Prior to viewing these scenes, half of the participants were given positive feedback to temporarily increase their self-esteem. Interestingly, the group that got the "self-esteem boost" showed less anxiety and less defensiveness in viewing the gruesome scenes than did a control group that didn't receive the prior positive feedback.

Thus, terror management theory has generated some interesting hypotheses about the role that self-esteem plays in modulating reactions to rumors and media discussion about the possibility of terrorist attacks. According to TMT, when the specter of future attacks is elevated, people should increase their self-esteem striving. In other words, they will be more likely than usual to engage in behaviors and patterns of thinking that are likely to bolster their self-esteem. TMT also posits that people who are relatively high in self-esteem should be somewhat less vulnerable to the threat of terrorism. That is, they should be less easily rattled and shaken by media speculation about possible terrorist strikes.

Although TMT offers an intriguing perspective on the function of self-esteem, there are alternative explanations as well (Leary, 2004). That said, there is quite a bit of empirical support for the specific idea that high self-esteem counteracts anxiety (Baumeister et al., 2003). This anxiety-buffering function of high self-esteem seems particularly relevant in these troubled times.

---

have the lowest self-esteem (Harter, 2003). For older children and adolescents, approval from parents and approval from classmates are the two strongest predictors of high self-esteem; by college age, peers have much more impact on self-esteem than parents do (Harter, 1993).

Children (and adults) also make their own judgments about themselves. Perceiving oneself as success-

ful in domains that are highly valued is important in these self-evaluations (Harter, 2003; MacDonald, Saltzman, & Leary, 2003). For instance, if Maria values success in the academic and social areas and sees herself as competent in these arenas, she will have higher self-esteem than Heather, who also values these domains but rates herself low on one or both of them. An important basis for self-judgments is how well one "stacks

Significant others play a key role in shaping self-esteem.

up" against a selected reference group (recall social comparison theory). A classic study reported that pre-adolescents' academic (but not global) self-esteem was affected by the quality of competition they faced in school (Marsh & Parker, 1984). In this study, children from schools in higher socioeconomic class areas with "high-quality" competition (high-ability reference group) were compared to children of similar ability from schools in lower-class areas with "low-quality" competition (low-ability reference group). Surprisingly, the children in the low-quality schools tended to display greater academic self-esteem than children of similar academic ability enrolled in the high-quality schools. This finding that academic self-esteem is boosted by being a "big fish in a small pond" has found widespread support, even in many other countries (Marsh & Hau, 2003). Thus, it seems that individuals compare themselves to others in their specific reference group (other students in their school), not to a general reference group (other students in the country). The fact that individuals with similar talents may vary in self-esteem depending on their reference group demonstrates the importance of social comparison in the development of self-esteem.

Ethnicity, Gender, and Self-Esteem

Because prejudice and discrimination are still pervasive in the United States, people commonly assume that members of minority groups have lower self-esteem than members of the majority group. Research both supports and contradicts this assumption. On the one hand, the self-esteem of Asians, Hispanics, and American Indians is lower than that of whites, although the differences are small (Twenge & Crocker, 2002). On the other, the self-esteem of blacks is higher than that of whites (Gray-Little & Hafdahl, 2000; Twenge & Crocker, 2002). Adding gender to the mix complicates the picture even more. White males have higher self-esteem than white females, but minority males have lower self-esteem than minority females (Twenge & Crocker, 2002).

Thus, ethnicity and gender interact in complex ways in self-esteem. The fact of cultural differences in the self-concept may provide some insight here. Recall our earlier discussion of individualism and collectivism. Note that differences on this dimension are found not only between different nations but also within a given country. And here's another fact: High individualism is associated with high self-esteem. What's interesting here is that the pattern of ethnic differences in individualism closely mirrors the pattern of ethnic differences in self-esteem (Twenge & Crocker, 2002). That is, blacks score higher than whites, whites do not differ significantly from Hispanics, and Hispanics score higher than Asian Americans. Thus, the ethnic differences in self-esteem are likely rooted in how the different groups view themselves, based on cultural messages.

Although females are not a minority group, they resemble ethnic minorities in that they tend to have lower status and less power than males. The popular press abounds with reports of low self-esteem in adolescent girls and women (Orenstein, 1994; Pipher, 1994). Is there any empirical basis for this assertion? In a massive undertaking, researchers examined gender differences in self-esteem by statistically summarizing the results of several hundred studies (with respondents ranging from 7 to 60 years of age) as well as the data from three nationally representative surveys of adolescents and young adults (Kling et al., 1999). In both analyses, males scored higher on self-esteem than females, although the differences were small for the most part. The largest difference occurred in the 15- to 18-year-old age group. Also, white girls have lower self-esteem than minority girls do. The fact that white girls have more negative body images than minority girls may be a factor in their lower self-esteem (Twenge & Crocker, 2002).

Basic Principles of Self-Perception

- *Distinguish between automatic and controlled processing.*
- *Define self-attributions, and identify the key dimensions of attributions.*
- *Explain how optimistic and pessimistic explanatory styles are related to adjustment.*
- *Discuss four motives that guide self-understanding.*
- *Describe four strategies people use to maintain positive feelings about the self.*

Now that you're familiar with some of the major aspects of the self, let's consider how people construct and maintain a coherent and positive view of the self.

Cognitive Processes

What do I want for breakfast? What shall I wear today? You're barely awake and you're already making decisions. People are faced with an inordinate number of decisions on a daily basis. How do they keep from being overwhelmed? The key lies in how people process information. According to Shelley Taylor (1981a), people are "cognitive misers." In this model, cognitive resources (attention, memory, and so forth) are limited, so the mind works to "hoard" them by taking cognitive short-cuts. For example, you probably have the same morning routine—shower, drink coffee, read the paper as you eat breakfast, check e-mail, and so forth. Because you do these things without a lot of thought, you can conserve your attentional, decision-making, and memory capacities for important cognitive tasks. This example illustrates the default mode of handling information: *automatic processing*. On the other hand, when important decisions arise or when you're trying to understand why you didn't get that job you wanted, you spend those precious cognitive resources. This mode is termed *controlled processing*. Ellen Langer (1989) describes these two states as *mindlessness* and *mindfulness*, respectively. In addition to guiding the processing of self-relevant information, these two modes of information processing operate in a variety of social situations, as you'll see in subsequent chapters.

Another way that cognitive resources are protected is through *selective attention*, with high priority given to information pertaining to the self (Bargh, 1997). An example of this tendency is a phenomenon known as the "cocktail party effect"—the ability to pick out the mention of your name in a roomful of chattering people (Moray, 1959; Wood & Cowan, 1995).

Another principle of self-cognition is that people strive to understand themselves. One way they do so, as you saw in our discussion of social comparison theory, is to compare themselves with others (Wood & Wilson, 2003). Yet another is to engage in attributional thinking, our next topic.

Self-Attributions

Let's say that you win a critical match for your school's tennis team. To what do you attribute your success? Is your new practice schedule starting to pay off? Did you have the home court advantage? Perhaps your opponent was playing with a minor injury? This example from everyday life illustrates the nature of the self-attribution process. *Self-attributions* are inferences that people draw about the causes of their own behavior. People routinely make attributions to make sense out of their experiences. These attributions involve inferences that ultimately represent guesswork on each person's part.

Fritz Heider (1958) was the first to assert that people tend to locate the cause of a behavior either within a person, attributing it to personal factors, or outside of a person, attributing it to environmental factors. He thus established one of the crucial dimensions along which attributions are made: internal versus external. The other two dimensions are stable/unstable and controllable/uncontrollable.

Internal or external. Elaborating on Heider's insight, various theorists have agreed that explanations of behavior and events can be categorized as internal or external attributions (Jones & Davis, 1965; Kelley, 1967; Weiner, 1974). *Internal attributions* ascribe the causes of behavior to personal dispositions, traits, abilities, and feelings. *External attributions* ascribe the causes of behavior to situational demands and environmental constraints. For example, if you credit your poor statistics grade to your failure to prepare adequately for the test or to getting overly anxious during the test, you are making internal attributions.

Whether one's self-attributions are internal or external can have a tremendous impact on one's personal adjustment. As you'll see in Chapter 8, lonely people tend to attribute the cause of their loneliness to internal, stable causes ("I'm unlovable"). Similarly, studies suggest that people who ascribe their setbacks to internal, personal causes while discounting external, situational explanations may be more prone to depression than people who display opposite tendencies (Riso et al., 2003).

Stable or unstable. A second dimension people use in making causal attributions is the stability of the causes underlying behavior (Weiner, 1986, 1994). A stable cause is one that is more or less permanent and unlikely to change over time. A sense of humor and intelligence are *stable internal* causes of behavior. *Stable external* causes of behavior include such things as laws and rules (speed limits, no smoking areas). Unstable causes of behavior are variable or subject to change. *Unstable internal* causes of behavior include such things as mood (good or bad) and motivation (strong or weak). *Unstable external* causes could be the weather and the presence or absence of other people. According to Bernard Weiner (1986, 1994), the stable-unstable dimension in attribution cuts across the internal-external dimension, creating four types of attributions for success and failure, as shown in Figure 5.10.

Let's apply Weiner's model to a concrete event. Imagine that you are contemplating why you just landed the job you wanted. You might credit your good fortune to internal factors that are stable (excellent ability) or unstable (hard work on your eye-catching résumé). Or you might attribute the outcome to external factors that are stable (lack of top-flight competition) or unstable (luck). If you didn't get the job, your explanations would fall in the same four categories: internal-stable (lack of ability), internal-unstable (inadequate effort on your résumé), external-stable (too much competition in your field), and external-unstable (bad luck).

Controllable or uncontrollable. A third dimension in the attribution process acknowledges the fact that sometimes events are under one's control and sometimes they are not (Weiner, 1986, 1994). For example, the amount of effort you expend on a task is typically perceived as something under your control, whereas an aptitude for music is viewed as something you are born with (beyond your control). Controllability can vary with each of the other two factors.

These three dimensions appear to be the central ones in the attribution process. Research has documented that self-attributions can influence future expectations (success or failure) and emotions (pride, hopelessness, guilt), and that these expectations and emotions combine to influence subsequent performance (Weiner, 1986, 1994). Thus, self-attributions play a key role in one's feelings, motivational state, and behavior.

Explanatory Style

Julio and Josh are freshmen who have just struck out trying to get their first college dates. After this disappointment, they reflect on the possible reasons for it. Julio speculates that his approach was too subtle. Look-

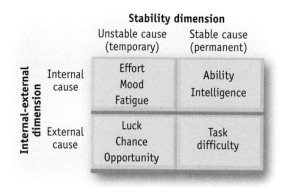

● FIGURE 5.10

Key dimensions of attributional thinking. Weiner's model assumes that people's explanations for success and failure emphasize internal versus external causes and stable versus unstable causes. For example, if you attribute an outcome to great effort or to lack of effort, you are citing causes that lie within the person. Since effort can vary over time, the causal factors at work are unstable. Other examples of causal factors that fit into each of the four cells in Weiner's model are shown in the diagram.

From Weiner, B., Frieze, I., Kukla, A., Reed, L.. & Rosenbaum, R. M. (1972). Perceiving the causes of success and failure. In E. E. Jones, D. E. Kanuouse, H. H. Kelly, R. E. Nisbett, S. Valins, & B. Weiner (Eds.), *Perceiving causes of behavior.* Morristown, NJ: General Learning Press. Reprinted by permission of the author.

ing back, he realizes that he wasn't very direct because he was nervous about asking the woman out. When she didn't reply, he didn't follow up for fear that she didn't really want to go out with him. On further reflection, he reasons that she probably didn't respond because she wasn't sure of his intentions. He vows to be more direct the next time. Josh, on the other hand, mopes, "I'll never have a relationship. I'm a total loser." On the basis of these comments, who do you think is likely to get a date in the future? If you guessed Julio, you are probably correct. Let's see why.

Explanatory style refers to the tendency to use similar causal attributions for a wide variety of events in one's life. According to Martin Seligman (1991), people tend to exhibit, to varying degrees, an *optimistic explanatory style* or a *pessimistic explanatory style* (see Figure 5.11 on the next page). The person with an optimistic explanatory style usually attributes setbacks to external, unstable, and specific factors. A person who failed to get a desired job, for example, might attribute this misfortune to factors in the interview situation ("The room was really hot," "The questions were slanted") rather than to personal shortcomings. This style can help people discount their setbacks and thus maintain a favorable self-image. It also helps people bounce back from failure. One study found that optimistic students had more confidence and performed better than pessimistic students after a sports failure (Martin-Krumm et al., 2003).

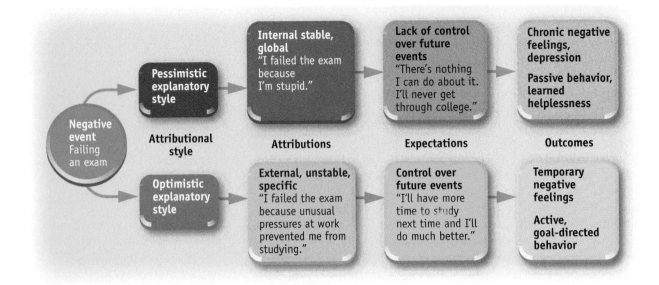

The effects of attributional style on expectations, emotions, and behavior. The pessimistic explanatory style is seen in the top set of boxes. This attributional style, which attributes setbacks to internal, stable, and global causes, tends to result in an expectation of lack of control over future events, depressed feelings, and passive behavior. A more adaptive, optimistic attributional style is shown in the bottom set of boxes.

In contrast, people with a pessimistic explanatory style tend to attribute their setbacks to internal, stable, and global (or pervasive) factors. These attributions make them feel bad about themselves and pessimistic about their ability to handle challenges in the future. Such a style can foster passive behavior and make people more vulnerable to learned helplessness and depression (Peterson, Maier, & Seligman, 1993). Luckily, cognitive-behavioral therapy appears to be successful in helping depressed individuals change their pessimistic explanatory style (Seligman et al., 1999). Thus, individuals can learn to stop always blaming themselves for negative outcomes (especially when they can't be avoided) and to take personal credit for positive outcomes.

Motives Guiding Self-Understanding

Whether people evaluate themselves by social comparisons, attributional thinking, or other means, they are highly motivated to pursue self-understanding. In seeking self-understanding, people are driven by four major motives: assessment, verification, improvement, and enhancement (Biernat & Billings, 2001; Sedikides & Strube, 1997).

Self-Assessment
The *self-assessment motive* is reflected in people's desire for truthful information about themselves (Trope,

1983, 1986). Individuals seek accurate feedback about many types of information—their personal qualities, abilities, physical features, and so forth. It's obvious why people look for accurate information. After all, it helps them set realistic goals and behave in appropriate ways (Oettingen & Gollwitzer, 2001). Still, the bald truth is not always welcome. Accordingly, people are also motivated by other concerns.

Self-Verification
The *self-verification motive* drives people toward information that matches what they already know about themselves, whether it is positive or negative. This tendency to strive for a consistent self-image ensures that individuals' self-concepts are relatively stable. Individuals maintain consistent self-perceptions in a number of subtle ways and are often unaware of doing so (Schlenker & Pontari, 2000). For example, people maintain consistency between their past and present behavior by erasing past memories that conflict with present ones. To illustrate, people who were once shy and who later became outgoing have been shown to recall memories about themselves that indicate that they perceive themselves as always having been outgoing (Ross & Conway, 1986). This inclination to revise the past in favor of the present may lie behind the oft-heard parental reproof, "When *I* was your age . . ." Here, parents conveniently erase memories of their childhood behavior—which was probably similar to that of their children—and, instead, compare their children's behavior to their

own *current* behavior (Ross, McFarland, & Fletcher, 1981).

Another way people maintain self-consistency is by seeking out feedback and situations that will confirm their existing self-perceptions and avoiding potentially disconfirming situations or feedback. According to William Swann's **self-verification theory, people prefer to receive feedback from others that is consistent with their own self-views.** Thus, those with positive self-concepts should prefer positive feedback from others and those with negative self-concepts should prefer negative feedback. Research usually finds this to be the case (Swann, Rentfrow, & Guinn, 2003). In one study, college men were divided into either a positive self-concept group or a negative self-concept group based on test scores. They were then asked to choose a partner for a subsequent 2- to 3-hour interaction. Participants were led to believe that one of the prospective partners held views of him that were consistent with his self-view and that the other held views of him that were inconsistent with his self-view. As predicted, subjects with positive self-views preferred partners who viewed them positively, whereas those with negative self-views chose partners who viewed them negatively (Swann, Stein-Seroussi, & Geisler, 1992).

Self-Improvement

What is your current self-improvement project? To study more? To get more exercise? When people seek to better themselves, the self-improvement motive comes into play. In trying to improve, individuals typically look to successful others for inspiration (Collins, 1996). Advertisers of personal care products (tooth whiteners, exercise machines, and so forth) tap into this motive by showing before-and-after photographs of individuals who have used the products.

Self-Enhancement

Finally, people are motivated by **self-enhancement,** or **the tendency to maintain positive feelings about the self.** One example of self-enhancement is the tendency to hold flattering views of one's personal qualities, a tendency termed the *better-than-average effect* (Alicke, 1985; Buckingham & Alicke, 2002). You've already seen an example of this effect in our earlier report that 70 percent of students who took the SAT rated themselves above average in leadership ability—a mathematical impossibility. Students can take perverse pleasure in knowing that faculty also succumb to this bias: 94 percent of them regard their teaching as above average (Cross, 1977)!

A second example of self-enhancement concerns *illusions of control* (Langer, 1975), in which people overestimate their degree of control over outcomes. Thus, individuals who pick their own "lucky" numbers

on lottery tickets falsely believe that they can influence the outcome of such random events. A third form of self-enhancement is the tendency to have *unrealistic optimism about future events* (Weinstein, 1980). For example, most people believe that they will have a brighter future and experience fewer negative events than others (Helweg-Larsen & Shepperd, 2001).

While self-enhancement is quite common, it is not universal. Individuals who have low self-esteem or who are depressed are less likely to use self-enhancement than others (Taylor & Brown, 1988, 1994). Culture also plays a role. A number of studies have found that self-enhancement is more pronounced in Western than in Eastern cultures (Kanagawa, Cross, & Markus, 2001). Still, self-enhancement motives are not entirely absent in collectivist cultures. It seems that American subjects self-enhance on individualistic attributes and Japanese participants on collectivist attributes (Sedikides, Gaertner, & Toguchi, 2003). In other words, people tend to self-enhance on the characteristics that their culture designates as important. Thus, people may self-enhance on different (culturally valued) attributes, but self-enhancement appears to be a universal motive.

The four self-motives of assessment, verification, improvement, and enhancement permit flexibility in making self-evaluations. Although you would think that accurate information would be the most useful to people, that doesn't seem to be the case. In a series of studies that pitted self-assessment, self-verification, and self-enhancement against each other, the self-enhancement motive was found to be the strongest, the self-verification motive a distant second, and the self-assessment motive an even more distant third (Sedikides, 1993).

Methods of Self-Enhancement

The powerful self-enhancement motive drives individuals to seek positive (and reject negative) information about themselves. Let's examine four cognitive strategies people commonly use.

Downward Comparisons

We've already mentioned that people compare themselves to others as a means of learning more about themselves (social comparison), whether or not they expect to receive esteem-threatening information. Once threat enters the picture, people often change their strategy and choose to compare themselves with someone who is worse off than they are (Wood, 1989). **This defensive tendency to compare oneself with someone whose troubles are more serious than one's own is termed** *downward social comparison.* Why do people switch strategies under threat? It seems that downward social comparisons are associated with increases in both mood and self-esteem (Reis, Gerrard, & Gibbons, 1993).

A dramatic example of downward comparison can be found in the aftermath of the terrorist attacks on the World Trade Center and the Pentagon in September 2001: Compared to the devastating losses suffered by the victims and families, most people's problems suddenly appeared insignificant. There are also more common examples. If you have ever been in a serious car accident in which your car was "totaled," you probably reassured yourself by reflecting on the fact that at least no one was seriously injured. Similarly, people with chronic illnesses may compare themselves with those who have life-threatening diseases. On television talk and "reality" shows (*Dr. Phil*, for example), people with assorted life tragedies provide numerous opportunities for downward social comparison. This aspect no doubt contributes to their popularity.

Self-Serving Bias

Suppose that you and three other individuals apply for a part-time job in the parks and recreation department and you are selected for the position. How do you explain your success? Chances are, you tell yourself that you were hired because you were the most qualified for the job. But how do the other three people interpret their negative outcome? Do they tell themselves that you got the job because you were the most able? Unlikely! Instead, they probably attribute their loss to "bad luck" or to not having had time to prepare for the interview. These different explanations for success and failure reflect the *self-serving bias,* or the tendency to attribute one's successes to personal factors and one's failures to situational factors (Miller and Ross, 1975).

Research indicates that people are more likely to take credit for their successes than they are to disavow their failures (Campbell & Sedikides, 1999). To illustrate: In an experiment, two strangers jointly took a test. They then received bogus success or failure feedback about their test performance and were asked to assign responsibility for the test results. Successful participants claimed credit, but those who failed blamed their partners (Campbell et al., 2000). Still, people don't always rush to take credit. In another experiment in the just-cited study, participants were actual friends. In this case, participants shared responsibility for both successful and unsuccessful outcomes. Thus, friendship places limits on the self-serving bias.

Although the self-serving bias has been documented in a variety of cultures (Fletcher & Ward 1988), it seems to be particularly prevalent in individualistic, Western societies, where the emphasis on competition and high self-esteem motivates people to try to impress others, as well as themselves. In contrast, Japanese subjects exhibit a *self-effacing bias* in explaining successes (Akimoto & Sanbonmatsu, 1999; Markus & Kitayama, 1991), as they tend to attribute their successes to the help they receive from others or to the ease of the task, while downplaying the importance of their ability. When they fail, Japanese subjects tend to be more self-critical than subjects from individualistic cultures (Heine & Renshaw, 2002). They are more likely to accept responsibility for their failures and to use their setbacks as an impetus for self-improvement (Heine et al., 2001). Studies have also failed to find the usual self-serving bias in Nepalese and Chinese samples (Lee & Seligman, 1997; Smith & Bond, 1994).

Basking in Reflected Glory

When your favorite sports team won the national championship last year, did you make a point of wearing the team cap? And when Ben, your best friend, won that special award, do you remember how often you told others the good news about him? If you played a role in someone's success, it's understandable that you would want to share in the recognition; however, peo-

People frequently claim association with others who are successful (bask in reflected glory) to maintain positive feelings about the self.

ple often want to share recognition even when they are on the sidelines of an outstanding achievement. *Basking in reflected glory* **is the tendency to enhance one's image by publicly announcing one's association with those who are successful.**

Robert Cialdini and his colleagues (1976) studied this phenomenon on college campuses with nationally ranked football teams. They predicted that, when asked how their team had fared in a recent football game, students would be more likely to say, "We won" (in other words, to bask in reflected glory, or to "BIRG"—pronounced with a soft "g") when the home team had been successful than to respond "We lost" when it had been defeated. As predicted, students were more likely to BIRG when their team won than when it lost. Also, subjects who believed that they had just failed a bogus test were more likely to use the words "we won" than those who believed they had performed well.

A related self-enhancement strategy is "CORFing," or *cutting off reflected failure.* Because self-esteem is partly tied to an individual's associations with others, people often protect their self-esteem by distancing themselves from those who are unsuccessful (Cialdini et al., 1976; Boen, Vanbeselaere, & Feys, 2002). Thus, if your cousin is arrested for drunk driving, you may tell others that you don't really know him very well.

Self-Handicapping

When people fail at an important task, they need to save face. In such instances, individuals can usually come up with a face-saving excuse ("I had a terrible stomachache"). Curiously, some people actually behave in a way that sets them up to fail so that they have a ready-made excuse for failure, should it occur. *Self-handicapping* **is the tendency to sabotage one's performance to provide an excuse for possible failure.** For example, when a big test is looming, they put off studying until the last minute or go out drinking the night before the test. If, as is likely, they don't do well

on the exam, they explain their poor performance by saying they didn't prepare. (After all, wouldn't you rather have others believe that your poor performance is due to inadequate preparation rather than lack of ability?) People use a variety of tactics for handicapping their performance: alcohol, drugs, procrastination, a bad mood, a distracting stimulus, anxiety, depression, and being overcommitted (Baumeister, 1998). A related tactic is *sandbagging,* in which people attempt to reduce performance expectations by playing down their abilities and predicting they'll fail (Gibson & Sachau, 2000).

Individuals differ in their reasons for self-handicapping. People with low self-esteem more often use it to maintain a positive impression (or to avoid failing), whereas those with high self-esteem are more likely to use it to enhance their image (Tice, 1991). That is, if they happen to do well, they can claim that they are especially capable because they performed so well with minimal preparation.

Self-handicapping seems like a "win-win" strategy: If you fail, you have a face-saving excuse ready, and if you happen to succeed, you can claim that you are unusually gifted! However, it probably has not escaped your attention that self-handicapping is highly risky. By giving yourself an attributional "out" in case of failure, your self-defeating behavior will likely result in poor performance (Zuckerman, Kieffer, & Knee, 1998). Moreover, while self-handicapping may save you from negative self-attributions about your ability, it does not prevent others from making different negative attributions about you. For example, people believe that individuals are less competent when they self-handicap than when they don't (Rhodewalt et al., 1995). Also, others may perceive you as lazy, inclined to drink too much, or highly anxious, depending on the means you use to self-handicap. Consequently, this self-enhancement tactic has serious drawbacks.

Self-Regulation

LEARNING OBJECTIVES

- Define self-regulation, and explain the ego-depletion model of self-regulation.
- Explain why self-efficacy is important to psychological adjustment.
- Describe how individuals develop self-efficacy.
- Describe the three categories of self-defeating behavior.

"Should I have that hot fudge sundae or not?" "I guess I'd better get started on that English paper." People are constantly trying to resist impulses and make themselves do things they don't want to do. They also determine the various goals they want to pursue and how to reach them. **This work of directing and controlling one's behavior is termed *self-regulation.*** Clearly, the ability to manage and direct what you think, how you feel, and how you behave is tied to your success at work, your relationships, and your mental and physical health (Baumeister & Vohs, 2003). Being able to forgo immediate gratification (studying instead of partying) and focus one's behavior toward important, longer-range goals (graduating and getting a good job) is of paramount importance if one is to be successful in life.

It's possible that people have a limited amount of self-control resources. So if you tax these resources resisting temptation in a given situation, you may have a hard time resisting the next immediate temptation or persisting at a new task. At least that's the idea behind the *ego-depletion model of self-regulation* (Baumeister et al., 1998). To investigate this hypothesis, researchers asked college students to participate in a study of taste perception (the study was actually on self-control) (Baumeister et al., 1998). Some participants were asked to eat two or three radishes in 5 minutes but not to touch the chocolate candy and chocolate chip cookies that were nearby. Others were asked to eat some candy or some cookies but were told not to eat any of the nearby radishes. A control group didn't participate in this part of the study. Then all subjects were asked to solve what were, unbeknownst-to-them, unsolvable puzzles while they supposedly waited for another part of the study. Researchers measured the subjects' self-control by the amount of time they persisted at the puzzles and the number of attempts they made. According to the ego-depletion model, the radish-eaters would use more self-control resources (resisting the chocolate) than would the chocolate-eaters (resisting the radishes) or the subjects in the no-food control group. Thus, this group should have the fewest self-control resources to use for persisting at a difficult task. As you can see in Figure 5.12, the radish-eaters gave up sooner and made fewer attempts on the puzzles than the chocolate-eaters or the control group. One of the rea-

sons people rely so often on habit and automatic processing is to conserve these important self-control resources (Baumeister, Muraven, & Tice, 2000).

Self-regulation seems to develop early and remain relatively stable. One study reported that 4-year-olds who were better at delaying gratification did better both in terms of academic performance and social competence some ten years later (Mischel, Shoda, & Peake, 1988; Shoda, Mischel, & Peake, 1990). In this section, we examine self-efficacy, a key aspect of self-regulation, as well as self-defeating behavior, a case of self-control failure.

Self-Efficacy

As explained in Chapter 2, *self-efficacy* **refers to people's conviction that they can achieve specific goals.** According to Albert Bandura (1997, 2000), efficacy beliefs vary according to the person's skills. You may have high

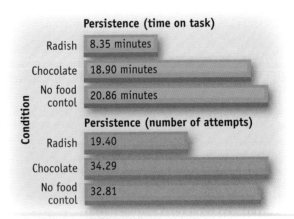

● FIGURE 5.12

Persistence on unsolvable puzzles. Participants who were instructed to eat radishes and not to eat chocolate chip cookies or chocolate candy used more self-control resources than participants who were instructed to eat the chocolate and not to touch the radishes or participants in the no-food control group. Because the radish-eaters had relatively few self-control resources to help them persist at a difficult task (unsolvable puzzles), they persisted for the shortest time and made the fewest attempts to solve the puzzles compared to the other two groups. (Adapted from Baumeister et al., 1998)

self-efficacy when it comes to making friends but low self-efficacy when it comes to speaking in front of a group. However, simply having a skill doesn't guarantee that you will be able to put it into practice. Like *The Little Engine that Could,* you must also *believe* that you are capable of doing so ("I *think* I can, I *think* I can . . ."). In other words, self-efficacy is concerned not with the skills you have, but with your *beliefs about what you can do* with these skills.

Albert Bandura

Courtesy, Albert Bandura

Correlates of Self-Efficacy

A number of studies have shown that self-efficacy affects individuals' commitments to goals, their performance on tasks, and their persistence toward goals in the face of obstacles (Maddux & Gosselin, 2003). In addition, people with high self-efficacy anticipate success in future outcomes and are able to tune out negative thoughts that can lead to failure. Self-efficacy is related to academic success (Schunk, 2003), career choice (Betz & Klein, 1996), and job performance (Stajkovic & Luthans, 1998).

Because of the importance of self-efficacy in psychological adjustment, it is worth keeping in mind that it is learned and can be changed. Research shows that increasing self-efficacy is an effective way to improve health (losing weight, stopping smoking) (Maddux & Gosselin, 2003) and to treat a variety of psychological problems, including test anxiety (Smith, 1989), phobias (Williams, 1995), fear of sexual assault (Ozer & Bandura, 1990), eating disorders (Goodrick et al., 1999),

and substance abuse (DiClemente, Fairhurst, & Piotrowski, 1995).

Developing Self-Efficacy

Self-efficacy is obviously a valuable quality. How does one acquire it? Bandura (1997, 2000) identifies four sources of self-efficacy: mastery experiences, vicarious experiences, persuasion/encouragement, and interpretation of emotional arousal.

Mastery experiences. The most effective path to self-efficacy is through mastering new skills. Sometimes new skills come easily—learning how to use the copy machine in the library, for instance. Some things are harder to master, such as learning how to use a spreadsheet program or how to play the piano. In acquiring more difficult skills, people usually make mistakes. How they handle these failure experiences is the key to learning self-efficacy. If you give up when you make mistakes, your failure instills self-doubts or low self-efficacy. On the other hand, if you persist through failure experiences to eventual success, you learn the lesson of self-efficacy: I *can* do it! A practical implication for parents, teachers, and coaches is that they should set high, but attainable, goals for children and encourage them to learn from their mistakes and to persevere until they succeed. This approach provides children with the mastery experiences they need to build self-efficacy and approach future challenges with confidence. Well-intentioned parents, teachers, and supervisors unwittingly deprive individuals of opportunities to develop self-efficacy when they do others' work or regularly allow others to opt out of obligations with no consequences.

Vicarious experiences. Another way to improve self-efficacy is by watching others perform a skill you want

© Mary Kate Denny/PhotoEdit

Ironically, difficulties and failures can ultimately contribute to the development of a strong sense of self-efficacy. Self-efficacy tends to improve when youngsters learn to persist through difficulties and overcome failures.

to learn. It's important that you choose a model who is competent at the task, and it helps if the model is similar to you (in age, gender, and ethnicity). For example, if you're shy about speaking up for yourself, observing someone who is good at doing so can help you develop the confidence to do it yourself. Picking successful role models is important—watching unsuccessful ones can undermine self-efficacy.

Persuasion and encouragement. Although it is less effective than the first two approaches, a third way to develop self-efficacy is through the encouragement of others. For example, if you're having a hard time asking someone for a date, a friend's encouragement might give you just the push you need. Of course, persuasion doesn't always work. And, unless encouragement is accompanied by specific and concrete suggestions, this tactic is unlikely to be successful.

Interpretation of emotional arousal. The physiological responses that accompany feelings and one's interpretations of these responses are another source of self-efficacy. Let's say you're sitting in class waiting for your professor to distribute an exam. You notice that your palms are moist and your heart is pounding. If you attribute these behaviors to fear, you can temporarily dampen your self-efficacy, thus decreasing your chances of doing well. Alternatively, if you attribute your sweaty palms and racing heart to the arousal everyone needs to perform well, you may be able to boost your self-efficacy and increase your chances of doing well. Of course, self-regulation doesn't always succeed. That's the case in self-defeating behavior, our next topic.

Self-Defeating Behavior

It's adaptable for people to act in their own self-interest, and typically they do. But sometimes people knowingly do things that are bad for them—such as smoking, having unprotected sex, and completing important assignments at the last minute. **Self-defeating behaviors are seemingly intentional actions that thwart a person's self-interest.** According to Roy Baumeister (1997; Baumeister & Scher, 1988), there are three categories of intentional self-defeating behaviors: deliberate self-destruction, tradeoffs, and counterproductive strategies. The key difference among these three behaviors lies in how intentional they are. As you can see in Figure 5.13, attempts at deliberate self-destruction involve the most intent; counterproductive strategies are the least intentional, and tradeoffs fall in between.

In *deliberate self-destruction,* people want to harm themselves and they choose courses of action that will forseeably lead to that result. Although this type of behavior may occur in individuals with psychological disorders, deliberate self-destruction appears to be infrequent in normal populations.

In *tradeoffs,* people foresee the possibility of harming themselves but accept it as a necessary accompaniment to achieving a desirable goal. Overeating, smoking, and drinking to excess are examples that come readily to mind. Other examples include procrastinating (putting off tasks feels good in the short-run, but the struggle to meet looming deadlines results in poor performance and increased stress and illness), failing to follow prescribed health care advice (it's easier to slack off now, but doing so leads to future problems), shyness (avoiding social situations protects against anxiety but makes loneliness more likely), and self-handicapping (getting drunk before an exam explains poor performance but increases the chances of failure).

One factor that underlies most self-defeating tradeoffs is poor judgment. That is, people choose immediate benefits (pleasant sensations, escape from painful thoughts or feelings) over long-term costs (heart disease, lung cancer, few intimate relationships). To bolster their choices, they usually ignore or downplay the long-term risks of their behavior. Two other factors that underlie tradeoffs are emotional distress (anxiety) and high self-awareness. Because negative emotions are distressing, people want quick escape. Thus, they light a cigarette or have a drink to bring immediate relief, and they tune out the long-term negative consequences of their actions. In short, people engage in tradeoffs because they bring immediate, positive, and reliable outcomes, not because they want to kill themselves.

In *counterproductive strategies,* a person pursues a desirable outcome but misguidedly uses an approach that is bound to fail. Of course, you can't always know in advance if a strategy will pay off. Thus, people must *habitually* use this strategy for it to qualify as self-defeating. For example, some people tend to persist in

Three Categories of Self-Defeating Behavior

Type of self-defeating behavior	Harm foreseen?	Harm desired?
Deliberate self-destruction	Yes	Yes
Tradeoffs	Yes	No
Counterproductive strategies	No	No

● **FIGURE 5.13**

Three categories of self-defeating behavior. Roy Baumeister and Steven Scher (1988) distinguished three categories of self-defeating behaviors, based on how intentional the behaviors are. Intentionality is determined by two factors: an individual's awareness that a behavior could bring possible harm and an individual's desire to harm himself or herself. Deliberate self-destruction is the most intentional, followed by tradeoffs, then counterproductive strategies. (Based on Baumeister & Scher, 1988)

Self-defeating behaviors come in many forms with many underlying motivations. Overeating is a matter of tradeoffs. People realize that excessive eating may be harmful in the long run, but it is enjoyable at the time.

unproductive endeavors, such as pursuing an unreachable career goal or an unrequited love. Such behavior costs valuable time, generates painful emotions, and blocks the discovery of productive approaches. The key cause of counterproductive behavior seems to be errors in judgment, such as misjudging one's abilities or the actions required to produce a desired result. People persist in these behaviors because they believe they'll be successful, not because they are intent on self-defeat.

To conclude, although most people engage in self-defeating behavior at some time, there is little evidence that they deliberately try to harm themselves or to fail at a task. Instead, self-defeating behavior appears to be the result of people's distorted judgments or strong desires to escape from immediate, painful feelings. If you're plagued by self-defeating behavior, the Recommended Reading titled *Self-Defeating Behaviors* (Cudney & Hardy, 1991) provides additional insights and suggestions for dealing with this frustrating problem

Self-Presentation

LEARNING OBJECTIVES

- *Explain why and when individuals engage in impression management.*
- *Cite some strategies people use to make positive impressions on others.*
- *Describe how high self-monitors are different from low self-monitors.*

Whereas your self-concept involves how you see yourself, your public self involves how you want others to see you. **A *public self* is an image presented to others in social interactions.** This presentation of a public self may sound deceitful, but it is perfectly normal, and everyone does it (Schlenker, 2003). Many self-presentations (ritual greetings, for example) take place automatically and without awareness. But when it really counts (job interviews, for example), people consciously strive to make the best possible impression.

Typically, individuals have a number of public selves that are tied to certain situations and certain people. For instance, you may have one public self for your parents and another for your peers. (Do you cover your tattoo when you go home?) You may have still others for your teachers, your boss, your co-workers, and so forth. Also, people differ in the degree of overlap or congruence among their various public selves (see Figure 5.14). Does it matter whether you perceive yourself to be essentially the same person in different situations? It seems so. People who see themselves as being similar across different social roles (with friends, at work, at school, with parents, with romantic partners) are better adjusted than those who perceive less integration in their self-views across these roles (Donahue et al., 1993; Lutz & Ross, 2003).

Impression Management

Interestingly, people think others notice and evaluate them more than is the actual case (Gilovich & Savitsky, 1999). This common tendency is aptly termed *the spotlight effect*. People also normally strive to make a positive impression on others to be liked, respected, hired, and so forth (Baumeister & Twenge, 2003). *Impression management refers to usually conscious efforts by people to influence how others think of them.* To see impression management in operation, let's look

at a study of behavior in simulated job interviews (von Baeyer, Sherk, & Zanna, 1981). In this study, female job applicants were led to believe that the man who would interview them held either traditional, chauvinistic views of women or just the opposite. The researchers found that applicants who expected a chauvinist presented themselves in a more traditionally feminine manner than subjects in the other condition. Their self-presentation efforts extended to both their appearance (they wore more makeup) and their communication style (they talked less and gave more traditional answers to a question about marriage and children). In a job interview, people are particularly attentive to making a good impression, but impression management also operates in everyday interactions, although

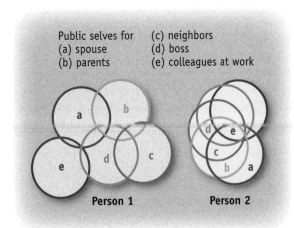

● **FIGURE 5.14**

Public selves and adjustment. Person 1 has very divergent public selves with relatively little overlap among them. Person 2, whose public selves are more congruent with each other, is likely to be better adjusted than Person 1.

Singer Christina Aguilera attracts press attention for her unusual self-presentation behavior.

individuals may be less aware of it (Schlenker, 2003). Let's look at some common impression management strategies.

Impression Management Strategies

One reason people engage in impression management is to claim a particular identity (Baumeister, 1998). Thus, you select a type of dress, hairstyle, and manner of speech to present a certain image of yourself. Tattoos and body piercings also create a specific image. A second motive for impression management is to gain liking and approval from others—by editing what you say about yourself and by using various nonverbal cues such as smiles, gestures, and eye contact. Because self-presentation is practiced so often, people usually do it automatically. At other times, however, impression management may be used intentionally—to get a job, a date, a promotion, and so forth. Some common self-presentation strategies include ingratiation, self-promotion, exemplification, intimidation, and supplication (Jones, 1990).

Ingratiation. Of all the self-presentation strategies, ingratiation is the most fundamental and most frequently used. **Ingratiation is behaving in ways to make oneself likable to others.** For example, *giving compliments* is effective, as long as you are sincere (people dislike insincerity and can often detect it). *Doing favors for others* is also a common tactic, as long as your gestures aren't so spectacular they leave others feeling indebted (Gordon, 1996). Other ingratiation tactics include *expressing liking for others* and *going along with others* (to get others to like you, it helps to do the things that they want to do).

Self-promotion. The motive behind self-promotion is earning respect. You do so by playing up your strong points so you will be perceived as competent. For instance, in a job interview, you might find ways to mention that you earned high honors at school and that you were president of the student body and a member of the soccer team. To keep from coming across as a braggart, you shouldn't go overboard with self-promotion. For this reason, false modesty often works well.

Exemplification. Because most people try to project an honest image, you have to demonstrate exemplary behavior to claim special credit for integrity or character. Danger-fraught occupations such as those in the military or law enforcement provide obvious opportunities to exemplify moral virtue. A less dramatic, but still effective, strategy is to behave consistently according to high ethical standards—as long as you don't come across as self-righteous. Also, your words and deeds need to match unless you want to be labeled a hypocrite.

Intimidation. This strategy sends the message, "Don't mess with me." Intimidation usually works only in nonvoluntary relationships—for instance, when it's

WEB LINK 5.4

Impression Management
This short article at TheFreeDictionary.com explains impression management and provides a number of links to other articles on related issues.

hard for workers to find another employer or for an economically dependent spouse to leave a relationship. Obvious intimidation tactics include threats and the withholding of valuable resources (salary increases, promotions, sex). A more subtle tactic is emotional intimidation—holding over a person's head the threat of an aggressive outburst if you don't get your way. The other self-presentation strategies work by creating a favorable impression; intimidation usually generates dislike. Nonetheless, it can work.

Supplication. This is usually the tactic of last resort. To get favors from others, individuals try to present themselves as weak and dependent—as in the song, "Ain't Too Proud to Beg." Students may plead or break into tears in an instructor's office in an attempt to get a grade changed. Because of the social norm to help those in need, supplication may work; however, unless the supplicator has something to offer the potential benefactor, it's not an effective strategy.

Individuals tailor their use of self-presentation strategies to match the situation. For instance, it's unlikely that you'd try intimidating your boss; you'd be more likely to ingratiate or promote yourself with her. As you can see in Figure 5.15 on the next page, all of these strategies carry risks. Thus, to make a good impression, you must use these strategies skillfully.

Perspectives on Impression Management

Curiously, almost all research on self-presentation has been conducted on first meetings between strangers, yet the vast majority of actual social interactions take place between people who already know each other. Noting the gap between reality and research, Dianne Tice and her colleagues (1995) investigated whether self-presentation varied in these two situations. They found that people strive to make positive impressions when they interact with strangers but shift toward modesty and neutral self-presentations when they are with friends. Why the difference? Because strangers don't know you, you want to give them positive information so they'll form a good impression of you. Besides, strangers have no way of knowing whether you are bending the truth. On the other hand, your friends already know your positive qualities. Thus, belaboring them is unnecessary and may make you seem immodest. Likewise, your friends know you well enough to know whether you are grandstanding, so you don't bother.

Strategic Self-Presentation Strategies

Presentation strategy	Impression sought	Emotion to be aroused in target	Negative impressions risked
Ingratiation	Likable	Affection	Boot-licker, conformist
Self-promotion	Competent	Respect	Conceited, defensive
Exemplification	Morally superior	Guilt	Hypocrite, sanctimonious
Intimidation	Dangerous	Fear	Blusterer, ineffectual
Supplication	Helpless	Obligation	Undeserving, lazy

● **FIGURE 5.15**

Strategic self-presentation strategies. Individuals rely on a variety of self-presentation strategies to present a certain image of themselves to others (Jones, 1990). To avoid the risks associated with the strategies, it's important to use the tactics skillfully.

Based on Jones, E. E. (1990). *Interpersonal perception.* New York: W. H. Freeman & Company, p. 198.

Sometimes the need to project a positive public image can lead to dangerous practices (Leary, Tchividjian, & Kraxberger, 1994). For instance, to avoid the embarrassment of buying condoms or talking with their sex partners, people will practice unprotected sex and heighten their risk of contracting AIDS. In pursuit of an attractive tan, people spend hours in the sun, thereby increasing their chances of getting skin cancer. To keep thin, many (especially women) use strong diet medications and develop full-blown eating disorders (see the Chapter 15 Application). To impress their peers, some adolescents take up drinking and smoking and even drug abuse. Finally, out of the desire to appear brave and daring, some people engage in reckless behavior that ends in accidents and death.

How good are people at discerning the results of their impression management attempts? As we noted earlier, individuals are much better judges of how people, in general, view them than they are of how specific persons evaluate them.

Self-Monitoring

According to Mark Snyder (1979, 1986), people vary in their awareness of how they are perceived by others. *Self-monitoring refers to the degree to which people attend to and control the impressions they make on others.* People who are high self-monitors seem to be very sensitive to their impact on others. Low

Courtesy, Mark Snyder

Mark Snyder

self-monitors, on the other hand, are less concerned about impression management and behave more spontaneously.

Compared to low self-monitors, high self-monitors want to make a favorable impression and try to tailor their actions accordingly; they are skilled at deciphering what others want to see. Because they control their emotions well and deliberately regulate nonverbal signals, they are talented at self-presentation (Gangestad & Snyder, 2000). In contrast, low self-monitors are more likely to express their true beliefs or, possibly, to try to convey the impression that they are sincere and genuine individuals.

As you might infer, these two personality types view themselves differently (Gangestad & Snyder, 2000). Low self-monitors see themselves as having strong principles and behaving in line with them, whereas high self-monitors perceive themselves as flexible and pragmatic. Because high self-monitors don't see a necessary connection between their private beliefs and their public actions, they aren't troubled by discrepancies between beliefs and behavior.

You may be wondering whether these groups differ on psychological adjustment. It seems that more adjustment problems are found among individuals who score either very high or very low on self-monitoring compared to those who score closer to the middle (Miller & Thayer, 1989). On a final note, we'll add that self-monitoring scores decline as people age—probably because individuals become more comfortable with themselves over time (Reifman, Klein, & Murphy, 1989). In the upcoming Application, we redirect our attention to the critical issue of self-esteem and outline seven steps for boosting it.

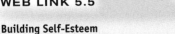

WEB LINK 5.5

Building Self-Esteem
The Counseling Center at the University of Florida offers tips on how to build self-esteem and self-confidence at this website.

Building Self-Esteem

LEARNING OBJECTIVES

- Explain when it is inadvisable to increase one's self-esteem and why this is so.
- List seven ways to build self-esteem.

Answer the following "yes" or "no."

___ **1.** I worry that others don't like me.
___ **2.** I have very little confidence in my abilities.
___ **3.** I often feel awkward in social situations and just don't know how to take charge.
___ **4.** I have difficulty accepting praise or flattery.
___ **5.** I have a hard time bouncing back from failure experiences.

If you answered "yes" to most of these questions, you may suffer from low self-esteem. As we noted earlier, people with low self-esteem are less happy and more prone to depression, become demoralized after failures, and are anxious in relationships. Too, people with high global self-esteem may have pockets of low self-esteem—for example, you may feel great about your "social self" but not so good about your "academic self." Thus, this Application can be useful to many people.

We have one caveat, however: It is possible for self-esteem to be too high—recall our earlier discussion about narcissism, ego threats, and violence. Better adjustment is associated with realistically high (and stable) self-esteem. Thus, our suggestions are directed to those whose self-esteem could use a legitimate boost, not to those whose self-esteem is inflated. The latter group can benefit from developing more realistic self-views.

As you saw in our discussion of self-efficacy, there is ample evidence that efforts at self-improvement can pay off by boosting self-esteem. Following are seven guidelines for building self-esteem. These suggestions are distilled from the advice of many experts, including Baumeister et al. (2003), Ellis (1989), McKay and Fanning (2000), Rogers (1977), and Zimbardo (1990).

1. Recognize That You Control Your Self-Image

The first thing you must do is recognize that *you* ultimately control how you see yourself. You *do* have the power to change your self-image. True, we have discussed at length how feedback from others influences your self-concept. Yes, social comparison theory suggests that people need such feedback and that it would

be unwise to ignore it completely. However, the final choice about whether to accept or reject such feedback rests with you. Your self-image resides in your mind and is a product of your thinking. Although others may influence your self-concept, you are the final authority.

2. Learn More About Yourself

People with low self-esteem don't seem to know themselves in as much detail as those with high self-esteem. Accordingly, to boost your self-esteem, you need to take stock of yourself. The Recommended Reading titled *Self-Esteem* (McKay & Fanning, 2000) contains a self-concept inventory that includes areas such as physical appearance, personality characteristics, relating to others, school and job performance, intellectual functioning, and sexuality. In taking inventory, you may discover that you're fuzzy about certain aspects of yourself. To get a clearer picture, pay careful attention to your thoughts, feelings, and behavior and utilize feedback from others.

3. Don't Let Others Set Your Goals

A common trap that many people fall into is letting others set the standards by which they evaluate themselves. Others are constantly telling you that you should do this or you ought to do that. Thus, you hear that you "should study computer science" or "ought to lose weight." Most of this advice is well intentioned and may contain good ideas. Still, it is important that you make your *own* decisions about what you will do and what you will believe in. For example, consider a business executive in his early forties who sees himself in a negative light because he has not climbed very high in the corporate hierarchy. The crucial question is: Did he ever *really* want to make that arduous climb? Perhaps he has gone through life thinking he should pursue that kind of success only because that standard was imposed on him by his family. Think about the source of and basis for your personal goals and standards. Do they really represent ideals that *you* value? Or are they beliefs that you have passively accepted from others without thinking?

4. Recognize Unrealistic Goals

Even if you truly value certain ideals and sincerely want to achieve certain goals, another question remains. Are your goals realistic? Many people demand too much of themselves. They want to always perform at their best, which is obviously impossible. For instance, you may have a burning desire to achieve national acclaim as an actress. However, the odds against such an achievement are enormous. It is important to recognize this reality so that you do not condemn yourself for failure. Some overly demanding people pervert the social comparison process by always comparing themselves against the *best* rather than against similar others. They assess their looks by comparing themselves with famous models, and they judge their finances by comparing themselves with the wealthiest people they know. Such comparisons are unrealistic and almost inevitably undermine self-esteem.

© Evan Agostini/Getty Images

© Pascal Le Segretain/Getty Images

If you like singing star Usher or actress Jennifer Aniston, that's fine, but they are not sensible benchmarks for evaluating your attractiveness or success. Some people distort the social comparison process.

5. Modify Negative Self-Talk

How you think about your life influences how you see yourself (and vice versa). People who are low in self-esteem tend to engage in various counterproductive modes of thinking. For example, when they succeed, they may attribute their success to good luck, and when they fail, they may blame themselves. Quite to the contrary, you should take credit for your successes and consider the possibility that your failures may not be your fault. As discussed in Chapter 4, Albert Ellis has pointed out that people often think irrationally and draw unwarranted negative conclusions about themselves. If someone breaks off a romantic relationship with you, do you think, "He doesn't love me. I must be a worthless, unlovable person?" The conclusion that you are a "worthless person" does *not* follow logically from the fact of the break-up. Such irrational thinking and negative self-talk breed poor self-esteem. Recognize the destructive potential of negative self-talk and bring it to a halt.

6. Emphasize Your Strengths

This advice may seem trite, but it has some merit. People with low self-esteem often derive little satisfaction from their accomplishments and virtues. They pay little heed to their good qualities while talking constantly about their defeats and frailties. The fact is that everyone has strengths and weaknesses. You should accept those personal shortcomings that you are powerless to change and work on those that are changeable, without becoming obsessed about it. At the same time, you should take stock of your strengths and learn to appreciate them.

7. Approach Others with a Positive Outlook

Some people with low self-esteem try to cut others down to their (subjective) size through constant criticism.

This faultfinding and negative approach does not go over well. Instead, it leads to tension, antagonism, and rejection. This rejection lowers self-esteem still further (see Figure 5.16). You can boost your esteem-building efforts by recognizing and reversing this self-defeating tendency. Cultivate the habit of maintaining a positive, supportive outlook when you approach people. Doing so will promote rewarding interactions and help you earn others' acceptance. There is probably nothing that enhances self-esteem more than acceptance and genuine affection from others.

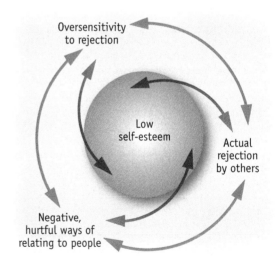

● FIGURE 5.16

The vicious circle of low self-esteem and rejection. A negative self-image can make expectations of rejection a self-fulfilling prophecy, because people with low self-esteem tend to approach others in negative, hurtful ways. Real or imagined rejections lower self-esteem still further, creating a vicious circle.

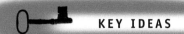

KEY IDEAS

Self-Concept

■ The self-concept is composed of a number of beliefs about what one is like, and it is not easily changed. It governs both present and future behavior. Discrepancies between one's ideal self and one's actual or ought self can produce negative emotions and lowered self-esteem. To cope with these negative states, individuals may bring their behavior in line with their ideal selves or blunt their awareness of self-discrepancies.

■ The self-concept is shaped by several factors, including individuals' observations of their own behavior, which often involve social comparisons with others. Self-observations tend to be biased in a positive direction. In addition, feedback from others shapes the self-concept; this information is also filtered to some extent. Cultural guidelines also affect the way people see themselves. Members of individualistic cultures usually have an independent view of the self, whereas those in collectivist cultures often have an interdependent view of the self.

Self-Esteem

■ Self-esteem is a person's global evaluation of his or her worth. Like the self-concept, it tends to be stable, but it can fluctuate in response to daily ups and downs.

■ Compared to those with high self-esteem, individuals with low self-esteem are less happy, are more likely to be depressed, are more prone to giving up after failure, and are less trusting of others.

■ Narcissistic individuals are prone to violence when their self-esteem is threatened. Self-esteem develops through interactions with significant others. Self-esteem, ethnicity, and gender interact in complex ways.

Basic Principles of Self-Perception

■ To avoid being overwhelmed with information, people use automatic processing; for important decisions, they use controlled processing. To explain the causes of their behavior, individuals make self-attributions. Generally, people attribute their behavior to internal or external factors and to stable or unstable factors. Controllability-uncontrollability is another key dimension of self-attributions. People tend to use either an optimistic explanatory style or a pessimistic explanatory style to explain various events that occur in their lives, and these attributional styles are related to psychological adjustment.

■ People are guided by four distinct motives in seeking to understand themselves. The self-assessment motive directs people toward accurate feedback about the self. The self-verification motive drives people toward information that matches their current self-views, even though doing so may involve some distortion of reality. The self-improvement motive underlies people's attempts to better themselves. The self-enhancement motive enables people to maintain positive views of themselves. Common self-enhancement strategies include downward comparisons, the self-serving bias, basking in reflected glory, and self-handicapping.

Self-Regulation

■ Self-regulation involves setting goals and directing behavior to meet those goals. A key aspect of self-regulation is self-efficacy—an individual's belief that he or she can achieve specific goals. Engaging in self-control can temporarily deplete what appears to be a limited underlying resource. Self-efficacy plays a key role in adjustment and can be learned through mastery experiences, vicarious experiences, persuasion, and positive interpretations of emotional arousal.

■ Sometimes normal people knowingly do things that are bad for them. These self-defeating actions fall into three categories: deliberate self-destruction, tradeoffs, and counterproductive strategies.

Self-Presentation

■ Public selves are the various images that individuals project to others. Generally, people try to manage the impressions they make by using a variety of strategies, including ingratiation, self-promotion, exemplification, intimidation, and supplication. Impression management can be dangerous to one's health. High self-monitors seem to be more concerned about making favorable impressions than low self-monitors are.

Application: Building Self-Esteem

■ The seven building blocks to higher self-esteem are (1) recognize that you control your self-image, (2) learn more about yourself, (3) don't let others set your goals, (4) recognize unrealistic goals, (5) modify negative self-talk, (6) emphasize your strengths, and (7) approach others with a positive outlook.

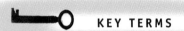

KEY TERMS

Basking in reflected glory
  p. 157
Collectivism   p. 145
Downward social comparison
  p. 155
Explanatory style   p. 153
External attributions   p. 152
Impression management
  p. 162
Individualism   p. 145
Ingratiation   p. 163
Internal attributions   p. 152
Narcissism   p. 148
Possible selves   p. 141
Public self   p. 161
Reference group   p. 143

Self-attributions   p. 152
Self-concept   p. 140
Self-defeating behaviors
  p. 160
Self-discrepancy   p. 141
Self-efficacy   p. 158
Self-enhancement   p. 155
Self-esteem   p. 146
Self-handicapping   p. 157
Self-monitoring   p. 164
Self-regulation   p. 158
Self-serving bias   p. 156
Self-verification theory
  p. 155
Social comparison theory
  p. 143

KEY PEOPLE

Albert Bandura   pp. 158–160
Roy Baumeister   p. 147

Hazel Markus   p. 140
Mark Snyder   p. 164

PRACTICE TEST

1. Which of the following statements about the self-concept is false?
   a. It is composed of one dominant belief about the self.
   b. It is composed of many self-beliefs.
   c. It is relatively stable over time.
   d. It influences present as well as future behavior.

2. Mismatches between one's actual and ought selves result in lower self-esteem and:
   a. dejection-related feelings.
   b. agitation-related feelings.
   c. feelings of self-enhancement.
   d. no particular feelings.

3. A person reared in a collectivist culture is likely to have a(n) _____ self-view, whereas a person reared in an individualistic culture is likely to have a(n) _____ self-view.
   a. self-discrepant; self-consistent
   b. self-consistent; self-discrepant
   c. independent; interdependent
   d. interdependent; independent

4. Low self-esteem is associated with:
   a. happiness.
   b. high trust of others.
   c. self-concept confusion.
   d. recovering after failure experiences.

5. Aggression in response to self-esteem threats is more likely to occur in people who are:
   a. high in self-esteem.
   b. low in self-esteem.
   c. narcissistic.
   d. self-defeating.

6. Which of the following is *not* a basic principle of self-perception?
   a. People are "cognitive spenders."
   b. People's explanatory style is related to adjustment.
   c. People most want to receive information that is consistent with their self-views.
   d. People most want to maintain positive feelings about the self.

7. Keisha is upset when a textbook is stolen, but she feels better after she hears that a classmate's book bag, including her cell phone, was stolen. This is an example of:
   a. the self-serving bias.
   b. basking in reflected glory.
   c. downward comparison.
   d. self-handicapping.

8. Which of the following statements about self-efficacy is true?
   a. It can be developed by persevering through failure until one achieves success.
   b. It is something that one is born with.
   c. It refers to a person's general self-confidence.
   d. It refers to conscious efforts to make a certain impression on others.

9. The self-presentation strategy of ingratiation involves trying to make others:
   a. respect you.
   b. fear you.
   c. feel sorry for you.
   d. like you.

10. Which of the following will *not* help you build higher self-esteem?
    a. Minimizing negative self-talk
    b. Comparing yourself with those who are the best in a given area
    c. Working to improve yourself
    d. Approaching others with positive expectations

Book Companion Website

Visit the Book Companion Website at **http://psychology.wadsworth.com/weiten_lloyd8e,** where you will find tutorial quizzes, flashcards, and weblinks for every chapter, a final exam, and more! You can also link to the Thomson Wadsworth Psychology Resource Center (accessible directly at **http://psychology.wadsworth.com**) for a range of psychology-related resources.

Personal Explorations Workbook

The following exercises in your *Personal Explorations Workbook* may enhance your self-understanding in relation to issues raised in this chapter. **Questionnaire 5.1:** Self-Monitoring Scale. **Personal Probe 5.1:** How Does Your Self-Concept Compare to Your Self Ideal? **Personal Probe 5.2:** Examining Your Self Evaluation. **Personal Probe 5.3:** Analyzing Your Emerging Self.

ANSWERS

1. a Page 140
2. b Pages 141–142
3. d Page 145
4. c Pages 146–147
5. c Pages 148–149
6. a Pages 152–155
7. c Pages 155–156
8. a Pages 158–159
9. d Page 163
10. b Pages 165–167

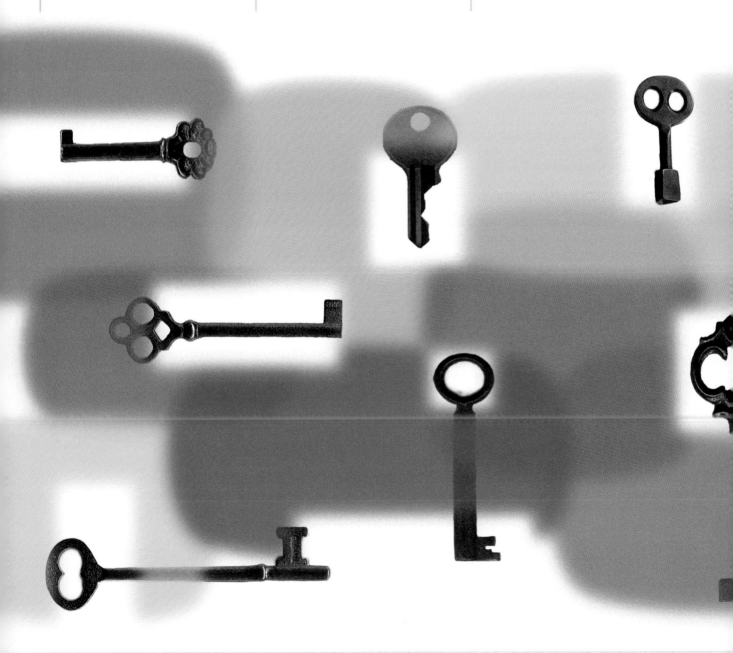

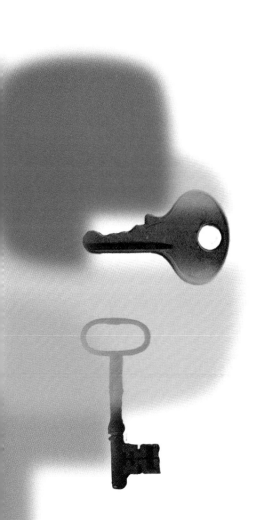

Social Thinking and Social Influence

You've had your eye on that attractive brunette in the first row of your English Lit class since the term began. Should you ask her out? As you ponder the wisdom of this action, you watch her, hoping to pick up some clues to help you make your decision. You notice a sorority decal on her notebook. But, you don't belong to a fraternity and you've never dated a sorority woman. You've heard that some of them can be snobbish, although she seems to be friendly and approachable. Still, you're only a sophomore; what if she's a senior? That could be awkward. As you contemplate what to do, similar thoughts flit through your mind.

In this scenario, you can see the process of person perception at work. People are constantly constructing impressions of others in order to understand them and predict their behavior. In this chapter, we explore what's involved in forming these impressions and how and why they can be inaccurate. Expanding our discussion of social cognition, we then turn to the problem of prejudice. Next, we look at how others try to influence your beliefs and behavior. Specifically, we focus on the power of persuasive messages and the pressures to conform and obey. As you'll see, social thinking and social influence play significant roles in personal adjustment.

Forming Impressions of Others

- Cite the five sources of information people use to form impressions of others.
- Describe the key differences between snap judgments and systematic judgments.
- Define attributions and explain when people are likely to make them.

- Describe two expectancies that can distort observer's perceptions.
- Describe four important cognitive distortions and how they operate.
- Describe some ways in which perceptions of others are efficient, selective, and consistent.

Do you recall the first time you met your current boss? She seemed pleasant, but distant, and you were worried that she might be difficult to work with. Thankfully, your concerns diminished as you got to know her better. As people interact with others, they constantly engage in *person perception,* **the process of forming impressions of others.** Because impression formation is usually such an easy and automatic process, people are unaware that it is taking place. Nonetheless, the process is a complex one. Let's review some of its essential aspects.

Key Sources of Information

Because you can't read other people's minds, you are dependent on *observations* of others to determine what they are like. In forming impressions of others, people rely on five key sources of observational information: appearance, verbal behavior, actions, nonverbal messages, and situational cues.

Appearance. Despite the admonition, "You can't judge a book by its cover," people frequently do exactly that. Physical features such as height, weight, skin color, and hair color are some of the cues used to "read" other people. Regardless of their accuracy, beliefs about physical features are used to form impressions of others (Hellström & Tekle, 1994). For example, Americans learn to associate the wearing of eyeglasses with studiousness. Style of dress, clothing or jewelry that designates religious beliefs, body piercings, and tattoos also provide clues about others.

Verbal behavior. Another obvious source of information about others is what they say. People form impressions based on what and how much others self-disclose, how often they give advice and ask questions, and how judgmental they are (Berry et al., 1997). If Tanisha speaks negatively about most people she knows, you will probably conclude that she is a critical person.

Actions. Because people don't always tell the truth, you have to rely on their behavior to provide insights about them. For instance, when you learn that Jamal volunteers five hours a week at the local homeless shelter, you are likely to infer that he is a caring person. In impression formation, "actions speak louder than words."

Nonverbal messages. Another key source of information about others is nonverbal communication: fa-

cial expressions, eye contact, body language, and gestures (Forrest & Feldman, 2000; Frank & Ekman, 1997). These nonverbal cues provide information about people's emotional states and dispositions. For example, in our culture a bright smile and good eye contact signal friendliness and openness. Also, because people know that verbal behavior is easily manipulated, they often rely on nonverbal cues to determine the truth of what others say (Frank & Ekman, 1997).

Situations. The setting in which behavior occurs provides crucial information about how to interpret a person's behavior (Trope & Gaunt, 2003). For instance, without situational cues, it would be hard to know whether a crying person is happy or sad.

Snap Judgments Versus Systematic Judgments

In their interactions with others, people are bombarded with more information than they can possibly handle. To avoid being overwhelmed, people rely on alternative ways to process information. *Snap judgments* about others are those made quickly and based on only a few bits of information and preconceived notions. Thus, they may not be particularly accurate. Nevertheless, people can get by with superficial assessments of others quite often. As Susan Fiske (1993) puts it: "People are

In forming impressions of others, people rely on cues such as appearance, actions, and verbal and nonverbal messages, as well as the nature of the situation.

good enough perceivers" (p. 156). Often, interactions with others are so fleeting or inconsequential that it makes little difference that such judgments are imprecise. Does it really matter that you mistakenly infer that the blonde postal clerk is a fun-loving person, or that your bespectacled restaurant server is an intellectual? You may never in-teract with them again, and even if you do, your interactions are not likely to be signifi-cant to either of you.

Courtesy, Susan Fiske

Susan Fiske

On the other hand, when it comes to selecting a friend, a mate, a boss, or an employee, it's essential that your impressions be as accurate as possible. Hence, it's not surprising that people are motivated to take more care in these assessments. In forming impressions of those who can affect their welfare and happiness, peo-ple make *systematic judgments* rather than snap deci-sions (see Figure 6.1). That is, they take the time to ob-serve the person in a variety of situations and to compare that person's behavior with that of others in similar situations.

In Chapter 5, we noted that people are "cognitive misers" (Taylor, 1981b). This fact has important impli-cations for impression formation. To conserve their time, energy, and cognitive resources (attention, mem-ory, and so forth), people often depend on automatic processing. Controlled processing, or *mindfulness,* which requires more cognitive effort, kicks in only when in-dividuals expect others to be personally relevant.

In assessing what a significant individual is like, people are particularly interested in learning why the person behaves in a certain way. This deeper level of understanding is vital if one is to make accurate pre-dictions about the person's future behavior. After all, when you're looking for a roommate, you don't want

to end up with an inconsiderate slob. To determine the cause of others' behavior, people engage in the process of causal attribution.

Attributions

As we have noted in earlier chapters, ***attributions* are inferences that people draw about the causes of their own behavior, others' behavior, and events.** In Chap-ter 5, we focused on self-attributions. Here, we'll apply attribution theory to the behavior of *other people.* For example, suppose that your boss bawls you out for doing a sloppy job on an insignificant project. To what do you attribute this tongue lashing? Was your work really that bad? Is your boss just in a grouchy mood? Is your boss under too much pressure?

In Chapter 5, we noted that attributions have three key dimensions: internal versus external, stable versus unstable, and controllable versus uncontrollable (Jones & Davis, 1965; Kelley, 1950; Weiner, 1974). For this discus-sion, we focus only on the internal/external dimension. When people ascribe the causes of someone's behavior to personal dispositions, traits, abilities, or feelings, they are making *internal* attributions. When they im-pute the causes of their behavior to situational de-mands and environmental constraints, they are mak-ing *external* attributions. For example, if a friend's business fails, you might attribute the failure to your friend's lack of business skills (an internal factor) or to

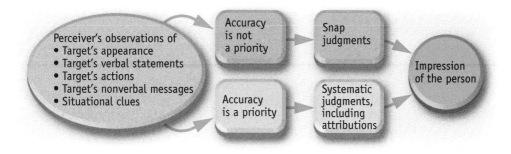

● FIGURE 6.1

The process of person perception. In forming impressions of others, perceivers rely on various sources of observational information. When it's important to form accurate impressions of others, people are motivated to make systematic judgments, including attributions. When accuracy isn't a priority, people make snap judgments about others.

Adapted from Brehm, S. S., & Kassin, S. M. (1993) *Social Psychology.* Boston: Houghton Mifflin. Copyright © 1993 by Houghton Mifflin Company. Adapted with permission.

DILBERT Reprinted by permission of United Feature Syndicate, Inc.

negative trends in the economy (an external factor). Parents who discover that their teenage son has banged up the family car may blame it on his carelessness (an internal attribution) or on slippery road conditions (an external attribution).

The types of attributions people make about others can have a tremendous impact on everyday social interactions. For example, blaming a friend's business failure on poor business "smarts" rather than on a poor economy will obviously affect how you view your friend—not to mention whether you'll lend her money! Likewise, if parents attribute their son's automobile accident to slippery road conditions, they are likely to deal with him very differently than if they attribute it to his carelessness. In addition, there is evidence that spouses' attributions for each other's behavior can affect their marital satisfaction (Fletcher & Thomas, 2000).

Obviously, people don't make attributions about every person they meet. Research suggests that people are relatively selective in this process (Jones, 1990; Malle & Knobe, 1997). It seems that people are most likely to make attributions (1) when others behave in unexpected or negative ways, (2) when events are personally relevant, and (3) when they are suspicious about another person's motives. For example, if Serena laughs loudly at the local student hangout, no one bats an eye. But if she does so in the middle of a serious lecture, it raises eyebrows and generates speculation about why she behaved this way.

Some aspects of the attribution process are logical (Trope & Gaunt, 2003). Nonetheless, research also shows that the process of person perception is sometimes illogical and unsystematic, as in the case of snap judgments. Other sources of error also creep into the process, a topic we take up next.

Perceiver Expectations

Remember Evan, that bully from the fourth grade? He made your life a total misery—constantly looking for opportunities to poke fun at you and beat you up. Now when you meet someone named Evan, your initial reaction is negative, and it takes a while to warm up to him. Why? Your negative past experiences with an Evan have led you to expect the worst, whether or not it's warranted. This is just one example of how *perceiver expectations* can influence the perception of others.

Confirmation Bias

Shortly after you begin interacting with someone, you start forming hypotheses about what the person is like. In turn, these hypotheses can influence your behavior toward that person in such a way as to confirm your expectations. Thus, if on your first encounter with Xavier, he has a camera around his neck, you will probably hypothesize that he has an interest in photography and question him selectively about his shutterbug activities. You might also neglect to ask more wide-ranging questions that would give you a more accurate picture of him. **This tendency to behave toward others in ways that confirm your expectations about them is termed *confirmation bias.***

Confirmation bias is a well-documented phenomenon (Snyder & Swann, 1978; Dougherty, Turban, & Callendar, 1994). It occurs in casual social interactions as well as in job interviews and in courtrooms, where the interviewer or attorney may ask leading questions (Fiske & Taylor, 1991). When it comes to forming first impressions of others, it is not so much that "seeing is believing" but rather that "believing is seeing."

Confirmation bias also occurs because individuals selectively recall facts to fit their views of others. In one experiment (Cohen, 1981), participants watched a

WEB LINK 6.2

Social Cognition Paper Archive and Information Center
Eliot R. Smith at Indiana University maintains a popular site that includes information about papers (abstracts, mostly) and people and that links to the wider social psychological research community.

videotape of a woman engaging in a variety of activities, including listening to classical music, drinking beer, and watching TV. Half of them were told that the woman was a waitress and the other half were told that she was a librarian. When asked to recall the woman's actions on the videotape, participants tended to remember activities consistent with their stereotypes of waitresses and librarians. Thus, those who thought that the woman was a waitress recalled her drinking beer; those who thought she was a librarian recalled her listening to classical music.

Although confirmation bias does occur, just how pervasive is it? Susan Fiske (1993) notes that when people have a high need for accuracy in their impression of someone, they are less likely to engage in selective questioning. Instead, they ask *diagnostic* questions such as, "Would you rather have a few close relationships or a lot of less intimate ones?" Diagnostic questions provide people with information about the accuracy of their expectations, in contrast to biased questions that seek mainly to confirm their initial hypotheses.

Normally, people remain unaware of the biases in their perceptions. They go blithely along, assuming that their version of reality is accurate. And, most of the time, this approach works (Fiske, 1993). It's only when someone disagrees that a perceiver is brought up short. When this happens, the individual may alter his or her views, conclude that the other person's perception is "off," or look for another satisfactory explanation for the difference in perceptions.

Self-Fulfilling Prophecies

Sometimes a perceiver's expectations can actually change another person's behavior. **A *self-fulfilling prophecy* occurs when expectations about a person cause the person to behave in ways that confirm the expectations.** This term was originally coined by sociologist Robert Merton (1948) to explain such phenomena as "runs" on banks that occurred during the Depression. That is, when unfounded rumors would circulate that a bank couldn't cover its deposits, people would rush to the bank and withdraw their funds, thereby draining the deposits from the bank and making real what was initially untrue. This phenomenon is also called *behavioral confirmation* or the *Pygmalion effect* (named after the Greek myth in which King Pygmalion carved a statue of the perfect woman and fell in love with it).

Figure 6.2 depicts the three steps in the self-fulfilling prophecy. First, the perceiver has an initial impression of someone. (A teacher believes that Jennifer is highly intelligent.) Then the perceiver behaves toward the target person in line with his or her expectations. (He asks her interesting questions and praises her answers.) The third step occurs when the target person adjusts his or her behavior to the perceiver's actions, which confirms the perceiver's hypothesis about the target person. (Jen-

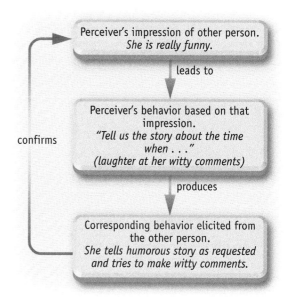

● FIGURE 6.2

The three steps of the self-fulfilling prophecy. Through a three-step process, your expectations about a person can cause that person to behave in ways that confirm those expectations. First, you form an impression of someone. Second, you behave toward that person in a way that is consistent with your impression. Third, the person exhibits the behavior you encourage, which confirms your initial impression.

Adapted from Smith, E. R., & Mackie, D. M. (1995). *Social Psychology*. New York: Worth, p. 103. Copyright © 1995 Worth Publishing. Reprinted with permission.

nifer performs well in class.) Note that both individuals are unaware that this process is operating. Also note that because perceivers are unaware of their expectations and of the effect they can have on others, they mistakenly attribute the target person's behavior to an internal cause (Jennifer is smart), rather than an external one (their own expectations).

The best-known experiments on the self-fulfilling prophecy have been conducted in classroom settings, looking at the effect of teachers' expectations on students' academic performance (Rosenthal, 1985). A review of 400 studies of this phenomenon over a period of 30 years reported that teacher expectations significantly influenced student performance in 36 percent of the experiments. The self-fulfilling prophecy also operates with adults and in noneducational settings such as the military, factories and businesses, courtrooms, and physicians' offices (Ambady et al., 2002; Halverson et al., 1997; Kierein & Gold, 2000; Rosenthal, 2003).

Although a perceiver's expectations can produce corresponding changes in another person's behavior, this outcome is not inevitable (Smith, Jussim, & Eccles, 1999). For one thing, self-fulfilling prophecies are less likely to operate if perceivers are motivated to form accurate impressions of others (Harris & Perkins, 1995).

Second, if target persons are aware of another's beliefs and these beliefs contradict their self-views, they work hard to change the perceiver's perceptions and are often successful (Hilton & Darley, 1985). Third, when target persons are confident about their self-views, they are less likely to be influenced by a perceiver with different perceptions (Swann & Ely, 1984).

Cognitive Distortions

Another source of error in person perception comes from distortions in the minds of perceivers. These errors in judgment are most likely to occur when a perceiver is in a hurry, is distracted, or is not motivated to pay careful attention to another person.

Social Categorization

One of the ways people efficiently process information is to classify objects (and people) according to their distinctive features (Fiske, 1998). Thus, people quite often categorize others on the basis of nationality, race, ethnicity, gender, age, religion, sexual orientation, and so forth. People frequently take the easy path of categorizing others to avoid expending the cognitive effort that would be necessary for a more accurate impression.

People perceive similar individuals to be members of their *ingroup* ("us") and those who are dissimilar to them, in the *outgroup* ("them"). Such categorizing has three important results. First, people usually have less favorable attitudes toward outgroup members than ingroup members (Brewer & Brown, 1998). Second, individuals usually see outgroup members as being much more alike than they really are, whereas they see members of the ingroup as unique individuals (Oakes, 2001). In other words, people frequently explain the behavior of outgroup members on the basis of the characteristic that sets them apart ("Those *Nerdians* are *all* drunks"), but attribute the same behavior by an ingroup member to individual personality traits ("*Brett's* a heavy drinker"). This phenomenon is termed the *outgroup homogeneity effect.* Anne Frank alluded to this tendency when she wrote, "What one Christian does is his own responsibility, what one Jew does is thrown back at all Jews."

A third result of categorizing is that it heightens the visibility of outgroup members when there are only a few of them within a larger group. In other words, minority group status in a group makes more salient the quality that distinguishes the person—ethnicity, gender, whatever. When people are perceived as being unique or distinctive, they are also seen as having more influence in a group, and their good and bad qualities are given extra weight (Crocker & McGraw, 1984). Significantly, distinctiveness also triggers stereotyping. This phenomenon explains why many people notice nagging women (but not men), noisy blacks (but not whites), and jolly fat (but not thin) people.

Stereotypes

Stereotypes **are widely held beliefs that people have certain characteristics because of their membership in a particular group.** For example, many people assume that Jews are shrewd and ambitious, that African Americans have special athletic and musical abilities, and that Muslims are religious fanatics. Although a kernel of truth may underlie some stereotypes, it should be readily apparent that not all Jews, African Americans, Muslims, and so forth behave alike. If you take the time to think about it, you recognize that there is enormous diversity in behavior within any group.

The most prevalent stereotypes in America are those based on gender, age, and ethnicity (Fiske, 1993). Gender stereotypes, although in transition, remain pervasive. For example, in a study of gender stereotypes in 30 countries, males were typically characterized as adventurous, powerful, and independent, while females were characterized as sentimental, submissive, and superstitious (Williams & Best, 1982, 1990). Because of their wide-ranging significance, gender stereotypes will be covered in detail in our chapter (10) on gender.

Stereotypes may also be based on physical appearance. In particular, there is plenty of evidence that physically attractive people are believed to have desirable personality traits. This widespread perception is termed the *"what-is-beautiful-is-good" stereotype* (Dion, Berscheid, & Walster, 1972). Specifically, beautiful people are usually viewed as more socially competent, more assertive, better adjusted, and more intellectually competent than those who are less attractive (Eagly et al., 1991). Yet most of these perceptions have little basis in fact.

Attractive people *do* have an advantage in the social arena. For example, they have better social skills, are more popular, are less socially anxious (especially about interactions with the other gender), are less lonely, and are more sexually experienced (Feingold, 1992b). However, they are not any different from others in intelligence, happiness, mental health, or self-esteem (Feingold, 1992b; Langlois et al., 2000). Thus, attractive people are perceived in a more favorable light than is actually justified. Unfortunately, the positive biases toward attractive people also operate in reverse. Thus, unattractive people are unjustifiably seen as less well adjusted and less intellectually competent than others. Most Americans believe that good looks are an advantage in everyday life (see Figure 6.3).

This tendency to associate attractiveness with positive qualities also occurs outside the United States—with an important twist. You'll recall from our discussion in Chapter 5 that Western societies tend to be *individualistic,* viewing people as autonomous individuals who

Most Americans Believe Good Looks Are an Advantage

Poll Question	"Fairly important" or "Very important" answers		
	Men	Women	Total
"How important do you think a person's physical attractiveness is in our society today in terms of his or her happiness, social life, and ability to get ahead?" 1990	82%	85%	84%
1999	76%	76%	76%

● **FIGURE 6.3**

Physical attractiveness as a social advantage. A Gallup poll reported that a large majority of men and women believe that physical attractiveness is an advantage when it comes to happiness, social life, and the ability to get ahead. Affirmative responses to the poll question decreased a little between 1990 and 1999, but it is clear that most people continue to believe that good looks are advantageous.

Data from Newport, F. (1999, September 15), *Americans agree that being attractive is a plus in American society.* Retrieved June 10, 2001 from http://gallup.com/poll/releases/pr990915.

are responsible for their actions. In contrast, members of *collectivist* societies value interdependence and obedience. In a study conducted in Korea, a collectivist culture, participants were asked to view photographs of Korean men and women and then to describe the personal qualities of those in the pictures (Wheeler & Kim, 1997). The participants described the attractive individuals as possessing qualities that are valued in collectivist cultures ("a concern for others" and "integrity," for instance), but they did not choose terms that are desirable in individualistic cultures ("dominant" and "assertive," for example). Thus, it is likely that although people in many cultures associate attractiveness with positive qualities, cultural values determine what characteristics are considered desirable.

Stereotypes can be spontaneously triggered when people encounter members of commonly stereotyped groups—even in those who are not prejudiced (Devine, 1989; Dunning & Sherman, 1997). Stereotypes can exist outside a person's awareness (Bodenhausen, Macrae, & Hugenberg, 2003; Greenwald & Banaji, 1995). Because stereotyping is automatic, some psychologists are pessimistic about being able to control it (Bargh, 1999); others take a more optimistic view (Uleman et al., 1996).

Why do stereotypes persist? For one thing, they are cognitively functional (Quinn, Macrae, & Bodenhausen, 2003). Recall that people are "cognitive misers." Because they are deluged with much more information than they can process, the tendency is to reduce complexity to simplicity. But, as we noted earlier, the tradeoff for simplification is inaccuracy. Stereotypes also endure because of confirmation bias. Thus, when

individuals encounter members of groups that they view with prejudice, they are likely to see what they expect to see. The self-fulfilling prophecy is a third reason stereotypes persist: Beliefs about another person may actually elicit the anticipated behavior and confirm biased expectations.

The Fundamental Attribution Error

When explaining the causes of others' behavior, people invoke personal attributions and discount the importance of situational factors. Although this tendency is not universal (Choi, Nisbett, & Norenzayan, 1999; Miyamoto & Kitayama, 2002), it is strong enough that Lee Ross (1977) called it the "*fundamental* attribution error." **The *fundamental attribution error* refers to the tendency to explain other people's behavior as the result of personal, rather than situational, factors.**

This tendency (sometimes termed *correspondence bias*) differs from stereotyping in that inferences are based on actual behavior. Nonetheless, those inferences may still be inaccurate. If Jeremy leaves class early, you may be correct in inferring that he is inconsiderate, but he might also have had a previously scheduled job interview. Thus, a person's behavior at a given time may or may not be reflective of his or her personality—but observers tend to assume that it is.

What's behind this tendency to discount situational influences on people's behavior? Once again, the culprit is people's tendency to be cognitive misers. It seems that making attributions is a two-step process (Gilbert & Malone, 1995). As you can see in Figure 6.4 (on the next page), in the first step, which occurs automatically, observers make an internal attribution because they are focusing on the person (not the situation). (At your bank, if you observe the man ahead of you yell at the teller, you might infer that he is a hostile person.) In the second step, observers weigh the impact of the situation on the target person's behavior and adjust their inference. (If you overhear the customer say that this is the third time in three weeks that the bank has made the same error in his account, you're likely to temper your initial judgment about his hostile tendencies.)

The first step in the attribution process occurs spontaneously, but the second step requires cognitive effort and attention. Thus, it is easy to stop after step one—especially, if one is in a hurry or distracted. Failure to take the effortful second step can result in the fundamental attribution error. However, when people are motivated to form accurate impressions of others (Webster, 1993) or when they are suspicious about another's motives (Fein, 1996), they do expend the effort to complete the second step. In these cases, they are more likely to make accurate attributions. Some evidence suggests that these two steps may be related to different types of brain activity (Lieberman et al., 2004).

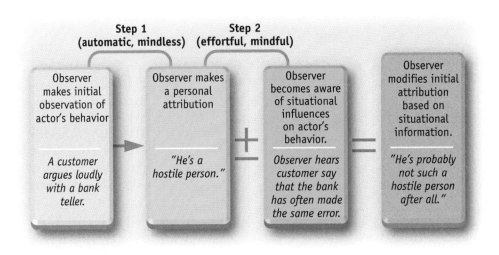

● **FIGURE 6.4**

Explaining the fundamental attribution error. People automatically take the first step in the attribution process (making a personal attribution). However, they often fail to take the second step (considering the possible influence of situational factors on a person's behavior) because that requires extra effort. The failure to consider situational factors causes observers to exaggerate the role of personal factors in behavior—that is, they make the fundamental attribution error. (Adapted from Brehm, Kassin, & Fein, 2002)

Step 1 (automatic, mindless)   **Step 2** (effortful, mindful)

Observer makes initial observation of actor's behavior

A customer argues loudly with a bank teller.

Observer makes a personal attribution

"He's a hostile person."

Observer becomes aware of situational influences on actor's behavior.

Observer hears customer say that the bank has often made the same error.

Observer modifies initial attribution based on situational information.

"He's probably not such a hostile person after all."

Cultural values seem to promote different attributional errors. In *individualistic* cultures, where independence is valued, it is assumed that people are responsible for their actions. In *collectivist* societies, conformity and obedience to group norms are valued, so it is assumed that one's behavior reflects adherence to group norms. Some experts speculate that different styles of thinking underlie cultural differences in attributional styles (Nisbett et al., 2001). They suggest that the Western mentality is *analytical* (attention is focused on an object and causality is ascribed to it), whereas the East Asian mentality is *holistic* (attention is focused on the field surrounding an object, and causality is understood to reside in the relationship between the object and its field). Consistent with both of these views, researchers have found that Americans explain others' behavior in terms of internal attributions more often than do Hindus (Miller, 1984), Chinese (Morris & Peng, 1994), Japanese (Weisz, Rothbaum, & Blackburn, 1984), or Koreans (Choi et al., 2003).

Defensive Attribution

Observers are especially likely to make internal attributions in trying to explain the calamities and tragedies that befall other people. Examples easily come to mind. When a woman is abused by a boyfriend or husband, people frequently blame the victim by remarking how stupid she is to stay with the man, rather than condemning the aggressor for his behavior. Similarly, rape victims are often judged to have "asked for it."

Defensive attribution is a tendency to blame victims for their misfortune, so that one feels less likely to be victimized in a sim-

ilar way. Blaming victims for their calamities also helps people maintain their belief that they live in a "just world" where people get what they deserve and deserve what they get (Lerner, 1980, 1998). Acknowledging that the world is not just—that unfortunate events can happen as a result of chance factors—would mean having to admit the frightening possibility that the catastrophes that happen to others could also happen to oneself. Defensive attributions are a self-protective, but irrational, strategy that allows people to avoid such unnerving thoughts and helps them feel in control of their lives (Hafer, 2000; Lipkus, Dalbert, & Siegler, 1996). Unfortunately, when victims are blamed for their setbacks, people unfairly attribute undesirable traits to them, such as incompetence, foolishness, and laziness.

A common example of defensive attribution is the tendency to blame the homeless for their plight.

LIVING IN TODAY'S WORLD

Beliefs, Revenge, and Intergroup Conflict

Knowing that terrorist attacks could come at any time and in any location in the country disturbs Americans' sense of control over their own and their loved ones' safety. This experience strikes at a fundamental need to see one's world as stable and predictable (Greenberg, Solomon, & Pyszczynski, 1997). A foundation of this need for order is the *belief in a just world (BJW)*. As we discuss elsewhere in this chapter, this belief is the idea that good things happen to good people and bad things happen to bad people. Individuals differ on how strongly they endorse BJW. Compared to weak endorsers, strong endorsers are more likely to have an internal locus of control (believe that their fate is under their own control versus chance), to espouse the Protestant work ethic, and to be more authoritarian and more politically conservative (Furnham & Procter, 1989).

Having to face incontrovertible evidence that the world is not just (the 9-11 attacks, for example) triggers fear, stress, and vulnerability, especially among strong endorsers of BJW. One way to deal with these painful feelings is to restore justice cognitively—by persuading themselves that the victims of tragedies actually deserve their fate (because they are "bad" people). These defensive attributions help individuals maintain the comforting, but false, belief that nothing bad will happen to them (because they are "good" people). "Blaming the victim" is reduced when individuals identify with the victim. For example, because the 9-11 attacks were perceived as an attack against the United States (versus an individual or a group), Americans identified and sympathized with the victims of the 9-11 attacks rather than blaming them.

A second response to challenges to BJW is to seek revenge—to punish those responsible for the perceived injustice (and for threatening their BJW). If the perpetrators can be punished, justice can be restored (when bad things do happen to good people, the perpetrators will get what they deserve). A recent study investigated the psychological dynamics involved in BJW after the 9-11 events (Kaiser, Vick, & Major, 2004). Prior to the 9-11 attacks, participants (college students) completed a test of BJW. Several months after 9-11, the subjects were assessed on a number of measures, including terrorism-related distress and the desire for revenge. The more strongly participants endorsed BJW, the more distressed they were about the attacks and the more they desired revenge against the terrorists.

Contrary to popular opinion, terrorists are not deranged; rather, they are usually enraged young males seeking revenge for perceived injustices (Silke, 2003). Therefore, it seems likely that some terrorists would have strong beliefs in a just world. Although we deplore the acts of terrorists, it is possible to understand them as attempts to seek revenge for perceived injustices perpetrated by other countries.

When some people feel vulnerable, they engage in aggression (revenge) to feel less vulnerable. Unfortunately, large-scale military strikes against terrorism can actually increase terrorist behavior when they "unwittingly reinforce terrorists' views of their enemies as aggressive, make it easier for terrorist groups to recruit new members, and strengthen alliances among terrorist organizations" (Plous & Zimbardo, 2004, p. B9). Ironically and tragically, engaging in vengeful aggression to reduce feelings of vulnerability may actually increase vulnerability when it perpetuates intergroup conflict.

Key Themes in Person Perception

The process of person perception is a complex one. Nonetheless, we can detect three recurrent themes in this process: efficiency, selectivity, and consistency.

Efficiency

In forming impressions of others, people prefer to exert no more cognitive effort or time than is necessary. Thus, much social information is processed automatically and effortlessly. According to Susan Fiske (1993), people are like government bureaucrats, who "only bother to gather information on a 'need to know' basis" (p. 175). After all, you're a busy person with many important things to do. It boggles the mind to consider what life would be like if you had to take the time to make careful observations and judgments of everyone you meet. Efficiency has two important advantages: People can make judgments quickly, and it keeps things simple. The big disadvantage is that judgments are error-prone. Still, on balance, efficiency works pretty well as an operating principle.

Selectivity

The old saying that "people see what they expect to see" has been confirmed repeatedly by social scientists. In a classic study, Harold Kelley (1950) showed how a person is preceded by his or her reputation. Students in a class at the Massachusetts Institute of Technology were told that a new lecturer would be speaking to them that day. Before the instructor arrived, the students were given a short description of him, with one important variation. Half the students were led to expect a "warm" person, while the other half were led to expect a "cold" one (see Figure 6.5). All the participants were exposed to exactly the same 20 minutes of lecture and interaction with the new instructor. However, those who were led to expect a warm person rated the instructor as significantly more considerate, sociable, humorous, good-natured, informal, and humane than those who were led to expect a cold person.

Especially if someone's behavior is ambiguous, people are likely to interpret what they see in a way that fits their expectations (Bodenhausen et al., 2003). Thus, after dealing with an assertive female customer, a salesman who holds traditional gender stereotypes might characterize the woman as "pushy." By contrast, he might fail to notice the same behavior in a man because he would have automatically interpreted it as appropriate male behavior.

Consistency

How many times did your parents remind you to be on your best behavior when you were meeting someone for the first time? As it turns out, they were onto something! Considerable research supports the idea that first impressions are powerful (Asch, 1956; Belmore, 1987). **A *primacy effect* occurs when initial information carries more weight than subsequent information.** It is worth noting that initial negative impressions may be especially hard to change (Mellers, Richards, & Birnbaum, 1992). Thus, getting off on the wrong foot may be particularly damaging.

First impressions tend to be particularly potent for several reasons. For one thing, it seems that once people believe that they have formed an accurate impression of someone, they tend to tune out later information (Belmore, 1987). But if people are motivated to form an accurate impression and are not tired, they are less likely to lock in their initial impressions (Webster, Richter, & Kruglanski, 1996). Also, confirmation biases may lead people to discount later information that con-

| Mr. Blank is a graduate student in the Department of Economics and Social Science here at M.I.T. He has had three semesters of teaching experience in psychology at another college. This is his first semester teaching Ec. 70. He is 26 years old, a veteran, and married. People who know him consider him to be a rather cold person, industrious, critical, practical, and determined. | Mr. Blank is a graduate student in the Department of Economics and Social Science here at M.I.T. He has had three semesters of teaching experience in psychology at another college. This is his first semester teaching Ec. 70. He is 26 years old, a veteran, and married. People who know him consider him to be a very warm person, industrious, critical, practical, and determined. |

● FIGURE 6.5

Descriptions of the guest lecturer in Kelley's (1950) study. These two descriptions, provided to two groups of students before the lecturer spoke, differ by only an adjective. But this seemingly small difference caused the two groups to form altogether different perceptions of the lecturer.

tradicts their initial impression. Of course, it is possible to override a primacy effect. If you're *actively* looking for change in a person or have compelling evidence that contradicts your initial impression, you can alter your opinion. Still, since people usually expect others to stay the same, their initial impressions don't change too often.

Thus far, our discussion of impression formation has been based on face-to-face encounters. What about impressions based on virtual encounters? In the first study to look at this issue, researchers reported that viewers of personal websites were able to form clear and coherent impressions of site authors and that there was general agreement on what the authors were like (Vazire & Gosling, 2004). The study also measured the accuracy of the observer's impressions by comparing the observers' trait ratings of the authors to criterion ratings of what the authors were really like. (The criterion ratings included the authors' scores on a test of five key personality traits as well as personality trait ratings by two friends of the authors.) Interestingly, the accuracy of observers' web-based impressions was comparable to the accuracy of impressions based on face-to-face encounters in both long-term and zero-acquaintance studies.

To conclude, although the process of person perception is highly subjective, people are relatively accurate perceivers of others (Fiske, 1998). Even when misperceptions occur, they are often harmless. However, there clearly are occasions when such inaccuracies are problematic. This is certainly true in the case of prejudice, which we consider next.

The Problem of Prejudice

LEARNING OBJECTIVES

- Explain how "old-fashioned" and modern discrimination differ.
- Describe some of the key determinants of prejudice, and explain how they work.
- Describe the operation of several strategies for reducing prejudice.

The terrorist attacks of September 11, 2001 were an extreme demonstration of the destructive power of prejudice—hatred of one group by another. Unfortunately, antagonism between groups continues to be a problem, both on the international scene and at home. For example, after the September 11 attacks, hate crimes increased against Americans presumed to be Muslims or Arabs. Why is it so hard for members of different groups to get along?

Let's begin our discussion by clarifying a couple of terms that are often confused. *Prejudice* **is a negative attitude toward members of a group;** *discrimination* **involves behaving differently, usually unfairly, toward the members of a group.** Prejudice and discrimination do tend to go together, but that is not always the case (see Figure 6.6). For example, a restaurant owner might be prejudiced against Chicanos and yet treat them like anyone else because he needs their business. This is an example of prejudice without discrimination. Although it is probably less common, discrimination without prejudice may also occur. For example, an executive who has favorable attitudes toward blacks may not hire them because his boss would be upset.

"Old-Fashioned" Versus Modern Discrimination

James Byrd Jr., a 49-year-old black man, was walking home from a family gathering in the summer of 1998 when he was offered a ride by three white men, one of whom he knew. Shortly thereafter, pieces of Byrd's savagely beaten body were found strewn along a rural road in Texas. Apparently, he had been beaten, then shackled by his ankles to the back of the truck and dragged to death over $2\frac{1}{2}$ miles of road. Police say that Byrd was targeted simply because he was black. Thankfully, such tragic events are relatively rare in the United States. Nonetheless, they remind us that discrimination still exists.

Over the past 40 years, prejudice and discrimination against minority groups have diminished in the United States. Racial segregation is no longer legal, and

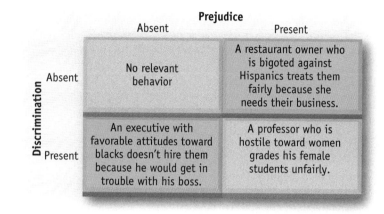

● **FIGURE 6.6**

Prejudice and discrimination. Prejudice and discrimination are highly correlated, but they don't necessarily go hand in hand. As the examples in the blue cells show, there can be prejudice without discrimination and discrimination without prejudice.

discrimination based on race, ethnicity, gender, and religion is much less common now than it was in the 1950s and 1960s. Thus, the good news is that overt, or *"old-fashioned," discrimination* against minority groups has declined (but not disappeared, as we noted above). The bad news is that a more subtle form of prejudice and discrimination has emerged (Dovidio & Gaertner, 1996; Gaertner & Dovidio, 1986). That is, people may privately harbor negative attitudes toward minority groups (including women) but express them only when they feel that such views are justified or that it's safe to do so. This new phenomenon has been termed *modern discrimination* (also called "modern racism"). Modern discrimination is also operating when people endorse equality as an abstract principle but oppose concrete programs intended to promote equality on the grounds that discrimination against minority groups no longer exists (Wright & Taylor, 2003). Similar distinctions between blatant and subtle discrimination have been found in European countries as well—for example, in British attitudes toward West Indians and Asians, in French attitudes toward North Africans and Asians, and in German attitudes toward Turks (Pettigrew & Meertens, 1995). In Figure 6.7 (on the next page), you can see the kinds of items used to measure old-fashioned and modern sexism.

Items Related to Old-Fashioned Sexism

1. Women are generally not as smart as men.

2. It is more important to encourage boys than to encourage girls to participate in athletics.

Items Related to Modern Sexism

1. Discrimination against women is no longer a problem in the United States.

2. Over the past few years, the government and news media have been showing more concern about the treatment of women than is warranted by women's actual experiences.

Scoring: Possible responses to the statements range from "strongly agree" to "strongly disagree." Individuals who moderately or strongly agree with the above items reflect old-fashioned or modern sexism, respectively.

● **FIGURE 6.7**

Measuring old-fashioned and modern sexism. Research shows similarities between old-fashioned and modern beliefs about both racism and sexism. Janet Swim and colleagues have developed a scale to measure the presence of both types of sexism. Four items from the 13-item scale are shown here. Old-fashioned sexism is characterized by endorsement of traditional gender roles and acceptance of stereotypes that portray females as less competent than males. In contrast, subtle, modern sexism is characterized by denial of continued discrimination and rejection of policies intended to help women.

From Swim, J. K., Aikin, K. J., Hall, W. S., & Hunter, B. A. (1995). Sexism and racism: Old-fashioned and modern prejudices. *Journal of Personality and Social Psychology, 68,* 199–214. Copyright © 1995 American Psychological Association. Reprinted by permission of the author.

While modern racists do not wish to return to the days of segregation, they also feel that minority groups should not push too fast for advancement or receive special treatment by the government. Individuals who endorse statements that favor "modern" discrimination ("Blacks are getting too demanding in their push for equal rights") are much more likely to vote against a black political candidate, to oppose school busing, and to favor tax laws that benefit whites at the expense of blacks, compared to those who do not endorse such views (Murrell et al., 1994). Interestingly, endorsing statements such as "I do not like black people" ("old-fashioned" racism) does *not* reliably predict an individual's political actions (because many people who might personally agree with such a statement are reluctant to publicly endorse it).

Causes of Prejudice

Prejudice is obviously a complex issue and has multiple causes. Although we can't thoroughly examine all of the causes of prejudice, we'll examine some of the major psychological and social factors that contribute to this vexing problem.

Authoritarianism

In some of the earliest research on prejudice, Robert Adorno and his colleagues (1950) identified the *authoritarian personality,* a personality type characterized by prejudice toward *any* group perceived to be different from oneself. Subsequent research found serious methodological weaknesses in the study, calling into question the validity of the personality type.

Over the past 50 years, both the definition and measurement of authoritarianism have evolved (Dion, 2003). The construct is now termed *right-wing authoritarianism* (RWA) (Altemeyer, 1988a, 1988b), and it is characterized by authoritarian submission (exaggerated deference to those in power), authoritarian aggression (hostility toward targets sanctioned by authorities), and conventionalism (strong adherence to values endorsed by authorities). Because authoritarians tend to support established authority, RWA is more commonly found among political conservatives than among political liberals (who are more likely to challenge the status quo).

Studies in Canada and the United States show that RWA correlates with prejudice and discrimination toward various minority groups—African Americans, ethnic minorities, women, homosexuals—(Altemeyer, 1998; Whitley, 1999). Among Russians and citizens of the former Soviet Union, authoritarianism is also correlated with prejudice (McFarland, Ageyev, & Abalakina-Paap, 1992; McFarland, Ageyev, & Djintcharadze, 1996).

What causes RWAs to be prejudiced? According to Robert Altemeyer (1998), there are two key factors. First, they organize their social world into ingroups and outgroups, and they view outgroups as threatening their cherished traditional values. Second, they tend to be self-righteous: They believe that they are more moral than others, and they feel justified in derogating groups that authority figures define as less moral than themselves. RWAs have typically been reared in highly religious and socially homogeneous groups, with little exposure to minority groups and unconventional behavior. They feel unduly threatened by social change—a fear picked up from their parents who believe that "the world is a dangerous and hostile place" (Altemeyer, 1988b, p. 38). Altemeyer also notes that fearful attitudes are reinforced by the mass media's emphasis on crime and violence. Exposure to various kinds of people and perspectives can reduce RWA (Peterson & Lane, 2001).

Cognitive Distortions and Expectations

Much of prejudice is rooted in cognitive processes that kick in automatically and operate without conscious intent (Wright & Taylor, 2003). As you recall, *social categorization* predisposes people to divide the social world into ingroups and outgroups. This distinction can trigger negativity toward outgroup members.

Perhaps no factor plays a larger role in prejudice than *stereotyping*. Many people subscribe to derogatory stereotypes of various ethnic groups. Although racial stereotypes have declined over the last 50 years, they're not entirely a thing of the past (Dovidio et al., 2003). Racial profiling, in which officials stop motorists, pedestrians, and airline passengers solely on the basis of skin color, is a case in point. Similarly, the events of September 11, 2001 caused some Americans to view all Muslims and Arabs as terrorists.

It seems that people are particularly likely to make the *fundamental attribution error* when evaluating targets of prejudice (Hewstone, 1990; Levy, Stroessner, & Dweck, 1998). Thus, when people take note of ethnic neighborhoods dominated by crime and poverty, they blame these problems on the residents (they're lazy and ignorant) and downplay or ignore situationally based explanations (job discrimination, poor police service, and so on). The old saying, "They should pull themselves up by their own bootstraps" is a blanket dismissal of how situational factors may make it especially difficult for minorities to achieve upward mobility. Similarly, in trying to understand why individuals in some countries hold negative views of the United States, many Americans depict such people as "crazy" or "evil" rather than looking at possible situational causes, such as the negative effects of American foreign policy on their countries or the negative portrayal of the United States in their media.

Defensive attributions, in which people unfairly blame victims of adversity to reassure themselves that the same thing won't happen to them, can also contribute to prejudice. For example, individuals who claim that people who contract AIDS deserve it may be trying to reassure themselves that they won't suffer a similar fate.

Expectations can also foster and maintain prejudice. You already know that once people have formed impressions, they are invested in maintaining them. For instance, people note and recall behavior that confirms their stereotypes better than information that is inconsistent with their beliefs (Bodenhausen, 1988). Also, when an outgroup member's behavior contradicts a stereotype, people often "explain away" such behavior to leave their stereotype intact. A study demonstrating this phenomenon involved male college students who were randomly assigned to pairs (Ickes et al., 1982). In one condition, one member of each pair was casually informed that his partner was extremely friendly; in a second condition, one man in each pair learned that his partner was just the opposite—very unfriendly. All the men were instructed to behave very positively toward each other during the study, which they did. After the interaction, the participants were asked to describe their partners. Those who expected their part-

ners to be very friendly described them this way. However, those who expected their partners to be very unfriendly described the friendly behavior as fake and merely a temporary response to their own friendly behavior. Thus, they interpreted their partner's behavior in line with their expectations.

Unfortunately, the fact that social thinking is automatic, selective, and consistent means that people usually see what they expect to see when they look through prejudiced eyes.

Competition Between Groups

Back in 1954, Muzafer Sherif and his colleagues conducted a now-classic study at Robbers' Cave State Park in Oklahoma to look at competition and prejudice (Sherif et al., 1961). In this study, 11-year-old white boys were invited, with parental permission, to attend a three-week summer camp. What the boys didn't know was that they were participants in an experiment. The boys were randomly assigned to one of two groups; at camp, they went directly to their assigned campsites and had no knowledge of the other group's presence. During the first week, the boys got to know the other members of their own group through typical camp activities (hiking, swimming, and camping out); each group also chose a name (the Rattlers and the Eagles).

In the second week, the Rattlers and Eagles were introduced to each other through intergroup competitions. Events included a football game, a treasure hunt, and a tug of war, with medals, trophies, and other desirable prizes for the winning team. Almost immediately after competitive games were introduced, hostile feelings erupted between the two groups and quickly escalated to highly aggressive behavior: Food fights broke out in the mess hall, cabins were ransacked, and group flags were burned.

This experimental demonstration of the effects of competition on prejudice is often mirrored in the real world. For example, disputes over territory often provoke antagonism, as is the case in the former Yugoslavia and in the Israeli-Palestinian conflict. The lack of jobs or other important resources can also create competition between social groups. Still, competition does not always breed prejudice. In fact, the *perception* of threats to one's ingroup (loss of status, for example) is much more likely to cause hostility between groups than actual threats to the ingroup are (Brown et al., 2001; Dovidio et al., 2003). Unfortunately, such perceptions are quite common because ingroup members usually assume that outgroup members are competitive and will try to thwart the ingroup's success (Fiske & Ruscher, 1993). To conclude, there is ample evidence that conflict over actual and perceived scarce resources can prejudice individuals toward outgroup members.

Threats to Social Identity

Although group membership provides individuals with a sense of identity and pride, it can also foster prejudice and discrimination, as we just noted. To explore a different facet of this idea, we turn to *social identity theory*, developed by Henri Tajfel (1982) and John Turner (1987). According to this theory, self-esteem is partly determined by one's *social identity*, or collective self, which is tied to one's group memberships (nationality, religion, gender, major, occupation, and so forth) (Luhtanen & Crocker, 1992). Whereas your personal self-esteem is elevated by individual accomplishments (you got an A on a history exam), your collective self-esteem is boosted when an ingroup is successful (your team wins the football game, your country wins a war). Likewise, your self-esteem can be threatened on both the personal level (you didn't get called for that job interview) and the collective level (your football team loses the championship game, your country is defeated in a war).

Threats to both personal and social identity motivate individuals to restore self-esteem, but threats to social identity are more likely to provoke responses that foster prejudice and discrimination (Crocker & Luhtanen, 1990). When collective self-esteem is threatened, individuals react in two key ways to bolster it. The most common response is to show *ingroup favoritism*—for example, tapping an ingroup member for a job opening or rating the performance of an ingroup member higher than that of an outgroup member (Branscombe et al., 1993). The second way to deal with threats to social identity is to engage in *outgroup derogation*—in other words, to "trash" outgroups that are perceived as threatening. This latter tactic is more often used by individuals who identify especially strongly with an ingroup (Perreault & Bourhis, 1999). Figure 6.8 depicts the various elements of social identity theory.

Significantly, it is "ingroup love," not "outgroup hate" that underlies most discrimination (Brewer, 1999). In other words, ingroups reward their own members and withhold rewards from outgroups, rather than deliberately blocking outgroups from desired resources (Fiske, 2002).

Reducing Prejudice

For decades, psychologists have searched for ways to reduce prejudice. Such a complicated problem requires solutions on a number of levels. Let's look at a few interventions that have been shown to work.

Cognitive Strategies

Because stereotypes are part of the social air that people breathe, practically everyone learns stereotypes about

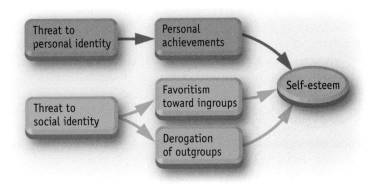

FIGURE 6.8

Social identity theory. According to Tajfel (1982) and Turner (1987), individuals have both a personal identity (based on a unique sense of self) and a social identity (based on group memberships). When social identity is threatened, people are motivated to restore self-esteem by either showing favoritism to ingroup members or derogating members of outgroups. These tactics contribute to prejudice and discrimination.

Adapted from Brehm, S. S., & Kassin, S. M. (1993). *Social psychology*. Boston: Houghton Mifflin. Copyright © 1993 by Houghton Mifflin Company. Adapted with permission.

various groups. This means that stereotyped thinking about others becomes a mindless habit—even for individuals who have been taught to be tolerant of those who are different from themselves (Devine, 1989; Fiske, 2002).

Although it's true that stereotypes kick in automatically, unintentionally, and unconsciously, individuals *can* override them—with some cognitive effort (Fiske, 2002). Thus, if you meet someone who speaks with an accent, your initial, automatic reaction might be negative. However, if you believe that prejudice is wrong and if you are aware that you are stereotyping, you can intentionally inhibit such thoughts. According to Patricia Devine's (1989) model of prejudice reduction, this process requires an intentional shift from *automatic processing* to *controlled processing*, or from *mindlessness* to *mindfulness*, in Ellen Langer's terms (see Chapter 5).

Research supports the idea that controlled, mindful thinking can actually reduce stereotyping and prejudice. In one study, children who were shown slides of handicapped individuals and who were asked questions that required them to think carefully about the disabled individuals showed less prejudice and more willingness to play with a handicapped peer than did children who saw the same slides but who were asked to make only mindless responses to the slides (Langer, Bashner, & Chanowitz, 1985). Thus, you can reduce prejudice if you are motivated to pay careful attention to what and how you think.

Intergroup Contact

Let's return to the Robbers' Cave study. When we left them, the Rattlers and Eagles were engaged in food fights and flag burning. Understandably, the experimenters were eager to restore peace. First, they tried speaking with each group, talking up the other group's good points and minimizing their differences. They also made the Eagles and the Rattlers sit together at meals and "fun" events like movies. Unfortunately, these tactics fell flat.

Next, the experimenters designed intergroup activities based on the principle of *superordinate goals—goals that require two or more groups to work together to achieve mutual ends.* For example, each boy had to contribute in some way (building a fire, preparing the food) on a cookout so that all could eat. After the boys had participated in a variety of such activities, the hostility between the two groups was much reduced. In fact, at the end of the three-week camping period, the Eagles and the Rattlers voted to ride the same bus back home.

Researchers have identified four necessary ingredients in the recipe for reducing intergroup hostility (Brewer & Brown, 1998). First, groups must *work together for a common goal* (merely bringing hostile groups into contact is not an effective way to reduce intergroup antagonism and may in fact worsen it). Second, cooperative efforts must have *successful outcomes* (if groups fail at a cooperative task, they are likely to blame each other for the failure). Third, group members must have the opportunity to establish *mean-*

ingful connections with one another and not merely go through the motions of interacting. The fourth factor of *equal status contact* requires bringing together members of different groups in ways that ensure that everyone has equal status. A large meta-analysis demonstrated clear support for intergroup contact as a means of reducing prejudice (Pettigrew & Tropp, 2000).

The "jigsaw classroom" uses these principles to reduce prejudice in schoolchildren (Aronson & Patnoe, 1997). In this intervention, six children are first assigned to an "expert group" in which they help each other learn specialized information prepared by the teacher about a study topic. Thus, each child becomes an "expert" on a subtopic. Then the children are assigned to ethnically mixed groups of six where they teach each other their school lessons. This arrangement puts all children on an equal footing (equal-status contact) and reduces competition for the teacher's attention and grades (scarce resources).

Children taught in a jigsaw classroom learn as much as peers taught in a traditional classroom setting. In addition, "jigsaw" children get an important bonus: Prejudice is replaced with positive feelings for ethnically different children, and the self-esteem of minority kids gets a big boost.

To conclude, although prejudice remains a complex and distressing social problem, a number of effective strategies are available to combat it.

The Power of Persuasion

LEARNING OBJECTIVES

- Cite the key elements in the persuasion process.
- Describe several source factors that influence persuasion.
- Discuss the evidence on one-sided versus two-sided messages and the value of arousing fear or positive feelings in persuasion.
- Describe several receiver factors that influence persuasion.
- Explain how the two cognitive routes to persuasion operate.

Every day you are bombarded by attempts to alter your attitudes through persuasion. You may not even be out of bed before you start hearing radio advertisements that are meant to persuade you to buy specific toothpastes, cell phones, and athletic shoes. When you watch the morning news, you hear statements from numerous government officials, all of which have been carefully crafted to shape your opinions. On your way to school, you see billboards showing attractive models draped over cars in the hopes that they can induce positive feelings that will transfer to the vehicles. Walking to class, a friend tries to get you to vote for his candidate for student body president. "Does it ever let up?" you wonder.

When it comes to persuasion, the answer is "no." As Anthony Pratkanis and Elliot Aronson (2000) note,

Americans live in the "age of propaganda." In light of this reality, let's examine some of the factors that determine whether persuasion works.

Persuasion **involves the communication of arguments and information intended to change another person's attitudes.** What are attitudes? For the pur-

WEB LINK 6.3

Social Influence and Persuasion
How are people influenced or affected by others? Shelley Wu has assembled a collection of web resources that seek to answer this question, covering such topics as cults, propaganda, and healthy approaches to influencing other people.

poses of our discussion, we'll define *attitudes* **as beliefs and feelings about people, objects, and ideas.** Let's look more closely at two of the terms in this definition. We use the term *beliefs* to mean thoughts and judgments about people, objects, and ideas. For example, you may *believe* that equal pay for equal work is a fair policy or that capital punishment is not an effec-

tive deterrent to crime. The "feeling" component of attitudes refers to the positivity and negativity of one's feelings about an issue as well as how strongly one feels about it. For example, you may *strongly favor* equal pay for equal work but only *mildly disagree* with the idea that capital punishment reduces the crime rate.

The Elements of the Persuasion Process

The process of persuasion includes four basic elements (see Figure 6.9). The *source* **is the person who sends a communication, and the** *receiver* **is the person to whom the message is sent.** Thus, if you watched a presidential address on TV, the president would be the source, and you and millions of other viewers would be the receivers in this persuasive effort. **The** *message* **is the information transmitted by the source; the** *channel* **is the medium through which the message is sent.** In examining communication channels, investigators have often compared face-to-face interaction against appeals sent via mass media (such as television and radio). Although the research on communication channels is interesting, we'll confine our discussion to source, message, and receiver variables.

Source Factors

Persuasion tends to be more successful when the source has high *credibility* (Petty, Wegener, & Fabrigar, 1997). Two subfactors make a communicator credible: expertise and trustworthiness. People try to convey their *expertise* by mentioning their degrees, their training, and their experience, or by showing an impressive grasp of the issue at hand (Wood & Kallgren, 1988). As to *trustworthiness*, whom would you believe if you were told that your state needs to reduce corporate taxes to stimulate its economy—the president of a huge corporation in your state or an economics professor from out of state? Probably the latter. Trustworthiness is undermined when a source, such as the corporation presi-

● FIGURE 6.9

Overview of the persuasion process. The process of persuasion essentially boils down to *who* (the source) communicates *what* (the message) *by what means* (the channel) *to whom* (the receiver). Thus, four sets of variables influence the process of persuasion: source, message, channel, and receiver factors. The diagram lists some of the more important factors in each category (including some that are not discussed in the text due to space limitations).

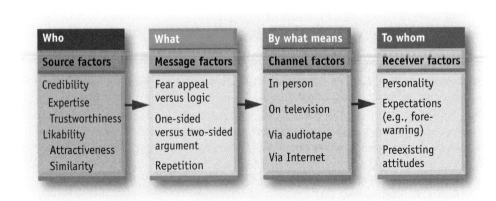

Who	What	By what means	To whom
Source factors	**Message factors**	**Channel factors**	**Receiver factors**
Credibility	Fear appeal versus logic	In person	Personality
Expertise		On television	Expectations (e.g., forewarning)
Trustworthiness	One-sided versus two-sided argument	Via audiotape	
Likability		Via Internet	Preexisting attitudes
Attractiveness	Repetition		
Similarity			

dent, appears to have something to gain. In contrast, trustworthiness is enhanced when people appear to argue against their own interests (Petty et al., 2001). This effect explains why salespeople often make remarks like "Frankly, my snowblower isn't the best and they have a better brand down the street if you're willing to spend a bit more . . ."

Likability is a second major source factor and includes a host of subfactors (Petty et al., 1997). A key consideration is a person's *physical attractiveness* (Petty et al., 1997). For example, one researcher found that attractive students were more successful than less attractive students in obtaining signatures for a petition (Chaiken, 1979). People also respond better to sources who are *similar* to them in ways that are relevant to the issue at hand (Mackie, Worth, & Asuncion, 1990). Thus, politicians stress the values they and their constituents hold in common.

Source variables are used to great effect in advertising. Many companies spend a fortune to obtain a spokesperson such as George Foreman, who combines trustworthiness, likability, and a knack for connecting with the average person. Companies quickly abandon spokespersons whose likability declines. For example, McDonald's and Sprite cancelled advertising contracts with basketball star Kobe Bryant after he was accused of rape. Thus, source variables are extremely important factors in persuasion.

Message Factors

Imagine that you are going to advocate the selection of a high-profile entertainer as the speaker at your commencement ceremony. In preparing your argument, you ponder the most effective way to structure your message. On the one hand, you're convinced that having a well-known entertainer on campus would be popular with students and would boost the image of your university in the community and among alumni. Still, you realize that this performer would cost a lot and that some people believe that an entertainer is not an appropriate commencement speaker. Should you present a *one-sided argument* that ignores the possible problems? Or should you present a *two-sided argument* that acknowledges concern about the problems and then downplays them?

In general, two-sided arguments seem to be more effective (Crowley & Hoyer, 1994). In fact, just men-

Advertisers frequently employ well-liked celebrities like James Earl Jones and Catherine Zeta-Jones to pitch their products, hoping that the positive feelings of the audience toward the source will transfer to the product.

tioning that there are two sides to an issue can increase your credibility with an audience (Jones & Brehm, 1970). One-sided messages work only when your audience is uneducated about the issue or when they already favor your point of view.

Persuaders also use emotional appeals to shift attitudes. Insurance companies show scenes of homes on fire to arouse fear. Antismoking campaigns emphasize the threat of cancer. Deodorant ads prey on the fear of embarrassment. Does *fear arousal* work? Yes, studies involving a wide range of issues (nuclear policy, auto safety, and dental hygiene among others) have shown that the arousal of fear often increases persuasion (Perloff, 1993). However, there are limiting conditions (Rogers & Prentice-Dunn, 1997). Fear appeals are most likely to work when your listeners view the dire consequences that you describe as exceedingly unpleasant, as fairly probable if they don't take your advice, and as avoidable if they do (Das, deWit, & Stroebe, 2003). If you induce strong fear in your audience without providing a workable solution to the problem (such as a surefire stop-smoking or weight-loss program), you may make your audience defensive, causing them to tune you out (Petty & Wegener, 1998).

Generating *positive feelings* is also an effective way to persuade people. Familiar examples of such tactics include the use of music and physically attractive actors in TV commercials, the use of laugh tracks in TV programs, and the practice of wining and dining prospective customers. Shortly after the terrorist attacks on America, you probably noticed that patriotic themes and images in ads increased dramatically. Producing positive feelings to win people over *can* be effective—

provided they don't care too much about the issue. If people do care about the topic, it takes more than good feelings to move them. For example, one study showed that the use of music in TV commercials was effective in persuading viewers, but only when the message concerned a trivial topic (Park & Young, 1986).

Receiver Factors

What about the receiver of the persuasive message? Are some people easier to persuade than others? Yes, but the answer is complicated. Transient factors, such as *forewarning* the receiver about a persuasive effort and a receiver's initial position on an issue, seem to be more influential than a receiver's personality. When you shop for a new TV, you expect salespeople to work at persuading you. To some extent, this forewarning reduces the impact of their arguments (Petty & Wegener, 1998). When receivers are forewarned about a persuasion attempt on a personally important topic, it is harder to persuade them than when they are not forewarned (Wood & Quinn, 2003). But when they are told to expect a persuasive message on an unimportant topic, their attitudes shift in the direction of the persuasive appeal even before it occurs—to avoid appearing gullible! Thus, the old saying, "To be forewarned is to be forearmed" is often, but not always, true.

Understandably, receivers are harder to persuade when they encounter a position that is incompatible with their existing beliefs. In general, people display a *disconfirmation bias* in evaluating such arguments (Edwards & Smith, 1996). Also, people from different cultures respond to different themes in persuasive messages. In one study, participants from an individualistic culture (the United States) preferred magazine ads that stressed the theme of uniqueness, while those from a collectivist culture (Korea) preferred ads that stressed conformity (Kim & Markus, 1999).

The Whys of Persuasion

In the previous section, we looked at a number of effective persuasion techniques. Clearly, you can't incorporate all of these factors into a single persuasive ap-

peal. Which ones should you use? To answer that important question, you need to understand *why* people change their attitudes. Thanks to the work of Richard Petty and John Cacioppo (1986), psychologists have a good understanding of the cognitive processes that underlie attitude change.

Richard Petty

According to the *elaboration likelihood model,* an individual's thoughts about a persuasive message (rather than the actual message itself) will determine whether attitude change will occur (Petty & Cacioppo, 1986). As we have noted, at some times people make quick, sloppy decisions (automatic processing, mindlessness, snap judgments), whereas at other times they process information carefully (controlled processing, mindfulness, systematic judgments). These processes also operate in persuasion.

John Cacioppo

When people are distracted, tired, or uninterested in a persuasive message, they fail to key in on the true merits of the product or issue. They process information, but not mindfully. Being in a happy mood produces the same effect (Sinclair, Mark, & Clore, 1994). Surprisingly, even when people do not carefully evaluate a message, attitude change can occur (Petty & Cacioppo, 1990). What happens is that the receiver is persuaded by cues that are peripheral to the message—hence the term the *peripheral route* (see Figure 6.10). Just because you're not mindfully analyzing a TV commercial for a new fruit drink doesn't mean that you're totally tuned out. You may not be paying attention to the substance of the commercial, but you are aware of superficial aspects of the ad—you like the music, your favorite basketball player is pitching the product, and so forth.

Although persuasion usually occurs via the peripheral route, senders can also use another route to attitude change—the *central route* (see Figure 6.10). In this

Courtesy, Richard E. Petty

Courtesy, John T. Cacioppo

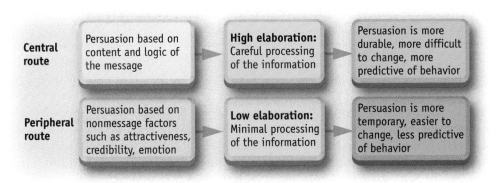

● FIGURE 6.10

The peripheral and central routes to attitude change. Persuasion can occur via two different routes. The central route, which results in high elaboration, tends to produce longer-lasting attitude change.

| **Central route** | Persuasion based on content and logic of the message | **High elaboration:** Careful processing of the information | Persuasion is more durable, more difficult to change, more predictive of behavior |
| **Peripheral route** | Persuasion based on nonmessage factors such as attractiveness, credibility, emotion | **Low elaboration:** Minimal processing of the information | Persuasion is more temporary, easier to change, less predictive of behavior |

Political candidates use music, flags, and slogans to persuade via the peripheral route; when they present their views on an issue, they are going for the central route.

letting biases influence their judgments, they overcorrected to the extent that a dislikable source was more persuasive than a likable one (Petty, Wegener, & White, 1998).

Ultimately, the two routes to persuasion are not equally effective. Attitudes formed via the central route are longer lasting and more resistant to challenge than those formed via the peripheral route (Petty & Wegener, 1998). They are also better predictors of a person's behavior (Petty, Priester, & Wegener, 1994).

To conclude, although we can't stem the tide of persuasive messages bombarding you every day, we hope we've alerted you to the need to be a vigilant recipient of persuasion attempts. Of course, persuasion is not the *only* method through which people try to influence you, as you'll see in the next section.

case, receivers process persuasive messages mindfully, by thinking about the logic and merits of the pertinent (or central) arguments. In other words, the receiver cognitively *elaborates* on the persuasive message—hence, the name of the model. If people have a favorable reaction to their thoughtful evaluation of a message, positive attitude change occurs; an unfavorable reaction results in negative attitude change.

For the central route to override the peripheral route, there are two requirements. First, receivers must be *motivated* to process the persuasive message carefully. Motivation is triggered when people are interested in the issue, find it personally relevant, and have time and energy to think about it carefully. For example, if your university is considering changing its grading system, you will probably make a point of thinking carefully about the various options and their implications. Second, receivers must have the *ability* to grasp the message that is, the message must be comprehensible, and individuals must be capable of understanding it. If people are distracted, tired, or find the message uninteresting or irrelevant, they will not pay careful attention to it, and superficial cues will become salient.

If people mindfully process persuasive messages, does doing so ensure that their decisions are objective or unbiased? It seems not. Biased processing can result from both motivational factors (having a vested interest) and ability factors (one-sided knowledge of an issue) (Wood, 2000). And alerting people to possible biases in their thinking doesn't necessarily help. For example, when participants were cautioned to avoid

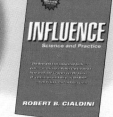

RECOMMENDED READING

Influence: Science and Practice
by Robert B. Cialdini
(Allyn and Bacon, 2001)

Cialdini, a social psychologist, has conducted extensive empirical research on influence tactics such as the door-in-the-face technique and lowballing (see the Application). As you might expect, Cialdini's book is based on his studies and his review of other scientific research on the topic. However, what makes his book unique is that he went far beyond laboratory research in his effort to better understand the ins and outs of social influence. For three years, he immersed himself in the real world of influence artists, becoming a "spy of sorts." As he puts it, "When I wanted to learn about the compliance tactics of encyclopedia (or vacuum cleaner, or portrait photography, or dance lessons) sales organizations, I would answer a newspaper ad for sales trainees and have them teach me their methods. Using similar but not identical approaches, I was able to penetrate advertising, public relations, and fundraising agencies to examine their techniques" (from the preface). The result is an insightful book that bolsters scientific data with anecdotal accounts of how influence artists ply their trade. Familiarity with their strategies can help you avoid being an easy mark, or "patsy."

Published by Allyn and Bacon, Boston, MA. Copyright © 2001 by Pearson Education. Reprinted by permission of the publisher.

The Power of Social Pressure

LEARNING OBJECTIVES

- Summarize what Asch discovered about conformity.
- Discuss the difference between normative and informational influence.
- Describe some conformity pressures in everyday life and how people can resist them.
- Describe some situational and personality factors involved in obedience to authority.
- Cite an important factor in resisting inappropriate demands of authority figures.
- Describe how culture can affect people's responses to social influence.

In the previous section, we showed you how others attempt to change your *attitudes*. Now you'll see how others attempt to change your *behavior*—by trying to get you to agree to their requests and demands.

Conformity and Compliance Pressures

If you extol the talent of popular singer Beyoncé Knowles or keep a well-manicured lawn, are you exhibiting conformity? According to social psychologists, it depends on whether your behavior is freely chosen or the result of group pressure. *Conformity* **occurs when people yield to real or imagined social pressure.** For example, if you like Beyoncé because you truly enjoy her music, that's not conformity. However, if you like her because it's "cool" and your friends would question your taste if you didn't, then you're conforming. Similarly, if you maintain a well-groomed lawn just to avoid complaints from your neighbors, you're yielding to social pressure.

The Dynamics of Conformity

To introduce this topic, we'll re-create a classic experiment devised by Solomon Asch (1955). The participants are male undergraduates recruited for a study of visual perception. A group of seven participants are shown a large card with a vertical line on it and asked to indicate which of three lines on a second card matches the original "standard line" in length (see Figure 6.11). All seven participants are given a turn at the task, and each announces his choice to the group. The subject in the sixth chair doesn't know it, but everyone else in the group is an accomplice of the experimenter.

The accomplices give accurate responses on the first two trials. On the third trial, line 2 clearly is the correct response, but the first five participants all say that line 3 matches the standard line. The genuine subject can't believe his ears. Over the course of the experiment, the accomplices all give the same incorrect response on 12 out of 18 trials. Asch wanted to see how the subject would respond in these situations. The line judgments are easy and unambiguous. Without group pressure, people make matching errors less than 1 per-

cent of the time. So, if the subject consistently agrees with the accomplices, he isn't making honest mistakes—he is conforming. Will the subject stick to his guns, or will he go along with the group? Averaging across 123 participants, Asch (1955) found that the men conformed (made mistakes) on 37 percent of the 12 trials. However, the participants varied considerably in their tendency to conform: 25 percent never caved in to the group, while 75 percent conformed on at least one trial. Although a meta-analysis of 133 Asch-type studies reported that conformity has declined over the past 50 years, it also concluded that majority influence remains a powerful force (Bond & Smith, 1996).

In subsequent studies, Asch (1956) determined that group size and group unanimity are key determinants of conformity. To examine group size, Asch repeated his procedure with groups that included 1 to 15 accomplices. Little conformity was seen when a subject was pitted against just one accomplice. Conformity increased rapidly as group size went from 2 to 4, peaked at a group size of 7, and then leveled off (see Figure 6.12). Thus, Asch concluded that as group size increases, conformity increases—up to a point. Subsequent research has confirmed this finding (Nemeth & Chiles, 1988). Significantly, Asch found that group size made little difference if just one accomplice "broke" with the others, wrecking their unanimous agreement. The presence of another dissenter lowered conformity to about one-quarter of its peak, even when the dis-

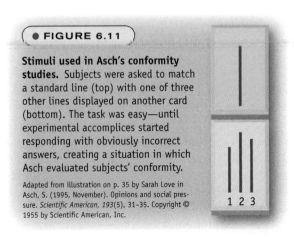

● FIGURE 6.11

Stimuli used in Asch's conformity studies. Subjects were asked to match a standard line (top) with one of three other lines displayed on another card (bottom). The task was easy—until experimental accomplices started responding with obviously incorrect answers, creating a situation in which Asch evaluated subjects' conformity.

Adapted from illustration on p. 35 by Sarah Love in Asch, S. (1995, November). Opinions and social pressure. *Scientific American, 193*(5), 31–35. Copyright © 1955 by Scientific American, Inc.

1 2 3

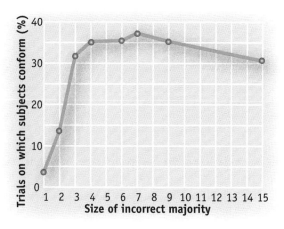

● FIGURE 6.12

Conformity and group size. This graph shows the percentage of trials on which subjects conformed as a function of the number of individuals with an opposing view. Asch found that conformity became more frequent as group size increased, up to about 7 persons, and then leveled off.

Adapted from illustration on p. 32 by Sarah Love in Asch, S. (1995, November). Opinions and social pressure. *Scientific American, 193*(5), 31–35. Copyright © 1955 by Scientific American, Inc.

senter made inaccurate judgments that happened to conflict with the majority view. Apparently, the participants just needed to hear a second person question the accuracy of the group's perplexing responses.

Conformity Versus Compliance

Did the conforming participants in Asch's study really change their beliefs in response to social pressure, or did they just pretend to change them? Subsequent studies asked participants to make their responses privately, instead of publicly (Deutsch & Gerard, 1955; Insko et al., 1985). Conformity declined dramatically when participants wrote down their responses. Thus, it is likely that Asch's participants did not really change their beliefs. Based on this evidence, theorists concluded that Asch's experiments evoked a particular type of conformity, called compliance. *Compliance* occurs **when people yield to social pressure in their public behavior, even though their private beliefs have not changed.**

The Whys of Conformity

People often conform or comply because they are afraid of being criticized or rejected. *Normative influence* **operates when people conform to social norms for fear of negative social consequences.** For example, around the time of the Supreme Court decision in 1954 that outlawed segregated schools, many ministers in Little Rock, Arkansas favored integration. However, they kept their opinions to themselves because they feared that they would lose church members and contributions if they went against the views of the majority (Campbell & Pettigrew, 1959). Compliance often results from subtle, implied pressure. For example, for fear of making a negative impression, you may remove your eyebrow ring for a job interview. However, compliance also occurs in response to explicit rules, requests, and commands. Thus, you'll probably follow your boss's directions even when you think they're lousy ideas.

People are also likely to conform when they are uncertain how to behave (Cialdini, 2001; Sherif, 1936). Thus, if you're at a nice restaurant and don't know which fork to use, you may watch others to see what they're doing. *Informational influence* **operates when people look to others for how to behave in ambiguous situations.** In situations like this, using others as a source of information about appropriate behavior is a good thing. But relying on others to know how to behave in unfamiliar situations can sometimes be problematic, as you'll see shortly.

It may have occurred to you that it is not always easy to distinguish normative from informational influence. Such concerns have prompted researchers to find alternative explanations for conformity (Martin & Hewstone, 2003). One viewpoint reconceptualizes normative and informational influence into three motives that underlie conformity (Cialdini & Goldstein, 2004): positive self-evaluations and having good relationships with others (normative-based motives) and better understanding a situation to reduce uncertainty (information-based motive). Another perspective looks at the role of group identification on conformity. For example, young adults who strongly identified with peer groups that endorsed smoking were more likely to smoke than were those who had a weak group identification (Schofield et al. 2001).

Resisting Conformity Pressures

Sometimes conforming is just harmless fun—such as participating in Internet-generated "flash mobs." At other times, people conform on relatively trivial matters—such as dressing up for a nice restaurant. In this case, conformity and compliance minimize the confusion and anxiety people experience in unfamiliar situations. However, when individuals feel pressured to conform to antisocial norms, tragic consequences may result. Negative examples of "going along with the crowd" include drinking more than one knows one should because others say, "C'mon, have just one more" and driving at someone's urging when under the influence of alcohol or drugs. Other instances include refusing to socialize with someone simply because the person isn't liked by one's social group and failing to come to another's defense when it might make one unpopular.

"Flash mobs" are an example of harmless conformity to social pressure. Participants follow instructions on the Internet to appear at a designated time and place to engage in specified, nonsensical behavior.

The above examples all concern normative influence, but pressure can come from informational influence as well. A useful example concerns a paradox called the *bystander effect*—the tendency for individuals to be less likely to provide help when others are present than when they are alone. Numerous studies have confirmed that people are less helpful in emergency situations when others are around (Latané and Nida, 1981; Levine et al., 1994). This effect even shows up on the Internet, when members of different-sized chat groups receive requests for assistance (Markey, 2000). Thankfully, the bystander effect is less likely to occur when the need for help is very clear.

What accounts for the bystander effect? A number of factors are at work, and conformity is one of them. The bystander effect is most likely to occur in *ambiguous situations,* because people look around to see whether others are acting as if there's an emergency (Harrison & Wells, 1991). If everyone hesitates, this inaction (in formational influence) suggests that help isn't needed. So the next time you witness what you think might be an emergency, don't automatically give in to the informational influence of inaction.

To resist conformity pressures, we offer these suggestions: First, make an effort to pay more attention to the social forces operating on you. Second, if you find yourself in a situation where others are pressuring you, try to identify someone in the group whose views match yours. Recall that just one dissenter in Asch's groups significantly reduced conformity pressures. And, if you know in advance that you're heading into this kind of situation, consider inviting a friend with similar views to go along.

Pressure from Authority Figures

Obedience is a form of compliance that occurs when people follow direct commands, usually from someone in a position of authority. In itself, obedience isn't good or bad; it depends on what one is being told to do. For example, if the fire alarm goes off in your classroom building and your instructor "orders" you to leave, obedience is a good idea. On the other hand, if your boss asks you to engage in an unethical or illegal act, *disobedience* is probably in order.

The Dynamics of Obedience

Stanley Milgram

Like many other people after World War II, social psychologist Stanley Milgram was troubled by how readily the citizens of Germany had followed the orders of dictator Adolf Hitler, even when the orders required morally repugnant actions, such as the slaughter of millions of Jews, as well as Russians, Poles, Gypsies, and homosexuals. This was Milgram's motivation to study the dynamics of obedience. Milgram's (1963) participants were a diverse collection of 40 men from the local community who volunteered for a study on the effects of punishment on learning. When they arrived at the lab, they drew slips of paper from a hat to get their assignments. The drawing was rigged so that the subject always became the "teacher" and an experimental accomplice (a likable 47-year-old accountant) became the "learner."

The teacher watched while the learner was strapped into a chair and as electrodes were attached to his arms (to be used to deliver shocks whenever he made a mistake on the task). The subject was then taken to an adjoining room that housed the shock generator that he would control in his role as the teacher. Although the apparatus looked and sounded realistic, it was a fake, and the learner was never shocked. The experimenter played the role of the authority figure who told the teacher what to do and who answered any questions that arose.

The experiment was designed such that the learner would make many mistakes, and the teacher was instructed to increase the shock level after each wrong answer. At 300 volts, the learner began to pound on the wall between the two rooms in protest and soon stopped responding to the teacher's questions. From this point forward, participants frequently turned to the experimenter for guidance. Whenever they did so, the experimenter (authority figure) firmly stated that the teacher should continue to give stronger and stronger shocks to the now-silent learner. Milgram wanted to know the maximum shock the teacher was willing to administer before refusing to cooperate.

As Figure 6.13 shows, 65 percent of the subjects administered all 30 levels of shock. Although they tended to obey the experimenter, many participants voiced and displayed considerable distress about harming the learner. They protested, groaned, bit their lips, trembled, and broke into a sweat—but they continued administering the shocks. Based on these findings, Milgram concluded that obedience to authority was even more common than he or others had anticipated.

The Causes of Obedience

After his initial demonstration, Milgram (1974) tried about 20 variations on his experimental procedure, looking for factors that influenced participants' obedience. For instance, he studied female participants to look at gender differences in obedience (he found no evidence of such differences). In another condition, two confederates played the role of teachers who defied the experimenter's demands to continue, one at 150 volts and one at 210 volts. In this condition, only 10 percent of the subjects shocked at the maximum level.

What caused the obedient behavior observed by Milgram? First, the demands on the participants (to shock the learner) escalated gradually so that very strong shocks were demanded only after the participant was well into the experiment. Second, participants were told that the authority figure, not the teacher, was responsible if anything happened to the learner. Third, subjects evaluated their actions in terms of how well they lived up to the authority figure's expectations, not by their harmful effects on the victim. Taken together, these findings suggest that human behavior is determined not so much by the *kind of person* one is as by the *kind of situation* one is in. Applying this insight to Nazi war crimes and other atrocities, Milgram made a chilling assertion: Inhuman and evil visions may originate in the disturbed mind of an authority figure like Hitler, but it is only through the obedient actions of normal people that such ideas can be turned into frightening reality.

Research has also identified personality variables that correlate with greater obedience. Authoritarianism is one of those (Elms & Milgram, 1966). Recall from our earlier discussion of this concept that, in addition to being prejudiced, those who score high on authoritarianism tend to be overly submissive to people in authority. On the other hand, individuals who have a strong sense of social responsibility and those who believe that they are in control of their destiny are less obedient than those with a weaker sense of social respon-

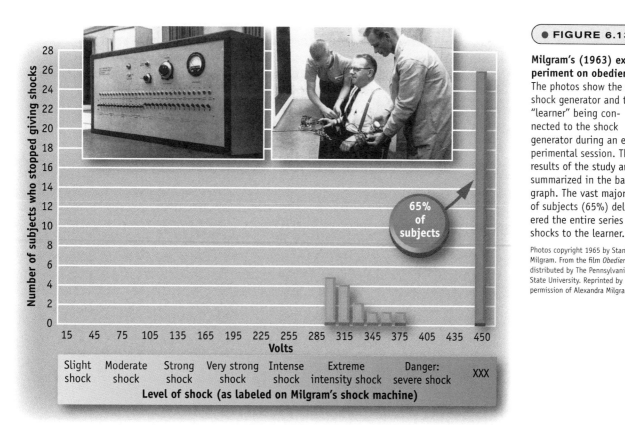

● FIGURE 6.13

Milgram's (1963) experiment on obedience.
The photos show the fake shock generator and the "learner" being connected to the shock generator during an experimental session. The results of the study are summarized in the bar graph. The vast majority of subjects (65%) delivered the entire series of shocks to the learner.

Photos copyright 1965 by Stanley Milgram. From the film *Obedience*, distributed by The Pennsylvania State University. Reprinted by permission of Alexandra Milgram.

65% of subjects

Number of subjects who stopped giving shocks

Volts

| Slight shock | Moderate shock | Strong shock | Very strong shock | Intense shock | Extreme intensity shock | Danger: severe shock | XXX |

Level of shock (as labeled on Milgram's shock machine)

sibility and those who believe that fate controls their destiny (Berkowitz, 1999; Blass, 1999). Thus, a few personality factors do play a role in obedient behavior. Still, the pervasive tendencies toward obedience demonstrate that situational factors have greater impact.

Milgram's study has been consistently replicated for many years, in diverse settings, with a variety of participants and procedural variations (Blass, 1999). Overall, the weight of evidence supports Milgram's results. Of course, critics have questioned the ethics of Milgram's procedure (Baumrind, 1964). Today, at most universities it would be difficult to obtain permission to replicate Milgram's study—an ironic epitaph for what may be psychology's best-known experiment.

To Obey or Not to Obey?

The findings of obedience research confront us with the chilling fact that most people can be coerced into engaging in actions that violate their morals and values. Recall the 1968 My Lai incident, an American "crime of obedience," in which U.S. military forces killed 400–500 Vietnamese women, children, and elderly men (Kelman & Hamilton, 1989). The Abu Ghraib prison scandal in Iraq is a more recent reminder that strong social pressures can produce morally repugnant behavior. Nonetheless, some individuals *are* able to resist pressure from authority figures. A dramatic example is Karen Silkwood, who probably died because she tried to report unsafe practices at the nuclear power plant where she worked. Thankfully, disobedience to authority is usually less dramatic and less dangerous, but "ethical resisters" also risk the loss of credibility, friends, and jobs for the sake of important principles (Glazer & Glazer, 1990). Examples of "whistleblowers" include Erin Brockovich, who helped expose hazardous-waste dangers, and Sherron Watkins, who warned Ken Lay, her boss at Enron Corporation, about accounting irregularities there.

In keeping with Milgram's finding that participants in the condition with two disobedient confederates found it easier to defy authority, it seems that social support plays a critical role in disobedient behavior. The findings of a study on college students' decisions to ride with an intoxicated driver are relevant here (Powell & Drucker, 1997). Participants were randomly assigned to one of four conditions: (1) driver with one beer, (2) intoxicated driver, (3) intoxicated driver and confederate who enters the car, and (4) intoxicated driver and confederate who refuses to enter the car. Participants consistently chose to enter the car in all conditions except when the confederate refused. Especially when disobedience involves risk, aligning oneself with

WEB LINK 6.4

The Stanford Prison Experiment: A Simulation Study of the Psychology of Imprisonment
The Stanford Prison experiment, conducted by Philip Zimbardo in 1971, is one of psychology's most famous studies. At this site, Zimbardo provides an in-depth set of online slides, supplemental materials, discussion questions, and links to other sites detailing all aspects of the original study and important reflections after more than 30 years.

supportive others (family, friends, labor unions, for example) can decrease anxiety and increase safety.

In dealing with pressure from authority figures, remember that social influence is a two-way street: You are not merely a helpless victim. Being mindful of how obedience pressures operate and of some strategies that make it easier to resist these pressures should make you a stronger player in these situations.

Culture and Social Influence

As we have discussed, Western cultures tend to have an individualistic orientation and other cultures, a collectivist orientation. This observed difference in orientations appears to influence people's *attitudes* about the desirability or undesirability of conformity, compliance, and obedience. For example, among East Asians, conformity is associated with the valued characteristics of harmony and connectedness; among Americans, uniqueness is associated with the positive values of freedom and interdependence (Kim & Markus, 1999). Thus, East Asians view conformity and obedience more positively than either Americans or citizens of some other Western countries (Matsumoto, 1994).

Is conformity *behavior* more common in collectivist than in individualistic cultures? Yes, as you might expect. A meta-analysis compared conformity rates in 17 countries and reported that conformity rates were higher in collectivist cultures than in individualistic cultures (Bond & Smith, 1996). Studies have found that both Japanese and Koreans are more conforming than Americans (Buck, Newton, & Muramatsu, 1984; Kim & Markus, 1999). Thus, beliefs about the desirability of yielding to social influence as well as conforming behavior are consistent with cultural orientations.

In the Application, we'll alert you to some social influence strategies that people use to get you and others to agree to their requests.

Seeing Through Compliance Tactics

LEARNING OBJECTIVES

- Describe two compliance strategies based on the principles of commitment and consistency.
- Describe several compliance strategies based on the principle of reciprocity.
- Discuss how the principle of scarcity can increase a person's desire for something.

Which of the following statements is true?

____ **1.** It's a good idea to ask for a small favor before soliciting the larger favor that you really want.

____ **2.** It's a good idea to ask for a large favor before soliciting the smaller favor that you really want.

Would you believe that *both* of the statements are true? Although the two approaches work for different reasons, both can be effective ways to get people to do what you want. It pays to understand these and other social influence strategies because advertisers, salespeople, and fundraisers (not to mention friends and neighbors) use them frequently to influence people's behavior. So you can see the relevance of these strategies to your own life, we've grouped them by the principles that make them work. Much of our discussion is based on the work of Robert Cialdini (2001), a social psychologist who spent several years observing social influence tactics used by salespeople, fundraisers, advertisers, and other compliance professionals. His book, *Influence: Science and Practice,* is an excellent and entertaining discussion of social influence principles in action.

Courtesy, Robert Cialdini

Robert Cialdini

The Consistency Principle

Once people agree to something, they tend to stick with their initial commitment (Cialdini, 2001). This principle is used to gain compliance in two ways. Both involve a person getting another individual to commit to an initial request and then changing the terms of the agreement to the requestor's advantage. Because people often stay with their initial commitments, the target will likely agree to the revised proposal, even though it may not be to his or her benefit.

The Foot-in-the-Door Technique

Door-to-door salespeople have long recognized the importance of gaining a *little* cooperation from sales targets (getting a "foot in the door") before hitting them with the real sales pitch. The *foot-in-the-door* **(FITD) *technique* involves getting people to agree to a small request to increase the chances that they will agree to a larger request later** (see Figure 6.14a on the next page). This technique is widely used. For example, groups seeking donations often ask people to simply sign a petition first. Salespeople routinely ask individuals to try a product with "no obligations" before they launch their hard sell. In a similar vein, a wife might ask her husband to get her a cup of coffee, and when he gets up to fetch it say, "While you're up, would you fix me a peanut butter sandwich?"

The FITD technique was first investigated by Jonathon Freedman and his colleagues. In one study (Freedman & Fraser, 1966), the large request involved telephoning homemakers to ask whether a team of six men doing consumer research could come into their home to classify all their household products. Imagine six strangers tramping through your home, pulling everything out of your closets and cupboards, and you can understand why only 22 percent of the subjects in the control group agreed to this outlandish request. Subjects in the experimental group were contacted three days before the unreasonable request was made and were asked to answer a few questions about the soaps used in their home. When the large request was made three days later, 53 percent of the experimental group complied with that request.

Of course, no strategy works all the time. A review of research reported that the FITD tactic increases compliance rates, on the average, about 13 percent (Burger, 1999). The technique may be ineffective if the second

┌───┐
│ **WEB LINK 6.5**   │
│   │
│ **Influence at Work**   │
│ This website, by researchers Robert Cialdini and Kelton │
│ Rhodes, offers an intriguing set of pages that explore │
│ a wide variety of social influence phenomena: persuasion, │
│ propaganda, brainwashing, and the tactics of various │
│ types of cults.   │
└───┘

The foot-in-the-door and door-in-the-face techniques. These two influence techniques are essentially the reverse of each other, but both can work. **(a)** In the foot-in-the-door technique, you begin with a small request and work up to a larger one. **(b)** In the door-in-the-face technique, you begin with a large request and work down to a smaller one.

request follows too quickly on the heels of the first one (Chartrand, Pinckert, & Burger, 1999), if the initial request is too trivial to register, or if the second request is so large it is unreasonable (Burger, 1999).

Why does this strategy work? The best explanation is rooted in Daryl Bem's *self-perception theory* or the idea that people sometimes infer their attitudes by observing their own behavior (Burger & Caldwell, 2003; Burger & Guadagno, 2003). When Joe agrees to sign a petition, he infers that he is a helpful person. So when he is confronted with a second, larger request to collect petition signatures, "helpful person" comes to mind, and Joe complies with the request.

The Lowball Technique

A second commitment-based strategy is the *lowball technique,* which involves getting someone to commit to an attractive proposition before its hidden costs are revealed. The name for this technique derives from a common practice in automobile sales, in which a customer is offered a terrific bargain on a car. The bargain price gets the customer to commit to buying, but soon after, the dealer starts revealing some hidden costs. Typically, the customer discovers that options apparently included in the original price are actually going to cost extra. Once they have committed to buying a car, most customers are unlikely to cancel the deal. Car dealers aren't the only ones who use this technique. For instance, a friend might ask if you want to spend a week with him at his charming backwoods cabin. After you accept this seemingly generous offer, he may add, "Of course, there's a little work to do. We need to paint the doors, repair the pier, and . . ." You might think that people would become angry and back out of a deal once its hidden costs are revealed. Sometimes this does happen, but once people make a public commitment, lowballing is a surprisingly effective strategy (Burger & Cornelius, 2003).

The Reciprocity Principle

Most people have been socialized to believe in the *reciprocity principle—the rule that one should pay back in kind what one receives from others.* Charities frequently make use of this principle. Groups seeking donations for the disabled, the homeless, and so forth routinely send "free" address labels, key rings, and other small gifts with their pleas for donations. The belief that we should reciprocate others' kindness is a powerful norm; thus, people often feel obliged to reciprocate by making a donation in return for the gift. According to Cialdini (2001), the reciprocity norm is so powerful that it often works even when (1) the gift is uninvited, (2) the gift comes from someone you dislike, or (3) the gift results in an uneven exchange. Let's review some reciprocity-based influence tactics.

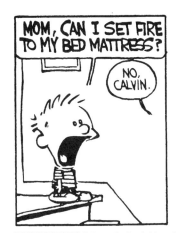

The Door-in-the-Face Technique

The door-in-the-face technique reverses the sequence of requests employed with the foot-in-the-door technique. The **door-in-the-face (DITF) technique involves making a large request that is likely to be turned down in order to increase the chances that people will agree to a smaller request later** (see Figure 6.14b). The name for this strategy is derived from the expectation that an initial request will be quickly rejected. For example, a wife who wants to coax her frugal husband into agreeing to buy a $25,000 sports car might begin by proposing that they purchase a $35,000 sports car. By the time he has talked his wife out of the pricier car, the $25,000 price tag may look quite reasonable to him. For the DITF to work, there must be no delay between the two requests (O'Keefe & Hale, 2001).

Other Reciprocity-Based Techniques

Salespeople who distribute free samples to prospective customers are also using the reciprocity principle. Cialdini (2001) describes the procedures used by the Amway Corporation, which sells such household products as detergent, floor wax, and insect spray. Amway's door-to-door salespeople give homemakers many bottles of their products for a "free trial." When they return a few days later, most of the homemakers feel obligated to buy some of the products.

The reciprocity norm is meant to promote fair exchanges in social interactions. However, when people manipulate the reciprocity rule, they usually give something of minimal value in the hopes of getting far more in return. For example, a person selling large computer systems may treat a potential customer at an exclusive restaurant in an effort to close a deal worth hundreds of thousands of dollars.

The Scarcity Principle

It's no secret that telling people they can't have something only makes them want it more. According to Cialdini (2001), this principle derives from two sources.

First, people have learned that items that are hard to get are of better quality than items that are easy to get. From there, they often assume, erroneously, that anything that is scarce must be good. Second, when people's choices (of products, services, romantic partners, job candidates) are constrained in some way, they often want what they can't have even more (Brehm & Brehm, 1981; Williams et al., 1993). The psychological term for this is *reactance* (Brehm, 1966).

Companies and advertisers frequently use the scarcity principle to drive up the demand for their products. Thus, you constantly see ads that scream "limited supply available," "for a limited time only," "while they last," and "time is running out."

In summary, people use a variety of methods to coax compliance from one another. Despite the fact that many of these influence techniques are more or less dishonest, they're still widely used. There is no way to completely avoid being hoodwinked by influence strategies. However, being alert to them can reduce the likelihood that you'll be a victim of influence artists. As we noted in our discussion of persuasion, "to be forewarned is to be forearmed."

Advertisers often try to artificially create scarcity to make their products seem more desirable.

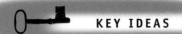

KEY IDEAS

Forming Impressions of Others

■ In forming impressions of other people, individuals rely on appearance, verbal behavior, actions, nonverbal messages, and situational cues. Individuals usually make snap judgments about others unless accurate impressions are important. To explain the causes of other people's behavior, individuals make attributions (either internal or external).

■ People often try to confirm their expectations about what others are like, which can result in biased impressions. Self-fulfilling prophecies can actually change a target person's behavior in the direction of a perceiver's expectations. Cognitive distortions are caused by categorizing, stereotyping, the fundamental attribution error, and defensive attributions. The process of person perception is characterized by the themes of efficiency, selectivity, and consistency.

The Problem of Prejudice

■ Prejudice is a particularly unfortunate outcome of the tendency to view others inaccurately. Blatant ("old-fashioned") discrimination occurs relatively infrequently today, but subtle expressions of prejudice and discrimination ("modern discrimination") have become more common. Common causes of prejudice include right-wing authoritarianism, cognitive distortions, competition between groups, and threats to social identity. Strategies for reducing prejudice are rooted in social thinking and intergroup contact.

The Power of Persuasion

■ The success of persuasive efforts depends on several factors. A source of persuasion who is expert, trustworthy, likable, physically attractive, and similar to the receiver tends to be relatively effective. Although there are some limitations, two-sided arguments, arousal of fear, and generation of positive feelings are effective elements in persuasive messages. Persuasion is undermined when receivers are forewarned or have beliefs that are incompatible with the position being advocated.

■ Persuasion takes place via two processes. The central route to persuasion requires a receiver to be motivated to process persuasive messages carefully (elaboration). A favorable reaction to such an evaluation will result in positive attitude change. When a receiver is unmotivated or unable to process persuasive messages carefully, persuasion may take place via the peripheral route (on the basis of simple cues such as a catchy tune).

The Power of Social Pressure

■ Asch found that subjects often conform to the group, even when the group reports inaccurate judgments. Asch's experiments may have produced public compliance while subjects' private beliefs remained unchanged. Both normative and informational influence can produce conformity. Being mindful of social pressures and getting support from others with similar views are ways to resist conformity pressures.

■ In Milgram's landmark study of obedience to authority, subjects showed a remarkable tendency to follow orders to shock an innocent stranger. Personality factors can influence obedient behavior, but situational pressures are more powerful determinants. Although people often obey authority figures, sometimes they are disobedient, usually because they have social support.

■ The value cultures place on conformity influences the extent to which individuals are likely to conform. Conformity tends to be greater in collectivistic cultures.

Application: Seeing Through Compliance Tactics

■ Although they work for different reasons, all compliance tactics have the same goal: getting people to agree to requests. The foot-in-the-door and the lowball technique are based on the principle of consistency, while the door-in-the-face technique and the tactic of offering "give-away" items rely on the principle of reciprocity. When advertisers suggest that products are in short supply, they are using the scarcity principle. Understanding these strategies can make you less vulnerable to manipulation.

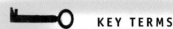

KEY TERMS

Attitudes   p. 186
Attributions   p. 173
Bystander effect   p. 192
Channel   p. 186
Compliance   p. 191
Confirmation bias   p. 174
Conformity   p. 190
Defensive attribution   p. 178
Discrimination   p. 181
Door-in-the-face technique
   p. 197
Elaboration likelihood model
   p. 188
Foot-in-the-door technique
   p. 195
Fundamental attribution
   error   p. 177

Informational influence
   p. 191
Lowball technique   p. 196
Message   p. 186
Normative influence   p. 191
Obedience   p. 192
Person perception   p. 172
Persuasion   p. 185
Prejudice   p. 181
Primacy effect   p. 180
Receiver   p. 186
Reciprocity principle   p. 196
Self-fulfilling prophecy
   p. 175
Source   p. 186
Stereotypes   p. 176
Superordinate goals   p. 185

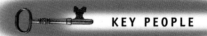

KEY PEOPLE

Solomon Asch   pp. 190–191
Robert Cialdini   pp. 189,
   195–197
Susan Fiske   pp. 172–173

Stanley Milgram
   pp. 192–194
Richard Petty and John
   Cacioppo   pp. 188–189
Muzafer Sherif   p. 183

PRACTICE TEST

1. Mindfulness operates when people:
   a. make snap judgments.
   b. are on "cognitive automatic pilot."
   c. make systematic judgments.
   d. are not concerned about forming accurate impressions.

2. Which of the following is *not* a type of cognitive distortion in perception?
   a. Categorizing
   b. "Old-fashioned" discrimination
   c. Stereotypes
   d. Defensive attribution

3. Which of the following is *not* a theme in person perception?
   a. Efficiency
   b. Selectivity
   c. Consistency
   d. Mindfulness

4. "Old-fashioned" discrimination is _____; modern discrimination is _____.
   a. blatant; subtle
   b. legal; illegal
   c. common; rare
   d. race-based; gender-based

5. Which of the following is a cause of prejudice?
   a. Mindfulness
   b. Right-wing authoritarianism
   c. Jigsaw classrooms
   d. Activities based on superordinate goals

6. Receivers who are forewarned that someone will try to persuade them will most likely
   a. be very open to persuasion.
   b. get up and stomp out of the room.
   c. not be very open to persuasion.
   d. heckle the persuader.

7. Compared to attitudes formed via the peripheral route, those formed via the central route
   a. operate subliminally.
   b. are hard to change.
   c. last only a short time.
   d. are poor predictors of behavior.

8. When people change their outward behavior but not their private beliefs, _____ is operating.
   a. conformity
   b. persuasion
   c. obedience
   d. compliance

9. Conformity is
   a. more common in collectivist countries.
   b. more common in individualistic countries.
   c. not affected by culture.
   d. viewed very positively in all cultures.

10. When charities send prospective donors free address labels and the like, which of the following social influence principles are they using?
    a. The consistency principle
    b. The scarcity principle
    c. The reciprocity principle
    d. The foot-in-the-door principle

Book Companion Website

Visit the Book Companion Website at **http://psychology.wadsworth.com/weiten_lloyd8e**, where you will find tutorial quizzes, flashcards, and weblinks for every chapter, a final exam, and more! You can also link to the Thomson Wadsworth Psychology Resource Center (accessible directly at **http://psychology.wadsworth.com**) for a range of psychology-related resources.

Personal Explorations Workbook

The following exercises in your *Personal Explorations Workbook* may enhance your self-understanding in relation to issues raised in this chapter. **Questionnaire 6.1:** Argumentativeness Scale. **Personal Probe 6.1:** Can You Identify Your Prejudicial Stereotypes? **Personal Probe 6.2:** How Do You Operate in a Group?

ANSWERS

1. c Page 173
2. b Page 176
3. d Pages 179–180
4. a Pages 181–182
5. b Page 182
6. c Page 188
7. b Page 189
8. d Page 191
9. a Page 194
10. c Page 196

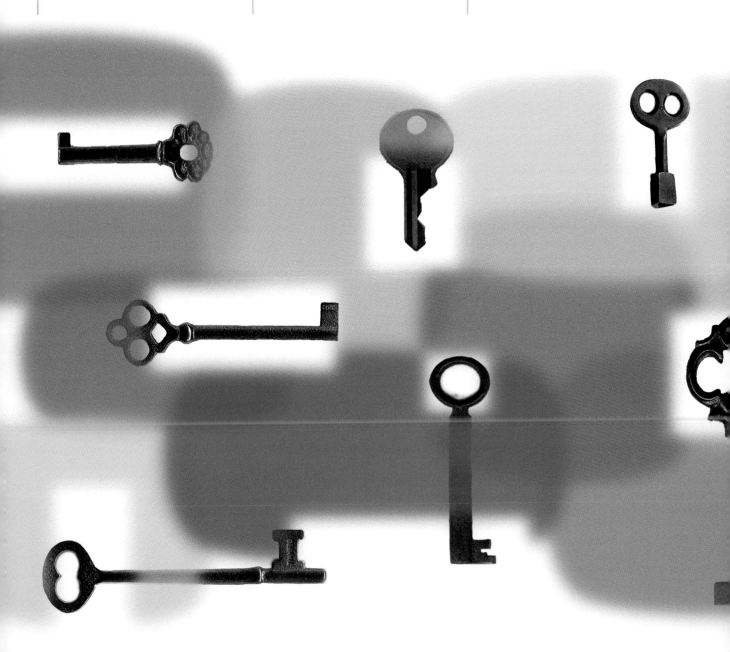

Interpersonal Communication

"Why don't you wear your new tie?" Robin suggests to Brian, as they are dressing to go out. "There you go again, telling me what to wear!" Brian retorts. To which Robin zings back with, "Oh, wear whatever you want. I don't care if you want to look like you're colorblind!" Could this couple have side-stepped the bad feelings and fight that are brewing? You bet! The keys to managing such encounters are recognizing the pitfalls of interpersonal communication and honing one's skills to deal effectively with them—two things you'll learn about in this chapter.

Communication skills are highly relevant to adjustment because they can be critical to happiness and success in life. In this chapter, we begin with an overview of the communication process and then turn to the important topic of nonverbal communication. Next, we discuss ways to communicate more effectively and examine common communication problems. Finally, we look at interpersonal conflict, including constructive ways to deal with it. In the Application, we consider ways to develop an assertive communication style.

The Process of Interpersonal Communication

LEARNING OBJECTIVES

■ List and explain the six components of the communication process.

■ List several important differences between face-to-face and computer-mediated communication.

■ Discuss how interpersonal communication is important to adjustment.

Communication can be defined as the process of sending and receiving messages that have meaning. Your personal thoughts have meaning, of course, but when you "talk to yourself," you are engaging in *intra*personal communication. In this chapter, we will focus on *inter*personal communication—the transmission of meaning between two or more people. For the most part, we'll concentrate on two-person interactions.

We define **interpersonal communication as an interactional process in which one person sends a message to another.** Note several points about this definition. First, for communication to qualify as *interpersonal,* at least two people must be involved. Second, interpersonal communication is a *process.* By this, we simply mean that it usually involves a series of actions: Kelli talks/Jason listens, Jason responds/Kelli listens, and so on. Third, this process is *interactional.* Communication is generally not a one-way street: Both participants send as well as receive information when they're interacting. A key implication of this fact is that you need to pay attention to both *speaking* and *listening* if you want to be an effective communicator.

Components of the Communication Process

Let's take a look at the essential components of the interpersonal communication process. The key elements are (1) the sender, (2) the receiver, (3) the message, (4) the channel through which the message is sent, (5) noise or interference, and (6) the context in which the message is communicated. As we describe these components, refer to Figure 7.1 to see how they work together.

The *sender* is the person who initiates the message. In a typical two-way conversation, both people serve as senders (as well as receivers). Keep in mind that each person brings a unique set of expectations and understandings to each communication situation. The *receiver* is the person to whom the message is targeted.

The *message* refers to the information or meaning that is transmitted from the sender to the receiver. The message is the content of the communication—that is, the ideas and feelings conveyed to another person. Two important cognitive processes underlie the transmission of messages: Speakers *encode* or transform their ideas and feelings into symbols and organize them into a message; receivers *decode* or translate a speaker's message into their own ideas and feelings (see Figure 7.1). Generally, fluent speakers of a language are unaware of these processes. If you've ever learned a new language, however, you have consciously experienced encoding (groping for the right word to express an idea) and decoding (trying to discover a word's meaning by how it is used).

The primary means of sending messages is language, but people also communicate to others nonverbally. Nonverbal communication includes the facial expressions, gestures, and vocal inflections used to supplement (and sometimes entirely change) the meaning of verbal messages. For example, when you say, "Thanks a lot," your nonverbal communication can convey either sincere gratitude or heavy sarcasm.

The *channel* refers to the sensory channel through which the message reaches the receiver. Typically, people receive information from multiple channels simultaneously. They not only hear what the other person

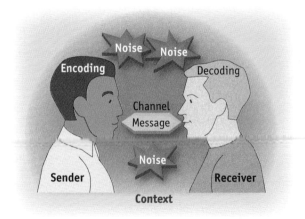

● **FIGURE 7.1**

A model of interpersonal communication. Interpersonal communication involves six elements: the sender, the receiver, the message, the channel through which the message is transmitted, distorting noise, and the context in which the message is sent. In conversations, both participants function as sender and receiver.

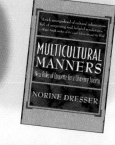
says, they also see the person's facial expressions, observe his or her gestures, experience eye contact, and sometimes feel the person's touch. Note that the messages in the various channels may be consistent or inconsistent with each other, making their interpretation more or less difficult. Sometimes sound is the only channel available for receiving information—when you talk on the telephone, for instance. Through sound, people hear both the literal content of messages and vocal inflections. In computer-mediated communication (e-mail, chat rooms, and so on), only the visual channel is called into play, as individuals communicate in writing.

Whenever two people interact, miscommunication can occur. **Any stimulus that interferes with accurately expressing or understanding a message is termed** *noise.* Sources of noise include environmental factors (street traffic, loud music) and physical factors (poor hearing, poor vision). Noise can also have semantic origins (Verderber & Verderber, 2005). For instance, profanity, ethnic slurs, or sexist language can cause a lis-

tener to disregard the larger message. In addition, psychological factors such as defensiveness and anxiety can contribute to noise, a topic we'll consider later in the chapter.

All social communication occurs in and is influenced by a *context,* **the environment in which communication takes place.** Context includes the *physical environment* (location, time of day, and noise level). Another aspect of the physical environment is how a conversation takes place: face to face, in a telephone call, or via the Internet. Other important aspects of context include the nature of the participants' *relationship* (work associates, friends, family), their *history* (previous interactions), their current *mood* (happy, stressed), and their *cultural backgrounds* (Verderber & Verderber, 2005). Culture is especially important in the United States because of the varieties of subcultures, many with different rules of communication. The Recommended Reading *Multicultural Manners* is an excellent guide to the cultural variety in communication practices in our diverse nation. Cultural context is also important in the global marketplace, as the marketers of Coca-Cola in China discovered too late (Petras & Petras, 1993). It seems that the symbols they used for the brand name translated to something like "Bite the wax tadpole" in Chinese!

Technology and Interpersonal Communication

The recent explosion in electronic and wireless communication technology has dramatically altered our notions of interpersonal communication. Today, communication via cellular telephones and the Internet must be considered along with face-to-face interactions.

Cell phones have both advantages and disadvantages (Verderber & Verderber, 2004). On the positive side, they are a convenient way to keep in touch with others, provide a sense of security, and can summon aid in an emergency. On the down side, they tie people to their jobs, can disrupt classrooms and public events, and bring private conversations into public places. Who hasn't been exasperated by being forced to listen to a loud-mouth yelling his or her personal business into a cell phone in a public place? New rules of etiquette have been devised to guide cell phone use in public. Three basic guidelines are (1) turn off your phone (or put it on "vibrate" mode) when the ringing will disturb others, (2) keep your calls short, and (3) make and receive calls unobtrusively or out of earshot from others (Farnsworth, 2002).

In the area of computer-mediated communication, e-mail is by far the most popular application, but newsgroups and chat rooms are also popular (Verderber & Verderber, 2004). As we have noted, face-to-face com-

Cell phone etiquette in public places calls for turning off your phone or putting it on vibrate mode, keeping your voice low and your calls short.

clarifying details, and describe your feelings, if necessary. It's also a good idea to review what you have written before you send it! The lack of nonverbal cues and the anonymous nature of computer-mediated communication also have important implications for relationship development (Bargh & McKenna, 2004), an issue we will take up in Chapter 8.

Communication and Adjustment

Before we plunge further into the topic of interpersonal communication, let's take a moment to emphasize its significance. Communication with others—friends, lovers, parents, spouses, children, employers, workers—is such an essential and commonplace aspect of everyday life that it's hard to overstate its role in adjustment. Many of life's gratifications (and frustrations and heartaches, as well) hinge on one's ability to communicate effectively with others. Numerous studies have shown that good communication can enhance satisfaction in relationships (Meeks, Hendrick, & Hendrick, 1998) and that poor communication ranks high as a cause of breakups among both straight and gay couples (Kurdek, 1994, 1998).

munication relies on the spoken word while Internet communication depends on the written word. You can see other important differences in Figure 7.2. The absence of nonverbal cues in computer-mediated communication means that you need to take special care that the other person understands your intended meaning. Thus, you should choose your words carefully, provide

Dimension	Face-to-Face	Internet
Physical distance	People need to be in the same place at the same time to meet.	People can meet and develop a relationship with someone thousands of miles away.
Anonymity	One can't be anonymous in real-life interactions.	People take greater risks in disclosing personal information than they otherwise do. Thus, feelings of intimacy can develop more quickly.
Richness of communication	People have access to nonverbal cues such as facial expressions and tone of voice to detect nuances in meaning or deception.	In cyberspace, these cues are absent.
Visual cues	Physical appearance and visual cues play a big role in attraction in face-to-face relationships.	These cues are generally absent on the Internet (although people can exchange photographs online).
Time	Two people have to connect at the same time.	There is no need for an immediate response, so time becomes relatively unimportant. On the Internet, you can take as long as you like to craft a response so you can more completely explain yourself.

● FIGURE 7.2

Differences between face-to-face and Internet communication. Computer-mediated communication applications (e-mail, chat rooms, news groups, and so forth) have dramatically changed the ways people interact and develop relationships. Internet communication differs from face-to-face communication in five important ways. (Adapted from Bargh & McKenna, 2004; Verderber & Verderber, 2004)

LIVING IN TODAY'S WORLD

Communication in Uncertain Times

The possibility of additional terrorist attacks in the United States continues to haunt many Americans. In such uncertain times, people have a strong need to be able to communicate with their family and friends. And for those who are employed on the front lines in emergencies, being in close communication with work sites is essential.

Luckily, recent advances in communications technology support individuals' needs to make fast contact with each other (Verderber & Verderber, 2004). Take cell phones, for example. Through both text-messaging and telephone mode, they provide a popular and convenient way for people to keep in touch. On college campuses, students with cell phones at their ears are a familiar sight. Cell phones also provide a sense of security for parents, children, and others who may want to contact each other or summon aid in an emergency. Recall that it was the cell phone calls between airline passengers and their loved ones that sparked the "Let's roll" rebellion on the hijacked plane that crashed in Pennsylvania on September 11. Of course, portable phones have their down sides, too, as

we discuss in the chapter. The computer is another important communication vehicle that connects people through e-mail, chat rooms, and newsgroups (Verderber & Verderber, 2004).

Mass communication has also assumed a higher profile in these unsettling times. People want to have fast access to the news in case of terrorist attacks or other disasters. Thus, in addition to their regular news programming, many radio stations and television channels provide hourly news updates and special bulletins. Some TV channels provide news on a 24-hour basis, and scrawls run continuously across the bottom of the screen to give viewers instant access to unfolding national and world events. The Internet is another source of news. An obvious advantage of computer–mediated news is that coverage of breaking events is much more timely than is possible with print newspapers.

Thus, both interpersonal and mass communication play a major role in helping people cope with the unfortunate and stressful reality of life in today's United States.

Nonverbal Communication

LEARNING OBJECTIVES

- List five general principles of nonverbal communication.
- Define proxemics and discuss personal space.
- Discuss display rules and what can be discerned from facial cues.
- Summarize the characteristics associated with effective eye contact.
- Describe the roles of body movement, posture, and gestures in communication.

- Summarize the research findings on touching and paralanguage.
- Discuss the difficulty of detecting deception and the nonverbal cues linked to deception.
- Explain what polygraphs do, and cite some problems with their use.
- Describe the significance of nonverbal messages in interpersonal interactions.

You're standing at the bar in your favorite hangout, gazing across a dimly lit room filled with people drinking, dancing, and talking. You signal to the bartender that you'd like another drink. Your companion comments on the loudness of the music, and you nod your head in agreement. You spot an attractive stranger across the bar; your eyes meet for a moment and you smile. In a matter of seconds, you have sent three messages with-

out uttering a syllable. To put it another way, you have just sent three nonverbal messages. **Nonverbal communication is the transmission of meaning from one person to another through means or symbols other than words.** Communication at the nonverbal level takes place through a variety of behaviors: interpersonal distance, facial expression, eye contact, body posture and movement, gestures, physical touch, and tone of voice.

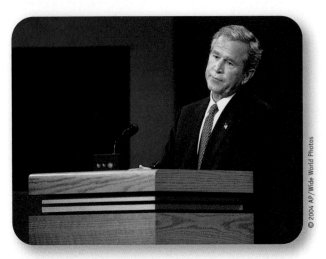

The power of nonverbal communication was dramatically illustrated during the first Presidential Debate of the 2004 election. President Bush's poor performance during the debate was attributed, in part, to facial expressions that conveyed a variety of negative emotions.

Clearly, a great deal of information is exchanged through nonverbal channels—probably more than most people realize. You can significantly enhance your communication skills by learning more about this important aspect of communication.

General Principles

Let's begin by examining some general principles of nonverbal communication.

1. *Nonverbal communication is multichanneled.* Nonverbal communication typically involves simultaneous messages sent through a number of channels. For instance, information may be transmitted through gestures, facial expressions, eye contact, and vocal tone at the same time. In contrast, verbal communication is limited to a single channel: speech. If you have ever tried to follow two people speaking at once, you understand how difficult it is to process multiple inputs of information. This means that many nonverbal transmissions can sail by the receiver unnoticed.

2. *Nonverbal communication is ambiguous.* A shrug or a raised eyebrow can mean different things to different people. Moreover, it can be difficult to know whether nonverbal messages are being sent intentionally. Although some popular books on body language imply otherwise, few nonverbal signals carry universally accepted meanings, even within the same culture. Thus, nonverbal cues are informative, but they are most reliable when accompanied by verbal messages and embedded in a familiar cultural and social context (Samovar & Porter, 2004).

3. *Nonverbal communication conveys emotions.* People often communicate their feelings without saying a word—for example, "a look that kills." Nonverbal demonstrations of positive feelings include sitting or standing close to those you care for, touching them often, and looking at them frequently. Still, nonverbal signals, on their own, are not the precise indicators of emotional states that they were once believed to be (Samovar & Porter, 2004), so you should be cautious in making inferences.

4. *Nonverbal communication may contradict verbal messages.* How often have you seen people proclaim "I'm not angry" even though their bodies shout that they are positively furious? When confronted with such an inconsistency, which message should you believe? Because of their greater spontaneity, you're probably better off heeding the nonverbal signs. Research shows that when someone is instructed to tell a lie, deception is most readily detected through nonverbal signals (DePaulo, LeMay, & Epstein, 1991).

5. *Nonverbal communication is culture-bound.* Like language, nonverbal signals are different in different cultures (Samovar & Porter, 2004). Sometimes cultural differences can be quite dramatic. For example, in Tibet people greet their friends by sticking out their tongues (Ekman, 1975).

Elements of Nonverbal Communication

Nonverbal signals can provide a great deal of information in interpersonal interactions. As we discuss specific nonverbal behaviors, we will focus on what they communicate about interpersonal attraction and social status.

Personal Space

Proxemics is the study of people's use of interpersonal space. *Personal space is a zone of space surrounding a person that is felt to "belong" to that person.* Personal space is like an invisible bubble you carry around with you in your social interactions. The size of this mobile zone is related to your cultural background, social status, personality, age, and gender.

The amount of interpersonal distance people prefer depends on the nature of the relationship and the

WEB LINK 7.1

Nonverbal Communication Research Page
Social psychologist Marvin A. Hecht, this site's editor, makes clear that the Internet is not an adequate realm for the preparation of a research paper on the topic of nonverbal communication. But the links provided here can serve to introduce students and others to major issues, researchers, current news, and examples drawn from this fascinating field.

situation (Darley & Gilbert, 1985; J. A. Hall, 1990). The appropriate distance between people is also regulated by social norms and varies by culture (J. A. Hall, 1990). For instance, people of Northern European heritage tend to engage in less physical contact and keep a greater distance between themselves than people of Latin or Middle Eastern heritage. The United States is usually characterized as a medium-contact culture, but there is a lot of variability among ethnic groups.

Anthropologist Edward T. Hall (1966) has described four interpersonal distance zones that are appropriate for middle-class encounters in American culture (see Figure 7.3). The general rule is that the more you like someone, the more comfortable you feel being physically close to that person. Of course, there are obvious exceptions, such as in crowded subways and elevators, but these situations are often experienced as stressful. Women seem to have smaller personal-space zones than men do (Remland, Jones, & Brinkman, 1995). When talking, women sit or stand closer together than men do.

Like other aspects of nonverbal communication, personal distance can convey information about status. People of similar status tend to stand closer together than people whose status is unequal (J. A. Hall, 1990). Moreover, it is the prerogative of the more powerful person in an interaction to set the "proper" distance (Henley, 1977).

Invasions of personal space usually produce discomfort and stimulate attempts to restore your privacy zone. To illustrate, if someone stands too close, you may back up. Or, if a stranger sits down at "your" table in the library and forces you to share it, you may reorient your body away from the intruder, place a barrier (for example, a stack of books) between you and the invader, or move to a different table. Invasions of personal space rarely go unnoticed, and they usually elicit a variety of reactions.

Facial Expression

More than anything else, facial expressions convey emotions. Paul Ekman and Wallace Friesen have identified six distinctive facial expressions that correspond with six basic emotions: anger, disgust, fear, happiness, sadness, and surprise (Ekman, 1994; Ekman & Friesen, 1984). Early research involving participants from many countries supported the idea that these six emotions are universally recognized (Ekman, 1972). In such studies, researchers show photographs depicting different emotions to subjects from a variety of Western and non-Western cultures and ask them to match the photographs with an emotion. Some representative results from this research are depicted in Figure 7.4 on the next page.

A recent meta-analysis of 97 studies (over 42 countries) looked at whether these six emotions are universally recognized or are culturally specific (Elfenbein &

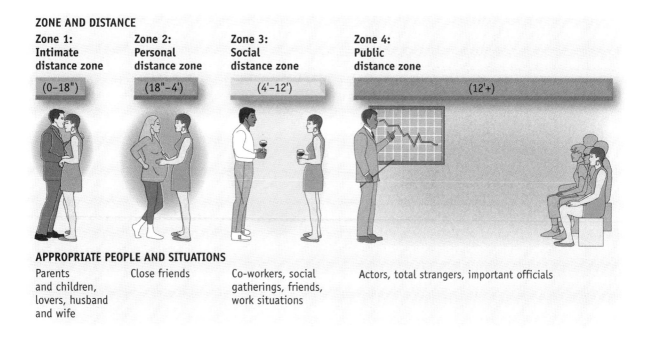

ZONE AND DISTANCE

Zone 1: Intimate distance zone	Zone 2: Personal distance zone	Zone 3: Social distance zone	Zone 4: Public distance zone
(0–18")	(18"–4')	(4'–12')	(12'+)

APPROPRIATE PEOPLE AND SITUATIONS

| Parents and children, lovers, husband and wife | Close friends | Co-workers, social gatherings, friends, work situations | Actors, total strangers, important officials |

● FIGURE 7.3

Interpersonal distance zones. According to Edward Hall (1966), people like to keep a certain amount of distance between themselves and others. The distance that makes one feel comfortable depends on whom one is interacting with and the nature of the situation.

Facial expressions and emotions.
Ekman and Friesen (1984) found that people in highly disparate cultures showed fair agreement on the emotions portrayed in these photos. This consensus across cultures suggests that the facial expressions associated with certain emotions may have a biological basis.

Photos from *Unmasking the Face,* © 1975 by Paul Ekman, photographs courtesy of Paul Ekman

Emotion Displayed			
Fear	Disgust	Happiness	Anger

Country	Agreement in judging photos (%)			
United States	85	92	97	67
Brazil	67	97	95	90
Chile	68	92	95	94
Argentina	54	92	98	90
Japan	66	90	100	90
New Guinea	54	44	82	50

Ambady, 2002). Interestingly, there was evidence for both perspectives. In support of the universal view, individuals do accurately recognize emotions in photographs of people from other cultures. Favoring cultural specificity, there was evidence of an "ingroup advantage." Thus, observers are better at recognizing the emotions in photographs from their own cultural groups than from cultural outgroups. A few basic facial expressions are universally recognizable, but other emotional expressions vary from culture to culture—as we noted in the earlier example of Tibetans sticking out their tongues to greet their friends.

Each society has rules that govern whether and when it is appropriate to express one's feelings. **These norms that govern the appropriate display of emotions are termed** *display rules.* In the United States, for instance, it is considered bad form to gloat over one's victories or to show envy or anger in defeat. This regulation of facial expression is an aspect of impression management that we discussed in Chapter 5. Is it possible to deliberately deceive others through facial expression? Absolutely. In fact, people are better at sending deceptive messages with their faces than with other areas of their bodies (Ekman & O'Sullivan, 1991). You are no doubt familiar with the term "poker face," an allusion to poker players who are experts at controlling their excitement about a good hand of cards (or their dismay about a bad one).

Besides cultural differences, there are gender differences in facial expression (Hall, Carter, & Horgan, 2000). For example, men typically show less facial expression than women do, a finding linked to social pressures for males to inhibit such displays (Kilmartin,

2000). Also, as you might expect, high self-monitors are better than low self-monitors at managing their facial expressions (Gangestad & Snyder, 2000).

Eye Contact

Eye contact (also called mutual gaze) is another major channel of nonverbal communication. The duration of eye contact is its most meaningful aspect. Because there is considerable research on "eye communication," we will summarize the most relevant findings.

Among European Americans, people who engage in high levels of eye contact are usually judged to have effective social skills and credibility. Similarly, speakers, interviewers, and experimenters receive higher ratings of competence when they maintain high rather than

Display rules require unsuccessful contestants in beauty pageants to suppress the display of resentful, envious, or angry feelings.

The eyes can be used to convey either very positive or very negative feelings.

low eye contact with their audience. As a rule, people engage in more eye contact when they're listening than when they're talking (Bavelas, Coates, & Johnson, 2002).

Gaze also communicates the *intensity* (but not the positivity or negativity) of feelings. For example, couples who say they are in love spend more time gazing at each other than other couples do (Patterson, 1988). Also, maintaining moderate (versus constant or no) eye contact with others typically generates positive feelings in them. These positive feelings may also translate into higher tips! One study found that food servers who squatted down next to their customers to take drink orders got higher tips than servers who stood next to their customers (Lynn & Mynier, 1993). Supposedly, the increased eye contact and closeness produced more positive feelings.

In a negative interpersonal context, a steady gaze becomes a stare that causes most people to feel uncomfortable (Kleinke, 1986). Moreover, like threat displays among nonhuman primates such as baboons and rhesus monkeys, a stare can convey aggressive intent (Henley, 1986). Thus, if you want to avoid road rage incidents, avoid making eye contact with hostile motorists ("Road rage plagues drivers," 1997). People also communicate by *reducing* eye contact with others. Unpleasant interactions, embarrassing situations, or invasions of personal space usually trigger this behavior (Kleinke, 1986).

Culture strongly affects patterns of eye contact (Samovar & Porter, 2004). For example, Americans should be sensitive to the fact that direct eye contact is perceived as an insult in some Native American tribes and in Mexico, Latin America, Japan, and Africa. By contrast, people from Arab countries look directly into the eyes of their conversational partners for longer periods than Americans are used to.

In the United States, gender and racial differences have been found in eye contact. For instance, women tend to gaze at others more than men do (Cegala & Sillars, 1989). However, the patterning of eye contact also

reflects status, and gender and status are often confounded. Higher-status individuals look at the other person more when speaking than when listening, while lower-status people behave just the opposite. Women usually show the lower-status visual pattern because they are typically accorded lower status than men. As you can see in Figure 7.5, when women are in high-power positions, they show the high-status visual pattern to the same extent that men do (Dovidio et al., 1988). African Americans use more continuous eye contact than European Americans when speaking, but less when listening (Samovar & Porter, 2004). Misunderstandings can arise if eye-gaze behaviors that are intended to convey interest and respect are interpreted as being disrespectful or dishonest.

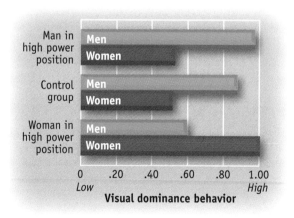

● **FIGURE 7.5**

Visual dominance, status, and gender. Women typically show low visual dominance (see control condition) because they are usually accorded lower status than men (Dovidio et al. 1988). However, when researchers placed women in a high-power position and measured their visual behavior, women showed the high visual dominance pattern and men showed the low visual dominance pattern. When men were placed in the high-power position, the visual dominance patterns reversed. Thus, visual dominance seems to be more a function of status than of gender.

Body Language

Body movements—those of the head, trunk, hands, legs, and feet—also provide nonverbal avenues of communication. *Kinesics* is the study of communication through body movements. Through a person's body movements, observers may be able to tell an individual's level of tension or relaxation. For instance, frequent touching or scratching suggests nervousness (Harrigan et al., 1991).

Posture also conveys information. Leaning back with arms or legs arranged in an asymmetrical or "open" position conveys a feeling of relaxation. Posture can also indicate someone's attitude toward you (McKay, Davis, & Fanning, 1995). When people lean toward you, it typically indicates interest and a positive attitude. When people angle their bodies away from you or cross their arms, their posture may indicate a negative attitude or defensiveness.

People in higher-status positions tend to adopt an "open" body posture, and those in lower-status roles usually adopt a "closed" position.

Posture can also convey status differences. Generally, a higher-status person will look more relaxed. By contrast, a lower-status person will tend to exhibit a more rigid body posture, often sitting up straight with feet together, flat on the floor, and arms close to the body (a "closed" position) (J. A. Hall, 1984; Vrugt & Luyerink, 2000). Again, status and gender differences are frequently parallel. That is, men are more likely to exhibit the high-status "open" posture and women the lower-status "closed" posture (J. A. Hall, 1990).

People use *hand gestures* to describe and emphasize the words they speak. You might point to give directions or slam your fist onto a desk to emphasize an assertion. As travelers frequently discover, the meaning of gestures is not universal (Samovar & Porter, 2004). For instance, a circle made with the thumb and forefinger means that everything is "OK" to an American but is considered an obscene gesture in some countries.

Touch

Touch takes many forms and can express a variety of meanings: support, consolation, and sexual intimacy (Anderson, 1999). Touch can also convey messages of status and power. In the United States, people typically "touch downward"—i.e., higher-status individuals are freer to touch subordinates than vice versa (Henley & Freeman, 1995). How people interpret the possible messages communicated by touch depends on the age and gender of the individuals involved, the setting in which the touching takes place, and the relationship between the toucher and recipient, among other things (Major, Schmidlin, & Williams, 1990). Also, there are strong norms about *where* people are allowed to touch friends. These norms are quite different for same-gender as opposed to cross-gender interactions, as can be seen in Figure 7.6.

Other findings about touching behavior come from an observational study of 4,500 pairs of Bostonians interacting in a variety of public places (shopping malls, hotel lobbies, subway stations) (Hall & Veccia, 1990, 1991). For one thing, female-female pairs touched each other significantly more than male-male pairs. Second, in younger pairs, men touched women more, but in older pairs, the pattern was reversed. Comparable age changes were not found for same-gender pairs.

Women typically perceive touch to be an expressive behavior signifying affection or support, whereas men often view touch as an instrumental behavior used to assert power or to show sexual interest. These gender differences in the meaning of touch can contribute to misunderstandings: In the workplace, touching is more likely to be perceived as sexual harassment by women than by men (LaPoire, Burgoon, & Parrott, 1992).

Paralanguage

The term *paralanguage* refers to *how* something is said rather than to *what* is said. Thus, *paralanguage* includes all vocal cues other than the content of the ver-

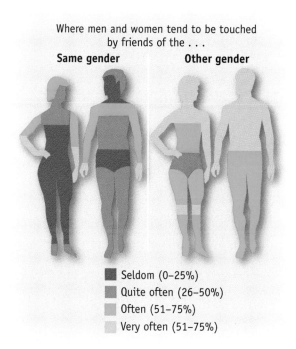

Where men and women tend to be touched
by friends of the . . .

Same gender   Other gender

■ Seldom (0–25%)
■ Quite often (26–50%)
■ Often (51–75%)
■ Very often (51–75%)

● **FIGURE 7.6**

Where friends touch each other. Social norms govern where
friends tend to touch each other. As these figures show, the
patterns of touching are different in same-gender as opposed
to cross-gender interactions.

Adapted from Marsh, P. (Ed.). (1988). *Eye to eye: How people interact.* Topsfield, MA: Salem
House. Copyright © 1988 by Andromeda Oxford Ltd. Reprinted by permission of HarperCollins,
Publishers, Inc. and Andromeda Oxford Ltd.

bal message itself. These cues include how loudly or
softly people speak, how fast they talk, and the rhythm
and quality of their speech. Each of these vocal characteristics can affect the message being transmitted.

Variations in vocal emphasis can give the same set
of words very different meanings. Consider the sentence "I really enjoyed myself" By varying the word that
is accented, you can speak this sentence in three ways,
each resulting in a different meaning:

- *I* really enjoyed myself! (Even though others may
not have had a good time, I did.)
- I *really* enjoyed myself! (My enjoyment was
exceptional.)
- I really *enjoyed* myself! (Much to my surprise, I
had a great time.)

As you can see from these examples, you can actually
reverse the literal meaning of a verbal message by how
you say it (such as with sarcasm).

Aspects of vocalization can also communicate emotions (Banse & Scherer, 1996). For example, rapid speech
may mean that a person is happy, frightened, or nervous.
Slower speech might be used when people are uncertain or when they want to emphasize a point. Loud vocalization often signals anger. A relatively high pitch

may indicate anxiety. Slow speech, low volume, and low
pitch are often associated with sadness. Thus, vocal quality provides another window on someone's true feelings. Keep in mind, however, that it is easy to assign
meanings to voice quality that aren't valid, such as associating a deep voice with masculinity and maturity
and a high, breathy voice with femininity and youth.

In cyberspace communication, e-mailers use various substitutes for the paralanguage cues used in spoken communication. For instance, capital letters are used
for emphasis ("I had a GREAT vacation"); however,
using capital letters throughout a message is viewed as
shouting and considered rude behavior. Using *emoticons*
(punctuation marks arranged to indicate the writer's
emotions) has also become a common practice; thus,
:-) indicates a smile and :-(indicates a frown. Interestingly, just as women display more emotion in their
faces than men, women are more likely than men to use
emoticons (Witmer & Katzman, 1999).

Detecting Deception

Like it or not, lying is a part of everyday life (DePaulo
et al., 2003). People typically tell one to two lies a day
(DePaulo et al., 1996). Most of these everyday lies are
inconsequential "white lies," such as claiming to be better than one actually is or lying to avoid hurting someone's feelings.

Is it possible to catch people in a lie? Yes, but it's difficult (DePaulo et al., 2003). In fact, even trained experts
are not spectacular lie detectors (Ekman & O'Sullivan,
1991). While it's true that people in occupations with
expertise or an interest in detecting deception (including
some types of psychologists) are more accurate judges
of liars than others (Ekman, O'Sullivan, & Frank, 1999),
even these individuals are not remarkably skilled at lie
detection. Regardless, people overestimate their ability
to detect liars (DePaulo et al., 1997).

The popular stereotypes about how liars give themselves away don't necessarily correspond to the actual
clues related to dishonesty. For example, observers tend
to focus on the face (the least revealing channel) and to
ignore more useful information (Burgoon, 1994). In
Figure 7.7 (on the next page), you can review the research findings on the nonverbal behaviors actually
associated with deception (based on DePaulo, Stone,
& Lassiter, 1985). By comparing the second and third
columns in the figure, you can see which cues are actually associated with deception and those that are erroneously linked with deception. Contrary to popular
belief, lying is *not* associated with slow talking, long
pauses before speaking, excessive shifting of posture,
reduced smiling, or lack of eye contact. A recent meta-
analysis of over 300 studies generally supported these
findings, concluding that liars say less, tell less compelling stories, make a more negative impression, are

Detecting deception from nonverbal behaviors. This chart summarizes evidence on which nonverbal cues are *actually* associated with deception and which are *believed* to be a sign of deception, based on a research review by DePaulo, Stone, and Lassiter (1985).

Nonverbal Cues and Deceptions

Kind of Cue	Are cues associated with actual deception?	Are cues believed to be a sign of deception?
Vocal Cues		
Speech hesitations	YES: Liars hesitate more	YES
Voice pitch	YES: Liars speak with higher pitch	YES
Speech errors (stutters, stammers)	YES: Liars make more errors	YES
Speech latency (pause before starting to speak or answer)	NO	YES: People think liars pause more
Speech rate	NO	YES: People think liars talk slower
Response length	YES: Liars give shorter answers	NO
Visual Cues		
Pupil dilation	YES: Liars show more dilation	(No research data)
Adapters (self-directed gestures)	YES: Liars touch themselves more	NO
Blinking	YES: Liars blink more	(No research data)
Postural shifts	NO	YES: People think liars shift more
Smile	NO	YES: People think liars smile less
Gaze (eye contact)	NO	YES: People think liars engage in less eye contact

more tense, and include less unusual content in their stories than truth tellers do (DePaulo et al., 2003).

So, how *do* liars give themselves away? As you may have noted in Figure 7.7, many of the clues "leak" from nonverbal channels, because speakers have a hard time controlling information from these channels (DePaulo & Friedman, 1998; Ekman and Friesen, 1974). Vocal cues include speaking with a higher pitch, giving relatively short answers, and excessive hesitations. Visual cues include dilation of the pupils. It's also helpful to look for inconsistencies between facial expressions and lower body movements. For example, a friendly smile accompanied by a nervous shuffling of feet could signal deception.

Bella DePaulo (1994), a noted researcher in this area, isn't too optimistic about the prospects of teaching people to spot lies, because the cues are usually subtle. If she's correct, perhaps *machines* can do better. **The *polygraph* is a device that records fluctuations in physiological arousal as a person answers questions.** Although called a "lie detector," it's really an emotion detector. The polygraph monitors key indicators of autonomic arousal such as heart rate, blood pressure, respiration rate, and perspiration, or galvanic skin response (GSR). The assumption is that when people lie, they

Courtesy, Bella DePaulo

Bella DePaulo

experience emotion that produces noticeable changes in these physiological indicators (see Figure 7.8).

Polygraph experts claim that lie detector tests are 85–90 percent accurate and that there is research support for the validity of polygraph testing (Iacono & Lykken, 1997; Iacono & Patrick, 1999). These claims are clearly not supported by the evidence. Methodologically sound research on this question is surprisingly sparse (largely because the research is difficult to do), and the limited evidence available is not very impressive (Lykken, 1998; Saxe & Ben-Shakhar, 1999). One problem is that when people respond to incriminating questions, they may experience emotional arousal even when they are telling the truth. Thus, polygraph tests often lead to accusations against the innocent. Another problem is that some people can lie without experiencing physiological arousal. Thus, because of high error rates, polygraph results are not admitted as evidence in most types of courtrooms. Yet, many companies require prospective and current employees to take lie detector tests to weed out thieves. In 1988, Congress passed a law curtailing this practice in certain occupations (Camara & Schneider, 1994). Perhaps computers will succeed where polygraphs have not—at least one laboratory is developing a computer program to detect the emotions underlying facial expressions (Bartlett et al., 1999).

To summarize, deception is potentially detectable, but the nonverbal behaviors that accompany lying are subtle and difficult to spot.

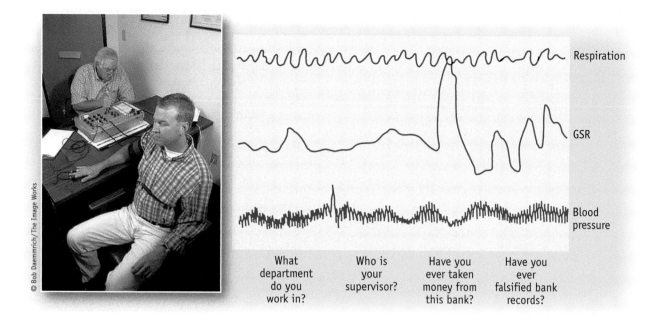

The polygraph measures emotional reactions. A lie detector measures the physiological arousal that most people experience when they tell a lie. After using nonthreatening questions to establish a baseline, a polygraph examiner looks for signs of arousal (such as the sharp change in GSR shown here) on incriminating questions.

The Significance of Nonverbal Communication

Although you are often unaware of nonverbal communication, you constantly use these cues to convey your own feelings to others and to "read" theirs. Let's consider some ways that nonverbal communication is linked to interpersonal relationships.

In our society, if you dislike someone, you don't usually say so. Instead, your negative feelings will leak out through nonverbal channels. Unfortunately, individuals with negative self-concepts attend to the positive verbal cues from others but disregard the negative nonverbal ones. Deprived of this important information, they may fail to learn why they alienate others, making it difficult for them to correct their behavior.

Accuracy in reading the emotions of others is related to social and academic competence even in children (Hubbard & Coie, 1994; Izard et al., 2001).

Is there any truth in the stereotype that females are better "readers" of nonverbal cues than men? Some researchers have found women to be better at this skill (1998; Hall & Matsumoto, 2004). However, motivation, rather than ability, may account for supposed gender differences in this area (Klein & Hodges, 2001). Some experts claim that this supposed gender difference is actually a status difference (Henley, 1977; Snodgrass, 1985, 1992). That is, people in subordinate roles are better at reading the nonverbal behaviors of those in dominant roles than vice versa. Later research has not supported this interpretation, however (Hall & Friedman, 1999; Snodgrass, Hecht, & Ploutz-Snyder, 1998).

Toward More Effective Communication

LEARNING OBJECTIVES

- List five suggestions for creating a positive interpersonal climate.
- Give five steps involved in making small talk.
- Cite some ways to reduce the risks of self-disclosure.

- Describe the role of self-disclosure in relationship development.
- Discuss cultural and gender differences in self-disclosure.
- Cite four points good listeners need to keep in mind.

As we've noted, the importance of communication in everyday life can hardly be exaggerated. In this section, we'll turn to some practical issues that will help you be-

come a more effective communicator with your family, friends, romantic partner, and co-workers. We'll review conversational skills, self-disclosure, and effective listening. Effective communication rests on the foundation of a positive interpersonal climate, so we'll start there.

Creating a Positive Interpersonal Climate

A positive interpersonal climate exists when people feel they can be open rather than guarded or defensive in their communication. You can do your part to create such an atmosphere by putting the following suggestions into practice.

■ *Learn to feel and communicate empathy.* **Empathy is adopting another's frame of reference so you can understand his or her point of view.** Being sensitive to others' needs and accepting of their feelings are hallmarks of empathy. Note that being accepting of others doesn't require you to condone or endorse their behavior. For example, if your roommate confides his concerns about his drinking, you can support him as a person by continuing to be his friend—without encouraging him to continue drinking.

■ *Practice withholding judgment.* You can promote an open climate by trying to be nonjudgmental. That doesn't mean that you can't express opinions and make judgments. It merely means that you should strive to interact with people in ways that don't make them feel inadequate or that put them down or force them to offer an opinion when they would rather not.

■ *Strive for honesty.* Mutual trust and respect thrive on authenticity and honesty. So-called hidden agendas don't stay hidden for long. Even if others don't know exactly what your underlying motives are, they often can sense that you're not being entirely honest. Of course, striving for honesty does not require you to communicate everything at any time to any person. For those conversations that are unavoidably painful—such as breaking up with a romantic partner—you should strive to be honest without being needlessly hurtful.

■ *Approach others as equals.* Most people don't like to be reminded of another's higher status or greater ability. When you have the higher status, it helps to approach people on equal terms.

■ *Express your opinions tentatively.* Instead of coming across as a know-it-all, let others know that your beliefs and attitudes are flexible and subject to revision. Using qualifying words or phrases is helpful. For instance, instead of announcing, "Here's the plan," you might say, "There seem to be several options; I lean toward . . . What do you think?"

Keep these points in mind as we delve further into the topic of interpersonal communication.

Conversational Skills

When it comes to meeting strangers, some people launch right into a conversation, while others break into a cold sweat as their minds go completely blank. If you fall into the second category, don't despair! The art of conversation is actually based on conversational *skills*. And these skills can be learned. To get you started, we'll offer a few general principles, gleaned primarily from *Messages: The Communication Skills Book* by McKay and associates (1995). If you want to explore this topic in greater depth, this book is an excellent source of practical advice.

RECOMMENDED READING

Messages: The Communication Skills Book
by Matthew McKay, Martha Davis, and Patrick Fanning (New Harbinger Publications, 1995)

In this short book, you will find a wealth of information by which to improve your communication skills in a wide variety of situations. *Messages* is organized according to six types of communication skills: basic, advanced, conflict, social, family, and public. Within each of these sections, chapters address important issues. For example, the section on family skills includes chapters on sexual communication, parent effectiveness, and family communications; the section on public skills addresses communication in small groups and public speaking; and "advanced skills" deals with hidden agendas, transactional analysis, and the role of culture and gender in communication. The authors have a breezy writing style and use lots of examples to illustrate their points. They have also included numerous exercises to help you assess your communication skills and practice more effective ways of interacting with others.

Cover design by Shelby Design & Associates. Reprinted by permission.

First, follow the Golden Rule: Give to others what you would like to receive from them. In other words, give others your attention and respect and let them know that you like them. Second, focus on the other person instead of yourself. Keep your attention focused on what the person is saying, rather than on how you look, what you're going to say next, or winning the argument. Third, as we have noted, use nonverbal cues to communicate your interest in the other person. Like you, others also find it easier to interact with a person who signals friendliness. A welcoming smile can make a big difference in initial contacts.

Now, how do you actually get the conversational ball rolling? Psychologist Bernardo Carducci (1999) suggests five steps for making successful small talk. We'll use his template and fill in with additional suggestions:

1. *Indicate that you are open to conversation by commenting on your surroundings.* ("This line sure is long."). Of course, you can begin with other topics, too, but you should be careful about your opening line. In one study, participants viewed videotapes of a man or a woman approaching an other-gender stranger and initiating a conversation using a cute/flippant, an innocuous, or a direct opening line (Kleinke, Meeker, & Staneski, 1986). The preferred openers were either innocuous ("Where are you from?") or direct ("Hi, I'm a little embarrassed about this, but I'd like to get to know you"). In contrast, the least preferred openers were of the cute/flippant variety ("Hi, I'm easy—are you?"). Because cute lines often backfire, your best bet is probably the conventional approach.

2. *Introduce yourself.* Do so early in the conversation and use specifics to give the other person information to relate to. ("I'm Jeremy Jackson. I'm a psychology major at the university.")

3. *Select a topic others can relate to.* ("I saw a great movie last night.") Keep an eye out for similarities and differences between you and your conversational partner (McKay et al., 1995). Thus, look for things you have in common—a tattoo, a class, a hometown—and build a conversation around that. Alternatively, work off of your differences. ("How did you get interested in science fiction? I'm a mystery fan myself.")

4. *Keep the conversational ball rolling.* You can keep things going by elaborating on your initial topic. ("After the movie, I met some friends at the new coffee house and tried their dessert special.") Alternatively, you can introduce a related topic or start a new one.

5. *Make a smooth exit.* Politely end the conversation. ("Well, I've got to be going, but I really enjoyed talking with you.")

After you've learned a little about another person, you may want to move the relationship to a deeper level.

This is where self-disclosure comes into play, the topic we'll address next.

Self-Disclosure

***Self-disclosure* is the act of sharing information about yourself with another person.** In other words, self-disclosure involves opening up about yourself to others. The information you share doesn't have to be a deep, dark secret, but it may be. Conversations with strangers and acquaintances typically start with superficial self-disclosure—the TV show you saw last night or your views on who will win the World Series. Only when people have come to like and trust each other do they begin to share private information—such as self-consciousness about one's weight, or jealousy of one's brother (Collins & Miller, 1994). Figure 7.9 illustrates how self-disclosure varies according to type of relationship.

Self-disclosure is critically important to adjustment for several reasons. First, sharing fears and problems with others who are trustworthy and supportive plays a key role in mental health. Recall from Chapter 4 that sharing your feelings can reduce stress. And after mutual self-disclosures, people experience a boost in positive feelings (Vittengl & Holt, 2000). Second, emotional (but not factual) self-disclosures lead to feelings of closeness, as long as disclosers feel that listeners are

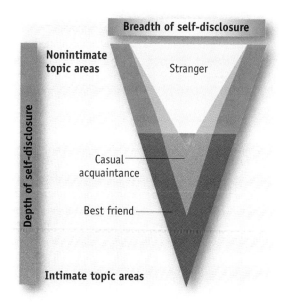

● FIGURE 7.9

Breadth and depth of self-disclosure. Breadth of self-disclosure refers to how many topics one opens up about; depth refers to how far one goes in revealing private information. Both the breadth and depth of one's disclosures are greater with best friends as opposed to casual acquaintances or strangers. (Adapted from Altman & Taylor, 1973)

understanding and accepting (Laurenceau, Barrett, & Pietromonaco, 1998; Reis & Shaver, 1988). And, as you saw in Chapter 1, having close relationships is an important ingredient of happiness.

Third, self-disclosure in romantic relationships correlates positively with relationship satisfaction (Meeks et al., 1998). More specifically, *equity* in self-disclosure, rather than high self-disclosure, may be the critical factor that helps couples avoid stress (Bowers, Metts, & Duncanson, 1985).

Reducing the Risks of Self-Disclosure

Let's face it: Disclosing private information to others is risky business. When you reveal private things about yourself to others, they might reject you or divulge your confidences to someone else. A study of European college students reported that they revealed others' personal emotional disclosures to third parties in 66–78 percent of the cases (Christophe & Rime, 1997). Although the researchers did not ask the students if they had been sworn to secrecy, in 85 percent of the cases the students were intimates (versus acquaintances) of the self-disclosers. Moreover, more emotionally intense disclosures were more likely to be shared—and with more people—than less emotionally intense revelations. Thus, if you have a secret you cannot risk others knowing but that is troubling you, it is probably safer to share it with a trained counselor. Alternatively, writing about an issue, such as in a journal, can help you feel better (Pennebaker, 1997; Sloan & Marx, 2004).

While it pays to be discriminating about sharing private business, limiting your conversations to superficial topics won't deepen a relationship. To safely steer the conversation toward more intimate topics, we advise using the strategy of *gradual* self-disclosure. Moving gradually gives you the chance to observe how the other person responds to your self-disclosures. Of course, the principle of gradual self-disclosure doesn't always hold. Many people can tell, early on, which relationships they want to remain relatively superficial and which they would like to become more intimate. But, for most sit-

uations, we advise gradual self-disclosure as the optimal route to close relationships, because it entails less risk and stress.

How can you gauge whether it's safe to share personal information with someone? It should reassure you to know that self-disclosure is *usually* reciprocated in depth and topic (Collins & Miller, 1994). Thus, a good strategy is to monitor your partners' verbal and nonverbal cues for their reactions to your disclosures. If you make a personal disclosure and the other person reciprocates with a parallel disclosure, this ordinarily signals comfort with more intimacy. Of course, some people who aren't comfortable engaging in self-disclosure themselves are sincerely willing to listen to you anyway. Thus, you can't depend on reciprocity alone as an indicator of another's interest.

That's why tuning in to nonverbal signals is of crucial importance. When people are uncomfortable, they will usually send you a nonverbal message to that effect to avoid embarrassing you with a more obvious verbal warning. "Stop" cues include reducing eye contact and displaying a puzzled, apprehensive, or pained facial expression. Your partner may angle his or her body away from you, increase the distance between you, or shuffle his or her feet impatiently. In contrast, when listeners lean forward, appear relaxed, and maintain good eye contact, they are likely interested in your self-disclosure.

What about the risk of self-disclosure in computer-mediated communication? Because of the relative anonymity of the Internet, self-disclosure in e-mail and chat rooms involves less risk (Bargh & McKenna, 2004). We'll explore the implications of this fact for relationship development in Chapter 8.

Self-Disclosure and Relationship Development

Earlier, we noted that self-disclosure leads to feelings of intimacy. Actually, the process is a little more complicated than that. Research suggests that only certain types of disclosures lead to feelings of closeness (Laurenceau et al., 1998). For instance, emotional self-disclosures do, but factual self-disclosures do not. Moreover, for inti-

© 2005 Dave Miller

macy to develop in a relationship, a discloser must feel understood and cared for (Reis & Patrick, 1996). In other words, self-disclosure alone doesn't lead to intimacy.

Self-disclosure varies over the course of relationships. At the beginning of a relationship, high levels of mutual disclosure prevail (Taylor & Altman, 1987). Once a relationship is well established, the level of disclosure tapers off, although responsiveness remains high (Reis & Patrick, 1996). Also, in established relationships, people are less likely to reciprocate disclosures. Thus, when a lover or a good friend reveals private information, you frequently respond with words of sympathy and understanding rather than a like disclosure. This movement away from equal exchanges of self-disclosure appears to be based on twin needs that emerge as intimate relationships develop: (1) the need for support and (2) the need to maintain privacy (Altman, Vinsel, & Brown, 1981). By reciprocating support (versus information), individuals can strengthen relationships while maintaining a sense of privacy. In fact, successfully balancing these two needs seems to be an important factor in relationship satisfaction (Finkenauer & Hazam, 2000).

When relationships are in distress, self-disclosure patterns change. For example, one or both individuals may decrease the breadth and depth of their self-disclosures, indicating that they are emotionally withdrawing (Baxter, 1988).

Self-disclosure can be a risky business. In many instances self-disclosure can lead to increased intimacy, but that depends on the nature of the relationship and the disclosure. Hence, when making disclosures it is important to pay attention to others' nonverbal reactions.

Culture, Gender, and Self-Disclosure

Americans generally assume that personal sharing is essential to close friendships and happy marriages. This view is consistent with an individualistic culture that emphasizes the individual and the expression of each person's unique feelings and experiences. In collectivist cultures such as China and Japan, people are open about their group memberships and status because these factors guide social interactions. However, sharing personal information is reserved for established relationships (Smith & Bond, 1999).

In the United States, it has been found that females tend to be more openly self-disclosing than males, although the disparity seems smaller than once believed (Dindia, 2000). This gender difference is strongest in *same-gender* friendships (Reis, 1998), with female friends

sharing more personal information than male friends. (As we'll discuss in Chapter 8, male friends tend to share activities versus personal talk.) In *other-gender* relationships, self-disclosure is more equal, although men with traditional gender-role attitudes are less likely to self-disclose, because they view sharing personal information as a sign of weakness. Also, women share more personal information and feelings, whereas men share more nonpersonal information (Dolgin, 2001).

Gender disparities in self-disclosure are attributed to socialization. In American culture, most men are taught to conceal tender emotions and feelings of vulnerability, especially from other men (Kilmartin, 2000). But different gender patterns are found in other countries (Reis & Wheeler, 1991). For example, in Jordan and Japan, where early intimacy between male and female friends is discouraged, close contacts between same-gender friends is encouraged.

And, in the early stages of other-gender relationships, American men often disclose more than women (Derlega et al., 1985). This finding is consistent with the traditional expectations that males should initiate relationships and females should encourage males to talk. Thus, it is an oversimplification to say that American women are always more open than men. (We will take up other aspects of gender and communication in the Chapter 10 Application.)

WEB LINK 7.4

Cross-Cultural Communication Strategies
Citizens of the 21st century are challenged to communicate sensitively with individuals from other cultural groups both within the United States and around the world. This site, maintained by the Conflict Research Consortium at the University of Colorado, provides commentaries by experts on a variety of intercultural communication settings.

Effective Listening

Effective listening is a vastly underappreciated skill. There's a lot of truth in the old saying, "We have two ears and only one mouth, so we should listen more than we speak." Because listeners process speech much more rapidly than people speak (between 500 and 1,000 words per minute versus 125–175 words per minute), it's easy for them to become bored, distracted, and inattentive (Hanna, 2003). Fatigue and preoccupation with one's own thoughts are other factors that interfere with effective listening.

To be a good listener, you need to keep four points in mind. First, *signal your interest in the speaker by using nonverbal cues.* Face the speaker squarely and lean toward him or her (rather than slouching or leaning back in a chair). This posture signals that you are interested in what the other person has to say. Try not to cross your arms and legs, as this posture can signal defensiveness. Maintaining eye contact with the speaker also indicates your attentiveness. (You know how annoying it is to talk with someone whose eyes are roaming around the room.) Communicate your feelings about what the speaker is saying by nodding your head or raising your eyebrows.

Second, *hear the other person out before you respond.* Listeners often tune out or interrupt a conversational partner when (1) they know someone well (because they believe that they already know what the speaker will say), (2) a speaker has mannerisms listeners find frustrating (stuttering, mumbling, speaking in a monotone), and (3) a speaker discusses ideas (abortion, politics) that generate strong feelings or uses terms (*welfare cheat, redneck*) that push "red buttons" (Verderber & Verderber, 2001). Although it is challenging not to tune out a speaker or to lob an insult in these situations, you'll be better able to formulate an appropriate response if you allow the speaker to complete his or her thought.

Third, *engage in active listening* (McKay et al., 1995). Pay careful attention to what the speaker is saying and mindfully process the information. Active listening also involves the skills of clarifying and paraphrasing. Inevitably, a speaker will skip over an essential point or say something that is confusing. When this happens, you need to ask for clarification. "Was Bill her boyfriend or her brother?" Clarifying ensures that you have an accurate picture of the message and also tells the speaker that you are interested.

Paraphrasing takes clarifying another step. To paraphrase means to state concisely what you believe the speaker said. You might say, "Let me see if I've got this

Being a good listener is an essential skill that contributes to success in relationships and on the job.

right . . ." or "Do you mean . . .?" It's obviously ludicrous to paraphrase every single thing the speaker says; you only need to paraphrase when the speaker says something important. Paraphrasing has a number of benefits: It reassures the speaker that you are "with" him or her, it derails misinterpretations, and it keeps you focused on the conversation.

Paraphrasing can take several forms (Verderber & Verderber, 2005). In *content paraphrasing,* you focus on the literal meaning of the message. In *feelings paraphrasing,* You focus on the emotions connected to the content of the message. If your friend declares, "I just can't believe he showed up at the party with his old girlfriend!," a feelings paraphrase is obviously in order ("You were really hurt by that").

To develop your skill at paraphrasing, try practicing it with a friend. Have the friend tell you about something; your job is to paraphrase from time to time to be sure that you really understand what your friend is trying to communicate. After each paraphrase, your friend can tell you whether he or she agrees with your interpretation. Don't be surprised if you have to re-paraphrase several times. Keep trying until you get it right. You'll probably discover that paraphrasing is harder than you think!

Finally, *pay attention to the other person's nonverbal signals.* Listeners use a speaker's words to get the "objective" meaning of a message, but they rely on non-

© Dana Hursey/Masterfile

verbal cues for the emotional and interpersonal meanings of a message. Your knowledge of body language, tone of voice, and other nonverbal cues can give you deeper understanding of what others are communicating. Remember that these cues are available not only when the other person is speaking but also when you are talking. If you often get signals that your listener is drifting away, you might be going overboard on irrelevant details or, perhaps, hogging the conversation. The antidote is active listening.

Most people are ineffective listeners because they are unaware of the elements of effective listening—information you now have. Also, effective listening hinges largely on your attitude. If you're willing to work at it, you can definitely become a good listener fairly quickly.

Communication Problems

LEARNING OBJECTIVES

- *Discuss four responses to communication apprehension.*
- *Describe five barriers to effective communication.*

In this section, we focus on two problems that can interfere with effective communication: anxiety and communication barriers.

Communication Apprehension

It's the first day of your child psychology class and you have just learned that 30-minute oral reports are a course requirement. Do you welcome this requirement as an opportunity to polish your public speaking skills or, panic-stricken, do you race to the registrar's office to drop the class? If you opted for the latter, you may suffer from **communication apprehension, or anxiety caused by having to talk with others.** Some people experience communication apprehension in all speaking situations (including one-on-one encounters), but most people who have the problem notice it only when they have to speak before groups.

Bodily experiences associated with communication apprehension can range from "butterflies" in the stomach to cold hands, dry mouth, and a racing heart rate. These physiological effects are stress-induced "fight or flight" responses of the autonomic nervous system (see Chapter 3). The physiological responses themselves aren't the root of communication apprehension; rather, the problem lies in the speaker's *interpretation* of these bodily responses. That is, high scorers on measures of communication apprehension frequently interpret the bodily changes they experience in public speaking situations as indications of fear. In contrast, low scorers often chalk up these reactions to the normal excitement in such a situation (Richmond & McCroskey, 1995).

Researchers have identified four responses to communication apprehension (Richmond & McCroskey, 1995). The most common is *avoidance,* or choosing not to participate when confronted with a voluntary com-

Being able to speak effectively before a group is a highly useful skill, so it is important to overcome communication apprehension.

WEB LINK 7.5

Effective Presentations
Students often tell teachers that they are terrified of making a presentation in front of a class. Professor Jeff Radel (University of Kansas Medical Center) has crafted an excellent set of guides to show the best ways of communicating by means of oral presentations, visual materials, and posters.

munication opportunity. If people believe that speaking will make them uncomfortable, they will typically avoid the experience. *Withdrawal* occurs when people unexpectedly find themselves trapped in a communication situation they can't escape. Here they may clam up entirely or say as little as possible. *Disruption* refers to the inability to make fluent oral presentations or to engage in appropriate verbal or nonverbal behavior. Of course, inadequate communication skills can produce this same behavioral effect, and it isn't always possible for the average person to identify the actual cause of the problem. *Overcommunication* is a relatively unusual response to high communication apprehension, but it does occur. An example would be someone who attempts to dominate social situations by talking nonstop. Although such individuals are seen as poor communicators, they are not usually perceived to have communication apprehension. That's because we expect to see it only in those who talk very little. Of course, overcommunication may be caused by other factors as well.

Obviously, avoidance and withdrawal tactics are merely short-term strategies for coping with communication apprehension (Richmond & McCroskey, 1995). Because it is unlikely that you can go though life without having to speak in front of a group, it is important to learn to cope with this stressful event rather than avoid it time and again. Allowing the problem to get out of hand can result in self-limiting behavior, such as refusing a job promotion that would entail public speaking. People with high communication apprehension are likely to have difficulties in relationships, at work, and at school (Richmond & McCroskey, 1995). Happily, both cognitive restructuring (Chapter 4) and systematic desensitization (Chapter 16) are highly effective methods for dealing with this problem.

Barriers to Effective Communication

Earlier in the chapter, we discussed noise and its disruptive effects on interpersonal communication. Now we want to check out some psychological factors that contribute to noise. These barriers to effective communication can reside in the sender, in the receiver, or sometimes in both. Common obstacles include defensiveness, motivational distortion, self-preoccupation and game playing.

Defensiveness

Perhaps the most basic barrier to effective communication is *defensiveness*—an excessive concern with protecting oneself from being hurt. People usually react defensively when they feel threatened, such as when they believe that others are evaluating them or trying to control or manipulate them. Defensiveness is also triggered when others act in a superior manner. Thus,

those who flaunt their status, wealth, brilliance, or power often put receivers on the defensive. Dogmatic people who project "I'm always right" also breed defensiveness.

A threat need not be real to elicit defensive behavior. If you persuade yourself that Brandon won't like you, your interactions with him will probably not be very positive. And, if the self-fulfilling prophecy kicks in, you may produce the negative reaction you fear. You want to cultivate a communication style that minimizes defensiveness in others. Still it's good to keep in mind that you don't have complete control over others' perceptions and reactions.

Motivational Distortion

In Chapter 6, we discussed distortions and expectancies in person perception. These same processes operate in communication. That is, people can hear what they want to hear instead of what is actually being said.

Each person has a unique frame of reference—certain attitudes, values, and expectations—that can influence what he or she hears. Information that contradicts an individual's own views often produces emotional discomfort. One way people avoid such unpleasant feelings is to engage in *selective attention,* or actively choosing to attend to information that supports their beliefs and ignoring information that contradicts them. Similarly, an individual may read meanings that are not intended into statements or jump to erroneous conclusions. This tendency to distort information occurs most often when people are discussing issues they feel strongly about, such as politics, racism, sexism, homosexuality, or abortion.

Self-Preoccupation

Who hasn't experienced the frustration of trying to communicate with someone who is so self-focused as to make two-way conversation impossible? These annoying individuals seem to talk to hear themselves talk. If you try to slip in a word about *your* problems, they cut you off by proclaiming, "That's nothing. Listen to what happened to me!" Further, self-preoccupied people are poor listeners. When someone else is talking, they're mentally rehearsing their next comments. Because they are self-focused, these individuals are usually oblivious to their negative impact on others.

Self-preoccupied people arouse negative reactions in others for several reasons. First, their remarks are usually so self-serving (seeking to impress, to gain unwarranted sympathy, and so on) that others find it offensive. Another problem is that they consistently take up more than their fair share of conversation time. Some individuals do both—talking only about themselves *and* going on at great length. After a "conversation" with someone like this, listeners feel ignored. No wonder people try to avoid such people if they can. If they can't, they usually respond only minimally to end the conversation quickly. Needless to say, you risk alienating others if you ignore the norm that conversations should involve a mutual sharing of information.

Game Playing

"Game playing" is another barrier to effective communication. Game playing was first described by Eric Berne (1964), who originated *transactional analysis,* a theory of personality and interpersonal relations that emphasizes patterns of communication. In Berne's scheme, *games* **are manipulative interactions with predictable outcomes, in which people conceal their real motives.** For instance, Yvonne knows that Carlos gets upset when her former boyfriend is mentioned. So when they're out with others, she "innocently" inquires, "Say, has anyone seen Rodrigo lately?" Here, the hidden agenda is to make Carlos feel bad. If Yvonne's behavior produces the desired response, she "wins." In the broadest sense, game playing can include the deliberate (or sometimes unintentional) use of ambiguous, indirect, or deceptive statements. Some game playing involves "verbal fencing" to avoid having to make clear one's meaning or intent. Particularly problematic are repetitive games that result in bad feelings and that erode the trust and respect that are essential to good relationships. Games interfere with effective communication and are a destructive element in relationships.

Interpersonal Conflict

LEARNING OBJECTIVES

- Cite some positive outcomes associated with constructive interpersonal conflict.
- Describe five personal styles of dealing with interpersonal conflict.
- List six tips for coping effectively with interpersonal conflict.
- Explain why Deborah Tannen characterizes America as "the argument culture."
- Describe some reasons for increased social contentiousness today.
- Describe what individuals and social institutions can do to reduce the level of public conflict.

People do not have to be enemies to be in conflict, and being in conflict does not make people enemies. *Interpersonal conflict* **exists whenever two or more people disagree.** By this definition, conflict occurs between friends and lovers as well as between competitors and enemies. The discord may be caused by a simple misunderstanding, or it may be a product of incompatible goals, values, attitudes, or beliefs. Because conflict is an unavoidable aspect of interactions, it's essential to know how to deal constructively with it.

Beliefs About Conflict

Many people assume that any kind of conflict is inherently bad and that it should be suppressed if at all possible. In reality, conflict is neither inherently bad nor inherently good. It is a natural phenomenon that may lead to either good or bad outcomes, depending on how people deal with it. When people see conflict as negative, they tend to avoid coping with it. Of course, sometimes avoiding conflict can be good. If a relationship or an issue is of little importance to you, or if you believe that the costs of confrontation are too high (your boss might fire you), avoidance might be the best way to handle a conflict. Also, cultures differ in how conflict should be handled. Collectivist cultures (such as China and Japan) often avoid conflict, whereas individualistic cultures tend to encourage direct confrontations (Ting-Toomey, 2000). In individualistic cultures, the consequences of avoiding conflict depend on the nature of the relationship. When relationships and issues are important to you, avoiding conflict is generally counterproductive. For one thing, it can lead to a self-perpetuating cycle (see Figure 7.10).

● FIGURE 7.10

The conflict avoidance cycle. Avoiding conflict can lead to a self-perpetuating cycle: (1) People think of conflict as bad, (2) they get nervous about a conflict they are experiencing, (3) they avoid the conflict as long as possible, (4) the conflict gets out of control and must be confronted, and (5) they handle the confrontation badly. In turn, this negative experience sets the stage for avoiding conflict the next time—usually with the same negative outcome. (Adapted from Lulofs, 1994)

Suppression of discord usually has a negative effect on a relationship in spite of efforts to conceal it. For example, people in distressed marriages use more avoidance than people in nondistressed or satisfied marriages (Noller et al., 1994).

When dealt with openly and constructively, interpersonal conflict can lead to a variety of valuable outcomes (Clark & Grote, 2003). Among other things, constructive confrontation may (1) bring problems out into the open where they can be solved, (2) put an end to chronic sources of discontent in a relationship, and (3) lead to new insights through the airing of divergent views.

Types of Conflict

To manage conflict effectively, you need to know what you're dealing with. A useful scheme categorizes conflicts into five types: pseudoconflicts, fact conflicts, policy conflicts, value conflicts, and ego conflicts (Verderber & Verderber, 2004).

A *pseudoconflict* is just what it says: a false conflict. The game playing between Yvonne and Carlos is one type of pseudoconflict. The goal of the game is to get the other person "hooked" so that an unresolved issue comes out. The "fight" between Brian and Robin that introduced the chapter is another example of a pseudoconflict. When Brian said, "There you go again, telling me what to wear," he intended to draw Robin into a fight about power issues in their relationship. Robin's comeback that Brian looked like he was colorblind was an acceptance of Brian's invitation to fight. Had Robin been able to identify the interchange as a pseudoconflict, she could have declined his invitation using a nondefensive tone of voice ("I was just making a suggestion. Wear what you like"). The key to managing such encounters is being able to recognize the game and not allowing yourself to be drawn in.

A second type of conflict occurs when people disagree about issues of a factual nature. For instance, Keisha and DeWayne disagree about whether they are supposed to meet another couple at the restaurant or be picked up so they can all drive in one car. The way to deal with such *fact based conflicts* is to check the facts and then not dwell on who was right and who was wrong. But, note that either party can escalate the disagreement into an argument with insulting comments ("Can't you ever get anything straight?").

Policy conflicts arise when people disagree about how to handle a particular situation. Take the case of Brad and Julia, who are planning their trip to Europe. Brad earns more than Julia. Should they split the expenses down the middle, or should they share the expenses based on the proportion of their incomes? Obviously, there is no right or wrong answer here. Successfully resolving a policy conflict depends on finding a solution that addresses the problem and the feelings of both people. Policy conflicts can reerupt when two people agree on a policy but one or both fail to follow through on it.

Differing personal values can also lead to conflicts. *Values* are beliefs people use to evaluate the worth of various aspects of life—religion, politics, and various social and aesthetic issues. Some values are obviously more important to people than others, and higher-ranked values usually have more influence on behavior. Thus, if you believe that your family's happiness is more important than your work, you may opt for a career with minimal stress and time demands. *Value-based conflicts* are a particular problem in intimate relationships. If couples can recognize conflicts as value based, they can understand that an issue is important to the other person and that he or she is not just being stubborn. When conflicts can't be resolved, two people may be willing to take turns obliging each other to maintain the relationship. For example, they might alternate going to each other's favorite hangout. Too, sometimes people can agree to disagree. Nonetheless, when unresolvable conflicts become an ongoing source of distress in relationships, they can lead to breakups. You can minimize value-based conflicts by matching up with a person who has similar values.

The most difficult conflicts to manage are those in which one or both parties view the outcome as a measure of self-worth—how competent one is, how much

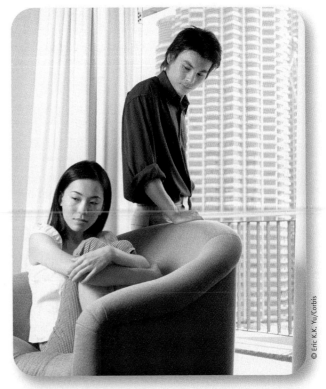

Disagreements are a fact of everyday life, so effective communicators need to learn how to deal with them constructively.

one knows, how much power one has, and so forth. In these *ego-based conflicts,* "winning" becomes more important than finding a fair solution to the problem. Ego-based conflicts often arise when one or both parties lapse into negative personal judgments about a content- or value-based issue under discussion. People most often slip into judgmental statements when they have expertise or a special stake in the discussion. Before you realize it, you are hooked by your emotions, lose the ability for rational thought, and find yourself saying things you can't take back. Because individuals perceive so much to be at stake, ego-based conflicts are difficult to manage. For this reason, the best way to handle them is to recognize them early on and to move the conflict back to a content level. Unfortunately, even minor disagreements can erupt into aggressive (and possibly lethal) confrontations. Thus, learning how to manage conflict is an essential skill in today's world.

Styles of Managing Conflict

How do you react to conflict? Most people have a habitual way or personal style of dealing with dissension. Studies have consistently revealed five distinct patterns of dealing with conflict: avoiding/withdrawing, accommodating, competing/forcing, compromising, and collaborating (Lulofs & Cahn, 2000). Two dimensions underlie these different styles: interest in satisfying one's own concerns and interest in satisfying others' concerns (Rahim & Magner, 1995). You can see the location of these five styles on these two dimensions in Figure 7.11. As you read about these styles, try to determine where you fit:

■ *Avoiding/withdrawing* (low concern for self and others). Some people simply find conflict extremely distasteful. When a conflict emerges, the avoider will change the subject, deflect discussion with humor, make a hasty exit, or pretend to be preoccupied with something else. People who prefer this style believe that ignoring a problem will make it go away. For minor problems, this tactic is often a good one—there's no need to react to every little annoyance. For bigger conflicts, avoiding/withdrawing is not a good strategy; it usually just delays the inevitable clash. If Maria consistently wants to discuss a problem and Tony consistently does not, relationship difficulties can arise. A particular problem occurs when an avoider has greater power in a relationship (parent, supervisor, romantic partner). This situation prevents the less powerful person from airing his or her concerns and breeds frustration and resentment. Of course, in some cases it is good to postpone a discussion, especially if one or both individuals is tired or rushed or needs time to cool off. Postponing qualifies as avoiding only if the promised discussion never takes place.

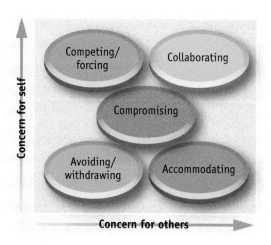

● FIGURE 7.11

Five styles of handling interpersonal conflict. In dealing with discord, individuals typically prefer one of five styles. The two dimensions of "concern for self" and "concern for others" underlie each of the five styles.

■ *Accommodating* (low concern for self, high concern for others). Like the avoider, the accommodator feels uncomfortable with conflict. However, instead of ignoring the disagreement, this person brings the conflict to a quick end by giving in easily. People who are overly concerned about acceptance and approval from others commonly use this strategy of surrender. Habitual accommodating is a poor way of dealing with conflict because it does not generate creative thinking and effective solutions. Moreover, feelings of resentment (on both sides) may develop because the accommodator often likes to play the role of a martyr. Of course, when you don't have strong preferences (for instance, where to eat out), occasional accommodating is perfectly appropriate. Also, in some cultures (such as Japan), it is the preferred style of dealing with conflict (Samovar & Porter, 2004).

■ *Competing/forcing* (high concern for self, low concern for others). The competitor turns every conflict into a black-and-white, win-or-lose situation. Competitors will do virtually anything to emerge victorious from confrontations; thus, they can be deceitful and aggressive—including using verbal attacks and physical threats. They rigidly adhere to one position and will use threats and coercion to force the other party to submit. Giving no quarter, competitors often get personal and "hit below the belt." This style is undesirable because, like accommodation, it fails to generate creative solutions to problems. Moreover, this approach is especially likely to lead to postconflict tension, resentment, and hostility.

■ *Compromising* (moderate concern for self and others). Compromising is a pragmatic approach to conflict that acknowledges the divergent needs of both parties. Compromisers are willing to negotiate and to meet the other person halfway. With this approach, each person gives up something so both can have partial satisfaction. Because both parties gain some satisfaction, compromising is a fairly constructive approach to conflict, especially when the issue is moderately important.

■ *Collaborating* (high concern for self and others). Whereas compromising simply entails "splitting the difference" between positions, collaborating involves a sincere effort to find a solution that will maximally satisfy both parties. In this approach, conflict is viewed as a mutual problem to be solved as effectively as possible. Collaborating thus encourages openness and honesty. It also stresses the importance of criticizing the other person's *ideas* in a disagreement rather than the other *person*. To collaborate, you have to work on clarifying differences and similarities in positions so that you can build on the similarities. Generally, this is the most productive approach for dealing with conflict. Instead of resulting in a postconflict residue of tension and resentment, collaborating tends to produce a climate of trust.

Dealing Constructively with Conflict

As you have seen, the most effective approach to conflict management is collaborating. To help you implement such an approach, we will offer some specific suggestions. But, before we get down to specifics, there are a few principles to keep in mind (Alberti & Emmons, 2001; Verderber & Verderber, 2004). First, in a conflict situation, try to give the other person the benefit of the doubt; don't automatically assume that those who disagree with you are ignorant or mean-spirited. Show respect for their position, and do your best to empathize with, and fully understand, their frame of reference. Second, approach the other person as an equal. If you have a higher status or more power (parent, supervisor), try to set this difference aside. Third, define the conflict as a mutual problem to be solved cooperatively, rather than as a win-lose proposition. Fourth, choose a mutually acceptable time to sit down and work on resolving the conflict. It is not always best to tackle the conflict when and where it first arises. Finally, communicate your flexibility and willingness to modify your position.

Here are some explicit guidelines for dealing effectively with interpersonal conflict (Alberti & Emmons, 2001; Johnson & Johnson, 1999; Verderber & Verderber, 2004):

■ *Make communication honest and open.* Don't withhold information or misrepresent your position. Avoid deceit and manipulation.

■ *Use specific behaviors to describe another person's annoying habits rather than general statements about their personality.* You'll probably get further with your roommate if you say something like, "Please throw your clothes in the hamper" rather than "You're such an inconsiderate slob." Remarks about specific actions are less threatening and are less likely to be taken personally. They also clarify what you hope will change.

■ *Avoid "loaded" words.* Certain words are "loaded" in the sense that they tend to trigger negative emotional reactions in listeners. For example, you can discuss politics without using terms such as "right-winger" and "knee-jerk liberal."

■ *Use a positive approach and help the other person save face.* Saying "I love it when we cook dinner together" will go over better than "You never help with dinner, and I resent it." Similarly, you can increase your chances of having a request accepted if you say, "I realize that you are very busy, but I'd really appreciate it if you would look at my paper again. I've marked the places I'd like you to reconsider."

■ *Limit complaints to recent behavior and to the current situation.* Dredging up past grievances only rekindles old resentments and distracts you from the current problem. And avoid saying things like "You *always* say you're too busy" or "You *never* do your fair share of the housework." Such categorical statements are bound to put the other person on the defensive.

■ *Assume responsibility for your own feelings and preferences.* Rather than "*You* make me mad," say "*I* am angry." Or, try "I'd appreciate it if you'd water the garden" instead of "Do you think the garden needs watering?"

Finally, if you can use an assertive (as opposed to submissive or aggressive) communication style, you will find it easier to head off and deal constructively with conflict situations. You can learn more about assertive communication in this chapter's Application.

Up to this point, we've been focusing on communication in the private sphere—interactions between people in personal relationships. To complete our discussion, we need to examine communication in the public sphere—interactions among members of the same society or community who do not personally know one another.

WEB LINK 7.6

The Conflict Resolution Information Source
This excellent resource on conflict management is provided by the University of Colorado's Conflict Research Consortium. The site is actually a gateway to a huge variety of resources on conflict management and is easy to navigate.

Public Communication in an Adversarial Culture

Political attack ads, vicious reality TV shows, "flame wars," hate-generating Internet sites, road rage—hostile incidents assault Americans on a daily basis. In fact, some universities have instituted speech and behavior codes to counteract hate speech and disrespectful behavior. Profanities and vulgarities in the workplace have become so commonplace that some employers have instituted anti-swearing policies (DuFrene & Lehman, 2002). Ominously, aggression among nonemotionally disturbed kindergartners is on the rise, including hitting, biting, and swearing at teachers; assaulting peers; and even carrying weapons (Wallis, 2003). What is going on?

RECOMMENDED READING

The Argument Culture: Moving from Debate to Dialogue
by Deborah Tannen (Random House, 1998)

In this thought-provoking work, Tannen claims that public interchanges in America are increasingly framed as battles or games. Hence, the focus has become trying to win arguments rather than trying to understand what is being said. While acknowledging that opposition can be useful and necessary, Tannen is concerned with what she sees as a trend for Americans to use an adversarial approach to the exclusion of other ways of communicating in public. And living in "the argument culture" is having negative effects on Americans and the larger society. With an easygoing style, Tannen brings in research and wide-ranging examples from politics, the media, the legal profession, the classroom, and the Internet to bolster her thesis.

To halt the growth of "the argument culture," Tannen advocates using nonadversarial ways to negotiate disagreements and mediate conflicts. For instance, she urges people to start looking for ways that both sides can win disagreements (as opposed to thinking in terms of one side "winning" and the other "losing"). In addition, she urges people to get out of the "dualism trap." Instead of asking, "What is the other *side*?" individuals can ask, "What are the other *sides*?" Tannen recommends setting up discussions with three or more people rather than using the debate-prone two-person format. She also suggests reducing the use of war metaphors (the battle of the sexes, the war on drugs, "annihilating" the other team, and so forth) and replacing them with less combative figures of speech.

Sociolinguist Deborah Tannen (1998) characterizes contemporary America as "the argument culture." According to Tannen, an atmosphere of "unrelenting contention" (p. 3) pervades American culture and is fueled by a growing tendency for Americans to automatically take an adversarial approach in almost any public situation. She worries that this constant exposure to public arguments is having a "corrosive" effect on Americans' spirits and is creating serious social problems. Hostile public debates confuse and frustrate listeners, inflame emotions, and alienate Americans from each other and their leaders.

Deborah Tannen

Contributing Factors

Obviously, numerous factors contribute to social contentiousness, and we can touch on only a few. We'll start with the fact that the United States is a strongly individualistic culture. This culture predisposes Americans to be adversarial because the self is perceived to be an isolated entity and in opposition to society. Second, Americans (and those in other Western cultures) have a dualistic view of nature and tend to see things in terms of opposites—good *versus* bad, strong *versus* weak, and so on (Tannen, 1998). On the other hand, most Eastern cultures have a nondualistic perspective, in which opposites are seen as complementary partners, both essential to a larger whole (good *and* bad, strong *and* weak).

A third factor is that face-to-face communication is on the decline, fed by economic pressures and advances in technology. Parents are working longer hours, and many come home exhausted. This can mean less "quality time" for children. Many families gather only rarely for meals. Instead, to accommodate busy schedules, family members each pop frozen dinners into the micro-

Road rage is one example of increased public conflict in American society.

wave. Whereas families used to gather around a single radio or television, now family members each have their own radios and TVs (as well as computers and cell phones). In the same vein, distance-learning classes permit many individuals to take classes they would not otherwise be able to attend, but students have limited social interactions with peers and instructors. Taken together, such changes mean that individuals spend more time on their own, rather than learning to interact effectively with others.

Excessive exposure to the high levels of physical and verbal aggression, especially in the media, is a fourth factor in the equation. Children spend from two to four hours a day watching television, with viewing time increasing up through early adolescence. The National Television Violence Study, a large-scale study of the content of network and cable television shows during the 1994–1997 viewing seasons, determined that 61 percent of programs airing between 6 A.M. and 11 P.M. contain violence (Center for Communication and Social Policy, 1998). By the time a child finishes grade school, he or she will have witnessed approximately 8,000 murders and 100,000 other acts of violence on TV (Huston et al., 1992). Of course, aggression also appears in other types of media: video games, the Internet, music videos, and music lyrics.

Over time, excessive exposure to these various forms of media violence takes its toll in a variety of ways. Numerous studies suggest that extensive exposure to media violence contributes to the development of aggressiveness in some children (Anderson et al., 2003), and aggressive children grow up to be aggressive adults (Broidy et al., 2003; Huesmann & Moise, 1998). In addition, repeated exposure to aggression causes viewers to become numb or *desensitized* to violence and its effects on victims (Anderson et al., 2003), causing viewers to be more accepting of it. Furthermore, there is evidence that some people come to believe that "television reality" depicts actual reality. Thus, people who are exposed to considerable TV violence come to believe that society is more hostile and dangerous than it actually is. In turn, they become more distrustful, view aggression as an acceptable way to solve problems, and are more likely to carry a weapon (Nabi & Sullivan, 2001).

Restoring Productive Public Communication

Must Americans resign themselves to living in an increasingly contentious society, or are there ways to reduce public hostility? Social institutions—the government, media, and schools, for instance—could institute broad-ranging changes that could significantly affect this problem (Anderson et al., 2003). Politicians could agree to desist from hostile campaign rhetoric, and governments could enact legislation to reduce access to

weapons and reduce poverty. Newspapers could encourage reporters to emphasize substance in their reporting and minimize sensationalism; producers could voluntarily reduce the amount of gratuitous violence portrayed on television and in films and increase the number of programs and movies with nonviolent and prosocial messages. And schools could institute programs that teach children social skills and nonviolent ways of resolving conflicts (Aber, Brown, & Jones, 2003).

But what can *individuals* do? By applying the principles of effective interpersonal communication discussed in this chapter, you can do a lot. Tune in to nonverbal signals, create a positive interpersonal climate, be a good listener, overcome the barriers to effective communication, and practice your conflict management skills. Practice these principles when you're on the phone or Internet, as well. When you're on the road, avoid antagonizing other drivers (see Figure 7.12). And minimize the amount of media violence you expose yourself to—be selective about the TV programs and movies you watch.

Efforts to reduce aggression in children are most effective when they occur at relatively young ages (Anderson & Huesmann, 2003). Therefore, parents have a special role to play. They can limit their children's exposure to physical and verbal aggression—on television, in movies, in video games, in books, and on the Internet. Also, parents can watch TV with their children and comment negatively about violent scenes. Children of such parents are less likely to have aggressive attitudes than children whose parents watch TV with them but say nothing about aggressive content (Nathanson, 1999). Too, parents can ensure that their kids are exposed to TV programs and movies that model

Tips for Avoiding Road Rage

Don't tailgate.

Don't use obscene gestures.

Don't lean on your horn; tap it lightly.

Signal before switching lanes and don't cut someone off when you change lanes.

Don't display bumperstickers or slogans that might antagonize others.

Avoid making eye contact with a hostile motorist.

Be polite and courteous even if the other driver is not.

Don't drive when you are angry, upset, or fatigued.

● **FIGURE 7.12**

Steering clear of road rage. Studies have shown that these strategies can reduce your chances of being a victim of road rage.

From Road Rage Plagues Drivers. (1997, November-December). *AAA Going Places*, 41–42. Copyright © 1997 by the American Automobile Association.

positive ways of interacting with others to increase helpfulness and cooperation in children (Huston & Wright, 1998). Parents can also help by encouraging and rewarding nonaggressive rather than aggressive ways of resolving childhood conflicts (especially in boys). Finally, they can use disciplinary methods that don't model aggressive behavior (for more information, see the Application for Chapter 11, on effective parenting).

In summary, individuals and social institutions can take many positive actions to reduce the level of conflictual communication in the public arena. In our upcoming Application, we will discuss *assertiveness,* a communication style that has proved extremely effective across a wide variety of interpersonal communication situations—for example, making acquaintances, developing relationships, and resolving conflicts.

APPLICATION

Developing an Assertive Communication Style

LEARNING OBJECTIVES
- *Differentiate assertive communication from submissive and aggressive communication.*
- *List five steps that lead to more assertive communication.*

Answer the following questions "yes" or "no."

____ **1.** When someone asks you for an unreasonable favor, is it difficult to say no?

____ **2.** Do you feel timid about returning flawed merchandise?

____ **3.** Do you have a hard time requesting even small favors from others?

____ **4.** When a group is hotly debating an issue, are you shy about speaking up?

____ **5.** When a salesperson pressures you to buy something you don't want, is it hard for you to resist?

If you answered "yes" to several of these questions, you may need to increase your assertiveness. Many people have a hard time being assertive; however, this problem is more common among females because they are socialized to be more submissive than males—for example, to "be nice." Consequently, assertiveness training is especially popular among women. Men, too, find assertiveness training helpful, both because some males have been socialized to be passive and because others want to learn to be less aggressive and more assertive. We'll elaborate on the differences between assertive, submissive, and aggressive behavior and discuss some procedures for increasing assertiveness.

Keep in mind that our perspective reflects an individualistic perspective. Other cultures may have different views on submissiveness, assertiveness, and aggressiveness (Samovar & Porter, 2004). For instance, some Native American tribes disdain both assertiveness and aggression. Similarly, such collectivist societies as China, Japan, Thailand, and the Philippines place a high value

on interpersonal harmony. By contrast, Israelis and members of the Jewish culture tend to have a confrontational interactional style in which vigorous debate is expected.

The Nature of Assertiveness

Assertiveness **involves acting in your own best interests by expressing your thoughts and feelings directly and honestly** (Alberti & Emmons, 2001; Bower & Bower, 1991, 2004). Essentially, assertiveness involves standing up for your rights when someone else is about to infringe on them. To be assertive is to speak out rather than pull your punches.

The nature of assertive communication can best be clarified by contrasting it with other types of communication. *Submissive communication* involves consistently giving in to others on points of possible contention. Submissive people often let others take advantage of them. Typically, their biggest problem is that they cannot say no to unreasonable requests. A common example is the college student who can't tell her roommate not to borrow her clothes. Submissive people also

---

WEB LINK 7.7

Assertiveness
In an online brochure, this site clarifies the nature of assertiveness and describes specific techniques for becoming more assertive. The site is maintained by the Counseling Center at the University of Illinois at Urbana–Champaign.

have difficulty voicing disagreement with others and making requests themselves. In traditional trait terminology, they are timid.

Although the roots of submissiveness have not been investigated fully, they appear to lie in excessive concern about gaining the social approval of others. However, the strategy of "not making waves" is more likely to garner others' contempt than their approval. Moreover, individuals who use this style often feel bad about themselves (for being "pushovers") and resentful of those whom they allow to take advantage of them. These feelings often lead the submissive individual to try to punish the other person by withdrawing, sulking, or crying (Bower & Bower, 1991, 2004). These manipulative attempts to get one's own way are sometimes referred to as "passive aggression" or "indirect aggression."

At the other end of the spectrum, *aggressive communication* focuses on saying and getting what you want, but at the expense of others' feelings and rights. With assertive behavior, you strive to respect others' rights and defend your own. The problem in real life is that assertive and aggressive behaviors *may* overlap. When someone is about to infringe on their rights, people often lash out at the other party (aggression) while defending their rights (assertion). The challenge, then, is to be firm and assertive without becoming aggressive.

Advocates of assertive communication argue that it is much more adaptive than either submissive or aggressive communication (Alberti & Emmons, 2001, Bower & Bower, 1991, 2004). They maintain that submissive behavior leads to poor self-esteem, self-denial, emotional suppression, and strained interpersonal relationships. Conversely, aggressive communication tends to promote guilt, alienation, and disharmony. In contrast, assertive behavior is said to foster high self-esteem, satisfactory interpersonal relationships, and effective conflict management.

The essential point with assertiveness is that you are able to state what you want clearly and directly. Being able to do so makes you feel good about yourself and will usually make others feel good about you, too. And, although being assertive doesn't guarantee your chances for getting what you want, it certainly enhances them.

Steps in Assertiveness Training

Numerous assertiveness training programs are available in book form, on CDs or videotapes, or through seminars. Some recommendations about books appear in the Recommended Readings box in this section. Most of the programs are behavioral and emphasize gradual improvement and reinforcement of appropriate behavior. Here we will summarize the key steps in assertiveness training.

1. Understand What Assertive Communication Is

To produce assertive behavior, you need to understand what it looks and sounds like. Thus, most programs begin by clarifying the nature of assertive communication. Assertiveness trainers often ask clients to imagine situations calling for assertiveness and compare hypothetical submissive (or passive), assertive, and aggressive responses. Let's consider one such comparison. In this example, a woman in assertiveness training is asking her roommate to cooperate in cleaning their apartment once a week. The roommate, who is uninterested in the problem, is listening to music when the conversation begins. In this example, the roommate is playing the role of the antagonist—called a "downer" in the following scripts (excerpted from Bower & Bower, 1991, 2004, pp. 8, 9, 11).

The Passive Scene

SHE: *Uh, I was wondering if you would be willing to take time to decide about the housecleaning.*

DOWNER: *(listening to the music) Not now, I'm busy.*

SHE: *Oh, okay.*

The Aggressive Scene

SHE: *Listen, I've had it with you not even talking about cleaning this damn apartment. Are you going to help me?*

DOWNER: *(listening to the music) Not now, I'm busy.*

SHE: *Why can't you look at me when you turn me down? You don't give a damn about the housework or me! You only care about yourself!*

DOWNER: *That's not true.*

SHE: *You never pay any attention to the apartment or to me. I have to do everything around here!*

DOWNER: *Oh, shut up! You're just neurotic about cleaning all the time. Who are you, my mother? Can't I relax with my stereo for a few minutes without you pestering me? This was my apartment first, you know!*

The Assertive Scene

SHE: *I know housework isn't the most fascinating subject, but it needs to be done. Let's plan when we'll do it.*

DOWNER: *(listening to music) Oh, c'mon—not now! I'm busy.*

SHE: *This won't take long. I feel that if we have a schedule, it will be easier to keep up with the chores.*

DOWNER: *I'm not sure I'll have time for all of them.*

SHE: *I've already drawn up a couple of rotating schedules for housework, so that each week we have an equal division of tasks. Will you look at them? I'd like to hear your decisions about them, say, tonight after supper?*

DOWNER: *[indignantly] I have to look at these now?*

SHE: *Is there some other time that's better for you?*

DOWNER: *Oh, I don't know.*

SHE: *Well, then let's discuss plans after supper for 15 minutes. Is that agreed?*

DOWNER: *I guess so.*

SHE: *Good! It won't take long, and I'll feel relieved when we have a schedule in place.*

Reading two or three books on assertiveness is a way to get a good picture of assertive behavior. A helpful way to distinguish among the three types of communication is in terms of how people deal with their own rights and the rights of others. Submissive people sacrifice their own rights. Aggressive people tend to ignore the rights of others. Assertive people consider both their own rights *and* the rights of others.

As we have noted, the nonverbal aspect of communication is extremely important. To ensure that your assertive words have impact, it is important to back them up with congruent nonverbal messages. Thus, you'll come across as more assertive if you face the person you're talking with, look directly at him or her, and maintain eye contact, rather than looking away from the other person, fidgeting, slouching, and shuffling your feet (Bower & Bower, 1991, 2004). You'll find some

additional guidelines for behaving assertively in Figure 7.13 (on the next page).

2. Monitor Your Assertive Communication

Most people's assertiveness varies from one situation to another. In other words, they may be assertive in some social contexts and timid in others. Consequently, once you understand the nature of assertive communication, you should monitor yourself and identify when you are nonassertive. In particular, you should figure out *who* intimidates you, on *what topics,* and in *which situations.*

3. Observe a Model's Assertive Communication

Once you have identified the situations in which you are nonassertive, think of someone who communicates

Guidelines for assertive behavior. Gordon and Sharon Bower (1991, 2004) outline a four-step program intended to help readers create successful assertive scripts for themselves. The four steps are (1) *describe* the unwanted behavior from another person (called your "Downer") that is troubling you, (2) *express* your feelings about the behavior to the other person, (3) *specify* the changes needed, and (4) try to provide rewarding *consequences* for the change. Using this framework, the table shown here provides some useful dos and don'ts for achieving effective assertive behavior.

Adapted from Bower, S. A., & Bower, G. H. (1991). *Asserting yourself: A practical guide for positive change* (2nd ed.). Reading, MA: Addison-Wesley. Copyright © 1991 by Sharon Anthony Bower and Gordon H. Bower. Reprinted by permission of Perseus Books Publishers, a member of Perseus Books, L.L.C.

Rules for Assertive Scripts

Do	Don't
Describe	
■ Describe the other person's behavior objectively.	Describe your emotional reaction to it.
■ Use concrete terms.	Use abstract, vague terms.
■ Describe a specified time, place, and frequency of the action.	Generalize for "all time."
■ Describe the action, not the "motive."	Guess at your Downer's motives or goals.
Express	
■ Express your feelings.	Deny your feelings.
■ Express them calmly.	Unleash emotional outbursts.
■ State feelings in a positive manner, as relating to a goal to be achieved.	State feelings negatively, making Downer attack.
■ Direct yourself to the specific offending behavior, not to the whole person.	Attack the entire character of the person.
Specify	
■ Ask explicitly for change in your Downer's behavior.	Merely imply that you'd like a change.
■ Request a small change.	Ask for too large a change.
■ Request only one or two changes at one time.	Ask for too many changes.
■ Specify the concrete actions you want to see stopped and those you want to see performed.	Ask for changes in nebulous traits or qualities.
■ Take account of whether your Downer can meet your request without suffering large losses.	Ignore your Downer's needs or ask only for your satisfaction.
■ Specify (if appropriate) what behavior you are willing to change to make the agreement.	Consider that only your Downer has to change.
Consequences	
■ Make the consequences explicit.	Be ashamed to talk about rewards and penalties.
■ Give a positive reward for change in the desired direction.	Give only punishments for lack of change.
■ Select something that is desirable and reinforcing to your Downer.	Select something that only you might find rewarding.
■ Select a reward that is big enough to maintain the behavior change.	Offer a reward you can't or won't deliver.
■ Select a punishment of a magnitude that "fits the crime" of refusing to change behavior.	Make exaggerated threats.
■ Select a punishment that you are actually willing to carry out.	Use unrealistic threats or self-defeating punishment.

assertively in those situations and observe that person's behavior closely. In other words, find someone to model yourself after. This is an easy way to learn how to behave assertively in situations crucial to you. Your observations should also allow you to see how rewarding assertive communication can be, which should strengthen your assertive tendencies. If an assertive model isn't available, you can adapt the relevant scenarios in most self-help books on assertiveness.

4. Practice Assertive Communication

The key to achieving assertive communication is to practice it and work toward gradual improvement. Your practice can take several forms. In *covert rehearsal*, you imagine a situation requiring assertion and the dialogue that you would engage in. In *role playing*, you ask a friend or therapist to play the role of an antagonist. Then practice communicating assertively in this artificial situation.

Eventually, of course, you want to transfer your assertiveness skills to real-life situations. Most experts recommend that you use *shaping* to increase your assertive communication gradually. As we discussed in the Chapter 4 Application, shaping involves rewarding yourself for making closer and closer approximations of a desired behavior. For example, in the early stages of your behavior-change program, your goal might be to make at least one assertive comment every day, while toward the end you might be striving to make at least eight such comments a day. Obviously, in designing a shaping program, it is important to set realistic goals for yourself.

5. Adopt an Assertive Attitude

Most assertiveness training programs have a behavioral orientation and focus on specific responses for specific situations (see Figure 7.14). However, it's ob-vious that real-life situations only rarely match those portrayed in books. Hence, some experts maintain that acquiring a repertoire of verbal responses for certain situations is not as important as developing a new attitude that you're not going to let people push you around (or let yourself push others around, if you're the aggressive type) (Alberti & Emmons, 2001). Although most programs don't talk explicitly about attitudes, they do appear to instill a new attitude indirectly. A change in attitude is probably crucial to achieving flexible, assertive behavior.

Assertive Responses to Some Common Putdowns

Nature of Remark	Put-Down Sentence	Suggested Assertive Reply
Nagging about details	"Haven't you done this yet?"	"No, when did you want it done?" (Answer without hedging, and follow up with a question.)
Prying	"I know I maybe shouldn't ask, but . . ."	"If I don't want to answer, I'll let you know." (Indicate that you won't make yourself uncomfortable just to please this person.)
Putting you on the spot socially	"Are you busy Tuesday?"	"What do you have in mind?" (Answer the question with a question.)
Pigeonholing you	"That's a woman for you!"	"That's one woman, not *all* women." (Disagree—assert your individuality.)
Using insulting labels for your behavior	"That's a dumb way to . . ."	"I'll decide what to call my behavior." (Refuse to accept the label.)
Basing predictions on an amateur personality analysis	"You'll have a hard time. You're too shy."	"In what ways do you think I'm too shy?" (Ask for clarification of the analysis.)

● FIGURE 7.14

Assertive responses to common put-downs. Having some assertive replies at the ready can increase your confidence in difficult social interactions.

Adapted from Bower, S. A., & Bower, G. H. (1991). *Asserting yourself: A practical guide for positive change* (2nd ed.). Reading, MA: Addison-Wesley. Copyright © 1991 by Sharon Anthony Bower and Gordon H. Bower. Reprinted by permission of Perseus Books Publishers, a member of Perseus Books, L.L.C.

KEY IDEAS

The Process of Interpersonal Communication

■ Interpersonal communication is the interactional process that occurs when one person sends a message to another. Communication takes place when a sender transmits a message to a receiver either verbally or nonverbally. The widespread use of cellular telephones and computers for communication has raised new issues in interpersonal communication. Although people often take it for granted, effective communication contributes to their adjustment in school, in relationships, and at work.

Nonverbal Communication

■ Nonverbal communication tends to be more spontaneous than verbal communication, and it is more ambiguous. Sometimes it contradicts what is communicated verbally. It is often multichanneled and, like language, is culturally bound. Nonverbal communication usually conveys emotions. Elements of nonverbal communication include personal space, facial expression, eye contact, body language, touch, and paralanguage.

■ Certain nonverbal cues are associated with deception, but many of these cues do not correspond to popular beliefs about how liars give themselves away. Discrepancies between facial expressions and other nonverbal signals may suggest dishonesty. The vocal and visual cues associated with lying are so subtle, however, that the detection of deception is difficult. Machines used to detect deception (polygraphs) are not particularly accurate.

■ Nonverbal communication plays an important role in adjustment, especially in the quality of interpersonal relationships.

Toward More Effective Communication

■ Effective communication rests on a foundation of a positive interpersonal climate. To promote a positive interpersonal climate, it helps to show empathy, treat people as equals, withhold judgment, strive for honesty, and express opinions tentatively. To be an effective communicator, it's important to develop good conversational skills, including knowing how to make small talk with strangers.

■ Self-disclosure—opening up to others—can foster emotional intimacy in relationships. Emotional (but not factual) self-disclosures lead to feelings of closeness. To reduce the risks of self-disclosure, it's best to self-disclose gradually. The receiver's nonverbal signals help the speaker know whether to continue or stop disclosing.

■ The level of self-disclosure varies over the course of relationships. Cultures vary in the preferred level of self-disclosure. American women tend to self-disclose more than men, but this disparity is not so large as it once was. Effective listening is an essential aspect of interpersonal communication.

Communication Problems

■ A number of problems can arise that interfere with effective communication. Individuals who become overly anxious when they talk with others suffer from communication apprehension. This difficulty can cause problems in relationships and in work and educational settings. Sometimes communication can produce negative interpersonal outcomes. Barriers to effective communication include defensiveness, motivational distortion, self-preoccupation, and game playing.

Interpersonal Conflict

■ Dealing constructively with interpersonal conflict is an important aspect of effective communication. Individualistic cultures tend to encourage direct confrontations, whereas collectivist cultures often avoid them. Nonetheless, many Americans have negative attitudes about conflict.

■ Conflicts can be classified as one of four types: pseudoconflicts, content conflicts, value conflicts, or ego conflicts. In dealing with conflict, most people have a preferred style: avoiding/withdrawing, accommodating, competing, compromising, or collaborating. The latter style is the most effective in managing conflict.

■ Public communication in America is becoming increasingly contentious. Contributing factors include living in an individualistic culture, having a dualistic perspective, having reduced face-to-face interactions, and being exposed to high levels of physical and verbal aggression, especially on television. Individuals and social institutions can institute a number of changes to restore productive communication in the public sphere.

Application: Developing an Assertive Communication Style

■ An assertive style enables individuals to stand up for themselves and to respect the rights of others. To become more assertive, individuals need to understand what assertive communication is, monitor assertive communication, observe a model's assertive communication, practice being assertive, and adopt an assertive attitude.

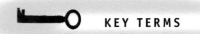

KEY TERMS

Assertiveness p. 227
Communication
    apprehension p. 219
Context p. 203
Display rules p. 208
Empathy p. 214
Games p. 221
Interpersonal
    communication p. 202
Interpersonal conflict p. 221

Kinesics p. 210
Noise p. 203
Nonverbal communication
    p. 205
Paralanguage pp. 210–211
Personal space p. 206
Polygraph p. 212
Proxemics p. 206
Self-disclosure p. 215

KEY PEOPLE

Sharon Anthony Bower and
    Gordon Bower
    pp. 228–231
Bella DePaulo pp. 211–212

Paul Ekman and Wallace
    Friesen pp. 207–208
Edward T. Hall p. 207
Deborah Tannen
    pp. 225–226

PRACTICE TEST

1. Which of the following is *not* a component of the interpersonal communication process?
   a. The sender
   b. The receiver
   c. The channel
   d. The monitor

2. Research shows that individuals from a variety of cultures:
   a. agree on the facial expressions that correspond with all emotions.
   b. agree on the facial expressions that correspond with 15 basic emotions.
   c. agree on the facial expressions that correspond with 6 basic emotions.
   d. do not agree on the facial expressions that correspond with any emotions.

3. Which of the following is *not* an aspect of body language?
   a. Body movement
   b. Personal space
   c. Posture
   d. Gestures

4. According to research, which of the following cues is associated with dishonesty?
   a. Speaking with a higher-than-normal pitch
   b. Speaking slowly
   c. Giving relatively long answers to questions
   d. Lack of eye contact

5. With regard to self-disclosure, it is best to:
   a. share a lot about yourself when you first meet someone.
   b. share very little about yourself for a long time.
   c. gradually share information about yourself.
   d. give no personal information on a first encounter, but share a lot the next time.

6. Regarding self-disclosure in same-gender friendships:
   a. most men disclose more to their friends than women.
   b. most women disclose more to their friends than men.
   c. men and women disclose about the same amount to their friends.
   d. men and women disclose about the same amount, but women start disclosing sooner.

7. When people hear what they want to hear instead of what is actually said, _____ is operating.
   a. defensiveness
   b. self-preoccupation
   c. motivational distortion
   d. game playing

8. The most difficult conflicts to manage are:
   a. pseudoconflicts.
   b. content-based conflicts.
   c. value-based conflicts.
   d. ego-based conflicts.

9. Generally, the most productive style for managing conflict is:
   a. collaboration.
   b. compromise.
   c. accommodation.
   d. avoidance.

10. Expressing your thoughts directly and honestly without trampling on other people is a description of which communication style?
    a. Aggressive
    b. Empathic
    c. Submissive
    d. Assertive

Book Companion Website

Visit the Book Companion Website at **http://psychology. wadsworth.com/weiten_lloyd8e,** where you will find tutorial quizzes, flashcards, and weblinks for every chapter, a final exam, and more! You can also link to the Thomson Wadsworth Psychology Resource Center (accessible directly at **http://psychology.wadsworth.com**) for a range of psychology-related resources.

Personal Explorations Workbook

The following exercises in your *Personal Explorations Workbook* may enhance your self-understanding in relation to issues raised in this chapter. **Questionnaire 7.1:** Opener Scale. **Personal Probe 7.1:** How Do You Feel about Self-Disclosure? **Personal Probe 7.2:** Reflections on Your Communication Style and Feelings about Conflict.

ANSWERS

1. d Pages 202–203
2. c Pages 207–208
3. b Page 210
4. a Pages 211–212
5. c Page 216
6. b Page 217
7. c Page 220
8. d Pages 222–223
9. a Page 225
10. d Pages 227–228

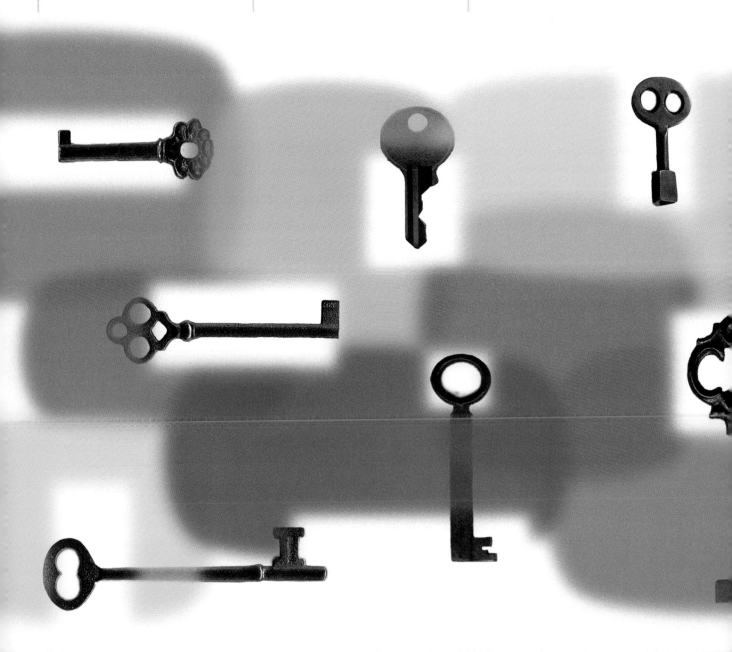

Friendship and Love

Antonio was so keyed up, he tossed and turned all night. When morning finally arrived, he was elated. In less than two hours, he would be meeting Sonia for coffee! In his first class that morning, thoughts and images of Sonia constantly distracted him from the lecture. When class was finally over, he had to force himself not to walk too fast to the Student Union, where they had agreed to meet. Sound familiar? Chances are that you recognize Antonio's behavior as that of someone falling in love.

Friendship and love play a major role in psychological adjustment. Recall from Chapter 1 that the strongest predictor of happiness, after personality, is social connectedness. And, social exclusion is associated with poor physical and mental health and antisocial behavior (Baumeister & Leary, 1995; Baumeister &Twenge, 2003). We begin this chapter by defining close relationships, including a discussion of how culture and the Internet influence relationships. Next, we consider why people are attracted to each other and why they stay in or leave relationships. Following that, we probe more deeply into friendship and romantic love. In the Application section, we focus on the painful problem of loneliness and how to overcome it.

Perspectives on Close Relationships

LEARNING OBJECTIVES

- Define close relationships and give some examples.
- Describe how members from individualistic cultures and collectivist cultures view love and marriage.
- Describe the differences between Internet and face-to-face interactions and how the Internet affects relationship development.

Before diving into the fascinating topic of romantic love, it would be helpful to have some background information. Let's examine the variety of close relationships, how culture influences people's views of relationships, and how the Internet affects relationships.

The Ingredients of Close Relationships

Typically, *close relationships* **are those that are important, interdependent, and long lasting.** In other words, people in close relationships spend a lot of time and energy maintaining the relationship, and what one person says and does affects the other. As you are aware, close relationships can arouse intense feelings—both positive (passion, concern, caring) and negative (rage, jealousy, despair).

Close relationships come in many forms: family relationships, friendships and work relationships, romantic relationships, and marriage. Although many close relationships are based on mutual, intimate self-disclosure, many are not. When college students were asked to identify that person to whom they felt closest, 47 percent named a romantic partner, 36 percent listed a friend, 14 percent mentioned a family member, and 3 percent named another individual such as a co-worker (Berscheid, Snyder, & Omoto, 1989). Thus, not all close relationships are characterized by emotional intimacy.

Marriages based on romantic love are the norm in Western cultures, whereas arranged marriages prevail in collectivist cultures.

Culture and Relationships

Cross-cultural research on close relationships is largely limited to romantic relationships, so we'll focus on them. Although it appears that romantic love is experienced in most cultures (Jankowiak & Fischer, 1992), cultures do vary in their emphasis on romantic love as a prerequisite for marriage. Interestingly, love as the basis for marriage goes back only to the 18th century of Western culture (Stone, 1977). According to Elaine Hatfield and Richard Rapson (1993), "Marriage-for-love represents an ultimate expression of individualism" (p. 2). By contrast, marriages arranged by families and other go-betweens remain common in cultures high in collectivism, including India (Gupta, 1992), Japan (Iwao, 1993), China (Xiaohe & Whyte, 1990), and West African countries (Adams, Anderson, & Adonu, 2004). This practice is declining in some societies as a result of Westernization. Still, when people in collectivist societies

contemplate marriage, they give strong consideration to the impact a relationship will have on their family rather than rely solely on what their heart says (Triandis, 1994). Studies show that attitudes about love in India, Pakistan, Thailand, and West African countries reflect these cultural priorities (Levine et al., 1995; Medora et al., 2002; Adams et al., 2004).

Cultural views of love and marriage are linked to both a culture's values and its economic health. In one study, researchers asked college students in 11 countries the following question: "If a man (woman) had all the other qualities you desired, would you marry this person if you were not in love with him (her)?" (Levine et al., 1995). Students in countries with more individualistic values and higher standards of living were significantly less likely to answer "yes" to the question than were those in countries with more collectivist values and lower standards of living (see Figure 8.1). And a different cross-cultural investigation of the meaning of various emotions found that Italians and Americans equated love with happiness, whereas Chinese respondents associated it with sadness and tended to envision unrequited love (Shaver, Wu, & Schwartz, 1991).

People from Western societies are often dumbfounded by collectivist cultures' deemphasis of romantic love and their penchant for arranged marriages. Most Westerners assume that the modern conception of romantic love as the basis for marriage must result in better marital relationships than collectivist cultures' "antiquated" beliefs and practices. However, there is little empirical support for this ethnocentric view (Dion & Dion, 1993; Triandis, 1994). Take, for example, a study of couples in India, which found that love grew over the years in arranged marriages, whereas it declined among couples who married for romantic love (Gupta & Singh, 1982). Also, the expectation that marriage will fill diverse psychological needs places greater pressure on marital relationships in individualistic societies than on those in collectivist cultures (Dion & Dion, 1993). These high expectations for personal fulfillment in marriage may be linked to the rapidly escalating divorce rates in these societies (Dion & Dion, 1993). The dearth of cross-cultural research on love means that we can only speculate on these matters. But smug assumptions about the superiority of Western ways look shaky, given our extremely high divorce rates.

The Internet and Relationships

To meet prospective friends and romantic partners, people used to be limited to school, work, and church settings. Then came the "bar scene," personal ads in newspapers, singles mixers, and video dating services. More recently, the Internet has dramatically expanded opportunities for people to meet and develop relationships through online dating services, e-mail, chat rooms, and news groups.

Critics see these trends as leading to the demise of face-to-face interactions, widespread loneliness and alienation, and millions being lured into dangerous liaisons by unscrupulous people. But research to date generally paints a very positive picture of the Internet's impact on people's connections with one another. For example, it offers a wealth of new opportunities to interact for those normally separated because of geography, physical infirmity, or social anxiety (McKenna & Bargh, 2000). Also, Internet groups provide a safer venue than real life for individuals with stigmatized identities (for example, gay people) to interact and receive support. Similarly, Internet groups for those with grave illnesses (cancer, multiple sclerosis, diabetes, AIDS) provide important support and information to their subscribers (Bargh & McKenna, 2004). Of course, the anonymous nature of Internet communication *does* make it easy for dishonest individuals to take advantage of others, so it's important to exercise caution in revealing personal information online.

In a relatively short period of time, the Internet has become an indispensable vehicle for making acquain-

Cross-Cultural Views on Love and Marriage			
Country	Yes	No	Undecided
Japan	2.3	62.0	35.7
United States	3.5	85.9	10.6
Brazil	4.3	85.7	10.0
Australia	4.8	80.0	15.2
Hong Kong	5.8	77.6	16.7
England	7.3	83.6	9.1
Mexico	10.2	80.5	9.3
Philippines	11.4	63.6	25.0
Thailand	18.8	33.8	47.5
India	49.0	24.0	26.9
Pakistan	50.4	39.1	10.4

● **FIGURE 8.1**

Cross-cultural views on love and marriage. College students in ten countries and Hong Kong responded to the following question: "If a man (woman) had all the other qualities you desired, would you marry this person if you were not in love with him (her)?" Generally, students in countries with higher standards of living and more individualistic values were significantly less likely to answer "yes" to the question than those in countries with lower standards of living and more collectivist values.

Adapted from Levine, R., Sato, S., Hashimoto, T., & Verma, J. (1995). Love and marriage in eleven cultures. *Journal of Cross-Cultural Psychology 26*(5), pp. 561, 564. Copyright © 1995 by Sage Publications, Inc. Adapted by permission of Sage Publications.

tances and developing relationships. One survey of several hundred randomly selected newsgroup users reported that 60 percent of the participants had formed an online personal relationship of some kind with another newsgroup user (Parks & Floyd, 1996). Are Internet relationships more superficial than face-to-face ones? Research to date suggests that virtual relationships are just as intimate as face-to-face ones and are sometimes even closer (McKenna, Green, & Gleason, 2002; Bargh, McKenna, & Fitzsimons, 2002). The relative anonymity of the Internet facilitates the formation of close relationships because it reduces the risks of self-disclosure (Bargh & McKenna, 2004). For example, people in chat rooms were better able to express their true selves (aspects of the self they felt were important but that they were usually unable to present in public) to the Internet partner than when in person (Bargh et al., 2002). The Internet also encourages relationship formation based on shared interests and values instead of on physical appearance, as is more often the situation in offline interactions (Bargh & McKenna, 2004).

In many cases virtual relationships move to face-to-face interactions. In a survey of participants from 20 randomly selected newsgroups, 54 percent reported that they had met face to face with an Internet friend (McKenna et al. 2002). When people do decide to move beyond an Internet-based relationship, they typically first exchange letters via "snail mail" or talk on the telephone. Actual meetings usually take place only after telephone contact. These researchers also found that romantic relationships that begin on the Internet seem to be just as stable over two years as traditional relationships (McKenna et al., 2002). This same study of Internet chat room users reported that 22 percent of the participants said that they were either living with, had become engaged to, or were married to someone they had first met on the Internet.

The Internet is playing a larger and larger role in the formation and maintenance of interpersonal relationships.

The Internet has also assumed importance in maintaining established relationships. In a poll of 1,000 Internet users, 94 percent reported that the Internet made it easier for them to communicate with friends and family who live far away, and 87 percent said that they use it regularly for that purpose (D'Amico, 1998). Some social critics have predicted that Internet use will reduce face-to-face interactions. However, it seems that heavy Internet users maintain their involvement with friends and family, but cut back on time devoted to television and newspapers (Nie & Erbring, 2000).

The differences between Internet and face-to-face communication (see Figure 7.2 in the previous chapter) require psychologists to reexamine the established theories and principles of relationship development that we discuss in this chapter (Bargh & McKenna, 2004). For example, good looks and close physical proximity are powerful factors in initial attraction in the real world. In Internet relationships, where people form relationships sight-unseen, these factors are irrelevant. Online, where people rely on self-disclosure to develop relationships, similarity of interests and values kicks in earlier and assumes more power than it does in face-to-face relationships. One study found that pairs of strangers who first interacted on the Internet and then talked face to face ended up liking each other more than did pairs of people who had two successive face-to-face encounters (McKenna & Bargh, 2000). But in another study of pairs randomly assigned to either face-to-face or Internet chat conversations, the face-to-face group felt more satisfied with the experience and felt a higher degree of closeness and self-disclosure with their partners (Mallen, Day, & Green, 2003).

Self-disclosure is another relationship issue affected by the differences in the two types of communication. Because the Internet is shrouded under the cloak of anonymity, people take greater risks in self-disclosure. Thus, feelings of intimacy can develop more quickly (McKenna & Bargh, 2000). Sometimes this experience can set up a false sense of intimacy, which can create uncomfortable feelings if a face-to-face meeting ensues—that is, meeting with a stranger who knows "too much" about you (Hamilton, 1999). Of course, face-to-face meetings can also go smoothly; some people even marry someone they met online. Anonymity also allows people to construct a virtual identity. Obviously, this can be a problem if one person adopts a fictional persona and another assumes that it is authentic and begins to take the relationship seriously.

Researchers have just begun to study the impact of the Internet on relationships. The findings in this fascinating area will not only provide much-needed information about virtual relationships, but should also reveal interesting new perspectives on face-to-face relationships.

Initial Attraction and Relationship Development

- Discuss the roles of proximity and familiarity in initial attraction.
- Summarize the findings on physical attractiveness in initial attraction.
- Discuss the role of reciprocal liking and similarity in getting acquainted.
- Describe the personality qualities that people like in others.

- Give some commonly used relationship maintenance strategies, and explain what is meant by "minding" relationships.
- Summarize interdependence theory and explain how rewards, costs, and investments influence relationship satisfaction and commitment.

Individuals use a multitude of factors to assess another person's appeal as a mate or a friend. Furthermore, because attraction is a two-way street, intricate interactions occur between variables. To simplify this complex issue, we'll divide our coverage into four segments. First, we'll review the factors that operate in initial encounters. Then we'll consider elements that come into play as relationships begin to develop. Next, we'll review what's involved in maintaining relationships. Finally, we'll look at what influences people to stay in or get out of relationships.

Our review of research in this section pertains to both friendships and romantic relationships. In some cases, a particular factor (such as physical attractiveness) may play a more influential role in love than in friendship, or vice versa. However, all the factors discussed in this section enter into both types of relationships. These factors also operate the same in the friendships and romantic relationships of gay and straight individuals (Garnets & Kimmel, 1991). But we should note that homosexuals face three unique dating challenges (Peplau & Spaulding, 2003). They have a small pool of potential partners, they are under pressure to conceal their sexual orientation, and they have limited ways to meet prospective partners. Also, fears of hos-

tility may cause them to limit their self-disclosures to acquaintances and friends.

Initial Encounters

Sometimes initial encounters begin dramatically with two strangers' eyes locking across a room. More often, two people become aware of their mutual interest, usually triggered by each other's looks and conversations. What draws two strangers together? Three factors stand out: proximity, familiarity, and physical attractiveness.

Proximity

Attraction usually depends on proximity: People have to be in the same place at the same time. **Proximity refers to geographic, residential, and other forms of spatial closeness.** Of course, proximity is not an issue in cyberspace interactions. But in everyday life people become acquainted with, and attracted to, someone who lives, works, shops, and plays nearby.

The importance of proximity was apparent in a classic study of friendship patterns among married graduate students living in a university housing project (Festinger, Schachter, & Back, 1950). People whose doors were close together were most likely to become friends.

Moreover, those whose homes faced the central court area had more than twice as many friends in the complex as those whose homes faced outward. Using the centralized court area apparently increased the likelihood that people would meet and befriend others.

Proximity effects were also found in a study of Maryland state police trainees (Segal, 1974). At the training academy, both dormitory rooms and classroom seats were assigned on the basis of alphabetical order. Six months after their arrival, participants were asked to name their three closest friends among the group of trainees. The trainees whose last names were closer together in the alphabet were much more likely to be friends than trainees whose names were widely separated in the alphabet.

Proximity effects may seem self-evident, but it is sobering to realize that your friendships and love interests are shaped by seating charts, apartment availability, shift assignments, and office locations (Berscheid & Reis, 1998).

Familiarity

You probably walk the same route to your classes several times a week. As the semester progresses, you begin to recognize some familiar faces on your route. Have you also found yourself nodding or smiling at these people? If so, you've experienced the *mere exposure effect,* **or an increase in positive feelings toward a novel stimulus (person) based on frequent exposure to it** (Zajonc, 1968). Note that the positive feelings arise just on the basis of seeing someone frequently—not because of any interaction.

The implications of the mere exposure effect on initial attraction should be obvious. Generally, the more familiar someone is, the more you will like him or her. And greater liking increases the probability that you will strike up a conversation and, possibly, develop a relationship with the person. And when it comes to actual interactions (versus mere exposure), more interchanges typically result in greater attraction, at least up to a point. There is, however, an important exception to the familiarity principle: If your initial reaction to someone is negative, increased exposure will only intensify your dislike (Swap, 1977).

Physical Attractiveness

Physical attractiveness plays a major role in initial face-to-face encounters (Peretti & Abplanalp, 2004). In other words, most people disregard the advice in statements such as "Beauty is only skin deep" and "You can't judge a book by its cover."

Research on the role of physical beauty in attraction has been conducted in a variety of settings, from college dances to get-acquainted dates to commercial dating services (Walster et al., 1966; Sprecher & Duck, 1994). All show that attractiveness is a key factor in dating. Good looks play a role in friendships as well. People, especially males, prefer attractiveness in their same- and other-gender friends (Aboud & Mendelson, 1996; Fehr, 2000).

On self-reports, women may downplay the importance of physical attractiveness compared to men (Feingold, 1990; Stevens, Owens, & Schaefer, 1990). However, when it comes to their actual behavior, women are as influenced by physical attractiveness as men. Because most of the research on physical attractiveness is based on self-reports, this gender difference is artificially heightened.

Do gays and straights differ in the importance they place on the physical attractiveness of prospective dating partners? Probably not, although the evidence is mixed and plagued by the same problems with self-reports just noted. Researchers often find gender rather than sexual orientation to be the more important factor in partner preferences (Hatala & Prehodka, 1996). For example, in the wording of gay and straight personal advertisements in newspapers, both heterosexual and homosexual men are more likely to request physically attractive partners than either heterosexual or homosexual women are (Bailey et al., 1997; Deaux & Hanna, 1984).

The emphasis on beauty may not be quite as great as the evidence reviewed thus far suggests. Figure 8.2 summarizes the results of a cross-cultural study conducted in 37 countries on the characteristics commonly sought in a mate (Buss, 1985). As you can see, personal qualities, such as kindness and intelligence, were ranked higher than physical attractiveness by both genders. These results are somewhat reassuring, but we know that verbal reports don't always predict people's actual priorities and behavior.

What makes someone attractive? Although there are some differences of opinion about what makes a person attractive, people tend to agree on the key elements of good looks. Researchers who study attractiveness focus almost exclusively on facial features and physique. Both are important in perceived attractiveness, but an unattractive body is seen as a greater liability than an unattractive face (Alicke, Smith, & Klotz, 1986). Males, whether gay or straight, place more emphasis on body build.

Even across different ethnic groups and countries, there seems to be strong agreement on attractive *facial features* (Cunningham et al., 1995; Langlois et al., 2000). Women who have "baby-faced" features such as large eyes, prominent cheekbones, a small nose, and full lips get high ratings (Jones, 1995). In particular, the combination of these youthful features with "mature" features (prominent cheekbones, narrow cheeks, wide smile) seems to be the winning ticket—picture Julia Roberts and Jennifer Lopez (Cunningham, Druen, & Barbee, 1997). Men who have a strong jaw and a broad forehead

Characteristics Commonly Sought in a Mate

Rank	Characteristics preferred by men	Characteristics preferred by women
1	Kindness and understanding	Kindness and understanding
2	Intelligence	Intelligence
3	*Physical attractiveness*	Exciting personality
4	Exciting personality	Good health
5	Good health	Adaptability
6	Adaptability	*Physical attractiveness*
7	Creativity	Creativity
8	Desire for children	*Good earning capacity*
9	College graduate	College graduate
10	Good heredity	Desire for children
11	*Good earning capacity*	Good heredity
12	Good housekeeper	Good housekeeper
13	Religious orientation	Religious orientation

● FIGURE 8.2

Characteristics sought in a mate. Buss (1989) surveyed individuals in three countries on the characteristics they sought in a mate. Kindness/understanding and intelligence were ranked higher than physical attractiveness by both males and females. Statistically significant gender differences in rankings were found for a variety of characteristics, which are shown in italics. For example, males ranked physical attractiveness higher than females did.

From Buss, D. M. (1989). Sex differences in human mate preferences: Evolutionary hypotheses tested in 37 cultures. *Behavioral and Brain Sciences, 12,* 1–14. Copyright © 1989 by Cambridge University Press. Reprinted with the permission of Cambridge University Press.

get high ratings on attractiveness (Mel Gibson and Denzel Washington come to mind) (Cunningham, Barbee, & Pike, 1990). On the other hand, softer- and finer-featured male faces are also rated attractive (Leonardo DiCaprio is the perfect example) (Perrett et al., 1998).

When it comes to *physique,* males who have broad shoulders, slim waists and legs, and small buttocks receive high attractiveness ratings (Singh, 1995). Tall men are also considered attractive (Lynn & Shurgot, 1984). Women of average weight with an "hourglass" figure and medium-sized breasts are rated high in attractiveness (Franzoi & Herzog, 1987; Singh, 1993). African American men and women prefer a larger body type than European American men and women do (Jackson & McGill, 1996; Rosenfeld et al., 1999). Nonetheless, being considerably overweight is viewed very negatively in the United States, despite the increasing incidence of obesity in the country (Hebl & Mannix, 2003).

Currently in the United States, there is heightened emphasis on thinness for girls and women. For example, one study reported that an overweight woman was viewed as significantly less sexually attractive, warm, and skilled than an average-weight woman (Regan, 1996); however, perceptions of an overweight versus an average-weight man didn't differ. A study of white college students found that women believed that their male and female peers preferred a much thinner female silhouette than was actually the case (and men exaggerated the extent to which others perceived large physiques as most desirable for males) (Cohn & Adler, 1992). This emphasis on thinness as the ideal female body shape may underlie the high incidence of eating disorders found among European American, Asian American, and Hispanic adolescent girls (Halpern et al., 1999). Eating disorders are less common among African Amer-

ican females because the ideal physique is larger for this group than that for European females (Polivy & Herman, 2002). We explore the important issue of eating disorders in the Chapter 15 Application.

Another response to "attractiveness pressure" is the increased rate of cosmetic surgery, especially among younger people. Between 2003 and 2004, the number of cosmetic surgeries performed on Americans 18 and younger increased 48 percent (Springen, 2004)! Most such surgeries are nose jobs and breast augmentations. The popularity of television shows like *Extreme Makeover* and *The Swan* no doubt accounts for some of this increase.

Because our culture particularly values attractiveness in females, physical attractiveness appears to be a more valued relationship quality for females than for males (Feingold, 1990; Regan, 2003). This gender gap was apparent in a study of the tactics heterosexual individuals used in pursuing romantic relationships. David Buss (1988) asked 208 newlywed individuals to describe the things they did when they first met their spouse, and during the remainder of their courtship, to make themselves more appealing to their partner. Buss found that men were more likely than women to emphasize their material resources by doing such things as flashing lots of money, buying nice gifts, showing off expensive possessions, and bragging about their importance at work (see Figure 8.3 on the next page). In contrast, women were more likely than men to work at enhancing their appearance by dieting, wearing stylish clothes, trying new hairstyles, and getting a tan. Although there were relative differences between the genders in emphasis on physical attractiveness, the data in Figure 8.3 show that both genders relied on tactics intended to enhance or maintain good looks.

Tactics of Attraction

Tactics used significantly more by males	Mean frequency	
	Men (N = 102)	Women (N = 106)
Display resources	0.67	0.44
Brag about resources	0.73	0.60
Display sophistication	**1.18**	0.88
Display strength	0.96	0.44
Display athleticism	**1.18**	0.94
Show off	0.70	0.47
Tactics used significantly more by females		
Wear makeup	0.02	**1.63**
Keep clean and groomed	**2.27**	**2.44**
Alter appearance—general	0.39	**1.27**
Wear stylish clothes	**1.22**	**2.00**
Act coy	0.54	0.73
Wear jewelry	0.25	**2.21**
Wear sexy clothes	0.68	0.91
Tactics for which no significant gender differences were found		
Act provocative	0.77	0.90
Flirt	**2.13**	**2.09**
Keep hair groomed	**2.20**	**2.31**
Increase social pressure	0.89	0.90
Act nice	**1.77**	**1.86**
Display humor	**2.24**	**2.28**
Act promiscuous	0.30	0.21
Act submissive	**1.24**	1.11
Dissemble (feign agreement)	**1.26**	1.09
Touch	**2.26**	**2.16**

● **FIGURE 8.3**

Similarities and differences between the genders in the tactics of attraction. Buss (1988) asked newlywed subjects to rate how often they had used 23 tactics of attraction to make themselves more appealing to their partner. The tactics used by one gender significantly more often than the other are listed in the first two sections of the figure. Although there were significant differences between the genders, there were also many similarities. The 11 tactics used most frequently by each gender (those above the median) are boldfaced, showing considerable overlap between males and females in the tactics they used most. (Note: Higher means in the data reflect higher frequency of use, but the numbers do not indicate frequency per day or week.)

Adapted from Buss, D. M. (1988). The evolution of human intrasexual competition: Tactics of mate attraction. *Journal of Personality and Social Psychology, 54*(4), 616–628. Copyright © 1988 by the American Psychological Association. Adapted by permission of the author.

Matching up on looks. Thankfully, people can enjoy rewarding social lives without being spectacularly good-looking. In the process of dating and mating, people apparently take into consideration their own level of

According to the matching hypothesis, we tend to wind up with someone similar to ourselves in attractiveness. However, other factors such as personality, intelligence, and social status also influence attraction.

attractiveness. **The *matching hypothesis* proposes that people of similar levels of physical attractiveness gravitate toward each other.** This hypothesis is supported by findings that both dating and married heterosexual couples tend to be similar in physical attractiveness (Feingold, 1988). There is some debate, however, about whether people match up by their own choice (Aron, 1988; Kalick & Hamilton, 1986). Some theorists believe that individuals mostly pursue highly attractive partners and that their matching is the result of social forces beyond their control, such as rejection by more attractive others. Researchers have also found evidence for matching effects in friendships between men, but not between women (Duck, 1994). The reasons for this gender difference are not readily apparent.

Resource exchange. Contradicting the matching hypothesis, several studies have shown that, in heterosexual dating, males "trade" occupational status for physical attractiveness in females, and vice versa (Deaux & Hanna, 1984; Feingold, 1992a; Green, Buchanan, & Heuer, 1984). This finding also holds true in many other cultures. As you already saw in the cross-cultural study summarized in Figure 8.2, men in most countries rate physical attractiveness in a prospective mate as more important than women do, whereas women rate "good financial prospects" and "ambitious and industrious" as more important characteristics than men do (Buss, 1989). In reviewing the content of personal ads in newspapers and magazines, Wiederman (1993) reported that women advertisers sought financial resources in prospective partners 11 times as often as men did.

Evolutionary social psychologists such as David Buss (1988) believe that these findings on age, status, and physical attractiveness reflect gender differences in inherited reproductive strategies that have been sculpted over thousands of generations by natural selection. Their thinking has been guided by parental investment theory, which maintains that a species' mating patterns depend on what each sex has to invest—in the way of time, energy, and survival risk—to produce and nurture offspring. According to this model, members of the gender that makes the smaller investment will compete with each other for mating opportunities with the gender that makes the larger investment, and the gender with the larger investment will tend to be more discriminating in selecting its partners.

Let's look at how this analysis applies to humans. Like many mammalian species, human males are required to invest little in the production of offspring beyond the act of copulation, so their reproductive potential is maximized by mating with as many females as possible. As well, males should prefer young and attractive females because these qualities are assumed to signal fertility, which should increase the chances of conception and passing genes on to the next generation. The situation for females is quite different. Females have to invest nine months in pregnancy, and our female ancestors typically had to devote at least several additional years to nourishing offspring through breast-feeding. These realities place a ceiling on the number of offspring women can produce, regardless of how many males they mate with. Hence, females have little or no incentive for mating with many males. Instead, females can optimize their reproductive potential by being selective in mating. They should also prefer reliable partners with good incomes (Buss, 1994). This ensures that a man will be committed to a long-term relationship and will be able to support the woman and their child, thus ensuring that her genes will be passed on.

Thus, in humans, males are thought to compete with other males for the relatively scarce and valuable "commodity" of reproductive opportunities. Parental investment theory predicts that in comparison to women, men will show more interest in sexual activity, more desire for variety in sexual partners, and more willingness to engage in uncommitted sex (see Figure 8.4). In contrast, females are thought to be the conservative, discriminating gender that is highly selective in choosing partners. This selectivity supposedly entails seeking partners who have more material resources that can be invested in feeding and caring for offspring. Why? Because in the world of our ancient ancestors, males' greater strength and agility would have been crucial assets in the never-ending struggle to find food and shelter and defend one's territory.

Although evolutionary psychologists assert that culture has little influence on gender differences in mate selection strategies (Buss, 1998), evidence contradicts this claim (Travis & Meginnis-Payne, 2001). Sociocultural models can also provide plausible explanations for gender differences in attraction and mate selection, including traditional gender-role socialization and men's greater economic power (Sprecher, Sullivan, & Hatfield, 1994). For instance, women's preferences for a physically attractive man appear to increase along with women's economic power (Gangestad, 1993). More-

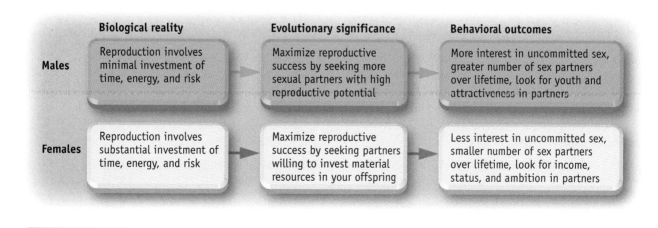

● FIGURE 8.4

Parental investment theory and mating preferences. Parental investment theory suggests that basic differences between males and females in parental investment have great adaptive significance and lead to gender differences in mating propensities and preferences, as outlined here.

Although most couples are similar in age and attractiveness, sometimes men exchange occupational status for physical attractiveness in women, and vice versa.

over, it is women in countries with limited educational and career opportunities for females who prefer men with high incomes (Eagly & Wood, 1999). Thus, both biological and environmental factors influence gender differences in mate selection strategies (Fitness, Fletcher, & Overall, 2003; Wood & Eagly, 2002).

Getting Acquainted

After several initial encounters, people typically begin the dance of getting to know each other. Is there any way to predict which budding relationships will flower and which will die on the vine? We'll examine three factors: reciprocal liking, perceived similarity, and desirable personality characteristics.

Reciprocal Liking

An old adage advises, "If you want to *have* a friend, *be* a friend." This suggestion captures the idea of the reciprocity principle in relationships. **Reciprocal liking refers to liking those who show that they like you.** Many studies have demonstrated that if you believe another person likes you, you will like him or her (Berscheid & Walster, 1978; Kenny, 1994). Think about it. Assuming

that others are sincere, you like it when they flatter you, do favors for you, and use nonverbal behavior to signal their interest in you (eye contact, leaning forward). Moreover, you usually reciprocate such behavior.

You can see the self-fulfilling prophecy at work here. If you believe that someone likes you, you behave in a friendly manner toward that person. Your behavior encourages him or her to respond positively, which confirms your initial expectation. A study by Rebecca Curtis and Kim Miller (1986) shows the self-fulfilling prophecy in action. College students who were strangers were divided into pairs for a 5-minute "get acquainted" conversation. Afterward, one member of each pair was led to believe that the other student either did or didn't like him or her. Then the pairs met again and talked about current events for 10 minutes. Raters, blind to the experimental condition of the participants, listened to tape recordings of the 10-minute interactions and rated the participants on a number of behaviors. As predicted, the individuals who believed that they were liked were rated as disclosing more about themselves, behaving more warmly, disagreeing less, and having a more positive tone of voice and general attitude than those who believed that they were disliked (see Figure 8.5).

The strategy of "playing hard to get" (nonreciprocity) seems at odds with the reciprocity principle. Is there any evidence that it works? You should probably avoid this tactic. People are usually turned off by others who reject them (Wright & Contrada, 1986). It also seems that individuals prefer those who are *moderately* selective in their liking for others. By contrast, people who like everyone are seen as having no standards, while those who like very few are perceived as arrogant.

Similarity

Do "birds of a feather flock together," or do "opposites attract"? Research offers far more support for the first

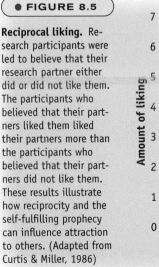

● FIGURE 8.5

Reciprocal liking. Research participants were led to believe that their research partner either did or did not like them. The participants who believed that their partners liked them liked their partners more than the participants who believed that their partners did not like them. These results illustrate how reciprocity and the self-fulfilling prophecy can influence attraction to others. (Adapted from Curtis & Miller, 1986)

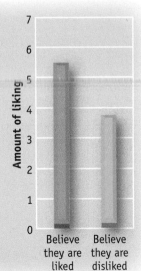

adage than for the second (Berscheid & Reis, 1998). Despite the increasing diversity in the United States, similarity continues to play a key role in attraction (Macionis, 1997), and the similarity principle operates in both friendships and romantic relationships regardless of sexual orientation (Aubé & Koestner, 1995; Peplau, Cochran, & Mays, 1997). Similarly, people who meet others via the Internet often narrow down prospects in advance by selecting individuals who are like them in key respects (sexual orientation, age, religion, and so forth).

Heterosexual married and dating couples tend to be similar in *demographic characteristics* (age, race, religion, socioeconomic status, and education), *physical attractiveness, intelligence, attitudes, and personality* (Hendrick & Hendrick, 1992). (To date, there are not enough data on the similarity of gay and lesbian couples to give a clear picture.) We've already explored similarity in physical attractiveness. Now, let's consider attitudes and personality.

It has been quite well established that similarity in *attitudes* promotes liking (Byrne, 1971; Byrne, Clore, & Smeaton, 1986). According to Donn Byrne's two-stage model, people first "sort" for dissimilarity, avoiding those who appear to be different. Then, from among the remaining group, individuals gravitate toward those who are most similar (Byrne, Clore, & Smeaton, 1986). Here's a typical laboratory experiment that demonstrates the impact of similarity on attraction. Subjects who have previously provided information on their own attitudes are led to believe that they will be meeting a stranger. They are given information about the stranger's views that has been manipulated to show various degrees of similarity to their own views. As attitude similarity increases, subjects' ratings of the likability of the stranger increase (see Figure 8.6). Once two people start dating, a phenomenon termed *attitude alignment* enhances attitudinal similarity. That is, when dating part-

WEB LINK 8.1

The Student Counseling Virtual Pamphlet Collection
The Student Counseling office at the University of Chicago had a great idea: gather together links to the very best online information from other counseling centers for the problems and issues faced by students. This "best of the best" resource includes helpful guides to love, friendship, relationships, and almost any issue an adult in school would face.

ners discover that they disagree on important values, couples typically modify their attitudes so they are more congruent (Davis & Rusbult, 2001).

People with similar *personality traits* are more likely to be attracted to each other than are those with dissimilar or complementary traits (Berscheid & Reis, 1998). For example, two people with "sunny" dispositions are more likely to pair up than a happy and an unhappy person are. This finding is true for both friends and romantic partners. Of course, sometimes opposites *do* attract. You probably know at least one couple with obvious dissimilarities—perhaps one tends to be quiet while the other is more domineering. Although such combinations sometimes work (Dryer & Horowitz, 1997), similarity is more often the rule, especially in the long run. For example, married couples with similar personalities are happier than couples with less similar personalities (Caspi & Herbener, 1990).

What is the appeal of similarity? For one thing, you assume that a similar person will probably like you (Condon & Crano, 1988). Second, when others share your beliefs, it validates them (Byrne & Clore, 1970).

Desirable Personality Characteristics

As you might expect, personal qualities are more important than physical characteristics for a future spouse or life partner, and the reverse is true for casual relationships. As you can see in Figure 8.7 (on the next page), for a marriage partner, both male and female college students highly ranked a good overall personality, honesty and trustworthiness, and kindness and compassion (Regan & Berscheid, 1997). For a sexual partner, both men and women ranked "attractive appearance" the highest. Other desirable personality qualities in relationship partners include warmth, friendliness, good sense of humor, and social assertiveness (Hatfield & Rapson, 1993; Regan, 2003).

Established Relationships

Over time, some acquaintanceships evolve into established relationships. Through conversation and shared activities, individuals mutually determine the desired level of intimacy they want in a relationship. Not all relationships need to be highly intimate to be satisfying.

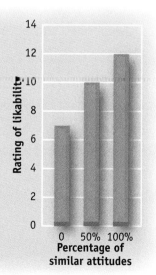

● **FIGURE 8.6**

Attitude similarity and attraction. When asked to rate the likability of a hypothetical stranger, subjects give progressively higher ratings to people who they are told share more attitudes with them.

Adapted from Gonzales, M. H., Davis, J. M., Loeny, G. L., Lukens, C. K., & Junghans, C. H. (1983). Interactional approach to interpersonal attraction. *Journal of Personality and Social Psychology, 44*, 1191–1197. Copyright © 1983 by the American Psychological Association. Adapted by permission of the author.

Rating of likability

Percentage of similar attitudes

	Sexual partner	Marriage partner
Women	Physically attractive	Honest or trustworthy
	Healthy	Sensitive/compassionate
	Attentive to my needs	Overall personality
	Sense of humor	Intelligent
	Overall personality	Attentive to my needs
Men	Physically attractive	Overall personality
	Healthy	Honest or trustworthy
	Overall personality	Physically attractive
	Attentive to my needs	Intelligent
	Self-confident	Healthy

● **FIGURE 8.7**

Characteristics men and women consider most important for a sexual partner and a marriage partner. Both men and women emphasize good looks when judging a sexual partner. When judging a marriage partner, both stress desirable personal qualities, although men also consider physical attractiveness to be important in a marriage partner.

From Regan, P. C., & Berscheid, E. (1997). Gender differences in characteristics desired in a potential sexual and marriage partner. *Journal of Psychology and Human Sexuality, 9*, 25–37.

For others, intimacy is an essential ingredient of relationship satisfaction. In either case, to continue, relationships need to be maintained.

Maintenance of Ongoing Relationships

Relationship maintenance **involves the actions and activities used to sustain the desired quality of a relationship.** In Figure 8.8, you can see a list of commonly used relationship maintenance behaviors. Often, these behaviors occur spontaneously (calling on the phone to check in, eating meals together); at other times, behaviors are more intentional and require more planning (traveling to visit family and friends) (Canary & Stafford, 2001). People use most of these strategies in their various relationships. Obviously, strategies vary depending on the nature of a relationship (familial, friendship, romantic) and its stage of development (new, developing, mature). For example, married couples engage in more assurances and social networking than dating partners do (Stafford & Canary, 1991). Both spontaneous and routine maintenance activities are correlated with relationship satisfaction and commitment (Dainton & Aylor, 2002). When the frequency of one partner's maintenance activities compares favorably with the other's expectations, relationship satisfaction is higher (Dainton, 2000). Gay and lesbian couples generally use the same maintenance behaviors as heterosexual couples (Haas & Stafford, 1998).

Another approach to relationship maintenance involves the process of "minding" relationships (Harvey & Omarzu, 1997). *Minding* is an active process that continues throughout a relationship and involves such things as mutual self-disclosure and relationship-enhancing beliefs and attributions about one's partner. According to this model, developing satisfying and intimate long-term relationships is associated with a high level of minding, and vice versa. To elaborate, a high degree of minding involves using good listening skills, having detailed knowledge about your partner's opinions, making generally positive attributions for your partner's behaviors, expressing feelings of trust and commitment, recognizing your partner's support and effort, and having an optimistic view of the future of the relationship. By contrast, a low degree of minding is characterized by a lack of interest in your partner's self-disclosures, generally negative attributions for your partner's behavior, dwelling on your partner's faults, and a pessimistic view of the future of the relationship. As you can see, this model has a strong cognitive flavor. Although Harvey and Omarzu focus on committed romantic relationships, they suggest that their model likely applies to family and friendship relationships as well.

Relationship maintenance strategies	
Strategy	**Behavioral Example**
Positivity	Try to act nice and cheerful
Openness	Encourage him/her to disclose thoughts and feelings to me
Assurances	Stress my commitment to him/her
Social networking	Show that I am willing to do things with his/her friends and family
Sharing tasks	Help equally with tasks that need to be done
Joint activities	Spend time hanging out
Mediated communication	Use e-mail to keep in touch
Avoidance	Respect each other's privacy and need to be alone
Antisocial behaviors	Act rude to him/her
Humor	Call him/her by a funny nickname
No flirting	Do not encourage overly familiar behavior (relevant in cross-gender friendships)

● **FIGURE 8.8**

Relationship maintenance strategies. College students were asked to describe how they maintained three different personal relationships over a college term. Their responses were grouped into 11 categories. You can see that, ironically, some people behave negatively in an attempt to enhance relationships. Openness was the most commonly nominated strategy. (Adapted from Canary & Stafford, 1994)

Relationship Satisfaction and Commitment

How do you gauge your satisfaction in a relationship? What determines whether you will stay in or get out of a relationship? *Interdependence or social exchange theory* **postulates that interpersonal relationships are governed by perceptions of the rewards and costs exchanged in interactions.** Basically, this model predicts that interactions between acquaintances, friends, and lovers will continue as long as the participants feel that the benefits they derive from the relationship are reasonable in comparison to the costs of being in the relationship. Harold Kelley and John Thibaut's interdependence theory (Kelley & Thibaut, 1978; Thibaut & Kelley, 1959) is based on B. F. Skinner's principle of reinforcement, which assumes that individuals try to maximize their rewards in life and minimize their costs (see Chapter 2).

Rewards include such things as emotional support, status, and sexual gratification (in romantic relationships); costs are such things as the time and energy that a relationship requires, emotional conflicts, and the inability to engage in other rewarding activities because of relationship obligations. According to interdependence theory, people assess a relationship by its *outcome*—their subjective perception of the rewards of the relationship minus its costs (see Figure 8.9).

Individuals gauge their *satisfaction* with a relationship by comparing the relationship outcomes (rewards minus costs) to their subjective expectations. **This personal standard of what constitutes an acceptable balance of rewards and costs in a relationship is called the** *comparison level.* It is based on the outcomes you have experienced in previous relationships and the outcomes you have seen others experience in their relationships. Your comparison level may also be influenced by your exposure to fictional relationships, such as those you have read about or seen on television. Consistent with the predictions of exchange theory, research shows that relationship satisfaction is higher when rewards are perceived to be high and costs, low.

To understand the role of *commitment* in relationships, we need to consider two additional factors. The first is the *comparison level for alternatives,* **or one's estimation of the available outcomes from alternative relationships.** In using this standard, individuals assess their current relationship outcomes in comparison to the potential outcomes of other similar relationships that are actually available to them. This principle helps explain why many unsatisfying relationships are not terminated until another love interest actually appears. The second factor that figures in relationship commitment is *investments,* **or things that people contribute to a relationship that they can't get back if the relationship ends.** Investments include past costs (time, money) that they can never recover if the relationship fails. Understandably, putting investments into a relationship strengthens one's commitment to it.

But what happens if individuals feel that they have invested a lot in a relationship that starts to have problems? Because they're unwilling to forfeit their investments, some people put even *more* into such a relationship. Others decide that they will probably have to forfeit their investment sooner or later, so they choose not to wait—especially if an attractive alternative comes into the picture.

Here's how interdependence theory works: If both members of a couple feel that they are getting a lot out of the relationship (lots of strokes, high status) compared to its costs (a few arguments, occasionally giving up preferred activities), they will probably perceive the relationship as satisfactory and will keep it going. However, if either one begins to feel that the ratio of rewards to costs is falling below his or her comparison level, dissatisfaction is likely to occur. The dissatisfied person may attempt to alter the balance of costs and rewards or try to ease out of the relationship. The likelihood of ending the relationship depends on the number of important investments a person has in the relationship and whether the person believes that an alternative relationship is available that could yield greater satisfaction.

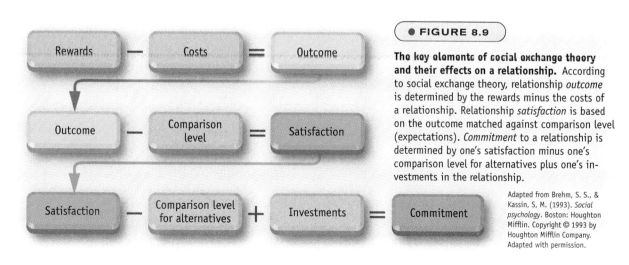

● FIGURE 8.9

The key elements of social exchange theory and their effects on a relationship. According to social exchange theory, relationship *outcome* is determined by the rewards minus the costs of a relationship. Relationship *satisfaction* is based on the outcome matched against comparison level (expectations). *Commitment* to a relationship is determined by one's satisfaction minus one's comparison level for alternatives plus one's investments in the relationship.

Adapted from Brehm, S. S., & Kassin, S, M. (1993). *Social psychology*. Boston: Houghton Mifflin. Copyright © 1993 by Houghton Mifflin Company. Adapted with permission.

Research generally supports interdependence theory and its extensions (Le & Agnew, 2003; Rusbult, Drigotas, & Verette, 1994). Social exchange principles seem to operate in a similar fashion regardless of a couple's sexual orientation (Peplau, 1991). Moreover, heterosexual and homosexual couples seem quite similar with regard to important aspects of relationships (Peplau & Spaulding, 2003). For example, studies of heterosexual males and females, gay males, and lesbians found that all groups report high satisfaction with their relationships (Duffy & Rusbult, 1986; Kurdek & Schmitt, 1986a, 1986b), as well as moderately high investments in their relationships, moderately poor alternatives, and strong commitment (Duffy & Rusbult, 1986).

This theory of an "interpersonal marketplace" provides a useful model for analyzing many relationships, particularly those in highly individualistic societies. The usefulness of interdependence theory appears more limited for people in collectivist cultures or those with interdependent self-views (Chapter 5).

Even in individualistic cultures, many people resist the idea that close relationships operate according to an economic model. Much of this resistance probably comes from discomfort with the idea that self-interest plays such an important role in the maintenance of relationships. Resistance may also stem from doubts about how well social exchange principles apply to close relationships. In fact, there is some empirical support for this position. Margaret Clark and her colleagues (Clark & Bennett, 1992) distinguish between *exchange relationships* (with strangers, acquaintances, co-workers) and *communal relationships* (with close friends, lovers, family members). Research suggests that in exchange relationships, the usual principles of social exchange dominate. Social exchange principles also operate in communal relationships, but seem to be applied differently. For example, in communal relationships, rewards are usually given freely, without any expectation of prompt reciprocation (Clark & Mills, 1993). Also, individuals pay more attention to the needs of a partner in a communal relationship than in an exchange relationship. In other words, you use a need-based norm with people who are close to you and help them without calculating whether and when they will reward you in kind (Clark & Grote, 2003).

Friendship

LEARNING OBJECTIVES

- *Summarize the research on what makes a good friend.*
- *Describe some key gender differences in friendships.*

It's hard to overestimate the importance of friends. They give help in times of need, advice in times of confusion, consolation in times of failure, and praise in times of achievement. The importance of friends was underscored by a finding we noted earlier: In identifying the person to whom they felt closest, 36 percent of college students named a friend (while 47 percent named a romantic partner, 14 percent named a family member, and 3 percent said "other").

Friends are important to adjustment. College students with strong friendships are more optimistic and deal better with stressful life events (Brissette, Scheirer, & Carver, 2002). Same-gender friendships between women are linked to positive mental and physical health (Knickmeyer, Sexton, & Nishimura, 2002). But friends can help or hinder adjustment, depending on relationship quality. Intimate and stable friendships are associated with less stress in adulthood and less troublesome behavior among teens, but the reverse is also true (Hartup & Stevens, 1999). So the absence of "problematic qualities" in your friends may be as significant as the presence of their positive qualities. Also, developing friendships with people who are different from oneself—in terms of ethnicity or sexual orientation, for example—can break down prejudice (Herek & Capitanio, 1996; Levin, van Laar, & Sidanius, 2003).

What Makes a Good Friend?

What *does* make a good friend? One approach to this question comes from a cross-cultural study of students in England, Italy, Japan, and Hong Kong (Argyle & Henderson, 1984). The investigators wanted to see whether they could find enough agreement on how friends should conduct themselves to permit the formulation of some informal rules governing friendships. On the basis of the students' responses, the authors

WEB LINK 8.2

SUNY Buffalo Counseling Center: Relationships Page
The Counseling Center at SUNY–Buffalo is recognized for its excellent guides to interpersonal relationships and to improving communication among college students. The online materials here focus on dozens of questions and issues stemming from people relating intimately to each other.

The Rules of Friendship

Share news of success with a friend

Show emotional support

Volunteer help in time of need

Strive to make a friend happy when in each other's company

Trust and confide in each other

Stand up for a friend in his or her absence

● FIGURE 8.10

Vital behaviors in friendship. A cross-cultural inquiry into the behaviors that are vital to friendship identified these six rules of friendship. (Adapted from Argyle & Henderson, 1984)

were able to identify six informal rules. As Figure 8.10 shows, the common thread running through these rules seems to be providing emotional and social support to friends.

We can also look at the common themes that underlie friendships of all ages to understand the nature of friendship. Researchers have identified three such themes (de Vries, 1996). The first involves the emotional dimension of friendship (self-disclosure, expressing affection and support, and so forth). A second theme concerns the communal nature of friendship (partici-

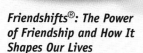

RECOMMENDED READING

Friendshifts®: The Power of Friendship and How It Shapes Our Lives
by Jan Yager (Hannacroix Creek Books, 1999)

The author of this useful self-help manual has coined the word "friendshifts®" to make the point that friendships change over the life span. In this readable book, sociologist Jan Yager traces the nature and role of friendships for children, teens, and adults (in both personal life and the workplace). At all ages, friendships play a vital role in mental health; thus the author urges readers to look carefully at the balance of positives and negatives in their various friendships. Drawing on psychological and sociological research as well as her own interviews, Yager offers excellent advice on making, keeping, and improving friendships. The book also includes a helpful resource section with websites and a bibliography.

pating in or supporting each other in mutually shared activities). A third dimension involves sociability and compatibility (friends are sources of fun and recreation). Thus, several lines of research indicate that the most important element of friendship is emotional support.

Gender Differences in Friendship

Men's and women's same-gender friendships have a lot in common, but there are some interesting differences that appear rooted in traditional gender roles and socialization.

In the United States, women's friendships are more often emotionally based, whereas men's tend to be activity based. Although some researchers have challenged this characterization (Walker, 1994), the current belief is that men's friendships are typically based on shared interests and doing things together, while women's friendships more often focus on talking—usually about feelings and relationships (Fehr, 1996, 2004). Obviously, female friends do engage in joint activities, but they often use these occasions to talk. And male friends talk, but their conversations are usually focused on activities and nonpersonal matters such as sports (Fehr, 1996, 2004).

We can also compare American men's and women's friendships on preferred topics of conversation. Women are far more likely than men to discuss personal issues: problems, people, relationships, and feelings (Fehr, 2004). Men, on the other hand, are much more likely to talk about sports, work, vehicles, and computers than personal concerns. E-mail communications also reflect this gender difference (Colley & Todd, 2002).

Whose friendships are more intimate, men's or women's? Currently, there is controversy over this question. One view is that men and women experience the same level of intimacy in their friendships but take different pathways to intimacy (closeness through doing versus closeness through self-disclosure, respectively) (Swain, 1989). A second perspective is that women achieve intimacy through self-disclosure and men, through both self-disclosure and joint activities (Helgeson, Shaver, & Dyer, 1987). A third, and the most widely accepted, view is that women's friendships are closer and more satisfying—because they involve more self-disclosure (Fehr, 2004; Reis, 1998).

In some other countries, men's same-gender friendships are more intimate (Reis, 1998). What short-circuits intimate connections between American men? Several factors stand out (Kilmartin, 2000; Bank & Hansford, 2000). First, men are socialized to be "strong and silent," which inhibits self-disclosure. Second, fear of homosexuality, which is stronger in males than females, is a barrier to intimacy between male friends. Third, traditional gender-role expectations encourage men to see each other as competitors. Why reveal weaknesses to someone who might take advantage of you?

Keep in mind that the gender differences we've reported may not hold for friendships in other cultures. Several studies have found gender differences in friendships to be more pronounced in the United States than in India (Berman, Murphy-Berman, & Pachauri, 1988) and among Chinese students in Hong Kong (Wheeler, Reis, & Bond, 1989). Thus, you should be cautious about generalizing the findings on gender differences in friendship beyond the United States at this point.

Romantic Love

LEARNING OBJECTIVES

- Summarize the research findings on the experience of love in gay and straight couples.
- Discuss some gender differences regarding love.
- Define passion, intimacy, and commitment, and describe Sternberg's eight types of love.
- Discuss adult attachment styles, including their correlates and stability.
- Discuss the course of romantic love over time.
- Explain why relationships fail and what couples can do to help relationships last.

Wander through a bookstore and you'll see an overwhelming array of titles such as *Men Who Can't Love*, *Women Who Love Too Much*, and *How to Survive the Loss of a Love*. Turn up your radio and you'll hear the refrains of "Crazy in Love," "I Will Always Love You," and "Dangerously in Love." Although there are other forms of love, such as parental love and platonic love, these books and songs are all about *romantic love*, a subject of consuming interest for almost everyone.

Love is difficult to define, difficult to measure, and frequently difficult to understand. Nonetheless, psychologists have conducted thousands of studies and developed a number of interesting theories on love and romantic relationships.

Sexual Orientation and Love

Sexual orientation **refers to a person's preference for emotional and sexual relationships with individuals of the same gender, the other gender, or either gender.** *Heterosexuals* seek emotional-sexual relationships with members of the other gender. *Homosexuals* seek emotional-sexual relationships with members of the same gender. *Bisexuals* seek emotional-sexual relationships with members of both genders. In recent years, the terms *gay* and *straight* have become widely used to refer to homosexuals and heterosexuals, respectively. *Gay* can refer to homosexuals of either gender, but most homosexual women prefer to call themselves *lesbians*.

Most studies of romantic love and relationships suffer from **heterosexism, or the assumption that all individuals and relationships are heterosexual.** For instance, most questionnaires on romantic love and romantic relationships fail to ask subjects about their sexual orientation. Thus, when data are analyzed, there is no way to know whether subjects are referring to same- or other-gender romantic partners. Assuming that their subjects are all heterosexuals, researchers proceed to describe their findings without any mention of homosexuals. Because many more people identify themselves as heterosexual, heterosexism in research isn't likely to distort conclusions about heterosexuals. Unfortunately, however, it renders homosexual relationships invisible. Consequently, psychologists don't know as much about sexual orientation as they would like to. However, since the 1990s, researchers have been devoting much more attention to this issue.

We *do* know that homosexual romances and relationships are essentially the same as those of heterosexuals. Both groups experience romantic and passion-

The experience of romantic love seems to be the same regardless of a person's sexual orientation.

ate love and make commitments to relationships (Kurdek, 1994, 1998). Both heterosexual and homosexual couples say they want their partners to have characteristics similar to theirs, hold similar values about relationships, report similar levels of relationship satisfaction, and perceive their relationships to be loving and satisfying (Peplau & Spaulding, 2003). When relationship differences are found, they are much more likely to be rooted in gender than in sexual orientation, as we'll see next.

Gender Differences Regarding Love

The stereotype holds that women are more romantic than men. Nonetheless, much of the research evidence suggests just the opposite—that men are the more romantic gender (Dion & Dion, 1988). For example, men hold more romantic beliefs ("Love lasts forever" or "There is one perfect love in the world for everyone") (Peplau, Hill, & Rubin, 1993). In addition, men fall in love more easily than women, whereas women fall out of love more easily than men (Hill, Rubin, & Peplau, 1976; Rubin, Peplau, & Hill, 1981). Also, women are more likely than men to say that they would marry someone they didn't love (Peplau & Gordon, 1985).

Thus, as a whole the evidence suggests that men are more romantic than women. However, there are several ways in which women seem more romantic. For one thing, women are more likely to report physical symptoms associated with being in love—for instance, feeling like they are "floating on a cloud" (Peplau & Gordon, 1985). Second, women are somewhat more likely to verbalize and display tender emotions (Dindia & Allen, 1992).

Research also supports the view that women are more selective in choosing a partner than men are (Kenrick et al., 1990). Evolutionary social psychologists would explain women's tendency to be more "picky" in terms of the parental investment model we discussed earlier in the chapter. The sociocultural explanation is based on the fact that heterosexual women are still more economically dependent on their partners than vice versa. This means that choosing a potential partner solely for romantic reasons may be a luxury that men (gay or straight) can more easily afford than heterosexual women. Support for this perspective comes from a previously mentioned study showing that women who prefer men with high incomes are those in countries with limited opportunities for females (Eagly & Wood, 1999).

Theories of Love

Can the experience of love be broken down into certain key components? How are romantic love relationships similar to other types of close relationships? These are the kinds of questions that two current theories of love address.

Triangular Theory of Love

Robert Sternberg's (1986, 1988) *triangular theory of love* posits that all love experiences are made up of three components: intimacy, passion, and commitment. Each of the components is represented as a point of a triangle, from which the theory derives its name (see Figure 8.11).

Intimacy **refers to warmth, closeness, and sharing in a relationship.** Signs of intimacy include giving and

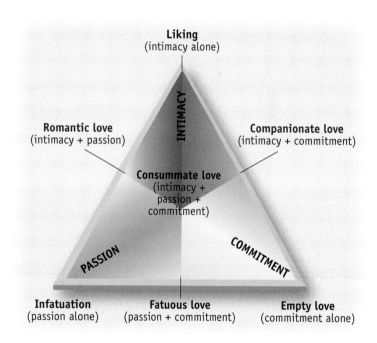

● FIGURE 8.11

Sternberg's triangular theory of love. According to Robert Sternberg (1986), love includes three components: intimacy, passion, and commitment. These components are portrayed here as points on a triangle. The possible combinations of these three components yield the seven types of relationships mapped out here. The absence of all three components is called nonlove, which is not shown in the diagram.

From Sternberg, R. J. (1986). A triangular theory of love. *Psychological Review, 93,* 119–135. Copyright © 1986 by the American Psychological Association. Reprinted by permission of the author.

receiving emotional support, valuing the loved one, wanting to promote the welfare of the loved one, and sharing one's self and one's possessions with another. As we've already discussed, self-disclosure is necessary to achieve and maintain feelings of intimacy in a relationship, whether platonic or romantic.

Robert Sternberg

Passion **refers to the intense feelings (both positive and negative) experienced in love relationships, including sexual desire.** Passion is related to drives that lead to romance, physical attraction, and sexual consummation. Although sexual needs may be dominant in many close relationships, other needs also figure in the experience of passion, including the needs for nurturance, self-esteem, dominance, submission, and self-actualization. For example, self-esteem is threatened when one experiences jealousy. Passion obviously figures most prominently in romantic relationships.

Commitment **involves the decision and intent to maintain a relationship in spite of the difficulties and costs that may arise.** According to Sternberg, commitment has both short-term and long-term aspects. The short-term aspect concerns the conscious decision to love someone. The long-term aspect reflects the determination to make a relationship endure. Although the decision to love someone usually comes before commitment, that is not always the case (in arranged marriages, for instance).

Sternberg has described eight types of relationships that can result from the presence or absence of each of the three components of love (see Figure 8.11). One of these relationship types, nonlove, is not pictured in the diagram because it is defined as the absence of any of the three components. Most casual interactions are of this type. When all three components are present, *consummate love* is said to exist.

Sternberg's model has generated a great deal of interest and some research. In support of his theory, researchers have demonstrated that Sternberg's three components characterize not only how people think about love in general but also how they personally experience love (Aron & Westbay, 1996). Also, measures of commitment and intimacy were found to be among the best predictors of whether dating couples continued their relationships (Hendrick, Hendrick, & Adler, 1988). A cross-cultural study of Chinese and American heterosexual couples in their 20s used questionnaires to measure intimacy, passion, and commitment (Gao, 2001). Scores on these three components of love increased as relationships became more serious. Although there were no significant differences between the two groups on intimacy and commitment scores, Americans scored

significantly higher on the passion scale than the Chinese. On the negative side, one study found little support for the idea that the various types of love can be accounted for by different weightings of intimacy, passion, and commitment (Hendrick & Hendrick, 1989). Although commitment is a key factor in romantic relationships, it is important in some friendships, as well.

Romantic Love as Attachment

In a groundbreaking theory of love, Cindy Hazan and Phillip Shaver (1987) asserted that romantic love can be conceptualized as an attachment process, with similarities to the bond between infants and their caregivers. According to these theorists, adult romantic love and infant attachment share a number of features: intense fascination with the other person, distress at separation, and efforts to stay close and spend time together. Of course, there are also differences: Infant-caregiver relationships are one-sided, whereas caregiving in romantic relationships works both ways. A second difference is that romantic relationships usually have a sexual component, whereas infant-caregiver relationships do not.

Cindy Hazan

Phillip Shaver

Hazan and Shaver's ideas build on earlier work in attachment theory by John Bowlby and Mary Ainsworth. Researchers who study attachment are keenly interested in the nature and development of *attachment styles,* **or typical ways of interacting in close relationships.** Their interest is fueled by the belief that attachment styles develop during the first year of life and strongly influence individuals' interpersonal interactions from then on.

Infant attachment. Based on actual observations of infants and their primary caregivers, earlier researchers identified three attachment styles (Ainsworth et al., 1978). Most infants develop a *secure attachment style* (see Figure 8.12). However, other infants develop insecure attachments. Some infants are very anxious when separated from their caretaker, a response characterized as an *anxious-ambivalent attachment style.* A third group of infants never connect very well with their caretaker and are classified in the *avoidant attachment style.* How do attachments in infancy develop? As you can see in Figure 8.12, three parenting styles have been identified as likely determinants of attachment quality. A *warm/responsive* approach seems to promote secure attach-

Infant attachment and romantic relationships. According to Hazan and Shaver (1987), romantic relationships in adulthood are similar in form to attachment patterns in infancy, which are determined in part by parental caregiving styles. The theorized relations between parental styles, attachment patterns, and intimate relations are outlined here. Hazan and Shaver's (1987) study sparked a flurry of follow-up research, which has largely supported the basic premises of their groundbreaking theory, although the links between infant experiences and close relationships in adulthood appear to be somewhat more complex than those portrayed here (Shaver & Hazan, 1992). (Based on Hazan and Shaver, 1986, 1987; Shaffer, 1989)

Parent's caregiving style	Infant attachment	Adult attachment style
Warm/responsive— She/he was generally warm and responsive; she/he was good at knowing when to be supportive and when to let me operate on my own; our relationship was always comfortable, and I have no major reservations or complaints about it.	**Secure attachment—** An infant-caregiver bond in which the child welcomes contact with a close companion and uses this person as a secure base from which to explore the environment.	**Secure—**I find it relatively easy to get close to others and am comfortable depending on them and having them depend on me. I don't often worry about being abandoned or about someone getting too close to me.
Cold/rejecting—She/he was fairly cold and distant, or rejecting, not very responsive; I wasn't her/his highest priority, her/his concerns were often elsewhere; it's possible that she/he would just as soon not have had me.	**Avoidant attachment—** An insecure infant-caregiver bond, characterized by little separation protest and a tendency for the child to avoid or ignore the caregiver.	**Avoidant—**I am somewhat uncomfortable being close to others; I find it difficult to trust them, difficult to allow myself to depend on them. I am nervous when anyone gets too close, and often love partners want me to be more intimate than I feel comfortable being.
Ambivalent/ inconsistent— She/he was noticeably inconsistent in her/his reactions to me, sometimes warm and sometimes not; she/he has her/his own agenda, which sometimes got in the way of her/his receptiveness and responsiveness to my needs; she/he definitely loved me but didn't always show it in the best way.	**Anxious/ambivalent attachment—**An insecure infant-caregiver bond, characterized by strong separation protest and a tendency of the child to resist contact initiated by the caregiver, particularly after a separation.	**Anxious/ambivalent—** I find that others are reluctant to get as close as I would like. I often worry that my partner doesn't really love me or won't want to stay with me. I want to merge completely with another person, and this desire sometimes scares people away.

ments, while a *cold/rejecting* style is associated with avoidant attachments. An *ambivalent/inconsistent* style seems to result in anxious-ambivalent attachments.

Adult attachment. What do these attachment styles look like in adulthood? To answer this question, we'll summarize the findings of a number of studies (Mickelson, Kessler, & Shaver, 1997; Shaver & Hazan, 1993). You can also see capsule summaries of adult attachment styles in Figure 8.12.

■ *Secure adults* (55 percent). These people trust others, find it easy to get close to them, and are comfortable with mutual dependence. They rarely worry about being abandoned by their partner. Secure adults have the longest-lasting relationships and the fewest di-

vorces. They describe their parents as behaving warmly toward them and toward each other.

■ *Avoidant adults* (25 percent). These individuals both fear and feel uncomfortable about getting close to others. They are reluctant to trust others and prefer to maintain emotional distance from others. They have the lowest incidence of positive relationship experiences of the three groups. Avoidant adults describe their parents as less warm than secure adults do and see their mothers as cold and rejecting.

■ *Anxious-ambivalent or preoccupied adults* (20 percent). These adults are obsessive and preoccupied with their relationships. They want more relationship closeness than their partners do and suffer extreme feelings of jealousy, based on fears of abandonment. Their relationships have the shortest duration of the three groups. Ambivalent adults describe their relationship with their parents as less warm than secure adults do and feel that their parents had unhappy marriages.

Cross-cultural studies in Australia and Israel have confirmed that people are distributed across the three styles with similar percentages in those countries (Feeney & Noller, 1990; Mikulincer, Florian, & Tolmacz, 1990). Also, males and females are distributed similarly across the three styles, and the proportions of gay men and lesbians in the different attachment styles match those of straight men and women (Ridge & Feeney, 1998).

Expanding on earlier work, Kim Bartholomew (Bartholomew & Horowitz, 1991) developed a four-category model of adult attachment styles. Her model stems from Bowlby's (1980) idea that individuals form abstract images about both the self and others, based on interactions with the primary caregiver. According to Bartholomew, people develop perceptions (positive or negative) of their own self-worth as well as perceptions (positive or negative) of others' trustworthiness and reliability. Depending on where people fall on these two dimensions, Bartholomew classifies them into one of four attachment styles: secure, preoccupied (anxious-ambivalent), fearful, or dismissing (see Figure 8.13). The main difference between the Bartholomew and the Hazan/Shaver models is that Bartholomew's delineates two avoidant attachment styles. Individuals of both types avoid close relationships to protect themselves against disappointment; however, fearful avoidants have

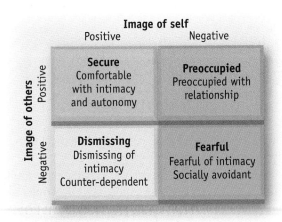

● **FIGURE 8.13**

Bartholomew's model of adult attachment. Drawing on Bowlby's (1980) pioneering work on attachment, Bartholomew conceptualizes adult attachment as rooted in abstract images of oneself (as worthy of love and support or not) and of others (as trustworthy and available versus unreliable and rejecting). Adults' self-views and views of others are assessed with a structured interview. Based on their responses, people are categorized into one of four attachment styles. (Adapted from Bartholomew & Horowitz, 1991)

WEB LINK 8.4

Phillip R. Shaver's Homepage
Phillip Shaver of the University of California–Davis has done pioneering research on adult attachment and its relationship to romantic relationships. His homepage provides a link to his Adult Attachment Lab, where visitors can view early and current work in the lab as well as links to other relevant sites.

negative self-views, whereas dismissing avoidants have positive self-views. While those in the former group need others to bolster self-validation, those in the latter group do not. The dismissing avoidant style emerged in Bartholomew's research but not in Hazan and Shaver's because of differences in the methodology used to classify subjects: Bartholomew uses a structured interview; Hazan and Shaver used a self-report measure. Bartholomew's four-category model has generally been supported by research (Brennan, Clark & Shaver, 1998; Collins & Feeney, 2004).

Correlates of attachment styles. The idea of adult attachment styles has triggered an avalanche of research. Among other findings, studies consistently show that securely attached individuals have more committed, satisfying, interdependent, and well-adjusted relationships compared to people with either anxious-ambivalent or avoidant attachment styles (Feeney, 1999; Mikulincer & Shaver, 2003). Studies have also found that an anxious-ambivalent style is associated with not being in a relationship and with being in relationships of shorter duration, and that an avoidant style is associated with shorter relationships (Shaver & Brennan, 1992).

Hoping to shed light on the connection between attachment style and relationship health, researchers have observed interactions between couples subjected to stress (Feeney, 2004). The findings generally support attachment theory predictions. That is, securely attached individuals both seek out and provide support under stress. By contrast, avoidant people withdraw from their partners and may become angry either when they are asked for support or don't receive the support they want. Anxious individuals become fearful and sometimes exhibit hostility. Thus, attachment style may play a role in whether relationship conflicts facilitate intimacy or worsen distress (Pietromonaco, Greenwood, & Barrett, 2004).

Individuals in the two insecure attachment styles are more vulnerable to a number of problems and symptoms, including low self-esteem, low self-confidence, self-consciousness, anger, resentment, anxiety, loneliness, and depression (Cooper et al., 2004; Mikulincer

Social Support and Stress

Immediately after the events of September 11, 2001, anxious Americans sought to contact and be near their family and friends. People at work called their family members; parents went to schools to collect their children; college students went home. In the anxious moments and hours of that terrifying time, people wanted to be with other people, especially those to whom they felt close.

Of course, other frightening life stresses exist besides fearing and dealing with terrorist attacks. Natural disasters such as tornadoes and hurricanes as well as life-threatening accidents and illnesses come to mind. Death, divorce, and romantic breakups are also difficult to deal with. Regardless of the type of traumatizing event, social support seems to serve as a protective buffer, as we noted in Chapter 3 (Uchino, Cacioppo, & Keicolt-Glaser, 1996; Wills & Fegan, 2001). For example, the survivors of Hurricanes Hugo and Andrew who best coped with the disasters were those who felt that they had the most social support (Norris & Kaniasty, 1996). Another example of the importance of social support comes from a study of breast cancer patients (Spiegel et al., 1989). Women with advanced breast cancer were randomly assigned to a social support or control condition. Those in the social support condition met weekly for 90 minutes with other patients and doctors to discuss their problems and fears; those in the control group had no access to this support system. Those in the social support condition showed improved moods and reduced fears, and, amazingly, they also lived an average of 18 months longer than did those in the no-support condition!

Social support also helps with everyday adjustment. Those who have a network of close relationships are happier and more satisfied with life than those who have fewer social connections (Diener et al., 1999). One study showed that those who have strong social support during final exams had a stronger immune response than those with weak social support (Jemmott & Magloire, 1988). Also, those with close social ties have better physical health and are less likely to die early (Cohen et al., 2002; Uchino et al., 1996).

Why is social support beneficial in times of stress? Although researchers are still working out definitive answers to this question, a number of factors are likely to come into play. At the cognitive level, sharing a stressful event with others helps individuals interpret the event as less monumental than if they had to face it on their own. Emotional support in the form of sympathy and reassurance also figures in. And social support may also reduce the physiological impact of stress.

In these stressful times, individuals' connections to their families, friends, lovers, mates, and co-workers form a life-sustaining web of interconnectedness. There is much truth in the Beatles lyrics, "I get by with a little help from my friends" (and other supportive people).

& Shaver, 2003). Attachment patterns may exert influence beyond romantic relationships. For instance, correlations have been found between attachment styles and friendships (Weimer, Kerns, & Oldenburg, 2004), gender roles (Steiner-Pappalardo & Gurung, 2002), religious beliefs (Kirkpatrick, 1998), and job satisfaction (Schirmer & Lopez, 2001).

Matching of attachment styles.   Does the "likes attract" principle extend to attachment styles? Bolstering the argument for similarity, there is evidence that people with a secure attachment style are more likely to have securely attached partners (Collins & Read, 1990; Feeney, 1994). On the other side, avoidant and ambivalent individuals are often paired with each other, but not with their mirror images (Collins & Read, 1990; Kirkpatrick & Davis, 1994). To date, it isn't clear whether these pairing patterns are present at the start of relationships or whether one or both individuals change their styles over time. Longitudinal studies are needed to sort this out. Approaching this issue in a different way, researchers have asked individuals about their preferred attachment style in a hypothetical partner. Here, all attachment groups rate securely attached individuals the highest (Chappell & Davis, 1998). For now, the evidence for similarity in attachment styles is mixed.

Stability of attachment styles. A number of studies have demonstrated that adult attachment styles parallel those in infancy (Shaver & Hazan, 1993). This pattern suggests that early bonding experiences do produce relatively enduring relationship styles. However, to conclude that an actual causal link exists between infant and adult attachment styles, we need longitudinal evidence. A meta-analysis of longitudinal studies concluded that attachment styles are moderately stable over the first 19 years of life (Fraley, 2002). Across adulthood, style stability appears to increase to some degree (Fraley & Brumbaugh, 2004). Despite the relative stability of attachment styles, they are not set in stone. In childhood, changes from secure to insecure attachment are typically related to negative life events (divorce or death of parents, parental substance abuse, maltreatment) (Waters et al., 2000; Weinfield, Sroufe, & Egeland, 2000). Experiences later in life may also lead to style changes (Baldwin & Fehr, 1995; Lopez & Gormley, 2002). One study reported that about 30 percent of individuals had changed their attachment style over a period of four years (Kirkpatrick & Hazan, 1994). In another, a significant number of individuals (aged 26–64 years) in short-term psychotherapy shifted from an insecure to a secure attachment style (Travis et al., 2001). Thus, psychotherapy may be a helpful option for those with attachment difficulties.

The Course of Romantic Love

Most people find being in love exhilarating and wish the experience could last forever. Must passion fade? Regrettably, the answer to this question seems to be "yes." Consistent with this view, Sternberg's (1986) theory holds that passion peaks early in a relationship and then declines in intensity. In contrast, both intimacy and commitment increase as time progresses, although they develop at different rates (see Figure 8.14). Research supports the idea that the intense attraction and arousal one feels for a lover does tend to subside over time (Sprecher & Regan, 1998; Lemieux & Hale, 2002).

Why does passion fade? It seems that three factors kick into high gear early, then fade in the stretch: fantasy, novelty, and arousal (Brehm et al., 2002). At first, love is "blind," so individuals usually develop a fantasy picture of their lover (often a projection of their own needs). However, as time passes, the intrusion of reality undermines this idealized view. Also, the novelty of a new partner fades with increased interactions and knowledge. Finally, people can't exist in a state of heightened physical arousal forever.

Might the loss of passion be a function of age? After all, people who stay in long relationships are also older.

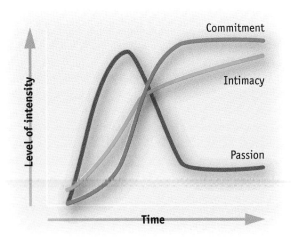

● FIGURE 8.14

The course of love over time. According to Sternberg (1986), the three components of love typically progress differently over time. He theorizes that passion peaks early in a relationship and then declines. In contrast, intimacy and commitment are thought to build gradually.

Some evidence argues against the age explanation. For example, people who change partners and remarry show an increase in the frequency of sex (Call, Sprecher, & Schwartz, 1995). So, while age probably plays some role, it isn't the sole explanation of this phenomenon.

Does the decline of passion mean the demise of a relationship? Not necessarily. Some relationships do dissolve when early passion fades. However, many others evolve into different, but deeply satisfying, mixtures of passionate-companionate love. And while passion *does* fade over time, it's important not to overemphasize or oversimplify this fact (Hatfield, 1988; Hendrick & Hendrick, 2000). Long-term relationships (and sexual feelings, as well) seem to be a complex amalgam of both passionate and companionate love. Significantly, both types of love are related to relationship satisfaction and commitment (Sprecher & Regan, 1998).

Why Relationships End

The question of why some relationships last while others end is a popular issue in relationship research. Nonetheless, the matter is complex, so easy answers have not been forthcoming (Berscheid & Reis, 1998).

If we were to follow seriously dating couples over several years, what proportion of them would split up over that period? If you guessed "about 50 percent," you'd be right. Consider the results of three longitudinal studies (all on heterosexual couples). One study tracked college couples who were either dating or engaged. Over a four-year period, 58 percent of them broke up (Sprecher, 1994). A second study of couples in "steady or serious" dating relationships reported that 51 percent had split at the end of 3 years (Kirkpatrick, & Davis, 1994). Similarly, the Boston Couples Study, a longitudinal study of dating couples in the Boston area, reported that almost half (45 percent) of the relationships had dissolved at the end of two years (Hill, Rubin, & Peplau, 1976). A 15-year follow-up to this study reported that 32 percent of the initial dating couples had married and that 64 percent of them had not (Peplau, Hill, & Rubin, 1993). Among the couples who had married at some time during the study, 68 percent were still together at the time of the follow-up.

To hone in on our key question as to why some relationships stand the test of time and some don't, let's take a closer look at the Boston Couples Study. Here, 200 couples (predominantly college students) were followed over two years. To participate in the study, couples had to be "going steady" and believe that they were in love. If couples split, researchers asked them to give their reasons (see Figure 8.15). The results of this and other studies (Brehm, 1992; Buss, 1989; Sprecher, 1994) suggest that four prominent factors contribute to romantic breakups:

What Causes Couples to Break Up?		
Factors	Women's reports (%)	Men's reports (%)
Interactive factors		
Becoming bored with relationship	77	77
Differences in interests	73	61
Differences in backgrounds	44	47
Differences in intelligence	20	10
Conflicting sexual attitudes	48	43
Conflicting marriage ideas	43	29
Noninteractive factors		
Woman's desire to be independent	74	50
Man's desire to be independent	47	61
Woman's interest in someone else	40	31
Man's interest in someone else	18	29
Living too far apart	28	41
Pressure from woman's parents	18	13
Pressure from man's parents	10	9

● **FIGURE 8.15**

Factors contributing to breakups. Couples who broke up after dating steadily were asked why by Hill, Rubin, and Peplau (1976). The factors commonly cited are listed here. The researchers distinguished between interactive factors, which consisted of problems that emerged out of the partners' ways of relating to each other, and noninteractive factors.

Adapted from Hill, C. T., Rubin, Z., & Peplau, L. A. (1976). Breakups before marriage: The end of 103 affairs. *Journal of Social Issues, 32,* 147–168. Basic Books Publishing Co., Inc. Adapted by permission of the author. All rights reserved.

1. *Premature commitment.* Virtually all the reasons for breakups involved things that could only be known after some sharing of personal information over time. Hence, it seems that many couples make romantic commitments without taking the time to get to know each other. These individuals may find out later that they don't really like each other or that they have little in common. For these reasons, "whirlwind courtships" are risky. Intimacy needs to be combined with commitment if relationships are to survive.

2. *Ineffective communication and conflict management skills.* The vast majority of couples have disagreements. Not surprisingly, disagreements increase as couples learn more about each other and become more interdependent (Buss, 1989). Poor conflict management skills are a key factor in relationship distress and can lead to romantic breakups (Sprecher, 1994). They are also associated with a greater likelihood of relationship aggression (see the Chapter 9 Application on intimate violence). As we discussed in Chapter 7, the solution to this problem is not to stifle all disagree-

ments, because conflict can be helpful to relationships. The key is to manage conflict constructively.

3. *Becoming bored with the relationship.* Couples who break up rank "boredom with the relationship" high on the list of reasons for splitting. As we have noted, novelty usually fades as people get to know each other, and boredom can set in. Individuals have needs for both novelty and predictability in close relationships (Sprecher, 1994). Balancing the two can be tricky for couples.

4. *Availability of a more attractive relationship.* Whether a deteriorating relationship actually ends depends, in great part, on the availability of a more attractive alternative (Felmlee, Sprecher, & Bassin, 1990; South & Lloyd, 1995). We all know of individuals who remained in unsatisfying relationships only until they met a more appealing prospect.

Helping Relationships Last

How can couples increase the likelihood that their relationships will last? Amazingly, researchers have only recently addressed this critical question. Still, there is enough research to support a few suggestions:

1. *Take plenty of time to get to know the other person before you make a long-term commitment.* Research based on Sternberg's theory found that the best predictors of whether dating couples' relationships would continue were their levels of intimacy and commitment (Hendrick et al., 1988). Regarding intimacy, we have already noted that self-disclosures that lead individuals to feel understood, cared for, and validated are crucial (Reis & Patrick, 1996). Other advice comes from long-married couples who were asked why they thought their relationship had lasted (Lauer & Lauer, 1985). The most frequently cited responses of 351 couples who had been married for 15 years or more were (1) friendship ("I like my spouse as a person"); (2) commitment to the relationship ("I want the relationship to succeed"); (3) similarity in values and relationship issues ("We agree on how and how often to show affection"); and (4) positive feelings about each other ("My spouse has grown more interesting"). Thus, early attention to the intimacy foundations of a relationship and ongoing, mutual efforts to build a com-

For Better or For Worse®   **by Lynn Johnston**

mitment can foster more enduring love. Figure 8.16 offers some key questions for couples to discuss before they decide to marry or partner (in the case of gay and lesbian couples).

2. *Emphasize the positive qualities in your partner and relationship.* It is essential to communicate more positive feelings than negative ones to your partner. Early in a relationship, people find this easy to do, but it gets harder as relationships continue. Once the initial glow of the relationship wears off, a common attributional error comes into play. The ***actor-observer effect*** **is the tendency to attribute one's own behavior to situational factors and the behavior of others to personal factors.** This tendency can set up the destructive habit of chronically blaming the other person for problems and not taking responsibility when one should. Ironically, married couples generally make more negative and fewer positive statements to their spouse than

1. What are our separate professional goals in terms of positions or jobs desired? One year from now? Five years? Fifteen years?

2. How do we decide to spend our money? Is there an amount ($50? $500? $5,000?) over which we need to discuss a purchase before committing to it?

3. Who is responsible for grocery shopping, cooking, and other tasks connected with meals? Do we eat out? A lot? A little?

4. Am I comfortable giving and receiving love, sexually? In sex, does my partner feel my love for him or her?

5. Who will take care of our child if we both work? How does each partner feel about day care?

● FIGURE 8.16

Key questions for dating couples to discuss before deciding to marry. To increase their chances for satisfying and long-lasting marriages and partnerships, experts advise dating couples to get to know each other well. Author Susan Piver (2000) has developed a list of 100 essential questions for couples to discuss before they make long-term commitments. The questions cover home, money, work, sex, health and food, family, children, community and friends, and spiritual life. Here is a sample of five questions to consider.

Piver, S. (2000). *The hard questions: 100 essential questions to ask before you say "I do."* New York: Jeremy P. Tarcher/Putnam.

to strangers, and we presume this situation holds for those in other types of committed relationships as well (Koren, Carlton, & Shaw, 1980; Miller, 1991). This tendency is more prevalent among distressed than among nondistressed couples (Bradbury & Fincham, 1990; Gottman, 1993). Unfortunately, when one partner engages in this behavior, the other usually responds in kind, which can set in motion a pattern of reciprocal negativity that makes things worse. Hence, as the old song advises, it helps to "accentuate the positive and eliminate the negative." Similarly, married couples who seek and grant forgiveness have better chances for longer and more satisfying relationships than those who avoid each other or retaliate in kind for a partner's negative behavior (Fincham, 2003).

3. *Find ways to bring novelty to long-term relationships.* As romantic partners learn more about each other and develop feelings of intimacy, they also become more predictable to

each other. But, too much predictability can translate into loss of interest and, possibly, boredom. One way "to keep the bloom on the rose" is to engage in novel activities together (Aron et al., 2000; Baumeister & Bratslavsky, 1999). For example, one study reported that couples who participated in exciting activities together (versus just spending time together) showed increases in relationship satisfaction over a 10-week period (Reissman, Aron, & Bergen, 1993).

4. *Develop effective conflict management skills.* Conflicts arise in all relationships, so it's important to handle them well. For one thing, it's helpful to distinguish between minor annoyances and significant problems. You need to learn to see minor irritations in perspective and recognize how little they matter. With big problems, however, it's usually best to avoid the temptation to sweep them under the rug in the hope that they'll disappear. Important issues rarely disappear on their own, and if you postpone the inevitable discussion, the "sweepings" will have accumulated, making it harder to sort out the various issues. An interaction pattern common to dissatisfied couples is "demand-withdraw" (Roberts & Krokoff, 1990). Typically, this pattern involves the woman pressing the man to discuss a relationship problem and the man avoiding or withdrawing from the interaction. This pattern is associated with the "closeness versus separateness dilemma," in which one partner wants more intimacy and closeness and the other wants more privacy and independence (Christensen & Heavey, 1990). For more specific suggestions on handling conflict, refer to our discussion in Chapter 7.

Engaging in novel activities together, like traveling to interesting destinations, contributes to long-term relationship satisfaction.

APPLICATION

Overcoming Loneliness

LEARNING OBJECTIVES

- Describe various types of loneliness.
- Discuss the prevalence of loneliness.
- Explain how early experiences and current social trends contribute to loneliness.
- Describe how shyness, poor social skills, and self-defeating attributions contribute to loneliness.
- Summarize the suggestions for conquering loneliness.

Answer the following "true" or "false."

___ **1.** Adolescents and young adults are the loneliest age group.

___ **2.** Many people who are lonely are also shy.

___ **3.** The seeds of loneliness are often sown early in life.

___ **4.** Effective social skills can be learned relatively easily.

All of the above are true, as you'll learn shortly. But first, we want to make a couple of points. For one thing, being alone doesn't necessarily trigger loneliness. In these fast-paced times, solitude can provide needed down time to recharge your batteries. Also, people need time alone to deepen self-understanding, wrestle with decisions, and contemplate important life issues. Second, people can feel lonely even when surrounded by others (at a party or concert, for instance). Similarly,

it's possible to have a large social network but not feel close to anyone in particular.

The Nature of Loneliness

Loneliness **occurs when a person has fewer interpersonal relationships than desired or when these relationships are not as satisfying as desired.** Of course, people vary in their needs for social connections. Thus, if you're not distressed by the quantity or quality of your social and emotional ties, you wouldn't be considered lonely.

We can think about loneliness in several ways. One approach is to look at the type of relationship deficit involved (Weiss, 1973). *Emotional loneliness* stems from the absence of an intimate attachment figure. For a child, this figure is typically a parent; for an adult, it is

Contrary to stereotypes, adolescents and young adults are more likely to feel lonely than people from older age groups.

© Michael Newman/PhotoEdit

usually a spouse or partner or an intimate friend. *Social loneliness* results from the lack of a friendship network (typically provided in school and work settings and in community groups). For example, a married couple who move to a new city will experience social loneliness until they make new social connections; however, because they have each other, they should not experience emotional loneliness. On the other hand, a recently divorced person will probably feel emotional loneliness but should not experience social loneliness, assuming that work and friendship networks remain intact (which is not always the case).

Emotional loneliness seems to be tied to the absence of a romantic partner in both college students and senior adults (Green et al., 2001). Social loneliness, however, seems to spring from different roots, depending on age. In college students, it's the *quantity* of friendship contacts that counts; among the older group, it's the *quality* of contacts. It's also worth noting that social support can't compensate for emotional loneliness—for example, the presence of friends and family cannot substitute for a loved one who has died (Stroebe et al., 1996). Of course, this is not to say that social support is unimportant. The point is that different types of loneliness require different responses; therefore, you need to pinpoint the exact nature of your social deficits to cope effectively with loneliness.

A second way to look at loneliness is in terms of its duration (Young, 1982). *Transient loneliness* involves brief and sporadic feelings of loneliness, which many people may experience even when their social lives are reasonably adequate. *Transitional loneliness* occurs when people who have had satisfying social relationships in the past become lonely after experiencing a disruption in their social network (the death of a loved one, say, or divorce or moving to a new locale). *Chronic loneliness* is a condition that affects people who have been unable to develop a satisfactory interpersonal network over a period of years. We'll focus on chronic loneliness for the most part.

Prevalence of Loneliness

How many people are tormented by loneliness? Although we don't have a precise answer to this question, anecdotal evidence suggests that the number of people plagued by loneliness is substantial. Telephone hotlines for troubled people report that complaints of loneliness dominate their calls. No doubt some of the popularity of cell phone calls, instant messaging, and chat rooms can be traced to loneliness.

The prevalence of loneliness in specific age groups actually contradicts stereotypes. For example, although many assume that the loneliest age group is the elderly, this "distinction" actually belongs to adolescents and young adults (Rubenstein & Shaver, 1982). Gay and lesbian adolescents are particularly likely to be lonely (Westefeld et al., 2001). Another vulnerable group is beginning college students. One study reported that 75 percent of those in this group experienced loneliness in their first few weeks on campus (Cutrona, 1982). It is likely that frequent changes of schools, jobs, and relationships during adolescence and young adulthood all contribute to the high rates of loneliness for this age group. A second unexpected finding is that loneliness decreases with age, at least until the much later years of adulthood when one's friends begin to die (Rubenstein & Shaver, 1982).

In line with expectations, single, divorced, and widowed adults are lonelier than their married or cohabiting counterparts (deJong-Gierveld, 1986; Stroebe et al., 1996), although some married people do feel lonely (Stack, 1998). Also, individuals whose parents have been divorced report feeling more lonely than those from intact families (Rubenstein & Shaver, 1982). Moreover, the earlier in their lives the divorce occurred, the stronger

Thanks to automation and online technology people today are able to take care of many of life's necessities without interacting with other human beings. These reduced opportunities for social interaction help to fuel increased loneliness.

the feelings of loneliness experienced in adulthood. In contrast, no differences in loneliness were noted between individuals who had lost a parent through death and those from intact families.

In keeping with gender differences in friendship patterns, college women are more apt to be lonely if they lack a close friend to confide in; college men experience more loneliness if they lack a group of friends to interact with (Cutrona, 1982). Women are found to be lonelier than men, but only on measures that use words such as "lonely" or "loneliness" (Borys & Perlman, 1985). Thus, it is likely that there is no actual gender difference but rather a reluctance by men to admit to feeling lonely.

The Roots of Loneliness

Any event that ruptures the social fabric of a person's life may lead to loneliness, so no one is immune. We'll consider the roles of early experiences and social trends.

Early Experiences

The seeds for chronic loneliness are likely sown early in life. A key problem seems to be early negative social behavior that leads to rejection by peers (Asher & Paquette, 2003). Children who are aggressive or withdrawn are likely to suffer peer rejection even in preschool (Ray et al., 1997). What prompts inappropriate social behavior in young children? One factor is insecure attachment styles. Because of difficult early parent-infant interactions, children often develop social behaviors (aggression, aloofness, competitiveness, overdependence) that "invite" rejection by adults and peers (Bartholomew, 1990; Duggan & Brennan, 1994). You can see how a vicious cycle gets set up. A child's inappropriate behavior prompts rejection by others, which in turn triggers negative expectations about social interactions in the child, along with more negative behavior, and so on. To help break this self-defeating cycle (and head off the loneliness that can result), it is crucial to help children learn appropriate social skills early in life.

Without intervention, insecurely attached children can grow into insecurely attached adults. And insecure attachment is correlated with loneliness in adulthood. Using the three-style model of attachment, anxious-ambivalent adults score the highest on loneliness, avoidant individuals score the next highest, and securely attached individuals score the lowest (Hazan & Shaver, 1987; Larose & Bernier, 2001). The high scores of the anxious-ambivalent group are in line with other research showing that these individuals want more intense and close relationships than they typically find. Good social skills are related to the lower loneliness scores of the "secures" (diTommaso et al., 2003).

Social Trends

Some social commentators and psychologists are concerned about recent trends that seem to be undermining social connections in our culture (Kraut et al., 1998; Putnam, 1996). Single working mothers and fathers may be so pressed for time that they have little time to cultivate adult relationships. Because of busy schedules, face-to-face interactions at home are reduced as family members eat on the run, on their own, or in front of the TV. And the fact that people watch television so much tends to diminish meaningful family conversation. While technology makes life easier in some respects and does provide opportunities for meaningful relationships, it has its down sides. For example, superficial social interactions become prevalent as people order their meals and do their banking at drive-up windows, purchase their groceries via automated checkout stations, and so forth. Finally, people are spending more time alone at computers in their offices and homes, reducing opportunities for face-to-face interactions.

RECOMMENDED READING

Shyness
by Philip G. Zimbardo
(Addison Wesley, 1977, 1990)

Zimbardo, a noted social psychologist, focuses his keen insight on the frustrations of being shy. A lack of jargon and ample use of actual case histories make this book highly readable. In Part I, Zimbardo explores the roots of shyness. Here he discusses various types of shyness and how shyness affects people, especially their social and intimate relationships. He also examines the origins of shyness and how family and school experiences can breed shyness. In Part II, Zimbardo turns to the practical question of how to cope with various types of shyness. Dealing with some forms of shyness requires examining and changing one's thinking about shyness and oneself. Other types require changes in behavior, especially social skills. The book includes numerous exercises and lots of sound advice to help readers implement the changes they need to make. For parents, teachers, and friends of shy individuals, Zimbardo includes a chapter on helping others to overcome their shyness.

Cover image reprinted by permission of Addison-Wesley Publishing Company, Inc. and Bart Goldman.

Correlates of Loneliness

For people who are chronically lonely, painful feelings are a fact of life. Three factors that figure prominently in chronic loneliness are shyness, poor social skills, and a self-defeating attributional style. Of course, the link between these factors and loneliness could go either way. Feeling lonely might cause you to make negative attributions about others, but making negative attributions can also lead to loneliness.

Shyness

Shyness is commonly associated with loneliness (Jackson et al., 2002). *Shyness* **refers to discomfort, inhibition, and excessive caution in interpersonal relations.** Specifically, shy people tend to (1) be timid about expressing themselves, (2) be overly self-conscious about how others are reacting to them, (3) embarrass easily, and (4) experience physiological symptoms of their anxiety, such as a racing pulse, blushing, or an upset stomach. In pioneering research on shyness, Philip Zimbardo (1977, 1990) and his associates report that 60 percent of shy people indicated that their shyness was *situationally specific*. That is, their shyness is triggered only in certain social contexts, such as asking someone for help or interacting with a large group of people (see Figure 8.17).

Poor Social Skills

Studies have also found that lonely people evaluate others negatively (Duck, Pond, & Leatham, 1995; Wittenberg & Reis, 1986), although this is not always the case (Christensen & Kashy, 1998). Either way, people who suffer from chronic loneliness typically have casual acquaintances rather than close friends, and they date infrequently (Bell, 1991). They spend much of their time in solitary activities such as listening to music or reading (Rubenstein & Shaver, 1982).

Often, these individuals are adults who were unable to break out of self-defeating patterns of social behavior developed early in life. A common finding is that lonely people show lower responsiveness to their conversational partners and are more self-focused (Rook, 1998). Similarly, researchers report that lonely people are relatively inhibited and unassertive, speaking less than nonlonely people. They also seem to disclose less about themselves than those who are not lonely. This (often unconscious) tendency has the effect of keeping people at an emotional distance and limits interactions to a relatively superficial level. These interactional problems are based, in part, on heightened fears of rejection (Jackson et al., 2002). It seems that people with "rejection anxiety" believe that their signaled interest is obvious to others when it is not (Vorauer et al., 2003). Thus, unaware that their signal was invisible,

"What Makes You Shy?"

	Percentage of shy students
Other people	
Strangers	70
Opposite sex	64
Authorities by virtue of their knowledge	55
Authorities by virtue of their role	40
Relatives	21
Elderly people	12
Friends	11
Children	10
Parents	8
Situations	
Where I am focus of attention—large group (as when giving a speech)	73
Large groups	68
Of lower status	56
Social situations in general	55
New situations in general	55
Requiring assertiveness	54
Where I am being evaluated	53
Where I am focus of attention—small group	52
Small social groups	48
One-to-one different-sex interactions	48
Of vulnerability (need help)	48
Small task-oriented groups	20
One-to-one same-sex interactions	14

● FIGURE 8.17

The situational determinants of shyness. Zimbardo (1977) asked subjects about the people and circumstances that made them feel shy. The results of his survey showed that shyness depends to a large degree on situational factors.

From Zimbardo, P. (1977). *Shyness: What is it, what to do about it.* Reading, MA: Addison-Wesley Copyright © 1977 by Philip Zimbardo, Inc. Reprinted by permission of Perseus Books Publishers, a member of Perseus Books, L.L.C.

WEB LINK 8.5

The Shyness Homepage
The Shyness Institute (Portola Valley, CA) offers a "gathering of network resources for people seeking information and services for shyness." The Institute is co-directed by psychologists Lynne Henderson and Philip Zimbardo.

those with rejection anxiety may perceive rejection where none exists.

Self-Defeating Attributional Style

It's easy to see how repeated rejections can foster negative expectations about social interactions. Thus, lonely people are prone to irrational thinking about their social skills, the probability of their achieving intimacy, the likelihood of being rejected, and so forth. Unfortunately, once people develop these negative ideas, they often behave in ways to confirm their expectations, setting up a vicious cycle of behavior.

Jeffrey Young (1982) points out that lonely people engage in *negative self-talk* that prevents them from pursuing intimacy in an active and positive manner. He has identified some clusters of ideas that foster loneliness. Figure 8.18 gives examples of typical thoughts from six of these clusters of cognitions and the overt behaviors that result. As you can see, several of the cognitions in Figure 8.18 are stable, internal self-attributions. This tendency to attribute loneliness to stable, internal causes constitutes a self-defeating attributional style (Anderson et al., 1994). In other words, lonely people tell themselves that they're lonely because they're basically unlovable individuals. Not only is this a devastating belief, it is also self-defeating because it offers no way to change the situation. Happily, it *is* possible to reduce loneliness, as you'll see.

Conquering Loneliness

The personal consequences associated with chronic loneliness can be painful and sometimes overwhelming: low self-esteem, hostility, depression, alcoholism, psychosomatic illness, and, possibly, suicide (McWhirter,

1990). Chronic loneliness is also a predictor of a number of diseases, including cardiovascular disease and cancer (Hawkley & Cacioppo, 2003). Although there are no simple solutions to loneliness, there are some effective ones. Let's look at four useful strategies.

One option is to use the Internet to overcome loneliness, although this approach can be a two-edged sword (McKenna & Bargh, 2000). On the plus side, the Internet is an obvious boon to busy people, those with stigmatized social identities, and those who find physical mobility difficult (the infirm and people with serious medical conditions). Moreover, shy people can interact without the anxiety involved in face-to-face communication. On the other hand, if lonely people spend a lot of time online, will they devote less time to face-to-face relationships? Will shy individuals develop the self-confidence to pursue relationships offline? Internet use in the general population is associated with generally positive effects (Bargh & McKenna, 2004). Among lonely persons, Internet use is also associated with benefits such as reduced loneliness, improved perceived social support, and formation of online friendships (Shaw, & Gant, 2002; Morahan-Martin & Schumacher, 2003). Still, one study found that lonely individuals more often reported that Internet use caused disturbances in their daily functioning (Morahan-Martin & Schumacher, 2003), raising concerns about Internet addiction (Nalwa & Anand, 2003). Research on these questions is in its infancy, so answers must await further research.

A second suggestion is to avoid the temptation to withdraw from social situations. A study that asked people what they did when they felt lonely found the top responses to be "read" and "listen to music" (Rubenstein & Shaver, 1982). If used occasionally, reading and lis-

From a paper presented at the annual convention of the American Psychological Association, 9/2/79. An expanded version of this paper appears in G. Emery, S. D. Hollan, & R. C. Bedrosian (Eds.). (1981). *New directions in cognitive therapy.* New York: Guilford Press and in L. A. Peplau & D. Perlman (Eds.). (1982). *Loneliness: A sourcebook of current theory, research and therapy.* New York: Wiley. Copyright © 1982 by John Wiley & Sons, Inc. and Jeffrey Young.

● **FIGURE 8.18**

Patterns of thinking underlying loneliness. According to Young (1982), negative self-talk contributes to loneliness. Six clusters of irrational thoughts are illustrated here. Each cluster of cognitions leads to certain patterns of behavior (right) that promote loneliness.

Clusters of Cognitions Typical of Lonely People

Clusters	Cognitions	Behaviors
A	1. I'm undesirable. 2. I'm dull and boring.	Avoidance of friendship
B	1. I can't communicate with other people. 2. My thoughts and feelings are bottled up inside.	Low self-disclosure
C	1. I'm not a good lover in bed. 2. I can't relax, be spontaneous, and enjoy sex.	Avoidance of sexual relationships
D	1. I can't seem to get what I want from this relationship. 2. I can't say how I feel, or he/she might leave me.	Lack of assertiveness in relationships
E	1. I won't risk being hurt again. 2. I'd screw up any relationship.	Avoidance of potentially intimate relationships
F	1. I don't know how to act in this situation. 2. I'll make a fool of myself.	Avoidance of other people

tening to music can be constructive ways of dealing with loneliness. However, as long-term strategies, they do nothing to help a lonely person acquire new "real-world" friends. This situation may be a particular problem for those with an avoidant attachment style. The importance of staying active socially cannot be overemphasized. Recall that proximity is a powerful factor in the development of close relationships. To make friends, you have to be around people.

A third strategy is to break out of the habit of the self-defeating attributional style we just discussed ("I'm lonely because I'm unlovable"). Recall from Chapter 5 that there are *other* attributions a lonely person could make and that these alternative explanations point to solutions (see Figure 8.19). If a person says, "My conversational skills are weak" (unstable, internal cause), the solution would be: "I'll try to find out how to improve them." Or, if someone thinks, "It always takes time to meet people when you move to a new location" (unstable, external cause), this attribution suggests the solution of trying harder to develop new relationships and giving them time to work. The attribution "I've really searched, but I just can't find enough compatible people at my workplace" (stable, external cause) may lead to the decision, "It's time to look for a new job." As you can see, the last three attributions lead to active modes of coping rather than the passivity fostered by a self-defeating attributional style.

Finally, to thwart loneliness, you need to cultivate your social skills. You'll find a wealth of information on this important topic in Chapter 7 (Interpersonal Communication). Lonely people, especially, should focus on reading others' nonverbal signals, deepening the level of their self-disclosure, engaging in active listening, improving their conversational skills, and developing an assertive communication style.

If you feel overwhelmed at the prospect of tackling loneliness on your own, consider paying a visit to your college counseling center. Dealing with loneliness

Stability dimension

	Unstable cause (temporary)	Stable cause (permanent)
Internal cause	I'm lonely now, but won't be for long. I need to get out and meet some new people.	I'm lonely because I'm unlovable. I'll never be worth loving.
External cause	My lover and I just split up. I guess some relationships work and some don't. Maybe I'll be luckier next time.	The people here are cold and unfriendly. It's time to look for a new job.

● FIGURE 8.19

Attributions and loneliness. Lonely people often have a self-defeating attributional style, in which they attribute their loneliness to stable, internal causes (see upper right quadrant). Learning to make alternative attributions (see other quadrants) can bring to light ways to deal with loneliness and facilitate active coping.

Based on Shaver, P., & Rubenstein, C. (1980). Childhood attachment experience and adult loneliness. In L. Wheeler (Ed.), *Review of personality and social psychology* (Vol.1, pp. 42–73). Thousand Oaks, CA: Sage Publications.

and shyness usually involves work on two fronts. First, counselors help people improve social skills through *social skills training*. (This approach can be used with socially isolated children, as well.) In this program, individuals learn and practice the skills involved in initiating and maintaining relationships. For example, they might watch videotapes of socially skilled models demonstrating appropriate social behavior in a variety of settings. They then practice these behaviors in the therapist's office. Sometimes these practice sessions are taped so people can actually see how they are coming across. Second, counselors can use *cognitive therapy* (see Chapter 16) to help lonely and shy individuals to break the habit of automatic negative thoughts and self-defeating attributions. Over a series of sessions, individuals learn to change their negative views of themselves ("I'm boring") and other people ("They're cold and unfriendly"). Both of these approaches have high success rates, and they can pave the way to more positive social interactions that are critical to adjustment.

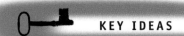

KEY IDEAS

Perspectives on Close Relationships

■ Close relationships are those that are important, interdependent, and long-lasting. They include friendships as well as work, family, and romantic relationships. People in individualistic cultures believe that romantic love is a prerequisite for marriage, whereas those in collectivist cultures are accustomed to arranged marriages.

■ The Internet offers many new vehicles for meeting others and developing relationships. The differences between Internet and face-to-face communication have important implications for established psychological theories and principles of relationship development.

Initial Attraction and Relationship Development

■ People are initially drawn to others who are nearby, who are seen often, and who are physically attractive. Although physical attractiveness plays a key role in initial attraction, people also seek other desirable characteristics, such as kindness and intelligence. People often match up on looks, but sometimes men trade status for physical attractiveness in women, and vice versa.

■ As people get acquainted, they prefer others who like them and those who have desirable personality characteristics. Similarity is a key factor in relationship development. Couples tend to be similar in age, race, religion, education, attitudes, and even some personality traits.

■ Once relationships are established, people engage in various maintenance behaviors and actions to sustain them. Interdependence (social exchange) theory uses principles of reinforcement to predict relationship satisfaction and commitment. How individuals apply social exchange principles depends on whether they are in exchange or communal relationships.

Friendship

■ The key ingredients of friendship are loyalty, emotional support, and letting friends be themselves. Women's same-gender friendships are usually characterized by self-disclosure and intimacy, whereas men's same-gender friendships typically involve doing things together.

Romantic Love

■ Research indicates that the experience of romantic love is the same for heterosexual and homosexual individuals. Contrary to stereotypes, men may be more romantic than women. In choosing a partner, women are more selective than men.

■ Sternberg's triangular theory of love proposes that passion, intimacy, and commitment combine into eight types of love. Hazan and Shaver theorize that love relationships follow the form of attachments in infancy, falling into three categories: secure, avoidant, and anxious-ambivalent. Bartholomew has proposed an alternative, four category model of adult attachment styles. Although attachment styles show stability over time, it is possible for them to change.

■ Initially, romantic love is usually characterized by passion, but strong passion appears to fade over time for a number of reasons. In relationships that continue, passionate love evolves into a less intense, more mature form of love.

■ The chief causes of relationship failure are the tendency to make premature commitments, ineffective conflict management skills, boredom with the relationship, and the availability of a more attractive relationship. To help relationships last, couples should take the time to know each other very well, emphasize the positive qualities in their partner and relationship, engage in new activities together, and develop effective conflict management skills.

Application: Overcoming Loneliness

■ Loneliness involves discontent with the extent and quality of one's interpersonal network. A surprisingly large number of people in our society are troubled by loneliness. The age groups most affected by loneliness contradict stereotypes.

■ The origins of chronic loneliness can often be traced to early negative behavior that triggers rejection by peers and teachers. Social trends may also promote loneliness. Loneliness is associated with shyness, poor social skills, and self-defeating attributions.

■ The keys to overcoming loneliness include avoiding the temptation to withdraw from social situations, avoiding self-defeating attributions, and working on one's social skills.

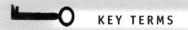

KEY TERMS

Actor-observer effect   p. 258
Attachment styles   p. 252
Close relationships   p. 236
Commitment   p. 252
Comparison level   p. 247
Comparison level for
   alternatives   p. 247
Heterosexism   p. 250
Intimacy   p. 251
Investments   p. 247
Loneliness   p. 260

Matching hypothesis   p. 242
Mere exposure effect   p. 240
Passion   p. 242
Proximity   p. 239
Reciprocal liking   p. 244
Relationship maintenance
   p. 246
Sexual orientation   p. 250
Shyness   p. 263
Social exchange theory
   p. 247

KEY PEOPLE

David Buss   pp. 243–244
Cindy Hazan and Philip
   Shaver   pp. 252–254

Harold Kelley and John
   Thibaut   pp. 247–248
Robert Sternberg
   pp. 251–252

PRACTICE TEST

1. Arranged marriages are most common in:
   a. individualistic cultures.
   b. collectivist cultures.
   c. unrequited cultures.
   d. both individualistic and collectivist cultures.

2. Which of the following is a relationship issue that operates differently in online versus face-to-face interactions?
   a. Physical proximity
   b. Physical attractiveness
   c. Self-disclosure
   d. All of the above

3. The mere exposure effect refers to an increase in positive feelings due to:
   a. seeing someone often.
   b. interacting with someone often.
   c. communicating via e-mail often.
   d. having similar attitudes.

4. The matching hypothesis suggests that people match up on the basis of:
   a. religion.
   b. personality.
   c. socioeconomic status.
   d. looks.

5. An individual's personal standard of what constitutes an acceptable balance of rewards and costs in a relationship is termed:
   a. social exchange.
   b. comparison level.
   c. comparison level for alternatives.
   d. relationship satisfaction.

6. Women's same-gender friendships are based on _____; men's are based on _____.
   a. shopping together; hunting together
   b. attending sports events; attending sports events
   c. shared activities; intimacy and self-disclosure
   d. intimacy and self-disclosure; shared activities

7. If a researcher fails to determine the sexual orientation of her research participants and reports her findings without any mention of homosexuals, her study suffers from:
   a. homosexism.
   b. social exchange.
   c. heterosexism.
   d. romantic bias.

8. A sociocultural explanation for the finding that women are more selective than men in choosing partners is that women:
   a. have better vision than men.
   b. have less economic power than men.
   c. are less superficial than men.
   d. have to compensate for being more romantic than men.

9. Adults who have positive views of themselves but negative views of others would be categorized in which of the following attachment styles?
   a. Secure
   b. Preoccupied
   c. Dismissive avoidant
   d. Fearful avoidant

10. A self-defeating attributional style associated with loneliness involves attributing loneliness to:
    a. internal, stable factors.
    b. internal, unstable factors.
    c. external, stable factors.
    d. external, unstable factors.

Book Companion Website

Visit the Book Companion Website at **http://psychology. wadsworth.com/weiten_lloyd8e**, where you will find tutorial quizzes, flashcards, and weblinks for every chapter, a final exam, and more! You can also link to the Thomson Wadsworth Psychology Resource Center (accessible directly at **http://psychology.wadsworth.com**) for a range of psychology-related resources.

Personal Explorations Workbook

The following exercises in your *Personal Explorations Workbook* may enhance your self-understanding in relation to issues raised in this chapter. **Questionnaire 8.1:** Social Avoidance and Distress Scale. **Personal Probe 8.1:** How Do You Relate to Friends? **Personal Probe 8.2:** Analyzing Your Views of Social Connectedness.

ANSWERS

1. b Pages 236–237
2. d Page 238
3. a Page 240
4. d Page 242
5. b Page 247
6. d Pages 249–250
7. c Page 250
8. b Page 251
9. c Page 254
10. a Page 264

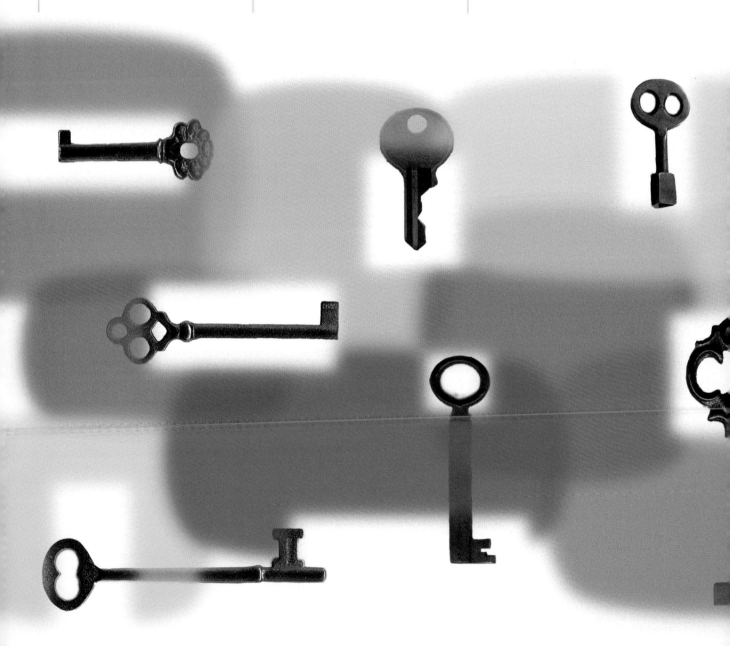

Marriage and Intimate Relationships

"My hands are shaky. I want to call her again but I know it is no good. She'll only yell and scream. It makes me feel lousy. I have work to do but I can't do it. I can't concentrate. I want to call people up, go see them, but I'm afraid they'll see that I'm shaky. I just want to talk. I can't think about anything besides this trouble with Nina. I think I want to cry."—A recently separated man quoted in Marital Separation *(Weiss, 1975, p. 48)*

This man is describing his feelings a few days after he and his wife broke up. He is still hoping for a reconciliation. In the meantime, he feels overwhelmed by anxiety, remorse, and depression. He feels very alone and is scared at the prospect of remaining alone. His emotional distress is so great that he can't think straight or work effectively. His reaction to the loss of an intimate relationship is not all that unusual. Marital breakups are devastating for most people—a reality that illustrates the enormous importance of intimate relationships in people's lives.

In this chapter we take a look at marriage and other intimate relationships. We discuss why people marry and how they progress toward the selection of a mate. To shed light on marital adjustment, we describe the life cycle of the family, highlighting key vulnerable spots in marital relations. We also address issues related to divorce, cohabitation, remaining single, and being gay. Finally, in the Application we examine the tragic problem of violence in intimate relationships. Let's begin by discussing recent challenges to the traditional concept of marriage.

Challenges to the Traditional Model of Marriage

LEARNING OBJECTIVES

- *Discuss recent trends relating to the acceptance of singlehood and cohabitation.*
- *Describe changing views on the permanence of marriage and gender roles.*
- *Explain how increased childlessness and the decline of the nuclear family have affected the institution of marriage.*

Marriage **is the legally and socially sanctioned union of sexually intimate adults.** Traditionally, the marital relationship has included economic interdependence, common residence, sexual fidelity, and shared responsibility for children. Although the institution of marriage remains popular, it sometimes seems to be under assault from shifting social trends. This assault has prompted many experts to ask whether marriage is in serious trouble (Cherlin, 2004; Lewin, 2004). Although it appears that the institution of marriage will weather the storm, it's worth looking at some of the social trends that are shaking up the traditional model of marriage:

1. *Increased acceptance of singlehood.* An increasing proportion of the adult population under age 35 is remaining single (Teachman, Polonko, & Scanzoni, 1999). In part, this trend reflects longer postponement of marriage than before. The median age at which people marry has been increasing gradually since the mid-1960s, as Figure 9.1 shows. Thus, remaining single is becoming a more acceptable lifestyle (DeFrain & Olson, 1999). Furthermore, the negative stereotype of people who remain single—which pictures them as lonely, frustrated, and unchosen—is gradually evaporating.

2. *Increased acceptance of cohabitation.* **Cohabitation is living together in a sexually intimate relationship without the legal bonds of marriage.** Negative attitudes toward couples living together have clearly declined (Cherlin, 2004), although many people continue to disapprove of the practice (Thornton & Young DeMarco, 2001). The prevalence of cohabitation has increased dramatically in recent decades. Census data, for instance, suggest that the number of couples living together increased more than tenfold between 1970 and 2000. Moreover, cohabiting relationships increasingly include children (Smock, 2000). (Cohabitation is discussed in further detail later in this chapter.)

3. *Reduced premium on permanence.* Most people still view marriage as a permanent commitment, but

an increasing number of people regard divorce as justifiable if their marriage fails to foster their interests as individuals (Bianchi & Casper, 2000). Accordingly, the social stigma associated with divorce has lessened, and divorce rates have risen. Some experts estimate that roughly 50 percent of marriages ultimately end in separation or divorce (Amato, 2004a; see pp. 285–286 for a more complete discussion of divorce rates).

4. *Transitions in gender roles.* The women's movement and economic pressures have led to substantial changes in the gender-role expectations of many people entering marriage today (Brewster & Padavic, 2000; Zuo & Tang, 2000). The traditional breadwinner and homemaker roles for the husband and wife are being discarded by many couples, as more and more married

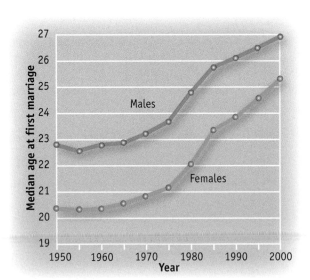

(● **FIGURE 9.1**)

Median age at first marriage. The median age at which people in the United States marry for the first time has been creeping up for both males and females since the mid-1960s. This trend indicates that more people are postponing marriage. (Data from U.S. Bureau of the Census)

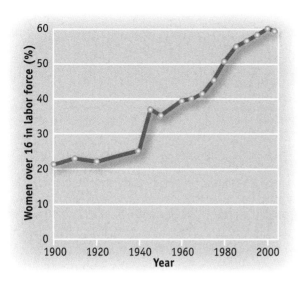

Women in the workforce. The percentage of women in the United States (over age 16) who work outside the home has been rising steadily throughout the 20th century, although it has leveled off in the last few years. (Data from U.S. Bureau of Labor Statistics)

Thanks in part to television portrayals of the family, such as that seen on the popular Cosby Show, *people cling to an idealized image of the traditional nuclear family, despite the fact that only a small minority of American families match this stereotype.*

women enter the workforce (see Figure 9.2). Role expectations for husbands and wives are becoming more varied, more flexible, and more ambiguous (Amato et al., 2003). Many people regard this trend as a step in the right direction. However, changing gender roles create new potential for conflict between marital partners (McGraw & Walker, 2004).

5. *Increased voluntary childlessness.* In the past two decades, the percentage of women without children has climbed in all age groups as an increasing number of married couples have chosen not to have children or to delay having children (Bulcroft & Teachman, 2004). This trend is a result of new career opportunities for women, the tendency to marry at a later age, and changing attitudes.

6. *Decline of the traditional nuclear family.* Thanks to endless reruns of television shows like *Leave It to Beaver, Father Knows Best, Happy Days, The Brady Bunch,* and *Family Ties,* in the eyes of most American adults the ideal family should consist of a husband and wife married for the first time, rearing two or more children, with the man serving as the sole breadwinner (Coontz, 2000). As McGraw and Walker (2004), put it, "Many people today, both in academic settings and popular culture, continue to idealize the image of the traditional nuclear family—one consisting of a breadwinner father and a homemaker mother . . . Because this ideology remains strong, a dearth of support exists for families

that do not conform to the image" (p. 177). In reality, this image was never all that accurate, and today it is estimated that only a small minority of American families match this ideal (Coontz, 2000). The increasing prevalence of single-parent households, stepfamilies, childless marriages, unwed parents, and working wives have conspired to make the traditional nuclear family a highly deceptive mirage that does not reflect the diversity of family structures in America.

In summary, the norms that mold marital and intimate relationships have been restructured in fundamental ways in recent decades. Traditional values have eroded as people have increasingly embraced more individualistic values (Bianchi & Casper, 2000; Popenoe, 1993). Thus, the institution of marriage is in a period of transition, creating new adjustment challenges for modern couples. Support for the concept of monogamy remains strong, but changes in the society are altering the traditional model of marriage. The impact of these changes can be seen throughout this chapter as we discuss various facets of married life.

Moving Toward Marriage

LEARNING OBJECTIVES

- Discuss several factors influencing the selection of a mate.
- Outline Murstein's stage theory of mate selection.
- Summarize evidence on predictors of marital success.

"I'm ashamed of being single, I have to admit it. I have grown to hate the word. The worst thing someone can say is, 'How come you're still not married?' It's like saying, 'What's wrong with you?' I look at women who are frumpy and physically undesirable and they're monochromatic and uninteresting and they don't seem unselfish and giving and I wonder, 'How did they become such an integral part of a man's life that he wanted to marry them and spend his life with them?' I'm envious. They're married and I date."—A woman quoted in Tales from the Front *(Kavesh & Lavin, 1988, p. 91)*

This woman desperately wants to be married. The intensity of her motivation for marriage may be a bit unusual, but otherwise she is fairly typical. Like most people, she has been socialized to believe that her life isn't complete until she finds a mate. Although alternatives to marriage are more viable than ever, experts project that over 90 percent of Americans will marry at least once. Some will do it several times! But why? What motivates people to marry? And how do individuals choose their partners? We'll address these questions as we discuss the factors that influence the movement toward marriage.

The Motivation to Marry

A great variety of motivational factors propel people into marriage. Foremost among them is the desire to participate in a socially sanctioned, mutually rewarding, intimate relationship. Another key factor is the social pressure exerted on people to marry. Getting married is still the norm in our society. Your parents, relatives, and friends expect you to marry eventually, and they often make this expectation abundantly clear with their comments and inquiries.

The popular view in our culture is that people marry because they have fallen in love. Although partially accurate, this view is oversimplified. A multitude of motivational factors are involved in the decision to marry. Peter Stein (1975, 1976) interviewed single men and women ages 22 to 45 who were judged to be neither unattractive nor socially inept. As you can see in Figure 9.3, he learned that many forces push and pull people toward marriage or singlehood.

Selecting a Mate

Modern Western cultures are somewhat unusual in permitting free choice of one's marital partner. Most societies rely on parental arrangements and severely restrict the range of acceptable partners along religious and class lines (Ingoldsby, 1995). Mate selection in American culture is a gradual process that begins with dating and moves on to sometimes lengthy periods of courtship. In this section, we will look at the impact of endogamy, homogamy, and gender on marital choice. We'll also discuss Bernard Murstein's S-V-R theory, which provides a good overview of the process of mate selection.

Endogamy

Endogamy **is the tendency of people to marry within their own social group.** Research demonstrates that people tend to marry others of the same race, religion, ethnic background, and social class (Jepsen & Jepsen, 2002; Kalmijn, 1998). This endogamy is promoted by cultural norms and by the way similarity fosters interpersonal attraction (see Chapter 8). Although endogamy appears to be declining, this trend has been gradual. For example, interracial marriages have become more common, but they only increased from 1.3 percent of marriages in 1980 to 2.4 percent in 1999 (Amato et al., 2003).

Homogamy

Homogamy **is the tendency of people to marry others who have similar personal characteristics.** Among other things, marital partners tend to be similar in age and education (Jepsen & Jepsen, 2002), physical attractiveness (Feingold, 1988), attitudes and values (Kilby, 1993), and even vulnerability to psychological disorders (Matthews & Reus, 2001). Interestingly, homogamy is associated with longer-lasting and more satisfying marital relations (Heaton, 2002).

Deviations from homogamy in age and education do not tend to be symmetrical, as husbands are usually older and better educated than their wives (South, 1991). The typical age gap is about three to four years (Surra, 1990). Cultural norms that discourage women from dating younger men may contribute to a "marriage squeeze" for women. Without the freedom to date younger men, women are likely to find their pool of po-

The Decision to Marry

Pushes toward marriage	Pulls toward marriage	Pushes toward singlehood	Pulls toward singlehood

Economic security	Influence of parents	Restrictions
		  Suffocating one-to-one rela-
		    tionships, feeling trapped
		  Obstacles to self-development
		  Boredom, unhappiness, anger
		  Role playing and conformity
		    to expectations
			Career opportunities

Influence from mass media	Desire for family		Variety of experiences
Pressure from parents	Example of peers		Self-sufficiency
Need to leave home	Romanticization of marriage		Sexual availability

Interpersonal and personal reasons
  Fear of independence
  Loneliness
  Alternative did not seem
    feasible
	Love
	  Physical attraction
	  Emotional attachment
		Poor communication with mate	Exciting lifestyle

	Security, social status, prestige	Sexual frustration	Freedom to change and experiment
Cultural expectations, socialization		Lack of friends, isolation, loneliness	Mobility
Regular sex		Limitations on mobility and available experience	Sustaining friendships

Guilt over singlehood		Influence of and participation in women's movement	Supportive groups
			  Men's and women's groups
			  Group living arrangements
			  Specialized groups

● FIGURE 9.3

The decision to marry. Stein (1975) interviewed single people ages 22 to 45 to determine the motivational factors that influence the decision to marry. *Pushes toward marriage* involve deficits supposedly felt by single persons. *Pushes toward singlehood* involve deficits felt by married people. *Pulls* are positive factors associated with marriage or being single. The two lists on the left identify the factors favoring marriage, while the two lists on the right identify those favoring singlehood. Not everyone weighs all these factors, but this list illustrates the complexity of the decision to marry.

Adapted from Stein, P. J. (1975). Singlehood: An alternative to marriage. *The Family Coordinator, 24*(4), 500. Copyright © 1975 by the National Council on Family Relations. Reprinted by permission.

tential partners dwindling more rapidly than men of similar age do.

Gender and Mate Selection Preferences

Research reveals that males and females exhibit both similarities and differences in what they look for in a marital partner. Many characteristics, such as emotional stability, dependability, and a pleasant disposition, are rated highly by both sexes (Buss et al., 2001). However, a few crucial differences between men's and women's priorities have been found, and these differences appear to be nearly universal across cultures. As we saw in Chapter 8, women tend to place a higher value than men on potential partners' socioeconomic status, intelligence, ambition, and financial prospects. In contrast, men consistently show more interest than women in potential partners' youthfulness and physical attractiveness (Buss & Kenrick, 1998).

Most theorists explain these gender disparities in terms of evolutionary concepts (Archer, 1996; Buss, 1996). According to evolutionary theories, all organisms, including humans, are motivated to enhance their chances of passing on their genes to subsequent generations. Human females

People tend to marry others who are similar in race, religion, social class, education, and other personal characteristics—a phenomenon called homogamy.

supposedly accomplish this end not by seeking larger or stronger partners, as in the animal kingdom, but by seeking male partners who possess or are likely to acquire more material resources that can be invested in children. Men, on the other hand, are assumed to maximize their reproductive outlook by seeking female partners with good breeding potential. Thus, men are thought to look for youth, attractiveness, good health, and other characteristics presumed to be associated with higher fertility. These evolutionary analyses of gender differences in mating are speculative and there are alternative explanations (see Chapter 8), but they fit with the evidence quite well.

Stimulus-Value-Role Theory

A number of theories have attempted to shed light on the process of mate selection and the development of premarital relationships. We'll focus on one particularly prominent model, Bernard Murstein's (1976, 1986) *stimulus-value-role (S-V-R) theory*. According to Murstein, couples generally proceed through three stages—the stimulus, value, and role stages—as they move toward marriage.

During the first stage, a person's attraction to members of the other gender depends mainly on their *stimulus value*. At this point, the individual focuses on relatively superficial and easily identifiable characteristics of the other person—especially the person's physical attractiveness, social status, occupational success, and reputation. Murstein borrows from *social exchange theory* (see Chapter 8) and argues that progress to the next stage depends on the pair's having relatively similar stimulus value, so as to produce an "even" exchange. The two persons may derive their stimulus value from different characteristics—one from wealth, say, and the other from beauty. However, progress to stage 2 is thought to depend on the couple's subjective perception that they possess similar stimulus value.

If a couple makes it to the second stage, involving *value comparison*, the significance of stimulus variables may be reduced. Further progress now depends on compatibility in values. Typically, the pair will begin to explore each other's attitudes about religion, politics, sex, gender roles, leisure activities, and so forth. If fundamental incompatibilities are uncovered, the relationship may stall at stage 2, or it may come to an end. However, if the two persons discover similarity in values, they are more likely to progress to stage 3.

In the *role stage*, people begin to think about getting married. Hence, they start evaluating whether the other person does a satisfactory job in the role of intimate companion. At this point, individuals focus on the distribution of power in their relationship, the reliability of emotional support, and the quality of their sexual liaison (if they have formed one). Although some people may marry after progressing through only the first two stages, Murstein maintains that marriage is generally delayed until couples are comfortable with role enactments in stage 3.

Murstein's theory has been questioned on the grounds that courtship relationships do not really evolve through distinct stages. Critics argue that individuals in romantic relationships acquire information about each other's stimulus characteristics, values, and roles continuously rather than in discrete stages (Leigh, Holman, & Burr, 1984, 1987). Although there is some merit to this criticism, S-V-R theory provides a useful overview of the factors that influence whether romantic relationships progress toward marriage.

Predictors of Marital Success

Are there any factors that reliably predict marital success? A great deal of research has been devoted to this question. This research has been plagued by one obvious problem: How do you measure "marital success"? Some researchers have simply compared divorced and intact couples in regard to premarital characteristics. The problem with this strategy is that many intact couples obviously do not have happy or successful marriages. Other researchers have used elaborate questionnaires to measure couples' marital satisfaction. Unfortunately, these scales are plagued by a number of problems. Among other things, they appear to measure complacency and lack of conflict more than satisfaction (Fowers et al., 1994). Although measures of marital quality are rather crude, some predictors of marital success have been found. The relations are all statistically weak, but they are intriguing nonetheless.

Family background. The marital adjustment of partners is correlated with the marital satisfaction of their parents. People whose parents were divorced are more likely than others to experience divorce themselves (Amato & DeBoer, 2001). For a number of reasons, marital instability appears to run in families.

Age. The ages of the bride and groom are also related to the likelihood of success. Couples who marry young have higher divorce rates (Bramlett & Mosher, 2001), as Figure 9.4 shows. Surprisingly, couples who marry late also have a higher propensity to divorce. Because they are selected from a smaller pool of potential mates, older newlyweds are more likely to differ in age, religion, social status, and education (Bitter, 1986). Such differences may make marriage more challenging regardless of age.

Length of courtship. Longer periods of courtship are associated with a greater probability of marital success (Cate & Lloyd, 1988). Longer courtships may allow

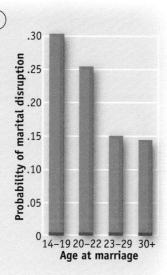

● FIGURE 9.4

Age at marriage and probability of marital disruption in the first five years. Martin and Bumpass (1989) estimated the likelihood of marital disruption (either divorce or separation) within five years for various groups. The data summarized here show that the probability of marital disruption is substantially higher among those who marry young.

couples to evaluate their compatibility more accurately. Alternatively, the correlation between courtship length and marital success may exist because people who are cautious about marriage have attitudes and values that promote marital stability.

Personality. Generally, studies have found that partners' specific personality traits are not very strong pre-

dictors of marital success. That said, there are some traits that show modest correlations with marital adjustment. For example, two negative predictors of marital success are perfectionism (Haring, Hewitt, & Flett, 2003) and insecurity (Crowell, Treboux, & Waters, 2002). In terms of the Big Five personality traits, there is evidence for a negative association between neuroticism and marital adjustment, and some preliminary evidence suggestive of a weak positive association between marital adjustment and both agreeableness and conscientiousness (Bouchard, Lussier, & Sabourin, 1999).

Premarital interaction. As you might expect, the degree to which couples get along well during their courtship is predictive of their marital adjustment. Premarital satisfaction is positively correlated with subsequent marital satisfaction. The quality of premarital communication appears especially crucial. For example, the more that prospective mates are negative, sarcastic, insulting and unsupportive during courtship, the greater the likelihood of marital distress and divorce (Clements, Stanley, & Markman, 2004).

In summary, research shows some thought-provoking correlations between couples' premarital characteristics and marital adjustment. However, most of the correlations are relatively small. Thus, there are no proven, reliable premarital predictors of marital success.

Marital Adjustment Across the Family Life Cycle

LEARNING OBJECTIVES

- *Explain what the family life cycle is.*
- *Describe the factors couples weigh in deciding to have children.*
- *Analyze the dynamics of the transition to parenthood.*
- *Identify common problems that surface as a family's children reach adolescence.*
- *Discuss the transitions that occur in the later stages of the family life cycle.*

"Jennifer has taken a lot of time away from us, the time that we normally spend doing things together or talking. It seems like maybe on a weekend when we would normally like to sleep in, or just have lazy sex, Jennifer wakes up and needs to be fed. . . . But I'm sure that will pass as soon as Jennifer gets a little older. We're just going through a phase."—A new mother quoted in American Couples *(Blumstein & Schwartz, 1983, p. 205)*

"We're just going through a phase." That statement highlights an important point: There are predictable patterns of development for families, just as there are for individuals. These patterns make up the ***family life cycle,*** **an orderly sequence of developmental stages**

that families tend to progress through. The institutions of marriage and family are inevitably intertwined. With the advent of marriage, two persons add a new member to their existing families and create an entirely new family. Typically, this new family forms the core of one's life as an adult.

Sociologists have proposed a number of models to describe family development. Our discussion is organized around a six-stage model of family development outlined by Carter and McGoldrick (1988, 1999). Figure 9.5 (on the next page) provides an overview of their model. It spells out the developmental tasks during each stage of the life cycle for families that eventually have children and remain intact. Although Carter and McGoldrick have

The Family Life Cycle

Family life cycle stage	Emotional process of transition: Key developmental task	Additional changes in family status required to proceed developmentally
1. Between families: The unattached young adult	Accepting parent/offspring separation	a. Differentiation of self in relation to family of origin b. Development of intimate peer relationships c. Establishment of self in work
2. The joining of families through marriage: The newly married couple	Commitment to new system	a. Formation of marital system b. Realignment of relationships with extended families and friends to include spouse
3. The family with young children	Accepting new members into the system	a. Adjusting marital system to make space for child(ren) b. Taking on parenting roles c. Realignment of relationships with extended family to include parenting and grandparenting roles
4. The family with adolescents	Increasing flexibility of family boundaries to include children's independence	a. Shifting of parent-child relationships to permit adolescent to move in and out of system b. Refocus on midlife marital and career issues c. Beginning shift toward concerns for older generation
5. Launching children and moving on	Accepting a multitude of exits from and entries into the family system	a. Renegotiation of marital system as a dyad b. Development of adult-to-adult relationships between grown children and their parents c. Realignment of relationships to include in-laws and grandchildren d. Dealing with disabilities and death of parents (grandparents)
6. The family in later life	Accepting the shifting of generational roles	a. Maintaining own and/or couple functioning and interests in face of physiological decline; exploration of new familial and social role options b. Support for a more central role for middle generation c. Making room in the system for the wisdom and experience of the elderly; supporting the older generation without over-functioning for them d. Dealing with loss of spouse, siblings, and other peers and preparation for own death; life review and integrations

● FIGURE 9.5

Stages of the family life cycle. The family life cycle can be divided into six stages, as shown here (based on Carter & McGoldrick, 1988). The family's key developmental task during each stage is identified in the second column. The third column lists additional developmental tasks at each stage.

described variations on this basic pattern that are associated with remaining childless or going through a divorce, we will focus primarily on the basic pattern in this section. Let's look at some of the key challenges that arise during each stage of the family life cycle.

Between Families: The Unattached Young Adult

As young adults become independent of their parents, they go through a transitional period during which they are "between families" until they form a new family through marriage. What is interesting about this stage is that it is being prolonged by more and more people. The percentage of young adults who are postponing marriage until their late twenties or early thirties has risen dramatically (DeFrain & Olson, 1999). The extension of this stage is probably due to a number of factors, including the availability of new career options for

women, increased educational requirements in the world of work, an increased emphasis on personal autonomy, and more positive attitudes about remaining single.

Joining Together: The Newly Married Couple

The next phase begins when the unattached adult becomes attached. The newly married couple gradually settle into their roles as husband and wife. This phase can be quite troublesome, as the early years of marriage are often marred by numerous problems and disagreements (McGoldrick, 1999). *In general, however, this stage tends to be characterized by great happiness—the proverbial "marital bliss."* Spouses' satisfaction with their relationship tends to be relatively high early in marriage, before the arrival of the first child.

This prechildren phase used to be rather short for most newly married couples, as they quickly went about the business of having their first child. Traditionally, couples simply *assumed* that they would proceed to have children. Remaining childless by choice used to be virtually unthinkable for wives, as having a child was viewed as the ultimate fulfillment of womanhood (Ulrich & Weatherall, 2000). This value system meant that women who remained childless often felt incomplete (Morell, 2000) or were viewed by others as selfish (Letherby & Williams, 1999).

In recent decades, however, ambivalence about the prospect of having children has clearly increased (T. W. Smith, 1999), and the percentage of childless couples has roughly doubled since 1980 (Bulcroft & Teachman, 2004). Thus, more and more couples find themselves struggling to *decide* whether to have children. Often, this decision occurs after numerous postponements, when the couple finally acknowledge that "the right time" is never going to arrive. Intentions about having children are not as stable over time as one might expect. In one study that followed adult participants over a span of six years, about one-quarter of the respondents changed their plans (Heaton, Jacobson, & Holland, 1999). These subjects were almost evenly split between those who planned to remain childless but subsequently decided they wanted to have children and those who intended to have children but subsequently expressed a preference for remaining child-free.

Couples who choose to remain childless cite the great costs incurred in raising children. In addition to the financial burdens, they mention such costs as giving up educational or career opportunities, loss of time for leisure activities and each other, loss of autonomy, worry about the responsibility associated with childrearing, and concerns about overpopulation (Bulcroft & Teachman, 2004; Connidis & McMullin, 1999). In contrast, couples who decide to have children cite many reasons for this choice, including the responsibility to procreate, the joy of watching youngsters mature, the sense of purpose that children create, and the satisfaction associated with emotional nurturance and the challenges of childrearing (Cowan & Cowan, 2000; Goetting, 1986). Clearly, parenthood is associated with both benefits and costs (Nomaguchi & Milkie, 2003). However, most parents report no regret about their choice. The vast majority of parents rate parenthood as a very positive and satisfying experience (Demo, 1992).

Family with Young Children

Although most parents are happy with their decision to have children, the arrival of the first child represents a major transition, and the disruption of routines can be emotionally draining (Bost et al., 2002; Carter, 1999). The transition to parenthood tends to have more impact on mothers than fathers (Nomaguchi & Milkie, 2003). The new mother, already physically exhausted

Although children can be unparalleled sources of joy and satisfaction, the transition to parenthood can be extremely stressful, especially for mothers.

by the birth process, is particularly prone to postpartum distress, and about 10 percent of new moms experience depression (Formichelli, 2001). The transition is more difficult when a wife's expectations regarding how much the father will be involved in child care are not met (Fox et al., 2000). A review of decades of research on parenthood and marital satisfaction found that (1) parents exhibit lower marital satisfaction than comparable nonparents, (2) mothers of infants report the steepest decline in marital satisfaction, and (3) the more children couples have, the lower their marital satisfaction tends to be (Twenge, Campbell, & Foster, 2003).

Crisis during the transition to first parenthood is far from universal, however (Cox et al., 1999). Couples with high levels of affection and commitment prior to the first child's birth are likely to maintain a stable level of satisfaction after the child's birth (Shapiro, Gottman, & Carrere, 2000). The key to making this transition less stressful may be to have *realistic expectations* about parental responsibilities (Belsky & Kelly, 1994). Studies find that stress tends to be greatest in new parents who have overestimated the benefits and underestimated the costs of their new role. Reactions to parenthood may also depend on how a couple's marriage is going. Involvement in and satisfaction with parenting tends to be higher when marital quality is higher (Gavin et al., 2002; Rogers & White, 1998). Although children bring their share of trials and tribulations to a marriage,

WEB LINK 9.1

American Academy of Child and Adolescent Psychiatry (AACAP): Facts for Families
Many new parents may need help coping with emerging problems in their children. The brochures here (in both English and Spanish) cover a wide range of psychological issues and psychiatric conditions.

divorce rates are clearly higher for those who remain childless (Shapiro et al., 2000).

Family with Adolescent Children

Although the adolescent years have long been viewed as a period of great stress and turmoil, research from the past decade has led to the conclusion that adolescence is not as turbulent or difficult as once believed (Steinberg & Levine, 1997). Ironically, though, studies indicate that it is an especially stressful period for the parents, who overwhelmingly rate adolescence as the most difficult stage of parenting (Gecas & Seff, 1990).

As adolescent children seek to establish their own identities, parental influence tends to decline while the influence of peer groups tends to increase. Parents tend to retain more influence than peers over important matters, such as educational goals and career plans, but peers gradually gain more influence over less critical matters, such as style of dress and recreational plans (Gecas & Seff, 1990). Thus, conflicts between adolescent children and their parents tend to involve everyday matters such as chores and dress more than substantive issues such as sex and drugs (Barber, 1994). Conflict is particularly likely to surface between adolescents (of both sexes) and their mothers. Adolescents tend to exhibit better adjustment in families in which they are encouraged to participate in decision making but parents ultimately maintain control (Preto, 1999). Parents apparently learn from their experience in dealing with an adolescent child, as they report less conflict with their second adolescent child than their first (Whiteman, McHale, & Crouter, 2003).

In addition to worrying about their adolescent children, middle-aged couples often worry about the care of their parents. Adults caught between these conflicting responsibilities have been called the *sandwich generation*. Thanks to increased longevity and decreased family size, today's average married couple has more parents than children, and an increasing number of adults provide care to their aging parents (Starrels et al., 1997). Females tend to assume most of the responsibility for elderly relatives, and it is estimated that in the future women can expect to spend more years caring for their aging parents than for their dependent children (Bromley & Blieszner, 1997). Many theorists are

concerned that these multigenerational caregiving responsibilities may prove burdensome. Supporting this concern, one study found that the number of hours spent caring for an aging parent was correlated with wives' psychological distress (Voydanoff & Donnelly, 1999). Another study found that becoming a caregiver for a parent was associated with declines in happiness, autonomy, and personal growth among women (Marks, Lambert, & Choi, 2002).

Launching Children into the Adult World

When children begin to reach their twenties, the family has to adapt to a multitude of exits and entries, as children leave and return, sometimes with their own spouses. This period, during which children normally progress from dependence to independence, brings a host of transitions. In many instances, conflict subsides and parent-child relations become closer and more supportive (Aquilino, 1997).

One might argue that launching children into the adult world tends to be a lengthier and more difficult process today than it once was (Furstenberg, 2001). The percentage of young adults who live with their parents has climbed in recent decades. The rapidly rising cost of a college education and the shrinking job market have probably led many young adults to linger in their parents' homes. Moreover, crises such as separation, divorce, job loss, and pregnancy out of wedlock force many children who have ventured out on their own to return to their parents. Young adults who return home after living independently have been characterized as the *boomerang generation*. Children from intact, two-parent homes are more likely to return than those with stepparents (Goldscheider & Goldscheider, 1998). Interestingly, young adults have more negative attitudes about returning home than their parents do (Veevers, Gee, & Wister, 1996). The repercussions of these new trends are the subject of current research. Preliminary data suggest that living with one's parents during adulthood has a modest negative impact on parent-child relations (White & Rogers, 1997). Conflicts are particularly likely when returning children have been unsuccessful in moving into autonomous adult roles (Treas & Lawton, 1999).

When parents do manage to get all their children launched into the adult world, they find themselves faced with an "empty nest." This period was formerly thought to be a difficult transition for many parents, especially mothers who were familiar only with the maternal role. In recent decades, however, more women have experience with other roles outside the home and look forward to their "liberation" from childrearing responsibilities. Most parents adjust effectively to the empty nest transition and are more likely to have problems if their children *return* to the once-empty nest

WEB LINK 9.2

The Whole Family Center
This lively site features reasonable advice and useful links for the issues that come up in families, such as rearing children and coping with family crises. A team of psychologists, social workers, educators, and marriage and family therapists, among others, serve as the experts at the center.

(Blacker, 1999). Hence, researchers have found that the empty nest is associated with improved mood and well-being for most women (Dennerstein, Dudley, & Guthrie, 2002). Middle-aged parents who have launched their children into the adult world report more enjoyment of life and higher marital satisfaction than similar-aged parents who still have children at home (White & Edwards, 1990).

The Family in Later Life

Marital satisfaction tends to climb in the postparental period as couples find they have more time to devote attention to each other (Brubaker, 1990). Whether this

trend is the result of reduced parental responsibilities, reduced work responsibilities, or other considerations remains unclear (Lee, 1988). In any case, many couples take advantage of their newfound freedom, traveling or developing new leisure interests. For many people this can be a period of increased intimacy. However, spouses do have to adapt to spending more time with each other and often need to renegotiate role expectations (Walsh, 1999). Of course, age-related considerations that are independent of the relationship, such as the increased likelihood of physical illness, can make the later years stressful. In general, however, the trend is for couples to report fairly high satisfaction until one of the spouses dies.

Vulnerable Areas in Marital Adjustment

LEARNING OBJECTIVES

- Discuss how gaps in role expectations may affect marital adjustment.
- Summarize how spouses' work affects their marital satisfaction and their children.
- Describe how financial issues are related to marital adjustment.
- Summarize evidence on the relationship between communication quality and marital adjustment.

"When we first got married, the first six months of conflicts were all about getting him to take account of what I had planned for him at home. . . . He would come waltzing in an hour and a half late for dinner, or cancel an evening with friends, because he had to close a deal. . . . We would argue and argue . . . not because I didn't want him to make a living . . . but because I thought he had to be more considerate."—A wife quoted in American Couples *(Blumstein & Schwartz, 1983, p. 174)*

An unavoidable reality of marriage is that couples must confront a legion of problems together. During courtship, couples tend to focus on pleasurable activities. But once couples are married, they deal with a variety

of problems, such as arriving at acceptable role compromises, paying bills, and raising a family. There is no such thing as a problem-free marriage. Successful marriages depend on couples' ability to handle their problems. In this section we will analyze the major kinds of difficulties that are likely to emerge. We can't offer simple solutions for these problems. However, in navigating your way through life, it helps to know where you're likely to encounter the most perilous reefs.

Gaps in Role Expectations

When a couple marry, they assume new roles—those of husband and wife. Each role comes with certain expectations that the partners hold about how wives and husbands should behave. These expectations may vary greatly from one person to another. Gaps between partners in their role expectations appear to have a negative effect on couples' marital satisfaction (Lye & Biblarz, 1993). Unfortunately, substantial differences in role expectations seem particularly likely in this era of transition in gender roles.

The traditional role expectations for husbands and wives used to be fairly clear. A husband was supposed to act as the principal breadwinner, make the important decisions, and take care of certain household chores, such as car or yard maintenance. A wife was supposed to raise the children, cook, clean, and follow the leadership of her husband. Spouses had different spheres of influence. The working world was the domain of the husband, the home the domain of the wife. In recent decades, however, the women's movement and other forces of social change have led to new expectations about marital roles. Thus, modern couples need to negotiate and renegotiate role responsibilities throughout the family life cycle (Zvonkovic et al., 1996).

Women may be especially vulnerable to ambivalence about shifting marital roles. More and more women are aspiring to demanding careers. Yet research shows that husbands' careers continue to take priority over their wives' vocational ambitions (Haas, 1999). It is wives who are expected to interrupt their career to raise young children, stay home when children are sick, and abandon their jobs when husbands' careers require relocation. Moreover, even when both spouses are employed, many husbands maintain traditional role expectations about housework, child care, and decision making.

Men's contribution to housework has increased noticeably since the 1960s, as you can see in Figure 9.6 (Bianchi et al., 2000). However, studies indicate that wives are still doing the bulk of the household chores in America, even when they work outside the home (Coltrane, 2001). For example, the data show that wives take responsibility for about 65 percent of total house-

● FIGURE 9.6

Housework trends since the 1960s. As these data show, the housework gap between husbands and wives has narrowed since the 1960s. Married men have more than doubled their housework, but it is the large reduction in wives' housework that has really shrunk the housework gap. (Data from Bianchi et al., 2000)

work (not including child care), whereas husbands account for the remaining 35 percent (see Figure 9.7). Moreover, wives still account for 78 percent of the essential "core housework" such as cooking, cleaning, and laundry, while men continue to handle more discretionary, traditional "male chores," such as yard or auto maintenance (Bianchi et al., 2000).

Although married women perform almost two-thirds of all housework, only about one-third of wives characterize their division of labor as unfair, because most women don't expect a 50-50 split (Coltrane, 2001). Although many couples accept these gender-driven expectations, the one-third of wives who perceive their division of labor as unfair constitute a sizable population of women for whom housework is a source of discontent. Research shows that women are more likely to

SALLY FORTH Reprinted with special permission of King Features Syndicate.

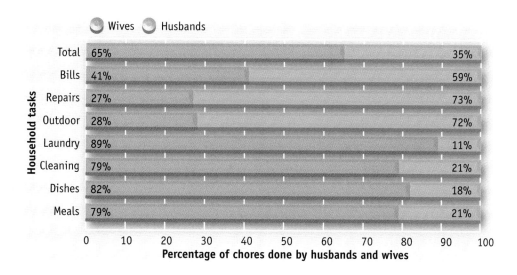

Wives   Husbands

Household tasks		
Total	65%	35%
Bills	41%	59%
Repairs	27%	73%
Outdoor	28%	72%
Laundry	89%	11%
Cleaning	79%	21%
Dishes	82%	18%
Meals	79%	21%

0   10   20   30   40   50   60   70   80   90   100
Percentage of chores done by husbands and wives

● FIGURE 9.7

Who does the housework? This chart breaks down the proportion of housework done by husbands and wives for specific tasks. The data show that wives continue to do a highly disproportionate share of most household tasks, especially the "core housework" tasks (cooking, cleaning, laundry) that are hard to ignore. Note also, that in spite of great changes in modern life, the division of labor in the household still largely meshes with traditional gender roles. (Data from Bianchi et al., 2000)

perceive their share of housework as unfair when they have nontraditional attitudes about gender roles and when they work outside the home (Coltrane, 2001). As you might expect, wives who perceive their housework burden to be unfair tend to report lower levels of marital satisfaction (Haas, 1999).

In light of this reality, it is imperative that couples discuss role expectations in depth before marriage. If they discover that their views are divergent, they need to take the potential for problems seriously. Many people casually dismiss gender-role disagreements, thinking they can "straighten out" their partner later on. But assumptions about marital roles, whether traditional or not, may be deeply held and not easily changed.

Work and Career Issues

The possible interactions between one's occupation and one's marriage are numerous and complex. Individuals' job satisfaction and involvement can affect their own marital satisfaction, their partner's marital satisfaction, and their children's development.

Work and Marital Adjustment

A host of studies have investigated the relationship between spouses' job satisfaction and their marital adjustment. We could speculate that these two variables might be either positively or negatively related. On the one hand, if a spouse is highly committed to a satisfying career, he or she may have less time and energy to devote

to marriage and family. On the other hand, the frustration and stress of an unsatisfying job might spill over to contaminate one's marriage.

The research on this question suggests that both scenarios are realistic possibilities. Both husbands and wives struggle to balance the demands of work and family, and both report that work commitments often interfere with family responsibilities (Hochschild, 1997; Milkie & Peltola, 1999). When pressures increase at work, husbands and wives report more role conflicts and often feel overwhelmed by their multiple commitments (Crouter et al., 1999). Furthermore, studies find that spouses' stress at work can have a substantial negative effect on their marital and family interactions (Perry-Jenkins, Repetti, & Crouter, 2001). For example, after highly stressful days at work, spouses tend to withdraw from family interactions (Crouter & Bumpus, 2001). The stress associated with working night shifts

WEB LINK 9.3

National Council on Family Relations (NCFR): Family Tips
The National Council on Family Relations has developed a subpage to reach out to families with practical advice from a cadre of experts on all sorts of family issues. Information is available on a host of topics, such as discussing terrorism with children, school violence, drugs, anger management, and so forth.

appears to be especially tough on spouses and families
(Presser, 2000).

Many studies have compared the marital adjustment of male-breadwinner versus dual-career couples. The interest in this comparison arises from traditional views that regard men's *lack* of employment, but
women's *employment*, as departures from the norm.
Typically, these studies simply categorize women as
working or nonworking and evaluate couples' marital
satisfaction. Most of these studies find little in the way
of consistent differences in the marital adjustment of
male-breadwinner versus dual-career couples (Haas,
1999; Perry-Jenkins & Turner, 2004). Although dual-
career couples do face special problems in negotiating
career priorities, child-care arrangements, and other
practical matters, their marriage need not be negatively
affected.

Although the difficulties involved in juggling work
and family roles can be challenging, some theorists have
argued that in the long run multiple roles are beneficial to both men and women. Barnett and Hyde (2001)
assert that negative effects of stress in one role can be
buffered by success and satisfaction in another role. They
also note that multiple roles can increase sources of social support and opportunities to experience success.
Moreover, when both parents work outside the home,
income tends to be greater and the spouses often find
they have more in common.

Parents' Work and Children's Development

Another issue of concern has been the potential impact
of parents' employment on their children. Virtually all
of the research in this area has focused on the effects of
mothers' employment outside the home. What does the
research on maternal employment show? Although
most Americans seem to believe that maternal employment is detrimental to children's development, the vast
majority of empirical studies have found little evidence
that a mother's working is harmful to her children
(Bianchi, 2000; Haas, 1999; Perry-Jenkins et al., 2001).
For instance, studies generally have not found a link
between mothers' employment status and the quality
of infant-mother emotional attachment (Etaugh, 1993;
NICHD Early Child Care Research Network, 1997).
Some studies have found that maternal employment
in the first year after a child's birth may have negative
effects on youngster's cognitive skills during early and
middle childhood (Han, Waldfogel, & Brooks-Gunn,
2001), but these effects are modest and inconsistent
across ethnic groups (Han et al., 2001; Harvey, 1999).

Financial Difficulties

How do couples' financial resources affect marital adjustment and family functioning? Neither financial
stability nor wealth can ensure marital satisfaction.
However, poverty can produce daunting challenges and
serious problems for married couples (Rank, 2004).
Without money, families live in constant dread of financial drains such as illness, layoffs, or broken appliances.
Husbands tend to view themselves as poor providers
and become hostile and irritable. Their hostility can
undermine the warm, supportive exchanges that help
sustain relationships. This problem is sometimes aggravated by disappointed wives who criticize their husbands. Spontaneity in communication may be impaired
by an understandable reluctance to talk about financial concerns.

Thus, it is not surprising that serious financial worries among couples are associated with increased hostility in husbands, increased depression in wives, and
lower marital happiness in both husbands and wives

(White & Rogers, 2001). Similarly, husbands' job insecurity is predictive of wives' reports of marital conflict and their thoughts of divorce (Fox & Chancey, 1998). Moreover, evidence consistently demonstrates that the risk of separation and divorce increases as husbands' income declines (Ono, 1998; South & Lloyd, 1995). The effects of low income on children are even more distressing. Children brought up in poverty exhibit poorer physical health, reduced mental health, lower academic performance, and increased delinquency in comparison to other children (Seccombe, 2001).

Even when financial resources are plentiful, money can be a source of marital strain. Quarrels about how to spend money are common and potentially damaging at all income levels. Pittman and Lloyd (1988), for instance, found that perceived financial stress (regardless of a family's actual income) was associated with decreased marital satisfaction. Another study examined how happily married couples handled their money in comparison to couples that eventually divorced (Schaninger & Buss, 1986). In comparison to the divorced couples, the happy couples engaged in more joint decision making on finances. Thus, the best way to avoid troublesome battles over money is probably to engage in extensive planning of expenditures together.

Inadequate Communication

Effective communication is crucial to the success of a marriage. Marital conflict is associated with a host of negative outcomes for partners and their family members, including increased depression, alcoholism, physical health problems, domestic violence, and divorce (Fincham, 2003). The damaging role that poor communication can play in marital relations was clearly demonstrated in a study of couples getting a divorce (Cleek & Pearson, 1985). In this study, communication difficulties were the most frequently cited problem among both husbands and wives (see Figure 9.8). Spouses' strategies for resolving conflicts may be particularly crucial to marital satisfaction (Crohan, 1992). Many partners respond to conflict by withdrawing and refusing to communicate—a pattern associated with deteriorating marital satisfaction over time (Heavey, Christensen, & Malamuth, 1995; Roberts, 2000).

A number of studies have compared communication patterns in happy and unhappy marriages. This research indicates that unhappily married spouses (1) find it difficult to convey positive messages, (2) misunderstand each other more often, (3) are less likely to recognize that they have been misunderstood, (4) use more frequent, and more intense, negative messages, and (5) often differ in the amount of self-disclosure they prefer in the relationship (Noller & Fitzpatrick, 1990; Noller & Gallois, 1988; Sher & Baucom, 1993). Above all else, unhappy couples tend to get caught up in escalating cycles of conflict from which they cannot escape, whereas happy couples find ways to exit the cycles (Fincham, 2003).

The importance of marital communication was underscored in a widely cited study by John Gottman and his colleagues that attempted to predict the likelihood of divorce in a sample of 52 married couples (Buehlman, Gottman, & Katz, 1992). Each couple

Photo by Sharon M. Fentiman

John Gottman

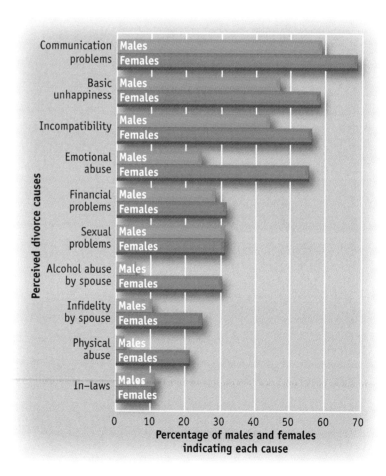

● FIGURE 9.8

Causes of divorce. When Cleek and Pearson (1985) asked divorcing couples about their perceptions regarding the causes of their divorce, both men and women cited communication difficulties more than any other cause.

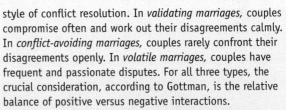

CATHY © Cathy Guisewite. Reprinted with permission of UNIVERSAL PRESS SYNDICATE. All rights reserved.

RECOMMENDED READING

Why Marriages Succeed or Fail . . . and How You Can Make Yours Last
by John Gottman (with Nan Silver)
(Simon & Schuster, 1994)

This book is about communication in intimate relationships—a subject that Gottman has studied intensively for over 20 years. A psychology professor at the University of Washington, Gottman is justifiably famous for his landmark research on the prediction of divorce. He has demonstrated that he can predict which couples will divorce with remarkable accuracy, based on careful examination of the couples' communication patterns. According to Gottman, the marriages that last are not those that appear to be free of conflict but those in which couples are able to resolve the conflicts that inevitably arise in intimate relationships. Gottman categorizes couples into three types based on their

style of conflict resolution. In *validating marriages,* couples compromise often and work out their disagreements calmly. In *conflict-avoiding marriages,* couples rarely confront their disagreements openly. In *volatile marriages,* couples have frequent and passionate disputes. For all three types, the crucial consideration, according to Gottman, is the relative balance of positive versus negative interactions.

In this practical, readable analysis of marital communication, the author provides plenty of case histories to make ideas come alive. The book also includes many thought provoking scales that readers can take to evaluate their own communication styles and tendencies. For example, there are scales to measure stonewalling, defensiveness, and the other communication tendencies Gottman characterizes as the "Four Horsemen of the Apocalypse." *Why Marriages Succeed or Fail* is an outstanding book loaded with exercises, quizzes, and tips that should help readers improve their marital communication. Gottman has written two other highly practical books on marriage that are worth consulting: *The Seven Principles for Making Marriage Work* (1999) and a more elaborate and detailed analysis titled *The Relationship Cure* (2001).

provided an oral history of their relationship and a 15-minute sample of their interaction style, during which they discussed two problem areas in their marriage. The investigators rated the spouses on a variety of factors that mostly reflected the subjects' ways of relating to each other. Based on these ratings, they were able to predict which couples would divorce within three years with 94 percent accuracy! Follow-up research has demonstrated that marital adjustment depends not on whether there is conflict (conflict is virtually inevitable), but rather on how conflict is handled when it occurs (Driver et al., 2003).

John Gottman, who is probably the world's foremost authority on marital communication, asserts that conflict and anger are normal in marital interactions and that they are not, in and of themselves, predictive of marital dissolution. Instead, Gottman (1994) identifies four other communication patterns, which he calls the "Four Horsemen of the Apocalypse," that are risk factors for divorce: contempt, criticism, defensiveness, and stonewalling. *Contempt* involves communicating

insulting feelings that one's spouse is inferior. *Criticism* involves constantly expressing negative evaluations of one's partner. *Defensiveness* involves responding to contempt and criticism with obstructive communication that escalates marital conflict. *Stonewalling* involves refusing to listen to one's partner, especially the partner's complaints. Gottman eventually added a fifth troublesome communication pattern, *belligerence,* which involves provocative, combative challenges to partners' power and authority (Gottman et al., 1998).

Given the importance of good communication, many approaches to marital therapy emphasize the development of better communication skills in partners (Gottman et al., 2002). However, poor marital communication is not simply a result of communication *skills* (Burleson & Denton, 1997). In many instances, spouses may have adequate or even excellent communication ability but be *unwilling* to make communication a priority, to avoid unnecessary criticism, to share in decision making, and so forth.

Divorce

LEARNING OBJECTIVES

- *Describe the evidence on changing divorce rates.*
- *Discuss how men and women tend to adjust to divorce.*

- *Analyze the evidence on the effects of divorce on children.*
- *Summarize data on the frequency and success of remarriage and its impact on children.*

"In the ten years that we were married I went from twenty-four to thirty-four and they were a very significant ten years. I started a career, started to succeed, bought my first house, had a child, you know, very significant years. And then all of a sudden, every goddamn thing, I'm back to zero. I have no house. I don't have a child. I don't have a wife. I don't have the same family. My economic position has been shattered. And nothing recoverable. All these goals which I had struggled for, every goddamn one of them, is gone."—A recently divorced man quoted in Marital Separation *(Weiss, 1975, p. 75)*

The dissolution of a marriage tends to be a bone-jarring event for most people, as this bitter quote illustrates. Any of the problems discussed in the previous section might lead a couple to consider divorce. However, people appear to vary in their threshold for divorce, just as they do in their threshold for marriage. Some couples will tolerate a great deal of disappointment and bickering without seriously considering divorce. Other couples are ready to call their attorney as soon as it becomes apparent that their expectations for marital bliss were somewhat unrealistic. Typically, however, divorce is the culmination of a gradual disintegration of the relationship brought about by an accumulation of interrelated

problems, which often date back to the beginning of couples' relationships (Huston, Niehuis, & Smith, 2001).

Increasing Rate of Divorce

Although relatively accurate statistics are available on divorce rates, it is still difficult to estimate the percentage of marriages that end in divorce. The usually cited ratio of marriages in a year to divorces in the same year is highly misleading. It is more informative to follow people married in a particular year over a period of time, but this type of research indicates a particular cohort's divorce rate 15–20 years after the marriages, so these findings may not be accurate for people currently entering into marriage. In any case, it is clear that divorce rates increased dramatically between the 1950s and 1980s, but they appear to have stabilized and even declined slightly since the 1980s (Amato et al., 2003). When divorce rates were at their peak, the most widely cited estimates of future divorce risk were around 50 percent (Bumpass, Raley, & Sweet, 1995). However, the modest reductions in divorce rates in recent years appear to have lowered the risk of divorce to 40–45 percent for today's couples (Bramlett & Mosher, 2001; Whitehead & Popenoe, 2001). The decline in divorce rates is encouraging, but the chances of marital dissolution remain quite high. Although most people realize that divorce rates are high, they have a curious tendency to underestimate the likelihood that they will personally experience a divorce. On the average, people peg their probability of divorce at about 10–11 percent, which is far below the actual probability for the population as a whole (Fowers et al., 2001).

Divorce rates are higher among blacks than whites or Hispanics, among lower-income couples, among couples who do not have children, among people who marry at a relatively young age, and among those whose parents divorced (Faust & McKibben, 1999; Kurdek, 1993). As Figure 9.9 shows, the vast majority of divorces occur during the first decade of a marriage (Hiedemann, Suhomlinova, & O'Rand, 1998). What types of marital problems are predictive of divorce? The most frequently cited problems include infidelity, jealousy, growing apart, foolish spending behavior, drinking and drug problems, and communication difficulties (not talking; being moody, critical, and easy to anger) (Amato & Previti, 2003; Amato & Rogers, 1997).

A wide variety of social trends have probably contributed to increasing divorce rates (Amato et al., 2003; Giddens, 2001; Sabatelli & Ripoll, 2004). The stigma attached to divorce has gradually eroded. Many religious denominations are becoming more tolerant of divorce, and marriage has thus lost some of its sacred quality. The declining fertility rate and the consequent smaller families probably make divorce a more viable possibil-

The high divorce rate has led to some novel ways of dealing with its worrisome legal aspects. Attorney Robert Nordyke discovered that the drive-up window at his new office—a former savings and loan branch in Salem, Oregon—was perfect for serving legal papers on his clients' spouses.

ity. The entry of more women into the workforce has made many wives less financially dependent on the continuation of their marriage. New attitudes emphasizing individual fulfillment seem to have counterbalanced older attitudes that encouraged dissatisfied spouses to suffer in silence. Reflecting all these trends, the legal barriers to divorce have also diminished.

Deciding on a Divorce

Divorces are often postponed repeatedly, and they are rarely executed without a great deal of agonizing forethought (Ahrons, 1999). Indecision is common, as roughly two out of five divorce petitions are eventually withdrawn (Donovan & Jackson, 1990). The decision to divorce is usually the outcome of a long series of smaller decisions that may take years to unfold, so divorce should be viewed as a process rather than a discrete event (Morrison & Cherlin, 1995). Wives' judgments about the likelihood of their marriages ending in divorce tend to be more accurate than husbands' judgments (South, Bose, & Trent, 2004). This finding may be related to

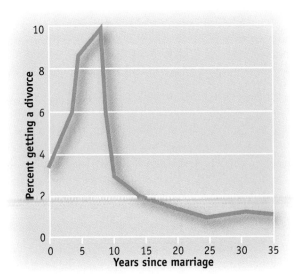

● **FIGURE 9.9**

Divorce rate as a function of years married. This graph shows the distribution of divorces in relation to how long couples have been married. As you can see, the vast majority of divorces occur in the early years, with divorce rates peaking between the fifth and tenth years of marriage. (Data from National Center for Health Statistics)

WEB LINK 9.4

Divorce Central
Divorce Central is one of a number of excellent sites that provide information and advice on legal, emotional, and financial issues for individuals contemplating or going through a divorce. Annotated links to the other outstanding divorce-related sites can also be found here.

Should the Government Promote Marriage?

As noted in the main body of the chapter, research evidence suggests that marriage is good for one's health and happiness (Waite & Gallagher, 2000). And studies show that children whose parents divorce exhibit an increased risk for quite a variety of negative outcomes (Amato, 2003). These findings suggest that both adults and children are most likely to flourish in stable, loving families, but social trends are clearly moving in just the opposite direction. Marriage rates are down and divorce rates are up, cohabitation rates are skyrocketing, and more and more children are being born out of wedlock (Bianchi & Casper, 2000). Concerns about these trends have led some religious leaders and public officials to argue that government entities ought to do more to promote a culture of marriage (Hackstaff, 1999; Popenoe, 1999; Wagner, 1998). At first glance, this sounds like a sensible, enlightened policy that everyone ought to be able to agree on, but in reality this issue turns out to be surprisingly complex and controversial.

The pro-marriage movement has been gathering momentum since the early 1990s. The advocates of this movement argue that people today are overly focused on their personal happiness and are unwilling to endure hardship and show loyalty when the going gets rough in a marriage (Fowers, 2000). They also assert that the emergence of no-fault divorce laws since the 1970s has made it too easy to get a divorce. Hence, the pro-marriage advocates campaign for policies that would make divorces more difficult to obtain. For example, several states have enacted *covenant marriage* laws. Couples who choose to enter into a covenant marriage agree to complete premarital education programs and pledge to divorce only in response to severe problems (such as spouse abuse or a lengthy prison term), and only after seeking extensive marriage counseling (Hawkins et al., 2002). Other advocated reforms have included waiting periods for divorces of up to five years and more demanding legal proceedings for divorces involving children. More proactive proposals have included mandating high school education programs touting the value of marriage, providing government subsidies for marriage counseling, and requiring couples to complete premarital relationship skills training (Amato, 2004b). Some pro-marriage proponents have also suggested giving married couples preferential treatment (over single, divorced, and cohabiting individuals) in regard to government benefits, such as welfare payments and housing subsidies (Murray, 2001).

Critics of the pro-marriage movement raise a variety of objections. First, they question the meaning of the research findings that serve as the rationale for this movement. Although they acknowledge that married people are somewhat healthier and happier than nonmarried adults, they point out that the data are correlational and that there is no solid evidence that being married *causes* this difference (Huston & Melz, 2004). They argue that causation probably runs the other way—that being healthy and happy causes people to have better marital opportunities and greater marital success. In a similar vein, they admit that experiencing divorce can be harmful for children but suggest that remaining in a home filled with bitter discord can be just as harmful (Booth & Amato, 2001). Second, the critics express concern that restricting access to divorce could leave some spouses and children stranded in homes riddled with alcoholism, drug abuse, or domestic violence (Gelles, 1996). Third, critics point out that making divorces harder to get just may not be a realistic option in today's society (Coontz, 1997). Although a majority of adults agree—in the abstract—that divorce laws should be tougher, they do not want *their own* personal freedom in this area to be impeded. Consistent with this finding, only 3 percent of couples have chosen covenant marriage in the state (Louisiana) that first offered this option (Licata, 2002). If divorces are made harder to get, critics argue that couples will simply revert back to the fraudulent practices of the past, when attorneys would coach spouses on how to submit fabricated testimony of adultery or mental cruelty to meet legal standards for a divorce.

Fourth, critics note that premarital relationship skills training and similar programs may have some genuine value for couples, but no research has been conducted on their efficacy in reducing the likelihood of divorce (Belluck, 2000). Thus, they argue that it is premature to *require* such training. Fifth, critics argue that if the government wants to promote marital success, it should focus more on making it *easier to stay married,* as opposed to harder to get a divorce. In particular, they note that divorce rates tend to be high in lower social classes where families could be better strengthened by improving social services (such as child care and job training). Finally, critics maintain that the pro-marriage movement treats the traditional nuclear family as the only legitimate family form and that pro-marriage programs will unfairly discriminate against single parents, divorced persons, cohabiting couples, and gay and lesbian partners (Coltrane, 2001; Scanzoni, 2004).

the fact that wives initiate two-thirds of divorce actions (Hetherington, 2003).

It is difficult to generalize about the relative merits of divorce as opposed to remaining in an unsatisfactory marriage. Extensive research clearly shows that people who are currently divorced suffer a higher incidence of both physical and psychological maladies and are less happy than those who are currently married (Amato, 2001; Waite & Gallagher, 2000). Furthermore, the process of getting divorced usually is extremely stressful for both spouses. We might guess that as divorce becomes more commonplace, it should also become less traumatic, but available evidence does not support this supposition (Kitson, 1992). As painful as marital dissolution may be, remaining in an unhappy marriage is also potentially detrimental. Research has shown that in comparison to divorced individuals, unhappily married people tend to show even poorer physical and emotional health (Wickrama et al., 1997).

Adjusting to Divorce

Objectively speaking, divorce appears to be more difficult and disruptive for women than for men (Clarke-Stewart & Bailey, 1989). Women are more likely to assume the responsibility of raising the children, whereas men tend to reduce their contact with their children. Within the first year after divorce, half of fathers basically lose contact with their kids (Carter & McGoldrick, 1999). Another key consideration is that divorced women are less likely than their ex-husbands to have adequate income or a satisfying job (Smock, Manning, & Gupta, 1999). For example, one well-designed study found that custodial mothers experienced a 36 percent decrease in their standard of living, whereas noncustodial fathers experienced a 28 percent *increase* (Bianchi, Subaiya, &

Kahn, 1999). The economic consequences of divorce clearly are more severe for women than for men, but in this era of two-income families, many men also experience a noticeable decline in their standard of living after going through a divorce (McManus & DiPrete, 2001).

Although divorce appears to impose greater stress on women than men, researchers do *not* find consistent gender differences in postdivorce adjustment (Amato, 2001). In the aggregate, the magnitude of the negative effects of divorce on individuals' psychological and physical well-being seems to be pretty similar for husbands and wives. Among both men and women, high preoccupation with one's ex-spouse is associated with poorer adjustment to divorce (Masheter, 1997). Factors associated with favorable postdivorce adjustment include having higher income, getting remarried, having more positive attitudes about divorce, and being the partner who initiated the divorce (Wang & Amato, 2000).

Effects of Divorce on Children

Roughly half of all divorces involve children. When couples have children, decisions about divorce must take into account the potential impact on their offspring. Widely publicized research by Judith Wallerstein and colleagues has painted a rather bleak picture of how divorce affects youngsters (Wallerstein & Kelly, 1980; Wallerstein & Blakeslee, 1989; Wallerstein, Lewis, & Blakeslee, 2000). This research has followed a sample of 60 divorced couples and their 131 children since 1971. At the 10-year followup, almost half of the participants were characterized as "worried, underachieving, self-deprecating, and sometimes angry young men and women" (Wallerstein & Blakeslee, 1989, p. 299). Even *25 years* after their parents' divorce, a majority of subjects were viewed as troubled adults who found it difficult to maintain stable and satisfying intimate relationships. The enduring, long-term effects of divorce reported by Wallerstein were particularly disturbing and generated great interest from the media, resulting in an abundance of TV interviews, magazine articles, and so forth.

Although the lengthy follow-up in Wallerstein's research is commendable, critics point out that her study suffers from a variety of flaws (Amato, 2003; Cherlin, 1999; Kelly & Emery, 2003). It was based on a small sample of children from a wealthy area in California that clearly was not representative of the population at large. There was no comparison group and conclusions were based on impressions from clinical interviews in which it is easy for interviewers to see what they want to see. Coltrane and Adams (2003) also note that Wallerstein is part of a conservative political-religious movement that favors traditional family arrangements and reforms that would make divorces more difficult to obtain. Hence, her conclusions may be shaped in part by a political agenda.

"That's right, Phil. A separation will mean—among other things—watching your own cholesterol."

Are Wallerstein's findings consistent with other research? Yes and no. The results of another long-running study by E. Mavis Hetherington (1993, 1999, 2003), which used a larger and more representative sample, a control group, and conventional statistical comparisons, suggest that Wallerstein's conclusions are unduly pessimistic. According to Hetherington, divorce

Courtesy, E. Mavis Hetherington

E. Mavis
Hetherington

can be traumatic for children, but a substantial majority adjust reasonably well after two to three years, and only about 25 percent show serious psychological or emotional problems in adulthood (versus 10 percent in the control group). Another complicated issue in assessing the effects of divorce is the choice of whom should be used as a baseline for comparison. One can argue that children of divorce should be compared to children from intact homes characterized by persistent marital discord, a group that also shows elevated rates of many types of adjustment problems (Morrison & Coiro, 1999; Papp, Cummings, & Schermerhorn, 2004).

Although Wallerstein's conclusions appear overly negative, *they differ from the results of other research only in degree* (Amato, 2003). After a divorce, many children exhibit depression, anxiety, nightmares, dependency, aggression, withdrawal, distractibility, lowered academic performance, reduced physical health, precocious sexual behavior and substance abuse (Hines, 1997; Kelly & Emery, 2003; Knox, 2000). Although these problems dissipate in most children after a few years, divorce can have a lasting impact that extends into adulthood. Experiencing divorce during childhood is a risk factor for many subsequent problems in one's adult years, including maladjustment, marital instability, and reduced occupational attainments (Amato, 1999). Children have more adjustment problems when their parents have a history of particularly bitter, acrimonious conflict (Amato, 2001).

So what can we conclude about the effects of divorce on children? *Overall, the weight of evidence suggests that divorce tends to have harmful effects on many children but can have beneficial effects for children if their parents' relationship is dominated by conflict* (Booth & Amato, 2001). However, the latter assertion is based on the assumption that the parents' divorce brings their bickering to an end. Unfortunately, the conflicts between divorcing spouses often continue for many years after they part ways (Hopper, 2001). For example, Goldberg (1985) describes a case history in which a man's ex-wife was still calling him 10 to 15 times a day to disturb and berate him three years after their divorce. It is also reasonable to conclude that *divorces have highly varied effects on children that depend on a complex constel-*

lation of interacting factors. As Furstenberg and Kiernan (2001) put it, "Many researchers have become increasingly wary about public discussions of divorce that treat it as an undifferentiated and uniform occurrence resulting in similar outcomes for all children" (p. 446).

Remarriage

Evidence that adequate courtship opportunities exist for the divorced is provided by the statistics on remarriage: Roughly three-quarters of divorced people eventually remarry (Bramlett & Mosher, 2001). The mean length of time between divorce and remarriage is a little less than 4 years (Coleman, Ganong, & Fine, 2001).

How successful are second marriages? The answer depends on your standard of comparison. Divorce rates *are* higher for second than for first marriages (Mason, 1998). However, this statistic may simply indicate that this group of people see divorce as a reasonable alternative to an unsatisfactory marriage. Nonetheless, studies of marital adjustment suggest that second marriages are slightly less successful than first marriages (Brown & Booth, 1996). Of course, if you consider that in this pool of people *all* the first marriages ran into serious trouble, then the second marriages look rather good by comparison.

Another major issue related to remarriage is its effect on children. Adaptation to remarriage can be difficult for children. Evidence suggests that on the average, interaction in stepfamilies appears to be somewhat less cohesive and warm than interaction in first-marriage families, and stepparent-stepchild relations tend to be more negative and distant than parent-child relations in first marriages (Pasley & Moorefield, 2004). Taken as a whole, the evidence suggests that children in stepfamilies are a little less well adjusted than children in first marriages and are roughly similar in adjustment to children in single-parent homes (Coleman, Ganong,

© Michelle D. Bridewell/PhotoEdit

Although remarried couples tend to have more open communication, the evidence suggests that second marriages are slightly less successful than first marriages, on the average.

& Fine, 2001). However, the differences between step-families and other types of families in the adjustment of their children tend to be modest. For example, Figure 9.10 highlights some representative results from one large-scale study (Acock & Demo, 1994).

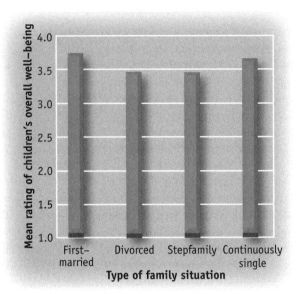

● FIGURE 9.10

Children's adjustment in four types of families. Acock and Demo (1994) assessed children's adjustment in four types of family structures: first marriages, divorced single-parent homes, step-families, and families in which the mother never married. The comparisons of 2457 families did turn up some statistically significant differences, as children's overall well-being was highest in intact first marriages. However, as you can see, the differences were rather small, and the authors concluded that "family structure has a modest effect on children's well-being."

Alternatives to Marriage

LEARNING OBJECTIVES

■ Describe stereotypes of single life, and summarize evidence on the adjustment of single people.
■ Discuss the prevalence of cohabitation and whether it improves the probability of marital success.
■ Discuss the stability and dynamics of intimate relationships among homosexual couples.
■ Outline some misconceptions about gay couples.

We noted at the beginning of the chapter that the traditional model of marriage has been undermined by a variety of social trends. More and more people are choosing alternatives to marriage. In this section we examine some of these alternatives, including remaining single, cohabitation, and gay relationships.

Remaining Single

The pressure to marry is substantial in our society (Berliner, Jacob, & Schwartzberg, 1999). People are socialized to believe that they are not complete until they have found their "other half" and have entered into a partnership for life. And reference is often made to people's "failure" to marry. In spite of this pressure, an increasing proportion of young adults are remaining single (Teachman, Tedrow, & Crowder, 2001), as Figure 9.11 shows.

Does the increased number of single adults mean that people are turning away

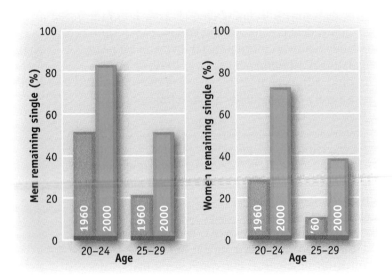

● FIGURE 9.11

The proportion of young people who remain single. This graph shows the percentage of single men and women, ages 20–24 or 25–29, in 2000 as compared to 1960 (based on U.S. Census data). The proportion of people remaining single has increased substantially for both sexes, in both age brackets. Single men continue to outnumber single women in these age brackets.

from the institution of marriage? Perhaps a little, but for the most part, no. A variety of factors have contributed to the growth of the single population. Much of this growth is a result of the increase in the median age at which people marry and the increased rate of divorce. The vast majority of single, never-married people *do* hope to marry eventually. In one study of never-married men and women (South, 1993), 87.4 percent of the 926 respondents ages 19 to 25 agreed with the statement "I would like to get married someday."

Singlehood has been plagued by two disparate stereotypes (DeFrain & Olson, 1999). On the one hand, single people are sometimes portrayed as carefree swingers who are too busy enjoying the fruits of promiscuity to shoulder marital responsibilities. On the other hand, they are seen as losers who have not succeeded in snaring a mate, and they may be portrayed as socially inept, maladjusted, frustrated, lonely, and bitter. These stereotypes do a great injustice to the diversity that exists among those who are single.

The "swinging single" stereotype appears to be a media-manufactured illusion designed to lure singles' spending power into nightclubs and bars. In reality, the bar circuit is usually described as an experience in alienation and disappointment. In comparison to married people, single people do have sex with more partners, but they have sex less frequently than their married counterparts (Michael et al., 1994).

As for the "maladjusted, bitter" stereotype, it is true that single people exhibit poorer mental and physical health than married people (Joung et al., 1997; Waite, 1995), and they rate themselves as less happy than their married counterparts (Stack & Eshleman, 1998; Waite, 2000). However, the differences are modest, and the happiness gap has shrunk, especially among women. Although popular stereotypes suggest that being single is more difficult for women than for men, the empirical data are mixed. The physical health benefits of being married appear to be greater for men than for women (Waite, 2000; Wu & Hart, 2002). But most studies find that single women are more satisfied with their lives and less distressed than comparable single men, and various lines of evidence suggest that women get along without men better than men get along without women (Davies, 1995; Marker, 1996).

Why is being married associated with greater health and happiness? The *health benefits* of marriage may result because spouses provide emotional and social support that buffers the negative effects of stress and because they discourage their partners' unhealthy habits (Joung et al., 1997; Murphy, Glaser, & Grundy, 1997). Another consideration is that married people tend to have a higher income (Hirschl, Altobelli, & Rank, 2003), and affluence is associated with better health (Adler & Snibbe, 2003). The *greater happiness* of married people has been attributed to the advantages they enjoy in so-

cial support, financial well-being, and physical health (Stack & Eshleman, 1998). Of course, the correlation between being married and health/happiness may be due in part to the effects of health and happiness on marital status. That is, it is likely that healthier and happier people are better able to attract and retain marital partners.

Cohabitation

As we noted earlier in the chapter, *cohabitation* refers to living together in a sexually intimate relationship outside of marriage. Recent years have witnessed a tremendous increase in the number of cohabiting couples (see Figure 9.12). Although cohabitation is still illegal in seven states (Fields, 2001), over 4.6 million couples were living together unmarried in the United States in 2000. However, the percentage of couples living together at any one time does not accurately convey how widespread this phenomenon has become, because cohabiting unions tend to be short (Seltzer, 2004). It is more instructive to study people getting married for the first time and determine the percentage of them who cohabited prior to their marriage (either with their spouse-to-be or someone else). Studies indicate that this percentage has increased dramatically, from around 11 percent in 1970 to over 50 percent in the mid-1990s (Bumpass & Lu, 2000). Increasing rates of cohabitation are not unique to the United States and are even higher in many

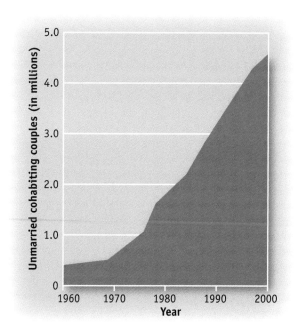

● **FIGURE 9.12**

Cohabitation in the United States. The number of unmarried couples living together has been increasing rapidly since 1970 (based on U.S. Census data). This increase shows no signs of leveling off.

European countries (Kiernan, 2004). In some places, cohabitation has become nearly as normative as marriage (Le Bourdais & Lapierre-Adamcyk, 2004).

Cohabitation tends to conjure up images of college students or other well-educated young couples without children, but these images are misleading. In reality, cohabitation rates have always been higher in the less-educated and lower-income segments of the population (Bumpass & Lu, 2000). Moreover, many cohabitating couples have children. About half of previously married cohabitants and 35 percent of never-married cohabitants have children in their household (Smock, 2000).

Although many people see cohabitation as a threat to the institution of marriage, many theorists see it as a new stage in the courtship process—a sort of trial marriage. Consistent with this view, about three-quarters of female cohabitants expect to marry their current partner (Lichter, Batson, & Brown, 2004). In spite of these expectations, however, cohabitants report that they are less satisfied with their relationships than married couples (Brown & Booth, 1996; Nock, 1995). Moreover, cohabitating relationships are notably less durable than marital relationships (Seltzer, 2004). Conceiving a child during cohabitation tends to increase couples' chances of staying together (Manning, 2004).

As a prelude to marriage, cohabitation should allow people to experiment with marital-like responsibilities and reduce the likelihood of entering marriage with unrealistic expectations. Living together may also permit people to identify incompatible mates more effectively than a traditional courtship would. These considerations suggest that couples who cohabit before they marry should go on to more successful marriages than those who do not.

Although this analysis sounds plausible, researchers have *not* found that premarital cohabitation increases the likelihood of subsequent marital success. In fact, studies have consistently found an association between premarital cohabitation and *increased* marital discord and divorce rates (Bumpass & Lu, 2000; Cohan & Kleinbaum, 2002; Teachman, 2003). What accounts for this finding? Many theorists argue that this nontraditional lifestyle has historically attracted a more liberal and less conventional segment of the population with a weak commitment to the institution of marriage and relatively few qualms about getting divorced. This explanation has considerable empirical support (Hall, 1996; Smock, 2000), but some support also exists for the alternative explanation—that the experience of cohabitation changes people's attitudes, values, or habits in ways that somehow increase their vulnerability to divorce (Kamp Dush, Cohan, & Amato, 2003; Seltzer, 2001).

Gay Relationships

Up until this point, we have, for purposes of simplicity, focused our attention on *heterosexuals,* those who seek

Despite the common stereotype that homosexuals rarely form long-term relationships, the fact is that they are similar to heterosexual couples in their attitudes and behaviors, and many enjoy long-term commitments in marriage-like arrangements.

© Ron Chapple/Thinkstock/Alamy

emotional-sexual relationships with members of the other gender. However, we have been ignoring a significant minority group: *homosexual* men and women, who seek emotional-sexual relationships with members of the same gender. (In everyday language, the term *gay* is used to refer to homosexuals of both genders, although many homosexual women prefer the term *lesbian* for themselves.)

How large is this minority group? No one knows for sure. Part of the problem is that this question is vastly more complex than it appears at first glance (LeVay, 1996). Sexual orientation is best represented as a continuum (see Chapter 13), so where do you draw the lines between heterosexuality, bisexuality, and homosexuality? And how do you handle the distinction between overt behavior and desire? Where, for instance, do you put a person who is married and has never engaged in homosexual behavior but who reports homosexual fantasies and acknowledges being strongly drawn to members of the same sex? The other part of the problem is that many people have extremely prejudicial attitudes about homosexuality, which makes gays cautious and reluctant to give candid information about their sexuality (Smith & Gates, 2001). Small wonder then that estimates of the portion of the population that is homosexual vary widely (Gonsiorek & Weinrich, 1991). A frequently cited estimate is 10 percent, but recent surveys suggest that this percentage may be an overestimate. Michaels (1996) has combined data from two of the better large-scale surveys to arrive at the estimates seen in Figure 9.13. As you can see, the numbers are open to varying interpretations, but as a whole they suggest that about 5–8 percent of the population could reasonably be characterized as homosexual.

Devoting a separate section to gay couples may seem to imply that the dynamics of their close relationships are different from those seen in heterosexual couples. Actually, this assumption appears to be much less true than widely thought, even though gays' close relationships unfold in a radically different social context than

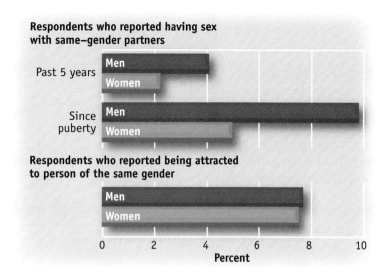

FIGURE 9.13

How common is homosexuality? The answer to this question is both complex and controversial. Michaels (1996) brought together data from large-scale surveys to arrive at the estimates shown here. If you look at how many people have actually had a same-sex partner in the last five years, the figures are relatively low, but if you count those who have had a same-sex partner since puberty, the figures more than double. Still another way to look at it is to ask people whether they are attracted to people of the same sex (regardless of their actual behavior). This approach suggests that about 8 percent of the population could be characterized as homosexual.

heterosexuals' marital relationships. As Garnets and Kimmel (1991) point out, gay relationships "develop within a social context of societal disapproval with an absence of social legitimization and support; families and other social institutions often stigmatize such relationships and there are no prescribed roles and behaviors to structure such relationships" (p. 170).

Attitudes about gay relationships have become more favorable in recent years, but over half of Americans still condemn homosexual relations as morally wrong (Yang, 1997) and oppose gay marriage and gays' right to adopt children (Herek, 2002). Gays continue to be victims of employment and housing discrimination, not to mention verbal and physical abuse and hate crimes (Herek, 2000; Herek, Cogan, & Gillis, 2002). With rare exceptions, gay couples cannot legally formalize their unions by getting married, and in fact, during the 1990s many states passed laws prohibiting same-gender marriages. Gay couples are also denied many economic benefits available to married couples. For example, they can't file joint tax returns, and gay individuals often can't obtain employer-provided health insurance for their partner.

Comparisons to Heterosexual Couples

Given the lack of moral, social, legal, and economic supports for gay relationships, are gay unions less stable than marital unions? Researchers have not yet been

WEB LINK 9.5

Partners Task Force for Gay and Lesbian Couples
Reflecting the belief that "same-gender couples deserve the same treatment as all other couples," this web page's resources address a wide range of issues, including relationships, parenting, domestic partnership, ceremonial marriage, and legal and civil rights matters.

able to collect adequate data on this question, but the limited data available suggest that gay couples' relationships *are* somewhat briefer and more prone to break-ups than heterosexual marriages (Kurdek, 1998; Peplau, 1991). If that's the case, it's probably because gay relationships face fewer barriers to dissolution—that is, fewer practical problems that make breakups difficult or costly (Kurdek, 1998; Peplau & Cochran, 1990). Married couples considering divorce often face a variety of such barriers—attorneys' fees, concerns about children, wrangling over joint investments, and the disapproval of their families—that may motivate them to salvage their deteriorating relationship. In contrast, gay couples do not have to wrestle with the legal formalities of divorce, and they are less likely to have children, joint investments, or family opposition to worry about.

Although gay relationships evolve in a different social context than marital relationships, recent studies have documented striking commonalities between heterosexual and homosexual couples. Both types of couples report similar levels of love and commitment in their relationships, similar levels of overall satisfaction with their relationships, and similar levels of sexual satisfaction (Bryant & Demian, 1994; Kurdek, 1998; Peplau, 1991). Resemblance is also apparent when researchers study what gays and heterosexuals want out of their relationships (Peplau, 1988; see Figure 9.14).

Homosexual and heterosexual couples are also similar in terms of the factors that predict relationship satisfaction, the sources of conflict in their relationships, and their patterns of conflict resolution (Kurdek, 2004).

Misconceptions About Gay Relationships

Although research indicates a considerable continuity between homosexual and heterosexual relationships, basic misconceptions about the nature of gay relationships remain widespread. Let's look at some of these inaccurate stereotypes.

First, many people assume that most gay couples adopt traditional masculine and feminine roles in their relationships, with one partner behaving in a cross-gendered manner. This appears to be true in only a small minority of cases. In fact, on the whole, gay couples appear to be more flexible about role expectations than heterosexuals (Reimann, 1997). In comparison to married couples, gay couples display a more equitable balance of power in their relationships and are less likely to adhere to traditional gender roles (Rosenbluth, 1997; Solomon, Rothblum, & Balsam, 2004).

Second, popular stereotypes suggest that gays only rarely get involved in long-term intimate relationships. In reality, most homosexual men, and nearly all homosexual women, prefer stable, long-term relationships, and at any one time roughly 40–60 percent of gay males and 45–80 percent of lesbians are involved in commit-

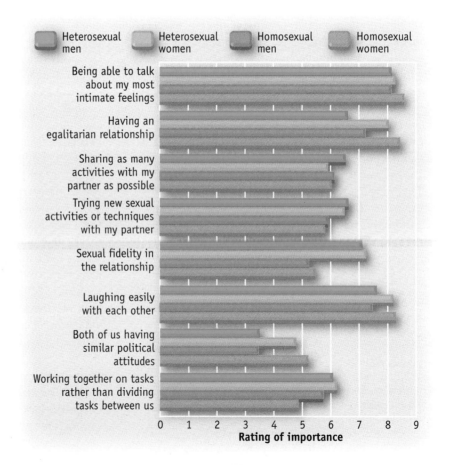

● FIGURE 9.14

Comparing priorities in intimate relationships. Peplau (1981) asked heterosexual men and women and homosexual men and women to rate the significance (9 = high importance) of various aspects of their intimate relationships. As you can see, all four groups returned fairly similar ratings. Peplau concludes that gays and heterosexuals largely want the same things out of their relationships.

From Peplau, L. A. (1981, March). What homosexuals want. *Psychology Today, 3,* 28–38. Reprinted with permission from Psychology Today Magazine. Copyright © 1981 Sussex Publishers, Inc.

ted relationships (Kurdek, 2004). Lesbian relationships are generally sexually exclusive. About half of committed male couples have "open" relationships, allowing for the possibility of sexual activity (but not affection) with outsiders. While intimate relationships among gays appear to be less stable than marriages among straights, they may compare favorably with heterosexual cohabitation, which would be a more appropriate baseline for comparison. Both gays and heterosexual cohabitants may face opposition to their relationship from their families and from society in general, and neither enjoys the legal and social sanctions of marriage.

Third, lesbians and gay men tend to be thought of as individuals rather than as members of families. This thinking reflects a bias that homosexuality and family just don't mesh (Allen & Demo, 1995). In reality, gays are very much involved in families as sons and daughters, as parents and stepparents, as aunts, uncles, and grandparents (Johnson & Colluci, 1999). Although exact data are not available, far more are parents than most people realize. Many of these parental responsi-

bilities are left over from previous marriages, as about 20–30 percent of gays have been heterosexually married (Kurdek, 2004). But an increasing number of homosexuals are opting to have children in the context of their gay relationships (Falk, 1994; Gartrell et al., 1999).

What do we know about gays and lesbians as parents? The evidence suggests that gays are similar to their heterosexual counterparts in their approaches to parenting and that their children are similar to the children of heterosexual parents in terms of personal development and peer relations (Patterson, 2001). The overall adjustment of children with gay parents appears similar in quality to that of children of heterosexual parents (Chan et al., 1998; Golombok et al., 2003). Moreover, the vast majority of children of gay parents grow up to identify themselves as heterosexual (Bailey & Dawood, 1998), and some studies suggest that they are no more likely than others to become homosexual (Flaks et al., 1995). In sum, children reared by gay and lesbian parents do not appear to suffer any special ill effects and do not seem noticeably different from other children.

APPLICATION

Understanding Intimate Violence

LEARNING OBJECTIVES

- *Discuss the incidence and consequences of date rape.*
- *Explain the factors that contribute to date rape.*
- *Discuss the incidence of partner abuse and the characteristics of batterers.*
- *Discuss why women stay in abusive relationships.*

Answer the following statements "true" or "false."

_____ **1.** Most rapes are committed by strangers.

_____ **2.** Research indicates that aggressive pornography does *not* contribute to sexual coercion.

_____ **3.** Most women in abusive relationships are attracted to violent men.

_____ **4.** Most men who have witnessed domestic violence as children will batter their intimate partners.

All of the above statements are false, as you will see in this Application, which examines the darker side of intimate relationships. Most of us assume that we will be safe with those whom we love and trust. Unfortunately, some people are betrayed by individuals to whom they feel closest. *Intimate violence is aggression toward those who are in close relationship to the aggressor.* Intimate violence takes many forms: psychological, physical, and sexual abuse. Tragically, this violence sometimes ends in homicide. In this Application, we'll

focus on two serious social problems: date rape and partner abuse.

Date Rape

Date rape refers to forced and unwanted intercourse in the context of dating. Date rape can occur on a first date, with someone you've dated for a while, or with someone to whom you're engaged. Many people confuse date rape with seduction. The latter occurs when a woman is persuaded *and agrees* to have sex. Date rape often occurs when seduction fails and the man goes on to have sex with the woman without her consent. The force used in date rape is typically verbal or physical coercion, but sometimes it involves a weapon.

Incidence and Consequences

How common is date rape? It's much more common than widely realized. Research suggests that 13–30 percent of women are likely to be victimized by date rape or attempted sexual coercion at some point in their lives (Abbey et al., 2004; Koss & Cook, 1993; Spitzberg, 1999). Most people naively assume that the vast majority of rapes are committed by strangers who leap from bushes or dark alleys to surprise their victims. In reality, research indicates that strangers are responsible for only a small minority of rapes and that over half of all rapes occur in the context of dating relationships (see Figure 9.15). Most rape victims are between the ages of 15 and 25.

How are women affected by date rape? All rape is traumatic, but it is particularly shattering for a woman to be raped by someone she has trusted. In the aftermath of date rape, women typically experience a variety of emotional reactions, including fear, anger, anxiety, self-blame, and guilt (Kahn & Andrioli Mathie, 1999). Many

rape victims suffer from depression, symptoms of post-traumatic stress disorder, and increased risk for suicide (Foa, 1998; Slashinski, Coker, & Davis, 2003; Ullman, 2004). Negative reactions can be exacerbated if the woman's family and friends are not supportive—particularly if family or friends blame the victim for the attack. In addition to the trauma of the rape, women also have to cope with the possibilities of pregnancy and sexually transmitted disease (Golding, 1996). Moreover, if the rape survivor presses charges against her attacker, she may have to deal with extremely difficult legal proceedings, negative publicity, and social stigma.

Contributing Factors

To understand the phenomenon of date rape, it's essential to know something about the factors that contribute to it. It probably comes as no surprise to learn that alcohol contributes to about half of sexually aggressive incidents (Abbey et al., 2004). Alcohol impairs judgment and reduces inhibitions, making men more willing to use force. Drinking also undermines men's ability to interpret ambiguous social cues, making them more likely to overestimate their date's interest in sex. The more intoxicated perpetrators are, the more aggressive they tend to be (Abbey et al., 2003). Alcohol also increases women's vulnerability to sexual coercion. Drinking can cloud women's assessments of their risk and their ability to mount firm resistance or find a way to escape the situation.

Increasingly, so-called "date rape drugs" are a cause for concern (Dyer, 2000; Pope & Shouldice, 2001). Rohypnol ("roofies") and gamma hydroxybutyrate (GHB) are two drugs used to subdue dates. Although these drugs are colorless, odorless, and tasteless, their effects are anything but benign, and they can even be fatal. Victims typically pass out and have no recall of what happened while they were under the influence of the drug. To make it easier to spike a drink, predators typically look for individuals who are already intoxicated.

Research on the effects of *aggressive pornography,* which depicts rape and other sexual violence against women, suggests that such material elevates some men's tendency to behave aggressively toward women (Donnerstein & Malamuth, 1997). It appears that aggressive pornography works *indirectly* by fostering callous attitudes toward women, making sexual coercion seem less offensive, and desensitizing males to the horror of sexual violence (Mullin & Linz, 1995). In particular, such pornography helps perpetuate the myth that women enjoy being raped and ravaged (Boeringer, 1994). That said, given the widespread dissemination of aggressive pornography, it is obvious that there are vast numbers of men who are exposed to it without becoming rapists. It seems likely that aggressive pornography contributes

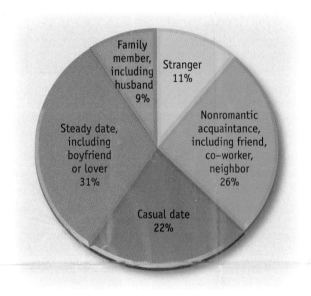

● **FIGURE 9.15**

Rape victim–offender relationships. Based on a national survey of 3187 college women, Mary Koss and her colleagues (1988) identified a sample of 468 women who indicated that they had been a victim of rape and who provided information on their relationship to the offender. Contrary to the prevailing stereotype, only a small minority (11 percent) had been raped by a stranger. As you can see, over half of rapes occur in the context of dating relationships. (Data based on Koss et al., 1988)

The rape allegations against basketball star Kobe Bryant focused a great deal of attention on the problem of date rape, which is far more common than most people realize.

to sexual violence only in a minority of men who are already predisposed to behave in sexually aggressive ways (Seto, Maric, & Barbaree, 2001).

Gender differences in sexual standards also contribute to date rape. Society still encourages a double standard for males and females. Men are encouraged to have sexual feelings, to act on them, and to "score," whereas women are socialized to be coy about their sexual desires. This double standard can promote sexual aggression by men who come to view dating as a "battle of the sexes" in which they are supposed to persist in their pursuit of sexual conquests (Abbey et al., 2001; Forbes, Adams-Curtis, & White, 2004).

Many date rapes are the result of miscommunication (Lim & Roloff, 1999). Social norms encourage game playing as part of flirting, so dating partners may not always say what they mean or mean what they say. Whereas the majority of women say "no" and mean it,

some women may say "no" to sexual activity when they actually mean "maybe" or "yes." Studies surveying the extent of token resistance among college women report that approximately 38 percent of them have acted this way (Muehlenhard & McCoy, 1991; Shotland & Hunter, 1995). Unfortunately, this behavior can backfire. For some men, it can cloud the issue of whether a woman has consented to sex (Osman, 2003).

In terms of personal characteristics, males who engage in sexual aggression tend to be relatively impulsive, low in empathy, hostile toward women, and heavy drinkers (Abbey et al., 2001, 2004). They tend to endorse traditional gender stereotypes about male dominance and tend to have had more (consensual) sex partners than their age-mates. They also tend to have poor anger management skills (Lundeberg et al., 2004).

A variety of situational factors influence the likelihood of date rape. Sexual assault is more likely (1) the more the man knows the woman, (2) the more isolated the setting they are in, (3) the more they have had some consensual sexual activity previously, and (4) the longer the man has misperceived the woman's sexual interest (Abbey et al., 2001). These factors can contribute to a man feeling that his date owes him sex because he has been "led on." He may then use his anger as an excuse to force the woman to have sex.

Reducing the Incidence of Date Rape

What can women do to reduce the likelihood of being victimized by date rape? Here are some suggestions: (1) Recognize date rape for what it is: an act of sexual aggression; (2) become familiar with the characteristics of men who are likely to engage in date rape (see Figure 9.16 on the next page) and be cautious about dating men who exhibit these traits; (3) beware of excessive alcohol and drug use, which may undermine self-control and self-determination in sexual interactions; (4) when dating someone new, agree to go only to public places and always carry enough money for transportation back home; (5) communicate feelings and expectations about sex by engaging in appropriate self-disclosure; and (6) be prepared to act *aggressively* if assertive refusals fail to stop unwanted advances.

Partner Abuse

The O. J. Simpson trial dramatically heightened public awareness of partner violence, particularly wife battering and homicide. People found it difficult to reconcile the image of the smiling sports hero with the fact that he was a convicted wife batterer with a history of terrorizing his former spouse. *Physical abuse* can include kicking, biting, punching, choking, pushing, slapping, hitting with an object, threatening with a weapon, using

Characteristics of Date Rapists

Sexual entitlement	Power and control	Hostility and anger	Acceptance of interpersonal violence
Touching women with no regard for their wishes	Interrupting people, especially women	Showing a quick temper	Using threats in displays of anger
Sexualizing relationships that are appropriately not sexual	Being a bad loser	Blaming others when things go wrong	Using violence in borderline situations
Engaging in conversation that is inappropriately intimate	Exhibiting inappropriate competitiveness	Tending to transform other emotions into anger	Approving observed violence
Telling sexual jokes at inappropriate times or places	Using intimidating body language		Justifying violence
Making inappropriate comments about women's bodies, sexuality, and so on	Game playing		

● FIGURE 9.16

Date rapists: Warning signs. According to Rozee, Bateman, and Gilmore (1991), four factors appear to distinguish date rapists: feelings of sexual entitlement, a penchant for exerting power and control, high hostility and anger, and acceptance of interpersonal violence. The presence of more than one of these characteristics is an important warning sign. When sexual entitlement is coupled with any other factor, special heed should be taken.

a weapon, and rape. Examples of *psychological abuse* include humiliation, name calling, controlling what the partner does and with whom the partner socializes, refusing to communicate, unreasonable withholding of money, and questioning of the partner's sanity. We will focus primarily on physical abuse of partners, or *battering*.

Incidence and Consequences

As with other taboo topics, obtaining accurate estimates of physical abuse is difficult. Research suggests that about 25 percent of women and 7 percent of men have been physically assaulted by an intimate partner at some point in their lives (Tjaden & Thoennes, 2000). Wives attack their husbands more than most people realize (P. Pearson, 1998), but much of wives' aggression appears to be retaliation for abuse and women tend to inflict less physical damage than men (Johnson, 2000). Thus, women are the principal victims of severe, dangerous abuse. A woman is the victim in 85 percent of nonfatal violent crimes committed by intimate partners and in 75 percent of murders by spouses (Rennison & Welchans, 2000). That said, women commit one-quarter of spousal murders, so it is an oversimplification to assume that partner abuse involves only male aggression against women. It is also inaccurate to assume that intimate violence is seen only in marital relationships. Partner abuse is also a significant problem for cohabiting heterosexual couples (DeMaris et al., 2003) and for gay and lesbian couples (Greenwood et al., 2002; Renzetti, 1995).

The effects of battering reverberate beyond the obvious physical injuries. Victims of partner abuse tend to suffer from severe anxiety, depression, feelings of helplessness and humiliation, stress-induced physical illness, symptoms of posttraumatic stress disorder, and increased vulnerability to suicide (Brewster, 2002; Campbell, 2002; Cohan et al., 2002). Children who witness marital violence also experience ill effects, such as anxiety, depression, reduced self-esteem, and increased delinquency (Johnson & Ferraro, 2001).

Characteristics of Batterers

Men who batter women are a diverse group, so a single profile has not emerged (Dixon & Browne, 2002). Some risk factors associated with an elevated risk for domestic violence include unemployment, drinking and drug problems, a tendency to anger easily, attitudes that condone aggression, and high stress (Stith et al., 2004). Males who were beaten as children or who witnessed their mothers being beaten are more likely to abuse their wives than other men are, although most men who grow up in these difficult circumstances do not become batterers (Stith et al., 2000). Battering appears to be somewhat more common in families of lower socioeconomic status, but no social class is immune (Roberts, 2002). In many instances, the motivation for battering is to use it as a tool to exert control over women (Johnson & Ferraro, 2001). Other relationship factors that are associated with domestic violence include having frequent disagreements, exhibiting a heated style of dealing with disagreements, and pairing a man holding traditional gender role attitudes with a woman who has nontraditional views of gender roles (DeMaris et al., 2003).

Why Do Women Stay in Abusive Relationships?

Women leave abusive partners more often than popular stereotypes suggest (Johnson & Ferraro, 2001), but people are still perplexed by the fact that many women remain in abusive relationships that seem horrible and degrading. However, research shows that this phenomenon is not really that perplexing. A host of seemingly compelling reasons explain why many women feel that leaving is not a realistic option. Many fear economic hardship and believe that they won't be able to survive financially without their husband (Choice & Lamke, 1997). Many simply have no place to go and fear becoming homeless (Browne, 1993a). Many feel guilty and ashamed about their failing relationship and don't want to face disapproval from family and friends, who are likely to fall into the trap of blaming the victim (Barnett & La Violette, 1993). Above all else, many fear that if they try to leave, they may precipitate more brutal violence and even murder (DeMaris & Swinford, 1996). Unfortunately, this fear is not an unrealistic one, in that many men have shown remarkable persistence in tracking down, stalking, threatening, beating, and killing their ex-partners. Despite the many difficulties of leaving abusive relationships (see Figure 9.17), attention is still focused on why women stay rather than on why men batter and on what interventions can prevent women from being brutalized or killed when they do leave (Koss et al., 1994). Treatment programs for men who batter their wives can be helpful in decreasing further violence, but the effectiveness of these programs is rather modest (Babcock, Green, & Robie, 2004; Roberts, 2002).

Although most of us would prefer not to think about this darker side of relationships, intimate violence is a reality we can ill-afford to ignore. It deeply touches the lives of millions of individuals. We can only hope that increased public awareness of intimate violence will help reduce its incidence and its tragic effects.

Perceived Reasons for Returning to Abusive Relationships

Reasons	Mean rating
Give the abuser one more chance	10.0
Lack of financial resources	9.1
Emotional dependency on the abuser	9.0
Lack of housing resources	8.7
Lack of job opportunities	7.7
Denial of cycle of violence	7.6
Lack of support or follow-through by the legal system	7.6
Lack of child-care resources	7.1
Lack of transportation	6.7
Fear that the abuser will find her and do her harm	6.7
Lack of support from other family members	6.6
Fear that the abuser will get custody of the children	5.8
Fear that the abuser will kidnap the children	5.8
Children miss the absent parent	5.6
Lack of professional counseling	5.1
Fear that the abuser will harm the children	4.6

● FIGURE 9.17

Perceived reasons for returning to abusive relationships. Shelters for battered wives generally report that the majority of their clients return to their partners. In one study (Johnson, Crowley, & Sigler, 1992), workers at ten shelters in Alabama were asked to rate the reasons that women returned to abusive relationships. The most frequently cited reasons are listed here in order of rated importance. As you can see, a diverse host of factors appear to propel women back into abusive relationships.

From Johnson, I. M., Crowley, J., & Sigler, R. T. (1992). Agency response to domestic violence: Services provided to battered women. In E. C. Viano (Ed.), *Intimate violence: Interdisciplinary perspectives* (pp 191–202, Table on p. 199). Philadelphia: Taylor & Francis. Copyright © 1992 Hemisphere Publishing. Reprinted with permission of Taylor & Francis, Inc.

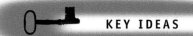

KEY IDEAS

Challenges to the Traditional Model of Marriage
■ The traditional model of marriage is being challenged by the increasing acceptability of singlehood, the increasing popularity of cohabitation, the reduced premium on permanence, changes in gender roles, the increasing prevalence of voluntary childlessness, and the decline of the traditional nuclear family. Nonetheless, marriage remains quite popular.

Moving Toward Marriage
■ A multitude of factors influence an individual's motivation to marry. Mate selection is influenced by endogamy, homogamy, and gender. Women place more emphasis on potential partners' ambition and financial prospects, whereas men are more interested in a partner's youthfulness and physical attractiveness.
■ According to Murstein, the process of mate selection goes through three stages, which emphasize the stimulus value of the potential partner, value compatibility, and adequacy of role enactments. There are some premarital predictors of marital success, such as family background, age, length of courtship, and personality, but the relations are weak. The nature of a couple's premarital interactions is a better predictor of marital adjustment.

Marital Adjustment Across the Family Life Cycle
■ The family life cycle is an orderly sequence of developmental stages that families tend to progress through. Newly married couples tend to be very happy before the arrival of children. Today more couples are struggling with the decision about whether to have children. The arrival of children is a major transition that is handled best by parents who have realistic expectations about the difficulties inherent in raising a family.
■ As children reach adolescence, parents should expect more conflict as their influence declines. They must learn to relate to their children as adults and help launch them into the adult world. Most parents no longer struggle with the empty nest syndrome. Adult children returning home may be more of a problem.

Vulnerable Areas in Marital Adjustment
■ Gaps in expectations about marital roles may create marital stress. Disparities in expectations about gender roles and the distribution of housework may be especially common and problematic. Work concerns can clearly spill over to influence marital functioning, but the links between parents' employment and marital adjustment are complex.
■ Wealth does not ensure marital happiness, but a lack of money can produce marital problems. Inadequate communication is a commonly reported marital problem, which is predictive of divorce.

Divorce
■ Divorce rates have increased dramatically in recent decades, but they appear to be stabilizing. Deciding on a divorce tends to be a gradual process marred by indecision. Unpleasant as divorce may be, the evidence suggests that toughing it out in an unhappy marriage can often be worse.

■ Wallerstein's research suggests that divorce tends to have extremely negative effects on children. Hetherington's research suggests that most children recover from divorce after a few years. The effects of divorce on children vary, but negative effects can be long-lasting.
■ A substantial majority of divorced people remarry. These second marriages have a somewhat lower probability of success than first marriages.

Alternatives to Marriage
■ An increasing proportion of the young population are remaining single, but this fact does not mean that people are turning away from marriage. Although singles generally have the same adjustment problems as married couples, evidence suggests that singles tend to be somewhat less happy and less healthy.
■ The prevalence of cohabitation has increased dramatically. Logically, one might expect cohabitation to facilitate marital success, but research has consistently found an association between cohabitation and marital instability.
■ Gay relationships develop in a starkly different social context than marital relationships. Nonetheless, studies have found that heterosexual and homosexual couples are similar in many ways. Gay relationships are characterized by great diversity. It is not true that gay couples usually assume traditional masculine and feminine roles, nor is it true that gays rarely get involved in long-term intimate relationships or family relations.

Application: Understanding Intimate Violence
■ Over half of rapes are committed in the context of dating. Estimates suggest that the chances of a woman being victimized by date rape at some time in her life range from 13 percent to 30 percent. Rape is a traumatic experience that has many serious consequences. Alcohol and drug use, violent pornography, and gender-based sexual standards all contribute to date rape. Miscommunication revolving around token resistance is particularly problematic.
■ Research suggests that about 25 percent of women and 7 percent of men have been victims of partner abuse. Women are the principal victims of serious, dangerous abuse. Men who batter their partners are diverse, but control is often the central issue. Women stay in abusive relationships for a variety of compelling, practical reasons, including economic realities.

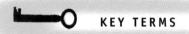

KEY TERMS

Cohabitation   p. 270
Date rape   p. 295
Endogamy   p. 272
Family life cycle   p. 275

Homogamy   p. 272
Intimate violence   p. 295
Marriage   p. 270

KEY PEOPLE

John Gottman   pp. 283–285
E. Mavis Hetherington
   p. 289

Bernard Murstein   p. 274
Judith Wallerstein   p. 288

PRACTICE TEST

1. Which of the following is *not* one of the social trends that are undermining the traditional model of marriage?
   a. Increased acceptance of singlehood
   b. Increased voluntary childlessness
   c. Increased acceptance of cohabitation
   d. Increased premium on permanence in marriage

2. Endogamy refers to:
   a. the tendency to marry within one's social group.
   b. the tendency to marry someone with similar characteristics.
   c. the final marriage in serial monogamy.
   d. norms that promote marriage outside one's social unit.

3. Which of the following is associated with a greater likelihood of marital success?
   a. Having parents who divorced.
   b. Perfectionism.
   c. Longer courtships.
   d. Younger age at marriage.

4. The transition to parenthood tends to be easier when:
   a. the newborn child was planned for.
   b. the parents have realistic expectations.
   c. the new parents are relatively young.
   d. the father is not heavily involved in child care.

5. Most research suggests that maternal employment is:
   a. very harmful to children.
   b. moderately harmful to children.
   c. generally not harmful to children.
   d. extremely beneficial to young male children.

6. When financial resources are plentiful in a marriage, arguments about money:
   a. may still be a problem.
   b. don't occur.
   c. are a big problem only if the wife earns more than her husband.
   d. are unrelated to marital satisfaction.

7. The evidence suggests that the negative effects of divorce on former spouses' psychological adjustment are:
   a. exaggerated for both sexes.
   b. greater for men than women.
   c. greater for women than men.
   d. about the same for men and women.

8. What is the most probable reason for the increase in the proportion of young people who are single?
   a. Loss of faith in the institution of marriage
   b. Increased individualism and declining collectivism

c. The median age at which people get married has increased
   d. An increase in the number of young people unwilling to undertake the financial burdens of marriage and family

9. Research on cohabitation indicates that:
   a. most cohabitants are just not interested in marriage.
   b. most cohabitants would eventually like to marry.
   c. cohabitation is declining.
   d. cohabitation experience improves the chances that one's marriage will be successful.

10. Which of the following has been supported by research on intimate relationships among gay men and lesbians?
   a. Gay couples adopt traditional male/female gender roles.
   b. Gays rarely become involved in long-term relationships.
   c. Gays have impoverished family relations.
   d. Gays want the same things out of intimate relationships that heterosexuals want.

Personal Explorations Workbook

The following exercises in your *Personal Explorations Workbook* may enhance your self-understanding in relation to issues raised in this chapter. **Questionnaire 9.1:** Self-Report Jealousy Scale. **Personal Probe 9.1:** How Do You Behave in Intimate Relationships? **Personal Probe 9.2:** Thinking About Your Attitudes About Marriage and Cohabitation.

ANSWERS

1. d Pages 270–271
2. a Page 272
3. c Pages 274–275
4. b Page 277
5. c Page 282
6. a Page 283
7. d Page 288
8. c Page 291
9. b Page 292
10. d Pages 294–295

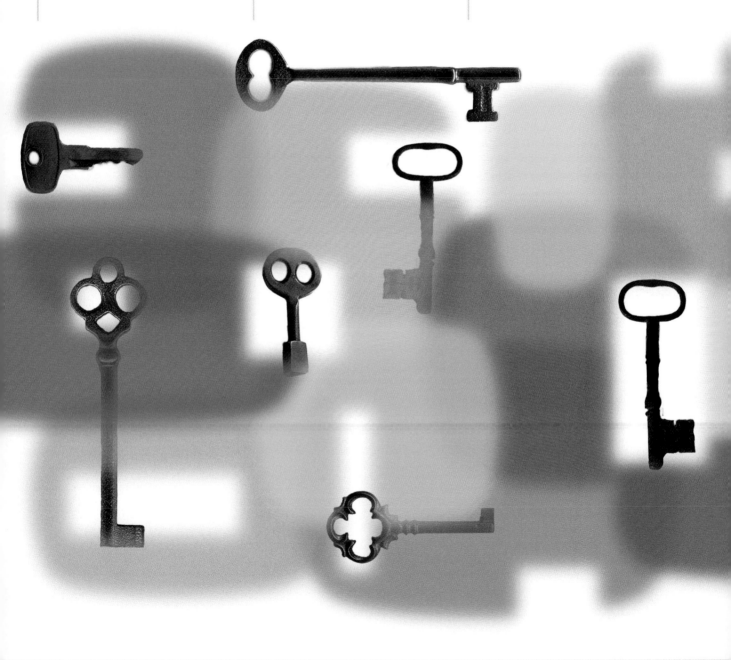

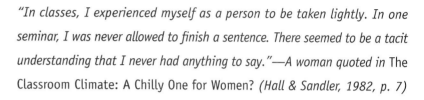

Gender and Behavior

"In classes, I experienced myself as a person to be taken lightly. In one seminar, I was never allowed to finish a sentence. There seemed to be a tacit understanding that I never had anything to say."—A woman quoted in The Classroom Climate: A Chilly One for Women? *(Hall & Sandler, 1982, p. 7)*

"I get a feeling, like I want to say 'I love you' or just put my arms around my girlfriend. But then, for some reason, I just shut down and I don't do anything. It seems like I am going to give up too much by getting too close. Maybe she'll want more than I have to give. This way I can cover myself. But I wind up feeling guilty about not showing her I care."—A man quoted in Man Alive: A Primer of Men's Issues *(Rabinowitz & Cochran, 1994, p. 55)*

The woman and man quoted here feel boxed in by gender roles. They're struggling with the limitations placed on their behavior because of their gender. They aren't unique or unusual—think about the times *you* have changed *your* behavior to bring it in line with society's concepts of masculinity and femininity.

Before continuing, we need to clarify some terms. Some scholars prefer to use the term *gender* to refer to male-female differences that are learned and *sex* to designate biologically based differences between males and females. However, as respected authority Janet Shibley Hyde (2004) points out, making this sharp distinction between *sex* and *gender* fails to recognize that biology and culture interact. Following this reasoning, we'll use **gender to mean the state of being male or female.** (When we use the term *sex,* we're referring to sexual behavior.) It's important to note that, as *we* use the term, *gender* says nothing about the *causes* of behavior. In other

Janet Shibley Hyde

FIGURE 10.1

Terminology related to gender. The topic of gender involves many closely related ideas that are easily confused. The gender-related concepts introduced in this chapter are summarized here for easy comparison.

Gender-Related Concepts	
Gender	The state of being male or female
Gender identity	An individual's perception of himself or herself as male or female
Gender stereotypes	Widely held and often inaccurate beliefs about males' and females' abilities, personality traits, and social behavior
Gender differences	Actual disparities in behavior between males and females, based on research observations
Gender roles	Culturally defined expectations about appropriate behavior for males and females
Gender-role identity	A person's identification with the traits regarded as masculine or feminine (one's sense of being masculine or feminine)
Sexual orientation	A person's preference for sexual partners of the other gender (heterosexual), the same gender (homosexual), or both genders (bisexual)

words, if we say that there are gender differences in aggressive behavior, we are simply stating that males and females differ in this area. This behavioral disparity might be caused by biological factors, by environmental factors, or by both. Figure 10.1 sorts out a number of gender-related terms that will be used in our discussions.

In this chapter, we take up some intriguing and controversial questions: Are there genuine behavioral differences between males and females? If so, what are their origins? Are traditional gender-role expectations healthy or unhealthy? Why are gender roles in our society changing, and what does the future hold? In the Application, we explore gender and communication styles.

Gender Stereotypes

LEARNING OBJECTIVES

- *Explain the nature of gender stereotypes and their connection with instrumentality and expressiveness.*
- *Discuss four important points about gender stereotypes.*

Obviously, males and females differ biologically—in their genitals and other aspects of anatomy, and in their physiological functioning. These readily apparent physical disparities between males and females lead people to expect other differences as well. Recall from Chapter 6 that *stereotypes* are widely held beliefs that people possess certain characteristics simply because of their membership in a particular group. Thus, **gender stereotypes** are widely shared beliefs about males' and females' abilities, personality traits, and social behavior.

cathy®

by Cathy Guisewite

CATHY © Cathy Guisewite. Reprinted with permission of UNIVERSAL PRESS SYNDICATE. All rights reserved.

Elements of Traditional Gender Stereotypes

Masculine	Feminine
Active	Aware of others' feelings
Adventurous	Considerate
Aggressive	Creative
Ambitious	Cries easily
Competitive	Devotes self to others
Dominant	Emotional
Independent	Enjoys art and music
Leadership qualities	Excitable in a crisis
Likes math and science	Expresses tender feelings
Makes decisions easily	Feelings hurt easily
Mechanical aptitude	Gentle
Not easily influenced	Home oriented
Outspoken	Kind
Persistent	Likes children
Self-confident	Neat
Skilled in business	Needs approval
Stands up under pressure	Tactful
Takes a stand	Understanding

● **FIGURE 10.2**

Traditional gender stereotypes. This is a partial list of the characteristics that college students associate with a typical man and a typical woman.

Adapted from Ruble, T. L. (1983). Sex stereotypes: Issues of change in the 70s. *Sex Roles, 9,* 397–402. Copyright © 1983 Plenum Publishing Co. Adapted by permission of Kluwer Academic/Plenum Publishers and the author.

Research finds a great deal of consensus on *supposed* behavioral differences between men and women (Bergen & Williams, 1991). For example, a survey of gender stereotypes in 25 countries revealed considerable similarity of views (Williams & Best, 1990; Williams, Satterwhite, & Best, 1999). Because of the widespread gains in educational and occupational attainment by American women since the 1970s, you might expect to find changes in gender stereotypes from then to now. However, gender stereotypes in this country have remained largely stable since the early 1970s, especially those for men (Diekman & Eagly, 2000; Spence & Buckner, 2000).

Gender stereotypes are too numerous to summarize here. Instead, you can examine Figure 10.2, which lists a number of characteristics people commonly link with femininity and masculinity. This list is based on a study in which subjects were asked to indicate the extent to which various traits are characteristic of each gender (Ruble, 1983). The stereotyped attributes for males generally reflect the quality of *instrumentality,* **an orientation toward action and accomplishment,** whereas the stereotypes for females reflect the qual-

ity of *expressiveness,* **an orientation toward emotion and relationships** (Eagly, Wood, & Diekman, 2000; Parsons & Bales, 1955).

When it comes to stereotypes, there are some important points to keep in mind. First, despite the general agreement on a number of gender stereotypes, variability also occurs (Williams & Best, 1990). The characteristics in Figure 10.2 represent the prototypic American male or female: white, middle-class, heterosexual, and Christian. But it is obvious that not everyone fits this set of characteristics. For example, the stereotypes for African American males and females are more similar on the dimensions of competence and expressiveness than those for white American males and females (Kane, 2000). Also, the stereotypes of white and Hispanic women are more positive than are those for African American women (Niemann et al., 1994).

A second point about gender stereotypes is that since the 1980s, the boundaries between male and female stereotypes have become less rigid (Deaux & Lewis, 1983, 1984). Earlier, the male and female stereotypes were seen as separate and distinct categories (for example, men are strong and women are weak). Now it seems that people perceive gender stereotypes as two overlapping categories.

A third consideration is that the traditional male stereotype is more complimentary than the conventional female stereotype. This fact is related to *androcentrism,* **or the belief that the male is the norm** (Bem, 1993). In other words, our society is organized in a way that favors "masculine" characteristics and behavior. Figure 10.3 provides some examples of how androcentrism can be manifested in the workplace.

Androcentrism in the Workplace

He's good on details.	She's picky.
He follows through.	She doesn't know when to quit.
He's assertive.	She's pushy.
He stands firm.	She's rigid.
He's a man of the world.	She's been around.
He's not afraid to say what he thinks.	She's outspoken.
He's close-mouthed.	She's secretive.
He exercises authority.	She's power-mad.
He climbed the ladder of success.	She slept her way to the top.
He's a stern taskmaster.	She's difficult to work for.

● **FIGURE 10.3**

Male bias on the job. In the world of work, women who exhibit traditional "masculine" characteristics are often perceived negatively. Thus, a man and a woman may display essentially the same behavior but elicit very different reactions.

Finally, keep in mind what you learned about stereotypes in Chapter 6: They can bias your perceptions and expectations of others as well as your interactions.

Let's shift from gender stereotypes to what males and females are actually like. Keep in mind that our discussion focuses on modern Western societies; the story may be different in other cultures.

Gender Similarities and Differences

LEARNING OBJECTIVES

- Summarize the research findings on gender similarities and differences in verbal, mathematical, and spatial abilities.
- Summarize the research on gender similarities and differences in personality and social behavior.
- Summarize the research on gender and psychological disorders.

- Summarize the situation regarding overall behavioral similarities and differences between males and females.
- Give two explanations for why gender differences appear larger than they actually are.

Are men more aggressive than women? Do more women than men suffer from depression? Hundreds of studies have attempted to answer these and related questions about gender and behavior. Moreover, new evidence is pouring in constantly, and many researchers report conflicting findings. Thus, it is almost an overwhelming task to keep up with trends in the field. Thankfully, a new statistical technique has come to the rescue. **Meta-analysis combines the statistical results of many studies of the same question, yielding an estimate of the size and consistency of a variable's effects.** This approach allows a researcher to assess the overall trends across all the previous studies of how gender is related to, say, math abilities or conformity. Meta-analysis has been a great boon to researchers, and quite a few meta-analyses on gender differences have now been conducted.

We'll do our best to thread our way through the available research. Here we examine three areas: cognitive abilities, personality traits and social behavior, and psychological disorders.

Cognitive Abilities

Perhaps we should first point out that gender differences have *not* been found in *overall* intelligence. Of course, this fact shouldn't be surprising, because intelligence tests are intentionally designed to minimize differences between the scores of males and females. But what about gender differences in *specific* cognitive skills? Let's start with *verbal abilities*.

Verbal Abilities
Verbal abilities include a number of distinct skills, such as vocabulary, reading, writing, spelling, and grammar abilities. Girls and women generally have the edge in the verbal area, although the gender differences are small (Halpern, 2000; Hyde & Kling, 2001; Hyde & Linn, 1988). Among the findings worth noting are the fact that girls usually start speaking a little earlier, have larger vocabularies and better reading scores in grade school, and are more verbally fluent (on tests of writing, for instance). Boys seem to fare better on verbal analogies. However, they are three to four times more likely to be stutterers (Skinner & Shelton, 1985) and five to ten times more likely than girls to be dyslexic (Vandenberg, 1987). Again, the gender differences in verbal abilities are small, but they generally favor females.

Mathematical Abilities
Researchers have also looked at gender differences in *mathematical abilities,* including performing computations and solving word and story problems. Meta-analyses of mathematical abilities show small gender differences favoring males (Hedges & Nowell, 1995; Hyde, Fennema, & Lamon, 1990; Nowell & Hedges, 1998). Interestingly, small gender differences favoring males appear for European Americans but not for African Americans, Hispanic Americans, or Asian Americans (Hyde, 1994b). In Canada, gender differences in mathematical abilities are minimal (Randhawa & Hunter, 2001).

Thus, the current view is that gender differences in mathematical abilities in the general population are essentially nil. However, this rule has several exceptions. In mathematical *problem solving,* boys start to slightly outperform girls when they reach high school. This difference is attributable in part to the fact that boys take more high school math courses (Halpern, 2000). Still, because problem-solving ability is essential for success in scientific courses and careers (arenas currently underpopulated by women), this finding is a concern. Males also outperform females at the high end of the mathematical ability distribution. For instance, when gifted seventh- and eighth-graders take the math subtest of the SAT, boys outnumber girls 17 to 1 in the group scoring over 700 (Benbow, 1988). To summarize, when all students are compared, gender differences in mathematical ability are small but favor males. In the area of problem solving, boys do a lot better, and many more boys than girls are precocious in math.

Spatial Abilities

In the cognitive area, the most compelling evidence for gender differences is in *spatial abilities,* which include perceiving and mentally manipulating shapes and figures. Males typically outperform females in most spatial abilities, and gender differences favoring males are consistently found in the ability to perform mental rotations of a figure in three dimensions—a skill important in occupations such as engineering, chemistry, and the building trades (see Figure 10.4). This gender gap in the ability to handle mental rotations is relatively large and has been found repeatedly (Halpern, 2000, 2004; Voyer, Voyer, & Bryden, 1995). Experience and training can improve mental rotation in both girls and boys (Sanz de Acedo & Garcia Ganuza, 2003).

Changes Over Time?

Have societal efforts to reduce sexism produced any changes in these gender patterns in cognitive abilities over the past 25 years? This is an important question, because any finding of changes would support the view that gender differences in cognitive abilities are largely attributable to environmental factors, as opposed to biological factors. There is evidence on both sides of the question (Feingold, 1988; Hyde et al., 1990; Halpern, 2000; Nowell & Hedges, 1998). To further complicate the issue, changes have occurred in how some mental abilities are measured—for instance, testing companies have eliminated items that show large gender differences (Halpern, 2000, 2004). Unfortunately, to date, not enough evidence exists to provide a definitive answer to the question.

To summarize, males and females in the general population seem to be basically similar regarding mental abilities; the exception is that males seem to excel in the spatial ability of mental rotation. The differences that do exist are relatively few—although some assert

that they are important ones (Halpern, 2000). We'll examine the possible causes of these differences after we examine gender comparisons in some other areas.

Personality Traits and Social Behavior

Turning to personality and social behavior, let's examine those factors for which gender differences are reasonably well documented.

Self-Esteem

As we noted in Chapter 5, females typically score lower than males on tests of self-esteem, but the difference in scores is generally small. For example, a meta-analysis of several hundred studies that included respondents from 7 to 60 years of age found only a small difference in self-esteem that favored males (Kling et al., 1999). The researchers also found that this gender difference increased somewhat during adolescence but returned to the smaller, preadolescent difference at about age 19. The authors found no support for claims in the popular press that girls' self-esteem drops dramatically during adolescence (Brody, 1997; Orenstein, 1994). A second meta-analysis also reported a small overall gender difference favoring males (Major et al., 1999).

Socioeconomic status and ethnicity also mediate gender differences in self-esteem (Major et al., 1999; Twenge & Crocker, 2002). Relatively large gender differences in self-esteem are found for lower- and middle-class males and females but not for upper-class males and females. Research consistently reports self-esteem

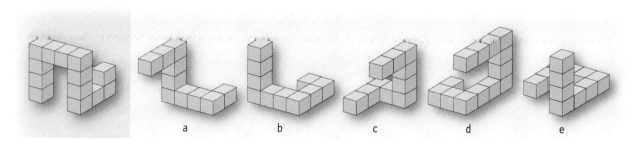

● FIGURE 10.4

Mental rotation test. If you mentally rotate the figure on the left, which of the five figures on the right would match it? The answer is "d." This problem illustrates how spatial rotation skills are measured. Researchers have uncovered some interesting gender differences in the ability to mentally rotate figures in space.

Adapted from Shepard, R. N., & Metzler, J. N. (1971). Mental rotation of three-dimensional objects. *Science, 171,* 701–703. Copyright © 1971 by American Association for the Advancement of Science. Adapted by permission of the publisher and author.

differences between white men and women, but findings are mixed for other ethnic groups (Major et al., 1999; Twenge and Crocker, 2002).

Aggression

Aggression **involves behavior that is intended to hurt someone, either physically or verbally** (see Chapter 4). Gender differences in aggression vary depending on the form aggression takes. A recent summary of cross-cultural meta-analyses reported that males consistently engage in more *physical aggression* than females (Archer, 2005). In the area of *verbal aggression* (insults, threats of harm), the findings are inconsistent (Geen, 1998; Harris, 1996). When it comes to *relational aggression,* such as giving someone the "silent treatment" to get one's way, talking behind another's back, or trying to get others to dislike someone, females are rated higher (Archer, 2005; Crick & Rose, 2000). Experts believe that the higher rates of relational aggression among girls and women result from the importance that females attach to close relationships (Crick, Casas, & Nelson, 2002).

This variable pattern of gender differences in aggression has also been found in cross-cultural research. In a study of 8-, 11-, and 15-year-olds from Finland, Israel, Italy, and Poland, researchers looked at gender differences in three types of aggression: physical, verbal, and indirect aggression (Oesterman et al., 1998). (*Indirect aggression* overlaps to some degree with relational aggression; it involves covert behaviors in which the target is not directly confronted—spreading rumors, for instance.) Across nations, boys were equally likely to use physical and verbal aggression and less likely to use indirect aggression. Girls most often used indirect aggression, followed by verbal aggression, then physical aggression.

Still, there is no getting around the fact that men commit a grossly disproportionate share of violent crimes. Figure 10.5 shows the stark gender differences in such crimes as assault, armed robbery, rape, and homicide.

Sexual Attitudes and Behavior

In the sexual domain, meta-analyses have found men to have more permissive attitudes than women about casual, premarital, and extramarital sex (Hyde & Oliver, 2000; Oliver & Hyde, 1993). Still, it's important to note that the analysis found many similarities between men and women—for example, both men and women were somewhat negative toward sexual permissiveness. Researchers also report that males are more sexually active and more likely to engage in masturbation than females are (Hyde & Oliver, 2000).

In a summary of gender differences in sexuality, Letitia Anne Peplau (2003) reported four key differences that hold for both gays and straights. First, men have more interest in sex than women (they think about sex more often and prefer to have sex more often, for example). Second, the connection between sex and intimacy is more important for women than for men (women typically prefer sex in the context of a relationship). Third, aggression is more often linked to sexuality for men than for women (men engage in coercive sex much more often). Finally, women's sexuality is more easily shaped by cultural and situational factors (their sexual attitudes are easier to change, for instance).

Conformity

Conformity **involves yielding to real or imagined social pressure.** Traditional beliefs hold that females are more conforming than males, who are viewed as more independent-minded. Nonetheless, research does not support the idea that females conform more to peer standards *unless* they are in a group pressure situation where they must openly disagree with others (Becker, 1986; Eagly & Carli, 1981; Hyde & Frost, 1993). As we noted earlier, race and gender often interact. For example, African American females seem to be less easily influenced and more assertive than either African American males or white females (Adams, 1980, 1983). The traditional explanation for gender differences in conformity is that women are more gullible than men, but there are alternative explanations as well: Women typically hold lower status in groups than men, and they may feel pressured to behave in line with female gender-role expectations (Eagly, 1987).

Emotional Expression

Conventional wisdom holds that women are more "emotional" than men. Does research support this be-

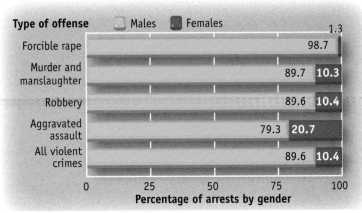

● FIGURE 10.5

Gender differences in violent crimes. Males are arrested for violent crimes far more often than females, as these statistics show. These data support the findings of laboratory studies indicating that males are more physically aggressive than females. (Data from U.S. Department of Justice, 2003)

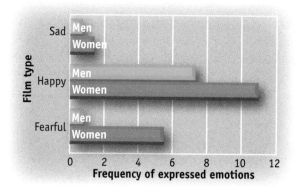

● **FIGURE 10.6**

Gender differences in emotional expression. Researchers calculated how often men and women showed facial expressions of various emotions as they viewed films. Women were judged to be more emotionally expressive than men on all three emotions studied. Men and women did not differ significantly in their reports of experienced emotion.

Adapted from Kring, A. M., & Gordon, A. H. (1998). Sex differences in emotions: Expression, experience and physiology. *Journal of Personality and Social Psychology, 74,* 686–703. Copyright © 1998 by the American Psychological Association. Adapted by permission of the author.

lief? If by being "emotional," we mean outwardly displaying one's emotions, the answer is yes. A number of studies have found that women express more emotion than men (Ashmore, 1990; Brody & Hall, 1993). Gender differences "favoring" women have been found on such emotions as sadness, disgust, fear, surprise, happiness, and anger.

Are women just more comfortable than men in publicly expressing emotion, or do women actually *experience* more emotion? To answer this question, Ann Kring and Albert Gordon (1998) had college students view films selected to evoke sadness, happiness, and fear. The researchers videotaped the participants' facial expressions and asked the subjects to describe their emotional experiences. As expected, they found gender differences in the facial expression of emotion (see Figure 10.6); however, they failed to find any gender differences in *experienced* emotions. Thus, gender differences in emotional functioning are limited to the outward expression of feelings and stem from the different display rules parents teach their sons and daughters (DeAngelis, 2001).

Communication

Popular stereotypes have it that females are much more talkative than males. In fact, the opposite seems to be true: Men talk more than women (Gleason & Ely, 2002). Men also tend to interrupt women more than women interrupt men, although this difference is small (Eckert & McConnell-Ginet, 2003). Yet when women have more power in work or personal relationships, women interrupt more (Aries, 1998). Thus, this supposed gender difference is probably better seen as a status difference.

Most studies have found that women speak more tentatively ("I may be wrong, but") than men (Carli & Bukatko, 2000). One explanation attributes women's greater use of tentative and polite language to lower status; another, to gender-specific socialization (Athenstadt, Haas, & Schwab, 2004).

Researchers have also studied how the genders compare in the realm of *non*verbal communication. A number of studies have shown women to be more sensitive to nonverbal cues (Hall, Carter, & Horgan, 2000). In an interesting twist, one study reported that women are better "readers" of happiness and that men are better "readers" of anger (Coats & Feldman, 1996). The researchers speculated that these gender differences in

encoding skills parallel the types of skills that members of each gender need in order to maintain their different social networks. Some claim that the gender difference in nonverbal sensitivity is actually a status difference (LaFrance, 2001), but others disagree (Hall & Friedman, 1999). For more on gender and communication, see this chapter's Application.

Psychological Disorders

In terms of the *overall* incidence of mental disorders, only minimal gender differences have been found. It seems that about one out of every three people will develop a psychological disorder over the course of their lives and that this statistic is roughly accurate for both males and females (Regier & Kaelber, 1995).

When researchers assess the prevalence of *specific* disorders, they *do* find some rather large gender differences (Regier et al., 1988; Nolen-Hoeksema & Keita, 2003). Antisocial behavior, alcoholism, and other drug-related disorders are far more prevalent among men than among women. On the other hand, women are about twice as likely as men to suffer from depression and anxiety disorders (phobias, for example). Females also show higher rates of eating disorders (see the Chapter 15 Application). In addition, women *attempt* suicide more often than men, but men *complete* suicides (actually kill themselves) more frequently than women (Maris, Berman, & Silverman, 2001).

What accounts for these gender differences in mental illnesses? One explanation is rooted in the obvious connection between the symptoms of "male" and "female" disorders and traditional gender roles

(Rosenfield, 1999). That is, women's disorders seem to reflect a turning *inward*—negative, hostile, anxious feelings and conflicts are directed against the self. In men, these same feelings and conflicts are typically directed *outward*—against either other individuals or society. (Suicide is one obvious exception.)

Putting Gender Differences in Perspective

Although research has uncovered some genuine gender differences in behavior, remember that these are *group* differences. That is, they tell us nothing about individuals. Essentially, we are comparing the "average man" with the "average woman." Furthermore, the differences between these groups are relatively small. Figure 10.7 shows how scores on a trait might be distributed for men and women. Although the group averages are detectably different, you can see that there is great variability within each group (gender) and huge overlap between the two group distributions. Thus, a gender difference that shows up on the average does not by itself tell us anything about you or any other unique individual. This is why such differences should not be used to restrict *individual* choices.

A second essential point is that gender accounts for a minute proportion of the differences between individuals. Using complicated statistical procedures, it is possible to gauge the influence of gender on behavior. These tests show that gender accounts for a very small amount of the variation among people. Thus, factors other than gender (for example, the social context in which behavior occurs) are far more important determinants of differences between individuals (Yoder & Kahn, 2003).

Another point to keep in mind is that when gender differences are found, they do not mean that one gender is better than the other (Halpern, 2004). When certain qualities are deemed superior to others by a particular society or group, the tendency is to perceive the group that performs less well in these valued areas as deficient, rather than as different. As Diane Halpern (1997) humorously notes, "It is about as meaningful to ask 'Which is the smarter sex?' . . . as it is to ask 'Which has the better genitals?'" (p. 1092). The problem is not with gender differences, but with how these differences are evaluated by the larger society.

To conclude, the behavioral differences between males and females are relatively few in number and small in size. Moreover, gender-relevant behavior often appears and disappears as gender-role expectations become more or less salient (Deaux & LaFrance, 1998). *Ultimately, the similarities between women and men greatly outweigh the differences.*

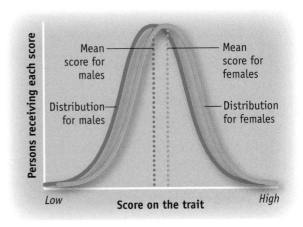

● **FIGURE 10.7**

The nature of group differences. Gender differences are group differences that tell us little about individuals because of the great overlap between the groups. For a given trait, one gender may score higher on the average, but there is far more variation within each gender than between the genders.

Alice Eagly

Although gender differences in personality and behavior are relatively few and modest, sometimes it seems otherwise. How come? One explanation focuses on gender-based differences in social roles. Alice Eagly's (1987) *social role theory* asserts that minor gender differences are exaggerated by the different social roles that males and females occupy. For example, because women are assigned the role of caregiver, they learn to behave in nurturing ways. Moreover, people come to associate such role-related behaviors with individuals of a given gender, not with the roles they play. In other words, people come to see nurturing as a female trait rather than a characteristic that anyone in a nurturing role would demonstrate. This is one way that stereotypes develop and persist.

Another explanation for discrepancies between beliefs and reality is that the differences actually reside in the eye of the beholder, not the beholdee. *Social constructionism* asserts that individuals construct their own reality based on societal expectations, conditioning, and self-socialization (Hyde, 1996; Maracek, 2001). According to social constructionists, the tendency to look for gender differences as well as specific beliefs about gender are rooted in the "gendered" messages and conditioning that permeate people's socialization experiences. To better understand these issues, we need to explore the role of biological and environmental factors as likely sources of gender differences.

Biological Origins of Gender Differences

LEARNING OBJECTIVES

- Summarize evolutionary explanations for gender differences.
- Review the evidence linking gender differences in cognitive abilities to brain organization.
- Review the evidence relating hormones to gender differences.

Are the gender differences that *do* exist biologically built in, or are they acquired through learning? This is the age-old issue of nature versus nurture. The "nature" theorists concentrate on how biological disparities between the genders contribute to differences in behavior. "Nurture" theorists, on the other hand, emphasize the role of learning and environmental influences. Although we will discuss biological and environmental influences separately, keep in mind that the distinctions between nature and nurture are less sharp today than they once were. Many contemporary researchers and theorists in this area are interested in how biological and environmental factors interact. We'll look at three biologically based lines of inquiry on this topic: evolutionary explanations, brain organization, and hormonal influences.

Evolutionary Explanations

Evolutionary psychologists suggest that gender differences in behavior reflect different natural selection pressures operating on the genders over the course of human history (Archer, 1996). That is, natural selection favors behaviors that maximize the chances of passing on genes to the next generation (reproductive success).

To support their assertions, evolutionary psychologists look for gender differences that are consistent across cultures (Kenrick & Trost, 1993). Is there consistency across cultures for the better-documented gender differences? Despite some fascinating exceptions, gender differences in cognitive abilities, aggression, and sexual behavior *are* found in many cultures (Beller & Gafni, 1996; Halpern, 2000). According to evolutionary psychologists, these consistent differences have emerged because males and females have been confronted with different adaptive demands. For example, males supposedly are more *sexually active and permissive* because they invest less than females in the process of procreation and can maximize their reproductive success by seeking many sexual partners (Buss & Kenrick, 1998).

The gender gap in *aggression* is also explained in terms of reproductive fitness. Because females are more selective about mating than males are, males have to engage in more competition for sexual partners than fe-

males do. Greater aggressiveness is thought to be adaptive for males in this competition for sexual access because it should foster social dominance over other males and facilitate the acquisition of the material resources emphasized by females when they evaluate potential partners (Kenrick & Trost, 1993). Evolutionary theorists assert that gender differences in *spatial abilities* reflect the division of labor in ancestral hunting-and-gathering societies in which males typically handled the hunting and females the gathering. Males' superiority on most spatial tasks has been attributed to the adaptive demands of hunting (Eals & Silverman, 1994).

Evolutionary analyses of gender differences are interesting, but controversial. While it is eminently plausible that evolutionary forces could have led to some divergence between males and females in typical behavior, evolutionary hypotheses are highly speculative and difficult to test empirically (Fausto-Sterling, 1992; Halpern, 2000). For example, it is quite a leap to infer that modern paper-and-pencil tests of spatial abilities assess a talent that would have made high scorers superior hunters million of years ago. In addition, evolutionary theory can be used to claim that the status quo in society is the inevitable outcome of evolutionary forces. Thus, if males have dominant status over females, natural selection must have favored this arrangement. The crux of the problem is that evolutionary analyses can be used to explain almost anything. For instance, if the situation regarding mental rotation were reversed—if females scored higher than males—evolutionary theorists might attribute females' superiority to the adaptive demands of gathering food, weaving baskets, and making clothes—and it would be difficult to prove otherwise.

WEB LINK 10.3

Great Ideas in Personality: Evolutionary Psychology and Sociobiology
Professor G. Scott Acton's excellent site in personality includes a major collection of resources supporting and opposing evolutionary psychology and sociobiology—the theory that human behavior is predominantly governed by biological forces, particularly those arising from one's genes.

Brain Organization

Some theorists propose that male and female brains are organized differently, which might account for gender differences in some cognitive abilities. As you may know, the human brain is divided into two halves. **The *cerebral hemispheres* are the right and left halves of the cerebrum, which is the convoluted outer layer of the brain.** The largest and most complicated part of the human brain, the cerebrum is responsible for most complex mental activities.

Some evidence suggests that the right and left cerebral hemispheres are specialized to handle different cognitive tasks (Sperry, 1982; Springer & Deutsch, 1998). For example, it appears that the *left hemisphere* is more actively involved in *verbal and mathematical processing*, while the *right hemisphere* is specialized to handle *visual-spatial and other nonverbal processing*. This pattern is generally seen in both right-handed and left-handed people, although it is less consistent among those who are left-handed.

After these findings on hemispheric specialization surfaced, some theorists began to wonder whether a connection might exist between this division of labor in the brain and the then-observed gender differences in verbal and spatial skills. Subsequently, researchers began looking for disparities between male and female brain organization.

Some thought-provoking findings *have* been reported. For instance, males exhibit more cerebral specialization than females (Bryden, 1988; Hines, 1990). In other words, males tend to depend more heavily than females on the left hemisphere in verbal processing and on the right hemisphere in spatial processing. Gender differences have also been found in the size of the *corpus callosum*, the band of fibers connecting the two hemispheres of the brain (Steinmetz et al., 1995). More specifically, some studies suggest that females tend to have a larger corpus callosum. This greater size might allow for better interhemispheric transfer of information, which in turn might underlie the more bilateral organization of female brains (Innocenti, 1994). Thus, some theorists have argued that these differences in brain organization are responsible for gender differences in verbal and spatial ability (Kimura & Hampson, 1993). Based on these findings, the popular press has often touted the idea that there are "male brains" and "female brains" that are fundamentally different (Bleier, 1984).

This idea is intriguing, but psychologists have a long way to go before they can attribute gender differences in verbal and spatial ability to right brain/left brain specialization. First, studies have not consistently found that males have more specialized brain organization than females (Fausto-Sterling, 1992), and the finding of a larger corpus callosum in females does not

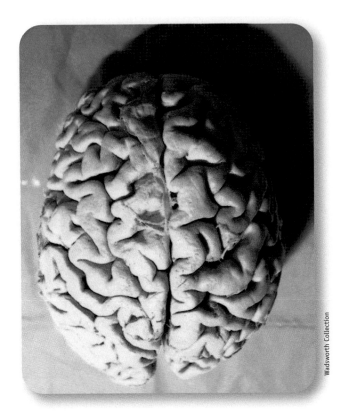

Studies have shown that the brain's cerebral hemispheres, shown here, are somewhat specialized in the kinds of cognitive tasks they handle and that such specialization is more pronounced in males than in females. Whether this difference bears any relation to gender differences in behavior is yet to be determined.

always show up (Hines, 1990). Second, because a significant amount of brain development occurs over the first five to ten years after birth, during which time males and females are socialized differently, it is possible that different life experiences may accumulate to produce slight differences in brain organization (Hood et al., 1987). In other words, the biological factors that supposedly cause gender differences in cognitive functioning may actually reflect the influence of environmental factors. Finally, it's important to remember that male and female brains are much more similar than they are different. Thus, the notion that cerebral specialization is linked to gender differences in mental abilities is still under debate.

Hormonal Influences

Biological explanations of gender differences have also focused on the possible role of hormones. ***Hormones are chemical substances released into the bloodstream by the endocrine glands.*** In this section we examine the effect of hormones on prenatal sexual differentiation and on sexual and aggressive behavior.

Prenatal Gender Differentiation

We know that hormones play a key role in gender differentiation during prenatal development. Biological gender is determined by sex chromosomes: An XX pairing produces a female, and an XY pairing produces a male. However, both male and female embryos are essentially the same until about 8 to 12 weeks after conception. Around this time, male and female gonads (sex glands) begin to produce different hormonal secretions. The high level of *androgens* (male hormones) in males and the low level of androgens in females lead to the differentiation of male and female genital organs.

The influence of prenatal hormones on gender differentiation becomes apparent when something interferes with normal prenatal hormonal secretions. About a half dozen endocrine disorders can cause overproduction or underproduction of specific gonadal hormones during prenatal development. Scientists have also studied children born to mothers given an androgen-like drug to prevent miscarriage. Two trends have been noted in this research (Collaer & Hines, 1995). First, females exposed prenatally to abnormally high levels of androgens exhibit more male-typical behavior than other females do. Second, males exposed prenatally to abnormally low levels of androgens exhibit more female-typical behavior than other males. For example, girls with *congenital adrenal hyperplasia* tend to show "tomboyish" interests in vigorous outdoor activities and in "male" toys and have elevated scores on measures of aggressiveness and spatial ability.

The findings suggest that prenatal hormones shape gender differences in humans. But there are a number of problems with this evidence (Basow, 1992; Fausto-Sterling, 1992). First, there is much more and much stronger evidence for females than for males. Second, it's always dangerous to draw conclusions about the general population based on small samples of people who have abnormal conditions. Third, most of the endocrine disorders studied have multiple effects (besides altering hormone level) that make it difficult to isolate actual causes. Finally, most of the research is necessarily correlational, and it is always risky to draw causal conclusions from correlational data.

Sexual and Aggressive Behavior

The hormone testosterone plays an important role in *sexual desire* for both men and women (Bancroft, 2002a). That is, when testosterone is reduced or eliminated, both men and women show decreases in sexual drive. A handful of studies have also reported associations between levels of male and female hormones and specific traits. So far, however, the results of these studies are equivocal and inconsistent (Fausto-Sterling, 1992; Hines, 1982). For instance, testosterone has been linked with higher levels of *aggression* (impulsive and antisocial behavior) in humans, but the picture is complicated because aggressive behavior can produce increases in testosterone (Dabbs, 2000).

To summarize, hormones probably do play a role in some aspects of sexual and aggressive behavior, although the nature of the connections is not well understood. Also, hormones have less influence on human behavior than they do on animal behavior, because humans are more susceptible to environmental influences. We still have much to learn about the complicated ways in which hormones interact with social and psychological factors.

The overall evidence suggests that biological factors play a relatively minor role in gender differences, creating predispositions that are largely shaped by experience. In contrast, efforts to link gender differences to disparities in the way males and females are reared have proved more fruitful. We consider this perspective next.

Environmental Origins of Gender Differences

LEARNING OBJECTIVES

- Define socialization and gender roles, and describe Margaret Mead's findings on the variability of gender roles and their implications.
- Explain how reinforcement and punishment, observational learning, and self-socialization operate in gender-role socialization.

- Describe how parents and peers influence gender-role socialization.
- Describe how schools and the media influence gender-role socialization.

Socialization **is the acquisition of the norms and roles expected of people in a particular society.** This process includes all the efforts made by a society to ensure that its members learn to behave in a manner that's considered appropriate. Teaching children about gender roles is an important aspect of the socialization process. *Gender roles* **are cultural expectations about what is appropriate behavior for each gender.** For example, in our culture women have been expected to rear children, cook meals, clean house, and do laundry. On the other hand, men have been expected to be the family breadwinner, do yardwork, and tinker with cars.

Are gender roles in other cultures similar to those seen in our society? Generally, yes—but not necessarily. Despite a fair amount of cross-cultural consistency in gender roles, some dramatic variability occurs as well (Gibbons, 2000). For instance, anthropologist Margaret Mead (1950) conducted a now-classic study of three tribes in New Guinea. In one tribe, *both* genders followed our masculine role expectations (the Mundugumor); in another, *both* genders approximated our feminine role (the Arapesh). In a third tribe, the male and female roles were roughly the *reverse* of our own (the Tchambuli). Such remarkable discrepancies between cultures existing within 100 miles of one another demonstrate that gender roles are not a matter of biological destiny. Instead, like other roles, gender roles are acquired through socialization.

As we noted earlier, Eagly's social role theory suggests that gender differences occur because males and females are guided by different role expectations. In the next section, we'll discuss how society teaches individuals about gender roles.

Processes in Gender-Role Socialization

How do people acquire gender roles? Several key learning processes come into play, including reinforcement and punishment, observational learning, and self-socialization.

Reinforcement and Punishment

In part, gender roles are shaped by the power of rewards and punishment—the key processes in operant conditioning (see Chapter 2). Parents, teachers, peers, and others often reinforce (usually with tacit approval) "gender-appropriate" behavior (Bussey & Bandura, 1999; Fagot & Hagan, 1991). For example, a young boy who has hurt himself may be told that "big boys don't cry." If he succeeds in inhibiting his crying, he may get a pat on the back or a warm smile—both potent reinforcers. Over time, a consistent pattern of such reinforcement will strengthen the boy's tendency to "act like a man" and suppress emotional displays.

Most parents take gender-appropriate behavior for granted and don't go out of their way to reward it. On the other hand, parents are much less tolerant of gender-inappropriate behavior, especially in their sons (Lytton & Romney, 1991; Sandnabba & Ahlberg, 1999). For instance, a 10-year-old boy who enjoys playing with dollhouses will probably elicit strong disapproval.

Parents typically reward "gender-appropriate" behavior in their children.

Reactions usually involve ridicule or verbal reprimands rather than physical punishment.

Observational Learning

Younger children commonly imitate the behavior of a parent or an older sibling. This imitation, or *observational learning,* occurs when a child's behavior is influenced by observing others, who are called *models.* Parents serve as models for children, as do siblings, teachers, relatives, and others who are important in children's lives. Note that models are not limited to real people; television, movie, and cartoon characters can also serve as models.

According to *social cognitive theory* (see Chapter 2), young children are more likely to imitate people who are nurturant, powerful, and similar to them (Bussey & Bandura, 1984, 1999). Children imitate both genders, but most children are prone to imitate same-gender models. Thus, observational learning often leads young girls to play with dolls, dollhouses, and toy stoves. By contrast, young boys are more likely to tinker with toy trucks, miniature gas stations, and tool kits. Interestingly, same-gender peers may be even more influential models than parents are (Maccoby, 2002).

Self-Socialization

Children are not merely passive recipients of gender-role socialization. Rather, they play an active role in this process, beginning early in life (Bem, 1993; Martin, Ruble, & Szkrybalo, 2002). Because society labels people, characteristics, behavior, and activities by gender, children learn that gender is an important social category. For example, they learn that females wear

Children learn behaviors appropriate to their gender roles very early in life. According to social learning theory, girls tend to do the sorts of things their mothers do, while boys tend to follow in their fathers' footsteps.

dresses and males don't. Around 2 to 3 years of age, children begin to identify themselves as male or female (Martin et al., 2002). In addition, they begin to organize the various pieces of gender-relevant information into gender schemas. **Gender schemas are cognitive structures that guide the processing of gender-relevant information.** Basically, gender schemas work like lenses that cause people to view and organize the world in terms of gender (Bem, 1993).

Self-socialization begins when children link the gender schema for their own gender to their self-concept. Once this connection is made, children are motivated to selectively attend to activities and information that are consistent with the schema for their own gender. For example, Jeremy knows that he is a boy and also has a "boy" schema that he attaches to his own sense of boyhood. Too, his self-esteem is dependent on how well he lives up to his boy schema. In this way, children get involved in their own socialization. They are "gender detectives," working diligently to discover the rules that are supposed to govern their behavior (Martin & Ruble, 2004).

Sources of Gender-Role Socialization

Four major sources of gender-role messages are parents, peers, schools, and the media. Keep in mind that gender-role socialization varies depending on one's socioeconomic status and ethnicity. For example, black families typically make fewer distinctions between girls

and boys when compared to white families (Hill, 2002). By contrast, gender roles are relatively rigidly defined in Asian and Hispanic families (Chia et al., 1994; Comas-Diaz, 1987). Also, gender roles are changing, so the generalizations that follow may say more about how *you* were socialized than about how your children will be.

Parents

A great deal of gender-role socialization takes place in the home. Nonetheless, a meta-analysis of 172 studies of parental socialization practices suggests that parents don't treat girls and boys as differently as one might expect (Lytton & Romney, 1991). Still, there are some important distinctions. For one thing, there is a strong tendency for both mothers and fathers to emphasize and encourage *play activities* that are "gender-appropriate." For example, studies show that parents encourage boys and girls to play with different types of toys (Wood, Desmarais, & Gugula, 2002). As Figure 10.8 (on the next page) shows, substantial gender differences are found in toy preferences. Generally, boys have less leeway to play with "feminine" toys than girls do with "masculine" toys. As children grow older, their leisure activities often vary by gender: Jaime plays in Little League and Alexis gets dancing lessons. Too, the picture books parents buy for their children typically depict characters engaging in gender stereotypic activities (Gooden & Gooden, 2001).

A second way parents emphasize gender is in the assignment of *household chores* (Lytton & Romney, 1991; Cunningham, 2001). Tasks are doled out on the basis of

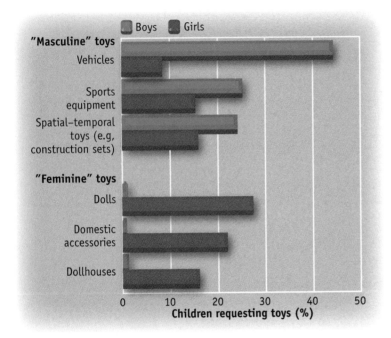

● FIGURE 10.8

Toy preferences and gender. This graph depicts the percentage of boys and girls asking for various types of toys in letters to Santa Claus (adapted from Richardson & Simpson, 1982). Boys and girls differ substantially in their toy preferences, which probably reflects the effects of gender-role socialization.

Adapted from Richardson, J. G., & Simpson, C. H. (1982). Children, gender and social structure: An analysis of the contents of letters to Santa Claus. *Child Development, 53,* 429–436. Copyright © 1982 by the Society for Research in Child Development, Inc. Adapted by permission.

gender stereotypes: Girls usually do laundry and dishes, whereas boys mow the lawn and sweep the garage.

Parents' attitudes about gender roles have been shown to influence the gender roles their children acquire (Fiese & Skillman, 2000). Importantly, gender expectations vary by ethnicity and socioeconomic status. African American families seem to place less emphasis on traditional gender roles than white American families do (Hill, 2002). By contrast, Hispanic families usually encourage traditional gender-role behavior, and Asian American families typically encourage subservience in their daughters (Tsai & Uemera, 1988). Also, middle-class parents may allow their children to deviate more from traditional gender roles than lower-class parents do (Reid & Paludi, 1993). Because social class cuts across ethnicity with regard to gender-role attitudes, the findings in this area are complex (Flannagan & Perese, 1998).

Peers

Peers form an important network for learning about gender-role stereotypes, as well as gender-appropriate and gender-inappropriate behavior. Between the ages of 4 and 6, children tend to separate into same-gender groups. From then to about age 12, boys and girls spend much more time with same-gender than other-gender

peers. Moreover, according to Eleanor Maccoby (1998, 2002), over time boys' and girls' groups develop different "subcultures" (shared understandings and interests) that strongly shape youngsters' gender-role socialization (Maccoby, 1998, 2002).

Play among same-gender peers takes different forms for boys and girls (Maccoby, 1998, 2002). Boys play in larger groups and roam farther away from home, whereas girls prefer smaller groups and stay near the house. In addition, high status in boys' groups tends to be achieved by engaging in dominant behavior (telling others what to do and enforcing orders). In contrast, girls usually express their wishes as suggestions rather than demands. Also, boys engage in rough-and-tumble play much more frequently than girls do.

Because both boys and girls are critical of peers who violate traditional gender norms, they perpetuate stereotypical behavior. Among children ages 3–11, boys are devalued more than girls for dressing like the

Boys are under more pressure than girls to behave in gender-appropriate ways. Little boys who show an interest in dolls are likely to be chastised by both parents and peers.

other gender, whereas girls are evaluated more negatively than boys for playing like the other gender (loudly and roughly versus quietly and gently) (Blakemore, 2003).

Schools

The school environment figures importantly in socializing gender roles (American Association of University Women, 1994; Sadker & Sadker, 1994). Children's grade-school *textbooks* have often ignored or stereotyped girls and women (AAUW Educational Foundation, 1992). Traditionally, these books have portrayed males as clever, heroic, and adventurous, whereas females have been shown performing domestic chores. Although the depiction of stereotypical gender roles has declined considerably since the 1970s, researchers still find significant differences in how males and females are portrayed, even in supposedly nonsexist books (Diekman & Murnen, 2004). Many high school and college textbooks also contain gender bias. The most common problems are using generic masculine language ("policeman" versus "police officer" and so forth) and portraying males and females in stereotypic roles. You might review your textbooks for instances of gender bias.

Gender bias in schools also shows up in *teachers' treatment of boys and girls*. Preschool and grade-school teachers often reward gender-appropriate behavior in their pupils (Fagot et al., 1985). Teachers also tend to pay greater attention to boys—helping them, praising them, and scolding them more than females (Sadker & Sadker, 1994). By contrast, girls tend to be less visible in the classroom and to receive less encouragement for academic achievement from teachers. Many teacher education textbooks still give little attention to gender equity (Zittleman & Sadker, 2002).

Gender bias also shows up in *academic and career counseling*. Despite the fact that females obtain higher grades than males (on the average) in all subjects from elementary school through college (Halpern, 2004), many counselors continue to encourage male students to pursue high-status careers in medicine or engineering while guiding female students toward less prestigious careers (Read, 1991).

The Media

Television is yet another source of gender-role socialization (Luecke-Aleksa et al., 1995). American youngsters spend a lot of time watching TV (see Figure 10.9). Children between the ages of 3 and 11 watch an average of 2 to 4 hours of TV per day (Huston et al., 1990). African American children and adolescents spend more time in front of the tube than their white peers (Roberts et al., 1999).

An analysis of male and female characters on prime-time *television programs* showed that the number and variety of roles of female TV characters have

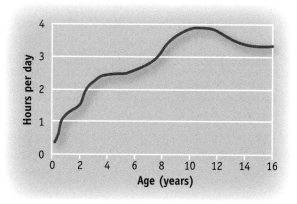

● **FIGURE 10.9**

Television viewing habits. As children grow up, they spend more and more time watching TV until viewing time begins to decline slightly around age 12. Research shows that children's conceptions of gender roles are influenced to a considerable degree by what they watch on television.

Adapted from Liebert, R. M., & Sprafkin, J. (1988). *The early window: Effects of television on children and youth.* Boston: Allyn & Bacon. Copyright © 1988 by Allyn & Bacon. Adapted by permission.

increased over the past 30 years but that these shifts lag behind the actual changes in women's lives (Glascock, 2001; Signorielli & Bacue, 1999). Compared to males, females appear less often, are less likely to be employed (especially in prestigious positions), are more likely to be younger, and are more likely to appear in secondary and comedy roles. In children's *cartoons,* male characters appear more often, have more prominent roles, talk more, and engage in more varied behaviors than female characters (Thompson & Zerbinos, 1995).

Television commercials are even more gender-stereotyped than TV programs (Furnham & Mak, 1999). Women are frequently shown worrying about trivial matters such as laundry and cleaning products, whereas men appear as bold outdoorsmen or energetic sports fans. In a study of gender stereotyping in TV commercials on five continents, the authors reported that, in all the countries studied, men appeared more often than women in both on- and off-screen announcer roles (Furnham & Mak, 1999).

Most *video games* push a hypermasculine stereotype featuring search-and-destroy missions, fighter pilot battles, and male sports (Lips, 2005). Of the few video games directed at girls, the great majority of them are highly stereotypic (shopping and Barbie games). Also, *music videos* frequently portray women as sex objects and men as dominating and aggressive (Sommers-Flanagan, Sommers-Flanagan, & Davis, 1993), and these portrayals appear to influence viewers' attitudes about sexual conduct (Hansen & Hansen, 1988).

A meta-analysis reported a link between the number and type of television programs children watch and the acquisition of gender-stereotyped beliefs: Children who watch a lot of television hold more stereotyped beliefs about gender than children who watch less TV (Herrett-Skjellum & Allen, 1996). Still, this research is correlational, so it is quite likely that other factors—such as parental values—come into play as well. Nonetheless, once gender stereotypes are learned, they are difficult to change.

Another manifestation of gender bias is television's inordinate *emphasis on women's physical appearance* (Lauzen & Dozier, 2002). Males on television may or may not be good-looking, but the vast majority of females are young, attractive, and sexy (Signorielli & Bacue, 1999). Overweight female characters are much more likely than male characters to receive negative comments about their weight (Fouts & Burggraf, 1999;

WEB LINK 10.4

Gender and Race in Media
The University of Iowa's Communications Studies Program offers a focused guide to the ways in which gender and racial differences are expressed in various media, including an excellent set of materials dealing with gender and advertising.

Fouts & Vaughan, 2002). As you'll see in the Chapter 15 Application, these cultural expectations have been cited as a cause of the disproportionately high incidence of eating disorders in females.

Gender Roles

LEARNING OBJECTIVES

- List five elements of the traditional male role, and contrast it with the modern male role.
- Describe three common problems associated with the traditional male role.
- List three major expectations of the female role.
- Describe three common problems associated with the female role.
- Describe two ways in which women are victimized by sexism.

Traditional gender roles are based on several unspoken assumptions: that all members of the same gender have basically the same traits, that the traits of one gender are very different from the traits of the other gender, and that masculine traits are more highly valued. In recent decades, many social critics and theorists in psychology and other fields have scrutinized gender roles, identifying the essential features and the ramifications of traditional roles. In this section, we review the research and

theory in this area and note changes in gender roles over the past 30 to 40 years. We begin with the male role.

Role Expectations for Males

A number of psychologists have sought to pinpoint the essence of the traditional male role (Brannon, 1976; Levant, 1996, 2003; Pleck, 1995). Many consider *antifemininity* to be the central theme that runs through the male gender role. That is, "real men" shouldn't act in any way that might be perceived as feminine. For example, men should not publicly display vulnerable emotions, should avoid feminine occupations, and should not show obvious interest in relationships—especially homosexual ones. Five key attributes constitute the traditional male role (Brannon, 1976; Jansz, 2000):

1. *Achievement.* To prove their masculinity, men need to beat out other men at work and at sports. Having a high-status job, driving an expensive car, and making lots of money are aspects of this element.
2. *Aggression.* Men should be tough and fight for what they believe is right. They should aggressively defend themselves and those they love against threats.
3. *Autonomy.* Men should be self-reliant and not admit to being dependent on others.
4. *Sexuality.* Real men are heterosexual and are highly motivated to pursue sexual activities and conquests.

"Sex brought us together, but gender drove us apart."

5. *Stoicism.* Men should not share their pain or express their "soft" feelings. They should be cool and calm under pressure.

Gender-role expectations for males have remained relatively stable for years. However, the male role may be undergoing some changes. According to Joseph Pleck (1995), who has written extensively on this issue, in the *traditional male role,* masculinity is validated by individual physical strength, aggressiveness, and emotional inexpressiveness. In the *modern male role,* masculinity is validated by economic achievement, organizational power, emotional control (even over anger), and emotional sensitivity and self-expression, but only with women.

Thus, in modern societies, the traditional male role coexists with some new expectations. Some theorists use the plural "masculinities" to describe these variations in the male gender role (Smiler, 2004). This flux in expectations means that males are experiencing role inconsistencies and pressures to behave in ways that conflict with traditional masculinity: to communicate personal feelings, to nurture children and share in housework, to integrate sexuality with love, and to curb aggression (Levant, 1996, 2003). Some psychologists believe that these pressures have shaken traditional masculine norms sufficiently that many men are experiencing a masculinity crisis (Levant, 1996, 2003). That is, they are feeling bewildered and confused, and their pride in being a man has been diminished. The rise in popularity of men's groups and organizations such as the Promise Keepers may reflect this confusion. The good news is that boys and men are beginning to get more attention from psychological theorists, researchers, and clinicians (see the Recommended Reading box).

Problems with the Male Role

It is often assumed that only females suffer from the constricting binds of traditional gender roles. Not so. Increasingly, the costs of the male role are a cause for concern (Levant, 1996; Pleck, 1995).

Pressure to Succeed

Most men are socialized to be highly competitive and are taught that a man's masculinity is measured by the size of his paycheck and job status. As Christopher Kilmartin (2000) notes, "There is always another man who has more money, higher status, a more attractive partner, or a bigger house. The traditional man . . . must constantly work harder and faster " (p. 13). Small wonder, then, that so many men pursue success with a fervor that is sometimes dangerous to their health. The extent of this danger is illustrated by men's life expectancy, which is about six years shorter than women's (of course, factors besides gender roles contribute to this difference).

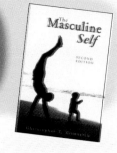

The majority of men who have internalized the success ethic are unable to fully realize their dreams. This is a particular problem for African American and Hispanic men, who experience more barriers to financial success than European American men do (Biernat & Kobrynowicz, 1997). How does this "failure" affect men? Although many are able to adjust to it, many are not. The latter group are likely to suffer from shame and poor self-esteem (Kilmartin, 2000). Men's emphasis on success also makes it more likely that they will spend long hours on the job. This pattern in turn decreases the amount of time families can spend together and increases the amount of time wives spend on housework and child care.

Interestingly, younger men seem less inclined to embrace the success ethic than older men. A significantly smaller proportion of men between the ages of 18 and 37 are work focused (they want to spend more time with their families) compared to men age 38 and older (Families and Work Institute, 2004).

The Emotional Realm

Most young boys are trained to believe that men should be strong, tough, cool, and detached (Brody, 2000; Jansz, 2000). Thus, they learn early to hide vulnerable emotions such as love, joy, and sadness because they believe that such feelings are feminine and imply weakness. Over time, some men become strangers to their own emotional lives (Levant, 1996). It seems that men with traditional views of masculinity are more likely to suppress outward emotions and to fear emotions, supposedly because they may lead to a loss of composure (Jakupcak et al., 2003).

The difficulty with "tender" emotions has serious consequences. First, as we saw in Chapter 3, suppressed emotions can contribute to stress-related disorders. And worse, men are less likely than women to seek help from health professionals (Addis & Mahalik, 2003). Second, men's emotional inexpressiveness can cause problems in their relationships with partners and children. For example, children whose fathers are warm, loving, and accepting toward them have higher self-esteem and lower rates of aggression and behavior problems, and the reverse is also true (Rohner & Veneziano, 2001). On a positive note, fathers are increasingly involving themselves with their children. And 30 percent of fathers report that they take equal or greater responsibility for their children than their working wives do (Bond et al., 2003).

One emotion males are allowed to express is anger. Sometimes this anger translates into physical aggression or violence. Men commit nearly 90 percent of violent crimes in the United States and almost all sexual assaults (U.S. Department of Justice, 2003).

Sexual Problems

Men often experience sexual problems that derive partly from their gender-role socialization, which gives them a "macho" sexual image to live up to. There are few things that men fear more than a sexual encounter in which they are unable to achieve an erection (Doyle, 1989). Unfortunately, these very fears often *cause* the dysfunction that men dread (see Chapter 13). The upshot is that men's obsession with sexual performance can produce anxiety that may interfere with their sexual responsiveness.

Another problem is that many men learn to confuse feelings of intimacy and sex. In other words, if a man experiences strong feelings of connectedness, he is likely to interpret them as sexual feelings. This confusion has a number of consequences (Kilmartin, 2000). For one thing, sex may be the only way some men can allow themselves to feel intimately connected to another. Thus, men's keen interest in sex may be driven, in part, by strong needs for emotional intimacy that don't get satisfied in other ways. The confusion of intimacy and sex may underlie the tendency for men (compared to women) to perceive eye contact, a compliment, an innocent smile, a friendly remark, or a brush against the arm as a sexual invitation (Kowalski, 1993). Finally, the sexualization of intimate feelings causes inappropriate anxiety when men feel affection for another man, thus promoting homophobia.

Homophobia **is the intense fear and intolerance of homosexuality.** Because homosexuality is still largely unaccepted, fear of being labeled homosexual keeps many people, who might otherwise be more flexible, adhering to traditional gender roles. This situation is particularly true for males. One reason that homophobia is more prevalent among males is that the male role is rooted in the fear of appearing feminine—and feminine characteristics are mistakenly associated with gay males (Maurer, 1999). Second, homophobia is much more common in men than in women because males feel more pressure to avoid any behavior characteristic of the other gender (Herek, 2003). Although they will tolerate "tomboyism" in girls, parents (especially fathers) are highly intolerant of any "sissy" behavior exhibited by their sons. This intense pressure against appearing feminine contributes not only to homophobia among heterosexual males but also to negative attitudes toward females (Friedman, 1989).

Role Expectations for Females

In the past 30 years, the role expectations for American women have undergone dramatic changes, especially when compared to male role expectations. Prior to the 1970s, a woman was expected to be a wife and a stay-at-home mother. Today, there are three major expectations:

1. *The marriage mandate.* Most women are socialized to feel incomplete until they find a mate. Women attain adult status when they get married. In the context of marriage, women are expected to be responsible for cooking, cleaning, and other housework.

2. *The motherhood mandate.* The imperative of the female role is to have children. This expectation has been termed the "motherhood mandate" (Russo, 1979). Preferably, a woman should have at least two children, and at least one of them should be a son. The prevailing ideology of today's motherhood mandate is that of "intensive mothering"—mothering should be wholly child-centered, and mothers should be self-

sacrificing rather than persons who also have needs and interests (Arendell, 2000).

3. *Work outside the home.* Most of today's young women, especially those who are college educated, expect to work outside the home, and they also want a satisfying family life (Family and Work Institute, 2004; Konrad, 2003). As you can see in Figure 10.10, the percentage of women in the labor force has been steadily rising over the last 30 years.

The marriage and motherhood mandates fuel women's focus on *heterosexual success*—learning how to attract and interest males as prospective mates. The resulting emphasis on dating and marriage can lead some women away from a challenging career—they worry about driving away a prospective mate who might be threatened by a high-achieving woman (Arnold, 1994). Because younger men are more supportive of their wives' working than older men, this conflict should ease for younger women (Family and Work Institute, 2004). The prospect of dealing with young children can also reduce women's career expectations.

Problems with the Female Role

Writers in the feminist movement generated some compelling analyses of the problems associated with the pre-1970s traditional role of wife and mother

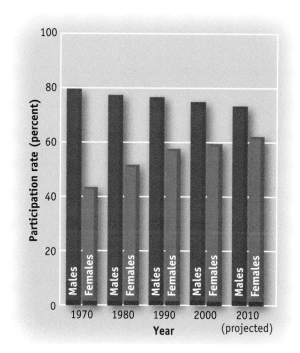

● **FIGURE 10.10**

Increases in women's workforce participation. The percentage of women who work outside the home has increased steadily over the past century, especially since 1970. In 2010, close to two-thirds of women are projected to be in the labor force, about 10 percent fewer than men. (Data from U.S. Bureau of the Census, 2000, 2003, 2004a)

Gender Stereotypes and "Appearance Pressure"

Currently in the United States, the ideal physique for women is an hourglass shape with medium-sized breasts packaged in a relatively thin body. For men, the ideal physique includes broad shoulders, narrow hips, narrow waist, and muscularity. Images of these gender ideals pervade "women's" and "men's" magazines as well as those that focus on fitness (Vartanian, Giant, & Passino, 2001). Physically attractive men and women dominate television programs and commercials. In an ironic use of the term, "reality" television shows such as *Extreme Makeover* and *The Swan* depict real men and women undergoing extensive plastic surgery to improve their lives. The media message for today's women: thin is "in"; for men: you need "six-pack abs" to be attractive.

Weight is particularly important for women because men generally prefer thinner women to those who are heavier. For many years, this concern with thinness has existed among white and Asian Americans, but it has been a lesser concern among Hispanics and black Americans (Polivy & Herman, 2002). Unfortunately, some recent evidence suggests that the thin female ideal may be spreading to these two groups as well (Barnett, Keel, & Conoscenti, 2001; Bay-Cheng et al., 2002, but also see Schooler et al. 2004).

Today, males also seem to be experiencing "appearance pressure." Recent studies show that adolescent boys, college men, and adult males all prefer to be more muscular (Morrison, Morrison, & Hopkins, 2003; Olivardia, Pope, & Phillips, 2000). Pressure on males also appears to be coming from women, who prefer a large torso with narrow waist and hips (Maisey et al., 1999). More men are dieting, working out, and seeking surgery than has been true in the past (Olivardia et al., 2000).

Do televised images of body ideals have any impact on viewers? Unfortunately, it seems that they do—negative ones. For example, in one study, college men and women were exposed to either sexist ads, nonsexist ads, or no ads (Lavine, Sweeney, & Wager, 1999). (The sexist ads portrayed both men and women as sex objects as part of a bogus marketing research study.) The results showed that both the men and women who were exposed to sexist ads had greater body dissatisfaction than students in the other two conditions. In a correlational study, the amount of exposure to ideal body images of women on television (based on viewing habits) was measured. Women with a lot of exposure to these ideal images were more likely to prefer a smaller waist and hips and a medium-sized bust for themselves (Harrison, 2003). Both women and men who viewed ideal body images of women were more likely to approve of cosmetic surgery for women. Other research on women has shown that internalized images of thinness have been linked to disordered eating (Harrison & Cantor, 1997).

The current social pressures for females to be thin and for males to be muscular cause both genders to have distorted perceptions of their peers' body ideals, thus increasing the pressure to conform. For example, a study of college students reported that the women believed that their male and female peers preferred a much thinner female silhouette than was actually the case; the men exaggerated the extent to which others perceived large physiques as most desirable for males (Cohn & Adler, 1992).

Also, social pressures to attain an ideal body shape push many individuals into unhealthy eating behaviors. Experts say that eating disorders are at an all-time high (Gleaves et al., 2000). And some males may turn to dangerous anabolic steroids to build up their muscle mass (Courtenay, 2000). Another response to "attractiveness pressure" is the increased rate of cosmetic surgeries. Between 2003 and 2004, a 48 percent increase occurred in the number of cosmetic surgeries performed on Americans who were 18 and younger (Springen, 2004).

Thus, the pressure to live up to an unrealistic, and sometimes unhealthy, ideal body shape is a significant adjustment challenge facing both males and females today.

(Friedan, 1964; Millett, 1970). Many criticized the assumption that women, unlike men, did not need an independent identity; it should be sufficient to be Jim Smith's wife and Jason and Robin's mother. Increasingly over the past 40 years, girls and women have been encouraged to develop and use their talents, and work opportunities for women have greatly expanded. Still, there are problems with the female role.

Diminished Career Aspirations

Despite recent efforts to increase women's opportunities for achievement, young women continue to have lower career aspirations than young men with comparable backgrounds and abilities (Wilgosh, 2001). Also, they are more likely to underestimate their achievement than boys (who overestimate theirs) (Eccles, 2001). This thinking is especially likely when estimating performance on "masculine" tasks such as science and math versus "feminine" (social skills, language) or gender-neutral tasks. This is a problem because science and math are the foundations for many high-paying, high-status careers. Higher intelligence and grades are generally associated with higher career aspirations, but this trend is less likely to hold true for girls than for boys (Kelly & Cobb, 1991).

The discrepancy between women's abilities and their level of achievement has been termed the *ability-achievement gap* (Hyde, 1996). The roots of this gap seem to lie in the conflict between achievement and femininity that is built into the traditional female role. Many women worry that they will be seen as unfeminine if they boldly strive for success. Of course, this is not a concern for all women. Still, gender discrimination remains a barrier for those who aim for prestigious careers.

Juggling Multiple Roles

Another problem with the female role is that societal institutions have not kept pace with the reality of women's lives. Women are able to successfully manage marriage and a career. But when children enter the picture, the emotional and time demands on women increase dramatically (Hoffnung, 2004).

Today 60 percent of married women with children under the age of 6 work outside the home (U.S. Bureau of the Census, 2004). Yet the workplace (and many husbands and fathers) still operate as if women were stay-at-home moms and as if there were no single-parent families. This gap between policies based on outdated assumptions about women's lives and reality means that women who "want it all" experience burdens and conflicts that most men do not. That's because most men typically have *major* day-to-day responsibilities in only *one* role: worker. But most women have major day-to-day responsibilities in *three* roles: spouse, parent, and worker.

Although more men, and especially younger men, are giving additional time to household chores and child care, women still do most of this work (Family & Work Institute, 2004). One way today's college-educated women deal with these conflicts is to postpone marriage and motherhood (and to have small families) to pursue more education or to launch their careers (Hoffnung, 2004). Once women in high-powered careers are established, some are temporarily "stopping out" of the workforce to focus on childbearing and rearing their young children (Wallis, 2004). Given the three-role reality of their lives, they trade off the worker role and income for a slower pace and less stress to rear young children, although they miss the stimulation and recognition from their work. (But keep in mind that these women have husbands who can support the family.) Their strategy: "You can have it all, just not all at the same time" (Wallis, 2004, p. 53).

Of course multiple roles, in themselves, are not inherently problematic. In fact, there is some evidence that multiple roles can be beneficial for mental health, as you'll see in Chapter 12. Rather, the problem stems from unequal sharing of role responsibilities. Greater participation in household tasks and child care by husbands or others as well as family-friendly workplaces and subsidized quality child-care programs would alleviate women's stress in this area.

Ambivalence About Sexuality

Like men, women may have sexual problems that stem, in part, from their gender-role socialization. For many women, the problem is difficulty in enjoying sex. Why? For one thing, many girls are still taught to suppress or deny their sexual feelings (Hyde & DeLamater, 2003).

RECOMMENDED READING

The Mismeasure of Woman
by Carol Tavris (Touchstone, 1993)

The title and thesis of this book refer to Protagoras's statement that "Man is the measure of all things." Tavris, a social psychologist, has written this book for the nonprofessional audience and uses her natural wit and humor to excellent advantage. She points out the fallacy of using a male-centered standard for evaluating "what is normal" for both men and women. Using research findings, she exposes numerous myths about males and females that are the source of misunderstanding and frustration for many.

Tavris is not interested in replacing a male-centered view with a female-dominant view but rather in expanding our view of what it means to be human. She urges people to move away from the tendency to think in "us versus them" terms about gender issues. Instead, she suggests that men and women need to work together and rethink how they need to be to have the kind of relationships and work that are life enhancing.

For another, they are told that a woman's role in sex is a passive one. In addition, girls are encouraged to focus on romance rather than on gaining sexual experience. As a result, many women feel uncomfortable (guilty, ashamed) with their sexual urges. The experience of menstruation (and its association with blood and pain) and the fear of pregnancy add another dimension of negativity to sex. And females' concerns about sexual exploitation and rape also foster negative emotions. Thus, when it comes to sexuality, women are likely to have ambivalent feelings instead of the largely positive feelings that men have (Tolman, 2002; Hyde, 2004).

Sexism: A Special Problem for Females

Intimately intertwined with the topic of gender roles is the issue of sexism. *Sexism* **is discrimination against people on the basis of their gender.** (Using our terminology, the term should be "genderism," but we'll stick with standard terminology for the sake of clarity.) Sexism usually refers to discrimination by men against women. However, sometimes *women* discriminate against other women and sometimes *men* are the vic-

tims of gender-based discrimination. In this section, we'll discuss two specific problems: economic discrimination and aggression toward women.

Economic Discrimination

Women are victimized by two forms of economic discrimination: differential access to jobs and differential treatment once on the job. Concerning *job access,* the problem is that women still lack the same employment opportunities as men. For example, in 2003, only 6 percent of mechanical engineers were women and only 30 percent of physicians and 14 percent of Congresspersons were women (U.S. Bureau of the Census, 2004a). Ethnic minority women were even less likely than white women to work in these occupations. On the other hand, women are overrepresented in "pink-collar ghetto" occupations, such as secretary and preschool and kindergarten teacher (see Figure 10.11).

The second aspect of economic discrimination is *differential treatment* on the job. For example, women typically earn lower salaries than men in the same jobs (see Figure 10.12). And when women demonstrate leadership qualities such as confidence, ambitiousness, and assertiveness, they are evaluated less favorably than

● **FIGURE 10.11**

Women in the world of work. Career opportunities for women have expanded dramatically in the past 40 years. Nonetheless, women remain underrepresented in many traditionally masculine occupations and overrepresented in many traditionally feminine occupations. (Data from U.S. Bureau of the Census, 2004a)

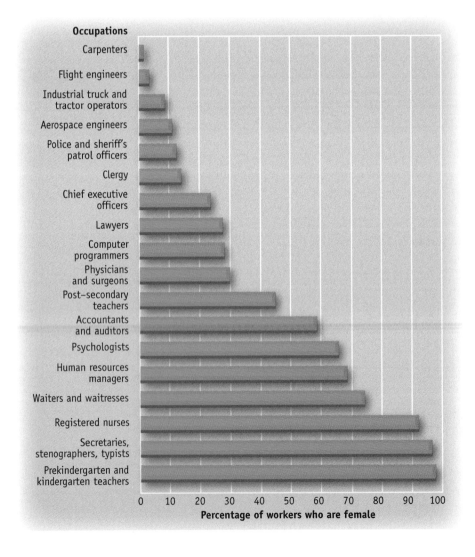

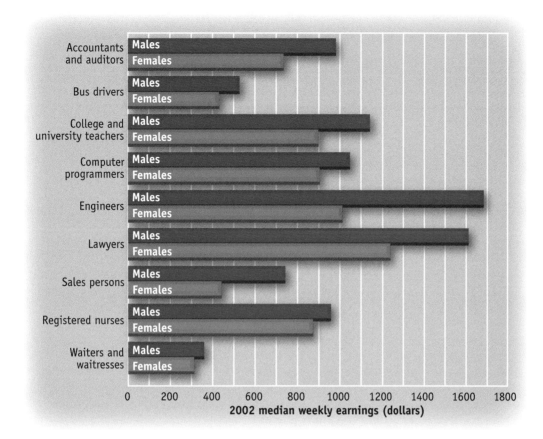

The gender gap in weekly wages. Women continue to earn less than men in all occupational categories, as these 2002 data for selected occupations make clear. Many factors can contribute to this gender gap in earned income, but economic discrimination is probably a major consideration. (Data from U.S. Bureau of Labor Statistics, 2003)

men because this behavior contradicts the female gender role (Eagly & Karau, 2002). There appears to be a *glass ceiling* that prevents most women and ethnic minorities from advancing beyond middle-management positions. For example, in 1996, only 4 of the top 1,000 corporations in America were headed by women (Valian, 1998). Ironically, men employed in traditionally female fields are promoted more quickly than their female counterparts, a phenomenon dubbed the *glass escalator* (Williams, 1998).

Aggression Toward Females

Forms of aggression toward girls and women include rape, intimate violence, sexual harassment, sexual abuse, incest, and violent pornography. We've discussed a number of these problems elsewhere (in particular, consult the Application for Chapter 9), so we'll focus on sexual harassment here. *Sexual harassment* has become recognized as a widespread problem that occurs not only on the job but also at home (obscene telephone calls), while walking outside (catcalls and whistles), and in medical and psychotherapy settings. It also takes place in schools and colleges. Figure 10.13 reports the results

Sexual Harassment in the Schools

Type of harassment	Percentage reporting
Received suggestive gestures, looks, comments, or jokes	89
Touched, pinched, or grabbed	83
Leaned over or cornered	47
Received sexual notes or pictures	28
Pressured to do something sexual	27
Forced to do something sexual	10
Other form of harassment	7

Note: Percentages do not add to 100 because readers could indicate more than one type of harassment.

Reported incidence of sexual harassment in the schools. This figure depicts common forms of sexual harassment in grades 2 through 12 and the percentage of girls reporting them. (Adapted from Stein, Marshall, & Tropp, 1993)

Adapted from Stein, N., Marshall, N. L., & Tropp, L. R. (1993). *Secrets in public: Sexual harassment in our schools,* p. 4. Copyright © 1993 Center for Research on Women at Wellesley College and the NOW Legal Defense and Education Fund.

of a survey on the most common forms of sexual harassment in grades 2 through 12. Teachers and professors who pressure students for sexual favors in exchange for grades have been singled out for strong criticism.

Although there are costs associated with gender roles for both males and females, sexism causes particularly serious problems in the lives of girls and women. In addition, when prejudice and discrimination prevent talented individuals from making contributions from which all could benefit, society as a whole suffers.

Gender in the Past and in the Future

LEARNING OBJECTIVES

- *Explain the basis for traditional gender roles and why they are changing.*
- *Define gender-role identity and discuss two alternatives to traditional gender roles.*

In Western society, gender roles are in a state of transition. As we have noted, sweeping changes in the female role have already occurred. It's hard to imagine today, but less than 100 years ago, women were not allowed to vote or to manage their own finances. Only a few decades ago, it was virtually unheard of for a woman to initiate a date, manage a corporation, or run for public office. In this section, we'll discuss why gender roles are changing and what the future might bring.

Why Are Gender Roles Changing?

Many people are baffled as to why gender roles are changing. They can't understand why age-old traditions are being flouted and discarded. A number of theories attempt to explain why gender roles are in transition. Basically, these theories look at the past to explain the present and the future. A key consideration is that gender roles have always constituted a division of labor. In earlier societies, the division of labor according to gender was a natural outgrowth of some simple realities. In most hunting-and-gathering societies, as well as most herding societies, an economic premium was put on physical strength. Men tend to be stronger than women, so they were better equipped to handle such jobs as hunting and farming. In most societies they got those assignments, whereas women were responsible for gathering, home maintenance, and childrearing (Nielsen, 1990). Another consideration was that women had to assume responsibility for nursing young children. Thus, although people might have worked out other ways of doing things (and some cultures did), there were some basic reasons for dividing labor according to gender in premodern societies.

Traditional gender roles are a carryover from the past. Once traditions are established, they have a way of perpetuating themselves. Over the past century or so in Western society, these divisions of labor have become increasingly antiquated. Therein lies the prime reason for changes in gender roles. *Traditional gender roles no longer make economic sense.* The widespread use of machines to do work has rendered physical strength relatively unimportant. Furthermore, as we

A division of labor based on gender no longer makes economic sense in our society. Relatively few jobs require great physical strength; the rest call for skills possessed by both men and women.

move toward a service economy, physical strength will become even less relevant.

The future is likely to bring even more dramatic shifts in gender roles. We can see the beginnings of these changes now. For example, although women still bear children, nursing responsibilities are now optional. Moreover, as women become more economically independent, they will have less need to get married solely for economic reasons. The possibility of developing a fetus outside the uterus may seem far-fetched now, but some experts predict that it is only a matter of time. If so, both men and women could be "mothers." In light of these and other changes in modern society, it is safe to say that gender roles are likely to remain in flux for some time to come.

Alternatives to Traditional Gender Roles

Gender-role identity **is a person's identification with the qualities regarded as masculine or feminine.** Initially, gender-role identity was conceptualized as either "masculine" or "feminine." All males were expected to develop masculine role identities and females, feminine gender-role identities. Individuals who did not identify with the role expectations for their gender or who identified with the characteristics for the other gender were judged to be few in number and to have psychological problems.

In the 1970s, social scientists began to rethink their ideas about gender-role identity. One assumption that was called into question is that males should be "masculine" and females should be "feminine." For one thing, it appears that the number of people who don't conform to traditional gender-role norms is higher than widely assumed, as is the amount of strain that some people experience trying to conform to conventional roles (Pleck, 1981, 1995). Research suggests that strong identification with traditional gender-role expectations is associated with a variety of negative outcomes. For example, high femininity in females is correlated with low self-esteem (Whitley, 1983) and increased psychological distress (Helgeson, 1994). High masculinity in males has been linked to increased Type A behavior (see Chapter 14), poor health care (Helgeson, 1994), greater likelihood of committing physical and sexual aggression in relationships (Mosher, 1991), and vulnerability to certain types of psychopathology (Evans & Dinning, 1982). Furthermore, relationship satisfaction tends to be lower in heterosexual couples with traditional gender-role identities (Ickes, 1993). Thus, contrary to earlier thinking, the evidence suggests that "masculine" males and "feminine" females may be less well adjusted, on the average, than those who are less traditional.

As people have become aware of the possible costs of conventional gender roles, there has been much debate about moving beyond them. A big question has been: What should we move toward? To date, two ideas have received the most attention: (1) androgyny and (2) gender-role transcendence. Let's examine these options.

Androgyny

Like masculinity and femininity, androgyny is a type of gender-role identity. *Androgyny* **refers to the coexistence of both masculine and feminine personality traits in a single person.** In other words, an androgynous person is one who scores above average on measures of *both* masculinity and femininity.

To help you fully appreciate the nature of androgyny, we need to briefly review other kinds of gender identity (see Figure 10.14). Males who score high on masculinity and low on femininity, and females who score high on femininity and low on masculinity, are said to be *gender-typed*. Males who score high on femininity but low on masculinity, and females who score high on masculinity but low on femininity, are said to be *cross-gender-typed*. Finally, males and females who score low on both masculinity and femininity are characterized as *gender-role undifferentiated*.

Keep in mind that we are referring to individuals' descriptions of themselves in terms of personality traits traditionally associated with each gender (dominance, nurturance, and so on). People sometimes confuse gender-role identity with sexual orientation, but they are not the same. A person can be homosexual, heterosexual, or bisexual (sexual orientation) and be

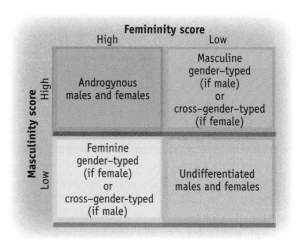

● **FIGURE 10.14**

Possible gender-role identities. This diagram summarizes the relations between subjects' scores on measures of masculinity and femininity and four possible gender identities.

androgynous, gender-typed, cross-gender-typed, or gender-role undifferentiated (gender-role identity).

In groundbreaking research three decades ago, Sandra Bem (1975) challenged the then-prevailing view that males who scored high in masculinity and females who scored high in femininity are better adjusted than "masculine" women and "feminine" men. She argued that traditionally masculine men and feminine women feel compelled to adhere to rigid and narrow gender roles that unnecessarily restrict their behavior. In contrast, androgynous individuals ought to be able to function more flexibly. She also advanced the idea that androgynous people are psychologically healthier than those who are gender-typed.

Courtesy, Sandra Bem
Sandra Bem

What about Bem's ideas? First, androgynous people do seem more flexible than others. That is, they can be nurturing (feminine) or independent (masculine), depending on the situation (Bem, 1975). In contrast, gender-typed males tend to have difficulty behaving nurturantly, while gender-typed females often have trouble with independence. Also, individuals whose partners are either androgynous or feminine (but not masculine or undifferentiated) report higher relationship satisfaction (Bradbury, Campbell, & Fincham, 1995). This finding holds for cohabiting heterosexuals, as well as for lesbian and gay couples (Kurdek & Schmitt, 1986b). Thus, in these areas, androgyny seems to be advantageous.

Bem's second assertion—that androgynous people are psychologically healthier than gender-typed individuals—requires a more complicated analysis. Since 1976, over a hundred studies have been conducted to try to answer this question. Some early studies *did* find a positive correlation between androgyny and mental health. Ultimately, however, the weight of the evidence did not support Bem's hypothesis that androgyny is especially healthy. In fact, several comprehensive surveys of the research concluded that *masculine* traits (in both males and females) were more strongly associated with psychological health than androgyny (Hyde & Frost, 1993;). These findings, as well as problems with the concept of androgyny and its measurement, have led Bem and other psychologists to take a different view of gender roles, as you'll see next.

Gender-Role Transcendence

As psychologists thought more about androgyny, they realized that the concept had some problems. For one thing, androgyny requires people to develop both masculine and feminine characteristics, rather than one or the other. Although it can be argued that androgyny is less restrictive than traditional gender roles, it may also lead people to feel that they have two potential sources of inadequacy to contend with, as opposed to only one (Bem, 1993).

More important, the idea that people should have both masculine and feminine traits reinforces the assumption that gender is an integral part of human behavior (Bem, 1983). In other words, the androgyny perspective presupposes that masculine and feminine traits actually exist within people. Another way of putting it is that the current system sets up self-fulfilling prophecies. That is, if people use gender-based labels ("masculine" and "feminine") to describe certain human characteristics and behavior, they are likely to associate these traits with one gender or the other. A final criticism of androgyny is that it implies that the solution to gender bias is to change the individual rather than to address the gender inequities in society and its institutions (Matlin, 2004).

Many gender theorists maintain that masculinity and femininity are really only arbitrary labels that we have learned to impose on certain traits through societal conditioning. This assertion is the foundation for the *gender-role transcendence* perspective (Bem, 1983, 1993; Spence, 1983). **The *gender-role transcendence* perspective proposes that to be fully human, people need to move beyond gender roles as a way of organizing their perceptions of themselves and others.** This goal requires that instead of dividing human characteristics into masculine and feminine categories (and then combining them, as the androgyny perspective suggests), we should dispense with the artificially constructed gender categories and labels altogether. How would this work? Instead of the labels "masculine" and "feminine," we would use gender-neutral terms such as "instrumental" and "expressive," respectively, to describe personality traits and behaviors. This "decoupling" of traits and gender could reduce the self-fulfilling prophecy problem.

The advocates of gender-role transcendence argue that this practice would help us break our current habits of "projecting gender into situations irrelevant to genitalia" (Bem, 1985, p. 222) and hasten the advent of a gender-free society. They believe that if gender were to be eliminated (or even reduced) as a means of

WEB LINK 10.5

Feminist Majority Foundation
This site brings together a massive set of resources dealing with issues from a feminist perspective.

categorizing traits, each individual's unique capabilities and interests would assume greater importance, and individuals would be more free to develop their own unique potentials.

Given that individuals today have had years of exposure to gender messages, moving toward gender-role transcendence would likely be a gradual process. According to James O'Neil and Jean Egan (1992), such a gender-role journey moves from initial acceptance of traditional gender roles (Stage 1) to a growing ambivalence about gender roles (Stage 2). From there, it evolves to anger about sexism (Stage 3) and then to actions to reduce sexist restrictions (Stage 4). Finally, in Stage 5, people integrate their gender-role beliefs, which enables them to see themselves and the world in less gender-stereotypic ways.

A Gender-Free Society?

Obviously, a gender-free society would require more than individuals changing their gender-based attitudes and behaviors. It would also be necessary to eliminate all gender discrimination in societal institutions as well, and such changes would take many years. While America is nowhere near being a gender-free society, the past 40 years show evidence of both individual and institutional changes in this direction.

Although many social scientists find the concept of a gender-free society appealing, some social critics are concerned about the decline of traditional gender roles. For instance, George Gilder (1992) maintains that conventional gender roles provide a fundamental underpinning for our economic and social order. Furthermore, he asserts that changes in gender roles will damage intimate relationships between women and men and have a devastating impact on family life. Gilder argues that women are needed in the home in their traditional homemaker role to provide for the socialization of the next generation. Without this traditional socialization, he predicts that our moral fabric will decay, leading to an increase in crime, violence, and drug abuse. Given these starkly contrasting projections, it will be interesting to see what developments unfold in the next few decades. Meanwhile, in the Application we'll take a look at how gender affects communication styles.

APPLICATION

Bridging the Gender Gap in Communication

LEARNING OBJECTIVES

- *Describe how the different socialization experiences of males and females contribute to communication problems between men and women.*
- *Describe expressive and instrumental styles of communication.*
- *Describe some common mixed-gender communication problems.*

Answer the following questions "true" or "false."

___ **1.** Men talk much more than women in mixed-gender groups.

___ **2.** Women are more likely to ask for help than men.

___ **3.** Women are more willing to initiate confrontations in relationships than men.

___ **4.** Men talk more about nonpersonal issues with their friends than women do.

If you answered true to all of these statements, you were correct. They are just some of the observed differences in communication styles between males and females. While not characteristic of all men and women or of all mixed-gender conversations, these style differences appear to be the source of many misunderstandings between males and females.

When people experience frustrating communication situations in their personal or work relationships, they often attribute them to the other person's quirks or failings. Instead, it seems that some of these frustrating experiences may result from gender differences in communication style. That is, many men and women learn to speak different "languages" in social interactions but don't realize it. In this Application, we explore the nature of these gender-based style differences, how they develop, and how they can contribute to interpersonal conflicts. We also offer some suggestions for dealing more effectively with these style differences.

The Clash of Two "Cultures"

According to sociolinguist Deborah Tannen (1990), males and females are typically socialized in different "cultures." That is, males are likely to learn a language of "status and independence," while females learn a language of "connection and intimacy" (p. 42). Tannen likens male/female communications to other "cross-cultural" communications—full of opportunities for misunderstandings to develop.

Photo by Sara Barrett, courtesy of Random House

Deborah Tannen

These differences in communication styles develop in childhood and are fostered by traditional gender stereotypes and the socializing influences of parents, teachers, media, and childhood social interactions—usually with same-gender peers. As we noted earlier, boys typically play in larger groups, usually outdoors, and farther away from home than girls (Feiring & Lewis, 1987). Thus, boys are less under the scrutiny of adults and are therefore more likely to engage in activities that encourage exploration and independence. Also, boys' groups are often structured in terms of high- and low-status roles. Boys achieve high status in their groups by engaging in dominant behavior (telling others what to do and enforcing compliance). The games that boys play often result in winners and losers, and boys frequently bid for dominance by interrupting each other, calling each other names, boasting to each other about their abilities, and refusing to cooperate with each other (Maccoby, 1998, 2002; Maltz & Borker, 1998).

In contrast, girls usually play in small groups or in pairs, often indoors, and gain high status through popularity—the key to which is intimacy with peers. Many of the games girls play do not have winners or losers.

"Norman won't collaborate."

© The New Yorker Collection 2002 Robert Weber from cartoonbank.com. All rights reserved.

And, while it is true that girls vary in abilities and skills, to call attention to oneself as better than others is frowned upon. Girls are likely to express their wishes as suggestions rather than as demands or orders (Maccoby, 1998, 2002; Maltz & Borker, 1998). Dominance tends to be gained by verbal persuasion rather than by the direct bids for power characteristic of boys' social interactions (Charlesworth & Dzur, 1987).

These two cultures shape the functions of speech in different ways. According to Eleanor Maccoby (1990), among boys, "speech serves largely egoistic functions and is used to establish and protect an individual's turf. Among girls, conversation is a more socially binding process" (p. 516).

Tannen contends that these different styles carry over into adult social interactions. Many males learn to see the social world as hierarchical. To maintain independence and avoid failure they have to jockey for high status. Hence, she says, men tend to approach conversations as "negotiations in which people try to achieve and maintain the upper hand if they can and protect themselves from others' attempts to put them down and push them around" (p. 25). Females, on the other hand, learn to see the social order as a community in which individuals are connected to others and one where the task is to preserve these connections. Consequently, women tend to approach conversations as "negotiations for closeness in which people try to seek and give confirmation and support, and to reach consensus. They try to protect themselves from others' attempts to push them away" (p. 25). These different views of the social order are the root of the often heard complaint, "You just don't understand"—the title of Tannen's book (see the Recommended Reading box).

The idea that there are two cultures founded on gender-based communication styles has intuitive appeal because it confirms people's stereotypes and reduces complex issues to simple explanations. But there's an important caveat here. As we have noted, status, power, and gender role differences can lurk behind what seem to be gender differences. Researchers have only recently tested Tannen's ideas; to date, the findings are mixed (Basow & Rubenfeld, 2003; Edwards & Hamilton, 2004; Michaud & Warner, 1997; MacGeorge et al., 2004). Although some gender differences in communication styles have been found, they are quite small (MacGeorge et al., 2004). Also, there are individual differences in preferred styles: Some women use the "male style" and some men use the "female style." As we have noted, the social context is a much stronger influence on behavior than gender, which means that many people use either style, depending on the situation. Therefore, we caution you not to reduce *all* communication problems between males and females to gender-based style differences. It is simply not true that men and women come from different planets.

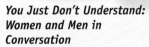
Instrumental and Expressive Styles

Because of the differences in their socialization experiences, men are more likely to use an "instrumental" style of communication and women, an "expressive" style (Block, 1973; Tannen, 1990). An *instrumental style* focuses on reaching practical goals and finding solutions to problems; an *expressive style* is characterized by being able to express tender emotions easily and being sensitive to the feelings of others. This gender difference has been found across a number of cultures (D'Andrade, 1966). Of course, many individuals use both styles, depending on the situation.

In conflict situations, men's instrumental style means that husbands are more likely to stay calm and problem oriented and to make more efforts to find compromise solutions to problems. However, an instrumental style can have a darker side. When the instrumental behavior of calmness changes to coldness and unresponsiveness, it becomes negative. Research has shown that this emotional unresponsiveness is characteristic of many men and that it seems to figure importantly in marital dissatisfaction (Larson & Pleck, 1998).

Many studies indicate that women are more skilled than men in nonverbal communication—a key component of the expressive style. For example, they are better at reading and sending nonverbal messages (Hall, 1998; Hall & Matsumoto, 2004). And women are better listeners (Miller, Berg, & Archer, 1983). But women engage in some "negative" expressive behaviors as well (Brehm, 1992). For example, during relationship conflicts, women are more likely to (1) display strong negative emotions (Noller, 1985, 1987); (2) use psychologically coercive tactics, such as guilt manipulations, verbal attacks, and power plays (Barnes & Buss, 1985); and (3) reject attempts at reconciliation (Barnes & Buss, 1985).

Common Mixed-Gender Communication Problems

In this section, we briefly review some common mixed-gender communication problems noted by Tannen. To keep things simple, we use "she" and "he" to illustrate various scenarios, but you should interpret these labels loosely for the reasons we have mentioned.

Mismatches

People expect their friends and partners to support and reassure them. When a mismatch occurs between their expectations and reality, they become confused, frustrated, and possibly hurt or angry. Consider a woman who tells her partner about a recurring problem she is having at work—not because she wants help with the problem but because she wants some sympathy. However, thinking that she is seeking a solution to the problem, he gives her advice. Not receiving the consolation she seeks, she believes he doesn't care. He is frustrated about her repeated complaining, because he has offered her the same advice in the past. Although neither wants to frustrate the other, that's exactly what happens because they are talking at cross-purposes. She wants him to commiserate with her, but he thinks she wants him to help her solve a problem. Each assumes the other knows what each wants, and neither does. These mismatches crop up quite frequently in intimate relationships.

Talking About People Versus Things

Women's conversations frequently involve sharing the details of their personal lives or talking *about* people. Talking about people isn't necessarily destructive, although it can be if it turns into talking *against* people. As they did in childhood, women share secrets with one another as a way of being close. Men are interested in details, too, but those of a different kind: politics, news, and sports. Women fear being left out by not knowing what is going on in friends' lives; men fear

cathy®

being left out by not knowing what is going on in the world (Tannen, 1990).

Tannen suggests that both women and men need to extend their communication strategies by adding aspects of the other style to their own. Thus, some men may need to learn to be more comfortable talking about their personal lives, whereas some women could benefit by talking more about impersonal topics and talking in a more assertive manner.

Lecturing and Listening

In many mixed-gender conversations, particularly those in public settings, women often end up playing the listener to the man's "lecture." Are men self-centered bigmouths? Are women meek, passive creatures? Instead of these interpretations, Tannen suggests that men and women are playing different games that are rooted in their childhood experiences. Men are playing "Do you respect me?" and women, "Do you like me?"

As we noted, males use conversation to jockey for status and challenge the authority of others—both men and women. A woman who lacks experience defending herself against these challenges can easily misinterpret an assertive man's style as an attack on her credibility. Similarly, women have been taught to hand off the conversational ball and expect that others will

do the same. While most women reciprocate, many men don't. When this happens, some women may feel awkward drawing the focus of the conversation back to themselves, because this style was frowned on during their childhood play with other girls.

To improve this kind of mixed-gender communication problem, Tannen suggests that women who tire of listening need to be more assertive and take some control of the conversation. Also, some men might be relieved to learn that they don't always have to talk. As we noted in Chapter 7, effective listening is a much-underrated communication skill.

The Woman's Double-Bind

According to Tannen, mixed-gender communication situations often place women at a disadvantage because males' instrumental style of communication tends to be used as the norm against which both women's and men's speech is evaluated (recall androcentrism). This fact means that a woman may be evaluated negatively regardless of which style (male or female) she adopts. The female style is devalued, but a woman who embraces the instrumental style will often evoke negative reactions. Women in positions of authority experience a special version of this double-bind. In Tannen's words, "If they speak in ways expected of women, they are seen as inadequate leaders. If they speak in ways expected of leaders, they are seen as inadequate women" (p. 244). Other research supports this view (Eagly & Karau, 2002).

Toward a "Shared Language"

Tannen asserts that many frustrations in personal and work relationships could be avoided if men and women were more aware of gender differences in communication styles. Many people misperceive style differences as the other's personal failings. If individuals could see

---

WEB LINK 10.6

Deborah Tannen's Homepage
Georgetown University Professor Deborah Tannen has won considerable recognition for her work on communication differences between men and women in diverse settings such as the home and office. Visitors to her "official" homepage will find a complete bibliography of professional and general interest publications by Tannen that explain her sociolinguistic theories.

---

the style differences for what they are, they could eliminate a lot of negative feelings. As Tannen (1990) says, "Nothing hurts more than being told your intentions are bad when you know they are good, or being told that you are doing something wrong when you know you're just doing it your way" (pp. 297–298). People need to understand that there are different ways of listening, talking, and having conversations, not just their own way. For some hints on how to improve gender-based communication, see Figure 10.15.

Hints to Improve Communication

Hints for Men

1. Notice whether or not you have a tendency to interrupt women. If you do, work on breaking this habit. When you catch yourself interrupting, say, "I'm sorry, I interrupted you. Go ahead with what you were saying."

2. Avoid responding to a woman's questions in monosyllables ("Yep," "Nope," "Uh-huh"). Give her more details about what you did and explain why.

3. Learn the art of conversational give and take. Ask women questions about themselves. And listen carefully when they respond.

4. Don't order women around. For example, don't say, "Get me the newspaper." First, notice whether it might be an inconvenience for her to do something for you. If it isn't, say, "Would you mind giving me the newspaper?" or "Would you please give me the newspaper?" If she's busy, get it yourself!

5. Don't be a space hog. Be more aware of the space you take up when you sit with others (especially women). Watch that you don't make women feel crowded out.

6. Learn to open up about personal issues. Talk about your feelings, interests, hopes, and relationships. Talking about personal things helps others know who you are (and probably helps you clarify your self-perceptions, too).

7. Learn to convey enthusiasm about things in addition to the victories of your favorite sports teams.

8. Don't be afraid to ask for help if you need it.

Hints for Women

1. When others interrupt you, politely but firmly redirect the conversation back to you. You can say, for example, "Excuse me. I haven't finished my point."

2. Look the person you're talking with directly in the eye.

3. A lower-pitched voice gets more attention and respect than a higher-pitched one, which is associated with little girls. Keeping your abdominal muscles firm as you speak will help keep your voice low.

4. Learn to be comfortable claiming more space (without becoming a space hog). If you want your presence to be noted, don't fold yourself up into an unobtrusive object.

5. Talk more about yourself and your accomplishments. This isn't offensive as long as others are doing the same and the circumstances are appropriate. If the conversation turns to photography and you know a lot about the topic, it's perfectly OK to share your expertise.

6. Make a point of being aware of current events so you'll be knowledgeable about what others are discussing and have an opinion to contribute.

7. Resist the impulse to be overly apologetic. Although many women say "I'm sorry" to convey sympathy or concern (not apology), these words are likely to be interpreted as an apology. Because apologizing puts one in a lower-power position, women who use apologetic words inappropriately put themselves at a disadvantage.

● **FIGURE 10.15**

Hints to improve communication. To have productive personal and work relationships in today's world demands that people be knowledgeable about gender and communication styles. Men and women may be able to benefit from the suggestions listed here. (Compiled by the authors based on insights from Tannen, 1990)

KEY IDEAS

Gender Stereotypes
■ Many stereotypes have developed around behavioral differences between the genders, although the distinctions between the male and female stereotypes are less rigid than they used to be. Gender stereotypes may vary depending on ethnicity, and they typically favor males.

Gender Similarities and Differences
■ There are no gender differences in general intelligence. When it comes to verbal abilities, gender differences are small, and they generally favor females. Gender differences in mathematical abilities are typically small as well, and they favor males. Males perform much better than females on the spatial ability of mental rotation.

■ Research shows that males typically are somewhat higher in self-esteem and more physically aggressive than females. Females are higher in relational aggression. Males and females are similar in the experience of emotions, but females are more likely to outwardly display emotions. Males have more permissive attitudes about casual sex and are more sexually active than females. Women seem to conform to group pressure a little more than men. Women are more sensitive to nonverbal cues. The genders are similar in overall mental health, but they differ in prevalence rates for specific psychological disorders.

■ The gender differences that do exist are quite small. Moreover, they are group differences that tell us little about individuals. Nonetheless, some people still believe that psychological differences between the genders are substantial. Social role theory and social constructionism provide two explanations for this phenomenon.

Biological Origins of Gender Differences
■ Biological explanations of gender differences include those based on evolution, brain organization, and hormones. Evolutionary psychologists explain gender differences on the basis of their purported adaptive value in ancestral environments. These analyses are speculative and difficult to test empirically.

■ Regarding brain organization, some studies suggest that males exhibit more cerebral specialization than females. However, linking this finding to gender differences in cognitive abilities is questionable for a number of reasons.

■ Efforts to tie hormone levels to gender differences have also been troubled by interpretive problems. Nonetheless, there probably is some hormonal basis for gender differences in aggression and in some aspects of sexual behavior.

Environmental Origins of Gender Differences
■ The socialization of gender roles appears to take place through the processes of reinforcement and punishment, observational learning, and self-socialization. These processes operate through many social institutions, but parents, peers, schools, and the media are the primary sources of gender-role socialization.

Gender Roles
■ Five key attributes of the traditional male role include achievement, aggression, autonomy, sexuality, and stoicism. The theme of antifemininity cuts across these dimensions. Problems associated with the traditional male role include excessive pressure to succeed, difficulty dealing with emotions, and sexual problems. Homophobia is a particular problem for men.

■ Role expectations for females include the marriage mandate, the motherhood mandate, and working outside the home. Among the principal costs of the female role are diminished aspirations, juggling of multiple roles, and ambivalence about sexuality. In addition to these psychological problems, women also face sexist hurdles in the economic domain and may be victims of aggression.

Gender in the Past and in the Future
■ Gender roles have always represented a division of labor. They are changing today, and they seem likely to continue changing because they no longer mesh with economic reality. Consequently, an important question is how to move beyond traditional gender roles. The perspectives of androgyny and gender-role transcendence provide two possible answers to this question.

Application: Bridging the Gender Gap in Communication
■ Because of different socialization experiences, many males and females learn different communication styles. These differences in experience and style seem to underlie a number of mixed-gender communication problems. Men and women need to understand these style differences to reduce interpersonal conflicts and the frustrations they cause.

■ Men are more likely to use an instrumental style of communication, whereas women tend toward an expressive style. Common mixed-gender communication problems include mismatches in expectations, differences in the tendency to talk about people versus things, falling into the lecture and listen trap, and the double-bind that women are often placed in.

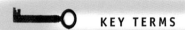

KEY TERMS

Aggression p. 308
Androcentrism p. 305
Androgyny p. 327
Cerebral hemispheres
  p. 312
Conformity p. 308
Expressiveness p. 305
Gender p. 303
Gender-role identity p. 327
Gender-role transcendence
  perspective p. 328
Gender roles p. 313

Gender schemas p. 315
Gender stereotypes p. 304
Homophobia p. 320
Hormones p. 312
Instrumentality p. 305
Meta-analysis p. 306
Sexism p. 324
Social constructionism
  p. 310
Social role theory p. 310
Socialization p. 313

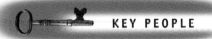

KEY PEOPLE

Sandra Bem p. 328
Alice Eagly p. 310
Janet Shibley Hyde p. 303

Joseph Pleck p. 319
Deborah Tannen
  pp. 330–332

1. Taken as a whole, gender differences in verbal abilities are:
   a. small and favor females.
   b. large and favor females.
   c. nonexistent.
   d. small and favor males.

2. Among the following traits, the largest gender differences are found in:
   a. verbal abilities.
   b. mathematical abilities.
   c. physical aggression.
   d. conformity.

3. Which of the following statements about gender differences is false?
   a. Males have higher self-esteem than females.
   b. Males are more physically aggressive than females.
   c. Females are more likely to yield to group pressure.
   d. Women talk more than men.

4. Of the three biologically based explanations for gender differences, which has the strongest support?
   a. Evolutionary theory
   b. Brain organization
   c. Hormones
   d. Social constructionism

5. Four-year-old Rachel seems to pay particular attention to what her mother and her older sister do, and she often imitates them. What is taking place?
   a. Self-socialization
   b. Observational learning
   c. Operant conditioning
   d. Androcentric bias

6. Parents tend to respond more to _____ behavior, especially in _____ .
   a. gender appropriate; boys
   b. gender appropriate; girls
   c. gender inappropriate; boys
   d. gender inappropriate; girls

7. Which of the following statements about peer socialization is true?
   a. Peer groups appear to influence gender-role socialization more in boys than girls.
   b. Girls play in smaller groups and boys in larger groups.
   c. High status in boys' groups is achieved by making suggestions to others.
   d. Peers have relatively little impact on gender-role socialization.

8. Which of the following is *not* a problem with the male role?
   a. Pressure to succeed
   b. Emotional inexpressiveness
   c. Sexual problems
   d. Androgyny

9. Which of the following is *not* a problem with the female role?
   a. Poor nonverbal communication skills
   b. Diminished aspirations
   c. Juggling multiple roles
   d. Ambivalence about sexuality

10. According to Deborah Tannen, men tend to use an _____ communication style, and women tend to use an _____ communication style.
    a. expressive; expressive
    b. expressive; instrumental
    c. instrumental; instrumental
    d. instrumental; expressive

Book Companion Website

Visit the Book Companion Website at **http://psychology. wadsworth.com/weiten_lloyd8e,** where you will find tutorial quizzes, flashcards, and weblinks for every chapter, a final exam, and more! You can also link to the Thomson Wadsworth Psychology Resource Center (accessible directly at **http://psychology.wadsworth.com**) for a range of psychology-related resources.

Personal Explorations Workbook

The following exercises in your *Personal Explorations Workbook* may enhance your self-understanding in relation to issues raised in this chapter. **Questionnaire 10.1:** Personal Attributes Questionnaire. **Personal Probe 10.1:** How Do You Feel about Gender Roles? **Personal Probe 10.2:** Reflecting on the Power of Gender Roles.

ANSWERS

1. a Page 306
2. c Pages 306–308
3. d Pages 307–309
4. c Pages 311–313
5. b Page 314
6. c Page 316
7. b Page 316
8. d Pages 319–320
9. a Pages 321–324
10. d Page 331

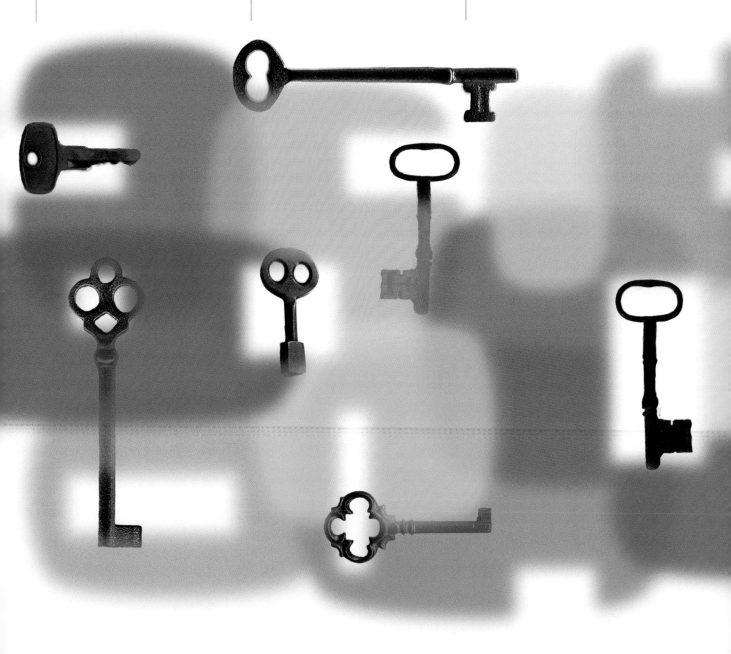

Development in Adolescence and Adulthood

"My mother always complains that I spend too much time on the telephone. She thinks that I'm just gossiping with my friends and feels that my time would be better spent studying. She can't seem to understand that my friends and I help each other through some pretty rough situations. She thinks that way because she doesn't believe that anything a teenager does besides homework is important. My Mom tells me to learn in school, but she doesn't realize that I'm actually trying to learn to survive school. Attending school is like a tryout for life. I know that it sounds silly to adults, but at times getting a date, being invited to a certain party, or being chosen to work on the school's newspaper can mean more than getting an A on a test."—"Tracy," quoted in Teenagers Talk About School *(Landau, 1988, p. 31)*

Do Tracy's—or her mother's—complaints sound familiar? Have you ever been frustrated by your parents' or your child's inability to understand your point of view? Psychologists attribute these contrasting perspectives to differences in development. In the above scenario, Tracy and her mother are at different levels of development in a number of areas: physical, cognitive, personality, and social. Thus, they have different perspectives on themselves and the world.

Until the 1970s, it was widely assumed that psychological development slowed to a crawl as people reached adulthood. Now, however, psychologists realize that important developmental changes continue throughout adult life. As a result, they are probing into these changes to identify crucial patterns and trends. In this chapter, we review the major changes that take place during adolescence and adulthood. We also examine the topics of dying and death. The Application offers some suggestions for effective parenting.

The Transition of Adolescence

- Define and discuss pubescence and secondary sex characteristics.
- Define and discuss puberty and primary sex characteristics.
- Summarize the findings on early and late maturation in boys and girls.

- Describe the cognitive changes that occur during adolescence.
- Explain Erikson's psychosocial crisis of adolescence and Marcia's four identity statuses.
- Discuss whether adolescence is a period of emotional turmoil and describe recent trends in adolescent suicide.

Adolescence is a transitional period between childhood and adulthood. Its age boundaries are not exact, but in our society adolescence begins at around age 13 and ends at about age 22. In some ways, adolescents resemble the children they were, yet the many changes they undergo during this stage ensure that they will be different from children in many respects. Similarly, we see glimpses of the adults that adolescents will become, but more often we observe that they don't behave much like adults. As adolescents mature, we see fewer resemblances to children and more similarities to adults.

Although most societies have at least a brief period of adolescence, this phenomenon is not universal across cultures (Schlegel & Barry, 1991). In some cultures, young people move almost directly from childhood to adulthood. A protracted period of adolescence is seen primarily in industrialized nations. In these societies, rapid technological progress has made lengthy education, and therefore prolonged economic dependence, the norm. Thus, in our own culture, middle school, high school, and college students often have a "marginal" status. They are capable of reproduction and are physiologically mature, yet they have not achieved the emotional and economic independence from their parents that are the hallmarks of adulthood.

Let's begin our discussion of adolescent development with its most visible aspect: the physical changes that transform the body of a child into that of an adult.

Physical Changes

Do you remember your middle school days when your body grew so fast that your clothes just couldn't "keep up"? This phase of rapid growth in height and weight is called the *adolescent growth spurt*—"spurt" because of the relatively sudden increases in body height and weight. Brought on by hormonal changes, it typically starts at about age 11 in girls and about two years later in boys (Malina, 1990). (Technically, this spurt should be called the *pre*adolescent growth spurt because it actually occurs *prior* to puberty, which is generally recognized as the beginning of adolescence.)

Psychologists use the term *pubescence* to describe the two-year span preceding puberty during which the changes leading to physical and sexual maturity take place. Besides growing taller and heavier during pubescence, children begin to take on the physical features that characterize adults of their respective genders. These bodily changes are termed *secondary sex characteristics*—physical features that distinguish one gender from the other but that are not essential for reproduction. For example, boys go through a voice change, develop facial hair, and experience greater skeletal and muscle growth in the upper torso, leading to broader shoulders and enhanced upper-body strength. Females experience breast growth and a widening of the pelvic bones, plus increased fat deposits in this area, resulting in wider hips (Susman, Dorn, & Schiefelbein, 2003). Figure 11.1 details these physical changes in boys and girls.

The physical changes we've been describing are triggered by the pituitary gland. This "master gland" of the endocrine system sends signals to the adrenal glands (on top of the kidneys) and gonads (ovaries and testes), which in turn secrete the hormones responsible for the changes in physical characteristics that differentiate males and females.

Note that the capacity to reproduce is not attained in pubescence. This ability develops during *puberty*, the stage that marks the beginning of adolescence and during which sexual functions reach maturity. During puberty, the *primary sex characteristics*—the structures necessary for reproduction—develop fully. In the male, these structures include the testes, penis, and related internal structures; in females, they include the ovaries, vagina, uterus, and other internal reproductive structures (see Figure 11.1).

WEB LINK 11.1

Adolescent Health and Mental Health
Visitors at this website will find links to resources about adolescence that cover many of the pressing health and mental health issues important to this phase of development. The site is edited by Michael Fenichel, a prominent psychologist in the use of the Internet to distribute quality professional information to the public.

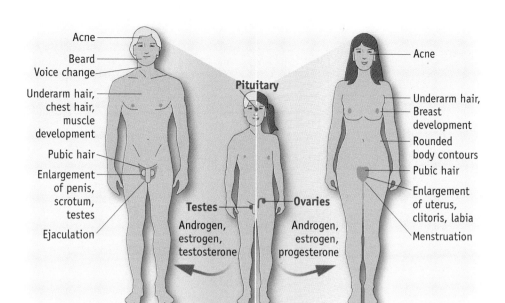

Physical development during pubescence and puberty. During pubescence, the two years prior to puberty, a growth spurt occurs and secondary sex characteristics develop. During puberty, the primary sex characteristics mature. These various physical changes are caused by hormonal secretions.

In females, the onset of puberty is typically signaled by *menarche*—**the first occurrence of menstruation.** American girls typically reach menarche between ages 12 and 13, with further sexual maturation continuing until approximately age 16 (Susman et al., 2003). Most girls are sterile for 12 to 18 months following menarche. (Pregnancy is a possibility for some girls at this age, so any girl who has begun to menstruate should assume that she can become pregnant.) Breast development and the presence of pubic hair serve as important social criteria of adolescence for girls.

In males, there is no clear-cut marker of the onset of sexual maturity, although the capacity to ejaculate is used as an index of puberty (the onset of sperm production not being a visible event). *Spermarche,* **or the first ejaculation,** usually occurs through masturbation, rather than nocturnal emissions (Hyde, 1994a). (In the latter, also called "wet dreams," ejaculation occurs during sleep and is sometimes accompanied by erotic dreams.) Experts note that ejaculation may not be a valid index of actual maturity, as early ejaculations may contain seminal fluid but not active sperm. The average age of spermarche in American boys is estimated to be age 14, with complete sexual maturation occurring at about 18 (Susman et al., 2003).

As we have noted, puberty arrives about two years later in boys than in girls. In fact, the major reason that adult males are taller than adult females is that males typically experience two additional years of development

before the onset of the growth spurt (Graber, Petersen, & Brooks-Gunn, 1996). Generational changes have occurred in the timing of puberty, at least for girls in industrialized countries (Anderson, Dallal, & Must, 2003). (To date, no valid method has been found for establishing the existence of a comparable trend among boys.) Today's girls begin puberty earlier, and complete it more rapidly, than their counterparts in earlier generations. This trend apparently reflects improvements in nutrition and medical care (Brooks-Gunn, 1991). In the United States and some other industrialized countries, this trend appears to have leveled off, probably

As they mature, adolescents look increasingly like adults, although boys typically lag two years behind girls in physical development.

For Better or For Worse®

by Lynn Johnston

because of the high standard of living (Tanner, 1990). Thus, the onset of sexual maturation may have a genetically predetermined age "floor."

Puberty also brings important changes in other body organs. For instance, the heart and lungs increase considerably in size, and the heart rate drops. These changes are more marked for boys than for girls and are responsible, in part, for the superior performance of males in certain physical activities relative to females. Before about age 12, boys and girls are similar in physical strength, speed, and endurance. After puberty, boys have clear advantage in all three areas (Smoll & Schutz, 1990). After sexual maturation has been attained, adolescents continue to mature physically until their secondary sex characteristics are fully developed and their body has reached adult height and proportions. In girls, such growth continues until about 17 years of age; in boys, it goes on until about age 20.

Variation in the onset of pubescence and puberty is normal. Still, the timing of these physical changes figures importantly in adjustment. More specifically, research suggests that girls who mature early and boys who mature late seem to feel particularly anxious and self-conscious about their changing bodies (Graber et al., 1997). The early-maturing girl is taller and heavier than most of the girls and nearly all of the boys her age. The late-maturing boy is shorter and slighter than most of the boys and nearly all of the girls his age. To make matters worse, both groups have body types that are at odds with the cultural ideals of extreme slenderness for females and muscular physique for males.

Compared to other girls, those who mature early fare more poorly in school, are less popular, have lower self-confidence, and have earlier sexual experiences and more unwanted pregnancies (Ge, Conger, & Elder, 1996; Stattin & Magnusson, 1990). They are also more likely to have tried alcohol, cigarettes, and marijuana

(Lanza & Collins, 2002), to have more negative body images (Striegel-Moore et al., 2001), and to be depressed (Rierdan & Koff, 1991). At age 24, early-maturing women have had more self-reported psychological disorders and current psychosocial symptoms compared to on-time maturers (Graber et al., 2004). Late-maturing boys have been found to feel more inadequate, to feel more insecure, and to think less of themselves than other boys do (Siegel, 1982). Still, early-maturing boys who were perceived by others to be well adjusted reported more emotional distress and hostile feelings than their less-developed peers (Ge, Conger, & Elder, 2001). At age 24, late-maturing males had engaged in significantly more deviant behavior and substance abuse than other men (Graber et al., 2004). Optimal adjustment for girls is associated with puberty coming "on time," whereas optimal adjustment for boys is most often related to early puberty. Girls' and boys' *perceptions* of the timing of their puberty and their feelings of attractiveness follow this same pattern (see Figure 11.2).

Cognitive Changes

Around the time of early adolescence, major changes take place in thinking and problem solving (Eccles, Wigfield, & Byrnes, 2003). Compared to those who are younger, adolescents can think abstractly (not merely concretely) and more efficiently. They also become more self-aware and self-reflective and can view problems from several perspectives rather than only one. Thus, the thinking of adolescents is qualitatively different from that of younger children. Whereas children go about solving problems on a trial-and-error basis, most adolescents are capable of solving problems by generating a number of possible hypotheses and systematically testing them.

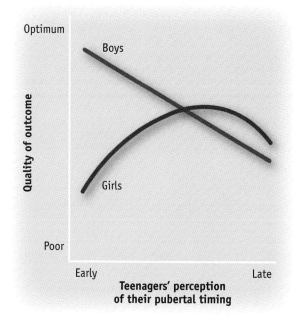

● FIGURE 11.2

Perceived timing of puberty and optimal adjustment. For girls, feelings of attractiveness and a positive body image are associated with the perception that puberty arrives "on time"; for boys, these feelings are associated with the perception that puberty arrives early.

Adapted from Tobin-Richards, M. H., Boxer, A. A., & Petersen, A. C. (1983). The psychological significance of pubertal change: Sex differences in perceptions of self during early adolescence. In J. Brooks-Gunn & A. C. Petersen (Eds.), *Girls at puberty: Biological and psychosocial perspectives.* New York: Plenum Publishing. Copyright © 1983 Plenum Publishing Co. Adapted by permission of Springer Science and Business Media and the authors.

As would be expected, adolescents show increases across several spheres of knowledge compared to children. For example, as individuals age, they know more facts (declarative knowledge), have more skills (procedural knowledge), and have a greater understanding of why one problem-solving approach works better than another (conceptual knowledge) (Byrnes, 2001; Eccles et al., 2003).

Adolescents are also more skilled than children in deductive reasoning skills (Eccles et al., 2003). These skills involve the ability to reach logical conclusions when given certain information (including that which is contrary to fact). Age-related increases have also been found in mathematical, spatial, and scientific reasoning ability, as well as in some memory processes (Byrnes, 2001; Eccles et al., 2003).

Another facet of cognitive functioning is decision making, specifically risk taking. Numerous studies have looked at age differences in the tendency to engage in physically harmful risky behavior: smoking, drinking, and unprotected sex (Byrnes, Miller, & Schafer, 1999). Most research shows that older adolescents are more likely than younger adolescents and children to engage in such behavior (DiClemente, Hansen, & Ponton,

RECOMMENDED READING

The Hurried Child: Growing Up Too Fast, Too Soon
by David Elkind
(Perseus Publishing, 2001)

In this eye-opening book, psychologist David Elkind shows how recent changes in the structure of family life have altered views of children and their needs. Earlier generations saw children as needing adult protection and guidance, a view consistent with the "traditional" family structure, in which at least one parent was available to the children at all times. Today, in many step-, single-parent, and dual-earner families, such nurturing is impossible for parents to provide. Many of these parents have alleviated their anxiety about parenthood by adopting a new conception of children as "superkids" who can take care of themselves.

This new view of children as "miniature adults" is mirrored in every facet of children's culture: education, television, movies, and music. Computer software for infants, video games for children, and the Internet also encourage the hurrying of intellectual and social development. Thus, society as a whole conspires with the parents to "hurry" children to outgrow their need for nurturance as quickly as possible.

According to Elkind, pressuring children to grow up fast can produce negative outcomes ranging from academic failure to psychosomatic illness to teenage suicide. Nevertheless, he maintains an attitude of optimism and hope that, with awareness of the pressures today's children face, parents can and will seek to alleviate their children's stress. Reading this book can help a concerned parent to do just that.

Cover Reprinted by permission of Perseus Books Publishers, a member of Perseus Books, L.L.C. Photo © Photonica.

1995; Eccles et al., 2003). Because "risky" adolescents are as knowledgeable about the possible negative outcomes of their behavior as "nonrisky" adolescents, psychologists speculate that the causes of risk-taking behavior are not cognitively rooted (Eccles et al., 2003). Instead, they probably involve other aspects of decision making, such as self-regulation (see Chapter 5).

Personality Changes

Adolescents are faced with a number of challenges in the realm of personality. They must grapple with identity questions and deal with the stresses of moving from childhood to adulthood.

The Search for Identity

As adulthood looms closer, adolescents turn their attention to their place in the larger social order. Erik Erikson (1968), an influential psychoanalytic theorist, used the term *identity* to express this important psychological connection between self and society. **Identity refers to having a relatively clear and stable sense of who one is in the larger society.** In Erikson's theory, the stage of adolescence is of pivotal importance; the challenge of this period is achieving identity. (Figure 11.3 depicts all eight of Erikson's stages, although in this chapter we will focus on only the last four.) Developing a sense of identity involves wrestling with such important issues as "Who am I?" "What do I stand for?" and "What kind of work do I want to do?" Gender, ethnicity, and sexual orientation are also important aspects of identity development. Although much of the process of identity formation is unconscious, a key point is that individuals create their identity; they do not just blindly accept the roles and beliefs designated for them by parents and society.

Erik Erikson

Ted Streshinsky/Corbis

WEB LINK 11.2

Erik Erikson Tutorial Homepage
Margaret Anderson, who teaches at Cortland College in New York, has developed a set of tutorials on major figures of importance to educational psychology. Her Erik Erikson tutorial includes a summary of his eight stages of development, biographical details, some controversies regarding his theories, and links to other online sources.

According to Erikson, identity emerges out of an "identity crisis," or a period of personal questioning during which individuals reflect on and experiment with various occupational possibilities and value choices (political, religious, sexual, and so forth). For most people, an identity crisis is not a sudden or agonizing experience but rather the gradual evolution of a sense of who one is. An identity crisis usually ends with a commitment to a specific career and personal value system. According to James Marcia (1980), these two factors of crisis and commitment combine in various ways to produce four identity statuses (see Figure 11.4) instead of just the two outcomes shown in Figure 11.3. Note that these are not stages that people pass through, but rather statuses that

Erikson's Stages of Psychosocial Development

Stage	Psychosocial crisis	Significant social relationships	Favorable outcome
1. First year of life	Trust versus mistrust	Mother or mother substitute	Trust and optimism
2. Second and third years	Autonomy versus doubt	Parents	A sense of self-control and adequacy
3. Fourth through sixth years	Initiative versus guilt	Basic family	Purpose and direction; ability to initiate one's own activities
4. Age 6 through puberty	Industry versus inferiority	Neighborhood, school	Competence in intellectual, social, and physical skills
5. Adolescence	Identity versus diffusion	Peer groups and outgroups; models of leadership	An integrated image of oneself as a unique person
6. Early adulthood	Intimacy versus isolation	Partners in friendship and sex; competition, cooperation	An ability to form close and lasting relationships, to make career commitments
7. Middle adulthood	Generativity versus stagnation	Divided labor and shared household	Concern for family, society, and future generations
8. The aging years	Integrity versus despair	"Humankind," "my kind"	A sense of fulfillment and satisfaction with one's life; willingness to face death

● **FIGURE 11.3**

Overview of Erikson's stages. Building on earlier work by Freud, Erik Erikson (1963) divided the life span into eight stages. Each stage involves a psychosocial crisis (column 2) that is played out in certain social relationships (column 3). If a crisis is handled effectively, a favorable outcome results (column 4).

Adapted from Erikson, E. H. (1963). *Childhood and society* (2nd ed.). New York: W. W. Norton. Copyright © 1950, 1963 by W. W. Norton & Co. Inc. Copyright renewed 1978, 1991 by Erik H. Erikson. Used by permission of W. W. Norton & Company, Inc.

Marcia's Four Identity Statuses

	Crisis present	Crisis absent
Commitment present	*Identity achievement* (successful achievement of a sense of identity)	*Identity foreclosure* (unquestioning adoption of parental or societal values)
Commitment absent	*Identity moratorium* (active struggling for a sense of identity)	*Identity diffusion* (absence of struggle for identity, with no obvious concern about this)

● **FIGURE 11.4**

Marcia's four identity statuses. According to James Marcia, the experience of an identity crisis and the development of personal commitments can combine into four possible identity statuses, as shown in this diagram.

Adapted from Marcia, J. E. (1980). Identity in adolescence. In J. Adelson (Ed.), *Handbook of adolescent psychology* (pp. 159–210). New York: Wiley. Copyright © 1980 by John Wiley & Sons. Inc. Adapted by permission of John Wiley & Sons, Inc.

characterize a person's identity orientation at any particular time. Thus, a person may never experience some of the statuses, including identity achievement.

The status of *identity foreclosure* is a premature commitment to visions, values, and roles prescribed by one's parents. *Moratorium* involves delaying commitment for a while to experiment with alternative ideologies. *Identity achievement* is arriving at a sense of self and direction after some consideration of alternative possibilities. Finally, *identity diffusion* is an inability to make identity commitments. In both identity achievement and foreclosure, the identity crisis is resolved because a sense of commitment is present. Of course, in foreclosure, the commitment is not an independently developed one, as is desirable. Individuals in both the moratorium and diffusion statuses have not resolved the identity crisis. While those experiencing identity diffusion have given up the search for identity, "moratoriums" are still pursuing it. As they move into their 20s, adolescents typically shift from the foreclosure and diffusion statuses to the moratorium or achievement statuses (Kroger, 1997; Meeus, 1996).

Considerable research has been done on identity statuses and their characteristics (Marcia, 1980, 1991). Compared to those in other statuses, adolescents in identity foreclosure are strongly connected to their families, cognitively rigid, conventional, and conservative in their values. Those going through a moratorium are conflicted between conforming and rebelling, have ambivalent feelings toward their parents, and are perceived by others to be intense. The identity diffused feel alienated from their parents, exhibit lower levels of moral reasoning, and show less emotional intimacy than those in the other statuses. Those who experience identity achievement are more cognitively flexible, function at higher levels of moral reasoning, and have more emotionally intimate relationships.

Erikson and many other theorists believe that identity achievement is a cornerstone of sound psychological health. Researchers find that long-term foreclosed and diffused individuals are likely to experience adjustment problems (Berzonsky & Kuk, 2000).

Time of Turmoil?

Is adolescence a period of emotional upheaval and turmoil? G. Stanley Hall (1904), the first psychologist to study adolescence, thought so. In fact, he specifically characterized adolescence as a period of "storm and stress." Hall attributed this turmoil to the conflicts between the physical changes of puberty and society's demands for social and emotional maturity.

Does research support Hall's idea? To answer this question, Jeffrey Arnett (1999) looked at the research on three relevant issues. First, there is evidence that *parent-adolescent conflicts* increase during (early) adolescence (Laursen, Coy, and Collins, 1998). Adolescents also experience more *volatile emotions and extremes of mood* than preadolescents or adults do (Larson & Richards, 1994). Finally, adolescents engage in *risk behaviors:* delinquent and antisocial behavior, alcohol and substance abuse, careless sexual practices, and school failure (Perkins & Borden, 2003).

Increases in these areas are not found in more traditional (preindustrial) cultures (Suarez-Orozco & Suarez-Orozco, 1995). Thus, Arnett argues that there is support for a modified storm-and-stress view that takes into account individual differences and cultural variations. Still, even for adolescents who do experience turmoil, it is important not to exaggerate the phenomenon. Based on her extensive studies of adolescents, Anne Petersen (1987) has concluded, "The adolescent's journey toward adulthood is inherently marked by change and upheaval, but need not be fraught with chaos or deep pain" (p. 34).

As young people progress through adolescence, the differences between the vast majority who can cope with the transition to adulthood and the small minority who cannot become increasingly obvious. Those in the latter group are prone to depression, suicidal behavior, drug and alcohol abuse, and chronic delinquency (Petersen, 1988; Takanishi, 1993). Of course, most teens who have a run-in with the law are not doomed to a life of crime, but repeated offenses are a cause for concern. As well, juvenile delinquents who have a childhood history of behavior problems are at high risk for adult criminal activity (Farrington & Loeber, 2000). Early professional attention in such cases can often forestall more serious trouble.

Adolescent Suicide

Adolescent suicide rates have risen alarmingly in recent decades. Suicide among 15- to 24-year-olds increased dramatically after 1960, while it rose only slightly in the general population during this time. Despite these increases, only a small minority of adolescents commit suicide (Meehan et al., 1992). Also, even with the steep increase in the 15–24 age group, the incidence of suicide in this group is about the same as or lower than that for any older age group.

Actually, the suicide crisis among teenagers involves *attempted suicide* more than *completed suicide*. Experts estimate that when all age groups are lumped together, suicide attempts outnumber actual suicidal deaths by a ratio of about 8 to 1 (Cross & Hirschfeld, 1986). However, the ratio of attempted to completed suicides among adolescents is much higher than that for any other age group—anywhere from 100:1 to 200:1 (Maris, Berman, & Silverman, 2000). Suicide attempts

by adolescents tend to be desperate cries for attention, help, and support. Gay and lesbian youth are much more likely to attempt suicide than their heterosexual peers. Experts estimate that 33 percent of homosexual youth have attempted suicide, compared to 13 percent of their heterosexual peers (Hershberger & D'Augelli, 2000). These high rates are not a result of homosexuality per se but are linked to other factors associated with psychological distress such as high stress, lack of social support, and so forth (Goldfried, 2001).

Girls are more likely to attempt suicide, and boys are more likely to complete suicide (Garland & Zigler, 1993). That's because girls use methods that are less lethal (overdosing on sleeping pills, for instance), whereas boys elect methods with a low likelihood of survival (shooting or hanging). Another factor may be lower tolerance for the perceived weakness implied in suicide attempts by males (Canetto & Sakinofsky, 1998). White adolescents have higher suicide rates than African American and Hispanic youth. Sadly, American Indian adolescents have a suicide rate that is more than twice the national average, a finding that is likely rooted in extreme poverty and a sense of hopelessness about the future (Strickland, 1997).

What drives an adolescent to such a dramatic, but dangerous, gesture? The "typical" suicidal adolescent has a long history of stress and personal problems extending back into childhood (de Wilde et al., 1992). Unfortunately, for some teenagers these problems—trouble at home, difficulties in school, problems with girlfriends and boyfriends—escalate during adolescence. As their efforts to cope with these problems fail, many teenagers rebel against parental authority, withdraw from social relationships, and make dramatic gestures such as running away from home. These actions

Most adolescents who attempt suicide have a long history of stress and personal problems and are socially isolated. A perceived failure at school or a perceived social slight can be the "final straw" that triggers a suicide attempt in such teens.

© Nancy Richmond/The Image Works

What to Do When You Fear Someone May Take Their Life

Determine whether the person is in imminent danger:

Ask the following questions in a nonjudgmental way:

1. Do you have a plan?
2. Do you know when you would do it (today, next week)?
3. Do you have access to what you would use?

If you believe that the person is in imminent danger:

Call 911 or get the person to a hospital emergency room or to the campus or local police station. If you are with the person, do not leave him or her alone.

If you believe that the threat is not imminent:

1. Do not discount the threat by telling the person that his or her problems are not that bad, or that the person has everything to live for, or that he or she is silly to contemplate suicide.
2. Reassure the person that help is available, that depression is treatable, and that suicidal feelings are temporary.
3. Let the person know that he or she is very important to you and how devastated you and others would be if he or she followed through with suicide.
4. Emphasize that there are alternative ways to deal with problems other than suicide. Often people fail to see other solutions to their problems.
5. Offer to go with the person to your campus counseling center, or to help him or her find a doctor or mental health professional.
6. Understandably, you may be frightened and worried when you learn such information. Consider going to the campus counseling center and asking for advice.

● FIGURE 11.5

Preventing suicide. If someone tells you that he or she is contemplating suicide, you should treat this information very seriously. Here are some suggestions for dealing with that difficult situation.

Based on American Foundation for Suicide Prevention (n.d.). *When you fear someone may take their life.* Retrieved January 10, 2005 from http://www.afsp.org/about/whattodo.htm

often lead to progressive social isolation. The experience of a humiliating event such as an arrest, a conflict with or a rejection by a parent or romantic partner, or a perceived failure at school or work can be the final thread in a tapestry of frustration and distress (Garland & Zigler, 1993; King, 1997). In Figure 11.5, we provide some suggestions for dealing with someone who tells you that he or she is contemplating suicide.

The Expanse of Adulthood

LEARNING OBJECTIVES

- *Summarize the key developmental transitions in early adulthood, including Erikson's views.*
- *Summarize the key developmental transitions in middle adulthood, including Erikson's views.*
- *Summarize the key developmental transitions in late adulthood, including Erikson's views.*

As people progress through adulthood, they periodically ask themselves, "How am I doing for my age?" In pondering this question, they are likely to be influenced by their social clocks (Helson, Mitchell, & Moane, 1984). **A *social clock* is a person's notion of a developmental schedule that specifies what he or she should have accomplished by certain points in life.** For example, if you feel that you should be married by the time you're 30, that belief creates a marker on your social clock. Although social clocks are a product of socialization, they do show individual variations.

Social clocks can exert considerable influence over decisions concerning education, career moves, marriage, parenting, and other life choices. Adhering to a social clock based on prevalent age norms brings social approval and is thus a way to evaluate one's own development. Important life events that come too early or too late according to one's social clock produce more stress than transitions that occur "on time" (Chiriboga, 1987). It is easy to imagine how an early marriage, delayed career promotion, or delayed retirement might be especially stressful. In particular, it seems that lagging behind one's personal schedule for certain achievements results in psychological distress (Antonucci & Akiyama, 1997). In short, most people listen carefully to their social clocks ticking in the background as they proceed through adulthood.

In recent years, psychologists have recognized that the time period in which a person is born can have significant effects on development (Stewart & Ostrove, 1998). Events such as the Great Depression, World War II, the Vietnam War, the women's movement, and the rise of the Internet can leave a lasting mark on the individuals who experience them. Complicating the picture further, developmental patterns are becoming increasingly diverse. That is, the boundaries between young, middle, and late adulthood are becoming blurred as more people have children later than one is "supposed" to, retire earlier than one is "supposed" to, and so forth. As we look at the major developmental transitions in adult life, keep in mind that there are many divergent pathways and timetables during these years.

Early Adulthood (From About Age 20 to 40)

Between the ages of about 20 and 30, adults must learn a number of new and important roles. Take Jack, for example: He graduated from college at age 22, then left his family and moved to Atlanta to start work as a management trainee. Over the next four years, he was involved in several serious relationships (which later broke up), and he changed jobs several times. At age 26, Jack got engaged and married. At age 28, he and his wife had their first child and he again changed jobs. Based on Jack's scenario, you can see why the years from 20 to 30 have been described as "demographically dense," referring to the fact that more role changes occur during this period than any other (Rindfuss, 1991). For some, early adulthood brings additional stress because it is a time for sorting out sexual orientation. As we discuss in Chapter 13, gay males and lesbians take longer than heterosexuals to recognize their sexual orientation (Garnets & Kimmel, 2003a).

To cope successfully with all these developmental challenges, young adults must have developed certain psychological and social competencies, including a set of personal values to guide their life decisions and enough self-control to reach their goals. In addition, they must have a sense of the kind of work they want to do, the job skills necessary for the position they want, and social skills by which to develop and maintain relationships at work and with friends and partners or mates. Also, most young adults are still struggling to become fully independent of their parents.

Erikson's Theory: Intimacy Versus Isolation

In Erikson's sixth stage, the psychosocial crisis centers on whether a person can develop the capacity to share *intimacy* with others (refer back to Figure 11.3). Erikson was not concerned simply with the young adult's need to find a marriage partner. Rather, he was concerned with more subtle issues, such as whether one can learn to open up to oth-

ers, truly commit to others, and give of oneself unselfishly. The person who can experience genuine intimacy is thought to be more likely to develop a mature and successful long-term relationship. Failure to resolve this psychosocial crisis favorably leads to difficulties in relating to others in an authentic fashion. The resulting sense of isolation can foster competitive interactions with friends and troublesome intimate relationships.

Jacob Orlofsky and his colleagues (1973) found support for five intimacy statuses, based on the quality of a person's relationships with others:

1. *Intimate.* Individuals in this status are capable of forming open and close relationships with both male and female friends and are involved in a committed relationship.

2. *Preintimate.* Although people in this category are capable of mature, reciprocal relationships, they haven't yet experienced a committed relationship because they are ambivalent about making commitments.

3. *Stereotyped.* Men and women in this status have relationships that are superficial and not very close. They often see others as objects to manipulate rather than to share with.

4. *Pseudointimate.* These individuals are typically involved in a relatively permanent relationship, but it resembles the stereotyped relationship in quality.

5. *Isolate.* Isolates avoid social situations and appear to be loners whose social interactions consist of casual conversations with a few acquaintances.

According to Erikson, the ability to establish and maintain intimate relationships depends on having successfully weathered the identity crisis of adolescence. The rationale here is that without a clear sense

The positive outcome of Erikson's sixth stage is intimacy or the capacity to relate openly to others and to make emotional commitments. Isolation, the negative outcome, is characterized by difficulties in forming relationships with others.

domains of sexuality and family roles are more salient for women than they are for men.

Going beyond Erikson's theory, two specific developmental tasks of early adulthood are adjusting to full-time work and adjusting to marriage and family life.

Adjusting to the World of Work

Young adults are confronted with several major challenges in their work lives (Super, 1957, 1985, 1988). To start, they need to complete their schooling and secure their first job. At this point in career development, many people are still only tentatively committed to their chosen occupational area. If their first experiences are not rewarding, they may shift to another area, where they continue to explore their work options. People in their twenties change jobs on the average of every two years (Peterson & Gonzales, 2005).

Ideally, people are able to find work that is gratifying and commit to an occupational area. Once individuals make a commitment to a particular kind of work, their future job moves usually take place within this area. During early adulthood, workers learn new skills and develop work attitudes that affect their job success. Effective mentors can play an important role in this process.

Once men begin working full-time, they tend to stay in the workforce until they retire (a continuous pattern). Women's work lives often have a discontinuous pattern—typically because women have greater child-care responsibilities. Thus, they may move in and out of the workforce at different points in their lives (Betz, 1993).

Adjusting to Marriage and Family Life

Although an increasing proportion of the population under 35 are remaining single (Teachman, Polonko, & Scanzoni, 1999), most people marry or become involved in committed relationships during early adulthood. Today, the average age of first marriage for women is about 25; for men, it is about 27 (U.S. Bureau, of the Census 2004a). As noted in Chapter 9, the first few years of married life tend to be very happy. The early years of committed gay and lesbian relationships also follow this pattern (Peplau & Spalding, 2003).

Compared to earlier generations, more of today's married couples are choosing not to have children

of yourself before you enter into an intimate relationship, you risk becoming overly dependent on another for your identity. Researchers typically find that college males and females in the more advanced identity statuses (achievement and moratorium) are most likely to be in the more advanced intimacy statuses (intimate and preintimate) (Fitch & Adams, 1983). Similarly, those experiencing identity foreclosure or diffusion predominate in the less advanced intimacy statuses (stereotyped, pseudointimate, and isolate). A similar pattern has been found in adults up to 35 years of age (Raskin, 1986; Tesch & Whitbourne, 1982).

Early research showed gender differences in the sequencing of Erikson's stages 5 and 6, such that non-career-oriented women seemed to resolve intimacy issues before they tackled identity issues (Dyk & Adams, 1990; Whitbourne & Tesch, 1985). (Career-oriented women showed the same pattern as men, passing though stage 5 before stage 6.) In a review of research on gender and identity, Jane Kroger (1997) found no gender differences in the key aspects of identity, except that men lagged behind women in attaining identity achievement. Kroger also reported that the identity

(Bulcroft & Teachman, 2004), but the vast majority plan to do so. The arrival of the first child represents a major transition. Among other things, it triggers a shift toward traditional roles for husband and wife (Cowan & Cowan, 1997). This shift is significant because greater discrepancies between the responsibilities of husband and wife after childbirth are associated with more marital conflict as well as declines in marital satisfaction and mental health, particularly for women (Perry-Jenkins, Repetti, & Crouter, 2001).

Even in dual-earner families, women typically bear greater responsibilities in the realms of child care and housework (Bond et al., 2003). Thus, mothers experience more work-family conflicts than fathers do. After the first few years of married life, marital satisfaction typically declines and continues at a lower level until middle adulthood, when it rises again (Glenn, 1998).

Like heterosexual married couples, most gay and lesbian couples are in dual-worker relationships. Unlike married couples, however, committed homosexual couples are more likely to have a flexible division of labor, where the workload is shared and tasks are completed based on personal preference (Peplau & Spaulding, 2003).

Middle Adulthood (From About Age 40 to 65)

Compared to early adulthood, which requires learning so many new roles, middle adulthood is an easier period.

Erikson's Theory: Generativity Versus Stagnation

The challenge of middle adulthood is acquiring *generativity,* or a concern for the welfare of future generations (refer to Figure 11.3). Adults demonstrate generativity when they provide unselfish guidance to younger people. The recipients of this guidance are often their own children, but not necessarily. For example, a middle-aged college professor may gain great satisfaction from working with students. Or a 50-year-old attorney might mentor a younger woman in her law firm. Thus, generativity and its opposite, stagnation, do not hinge on a person's having children. Stagnation is characterized by self-absorption and self-indulgent preoccupation with one's own needs.

A number of studies support Erikson's views on generativity and middle adulthood. For example, researchers have found that generativity increases between young adulthood and middle age (McAdams, de St. Aubin, & Logan, 1993; Stewart, Ostrove, & Helson, 2001). Studies also report that highly generative individuals are well adjusted (low levels of anxiety and depression) and high in life satisfaction (Ackerman, Zuroff, & Moskowitz, 2000; Grossbaum & Bates, 2002).

More specific challenges of middle age include confronting the aging process and making transitions in work and family roles.

Confronting the Aging Process

Chief among the challenges of middle adulthood is coming to terms with the aging process. Middle-aged adults notice a number of physical transformations: changes in vision that often require glasses or bifocals for reading, the onset of wrinkles and sagging skin, weight gain, tooth and gum problems, and more bodily aches and pains and general "creakiness" (Lachman, 2004; Whitbourne, 2001). In addition, people are forced to acknowledge their mortality as they witness the deaths of parents, colleagues, and friends.

After early adulthood, people perceive themselves to be younger than they actually are (Montepare & Lachman, 1989). In Figure 11.6, you can see that the gap between actual and subjective age widens over time, especially among women, suggesting that women find it harder to accept growing older. This attitude no doubt reflects the "double standard of aging"—the perception that women's attractiveness declines more with age than men's does (Zebrowitz & Montepare, 2000). On a positive note, feeling younger than one's

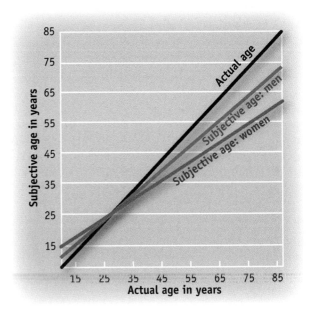

● FIGURE 11.6

Discrepancies between actual and subjective age. After early adulthood, people see themselves as younger than they really are. This gap between reality and perception increases with age, especially among women. This graph also shows that adolescents perceive themselves to be older than they really are, while the age perceptions of young adults match reality fairly closely.

Adapted from Montepare, J., & Lachman, M. E. (1989). You're only as old as you feel: Self-perceptions of age, fears of aging, and life satisfaction. *Psychology and Aging, 4,* 73–78. Copyright © 1989 American Psychological Association. Adapted by permission of the author.

actual age is correlated with greater psychological adjustment and health (Lachman, 2004).

Transitions in the Parenting Role

As children grow up, parental influence tends to decline, and the early years of parenting—which once seemed so difficult—are often recalled with fondness. When children reach adolescence and seek to establish their own identities, gradual realignment occurs in parent-child relationships. As a result, conflicts over values are common, and power struggles frequently ensue (Arnett, 1999). Parents overwhelmingly rate adolescence as the most difficult stage of childrearing (Steinberg, 2001). Still, on balance, most parents have little regret about their decision to have children and rate parenthood as a positive experience (Demo, 1992).

Although "emptying of the nest" is widely believed to be a traumatic event for parents, especially mothers, only about 25 percent of mothers and fathers report being very sad or unhappy when the last child leaves home (Lewis & Lin, 1996). In fact, the "empty nest" is associated with improved mood and well-being for most women (Dennerstein, Dudley, & Guthrie, 2002). An interesting phenomenon is that in recent decades, the percentage of young adults who return home to live with their parents has increased. Returning home is due to a number of factors: inability to find a job, marital separation, divorce, or job loss. To date, research indicates that young adults living with their parents has a small negative impact on parent-child relationships (White & Rogers, 1997).

The postparental period often provides couples with more freedom and time to devote to each other, to travel, and to new leisure interests. As offspring strike out on their own, couples' marital satisfaction starts climbing to higher levels once again (Glenn, 1998). It tends to remain fairly high until one of the spouses (usually the husband) dies.

A related challenge for most middle-aged adults is learning the grandparent role. In addition, some individuals (typically women) may assume responsibility for the care of aging parents and relatives (Putney & Bengtson, 2001).

Transitions in the Work Role

Work plays a central role in the midlife years (Lachman, 2004). At midlife, workers seem to follow one of two patterns (Papalia & Olds, 1995). Those in the *stable career pattern* are at the peak of their careers. They have more responsibility, earn more money, and wield more influence than their younger co-workers. As we noted, many take the opportunity to mentor younger workers, an expression of generativity. Some workers in this group continue to work at a frantic pace, struggling to accomplish their goals as they hear their social clocks ticking. Others seem content with their work achievements and begin to shift some of their attention and energy to family and leisure activities.

Workers in the *changing careers pattern* make up a more varied group. Whereas all are seeking to begin a different type of work, their reasons for doing so are quite varied. Some are looking for a new line of work because they have been forced out of a job by cutbacks. Others are seeking new careers because they want new challenges at this time in their lives. A third group is composed of women who are entering or reentering the workforce because family concerns now occupy less of their time and energy.

Is There a Midlife Crisis?

Much has been made about whether most people go through a **midlife crisis**—**a turbulent period of doubts and reappraisal of one's life.** Two influential studies of adult development in the 1970s both concluded that a midlife crisis is a normal transition experienced by a majority of people. Daniel Levinson and his colleagues (1978) found that most of their subjects (all men) went through a midlife crisis around the ages of 40 to 45. This transition was marked by life reevaluation and emotional turmoil. Roger Gould (1978) found that

Do most adults go through a midlife crisis in their 40s? The research on this question is contradictory, but overall, the evidence suggests that only a minority of people in their 40s struggle with a midlife crisis.

people tended to go through a midlife crisis between the ages of 35 and 45. His subjects reported feeling pressed by time. They heard their social clocks ticking loudly as they struggled to achieve their life goals.

Since the landmark studies of Levinson and Gould, many other researchers have questioned whether the midlife crisis is a normal developmental transition. A host of studies have failed to detect an increase in emotional turbulence at midlife (Baruch, 1984; Eisler & Ragsdale, 1992; Roberts & Newton, 1987). How can we explain this discrepancy? Levinson and Gould both depended primarily on interview and case study methods to gather their data. However, when knitting together impressionistic case studies, it is easy for investigators to see what they expect to see. Given that the midlife crisis has long been a part of developmental folklore, Levinson and Gould may have interpreted their case study data in this light (McCrae & Costa, 1984). In any case, investigators relying on more objective measures of emotional stability have found signs of midlife crises in only a tiny minority (2–5 percent) of subjects (Chiriboga, 1989; McCrae & Costa, 1990). Typically, these are individuals whose circumstances in early adulthood (family pressures, poverty, and so forth) severely limited their chances to achieve life satisfaction (McAdams, 1988). To summarize, midlife may bring a period of increased reflection as people contemplate the remainder of their lives, but it's clear that the fabled midlife crisis is not typical (Lemme, 1999).

Of course, this finding doesn't mean that people don't make major changes in midlife. Nearly everyone knows someone who has embarked on a new career or committed relationship during middle age. Nonetheless, researchers find that such "turning points" are more often caused by unexpected events (divorce, job transfers, serious illness), which can occur at any time in adulthood (Lachman & Bertrand, 2001; Wethington, Kessler, & Pixley, 2004). In fact, some evidence exists for a "quarter-life" crisis (mid-20s and early 30s)

involving the search for meaningful work and relationships (Lachman, 2004; Robbins & Wilner, 2001).

Late Adulthood (After Age 65)

Late adulthood also has its share of developmental transitions. These challenges include adjusting to retirement, adapting to changes in one's support network, coping with health problems, and confronting death. Let's begin by discussing Erikson's views of late adulthood.

Erikson's Theory: Integrity Versus Despair

The challenge of Erikson's last stage is to achieve *ego integrity* (refer to Figure 11.3). People who achieve integrity are able to look back on their lives with a sense of satisfaction and to find meaning and purpose there. The opposite, despair, is the tendency to dwell on the mistakes of the past, bemoan paths not chosen, and contemplate the approach of death with bitterness. Erikson asserts that it is better to face the future in a spirit of acceptance than to wallow in regret and resentment. In a test of Erikson's theory, researchers studied male and female adults over a 20-year span (Whitbourne et al., 1992). Among other things, they found that favorable resolutions of earlier stages lead to favorable resolutions of later stages. Another study of participants ages 17 to 82 reported that subjective well-being was correlated with increasing age and psychological maturity and that the factors of generativity and ego integrity accounted for most of the relationship between age and well-being (Sheldon & Kasser, 2001a).

Key developmental challenges in late adulthood include retirement and changes in support networks.

Retirement

As retirement looms near, people prepare to leave the workplace. Over the years, the average age of retirement has been decreasing, and it is now 62. Still, this number is misleading because it falsely implies that retirement is an abrupt event. In fact, retirement these days is usually a gradual process during which people cut back on their work hours over some years rather than stopping work altogether (Mutchler et al., 1997).

Individuals approach retirement with highly variable attitudes. Chief concerns include having adequate retirement income and being able to fill the hours previously devoted to paid work. Happily, many studies have shown that retirement has no adverse effect on overall health or life satisfaction (Bossé, Spiro, & Kressin, 1996). Retirement can pose a problem, however, for those who are forced to leave work because of ill health, mandatory retirement policies, or job elimination or whose incomes are inadequate. Those most likely to be so affected are blacks, Hispanics, and women (Flippen & Tienda, 2000). Retirement can also be stressful if it comes at the same time as other life changes, such as widowhood. Although retirement may result in decreased income, it also provides more time for travel, hobbies, and friends. Through volunteer work, retirees can share their knowledge and skills and interact with others in meaningful ways (Moen et al., 2000). Retirees who make the best adjustment have an adequate income, good health, and an extended social network of friends and family (Gall, Evans, & Howard, 1997).

Changes in Support Networks

As we noted, relationship satisfaction starts rising later in life and remains fairly high until one of the spouses or partners dies. In addition, most older adults maintain their ties to their children and grandchildren. In one large study of over 11,000 adults age 65 and over, 63 percent of the participants reported that they saw at least one of their children at least once a week, and another 16 percent saw a child one to three times a month. Only 20 percent indicated that they saw their children once a month or less (Crimmins & Ingegneri, 1990). Surprisingly, elderly parents who see their children regularly or who report positive interactions with them don't describe themselves as happier than those who see their children less often or who have less positive relationships with their offspring (Markides & Krause, 1985; Seccombe, 1987).

Older adults report that siblings become more important than they were earlier (White, 2001). Relationships with sisters (sister-sister or sister-brother) seem to be especially important in old age (Cicirelli, 1996).

A few studies have explored family relationships in ethnic minority families. This research indicates that Hispanics have extensive family relationships, with frequent visiting and exchanges not only with the immediate family but also with grandparents and cousins (Keefe, 1984). There is also evidence that Italian American and African American siblings have closer relationships than siblings from nonethnic families, although the number of these intimate relationships appears to be relatively small (Gold, 1990).

Friends seem to play a more significant role in life satisfaction for older adults than family members do, at least for most white Americans (Pruchno & Rosenbaum, 2003). Friendships provide companionship, as well as opportunities for engaging in leisure activities and sharing thoughts and feelings. Although the elderly have fewer friends than those who are younger, they are happier with their current number of friends than younger adults are (Lansford, Sherman & Antonucci, 1998). The elderly have fewer friends in part because they have lost friends through death, but also because they are more selective about their friends (Carstensen, 1995). In contrast to younger adults, older adults particularly prefer friends who help them avoid stress and make them feel good. The gender differences in friendships we noted in Chapter 8 continue throughout adulthood. Thus, older men may have a larger network of friends than women do, but women's friendships are more intimate (Sherman, deVries, & Lansford, 2000). Men rely heavily on their wives for emotional support, whereas women derive support from children and friends, along with their spouse (Umberson, Wortman, & Kessler, 1992). This difference in social support puts husbands at greater risk than wives for health and adjustment problems when a spouse dies (Lee, Willetts, & Seccombe, 1998).

For African American elders, *ritual kin* are an important component of social support networks. In

For older adults, friendships provide companionship and opportunities for shared activities.

these relationships, certain neighbors or peers acquire the status of a close family member and render mutual aid and support (Taylor et al., 1990). Also, for elderly African Americans, participation in church activities plays a central role in psychological adjustment (Bryant & Rakowski, 1992).

Other significant challenges for older adults include coping with health problems, dealing with the deaths of friends and partners, and confronting one's own mortality. We'll address these issues in the last two sections of the chapter.

Aging: A Gradual Process

LEARNING OBJECTIVES

- Discuss age-related changes in appearance and their psychological significance.
- Describe the sensory, neurological, and endocrine changes that accompany aging.
- Discuss health changes as people age and two things people can do to maintain health.

- Describe age-related changes in intelligence, information processing, and memory.
- Summarize evidence on personality change and stability in adulthood.

As an alternative to the ages-and-stages approach to adult development, many psychologists take the approach of identifying the physical, cognitive, and personality changes that occur across the expanse of adulthood. Whereas some of these age-related developments are quite obvious, others are very subtle. In either case, the changes take place gradually.

Physical Changes

The physical changes that occur in adulthood affect appearance, the nervous system, vision and hearing, hormone functioning, and health. Unless we indicate otherwise, the following summary of trends is based on the work of Susan Krauss Whitbourne (1996, 2001), a leading researcher in adult psychology and aging.

Susan Krauss Whitbourne

Changes in Appearance

Height is stable in adulthood, although it does tend to decline by an inch or so after age 55, as the spinal column "settles." Weight is more variable and tends to increase in most adults up through the mid-50s, when a gradual decline typically begins. Although weight often goes down late in life, the percentage of body weight that is fat tends to increase throughout adulthood, to the chagrin of many. The skin of the face and body tends to wrinkle and sag. The appearance of the face may change, as the nose and ears tend to become longer and wider, and the jaw appears to shrink. Hair tends to thin out and become gray in both genders, and many males have to confront receding hairlines and baldness.

The net impact of these changes is that many older people view themselves as less attractive. This unfortunate reality is probably aggravated by the media's obsession with youthful attractiveness. Older women suffer more than older men as a result of the decline in physical attractiveness because of the "double standard of aging." That is, because much of a woman's worth is determined by her physical attractiveness to men, her social status declines along with her attractiveness. In contrast, older men don't have to rely on their looks for social status; instead, they can use their occupational achievements and money.

Sensory Changes

The most important changes in sensory reception occur in hearing and vision. Hearing problems and visual impairments become common, with men exhibiting higher frequencies of both. Noticeable hearing losses do not usually show up until people reach their 50s. Whereas the vast majority of the elderly require corrective treatment for visual losses, only about a third of older adults suffer hearing losses that require corrective treatment.

The proportion of people with 20/20 vision declines steadily as age increases. From about age 30 to the mid-60s, most people become increasingly far-sighted. After the mid-60s, the trend is toward greater nearsightedness. Depth perception begins to decline in the mid-40s. As well, older people commonly have difficulty adapting to darkness, experience poor recovery from glare, and have reduced peripheral vision. These changes in vision may be responsible for accidents in and outside the home, but they most seriously affect driving ability (particularly at night). Drivers over age 65 have a high proportion of car accidents (except compared to males under 25), which are typically caused by failing to obey traffic signs, not yielding the right of way, and making improper turns, rather than speeding (Kline et al., 1992).

In addition, small sensory losses in touch, taste, and smell have been detected, usually after age 50. These losses generally have little impact on day-to-day functioning, although older people often complain that their food is somewhat tasteless. In contrast, visual and hearing losses often make interpersonal interaction more awkward and difficult, promoting social withdrawal in some.

Neurological Changes

The nervous system is composed of *neurons,* **individual cells that receive, integrate, and transmit information.** The number of active neurons in the brain declines steadily during adulthood. As neurons die, the brain decreases in both weight and volume, especially after age 50. Although this progressive neuronal loss sounds alarming, it is a normal part of the aging process. Its functional significance is the subject of some debate, but it doesn't appear to contribute to any of the age-related dementias. *Dementia* **is an abnormal condition marked by multiple cognitive deficits that include memory impairment.** Dementia can be caused by a variety of disorders, such as Alzheimer's disease, Parkinson's disease, and AIDS, to name just a few. Because some of these diseases are more prevalent in older adults, dementia is seen in about 15 percent of people over age 65 (Elias, Elias, & Elias, 1990). However, it is important to emphasize that dementia and "senility" are not part of the normal aging process. As Cavanaugh (1993) notes, "The term *senility* has no valid medical or psychological meaning, and its continued use simply perpetuates the myth that drastic mental decline is a product of normal aging" (p. 85).

Alzheimer's disease accounts for about 50–60 percent of all cases of dementia. Some 5–7 percent of adults over age 65 have the disease; this number grows to about 25 percent for those 85 and older (Gatz & Smyer, 2001; Gurland et al., 1999). Although the precise causes of Alzheimer's disease are not yet known, it is associated with changes in brain chemistry (Davis et al., 1999) and structure (Knowles et al., 1999). It is a vicious affliction that can strike during middle age (40–65) or later in life (after 65). The disease is one of progressive deterioration, ending in death, and it takes from 8 to 10 years, on average, to run its course.

Although it will be many years before drugs and vaccines are available to safely slow or stop the disease, federally funded research programs around the country are making progress on the Alzheimer's puzzle (Siegler, Bosworth, & Poon, 2003). For example, older adults who engage frequently in cognitively stimulating activities may reduce their risk of Alzheimer's disease (Wilson & Bennett, 2003). One research project involves a group of elderly Catholic nuns in a Minnesota convent (Nash, 1997). About 20 years ago, these women agreed to serve as research subjects in a longitudinal study of Alzheimer's disease and, on death, to donate their brains to this scientific project. Among other findings from the ongoing Nun Study is a strong association between a high frequency of small strokes and severe confusion and memory loss (Snowdon, 2001). It also seems that folic acid may exert a protective effect against Alzheimer's disease. For more information on the Nun Study, see the Recommended Reading box on the next page and Web Link 11.6.

The beginnings of Alzheimer's disease are so subtle that they are difficult to detect. Individuals often forget common words, may report reduced energy, and may lose their temper. Early on, depression often appears (Espiritu et al., 2001). Later, obvious problems begin to emerge, including difficulties in speaking, comprehending, and performing complicated tasks. Individuals don't seem to have trouble with familiar activities. However, profound memory loss develops, especially for recent events. For example, patients may forget the time, date, current season of the year, and where they are. They may also fail to recognize familiar people, something particularly devastating to family and friends. Sometimes, they experience hallucinations, delusions, and paranoid thoughts. Later, victims become completely disoriented and lose control of bladder and bowel functions. At this point, they are unable to care for themselves at all. The disease is eventually fatal.

Hormonal Changes

Although age-related changes occur in hormonal functioning, their significance is not well understood.

They do not appear to be the chief cause of declining sexual activity during the later years. Rather, this decline reflects the acceptance of social norms that older people don't have sexual desires and that sexual activity in the elderly is "inappropriate." For women, decreased sexual activity may simply reflect lack of opportunity, as the proportion of widows increases dramatically with age. The vast majority of older adults remain physically capable of engaging in rewarding sexual encounters, although arousal tends to be somewhat slower and less intense.

Among women, menopause is a key transition that typically occurs in the early 50s. **Menopause is the time when menstruation ceases.** It is tied to a decrease in the production of estrogen. Episodes of moderate physical discomfort ("hot flashes" and "night sweats") dur-

ing the transitional phase are fairly common but are usually no more troublesome than menstruation itself. Vaginal dryness, which can make intercourse painful, can be relieved by a water-based lubricant (K-Y Jelly, for example). The decrease in estrogen is also tied to loss of bone density, which makes women more susceptible than men to osteoporosis and bone fractures (Masi & Bilezikian, 1997). Not so long ago, menopause was almost universally associated with severe emotional strain. However, it is now clear that women's reactions to menopause vary greatly, depending on their expectations (Matthews, 1992). Most women suffer little psychological distress (George, 2002). In fact, many feel liberated from menstrual periods, childbearing, and worrying about birth control (Walter, 2000).

Although the idea of a "male menopause," has generated much discussion in recent years, there really is no equivalent experience among men (Jacobs, 2001). Significant endocrine changes do occur in males in their later years, but these changes are gradual and are largely unrelated to physical or psychological distress. Although sperm production declines between the ages of 25 and 60, older men are still capable of fathering children (Morley, 2001).

Changes in Health Status

The quality of health diminishes with increasing age. There are many reasons for this trend. Vital organ systems lose some of their functional capacity. Vulnerability to some diseases (such as heart disease) increases with age. For other diseases (such as pneumonia), the vulnerability may remain unchanged, but their effects may be more serious. In any case, the proportion of people with a chronic health problem climbs steadily with age. As you can see in Figure 11.7, common chronic health problems among those over 65 are hypertension, arthritis, heart disease, cancer, and diabetes.

Factors such as lifestyle differences and access to and affordability of health care obviously play an important role in maintaining good health. Among the elderly, the affluent have better health than the poor, and whites are healthier than African Americans (Berkman & Gurland, 1998). The health of elderly Hispanics seems to fall between that of whites and African Americans. Native Americans fare the worst.

Most older people live independently—at least until they reach 85. However, with "the graying of America" because of the aging of the baby boomer generation, the number of elderly individuals needing assistance with activities of daily living is expected to soar. Home health care and assisted living facilities are cost-effective alternatives to nursing homes (Maddox, 2001). They also have the important added advantage of permitting individuals to function relatively independently. Although relatively few elderly Americans live in nursing homes, these numbers do increase with

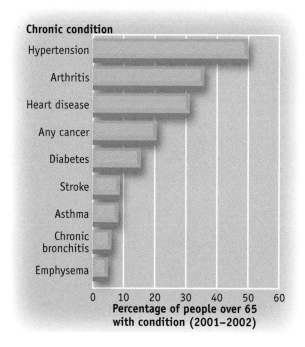

● FIGURE 11.7

Chronic health problems in those over age 65. Although most people over age 65 are in good health, they suffer from a number of chronic conditions. Note: These data refer only to noninstitutionalized individuals. (Federal Interagency Forum on Aging-Related Statistics, 2004)

age (U.S. Bureau of the Census, 2004b). Nursing home use varies across ethnic groups, typically because of the availability of family members to care for the frail elderly. For instance, African American, Hispanic, and Asian American families are more likely to care for the elderly at home than white families are (Gabrel, 2000).

Although it's a given that everyone ages, people can improve their health regardless of age. For one thing,

those who engage in exercise and physical activity tend to be healthier and live longer than those who do not (Connell & Janevic, 2003). Regular exercise during adulthood has been shown to protect against hypertension, heart disease, cancer, and osteoporosis. Because it increases the strength and flexibility of joints and muscles, exercise also reduces the chance of injuries. Regular aerobic exercise also promotes lower stress levels, more positive moods, and better cognitive functioning. People can also increase their chances of maintaining their health by eating a healthy diet. You can learn more about exercise and nutrition in Chapter 14.

Cognitive Changes

It is commonly believed that intelligence drops during middle age and that memory lapses become more frequent in the later years. Are these notions accurate? Let's review the evidence.

Intelligence

Researchers have long been interested in whether general intelligence, as measured by IQ tests, remains stable throughout the adult years. The current evidence suggests that IQ is fairly stable throughout most of adulthood, with most declines beginning after age 60 (Schaie, 1994). Still, there are large individual differences in IQ fluctuations. It's important to note that findings are typically based on *average* test scores, which can be dragged down by a small group of people who experience declines. When Schaie (1990) calculated the percentage of people who maintained stable performance on various mental abilities (see Figure 11.8), he found that about 80 percent showed no declines by age 60 and that about two-thirds were still stable through age 81. Older individuals who maintain

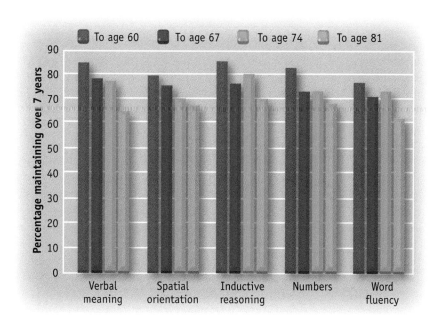

● FIGURE 11.8

Age and the stability of primary mental abilities. In his longitudinal study of cognitive performance begun in 1956, Schaie (1983, 1994) has repeatedly assessed the five basic mental abilities shown along the bottom of this chart. The data graphed here show the percentage of subjects who maintained stable levels of performance on each ability through various ages up to age 81. As you can see, even at the oldest ages, the majority of subjects show no significant decline on most abilities.

From Schaie, K. W. (1990). Intellectual development in adulthood. In J. E. Birren & K. W. Schaie (Eds.), *Handbook of the psychology of aging* (3rd ed). San Diego: Academic Press. Copyright © 1990, reproduced with permission of Elsevier.

Many people, such as scientist Jane Goodall (forefront in the left photo) and former President Jimmy and First Lady Rosalyn Carter, remain active and productive in their 70s, 80s, and even beyond.

higher levels of cognitive functioning have good physical health, above-average education and occupations, plenty of intellectual and social stimulation, and are satisfied with their life accomplishments in midlife or early old age (Schaie, 1994).

Information Processing and Problem Solving

Although intelligence is more stable during adulthood than widely believed, some significant cognitive changes do take place. These changes are most apparent in specific aspects of information processing and problem solving.

There is ample evidence that the ability to narrow one's focus of attention diminishes somewhat with increasing age, as does the ability to handle simultaneous multiple inputs (Hartley & McKenzie, 1991; Kausler, 1994). These changes may be due to decreased efficiency in filtering out irrelevant stimuli. Most of the studies have simply compared extreme age groups (very young participants against very old participants). Thus, it's not clear at what age these changes tend to emerge.

In the cognitive domain, age seems to take its toll on speed first. Many studies indicate that speed in learning, solving problems, retrieving memories, and processing information tends to decline with age, probably beginning in middle adulthood (Salthouse, 2000, 2004). The general nature of this trend (across differing tasks) suggests that it may be a result of age-related changes in neurological functioning.

Overall success on both practical and laboratory problem-solving tasks appears to decrease as people grow older (Sinnott, 1989). For the most part, problem-solving ability is unimpaired if older people are given adequate time to compensate for their reduced speed in information processing. Furthermore, many of the age-related decrements in cognitive functioning can

be partly compensated for by increases in older adults' knowledge.

It should be emphasized that many people remain capable of great intellectual accomplishment in their later years (Simonton, 1997). This fact was verified in a study of scholarly, scientific, and artistic productivity that examined lifelong patterns of work among 738 men who lived at least through the age of 79 (Dennis, 1966). Figure 11.9 plots the percentage of professional works completed by these men in their 20s, 30s, 40s, 50s, 60s, and 70s. As you can see, in most professions the 40s decade was the most productive. However, in many areas productivity was remarkably stable through the 60s and even the 70s. Other researchers have focused on the quality, rather than the quantity, of output. They typically find that "masterpieces" occur at the same relative frequency among the works of creators of all ages (Simonton, 1997).

Memory

Many older people complain about problems with their memory. And it does seem that the capacity of short-term or working memory decreases as people age (Dixon & Cohen, 2003). Also, as we noted, the speed of processing information slows with age. This combination of less working memory capacity and slower processing seems to underlie older adults' poorer performance on complex tasks that demand considerable cognitive effort and resources. Older adults also experience frustrating declines in episodic memory (Dixon &

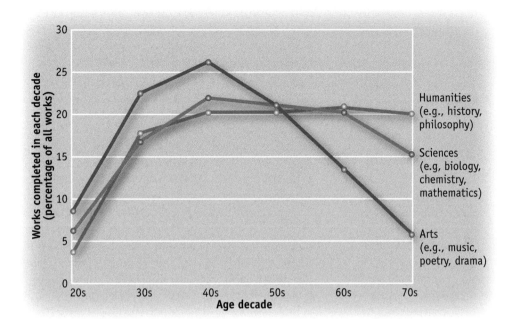

● FIGURE 11.9

Age trends in professional productivity. Dennis (1966) compiled the percentage of professional works completed in each decade of life by 738 men who lived to at least age 79. Productivity peaked in the 40s decade, but professional output remained strong through the 60s decade, and even lasted through the 70s decade for the humanities and sciences.

Based on data from Dennis, W. (1966). Creative productivity between the ages of 20 and 80 years. *Journal of Gerontology, 2*(1), 1–8. Copyright © 1966 the Gerontological Society of America. Adapted by permission.

Cohen, 2003). For example, sometimes they may have difficulties remembering individuals' names or where the car is parked. On tasks that don't require much mental effort (recognizing a familiar face, for example), age-related declines are minimal.

The memory losses associated with aging are moderate and are not universal. However, individuals' beliefs about their memory abilities can produce self-fulfilling prophecies. In one study, individuals who believed that memory gets worse with age estimated larger self-declines in memory compared to people who believed that memory declines only a little with age (Cavanaugh, Feldman, & Hertzog, 1998). Self-beliefs are also important because they are tied to the use of compensatory strategies (for example, investing extra time and effort in learning new skills) to offset memory problems (Cavanaugh, 2000).

Cultural attitudes about aging have been shown to affect memory in the elderly. In an interesting study, researchers looked at memory performance in younger people (20s) and older people (late 50s to 90s). The participants were selected from three cultural groups with differing views of older people: hearing Americans (who hold negative views about aging), deaf Americans (who have generally positive views about aging), and hearing Chinese (who hold positive views about aging). As you can see in Figure 11.10, basically no differences were seen in memory among the younger participants from the three different cultures. In contrast, older Chinese participants performed significantly better than older hearing and deaf Americans. Thus, as we noted in Chapter 6, stereotypes (in this case, about the elderly) can produce self-fulfilling prophecies, for better and for worse.

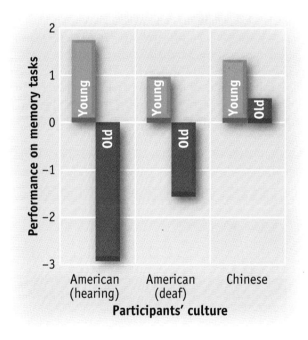

● FIGURE 11.10

Cultural attitudes about aging and memory performance in older persons. Levy and Langer (1994) found that the memory performance of older mainland Chinese, whose culture has positive attitudes about aging, was significantly better than that of older hearing and deaf Americans. Although the differences were not statistically significant, older deaf Americans, whose culture generally has positive views about aging, performed better than older hearing Americans, whose culture has more negative attitudes about aging. The memory performance of young people from these three groups did not differ. (Data from Levy & Langer, 1994)

Adapted from Baron, R., & Byrne, D. (1997). *Social psychology*. Boston, MA: Allyn & Bacon. Copyright © 1997 by Pearson Education. Adapted by permission of the publisher.

A popular misconception is that older people have vivid recollections of events in the distant past while being forgetful about recent events. In actuality, there is no evidence that the elderly have more numerous, or more vivid, early memories (Kausler, 1994; Rabbitt & McGinnis, 1988). In fact, memories of events long ago may be loose reconstructions that are less accurate than people assume.

Personality Changes

Is a grouchy 20-year-old destined to be crotchety at 40 or 65? Or can the cranky young adult become a mellow senior citizen? Psychologists have engaged in lively debate about whether personality remains stable in adulthood, and both sides have been able to cite supportive research. On the one hand, a number of large-scale longitudinal studies using objective assessments of personality traits provide evidence for long-term stability in personality. The general conclusion that emerges from these longitudinal studies is that personality tends to be quite stable over periods of 20 to 40 years (Costa & McCrae, 1994, 1997). For example, Paul Costa and Robert McCrae (1988) conducted a six-year longitudinal study of 983 men who were ages 21 to 76 at the time of the first testing. Over this six-year period, the researchers looked at the stability of the traits in their five-factor model of personality (see Chapter 2). The stability of the participants' self-ratings on these five traits over six years was quite high. Costa and McCrae also asked the spouses of the participants to rate the subjects over the same six-year interval. They found that the stability of the spousal ratings closely matched that of the participants' self-ratings. Also, a recent meta-analysis of 150 studies, involving almost 50,000 participants, concluded that personality in early adulthood was a good predictor of personality in late adulthood and that the stability of personality increases with age up to about age 50 (Roberts & DelVecchio, 2000).

On the other hand, some studies suggest that substantial personality changes continue to occur throughout the life span (Haan, Millsap, & Hartka, 1986; Helson & Moane, 1987; Whitbourne et al., 1992). For example, in a study of women graduates of Mills College, few personality changes were found between the ages of 21 and 27; however, between the ages of 27 and 43, the women increased in dominance (including confidence) and independence (Helson and Moane, 1987; Helson, Mitchell, & Moane, 1984). According to Susan Krauss Whitbourne and her colleagues (1992), "there is a growing body of evidence indicating the existence of adult personality changes on a variety of ... variables" (p. 268).

In sum, researchers assessing the stability of personality in adulthood have reached contradictory conclusions. How can they be reconciled? This appears to be one of those debates in which researchers are eyeing the same findings from different perspectives. Hence, some conclude that the glass is half full, whereas others conclude that it's half empty. In his discussion of this controversy, Lawrence Pervin (1994) concludes that personality is characterized by *both* stability and change. Thus, some personality traits (such as emotional stability, extraversion, and assertiveness) tend to remain stable, while others (such as masculinity and femininity) tend to change as people grow older (Helson & Stewart, 1994).

Death and Dying

LEARNING OBJECTIVES

- *Discuss cultural and individual attitudes about death, including death anxiety.*
- *Describe Kübler-Ross's five stages of dying and research findings about the dying process.*
- *Describe cultural variations in mourning practices and discuss the grieving process.*
- *Discuss different types of loss and what helps people cope with bereavement.*

Dealing with the deaths of close friends and loved ones is an increasingly frequent adjustment problem as people move through adulthood. Moreover, the final challenge of life is to confront one's own death.

Attitudes About Death

Because death is a taboo topic in modern Western society, the most common strategy for dealing with it is *avoidance*. There is abundant evidence of Americans' inability to confront death comfortably. People often use euphemisms such as "passed away" to avoid even the word itself. To minimize exposure to the specter of death, individuals sometimes unnecessarily quarantine the dying in hospitals and nursing homes. Professionals take custody of the body at death and manage funeral arrangements for families. These are all manifestations of what Kastenbaum (2001) calls a ***death*** *system*—**the collection of rituals and procedures used by a culture to handle death.** Death systems vary from culture to culture. Ours happens to be rather negative and evasive.

Negativism and avoidance are *not* universal features of death systems. In Mexican culture, death is discussed frequently and is even celebrated on a national feast day, the Day of the Dead (DeSpelder & Strickland, 1983). Also, the Amish view death as a natural transition rather than a dreaded adversary (Bryer, 1979). Thus, some cultures and subcultures display less fear of death than others.

***Death anxiety* is the fear and apprehension about one's own death.** In Chapters 2 and 5, we noted that terror management theory asserts that death anxiety stems from the conflict between humans' instinct for self-preservation and their awareness of the inevitability of death. According to terror management theory, cultures provide traditions and institutions to help people deal with death anxiety. In support of the theory, adults who have a strong faith in a higher force or being have low death anxiety (Cicirelli, 1999, 2002). Having a well-formulated personal philosophy of death, rather than having a particular religious affiliation, is associated with low death anxiety. For instance, one study found that both devout Christians and devout atheists were less anxious about death than those with ambivalent religious views (Moore, 1992). Also, individuals who haven't accomplished all that they had hoped are more likely to fear death, as are those who are anxious and depressed (Neimeyer & Van Brunt, 1995).

Although death anxiety is uncommon in children, it does appear in those who live in dangerous neighborhoods or war zones. Death anxiety is high in terminally ill children whose parents don't tell them of their impending death (O'Halloran & Altmaier, 1996). Death anxiety typically declines from early to late adulthood (Thorson & Powell, 2000). In fact, elderly adults are more likely to fear the period of uncertainty that comes before death than death itself. They worry about where they will live, who will take care of them, and how they will cope with the loss of control and independence they may experience before death.

The Process of Dying

Pioneering research on the experience of dying was conducted by Elisabeth Kübler-Ross (1969, 1970) during the 1960s. At first, her project met with immense resistance. Fellow physicians at the hospital where she worked were initially unresponsive to her requests to interview dying patients. Gradually, however, it became apparent that

Elisabeth Kübler-Ross

© Roos/Gamma Liaison-Getty Images

WEB LINK 11.7

The End of Life: Exploring Death in America
Since late 1997, National Public Radio (NPR) has regularly aired a range of programs relating to dying and death as experienced in American culture. This companion website at NPR offers not only printed and audio transcripts of each program but many bibliographical and organizational resources as well.

many such patients were enthusiastic about the discussions. They were frustrated by the "conspiracy of silence" that surrounds death and were relieved to get things out in the open.

Eventually, Kübler-Ross interviewed over 200 terminally ill patients and developed a model of the process of dying. According to her model, people evolve through a series of five stages as they confront their own death:

Stage 1: Denial. Denial, shock, and disbelief are the first reactions to being informed of a serious, life-terminating illness. According to Kübler-Ross, few patients maintain this stance to the end.

Stage 2: Anger. After denial, the patient often becomes nasty, demanding, difficult, and hostile. Asking and resolving the question "Why me?" can help the patient reduce resentment.

Stage 3: Bargaining. In this stage the patient wants more time and asks for favors to postpone death. The bargaining may be carried out with the physician or, more frequently, with God.

Stage 4: Depression. Depression is a signal that the acceptance process has really begun. Kübler-Ross has referred to this stage as "preparatory grief"—the sadness of anticipating an impending loss.

Stage 5: Acceptance. The person who achieves acceptance has taken care of unfinished business. The patient has relinquished the unattainable and is now ready to die. He or she will want to be with close family members, usually a wife or husband and children; dying children want to be with their parents. Although patients desire the presence of someone warm, caring, and accepting at this time, verbal communication may be totally unnecessary.

Although Kübler-Ross asserted that people do not necessarily progress through these five stages in lockstep sequence, her use of the term "stages" implies otherwise. Thus, it is not surprising that her theory has been criticized on this confusing point (Kastenbaum, 1999). Systematic studies of dying patients have not always observed the same five emotions or the same progression of emotions she described (Corr, 1993). Instead of progressing though a common, five-stage process, dying people seem to show "a jumble of conflicting or alternating reactions running the gamut from denial to acceptance, with tremendous variation affected by age, sex, race, ethnic group, social setting, and personality" (Butler & Lewis, 1982, p. 370). Nonetheless, Kübler-Ross greatly improved our understanding of the process of dying and stimulated research that continues to add to our knowledge.

Bereavement and Grieving

When a friend, spouse, or relative dies, individuals must cope with *bereavement,* **or the painful loss of a loved one through death.** The death of someone close typically brings forth the painful and complex emotions of grief. *Mourning* **refers to the formal practices of an individual and a community in response to a death.** Many cultural and religious rituals help survivors adjust to and cope with their loss.

Cultural Variations

Considerable variation exists among and within cultures as to how this major life event is acknowledged. In America and Western European countries, the bereaved are typically encouraged to break their emotional ties with the deceased relatively quickly and to return to their regular routines. Nonetheless, research has found support for "continued bonds" with the deceased among American widows and widowers (Bonanno & Kaltman, 1999). Based on interviews of men and women during the first two months of bereavement, one study reported that 71 percent felt that their deceased spouses were still with them at times and that 61 percent felt that their deceased spouses were watching out for them (Shuchter & Zisook, 1993). Moreover, 39 percent reported that they talked regularly with their deceased spouses. In Asian, African, and Hispanic cultures, the bereaved are encouraged to maintain emotional ties to their dead loved ones (Bonanno, 1998). Almost all Japanese homes have altars dedicated to family ancestors, and family members routinely talk to the deceased and offer them food. Regardless of the particular form that mourning takes, all such rituals are designed to make death meaningful and to help the bereaved cope with the pain and disruption of death.

The Grieving Process

The common view of bereavement asserts that distress is an inevitable response to loss and that failure to experience distress is a sign that the individual has not grieved "properly" (Bonanno & Kaltman, 1999). As a result, the person is expected to suffer negative consequences later. In keeping with this view, John Bowlby (1980) characterizes grieving as a four-stage process:

Stage 1: Numbness. In this initial phase, survivors are typically dazed and confused. They may experience physical reactions such as nausea or tightness in the chest or throat. This phase may last several days or, in cases when death has been unexpected, several weeks.

Stage 2: Yearning. Here, survivors try to recover the lost person. Individuals may report that they see the deceased and may wander as if they are searching for the loved one. They often feel frustration, anger, and guilt. In addition, they may experience intense feelings of sadness and may cry and sob uncontrollably. They may also suffer loss of appetite and insomnia.

Stage 3: Disorganization and despair. Searching for the loved one ceases as the loss is accepted as real. However, accepting the loss brings feelings of helplessness, despair, and depression. Survivors often experience extreme fatigue and a need to sleep much more than usual.

Stage 4: Reorganization. Individuals are able to resume their normal routines at home and at work. Depression lifts, regular sleeping habits return, and energy increases. Thoughts of the loved one may bring sadness, but these feelings are no longer overwhelming.

Although Bowlby's model is certainly plausible, research suggests that most grief reactions do not follow this straightforward path (Wortman, Wolff, & Bonanno, 2004). Just as people react differently to the experience of dying, they also show variable responses to bereavement. For instance, one study examined the patterns of change in depression in a sample of older adults prior to a spouse's death and at 6 and 18 months

The grieving process is more variable among people than widely appreciated.

after spousal loss (Bonanno et al., 2002). By measuring depression both before and after a spouse's death, researchers could separate preloss depression from loss-induced depression. Participants' grief reactions fell into five patterns. *Absent grief* or the *resilient pattern* is characterized by low levels of depression before and after the spouse's death. In *chronic grief*, depression exists before and after the spouse's death. *Common grief* is characterized by an increase in depression shortly after the spouse's death and a decrease in depression over time. The *depressed-improved* pattern reflects a decrease in depression after the spouse's death. *Chronic depression* describes those who are depressed both before and after spousal loss.

When you examine Figure 11.11, you may be surprised to find that common grief is *not* the most frequent pattern. In fact, absent grief occurs much more frequently—almost half of the participants follow this pattern. As we noted earlier, many (including some mental health professionals) believe that individuals who fail to engage in "grief work" will suffer long-term adjustment problems. However, this view is contradicted by many studies (Bonanno et al., 2002; Wortman et al., 2004). In the current study, resilience was found to be associated with preloss acceptance of death, whereas

chronic grief was associated with preloss dependency on the spouse. To counter the traditional "negative" view of bereavement, some researchers are investigating how positive emotions and laughter can ameliorate the stress of grieving (Bonanno & Keltner, 1997).

Coping with Different Types of Loss

The research we have been discussing looked only at the experiences of widows and widowers. The researchers would probably have obtained quite different findings if the subjects had been parents who had lost a child, the most difficult type of death adults must cope with (Stillion, 1995). Coping with miscarriage and stillbirth can also be painful (Klass, 1996). One study compared the grief reactions of 255 middle-aged women who had experienced the death of a spouse, a parent, or a child in the two years preceding the study (Leahy, 1993). As you might expect, mothers who had lost children had the highest levels of depression. And women whose husbands had died were significantly more depressed than women who had lost a parent. Other studies of bereaved persons (including men) have also found that they score higher on depression than the nonbereaved (Wortmann & Silver, 1990). They also score lower on life satisfaction and are at greater risk for illness. Thus, the death of an intimate is an adjustment challenge for most people, even though individuals' reactions to the experience may vary.

A particularly difficult bereavement situation occurs when a child or an adolescent loses a parent to death. In these cases, grieving typically involves frequent crying, angry outbursts, trouble concentrating at school, and sleep problems. These symptoms may last from several months to a year (Silverman & Worden, 1992). It is important for adults to take the time to talk with grieving children. In particular, children need to be assured that the parent did not leave out of anger and that the remaining parent will not disappear (Furman, 1984).

Although the numbers are small, some children and adolescents have lost schoolmates and teachers in schoolyard killings and may also have witnessed such traumatic acts of violence. These individuals are likely to suffer from posttraumatic stress disorder (see Chapter 3). Typical reactions to these disturbing and tragic events include shock, prolonged grief, flashbacks, and fear of returning to school (Nader, 1997).

Bereavement overload occurs when individuals experience several deaths at the same time or in close succession. As an example, the tens of thousands of individuals who lost all or most of their families and friends during the December 26, 2004 earthquake and tsunami disaster in Southeast Asia come quickly to mind. On a less dramatic scale, other groups who are likely to suffer bereavement overload include members of the gay community, who have lost lovers and friends to AIDS,

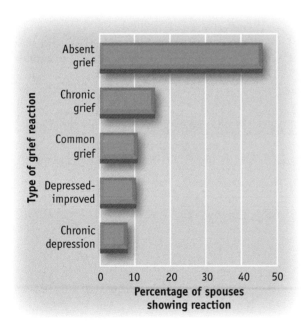

● **FIGURE 11.11**

Five reactions to spousal loss. Researchers gathered data on 205 older individuals prior to spousal loss and 6 months and 18 months following spousal loss. Ninety percent of the subjects exhibited one of the five bereavement patterns shown in the figure. Contrary to popular belief, "absent grief" or the "resilient pattern" was the most frequently experienced reaction, while "common grief" occurred relatively infrequently. Traditional views of grief hold that the "common grief" reaction is the only healthy response to loss, but numerous studies contradict that view. (Adapted from Bonanno et al., 2002)

The Southeast Asian tsunami disaster was a rare and dramatic example of bereavement overload, the devastating experience of having to cope with several or more deaths at the same time.

© Arko Datta/Reuters/Corbis

and the elderly, who must deal with the loss of spouses, friends, and siblings because of advancing years.

To cope with loss, people need the sympathy and support of family and friends as well as the passage of time. Still, the presence of friends and family can't substitute for a loved one who has died (Stroebe et al., 1996). Parents who have lost a child may find it helpful to talk with others who have been through this experi-ence (Lieberman, 1993). Groups for bereaved children and adolescents can be particularly helpful (Bacon, 1996). Tragically, because of the immensity of the losses in the Southeast Asian tsunami disaster, survivors will take years to recover, and some may never do so.

In the Application, we look at some ways parents can facilitate their children's development by provid-ing optimal combinations of affection and discipline.

APPLICATION

Becoming an Effective Parent

LEARNING OBJECTIVES

- *Describe Ainsworth's three attachment styles and how caregivers can promote secure attachment in their infants.*
- *Summarize the research on the effects of day care on infants and children.*
- *Discuss Baumrind's parenting styles and their effects on children's development.*
- *Discuss issues related to the effective parenting of adolescents.*
- *List five suggestions for more effective parenting.*
- *List five suggestions for the effective use of punishment.*

Are the following statements "true" or "false?"

___ **1.** Infant-mother emotional attachments are formed automatically.

___ **2.** Placing infants and children in day care nega-tively affects their development.

___ **3.** Extensive use of punishment is the key to effec-tive discipline.

___ **4.** Parents shouldn't have to explain their reasons for punishing their children.

All these statements are false. All represent popular myths about childrearing that we address in this Ap-plication. Many parents are eager to learn all they can about children's development. They search to find new and better ways to ensure optimal social, emotional, and cognitive development in their children. What kinds of answers can psychology provide?

Maternal Behavior and Infant-Mother Attachment

During the first few months of life, infants rely on built-in behaviors such as crying, cooing, and smiling to initiate and maintain contact with adult caregivers. Before long, infants start to recognize their most frequent caregiver (typically, the mother) and are more easily soothed by that person. By the age of 8 months, most babies develop a strong emotional connection to a single familiar caregiver (hereafter assumed to be the mother, to simplify our discussion). **This emotional bond between infant and mother is termed** *infant attachment.*

Contrary to popular belief, infants' attachment to their mothers is not automatic. Indeed, as we noted in Chapter 8, not all infants develop a secure attachment to their mothers. Sometimes, mothers are insensitive or inconsistent in responding to their infants' needs (Pederson & Moran, 1996). "Difficult" infants whose mothers are unable to respond sensitively to them are at risk for developing an insecure attachment style (Vaughn & Bost, 1999). For instance, some babies are prone to distress, spit up most of their food, make bathing a major battle, refuse to go to sleep, and rarely smile. It is easy to see that such behavior could undermine a mother's responsiveness to an infant.

After extensive study, Mary Ainsworth and her colleagues (1978) concluded that infants could be classified into one of three attachment styles by about 8 months of age. These different styles develop out of parent-infant interactions during the early months of life. Babies with an *avoidant* attachment style tend to ignore their mothers. Those with an *anxious-ambivalent* style seem to desire contact with the mother, yet they actively resist her when she comes near.

Fortunately, the majority of infants are *securely attached* and welcome contact with their mothers. A secure attachment to a caregiver during infancy is important because it provides a basis for successful social relationships later in life. A meta-analysis of 63 studies reported that those who were securely attached had more positive peer relationships than those who were insecurely attached (Schneider, Atkinson, & Tardif, 2001). In Erik Erikson's terms, the securely attached baby has developed a sense of basic trust in the mother and toward the world at large.

Researchers are also studying a fourth—*disorganized/disoriented*—attachment style, in which infants are both drawn to their caregivers and fear them because of past negative interactions (Main & Solomon, 1990). This style appears to be common among neglected and abused children (Barnett, Ganiban, & Cic-

chetti, 1999). A longitudinal study reported that this attachment style is associated with dissociative disorders (see Chapter 15) in childhood and adolescence (Carlson, 1998).

How can caregivers promote a secure attachment in infants? Ainsworth and her associates reported that the mothers of securely attached infants were perceptive about the baby's needs, responded to those needs relatively quickly and consistently, and enjoyed physical contact with the baby. Other research has confirmed that these are among the key attributes of effective parenting of infants (DeWolff & van Ijzendoorn, 1997).

Day Care and Attachment

The impact of day care on attachment is a hotly debated topic these days. The crucial question is whether daily infant-mother separations might disrupt the attachment process. The issue is an important one, given that 55 percent of mothers with an infant under the age of 1 and 67 percent of mothers with a child under the age of 5 work outside the home (U.S. Bureau of the Census, 2004a). Research by Jay Belsky (1992) suggests that babies under a year who receive nonmaternal care for more than 20 hours per week have an increased risk of developing insecure attachments to their mothers. Belsky's findings have raised many eyebrows, but they need to be put in perspective. First, the data reveal that the proportion of day-care infants who exhibit insecure attachment is only slightly higher than the norm in American society and even lower than the norm in some other societies (Lamb, Sternberg, & Prodromidis, 1992). Second, many studies have found no differences in attachment between children reared in day care or at home (Roggman et al., 1994), and some studies have even found that day care can have beneficial effects on youngsters' intellectual and social development (Caldwell, 1993; Egeland & Hiester, 1995). Third, the effects of day care depend on the quality of the care provided. Negative effects are minimal and may even be outweighed by positive effects in safe, clean, spacious, well-equipped, adequately staffed facilities that provide lots of individual attention and carefully planned activities (Fitzgerald et al., 2003). Nonetheless, infants and young children who spend many hours in day care with poorly trained child-care workers and large child-caregiver ratios are at risk for developing insecure attachment, especially if their mothers are insensitive caregivers.

Dimensions of Childrearing

As children grow from infancy into toddlerhood, the role of parenting broadens. How parents react to a child's actions communicates their standards of appropriate and inappropriate behavior. Parents fulfill this role with varying degrees of conscious awareness.

As we mentioned in Chapter 5, two major dimensions underlie parenting behavior (Maccoby & Martin, 1983). The first, and most important, is *parental acceptance.* Although most parents are at least moderately accepting of their children, some are indifferent or even hostile and rejecting. Parental acceptance and warmth appear to influence the degree to which children internalize the standards and expectations of their parents (Eccles et al, 1997). Children whose parents hold them in high regard develop high self-esteem and self-control (behave appropriately even if the parents are not present). In contrast, children whose parents are less accepting may develop lower self-esteem and less self-control. Thus, they may behave when the parents are around (out of fear of punishment) but misbehave when on their own.

The second dimension of parenting behavior is *parental control,* or strictness of parental standards. For example, a parent who is moderately controlling sets high performance standards and expects increasingly mature behavior. A parent who is uncontrolling expects little of the child. The absence of control is associated with maladjustment and high levels of aggression.

Courtesy, Diana Baumrind

Diana Baumrind

Diana Baumrind (1967, 1971, 1978) looked at specific parenting styles as interactions between the two dimensions of acceptance and control. In addition, she wanted to know the effects of these parenting styles on children's social and intellectual competence. In her initial study, Baumrind observed a sample of preschool children and their parents and rated both groups on a number of dimensions. Additional data were obtained through interviews with the parents. Baumrind was able to identify four distinct parenting styles: authoritarian, permissive, authoritative, and neglectful.

Authoritative parents (high acceptance, high control) set high goals for their children but are also accepting of their children and responsive to their needs. They also provide age-appropriate explanations that emphasize the consequences of "good" and "bad" behavior. They encourage verbal give-and-take and allow their children to question parental requests. Authoritative parents maintain firm control but take into account each child's unique and changing needs. They are willing to negotiate with their children, setting new and less restrictive limits when appropriate, particularly as children mature.

Authoritarian parents (low acceptance, high control) are highly demanding and controlling and use physical punishment or the threat of it with their children. By virtue of their higher status, they issue com-

WEB LINK 11.8

The ChildTrauma Academy
Founded by Bruce Perry, a psychiatrist, The ChildTrauma Academy develops programs that seek to nurture, protect, and enrich children. Its website is rich with information on basic child development topics, such as attachment, curiosity, and language development. However, its foremost strength is its collection of materials on how to help children victimized by physical, psychological, or sexual abuse or other types of severe trauma.

mands that are to be obeyed without question ("Do it because I said so"). These parents rigidly maintain tight control even as their children mature. They also tend to be somewhat emotionally distant and may be rejecting.

Permissive parents (high acceptance, low control) make few or no demands of their children. They allow children free expression of impulses and set few limits on appropriate behavior. Permissive parents are responsive and warmly accepting and indulge their children's desires.

Neglectful parents (low acceptance, low control) provide for the basic physical and emotional needs of their children, but not much else. They convey the impression that they don't really care for their children: They are not particularly involved with or supportive of their children (no help with homework, minimal supervision, little time spent together).

Correlates of Parenting Styles

Baumrind and others have found that parenting styles are associated with different traits in children, as summarized in Figure 11.12. As you might expect, *authoritative* parenting is associated with the most positive outcomes. Children whose parents use this style do the best in school and tend to be self-reliant, friendly, and cooperative. In contrast, the children of *authoritarian* parents tend to do less well in school and to have lower self-esteem and poorer social skills. *Permissive* parents often have children whose grades are lower and who are undisciplined, impulsive, and easily frustrated. Although Baumrind didn't report on children of *neglectful* parents, other researchers have found them to have low self-esteem and to be moody, impulsive, and aggressive (Maccoby & Martin, 1983). This style also predicts the most maladaptive outcomes of the four parenting styles (Baumrind, 1991; Patterson, DeBaryshe, & Ramsey, 1989). Problems include low academic and social competence, delinquency, and alcohol and substance abuse.

Of course, these data are correlational and do not establish that the parenting style is the *cause* of the chil-

Parenting Styles and Children's Traits

Parenting style	Authoritative	Authoritarian	Permissive
Children's behavioral profile	**Energetic-friendly**	**Conflicted-irritable**	**Impulsive-aggressive**
	Self-reliant	Fearful, apprehensive	Rebellious
	Self-controlled	Moody, unhappy	Low in self-reliance and self-control
	Cheerful and friendly	Easily annoyed	Impulsive
	Copes well with stress	Passively hostile	Aggressive
	Cooperative with adults	Vulnerable to stress	Domineering
	Curious	Aimless	Aimless
	Purposive	Sulky, unfriendly	Low in achievement
	Achievement-oriented		

● FIGURE 11.12

Baumrind's findings on parenting styles and children's traits. Diana Baumrind (1977) has studied three styles of parenting and their relations to children's social and intellectual competence. As you can see, authoritative parenting is associated with the most desirable outcomes. (Summary adapted from Schaffer, 1989)

Based on Baumrind, D. (1977). *Socialization determinants of personal agency.* Paper presented at the meeting of the Society for Research in Child Development, New Orleans, LA.

dren's traits. The direction of influence goes both ways (Cummings, Braungart-Rieker, & DuRocher-Schudlich, 2003). For instance, parents may become increasingly authoritarian *in response to* their child's increasing resentment and irritability. Even so, Baumrind's results imply that authoritative parenting is most likely to foster social and cognitive competence in children.

Rearing Adolescents

Adolescents' emerging cognitive abilities enable them to question parental values and to formulate a personal philosophy to guide their own behavior. Although this process is necessary, it often drives intergenerational conflicts. Parents seem to have a harder time dealing with these conflicts than adolescents do (Steinberg, 2001).

One of the undercurrents in parent-adolescent relationships is that the balance of power between parent and child is shifting. Younger children accept their parents' power as a legitimate source of authority, especially if they have a warm relationship. The increasing autonomy of adolescents, however, requires a more equal parent-child relationship. While this is a necessary step on the road to autonomous adulthood, negotiating such shifts in power can be difficult. Authoritative parents who are willing to respond to their teenagers' input are most likely to avoid such turmoil (Steinberg, 2001). Authoritarian parents who are unwilling to relinquish their control promote hostility and rebellion in adolescents. Permissive and neglectful parents, who never exercised much control over their children, may find themselves faced with adolescents

Research has uncovered some interesting correlations between parents' disciplinary style and their children's personality traits. An authoritative parenting style seems to be associated with the most desirable traits.

Promoting Resilience in Children

Peoples' coping abilities are overwhelmed when they are exposed to traumatic events such as the Oklahoma City bombing, a space shuttle explosion, the 9/11 terrorist attacks, a violent homicide or suicide, rape, or a natural disaster. Other events that traumatize individuals include exposure to acts of war, domestic or community violence, and child abuse or neglect.

Psychologists are particularly interested in how children react to traumatic events to understand how to protect them from long-term damage. Children's reactions to traumatic events are likely to vary depending on their age (National Institute of Mental Health, 2001; Gallagher & Chase, 2002). The responses of children under the age of 6 tend to be muted unless their parents exhibit strong distress that disturbs the children. If children between the ages of 6 and 11 are troubled, parents may observe regressive or disruptive behaviors, nightmares, irrational fears, reluctance to go to school, and vague bodily complaints (stomachaches, headaches, and so forth). The responses of youngsters in the 12–17 age bracket tend to resemble the responses seen in adults, such as flashbacks, emotional numbing, and avoidance of any reminders of the traumatic event. Sleep disturbances and difficulties at school are also common. Adolescents may increase their use of alcohol or cigarettes.

Following a traumatic experience, most children return to their normal level of functioning after the acute phase of distress passes (Cloitre, Morin, & Lanares, 2004). Unfortunately, a few have difficulties getting back on track. Children and adolescents who have experienced at least one of the following risk factors are more likely to have long-term difficulties coping with a traumatic event (Cloitre, et al., 2004):

- Directly witnessed an event or have a family member who observed an event
- Survived the death of a parent or another important person
- Had mental health problems before the event
- Experienced an earlier traumatic event
- Lacked a strong support network
- Had a parent whose levels of stress and fear are on the increase

Although exposure to a traumatic event heightens the risk for psychological problems, many children have an amazing ability to overcome adversity. This ability to bounce back from traumatic experiences is termed *resilience*. Researchers have tracked the adjustment of children who have (1) been exposed to war, (2) lived in areas of high terrorist activity, (3) experienced traumatic events such as the 9/11 attacks, (4) lived in American slums, (5) lost loved ones through death, (6) witnessed life-threatening natural disasters, and (7) lived with a parent with a serious psychological disorder such as schizophrenia (Gallagher & Chase, 2002; Cloitre, et al., 2004).

According to Richard Gallagher and Ayana Chase (2002), "Many children who have experienced tragedy or witnessed life-threatening events emerge with a positive outlook on life, have a good capacity to form positive, fulfilling relationships, achieve a high level of personal success, and develop effective resources for dealing with future negative events" (p. 2). Parents, teachers, and others who work with children and adolescents can do a lot to foster such positive outcomes in the face of traumatic events. The following advice, adapted from Gallagher & Chase (2002), may be helpful:

- *Take steps to ensure children's safety.* Make sure that settings where children gather are safe and secure. Secure environments enable children to spend their time on playing and learning.
- *Help children establish and maintain a close relationship with an adult.* Children who experience the harshest circumstances can do well if they have a relationship with at least one very supportive adult. Nonparental figures can fill this role if parents cannot.
- *Be sure that children and teens know ways to calm themselves.* Help children relax through play, talk, art activities, music, or physical comforting. Teens should be encouraged to engage in exercise, muscle relaxation, or deep breathing to reduce stress, as opposed to unhealthy stress-reduction methods such as smoking, drinking, and drugs.
- *Help children understand the real statistical probability of tragedy and disaster.* Children need to understand that traumatic events are very unlikely to happen to them or to their family members. A realistic outlook will help children remain alert to dangers, but free from constant worries that they are in danger.
- *Watch for negative reactions and provide early assistance, or treatment, when necessary.* Reactions to traumatic events may appear months after rather than immediately following the event. Chronic irritability, avoiding

anxiety-inducing situations, fatigue, and inability to concentrate may signal problems, especially if these symptoms interfere with daily functioning and last for more than a week.

• *Keep children informed about related events.* Children may overhear information about a traumatic event and misinterpret it. Adults should provide age-appropriate facts about frightening situations. Repeated exposure to violent images and those related to destruction and death is especially harmful to children.

• *Help children establish a set of values to guide their actions.* Children who have values for relating to the world show less depression and anxiety than others.

Prosocial values help them feel connected to a larger social group and engage in positive behavior.

• *Help children develop a positive outlook for the future.* Traumatic events can shake children's natural optimism about the future. Parents can help children recover their optimism by reminding them that negative events are temporary. They can also help their kids develop self-efficacy (see Chapter 5) so that the children believe they are able to cope with stressful situations and can make contributions to better the world.

• *Take care of your own physical and mental health.* Adults need to get rest and support so they can be a calming influence on their children and be emotionally available and supportive to them.

---

whose behavior is completely out of hand. Compared to the other parenting styles, authoritative parenting is also associated with greater resistance to unfavorable peer pressure (Masten, 2001).

Researchers who have studied parenting styles in adolescence have found essentially the same pattern of outcomes we noted earlier, although the differences among the four groups are not always dramatic (Baumrind, 1989; Steinberg, 2001). Authoritatively reared

adolescents show the highest competence and adjustment, while neglectfully reared adolescents generally show the lowest. Adolescents reared with authoritarian or permissive styles generally fall between the other two groups. Figure 11.13 depicts the high school grades and school misconduct of adolescents in these four groups. These findings are consistent across a number of ethnic groups, including African American, Hispanic, and Asian American (Steinberg, 2001).

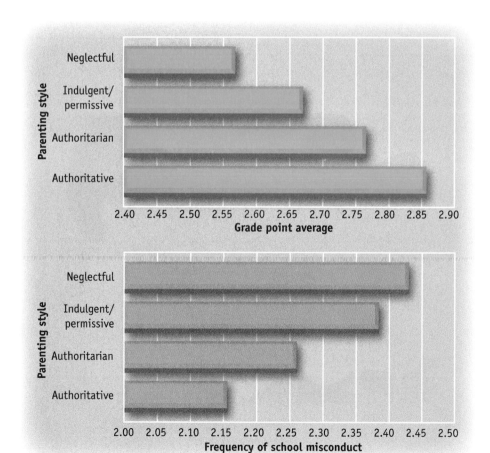

● **FIGURE 11.13**

Parenting styles, school performance, and school misconduct. Lamborn and colleagues (1991) classified the families of over 4,000 14- to 18-year-olds into four parenting styles, based on adolescents' ratings of their parents. They then compared the youths on a number of outcomes, including high school grade point average and frequency of school misconduct. Adolescents from authoritative families showed the highest competence and adjustment (higher grades, less misconduct), while those from neglectful families showed the lowest.

Data from Lamborn, S. D., Mounts, N. S., Steinberg, L., & Dornbusch, S. M. (1991). Patterns of competence and adjustment among adolescents from authoritative, authoritarian, indulgent, and neglectful families. *Child Development, 62,* 1049-1065. Copyright © 1991 by the Society for Research in Child Development. Used with permission of SRCD.

Toward Effective Parenting

Are there some "basic rules" for effective parenting? We offer five key principles here. Of course, it's essential to tailor these suggestions to the age and developmental level of a specific child. For an additional perspective, see the Recommended Reading box on Laurence Steinberg's (2004) book on effective parenting.

Laurence Steinberg

1. *Set high, but reasonable standards.* Children should be expected to behave in a socially appropriate manner for their age and to do as well as they can in school and in other activities. Parents who don't expect much from their children are teaching them not to expect much from themselves.

2. *Stay alert for "good" behavior and reward it.* Most parents pay attention to children when they are misbehaving and ignore them when they're being good. This approach is backward! Develop the habit of praising good behavior so a child knows what you want.

3. *Explain your reasons when you ask a child to do something.* Don't assume that a child can read your mind. Explaining the purpose of a request can transform what might appear to be an arbitrary request into a reasonable one. It also encourages self-control in a child.

4. *Encourage children to take the perspective of others.* Talk to children about the effects of their behavior on others ("How would you feel if Keisha did that to

you?"). This role-playing approach fosters moral development and empathy in children.

5. *Enforce rules consistently.* Children need to have a clear idea about what is expected of them and to know that there will be consequences when they fail to meet your standards. This practice also fosters self-control in children.

Parents often wonder how punishment can be used more effectively in disciplinary efforts.

Using Punishment Effectively

To use punishment effectively, parents should use it less often. That's because punishment often has unintended, negative side effects. A recent meta-analysis of 88 studies on corporal punishment reported that it *is* associated with stopping the punished behavior (Gershoff, 2002). Still, the bad news is that punishment is also associated with host of problematic outcomes: reduced quality of parent-child relationships, poorer mental health in childhood and adulthood, increased delinquency and aggression in childhood, and increased aggression and criminal behavior in adulthood.

Many professionals decry the use of punishment for these reasons. Others assert that occasional, mild spankings should not be conflated with harsher punishment (which was the case in Gershoff's meta-analysis). Advocates of this position argue that infrequent, mild spankings can reduce disobedience and fighting and are not associated with negative outcomes (Baumrind, Larzelere, & Cowan, 2002; Larzelere, 2000). As an al-

Although physical punishment is frequently administered to suppress aggressive behavior, in the long run it actually is associated with an increase in aggressive behavior.

ternative to punishment, most psychologists favor a combination of negative reinforcement ("time out" or the loss of privileges) of unwanted behavior and positive reinforcement (praise) of alternative, positive behavior (Kazdin & Benjet, 2003). The following guidelines summarize research evidence on how to make punishment effective while minimizing its side effects (Berkowitz, 1993):

1. *Punishment should not damage the child's self-esteem.* To be effective, punishment should get across the message that it is the behavior that is undesirable, not the child. Unduly harsh physical punishment, derogatory accusations, and other hurtful words erode the child's self-esteem.

2. *Punishment should be swift.* A delay in delivering punishment undermines its impact. A parent who says, "Wait until your father (or mother) gets home . . ." is making a fundamental mistake. (He or she is also unfairly setting up the other parent as the "heavy.") Quick punishment highlights the connection between the prohibited behavior and its negative outcome.

3. *Punishment should be consistent.* If you want to eliminate an undesirable behavior, you should punish it every time it occurs. When parents are inconsistent about punishing a particular behavior, they only create confusion in the child.

4. *Punishment should be explained.* When children are punished, the reason for their punishment should be explained as fully as possible, given the constraints of their age. The more children that understand the reason they are punished, the more effective the punishment tends to be. These explanations, characteristic of the authoritative style, also foster the development of self-control.

5. *Point out alternative, positive ways for your child to behave and reinforce these actions.* One shortcoming of punishment is that it only tells a child what not to do. A better strategy is to punish an undesirable response and reward a positive alternative behavior. Children usually engage in undesirable behavior for a reason. Suggest another response that serves the same purpose and reward a child for doing it. For example, many troublesome behaviors exhibited by children are primarily attention-seeking devices. Punishment of these responses will be more effective if you can provide a child with more acceptable ways to gain attention.

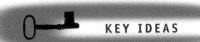

KEY IDEAS

The Transition of Adolescence

■ During pubescence, the adolescent growth spurt takes place and secondary sex characteristics develop. During puberty, which begins a few years later, the primary sex characteristics mature. The onset of puberty marks the beginning of adolescence. Girls typically mature two years earlier than boys. Boys who mature late and girls who mature early may find puberty particularly stressful.

■ During adolescence, cognitive changes also occur, including development of the ability to apply logic to hypothetical situations, increases in knowledge, and greater skills in deductive reasoning. Despite greater cognitive sophistication, older adolescents are more likely to engage in physically harmful risky behavior, suggesting that this behavior is governed by noncognitive factors.

■ In the realm of personality, adolescents must develop a clear sense of identity. Some theorists assert that adolescence is a period of turmoil, and there is research support for a modified storm-and-stress view that recognizes cultural and individual differences. Attention should be paid to youths who display symptoms of serious problems such as depression, suicidal behavior, drug and alcohol abuse, and chronic delinquency. Suicide among adolescents has greatly increased since 1960, but very few young people actually take their lives.

The Expanse of Adulthood

■ During early adulthood, individuals make more major role changes than in any other developmental stage. In Erikson's theory, the key psychosocial crisis for young adults is intimacy versus isolation. Specific developmental tasks of young adulthood include leaving one's family, entering the workplace and developing a career, finding a mate, having and rearing children, and adjusting to family life.

■ In middle adulthood, the major psychosocial crisis is generativity versus stagnation, according to Erikson. Additional tasks for this group include confronting the aging process and dealing with transitions in the parental role as children mature and leave home. Midlife adults also experience changes in their work roles. Typically, they follow either the stable career pattern or the changing careers pattern. Few individuals seem to experience a midlife crisis.

■ The key psychosocial crisis for older adults, according to Erikson, is integrity versus despair. Older adults must adjust to retirement, adapt to changes in their social networks, cope with health problems, and confront their own death.

Aging: a Gradual Process

■ Physical development during adulthood leads to many obvious changes in physical appearance and sensory acuity. After age 30 there is a steady loss of active brain cells; however, this loss does not appear to underlie reductions in cognitive functioning. Similarly, hormonal changes appear to be only modestly related to midlife distress or declining sexual activity. Unfortunately, health does tend to decline with increasing age for a variety of reasons. Engaging in regular exercise and eating a nutritious diet can help maintain health.

■ Intelligence seems to remain fairly stable during most of adulthood. Attentional capacity, speed of learning, and success in problem solving all tend to decline slightly during old age. Memory processes also deteriorate but can be exacerbated by self-fulfilling prophecies. However, most people remain capable

of sound intellectual functioning in their later years. The adult personality seems to be characterized by both stability and change.

Death and Dying

■ Attitudes about death vary from one culture to another. Attitudes in this culture are characterized by negativism, avoidance, and fear. Kübler-Ross's research on the process of dying indicated that individuals progress through a sequence of five stages. Later research has called into question the idea that people's reactions to dying follow such a straightforward path.

■ A wide variation exists between and within cultures regarding how death is acknowledged. Research has revealed a variety of patterns of grieving, calling into question traditional views of the process of mourning. The loss of a child is the most difficult type of death adults must cope with. In coping with bereavement, people need the support of family and friends. Support groups can also be helpful.

Application: Becoming an Effective Parent

■ Attachment between infants and their primary caregivers develops early in life. According to Mary Ainsworth, infants develop one of three attachment styles with their caregivers: secure, anxious-ambivalent, and avoidant. Of Diana Baumrind's four parenting styles, authoritative parenting is associated with the most positive outcomes in children.

■ Intergenerational conflicts typically increase during adolescence, and parents seem to find these conflicts more difficult to deal with than adolescents do.

■ Effective parenting involves following five key principles, as well as knowing how to use punishment effectively.

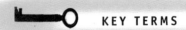

KEY TERMS

Bereavement   p. 360
Death anxiety   p. 359
Death system   pp. 358–359
Dementia   p. 353
Identity   p. 342
Infant attachment   p. 363
Menarche   p. 339
Menopause   p. 354
Midlife crisis   p. 349
Mourning   p. 360

Neurons   p. 353
Primary sex characteristics p. 338
Puberty   p. 338
Pubescence   p. 338
Secondary sex characteristics p. 338
Social clock   p. 345
Spermarche   p. 339

KEY PEOPLE

Mary Ainsworth   p. 363
Diana Baumrind pp. 364–365
Erik Erikson   p. 342
Elisabeth Kübler-Ross pp. 359–360

Laurence Steinberg pp. 368–369
Susan Krauss Whitbourne pp. 352–365

1. Primary sex characteristics develop during _____; secondary sex characteristics develop during _____.
   a. menarche, menopause
   b. puberty, pubescence
   c. the sexual stage; the physical stage
   d. adulthood; adolescence

2. Optimal adjustment is associated with puberty arriving _____ for girls and _____ for boys.
   a. late; on time
   b. early; on time
   c. on time; early
   d. late; early

3. Compared to those who are younger, adolescents:
   a. can think abstractly.
   b. have greater knowledge.
   c. show greater self-awareness.
   d. all of the above.

4. Which of the following statements about storm and stress in adolescence is false?
   a. Conflicts with parents increase during adolescence.
   b. Adolescents experience more volatile emotions than younger or older individuals do.
   c. Adolescents engage in more risk behaviors than children do.
   d. Heightened emotional turmoil in adolescence is found in all cultures.

5. The life stage that involves more role changes than any other is:
   a. adolescence.
   b. early adulthood.
   c. middle adulthood.
   d. later adulthood.

6. According to Erikson, the psychosocial conflict of middle adulthood is:
   a. identity versus identity diffusion.
   b. intimacy versus isolation.
   c. generativity versus stagnation.
   d. integrity versus despair.

7. Which of the following is a false statement about retirement?
   a. Retirement typically has a negative impact on overall health and life satisfaction.
   b. The best-adjusted retirees have an adequate income, good health, and a social network.
   c. Most older adults maintain their ties to their children.
   d. Retirement is typically a gradual process of cutting back on work hours over a period of years.

8. With regard to whether personality changes with age, it can be concluded that:
   a. a pattern of change is most typical.
   b. a pattern of stability is most typical.
   c. some traits change over time and some traits remain stable.
   d. no pattern can be discerned.

9. Less anxiety about death is found among those who:
   a. feel they haven't accomplished all that they had hoped.
   b. have a particular religious affiliation.
   c. have ambivalent religious views.
   d. have a well-formulated philosophy of death.

10. Baumrind's authoritative parenting style is characterized by:
    a. high acceptance and high control.
    b. low acceptance and high control.
    c. high acceptance and low control.
    d. low acceptance and low control.

Book Companion Website

Visit the Book Companion Website at **http://psychology.wadsworth.com/weiten_lloyd8e,** where you will find tutorial quizzes, flashcards, and weblinks for every chapter, a final exam, and more! You can also link to the Thomson Wadsworth Psychology Resource Center (accessible directly at **http://psychology.wadsworth.com**) for a range of psychology-related resources.

Personal Explorations Workbook

The following exercises in your *Personal Explorations Workbook* may enhance your self-understanding in relation to issues raised in this chapter. **Questionnaire 11.1:** Death Anxiety Scale. **Personal Probe 11.1:** How Do You Feel about Age Roles? **Personal Probe 11.2:** How Flexible Is Development?

ANSWERS

1. b Page 338
2. c Page 340
3. d Pages 340–341
4. d Page 343
5. b Page 346
6. c Page 348
7. a Pages 350–351
8. c Page 358
9. d Page 359
10. a Page 364

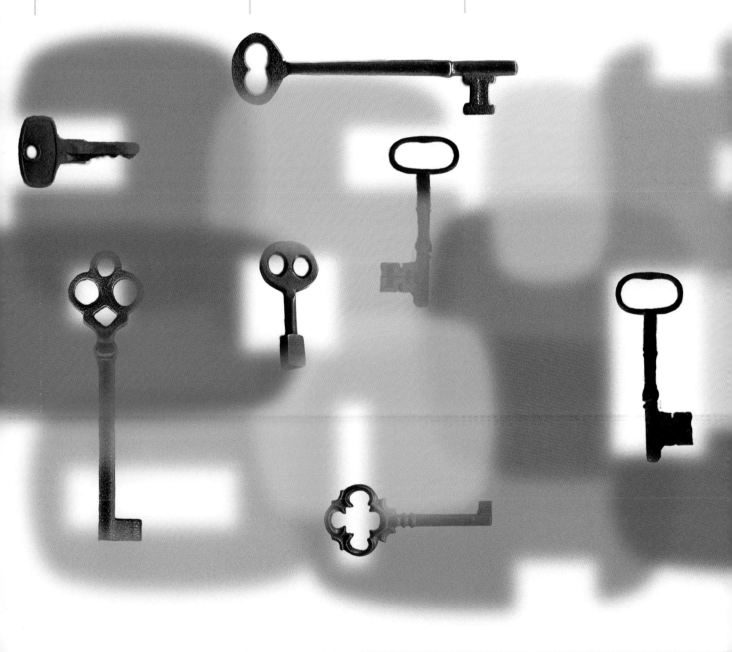

Careers and Work

When adults meet for the first time, their initial "How do you do?" is usually followed by the more crucial question, "What do you do for a living?" The answer may convey information not only about one's occupation but also about one's social status, lifestyle, personality, interests, and aptitudes. In other words, work plays a pivotal role in adult life. According to a recent Gallup poll, 73 percent of Americans rated work as either "extremely" or "very important" in their life (Moore, 2003). In Figure 12.1 on the next page, you can see that how people view their jobs is strongly correlated with their income.

Because work is such a significant aspect of life, psychologists take a great interest in it. *Industrial/organizational (I/O) psychology* **is the study of human behavior in the workplace.** Among other issues, I/O psychologists study worker motivation and satisfaction, job performance, leadership, personnel selection, and diversity in organizations. A recent concern is how individuals balance work and family life (Borman, Klimoski, & Ilgen, 2003).

We begin this chapter by reviewing some important considerations in choosing a career. Then we explore two models of career development and discuss women's career issues. Next, we examine how the workplace and workforce are changing and look at some occupational hazards such as job stress, sexual harassment, and unemployment. Finally, we address the important issue of balancing work, relationships, and leisure. In the Application, we offer some concrete suggestions for enhancing your chances of landing a desirable job.

Choosing a Career

LEARNING OBJECTIVES

- Describe personal and family influences on job choice.
- Cite several helpful sources of career information.
- List some aspects of potential occupations that are important to know about.

- Explain the role of occupational interest inventories in career decisions.
- List five important considerations in choosing an occupation.

One of your biggest decisions in life is choosing a career. The importance of this decision is enormous. It may determine whether you are employed or unemployed, financially secure or insecure, happy or unhappy. Rapidly advancing technology and the increased training and education required to break into most fields make it more important than ever to choose thoughtfully. In theory, what's involved in making a successful career choice is pretty straightforward. First, you need to have a clear grasp of your personal characteristics. Second, you need realistic information about potential careers. From there, it's just a matter of selecting an occupation that is a good match with your personal characteristics. In reality, the process is a lot more complicated. Let's take a closer look.

Examining Personal Characteristics and Family Influences

People who have limited job skills and qualifications have limited job options. Thus, they usually must take whatever job is available rather than a job that is well suited for them. Actually *choosing* a career is a luxury usually afforded to the middle and upper classes. For those who are able to select a career, personal qualities and family influences come into play.

Personal Characteristics

Making career decisions can be scary. Individuals who exhibit *secure attachment* and who have achieved a solid sense of *identity* thus seem better able to take the risks associated with making career choices (Blustein, Prezioso, & Schultheiss, 1995).

What other personal characteristics affect career choice? Although *intelligence* does not necessarily predict occupational success, it does predict the likelihood of entering particular occupations. That's because intelligence is related to academic success—the ticket required to enter certain fields. Professions such as law, medicine, and engineering are open only to those who can meet increasingly selective criteria as they advance from high school to college to graduate education and professional training. This relationship between intel-

ligence and occupational level generally holds well for men, but an ability-achievement gap exists for women, as we noted in Chapter 10.

In many occupations, special talents are more important than general intelligence. *Specific aptitudes* that might make a person well suited for certain occupations include creativity, artistic or musical talent, mechanical ability, clerical skill, mathematical ability, and persuasive talents. A particularly crucial characteristic is *social skills,* since the use of teams to accomplish work tasks is increasingly important in a wide variety of organizations (Kozlowski & Bell, 2003).

As people travel through life, they acquire a variety of *interests.* Are you intrigued by the business

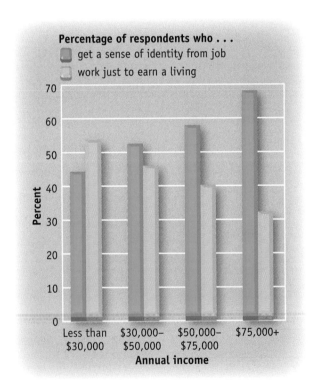

● FIGURE 12.1

How workers view their jobs. The way workers view their jobs is strongly related to their income. Those who earn higher salaries are more likely to obtain a sense of identity from their work; whereas those who earn lower salaries typically see their jobs merely as a way to make a living. (Data from Moore, 2001)

world? the academic world? international affairs? the outdoors? physical sciences? music? athletics? human services? The list of potential interests is virtually infinite. Because interests underlie your motivation for work and your job satisfaction, they should definitely be considered in your career planning.

Finally, it is important to choose an occupation that is compatible with your personality (Swanson & D'Achiardi, 2005). In assessing your personality, pay special attention to your dominant abilities and interests.

Family Influences

Individuals' career choices are strongly influenced by their family background (Whiston & Keller, 2004). That is, the jobs that appeal to people tend to be like those of their parents. For instance, people who grow up in middle-class homes are likely to aspire to high-paying professions in law, medicine, or engineering. On the other hand, individuals from low-income families often lean toward blue-collar jobs in construction work, office work, and food services.

Family background influences career choice for several reasons. For one thing, a key predictor of occupational status is the number of years of education an individual has completed (Arbona, 2005). And, because parents and children often attain similar levels of education, they are likely to have similar jobs. Second, career attainment is related to socioeconomic sta-

tus. The factors that mediate this relationship are educational aspirations and attainment during the school years (Schoon & Parsons, 2002). Thus, parents and teachers can help boost their children's career aspirations and opportunities by encouraging them to do well in school. Although socioeconomic status seems to have more influence on career aspirations than ethnicity (Rojewski, 2005), ethnic differences in aspirations are still found. For example, a cross-cultural and multi-ethnic study reported that Chinese and Asian American college students' more often choose investigative occupations, and their career decisions are more influenced by their parents than those of European American college students (Tang, 2002).

Finally, parenting practices come into play. As we noted in Chapter 11's Application on parenting, parenting styles are correlated with socioeconomic status. They also shape work-related values. Thus, most children from middle-class homes are encouraged to be curious and independent, qualities that are essential to success in many high-status occupations. By contrast, most children from lower-status families are often taught to conform and obey. As a result, they may have less opportunity to develop the qualities demanded in high-status jobs. As we noted in Chapter 10, parents' gender-role expectations also influence their children's aspirations and sometimes interact with socioeconomic status and ethnicity.

Family background plays an important role in children's later career choices.

Researching Job Characteristics

The second step in selecting an occupation is seeking out information about jobs. Over 20,000 occupations are listed in the U.S. Department of Labor's *Dictionary of Occupational Titles*. The sheer number of jobs is overwhelming. Obviously, you have to narrow the scope of your search before you can start gathering information.

Sources of Career Information

Once you have selected some jobs that might interest you, the next question is, Where do you get information on them? A helpful place to start is the *Occupational Outlook Handbook*, available in most libraries and on the World Wide Web (see Web Link 12.1). This government document, published every two years by the U.S. Bureau of Labor Statistics, is a comprehensive guide to occupations. It includes job descriptions, education and training requirements, advancement possibilities, salaries, and employment outlooks for 250 occupations. In addition, it details numerous career information resources, including those for the handicapped, veterans, women, and minorities. You can also find tips on locating jobs and accepting salary offers in this useful resource.

If you want more detailed information on particular occupations, you can usually get it from government agencies, trade unions, and professional organizations. For example, if you're interested in a career in psychology, you can obtain a number of pamphlets or books from the American Psychological Association (APA). Also, the APA website provides links to other sites describing more than 50 subfields in psychology, many of which provide useful career information. Related professions (social work, school psychology, and so on) also have Web pages. You will find the addresses of these pages on Marky Lloyd's Careers in Psychology Web site (see Web Link 12.3).

After you've read the available literature about an occupation, it's helpful to talk to some individuals working in that area. People in the field can provide you with more down-to-earth information than you can get by reading. Keep in mind, though, that the people you talk to may not be a representative sample of those who work in an occupation. Don't make the mistake of rejecting a potentially satisfying career just because one person hates it.

Essential Information About Occupations

When you examine occupational literature and interview people, what kinds of information should you seek? To some extent, the answer depends on your unique interests, values, and needs. However, some things are of concern to virtually anyone. Workers typically rate highest in importance good health insurance, retirement plans, limited job stress, and recognition for performing well (Saad, 1999). Some key issues you need to know about include:

The nature of the work. What would your duties and responsibilities be on a day-to-day basis?

Working conditions. Is the work environment pleasant or unpleasant, low key or high pressure?

Job entry requirements. What education and training are required to break into this occupational area?

Potential earnings. What are entry-level salaries, and how much can you hope to earn if you're exceptionally successful? What does the average person earn? What are the fringe benefits?

Potential status. What is the social status associated with this occupation? Is it personally satisfactory for you?

Opportunities for advancement. How do you move up in this field? Are there adequate opportunities for promotion and advancement?

Intrinsic job satisfaction. Apart from money and formal fringe benefits, what can you derive in the way of personal satisfaction from this job? Will it allow you to help people, to have fun, to be creative, or to shoulder responsibility?

Future outlook. What is the projected supply and demand for this occupational area?

By the way, if you're wondering whether your college education will be worth the effort in terms of dollars and cents, the answer is yes. As we'll discuss shortly, the jobs that you can obtain with a college degree typically yield higher pay than those that require less education (U.S. Bureau of Labor Statistics, 2004). The ex-

---

WEB LINK 12.1

Occupational Outlook Handbook (OOH) Online
Every two years the Bureau of Labor Statistics publishes the OOH, now available via the Internet. This guide to every occupation in the United States includes descriptions of the nature of each job and its working conditions, educational requirements, future employment, and earnings prospects.

WEB LINK 12.2

The Riley Guide: Employment Opportunities and Job Resources on the Internet
This site, developed by the well-regarded career expert Margaret F. Dikel, complements her excellent book, the *Guide to Internet Job Searching*. Her website contains hundreds of annotated links regarding almost any topic related to employment and careers.

perts also agree that the future belongs to those who are better educated (U.S. Department of Labor, 2000).

Using Psychological Tests for Career Decisions

If you are undecided about an occupation, you might consider taking some tests at your campus counseling center. *Occupational interest inventories* **measure your interests as they relate to various jobs or careers.** Three widely used tests of this type are the Strong Interest Inventory (SII), the Self-Directed Search (SDS), and the Campbell Interest and Skill Survey (CISS) (Hansen, 2005).

Occupational interest inventories do not attempt to predict whether you would be successful in various occupations. Rather, they focus more on the likelihood of job *satisfaction* than job *success*. When you take an occupational interest inventory, you receive many scores indicating how similar your interests are to the typical interests of people in various occupations. For example, a high score on the accountant scale of a test means that your interests are similar to those of the average accountant. This correspondence in interests does not ensure that you would enjoy a career in accounting, but it is a moderately good predictor of job satisfaction (Hackett & Watkins, 1995).

Interest inventories like the SII can provide worthwhile food for thought about possible careers. The results may confirm your subjective guesses about your interests and strengthen already-existing occupational preferences. Additionally, the test results may inspire you to investigate career possibilities that you had never thought of before. Unexpected results may stimulate you to rethink your career plans.

Although interest inventories can be helpful in working through career decisions, several cautions are worth noting. First, you may score high on some occupations that you're sure you would hate. Given the sheer number of occupational scales on the tests, this can easily happen by chance. However, you shouldn't dismiss the remainder of the test results just because you're sure that a few specific scores are "wrong." Second, don't let the test make career decisions for you. Some students naïvely believe that they should pursue whatever occupation yields their highest score. That is not how the tests are meant to be used. They merely provide information for you to consider. Ultimately, you have to think things out for yourself.

Third, you should be aware that most occupational interest inventories have a lingering gender bias. Many of these scales were originally developed 30 to 40 years ago when outright discrimination or more subtle discouragement prevented women from entering many traditionally "male" occupations. Critics assert that

WEB LINK 12.3

Marky Lloyd's Careers in Psychology Page
For those who think they might want a job or career in psychology or allied fields, Professor Marky Lloyd, one of this textbook's authors, has put together a fine set of resources to help in both planning and making the choice. Many of the resources are helpful to any student seeking career guidance and employment tips.

interest inventories have helped channel women into gender-typed careers, such as nursing and teaching, while guiding them away from more prestigious "male" occupations, such as medicine and engineering. Undoubtedly, this was true in the past. Recently, progress has been made toward reducing gender bias in occupational tests, although it has not been eliminated (Hansen, 2005). Research suggests that ethnic bias on interest tests is less of a concern than gender bias (Hansen, 2005; Worthington, Flores, & Navarro, 2005). In interpreting interest inventory results, be wary of letting gender stereotypes limit your career options. A good career counselor can help you sort through the effects of gender bias on your test results.

Taking Important Considerations into Account

As you contemplate your career options, here are some important points to keep in mind.

1. *You have the potential for success in a variety of occupations.* Career counselors stress that people have multiple potentials (Bolles, 2005). As we have noted, you have over 20,000 occupations to choose from. Considering the huge variety in job opportunities, it's foolish to believe that only one career would be right for you. If you expect to find one job that fits you perfectly, you may spend your entire lifetime searching for it.

2. *Be cautious about choosing a career solely on the basis of salary.* Because of the tremendous emphasis on material success in America, people are often tempted to choose a career solely on the basis of income or status. Experts advise against this strategy (Lowman, 1991). When people ignore personal characteristics in choosing a career, they risk being mismatched. Such job mismatching can result in boredom, frustration, and unhappiness with one's work, and these negative feelings can spill over into other spheres of life.

3. *There are limits on your career options.* Entry into a particular occupation is not simply a matter of choosing what you want to do. It's a two-way street. You get to make choices, but you also have to persuade schools and employers to choose you. Your career options will be limited to some extent by factors beyond your control, including fluctuations in the economy and the job market.

4. *Career choice is a developmental process that extends throughout life.* Occupational choice involves not a single decision but a series of decisions. Although this process was once believed to extend only from prepuberty to one's early 20s, it is now recognized that the process continues throughout life. Some experts predict that the average person will have 12 to 15 jobs over the course of his or her working life (Smith, 2000). Moreover, labor analysts now project that individuals will change their careers—not just their jobs—three to four times during their working lives (Naisbitt & Aburdene, 1991). Nonetheless, middle-aged people may underestimate the options available to them and

therefore miss opportunities to make constructive changes. We want to emphasize that making occupational choices is not limited to youth.

5. *Some career decisions are not easily undone.* Although it's never too late to strike out in new career directions, it is important to recognize that many decisions are not readily reversed. Once you invest time, money, and effort in moving along a particular career path, it may not be easy to change paths. And family responsibilities can make major career changes difficult. This potential problem highlights why it is important to devote careful thought to your occupational choice.

In the next section, we explore in greater detail how personal characteristics are related to career choice and career development.

Models of Career Choice and Development

LEARNING OBJECTIVES
- *Summarize Holland's hexagonal model of career choice.*
- *Summarize Super's five-stage model of career development.*
- *Discuss women's career development.*

Psychologists have long been interested in understanding how individuals make career choices and how their careers evolve over time. Theorists have developed several approaches to these issues. Here we examine two influential models.

Holland's Trait Measurement and Matching Model

The most influential trait model of career choice is that developed by John Holland (1985, 1996). According to Holland, career choice is related to an individual's personality characteristics, which are assumed to be relatively stable over time. In Holland's system, people can be classified into one of six personality types, called *personal orientations.* Similarly, occupations can be classified into six ideal *work environments.* For obvious reasons, this model is often called the *hexagonal model.* According to Holland, people flourish when their personality type is matched with a work environment that is congruent with their abilities, interests, and self-beliefs. A good match typically results in career satisfaction, achievement, and stability. Here are the six personal orientations and their optimal work environments:

■ *Realistic* people describe themselves as good at mechanical tasks and weak in social skills. They prefer jobs with tasks that are physical or mechanical and that

are clearly defined, such as farming, auto mechanics, and engineering. They tend to avoid tasks that involve social skills, abstract thinking, subjectivity, or verbal skill.

■ *Investigative* people enjoy abstract thinking and logical analysis, preferring understanding to action. They like working with ideas rather than with things or people. Investigative individuals can often be found working in research laboratories or libraries.

■ *Artistic* people see themselves as imaginative and independent. They tend to be impulsive and creative and are socially aloof. These individuals dislike structured tasks, preferring instead to rely on their subjective impressions in dealing with the environment. They have a high need for emotional expression and often seek careers in art, music, or drama.

■ *Social* people describe themselves as being understanding and wanting to help others. They prefer to interact with people, and they have the necessary social skills to do so comfortably. They typically have greater verbal ability than mathematical ability. Social types are often found in the helping professions, such as teaching, nursing, and social work.

■ *Enterprising* people perceive themselves as happy, self-confident, sociable, and popular. They like to use their social skills to lead or persuade others. They prefer sales or supervisory positions, in which they can express these characteristics.

■ *Conventional* people are conforming, systematic, and orderly. They typically have greater clerical and mathematical ability than verbal ability. They prefer working environments that are structured and predictable and may be well suited to occupations in the business world.

Holland has developed several tests to measure the six basic personal orientations. One of them, the Self-Directed Search (SDS), is a self-scoring test. Once individuals identify their personality type on the SDS, they can match it with various relevant occupations. Studies have shown the SDS to be a useful career assessment tool (Spokane & Cruza-Guet, 2005).

Obviously, these six personal orientations are ideal types, and no one person will fit perfectly into any one type. In fact, most people are a combination of two or three types (Holland, 1996). You can take a rough stab at categorizing your own personal orientation by studying Figure 12.2. Look at the matching work environments to get some ideas for possible career options.

More research has been conducted on Holland's hexagonal model than any other theory in vocational psychology, and much of this research is supportive (Spokane & Cruza-Guet, 2005). For instance, researchers report that Holland's model describes relatively accurately the career preferences of college-bound male and female white, black, Hispanic, Asian, and American Indian adolescents (Day & Rounds, 1998; Day, Rounds, & Swaney, 1998). Also, people with good job-personality matches are more satisfied with their jobs and are likely to remain in these jobs longer than those who are less well matched (Holland, 1996).

In contrast to trait models such as Holland's that view occupational choice as a specific event, stage theories view occupational choice as a developmental process. We look at that approach next.

Super's Developmental Model

Donald Super

A highly influential developmental model of career choice is one outlined by Donald Super (1957, 1985, 1988). He views occupational development as a process that begins in childhood, unfolds gradually across

---

Holland's Personal Orientations and Related Work Environments

Themes	Personal orientations	Work environments
Realistic	Values concrete and physical tasks. Perceives self as having mechanical skills and lacking social skills.	*Settings:* concrete, physical tasks requiring mechanical skills, persistence, and physical movement *Careers:* machine operator, truck driver, draftsperson, barber
Investigative	Wants to solve intellectual, scientific, and mathematical problems. Sees self as analytical, critical, curious, introspective, and methodical.	*Settings:* research laboratory, diagnostic medical case conference, work group of scientists *Careers:* marine biologist, computer programmer, clinical psychologist, architect, dentist
Artistic	Prefers unsystematic tasks or artistic projects: painting, writing, or drama. Perceives self as imaginative, expressive, and independent.	*Settings:* theater, concert hall, library, radio or TV studio *Careers:* sculptor, actor, designer, musician, author, editor
Social	Prefers educational, helping, and religious careers. Enjoys social involvement, church, music, reading, and dramatics. Is cooperative, friendly, helpful, insightful, persuasive, and responsible.	*Settings:* school and college classrooms, psychiatrist's office, religious meetings, mental institutions, recreational centers *Careers:* counselor, nurse, teacher, social worker, judge, minister, sociologist
Enterprising	Values political and economic achievements, supervision, and leadership. Enjoys leadership control, verbal expression, recognition, and power. Perceives self as extraverted, sociable, happy, assertive, popular, and self-confident.	*Settings:* courtroom, political rally, car sales room, real estate firm, advertising company *Careers:* realtor, politician, attorney, salesperson, manager
Conventional	Prefers orderly, systematic, concrete tasks with verbal and mathematical data. Sees self as conformist and having clerical and numerical skills.	*Settings:* bank, post office, file room, business office, Internal Revenue office *Careers:* banker, accountant, timekeeper, financial counselor, typist, receptionist

---

● **FIGURE 12.2**

Overview of Holland's theory of occupational choice. According to John Holland (1985), people can be divided into six personality types (personal orientations) that prefer different work environments.

Adapted from Holland, J. L. (1985). *Making occupational choices: A theory of occupational personalities and work environments* (2nd ed.). Englewood Cliffs, NJ: Prentice-Hall. Adapted by permission of Prentice-Hall, Inc.

most of the life span, and ends with retirement. Super asserts that the person's *self-concept* is the critical factor in this process. In other words, decisions about work and career commitments reflect people's attempts to express their changing views of themselves. To map these changes, Super breaks the occupational life cycle into five major stages and a variety of substages (see Figure 12.3).

Growth Stage

The growth stage encompasses childhood, during which youngsters fantasize about exotic jobs they would enjoy. Generally, they imagine themselves as detectives, airplane pilots, and brain surgeons rather than plumbers, grocers, and bookkeepers. Until near the end of this period, children are largely oblivious to realistic considerations such as the abilities or education required for specific jobs. Instead, they base their fantasies purely on their likes and dislikes.

Exploration Stage

Pressures from parents, teachers, and peers to develop a general career direction begin to intensify during high school. By the end of high school, individuals are expected to have narrowed a general career direction into a specific one. Whether through studying about it or through part-time work, young people try to get a real taste of the projected occupation. During the later part of this stage, individuals typically attempt to enter the world of work on a full-time basis. Many people in this phase are still only tentatively committed to their chosen occupation. If their initial work experiences are gratifying, their commitment will be strengthened. However, if their first experiences are not rewarding, they may shift to another occupation, where they will continue the exploration process.

Establishment Stage

Vacillation in career commitment continues to be common during the first part of the establishment stage. For some, doubts begin to surface for the first time as they reappraise the match between their personal attributes and their current position. Others simply carry earlier doubts into this stage. If a person's career choice turns out to be gratifying, however, the individual firmly commits to an occupation. With few exceptions, future job moves will take place *within* this occupational area. Having made a commitment, the

● FIGURE 12.3

Overview of Super's theory of occupational development. According to Donald Super, people go through five major stages (and a variety of substages) of occupational development over the life span.

Adapted from Zaccaria, J. (1970). *Theories of occupational choice and vocational development.* Boston: Houghton Mifflin. Copyright © 1970 by Time Share Corporation, New Hampshire.

Stages of Occupational Development

Stage	Approximate ages	Key events and transitions
Growth stage	**0–14**	**A period of general physical and mental growth**
Prevocational substage	0–3	No interest or concern with vocations
Fantasy substage	4–10	Fantasy is basis for vocational thinking
Interest substage	11–12	Vocational thought is based on individual's likes and dislikes
Capacity substage	13–14	Ability becomes the basis for vocational thought
Exploration stage	**15–24**	**General exploration of work**
Tentative substage	15–17	Needs, interests, capacities, values, and opportunities become bases for tentative occupational decisions
Transition substage	18–21	Reality increasingly becomes basis for vocational thought and action
Trial substage	22–24	First trial job is entered after the individual has made an initial vocational commitment
Establishment stage	**25–44**	**Individual seeks to enter a permanent occupation**
Trial substage	25–30	Period of some occupational change due to unsatisfactory choices
Stabilization substage	31–44	Period of stable work in a given occupational field
Maintenance stage	**45–65**	**Continuation in one's chosen occupation**
Decline stage	**65+**	**Adaptation to leaving workforce**
Deceleration substage	65–70	Period of declining vocational activity
Retirement substage	71+	A cessation of vocational activity

person's task is now to demonstrate the ability to function effectively in the chosen occupation. To succeed, individuals must use previously acquired skills, learn new skills as necessary, and display flexibility in adapting to organizational changes.

Maintenance Stage

As the years go by, opportunities for further career advancement and occupational mobility decline. Around their mid-40s, many people cross into the maintenance stage, during which they worry more about *retaining* their achieved status than *improving* it. Rapidly changing technology may compel middle-aged employees to enhance and update their skills as they face competition from younger, more recently educated workers. The primary goal in this stage, however, is simply to protect the security, power, advantages, and perks that one has attained. With decreased emphasis on career advancement, many people shift energy and attention away from work in favor of family or leisure activities.

Decline Stage

Deceleration involves a decline in work activity during one's later years as retirement looms near. People redirect their energy and attention toward planning for this major transition. In his original formulation, which was based on research in the 1950s, Super projected that deceleration ought to begin at around age 65. Since the 1970s, however, the entry of the large baby boom cohort into the workforce has created an oversupply of skilled labor and professional talent. This social change has created pressures that promote early retirement. Because of these conditions, deceleration often begins earlier than Super initially indicated.

Retirement brings work activity to a halt. People approach this transition with highly varied attitudes. Many individuals look forward to it eagerly. Others approach it with apprehension, unsure about how they will occupy themselves and worried about their financial viability. Still others approach retirement with a combination of hopeful enthusiasm and anxious concern. Although anxiety about the unknown is understandable, many studies have shown that retirement typically has no adverse effect on psychological distress (Ross & Drentea, 1998). Although retirement may mean less income, it can also mean more time to spend with friends and on hobbies, travel, and meaningful volunteer work.

As a stage theorist, Super deserves credit for acknowledging that people follow different patterns in their career development. He identified several patterns for both men and women that do not coincide with the conventional pattern we have described. In support of Super's model, it has been found that self-esteem and career maturity are positively correlated (Crook, Healy,

& O'Shay, 1984). On the other hand, a study of adolescents reported that identity status was a stronger predictor of career maturity than self-esteem (Wallace-Broscious, Serafica, & Osipow, 1994). A more serious problem with Super's theory is that it assumes that people will remain in the same careers all of their working lives. But today's American workers are likely to have a number of career changes, a reality that is incompatible with the assumptions of long-term models like Super's. The current thinking about career stages or cycles is that they are shorter and recur periodically over the course of a person's career (Greenhaus, 2003). To be useful, stage models must reflect today's workplace realities.

Women's Career Development

It is currently estimated that 60 percent of adult women (versus 74 percent of men) are in the labor force (U.S. Bureau of the Census, 2004a). Moreover, the odds that a woman will work outside the home during her adult life are greater than 90 percent (U. S. Department of Labor, 2003). Although women's labor force participation is approaching that of men's, important gender differences remain when it comes to career choice and development. For one thing, most women still subordinate their career goals to their husbands' (Betz, 2005). This is even the case with academically gifted women (Arnold, 1995). If a married man wants or needs to move to another job, his wife typically follows him and takes the best job she can find in the new location. Hence, married women usually have less control over their careers than married men do. Also, the high divorce rate (50 percent) means that many women will have to provide for themselves and their children. One study reported that after a divorce, the woman's standard of living drops 27 percent (Weitzman, 1996). Today's women need to take these factors into account as they consider their career options.

Another gender difference concerns career paths. Men's career paths are usually *continuous,* whereas women's tend to be *discontinuous* (Betz, 1993). In other words, once men start working full-time, they usually continue to work. Women are more likely to interrupt their careers to concentrate on childrearing or family crises (Hattery, 2001). Still, because women are having fewer children and are returning to work sooner, the amount of time they are out of the labor force is decreasing (Han & Moen, 1999). Some researchers report that labor force discontinuity is a factor in women's lower salaries and status (Waldfogel, 1997), while others fail to find a "family penalty" (Schneer & Reitman, 1993). Women who do not have children usually remain in the labor force and tend to have a pattern of career advancement (Felmlee, 1995).

The Changing World of Work

- List six work-related trends.
- Describe the relationship between education and salary.
- Summarize important demographic changes that are transforming the workforce.

- Cite some problems that women and minorities face in today's workplace.
- Describe some challenges presented by workforce diversity to organizations and workers.

Before you enter the working world, it's important to get your bearings. In this section we look at several important background issues: contemporary trends in the workplace, the relationship between education and earnings, and diversity in the workforce.

Workplace Trends

Work **is an activity that produces something of value for others.** For some people, work is just a way to earn a living; for others, work is a way of life. For both types of workers, the nature of work is undergoing dramatic changes. Because trends in the workplace can affect your future job prospects, you need to be aware of six important trends:

1. *Technology is changing the nature of work.* Computers have dramatically transformed the workplace. From the worker's point of view, these changes are having both negative and positive effects. On the negative side, computers have been used to automate many jobs that people perform, reducing the need for some workers. The digital workplace also demands that employees have more education and skills than were previously required. Workers also have to keep upgrading their technology skills, which can be stressful. On the positive side, computer technology makes it possible for employees to work at home and to communicate with others in distant offices and while traveling. Another consideration is that computer-driven machines require workers to design, manufacture, sell, and service them.

2. *New work attitudes are required.* Yesterday's workers could usually count on job security. Thus, many could afford a somewhat passive attitude in shaping their careers. But today's workers have job security only as long as they can add value to a company. This situation means that workers must take a more active role in shaping their careers (Smith, 2000). In addition, they must develop a variety of valuable skills, be productive workers, and skillfully market themselves to prospective employers. In the new work environment, the keys to job success are self-direction, self-management, up-to-date knowledge and skills, flexibility, and mobility (Smith, 2000).

3. *Lifelong learning is a necessity.* Experts predict that today's jobs are changing so rapidly that in many cases, work skills will become obsolete over a 10- to 15-year period (Lock, 2000). Thus, lifelong learning and training will become essential for employees. Every year, nearly one-third of American workers take courses to improve their job skills (American Council on Education, 1997). In some cases, retraining occurs on the job; in others, community colleges and technical institutes provide continuing education (Kasper, 2002). Distance learning courses and programs are also available, although you have to watch out for bogus programs (Mariani, 2001). For suggestions on how to evaluate the quality and accreditation claims of distance education programs, see Web Link 12.4. Workers who know "how to learn" will be able to keep pace with the rapidly changing workplace and will be highly valued. Those who cannot will be left behind.

4. *Independent workers are increasing.* Corporations are downsizing and restructuring to cope with the changing economy and to be competitive globally. In doing so, they are slashing thousands of permanent

The growth of technology is significantly changing the nature of work, with both positive and negative effects.

jobs and doling out the work to temporary employees or to workers in other countries, a practice termed "outsourcing." By reducing the number of regular workers, companies can dramatically cut their expenditures on payroll, health insurance, and pension plans, as temporary employees don't typically receive such benefits. A leaner workforce also enables organizations to respond quickly to fast-changing markets. According to Daniel Pink (2001), one way to survive in this new environment is to become a "free agent" and hire out your skills to one or more organizations on a contract basis (see Recommended Reading). To characterize the "free agent" work pattern, Pink suggests the metaphor of the "LEGO career" instead of the "career ladder." Just as you can construct a variety of structures by assembling LEGO blocks, "free agents" assemble and reassemble the building blocks of their work life (values, interests, aptitudes, and skills) in different combinations to match career opportunities that emerge over time. Many professionals thrive on contract work; they have freedom, flexibility, and high incomes. But for those who are short on skills and entrepreneurial spirit, this work can be stressful and risky. About a third of independent employees would prefer to work for someone else than to work for themselves (Bond et al., 2003).

5. *The boundaries between work and home are breaking down.* Computer technology is one force driving this change, because people can work at home and stay in touch with the office via high-speed Internet, telephone, and fax machine. Working at home is convenient—workers save time (no commuting) and money (on gas, parking, clothes). Still, family members and friends may interrupt home-workers, necessitating setting rules to protect work time. And the advent of cell phones and pagers means that employees can be contacted any time and any place, making some workers feel as though they are on an "electronic leash." On the other side, the availability of onsite day care in some large companies shows that a traditional home function has moved to the office (Rousseau, 1997). This development is largely a response to increases in the number of single-parent families and

dual-earner households, **in which both partners are employed.** Quality onsite day care is a big draw to workers because it allows parents to interact with their children during the day.

6. *The highest job growth will occur in the professional and service occupations.* The United States, like many other industrialized nations, continues to shift from a manufacturing, or "goods-producing," economy to a service-producing one (U.S. Bureau of Labor Statistics, 2004). Whereas the bulk of yesterday's jobs were in manufacturing, construction, agriculture, and mining, the jobs of the next decade will be in the professional (and related technical) occupations and service occupations. Among the professional occupations, jobs in the computer and health care industries are expected to expand dramatically. (In psychology, jobs in health, counseling, and school psychology are expected to show strong growth.) In the service occupations, strong

High-growth, high-salary occupations. According to the U.S. Department of Labor (2004), between 2002 and 2012 these 19 occupations will have the largest number of job openings and will provide high pay. (Adapted from *Occupational Outlook Quarterly,* Spring 2004)

"Best Bet" Occupations, 2002–2012

Registered nurses	Executive secretaries and administrative assistants
Postsecondary teachers	First-line supervisors or managers of office and administration support workers
General and operations managers	
Sales representatives, wholesale and manufacturing, except technical and scientific products	Accountants and auditors
	Carpenters
Truck drivers, heavy and tractor-trailer	Automotive service technicians and mechanics
Elementary school teachers	Police and sheriff's patrol officers
First-line supervisors or managers of retail sales workers	Licensed practical and licensed vocational nurses
Secondary school teachers, except vocational education	Electricians
	Management analysts
General maintenance and repair workers	Computer systems analysts

job growth should occur in education (at all levels), social services, and business services. Figure 12.4 depicts those occupations expected to grow the most and pay the most between now and 2012.

Education and Earnings

Although many jobs exist for individuals without a college degree, these jobs usually offer the lowest pay and benefits. In fact, all but 1 of the 50 highest-paying occupations require a college degree or higher (U.S. Bureau of Labor Statistics, 2004). (By the way, the high-paying job that doesn't require a college degree is air traffic controller.) In Figure 12.5, you can see that the more you learn, the more you earn. This relationship holds for both males and females, although, as you can see, men are paid approximately $5,000 to $28,000 more than women with the same educational credentials.

On the other hand, a college diploma is no guarantee of a great job. In fact, many college graduates are underemployed. **Underemployment is settling for a job that does not fully utilize one's skills, abilities, and training.** About 18 percent of college graduates take jobs that don't usually require a college degree, and experts predict that this situation is unlikely to change in the near future (Lock, 2005a; Mittlehauser, 1998). And while it's true that the jobs you can obtain with a college degree pay more than those requiring less education, the higher-paying jobs go to college graduates with *college-level* reading, writing, and quantitative skills. College graduates without these skills more often end up in high-school-level jobs (Pryor & Schaffer, 1997).

Current employers are not very happy with the academic skills of many of their employees. According to a survey by the College Board's National Commission on Writing, a majority of U.S. employers say that about a third of their workers do not meet the writing require-

ments of their positions ("Employers Bemoan," 2004). As new jobs develop, they will require more education and higher skill levels. International competition and technology are the two driving forces here (U.S. Depart-

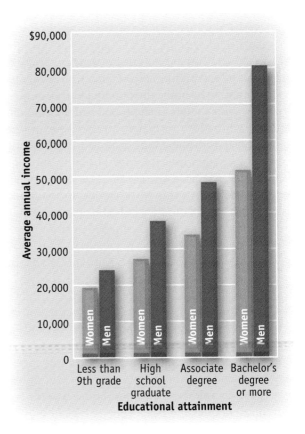

● FIGURE 12.5

Education and income. This graph shows the average incomes of year-round, full-time workers age 18 and over, by gender and educational attainment. As you can see, the more education people have, the higher their income tends to be. However, at all levels women earn less than men with comparable education. (Data from U.S. Bureau of the Census, 2004a)

ment of Labor, 2000). Thus, computer literacy is an essential complement to a good basic education.

The Changing Workforce

The *labor force* **consists of all those who are employed as well as those who are currently unemployed but are looking for work.** In this section, we look at some of the changes affecting the workforce and consider how women and other minorities fare in the workplace.

Demographic Changes

The workforce is becoming increasingly diverse, with regard to both gender and ethnicity. In 2003, 62 percent of married women worked, compared to 41 percent in 1970 (U.S. Census Bureau, 2004). This increase holds even for women with very young children. For instance, in 1975 only 33 percent of women with children under the age of 3 worked outside the home. By 2003, this number had grown to 57 percent (U.S. Bureau of the Census, 2004a). These changes have implications not only for work and family life but also for men's and women's roles.

The workforce is also becoming more ethnically diversified (see Figure 12.6) (U.S. Bureau of Labor Statistics, 2002). High school graduation rates for Asian Americans about match those for European Americans, and college graduation rates for Asian Americans exceed those of European Americans. By contrast, the high school and college graduation rates of Hispanics and African Americans lag behind those of European Americans, although they have been improving in re-

Today's workforce is becoming increasingly diverse.

cent decades (Worthington et al., 2005). Consequently, both groups are at a disadvantage when it comes to competing for the better jobs.

Although gay, lesbian, and bisexual workers have been long-standing participants in the workplace, they are often "closeted" for fear of discrimination. Unfortunately, most of these workers do not have the same legal protections against employment discrimination as their heterosexual counterparts (Badgett, 2003). Thus, disclosing one's sexual orientation may cause a homophobic supervisor to fire, refuse to promote, or reduce the income of a gay or lesbian employee. Predictably, factors associated with the decision to disclose one's sexual orientation at work include employer poli-

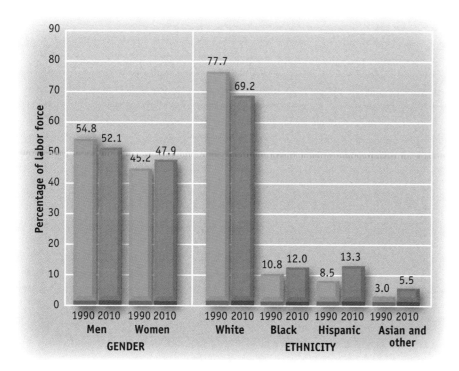

● FIGURE 12.6

Increasing diversity in the work force. Women and minority group members are entering the workforce in greater numbers than before. This graph projects changes in the share of the labor force by gender and by ethnicity between 1990 and 2010. (Data from U.S. Bureau of Labor Statistics, 2002)

cies and perceived employer gay-supportiveness (Griffith & Hebl, 2002). We are unaware of reliable data on the effects of sexual orientation disclosure and employment discrimination

Today's Workplace for Women and Minorities

Recent years have seen a dramatic upsurge in the number of females and ethnic minorities in the workplace. Is today's workplace essentially the same for these groups as it is for white males? In many respects, the answer appears to be no. Although job discrimination on the basis of race and gender has been illegal for more than 25 years, women and minority group members continue to face obstacles to occupational success, as evidenced by recent court decisions that found Morgan Stanley and Wal-Mart guilty of sex discrimination. Foremost among these obstacles is *job segregation.* Jobs are simultaneously typed by gender and by race. For example, skycaps are typically African American males. Most white women and people of color tend to be concentrated in female-dominated jobs where there is little opportunity for advancement or increase in salary. As we discussed in Chapter 10, workers in female-dominated fields typically earn less than employees in male-dominated fields, even when the jobs require similar levels of training, skill, and responsibility.

Still, more women and ethnic minorities are entering higher-status occupations, even if at a low rate (Jacobs, 1999). Unfortunately, they still face discrimination because they are frequently *passed over for promotion* in favor of white men (Maume, 1999). This seems to be a problem especially at higher levels of management. For example, the U.S. government's 1995 Glass Ceiling Commission reported that 95 percent of the senior-level managers of Fortune 1000 industries and Fortune 500 companies are men and that 97 percent are white (Swoboda, 1995). There appears to be a **glass ceiling, or invisible barrier that prevents most women and ethnic minorities from advancing to the highest levels of occupations** (see Figure 12.7). In fact, the Commission termed this barrier a "concrete wall" for women of color. Largely because of these reduced opportunities for career advancement, almost twice as many female corporate managers as males quit their

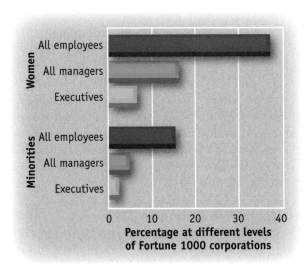

● FIGURE 12.7

The glass ceiling for women and minorities. A government survey of Fortune 1000 corporations found that women and minorities are underrepresented in management and executive positions. (U.S. Department of Labor, 1992)

jobs (Stroh, Brett, & Reilly, 1996). At the other end of the job spectrum, there seems to be a "sticky floor" that causes women and minorities to get stuck in low-paying occupations (Brannon, 2005).

When there is only one woman or minority person in an office, that person becomes a **token—or a symbol of all the members of that group.** Tokens are more distinctive than members of the dominant majority. And, as we discussed in Chapter 6, distinctiveness makes a person's actions subject to intense scrutiny, stereotyping, and judgments. Thus, if a white male makes a mistake, it is explained as an *individual* problem. When a token woman or minority person makes a mistake, it is seen as evidence that *all* members of that group are incompetent. Hence, tokens experience a great deal of *performance pressure,* an added source of job stress (Thomas, 2005). Interestingly, if tokens are perceived as being "too successful," they may be labeled "workaholics" or may be accused of trying to "show up" members of the dominant majority. These unfavorable perceptions may be reflected in performance appraisals. The performance of successful white men is less likely to be interpreted in these negative ways.

Another way the world of work is different for women, ethnic, and gay and lesbian minorities is that they have *less access to same-gender or same-group role models and mentors* (Murrell & James, 2001). Finally, *sexual harassment,* a topic we'll take up later, is much more likely to be a problem for working women than for working men. In sum, women and minority individuals must contend with discrimination on the job in a number of forms.

WEB LINK 12.5

U.S. Department of Labor
With primary responsibility for many job- and work-related matters in the U.S. government, the Labor Department offers a site that can serve as a base to explore a variety of topics, including wages and compensation, worker productivity, and the legal rights of workers (such as protection from sexual harassment).

The Challenges of Change

The increasingly diverse workforce presents challenges to both organizations and workers. Important cultural differences exist in managing time and people, in identification with work, and in making decisions (Thomas, 2005). These differences can contribute to conflict. Another challenge is that some individuals feel that they are personally paying the price of prejudice in the workplace, and this perception causes resentment. Recognizing the problem, some corporations offer diversity training programs for their employees. Ironically, these programs can make the problem worse if they take a blaming stance toward white males or if they stir up workers' feelings but provide no ongoing support for dealing with them (Baker, 1996). Thus, it is essential that such programs be carefully designed. The strong support of top management is also critical to their success (Rynes & Rosen, 1995).

Many who advocate abandoning affirmative action programs argue that these programs promote "reverse discrimination" through the use of unfair hiring and promotion practices. For some, this perception may reflect a sense of *privilege,* an unquestioned assumption that white males should be guaranteed a place in society and that others should compete for the remaining jobs (Jacques, 1997). Some also argue that affirmative action undercuts the role of merit in employment decisions and sets up (supposedly) under-prepared workers for failure (Sowell, 1994). Negative feelings about affirmative action prompt some to automatically assume that *all* women and ethnic minority co-workers have been hired *only* because of their gender or ethnicity (Thomas, 2005). Obviously, these assumptions can be quite harmful to an employee's success. For instance, several studies have demonstrated that attaching an affirmative action label to an employee results in negative attributions and perceptions of incompetence (Sagrestano, 2004). The good news is that this potential negative effect can be eliminated when people know that decisions are based on merit as well as on group membership.

To minimize conflict and to maintain worker productivity and satisfaction, companies can provide well-designed diversity programs and managers can educate themselves about the varied values and needs of their workers. Similarly, both majority and minority employees must be willing to learn to work comfortably with those who come from other backgrounds.

Coping with Occupational Hazards

LEARNING OBJECTIVES

- *List some important sources of job stress.*
- *Summarize the effects of job stress on physical and mental health.*
- *Describe actions organizations are taking to reduce job stress.*
- *Describe the prevalence and consequences of sexual harassment.*
- *Cite some ways that organizations and individuals can reduce sexual harassment.*
- *Describe some causes and effects of unemployment.*

Work can bring people deep satisfaction, but it can also be a source of frustration and conflict. In this section, we explore three challenges to today's workers: job stress, sexual harassment, and unemployment.

Job Stress

You saw in Chapter 3 that stress can emerge from any corner of your life. However, many theorists suspect that the workplace is the primary source of stress in modern society. Let's examine job stress and what employers and workers can do about it.

Sources of Stress on the Job

Americans today are working harder and longer than they were a decade ago, causing experts to cite overwork as a major source of job stress (McGuire, 1999). Current estimates clock the average full-time workweek at 48 hours; in law and finance, 60-hour weeks are common (Hodge, 2002). According to a United Nations report, the average American worked 1,978 hours in 2000, up from 1,942 hours in 1990 (International Labour Office, 2002). That's an increase of nearly a full week over the past decade. Compare this situation to that in Canada, Japan, and Mexico, where the average worker put in about 100 hours, or 2.5 weeks, less than American workers in 2000. Germans worked nearly 12.5 weeks less than Americans in 2000. Also, among affluent nations, only the United States does not require a minimum number of sick days for workers (Heymann et al., 2004).

In addition to long hours, common job stressors include lack of privacy, high noise levels, unusual hours (such as rotating shifts), the pressure of deadlines, lack of control over one's work, inadequate resources to do a job, and perceived inequities at work (Fairbrother & Warn, 2003). Fears of being "downsized" and concerns about health care benefits (losing them or paying increasingly higher premiums) also dog workers in today's economy. Office politics and

Firefighters obviously face a great deal of stress in their work, but so do people in many other jobs. Work stress is a major issue in a diverse array of occupations.

conflict with supervisors, subordinates, and co-workers also make the list of job stressors. Workers who must adapt to computers and automated offices experience "technostress" (Brod, 1988). Firefighters and coal miners face frequent threats to their physical safety. High-pressure jobs such as air traffic controller and surgeon demand virtually perfect performance, as errors can have disastrous consequences. Ironically, "underwork" (boring, repetitive tasks) can also be stressful.

Women may experience certain workplace stressors, such as sex discrimination and sexual harassment, at higher rates than men (Davidson & Fielden, 1999). African Americans and ethnic minorities must cope with racism and other types of discrimination on the job (Davidson & Fielden, 1999). Discrimination is also a problem for gay and lesbian employees (Badgett, 2003). Workers from lower socioeconomic groups typically work in more dangerous jobs than workers from higher socioeconomic status do.

Why are American workers so stressed out? According to Gwendolyn Keita and Joseph Hurrell (1994), four factors are the culprits:

1. *More workers are employed in service industries.* Workers in these jobs must interact with a variety of individuals on a daily basis. While most customers are civil and easy to deal with, some are decidedly difficult. Nonetheless, even obnoxious and troublesome customers "are always right," so workers have to swallow their frustration and anger, and this situation is stressful.

2. *The economy is unpredictable.* In the age of restructuring, downsizing, takeovers, and bankruptcies, even excellent workers aren't assured of keeping their jobs like workers in the past. Thus, the fear of job loss may lurk in the back of workers' minds.

3. *Rapid changes in computer technology tax workers' abilities to keep up.* Computers have taken over some jobs, forcing workers to develop new skills and to do so quickly. In other jobs, the stress comes from rapid and ongoing advances in technology that force workers to keep pace with the changes.

4. *The workplace is becoming more diverse.* As more women and minority group members enter the workplace, individuals from all groups must learn to interact with those who are unfamiliar. Developing these skills takes time and may be stressful.

Taking a broader view, Robert Karasek contends that the two key factors in occupational stress are the *psychological demands* made on a worker and a worker's amount of *decision control* (Karasek, 1979; Karasek & Theorell, 1990). Psychological demands are measured by asking employees questions such as "Is there excessive work?" and "Must you work fast (or hard)?" To measure decision control, employees are asked such questions as "Do you have a lot of say in your job?" and "Do you have freedom to make decisions?" In Karasek's demand-control model, *stress is greatest in jobs characterized by high psychological demands and low decision control.* Based on survey data obtained from workers, he has tentatively mapped out where various jobs fall on these two key dimensions of job stress, as shown in Figure 12.8. The jobs thought to be most stressful are those with heavy psychological demands and little control over decisions (see the lower right area of the figure). Considerable research has been conducted on the demand-control model, most of which has been supportive (Sonnentag & Frese, 2003).

Effects of Job Stress

As with other forms of stress, occupational stress is associated with a host of negative effects. In the work arena itself, job stress has been linked to an increased number of industrial accidents, increased absenteeism (Allegro & Veerman, 1998), poor job performance, and higher turnover rates (Buunk et al., 1998). Experts estimate that stress-related reductions in workers' pro-

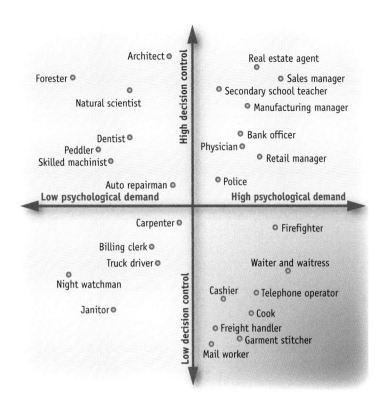

● FIGURE 12.8

Karasek's model of occupational stress as related to specific jobs. Robert Karasek (1979) theorizes that occupational stress is greatest in jobs characterized by high psychological demands and low decision control. Based on survey data, this chart shows where various familiar jobs fall on these two dimensions. According to Karasek's model, the most stressful jobs are those shown in the shaded area on the lower right.

ductivity may cost American industry hundreds of billions per year (Karasek & Theorell, 1990).

When job stress is temporary, as when important deadlines loom, workers usually suffer only minor and brief effects of stress, such as sleeplessness or anxiety. Prolonged, high levels of stress are more problematic, as those who work in people-oriented jobs such as human services, education, and health care can attest (Maslach

& Goldberg, 1998). As we noted in Chapter 3, prolonged stress can lead to *burnout,* characterized by exhaustion, cynicism, and poor job performance (Maslach, 2003).

Of course, the negative effects of occupational stress extend beyond the workplace. Foremost among these adverse effects are those on employees' *physical health.* Work stress has been related to a variety of physical maladies, including heart disease, high blood pressure, ulcers, arthritis, asthma, and cancer (Thomas, 2005). In a test of Karasek's model of work stress, symptoms of heart disease were more prevalent among Swedish men whose jobs were high in psychological demands and low in decision control (Karasek et al., 1981; see Figure 12.9 on the next page). Job stress can also have a negative impact on workers' *psychological health.* Occupational stress has been related to distress, anxiety, and depression (Sonnentag & Frese, 2003) as well as abuse of alcohol or drugs (Maslach & Goldberg, 1998).

Dealing with Job Stress

There are essentially three avenues of attack for dealing with occupational stress (Ivancevich et al., 1990). The first is to intervene at the *individual* level by modifying workers' ways of coping with job stress. The second is to intervene at the *organizational* level by redesigning the work environment itself. The third is to intervene at the *individual-organizational interface* by improving the fit between workers and their companies.

Interventions at the *individual* level are the most widely used strategy for managing work stress in the United States (Sonnenberg & Frese, 2003). Many companies have instituted programs designed to improve their employees' coping skills. These programs usually focus on relaxation training, time management, cognitive approaches to reappraising stressful events, and

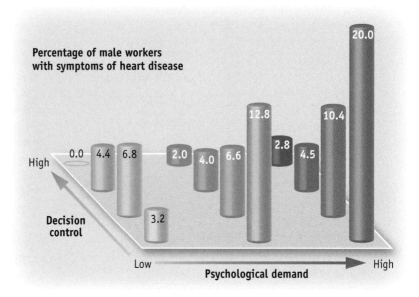

● FIGURE 12.9

Job characteristics in Karasek's model and heart disease prevalence. Karasek et al. (1981) interviewed 1,621 Swedish men about their work and assessed their cardiovascular health. The vertical bars in this figure show the percentage of the men with symptoms of heart disease as a function of the characteristics of their jobs. The highest incidence of heart disease was found among men who had jobs high in psychological demands and low in decision control, just as Karasek's model of occupational stress predicts.

Redrawn from Karasek, R. A., Baker, D., Marxer, F., Ahlbom, A., & Theorell, T. (1981). Job decision latitude, job demand, and cardiovascular disease: A prospective study of Swedish men. *American Journal of Public Health, 71*, 694–705. Reprinted by permission.

other constructive coping strategies that we discussed in Chapter 4. Also popular are *workplace wellness programs* that seek to improve employees' physical health (Nurminen et al., 2002). These programs usually focus on exercise and fitness training, health screening, nutritional education, and reduction of health-impairing habits, such as smoking and overeating.

Interventions at the *organizational* level are intended to make work environments less stressful. Some companies attempt to reduce occupational stress by reducing noise levels, instituting rest periods, making surroundings more attractive, and giving workers different tools or responsibilities. Decentralizing management and giving workers greater participation in decision making may also help reduce occupational stress (Wilpert, 1995).

Interventions at the *individual-organizational* interface can take many forms. Now and for the foreseeable future, the biggest challenge is probably to accommodate the changing nature of the workforce, which increasingly includes dual-earner couples and single parents rather than married men who are the sole wage earners in their families. What kinds of accommodations are companies making in response to the changing needs of their workers? In the important area of child care, the workplace has not been particularly responsive, according to a national survey based on a representative sample of American workers that looked at various aspects of work life in 1992 and 2002 (Bond et al., 2003). Only 10 percent of employers offered child-care services to their employees both in 1992 and in 2002. The survey also reported that only 18 percent of employees in 2002 had access to job-based child-care resource and referral services (24 percent had access to elder-care resource and referral services).

The most notable increase in family-friendly employer policies during the 10-year period was in flexible working hours. In 2002, 43 percent of employees were able to set their own starting and quitting times within some range of hours, compared to 29 percent in 1992. Among other things, flexible work times help parents manage child care and other family responsibilities. Thus, it is not surprising that workers who

Sally Forth by Francesco Marciuliano

SALLY FORTH. Reprinted with special permission of King Features Syndicate

have flexible work arrangements report higher job satisfaction than employees whose jobs are less flexible. We'll return to the issue of family-friendly work benefits in our discussion of "Work and Family Roles."

As we noted, workers from lower socioeconomic groups typically experience more work stress than those from higher-status groups. Ironically, these are the workers who receive less attention through stress management and other programs (Ilgen, 1990). Researchers also pay limited attention to gender, race, and socioeconomic status in their research on job stressors and intervention programs (Davidson & Fielden, 1999).

Sexual Harassment

Sexual harassment burst into the American consciousness in the fall of 1991 during the televised confirmation hearings for the nomination of Clarence Thomas as a Justice of the U.S. Supreme Court. Although Justice Thomas survived the confirmation process, many would argue that his reputation was damaged by Anita Hill's public allegations of sexual harassment, and so was Hill's. Allegations of sexual harassment also caused serious problems for President Bill Clinton. These highly publicized examples of sexual harassment charges have served as a wake-up call to individuals and companies, as both can be sued for harassment (regulations were instituted in 1980). Although most workers recognize that they need to take the problem of sexual harassment seriously, many people remain relatively naïve about what constitutes sexual harassment.

Sexual harassment occurs when employees are subjected to unwelcome sexually oriented behavior. According to law, there are two types of sexual harassment. The first is *quid pro quo* (from the Latin expression that translates as "something given or received in exchange for something else"). In the context of sexual harassment, quid pro quo involves making submission to unwanted sexual advances a condition of hiring, advancement, or not being fired. In other words, the worker's survival on the job depends on agreeing to engage in unwanted sex. The second type of harassment is *hostile environment,* or any type of unwelcome sexual behavior that creates a hostile work environment that can inflict psychological harm and interfere with job performance.

Sexual harassment can take a variety of forms: unsolicited and unwelcome flirting, sexual advances, or propositions; insulting comments about an employee's appearance, dress, or anatomy; unappreciated dirty jokes and sexual gestures; intrusive or sexual questions about an employee's personal life; explicit descriptions of the harasser's own sexual experiences; abuse of familiarities such as "honey" and "dear"; unnecessary and unwanted physical contact such as touching, hugging, pinching, or kissing; catcalls; exposure of geni-

tals; physical or sexual assault; and rape. As experts have pointed out, sexual harassment is an abuse of power by a person in authority. To determine what legally constitutes sexual harassment, the courts take into account "whether the behavior is motivated by the gender of the victim, whether it is unwelcome, whether it is repetitive, and whether it could lead to negative psychological or organizational outcomes" (Goldberg & Zhang, 2004, p. 823). Same-gender sexual harassment also occurs and is tried according to the same standards applied in cross-sex sexual harassment although little research has been done on the topic.

Prevalence and Consequences

Sexual harassment in the workplace is more widespread than most people realize. A review of 18 studies suggested that approximately 42 percent of female workers in the United States report having been sexually harassed (Gruber, 1990). A liberal estimate for male workers is 15 percent (Gutek, 1993). The typical female victim is young, divorced or separated, in a nonsenior position, and in a masculine-stereotyped field (Davidson & Fielden, 1999). A survey of women in the military reported that 76 percent had experienced sexual harassment in the previous year (Yoder, 2001). Women in blue-collar jobs are also at high risk, but sexual harassment also occurs in the professions. For example, in a

RECOMMENDED READING

Sexual Harassment on the Job: What It Is and How to Stop It
by William Petrocelli and Barbara Kate Repa
(Nolo Press, 1998)

Employees and employers now recognize that they need to know what constitutes sexual harassment and what does not. In addition, those who believe that they are being sexually harassed want to know how to stop it. As the title of this book indicates, it addresses both issues. The authors clearly define the varieties of sexual harassment and provide examples from the workplace and from court cases to reinforce their points. Petrocelli and Repa view the alternatives to ending sexual harassment as a series of escalating steps, and they helpfully guide readers through their various options. For employers, there is a chapter on workplace policies and programs to reduce occurrences of sexual harassment.

Cover image reproduced by permission of Nolo Press. Copyright © 2002. http://www.nolo.com

survey of United Methodist clergywomen, 77 percent reported that they had experienced sexual harassment—with 41 percent of these incidents perpetrated by colleagues and other ministers ("Women Clerics," 1990).

Experiencing sexual harassment can have negative effects on psychological and physical health (Norton, 2002). Problematic reactions include anger, reduced self-esteem, depression, and anxiety. Victims may also have difficulties in their personal relationships and in sexual adjustment (loss of desire, for example). Increased alcohol consumption, smoking, and dependence on drugs are also reported (Davidson & Fielden, 1999). Sexual harassment can also produce fallout on the job: Women who are harassed may be less productive, less satisfied with their jobs, and less committed to their work and employer.

Stopping Sexual Harassment

To predict the occurrence of sexual harassment, researchers have developed a two-factor model based on the person (prospective harasser) and the social situation (Pryor, Giedd, & Williams, 1995). According to this model, individuals vary in their proclivity for sexual harassment, and organizational norms regarding the acceptability of sexual harassment also vary. Research suggests that sexual harassment is most likely to occur when individual proclivity is high and organizational norms are accepting. Thus, it follows that organizations can reduce the incidence of sexual harassment by promoting norms that are intolerant of it.

Acknowledging the prevalence and negative impact of sexual harassment, many organizations have taken steps to educate and protect their workers. Managers are publicly speaking out against sexual harassment, supporting programs designed to increase employees' awareness of the problem, issuing policies expressly forbidding harassment, and implementing formal grievance procedures for handling allegations of harassment.

Responses to sexual harassment may be personal as well as organizational. Research-ers have developed a typology of possible responses to this problem (see Figure 12.10) and have studied their relative effectiveness (Bowes-Sperry & Tata, 1999; Knapp et al., 1997). Ironically, the most frequently used strategy—avoiding/denial—is also the least effective one. Confrontation and advocacy seeking are two effective strategies but are infrequently used. In the Recommended Reading box on page 391, we describe a book that both employers and employees should find helpful in ridding the workplace of sexual harassment.

Unemployment

People with little education and training have always been vulnerable to unemployment. In today's economic market, however, even those with a good education and excellent job skills are not immune to unemployment. What's going on?

Causes of Unemployment

Unemployment today is caused primarily by the dramatic economic changes we have already discussed. First, the shift from a manufacturing to a service economy has significantly transformed the nature of work. On the positive side, this means that many new jobs are being created; on the negative side, it means that workers in high-paying manufacturing jobs are being laid off

● FIGURE 12.10

Effectiveness of responses to sexual harassment. Responses to sexual harassment can be classified into four categories based on the focus of the response (directed toward self or toward the harasser) and the mode of the response (involving the self or others). Unfortunately, the most frequent reactions turn out to be the least helpful. Effective strategies are available, but they are infrequently used.

From Bowes-Sperry, L., & Tata, J. (1999). A multiperspective framework of sexual harassment. In G. N. Powell (Ed.), *Handbook of gender and work* (pp. 263–280). Thousand Oaks, CA: Sage Publications. Copyright © 1999 by Sage Publications. Reprinted with permission of Sage Publications, Inc.

MODE OF RESPONSE

	SELF-RESPONSE	SUPPORTED RESPONSE
SELF-FOCUS	**Avoidance/Denial** Most frequently used, yet least effective for ending harassment. • avoiding the harasser • altering the job situation by transferring/quitting • ignoring the behavior • going along with the behavior • treating the behavior as a joke • blaming self	**Social Coping** Not effective for ending harassment, but may assist in coping with negative consequences resulting from harassment. • bringing along a friend when harasser will be present • discussing the situation with sympathetic other • seeking medical and/or emotional counseling
INITIATOR FOCUS	**Confrontation/Negotiation** Not frequently used, but very effective for ending harassment. • asking or telling the harasser to stop • threatening the harasser • disciplining the harasser (if in a position to do so)	**Advocacy Seeking** Not frequently used, but very effective for ending harassment. • reporting the behavior to a supervisor, other internal official body, or outside agency • asking another person (e.g., friend) to intervene • seeking legal remedies through the court system

FOCUS OF RESPONSE

(robots are now assembling cars, for instance). A second economic change is the globalization of the marketplace. For corporations, this means restructuring and downsizing to increase efficiency and profits—at the expense of workers, including those in white-collar jobs. Thus, a major consequence of these economic upheavals is *displaced workers—individuals who are unemployed because their jobs have disappeared.* Between 1999 and 2001, about 4 million workers with three or more years of experience were displaced as a result of plant closings, slack or insufficient work, or positions being eliminated (U.S. Bureau of the Census, 2004a).

Effects of Unemployment

Losing one's job is difficult at best and devastating at worst. Not only can it cause economic distress, it can also cause health problems and such psychological difficulties as loss of self-esteem, depression, and anxiety (Bobek & Robbins, 2005). Also, the rate of attempted and completed suicides increases with unemployment. The amount of distress experienced as the result of job loss is not affected by gender (Kulik, 2000).

While losing a job at any age is highly stressful, those who are laid off in middle age seem to find the experience most difficult (Kulik, 2000). For one thing, they typically have more financial responsibilities than those in other age groups. Second, if other family members aren't able to provide health insurance, the entire family's health and welfare is jeopardized (Couch, 1998). Third, older workers typically remain out of work for a longer time than younger workers. Thus, economic hardship can be a real possibility and can threaten quality of life for the worker's whole family. Finally, middle-aged workers have been on the job for a number of years. Because they typically feel highly involved in their work, being cut off from this important source of life satisfaction is painful (Broomhall & Winefield, 1990). Of course, not all middle-aged workers are affected negatively by loss of work (Leana & Feldman, 1992). Individuals who are in their 50s and close to retirement and those who are motivated to try their hand at something new seem the least affected.

Sometimes the stress of job loss leads to violence. Occasionally, such violent episodes occur in the workplace (Sygnatur & Toscano, 2000). As you can see in Figure 12.11 the overriding cause of on-the-job homicides is robberies (67 percent). Of the remaining causes, the next highest is disputes between co-workers (15 percent). These situations often involve a displaced worker who lashes out in rage and desperation at a supervisor or co-workers. Employees who lose their jobs because of downsizing—instead of poor job performance—are likely to believe they have been treated arbitrarily and unfairly—a situation associated with increased aggression (Baron, Neuman, & Geddes, 1999; LeBlanc & Barling, 2004). Workplace murderers are

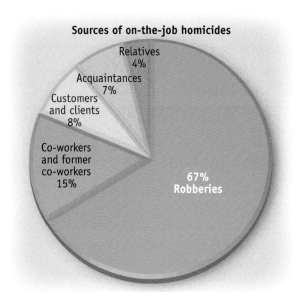

Sources of on-the-job homicides

- Relatives 4%
- Acquaintances 7%
- Customers and clients 8%
- Co-workers and former co-workers 15%
- 67% Robberies

● FIGURE 12.11

Violence at work. Business-related disputes with work colleagues, such as retaliation for being fired, account for a relatively small portion of homicides at work, even though they are the second leading cause of on-the-job homicides. Homicides in the workplace are not the largest source of fatalities in the workplace (accidents are); nonetheless, they occur often enough to be a source of concern to workers. (Data from U.S. Bureau of Labor Statistics, 1998)

typically middle-aged white males, loners at work, owners of gun collections, and fascinated by exotic weapons (Stuart, 1992). They are often angry and paranoid and may signal their intentions by making violent threats. Incidents of workplace violence and recent concerns about terrorism have prompted some organizations to make an effort to identify potentially dangerous individuals (Auerbach & Gramling, 1998).

Job loss can also generate anger among people who are dependent on the displaced workers. For example, a study of over 800 employed individuals and their partners reported that job loss led partners to withdraw social support from each other and to be increasingly critical, insulting, and angry (Vinokur, Price, & Caplan, 1996).

Coping with Unemployment

Support from friends and family is essential in coping with unemployment. When a person is out of work for an extended period of time or has little social support, counseling may also be helpful. Some companies offer programs for laid-off workers. These programs typically teach employees how to search for jobs, manage stress, and cultivate social support. In the "Living in Today's World" box on page 394, we offer some specific suggestions for coping with unemployment.

LIVING IN TODAY'S WORLD

Coping with Unemployment

Mental health experts view job loss as a devastating life experience—similar to death, divorce, and serious illness or disability. Foremost, people are hit with the frightening prospect of loss of income and must deal with the stressful practicalities of how to live on less. Job loss also deals a psychological blow because it strikes at a key component of adult identity—having a job. If you're a victim of downsizing, you must deal with the anger and resentment that stem from the unfairness of the situation. Understandably, job loss is associated with decreases in self-confidence, feelings of failure and rejection, and increases in anxiety and depression (Bobek & Robbins, 2005). Unfortunately, job loss also increases the likelihood of marital problems. Being aware of the psychological aspects of job loss can help you cope with the experience.

Some experts suggest that individuals' reactions to job loss are similar to what they experience when they confront their own death (Bobek & Robbins, 2005; Lock, 2005b). Both of these experiences involve coming to terms with loss (although the losses are obviously quite different). In contemplating one's death, Elisabeth Kübler-Ross (1969) asserted that people experience a variety of reactions. These include *denial* ("I can't believe this is happening to me."), *anger* ("How could they do this to me?"), *bargaining* ("Maybe if I offer to work overtime for free, my boss will change her mind."), *depression* ("How can I look my kids in the eye?"), and *acceptance* ("I can learn from this painful experience and will be able to provide for myself and my family again."). As we noted in Chapter 11, people don't necessarily go through these five reactions in lockstep sequence. Individuals often move in and out of these emotional states as they strive to recover their psychological equilibrium. Interestingly, one author of a survival guide for the unemployed advises those who have been "downsized" to get angry—and then to move on (Laskoff, 2004).

For some practical suggestions for coping with job loss, we draw on the advice of career experts Michael Laskoff (2004) and Robert Lock (2005b).

Apply for unemployment benefits as soon as possible. You may be able to collect benefits for 26 weeks (or longer in some cases). Contact the nearest office of your state's Employment Security Commission or Department of Labor.

Determine your income and expenses. Determine precisely your sources of income (unemployment benefits, spouse or partner's income, savings) and how much you can count on per week/month. Itemize your weekly/monthly expenses. Set up a realistic budget and stick to it. Talk with your creditors if you need to.

Lower your expenses and think of ways to bring in extra income. Cut out unnecessary expenses for now. Minimize your credit card purchases and pay the bills off every month to avoid building up huge debt and becoming a slave to high interest payments. For extra income, consider selling a car, or having a garage sale, or putting items up for auction on eBay. Use your skills as a temporary worker.

Stay healthy. To save money on medical expenses, eat well-balanced meals and get adequate sleep. Use relaxation techniques to manage your stress (see Chapter 4). Keep yourself in a positive frame of mind by recalling past successes and imagining future ones.

Reach out for support. Although it is difficult to do, explain your situation to your family. You need their support and they need to know how your unemployment will affect them. If you are having relationship problems, consult a counselor. Let your friends know that you are looking for work; they may have job leads. Consider attending a support group or consulting a career counselor. Attend religious services or make time for daily meditation or spiritual reading.

Get organized and get going. Start by setting aside time and space to work on your job search. Then consider your situation. Can you find the same type of job or do you need to think about other options? Do you need to relocate? Do you need more education or retraining? Visit the library and check out some of the excellent career planning books (*What Color Is Your Parachute?*, for example). Once you're clear about your options, get busy. Expect to spend 15–25 hours a week on job-searching activities. Spend some time every week on volunteer activities in an area you would like to pursue.

Balancing Work and Other Spheres of Life

LEARNING OBJECTIVES

■ *Summarize current perspectives on workaholism.*
■ *Define work-family conflict, and discuss the benefits of multiple roles.*
■ *List several types of leisure activities and summarize their benefits.*

A major challenge for individuals today is balancing work, family, and leisure activities in ways that are personally satisfying. We noted that dual-earner families are becoming increasingly common and that the traditional boundaries between family and paid work life are breaking down. These two developments are related. Historically, traditional gender roles assigned women's work to the home and men's work outside the home. This division of labor created boundaries between family and work life. With more women entering the workforce, these boundaries have become blurred. The technology-based changes in the workplace are also eroding these distinctions between family and work life. Here we examine three issues related to balancing various life roles.

Workaholism

Most people cherish their leisure activities and relationships with their families and friends. However, *workaholics* devote nearly all their time and energy to their jobs. They put in lots of overtime, take few vacations, regularly bring work home from the office, and think about work most of the time. They are energetic, intense, and ambitious. In addition to personal factors, situational forces can also promote workaholism. Thus, workaholism is more common where the organizational climate supports imbalances between work and personal life (Burke, 2001).

Although workaholism has received considerable attention in the popular press, empirical research on the topic is relatively limited (Harpaz & Snir, 2003). A survey of 800 senior-level managers reported that nearly one in four considered themselves to be workaholics (Joyner, 1999). Psychologists are divided on the issue of whether workaholism is problematic. Should workaholics be praised for their dedication and encouraged in their single-minded pursuit of fulfillment through work? Or is workaholism a form of addiction, a sign that an individual is driven by compulsions he or she cannot control? In support of the former view is evidence that some workaholics tend to be highly satisfied with their jobs and with their lives (Bonebright, Clay, & Ankenmann, 2000). They work hard simply because work is the most meaningful activity they know.

Yet other evidence suggests that workaholics may have poorer emotional and physical well-being than non-workaholics (Bonebright et al., 2000; Burke, 2000). How can these conflicting findings be reconciled?

It seems that there are two types of workaholics (Buelens & Poelmans, 2004; Spence & Robbins, 1992). One type, the *enthusiastic workaholic,* works for the pure joy of it. Such people derive immense satisfaction from work and generally perform well in highly demanding jobs. The other type, the *nonenthusiastic workaholic,* feels driven to work but reports low job enjoyment. Moreover, these workaholics tend to report lower life satisfaction and less purpose in life than enthusiastic workaholics. Thus, it is not surprising that the nonenthusiastic group is more likely to develop *burnout* (Porter, 1996).

Both types of workaholics experience an imbalance between work and personal time. Not surprisingly, this situation translates into a high degree of work-family conflict for both groups (Bonebright et al., 2000). Moreover, the families of both groups suffer (Robinson, 1998). So, although enthusiastic workaholics really love their work, their devotion to their jobs has a price, one often paid by their families.

Work and Family Roles

One of the biggest recent changes in the labor force has been the emergence of dual-earner households, now the dominant family form in the United States (U.S. Bureau of the Census, 2004a). Dual-earner couples are struggling to discover better ways of balancing family life and the demands of work. These changes in work and family life have sparked the interest of researchers in many disciplines, including psychology.

An important fact of life for dual-earner couples is that they juggle *multiple roles:* spouse or partner and employee. TICKS (two-income couples with kids) add a third role: parent. Thus, today's working parents experience **work-family conflict or the feeling of being pulled in multiple directions by competing demands from the job and the family.** In heterosexual dual-earner families, men are taking on more household chores and child care, but most wives still have greater responsibilities in these areas (Bond et al., 2003). In gay and lesbian dual-earner households, responsibilities are more evenly divided (Kurdek, 1993b; Patterson, 2003). Single parents are especially likely to have work-family conflicts.

Given the tight economic conditions, employers seem to be cutting back on family-friendly benefits (Geller, 2003). Some believe that this situation is partly to blame for the downward slide in the percentage of mothers with infant children who are in the labor force (Armour, 2004). In 1998, the participation rate for this group had reached a high of 59 percent; by 2003, it had fallen to 55 percent. According to Ellen Galinsky, president of the Families and Work Institute, "They're not fleeing work—they're fleeing the demanding way of work" (Armour, 2004). To gain more control over their lives, some women are temporarily opting out of the workforce; others are going into business for themselves.

To be fair, some of the decline in women's labor force participation rates can probably also be attributed to generational shifts in the views of the optimal balance of work and family roles. As you can see in Figure 12.12, more Gen-X employees with children endorse a family-centric view over a work-centric view compared to a comparable group of Boomers (Families and Work Institute, 2004). Some suggest that these generational differences are due, in part, to many Gen-Xers seeing their hardworking parents lose their jobs due to downsizing (Families and Work Institute, 2004).

Although today's working parents may feel stressed, researchers find that multiple roles are beneficial for both men's and women mental, physical, and relationship health (Barnett & Hyde, 2001). For women, the benefits of multiple roles are attributed primarily to

The Time Bind: When Work Becomes Home and Home Becomes Work
by Arlie Russell Hochschild (Owl Books, 2001)

Sociologist Hochschild addresses the difficulties of balancing work and family life. She makes the disturbing claim that many adult workers are spending more time at work than at home because they actually prefer it that way. For the children of these parents, it means spending more time in day care or afterschool activities.

Hochschild's unsettling thesis is based on a case study of an anonymous Fortune 500 corporation ("Americo"). In three summers of field research, she interviewed employers and employees, attended business meetings, and shadowed working parents and their children. She observed that although Americo offered a number of "family friendly" programs (flextime, paternity leave), employees rarely made use of them. For many workers, lack of participation was rooted in concerns about career advancement and fears about job security in the age of downsizing. The shocker was that many workers actually preferred office life to home life! In other words, workers saw the office as a structured, supportive refuge compared to the conflicts, hassles, and pressures at home.

To address the problem, the author urges parents to start a "time movement" by organizing to reduce work hours. Ironically, her data give little reason to believe that working parents would want to join such a movement. Moreover, she fails to address the really significant implication of her findings—namely, that Americans really need to reconsider what a satisfying adult life encompasses. Despite such weaknesses in her analysis, the findings are provocative and well worth thinking about.

Generational Differences in Work and Family Priorities

Relative emphasis on work and family	2002 Ages	
	Gen-X (23–37)	Boomers (38–57)
Family-centric	55%	46%
Dual-centric	33%	35%
Work-centric	13%	20%

● FIGURE 12.12

Generational differences in work and family priorities. Gen-X parents are significantly more likely than Boomer parents to be family-centric (place more emphasis on family than work), whereas Boomer parents are significantly more likely than Gen-Xers to be work-centric (place greater emphasis on work than family). The fact that both groups have children under 18 living at home suggests that this is a generational, rather than a life cycle, difference.

From Families and Work Institute (2004, October). *Generation and gender in the workplace.* New York: Author.

the effects of the employee role. For men, family involvement is important, especially in the area of relationship health. According to Rosalind Barnett and Janet Hyde (2001), a number of factors contribute to the positive outcomes associated with multiple roles, including added income, social support, opportunities to experience success, and buffering. The latter refers to the idea that successes and satisfactions in one role provide a buffer against the negative effects of stress or failure in another role. Of course, there are outside limits to the number of roles and the amount of work that people can take on before they sacrifice the benefits of multiple roles (Barnett & Hyde, 2001). Role overload likely causes psychological distress.

Leisure and Recreation

Most Americans are working 48-hour workweeks, and many put in more paid work hours than that. Some workers put in extra hours because their employers mandate it. Others choose to work more hours to maintain their standard of living, because real earning power, especially for low-wage workers, has fallen behind what it was 25 years ago (Joyner, 2001). And when workers arrive home, unpaid family work awaits them. Given the pace of contemporary American life, it's no surprise that almost 60 percent of Americans say that having leisure time is either "extremely important" or "very important" in their lives, according to a Gallup poll (Moore, 2003).

American workers take an average of 16 days of paid annual vacation (Mishel, Bernstein, & Schmitt, 2001). The paid vacation time of American workers lags far behind that of many European workers (see Figure 12.13). Moreover, workers in most European Union countries get four weeks of vacation time by law (Roughton, 2001). A generous number of public holi-

days pushes the average vacation time in the E.U. to about seven weeks! Interestingly, those long European vacations don't seem to cut into worker productivity. In contrast, Americans worked longer hours over the past decade, but productivity slipped (Mishel et al., 2001). Perhaps more leisure time would improve the situation.

We define *leisure* as unpaid activities people choose to engage in because the activities are personally meaningful. How might we distinguish activities that are meaningful from those that aren't? Although people may lounge in front of the TV set for hours at a time, most would also acknowledge that an important difference exists between this use of time and, say, hiking around a nearby lake. While one activity merely provides respite from a boring or exhausting day (which you sometimes need), the other can be genuinely revitalizing. Being a couch potato will probably contribute nothing to your state of mind and may even contribute to your feeling apathetic and depressed. On the other hand, participating in activities that are meaningful and fulfilling can contribute to your feeling of well-being (Ragheb, 1993).

Types of Leisure Activities

The types of leisure activities that people prefer are quite diverse (see Figure 12.14 on the next page). Popular leisure pursuits include:

- *Hobbies.* Among the most popular hobbies are photography; acting; music (playing and listening); gardening; knitting; drawing; collecting stamps, autographs, and so forth; hiking; camping; fishing; and birdwatching.
- *Reading.* Although fewer individuals read now than in the past, plenty of people still love to curl up with a good book. Books allow readers to escape from daily cares, solve mysteries, travel to real or imaginary places, learn useful information, and find inspiration. Mysteries, romances, science fiction, historical novels, biographies, graphic novels, self-help books, magazines—the variety of available reading material is truly astounding.
- *Surfing the Internet.* A relatively new entry into the world of leisure, the Internet offers an amazing array of activities: e-mailing friends and relatives, meeting new people, visiting chat rooms on topics of interest, playing multiuser games, listening to music, visiting world-class museums, and taking tours through ancient historic sites are just a few options.
- *Travel.* Many choose their destinations spontaneously, but others are more systematic in their travel plans. For example, some individuals want to travel to all the U.S. national parks or all the major Civil War battlefields. Those who can afford it may travel to other countries—to get a taste of real French cooking or a firsthand look at what remains of ancient Egyptian civilization.

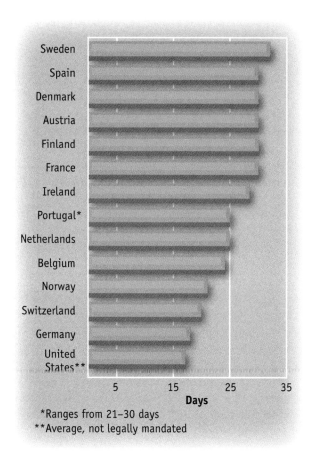

*Ranges from 21–30 days
**Average, not legally mandated

● FIGURE 12.13

American and European vacation days. American workers average 16 paid vacation days a year. Most European workers get considerably longer vacations. Moreover, these are benefits mandated by law.

Participation in leisure activities. Americans enjoy participating in quite a variety of leisure activities. The percentage of men and women engaging in popular leisure pursuits is summarized here. (Data from U.S. Bureau of the Census, 2004a)

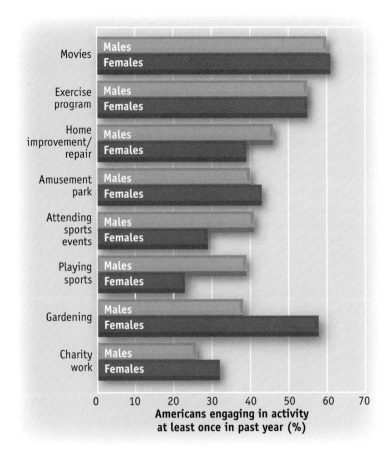

Americans engaging in activity at least once in past year (%)

■ *Games and puzzles.* Some individuals enjoy playing bridge for relaxation; others like to play board games such as Scrabble or chess. Computerized and video games are highly popular, especially with children and adolescents. For some, the day isn't complete without the daily crossword puzzle. Others like to assemble jigsaw puzzles.

■ *Sports.* Many people like to play team sports such as bowling or softball, enjoying the benefits of both physical exercise and social interaction. Others enjoy individual sports such as jogging, swimming, surfing, ice skating, or skiing. Kayaking is a popular option that can be done solo or with another.

■ *Volunteer activities.* Helping others appeals to individuals in almost all age groups. Moreover, you can use your skills to help others in an incredibly diverse array of settings: homeless shelters, hospitals, schools, battered women's shelters, boys' and girls' clubs, and sports teams, for example.

Being aware of the broad range of leisure activities heightens your chances of selecting those that are most meaningful to you.

Benefits of Leisure Activities

The idea that a satisfying balance of work, relationships, and leisure activities will lead to a more reward-ing and healthy life has intuitive appeal. Happily, research generally supports this notion. In one study of adult males, both job satisfaction and leisure satisfaction were significant predictors of psychological health (Pearson, 1998). College students who participate at high levels in a variety of leisure activities report higher rates of perceived physical, mental, and social health than students who are less involved (Caldwell, Smith & Weissinger, 1992). Among adults age 55 and older, regular participation in a variety of leisure activities is positively correlated with psychological well-being and negatively related to depression (Dupuis & Smale, 1995). Interestingly, this study found that one leisure activity was *negatively* related to perceived well-being: viewing television. Getting up off the couch is beneficial. Regular exercise can reduce the effects of stress, improve your mood and self-esteem, and help you shed unwanted pounds, as you'll see in Chapter 14.

To summarize, meaningful work, rewarding family interactions and friendships, and revitalizing leisure pursuits are three components of a rewarding life. Maintaining a satisfying balance among these three components is a major challenge in contemporary times.

In the Application, we describe how to conduct an effective job search and offer a few interviewing tips.

Getting Ahead in the Job Game

LEARNING OBJECTIVES

- Summarize the guidelines for putting together an effective résumé.
- Discuss strategies for targeting companies you would like to work for.
- Describe several strategies for landing a job interview.

- List some factors that can influence an interviewer's rating of a job candidate.
- List the dos and don'ts of interviewing for jobs.

Answer the following statements "true" or "false."

____ 1. The most common and effective job search method is answering classified ads.

____ 2. Your technical qualifications will determine the success of your job search.

____ 3. Employment agencies are a good source of leads to high-level professional jobs.

____ 4. Your résumé should be very thorough and include everything you have ever done.

____ 5. It's a good idea to inject some humor into your job interviews to help you and your interviewer relax.

Most career counselors would agree that all these statements are generally false. Although there is no one "tried and true" method for obtaining desirable jobs, experts do have guidelines that can increase your chances of success. Their insights are summarized in this Application. To ensure that you get the best job you can, you'll need to know more details than we can provide here. A good place to start is to read *What Color Is Your Parachute?*, one of the best job search manuals available (see the Recommended Reading box).

Above all else, it is important to conduct a job search that is well organized, thorough, and systematic. Sending out a hastily written résumé to a few randomly selected companies is a waste of effort. An effective job search requires lots of time and careful planning. People who are desperate for a job tend to behave in ways that cause prospective employers to see them as bad risks. Thus, it is crucial that you begin your search well in advance of the time when you will need a job. The best time to look for a job is when you don't need one. Then you can select an employer, rather than seeking an employer who will select you.

Of course, no amount of planning and effort can guarantee favorable results in a job search. Luck is definitely a part of the picture. Success may hinge on being in the right place, or meeting the right person at the right time. Moreover, becoming a top candidate for a position will depend on factors other than your technical competence. This is not to say that technical competence isn't necessary; it is. But given the realities of today's job market, employers are often inundated with applicants who have all of the required training and experience. The one who is ultimately selected may not be the one with the best technical qualifications. Rather,

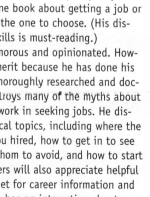

RECOMMENDED READING

What Color Is Your Parachute? A Practical Manual for Job-Hunters and Career-Changers
by Richard Nelson Bolles (Ten Speed Press, 2005)

Richard Bolles is a clever, creative writer who has put together a landmark book on the process of hunting for a job. "Parachute" was first published in 1970 and has become so successful that it's updated yearly. If you have time to read only one book about getting a job or changing careers, this is the one to choose. (His discussion of transferable skills is must-reading.)

Bolles's writing is humorous and opinionated. However, his opinions have merit because he has done his homework. The book is thoroughly researched and documented. The author destroys many of the myths about what does and does not work in seeking jobs. He discusses a variety of practical topics, including where the jobs are, what will get you hired, how to get in to see the boss, whom to see, whom to avoid, and how to start your own business. Readers will also appreciate helpful hints on using the Internet for career information and job searching. Bolles also has an interesting chapter on integrating work and faith. The book contains a number of useful appendixes, including exercises to help people determine their ideal job and locating a career counselor or coach.

Reproduced by permission of the publisher.

most hiring decisions are made on the basis of subjective impressions gleaned from résumés, telephone conversations, and face-to-face interviews. These impressions are based on perceptions of personality, appearance, social skills, and body language. Knowing this situation, you can practice certain strategies that may increase the odds in your favor.

No matter what type of job you're looking for, successful searches have certain elements in common. First, you must prepare a résumé. Next, you need to target specific companies or organizations you would like to work for. Then, you must inform these companies of your interest in such a way as to get them interested in you.

Putting Together a Résumé

No matter what your job search strategy, an excellent résumé is a critical ingredient. The purpose of a résumé is not to get you a job, but to get you an interview. To be effective, your résumé must show that you have at least the minimum technical qualifications for the position, know the standard conventions of the work world, and are a person who is on the fast track to success. Furthermore, it must achieve these goals without being flashy or gimmicky. Especially, it must contain no spelling or grammatical mistakes. Consider these two "fatal flaws" that appeared on cover letters: "I am a *rabid* typist" and "Thank you for your consideration. Hope to hear from you *shorty*"!

Your résumé should project the desired positive, yet conservative, image if you follow these guidelines (Lock, 2005a):

1. Use white, ivory, or beige (*never* any other color) paper high in rag content.

2. Make sure the résumé contains not a single typographical error.

3. Use the best professional printing service available.

4. Keep it short. One side of an 8.5" X 11" sheet of paper will suffice for most college students; do not go over two pages.

5. Don't write in full sentences, and avoid using the word *I*. Instead, begin each statement with an "action" word that describes a specific achievement, such as "Supervised a staff of fifteen" or "Handled all customer complaints."

6. Avoid giving any personal information that is superfluous to the job. Such information is an unnecessary distraction and may give the reader cause to dislike you and therefore reject your application.

An effective résumé will generally contain the following information, laid out in an easy-to-read format (Figure 12.15 shows an attractively prepared résumé):

Heading. At the top of the page, give your name, address, and phone number. This is the only section of the résumé that is not given a label. (You do not need to label the document "Résumé.")

Objective. State precisely and concisely the kind of position you are seeking, remembering to use action words and to avoid the use of *I*. An example might be "Challenging, creative position in the communication field requiring extensive background in newspaper, radio, and television."

Education. List any degrees you've earned, giving major field of study, date, and granting institution for each. (List the highest degree you received first. If you have a college degree, you don't need to mention your high school diploma.) If you have received any *academic* honors or awards, mention them in this section.

Experience. This section should be organized chronologically, beginning with your most recent job and working backward. For each position, give the dates of employment and describe your responsibilities and your accomplishments. Be specific, and make sure your most recent position is the one with the greatest achievements. Don't bother listing trivial attainments. Readers find such material annoying, and it just calls attention to the fact that you don't have more important items to list.

Also, although it may be tempting, beware of padding your résumé with misrepresentations or outright untruths. Although false information may help you get an interview, a good interviewer can usually detect a fraud. Also, background checking is relatively common today (Kluger, 2002). Thus, the truth is likely to come out—either before or during the interview—and then the irreparable damage is done. If you are wondering whether to include a questionable entry on your résumé, use the "sniff test" (Theisen, 2002). Could you talk easily with an interviewer about what you claim on your résumé without feeling nervous? If not, delete the information.

If you are currently a student or are a recent graduate, your schooling will provide the basis for both

---

WEB LINK 12.6

JobWeb
The National Association of Colleges and Employers has assembled a comprehensive set of resources for both students and career guidance professionals. The site includes information on job searching, employment listings, educational updating, and college- and university-based resources.

your experience and your qualifications. You can give yourself a boost over the competition by taking part-time or summer jobs in the field in which you plan to work. If this option isn't feasible, do some volunteer work in this area and list it under an "Honors and Activities" section on your résumé.

Technology is changing a number of aspects of the job search process, including the preparation and screening of résumés. Increasingly, companies are likely to electronically scan résumés for key words that match job specifications (Lock, 2005a). Thus, it's helpful to know how to create an electronic résumé in addition to the traditional paper version. You can get information about doing so at your campus Career Services office. Also, many organizations post formatting instructions on their websites for people who want to submit electronic résumés.

Finding Companies You Want to Work For

Initially, you need to determine what general type of organization will best suit your needs. Do you want to work in a school? a hospital? a small business? a large corporation? a government agency? a human services agency? If you want to select an appropriate work environment, you need an accurate picture of your personal qualities and knowledge of various occupations and their characteristics. Job search manuals like *Parachute* can provide you with helpful exercises in self-exploration. To learn about the characteristics of different occupations, look them up in the *Occupational Outlook Handbook,* visit your Career Services office, or see a reference librarian.

Once you've decided on a setting, you need to target specific companies. That's easy—you simply look

---

Example of an Attractively Formatted Résumé

TERESA M. MORGAN

Campus Address	Permanent Address
1252 River St., Apt. 808	1111 W. Franklin
East Lansing, MI 48823	Jackson, MI 49203
(517)332-6086	(517)782-0819

OBJECTIVE
To pursue a career in interior design, or a related field, in which I can utilize my design training. Willing to relocate after June 2005.

EDUCATION
Sept. 2003–June 2005
Michigan State University, East Lansing, MI 48825.
Bachelor of Arts–Interior Design, with emphasis in Design Communication and Human Shelter. Courses include Lighting, Computers, Public Relations and History of Art.
(F.I.D.E.R. accredited) 3.0 GPA (4.0 = A).

July 2003–Aug. 2003
Michigan State University overseas study, England and France, Decorative Arts and Architecture. 4.0 GPA (4.0 = A).

Sept. 2001–June 2003
Jackson Community College, Jackson, MI 49201.
Associate's Degree. 3.5 GPA (4.0 = A).

EMPLOYMENT
Dec. 2004–June 2005
Food Service and Maintenance, Owen Graduate Center, Michigan State University.
• Prepared and served food.
• Managed upkeep of adjacent Van Hoosen Residence Hall.

Sept. 2003–June 2004
Food Service and Maintenance, McDonel Residence Hall, Michigan State University.
• Served food and cleaned facility.
• Handled general building maintenance.

June 2002–Dec. 2002
Waitress, Charlie Wong's Restaurant, Jackson, MI.
• Served food, dealt with a variety of people on a personal level.
• Additional responsibilities: cashier, hostess, bartender, and employee trainer.

HONORS AND ACTIVITIES
• Community College Transfer scholarship from MSU.
• American Society of Interior Design Publicity Chairman; Executive Board, MSU Chapter.
• Sigma Chi Little Sisters.
• Independent European travel, summer 2003.
• Stage manager and performer in plays and musicals.

REFERENCES and PORTFOLIO available upon request.

● FIGURE 12.15

Example of an attractively formatted résumé. The physical appearance of a résumé is very important. This example shows what a well-prepared résumé should look like. (Adapted from Lock, 2005b)

for companies that have advertised openings in your field, right? Not necessarily. If you restrict yourself to this approach, you may miss many valuable opportunities. Experts estimate that up to 80 percent of all vacancies, especially those above entry level, are never advertised (Bolles, 2005).

How should you proceed? Certainly you should check the classified section in newspapers to identify the many positions that are advertised. If you are willing to relocate anywhere, a good source for business and professional jobs is the *National Business Employment Weekly*. You should also consult any trade or professional newspapers, magazines, or journals in your field. You can also search for job openings on the Internet (see several of the Web Links in this chapter). But you should note that using Internet job boards is one of the least effective ways of getting a job (Bolles, 2005; Kleiman, 2003).

You could also go to an employment agency, but keep in mind that these agencies generally handle only entry-level, hourly wage jobs. In addition, they can cost you thousands of dollars. If you're interested in professional jobs, you might consider contacting executive recruiters, widely known as "headhunters." Executive recruiters work on commission for organizations that have vacancies to fill. They earn their livelihood by actively looking for people who have the qualifications being sought by the hiring organization. You can locate headhunters nationwide by consulting *The Directory of Executive Recruiters*.

What about that 80 percent of openings that are not advertised? Actually, this statistic is somewhat misleading, because it includes a large number of vacancies that are filled by promotions within organizations. Nonetheless, many organizations do have openings that are not accessible through traditional channels. If you have targeted companies that haven't advertised any vacancies, you may want to initiate the contact yourself. Richard Bolles, author of *What Color Is Your Parachute?*, suggests the following strategy. First, identify a specific problem that the organization has, then devise a strategy to solve it. Next, find out who has the power to hire and fire (either through library research or a network of personal contacts). Finally, approach this person directly to convince him or her of your unique capability to help.

Landing an Interview

No one is going to hire you without first "checking out the goods." This inspection process typically involves one or more formal interviews. How do you go about getting yourself invited for an interview? If you are applying for an advertised vacancy, the traditional approach is to send a résumé with a cover letter to the hiring organization. If your letter and résumé stand out from the crowd, you may be invited for an interview. One way to increase your chances is to persuade the prospective employer that you are interested enough in the company to have done some research on the organization. By taking the time to learn something about a company, you should be in a better position to make a convincing case about the ways in which your expertise will be particularly useful to the organization.

If you are approaching an organization in the absence of a known position opening, your strategy may be somewhat different. You may still opt to send a résumé, along with a more detailed cover letter explaining why you have selected this particular company. Another option, suggested by Bolles (2005), is to introduce yourself (by phone or in person) directly to the person in charge of hiring and request an interview. You can increase your chances of success by using your network of personal contacts to identify some acquaintance that you and the person in charge have in common. Then, you can use this person's name to facilitate your approach. After you have an interview, you should follow up with a thank-you note and a résumé that will jog the prospective employer's memory about your training and talents.

Polishing Your Interview Technique

The final, and most crucial, step in the process of securing a job is the face-to-face interview. If you've gotten this far, the employer already knows that you have the necessary training and experience to do the job. Your challenge is to convince the employer that you're the kind of person who would fit well in the organization. Your interviewer will attempt to verify that you have the intangible qualities that will make you a good team player. Even more important, he or she will try to identify any "red flag" behaviors, attitudes, or traits that mark you as an unacceptable risk.

Because interviews are so important, you would think that interviewers' ratings of job applicants are

WEB LINK 12.7

CareerJournal
Compiled by an editorial team from *The Wall Street Journal*, CareerJournal contains both daily updates on employment issues (particularly for executive, managerial, and professional positions) and a vast array of job-seeking and employment articles online. Students can find an extraordinary wealth of tips and strategies on résumé and cover letter preparation, effective interviewing, and similar practical matters.

heavily based on job-relevant considerations. Unfortunately, research shows that this is not usually the case. For one thing, confirmation bias (Chapter 6) can operate in interview situations. That is, interviewers who have formed expectations about a job candidate (based on the résumé, letters of recommendation, and the like) often behave in ways that tend to confirm these expectations, whether positive or negative (Dipboye, 1992).

In addition, researchers find that more attractive candidates are usually rated higher than less attractive ones, as are those who dress in a manner consistent with the dress norms in an organization (Forsythe, Drake, & Cox, 1985). Also, visible tattoos or body piercings can create a negative impression at a job interview (Mallory, 2001). And remember to go easy on the aftershave lotion or perfume. A strong scent can be a real turnoff. Researchers also find that job candidates who are overweight are rated lower (especially if they are women) than those of average weight (Pingitore et al., 1994). Finally, it has been found that interviewees who emit positive nonverbal cues—leaning forward, smiling, and nodding—are rated higher than those who do not (Riggio & Throckmorton, 1988). Thus, to do your best in an interview, you should brush up on your nonverbal communication skills (Chapter 7) and your impression management tactics (Chapter 5). And remember, because of primacy effects (Chapter 6), the first few minutes of the interview are crucial.

To create the right impression, you must come across as confident, enthusiastic, and ambitious. By the way, a firm (not wishy-washy or bone-crushing) handshake helps create a positive first impression, especially for women (Chaplin et al., 2000). Your demeanor

WEB LINK 12.8

Salary.com
This useful site allows you to determine median salaries for numerous occupations at different experience levels and in different geographical areas and compare them to national averages. You can probably get all the information you need for free, but you can also pay (a lot) for a customized salary report.

should be somewhat formal and reserved, and you should avoid any attempts at humor—you never know what might offend your interviewer. Above all, never give more information than the interviewer requests, especially negative information. If asked directly what your weaknesses are—a common ploy—respond with a "flaw" that is really a positive, as in "I tend to work too hard at times." Don't interrupt or contradict your interviewer. And don't ever blame or criticize anyone, especially previous employers, even if you feel that the criticism is justified (Lock, 2005b).

Developing an effective interview technique requires practice. Many experts suggest that you never turn down an interview, because you can always benefit from the practice even if you don't want the job. Advance preparation is also crucial. Never go into an interview cold. Find out all you can about the company before you go. Try to anticipate the questions that will be asked and have some answers ready. In general, you will not be asked simply to reiterate information from your résumé. Remember, it is your personal qualities that are being assessed at this point. A final word of advice: If possible, avoid any discussion of salary in an initial interview. The appropriate time for salary negotiation is *after* a firm offer of employment has been extended. By the way, you can scope out salary information for many jobs by visiting Web Link 12.8. And you can find additional tips on interviewing at some of the other Web Links in this chapter.

To be successful on a job interview, candidates need to dress appropriately and convey confidence, enthusiasm, and interest in the job.

KEY IDEAS

Choosing a Career

■ Ideally, people look for jobs that are compatible with their personal characteristics. Thus, individuals need to have a sense of their own abilities, interests, and personality. Family background also influences career choices.

■ There are abundant resources for those who want to learn about possible career options. In researching prospective careers, it is important to find out about the nature of the work, working conditions, entry requirements, potential earnings, potential status, opportunities for advancement, intrinsic satisfactions, and the future outlook for jobs.

■ Individuals who have trouble making career decisions may find it helpful to take an occupational interest inventory. People have the potential for success in a variety of occupations, and they need to keep this and other considerations in mind as they make career decisions.

Models of Career Choice and Development

■ John Holland's hexagonal model of career development asserts that people select careers based on their own personality characteristics. Holland's well-supported theory includes six personal orientations and matching work environments.

■ Super's stage theory holds that self-concept development is the basis for career choice. According to this model, there are five stages in the occupational life cycle: growth, exploration, establishment, maintenance, and decline. The assumption that people will remain in the same career all of their working lives is out of sync with current workplace realities.

■ Models of career development in women are still being developed. Women's career paths are often less orderly and predictable than men's because of the need to juggle multiple roles and because many women interrupt their careers to devote time to childrearing.

The Changing World of Work

■ Work is an activity that produces something of value for others. A number of contemporary trends are changing the world of work. Generally, the more education individuals obtain, the higher their salaries will be.

■ Between now and the year 2012, more women and minorities will join the labor force. Although women and minorities are participating in the workforce at all occupational levels, they tend to be concentrated in the lower-paying and lower-status positions. Furthermore, women and minorities face discrimination in a number of areas. Increasing diversity in the workforce presents challenges to both organizations and workers.

Coping with Occupational Hazards

■ Major hazards related to work include job stress, sexual harassment, and unemployment. The negative effects of stress affect both employers and employees. Interventions to manage stress in the workplace can be made at the individual level, the organizational level, and the individual-organizational interface.

■ Victims of sexual harassment often develop physical and psychological symptoms of stress that can lead to decreased work motivation and productivity. Many organizations are educating their workers about this problem. Individuals can also take steps to reduce sexual harassment, although the most popular strategies tend to be the least effective.

■ Because of dramatic changes in the economy, unemployment is a problem for both skilled and unskilled workers. Job loss is highly stressful; middle-aged workers are most distressed by the experience. Unemployed workers who believe that they have been treated unfairly and arbitrarily often feel angry; a few of these individuals may resort to violence in the workplace. In coping with unemployment, social support is critical.

Balancing Work and Other Spheres of Life

■ A major challenge for workers today is balancing work, family, and leisure activities in ways that are personally satisfying. Workaholism may be based on positive or negative motives, but it still creates work-family conflict for workaholics and their families.

■ As dual-earner families have become the family norm, juggling multiple roles has emerged as a challenge, especially for women. Nonetheless, multiple roles are generally beneficial to mental, physical, and relationship health. Leisure plays an important role in psychological and physical health.

Application: Getting Ahead in the Job Game

■ Career counselors agree about the essential elements of a successful job search. The key factors include (1) determining the type of organization that will best suit one's needs, (2) constructing an effective résumé, (3) winning a job interview, and (4) developing an effective interview technique.

■ Before interviewing with a company, it is wise to do some research on the company to demonstrate your interest in the organization. Nonverbal communication skills can be crucial in job interviews. You should try to appear confident and enthusiastic. Try to avoid salary discussions in your initial interview.

KEY TERMS

Displaced workers   p. 393
Dual-earner households
   p. 383
Glass ceiling   p. 386
Industrial/organizational
   (I/O) psychology   p. 373
Labor force   p. 385
Leisure   p. 397

Occupational interest
   inventories   p. 377
Sexual harassment   p. 391
Token   p. 386
Underemployment   p. 384
Work   p. 382
Work-family conflict   p. 395

KEY PEOPLE

Richard Nelson Bolles
   p. 399
John Holland   pp. 378–379

Robert Karasek   pp. 388–390
Donald Super   pp. 379–381

1. Individuals' career choices are often:
    a. much higher in status than those of their parents.
    b. similar to those of their parents.
    c. much lower in status than those of their parents.
    d. unrelated to their family background.

2. Findings on education and earnings show that:
    a. at all levels of education, men earn more than women.
    b. at all levels of education, women earn more than men.
    c. there are no gender differences in education and earnings.
    d. there is no relationship between education and earnings.

3. Occupational interest inventories are designed to predict:
    a. how successful an individual is likely to be in a job.
    b. how long a person will stay in a career.
    c. how satisfied a person is likely to be in a job.
    d. all of the above.

4. Holland's hexagonal theory of occupational choice emphasizes:
    a. the role of self-esteem in job choice.
    b. the unfolding of career interests over time.
    c. parental influences and job choice.
    d. matching personality traits and job environments.

5. Which of the following is *not* a work-related trend?
    a. Technology is changing the nature of work.
    b. New work attitudes are required.
    c. Most new jobs will be in the manufacturing sector.
    d. Life-long learning is a necessity.

6. When there is only one woman or minority person in a workplace setting, that person becomes a symbol of his or her group and is referred to as a _____.
    a. token.
    b. scapegoat.
    c. sex object.
    d. protected species.

7. Job stress has been found to lead to all but which of the following negative effects?
    a. Burnout
    b. Bipolar disorder
    c. High blood pressure
    d. Anxiety

8. According to law, the two types of sexual harassment are:
    a. quid pro quo and environmental.
    b. legal and illegal.
    c. caveat emptor and confrontational.
    d. industrial and organizational.

9. Compared to European workers, American workers receive:
    a. much less paid vacation time.
    b. about the same amount of paid vacation time.
    c. much more paid vacation time, but less sick leave.
    d. much more paid vacation and more sick leave.

10. Which of the following is a good tip for preparing an effective résumé?
    a. Make your résumé as long as possible.
    b. Use complete sentences.
    c. Keep it short.
    d. Provide a lot of personal information.

Book Companion Website

Visit the Book Companion Website at **http://psychology.wadsworth.com/weiten_lloyd8e**, where you will find tutorial quizzes, flashcards, and weblinks for every chapter, a final exam, and more! You can also link to the Thomson Wadsworth Psychology Resource Center (accessible directly at **http://psychology.wadsworth.com**) for a range of psychology-related resources.

Personal Explorations Workbook

The following exercises in your *Personal Explorations Workbook* may enhance your self-understanding in relation to issues raised in this chapter. **Questionnaire 12.1:** Assertive Job-Hunting Survey. **Personal Probe 12.1:** What Do You Know about the Career That Interests You? **Personal Probe 12.2:** How Will Your Job or Career Fit with Your Life Needs?

ANSWERS

1. b Page 375
2. a Page 384
3. c Page 377
4. d Pages 378–379
5. c Pages 382–384
6. a Page 386
7. b Pages 387–391
8. a Pages 391–392
9. a Page 397
10. c Pages 400–401

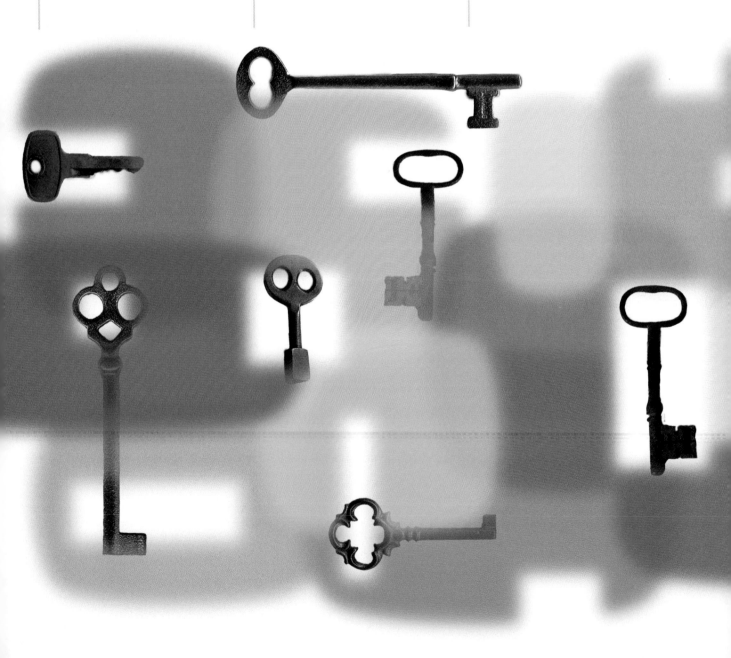

Development
and Expression
of Sexuality

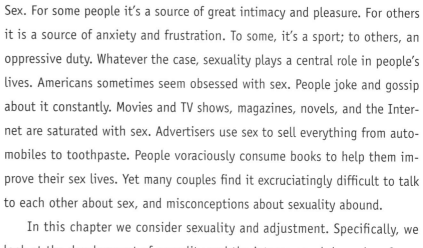

CHAPTER

13

Sex. For some people it's a source of great intimacy and pleasure. For others it is a source of anxiety and frustration. To some, it's a sport; to others, an oppressive duty. Whatever the case, sexuality plays a central role in people's lives. Americans sometimes seem obsessed with sex. People joke and gossip about it constantly. Movies and TV shows, magazines, novels, and the Internet are saturated with sex. Advertisers use sex to sell everything from automobiles to toothpaste. People voraciously consume books to help them improve their sex lives. Yet many couples find it excruciatingly difficult to talk to each other about sex, and misconceptions about sexuality abound.

In this chapter we consider sexuality and adjustment. Specifically, we look at the development of sexuality and the interpersonal dynamics of sexual relationships. Then we discuss sexual arousal and the varieties of sexual expression. We also address the important topics of contraception and sexually transmitted diseases. In the Application, we offer some suggestions for enhancing sexual relationships.

Before beginning, we should note that sex research has some unique problems. Given the difficulties in doing direct observation, sex researchers depend mostly on interviews and questionnaires. And people who are willing to volunteer information are more liberal and more sexually experienced than the general population (Wiederman, 2004). In addition, respondents may shade the truth about their sex lives because of shame, embarrassment, boasting, or wishful thinking. Researchers also have difficulty getting representative samples, so most studies of American sexuality are overrepresented with white, middle-class volunteers. Thus, you need to evaluate the results of sex research with more than the usual caution.

Becoming a Sexual Person

- List four key aspects of sexual identity.
- Discuss how hormones influence sexual differentiation and sexual behavior.
- Discuss how families, peers, schools, and the media shape sexual attitudes and behavior.
- Discuss gender differences in sexual socialization and how they affect individuals.

- Summarize the current thinking on the origins of sexual orientation and attitudes toward homosexuality.
- Discuss the identity development and adjustment of lesbians and gay males.

People vary greatly in how they express their sexuality. While some eagerly reveal the intimate details of their sex lives, others can't even use sexual words without embarrassment. Some people need to turn out the lights before they can have sex; others would like to be on camera with spotlights shining. To understand this diversity, we need to examine developmental influences on human sexual behavior.

Key Aspects of Sexual Identity

Identity refers to a clear and stable sense of who one is in the larger society (see Chapter 11). We'll use the term **sexual identity to refer to the complex of personal qualities, self-perceptions, attitudes, values, and preferences that guide one's sexual behavior.** In other words, your sexual identity is your sense of yourself as a sexual person. It includes four key features: sexual orientation, body image, sexual values and ethics, and erotic preferences.

1. *Sexual orientation.* Sexual orientation is an individual's preference for emotional and sexual relationships with individuals of one gender or the other. **Heterosexuals seek emotional-sexual relationships with members of the other gender. Homosexuals seek emotional-sexual relationships with members of the same gender. Bisexuals seek emotional-sexual relationships with members of both genders.** In recent years, the terms *gay* and *straight* have become widely used to refer to homosexuals and heterosexuals, respectively. Male homosexuals are called *gay*, whereas female homosexuals prefer to be called *lesbians*. As a social issue, sexual orientation has only recently come out of the closet. Because many people are ignorant about this issue, we give it a closer look a little later in this chapter.

2. *Body image.* Your body image is how you see yourself physically. Your view of your physical self definitely affects how you feel about yourself in the sexual domain. A positive body image is correlated with greater sexual activity and higher sexual satisfaction (Hatfield & Rapson, 1996). While ultra-thinness for women has been a long-time media message, muscular body types

for men are getting more promotion (Pope, Phillips, & Olivardia, 2000). The increasing popularity of gym memberships and the recent dramatic increases in facelifts and breast enhancements testifies to the importance of body image (Springen, 2004).

3. *Sexual values and ethics.* All cultures impose constraints on how people are expected to behave sexually. People are taught that certain expressions of sexuality are "right" while others are "wrong." The nature of these sexual messages varies depending on gender, race, ethnicity, and socioeconomic status. For example, the double standard encourages sexual experimentation in males, but not females. Individuals are faced with the daunting task of sorting through these often-conflicting messages to develop their own sexual values and ethics.

4. *Erotic preferences.* Within the limits imposed by sexual orientation and values, people still differ in what they find enjoyable. Your erotic preferences encompass your attitudes about self-stimulation, oral sex, intercourse, and other sexual activities. They develop through a complex interplay of physiological and psychosocial influences—issues we take up next.

Physiological Influences

Among the various physiological factors involved in sexual behavior, hormones have been of particular interest to researchers.

Hormones and Sexual Differentiation

During prenatal development, a number of biological developments result in a fetus that is a male or a female. Hormones play an important role in this process, which is termed *sexual differentiation*. Around the third month of prenatal development, different hormonal secretions begin to be produced by male and female *gonads*—the sex glands. In males, the testes produce *androgens,* **the principal class of male sex hormones.** Testosterone is the most important of the androgens. In females, the ovaries produce *estrogens,* **the principal class of female sex hormones.** Actually, both classes of hormones are present in both genders, but in different proportions. During prenatal development, the differentiation of the genitals depends primarily on the level of testosterone produced—high in males, low in females.

At puberty, hormones reassert their influence on sexual development. As you saw in Chapter 11, adolescents attain reproductive capacity as hormonal changes trigger the maturation of the *primary sex characteristics* (sex organs). Hormonal shifts also regulate the development of *secondary sex characteristics* (physical features that distinguish the genders but are not directly involved in reproduction). In females, more estrogen leads to breast development, widened hips, and more rounded body contours. In males, more androgen results in developing facial hair, a deeper voice, and angular body contours.

Hormones and Sexual Behavior

Hormonal fluctuations clearly regulate sex *drive* in many species of animals. Hormones also play a role in human sexuality, but their influence is much more modest. *Androgen* does seem related to sexual motivation in *both* men and women, although the effect is less strong in women (Apperloo et al., 2003; Freeman, Bloom, & McGuire, 2001). Also, high levels of testosterone in female and male subjects correlate with higher rates of sexual activity (Morley & Perry, 2003). Curiously, *estrogen* levels among women do not correlate well with sexual interest.

In summary, physiological factors have important effects on sexual development. Their influence on sexual *anatomy*, however, is much greater than their influence on sexual *activity*.

Psychosocial Influences

The principal psychosocial influences on sexual identity are essentially the same as the main sources of gender-role socialization discussed in Chapter 10. Sexual identity is shaped by families, peers, schools, and the media.

Families

Parents and the home environment are significant influences on sexual identity in the early years. Before they reach school age, children usually engage in some sex play and exploration, often under the guise of "playing doctor." They also display curiosity about sexual matters, asking questions such as "Where do babies come from?" Parents who punish innocent, exploratory sex play and who stutter and squirm when kids ask sexual questions convey the idea that sex is "dirty." As a result, children may begin to feel guilty about their sexual urges and curiosity.

Most adolescents want both their parents to be their primary source of sex information (Kreinin,

Rodriguez, & Edwards, 2001). According to a 2003 Gallup Youth Survey, 63 percent of teenagers (ages 13 to 17) reported that their parents talked to them about sex, while 36 percent said that their parents mostly left this discussion up to the schools (Mazzuca, 2003). In another national survey of adolescents and young adults (ages 13 to 24), only 37 percent felt that they learned "a lot" of information about relationships and sexual health from their parents (see Figure 13.1). Children definitely benefit from having positive and

Main Sources of Sex Information Among Youth

Source	Male	Percentage Female	Total
Friends	46	48	47
Sex education classes	42	39	40
Boyfriends, girlfriends, partners	40	39	39
Media (TV, movies, magazines, the Internet)	33	42	38
Parents	34	40	37
Doctors, other health care providers	21	50	36
Brothers and sisters	24	19	22

● FIGURE 13.1

Main sources of sex information among youth. Adolescents and young adults (ages 13 to 24) said they had learned "a lot" from the following sources, according to a national survey.

Adapted from Kaiser Family Foundation, Holt, T., Greene, L., & Davis, J. (2003). *National survey of adolescents and young adults: Sexual health knowledge, attitudes, and experience.* Menlo Park, CA: Henry J. Kaiser Family Foundation. (Question 2, p. 97).

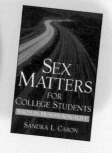
open conversations about sex with their parents. For example, adolescents who receive most of their sex education from a parent engage in sex later, less often, and with fewer sexual partners than adolescents whose parents avoid the subject (Jaccard, Dittus, & Gordon, 2000; Meschke, Bartholomae, & Zentall, 2000). Moreover, they are more likely to use contraceptives if they *are* sexually active (Whitaker et al., 1999).

Parents who make sex a taboo topic end up reducing their influence on their kids' evolving sexual identity, as the children turn elsewhere for information.

Peers

As you can see in Figure 13.1, friends are a leading source of relationship and sexual health information. (Only health care providers are rated higher, and only by females.) Unfortunately, peers can be a source of highly misleading information and often champion sexual ethics at odds with parents' views.

However, peers can also be a highly effective force for sexually responsible behavior. Some programs train selected high school seniors to educate younger students to postpone sexual involvement until they are mature enough to be sexually responsible (Howard & McCabe, 1990). Among other things, students practice effective responses to the "lines" teens encounter. Teens

who participate in such programs are less likely to have sex, and when they do have sex, they are more likely to use contraceptives.

Schools

Surveys show that the vast majority of parents and other adults support sex education programs in the schools, despite the media attention given to isolated, vocal protests (SIECUS, 2004). Also, most teenagers want their schools to offer sex education (McKay & Holoway, 1997). Because they fear protests by vocal minorities, many schools offer sex education programs that are nothing more than "an organ recital—what is connected to what in the body with no discussion of how or why two bodies might connect with each other" (Zellman & Goodchilds, 1983, p. 53).

Researchers who surveyed a nationally representative sample of American public, middle, junior, and senior high schools reported that 90 percent of schools offered *some* type of sex education (Kaiser Family Foundation, 2004). Among the surveyed schools, 30 percent offer "abstinence only" programs (no information about contraceptive methods), 47 percent offer "abstinence plus" programs (information about contraception and sexually transmitted diseases), and 20 percent offer comprehensive programs (information on such topics as contraception, abortion, sexually transmitted diseases, relationships, sexual orientation, and responsible decision making).

What is the effectiveness of these various programs? Unfortunately, "abstinence only" programs do not deter adolescents from engaging in sex, nor do they change teens' attitudes about their sexual intentions (Kirby, 2000; Thomas, 2000). In contrast, comprehensive programs result in a wide range of positive outcomes: increased use of contraception, reduced pregnancies, and reduced high-risk sexual behavior (Kirby, 2000). Also, these programs do not promote (and may delay) having early sex and do not increase (and may decrease) the number of sexual partners.

The Media

Americans see thousands of sexual encounters a year on television, videos, and DVDs. Among the top 20 teen television programs, 83 percent contain sexual

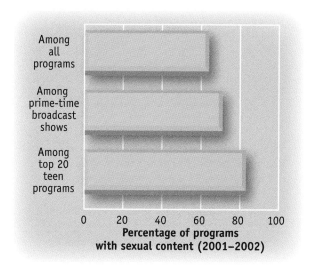

Percentage of programs
with sexual content (2001–2002)

● FIGURE 13.2

Sexual content in television programs. Sexual content pervades television programs and is especially high in the top 20 teen programs, according to this survey of programs that aired in 2001–2002.

From *A Biennial Report of the Kaiser Family Foundation: Sex on TV 3, Executive Summary*, (#3324), The Henry J. Kaiser Family Foundation. This information was reprinted with permission from the Henry J. Kaiser Family Foundation.

content (see Figure 13.2). Although it is still unusual to see TV characters talking about the consequences of unprotected sex or "using protection," TV sex is slowly getting "safer." For example, in shows that talked about or depicted sexual intercourse, 26 percent made some reference to a safer sex issue, nearly double the rate four years prior (14 percent) (Kaiser Family Foundation, 2003). Television portrayals of sexual relationships can influence young people's emerging sexual values. For example, one experiment reported that teens who watched 15 hours of TV shows containing casual sex had more permissive attitudes toward nonmarital sex than teens who saw 15 hours of TV depicting nonsexual relationships (Bryant & Rockwell, 1994). On the other hand, television can promote responsible sexual behavior and tolerance of homosexuality (Keller & Brown, 2002; Silver, 2002).

Books and magazines are another source of information on sex. Some 20 percent of adolescents and young adults reported that they had learned "a lot" about relationships and sexual health from magazines (Kaiser Family Foundation, 2003). Of course, some publications provide accurate and useful information, but many perpetuate myths about sex and miseducate young readers. The lyrics of rock music also contain extensive references to sexual behavior and norms of sexual conduct. Some rap music has come under fire because it portrays women as sex objects and advocates sexual violence against women. Approximately two-thirds of music videos contain sexual imagery (Pardun & McKee, 1995).

Turning to cyberspace, experts estimate that there will be 1.2 billion Internet users worldwide by 2005 (Cooper, 2002). Newsgroups with sexually explicit images are extremely popular, especially among males. But parents are understandably alarmed about young children having easy access to sexually explicit material. Among 10- to 17-year-olds, 25 percent have encountered unwanted pornography, and 20 percent have been exposed to unwanted sexual solicitations (Finkelhor, Mitchell, & Wolak, 2000). On the other hand, the Internet provides easy and private access to useful information on a host of sexual topics, including contraceptive methods and resources for gays and lesbians. The "Living in Today's World" sidebar expands on the issue of sex and the Internet.

To conclude, sexual identities are shaped by a host of intersecting influences. Given the multiplicity of factors at work, people bring highly diverse expectations to their sexual relationships. As you'll see, this variability can complicate sexual interactions.

Gender Differences in Sexual Socialization

Summarizing the research on gender differences in sexuality, Letitia Anne Peplau (2003), a major researcher on gender and relationships, concludes that there are four key differences, and that these hold for both gays and straights. First, men have more interest in sex than women (they think about and want to have sex more often). Second, the connection between sex and intimacy is more important for women than for men (women typically prefer sex in the context of a relationship). Third, aggression is more often linked to sexuality for men than for women (men engage in coercive sex much more often). Finally, women's sexuality is more easily shaped by cultural and situational factors (their sexual attitudes are easier to change and they are more likely to change their sexual orientation over time).

Letitia Anne Peplau

Societal values obviously come into play here. American males are encouraged to experiment sexually, to initiate sexual activities, and to enjoy sex without emotional involvement (Townsend, 1995). They also get the message to be conquest-oriented regarding sex ("scoring"). Thus, men may emphasize "sex for fun" in casual relationships and reserve "sex with love" for committed relationships (Oliver & Hyde, 1993).

Girls are typically taught to view sex in the context of a loving relationship (Hatfield & Rapson, 1996). They learn about romance and the importance of physical attractiveness and catching a mate. It isn't

Sex and the Internet

The Internet is playing an increasingly important role in sexuality. In fact, some experts say that "the influence of the Internet on sexuality is likely to be so significant that it will ultimately be recognized as the next 'sexual revolution'" (Cooper et al., 2000). Researchers estimate that between 20 percent and 33 percent of Internet users engage in some form of online sexual activity (Egan, 2000).

Online sexual activity involves the use of the Internet for any activity (text, audio, or graphics) that involves sexuality (Cooper et al, 2002). These activities are quite diverse and include using the Internet for information or entertainment, as well as for purchasing sexual materials, searching for sexual partners, and having sexually explicit discussions.

The first large-scale survey of adults who used the Internet for sexual pursuits (Cooper et al., 1999) described the respondents:

- Males outnumbered females by about 6 to 1.
- The average age was about 35.
- Most (87 percent) identified themselves as heterosexual; 7 percent, as gay or lesbian; 7 percent, as bisexual.
- Most (64 percent) were either married (47 percent) or in committed relationships (17 percent).
- Most (59 percent) were managers or professionals; 27 percent were in sales or clerical work or in the trades; 13 percent were students; 2 percent were unemployed.

Cybersex, a subcategory of online sexual activity, involves the use of computerized content for sexual stimulation and gratification (Maheu & Subotnik, 2001). People look at erotic pictures, engage in sexual chat, exchange sexually explicit e-mail messages, and share mutual sexual fantasies while masturbating. In a large online survey, 39 percent of the respondents said that they had engaged in cybersex, although fewer than 3 percent engaged in it "often" or "all the time" (Cooper et al., 2002). Interestingly, 60 percent of people in this survey did not believe that cybersex violated a person's marriage vows. However, spouses of individuals who are involved in Internet sexual affairs say that online affairs are as emotionally painful as those offline (Schneider, 2003).

The large online survey also reported that 25 percent of respondents had had an in-person meeting for a date or sexual experience with someone whom they had met online (Cooper et al., 2002). (More women than men reported engaging in this behavior, since women are more likely to use the Internet to explore online sexual relationships.) Because people who make these arrangements are more likely to engage in risky sexual behavior, they expose themselves to potential sexual assault and contracting STDs (McFarlane, Bull, & Reitmeijer, 2000).

Actual *cybersex addiction* or *Internet sex addiction* is a specific form of Internet addiction (see Chapter 4). People with this problem engage in online sex so often that it interferes with their personal and work life, they are unable to refrain from the activity (except temporarily), and they deny its negative effects on their lives. Most professionals view cybersex addiction as a type of compulsion (see Chapter 15). This behavior can have serious consequences for addicted individuals and their families (Cooper, 2002). Internet sex addicts may neglect their spouses and children, sow feelings of betrayal in their mates, and break up their marriages (Schneider, 2003). They can also lose their jobs if they neglect their work or are discovered engaging in cybersex at the office. (About 20 percent who engage in online sex use an office computer for this activity, risky behavior in that many organizations now monitor the online activities of their employees.)

Because Internet sexuality is a relatively new phenomenon, mental health professionals are still developing their views about it (Cooper et al., 1999). Some see it as just another form of sexual expression. Others are alarmed that Internet sex addiction is a growing problem. To date, research supports both of these perspectives (Cooper et al., 1999; 2002). Online sex does seem to be a form of sexual expression for light users (less than 1 hour per week) and moderate users (1 to 10 hours per week). They typically use sexual material on the Internet for entertainment more than for sexual release—akin to reading *Playboy* or viewing TV programs with lots of "skin." These individuals make up about 92 percent of all Internet sex users. Unfortunately it is quite a different story for high users (11 to 80 hours per week), who make up 8 percent of all those involved in online sexual activity. These people report significantly more psychological distress and score higher on measures of compulsivity and sensation seeking (see Chapter 2 Application). They are at high risk for developing psychological problems. Research needs to substantiate these findings and to determine which activities increase risk for heavy users.

The Internet can obviously have a positive influence on sex. Among other things, it is an excellent source of helpful information. And gay, lesbian, and bisexual individuals can use it to locate virtual support communities. On the other hand, the anonymity, affordability, and accessibility of the Internet lead some individuals to become hooked on cybersex, resulting in serious negative consequences (Cooper & Sportolari, 1997). We look to researchers and mental health professionals for much-needed insights into this emerging and significant area of sexuality.

Because of gender differences in sexual socialization, females tend to begin seeing themselves as sexual persons at a later age than males.

until women actually begin having sexual experiences that they start to see themselves as sexual persons.

Sexual socialization usually takes longer for females than for males because women usually have more emotional baggage connected with sex than men do. One factor is the *fear of pregnancy.* Concerns about becoming pregnant inhibit a woman's enthusiasm for sex. Second, girls hear *negative messages about sex and men* ("Men only want one thing") from their mothers, siblings, and female peers. They are also aware of rape and incest. Third, women typically develop *negative associations about their genitals and sex* that males don't experience: blood and pain associated with menstruation and fears of penetration. A fourth factor is *sexual guilt.* Whereas social norms encourage males to be sexually active, these norms discourage such behavior in females—sexually active women may be looked on as "loose." All these negative associations with sex are combined with the positive rewards of dating and emotional intimacy. Hence, it's no surprise that many women feel ambivalent about sex (Hyde, 2004). These feelings can tilt in the negative direction if early sexual partners are unskilled, impatient, or selfish.

With differing views of sexuality and relationships, males and females can be out of sync with each other—particularly in adolescence and early adulthood. In adulthood, women become more comfortable with themselves as sexual persons, while males become more comfortable with emotional intimacy and commitment. These gender differences mean that communication is essential for mutually satisfying sexual relationships.

Because both members of *same-gender couples* have been socialized similarly, they are less likely than straight couples to have compatibility problems. Like heterosexual women, lesbians typically experience emotional attraction to their partners before experiencing sexual feelings (Peplau & Spaulding, 2003). By contrast, gay men (like heterosexual men) tend to

place much more importance on physical appearance and sexual compatibility in selecting partners (Blumstein & Schwartz, 1983) and to develop emotional relationships out of sexual ones (Harry, 1983).

Sexual Orientation

Gay, straight, or in between? In this section, we'll explore the intriguing and controversial topic of sexual orientation.

Key Considerations

Most people view heterosexuality and homosexuality as two distinct categories: you're either one or the other. However, many individuals who define themselves as heterosexuals have had homosexual experiences, and vice versa (Kinsey, 1948, 1953; Laumann et al., 1994). Thus, it is more accurate to view heterosexuality and homosexuality as end points on a continuum. Indeed, Alfred Kinsey devised a seven-point scale, shown in Figure 13.3 on the next page, to characterize sexual orientation.

Alfred Kinsey

How are people distributed on this scale? No one knows for sure, because it's hard to get accurate data. Furthermore, there's some debate about where to draw the lines between heterosexuality, bisexuality, and homosexuality on the Kinsey scale. A frequently cited estimate of the number of people who are predominantly homosexual is 10 percent; however, several recent surveys have all reported lower estimates (ACFS Investigators, 1992; Johnson et al., 1992; Laumann et al., 1994). The overall evidence suggests that about 5 percent–8 percent of the population could reasonably be characterized as homosexual (Michaels, 1996; see Chapter 9).

Now let's complicate things a little more. Using Kinsey's model, how would you characterize a person who was married for 10 years, has children, got a divorce, and is now involved in a committed homosexual relationship? And what about a person who is married but who has homosexual fantasies and feels strongly drawn to members of the same gender? Clearly, these complex situations require more elaborate models. One such model portrays sexual orientation as a cluster of seven factors that can be rated along Kinsey's seven-point scale: sexual behavior; emotional preference; sexual fantasies; sexual attraction; social preference; lifestyle, social world, and community; and self-identification (Klein, Sepekoff, & Wolff, 1986). In this view, individuals' ratings on the seven factors may or may not be congruent, and ratings may change over time to match shifts in people's understanding of their

0	1	2	3	4	5	6
Exclusively heterosexual behavior	Incidental homosexual behavior	More than incidental homosexual behavior	Equal amount of heterosexual and homosexual behavior	More than incidental heterosexual behavior	Incidental heterosexual behavior	Exclusively homosexual behavior

Ambisexual behavior

● FIGURE 13.3

Heterosexuality and homosexuality as end points on a continuum. Kinsey and other sex researchers view heterosexuality and homosexuality as ends of a continuum rather than as all-or-none distinctions. Kinsey created this seven-point scale (from 0 to 6) for describing sexual orientation. He used the term *ambisexual* to describe those falling in the middle of the scale, but *bisexual* is more widely used today.

sexual orientation. It's obvious that sexual orientation is a complex concept we need to know a lot more about.

Origins

Why do some people become straight and others, gay? A number of *environmental explanations* have been suggested as causes of homosexuality. Freud believed that homosexuality originates from an unresolved Oedipus complex (see Chapter 2). That is, instead of coming to identify with the parent of the same gender, the child continues to identify with the parent of the other gender. Learning theorists assert that homosexuality results from early negative heterosexual encounters or early positive homosexual experiences. Sociologists propose that homosexuality develops because of poor relationships with same-gender peers or because being labeled a homosexual sets up a self-fulfilling prophecy. Surprisingly, a comprehensive review of the causes of sexual orientation found no compelling support for *any* of these explanations of homosexuality (Bell, Weinberg, & Hammersmith, 1981).

Similarly, there is no evidence that parents' sexual orientation is linked to that of their children (Patterson, 2003). That is, heterosexual parents are as likely to produce homosexual (or heterosexual) offspring as homosexual parents are. Children who grow up in gay or lesbian families are predominantly heterosexual.

Researchers have found that extremely feminine behavior in young boys and masculine behavior in young girls is correlated with subsequent homosexuality (Bailey, 2003; Bem, 2000). Consistent with this finding, many gay men and some gay women report that they can trace their homosexual leanings back to their early childhood (Bailey, 2003). The evidence for this connection in lesbians is less strong than it is in males, supporting the emerging view that female sexuality is more fluid than that of males (Baumeister, 2000; Peplau & Garnets, 2000).

Some theorists speculate that *biological factors* are involved in the development of homosexuality, because many gay men and some lesbians can trace their homosexual leanings back to their childhood years (Bell, Weinberg, & Hammersmith, 1981; Garnets & Kimmel, 1991). Several lines of research suggest that hormonal secretions during prenatal development may shape sexual development, organize the brain in a lasting manner, and influence subsequent sexual orientation (Berenbaum & Snyder, 1995; Ellis & Ebertz, 1997). To date, however, the research is inconclusive, so this theory must be viewed with caution. Other researchers have explored the relationship between circulating hormone levels in adults and sexual orientation, but there is no convincing evidence of an association (Bailey, 2003; Banks & Gartrell, 1995).

Genetic factors are also of interest. In an important study, investigators identified gay and bisexual men who had a twin brother or an adopted brother (Bailey & Pillard, 1991). They found that 52 percent of the subjects' identical twins were gay, that 22 percent of their fraternal twins were gay, and that 11 percent of their adoptive brothers were gay. A companion study of lesbian women with twin or adopted sisters reported a similar pattern of results (Bailey et al., 1993; see Figure 13.4). More recent twin studies, with larger and more representative samples, have provided further support for the conclusion that heredity influences sexual orientation, although these studies have yielded smaller estimates of genetic influence (Bailey, Dunne, & Martin, 2000; Kendler et al., 2000). Thus, there may be genetic links to homosexuality.

The bottom line is that it isn't yet clear what determines sexual orientation. Moreover, it appears that different paradigms are needed to explain male and female homosexuality (Peplau & Garnets, 2000). It is likely that there are a variety of types of homosexuality—and heterosexuality—that will require a variety

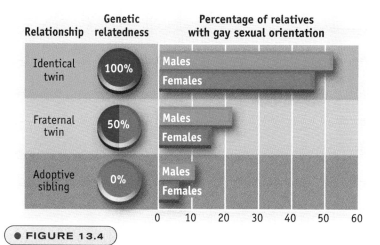

Relationship	Genetic relatedness	Percentage of relatives with gay sexual orientation
Identical twin	100%	Males / Females
Fraternal twin	50%	Males / Females
Adoptive sibling	0%	Males / Females

0   10   20   30   40   50   60

● FIGURE 13.4

Genetics and sexual orientation. A concordance rate indicates the percentage of twin pairs or other pairs of relatives that exhibit the same characteristic. If relatives who share more genetic relatedness show higher concordance rates than relatives who share less genetic overlap, this evidence suggests a genetic predisposition to the characteristic. Recent studies of both gay men and lesbian women have found higher concordance rates among identical twins than fraternal twins, who, in turn, exhibit more concordance than adoptive siblings. These findings are consistent with the hypothesis that genetic factors influence sexual orientation. If only genetic factors were responsible for sexual orientation, the identical twin concordance rates would be 100 percent; because they are much lower, environmental factors must also play a role. (Data from Bailey & Pillard, 1991; Bailey et. al., 1993)

of explanations rather than a single account (Hyde & DeLamater, 2003). This issue is exceedingly complex and research is still in its infancy. The best we can say is that the explanations must lie in some complex interaction of biological and environmental factors.

Attitudes Toward Homosexuality

The legalization of same-gender marriage in parts of the United States in 2004 set off a contentious public debate. Fueling the controversy, constitutional amendments banning gay marriage were introduced in the U.S. Congress and in many state legislatures. At the end of 2004, 15 states had approved constitutional amendments barring gay marriage, and many others had legislative bans on marriage rights for gays (Sullivan, 2004). Nonetheless, civil unions are legal in California, Hawaii, and Vermont, and "domestic partnerships" are legal in Maine and New Jersey (Larson, 2004).

Although the public discussion over gay marriage is difficult, some believe that it has value (Garnets & Kimmel, 2003a). First, it has allowed the gay community to educate straight citizens about the realities and diversity of same-gender couples and their family relationships. Second, it has helped to raise the nation's awareness about the facets of discrimination against gays. Although many Americans are opposed to gay marriage, they are much more accepting of other issues related to homosexuality (see Figure 13.5 on the next

page). Greater acceptance is due, in part, to the increasing visibility of lesbians and gays in society, including likable gay characters (*Will and Grace*) and individuals (*Queer Eye for the Straight Guy*) on television.

Homophobia **is the intense fear and intolerance of homosexuals.** Because few people with negative attitudes toward homosexuals have the psychopathology that "phobia" implies, some psychologists believe that *sexual prejudice* is a more appropriate term (Herek, 2003). The lowest levels of sexual prejudice are associated with individuals who personally know someone who is gay (Herek & Capitanio, 1996). Higher levels of sexual prejudice are associated with being older, male, less educated, and living in the South or Midwest and in rural areas (Herek & Capitanio, 1996). Sexual prejudice is also correlated with such psychological factors as authoritarianism (see Chapter 6) and conservative religious and political beliefs (Altemeyer, 1996; Herek & Capitanio, 1996). Un-

TV personality Rosie O'Donnell and partner Kelli Carpenter were among many gay and lesbian couples who married when San Francisco permitted gay marriages in 2004. (As of April 2005, the legal status of gay marriages in California was not yet resolved.)

© Justin Sullivan/Getty Images

Attitudes Toward Homosexuals	
Poll Question*	**Percent endorsing**
1. Homosexuals should have equal rights in terms of job opportunities.	89
2. Gay partners should have the same inheritance rights as married couples.	60
3. Gay partners should have the same health insurance and other employee benefits as married couples.	60
4. Gay partners should have the same social security benefits as married couples.	55
5. Gay and lesbian partners should have the same adoption rights as married couples.	45
6. Which of the following do you support for gay couples?	
a. Marriage rights	28
b. Civil unions	23
c. No legal recognition	43
d. Don't know	6

*Item 1 is based on a May 2–4, 2004 Gallup survey. Items 2–5 are based on a February 5–6, 2004 *Newsweek* survey. Item 6 is based on a May 13–14, 2004 *Newsweek* survey. All surveys are based on randomly selected national samples.

● **FIGURE 13.5**

Attitudes toward homosexuals. Americans' attitudes toward gays are highly variable, depending on the specific issue. Women generally have more accepting attitudes than men.

fortunately, negative attitudes sometimes translate into hate crimes. Approximately 25 percent of gay men and 20 percent of lesbians have been victims of hate crimes, and this estimate is likely low (Herek, Gillis, & Cogan, 1999).

Popular television programs like Queer Eye for the Straight Guy *have contributed to the increased acceptance of gays and lesbians.*

Not all societies view homosexuality negatively. A review of anthropological studies of 294 societies reported that 59 societies had a clear opinion of homosexuality; within this group, 69 percent approved of it and 31 percent condemned it (Gregerson, 1982).

Sexual Identity Development

Developing one's sexual identity is complicated and difficult when it must take place in a climate of sexual prejudice. In discussing that process, we draw heavily on the work of psychologists Linda Garnets and Douglas Kimmel (1991, 2003b). For gays, lesbians, and bisexuals, sexual identity development involves acknowledging, recognizing, and labeling one's sexual orientation; conceptualizing it in positive terms; and disclosing it to others. Gay people of color may need to create a dual identity that integrates their sexual orientation and their culture; gay women of color may need to create a triple identity.

Linda Garnets

In deciding to disclose one's sexual orientation to others, people must balance the psychological and social benefits against the costs (being fired, losing friends, losing custody of children, falling victim to hate crimes). A pragmatic solution to this conflict is *rational outness*—being "as open as possible, because it feels healthy to be honest, and as closed as necessary to protect against discrimination" (Bradford & Ryan, 1987, p. 77). People are more likely to disclose their sex-

Douglas C. Kimmel

ual orientation to close heterosexual friends and siblings than to parents, co-workers, or employers.

Coming to terms with one's homosexuality in a hostile environment is difficult. Some parents throw their gay children out of the house, and some teachers and peers harass and assault gay and lesbian youth. A survey of 165 15- to 21-year-old gay and bisexual youth reported that over half feared disclosing their sexual orientation to their parents (D'Augelli & Hershberger, 1993). This same study reported that, among parents who knew about their children's homosexuality, 12 percent of mothers were perceived by their children to be rejecting and 8 percent to be intolerant but not rejecting; comparable figures for fathers were 18 percent and 10 percent, respectively. At least half of gay and lesbian teenagers reported that they had lost at least one friend because of their sexual orientation (Ryan & Futterman, 1997). High schools and colleges increasingly support groups for gay, lesbian, and bisexual students. And the Internet offers a wealth of resources for gay, lesbian, and bisexual people (see Web Link 13.2). These developments should relieve some of the stress that homosexuals experience (see the Recommended Reading box).

Adjustment

The mental health community initially classified homosexuality as a psychological disorder. The pioneering research of Evelyn Hooker (1957) and others, however, demonstrated that view to be a myth: Gays and straights do not differ on overall measures of psychological adjustment (Bell & Weinberg, 1978; Rosen, 1974). As a result of research, changes in public attitudes, and political lobbying, homosexuality was deleted from the official list of psychological disorders in 1973. Since then, research continues to demonstrate comparable psychological adjustment in gay and straight individuals, couples, and parents (Gonsiorek, 1991; Patterson & Redding, 1996; Peplau & Spaulding, 2003). Similarly, there is no evidence of psychopathology in nonclinical samples of bisexual men and women (Fox, 1996).

Although there is no reliable evidence that homosexual orientation per se impairs psychological functioning, exposure to sexual prejudice and discrimination can cause acute distress (Meyer, 2003). Some recent studies suggest that gay males and lesbians are at

RECOMMENDED READING

Loving Someone Gay
by Don Clark (Celestial Arts, 1997)

Now in its 20th anniversary edition, this book speaks both to those who are gay and to those who know someone gay. The author, a clinical psychologist who is gay, writes in a personal and informal style that draws the reader in. He also easily weaves in real-life examples to illustrate his points. The first two sections address questions of special interest to homosexuals. For example, Clark discusses the impact of invisibility and oppression on one's self-concept, as well as the rewards of being gay. Other topics include coming out, meeting other gay people, the emotional and sexual aspects of relationships, and dealing with break-ups. The third section, "Loving Someone Gay," contains advice for people who know someone gay: parents, wives, husbands, sons, daughters, other relatives, friends, and neighbors. In "Professional Help," the fourth section, Clark provides suggestions for those who interact, often unknowingly, with gays (teachers, librarians, physicians, nurses, clergy, counselors, police, judges, legislators, and researchers).

Another excellent book in this area is *Positively Gay: New Approaches to Gay and Lesbian Life* edited by Betty Berzon (Celestial Arts, 2001). In this book, experts explore a variety of topics of interest to gay individuals: special issues in same-gender relationships, family relationships, children, aging, religion, work, and people of color. For a book that deals specifically with gays and their parents, try *Coming Out to Parents: A Two-Way Survival Guide for Lesbians and Gay Men and Their Parents* by Mary Borhek (Pilgrim Press, 1993).

Cover image reprinted by permission of the publisher.

greater risk than their straight peers for anxiety, depression, substance dependence, and suicide attempts (Cochran, 2001; DeAngelis, 2002).

According to the 2000 U.S. Census, 33 percent of female same-gender couples and 22 percent of male same-gender couples are rearing children. The children of some couples are their own from previous heterosexual relationships or artificial insemination; other children have been adopted. Studies to date indicate that children of gay or lesbian parents are no different than children of heterosexual parents in terms of self-esteem, gender roles, sexual orientation, peer group relationships, or social adjustment (Golombok et al., 2003; Patterson, 2003).

WEB LINK 13.2

American Psychological Association's Public Affairs Site
APA's Office of Public Affairs website offers information and resources on important contemporary psychological issues. The site provides answers to common questions about sexual orientation and homosexuality as well as links to additional web resources.

Interaction in Sexual Relationships

LEARNING OBJECTIVES

- *List some common sexual motives.*
- *Describe four common barriers in communicating about sex.*

Sexual relationships stir up intense emotions. When things are going well, you feel on top of the world; when they're not, you feel in the grip of despair. In this section, we'll briefly discuss the interpersonal dynamics of sexual relationships.

Motives for Engaging in Sex

What motivates individuals to engage in sexual encounters? As you might surmise, sexual motives are quite diverse. Hill (1997) has described eight distinct sexual motives: (1) feeling valued by one's partner, (2) showing value for one's partner, (3) obtaining relief from stress, (4) providing nurturance to one's partner, (5) enhancing feelings of personal power, (6) experiencing the power of one's partner, (7) experiencing pleasure, and (8) procreating. Individuals differ in the strength of these motives (Hill & Preston, 1996). Obviously, motives for sexual encounters vary depending on the circumstances.

On a related issue—the relationship between sex and love—men and women often have somewhat different views. Women are more likely than men to associate sex with love and to "romanticize" sexual desire (Peplau, 2003). These gender differences transcend sexual orientation, as they are observed in gays as well as straights (Peplau, Fingerhut, & Beals 2004).

Some experts speculate that these differences stem from gender-role socialization (Carroll, Volk, & Hyde, 1985). Still other researchers believe that these gender differences are a product of biological influences (Buss, 1999). It is possible that both influences play a role.

Communicating About Sex

Because individuals differ in sexual motives, attitudes, and appetites, disagreements about sex are commonplace (Laumann et al., 1994). Couples have to negotiate whether, how often, and when they will have sex. They also have to decide what kinds of erotic activities will take place and what sexual behavior means to their relationship. This negotiation process may not be explicit, but it's there. Unresolved disparities can be an ongoing source of frustration in a relationship. Still, many people find it difficult to talk with their partner about sex. Couples can encounter four common barriers to sexual communication:

1. *Fear of appearing ignorant.* According to a Kinsey Institute/Roper poll, most Americans are woefully ignorant about sex. That is, on an 18-item test of basic sexual knowledge, 55 percent of adults responded incorrectly to at least half of the questions (Reinisch, 1990). (You can test your own knowledge about some aspects of sex by responding to the questions in Figure 13.6.) Because most people feel that they should be experts about sex and know that they are not, they feel ashamed. To hide their ignorance, they avoid talking about sex.

2. *Concern about partner's response.* Both men and women say they want their partners to tell them what they want sexually (see Figure 13.7). Ironically, neither

---

How Knowledgeable About Sex Are You?

1. Massage oil, petroleum jelly, and body lotions are good lubricants to use with a condom or diaphragm.
   ____ True ____ False ____ Don't know

2. Adult male homosexuals have lower than normal levels of male hormones.
   ____ True ____ False ____ Don't know

3. A teenage girl or woman can get pregnant during her menstrual period.
   ____ True ____ False ____ Don't know

4. Most cases of sexually transmitted diseases occur in people aged 26-50.
   ____ True ____ False ____ Don't know

5. In the United States, heterosexually-transmitted HIV infections rarely occur.
   ____ True ____ False ____ Don't know

Scoring: 1. False. (Oil-based creams, lotions, and jellies can produce microscopic holes in rubber products within 60 seconds of their application.) 2. False. (Research does not support this view.) 3. True. (While the chance of a woman's becoming pregnant during her menstrual period is lower than at other times, pregnancy can occur if she has unprotected sex during her period. Sperm can live for up to 8 days in a woman's reproductive tract, and if the menstrual cycle is irregular, as it is likely to be in adolescence, sperm may still be present in the reproductive tract a week later to fertilize a new egg.) 4. False. (Most cases of sexually transmitted diseases occur in the under-25 age group.) 5. False. (There is currently an upsurge in heterosexually-transmitted HIV infections in the U.S.)

● **FIGURE 13.6**

How knowledgeable about sex are you? Check your basic sexual knowledge by answering these five questions. Information about each of the questions is discussed in this chapter.

feels comfortable doing so (Hatfield & Rapson, 1996). People usually hold back because they're afraid of hurting the other's feelings. Or they fear that their partner won't respect and love them if they are truthful. Research shows that more extensive disclosure of sexual likes and dislikes positively predicts sexual and relationship satisfaction in committed relationships (Sprecher & Cate, 2004). Thus, if you keep your preferences to yourself, you are likely to remain frustrated and unsatisfied.

3. *Conflicting attitudes about sex.* Many people, particularly women, are burdened with the negative sexual messages they learned as children. Also, most individuals have contradictory beliefs about sex ("Sex is 'beautiful'" and "Sex is 'dirty'"), and this dissonance produces psychological conflicts. It may also cause individuals to feel uncomfortable with themselves as sexual persons and to have difficulty talking about sex.

4. *Early negative sexual experiences.* Some people have had negative sexual experiences that inhibit their enjoyment of sex. If these experiences are due to ignorant or inconsiderate sexual partners, subsequent positive sexual interactions will usually resolve the problem over time. If earlier sexual experiences have been traumatic, as in the case of rape or incest, counseling may be required to help the individual view sex positively and enjoy it.

To communicate more easily and effectively about sex, you may want to review Chapter 7. Most of the advice on how to improve verbal and nonverbal communication can be applied to sexual relationships. Assertive communication and constructive conflict-resolution strategies can keep sexual negotiations healthy. A basic rule is to accentuate the positive ("I like it when you ...") rather than the negative ("I don't like it when you ...").

What Men and Women Want More of During Sex

Dating couples	
Men	**Women**
Wish their partners would:	
Be more experimental	Talk more lovingly
Initiate sex more often	Be more seductive
Try more oral-genital sex	Be warmer and more involved
Give more instructions	Give more instructions
Be warmer and more involved	Be more complimentary

Married couples	
Men	**Women**
Wish their partners would:	
Be more seductive	Talk more lovingly
Initiate sex more	Be more seductive
Be more experimental	Be more complimentary
Be wilder and sexier	Be more experimental
Give more instructions	Give more instructions
	Be warmer and more involved

● **FIGURE 13.7**

What men and women want more of during sex. Dating and married couples were asked which sexual activities they wanted more of in their relationships. Men and women all agreed that they wanted more instructions from their partners. They also generally agreed that they wanted warmer, more involved sexual relationships and more experimentation. In terms of gender differences, men wanted their partners to take the initiative and to be wilder and sexier; women wanted more emotional reassurance.

From Hatfield, E., & Rapson, R. L. (1997). *Love, sex, and intimacy: Their psychology, biology, and history.* Boston: Allyn & Bacon. Copyright © 1997 by Pearson Education. Reprinted by permission of the publisher.

The Human Sexual Response

LEARNING OBJECTIVES

- *Describe the four phases of the human sexual response cycle*
- *Discuss gender differences in patterns of orgasm and some reasons for them.*

When people engage in sexual activity, exactly how does the body respond? Surprisingly, until William Masters and Virginia Johnson conducted their groundbreaking research in the 1960s, little was known about the physiology of the human sexual response. Masters and Johnson used physiological recording devices to monitor the bodily changes of volunteers engaging in sex. Their observations and interviews with their subjects yielded a detailed description of the human sexual response that won them widespread acclaim.

Nonetheless, critics note that the model focuses entirely on genital changes during sex and ignores cognitive factors. Other models include these subjective factors. For example, the three-stage model of noted sex therapist Helen Singer Kaplan (1979) begins with desire, followed by excitement and orgasm. Since people's thoughts and views about sex underlie many sexual problems, a cognitive approach is helpful. Because of the historical importance of Masters and Johnson's model, we describe it here. But you should be mindful of cognitive factors as you read about it.

The Sexual Response Cycle

Masters and Johnson's (1966, 1970) description of the sexual response cycle is a general one, outlining typical rather than inevitable patterns—people vary considerably. Figure 13.8 shows how the intensity of sexual arousal changes as women and men progress through the four phases of the sexual response cycle.

Excitement Phase

During the initial phase of excitement, the level of arousal usually escalates rapidly. In both sexes, muscle tension, respiration rate, heart rate, and blood pressure increase quickly. In males *vasocongestion*—**engorgement of blood vessels**—produces penile erec-

tion, swollen testes, and the movement of the scrotum (the sac containing the testes) closer to the body. In females, vasocongestion leads to a swelling of the clitoris and vaginal lips, vaginal lubrication, and enlargement of the uterus. Most women also experience nipple erection and a swelling of the breasts.

Plateau Phase

The name given to the "plateau" stage is misleading because physiological arousal does not level off. Instead, it continues to build, but at a much slower pace. In women, further vasocongestion produces a tightening of the lower third of the vagina and a "ballooning" of the upper two-thirds, which lifts the uterus and cervix away from the end of the vagina. In men, the head of the penis may swell, and the testicles typically enlarge and move closer to the body. Many men secrete a bit of pre-ejaculatory fluid from the tip of the penis that may contain sperm.

Distractions during the plateau phase can delay or stop movement to the next stage. These include ill-

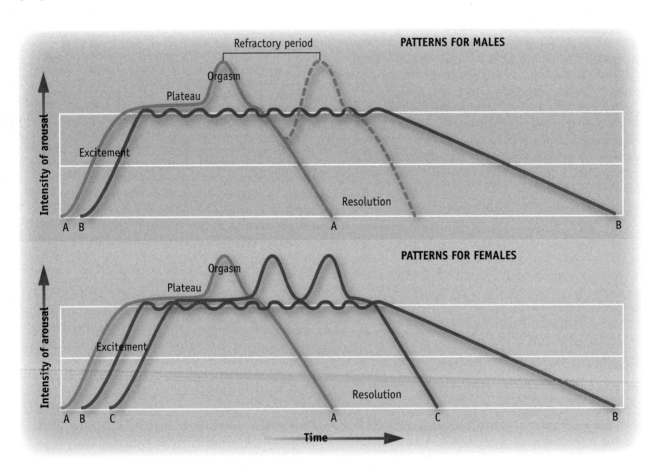

● FIGURE 13.8

The human sexual response cycle. There are similarities and differences between men and women in patterns of sexual arousal. Pattern A, which culminates in orgasm and resolution, is the most typical sequence for both sexes. Pattern B, which involves sexual arousal without orgasm followed by a slow resolution, is also seen in both genders, but it is more common among women. Pattern C, which involves multiple orgasms, is seen almost exclusively in women, as men go through a refractory period before they are capable of another orgasm. (Based on Masters & Johnson, 1966)

timed interruptions like a telephone or doorbell ringing, or a child's knocking—or not!—on the bedroom door. Equally distracting can be such things as physical discomfort, pain, guilt, frightening thoughts, feelings of insecurity or anger toward one's partner, and anxiety about not having an orgasm.

Orgasm Phase

Orgasm **occurs when sexual arousal reaches its peak intensity and is discharged in a series of muscular contractions that pulsate through the pelvic area.** Heart rate, respiration rate, and blood pressure increase sharply during this exceedingly pleasant spasmodic response. The male orgasm is usually accompanied by ejaculation of seminal fluid. Some women report that they ejaculate some kind of fluid at orgasm. How common this is and the source and nature of the fluid are matters still under debate (Darling, Davidson, & Conway-Welch, 1990). The subjective experience of orgasm appears to be essentially the same for men and women.

Resolution Phase

During the resolution phase, the physiological changes produced by sexual arousal subside. If one has not had an orgasm, the reduction in sexual tension may be relatively slow and sometimes unpleasant. After orgasm, men generally experience a *refractory period,* **a time following male orgasm during which males are largely unresponsive to further stimulation.** The refractory period varies from a few minutes to a few hours and increases with age.

Gender Differences in Patterns of Orgasm

As a whole, the sexual responses of women and men parallel each other fairly closely. The similarities clearly outweigh the differences. Nonetheless, there are some interesting differences between the genders in their patterns of experiencing orgasm. During *intercourse,* women are less likely than men to reach orgasm (that is, they are more likely to follow pattern B in Figure 13.8). According to one survey of American sexual behavior (Laumann et al., 1994), about 29 percent of women reported that they always reached orgasm in their primary

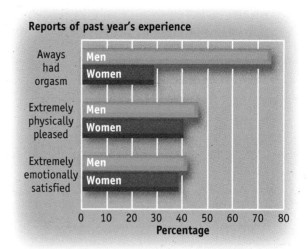

Reports of past year's experience

● FIGURE 13.9

Sexual satisfaction with primary partner. A major survey of American sexual behavior showed large gender differences in the consistency of orgasm, a physical measure of sexual satisfaction. Men's and women's subjective evaluations of physical and emotional sexual satisfaction are much more similar. These data indicate that not everyone who has an orgasm every time has a blissful sex life and that factors other than orgasm contribute to a satisfying sex life.

From Laumann, E. O., Gagnon, J. H., Michael, R. T., & Michaels, S. (1994). *The social organization of sexuality: Sexual practices in the United States.* Chicago: University of Chicago Press. Copyright © 1994 by University of Chicago Press. Reprinted by permission.

sexual relationships, compared to 75 percent of men (see Figure 13.9). Apparently, about 10 percent of American women have never had an orgasm by any means (Spector & Carey, 1990).

In their laboratory, Masters and Johnson found that the men they studied took about 4 minutes to reach a climax with their partners. Women took about 10–20 minutes to reach orgasm with their partners, but they reached orgasm in about 4 minutes when they masturbated. Clearly, then, women are capable of reaching orgasm more quickly than they typically do. Our point here is not that men and women should race each other to the finish line but that physiological factors are not the likely cause of gender differences related to orgasm.

How do we account for these disparities? First, although most women report that they enjoy intercourse, it is not the optimal mode of stimulation for them. This is because intercourse provides rather indirect stimulation to the clitoris, the most sexually sensitive genital area in most women. Thus, more lengthy *foreplay,* including manual or oral stimulation of the clitoris, is usually the key to enhancing women's sexual pleasure. Many men mistakenly assume that women experience the same degree of pleasurable sensations that they do during sexual intercourse. But this is not the case, as the upper two-thirds of the vagina has relatively few nerve endings—a good thing, since the vagina serves as the birth canal! Manual or oral stimulation of the

WEB LINK 13.3

Kaiser Family Foundation
This foundation sponsors multiple programs and educational efforts in the United States and South Africa to promote health generally, and its site provides a large set of resources regarding human sexuality, one major focus of its educational efforts.

clitoris is more effective in producing female orgasm than sexual intercourse alone (Bancroft, 2002b). Unfortunately, many couples are locked into the idea that orgasms should be achieved only through intercourse. (Even the word *foreplay* suggests that any other form of sexual stimulation is merely preparation for the "main event.") Also, most women associate sex with affection, so they want to hear some tender words during a sexual encounter. Men who verbally express their love and affection usually find their partners more responsive.

Research suggests that lesbians have orgasms more often and more easily in sexual interactions than heterosexual women do (Peplau et al., 2004). Kinsey (1953) attributed this difference to female partners' knowing more about women's sexuality and how to optimize women's sexual satisfaction than male part-

ners do. Also, female partners are more likely to emphasize the emotional aspects of lovemaking than male partners (Peplau et al., 2004). Taken together, these facts support a socialization-based explanation of gender differences in orgasmic consistency.

Because women reach orgasm through intercourse less consistently than men, they are more likely than men to fake an orgasm. Surveys reveal that more than half of all adult women (straight and lesbian) have faked an orgasm (Elliott & Brantley, 1997). Men (straight and gay) also fake them, but much less frequently. People typically do so to make their partner feel better or to bring sexual activity to an end when they're tired. Frequent faking is not a good idea, because it can become a vicious cycle and undermine communication about sex (Crooks & Bauer, 2005).

Sexual Expression

LEARNING OBJECTIVES

- Discuss fantasy as well as kissing and touching as aspects of sexual expression.
- Discuss the prevalence of self-stimulation and attitudes about it.

- Discuss oral and anal sex as forms of sexual expression.
- Discuss intercourse and the preferred sexual activities of gay males and lesbians.

People experience and express sexuality in myriad ways. ***Erogenous zones* are areas of the body that are sexually sensitive or responsive.** The genitals and breasts usually come to mind when people think of erogenous zones, as these areas are particularly sensitive for most people. But it's worth noting that many individuals fail to appreciate the potential that lies in other areas of the body. Virtually any area of the body can function as an erogenous zone.

Indeed, the ultimate erogenous zone may be the mind. That is, an individual's mental set is extremely important to sexual arousal. Skillful genital stimulation by a partner may have absolutely no impact if a person is not in the mood. Yet fantasy in the absence of any other stimulation can produce great arousal. In this section, we'll consider the most common forms of sexual expression.

Fantasy

Have you ever fantasized about having sex with someone other than your partner? If so, you've had one of the most commonly reported fantasies (see Figure 13.10). There's no need to feel guilty about this; more than 90 percent of men and women have fantasies during sexual activities with another person (Leitenberg & Henning, 1995). As you might expect, women's fan-

tasies tend to be more romantic, while men's tend to contain more explicit imagery. Most sex therapists view sexual fantasies as harmless ways to enhance sexual excitement and achieve orgasm.

As you can see in Figure 13.10, dominance and submission fantasies are not uncommon. Still, just because you fantasize about a particular encounter, such as forced sex, doesn't mean that you really want to have such an experience. Only one-tenth of 1 percent of women say that they enjoy forced sex, and only one-third of 1 percent of men say that they enjoy forcing a partner to have sex (Laumann et al., 1994).

Kissing and Touching

Most two-person sexual activities begin with kissing. Kissing usually starts at the lips but may be extended to almost any area of the partner's body. Mutual caressing is also an integral element of sexual stimulation for most couples. Like kissing, this tactile stimulation may be applied to any area of the body. Manual and oral stimulation of the other partner's genitals are related sexual practices.

Men often underestimate the importance of kissing and touching (including clitoral stimulation). It is not surprising, therefore, that heterosexual women commonly complain that their partners are in too much of

Fantasies During Intercourse

Theme	Subjects reporting fantasy (%)	
	Males	Females
A former lover	42.9	41.0
An imaginary lover	44.3	24.3
Oral-genital sex	61.2	51.4
Group sex	19.3	14.1
Being forced or overpowered into a sexual relationship	21.0	36.4
Others observing you engage in sexual intercourse	15.4	20.0
Others finding you sexually irresistible	55.2	52.8
Being rejected or sexually abused	10.5	13.2
Forcing others to have sexual relations with you	23.5	15.8
Others giving in to you after resisting you at first	36.8	24.3
Observing others engaging in sex	17.9	13.2
A member of the same sex	2.8	9.4
Animals	0.9	3.7

Note: For comparison, the responses of "frequently" and "sometimes" were combined for both males and females to obtain these percentages. The number of respondents answering for a specific fantasy ranged from 103 to 106 for males and from 105 to 107 for females.

● **FIGURE 13.10**

Common sexual fantasies. The percentage of men and women reporting various sexual fantasies during intercourse is shown here. Sue (1979) concluded that people fantasize about experiences they wouldn't seek out in real life.

Adapted from Sue, D. (1979). The erotic fantasies of college students during coitus. *Journal of Sex Research, 15*(4), 299–305. Copyright © 1979 for the Society for the Scientific Study of Sexuality. Reprinted by permission.

a hurry (King, 2005). Partners who seek to learn about each other's preferences and who try to accommodate each other are much more likely to have mutually satisfying sexual experiences than those who don't.

Self-Stimulation

Masturbation, or the stimulation of one's own genitals, has traditionally been condemned as immoral because it is nonreproductive. Disapproval and suppression of masturbation were truly intense in the 19th and early 20th centuries, when people believed that the practice was harmful to physical and mental health. Because the term *masturbation* has acquired negative connotations, many modern experts prefer to use *self-stimulation* or *autoeroticism*. Sometimes people, more often women, use vibrators or other "sex toys" for self-stimulation.

Kinsey discovered over four decades ago that most people masturbate with no ill effects. Sexologists now recognize that self-stimulation is normal and healthy. In fact, sex therapists often prescribe masturbation to treat both male and female sexual problems (see this Chapter's Application). Nonetheless, nearly half of those who engage in the practice feel guilty about it (Laumann et al., 1994).

Self-stimulation is common in our society: By adulthood, nine out of ten males and eight out of ten females report having masturbated at least once (Atwood & Gagnon, 1987). African American males masturbate less than Asian, white, and Hispanic men. Also, masturbation is less common among those with less education (Laumann et al., 1994).

Among married couples, 57 percent of husbands and 37 percent of wives report engaging in self-stimulation (Laumann et al., 1994). In fact, masturbation in marriage is often associated with a greater degree of marital and sexual satisfaction (Leitenberg, Detzer, & Srebnik, 1993). Still, couples usually don't talk about it, probably for fear that it will be viewed as a sign of sexual discontent.

Oral and Anal Sex

Oral sex refers to oral stimulation of the genitals. ***Cunnilingus*** **is oral stimulation of the female genitals;** ***fellatio*** **is oral stimulation of the penis.** Partners may stimulate each other simultaneously, or one partner may stimulate the other without immediate reciprocation. Oral-genital sex may be one of several activities in a sexual encounter, or it may be the main event. Oral sex is a major source of orgasms for many heterosexual couples, and it plays a central role in homosexual relationships. A positive aspect of oral sex is that it does not result in pregnancy. (This fact partly accounts for the finding that younger teens are more likely to engage in oral sex than sexual intercourse [Willetts, Sprecher, & Beck, 2004]. Among older teens, sexual intercourse is at least as common as oral sex.) However, some sexually transmitted diseases (human immunodeficiency virus or HIV, for example) can be contracted through mouth-genital stimulation, especially if there are small cracks in the mouth or if the mouth is exposed to semen (Guest, 2004).

Negative attitudes persist about oral sex, particularly among African Americans, Hispanics, religious conservatives, and those with less education (Laumann et al., 1994). About 80 percent of men and 70 percent of women (both gay and straight) report that they have either given or received oral sex at least once (Laumann et al., 1994). Oral sex is now a component in most couples' sexual relationships.

Anal intercourse involves insertion of the penis into a partner's anus and rectum. Legally, it is termed *sodomy* (and is still considered illegal in some states). About 25 percent of men and women report that they have practiced anal sex at least once (Laumann et al., 1994). Anal intercourse is more popular among homosexual male couples than among heterosexual couples. However, even among gay men it ranks behind oral sex and mutual masturbation in prevalence. Anal sex is risky as rectal tissues are easily torn, facilitating HIV transmission.

Intercourse

Vaginal intercourse, known more technically as *coitus,* **involves inserting the penis into the vagina and (typically) pelvic thrusting.** It is the most widely endorsed and widely practiced sexual act in our society. In the recent American sex survey, 95 percent of heterosexual respondents said that they had practiced vaginal sex the last time they had sex (Laumann et al., 1994). Inserting the penis generally requires adequate vaginal lubrication, or intercourse may be difficult and painful for the woman. This is another good reason for couples to spend plenty of time on mutual kissing and touching, since as we saw with Masters and Johnson's findings, sexual excitement causes vaginal lubrication in women. In the absence of adequate lubrication,

partners may choose to use artificial lubricants such as Astroglide or K-Y Warming Liquid.

Couples use a variety of positions in intercourse, and may use more than one position in a single encounter. The man-above, or "missionary," position is the most common, but the woman-above, side-by-side, and rear-entry positions are also popular. Each position has its advantages and disadvantages. Although people are fascinated by the relative merits of various positions, specific position may not be as important as the tempo, depth, and angle of movements in intercourse. As with other aspects of sexual relations, the crucial consideration is that partners talk to each other about their preferences.

What kinds of sexual activities do homosexuals prefer in the absence of coitus (which is, by definition, a heterosexual act)? As is true with heterosexual couples, the preliminary activities of gay and lesbian couples include kissing, hugging, and petting. Gay men also engage in fellatio, mutual masturbation, and anal intercourse, in that order (Lever, 1994). Lesbians engage in cunnilingus, mutual masturbation, and *tribadism,* in which one partner lies on top of the other and makes thrusting movements so that both receive genital stimulation at the same time. Contrary to stereotype, a dildo (an artificial penis) is rarely used by lesbian couples (Jay & Young, 1979).

Patterns of Sexual Behavior

LEARNING OBJECTIVES

- *Describe how the fear of contracting AIDS has influenced sexual attitudes and practices.*
- *Summarize attitudes toward and prevalence of early sexual experiences.*
- *Summarize the findings on sex patterns in dating couples and married couples.*
- *Compare and contrast sexual behavior in married couples versus committed homosexual couples.*
- *Summarize the evidence on infidelity in committed relationships.*

In this section we consider whether fears of contracting acquired immune deficiency syndrome (AIDS) have influenced sexual attitudes and behaviors, then see how age and type of relationship are related to sexual behavior, and consider the issue of infidelity.

Sex in the Age of AIDS

Over the past 30 years, American sexual attitudes and behaviors have become more liberal. Although the media have labeled these changes a "sexual revolution," it is probably more accurate to characterize them as an evolution in attitudes and behavior. This trend toward more permissive sexual behavior appears to have slowed during the 1990s (Christopher & Sprecher, 2000).

While heralded by some, the liberal trends have had several serious drawbacks. Two troublesome problems are teenage pregnancy and sexually transmitted diseases (Trussell, Brown, & Hogue, 2004). The spread of HIV infection that leads to AIDS was, and remains, a special concern. Has public awareness of AIDS put the brakes on the liberalizing trends?

For both pregnancy rates and sexually transmitted diseases, the news is mixed. Although the teenage birth rate declined 26 percent between 1991 and 2001, the rate remains one of the highest in the world (Trussell et al, 2004; U.S. Department of Health and Human Services, 2002). Regarding sexually transmitted diseases, rates of genital infections among adolescents remain at high levels. Twenty-five percent of all cases of sexually

transmitted diseases occur among teenagers (and two-thirds are among people under 25 years of age) (Trussell et al., 2004). The good news is that most young people are knowledgeable about HIV and AIDS. Also, between 1991 and 2001, the percentage of high school students who had ever had sexual intercourse decreased, the average number of sex partners decreased, and the incidence of condom use increased, as you can see in Figure 13.11. Unfortunately, these positive patterns do not hold for all teens. Thus, in the age of AIDS, there is both good and bad news about patterns of sexual behavior.

Early Sexual Experiences

By age 22, 90 percent of Americans have had sexual intercourse. With the average age for marriage being 27 for men and 25 for women, it is obvious that most people are not virgins when they enter committed relationships. Thus, the term *premarital sex* is losing relevance. Another problem with the term is that it doesn't apply to homosexuals, who aren't permitted to marry under

Sexual Risk Behavior in High School Students

Grade	Survey year	Ever had intercourse (%)	Four or more sexual partners in lifetime (%)	Condom use during last sexual intercourse (%)
9	1991	39	13	53
	2001	34	10	68
10	1991	48	15	46
	2001	41	13	60
11	1991	62	22	49
	2001	52	15	59
12	1991	67	25	41
	2001	61	22	49

Note: Percentages are rounded to the nearest whole number.

● **FIGURE 13.11**

Sexual risk behavior in high school students. In national surveys over a ten-year period, high school students reported on their sexual behavior: whether they had ever had sexual intercourse, the number of sex partners they had had, and whether they had used a condom during their last intercourse. Between 1991 and 2001, sexual risk behavior declined: Fewer students had sex, fewer had four or more sex partners, and more had used a condom during their last sexual encounter. Still, risky behavior increased as students progressed in school.

From Centers for Disease Control. (2002). Trends in sexual risk behaviors among high school students—United States, 1991–2001. *Morbidity and Mortality Weekly Report, 51*(38), 856–859. (Figure based on data in table on p. 858)

the law (except in Massachusetts as of 2004). Thus, we have chosen to characterize youthful sexual encounters as "early sexual experiences" instead of "premarital sex."

Attitudes

Compared to a generation ago, more people believe that sex before marriage is acceptable, especially if the two people are emotionally committed to each other. Nonetheless, a sexual double standard still exists. Both men and women are less approving of sexual activity for women than men, especially in the early stages of relationships (Willetts et al., 2004).

Prevalence

In Figure 13.11, you can see that 61 percent of high school seniors have had sexual intercourse (Centers for Disease Control, 2002a). This same survey reported that African American teenagers are likely to engage in sex earlier than their Hispanic or European American peers. Studies also find that African American teens from affluent families are less likely to engage in sex than their less affluent counterparts are (Leadbeater & Way, 1995; Murry, 1996). Thus these apparent ethnic differences are probably actually differences in socioeconomic status. Early sexual activity is also correlated with parents' lack of education, poor academic performance, and low educational expectations (Davis & Lay-Yee, 1999; Lammers et al., 2000). Interestingly, adult homosexuals report rates of *heterosexual* premarital intercourse that are nearly identical to those reported by heterosexuals (Saghir & Robbins, 1973). These findings support the view that adolescence is an important period for working out answers to questions about sexual orientation.

"Hooking up," a phenomenon that has arisen since the late 1990s, involves two strangers or briefly acquainted people having a single sexual encounter. Unlike a one-night-stand, hookups don't always involve intercourse (petting below the waist and oral sex are common). According to one study, 78 percent of college students have had at least one hookup (Paul, McManus, & Hayes, 2000). And 46 percent of men and 33 percent of women in this study had sexual intercourse when they hooked up. Casual sex is risky: People don't always practice safer sex, and the risk of contracting sexually transmitted diseases increases with multiple partners.

Sex in Committed Relationships

Sex is a key aspect of most committed, romantic relationships. In this section, we examine patterns of sexual activity in dating couples, married couples, and gay couples.

Sex Between Dating Partners

At some point, couples confront the question of whether or when they should have sex. Some worry that sex

Sexual encounters with casual acquaintances are common in today's society. Nonetheless, casual sex can be risky for a variety of reasons.

might adversely affect the relationship; others fear that not having sex will cause trouble. Is there evidence to support either view? As it turns out, sexual intimacy is a positive predictor of relationship stability (Sprecher & Cate, 2004). However, gender and sexual and relationship satisfaction are also part of this equation. For men, sexual (but not relationship) satisfaction is significantly correlated with relationship stability; for women, relationship (but not sexual) satisfaction is significantly associated with relationship stability (Sprecher, 2002).

Marital Sex

Couples' overall marital satisfaction is strongly related to their satisfaction with their sexual relationship (Sprecher & Cate, 2004). Of course, it is difficult to know whether good sex promotes good marriages or good marriages promote good sex. In all probability, it's a two-way street. Relationship satisfaction is also correlated with satisfaction in other areas of a relationship (fairness in distribution of household labor, for example) (Sprecher & Cate, 2004).

Married couples vary greatly in how often they have sex (see Figure 13.12). *On the average,* couples in their 20s and 30s engage in sex about two or three times a week. The frequency of sex among married couples tends to decrease as the years wear on (Sprecher & Cate, 2004). Biological changes play some role in this trend, but social factors seem more compelling. Most couples attribute this decline to increasing fatigue from work and childrearing and to growing familiarity with their sexual routine.

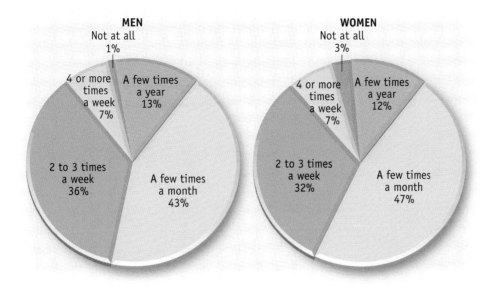

MEN

- Not at all 1%
- 4 or more times a week 7%
- A few times a year 13%
- 2 to 3 times a week 36%
- A few times a month 43%

WOMEN

- Not at all 3%
- 4 or more times a week 7%
- A few times a year 12%
- 2 to 3 times a week 32%
- A few times a month 47%

● **FIGURE 13.12**

Frequency of sex among married men and women. A well-sampled survey asked Americans, "How often have you had sex in the past 12 months?" Married individuals' responses to the question were wide ranging. The most frequent response was "a few times per month" followed by "2 to 3 times a week."

From Michael, R. T., Gagnon, J. H., Laumann, E. O., & Kolata, G. (1994) *Sex in America: A definitive survey.* Boston: Little, Brown. Copyright © 1994 by CSG Enterprises, Inc. Edward O. Lauman, Robert T. Michael, and Gina Kolata. By permission of Little, Brown and Company, Inc.

As men and women age, sexual arousal tends to build more slowly and orgasms tend to diminish in frequency and intensity. Males' refractory periods lengthen, and females' vaginal lubrication and elasticity decrease. Nevertheless, older people remain capable of rewarding sexual encounters (Burgess, 2004). A national survey of couples reported that those in the 75 and older age group had sex slightly less than once a month (Call, Sprecher, & Schwartz, 1995).

Sex in Homosexual Relationships

Regarding the relative frequency of sex among lesbian, gay, and heterosexual couples, Peplau and her colleagues (2004) report three patterns. First, there is a general decline in the frequency of sexual behavior over time. Second, in the early stages of a relationship, gay males engage in sex more frequently than the other couples. For example, among couples who had been together for 2 years or less, 67 percent of gay men reported having sex three or more times a week, compared to 45 percent of married couples and 33 percent of lesbian couples (Blumstein & Schwartz, 1983). Third, lesbian couples have sex less often than the other couples.

Like heterosexual women, most lesbians believe that sex and love are intertwined. In contrast (and like straight males), gay men find casual sex more acceptable (Sanders, 2000). Comparative studies find comparable levels of sexual satisfaction in gay, lesbian, and heterosexual couples (Peplau et al., 2004). And for both lesbians and gay men, sexual satisfaction is correlated with overall relationship satisfaction.

Infidelity in Committed Relationships

Sexual infidelity occurs when a person who is in a committed relationship engages in erotic activity with someone other than his or her partner. Among married couples, this behavior is also called "adultery" or "extramarital sex." Infidelity among couples in committed relationships (straight and gay) is termed "extradyadic sex." The vast majority of people (90 percent) in our society believe that extramarital sex is "always" or "almost always wrong" (Treas & Giesen, 2000). Nonetheless, Americans are fascinated by infidelity, if the popularity of the TV series *Desperate Housewives* is any gauge!

Although it's not common, extramarital sex can be consensual. Two examples include "swinging" and "open marriage." Swinging typically involves married couples exchanging partners for sex or both partners having sex with a third person (Atwood & Seifer, 1997). In "open marriage," both partners agree that it is okay for each to have sex with others (O'Neill & O'Neill, 1972). As we noted, gay male couples are more likely to have "open 'marriages'" than are lesbian or married couples.

The popularity of the TV series *Desperate Housewives* *suggests that Americans are fascinated by infidelity.*

What Constitutes Infidelity?

Does this constitute cheating in a marriage?	Answered "yes"	
	Married men	Married women
Kissing someone else	59%	75%
Having a sexually explicit conversation on the phone	64%	74%
Having a sexually explicit conversation on the Internet	62%	72%
Holding hands with someone else	40%	49%
Fantasizing about having sex with someone else	39%	43%
Casually flirting with someone else	32%	38%

● **FIGURE 13.13**

What constitutes infidelity? A 1998 *Time*/CNN poll asked 397 married men and 431 married women whether various actions constituted cheating in a marriage. Men's responses were more liberal than women's, especially regarding "kissing someone else."

From Handy, B. (1998, August 3). How we really feel about infidelity. *Time*, pp. 52–53. Copyright © 1998 by Time Inc. Reprinted by permission.

Precisely what kind of erotic activity qualifies as "cheating" is debatable, especially between men and women, as you can see in Figure 13.13. Are you unfaithful if you develop a deep emotional involvement without sex? No doubt many people would say "yes." The Internet has added confusion to an already complex issue. For example, is it "cheating" if a person in a committed relationship uses the Internet for sexual arousal or masturbation? What about exchanging sexually explicit e-mail with someone you've never met face to face? Therapists are seeing more couples for problems related to Internet-initiated affairs (Cooper & Griffin-Shelley, 2002).

Prevalence

Despite the fact that most people disapprove of infidelity, a number of people get involved in it. Because of the associated stigma and secrecy, accurate estimates of infidelity are difficult to come by. Several recent surveys on sex reported that about 25 percent of married men and about 10 percent of married women had engaged in an extramarital affair at least once (Laumann et al., 1994; Wiederman, 1997).

In straight cohabiting relationships, about a third of men and women have engaged in extradyadic sex (Blumstein & Schwartz, 1983). As we noted, sexual openness is the norm in committed gay male relationships, and the rates of extradyadic sex for this group are higher than for all other groups (Peplau et al., 2004). Committed lesbian relationships are much more exclusive, in principle and in practice, than gay male relationships (Peplau et al., 2004). Rates of lesbian extradyadic sex are also lower than those for married women.

Motivations

Why do people pursue extramarital sexual encounters? Common reasons include dissatisfaction with a relationship, anger toward a partner, and boredom (Willetts et al., 2004). Sometimes people need to confirm that they are still desirable, or they want to trigger the end of an unsatisfying relationship. Then again, extramarital sexual activity can occur simply because two people are attracted to each other. Erotic reactions to people other than one's partner do not cease when one makes a permanent commitment. Most people suppress these sexual desires because they disapprove of adultery.

The gender differences in motivations for infidelity parallel gender differences in sexual socialization. Men tend to engage in extradyadic affairs to obtain sexual variety, while women usually seek an emotional connection (Blumstein & Schwartz, 1983).

Age is also a factor. People between the ages of 18 and 30 are twice as likely to engage in sex outside a marriage or committed relationship than people over 50 (Treas & Giesen, 2000).

Impact

The impact of extramarital sexual activity on marriages has not been investigated extensively. Experts speculate that approximately 20 percent of all divorces are caused by infidelity (Reinisch, 1990). Still, it's hard to know in these cases whether extramarital sex is a symptom of a disintegrating relationship or its cause. Occasionally, extramarital affairs can have a positive effect on a marriage if they motivate a couple to resolve relationship problems. Participants in extramarital affairs, whether or not they are discovered, may experience loss of self-respect, guilt, stress, and complications of sexually transmitted diseases. Sexual fidelity is positively correlated with relationship satisfaction for lesbian and heterosexual couples, but not for gay male couples (Kurdek, 1991).

Practical Issues in Sexual Activity

LEARNING OBJECTIVES

- *Describe constraints on effective contraception and discuss the merits of hormone-based contraceptives and condoms.*
- *Describe the various types of STDs, and discuss their prevalence and means of transmission.*
- *List some suggestions for safer sexual practices.*

Regardless of the context of sexual activity, two practical issues are often matters of concern: contraception and sexually transmitted diseases. These topics are more properly in the domain of medicine than of psychology, but birth control and sex-related infections certainly do have their behavioral aspects.

Contraception

Most people want to control whether and when they will conceive a child, so they need reliable contraception. Despite the availability of effective contraceptive methods, however, many people fail to exercise much control.

Constraints on Effective Contraception

Effective contraception requires that intimate couples negotiate their way through a complex sequence of steps. First, both people must define themselves as sexually active. Second, both must have accurate knowledge about fertility and conception. Third, their chosen method of contraception must be readily accessible. Finally, both must have the motivation and skill to use the method correctly and consistently. Failure to meet even one of these conditions can result in an unintended pregnancy.

Despite the threat of AIDS, only about two out of three sexually active females age 15 to 19 use contraception—but not every time they have sex (Glei, 1999). Why this risky behavior? First, many believe that if they aren't gay, aren't intravenous drug users, and don't have frequent sex, they don't need to take precautions (Tucker & Cho, 1991). Second, those who feel guilty about planned sex rationalize their sexual behavior by telling themselves that "we got carried away."

A third factor is conflicting norms about gender and sexual behavior. Men are socialized to be the initiators of sexual activity, but when it comes to birth control, they often rely on women to take charge. It is hard for a woman to maintain an image of sexual naïveté and also be responsible for contraception. Telling her partner that she is "on the pill" or whipping out a condom conveys quite a different image. Unfortunately, a woman's decision to use a condom may be influenced more by concerns about how her partner might perceive her than her perceived susceptibility to infections and attitudes about condom use (Bryan, Aiken, & West, 1999). Finally, alcohol is a factor. It doesn't increase sexual desire, but it does typically impair judgment (MacDonald, Zanna, & Fong, 1996). In addition, many college students drink as a socially acceptable way to avoid potentially embarrassing discussions about sex.

Selecting a Contraceptive Method

If a couple is motivated to control their fertility, how should they go about selecting a technique? A rational

WEB LINK 13.5

Sexual Health Network
The health professionals who staff this Connecticut-based site have assembled a comprehensive set of resources related to all aspects of human sexual health. Especially notable are materials discussing sexual functioning for persons with physical injuries or disabilities.

Contraceptive Methods

Method	Ideal failure rate (%)	Actual failure rate (%)	Advantages	Disadvantages
Birth control pills (combination)	0.3	8	Highly reliable; coitus-independent; has some health benefits	Side effects; daily use; continual cost; health risks for some women; no protection against STDs
Minipill (progestin only)	0.3	8	Thought to have low risk of side effects; coitus-independent; has some health benefits	Breakthrough bleeding; daily use; continual cost; health risks for some women; no protection against STDs
IUD	0.6	0.8	No memory or motivation required for use; very reliable; some health benefits	Cramping, bleeding, expulsion; risk of pelvic inflammatory disease; no protection against STDs
Diaphragm with spermicidal cream or jelly	6	16	No major health risks; inexpensive	Aesthetic objections; initial cost
Condom (male)	2	15	Protects against STDs; simple to use; male responsibility; no health risks; no prescriptions required	Unaesthetic to some; requires interruption of sexual activity; continual cost
Sponge	9	16	24-hour protection; simple to use; no taste or odor; inexpensive; effective with several acts of intercourse	Aesthetic objections; continual cost; no protection against STDs
Cervical cap with spermicidal cream or jelly	9	16	48-hour protection; no major health risks	May be difficult to insert; may irritate cervix; initial cost
Spermicides	18	29	No major health risks; no prescription required	Unaesthetic to some; must be properly inserted; continual cost; no protection against STDs
Fertility awareness (rhythm)	1–9	25	No cost; acceptable to Catholic church	Requires high motivation and periods of abstinence; unreliable; no protection against STDs
Withdrawal	4	27	No cost or health risks	Reduces sexual pleasure; unreliable; requires high motivation; no protection against STDs
Transdermal patch	.03	8	No memory or motivation required to use; coitus-independent; very reliable; has some health benefits	Continual cost; skin irritation for some women; no protection against STDs
No contraception	85	85	No immediate monetary cost	High risk of pregnancy and STDs

Note: STDs = Sexually transmitted diseases

● FIGURE 13.14

A comparison of widely used contraceptive techniques. Couples can choose from a variety of contraceptive methods. This chart summarizes the advantages and disadvantages of each method. Note that the typical failure rate is much higher than the ideal failure rate for all methods, because couples do not use contraceptive techniques consistently and correctly. (Based on Hatcher et al., 2004; Crooks and Baur, 2005)

choice requires accurate knowledge of the effectiveness, benefits, costs, and risks of the various methods. Figure 13.14 summarizes information on most of the methods currently available. The *ideal failure rate* estimates the probability of conception when the technique is used correctly and consistently. The *actual failure rate* is what occurs in the real world, when users' negligence is factored in.

Besides being informed about the various types of contraceptive methods, couples must also put this information to use. Contraception is a joint responsibil-

ity. Hence, it's essential for partners to discuss their preferences, to decide what method(s) they are going to use, and to *act* on their decision. Let's look in more detail at the two most widely used birth control methods in the Western world: hormone-based contraceptives and condoms.

Hormone-based contraceptives contain synthetic forms of estrogen and progesterone (or progesterone only, in the minipill), which inhibit ovulation in women. Types of hormone-based contraceptives include "the pill," the transdermal patch (worn on the skin), and the vaginal ring (inserted once a month). Many couples prefer these birth control options because contraceptive use is not tied to the sex act. Only the interuterine device permits a similar degree of sexual spontaneity.

Use of hormone-based contraceptives does not appear to increase a woman's overall risk for cancer (Trussell, 2004). In fact, the likelihood of certain forms of cancer (such as uterine and ovarian cancer) is reduced in women who use low-dosage oral contraceptives. These methods do slightly increase the risk of certain cardiovascular disorders, such as heart disease and stroke. Thus, alternative methods of contraception should be considered by women who smoke, are over age 35, or have any suspicion of cardiovascular disease.

A *condom* is a sheath worn over the penis during intercourse to collect ejaculated semen. The condom is the only widely available contraceptive device for use by males. A condom slightly reduces a man's sensitivity, but many men see this dulling as a plus because it can make sex last longer. Condoms can be purchased in any drugstore without a prescription. If used correctly, the condom is highly effective in preventing pregnancy (Warner, Hatcher, & Steiner, 2004). It must be placed over the penis after erection but before any contact with the vagina, and space must be left at the tip to collect the ejaculate. The man should withdraw before completely losing his erection and hold the rim of the condom during withdrawal to prevent any semen from spilling into the vagina.

Condoms are made of polyurethane, latex rubber, and animal membranes ("skin"). Polyurethane condoms are thinner than latex condoms; however, they are more likely to break and to slip off than latex condoms. The FDA still requires that the box say that the risks of pregnancy and infection are "unknown." The use of latex condoms definitely reduces the chances of contracting or passing on various sexually transmitted diseases. However, oil-based creams and lotions (petroleum jelly, massage oil, baby oil, and hand and body lotions, for example) should never be used with *latex* condoms (or diaphragms) (Warner et al., 2004). Within 60 seconds, these products can make microscopic holes in the rubber membrane that are large enough to allow passage of HIV and organisms produced by other sexually transmitted diseases. Water-based lubricants such as Astroglide or K-Y warming jelly don't cause this problem. Polyurethane condoms are impervious to oils. Skin condoms do *not* offer protection against sexually transmitted diseases.

In closing, we should mention emergency contraception. Women may seek emergency contraception in cases of sexual assault, contraceptive failure, or unprotected sex. Progestin pills (Plan B), which are available by prescription, can prevent a pregnancy if they are taken within 72 hours after intercourse. The drug works like birth control pills, by preventing ovulation or fertil-

ization and implantation of the fertilized egg into the uterine wall ("Condoms—Extra Protection," 2005). If the fertilized egg is already implanted into the wall of the uterus, progestin will not harm it. By contrast, mifepristone (RU 486) is a drug that can induce a miscarriage in the first seven weeks of a pregnancy (Stewart, Ellertson, & Cates, 2004). Prescribed by a physician, mifepristone is typically administered in the form of two pills taken several days apart. Although no substitute for regular birth control, the drug can be used after unprotected sex and is particularly helpful in cases of rape.

Sexually Transmitted Diseases

A *sexually transmitted disease* (STD) **is a disease or infection that is transmitted primarily through sexual contact.** When people think of STDs, they typically think of syphilis and gonorrhea, but these diseases are only the tip of the iceberg. There are actually about 20 sexually transmitted diseases. Some of them—for instance, pubic lice—are minor nuisances that can readily be treated. Others, however, are severe afflictions that are difficult to treat. For instance, if it isn't detected early, syphilis can cause heart failure, blindness, and brain damage, and AIDS is eventually fatal. (We'll discuss AIDS in detail in Chapter 14.)

Prevalence and Transmission

No one is immune to sexually transmitted diseases. Even monogamous partners can develop some STDs (yeast infections, for instance). Health authorities estimate that about 15 million new cases occur in the United States each year (Cates, 2004). The highest incidence of STDs occurs in the under-25 age group (Cates, 2004). About one person in four contracts an STD by age 21 (Feroli & Burstein, 2003).

The United States has seen a recent surge of HIV infections stemming from heterosexual transmission (Centers for Disease Control, 2003). AIDS is increasing more rapidly among women than among men, especially among women of color (Centers for Disease Control, 2002b). Women whose sexual partners have multiple sex partners or who inject drugs are especially at risk. An increasing concern is that a woman's partner may be secretly having sex with other men and may deny that he is gay or bisexual (King, 2004). Infected women are more likely to be poor and less likely to get treatment (Cowley & Murr, 2004). The rate of HIV infections is also up among young gay and bisexual men, especially those of color (Gross, 2003).

Women suffer more severe long-term consequences of STDs than men, including chronic pelvic pain, infertility, and cervical cancer (Cates, 2004). Because of the transmission dynamics of sexual intercourse, they are also more likely to acquire an STD from any single sexual encounter. But women are less likely to seek treatment because more of their STDs are asymptomatic or not perceived to be serious.

The principal types of sexually transmitted diseases are listed in Figure 13.15, along with their symptoms and modes of transmission. Most of these infections are spread from one person to another through intercourse, oral-genital contact, or anal-genital contact. Concerning the transmission of STDs, six points are worth emphasizing:

1. You should consider *any* activity that exposes you to blood (including menstrual blood), semen, vaginal secretions, urine, feces, or saliva as high-risk behavior *unless* you and your partner are in a mutual, sexually exclusive relationship and neither of you is infected.

2. The more sexual partners you have, the higher your chances of exposure to a sexually transmitted infection.

3. Don't assume that the labels people attach to themselves (heterosexual or homosexual) accurately describe their actual sexual behavior. According to the director of the Kinsey Institute, "Studies of men from the general population show that more than 30 percent have had at least one sexual experience with another male since puberty" (Reinisch, 1990).

4. People can be carriers of sexually transmitted diseases without knowing it. For instance, in its early stages gonorrhea may cause no readily apparent symptoms in women, who may unknowingly transmit the infection to their partners.

5. Even when people know they have a sexually transmitted infection, they may fail to refrain from sex or inform their partners. Guilt and embarrassment cause many people to ignore symptoms of sexually transmitted diseases and continue their normal sexual activities. Close to half of the subjects in one study admitted that they had told dates that they had had fewer sexual partners than was actually the case (Reinisch, 1990). People are even more likely to lie about homosexual activity, sex with prostitutes, and drug use. So don't assume that sexual partners will warn you that they may be contagious.

6. Engaging in anal intercourse (especially being the receiving partner) puts one at high risk for AIDS. Rectal tissues are delicate and easily torn, thus letting the virus pass through the membrane. Oral-genital sex may also transmit HIV, particularly if semen is swallowed.

Prevention

Abstinence is obviously the best way to avoid acquiring sexually transmitted diseases. Of course, this is not an appealing or realistic option for most people. Short of abstinence, the best strategy is to engage in sexual activity only in the context of a long-term relationship,

where you have an opportunity to know your partner reasonably well. Casual sex greatly increases your risk for STDs, including HIV. To decrease this risk, you should use condoms with spermicides.

Along with being judicious about sexual relations, you need to talk openly about safer sexual practices with your partner. But if you don't carry the process one step further and practice what you preach, you remain at risk. As we noted, many people engage in risky sexual behavior—a practice they can ill afford while we are still in the grip of the deadly AIDS epidemic.

Unfortunately, the availability of new drug treatments for HIV seems to have increased risk taking among drug users, gay men, and heterosexuals who frequent STD clinics (Centers for Disease Control, 2000). Although these new drugs are welcome news, they cost over $10,000 per year—well out of the reach of those without health insurance (Freedberg et al., 2001). And they require a patient to follow a strict and complicated regimen of medication.

We offer the following suggestions for safer sex (Hyde & DeLamater, 2003; King, 2005):

■ Don't have sex with lots of people. You increase your risk of contracting STDs.

■ Don't have sex with someone who has had lots of previous partners. People won't always be honest about their sexual history, so it's important to know whether you can trust a prospective partner's word.

■ If you are not involved in a sexually exclusive relationship, always use latex condoms with spermicides. They have a good track record of preventing STDs and offer effective protection against the AIDS virus. (And never use oil-based lubricants with latex condoms; use water-based lubricants instead.)

■ If there is any possibility that you or your partner has an STD, abstain from sex, always use condoms, or use other types of sexual expression such as hand-genital stimulation. (Remember that mouth-genital sex may transmit HIV, especially if semen enters the mouth.)

■ Wash your genitals with soap and warm water before and after sexual contact.

■ Urinate shortly after intercourse.

■ Because HIV is easily transmitted through anal intercourse, it's a good idea to avoid this type of sex.

■ Watch for sores, rashes, or discharge around the vulva or penis, or elsewhere on your body, especially the mouth. If you have cold sores, avoid kissing or oral sex.

If you have any reason to suspect that you have an STD, find a good health clinic and get tested *as soon as possible.* (It's normal to be embarrassed or afraid of getting bad news, but don't delay. Health professionals are in the business of helping people, not judging them.) To be really sure, get tested twice. If both tests are negative,

Sexually Transmitted Diseases (STDs)

STD	Transmission	Symptoms
Acquired immune deficiency syndrome (AIDS)	The AIDS virus is spread by coitus or anal intercourse. There is a chance the virus may also be spread by oral-genital sex, particularly if semen is swallowed. (AIDS can also be spread by nonsexual means: contaminated blood, contaminated hypodermic needles, and transmission from an infected woman to her baby during pregnancy or childbirth.)	Most people infected with the virus show no immediate symptoms; antibodies usually develop in the blood 2-8 weeks after infection. People with the virus may remain symptom-free for 5 years or more. No cure for the disease has yet been found. Common symptoms include fevers, night sweats, weight loss, chronic fatigue, swollen lymph nodes, diarrhea and/or bloody stools, atypical bruising or bleeding, skin rashes, headache, chronic cough, and a whitish coating on the tongue or throat.
Chlamydia infection	The *Chlamydia trichomatis* bacterium is transmitted primarily through sexual contact. It may also be spread by fingers from one body site to another.	In men, chlamydial infection of the urethra may cause a discharge and burning during urination. Chlamydia-caused epididimitis may produce a sense of heaviness in the affected testicle(s), inflammation of the scrotal skin, and painful swelling at the bottom of the testicle. In women, pelvic inflammatory disease caused by chlamydia may disrupt menstrual periods, elevate temperature, and cause abdominal pain, nausea, vomiting, headache, infertility, and ectopic pregnancy.
Genital warts	The virus is spread primarily through penile-vaginal, oral-genital, oral-anal, or genital-anal contact.	Warts are hard and yellow-gray on dry skin areas, soft pinkish red and cauliflowerlike on moist areas.
Gonorrhea ("clap")	The *Neisseria gonorrhoeae* bacterium (gonococcus) is spread through penile-vaginal, oral-genital, or genital-anal contact.	Most common symptoms in men are a cloudy discharge from the penis and burning sensations during urination. If the disease is untreated, complications may include inflammation of the scrotal skin and swelling at the base of the testicle. In women, some green or yellowish discharge is produced, but the disease commonly remains undetected. At a later stage, pelvic inflammatory disease may develop.
Herpes	The genital herpes virus (HSV-2) appears to be transmitted primarily by penile-vaginal, oral-genital, or genital-anal contact. The oral herpes virus (HSV-1) is transmitted primarily by kissing, or oral-genital contact.	Small red, painful bumps (papules) appear in the region of the genitals (genital herpes) or mouth (oral herpes). The papules become painful blisters that eventually rupture to form wet, open sores.
Pubic lice ("crabs")	*Phthirus pubis,* the pubic louse, is spread easily through body contact or through shared clothing or bedding.	Persistent itching. Lice are visible and may often be located in pubic hair or other body hair.
Syphilis	The *Treponema pallidum* bacterium (spirochete) is transmitted from open lesions during penile-vaginal, oral-genital, oral-anal, or genital-anal contact.	*Primary stage:* A painless chancre (sore) appears at the site where the spirochetes entered the body. *Secondary stage:* The chancre disappears and a generalized skin rash develops. *Latent stage:* There may be no observable symptoms. *Tertiary stage:* Heart failure, blindness, mental disturbance, and many other symptoms may occur. Death may result.
Trichomoniasis	The protozoan parasite *Trichomonas vaginalis* is passed through genital sexual contact or less frequently by towels, toilet seats, or bathtubs used by an infected person.	In women, white or yellow vaginal discharge with an unpleasant odor; vulva is sore and irritated. Men are usually asymptomatic.
Viral hepatitis	The hepatitis B virus may be transmitted by blood, semen, vaginal secretions, and saliva. Manual, oral, or penile stimulation of the anus is strongly associated with the spread of this virus. Hepatitis A seems to be spread primarily via the fecal-oral route. Oral-anal sexual contact is a common mode of sexual transmission for hepatitis A.	Vary from nonexistent to mild, flulike symptoms to an incapacitating illness characterized by high fever, vomiting, and severe abdominal pain.

● FIGURE 13.15

Overview of common sexually transmitted diseases (STDs). This chart summarizes the symptoms and modes of transmission of 9 STDs. Note that intercourse is not required to transmit all STDs—many STDs can be contracted through oral-genital contact or other forms of physical intimacy. (Adapted from Hatcher et al., 2004; Crooks and Baur, 2005)

you can stop worrying. If you have several sexual partners in a year, you should have regular STD checkups. You will have to ask for them, as most doctors and health clinics won't perform them otherwise.

Remember that the symptoms of some STDs disappear as the infection progresses. If your test results are positive, it's essential to get the proper treatment *right away.* Notify your sexual partner(s) so they can be tested immediately, too. And avoid sexual intercourse and oral sex until you and your partner are fully treated and a physician or clinic says you are no longer infectious.

In the Application, we focus on enhancing sexual satisfaction and treating common sexual problems.

APPLICATION

Enhancing Sexual Relationships

LEARNING OBJECTIVES

- List six general suggestions for enhancing sexual relationships.
- Discuss the nature, prevalence, and causes of common sexual dysfunctions.
- Describe the strategies for coping with erectile difficulties, premature ejaculation, orgasmic difficulties, and hypoactive sexual desire.

Answer the following statements "true" or "false."

_____ **1.** Sexual problems are unusual.

_____ **2.** Sexual problems belong to couples rather than individuals.

_____ **3.** Sexual problems are highly resistant to treatment.

_____ **4.** Sex therapists sometimes recommend masturbation as a treatment for certain types of problems.

The answers are (1) false, (2) true, (3) false, and (4) true. If you missed several of these questions, you are by no means unusual. Misconceptions about sexuality are the norm rather than the exception. Fortunately, there is plenty of useful information on how to improve sexual relationships.

For the sake of simplicity, our advice is directed to heterosexual couples, but much of what we have to say is also relevant to same-gender couples. For advice aimed specifically at same-gender couples, we recommend *Permanent Partners: Building Gay and Lesbian Relationships That Last* by Betty Berzon (2004).

General Suggestions

Let's begin with some general ideas about how to enhance sexual relationships, drawn from several excellent books on sexuality (Crooks & Baur, 2005; Hyde & DeLamater, 2003; King, 2005). Even if you are satisfied with your sex life, these suggestions may be useful as "preventive medicine."

1. *Pursue adequate sex education.* A surprising number of people are ignorant about the realities of sexual functioning. So the first step in promoting sexual satisfaction is to acquire accurate information about sex. The shelves of most bookstores are bulging with popular books on sex, but many of them are loaded with inaccuracies. A good bet is to pick up a college textbook on human sexuality. The Recommended Readings in this chapter describe books that we think are excellent. Enrolling in a course on sexuality is also a good idea. Most colleges offer such courses today.

2. *Review your sexual values system.* Many sexual problems stem from a negative sexual values system that associates sex with immorality. The guilt feelings caused by such an orientation can interfere with sexual functioning. Thus, sex therapists often encourage adults to examine the sources and implications of their sexual values.

3. *Communicate about sex.* As children, people often learn that they shouldn't talk about sex. Many people carry this edict into adulthood and have great difficulty discussing sex, even with their partner. Good communication is essential in a sexual relationship. Figure 13.16 lists common problems in sexual relations. Many of these problems—such as choosing an inconvenient time, too little erotic activity before intercourse, and too little tenderness afterward—are traceable largely to poor communication. Both men and women say they want more instructions from their partner (refer back to Figure 13.7). But your partner is not a mindreader! You have to share your thoughts and feel-

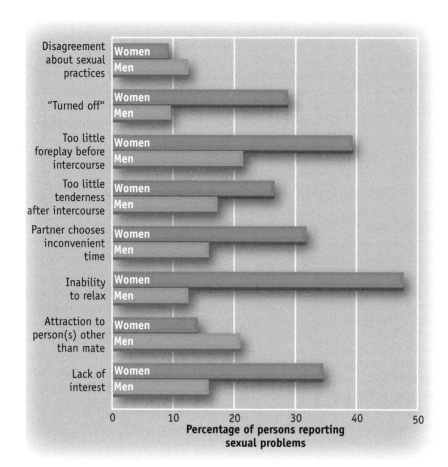

● **FIGURE 13.16**

Common problems in sexual relations.
The percentage of men and women reporting various types of problems in their sexual relationships is shown here, based on a sample of 100 couples.

Adapted from Frank, E., Anderson, C., & Rubenstein, D. (1978). Frequency of sexual dysfunction in "normal" couples. *New England Journal of Medicine, 299*, 111–115. Copyright © 1978 by the New England Journal of Medicine. Reprinted by permission.

ings. If you are unsure about your partner's preferences, ask. And provide candid (but diplomatic) feedback when your partner asks for your reactions.

4. *Avoid goal setting.* Sexual encounters are not tests or races. Sexual experiences are usually best when people relax and enjoy themselves. People get overly concerned about orgasms or about both partners reaching orgasm simultaneously. A grim determination to climax typically makes it harder to do so. This mental set can lead to disruptive habits like *spectatoring,* or stepping outside the sexual act to judge one's performance. It's better to adopt the philosophy that getting there is at least half the fun.

5. *Enjoy your sexual fantasies.* As we noted earlier, the mind is the ultimate erogenous zone. Although Freudian theory originally saw sexual fantasy as an unhealthy by-product of sexual frustration and immaturity, research shows that sexual fantasies are most

Unresolved sexual problems can be a source of tension and frustration in relationships. Physical, psychological, and interpersonal factors can contribute to sexual difficulties.

common among those who have the fewest sexual problems (Leitenberg & Henning, 1995; Renaud & Byers, 2001). Men and women both report that their sexual fantasies increase their excitement. So don't be afraid to use fantasy to enhance your sexual arousal.

6. *Be selective about sex.* Sexual encounters generally work out better when you have privacy and a relaxed atmosphere, when you are well rested, and when you are enthusiastic. Of course, you can't count on (or insist on) having ideal situations all the time, but you should be aware of the value of being selective. If your heart just isn't in it, it may be wise to wait. Partners often differ about when, where, and how often they should have sex. Such differences are normal and should not be a source of resentment. Couples simply need to work toward reasonable compromises—through open communication.

Understanding Sexual Dysfunction

Many people struggle with *sexual dysfunctions*—**impairments in sexual functioning that cause subjective distress.** Figure 13.17 shows the prevalence of some of the most common sexual problems (Laumann et al., 1994).

Physical, psychological, and interpersonal factors can contribute to sexual problems. *Physical factors* include chronic illness, disabilities, some medications, alcohol, and drugs. *Individual psychological factors* include anxieties around fear of failure, negative attitudes about sexuality learned during childhood, spectatoring, fears of pregnancy and STDs, life stresses such as unemployment, and prior sexual abuse. *Interpersonal factors* include ineffective communication about sexual matters and unresolved relationship issues that fuel anger and resentment.

People commonly assume that a sexual problem resides in just one partner (physical or individual psychological factors). While this is sometimes the case, most sexual problems emerge out of partners' unique ways of relating to each other (interpersonal factors). Moreover, even in those cases where a problem may lie more with one partner than another, the couple needs to work together for an acceptable solution. In other words, sexual problems belong to couples rather than to individuals.

Now let's examine the symptoms and causes of four common sexual dysfunctions: erectile difficulties, premature ejaculation, orgasmic difficulties, and low sexual desire.

Erectile difficulties occur when a man is persistently unable to achieve or maintain an erection ade-

● **FIGURE 13.17**

Sexual dysfunction in normal couples.
This graph shows the prevalence of various sexual dysfunctions during a year in a probability sample of American men and women. The most common problems among men are premature ejaculation and anxiety about performance; in women, they are lack of interest in sex and orgasmic difficulties.

From Laumann, E. O., Gagnon, J. H., Michael, R. T., & Michaels, S. (1994). *The social organization of sexuality: Sexual practices in the United States.* Chicago: University of Chicago Press. Copyright © 1994 by University of Chicago Press. Reprinted by permission.

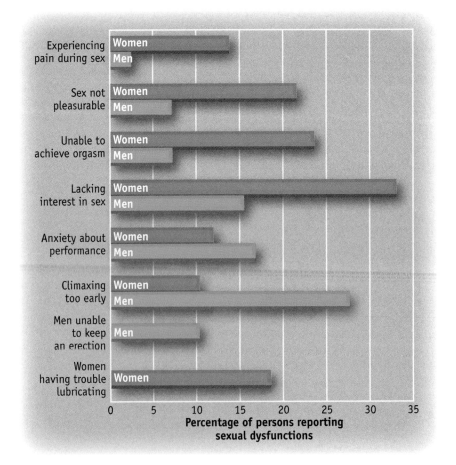

WEB LINK 13.6

Sexual Disorders Information Sites on the Web
In writing a 1997 article for the *Journal of Sex Education and Therapy,* David A. Gotlib and Peter Fagan at Johns Hopkins University surveyed the web for the best online resources about sexuality. This April 2001 revision of their recommended links was prepared with the help of Cynthia Osborne.

quate for intercourse. The traditional name for this problem is *impotence,* but sex therapists have discarded the term because of its demeaning connotation. A man who has never had an erection sufficient for intercourse is said to have *lifelong erectile difficulties.* A man who has had intercourse in the past but who is currently having problems achieving erections is said to have *acquired erectile difficulties.* The latter problem is more common and easier to overcome.

Some 30 million American men are estimated to suffer from erectile difficulties if a broad criterion (the inability to get an erection adequate for satisfactory sexual performance) is used (Levine, 2003). Erectile difficulties affect about 1 in 20 men age 40 and over, and about 1 in 4 over age 65.

Physical factors can play a role in erectile dysfunction. For example, experts estimate that as many as 25 percent of all cases may be due to side effects of medication (Miller, 2000). A host of common diseases (such as diabetes) can produce erectile problems as a side effect (Althof, 2000). Many temporary conditions, such as fatigue, worry about work, an argument with your partner, a depressed mood, or too much alcohol can cause such incidents. The most common psychological cause of erectile difficulties is anxiety about sexual performance. Anxiety may stem from doubts about virility or conflict about the morality of sexual desires. Interpersonal factors can enter in if the partner turns an incident into a major catastrophe. If the man allows himself to get unduly concerned about his sexual response, the seeds of anxiety may be sown.

Premature ejaculation occurs when sexual relations are impaired because a man consistently reaches orgasm too quickly. What is "too quickly"? Obviously, any time estimate is hopelessly arbitrary. The critical consideration is the subjective feelings of the partners. If either partner feels that the ejaculation is persistently too fast for sexual gratification, they have a problem. Approximately 29 percent of men repeatedly experience premature ejaculation (Laumann et al, 1994).

What causes premature ejaculation? Some men who have a lifelong history of quick ejaculation may have a neurophysiological predisposition to this condition (Metz & Pryor, 2000). But psychological factors

are the typical cause. Some men simply don't exert much effort to prolong intercourse. Most of these men do not view their ejaculations as premature, even if their partners do. Other causes can include stress, depression, or anger at one's partner. Many therapists believe that this problem is rooted in early sexual experiences in which a rapid climax was advantageous. Furtive sex in the backseat of a car, quick efforts at masturbation, and experiences with prostitutes are situations in which men typically attempt to achieve orgasm quickly. A pattern of rapid ejaculation established by these formative experiences can become entrenched.

Orgasmic difficulties occur when people experience sexual arousal but have persistent problems in achieving orgasm. When this problem occurs in men, it is often called *male orgasmic disorder.* The traditional name for this problem in women, *frigidity,* is no longer used because of its derogatory implications. Since this problem is much more common among women, we'll limit our discussion to them. A woman who has never experienced an orgasm through any kind of stimulation is said to have *generalized lifelong orgasmic difficulties.* Women who experience orgasms in some situations or only rarely are said to have *situational orgasmic difficulties.* This category includes women who experience orgasm only through noncoital techniques (oral, manual, and self-stimulation). Although lifelong orgasmic difficulties would seem to be the more severe problem, they are actually more responsive to treatment than situational orgasmic difficulties.

Physical causes of orgasmic difficulties are rare (medications can be a problem). One of the leading psychological causes is a negative attitude toward sex. Women who have been taught that sex is dirty or sinful are likely to approach it with shame and guilt. These feelings can undermine arousal, inhibit sexual expression, and impair orgasmic responsiveness. Arousal may also be inhibited by fear of pregnancy or excessive concern about achieving orgasm.

Some women have orgasmic difficulties because intercourse is too brief. Others fail to experience orgasms because their partners are unconcerned about their needs and preferences. But many couples simply need to explore sexual activities such as manual or oral stimulation of the clitoris that are more effective in producing female orgasm than sexual intercourse, alone (Bancroft, 2002b).

Hypoactive sexual desire, or the lack of interest in sexual activity, seems to be on the rise. Individuals with this problem rarely initiate sex or tend to avoid sexual activities with their partner (Aubin & Heiman, 2004). It occurs in both men and women, but it is more common among women (see Figure 13.17). Many attribute the recent increases in this problem to the fast pace of contemporary life and to couples' heavy workloads both at home and the office. In men, low sexual desire is often related to embarrassment about erectile dysfunction (McCarthy, Bodnar, & Handal, 2004). In women, it is most often associated with relationship difficulties (Aubin & Heiman, 2004). Sometimes the problem arises when a person is trying to sort out his or her sexual orientation.

Coping with Specific Problems

William Masters and Virginia Johnson

With the advent of modern sex therapy, sexual problems no longer have to be chronic sources of frustration and shame. *Sex therapy involves the professional treatment of sexual dysfunctions.* Masters and Johnson reported high success rates for their treatments of specific problems, as Figure 13.18 shows. Some critics argue that the cure rates reported by Masters and Johnson are overly optimistic in comparison with those reported by other investigators (Zilbergeld & Evans, 1980). Nonetheless, there is a consensus that sexual dysfunctions can be overcome with encouraging regularity (McCarthy et al., 2004). The advent of medications to treat sexual problems (Viagra) has resulted in an increased emphasis on medical and individual treatments over relationship interventions (Aubin & Heiman, 2004). Nonetheless, couple-based treatment approaches definitely have their place and

are effective. If you're in the market for a sex therapist, be sure to get someone who is qualified to work in this specialized field. One professional credential to look for is that provided by the American Association of Sex Educators, Counselors, and Therapists (AASECT).

Of course, sex therapy isn't for everyone. It can be expensive and time-consuming. In some areas, it is difficult to find. However, many people can benefit from ideas drawn from the professional practice of sex therapy.

Erectile Difficulties

Viagra, the much-touted pill for treating erectile disorders, is about 80 percent effective (Handy, 1998a). Still, it is not without its drawbacks—some of them life threatening. Cialis and Levitra are two similar pills that enhance erections over a longer time period (24 to 36 hours) than Viagra. To work effectively, these pills must be incorporated into the couple's love-making style (Rosen, 2000). The expectation that a pill alone will solve sexual problems that stem from relationship or psychological issues can set men up for additional sexual dysfunction (McCarthy et al., 2004).

To overcome psychologically based erectile difficulties, the key is to decrease the man's performance anxiety. It is a good idea for a couple to discuss the problem openly. The woman should be reassured that the difficulty does not reflect lack of affection by her partner. Obviously, it is crucial for her to be emotionally supportive rather than hostile and demanding.

Masters and Johnson introduced a procedure called sensate focus in the treatment of erectile difficul-

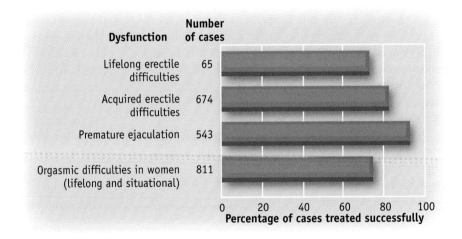

● FIGURE 13.18

Success rates reported by Masters and Johnson in their treatment of sexual dysfunctions. This figure shows the success rates for cases treated between 1959 and 1985. Treatment was categorized as successful only if the change in sexual function was clear and enduring. The minimum follow-up period was two years, and in many cases follow-up was five years later.

Adapted from Masters, W. H., Johnson, V. E., & Kolodny, R. C. (1988). *Human sexuality* (3rd ed.). Boston: Allyn & Bacon. Copyright © 1988 by Pearson Education. Adapted by permission of the publisher.

ties and other dysfunctions. ***Sensate focus* is an exercise in which partners take turns pleasuring each other while giving guided verbal feedback and in which certain kinds of stimulation are temporarily forbidden.** One partner stimulates the other, who simply lies back and enjoys it while giving instructions and feedback about what feels good. Initially, the partners are not allowed to touch each other's genitals or to attempt intercourse. This prohibition should free the man from feelings of pressure to perform. Over a number of sessions, the couple gradually includes genital stimulation in their sensate focus, but intercourse is still banned. With the pressure to perform removed, many men spontaneously get erections. Repeated arousals should begin to restore the man's confidence in his sexual response. As his confidence returns, the couple can move on gradually to attempts at intercourse.

Premature Ejaculation

Men troubled by premature ejaculation range from those who climax almost instantly to those who cannot last the time that their partner requires. In the latter case, simply slowing down the tempo of intercourse may help. Sometimes the problem can be solved indirectly by discarding the traditional assumption that orgasms should come through intercourse. If the female partner enjoys oral or manual stimulation, these techniques can be used to provide her with an orgasm either before or after intercourse. This strategy can reduce the performance pressure for the male partner, and couples may find that intercourse starts to last longer.

For the problem of instant ejaculation, two treatments are very effective: the *stop-start method* (Semans, 1956) and the *squeeze technique* (Masters & Johnson, 1970). With both, the woman brings the man to the verge of orgasm through manual stimulation. Then, she either stops stimulating him (stop-start technique) or squeezes the end of his penis firmly for 3–5 seconds (squeeze technique) until he calms down. She repeats this procedure three or four times before bringing him to orgasm. These exercises can help a man recognize preorgasmic sensations and teach him that he can delay ejaculation. Medication may also help (Polonsky, 2000).

Orgasmic Difficulties

Negative attitudes and embarrassment about sex are often at the root of women's orgasmic difficulties. Thus, therapeutic discussions are usually geared toward helping nonorgasmic women to reduce their ambivalence about sexual expression, become more clear about their sexual needs, and become more assertive about them. Sex therapists often suggest that women who have never had an orgasm try to have one by using a vibrator and then shifting to masturbation, as the latter more closely approximates stimulation by a partner (Crooks & Baur, 2005). Many women achieve orgasms in intercourse after an initial breakthrough with self-stimulation. To make this transition, it is essential that the woman express her sexual wishes to her partner. Sensate focus is also an effective technique for treating orgasmic difficulties (Heiman & Meston, 1997).

When a woman's orgasmic difficulties stem from not feeling close to her partner, treatment usually focuses on couples' relationship problems more than on sexual functioning per se. Therapists also focus on helping couples improve their communication skills.

Hypoactive Sexual Desire

Therapists consider reduced sexual desire the most challenging sexual problem to treat (Aubin & Heiman, 2004). This is because the problem usually has multiple causes, which can also be difficult to identify. If the problem is a result of fatigue from overwork, couples may be encouraged to allot more time to personal and relationship needs. But hypoactive sexual desire can also masquerade as effects of relationship issues. Treatment for this problem is usually more intensive than that for more specific sexual disorders, and it is usually multifaceted to deal with the multiple aspects of the problem. Some medications can help with low sexual desire, but drugs will not solve relationship problems. For these, couples therapy is needed.

KEY IDEAS

Becoming a Sexual Person

■ One's sexual identity is made up of sexual orientation, body image, sexual values and ethics, and erotic preferences. Physiological factors such as hormones influence sexual differentiation, maturation, and anatomy more than they do sexual activity. Psychosocial factors appear to have more impact on sexual behavior. Sexual identity is shaped by families, peers, schools, and the media. Because of differences in sexual socialization, sexuality usually has different meanings for males and females.

■ Experts believe that sexual orientation is best viewed as a continuum, with end points of heterosexuality and homosexuality. The determinants of sexual orientation are not yet known but appear to be a complex interaction of biological and environmental factors. Attitudes toward homosexuals are negative, but moving in a positive direction. Coming to terms with a homosexual orientation is a process. Recent evidence suggests that homosexuals are at greater risk for depression and suicide attempts than are heterosexuals, a phenomenon linked to their membership in a stigmatized group.

Interaction in Sexual Relationships

■ People frequently enter into sexual interactions with differing motivations. Men tend to be motivated more by physical gratification, whereas women are more likely to have emotional motives. Variations among people in erotic preferences are also shaped by their attitudes.

■ Disparities between partners in sexual interest and erotic preferences lead to disagreements that require negotiation. Effective communication plays an important role in sexual and relationship satisfaction.

The Human Sexual Response

■ The physiology of the human sexual response was described by Masters and Johnson. They analyzed the sexual response cycle into four phases: excitement, plateau, orgasm, and resolution. For a more complete view of this process, individuals' subjective experiences during sexual encounters also need to be factored in.

■ Women reach orgasm in intercourse less consistently than men, usually because foreplay and intercourse are too brief and because of gender differences in sexual socialization.

Sexual Expression

■ Sexual fantasies are normal and are an important aspect of sexual expression. Kissing and touching are important erotic activities, but their importance is often underestimated by heterosexual males. Despite the strongly negative attitudes about masturbation that are traditional in our society, this practice is quite common, even among married people. Oral-genital sex has become a common element in most couples' sexual repertoires.

■ Coitus is the most widely practiced sexual act in our society. Four coital positions are commonly used, each with its advantages and disadvantages. Sexual activities between gay males include mutual masturbation, fellatio, and, less often, anal intercourse. Lesbians engage in mutual masturbation, cunnilingus, and tribadism.

Patterns of Sexual Behavior

■ American sexual attitudes and behavior have become more liberal over the past 30 years, although this trend appeared to slow in the 1990s. Teen pregnancy rates have declined recently, but they still remain high. STD rates are highest among young people. The incidence of sexually risky behavior among teens has declined in recent years.

■ The acceptability and prevalence of premarital sex have increased since the 1960s. Unprotected casual sex remains a problem among high school and college students.

■ Satisfaction with the sexual aspect of a relationship is correlated with overall relationship satisfaction in both gay and straight couples. Younger married couples tend to have sex about two or three times a week. This frequency declines with age in both heterosexual and same-gender couples.

■ Most Americans strongly disapprove of extramarital sex. Infidelity is uncommon among married couples and lesbians and more common among gay male couples. People become involved in extradyadic relationships for a variety of reasons.

Practical Issues in Sexual Activity

■ Contraception and sexually transmitted diseases are two practical issues that concern many couples. Many people who do not want to conceive a child fail to use contraceptive procedures effectively, if at all. Contraceptive methods differ in effectiveness and have various advantages and disadvantages.

■ STDs are increasing in prevalence, especially among those under 25. The danger of contracting STDs is higher among those who have had more sexual partners. In the United States, the rates of HIV infections stemming from heterosexual sex are on the rise, particularly among women. HIV rates are also up among young gay and bisexual men. Using condoms decreases the risk of contracting STDs. Early treatment of STDs is important.

Application: Enhancing Sexual Relationships

■ To enhance their sexual relationships, individuals need to have adequate sex education and positive values about sex. They also need to be able to communicate with their partners about sex and avoid goal setting in sexual encounters. Enjoying sexual fantasies and being selective about their sexual encounters are also important.

■ Common sexual dysfunctions include erectile difficulties, premature ejaculation, orgasmic difficulties, and hypoactive sexual desire. Treatments for low sexual desire are less effective than those for more specific sexual problems.

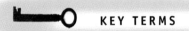

KEY TERMS

Anal intercourse   p. 424
Androgens   p. 408
Bisexuals   p. 408
Coitus   p. 424
Cunnilingus   p. 423
Erectile difficulties
    pp. 436–437
Erogenous zones   p. 422
Estrogens   p. 408
Fellatio   p. 423
Gonads   p. 408
Heterosexuals   p. 408
Homophobia   p. 415
Homosexuals   p. 408

Hypoactive sexual desire
    p. 437
Orgasm   p. 421
Orgasmic difficulties   p. 437
Premature ejaculation
    p. 437
Refractory period   p. 421
Sensate focus   p. 439
Sex therapy   p. 438
Sexual dysfunctions   p. 436
Sexual identity   p. 408
Sexually transmitted disease
    (STD)   p. 431
Vasocongestion   p. 420

KEY PEOPLE

Linda Garnets and Douglas
    Kimmel   pp. 416–417
Alfred Kinsey   pp. 413–414

William Masters and Virginia
    Johnson   pp. 419–421
Letitia Anne Peplau   p. 411

PRACTICE TEST

1. Young men typically feel _____ about sex; young women typically feel _____ about sex.
   a. positive; positive
   b. positive; negative
   c. ambivalent; ambivalent
   d. positive; ambivalent

2. Which of the following statements about sexual orientation is true?
   a. Heterosexuality and homosexuality are best viewed as two distinct categories.
   b. Heterosexuality and homosexuality are best viewed as end points on a continuum.
   c. Biological factors alone probably determine sexual orientation.
   d. Environmental factors alone probably determine sexual orientation.

3. Which of the following describes the correct order of the four phases of Masters and Johnson's sexual response cycle?
   a. Resolution, plateau, excitement, orgasm
   b. Plateau, excitement, orgasm, resolution
   c. Excitement, plateau, orgasm, resolution
   d. Excitement, orgasm, plateau, resolution

4. Sexual fantasies:
   a. are signs of abnormality.
   b. are quite normal.
   c. rarely include having sex with someone other than one's partner.
   d. are an excellent indication of what people want to experience in reality.

5. Which of the following characterizes teen sexual behavior in the "age of AIDS"?
   a. Fewer teens are engaging in risky sexual behavior now than 10 years ago.
   b. The teen pregnancy rate has increased since the early 90s.
   c. About 75 percent of sexually active teens use condoms regularly.
   d. The teen pregnancy rate in America is among the lowest in the world.

6. Regarding overall marital satisfaction and sexual satisfaction, research indicates there is:
   a. a strong relationship.
   b. a weak relationship.
   c. no relationship.
   d. a strong relationship, but only in the first year of marriage.

7. About what percent of Americans strongly disapprove of sexual infidelity?
   a. 0 percent
   c. 60 percent
   b. 30 percent
   d. 90 percent

8. Which of the following statements about condom use is false?
   a. It's okay to use oil-based lubricants with polyurethane condoms.
   b. It's okay to use oil-based lubricants with rubber condoms.
   c. Skin condoms do not protect against STDs.
   d. It's okay to use water-based lubricants with rubber or polyurethane condoms.

9. Sexually transmitted diseases:
   a. are all very serious.
   b. always cause symptoms right away.
   c. are most common among people under age 25.
   d. are most common among people between 26 and 40.

10. Which of the following is *not* one of the text's suggestions for enhancing your sexual relationships?
    a. Pursue adequate sex education.
    b. Review your sexual values system.
    c. Communicate about sex.
    d. Set clear goals for each sexual encounter.

Book Companion Website

Visit the Book Companion Website at **http://psychology.wadsworth.com/weiten_lloyd8e,** where you will find tutorial quizzes, flashcards, and weblinks for every chapter, a final exam, and more! You can also link to the Thomson Wadsworth Psychology Resource Center (accessible directly at **http://psychology.wadsworth.com**) for a range of psychology-related resources.

Personal Explorations Workbook

The following exercises in your Personal Explorations Workbook may enhance your self-understanding in relation to issues raised in this chapter. **Questionnaire 13.1:** Sexuality Scale. **Personal Probe 13.1:** How Did You Acquire Your Attitudes about Sex? **Personal Probe 13.2:** Reflecting on the Place of Sexuality Throughout Your Life.

ANSWERS

1. d Pages 411–412
2. b Pages 413–414
3. c Pages 420–421
4. b Page 422
5. a Pages 424–425
6. a Page 426
7. d Page 427
8. b Page 431
9. c Pages 431–432
10. d Pages 434–436

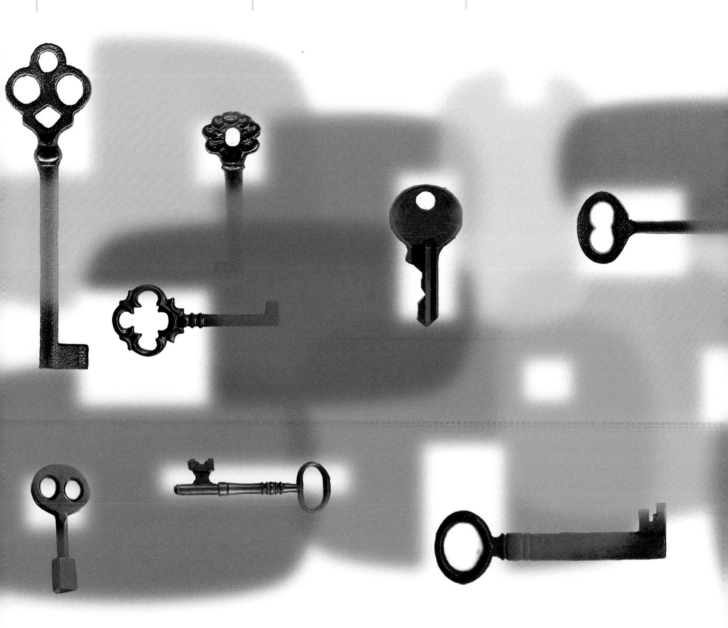

Psychology and Physical Health

The patterns of illness found in a society tend to fluctuate over time. In our society, some interesting trends have occurred during the last century or so. Before the 20th century, the principal threats to health were *contagious diseases* caused by specific infectious agents. Because such diseases can be transmitted readily from one person to another, people used to live in fear of epidemics. The leading causes of death were diseases such as the plague, smallpox, typhoid fever, influenza, diphtheria, yellow fever, malaria, cholera, tuberculosis, polio, and scarlet fever. Today, the incidence of these diseases has declined to the point where none of them is among the leading killers in the United States (see Figure 14.1 on the next page).

What neutralized these dreaded diseases? The general public tends to attribute the conquest of contagious diseases to advances in medical treatment. Although progress in medicine certainly played a role, Grob (1983) marshals evidence that the significance of such progress has been overrated. Of greater significance, according to Grob, have been (1) improvements in nutrition, (2) improvements in public hygiene and sanitation (water filtration, treatment of sewage, and so forth), and (3) evolutionary changes in human immune resistance to the diseases. Whatever the causes, infectious diseases are no longer the major threat to physical health in the industrialized nations of the world (although many remain quite prevalent in Third World countries).

Unfortunately, the void left by contagious diseases has been filled all too quickly by various *chronic diseases*—illnesses that develop gradually over many years (refer to Figure 14.1). Psychosocial factors, such as lifestyle and stress, play a much larger role in the development of chronic diseases than they do in contagious diseases. Today, the three leading chronic diseases (heart disease, cancer, and stroke) account for 63 percent of all

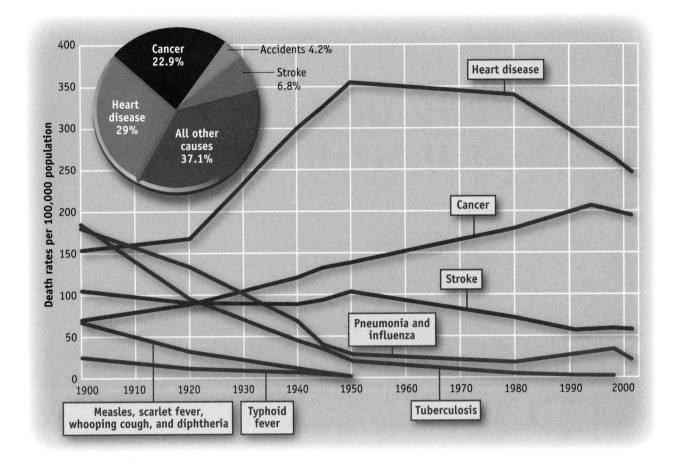

● FIGURE 14.1

Changing patterns of illness. Trends in the death rates for various diseases during the 20th century reveal that contagious diseases (shown in blue) have declined as a threat to health. However, the death rates for stress-related chronic diseases (shown in red) have remained quite high. The pie chart (inset), which depicts the percentage of deaths caused by most of the leading killers today, shows the results of these trends: Three chronic diseases (heart disease, cancer, and stroke) account for almost 60 percent of all deaths.

deaths in the United States, and these mortality statistics reveal only the tip of the iceberg. Psychosocial factors contribute to many other, less serious illnesses, such as headaches, backaches, skin disorders, asthma, and ulcers.

In light of these trends, it is not surprising that the way we think about illness is changing. Traditionally, illness has been thought of as a purely biological phenomenon produced by an infectious agent or some internal physical breakdown. However, the shifting patterns of disease and new findings relating stress to physical illness have rocked the foundation of this biological model. In its place a new model has gradually emerged (Suls & Rothman, 2004). The *biopsychosocial* model holds that physical illness is caused by a complex interaction of biological, psychological, and sociocultural factors. This new model does not suggest that biological factors are unimportant. Rather, it

simply asserts that biological factors operate in a psychosocial context that can also be highly influential.

The growing recognition that psychological factors influence physical health led to the development of a new specialty within psychology. *Health psychology is concerned with how psychosocial factors relate to the promotion and maintenance of health and with the causation, prevention, and treatment of illness.* This specialty is relatively young, having emerged in the late 1970s. In this chapter we focus on the rapidly growing domain of health psychology. The chapter's first section analyzes the link between stress and illness. The second section examines common health-impairing habits, such as smoking and overeating. The third section discusses how people's reactions to illness can affect their health. The Application expands on one particular type of health-impairing habit: the use of recreational drugs.

Stress, Personality, and Illness

LEARNING OBJECTIVES

- Describe the Type A personality and evidence regarding its most toxic element.
- Discuss possible explanations for the link between hostility and heart disease.
- Summarize evidence relating emotional reactions and depression to heart disease.
- Describe the evidence linking stress and personality to cancer.
- Summarize evidence linking stress to a variety of diseases and immune functioning.
- Evaluate the strength of the relationship between stress and illness.

As we noted in Chapter 3, during the 1970s health researchers began to uncover new links between stress and a variety of diseases previously believed to be purely physiological in origin. In this section, we'll look at the evidence on the apparent link between stress and physical illness and discuss how personality factors contribute to this relationship. We begin with heart disease, which is far and away the leading cause of death in North America.

Personality, Emotions, and Heart Disease

Heart disease accounts for nearly 40 percent of the deaths in the United States every year. **Coronary heart disease results from a reduction in blood flow through the coronary arteries, which supply the heart with blood.** This type of heart disease causes about 90 percent of heart-related deaths. Atherosclerosis is the principal cause of coronary disease. **Atherosclerosis is a gradual narrowing of the coronary arteries,** usually caused by a buildup of fatty deposits and other debris on the inner walls (see Figure 14.2). Atherosclerosis

progresses slowly over many years. Narrowed coronary arteries may eventually lead to situations in which the heart is temporarily deprived of adequate blood flow, causing a condition known as *myocardial ischemia.* This ischemia may be accompanied by brief chest pain, called *angina.* If a coronary artery is blocked completely (by a blood clot, for instance), the abrupt interruption of blood flow can produce a full-fledged heart attack, or *myocardial infarction.* Atherosclerosis is more prevalent in men than women and tends to increase with age. Other established risk factors for coronary disease include smoking, diabetes, high cholesterol levels, and high blood pressure (Greenland et al., 2003; Khot et al., 2003). Smoking and diabetes are somewhat stronger risk factors for women than for men (Stoney, 2003). Contrary to public perception, cardiovascular diseases kill women just as much as men, but these diseases tend to emerge in women about 10 years later in life than in men (Stoney, 2003).

Recently, attention has shifted to the possibility that inflammation may contribute to atherosclerosis and elevated coronary risk (Hackam & Anand, 2003). Evidence is mounting that inflammation plays a key role in the initiation and progression of atherosclerosis, as well as the acute complications that trigger heart attacks (Albert et al., 2002; Libby, Ridker, & Maseri, 2002). Fortunately, researchers have found a marker— levels of C-reactive protein (CRP) in the blood—that may help physicians estimate individuals' coronary risk more accurately than was possible previously (Ridker, 2001). Figure 14.3 (on the next page) shows how combined levels of CRP and cholesterol appear to be related to coronary risk. CRP levels are also predictive of the development of high blood pressure, which suggests that hypertension may be part of an inflammatory syndrome (Sesso et al., 2003).

Hostility and Coronary Risk

In the 1960s and 1970s a pair of cardiologists, Meyer Friedman and Ray Rosenman (1974), were investigating the causes of coronary disease. Originally, they were interested in the usual factors thought to produce

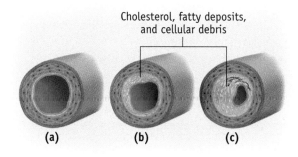

● **FIGURE 14.2**

Atherosclerosis. Atherosclerosis, a narrowing of the coronary arteries, is the principal cause of coronary disease. **(a)** A normal artery. **(b)** Fatty deposits, cholesterol, and cellular debris on the walls of the artery have narrowed the path for blood flow. **(c)** Advanced atherosclerosis. In this situation, a blood clot might suddenly block the flow of blood through the artery.

The relationship of cholesterol and inflammation to coronary risk. Levels of C-reactive protein (CRP) in the blood appear to be a useful index of the inflammation that contributes to atherosclerosis (Ridker, 2001). This graph shows how increasing CRP levels and increasing cholesterol levels combine to elevate cardiovascular risk (for a heart attack or stroke). The relative risks shown are for successive quintiles on each measure (each quintile represents one-fifth of the sample, ordered from those who scored lowest to those who scored highest). The relative risks are in relation to those who fall in the lowest quintile on both measures.

Adapted from Ridker, P. M. (2001). High sensitivity C-reactive protein: Potential adjunct for global risk assessment in primary prevention of cardiovascular disease. *Circulation, 103,* 1813–1818. Copyright © 2001 American Heart Association. Adapted by permission of the publisher Lippincott Williams & Wilkins and the author.

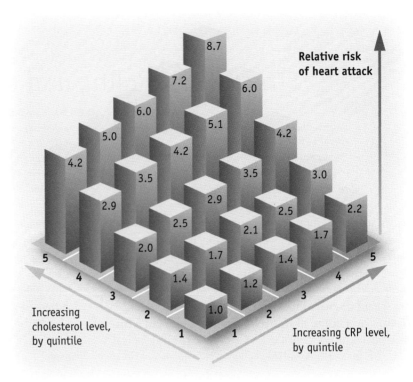

a high risk of heart attack: smoking, obesity, physical inactivity, and so forth. Although they found these factors to be important, they eventually recognized that a piece of the puzzle was missing. Many people who smoked constantly, got little exercise, and were severely overweight still managed to avoid the ravages of heart disease. Meanwhile, others who seemed to be in much better shape with regard to these risk factors experienced the misfortune of a heart attack. What was their explanation for these perplexing findings? Stress! Specifically, they identified an apparent connection between coronary risk and a pattern of behavior they called the *Type A personality,* which involves self-imposed stress and intense reactions to stress.

Friedman and Rosenman divided people into two basic types (Friedman, 1996; Rosenman, 1993). **The Type A personality includes three elements: (1) a strong competitive orientation, (2) impatience and time urgency, and (3) anger and hostility. In contrast, the Type B personality is marked by relatively relaxed, patient, easygoing, amicable behavior.** Type A's are ambitious, hard-driving perfectionists who are exceedingly time conscious. They routinely try to do several things at once. They fidget frantically over the briefest delays. They tend to be highly competitive, achievement-oriented workaholics who drive themselves with many deadlines. They are easily aggravated and get angry quickly. Type B's are less hurried, less competitive, and less easily angered than Type A's.

Decades of research uncovered a tantalizingly modest correlation between Type A behavior and increased coronary risk. More often than not, studies found an association between Type A personality and an elevated incidence of heart disease, but the findings were not as strong or as consistent as expected (Ragland & Brand, 1988; Smith & Gallo, 2001). However, in recent years, researchers have found a stronger link between personality and coronary risk by focusing on a specific component of the Type A personality: anger and hostility (Rozanski, Blumenthal, & Kaplan, 1999). For example, in one study of almost 13,000 men and women who had no prior history of heart disease (Williams et al., 2000), investigators found an elevated incidence of heart attacks among participants who exhibited an angry temperament. The participants, who were followed for a median period of 4.5 years, were classified as being low (37.1 percent), moderate (55.2 percent), or high (7.7 percent) in anger. Among participants with normal blood pressure, the high-anger subjects experienced almost three times as many coronary events as the low-anger subjects (see Figure 14.4). In another study, CT scans were used to look for signs of atherosclerosis in a

WEB LINK 14.1

healthfinder
Through the U.S. Department of Health and Human Services, the government has opened an ambitious online gateway to consumer-oriented information about health in all its aspects. Annotated descriptions are available for all resources identified in no-cost searches of this database.

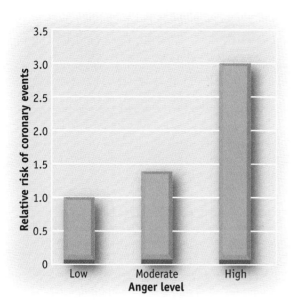

Research suggests that excessive anger and hostility are associated with an increased risk for various types of heart disease.

● **FIGURE 14.4**

Anger and coronary risk. Working with a large sample of healthy men and women who were followed for a median of 4.5 years, Williams et al. (2000) found an association between trait anger and the likelihood of a coronary event. Among subjects who manifested normal blood pressure at the beginning of the study, a moderate anger level was associated with a 36 percent increase in coronary attacks, and a high level of anger nearly tripled participants' risk for coronary disease. (Based on data in Williams et al., 2000)

sample of 374 young men and women whose cynical hostility had been assessed a decade earlier when they were 18 to 30 years old (Irabarren et al., 2000). Participants with above-average hostility scores were twice as likely to exhibit atherosclerosis as participants with below-average hostility scores.

Many other studies have also found an association between hostility and various aspects of cardiovascular disease (Eaker et al., 2004; Niaura et al, 2002), including CRP levels (Suarez, 2004). Thus, recent research trends suggest that hostility may be the crucial toxic element in the Type A syndrome that accounts for the correlation between Type A behavior and heart disease. Why are anger and hostility associated with coronary risk? Research has uncovered a number of possible explanations (see Figure 14.5).

First, anger-prone individuals appear to exhibit greater physiological reactivity than those who are lower in hostility (Smith & Gallo, 1999; Suarez et al.,

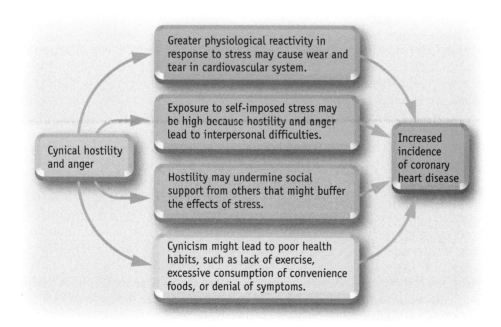

● **FIGURE 14.5**

Mechanisms that may link hostility and anger to heart disease. Explanations for the apparent link between cynical hostility and heart disease are many and varied. Four widely discussed possibilities are summarized in the middle column of this diagram.

1998). The frequent ups and downs in heart rate and blood pressure may create wear and tear in their cardiovascular systems.

Second, hostile people probably create additional stress for themselves (Felsten, 1996; Smith & Gallo, 2001). For example, their quick anger may provoke many arguments and conflicts with others. Consistent with this line of thinking, Smith and colleagues (1988) found that subjects high in hostility reported more hassles, more negative life events, more marital conflict, and more work-related stress than subjects who were lower in hostility.

Third, thanks to their antagonistic ways of relating to others, hostile individuals tend to have less social support than others (Brummett et al., 2001; Hart, 1999). As we noted in Chapter 3, research suggests that social support may be an important coping resource that promotes health and buffers the effects of stress (Wills & Fegan, 2001). Moreover, research indicates that low social support may be an independent risk factor for coronary disease (Rozanski, Blumenthal, & Kaplan, 1999).

Fourth, perhaps because of their cynicism, people high in anger and hostility seem to exhibit a higher prevalence of poor health habits that may contribute to the development of cardiovascular disease. For example, people high in hostility are more likely to smoke, drink alcohol and coffee, and be overweight than others (Everson et al., 1997; Siegler et al., 1992).

In sum, there are a variety of plausible explanations for the connection between hostility and heart disease. With all these mechanisms at work, it's not surprising that anger is associated with increased coronary risk.

Emotional Reactions and Heart Disease

Although work on personality risk factors has dominated research on how psychological functioning contributes to heart disease, recent studies suggest that emotional reactions may also be critical. *One line of research has supported the hypothesis that transient mental stress and the resulting emotions that people experience can tax the heart.* Based on anecdotal evidence, cardiologists and laypersons have long voiced suspicions that strong emotional reactions might trigger heart attacks in individuals with coronary disease, but it has been difficult to document this connection. However, advances in cardiac monitoring have facilitated investigation of the issue. As suspected, laboratory experiments with cardiology patients have shown that brief periods of mental stress can trigger acute symptoms of heart disease, such as myocardial ischemia and angina (Gottdiener et al., 1994). Overall, the evidence suggests that mental stress can elicit ischemia in about 30–70 percent of patients with stable coronary disease (Kop, Gottdiener, & Krantz, 2001).

RECOMMENDED READING

Is It Worth Dying For?
by Robert S. Eliot &
Dennis L. Breo
(Bantam Books, 1984, 1991)

Robert S. Eliot is a cardiologist whose work on "hot reactors" has attracted attention. Eliot believes that some people are particularly vulnerable to heart attacks because they have an overly reactive cardiovascular response to stress. These people may or may not exhibit Type A behavior or cynical hostility. Hot reacting involves a *physiological* tendency that is probably affected by genetic inheritance. Those who are both a hot reactor and an anger-prone Type A personality probably have a *very* elevated risk of coronary problems. Eliot and Breo explain all this and much more in their highly readable book, which focuses on the connections between stress and coronary risk. In addition to explaining how stress, hot reacting, and Type A behavior influence the risk of heart attack, they discuss the significance of health-impairing habits such as physical inactivity, poor eating, and smoking. They construct a handy overview of how a diverse array of factors govern cardiac vulnerability and then offer a great deal of useful advice on how to minimize your susceptibility to a heart attack.

Cover image copyright © 1984, 1989 Bantam Books. Reprinted by permission.

Moreover, research indicates that these patients have a higher risk for heart attack than the cardiology patients who do not manifest ischemia in response to mental stress (Krantz et al., 2000).

Researchers have also examined the importance of emotional reactions by having patients keep a diary of their emotions while their cardiac functioning is monitored continuously as they go about their business. For example, Gullette and colleagues (1997) found that the likelihood of ischemia increased two- or three-fold when people reported negative emotions, such as tension, frustration, and sadness. In another study, 660 patients who experienced a nonfatal myocardial infarction were subsequently interviewed about events that occurred in the 6 hours prior to the onset of their heart attack (Moller et al., 1999). The interviews suggested that episodes of anger were a frequent trigger for the participants' heart attacks. Consistent with this evidence, studies that have provided stress management training for coronary patients have shown promising results in efforts to reduce the likelihood of additional heart attacks (Claar & Blumenthal, 2003). Taken together, these studies suggest that emotional

Coping with Traumatic Events

A principal theme of this chapter is that stress can affect one's physical health. In today's world, a major new source of stress is living with the ominous threat of further terrorist attacks and the emotional fallout that results. Aware of these problems, a variety of health organizations have consulted their top experts and posted advice on the Internet about how to cope with terrorism-related anxiety and emotional reactions to traumatic events. The advice on these sites is fairly similar, with a great deal of overlap in content. The best overall list of suggested coping strategies, found at the website of the National Center for PTSD, is provided here. These strategies may be helpful in dealing with this new form of stress:

• Spend time with other people. Coping with stressful events is easier when people support each other.

• If it helps, talk about how you are feeling. Be willing to listen to others who need to talk about how they feel.

• Get back to your everyday routines. Familiar habits can be comforting.

• Take time to grieve and cry if you need to. To feel better in the long run, you need to let these feelings out instead of pushing them away or hiding them.

• Ask for support and help from your family, friends, church, or other community resources. Join or develop support groups.

• Eat healthy food and take time to walk, stretch, exercise, and relax, even if just for a few minutes at a time.

• Make sure you get enough rest and sleep. You may need more sleep than usual when you are highly stressed.

• Do something that just feels good to you, such as taking a warm bath, taking a walk, sitting in the sun, or petting your cat or dog.

• If you are trying to do too much, cut back by putting off or giving up a few things that are not absolutely necessary.

• If TV news reports get too distressing, turn them off and distract yourself by doing something you enjoy.

reactions to stressful events may precipitate heart attacks in people with coronary disease and that learning to better manage one's emotions may reduce one's coronary risk.

Depression and Heart Disease

Another line of research has recently implicated depression as a major risk factor for heart disease. *Depressive disorders,* which are characterized by persistent feelings of sadness and despair, are a fairly common form of psychological disorder (see Chapter 15). Over the years, many studies have found elevated rates of depression among patients suffering from heart disease, but most theorists have explained this correlation by asserting that being diagnosed with heart disease makes people depressed. However, studies conducted in the last decade or so have suggested that the causal relations may also flow in the opposite direction—*that the emotional dysfunction of depression may cause heart disease* (Thomas, Kalaria, & O'Brien, 2004). For example, Pratt and colleagues (1996) examined a large sample of people 13 years after they were screened for de-

pression. They found that participants who had been depressed at the time of the original study were four times more likely than others to experience a heart attack during the intervening 13 years. Because the participants' depressive disorders preceded their heart attacks, one cannot argue that their heart disease caused their depression. Overall, studies have found that depression roughly doubles one's chances of developing heart disease (Lett et al., 2004; Rudisch & Nemeroff, 2003). Moreover, depression also appears to influence how heart disease progresses, as it is associated with a worse prognosis among cardiology patients (Glassman et al., 2003). Although the new emphasis is on how depression contributes to heart disease, experts caution that the relationship between the two conditions is surely bidirectional and that heart disease also increases vulnerability to depression (Sayers, 2004).

Stress and Cancer

If one single word can strike terror into most people's hearts, it is probably *cancer.* People generally view cancer as the most sinister, tragic, loathsome, and unbearable of diseases. In reality, cancer is actually a *collection* of over 200 related diseases that vary in their characteristics and amenability to treatment (Nezu et al., 2003). **Cancer refers to malignant cell growth, which may occur in many organ systems in the body.** The core problem in cancer is that cells begin to reproduce in a rapid, disorganized fashion. As this reproduction process lurches out of control, the teeming new cells clump together to form tumors. If this wild growth continues unabated, the spreading tumors cause tissue damage and begin to interfere with normal functioning in the affected organ systems.

It is widely believed by the general public that stress and personality play major roles in the development of cancer (McKenna et al., 1999). However, the research linking psychological factors to the *onset* of cancer is extremely weak. A few retrospective studies have found evidence that high stress precedes the development of cancer (Cohen, Kunkel, & Levenson, 1998), but many others have failed to find any connection, and there is no convincing evidence that stress contributes to the causation of cancer (Newell, 1991; Petticrew, Fraser, & Regan, 1999). That said, Delahanty and Baum (2001) note that researchers trying to link stress to cancer face a daunting task. Most types of cancer develop slowly over periods of many years before a tumor is detectable. For most patients it is impossible to know when their cancer began to develop. If you can't pinpoint the onset of a disease, how can you link its onset to stressful events? Should you look into stress that occurred two years ago, or five years ago, or ten years ago? Thus, the failure to find an association between stress and cancer onset may not reflect the absence of such a link; it may only mean that insurmountable difficulties exist in detecting the association.

Investigators have also attempted to determine whether there is a *cancer-prone personality* that might reflect unsuccessful patterns of coping with stress. These studies have yielded some intriguing threads of consistency, suggesting that lonely, depressed people who depend on repressive, avoidant coping strategies may have a slightly elevated risk for cancer (Eysenck, 1988, 1993b; McKenna et al., 1999; Temoshok, 1987). However, this research must be viewed with great caution, given the possibility that someone's personality may change after discovering that he or she has cancer.

Although efforts to link psychological factors to the onset of cancer have largely failed, more convincing evidence has shown that stress and personality influence the *course* of the disease. The onset of cancer frequently sets off a chain reaction of stressful events (Anderson, Golden-Kreutz, & DiLillo, 2001). Patients typically have to grapple with fear of the unknown; difficult and aversive treatment regimens; nausea, fatigue, and other treatment side effects; dislocations in

WEB LINK 14.2

Centers for Disease Control and Prevention (CDC)
The CDC is the federal agency charged with monitoring and responding to serious threats to the nation's health as well as taking steps to prevent illness. This site's "Health Information from A to Z" offers the public in-depth medical explanations of many health problems both common (flu, allergies) and unusual (fetal alcohol syndrome, meningitis).

intimate relationships; career disruptions; job discrimination; and financial worries. Such stressors may often contribute to the progress of the disease, perhaps by impairing certain aspects of immune system functioning (Andersen, Kiecolt-Glaser, & Glaser, 1994). The impact of all this stress may depend in part on one's personality. Research suggests that mortality rates are somewhat higher among patients who respond with depression, repressive coping, and other negative emotions (Friedman, 1991). In contrast, prospects appear to be better for patients who can maintain their emotional stability and enthusiasm.

Stress and Other Diseases

The development of questionnaires to measure life stress has allowed researchers to look for correlations between stress and a variety of diseases. For example, Zautra and Smith (2001) found an association between life stress and the course of rheumatoid arthritis. Another study found an association between stressful life events and the emergence of lower back pain (Lampe et al., 1998). Other researchers have connected stress to the occurrence of asthmatic reactions (Ritz et al., 2000) and periodontal disease (Marcenes & Sheiham, 1992). Studies have also found an association between high stress and flareups of irritable bowel syndrome (Blanchard & Keefer, 2003) and peptic ulcers (Levenstein, 2002).

These are just a handful of representative examples of research relating stress to physical diseases. Figure 14.6 provides a longer list of health problems that have been linked to stress. Many of these stress-illness connections are based on tentative or inconsistent findings, but the sheer length and diversity of the list is remarkable. Why should stress increase the risk for so many kinds of illness? A partial answer may lie in immune functioning.

Stress and Immune Functioning

The apparent link between stress and many types of illness probably reflects the fact that stress can undermine the body's immune functioning. **The *immune response* is the body's defensive reaction to invasion**

Health Problems That May Be Linked to Stress

Health Problem	Representative evidence
Common cold	Mohren et al. (2001)
Ulcers	Levenstein (2002)
Asthma	Lehrer et al. (2002)
Migraine headaches	Ramadan (2000)
Premenstrual distress	Stanton et al. (2002)
Vaginal infections	Williams & Deffenbacher (1983)
Herpes virus	Padgett & Sheridan (2000)
Skin disorders	Arnold (2000)
Rheumatoid arthritis	Keefe et al. (2002)
Chronic back pain	Lampe et al. (1998)
Diabetes	Landel-Graham, Yount, & Rudnicki (2003)
Complications of pregnancy	Dunkel-Schetter et al. (2001)
Hyperthyroidism	Yang, Liu, & Zang (2000)
Hemophilia	Buxton et al. (1981)
Stroke	Harmsen et al. (1990)
Appendicitis	Creed (1989)
Multiple sclerosis	Grant et al. (1989)
Periodontal disease	Marcenes & Sheiham (1992)
Hypertension	O'Callahan, Andrews, & Krantz (2003)
Cancer	Holland & Lewis (1993)
Coronary heart disease	Orth-Gomer et al. (2000)
AIDS	Ironson et al. (2000)
Inflammatory bowel disease	Searle & Bennett (2001)
Epileptic seizures	Kelly & Schramke (2000)

● FIGURE 14.6

Stress and health problems. The onset or progress of the health problems listed here *may* be affected by stress. Although the evidence is fragmentary in many instances, it's alarming to see the number and diversity of problems on this list.

by bacteria, viral agents, or other foreign substances. The human immune response works to protect the body from many forms of disease. Immune reactions are remarkably complex and multifaceted (Chiappelli & Liu, 2000). Hence, there are a great many ways to measure immune function in an organism, and these multiple measures can sometimes produce conflicting, confusing results in research.

Nonetheless, a wealth of studies indicate that experimentally induced stress can impair immune functioning *in animals* (Moynihan & Ader, 1996). That is, stressors such as crowding, shock, food restriction, and restraint reduce various aspects of immune reactivity in laboratory animals (Chiappelli & Hodgson, 2000).

Janice Kiecolt-Glaser

Studies by Janice Kiecolt-Glaser and her colleagues have also related stress to suppressed immune activity *in humans* (Kiecolt-Glaser & Glaser, 1995). In one study, medical students provided researchers with blood samples so that their immune response could be assessed at various points (Kiecolt-Glaser et al., 1984). The students provided the baseline sample a month before final exams and contributed the "high-stress" sample on the first day of their finals. The subjects also responded to the Social Readjustment Rating Scale (SRRS; see Chapter 3) as a measure of recent stress. Reduced levels of immune activity were found during the extremely stressful finals week. Reduced immune activity was also correlated with higher scores on the SRRS.

Many other studies have also shown a link between stress and suppressed immune response (Ader, 2001; Segerstrom & Miller, 2004). For example, when quarantined volunteers were exposed to respiratory viruses that cause the common cold, those under high stress were more likely to be infected by the viruses (Cohen, Tyrrell, & Smith, 1993). Other studies have found evidence of reduced immune activity among people who scored relatively high on a stress scale measuring daily hassles (Levy et al., 1989), among men who were recently divorced or separated (Kiecolt-Glaser et al., 1988), among husbands and wives grappling with a high level of marital conflict (Kiecolt-Glaser et al., 1997), among people recently traumatized by a hurricane (Ironson et al., 1997), and among men who recently experienced the death of an intimate partner (Kemeny et al., 1995). Unfortunately, evidence suggests that susceptibility to immune suppression in the face of stress increases as people grow older (Kiecolt-Glaser & Glaser, 2001). To summarize, scientists have assembled impressive evidence that stress can temporarily suppress human immune functioning, which can make people more vulnerable to infectious disease agents.

Conclusions

A wealth of evidence suggests that stress influences physical health. However, virtually all of the relevant research is correlational, so it cannot demonstrate conclusively that stress *causes* illness (Smith & Gallo, 2001; Watson & Pennebaker, 1989). The association between stress and illness could be due to a third variable. Perhaps some aspect of personality or some type of physiological predisposition makes people overly prone to interpret events as stressful *and* overly prone to interpret unpleasant physical sensations as symptoms of illness (see Figure 14.7 on the next page). For instance, in the Chapter 3 Application we discussed how neuroticism might increase individuals' sensitivity to both stress and illness. Moreover, critics of this research note that many of the studies used research designs that may have inflated the apparent link between stress and illness (Schwarzer & Schulz, 2003; Turner & Wheaton, 1995).

In spite of methodological problems favoring inflated correlations, the research in this area consistently indicates that the *strength* of the relationship between stress and health is modest. The correlations typically fall in the .20s and .30s (Cohen, Kessler, & Gordon, 1995). Clearly, stress is not an irresistible force that produces inevitable effects on health. Actually, this fact should come as no surprise. As we saw in Chapter 3, some people handle stress better than others. Furthermore, stress is only one actor on a crowded stage. A complex network of biopsychosocial factors influence health, including genetic endowment, exposure to infectious agents and environmental toxins, nutrition, exercise, alcohol and drug use, smoking, use of medical care, and cooperation with medical advice. In the next section we look at some of these factors as we examine health-impairing habits and lifestyles.

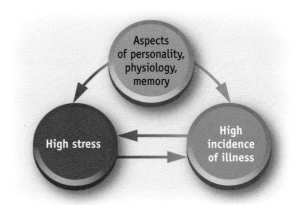

● FIGURE 14.7

The stress/illness correlation. Based on the evidence as a whole, most health psychologists would probably accept the assertion that stress often contributes to the causation of illness. However, some critics argue that the stress-illness correlation could reflect other causal processes. One or more aspects of personality, physiology, or memory might contribute to the correlation between high stress and a high incidence of illness (see Chapter 3 for additional discussion of this complex issue).

Habits, Lifestyles, and Health

LEARNING OBJECTIVES

- *Give some reasons for why people develop health-impairing habits.*
- *Discuss the health effects of smoking and the dynamics of giving up smoking.*
- *Summarize data on patterns of alcohol use and the short-term risks of drinking.*
- *Describe the major long-term health risks and social costs of drinking.*
- *Discuss the health risks and determinants of obesity.*
- *Outline the key elements in effective weight loss efforts.*

- *Provide examples of links between nutrition and health and discuss the basis for poor nutrition.*
- *List three general goals intended to foster sound nutrition.*
- *Summarize evidence on the benefits and risks of exercise.*
- *List four guidelines for embarking on an effective exercise program.*
- *Describe AIDS and summarize evidence on the transmission of the HIV virus.*
- *Identify some common misconceptions about AIDS and discuss the prevention of AIDS.*

Some people seem determined to dig an early grave for themselves. They do precisely those things they have been warned are particularly bad for their health. For example, some people drink heavily even though they know they're corroding their liver. Others eat all the wrong foods even though they know they're increasing their risk for a heart attack. Unfortunately, health-impairing habits contribute to far more deaths than most people realize. In a recent analysis of the causes of death in the United States, Mokdad and colleagues (2004) estimate that unhealthy behaviors are responsible for about half of all deaths each year. The unhealthy habits that account for the most premature mortality, by far, are smoking and poor diet/physical inactivity (see Figure 14.8). Other leading behavioral causes of

death include alcohol consumption, unsafe driving, sexually transmitted diseases, and illicit drug use.

It may seem puzzling that people behave in self-destructive ways. Why do they do it? Several factors are involved. First, many health-impairing habits creep up on people slowly. For instance, drug use may grow imperceptibly over years, or exercise habits may decline ever so gradually. Second, many health-impairing habits involve activities that are quite pleasant at the time. Actions such as eating favorite foods, smoking cigarettes, and getting "high" are potent reinforcing events. Third, the risks associated with most health-impairing habits are chronic diseases such as cancer that usually take 10, 20, or 30 years to develop. It is relatively easy to ignore risks that lie in the distant fu-

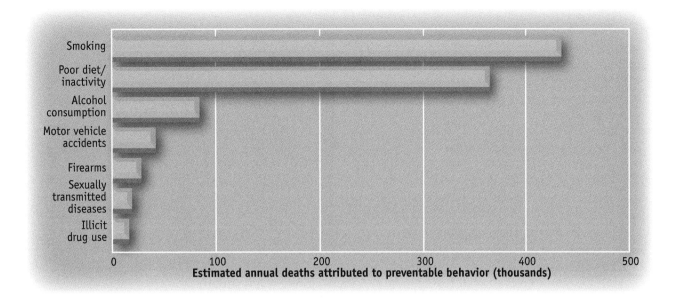

Mortality due to health-impairing behaviors. Synthesizing data from many sources, Mokdad and colleagues (2004) estimated the number of annual deaths in the United States attributable to various health-impairing behaviors in an interesting article published in *The Journal of the American Medical Association*. As you can see, their calculations suggest that smoking and obesity are the leading causes of preventable mortality. However, their mortality estimate for obesity has proven controversial and is the subject of some debate (some experts argue that their estimate is too high). (Data from Mokdad et al., 2004)

ture. Fourth, it appears that *people have a tendency to underestimate the risks associated with their own health-impairing habits* while viewing the risks associated with others' self-destructive behaviors much more accurately (Weinstein, 2003; Weinstein & Klein, 1996). In other words, most people are aware of the dangers

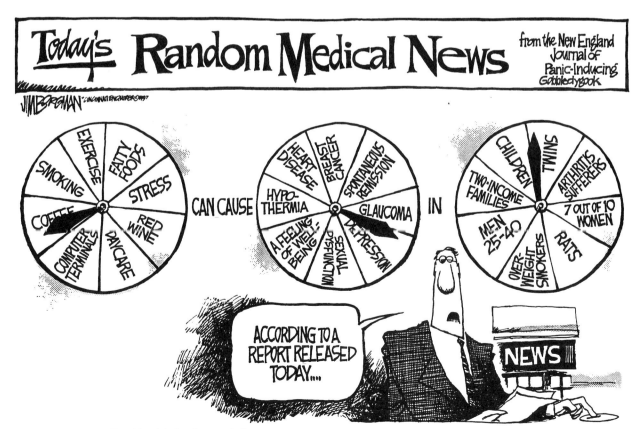

Cartoon by Borgman Reprinted with special permission from King Features Syndicate.

associated with certain habits, but they often engage in *denial* when it is time to apply this information to themselves. Yet another problem is that people are exposed to so much conflicting information about what's healthy and what isn't. It seems like every week a report in the media claims that yesterday's standard health advice has been contradicted by new research. This apparent inconsistency confuses people and undermines their motivation to pursue healthy habits.

In this section we discuss how health is affected by smoking, drinking, overeating and obesity, poor nutrition, and lack of exercise. We also look at behavioral factors that relate to AIDS. The health risks of recreational drug use are covered in the Application.

Smoking

The percentage of people who smoke has declined noticeably since the mid-1960s (see Figure 14.9). Nonetheless, about 25.7 percent of adult men and 21 percent of adult women in the United States continue to smoke regularly. Unfortunately, these percentages are slightly higher (28 percent for both sexes) among college students (Rigotti, Lee, & Wechsler, 2000). Moreover, smoking is even more common in many other societies.

Health Effects

Suspicions about the health risks associated with tobacco use were voiced in some quarters early in the 20th century. However, the risks of smoking were not widely appreciated until the mid-1960s. Since then, accumulating evidence has clearly shown that smokers face a much greater risk of premature death than nonsmokers. For example, the average smoker has an esti-

mated life expectancy *13–14 years shorter* than that of a similar nonsmoker (Schmitz & Delaune, 2005). The overall risk is positively correlated with the number of cigarettes smoked and their tar and nicotine content. Cigar smoking, which has increased dramatically in recent years, elevates health risks almost as much as cigarette smoking (Baker et al., 2000).

Why are mortality rates higher for smokers? Smoking increases the likelihood of developing a surprisingly large range of diseases, as you can see in Figure 14.10 (Schmitz & Delaune, 2005; Woloshin, Schwartz, & Welch, 2002). Lung cancer and heart disease kill the largest number of smokers. However, smokers also have an elevated risk for oral, bladder, and kidney cancer, as well as cancers of the larynx, esophagus, and pancreas; for atherosclerosis, hypertension, stroke, and other cardiovascular diseases; and for bronchitis, emphysema, and other pulmonary diseases. Most smokers know about the risks associated with tobacco use, but they tend to underestimate the actual risks as applied to themselves (Ayanian & Cleary, 1999).

Giving Up Smoking

Studies show that if people can give up smoking, their health risks decline reasonably quickly (Williams et al., 2002). Five years after people stop smoking, their health risk is already noticeably lower than that for people who continue to smoke. The health risks for people who give up tobacco continue to decline until they reach a normal level after about 15 years (see Figure 14.11). Evidence suggests that 70 percent of smokers would like to quit, but they are reluctant to give up a major source of pleasure and they worry about craving cigarettes, gaining weight, becoming anxious and

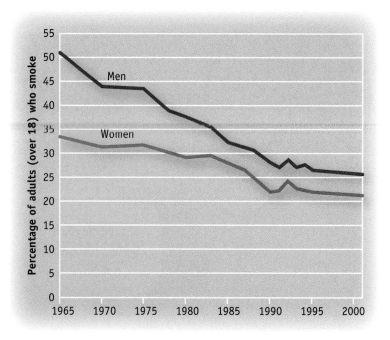

● FIGURE 14.9

The prevalence of smoking in the United States. This graph shows how the percentage of U.S. adults who smoke has declined steadily since the mid-1960s. Although considerable progress has been made, smoking still accounts for about 435,000 premature deaths each year. (Data from Centers for Disease Control)

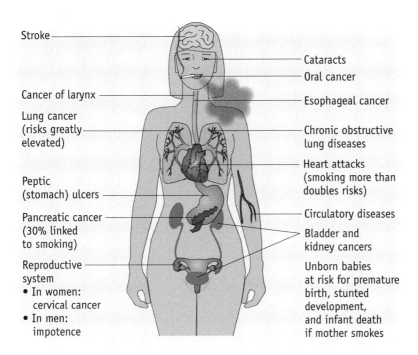

Stroke

Cataracts

Oral cancer

Cancer of larynx

Esophageal cancer

Lung cancer
(risks greatly
elevated)

Chronic obstructive
lung diseases

Peptic
(stomach) ulcers

Heart attacks
(smoking more than
doubles risks)

Pancreatic cancer
(30% linked
to smoking)

Circulatory diseases

Bladder and
kidney cancers

Reproductive
system
• In women:
cervical cancer
• In men:
impotence

Unborn babies
at risk for premature
birth, stunted
development,
and infant death
if mother smokes

Health risks associated with smoking. This graphic provides an overview of the various diseases that are more common among smokers than nonsmokers. As you can see, tobacco elevates one's vulnerability to a remarkably diverse array of diseases, including the three leading causes of death in the modern world—heart attack, cancer, and stroke.

irritable, and feeling less able to cope with stress (Grunberg, Faraday, & Rahman, 2001).

There are nearly 40 million ex-smokers in the United States. Collectively, they clearly demonstrate that it is possible to give up smoking successfully. But many didn't succeed until their third, fourth, or fifth attempt, and most would testify that quitting isn't easy.

Research shows that long-term success rates for efforts to quit smoking are in the vicinity of only 25 percent (Cohen et al., 1989). Light smokers are somewhat more successful at quitting than heavy smokers. Discouragingly, people who enroll in formal smoking-cessation programs are only slightly more successful than people who try to quit on their own (Swan, Hudman, & Khroyan, 2003). In fact, it is estimated that the vast majority of people who successfully give up smoking quit on their own, without professional help (Niaura & Abrams, 2002).

No single approach to quitting smoking is most effective for everyone. However, if you attempt to give up smoking on your own (without entering a formal treatment program), the self-modification techniques described in the Application for Chapter 4 can be invaluable. A good program should include careful monitoring of smoking habits, ample rewards for going without cigarettes, and control of antecedents to avoid situations that trigger smoking. It is also important to set a specific target date for quitting, to have specific plans for coping with temptation, and to arrange cooperation and encouragement from family and friends

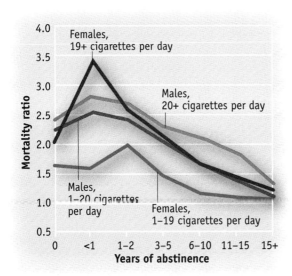

● FIGURE 14.11

Quitting smoking and mortality. Research suggests that various types of health risks associated with smoking decline gradually after people give up tobacco. The data shown here, from the 1990 U.S. Surgeon General's report on smoking, illustrate the overall effects on mortality rates. (Data from U.S. Department of Health and Human Services, 1990)

WEB LINK 14.3

The QuitNet Community
The Boston University School of Public Health sponsors an online community of individuals who seek to quit smoking and tobacco use. A range of excellent resources, including an online support "community" available 24 hours a day, can help make this behavioral health change a reality.

(Fisher et al., 2004). Keep in mind, too, that people attempting to give up smoking often fail several times before eventually succeeding. Evidence suggests that the readiness to quit builds gradually as people cycle through periods of abstinence and relapse (Herzog et al., 1999; Prochaska, 1994). Hence, if your effort to quit smoking ends in failure, don't give up hope—try again in a few weeks or a few months.

In recent years attention has focused on the potential value of *nicotine substitutes,* which can be delivered via gum, skin patches, nasal sprays, or inhalers. The rationale for nicotine substitutes is that insofar as nicotine is addictive, using a substitute might be helpful during the period when the person is trying to give up cigarettes. Do these substitutes work? They do help. Controlled studies have demonstrated that nicotine substitutes increase long-term rates of quitting in comparison to placebos (Swan et al., 2003). However, the increases are modest and the success rates are still discouragingly low. Nicotine substitutes are not a magic bullet or a substitute for a firm determination to quit. The various methods of nicotine delivery seem to be roughly equal in effectiveness, but combining a couple methods of delivery appears to increase the chances of quitting successfully (Schmitz & Delaune, 2005).

Drinking

Alcohol rivals tobacco as one of the leading causes of health problems in Americans. Alcohol encompasses a variety of beverages containing ethyl alcohol, such as beers, wines, and distilled spirits. The concentration of alcohol in these drinks varies from about 4 percent in most beers up to 40 percent in 80-proof liquor (or more in higher-proof liquors). Survey data indicate that about half of adults in the United States drink. As Figure 14.12 shows, per capita consumption of alcohol in the United States declined in the 1980s and 1990s, but this decrease followed decades of steady growth, and alcohol consumption remains relatively high, although certainly not the highest in the world.

Drinking is particularly prevalent on college campuses. Researchers from the Harvard School of Public Health (Wechsler et al., 2002) surveyed nearly 11,000 undergraduates at 119 schools and found that 81 percent of the students drank. Moreover, 49 percent of the men and 41 percent of the women reported that they engage in binge drinking with the intention of getting drunk. Perhaps most telling, college students spend far more money on alcohol ($5.5 billion annually) than they do on their books.

RECOMMENDED READING

The Stop Smoking Workbook: The Definitive Step-by-Step Guide to Healthy Quitting
by Lori Stevic-Rust & Anita Maximin (MJF Books, 1996)

The title says it all—this highly practical book is intended to help smokers through the challenging process of giving up tobacco. Written by two health psychologists, the book begins with a review of facts and myths about smoking, including a detailed review of the habit's physiological effects. Then the authors take the reader through a series of self-assessments intended to help them better understand when and why they smoke. The authors go on to outline strategies for setting a quit date and getting through the first few weeks. They also discuss how to deal with the urge to smoke and how to reduce the likelihood of relapse. The book is loaded with exercises and questionnaires that really make it something of a "workbook." The information is scientifically sound and the coverage of smoking-related issues is thorough.

Cover reprinted by permission of New Harbinger, Oakland, CA. 800/748-6273. www.newharbinger.com

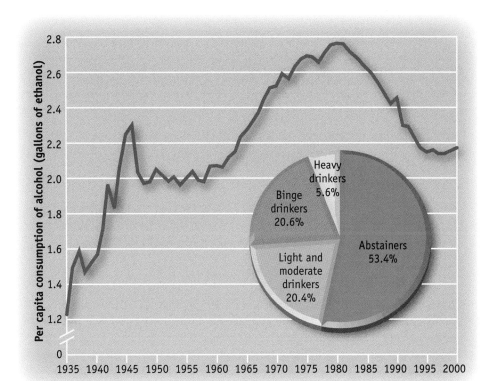

● FIGURE 14.12

Drinking in America. Drinking in the United States, as indexed by per capita consumption of ethanol in gallons, rose steadily through most of the 20th century, although notable declines occurred during the 1980s and 1990s. The inset shows the percentage of American adults who are abstainers, light drinkers, binge drinkers (people who have consumed five or more drinks on the same occasion at least once in the past month), and heavy drinkers (people who have consumed five or more drinks on the same occasion at least five times in the past month). The highest rates of binge drinking and heavy drinking are seen among young adults. (Data from National Institute on Alcohol Abuse and Alcoholism and U.S. Department of Health and Human Services)

Why Do People Drink?

The effects of alcohol are influenced by the user's experience, motivation, and mood, as well as by the presence of food in the stomach, the proof of the beverage, and the rate of drinking. Thus, we see great variability in how alcohol affects different people on different occasions. Nonetheless, the central effect is a "Who cares?" brand of euphoria that temporarily boosts self-esteem as one's problems melt away. Negative emotions such as tension, worry, anxiety, and depression are dulled, and inhibitions may be loosened (Johnson & Ait-Daoud, 2005). Thus, when first-year college students are asked why they drink, they say it's to relax, to feel less tense in social situations, to keep friends company, and to forget their problems. Of course, many other factors are also at work (Wood, Vinson, & Sher, 2001). Families and peer groups often encourage alcohol use. Drinking is a widely endorsed and encouraged social ritual in our culture. Its central role is readily apparent if you think about all the alcohol consumed at weddings, sports events, holiday parties, and so forth. Moreover, the alcohol industry spends hundreds of millions of dollars on advertising to convince us that drinking is cool, sexy, sophisticated, and harmless.

Short-Term Risks and Problems

Alcohol has a variety of side effects, including some that can be very problematic. To begin with, we have that infamous source of regret, the "hangover," which may include headaches, dizziness, nausea, and vomiting. In the constellation of alcohol's risks, however, hangovers are downright trivial. For instance, life-threatening overdoses are more common than most people realize. Although it's possible to overdose with alcohol alone, a more common problem is overdosing on combinations of alcohol and sedative or narcotic drugs.

In substantial amounts, alcohol has a decidedly negative effect on intellectual functioning and perceptual-motor coordination. The resulting combination of

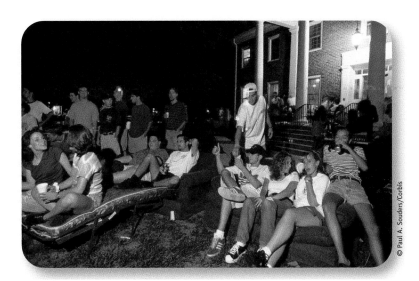

Overindulging in alcohol is particularly widespread among college students.

Drinking and impaired driving. The chart shown here estimates how many drinks it takes to impair driving ability in people of various weights. As you can see, as few as three drinks in a two-hour period can elevate blood alcohol content (BAC) to a dangerous level.

	BAC to .05% Be careful driving			.05–.09% Driving will be impaired					.10% and up Do not drive			

Weight (lbs.)

	1	2	3	4	5	6	7	8	9	10	11	12
100	1	2	3	4	5	6	7	8	9	10	11	12
120	1	2	3	4	5	6	7	8	9	10	11	12
140	1	2	3	4	5	6	7	8	9	10	11	12
160	1	2	3	4	5	6	7	8	9	10	11	12
180	1	2	3	4	5	6	7	8	9	10	11	12
200	1	2	3	4	5	6	7	8	9	10	11	12
220	1	2	3	4	5	6	7	8	9	10	11	12
240	1	2	3	4	5	6	7	8	9	10	11	12

Drinks (1¹/₂ oz. liquor or 12 oz. beer) in two-hour period

tainted judgment, slowed reaction time, and reduced coordination can be deadly when people attempt to drive after drinking. As Figure 14.13 shows, depending on body weight, it may take only a few drinks for driving to be impaired. It's estimated that alcohol contributes to 30 percent of all automobile fatalities in the United States (Yi et al., 1999). Drunk driving is a major social problem and the leading cause of death in young adults. Alcohol is also implicated in many other types of accidents. Victims test positive for alcohol in 38 percent of fire fatalities, 49 percent of drownings, and 63 percent of fatal falls (Smith, Branas, & Miller, 1999).

With their inhibitions released, some drinkers become argumentative and prone to aggression. In the Harvard survey of undergraduates from 119 schools, 29 percent of the students who did *not* engage in binge drinking reported that they had been insulted or humiliated by a drunken student, 19 percent had experienced serious arguments, 9 percent had been pushed, hit, or assaulted, and 19.5 percent had been the target of unwanted sexual advances (Wechsler et al., 2002). Worse yet, alcohol appears to contribute to about 90 percent of student rapes and 95 percent of violent crime on campus. In society at large, alcohol is associated with a variety of violent crimes, including murder, assault, rape, child abuse, and spouse abuse (Wood et al., 2001). Finally, alcohol can also contribute to reckless sexual behavior, which may have ramifications for one's health. In the Harvard survey, 21 percent of students who drank reported that they had unplanned sex as a result of drinking, and 10 percent indicated that their drinking had led to unprotected sex.

Long-Term Health Effects and Social Costs

Alcohol's long-term health risks are mostly (but not exclusively) associated with chronic, heavy consumption of alcohol. Estimates of the number of people at risk vary considerably. According to Schuckit (2000) ap-

proximately 5–10 percent of American men and women engage in chronic alcohol abuse and another 10 percent of men and 3–5 percent of women probably suffer from *alcohol dependence,* or *alcoholism.* **Alcohol dependence (alcoholism) is a chronic, progressive disorder marked by a growing compulsion to drink and impaired control over drinking that eventually interfere with health and social behavior.** Whether alcoholism is best viewed as a disease or as a self-control problem is the source of considerable debate, but experts have reached a reasonable consensus about the warning signs of alcoholism. These signs include preoccupation with alcohol, drinking to relieve uncomfortable feelings, gulping drinks, clandestine drinking, and the other indicators listed in Figure 14.14.

Alcoholism and problem drinking are associated with an elevated risk for a wide range of serious health problems, which are summarized in Figure 14.15 (Mack, Franklin, & Frances, 2003; Moak & Anton, 1999). Although there is some thought-provoking evidence that moderate drinking may reduce one's risk for coronary disease (Chick, 1998; Mukamal et al., 2003), it is clear that heavy drinking increases the risk for heart disease, hypertension, and stroke. Excessive drinking is also correlated with an elevated risk for various types of cancer, including oral, stomach, pancreatic, colon, and rectal cancer. Moreover, serious drinking problems can lead to cirrhosis of the liver, malnutrition, pregnancy

WEB LINK 14.4

National Institute on Alcohol Abuse and Alcoholism
Just two of the many scientific research sources from this NIH agency include the entire collection of the bulletin *Alcohol Alert,* issued since 1988 on specific topics related to alcoholism (e.g., "Alcohol and Sleep" or "Youth Drinking") and the ETOH Database, a searchable repository of more than 100,000 records on alcoholism and alcohol abuse.

● FIGURE 14.14

Detecting a drinking problem. Facing the reality that one has a problem with alcohol is always difficult. This list of the chief warning signs associated with problem drinking is intended to help with this process.

Adapted from Edlin, G., & Golanty, E. (1992). *Health and wellness*. Boston: Jones & Bartlett. Copyright © 1992 Jones & Bartlett Publishers, Inc. Reprinted with permission.

complications, brain damage, and neurological disorders. Finally, alcoholism can produce severe psychotic states, characterized by delirium, disorientation, and hallucinations.

We have focused on the personal risks of alcohol abuse, but the enormous social costs of alcohol should also be emphasized (Wood et al., 2001). Drinking problems wreak havoc in millions of families. Children of alcoholics grow up in dysfunctional environments in which the risk of physical or sexual abuse is much higher than normal (Mathew et al., 1993). In the world of work, alcohol-related absenteeism and reduced efficiency on the job cost American industry billions of dollars annually. It is hard to put a dollar value on the diverse social costs of alcohol abuse, but experts estimate that alcohol costs the U.S. economy about $185 billion annually (Johnson & Ait-Daoud, 2005). Thus, the social costs of alcohol are staggering.

Overeating

Obesity is a common health problem. The criteria for obesity vary considerably. One simple, intermediate criterion is to classify people as obese if their weight exceeds their ideal body weight by 20 percent. If this criterion is used, 31 percent of men and 35 percent of women in the United States qualify as obese (Brownell & Wadden, 2000). Many experts prefer to assess obesity in terms of *body mass index (BMI)*—weight (in kilograms) divided by height (in meters) squared (kg/m^2). This increasingly used index of weight controls for variations in height. A BMI of 25.0–29.9 is typically regarded as overweight, and a BMI over 30 is considered obese (Bjorntorp, 2002). Although American culture seems to be obsessed with slimness, recent

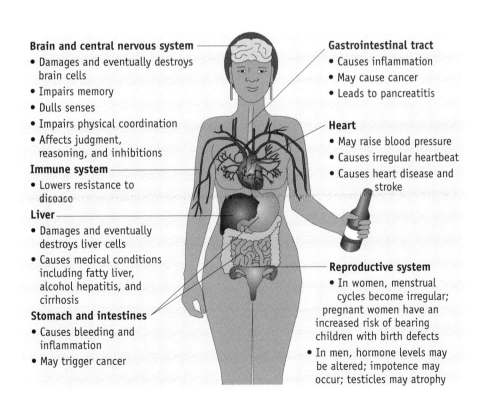

Brain and central nervous system
- Damages and eventually destroys brain cells
- Impairs memory
- Dulls senses
- Impairs physical coordination
- Affects judgment, reasoning, and inhibitions

Immune system
- Lowers resistance to disease

Liver
- Damages and eventually destroys liver cells
- Causes medical conditions including fatty liver, alcohol hepatitis, and cirrhosis

Stomach and intestines
- Causes bleeding and inflammation
- May trigger cancer

Gastrointestinal tract
- Causes inflammation
- May cause cancer
- Leads to pancreatitis

Heart
- May raise blood pressure
- Causes irregular heartbeat
- Causes heart disease and stroke

Reproductive system
- In women, menstrual cycles become irregular; pregnant women have an increased risk of bearing children with birth defects
- In men, hormone levels may be altered; impotence may occur; testicles may atrophy

● FIGURE 14.15

Health risks associated with drinking. This graphic provides an overview of the various diseases that are more common among drinkers than abstainers. As you can see, alcohol elevates one's vulnerability to a remarkably diverse array of diseases.

surveys show surprisingly sharp increases in the incidence of obesity (Corsica & Perri, 2003). If a BMI over 25 is used as the cutoff, almost two-thirds of American adults are struggling with weight problems (Sarwer, Foster, & Wadden, 2004). Moreover, they are not alone—they have plenty of company from their children, as weight problems among children and adolescents have increased 15–22 percent in recent decades (West et al., 2004).

Obesity is similar to smoking in that it exerts a relatively subtle impact on health that is easy for many people to ignore. Nevertheless, the long-range effects of obesity can be quite dangerous. Obesity is a significant health problem that elevates one's mortality risk (Allison et al., 1999; Bender et al., 1999). Overweight people are more vulnerable than others to heart disease, diabetes, hypertension, respiratory problems, gallbladder disease, stroke, arthritis, muscle and joint pain, and back problems (Manson, Skerrett, & Willet, 2002; Pi-Sunyer, 2002). For example, Figure 14.16 shows how the prevalence of diabetes, hypertension, coronary disease, and musculoskeletal pain are elevated as BMI increases.

Evolution-oriented researchers have a plausible explanation for the dramatic increase in the prevalence of obesity (Pinel, Assanand, & Lehman, 2000). They point out that over the course of history, most animals and humans have lived in environments in which there was fierce competition for limited, unreliable food resources and starvation was a very real threat. Hence, warm-blooded, foraging animals evolved a propensity to consume more food than immediately necessary when the opportunity presented itself because food might not be available later. Excess calories were stored in the body to prepare for future food shortages. This approach to eating remains adaptive for most species of animals that continue to struggle with the ebb and flow of unpredictable food supplies. However, in today's modern, industrialized societies, the vast majority of humans live in environments that provide an abundant, reliable supply of tasty, high-calorie food. In these environments, humans' evolved tendency to overeat when food is plentiful leads most people down a pathway of chronic, excessive food consumption. According to this line of thinking, most people in food-replete environments tend to overeat in relation to their physiological needs, but because of variations in genetics, metabolism, and other factors only some become overweight.

Determinants of Obesity

A few decades ago it was widely believed that obesity is a function of personality. Obesity was thought to occur mostly in depressed, anxious, compulsive people who overate to deal with their negative emotions or in lazy, undisciplined individuals. However, research eventu-

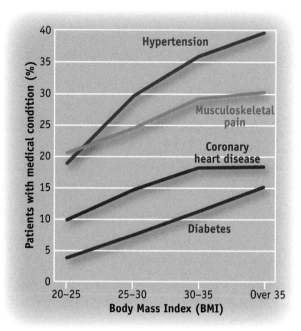

● FIGURE 14.16

Weight and the prevalence of various diseases. This graph shows how obesity, as indexed by BMI, is related to the prevalence of four common types of illness. The prevalence of diabetes, heart disease, muscle pain, and hypertension all increase as BMI goes up. Clearly, obesity is a significant health risk. (Data from Brownell & Wadden, 2000)

ally showed that there is no such thing as an "obese personality" (Rodin, Schank, & Striegel-Moore, 1989). Instead, research showed that a complex network of interacting factors determine whether people develop weight problems.

Heredity. Chief among the factors contributing to obesity is *genetic predisposition* (Bouchard, 2002). In one influential study, adults raised by foster parents were compared with their biological and foster parents in regard to body mass index (Stunkard et al., 1986). The investigators found that the adoptees resembled their biological parents much more than their adoptive parents. In a subsequent *twin study,* Stunkard and associates (1990) found that identical twins reared apart were far more similar in body mass index than fraternal twins reared together (see Chapter 2 for a discussion of the logic underlying twin studies). Based on a study of over 4000 twins, Allison and colleagues (1994) estimate that genetic factors account for 61 percent of the variation in weight among men and 73 percent of the variation among women. These genetic factors probably explain why some people can eat constantly without gaining weight whereas other people grow chubby eating far less. Thus, it appears that some people inherit a genetic vulnerability to obesity (Cope, Fernandez, & Allison, 2004).

Excessive eating and inadequate exercise. The bottom line for overweight people is that their energy intake from food consumption chronically exceeds their energy expenditure from physical activities and resting metabolic processes. In other words, they eat too much in relation to their level of exercise (Wing & Polley, 2001). In modern America, the tendency to overeat and exercise too little is easy to understand (Henderson & Brownell, 2004). Tasty, caloric, high-fat foods are readily available nearly everywhere, not just in restaurants and grocery stores, but in shopping malls, airports, gas stations, schools, and workplaces. And when people eat out, they tend to eat larger meals and consume more high-fat food than they would at home (French, Harnack, & Jeffery, 2000). Unfortunately, the increased availability of highly caloric food in America has been paralleled by declining physical activity. Modern conveniences, such as cars and elevators, and changes in the world of work, such as the shift to more desk jobs, have conspired to make American lifestyles more sedentary then ever before.

Set point. People who lose weight on a diet have a rather strong (and depressing) tendency to gain back all the weight they lose. The reverse is also true. People who have to work to put weight on often have trouble keeping it on. According to Richard Keesey (1995), these observations suggest that your body may have a *set point,* or a natural point of stability in body weight. **Set-point theory proposes that the body monitors fat-cell levels to keep them (and weight) fairly stable.** When fat stores slip below a crucial set point, the body supposedly begins to compensate for this change (Keesey, 1993). This compensation apparently leads to increased hunger and decreased metabolism.

Studies have raised some doubts about various details of set-point theory, leading some researchers to propose an alternative called *settling-point theory* (Pinel et al., 2000). ***Settling-point theory* proposes that weight tends to drift around the level at which the constellation of factors that determine food consumption and energy expenditure achieve an equilibrium.** According to this view, weight tends to remain stable as long as there are no durable changes in any of the factors that influence it. Settling-point theory casts a much wider net than set-point theory, which attributes weight stability to specific physiological processes. Another difference is that set-point theory asserts that an obese person's body will initiate processes that actively defend an excessive weight, whereas settling-point theory suggests that if an obese person makes long-term changes in eating or exercise that person's settling point will drift downward without active resistance. Thus, settling-point theory is a little more encouraging to those who hope to lose weight.

Losing Weight

Whether out of concern about their health or just old-fashioned vanity, an ever-increasing number of people are trying to lose weight. At any given time, about 21 percent of men and 39 percent of women are dieting (Hill, 2002). Although concerns have been raised that dieting carries its own risks, the evidence clearly indicates that weight loss efforts involving moderate changes in eating and exercise are more beneficial than harmful to people's health (Devlin, Yanovski, & Wilson, 2000). Research has provided some good news for those who need to lose weight. Studies have demonstrated that relatively modest weight reductions can significantly diminish many of the health risks associated with obesity. For example, a 10 percent weight loss is associated with reduced medical risks (Jeffery et al., 2000). Thus, the traditional objective of obesity treatment—reducing to

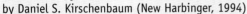
one's ideal weight—has been replaced by more modest and realistic goals (Sarwer et al., 2004).

While many factors may contribute to obesity, there is only one way to lose weight. You must change your ratio of energy intake (food consumption) to energy output (physical activities). To be quite specific, to lose one pound you need to burn up 3500 more calories than you consume. You have three options in trying to change your ratio of energy input to energy output: (1) You can sharply reduce your food consumption, (2) you can sharply increase your exercise output, or (3) or you can simultaneously decrease your food intake and step up your exercise output in more moderate ways. Virtually all experts recommend the third option. Brownell (1995) emphasizes that exercise is an essential ingredient of an effective weight-loss regimen. Exercise seems especially important for *maintaining* reduced weight, as it is the single best predictor of long-term weight loss (Wing & Polley, 2001). Moreover, exercise can yield many other benefits, which we will discuss momentarily.

Self-modification techniques (see the Chapter 4 Application) can be helpful in achieving gradual weight loss. Indeed, behavior modification procedures represent the cornerstone of most reputable, professional weight-loss programs. Overall, the evidence on weight-loss programs suggests that they are moderately successful in the short term (the first 6 months), but in the long run the vast majority of people regain most of the weight that they lose (Jeffery et al., 2000). Diet medications can be a useful adjunct in weight loss efforts that can contribute to success, but only if they are part of a conventional program that alters eating and exercise habits (Brownell & Wadden, 2000). Reliance on medication alone does not lead to durable weight loss, and diet drugs carry risks of their own.

Poor Nutrition

Nutrition is a collection of processes (mainly food consumption) through which an organism utilizes the materials (nutrients) required for survival and growth. The term also refers to the *study* of these processes. Unfortunately, most of us don't study nutrition very much. Moreover, the cunning mass marketing of nutritionally worthless foods makes maintaining sound nutritional habits more and more difficult.

Nutrition and Health

Evidence is accumulating that patterns of nutrition influence susceptibility to a variety of diseases and health problems. For example, in a study of over 42,000 women, investigators found an association between a measure of overall diet quality and mortality. Women who reported poorer quality diets had elevated mortality rates (Kant et al., 2000). What are the specific links between diet and health? In addition to the problems associated with obesity, which we have already discussed, other possible connections between eating patterns and health include the following:

1. Heavy consumption of foods that elevate serum cholesterol level (eggs, cheeses, butter, shellfish, sausage, and the like) appears to increase the risk of cardiovascular disease (Stamler et al., 2000; see Figure 14.17). Eating habits are only one of several factors that influence serum cholesterol level, but they do make an important contribution.

2. Vulnerability to cardiovascular diseases may also be influenced by other dietary factors. For example, low-fiber diets may increase the likelihood of coronary disease (Ludwig et al., 1999; Wolk et al., 1999) and high intake of red and processed meats, sweets, potatoes, and refined grains is associated with increased cardiovascular risk (Hu & Willett, 2002). Recent research indicates that the omega 3 fatty acids found in

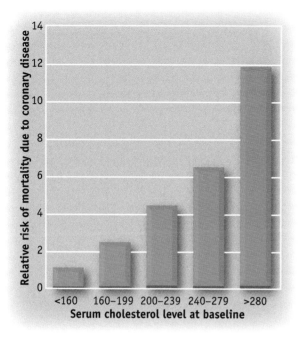

● **FIGURE 14.17**

The link between cholesterol and coronary risk. In a review of several major studies, Stamler et al. (2000) summarize crucial evidence on the association between cholesterol levels and the prevalence of cardiovascular disease. This graph is based on a sample of over 11,000 men who were 18 to 39 at the beginning of the study (1967–1973) when their serum cholesterol level was measured. The data shown here depict participants' relative risk for coronary heart disease during the ensuing 25 years, as a function of their initial cholesterol level. (Data from Stamler et al., 2000)

fish and fish oils offer protection against coronary disease (Din, Newby, & Flapan, 2004).

3. High salt intake is thought to be a contributing factor in the development of hypertension (Vollmer et al., 2001), although there is still some debate about its exact role.

4. High caffeine consumption may elevate one's risk for hypertension (James, 2004) and for coronary disease (Happonen, Voutilainen, Salonen, 2004), although the negative effects of caffeine appear relatively modest.

5. High-fat diets have been implicated as possible contributors to some forms of cancer, especially prostate cancer (Rose, 1997), colon and rectal cancer (Shike, 1999), and breast cancer (Wynder et al., 1997). Some studies also suggest that high-fiber diets may reduce one's risk for colon and rectal cancer (Reddy, 1999), but the evidence is not conclusive.

6. Vulnerability to osteoporosis, an abnormal loss of bone mass observed most commonly in post-menopausal women, appears to be elevated by a life-long pattern of inadequate calcium intake (Kalkwarf, Khoury, Lanphear, 2003).

7. Although the research findings are mixed, there is some evidence that vitamin E may reduce one's risk for coronary disease and some types of cancer (Friedrich, 2004).

Of course, nutritional habits interact with other factors—genetics, exercise, environment, and so on—to determine whether someone will develop a particular disease. Nonetheless, the examples just described indicate that eating habits *can* influence physical health.

The Basis for Poor Nutrition

Nutritional deficiencies are more widespread in the United States than most people realize. One study found that 70 percent of men and 80 percent of women consumed a diet deficient in at least one of 15 essential nutrients (Murphy et al., 1992). For the most part, these deficiencies are not a result of low income or an inability to afford appropriate foods. Instead, most malnutrition in America is attributable to lack of knowledge about nutrition and lack of effort to ensure good nutrition (West et al., 2004).

In other words, our nutritional shortcomings are the result of ignorance and poor motivation. Americans are remarkably naive about the basic principles of nutrition. Schools tend to provide little education in this area, and most people are not highly motivated to make sure their food consumption is nutritionally sound. Instead, people approach eating very casually, guided not by nutritional needs but by convenience, palatability, and clever advertising.

For most people, then, the first steps toward improved nutrition involve changing attitudes and acquiring information. First and foremost, people need to recognize the importance of nutrition and commit themselves to making a real effort to regulate their eating patterns. Second, people should try to acquire a basic education in nutritional principles.

Nutritional Goals

The most healthful approach to nutrition is to follow well-moderated patterns of food consumption that ensure nutritional adequacy while limiting the intake of

The food guide pyramid. The food pyramid, endorsed in 1992 by the U.S. Department of Agriculture, is intended to provide a simple and easy guide to nutritionally balanced eating. It identifies key categories of food and makes recommendations about how many daily servings one should have in each category. As your text explains, it has been subjected to criticism and currently is under revision.

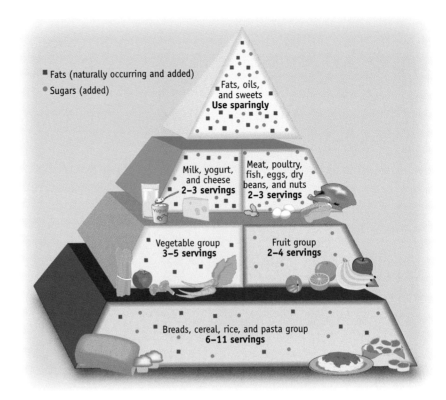

certain substances that can be counterproductive. Here are some general guidelines for achieving these goals:

1. *Consume a balanced variety of foods.* Food is made up of a variety of components, six of which are essential to your physical well-being. These six *essential nutrients* are proteins, fats, carbohydrates, vitamins, minerals, and fiber. Proteins, fats, and carbohydrates supply the body with its energy. Vitamins and minerals help release that energy and serve other important functions as well. Fiber provides roughage that facilitates digestion. Educational efforts to promote adequate intake of all essential nutrients have generally suggested that people should be guided by the classic food pyramid published by the U. S. Department of Agriculture (see Figure 14.18). Although the food pyramid remains a useful benchmark, it has been subjected to considerable criticism, and hotly debated revisions are under way (Norton, 2004). The principal problem with the food pyramid is its failure to distinguish between different types of fat, different forms of carbohydrates, and different sources of protein (Willett & Stampfer, 2003). For example, the current thinking is that monounsaturated and polyunsaturated fats are healthy, whereas saturated fats should be consumed sparingly. A revised food pyramid, which takes distinctions such as these into consideration, is shown in Figure 14.19.

2. *Avoid excessive consumption of saturated fats, cholesterol, refined-grain carbohydrates, sugar, and salt.*

These commodities are all overrepresented in the typical American diet. It is particularly prudent to limit the intake of saturated fats by eating less beef, pork, ham, hot dogs, sausage, lunch meats, whole milk, and fried foods. Consumption of many of these foods should also be limited to reduce cholesterol intake, which influences vulnerability to heart disease. In particular, beef, pork, lamb, sausage, cheese, butter, and eggs are high in cholesterol. Refined-grain carbohydrates, such as white bread, pasta, and white rice, are problematic because they increase glucose levels in the blood too quickly. Refined (processed) sugar is believed to be grossly overconsumed. Hence, people should limit their dependence on soft drinks, chocolate, candy, pastries, and high-sugar cereals. Finally, many people should cut down on their salt intake. Doing so may require more than simply ignoring the salt shaker, as many prepackaged foods are loaded with salt.

3. *Increase consumption of polyunsaturated fats, whole-grain carbohydrates, natural sugars, and foods with fiber.* To substitute polyunsaturated fats for saturated ones, you can eat more fish, chicken, turkey, and veal; trim meats of fat more thoroughly; use skim (nonfat) milk; and switch to vegetable oils that are high in polyunsaturated fats. Healthy carbohydrates include whole grain foods such as whole wheat bread, oatmeal, and brown rice, which are digested more slowly than refined-grain carbohydrates. Fruits and vegetables tend to provide natural sugars and ample fiber. Healthy sources of protein include fish, poultry, eggs, and nuts.

● FIGURE 14.19

The healthy eating pyramid. This alternative food pyramid was developed by Walter Willett and colleagues at the Harvard Medical School. It corrects a variety of flaws that were apparent in the USDA food pyramid and incorporates recent scientific findings on healthy versus unhealthy fats and carbohydrates.

Adapted from Willett, W. C. (2001). *Eat, drink, and be healthy: The Harvard Medical School guide to healthy eating.* New York: Free Press. Copyright © 2001 by the President and Fellows at Harvard College. Adapted with permission of Simon & Schuster Adult Publishing Group.

RECOMMENDED READING

Eat, Drink, and Be Healthy: The Harvard Medical School Guide to Healthy Eating
by Walter C. Willett (Free Press, 2001)

Harvard Medical School professor Walter Willett is a renowned nutrition researcher who has written a superb book on healthy eating. Willett has been one of the more vocal critics of the food pyramid released by the U.S. Department of Agriculture in 1992. He asserts that "It was built on shaky scientific ground back in 1992. Since then it has been steadily eroded by new research from all parts of the globe" (pp. 15–16). Willett explains that the food pyramid was the product of extensive wrangling between scientists, bureaucrats, and special interest lobbies, such as the meat, dairy, and sugar industries. Given all the compromises that were struck, it never was an optimal guide for healthy eating. Moreover, the food pyramid does not reflect many important, recent scientific findings on nutrition. Willett reviews these findings and their practical implications in an easy-to-understand, readable style. He sifts through the often contradictory evidence on nutrition and health and makes sense of it all. He describes an alternative healthy eating pyramid and then provides extensive advice on how to eat in a sensible manner.

Cover reprinted with permission of Simon & Schuster Adult Publishing Group. Copyright © 2001 by President and fellows at Harvard College.

Lack of Exercise

A great deal of evidence suggests that there is a link between exercise and health. Research indicates that regular exercise is associated with increased longevity (Lee & Skerrett, 2001). Moreover, you don't have to be a dedicated athlete to benefit from exercise. Even a moderate level of reasonably regular physical activity is associated with lower mortality rates (Richardson et al., 2004; see Figure 14.20 on the next page). Unfortunately, physical fitness appears to be declining in the United States. Only 25 percent of American adults get an adequate amount of regular exercise (Dubbert et al., 2004).

Benefits and Risks of Exercise

Exercise is correlated with greater longevity because it promotes a diverse array of specific benefits. First, an appropriate exercise program can enhance cardiovascular fitness and thereby reduce one's susceptibility to cardiovascular problems. Fitness is associated with reduced risk for coronary disease, stroke, and hypertension

WEB LINK 14.6

About.Com: Health and Fitness
About.Com is a commercial endeavor enlisting subject experts to edit topic-specific directories with annotated links and other information resources. More than 60 directories related to topics of health and fitness—including alcoholism, substance abuse, and smoking cessation—are now available at About.Com.

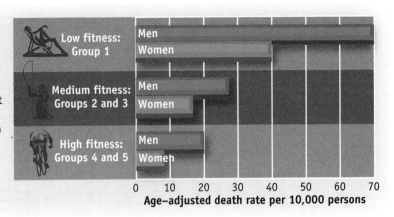

Fitness category
Participants were divided into five categories based on their fitness, ranging from least fit (group 1) to most fit (group 5)

- Low fitness: Group 1 — Men / Women
- Medium fitness: Groups 2 and 3 — Men / Women
- High fitness: Groups 4 and 5 — Men / Women

0 10 20 30 40 50 60 70
Age–adjusted death rate per 10,000 persons

● **FIGURE 14.20**

Physical fitness and mortality. Blair et al. (1989) studied death rates among men and women who exhibited low, medium, or high fitness. Even medium fitness was associated with lower mortality rates in both genders. The investigators note that one could achieve this level of fitness by taking a brisk half-hour walk each day. (Data from Blair et al., 1989)

(Blair, Cheng, & Holder, 2001; Lee et al., 2001). Second, regular physical activity can contribute to the avoidance of obesity (Corsica & Perri, 2003). Hence, fitness may indirectly reduce one's risk for a variety of obesity-related health problems, including diabetes, respiratory difficulties, arthritis, and back pain. Third, some recent studies suggest that physical fitness is also associated with a decreased risk for colon cancer and for breast and reproductive cancer in women (Thune & Furberg, 2001). The apparent link between exercise and reduced cancer risk has been a pleasant surprise for scientists, who are now scrambling to replicate the findings and figure out the physiological mechanisms underlying this association.

Fourth, exercise may serve as a buffer that reduces the potentially damaging effects of stress (Plante, 1999b; Plante, Caputo, & Chizmar, 2000). This buffering effect may occur because people high in fitness show less physiological reactivity to stress than those who are less fit. Fifth, exercise may have a favorable impact on mental health, which in turn may have positive effects on physical health. Studies have found a consistent association between regular exercise over a period of at least eight weeks and reduced depression (Phillips, Kiernan, & King, 2001), which is important given the evidence that depression is correlated with increased vulnerability to heart disease. Sixth, successful participation in an exercise program can produce desirable personality changes that may promote physical wellness. Research suggests that fitness training can lead to improvements in one's mood, self-esteem, and work efficiency, as well as reductions in tension and anxiety (Dunn, Trivedi, & O'Neal, 2001; Hays, 1999; Sonstroem, 1997).

Devising an Exercise Program

Putting together a good exercise program is difficult for many people. Exercise is time-consuming, and if you're out of shape, your initial attempts may be painful, aversive, and discouraging. People who do not get enough exercise cite lack of time, lack of convenience, and lack of enjoyment as the reasons (Jakicic & Gallagher, 2002). To circumvent these problems, it is wise to heed the following advice (Greenberg, 2002; Jakicic & Gallagher, 2002; Phillips et al., 2001):

1. *Look for an activity that you will find enjoyable.* You have a great many physical activities to choose from (see Figure 14.21). Shop around for one that you find intrinsically enjoyable. Doing so will make it much easier for you to follow through and exercise regularly.

2. *Increase your participation gradually.* Don't try to do too much too quickly. An overzealous approach can lead to frustration, not to mention injury. An exercise regimen should build gradually. If you experience injuries, avoid the common tendency to ignore them. Consult your physician to see whether continuing your exercise program is advisable.

3. *Exercise regularly without overdoing it.* Sporadic exercise will not improve your fitness. A widely cited rule of thumb is that you should plan on exercising for a minimum of 30 minutes three to five times a week, or you will gain little benefit from your efforts. At the other extreme, don't try to become fit overnight by working out too vigorously. One recent study found that people are more likely to stick to an exercise regimen consisting of more frequent workouts of moderate intensity than a regimen of less frequent but more intense workouts (Perri et al., 2002).

How Beneficial Is Your Favorite Sport?

	Jogging	Bicycling	Swimming	Skating (ice or roller)	Handball/Squash	Skiing—Nordic	Skiing—Alpine	Basketball	Tennis	Calisthenics	Walking	Golf	Softball	Bowling
Physical fitness														
Cardiorespiratory endurance (stamina)	21	19	21	18	19	19	16	19	16	10	13	8	6	5
Muscular endurance	20	18	20	17	18	19	18	17	16	13	14	8	8	5
Muscular strength	17	16	14	15	15	15	15	15	14	16	11	9	7	5
Flexibility	9	9	15	13	16	14	14	13	14	19	7	9	9	7
Balance	17	18	12	20	17	16	21	16	16	15	8	8	7	6
General well-being														
Weight control	21	20	15	17	19	17	15	19	16	12	13	6	7	5
Muscle definition	14	15	14	14	11	12	14	13	13	18	11	6	5	5
Digestion	13	12	13	11	13	12	9	10	12	11	11	7	8	7
Sleep	16	15	16	15	12	15	12	12	11	12	14	6	7	6
Total	**148**	**142**	**140**	**140**	**140**	**139**	**134**	**134**	**128**	**126**	**102**	**67**	**64**	**51**

● **FIGURE 14.21**

A scorecard on the benefits of 14 sports and exercises. Here is a summary of how seven experts rated the value of 14 sporting activities (the highest rating possible on any one item was 21). The ratings were based on vigorous participation four times per week.

Adapted from Conrad, C. C. (1976, May). How different sports rate in promoting physical fitness. *Medical Times,* pp. 45. Copyright 1976 by Romaine Pierson Publishers. Reprinted by permission.

Regular exercise has many physical and psychological benefits that promote increased longevity.

4. *Reinforce yourself for your participation.* To offset the inconvenience or pain that may be associated with exercise, it is a good idea to reinforce yourself for your participation. The behavior modification procedures discussed in Chapter 4 can be helpful in devising a viable exercise program.

Behavior and AIDS

At present, some of the most problematic links between behavior and health may be those related to AIDS. AIDS stands for *acquired immune deficiency syndrome,* **a disorder in which the immune system is gradually weakened and eventually disabled by the human immunodeficiency virus (HIV).** Being infected with the HIV virus is *not* equivalent to having AIDS. AIDS is the final stage of the HIV infection process, typically manifested about 7–10 years after the original infection (Carey & Vanable, 2003). With the onset of AIDS, one is left virtually defenseless against a host of opportunistic infectious agents. The symptoms of AIDS vary widely depending on the specific constellation of diseases that one develops (Cunningham & Selwyn, 2005). Unfortunately, the worldwide prevalence of this deadly disease continues to increase at an alarming rate, especially in certain regions of Africa (De Cock & Janssen, 2002).

Prior to 1996–1997, the average length of survival for people after the onset of the AIDS syndrome was about 18 to 24 months. Encouraging advances in the treatment of AIDS with drug regimens referred to as *highly active antiretroviral therapy* hold out promise for *substantially* longer survival (Sande & Ronald, 2004). But these drugs are being rushed into service and their long-term efficacy is yet to be determined. Medical experts are concerned that the general public has gotten the impression that these treatments have transformed AIDS from a fatal disease to a manageable one, which is a premature conclusion. HIV strains are evolving and many have developed resistance to the currently available antiretroviral drugs (Trachtenberg & Sande, 2002). Moreover, many patients do not respond well to the new drugs and many patients who are responsive have difficulty sticking to the complicated drug administration regimens that often require people to take 20–30 pills daily and that often have adverse side effects (Catz & Kelly, 2001; Sorenson, Haug, & Batki, 2005). Another daunting problem is that these expensive new drugs remain largely unavailable in developing nations, which have not seen progress in treatment. In some African nations the impact of AIDS has reduced life expectancy to levels not seen for hundreds of years. In Botswana, for instance, projections suggest that life expectancy has declined from 66 to 33 years (Carey & Vanable, 2003).

Transmission

As mentioned in Chapter 13, the HIV virus is transmitted through person-to-person contact involving the exchange of bodily fluids, primarily semen and blood. The two principal modes of transmission in the United States have been sexual contact and the sharing of needles by intravenous (IV) drug users. In the United States, sexual transmission has occurred primarily among gay and bisexual men, but heterosexual transmission has increased in recent years (Catania et al., 2001). In the world as a whole, infection through heterosexual relations has been more common from the beginning. In heterosexual relations, male-to-female transmission is estimated to be about eight times more likely than female-to-male transmission (Ickovics, Thayaparan, & Ethier, 2001). The HIV virus can be found in the tears and saliva of infected individuals, but the concentrations are low, and there is no evidence that the infection can be spread through casual contact. Even most forms of noncasual contact, including kissing, hugging, and sharing food with infected individuals, appear safe (Kalichman, 1995).

Misconceptions

Misconceptions about AIDS are widespread. Ironically, the people who hold these misconceptions fall into two polarized camps. On the one hand, a great many people have unrealistic fears that AIDS can be readily transmitted through casual contact with infected individuals. These people worry unnecessarily about contracting AIDS from a handshake, a sneeze, or an eating utensil. They tend to be paranoid about interacting with homosexuals, thus fueling discrimination against gays. Some people also believe that it is dangerous to donate blood when, in fact, blood donors are at no risk whatsoever.

On the other hand, many young heterosexuals who are sexually active with a variety of partners foolishly downplay their risk for HIV, naively assuming that they are safe as long as they avoid IV drug use and sexual relations with gay or bisexual men. They greatly underestimate the probability that their sexual partners may have previously used IV drugs or had unprotected sex with an infected individual. They don't understand, for instance, that most bisexual men do not disclose their bisexuality to their female partners (Kalichman et al., 1998). Also, because AIDS is usually accompanied by discernible symptoms, many young people believe that prospective sexual partners who carry the HIV virus will exhibit telltale signs of illness. However, as we have already noted, having AIDS and being infected with HIV are not the same thing, and HIV carriers often remain healthy and symptom-free for many years after they are infected. In sum, many myths about AIDS persist, despite extensive efforts to educate the public about this complex and controversial disease. Figure 14.22 contains a short quiz to test your knowledge of the facts about AIDS.

Prevention

The behavioral changes that minimize the risk of developing AIDS are fairly straightforward, although making the changes is often much easier said than done (Coates & Collins, 1998). In all groups, the more sexual partners a person has, the higher the risk that he or she will be exposed to the HIV virus. Thus, people can reduce their risk by having sexual contacts with fewer partners and by using condoms to control the exchange of semen. It is also important to curtail certain sexual practices (in particular, anal sex) that increase the probability of semen/blood mixing. The 1980s and early 1990s saw considerable progress toward wider use of safe sex practices, but new cohorts of young people appear to be much less concerned about the risk of HIV infection than the generation that witnessed the original emergence of AIDS (Catania et al., 2001). In particular, experts are concerned that recent advances in treatment may lead to more casual attitudes about risky sexual practices, a development that would not bode well for public health efforts to slow the spread of AIDS (Crepaz, Hart, & Marks, 2004).

AIDS Risk Knowledge Test

Answer the following "true" or "false."

T F **1.** The AIDS virus cannot be spread through kissing.

T F **2.** A person can get the AIDS virus by sharing kitchens and bathrooms with someone who has AIDS.

T F **3.** Men can give the AIDS virus to women.

T F **4.** The AIDS virus attacks the body's ability to fight off diseases.

T F **5.** You can get the AIDS virus by someone sneezing, like a cold or the flu.

T F **6.** You can get AIDS by touching a person with AIDS.

T F **7.** Women can give the AIDS virus to men.

T F **8.** A person who got the AIDS virus from shooting up drugs cannot give the virus to someone by having sex.

T F **9.** A pregnant woman can give the AIDS virus to her unborn baby.

T F **10.** Most types of birth control also protect against getting the AIDS virus.

T F **11.** Condoms make intercourse completely safe.

T F **12.** Oral sex is safe if partners "do not swallow."

T F **13.** A person must have many different sexual partners to be at risk for AIDS.

T F **14.** It is more important to take precautions against AIDS in large cities than in small cities.

T F **15.** A positive result on the AIDS virus antibody test often occurs for people who do not even have the virus.

T F **16.** Only receptive (passive) anal intercourse transmits the AIDS virus.

T F **17.** Donating blood carries no AIDS risk for the donor.

T F **18.** Most people who have the AIDS virus look quite ill.

Answers: 1. T 2. F 3. T 4. T 5. F 6. F 7. T 8. F 9. T 10. F 11. F 12. F 13. F 14. F 15. F 16. F 17. T 18. F

● **FIGURE 14.22**

A quiz on knowledge of AIDS. Because misconceptions about AIDS abound, it may be wise to take this brief quiz to test your knowledge of AIDS.

Adapted from Kalichman, S. C. (1995). *Understanding AIDS: A guide for mental health professionals.* Washington, DC: American Psychological Association. Copyright © 1995 by the American Psychological Association. Adapted with permission of the author.

Reactions to Illness

LEARNING OBJECTIVES

- Summarize evidence on patterns of treatment-seeking behavior.
- Explain the appeal of the "sick role."
- Identify the factors that tend to undermine doctor-patient communication and how to improve it.
- Discuss the prevalence of nonadherence to medical advice and its causes.

So far we have emphasized the psychosocial aspects of maintaining health and minimizing the risk of illness. Health is also affected by how individuals respond to physical symptoms and illnesses. Some people engage in denial and ignore early-warning signs of developing diseases. Others engage in active coping efforts to conquer their diseases. In this section, we discuss the decision to seek medical treatment, the sick role, communication with health providers, and compliance with medical advice.

The Decision to Seek Treatment

Have you ever experienced nausea, diarrhea, stiffness, headaches, cramps, chest pains, or sinus problems? Of course you have; everyone experiences some of these problems periodically. However, whether you view these sensations as *symptoms* is a matter of individual interpretation. When two persons experience the same unpleasant sensations, one may shrug them off as a nuisance, while the other may rush to a physician (Martin & Leventhal, 2004). Studies suggest that those who are relatively high in anxiety and neuroticism tend to report more symptoms of illness than others do (Feldman et al., 1999). Those who are extremely attentive to bodily sensations and health concerns also report more symptoms than the average person (Barsky, 1988).

Variations in the perception of symptoms help explain why people vary so much in their readiness to seek medical treatment (Cameron, Leventhal, &

Leventhal, 1993). Generally, people are more likely to seek medical care when their symptoms are unfamiliar, appear to be serious, last longer than expected, or disrupt their work or social activities (Bernard & Krupat, 1994; Martin et al., 2003). Another key consideration is how friends and family react to the symptoms. Medical consultation is much more likely when friends and family view symptoms as serious and encourage the person to seek medical care, although nagging a person about seeking care can sometimes backfire (Martin et al., 2003). Gender also influences decisions to seek treatment, as women are much more likely than men to utilize medical services (Bertakis et al., 2000).

The time that elapses between the first perception of physical distress and the actual provision of health care is not necessarily a period of passive waiting. The process of seeking medical treatment can be divided into three stages of active, complex problem-solving (Martin et al., 2003). First, people have to decide that their physical sensations *are* symptoms—that they are indicative of illness. Second, they have to decide that their apparent illness warrants medical attention. Third, they have to go to the trouble to make the actual arrangements for medical care, which can be complicated and time-consuming. The task of checking insurance coverage, finding an appropriate doctor, negotiating an appointment, arranging to get off work or take care of children, and so forth can be a huge series of hassles.

Courtesy, Robin DiMatteo

Robin DiMatteo

Small wonder then, that the biggest problem in regard to treatment seeking is the tendency of many people to delay the pursuit of needed professional consultation. Delays can be important, because early diagnosis and quick intervention can facilitate more effective treatment of many health problems. Unfortunately, procrastination is the norm even when people are faced with a medical emergency, such as a heart attack (Martin & Leventhal, 2004). Why do people dawdle in the midst of a crisis? Robin DiMatteo (1991) mentions a number of reasons, noting that people delay because they often (1) misinterpret and downplay the significance of their symptoms, (2) fret about looking silly if the problem turns out to be nothing, (3) worry about "bothering" their physician, (4) are reluctant to disrupt their plans (to go out to dinner, see a movie, and so forth), and (5) waste time on trivial matters (such as taking a shower, gathering personal items, or packing clothes) before going to a hospital emergency room.

The Sick Role

Although many people tend to delay medical consultations, some people are actually eager to seek medical care. Given this reality, it is not surprising that up to 60 percent of patients' visits to their primary care physicians appear to have little medical basis (Ellington & Wiebe, 1999). Many of the people who are quick to solicit medical assistance probably have learned that there are potential benefits in adopting the "sick role" (Hamilton, Deemer, & Janata, 2003; Lubkin, 1990). For instance, the sick role absolves people from responsibility for their incapacity and can be used to exempt them from many of their normal duties and obligations (Segall, 1997). Fewer demands are placed on sick people, who can often be selective in deciding which demands to ignore. Illness can provide a convenient, face-saving excuse for one's failures (Wolinksky, 1988). Sick people may also find themselves receiving lots of attention (affection, concern, sympathy) from friends and relatives. This positive attention can be rewarding and can encourage the maintenance of symptoms (Walker, Claar, & Garber, 2002).

Thus, some people grow to *like* the sick role, although they may not be aware of it. Such people readily seek professional care, but they tend to behave in subtle ways that prolong their illness (Kinsman, Dirks, & Jones, 1982). For example, they may only pretend to go along with medical advice, a common problem that we discuss momentarily.

Communicating with Health Providers

When people seek help from physicians and other health care providers, many factors can undermine effective communication. A large portion of medical patients leave their doctors' offices not understanding what they have been told and what they are supposed to do (Johnson & Carlson, 2004). This situation is unfortunate, because good communication is a crucial requirement for sound medical decisions, informed choices about treatment, and appropriate follow-through by patients (Buckman, 2002; Gambone, Reiter, & DiMatteo, 1994).

There are many barriers to effective provider-patient communication (Beisecker, 1990; DiMatteo, 1997). Economic realities dictate that medical visits be generally quite brief, allowing little time for discus-

WEB LINK 14.7

MedFriendly
Do you ever wonder what complicated medical terms really mean? Have you tried to read a medical report from a doctor and found yourself not knowing what the doctor was talking about? The MedFriendly site may be your answer in its often humorous, but always clear and helpful definitions of many terms, concepts, and abbreviations used in medicine and health care generally.

sion. Illness and pain are subjective matters that may be difficult to describe. Many providers use too much medical jargon and overestimate their patients' understanding of technical terms. Some providers are uncomfortable being questioned and discourage their patients' information seeking. Patients who are upset and worried about their illness may simply forget to report some symptoms or to ask questions they meant to ask. Other patients are evasive about their real concerns because they fear a serious diagnosis. Many patients are reluctant to challenge doctors' authority and are too passive in their interactions with providers.

What can you do to improve your communication with health care providers? The key is to not be a passive consumer of medical services (Ferguson, 1993; Kane, 1991). Arrive for an appointment on time, with your questions and concerns prepared in advance. Try to be accurate and candid in replying to your doctor's questions. If you don't understand something the doctor says, don't be embarrassed to ask for clarification. If you have doubts about the suitability or feasibility of your doctor's recommendations, don't be afraid to voice them.

Adherence to Medical Advice

Many patients fail to adhere to the instructions they receive from physicians and other health care professionals. The evidence suggests that noncompliance with medical advice may occur 30 percent of the time when short-term treatments are prescribed for acute conditions and 50 percent of the time when long-term treatments are needed for chronic illness (Johnson & Carlson, 2004). Nonadherence takes many forms. Patients may fail to begin a treatment regimen, stop the regimen early, reduce or increase the levels of treatment that were prescribed, or be inconsistent and unreliable in following treatment procedures (Dunbar-Jacob & Schlenk, 2001). Nonadherence is a major problem that has been linked to increased sickness, treatment failures, and higher mortality (Christensen & Johnson, 2002; DiMatteo et al., 2002). Moreover, nonadherence wastes expensive medical visits and medications and increases hospital admissions, leading to enormous economic costs. Robin DiMatteo (2004b) speculates that in the United States alone, nonadherence may be a $300 billion a year drain on the health care system.

Our concern about adherence is not intended to suggest that you passively accept all professional advice from medical personnel. However, when you have doubts about a prescribed treatment, you should speak up. Passive resistance can backfire. For instance, if a physician sees no improvement in a patient who falsely insists that he has been tak-

ing his medicine, the physician may abandon an accurate diagnosis in favor of an inaccurate one. The inaccurate diagnosis could lead to inappropriate treatments that might be harmful to the patient.

Why don't people comply with the advice that they've sought out from highly regarded health care professionals? Physicians tend to attribute noncompliance to patients' personal characteristics, but research indicates that personality traits and demographic factors are surprisingly unrelated to adherence rates (DiMatteo, 2004b). One factor that *is* related to adherence is patients' *social support*. Adherence is improved when patients have family members, friends, or coworkers who remind them and help them to comply with treatment requirements (DiMatteo, 2004a). Here are some other considerations that influence the likelihood of adherence (Dunbar-Jacob & Schlenk, 2001; Johnson & Carlson, 2004):

1. *Frequently, noncompliance is due to patients simply forgetting instructions or failing to understand the instructions as given.* Highly trained professionals often forget that what seems obvious and simple to them may be obscure and complicated to many of their patients.

2. *Another key factor is how aversive or difficult the treatments are.* If the prescribed regimen is unpleasant, compliance will tend to decrease. For example, adherence is reduced when prescribed medications have many severe side effects. And the more that following instructions interferes with routine behavior, the less likely it is that the patient will cooperate successfully.

3. *If a patient has a negative attitude toward a physician, the probability of noncompliance will increase.* When patients are unhappy with their interactions with the doctor, they're more likely to ignore the medical advice provided.

Communication between health care providers and patients tends to be far from optimal for a variety of reasons.

In response to the noncompliance problem, researchers have investigated many methods of increasing patients' adherence to medical advice. Interventions have included simplifying instructions, providing more rationale for instructions, reducing the complexity of treatment regimens, helping patients with emotional distress that undermines adherence, and training patients in the use of behavior modification strategies. All of these interventions can improve adherence, although their effects tend to be modest (Christensen & Johnson, 2002; Roter et al., 1998).

APPLICATION

Understanding the Effects of Drugs

LEARNING OBJECTIVES

- *Explain the concepts of drug tolerance, physical and psychological dependence, and overdose.*
- *Summarize the main effects and risks of narcotics.*
- *Summarize the main effects and risks of sedatives.*
- *Summarize the main effects and risks of stimulant drugs.*
- *Summarize the main effects and risks of hallucinogens.*
- *Summarize the main effects and risks of marijuana and ecstasy (MDMA).*

Answer the following "true" or "false."

___ 1. Smoking marijuana can make men impotent and sterile.
___ 2. Overdoses caused by cocaine are relatively rare.
___ 3. It is well documented that LSD causes chromosome damage.
___ 4. Hallucinogens are addictive.
___ 5. Ecstasy is a relatively harmless drug.

As you will learn in this Application, all of these statements are false. If you answered all of them accurately, you may already be well informed about drugs. If not, you *should* be. Intelligent decisions about drugs require an understanding of their effects and risks.

This Application focuses on the use of drugs for their pleasureable effects, commonly referred to as *drug abuse* or *recreational drug use*. Drug abuse reaches into every corner of our society and is a problematic health-impairing habit. Although small declines appear to have occurred in the overall abuse of drugs in recent years, survey data show that illicit drug use has mostly been increasing since the 1960s (Winick & Norman, 2005).

Like other controversial social problems, recreational drug use often inspires more rhetoric than reason. For instance, a former president of the American Medical Association made headlines when he declared that marijuana "makes a man of 35 sexually like a man of 70." In reality, the research findings do not support this assertion. This influential physician later retracted his statement, admitting that he had made it simply to campaign against marijuana use (Leavitt, 1995). Unfortunately, such scare tactics can backfire by undermining the credibility of drug education efforts.

Recreational drug use involves personal, moral, political, and legal issues that are not matters for science to resolve. However, the more knowledgeable you are about drugs, the more informed your decisions and opinions about them will be. Accordingly, this Application is intended to provide you with nonjudgmental, realistic coverage of issues related to recreational drug use. We begin by reviewing key drug-related concepts.

Recreational drug users come from all ages and all walks of life.

Then we examine the effects and risks of five types of widely abused drugs: narcotics, sedatives, stimulants, hallucinogens, and marijuana. We wrap up our coverage with a brief discussion of ecstasy (MDMA), which has stirred up controversy in recent years.

Drug-Related Concepts

The principal types of recreational drugs are described in Figure 14.23. This table lists representative drugs in each of the five categories and indicates how the drugs are taken, their principal medical uses, their desired effects, and their common side effects.

Most drugs produce tolerance effects. *Tolerance* is **a progressive decrease in a person's responsiveness to a drug with continued use.** Tolerance effects usually lead people to consume larger and larger doses of a drug to attain the effects they desire. Tolerance builds more rapidly to some drugs than to others. The first column in Figure 14.24 on the following page (which lists the risks associated with drug abuse) indicates whether various categories of drugs tend to produce rapid or gradual tolerance.

In evaluating the potential problems associated with the use of specific drugs, a key consideration is the likelihood of either physical or psychological dependence. Although both forms of drug dependence have a physiological basis (Di Chiara, 1999; Self, 1998), important differences exist between the two syndromes. *Physical dependence* **exists when a person must continue to take a drug to avoid withdrawal illness (which occurs when drug use is terminated).** The symptoms of withdrawal illness (also called abstinence syndrome) vary depending on the drug. Withdrawal from heroin and barbiturates can produce fever, chills, tremors, convulsions, seizures, vomiting, cramps, diarrhea, and severe aches and pains. The agony of withdrawal from these drugs virtually compels addicts to continue using them. Withdrawal from stimulants leads to a different and somewhat milder syndrome dominated by fatigue, apathy, irritability, depression, and disorientation.

Psychological dependence **exists when a person must continue to take a drug to satisfy intense mental and emotional craving for it.** Psychological dependence is more subtle than physical dependence, as it is not marked by a clear withdrawal reaction. However, psychological dependence can create a powerful, overwhelming need for a drug. The two types of dependence often coexist—that is, many people manifest

Comparison of Major Categories of Abused Drugs

Drugs	Methods of administration	Principal medical uses	Desired effects	Short-term side effects
Narcotics (opiates) Morphine Heroin	Injected, smoked, oral	Pain relief	Euphoria, relaxation, anxiety reduction, pain relief	Lethargy, drowsiness, nausea, impaired coordination, impaired mental functioning, constipation
Sedatives Barbiturates (e.g., Seconal) Nonbarbiturates (e.g., Quaalude)	Oral, injected	Sleeping pill, anticonvulsant	Euphoria, relaxation, anxiety reduction, reduced inhibitions	Lethargy, drowsiness, severely impaired coordination, impaired mental functioning, emotional swings, dejection
Stimulants Amphetamines Cocaine	Oral, sniffed, injected, freebased, smoked	Treatment of hyperactivity and narcolepsy; local anesthetic (cocaine only)	Elation, excitement, increased alertness, increased energy, reduced fatigue	Increased blood pressure and heart rate, increased talkativeness, restlessness, irritability, insomnia, reduced appetite, increased sweating and urination, anxiety, paranoia, increased aggressiveness, panic
Hallucinogens LSD Mescaline Psilocybin	Oral		Increased sensory awareness, euphoria, altered perceptions, hallucinations, insightful experiences	Dilated pupils, nausea, emotional swings, paranoia, jumbled thought processes, impaired judgment, anxiety, panic reaction
Cannabis Marijuana Hashish THC	Smoked, oral	Treatment of glaucoma; other uses under study	Mild euphoria, relaxation, altered perceptions, enhanced awareness	Bloodshot eyes, dry mouth, reduced memory, sluggish motor coordination, sluggish mental functioning, anxiety

● FIGURE 14.23

Major categories of abused drugs. This chart summarizes the methods of ingestion, chief medical uses, and principal effects of five major types of recreational drugs. Alcohol is covered in the main body of the chapter. (Based on Julien, 2001; Levinthal, 2002; Lowinson, et al., 2005)

● FIGURE 14.24

Specific risks for various categories of drugs. This chart shows estimates of the risk potential for tolerance, dependence, and overdose for the five major categories of drugs discussed in this Application.

Risks Associated with Major Categories of Abused Drugs

Drugs	Tolerance	Risk of physical dependence	Risk of psychological dependence	Fatal overdose potential
Narcotics (opiates)	Rapid	High	High	High
Sedatives	Rapid	High	High	High
Stimulants	Rapid	Moderate	High	Moderate to high
Hallucinogens	Gradual	None	Very low	Very low
Cannabis	Gradual	None	Low to moderate	Very low

both psychological and physical dependence on a specific drug. Both types of dependence are established gradually with repeated use of a drug. However, specific drugs vary greatly in their potential for creating dependence. The second and third columns in Figure 14.24 provide estimates of the risk of each kind of dependence for the drugs covered in our discussion.

An *overdose* is an excessive dose of a drug that can seriously threaten one's life. Any drug can be fatal if a person takes enough of it, but some drugs carry more risk of overdose than others. In Figure 14.24, column 4 estimates the risk of accidentally consuming a lethal overdose of various drugs. Drugs that are central nervous system (CNS) depressants—narcotics and sedatives—carry the greatest risk of overdose. It's important to understand that the effects of these drugs are additive. Many overdoses involve lethal *combinations* of CNS depressants. What happens when people overdose on these drugs? Their respiratory system usually grinds to a halt, producing coma, brain damage, and death within a brief period. In contrast, fatal overdoses with CNS stimulants (cocaine and amphetamines) usually involve a heart attack, stroke, or cortical seizure.

Now that our basic vocabulary is spelled out, we can begin to examine the effects and risks of major recreational drugs. Of course, we'll be describing the *typical* effects of each drug. Please bear in mind that the effects of any drug depend on the user's age, body weight, physiology, personality, mood, expectations, and previous experience with the drug. The dose and potency of the drug, the method of administration, and the setting in which the drug is taken also influence its effects (Leavitt, 1995). Our coverage is based largely on comprehensive books by Levinthal (2002), Julien (2001), and Lowinson and colleagues (2005), but we cite additional sources when discussing specific studies or controversial points.

Narcotics

Narcotics (or opiates) are drugs derived from opium that are capable of relieving pain. In legal regulations, the term *narcotic* is used in a haphazard way to refer to a variety of drugs besides opiates. The most widely abused opiates are heroin, morphine, and a relatively new painkiller called Oxycontin. However, less potent opiates, such as codeine, Demerol, and Vicodin, are also subject to misuse.

Effects

The most significant narcotics problem in modern, Western society is the use of heroin. Most users inject this drug intravenously with a hypodermic needle. The main effect is an overwhelming sense of euphoria. This euphoric effect has a "Who cares?" quality to it that makes the heroin high an attractive escape from reality. Common side effects include nausea, lethargy, drowsiness, constipation, and slowed respiration.

Risks

Narcotics carry a high risk for both *psychological and physical dependence* (Knapp, Ciraulo, & Jaffe, 2005). It is estimated that there are about 600,000 heroin addicts in the United States (Winick & Norman, 2005). Although heroin withdrawal usually isn't life threatening, it can be terribly unpleasant, so that "junkies" have a desperate need to continue their drug use. Once dependence is entrenched, users tend to develop a *drug-centered lifestyle* that revolves around the need to procure more heroin. This lifestyle occurs because the drug is expensive and available only through highly undependable black market channels. Obviously, it is difficult to lead a productive life if one's existence is dominated by a desperate need to "score" heroin. The inordinate cost of the drug forces many junkies to resort to criminal activities to support their habit.

Heroin is blamed for over 4,000 deaths annually in the United States, so *overdose* is a very real danger. Opiates are additive with other CNS depressants, and most narcotic overdoses occur in combination with the use of sedatives or alcohol. Junkies also risk *contracting infectious disease* because they often share hypodermic needles and tend to be sloppy about sterilizing them. The most common of these diseases used to be hepatitis, but in recent years AIDS has been transmitted at an alarming rate through the population of intravenous drug users (Des Jarlais, Hagan, & Friedman, 2005).

Sedatives

Sedatives **are sleep-inducing drugs that tend to decrease central nervous system and behavioral activity.** In street jargon, they are often called "downers." Over the years, the most widely abused sedatives have been the barbiturates, which are compounds derived from barbituric acid. However, barbiturates have gradually become medically obsolete and diminished in availability, so sedative abusers have had to turn to drugs in the benzodiazepine family, such as Valium (Wesson et al., 2005).

Effects

People abusing sedatives generally consume larger doses than are prescribed for medical purposes. These overly large doses have a euphoric effect similar to that produced by drinking large amounts of alcohol (Wesson et al., 2005). Feelings of tension, anxiety, and depression are temporarily replaced by a relaxed, pleasant state of intoxication, in which inhibitions may be loosened. Sedatives carry a truckload of dangerous side effects. Motor coordination suffers badly, producing slurred speech and a staggering walk, among other things. Intellectual functioning also becomes sluggish, and judgment is impaired. One's emotional tone may become unstable, with feelings of dejection often intruding on the intended euphoric mood.

Risks

Sedatives have the potential to produce *both psychological and physical dependence.* They are also among the leading causes of *overdoses* in the United States because of their additive interactions with other CNS depressants (especially alcohol) and because of the degree to which they impair judgment. In their drug-induced haze, sedative abusers are likely to take doses they would ordinarily recognize as dangerous. Sedative users also elevate their risk for *accidental injuries* because these drugs can have significant effects on motor coordination. Many users trip down stairs, fall off bar stools, get into automobile accidents, and so forth.

Stimulants

Stimulants **are drugs that tend to increase central nervous system and behavioral activity.** They range from mild, widely available forms, such as caffeine and nicotine, to stronger, carefully regulated stimulants, such as cocaine and amphetamines ("speed"). Here we focus on the latter two drugs.

Cocaine is an organic substance extracted from the coca shrub, which grows most prominently in South America. It is usually consumed as a crystalline powder that is snorted through the nasal cavities, although it can be consumed orally or intravenously. "Crack" is a processed variant of cocaine, consisting of little chips of cocaine that are usually smoked. Smoking crack tends to be more dangerous than snorting cocaine powder because smoking leads to a more rapid absorption of the drug into the bloodstream and more concentrated delivery of cocaine to the brain. That said, all the forms of cocaine and all the routes of administration can deliver highly toxic amounts of the drug to the brain (Repetto & Gold, 2005).

Synthesized in a pharmaceutical laboratory, amphetamines are usually consumed orally. However, speed is also sold as a crystalline powder (called "crank" or "crystal meth") that may be snorted or injected intravenously. A smokable form of methamphetamine, called "ice," is seen in some regions.

Effects

Amphetamines and cocaine have almost indistinguishable effects, except that cocaine produces a very brief high (20–30 minutes unless more is taken), while a speed high can last many hours (Gold, Miller, & Jonas, 1992). Stimulants produce a euphoria very different from that created by narcotics or sedatives. They produce a buoyant, elated, enthusiastic, energetic, "I can conquer the world!" feeling accompanied by increased alertness. Common side effects include increased blood pressure, muscle tension, sweating, and restlessness. Some users experience unpleasant feelings of irritability, anxiety, and paranoia.

Risks

Stimulants can cause physical dependence, but the physical distress caused by stimulant withdrawal is mild compared to that caused by narcotic or sedative withdrawal. Psychological dependence on stimulants is a more common problem. Cocaine can create an exceptionally *powerful psychological dependence* that compels the user to pursue the drug with a fervor normally seen only when physical dependence exists (Gold & Jacobs, 2005).

Both cocaine and amphetamines can suppress appetite and disrupt sleep. Thus, heavy use of stimulants may lead to poor eating, poor sleeping, and ultimately, a *deterioration in physical health.* Furthermore, stimulant use increases one's risk for stroke, heart attack, and other forms of cardiovascular disease, and crack smoking is associated with a host of respiratory problems (Gourevitch & Arnsten, 2005; Weaver & Schnoll, 1999).

Heavy stimulant use occasionally leads to the onset of a severe psychological disorder called *amphetamine* or *cocaine psychosis* (depending on the drug involved), which is dominated by intense paranoia (King & Ellinwood, 2005). All of the risks associated with stimulant use increase when more potent forms of the drugs (crack and ice) are used. Overdoses on stimulants used to be relatively infrequent (Kalant & Kalant, 1979). However, in recent years, *cocaine overdoses have increased sharply* as more people experiment with more dangerous modes of ingestion. In 2001, cocaine was the leading cause of drug-related emergency room visits (Gold & Jacobs, 2005).

Hallucinogens

Hallucinogens **are a diverse group of drugs that have powerful effects on mental and emotional functioning, marked most prominently by distortions in sensory and perceptual experience.** The principal hallucinogens are LSD, mescaline, and psilocybin, which have similar effects, although they vary in potency. Mescaline comes from the peyote plant, psilocybin comes from a particular type of mushroom, and LSD is a synthetic drug.

Effects

Hallucinogens intensify and distort perception in ways that are difficult to describe, and they temporarily impair intellectual functioning as thought processes become meteoric and jumbled. These drugs can produce awesome feelings of euphoria that sometimes include an almost mystical sense of "oneness" with the human race. This is why they have been used in religious ceremonies in various cultures. Unfortunately, at the other end of the emotional spectrum, they can also produce nightmarish feelings of anxiety, fear, and paranoia, commonly called a "bad trip."

Risks

There is no potential for physical dependence on hallucinogens, and no deaths attributable to overdose are known to have occurred. Psychological dependence has been reported but appears to be rare. Research reports that LSD increases chromosome breakage were based on poor methodology (Dishotsky et al., 1971). However, like most drugs, hallucinogens may be harmful to a fetus if taken by a pregnant woman.

Although the dangers of hallucinogens have probably been exaggerated in the popular press, there are some significant risks (Pechnick & Ungerleider, 2005). Emotion is highly volatile with these drugs, so users can never be sure that they won't experience *acute panic* from a terrifying bad trip. Generally, this disorientation subsides within a few hours, leaving no permanent emotional scars. However, in such a severe state of disorientation, *accidents and suicide* are possible. *Flashbacks* are vivid hallucinogenic experiences occurring months after the original drug ingestion. They do not appear to be a common problem, but repetitious flashbacks have proved troublesome for some individuals. In a small minority of users, hallucinogens may contribute to the emergence of a *variety of psychological disorders* (psychoses, depressive reactions, paranoid states) that may be partially attributable to the drug (Pechnick & Ungerleider, 2005).

Marijuana

Cannabis **is the hemp plant from which marijuana, hashish, and THC are derived.** Marijuana is a mixture of dried leaves, flowers, stems, and seeds taken from the plant, while hashish comes from the plant's resin. THC, the active chemical ingredient in cannabis, can be synthesized for research purposes (for example, to give to animals).

Effects

When smoked, cannabis has an almost immediate impact that may last several hours. The effects of the drug vary greatly, depending on the user's expectations and experience with it, the drug's potency, and the amount smoked. The drug has subtle effects on emotion, perception, and cognition (Grinspoon, Bakalar, & Russo, 2005). Emotionally, the drug tends to create a mild, relaxed state of euphoria. Perceptually, it enhances the impact of incoming stimulation, thus making music sound better, food taste better, and so on. Cannabis tends to produce a slight impairment in cognitive functioning (especially short-term memory) and perceptual-motor coordination while the user is high. However, there are huge variations among users.

Risks

Overdose and physical dependence are not problems with marijuana, but as with any other drug that produces pleasant feelings, it has the potential to produce *psychological dependence* (Grinspoon, Bakalar, & Russo, 2005). There is no solid evidence that cannabis causes psychological disorders. However, marijuana can cause *transient problems with anxiety and depression* in some people. Studies also suggest that cannabis may have a more *negative effect on driving* than has been widely believed (Ramaekers, Robbe, & O'Hanlon, 2000). Like tobacco smoke, marijuana smoke carries carcinogens and impurities into the lungs, thus increasing one's chances for *respiratory and pulmonary diseases, and probably lung cancer* (Stephens, 1999). However, the evidence on other widely publicized risks remains controversial. Here is a brief overview of the evidence on some of these controversies:

■ *Does marijuana reduce the user's immune response?* Research with animals suggests that cannabis may suppress the body's natural immune response slightly. However, infectious diseases do *not* appear to be more common among marijuana smokers than among nonsmokers. Hence, marijuana's effect on immune functioning apparently is too small to have any practical importance (Hall, Solowij, & Lemon, 1994; Hollister, 1988).

- *Does marijuana lead to impotence and sterility in men?* Cannabis appears to produce a small, reversible decline in sperm count among male smokers and may have temporary effects on hormone levels (Bloodworth, 1987). Citing these findings, the popular media have frequently implied that marijuana therefore makes men sterile and impotent. However, the evidence suggests that marijuana has little lasting impact on male smokers' fertility or sexual functioning (Grinspoon & Bakalar, 1997).

- *Does marijuana have long-term negative effects on cognitive functioning?* It has long been known that marijuana has a negative impact on attention and memory while users are high, but until recently studies had failed to find any permanent cognitive deficits attributable to cannabis use. However, a spate of recent studies using more elaborate and precise assessments of cognitive functioning *have* found an association between chronic, heavy marijuana use and measureable impairments in attention and memory (see Figure 14.25) that show up when users are not high (Ehrenreich et al., 1999; Solowij et al., 2002). That said, the cognitive deficits that have been observed are modest and certainly not disabling, and one study found that the deficits vanished after a month of marijuana abstinence (Pope, Gruber, & Yurgelun-Todd, 2001; Pope et al., 2001). More research is needed, but the recent studies in this area provide some cause for concern.

Ecstasy (MDMA)

The newest drug controversy in Western society centers on MDMA, better known as "ecstasy." MDMA was originally formulated in 1912 but was not widely used in the United States until the 1990s, when it became popular in the context of "raves" and dance clubs (Millman & Beeder, 1994). This compound is related to both amphetamines and hallucinogens, especially mescaline. It produces a high that typically lasts a few hours or more. Users report that they feel warm, friendly, euphoric, sensual, insightful, and empathetic, yet alert and energetic. Problematic side effects include increased blood pressure, muscle tension, sweating, blurred vision, insomnia, and transient anxiety.

Empirical research on ecstasy is still in its infancy, so assertions about its risks and dangers must be tentative and provisional. Data on adverse effects are also complicated by the fact that the vast majority of MDMA users ingest it in conjunction with many other drugs (Hammersley et al., 1999; Pedersen & Skrondal, 1999). Yet another complicating factor is that MDMA often contains potentially harmful impurities, contaminants, and toxic by-products introduced during its illicit manufacture (Grob & Poland, 2005).

MDMA does not appear to be especially addictive, but psychological dependence can clearly become a

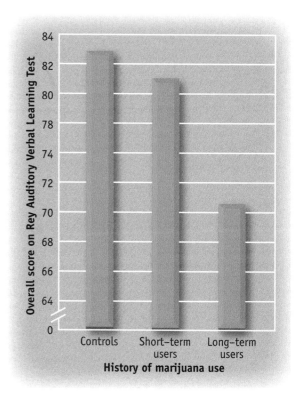

● FIGURE 14.25

Chronic cannabis use and cognitive performance. Solowij and associates (2002) administered a battery of neuropsychological tests to 51 long-term cannabis users, who had smoked marijuana regularly for an average of 24 years; 51 short-term cannabis users, who had smoked marijuana regularly for an average of 10 years; and 33 control subjects who had little or no history of cannabis use. The cannabis users were required to abstain from smoking marijuana for a minimum of 12 hours prior to their testing. The study found evidence suggestive of subtle cognitive impairments among the long-term cannabis users on many of the tests. The graph shown here depicts the results observed for overall performance on the Rey Auditory Verbal Learning Test, which measures several aspects of memory functioning.

problem for some people. MDMA has been implicated in cases of stroke and heart attack, seizures, heat stroke, and liver damage, but its exact contribution is hard to gauge given all the other drugs that MDMA users typically consume (Burgess, O'Donohoe, & Gill, 2000; Grob & Poland, 2005). Chronic, heavy use of ecstasy appears to be associated with sleep disorders, depression, and elevated anxiety and hostility (Morgan, 2000). Moreover, studies of former MDMA users suggest that ecstasy may have subtle, long-term effects on cognitive functioning (Parrott, 2000). Quite a few studies have found memory deficits in former users (Bhattachary & Powell, 2001; Zakzanis & Young, 2001). Other studies have found decreased performance on laboratory tasks requiring attention and learning (Gouzoulis-Mayfrank et al., 2000). Thus, although more research is needed, there are many reasons to be concerned about the possible effects of ecstasy.

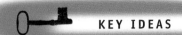

KEY IDEAS

Stress, Personality, and Illness

■ The biopsychosocial model holds that physical health is influenced by a complex network of biological, psychological, and sociocultural factors. Stress is one of the psychological factors that can affect physical health. In particular, cynical hostility has been implicated as a contributing cause of coronary heart disease. A number of mechanisms may contribute to this connection.

■ Emotional reactions may also influence susceptibility to heart disease. Recent research has suggested that transient mental stress and the negative emotions that result may tax the heart. Yet another line of research has identified the emotional dysfunction of depression as a risk factor for heart disease.

■ The connection between psychological factors and the onset of cancer is not well documented, but stress and personality may influence the course of the disease. Researchers have found associations between stress and the onset of a variety of other diseases. Stress may play a role in a variety of diseases because it can temporarily suppress immune functioning. While there's little doubt that stress can contribute to the development of physical illness, the link between stress and illness is modest.

Habits, Lifestyles, and Health

■ People commonly engage in health-impairing habits and lifestyles. These habits creep up slowly, and their risks are easy to ignore because the dangers often lie in the distant future.

■ Smokers have much higher mortality rates than nonsmokers because they are more vulnerable to a variety of diseases. Giving up smoking can reduce one's health risks, but it is difficult and relapse rates are high.

■ Drinking rivals smoking as a source of health problems. In the short term, drinking can impair driving, cause various types of accidents, and increase the likelihood of aggressive interactions or reckless sexual behavior. In the long term, chronic, excessive alcohol consumption increases one's risk for numerous health problems, including cirrhosis of the liver, heart disease, hypertension, stroke, and cancer.

■ Obesity elevates one's risk for many health problems. Body weight is influenced by genetic endowment, eating and exercise habits, and perhaps set point or setting point. Weight loss is best accomplished by decreasing caloric consumption while increasing exercise.

■ Poor nutritional habits have been linked to many health problems, including cardiovascular diseases and some types of cancer, although some of the links are tentative. One's health can best be served by following balanced food consumption patterns while limiting the intake of saturated fats, cholesterol, refined carbohydrates, sugar, and salt.

■ Lack of exercise is associated with elevated mortality rates. Regular exercise can reduce one's risk for cardiovascular disease, cancer, and obesity-related diseases; buffer the effects of stress; and lead to desirable personality changes.

■ Although misconceptions abound, HIV is transmitted almost exclusively by sexual contact and the sharing of needles by IV drug users. One's risk for HIV infection can be reduced by avoiding IV drug use, having fewer sexual partners, using condoms, and curtailing certain sexual practices.

Reactions to Illness

■ Variations in seeking treatment are influenced by the severity, duration, and disruptiveness of one's symptoms and by the reactions of friends and family. The biggest problem is the tendency of many people to delay needed medical treatment. At the other extreme, a minority of people learn to like the sick role because it earns them attention and allows them to avoid stress.

■ Good communication is crucial to effective health services, but many factors undermine communication between patients and health providers, such as short visits, overuse of medical jargon, and patients' reluctance to ask questions.

■ Noncompliance with medical advice is a major problem, which appears to occur 30–50 percent of the time. The likelihood of nonadherence is greater when instructions are difficult to understand, when recommendations are difficult to follow, and when patients are unhappy with their doctor.

Application: Understanding the Effects of Drugs

■ Recreational drugs vary in their potential for tolerance effects, psychological dependence, physical dependence, and overdose. The risks associated with narcotics use include both types of dependence, overdose, and the acquisition of infectious diseases.

■ Sedatives can also produce both types of dependence, are subject to overdoses, and elevate the user's risk for accidental injuries. Stimulant use can lead to psychological dependence, overdose, psychosis, and a deterioration in physical health. Cocaine overdoses have increased greatly in recent years.

■ Hallucinogens can in some cases contribute to accidents, suicides, and psychological disorders, and they can cause flashbacks. The risks of marijuana use include psychological dependence, impaired driving, transient problems with anxiety and depression, and respiratory and pulmonary diseases. Recent studies suggest that marijuana may have some long-term negative effects on cognitive processes.

■ More research is needed, but it appears that the use of ecstasy (MDMA) may contribute to a variety of acute and chronic physical maladies. MDMA may also have subtle, negative effects on cognitive functioning.

KEY TERMS

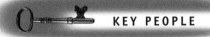

KEY PEOPLE

PRACTICE TEST

1. The greatest threats to health in our society today are:
   a. environmental toxins.
   b. accidents.
   c. chronic diseases.
   d. contagious diseases caused by specific infectious agents.

2. Which of the following is *not* associated with elevated coronary risk?
   a. Cynical hostility
   b. Strong emotional reactions to transient mental stress
   c. Obsessive-compulsive disorder
   d. Depression

3. Why do people tend to act in self-destructive ways?
   a. Because many health-impairing habits creep up on them
   b. Because many health-impairing habits involve activities that are quite pleasant at the time
   c. Because the risks tend to lie in the distant future
   d. All of the above

4. Some short-term risks of alcohol consumption include all but which of the following?
   a. Hangovers and life-threatening overdoses in combination with other drugs
   b. Poor perceptual coordination and driving drunk
   c. Increased aggressiveness and argumentativeness
   d. Transient anxiety from endorphin-induced flashbacks

5. Twin studies and other behavioral genetics research suggest that:
   a. genetic factors have little impact on people's weight.
   b. heredity has scant influence on BMI but does influence weight.
   c. heredity accounts for 60 percent or more of the variation in weight.
   d. heredity is responsible for severe, morbid obesity but has little influence over the weight of normal people.

6. Which of the following has *not* been found to be a mode of transmission for AIDS?
   a. Sexual contact among homosexual men
   b. The sharing of needles by intravenous drug users
   c. Sexual contact among heterosexuals
   d. Sharing food

7. Regarding the seeking of medical treatment, the biggest problem is:
   a. the tendency of many people to delay treatment.
   b. the tendency of many people to rush too quickly for medical care for minor problems.

c. not having enough doctors to cover peoples' needs.
   d. the tendency of people in higher socioeconomic categories to exaggerate their symptoms.

8. In which of the following cases are people most likely to follow the instructions they receive from health care professionals?
   a. When the instructions are complex and punctuated with impressive medical jargon
   b. When they do not fully understand the instructions but still feel the need to do something
   c. When they like and understand the health care professional
   d. All of the above

9. Which of the following risks is *not* typically associated with narcotics use?
   a. Overdose
   b. Infectious disease
   c. Physical dependence
   d. Flashbacks

10. The use of sedatives may result in personal injury because they:
    a. cause motor coordination to deteriorate.
    b. produce a strong physical dependence.
    c. suppress pain warnings of physical harm.
    d. trigger hallucinations such as flying.

Book Companion Website

Visit the Book Companion Website at **http://psychology. wadsworth.com/weiten_lloyd8e,** where you will find tutorial quizzes, flashcards, and weblinks for every chapter, a final exam, and more! You can also link to the Thomson Wadsworth Psychology Resource Center (accessible directly at **http://psychology.wadsworth.com**) for a range of psychology-related resources.

Personal Explorations Workbook

The following exercises in your *Personal Explorations Workbook* may enhance your self-understanding in relation to issues raised in this chapter. **Questionnaire 14.1:** Chronic Self-Destructiveness Scale. **Personal Probe 14.1:** How Do Your Health Habits Rate? **Personal Probe 14.2:** Examining Specific Health Habits.

ANSWERS

1. c Pages 443–444
2. c Pages 445–448
3. d Pages 452–454
4. d Pages 457–458
5. c Pages 460–461
6. d Page 468
7. a Pages 469–470
8. c Pages 471–472
9. d Pages 474–475
10. a Page 475

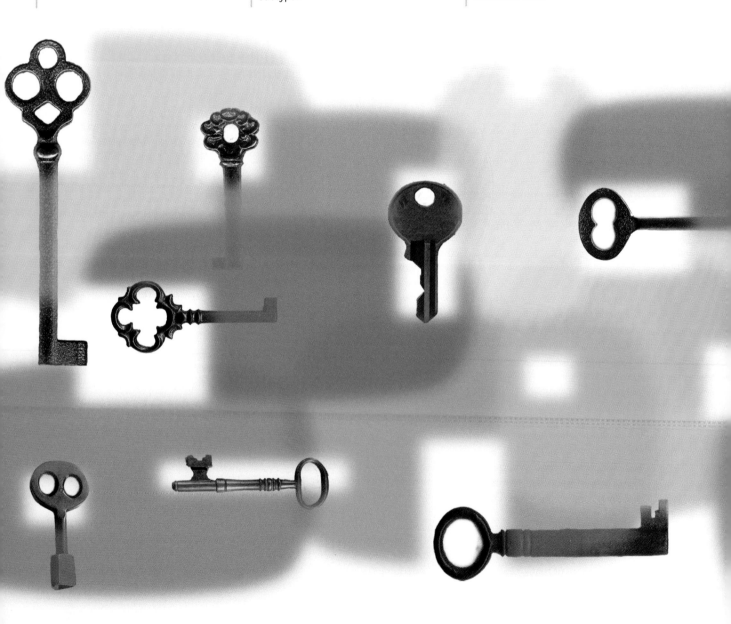

Psychological Disorders

"The government of the United States was overthrown more than a year ago! I'm the president of the United States of America and Bob Dylan is vice president!" So said Ed, the author of a prominent book on journalism, who was speaking to a college journalism class, as a guest lecturer. Ed also informed the class that he had killed both John and Robert Kennedy, as well as Charles de Gaulle, the former president of France. He went on to tell the class that all rock music songs were written about him, that he was the greatest karate expert in the universe, and that he had been fighting "space wars" for 2000 years. The students in the class were mystified by Ed's bizarre, disjointed "lecture," but they assumed that he was putting on a show that would eventually lead to a sensible conclusion. However, their perplexed but expectant calm was shattered when Ed pulled a hatchet from the props he had brought with him and hurled the hatchet at the class! Fortunately, he didn't hit anyone, as the hatchet sailed over the students' heads. At that point, the professor for the class realized that Ed's irrational behavior was not a pretense. The professor evacuated the class quickly while Ed continued to rant and rave about his presidential administration, space wars, vampires, his romances with female rock stars, and his personal harem of 38 "chicks." (Adapted from Pearce, 1974)

Clearly, Ed's behavior was abnormal. Even *he* recognized that when he agreed later to be admitted to a mental hospital, signing himself in as the "President of the United States of America." What causes such abnormal behavior? Does Ed have a mental illness, or does he just behave strangely? What is the basis for judging behavior as normal versus abnormal? How common are such disorders? These are just a few of the questions we address in this chapter as we discuss psychological disorders and their complex causes.

Abnormal Behavior: Myths and Realities

- *Describe and evaluate the medical model of abnormal behavior.*
- *Explain the most commonly used criteria of abnormality.*

- *Discuss the history of the DSM system, and describe the five axes of DSM-IV.*
- *Summarize data on the prevalence of various psychological disorders.*

Misconceptions about abnormal behavior are common. We therefore need to clear up some preliminary issues before we describe the various types of psychological disorders. In this section, we discuss (1) the medical model of abnormal behavior, (2) the criteria of abnormal behavior, (3) the classification of psychological disorders, and (4) the prevalence of such disorders.

The Medical Model Applied to Abnormal Behavior

In Ed's case, there's no question that his behavior was abnormal. But does it make sense to view his unusual and irrational behavior as an *illness*? This is a controversial question. **The *medical model* proposes that it is useful to think of abnormal behavior as a disease.** This point of view is the basis for many of the terms used to refer to abnormal behavior, including mental *illness*, psychological *disorder*, and psycho*pathology* (*pathology* refers to manifestations of disease). The medical model gradually became the dominant way of thinking about abnormal behavior during the 19th and 20th centuries, and its influence remains strong today.

The medical model clearly represented progress over earlier models of abnormal behavior. Prior to the 18th century, most conceptions of abnormal behavior were based on superstition. People who behaved strangely were thought to be possessed by demons, to be witches in league with the devil, or to be victims of God's punishment. Their disorders were "treated" with chants, rituals, exorcisms, and such. If the people's behavior was seen as threatening, they were candidates for chains, dungeons, torture, and death (see Figure 15.1).

The rise of the medical model brought improvements in the treatment of those who exhibited abnormal behavior. As victims of an illness, they were viewed with more sympathy and less hatred and fear. Although living conditions in early asylums were often deplorable, gradual progress was made toward more humane care of the mentally ill. It took time, but ineffectual approaches to treatment eventually gave way to scientific investigation of the causes and cures of psychological disorders.

However, in recent decades, some critics have suggested that the medical model may have outlived its usefulness (Kiesler, 1999). A particularly vocal critic has been Thomas Szasz (1974, 1993). He asserts that "strictly speaking, disease or illness can affect only the body; hence there can be no mental illness. . . . Minds can be 'sick' only in the sense that jokes are 'sick' or economies are 'sick'" (1974, p. 267). He further argues that abnormal behavior usually involves a deviation from social norms rather than an illness. He contends that such deviations are "problems in living" rather than medical problems. According to Szasz, the medical model's disease analogy converts moral and social questions about what is acceptable behavior into medical questions.

Thomas Szasz

● FIGURE 15.1

Historical conceptions of mental illness. Throughout most of history, psychological disorders were thought to be caused by demonic possession, and the mentally ill were candidates for chains and torture.

Although the criticism of Szasz has some merit, we'll take the position that the disease analogy continues to be useful, although you should keep in mind that it is *only* an analogy. Medical concepts such as *diagnosis, etiology,* and *prognosis* have proven valuable in the treatment and study of abnormality. **Diagnosis involves distinguishing one illness from another. Etiology refers to the apparent causation and developmental history of an illness. A *prognosis* is a forecast about the probable course of an illness.** These medically based concepts have widely shared meanings that permit clinicians, researchers, and the public to communicate more effectively in their discussions of abnormal behavior.

Criteria of Abnormal Behavior

If your next-door neighbor scrubs his front porch twice every day and spends virtually all his time cleaning and recleaning his house, is he normal? If your sister-in-law goes to one physician after another seeking treatment for ailments that appear imaginary, is she psychologically healthy? How are we to judge what's normal and what's abnormal? More important, who's to do the judging?

These are complex questions. In a sense, *all* people make judgments about normality in that they all express opinions about others' (and perhaps their own) mental health. Of course, formal diagnoses of psychological disorders are made by mental health professionals. In making these diagnoses, clinicians rely on a variety of criteria, the foremost of which are the following:

1. *Deviance.* As Szasz has pointed out, people are often said to have a disorder because their behavior deviates from what their society considers acceptable. What constitutes normality varies somewhat from one culture to another, but all cultures have such norms. When people ignore these standards and expectations, they may be labeled mentally ill. For example, *transvestic fetishism* is a sexual disorder in which a man achieves sexual arousal by dressing in women's clothing. This behavior is regarded as disordered because a man who wears a dress, brassiere, and nylons is deviating from our culture's norms. This example illustrates the arbitrary nature of cultural standards regarding normality, as the same overt behavior (cross-gender dressing) is acceptable for women yet deviant for men.

2. *Maladaptive behavior.* In many cases, people are judged to have a psychological disorder because their everyday adaptive behavior is impaired. This is the key criterion in the diagnosis of substance use (drug) disorders. In and of itself, alcohol and drug use is not terribly unusual or deviant. However, when the use of cocaine, for instance, begins to interfere with a person's

This man clearly exhibits a certain type of deviance, but does that mean that he has a psychological disorder? The criteria of mental illness are more subjective and complicated than most people realize, and to some extent, judgments of mental health represent value judgments.

social or occupational functioning, a substance use disorder exists. In such cases, it is the maladaptive quality of the behavior that makes it disordered.

3. *Personal distress.* Frequently, the diagnosis of a psychological disorder is based on an individual's report of great personal distress. This is usually the criterion met by people who are troubled by depression or anxiety disorders. Depressed people, for instance, may or may not exhibit deviant or maladaptive behavior. Such people are usually labeled as having a disorder when they describe their subjective pain and suffering to friends, relatives, and mental health professionals.

Although two or three criteria may apply in a particular case, people are often viewed as disordered when only one criterion is met. As you may have already noticed, diagnoses of psychological disorders involve *value judgments* about what represents normal or abnormal behavior (Widiger & Sankis, 2000). The criteria of mental illness are not nearly as value-free as the criteria of physical illness. In evaluating physical

can be divided neatly into two distinct groups: those who are normal and those who are not. In reality, it is often difficult to draw a line that clearly separates normality from abnormality. On occasion, everyone experiences personal distress. Everybody acts in deviant ways once in a while. And everyone displays some maladaptive behavior. People are judged to have psychological disorders only when their behavior becomes *extremely* deviant, maladaptive, or distressing. Thus, normality and abnormality exist on a continuum. It's a matter of degree, not an either-or proposition (see Figure 15.2).

David Rosenhan

For the most part, people with psychological disorders do *not* behave in bizarre ways that are very different from the behavior of normal people. At first glance, people with psychological disorders are usually indistinguishable from those without disorders. A study by David Rosenhan (1973) showed that even mental health professionals may have difficulty distinguishing normality from abnormality. To study diagnostic accuracy, Rosenhan arranged for a number of normal people to seek admission to mental hospitals. These "pseudopatients" arrived at the hospitals complaining of one false symptom—hearing voices. Except for this single symptom, they acted as they normally would and gave accurate information when interviewed about their personal histories. *All* the pseudopatients

diseases, people can usually agree that a weak heart or a malfunctioning kidney is pathological, regardless of their personal values. However, judgments about mental illness reflect prevailing cultural values, social trends, and political forces, as well as scientific knowledge (Kutchins & Kirk, 1997; Mechanic, 1999).

Antonyms such as *normal* versus *abnormal* and *mental health* versus *mental illness* imply that people

● FIGURE 15.2

Normality and abnormality as a continuum. No sharp boundary divides normal and abnormal behavior. Behavior is normal or abnormal in degree, depending on the extent to which it is deviant, personally distressing, or maladaptive.

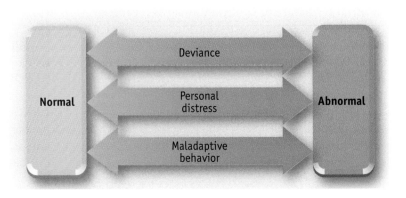

were admitted, and the average length of their hospitalization was 19 days!

Why is it so hard to distinguish normality from abnormality? The pseudopatients' observations about life on the psychiatric wards offer a clue. They noted that the real patients acted normal most of the time and only infrequently acted in a deviant manner. As you might imagine, Rosenhan's study evoked quite a controversy about our diagnostic system for mental illness. Let's take a look at how this diagnostic system has evolved.

Psychodiagnosis: The Classification of Disorders

Obviously, we cannot lump all psychological disorders together without giving up all hope of understanding them better. A sound taxonomy of mental disorders can facilitate empirical research and enhance communication among scientists and clinicians (First, 2003). Hence, a great deal of effort has been invested in devising an elaborate system for classifying psychological disorders.

Guidelines for psychodiagnosis were extremely vague and informal prior to 1952, when the American Psychiatric Association unveiled its *Diagnostic and Statistical Manual of Mental Disorders* (Nathan & Langenbucher, 2003). This classification scheme described about 100 disorders. Revisions intended to improve the system were incorporated into the second edition (DSM-II) published in 1968, but the diagnostic guidelines were still pretty sketchy. However, the third edition (DSM-III), published in 1980, represented a major advance, as the diagnostic criteria were made much more explicit, concrete, and detailed to facilitate more consistent diagnoses across clinicians (Blacker & Tsuang, 1999). The current, fourth edition (DSM-IV), which was released in 1994, made use of intervening research to refine the critieria introduced in DSM-III. Each revision of the DSM system has expanded the list of disorders covered. The current version describes about three times as many types of psychological disorders as DSM-I (Houts, 2002).

The publication of DSM-III in 1980 introduced a new multiaxial system of classification, which asks for judgments about individuals on five separate dimensions, or "axes." Figure 15.3 on the next page provides an overview of the entire system and the five axes. The diagnoses of disorders are made on Axes I and II. Clinicians record most types of disorders on Axis I. They use Axis II to list long-running personality disorders or mental retardation. People may receive diagnoses on both Axes I and II.

The remaining axes are used to record supplemental information. A patient's physical disorders are listed on Axis III (General Medical Conditions). On Axis IV (Psychosocial and Environmental Problems), the clinician makes notations regarding the types of stress experienced by the individual in the past year. On Axis V (Global Assessment of Functioning), estimates are made of the individual's current level of adaptive functioning (in social and occupational behavior, viewed as a whole), and of the individual's highest level of functioning in the past year. Most theorists agree that the multiaxial system is a step in the right direction because it recognizes the importance of information besides a traditional diagnostic label.

The Prevalence of Psychological Disorders

How common are psychological disorders? What percentage of the population is afflicted with mental illness? Is it 10 percent? Perhaps 25 percent? Could the figure range as high as 40 percent or 50 percent?

Such estimates fall in the domain of *epidemiology—the study of the distribution of mental or physical disorders in a population.* In epidemiology, *prevalence* refers to the percentage of a population that exhibits a disorder during a specified time period.* In the case of mental disorders, the most interesting data are the estimates of *lifetime prevalence,* the percentage of people having a specific disorder at any time in their lives.

Studies published in the 1980s and early 1990s found psychological disorders in roughly *one-third* of the population (Regier & Kaelber, 1995; Robins, Locke, & Regier, 1991). Subsequent research, which has focused on a somewhat younger sample (age 18–54 instead of over age 18), suggests that about 44 percent of the adult population will struggle with some sort of psychological disorder (Kessler & Zhao, 1999; Regier & Burke, 2000). Obviously, all these figures are *estimates* that depend to some extent on the sampling and assessment techniques used (Wakefield, 1999). Some of the increase in the prevalence of mental illness is more apparent than real, as it is partly attributable to more effective tabulation of certain disorders. However, research also suggests that there has been a genuine increase in the prevalence of mental disorders

WEB LINK 15.2

NAMI: The National Alliance for the Mentally Ill
Professional and lay evaluators have consistently found NAMI among the most helpful and informative organizations dealing with the entire spectrum of mental disorders, including schizophrenia and depression. The NAMI site offers a particularly rich array of information on specific mental disorders and on how patients and their families can find support.

Axis I
Clinical Syndromes

1. *Disorders usually first diagnosed in infancy, childhood, or adolescence*
   This category includes disorders that arise before adolescence, such as attention deficit disorders, autism, mental retardation, enuresis, and stuttering.

2. *Organic mental disorders*
   These disorders are temporary or permanent dysfunctions of brain tissue caused by diseases or chemicals. Examples are delirium, dementia, and amnesia.

3. *Substance-related disorders*
   This category refers to the maladaptive use of drugs and alcohol. Mere consumption and recreational use of such substances are not disorders. This category requires a maladaptive pattern of use, as with alcohol abuse and cocaine dependence.

4. *Schizophrenia and other psychotic disorders*
   The schizophrenias are characterized by psychotic symptoms (for example, grossly disorganized behavior, delusions, and hallucinations) and by over 6 months of behavioral deterioration. This category also includes delusional disorder and schizoaffective disorder.

5. *Mood disorders*
   The cardinal feature is emotional disturbance. Patients may, or may not, have psychotic symptoms. These disorders include major depression, bipolar disorder, dysthymic disorder, and cyclothymic disorder.

6. *Anxiety disorders*
   These disorders are characterized by physiological signs of anxiety (for example, palpitations) and subjective feelings of tension, apprehension, or fear. Anxiety may be acute and focused (panic disorder) or continual and diffuse (generalized anxiety disorder).

7. *Somatoform disorders*
   These disorders are dominated by somatic symptoms that resemble physical illnesses. These symptoms cannot be accounted for by organic damage. There must also be strong evidence that these symptoms are produced by psychological factors or conflicts. This category includes somatization, conversion disorder, and hypochondriasis.

8. *Dissociative disorders*
   These disorders all feature a sudden, temporary alteration or dysfunction of memory, consciousness, identity, and behavior, as in dissociative amnesia and multiple personality.

9. *Sexual and gender-identity disorders*
   There are three basic types of disorders in this category: gender identity disorders (discomfort with identity as male or female), paraphilias (preference for unusual acts to achieve sexual arousal), and sexual dysfunctions (impairments in sexual functioning).

(● FIGURE 15.3)

Overview of the DSM diagnostic system. Published by the American Psychiatric Association, the *Diagnostic and Statistical Manual of Mental Disorders* is the formal classification system used in the diagnosis of psychological disorders. It is a *multiaxial* system, which means that information is recorded on the five axes described here.

Adapted with permission from the *Diagnostic and Statistical Manual of Mental Disorders*, 4th ed. *Text revision*. Copyright © 2000 American Psychiatric Association.

Axis II
Personality Disorders

These disorders are patterns of personality traits that are longstanding, maladaptive, and inflexible and involve impaired functioning or subjective distress. Examples include borderline, schizoid, and antisocial personality disorders.

Axis III
General Medical Conditions

Physical disorders or conditions are recorded on this axis. Examples include diabetes, arthritis, and hemophilia.

Axis IV
Psychosocial and Environmental Problems

Axis IV is for reporting psychosocial and environmental problems that may affect the diagnosis, treatment, and prognosis of mental disorders (Axes I and II). A psychosocial or environmental problem may be a negative life event, an environmental difficulty or deficiency, a familial or other interpersonal stress, an inadequacy of social support or personal resources, or another problem that describes the context in which a person's difficulties have developed.

Axis V
Global Assessment of Functioning (GAF) Scale

Code	Symptoms
100	Superior functioning in a wide range of activities
90	Absent or minimal symptoms, good functioning in all areas
80	Symptoms transient and expectable reactions to psychosocial stressors
70	Some mild symptoms or some difficulty in social, occupational, or school functioning, but generally functioning pretty well
60	Moderate symptoms or difficulty in social, occupational, or school functioning
50	Serious symptoms or impairment in social, occupational, or school functioning
40	Some impairment in reality testing or communication or major impairment in family relations, judgment, thinking, or mood
30	Behavior considerably influenced by delusions or hallucinations, serious impairment in communication or judgment, or inability to function in almost all areas
20	Some danger of hurting self or others, occasional failure to maintain minimal personal hygiene, or gross impairment in communication
10	Persistent danger of severely hurting self or others
1	

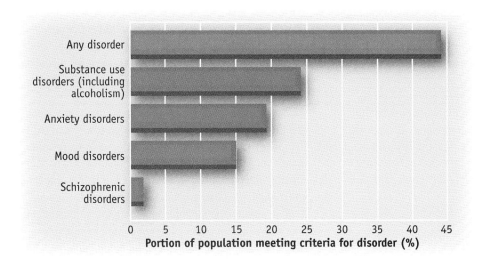

Portion of population meeting criteria for disorder (%)

Lifetime prevalence of psychological disorders. The estimated percentage of people who have, at any time in their life, suffered from one of four types of psychological disorders or from a disorder of any kind (top bar) is shown here. Prevalence estimates vary somewhat from one study to the next, depending on the exact methods used in sampling and assessment. The estimates shown here are based on pooling data from Waves 1 and 2 of the Epidemiological Catchment Area studies and the National Comorbidity Study, as summarized by Regier and Burke (2000) and Dew, Bromet, and Switzer (2000). These studies, which collectively evaluated over 28,000 subjects, provide the best data to date on the prevalence of mental illness in the United States.

among more recent age cohorts (Smith & Weissman, 1992). In any event, as Figure 15.4 shows, the most common classes of disorders are (1) substance (alcohol and drugs) use disorders, (2) anxiety disorders, and (3) mood disorders.

We are now ready to start examining the specific types of psychological disorders. Obviously, we cannot cover all of the diverse disorders listed in DSM-IV. However, we will introduce most of the major cate-gories of disorders to give you an overview of the many forms abnormal behavior takes. In discussing each set of disorders, we begin with brief descriptions of the specific syndromes or subtypes that fall in the category. Then we focus on the *etiology* of the disorders in that category. Although many paths can lead to specific disorders, some are more common than others. We highlight some of the common paths in order to enhance your understanding of the roots of abnormal behavior.

Anxiety Disorders

LEARNING OBJECTIVES

- List and describe four types of anxiety disorders.
- Discuss the contribution of biological factors and conditioning to the etiology of anxiety disorders.
- Explain the contribution of cognitive factors and stress to the etiology of anxiety disorders.

Everyone experiences anxiety from time to time. It is a natural and common reaction to many of life's difficulties. For some people, however, anxiety becomes a chronic problem. These people experience high levels of anxiety with disturbing regularity. *Anxiety disorders* **are a class of disorders marked by feelings of excessive apprehension and anxiety.** There are four principal types of anxiety disorders: generalized anxiety disorder, phobic disorder, obsessive-compulsive disorder, and panic disorder. They are not mutually exclusive, as many people who develop one anxiety syndrome often suffer from another at some point in their lives (Hunt & Andrews, 1995).

Generalized Anxiety Disorder

The *generalized anxiety disorder* **is marked by a chronic, high level of anxiety that is not tied to any** specific threat. People with this disorder worry constantly about yesterday's mistakes and tomorrow's problems. They worry excessively about minor matters related to family, finances, work, and personal illness (Sanderson & Barlow, 1990). In particular, they worry about how much they worry (Barlow et al., 2003). Their anxiety is frequently accompanied by physical symptoms, such as muscle tension, diarrhea, dizziness, faintness, sweating, and heart palpitations. Generalized anxiety disorder tends to have a gradual onset and is seen more frequently in females than males (Brown, 1999).

Phobic Disorder

In a phobic disorder, an individual's troublesome anxiety has a specific focus. *A phobic disorder* **is marked by a persistent and irrational fear of an object or situation that presents no realistic danger.** Although mild phobias are extremely common, people are said to have a phobic disorder only when their fears seriously interfere with their everyday behavior. Phobic reactions tend to be accompanied by physical symptoms of anxiety, such as trembling and palpitations (Rapee & Barlow, 2001). The following case provides an example of a phobic disorder:

Hilda is 32 years of age and has a rather unusual fear. She is terrified of snow. She cannot go outside in the snow. She cannot even stand to see snow or hear about it on the weather report. Her phobia severely constricts her day-to-day behavior. Probing in therapy revealed that her phobia was caused by a traumatic experience at age 11. Playing at a ski lodge, she was buried briefly by a small avalanche of snow. She had no recollection of this experience until it was recovered in therapy. (Adapted from Laughlin, 1967, p. 227)

As Hilda's unusual snow phobia illustrates, people can develop phobic responses to virtually anything. Nonetheless, certain types of phobias are relatively common, as the data in Figure 15.5 show. Particularly common are acrophobia (fear of heights), claustrophobia (fear of small, enclosed places), brontophobia (fear of storms), hydrophobia (fear of water), and various animal and insect phobias (Eaton, Dryman, & Weissman, 1991). People troubled by phobias typically realize that their fears are irrational, but they still are unable to calm themselves when they encounter a phobic object.

Panic Disorder and Agoraphobia

A panic disorder **is characterized by recurrent attacks of overwhelming anxiety that usually occur suddenly and unexpectedly.** These paralyzing attacks are accompanied by physical symptoms of anxiety. After a number of anxiety attacks, victims often become apprehensive, wondering when their next panic attack will occur. Their concern about exhibiting panic in public may escalate to the point where they are afraid to leave home. This creates a condition called *agoraphobia*.

Agoraphobia **is a fear of going out to public places** (its literal meaning is "fear of the marketplace or open

● **FIGURE 15.5**

Common phobias. Frequently reported phobias are listed here, along with their typical age of onset and information on gender differences in phobias.

From Marks, I. M. (1969). *Fears and phobias.* San Diego: Academic Press. Copyright 1969 by Isaac Marks. Reprinted by permission.

Common Phobias

	Percent of all phobias	Gender difference	Typical age of onset
Agoraphobia (fear of places of assembly, crowds, open spaces)	10%–50%	Large majority are women	Early adulthood
Social phobia (fear of being observed doing something humiliating)	10%	Majority are women	Adolescence
Specific phobias			
Animals	5%–15%	Vast majority are women	Childhood
Cats (ailurophobia) Dogs (cynophobia)			
Insects (insectophobia) Spiders (arachnophobia)			
Birds (avisophobia) Horses (equinophobia)			
Snakes (ophidiophobia) Rodents (rodentophobia)			
Inanimate objects	20%	None	Any age
Dirt (mysophobia) Storms (brontophobia)			
Heights (acrophobia) Darkness (nyctophobia)			
Closed spaces (claustrophobia)			
Illness-injury (nosophobia)	15%–25%	None	Middle age
Death (thanatophobia)			
Cancer (cancerophobia)			
Venereal disease (venerophobia)			

© 1990 by Sidney Harris

places"). Because of this fear, some people become prisoners confined to their homes, although many can venture out if accompanied by a trusted companion (Hollander & Simeon, 2003). As its name suggests, agoraphobia has traditionally been viewed as a phobic disorder. However, more recent evidence suggests that agoraphobia is mainly a complication of panic disorder. About two-thirds of people who suffer from panic disorder are female (Horwath & Weissman, 2000). The onset of panic disorder typically occurs during late adolescence or early adulthood (Pine, 2000).

Obsessive-Compulsive Disorder

Obsessions are *thoughts* that repeatedly intrude on one's consciousness in a distressing way. Compulsions are *actions* that one feels forced to carry out. Thus, **an obsessive-compulsive disorder (OCD) is marked by persistent, uncontrollable intrusions of unwanted thoughts (obsessions) and urges to engage in senseless rituals (compulsions).** To illustrate, let's examine the bizarre behavior of a man once reputed to be the wealthiest person in the world:

The famous industrialist Howard Hughes was obsessed with the possibility of being contaminated by germs. This led him to devise extraordinary rituals to minimize the possibility of such contamination. He would spend hours methodically cleaning a single telephone. He once wrote a three-page memo instructing assistants on exactly how to open cans of fruit for him. The following is just a small portion of the instructions that Hughes provided for a driver who delivered films to his bungalow. "Get out of the car on the traffic side. Do not at any time be on the side of the car between the car and the curb. . . . Carry only one can of film at a time. Step over the gutter opposite the place where the sidewalk dead-ends into the curb

from a point as far out into the center of the road as possible. Do not ever walk on the grass at all, also do not step into the gutter at all. Walk to the bungalow keeping as near to the center of the sidewalk as possible." (Adapted from Barlett & Steele, 1979, pp. 227–237)

Obsessions often center on fear of contamination, inflicting harm on others, suicide, or sexual acts. Compulsions usually involve stereotyped rituals that temporarily relieve anxiety. Common examples include constant handwashing; repetitive cleaning of things that are already clean; endless rechecking of locks, faucets, and such; and excessive arranging, counting, and hoarding of things (Pato, Eisen, & Phillips, 2003). Specific types of obsessions tend to be associated with specific types of compulsions. For example, obsessions about contamination tend to be paired with cleaning compulsions, and obsessions about symmetry tend to be paired with ordering and arranging compulsions (Leckman et al., 1997). Although many of us can be compulsive at times, full-fledged obsessive-compulsive disorders occur in roughly 2.5 percent of the population (Turner et al., 2001). The prevalence of obsessive-compulsive disorder

Repetitive handwashing is an example of a common compulsive behavior.

seems to be increasing, but this trend may simply reflect changes in clinicians' and researchers' diagnostic tendencies (Stein et al., 1997a). Most cases of OCD emerge before the age of 35 (Otto et al., 1999).

Etiology of Anxiety Disorders

Like most psychological disorders, anxiety disorders develop out of complicated interactions among a variety of factors. Conditioning and learning appear especially important, but biological factors may also contribute to anxiety disorders.

Biological Factors

Recent studies suggest that there may be a weak to moderate genetic predisposition to anxiety disorders, depending on the specific type of disorder (Fyer, 2000; Hettema, Neale, & Kendler, 2001). These findings are consistent with the idea that inherited differences in temperament might make some people more vulnerable than others to anxiety disorders. Kagan and his colleagues (1992) have found that about 15–20 percent of infants display an *inhibited temperament,* characterized by shyness, timidity, and wariness, which appears to have a strong genetic basis. Research suggests that this temperament is a risk factor for the development of anxiety disorders (Rosenbaum, Lakin, & Roback, 1992).

One influential theory holds that *anxiety sensitivity* may make people vulnerable to anxiety disorders (Reiss, 1991; Weems et al., 2002). According to this notion, some people are very sensitive to internal physiological symptoms of anxiety and are prone to overreact with fear when they experience these symptoms. Anxiety sensitivity may fuel an inflationary spiral in which anxiety breeds more anxiety, which eventually spins out of control in the form of an anxiety disorder.

Recent evidence suggests that a link may exist between anxiety disorders and neurochemical activity in the brain. *Neurotransmitters* **are chemicals that carry signals from one neuron to another.** Therapeutic drugs (such as Valium) that reduce excessive anxiety appear to alter activity at synapses for a neurotransmitter called GABA. This finding and other lines of evidence suggest that disturbances in the neural circuits using GABA may play a role in some types of anxiety disorders (Skolnick, 2003). Abnormalities in other neural circuits using the transmitter serotonin have been implicated in panic and obsessive-compulsive disorders (Sullivan & Coplan, 2000). Thus, scientists are beginning to unravel the neurochemical bases for anxiety disorders.

Conditioning and Learning

Many anxiety responses may be *acquired through classical conditioning* and *maintained through operant conditioning* (see Chapter 2). According to Mowrer (1947), an originally neutral stimulus (the snow in Hilda's case, for instance) may be paired with a frightening event (the avalanche) so that it becomes a conditioned stimulus eliciting anxiety (see Figure 15.6). Once a fear is acquired through classical conditioning, the person may start avoiding the anxiety-producing stimulus. The avoidance response is negatively reinforced because it is followed by a reduction in anxiety. This process involves operant conditioning (also shown in Figure 15.6). Thus, separate conditioning processes may create and then sustain specific anxiety responses (Levis, 1989). Consistent with this view, studies find that a substantial portion of people suffering from phobias can identify a traumatic conditioning experience that probably contributed to their anxiety disorder (Antony & McCabe, 2003; King, Eleonora, & Ollendick, 1998).

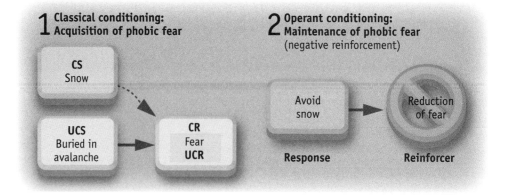

• FIGURE 15.6

Conditioning as an explanation for phobias. (1) Many phobias appear to be acquired through classical conditioning when a neutral stimulus is paired with an anxiety-arousing stimulus. **(2)** Once acquired, a phobia may be maintained through operant conditioning, because avoidance of the phobic stimulus leads to a reduction in anxiety, resulting in negative reinforcement.

The tendency to develop phobias of certain types of objects and situations may be explained by Martin Seligman's (1971) concept of *preparedness.* Like many theorists, Seligman believes that classical conditioning creates most phobic responses. *However, he suggests that people are biologically prepared by their evolutionary history to acquire some fears much more easily than others.* His theory would explain why people develop phobias of ancient sources of threat (such as snakes and spiders) much more readily than modern sources of threat (such as electrical outlets or hot irons). Some laboratory studies have yielded evidence consistent with the idea that we are wired by evolution to readily develop certain conditioned fears, but the evidence is inconsistent (Ohman & Mineka, 2003; Rapee & Barlow, 2001).

There are a number of problems with conditioning models of phobias (Rachman, 1990). For instance, many people with phobias cannot recall or identify a traumatic conditioning experience that led to their phobia. Conversely, many people endure extremely traumatic experiences that should create a phobia but do not. To provide better explanations for these complexities, conditioning models of anxiety disorders are currently being revised to include a larger role for cognitive factors (de Jong & Merckelbach, 2000).

Cognitive Factors

Cognitive theorists maintain that certain styles of thinking make some people particularly vulnerable to anxiety disorders. According to these theorists, some people are prone to suffer from problems with anxiety because they tend to (a) misinterpret harmless situations as threatening, (b) focus excessive attention on perceived threats, and (c) selectively recall information that seems threatening (Beck, 1997; McNally, 1994, 1996). In one intriguing test of the cognitive view, anxious and nonanxious subjects were asked to read 32 sentences that could be interpreted in either a threatening or a nonthreatening manner (Eysenck et al., 1991). For instance, one such sentence was "The doctor examined little Emma's growth," which could mean that the doctor checked her height or the growth of a tumor. As Figure 15.7 shows, the anxious subjects interpreted the sentences in a threatening way more often than the nonanxious subjects did. Thus, the cognitive view holds that some people are prone to anxiety disorders because they see threat in every corner of their lives (Williams et al., 1997).

Stress

Finally, studies have supported the long-held suspicion that anxiety disorders are stress related. For instance, Faravelli and Pallanti (1989) found that patients with panic disorder had experienced a dramatic increase in stress in the month prior to the onset of their disorder. In another study, Brown et al. (1998) found an association between stress and the development of social phobia. Thus, there is reason to believe that high stress often helps precipitate the onset of anxiety disorders.

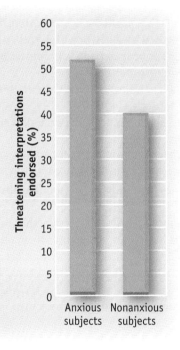

● **FIGURE 15.7**

Cognitive factors in anxiety disorders. Eysenck and his colleagues (1991) compared how subjects with anxiety problems and nonanxious subjects tended to interpret sentences that could be viewed as threatening or nonthreatening. Consistent with cognitive models of anxiety disorders, anxious subjects were more likely to interpret the sentences in a threatening light.

Somatoform Disorders

LEARNING OBJECTIVES

■ *Describe three types of somatoform disorders.*
■ *Summarize what is known about the causes of somatoform disorders.*

Chances are, you have met people who always seem to be complaining about aches, pains, and physical maladies of doubtful authenticity. When physical illness appears *largely* psychological in origin, people are said to suffer from somatoform disorders. **Somatoform disorders are physical ailments that cannot be fully explained by organic conditions and are largely due to psychological factors.** Although their symptoms are more imaginary than real, victims of somatoform disorders are *not* simply faking illness. Deliberate feigning of illness for personal gain is another matter altogether, called *malingering*.

People with somatoform disorders typically seek treatment from physicians practicing neurology, internal medicine, or family medicine, instead of from psychologists or psychiatrists. Making accurate diagnoses of somatoform disorders can be difficult, because the causes of physical ailments are sometimes hard to identify. In some cases, a problem is misdiagnosed as a somatoform disorder when a genuine organic cause for a person's physical symptoms goes undetected despite medical examinations and tests (Yutzy, 2003).

Let's look at three specific types of somatoform disorders: somatization disorder, conversion disorder, and hypochondriasis. Diagnostic difficulties make it hard to obtain sound data on the prevalence of somatoform disorders (Bouman, Eifert, & Lejuez, 1999).

Somatization Disorder

Individuals with somatization disorders are often said to "cling to ill health." **A *somatization disorder* is marked by a history of diverse physical complaints that appear to be psychological in origin.** Somatization disorder occurs mostly in women (Guggenheim, 2000) and often coexists with depression or anxiety disorders (Gureje et al., 1997). Victims report an endless succession of minor physical ailments that seem to wax and wane in response to the stress in their lives (Servan-Schreiber, Kolb, & Tabas, 1999). They usually have a long and complicated history of medical treatment from many doctors. The distinguishing feature of this disorder is the diversity of victims' physical complaints. Over the years, they report a mixed bag of cardiovascular, gastrointestinal, pulmonary, neurological, and genitourinary symptoms. The unlikely nature of such a mixture of symptoms occurring together often alerts a physician to the possible psychological basis for the patient's problems.

Conversion Disorder

Conversion disorder is characterized by a significant loss of physical function with no apparent organic basis, usually in a single organ system. Common symptoms include partial or complete loss of vision, partial or complete loss of hearing, partial paralysis, severe laryngitis or mutism, seizures, vomiting, and loss of feeling or function in limbs, such as that seen in the following case:

Mildred was a rancher's daughter who lost the use of both of her legs during adolescence. Mildred was at home alone one afternoon when a male relative attempted to

WEB LINK 15.3

National Institute of Mental Health: For the Public
A wealth of information on psychological disorders is available at this subpage of the U.S. National Institute of Mental Health's massive website. Visitors will find detailed online booklets on generalized anxiety disorder, obsessive-compulsive disorder, panic disorder, depression, bipolar disorder, and so forth. Brief fact sheets, dense technical reports, and many other resources are also available.

assault her. She screamed for help, and her legs gave way as she slipped to the floor. She was found on the floor a few minutes later when her mother returned home. She could not get up, so she was carried to her bed. Her legs buckled when she made subsequent attempts to walk on her own. Due to her illness, she was waited on hand and foot by her family and friends. Neighbors brought her homemade things to eat or to wear. She became the center of attention in the household. (Adapted from Cameron, 1963, pp. 312–313)

People with conversion disorder are usually troubled by more severe ailments than people with somatization disorder. In some cases of conversion disorder, there are telltale clues about the psychological origins of the illness because the patient's symptoms are not consistent with medical knowledge about their apparent disease. For instance, the loss of feeling in one hand that is seen in "glove anesthesia" is inconsistent with the known facts of neurological organization (see Figure 15.8).

Hypochondriasis

Hypochondriacs constantly monitor their physical condition, looking for signs of illness. Any tiny alteration from their physical norm leads them to conclude that

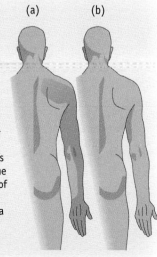

● **FIGURE 15.8**

Glove anesthesia. In conversion disorders, the physical complaints are sometimes inconsistent with the known facts of physiology. Such is the case in *glove anesthesia,* in which the patient complains of losing feeling in a hand. Given the patterns of nerve distribution in the arm shown in **(a)**, a loss of feeling in the hand exclusively as shown in **(b)** is a physical impossibility, indicating that the patient's problem is psychological in origin.

"THE WAY HE MOANS AND GROANS WHEN HE GETS A LITTLE COLD... I CAN'T DECIDE WHETHER HE SHOULD CALL A DOCTOR OR A DRAMA CRITIC."

Reprinted by permission of Edgar Argo.

they have contracted a disease. *Hypochondriasis* (more widely known as *hypochondria*) is characterized by excessive preoccupation with health concerns and incessant worry about developing physical illnesses. The following case illustrates the nature of hypochondria:

Jeff is a middle-aged man who works as a clerk in a drug store. He spends long hours describing his health problems to anyone who will listen. Jeff is an avid reader of popular magazine articles on medicine. He can tell you all about the latest medical discoveries. He takes all sorts of pills and vitamins to ward off possible illnesses. He's the first to try every new product on the market. Jeff is constantly afflicted by new symptoms of illness. His most recent problems were poor digestion and a heartbeat that he thought was irregular. He frequently goes to physicians who can find nothing wrong with him physically. They tell him that he is healthy. He thinks they use "backward techniques." He suspects that his illness is too rare to be diagnosed successfully. (Adapted from Suinn, 1984, p. 236)

When hypochondriacs are assured by their physician that they do not have any real illness, they often are skeptical and disbelieving (Starcevic, 2001). As in Jeff's case, they frequently assume that the physician must be incompetent, and they go shopping for another doctor. Hypochondriacs don't subjectively suffer from physical distress as much as they overinterpret every conceivable sign of illness. Hypochondria frequently appears alongside other psychological disorders, especially anxiety disorders and depression (Iezzi, Duckworth, & Adams, 2001). For example, Howard Hughes's obsessive-compulsive disorder was coupled with profound hypochondria.

Etiology of Somatoform Disorders

Inherited aspects of physiological functioning, such as a highly reactive autonomic nervous system, may predispose some people to somatoform disorders (Weiner, 1992). However, available evidence suggests that these disorders are largely a function of personality and learning.

Personality Factors

People with certain types of personality traits seem to be particularly prone to develop somatoform disorders. The prime candidates appear to be people with *histrionic* personality characteristics (Nemiah, 1985; Slavney, 1990). The histrionic personality tends to be self-centered, suggestible, excitable, highly emotional, and overly dramatic. Such people thrive on the attention that they get when they become ill. The personality trait of *neuroticism* also seems to elevate individuals' susceptibility to somatoform disorders (Kirmayer, Robbins, & Paris, 1994).

Cognitive Factors

In recent years, theorists have devoted increased attention to how cognitive peculiarities might contribute to somatoform disorders. For example, Barsky (2001) asserts that some people focus excessive attention on their internal physiological processes and amplify normal bodily sensations into symptoms of distress, which lead them to pursue unnecessary medical treatment. Recent evidence suggests that people with somatoform disorders tend to draw catastrophic conclusions about minor bodily complaints (Salkovskis & Warwick, 2001). They also seem to apply a faulty standard of good health, equating health with a complete absence of symptoms and discomfort, which is unrealistic (Barsky et al., 1993).

The Sick Role

As we discussed in Chapter 14, some people grow fond of the role associated with being sick (Pilowsky, 1993). Their complaints of physical symptoms may be reinforced by indirect benefits derived from their illness (Schwartz, Slater, & Birchler, 1994). One payoff is that becoming ill is a superb way to avoid having to confront life's challenges. Many people with somatoform disorders are avoiding facing up to marital problems, career frustrations, family responsibilities, and the like. After all, when you're sick, others cannot place great demands on you. Another benefit is that physical problems can provide a convenient excuse when people fail, or worry about failing, in endeavors that are critical to their self-esteem (Organista & Miranda, 1991).

Attention from others is another payoff that may reinforce complaints of physical illness. When people become ill, they command the attention of family, friends, co-workers, neighbors, and doctors. The sympathy that illness often brings may strengthen the person's tendency to feel ill. This clearly occurred in Mildred's case of conversion disorder. Her illness paid handsome dividends in terms of attention, consolation, and kindhearted assistance from others.

Dissociative Disorders

LEARNING OBJECTIVES

- *Describe three types of dissociative disorders.*
- *Summarize what is known about the causes of dissociative disorders.*

Dissociative disorders are among the more unusual of psychological syndromes. ***Dissociative disorders* are a class of disorders in which people lose contact with portions of their consciousness or memory, resulting in disruptions in their sense of identity.** Here we describe three dissociative syndromes—dissociative amnesia, dissociative fugue, and dissociative identity disorder—all of which are relatively uncommon.

Dissociative Amnesia and Fugue

Dissociative amnesia and fugue are overlapping disorders characterized by serious memory deficits. ***Dissociative amnesia* is a sudden loss of memory for important personal information that is too extensive to be due to normal forgetting.** Memory losses may occur for a single traumatic event (such as an automobile accident or home fire) or for an extended period of time surrounding the event. Cases of amnesia have been observed after people have experienced disasters, accidents, combat stress, physical abuse, and rape, or after they have witnessed the violent death of a parent, among other things (Arrigo & Pezdek, 1997; Loewenstein, 1996). **In *dissociative fugue,* people lose their memory for their sense of personal identity.** Having forgotten their name, their family, where they live, and where they work, these people typically wander away from their home area. In spite of this wholesale forgetting, they remember matters unrelated to their identity, such as how to drive a car and how to do math.

Dissociative Identity Disorder

***Dissociative identity disorder (DID)* involves the coexistence in one person of two or more largely complete, and usually very different, personalities.** The name for this disorder used to be *multiple personality disorder,* which still enjoys informal usage. In dissociative identity disorder, the divergences in behavior go far beyond those that people normally display in adapting to different roles in life. People with "multiple personalities" feel that they have more than one identity. Each personality has his or her own name, memories, traits, and physical mannerisms. Although rare, this "Dr. Jekyll and Mr. Hyde" syndrome is frequently portrayed in novels, movies, and television

shows. In popular media portrayals, the syndrome is often mistakenly called *schizophrenia*. As you will see later, schizophrenic disorders are entirely different and do not involve "split personality."

In dissociative identity disorder, the various personalities are often unaware of each other (Eich et al., 1997). In other words, the experiences of a specific personality are only recalled by that personality and not the others. The alternate personalities commonly display traits that are quite foreign to the original personality. For instance, a shy, inhibited person might develop a flamboyant, extraverted alternate personality. Transitions between identities often occur suddenly. The disparities between identities can be bizarre, as personalities may assert that they are different in age, race, gender, and sexual orientation (Kluft, 1996). Dissociative identity disorder rarely occurs in isolation. Most DID patients also have a history of anxiety, mood, or personality disorders (Ross, 1999).

Starting in the 1970s, a dramatic increase was seen in the diagnosis of dissociative identity disorder (Kihlstrom, 2001). Some theorists believe that this disorder used to be underdiagnosed—that is, it often went undetected (Maldonado & Spiegel, 2003; Saxe et al., 1993). However, other theorists argue that a handful of clinicians have begun overdiagnosing the condition and that some clinicians even contribute to the emergence of DID (McHugh, 1995; Powell & Gee, 1999). Consistent with this view, a survey of all the psychiatrists in Switzerland found that 90 percent of them had never seen a case of dissociative identity disorder, whereas three of the psychiatrists had each seen more than 20 patients with dissociative identity disorder (Modestin, 1992). The data from this study suggest that 6 psychiatrists (out of 655 surveyed) accounted

WEB LINK 15.4

International Society for the Study of Dissociation
Dissociative disorders, including dissociative identity disorder, are the focus of this organization of research and clinical professionals. In addition to a selective bibliography and a set of treatment guidelines, the site provides an impressive set of links to other professional groups involved in studying and treating dissociation.

Risk Factors for Posttraumatic Stress Disorder in the Aftermath of Trauma

The threat of terrorism in contemporary life raises concerns about its psychological fallout. Epidemiologists are still trying to determine exactly how many people developed posttraumatic stress disorder and other psychological disorders in the wake of the terrorist attacks that took place on September 11, 2001 (DeRoma et al., 2003; Lating et al., 2004; Piotrkowski & Brannen, 2002). As you may recall from Chapter 3, *posttraumatic stress disorder (PTSD)* involves enduring psychological disturbance attributed to the experience of a major traumatic event. Although PTSD is fairly common in the wake of major disasters, the vast majority of people who experience such events do *not* develop PTSD (Ozer & Weiss, 2004). Hence, a current focus of research is to ask why—what factors make certain people more vulnerable than others to PTSD? Two recent reviews of hundreds of studies on predictors of PTSD suggest that the major risk factors are as follows (Brewin, Andrews, & Valentine, 2000; Ozer et al., 2003).

Severity of exposure to the traumatic event. As one would expect, the probability of PTSD is an increasing function of the intensity of one's exposure to the traumatic event. For example, studies have found that the closer people were to an explosion, fire, flood, or combat zone, the higher the risk of PTSD. And the more people perceived that their life was in danger, the greater the likelihood of PTSD.

Pretrauma adjustment. Research consistently shows susceptibility to PTSD is influenced by the quality of one's pretrauma adjustment. The likelihood of PTSD is much higher among people who are already struggling with psychological problems and among people who have a history of previous exposures to trauma, including abuse during their childhood.

Gender. Research suggests that women are more vulnerable to PTSD than men. This gender disparity is seen when men and women are exposed to the same traumatic stressor. For example, female survivors of the 1995 bombing of the Murrah Federal Building in Oklahoma City (which killed 168 people) were twice as likely as male survivors to develop PTSD. The reasons for this gender gap are not readily apparent.

Posttrauma social support. A surprisingly strong predictor of whether people develop PTSD is the quality of their social support after their exposure to the traumatic event. Strong social support from family and friends reduces the likelihood of PTSD.

Intensity of one's reaction at the time of the traumatic event. Individuals who have especially intense emotional reactions during or immediately after the traumatic event show increased susceptibility to PTSD. Vulnerability seems to be greatest among people whose reactions are so intense that they report dissociative experiences (a sense that things are not real, that time is stretching out, that one is watching oneself in a movie).

---

for two-thirds of the dissociative identity disorder diagnoses in Switzerland.

Etiology of Dissociative Disorders

Psychogenic amnesia and fugue are usually attributed to excessive stress. However, relatively little is known about why this extreme reaction to stress occurs in a tiny minority of people but not in the vast majority who are subjected to similar stress. Some theorists speculate that certain personality traits—fantasy-proneness and a tendency to become intensely absorbed in personal experiences—may make some people more susceptible to dissociative disorders, but adequate evidence is lacking on this line of thought (Kihlstrom, Glisky, & Angiulo, 1994).

The causes of dissociative identity disorder are particularly obscure. Some skeptical theorists, such as Nicholas Spanos (1994, 1996) and Lilienfeld and colleagues (1999), believe that people with multiple personalities are engaging in intentional role playing to use mental illness as a face-saving excuse for their personal failings. Spanos also argues that a small minority of therapists help create multiple personalities in their patients by subtly encouraging the emergence of alternate personalities. According to Spanos, dissociative identity disorder is a creation of modern North American culture, much as demonic possession was a creation of early Christianity. To bolster his argument, he discusses how DID patients' symptom presentations seem to have been influenced by popular media. For example, the typical patient with dissociative identity disorder used to report having two or three personalities, but since the publication of *Sybil* (Schreiber, 1973) and other books describing patients with many personalities, the average number of alternate personalities has climbed to about 15. In a similar vein, a dramatic upsurge occurred in the number of dissociative patients reporting that they were victims of ritual satanic abuse during childhood after the publication of *Michelle Remembers* (Smith & Pazder, 1980), a book about a DID patient who purportedly was tortured by a satanic cult.

In spite of these concerns, many clinicians are convinced that DID is an authentic disorder (Gleaves, May,

& Cardena, 2001). They argue that there is no incentive for either patients or therapists to manufacture cases of multiple personalities, which are often greeted with skepticism and outright hostility. They maintain that most cases of DID are rooted in severe emotional trauma that occurred during childhood (Draijer & Langeland, 1999). A substantial majority of people with DID report a history of disturbed home life, beatings and rejection from parents, and sexual abuse (Lewis et al., 1997; Scroppo et al., 1998). However, this link is not unique to DID, as a history of child abuse elevates the likelihood of *many* disorders, especially among females (MacMillan et al., 2001). In the final analysis, however, very little is known about the causes of dissociative identity disorder, which remains a controversial diagnosis. In one survey of American psychiatrists, only one-quarter of the respondents indicated that they felt there was solid evidence for the scientific validity of the DID diagnosis (Pope et al., 1999).

Mood Disorders

LEARNING OBJECTIVES

- Describe the two major mood disorders and discuss their prevalence.
- Explain how genetic and neurochemical factors may be related to the development of mood disorders.

- Discuss how cognitive processes may contribute to mood disorders.
- Explain how interpersonal behavior and stress may contribute to mood disorders.

What might Abraham Lincoln, Leo Tolstoy, Marilyn Monroe, Vincent Van Gogh, Ernest Hemingway, Winston Churchill, Virginia Woolf, Janis Joplin, Irving Berlin, Kurt Cobain, Francis Ford Coppola, Carrie Fisher, Ted Turner, Sting, Mike Wallace, Larry Flynt, Jane Pauley, and Ben Stiller have in common? Yes, they

all achieved great prominence, albeit in different ways at different times. But, more pertinent to our interest, they all suffered from severe mood disorders. Although mood disorders can be terribly debilitating, people with mood disorders may still achieve greatness, because such disorders tend to be *episodic*. In other words,

Mood disorders are common and have afflicted many successful, well-known people, such as Jane Pauley, Ben Stiller and Sting.

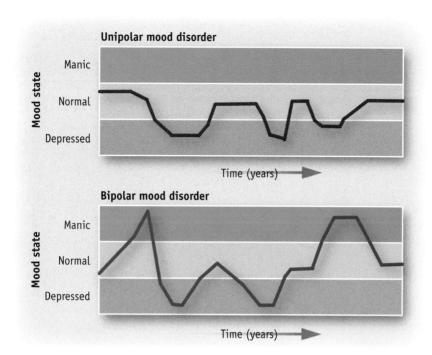

● FIGURE 15.9

Episodic patterns in mood disorders. Episodes of emotional disturbance come and go unpredictably in mood disorders. People with unipolar disorders suffer from bouts of depression only, while people with bipolar disorders experience both manic and depressive episodes. The time between episodes of disturbance varies greatly.

emotional disorders often come and go. Thus, episodes of disturbance are interspersed among periods of normality. These episodes of disturbance can vary greatly in length, but they typically last 3 to 12 months (Akiskal, 2000).

Of course, we all have our ups and downs in terms of mood. Life would be dull indeed if emotional tone were constant. Everyone experiences depression occasionally and has other days that bring an emotional high. Such emotional fluctuations are natural, but some people are prone to extreme distortions of mood. *Mood disorders* **are a class of disorders marked by emotional disturbances that may spill over to disrupt physical, perceptual, social, and thought processes.**

Mood disorders include two basic types: unipolar and bipolar (see Figure 15.9). People with *unipolar disorders* experience emotional extremes at just one end of the mood continuum—depression. People with *bipolar disorders* experience emotional extremes at both ends of the mood continuum, going through periods of both *depression* and *mania* (excitement and elation). The mood swings in bipolar disorders can be patterned in many ways.

Major Depressive Disorder

The line between normal and abnormal depression can be difficult to draw (Kendler & Gardner, 1998). Ultimately, a subjective judgment is required. Crucial considerations in this judgment include the duration of the depression and its disruptive effects. When a depression significantly impairs everyday adaptive be-

havior for more than a few weeks, there is reason for concern.

In *major depressive disorder* **people show persistent feelings of sadness and despair and a loss of interest in previous sources of pleasure.** Figure 15.10 on the next page summarizes the most common symptoms of depressive disorders and compares them to the symptoms of mania. Negative emotions form the heart of the depressive syndrome, but many other symptoms may also appear. Depressed people often give up activities that they used to find enjoyable. For example, a depressed person might quit going bowling or give up a favorite hobby like photography. Reduced appetite and insomnia are common. People with depression often lack energy. They tend to move sluggishly and talk slowly. Anxiety, irritability, and brooding are frequently observed. Self-esteem tends to sink as the depressed person begins to feel worthless. Depression plunges people into feelings of hopelessness, dejection, and boundless guilt. The severity of abnormal depression varies considerably. The onset of unipolar disorder can occur at any point in the life span, but a substantial majority of cases emerge before age 40 (Hammen, 2003). Depression does occur in children, as well as

WEB LINK 15.5

Dr. Ivan's Depression Central
Some might suggest that psychiatrist Ivan Goldberg's site would be better titled "Everything You Ever Wanted to Know About Depression . . ." He offers visitors a great depth of resources regarding depression and mood disorders.

Common symptoms in manic and depressive episodes. The emotional, cognitive, and motor symptoms exhibited in manic and depressive illnesses are largely the opposite of each other.

From Sarason, I. G., & Sarason, B. R. (1987). *Abnormal psychology: The problem of maladaptive behavior* (5th ed., p. 283). Englewood Cliffs, NJ: Prentice-Hall. © 1987 Prentice-Hall. Reprinted by permission of Prentice-Hall, Inc.

Comparison of Manic and Depressive Symptoms

Characteristics	Manic episode	Depressive episode
Emotional	Elated, euphoric, very sociable, impatient at any hindrance	Gloomy, hopeless, socially withdrawn, irritable
Cognitive	Characterized by racing thoughts, flight of ideas, desire for action, and impulsive behavior; talkative, self-confident; experiencing delusions of grandeur	Characterized by slowness of thought processes, obsessive worrying, inability to make decisions, negative self-image, self-blame, and delusions of guilt and disease
Motor	Hyperactive, tireless, requiring less sleep than usual, showing increased sex drive and fluctuating appetite	Less active, tired, experiencing difficulty in sleeping, showing decreased sex drive and decreased appetite

adolescents and adults (Gruenberg & Goldstein, 2003). The median duration of depressive episodes is 5 months (Solomon et al., 1997). The vast majority (75–95 percent) of people who suffer from depression experience more than one episode over the course of their lifetime (Dubovsky, Davies, Dubovsky, 2003). The median number of depressive episodes is four.

How common are depressive disorders? Very common. A recent, large-scale study of a nationally representative sample of over 9000 adults found that the lifetime prevalence of depressive disorder was 16.2 percent (Kessler et al., 2003). That estimate suggests that over 30 million people in the United States have suffered from depression! That said, estimates of the prevalence of depression vary quite a bit from one study to another because of the previously mentioned difficulty in drawing a line between normal dejection and abnormal depression. Hence, researchers using different procedures and cutoff points obtain different estimates. Nonetheless, evidence suggests that the prevalence of depression is increasing, as it is higher in more recent age cohorts (Rehm, Wagner, & Ivens-Tyndal, 2001). In particular, age cohorts born since World War II appear to have an elevated risk for depression (Kessler, 2002). The factors underlying this rise in depression are not readily apparent, and researchers are scrambling to collect data that might shed light on this unanticipated trend.

Researchers also find that the prevalence of depression is about twice as high in women as it is in men (Nolen-Hoeksema, 2002). The many possible explanations for this gender gap are the subject of considerable debate. The gap does *not* appear to be attributable to differences in genetic makeup or other biological factors (Kessler et al., 2003). Susan Nolen-Hoeksema (2001) argues that women experience more depression than

Susan Nolen-Hoeksema

Courtesy, Susan Nolen-Hoeksema

men because they are far more likely to be victims of sexual abuse and somewhat more likely to endure poverty, harassment, and role constraints. In other words, she attributes the higher prevalence of depression among women to their experience of greater stress and adversity. Nolen-Hoeksema also believes that women have a greater tendency than men to *ruminate* about setbacks and problems. Evidence suggests that this tendency to dwell on one's difficulties elevates vulnerability to depression, as we will discuss momentarily.

Bipolar Disorder

Bipolar disorder (formerly known as *manic-depressive disorder*) is marked by the experience of both depressed and manic periods. The symptoms seen in manic periods generally are the opposite of those seen in depression (see Figure 15.10 for a comparison). In a manic episode, a person's mood becomes elevated to the point of euphoria. Self-esteem skyrockets as the person bubbles over with optimism, energy, and extravagant plans. People become hyperactive and may go for days without sleep. They talk rapidly and shift topics wildly as their minds race at breakneck speed. Judgment is often impaired. Some people in manic periods gamble impulsively, spend money frantically, or become sexually reckless. Like depressive disorders, bipolar disorders vary considerably in severity.

You may be thinking that the euphoria in manic episodes sounds appealing. If so, you are not entirely wrong. In their milder forms, manic states can seem attractive. The increases in energy, self-esteem, and optimism can be deceptively seductive. Because of the increase in energy, many bipolar patients report temporary surges of productivity and creativity (Goodwin & Jamison, 1990).

Although manic episodes may have some positive aspects, bipolar disorder ultimately proves to be troublesome for most victims. Manic periods often have a paradoxical negative undertow of uneasiness and irritability (Dilsaver et al., 1999). Moreover, mild manic episodes usually escalate to higher levels that become scary and disturbing. Impaired judgment leads many victims to do things that they greatly regret later, as illustrated in the following case:

Robert, a dentist, awoke one morning with the idea that he was the most gifted dental surgeon in his tri-state area. He decided that he should try to provide services to as many people as possible, so that more people could benefit from his talents. Thus, he decided to remodel his two-chair dental office, installing 20 booths so that he could simultaneously attend to 20 patients. That same day he drew up plans for this arrangement, telephoned a number of remodelers, and invited bids for the work. Later that day, impatient to get going on his remodeling, he rolled up his sleeves, got himself a sledgehammer, and began to knock down the walls in his office. Annoyed when that didn't go so well, he smashed his dental tools, washbasins, and X-ray equipment. Later, Robert's wife became concerned about his behavior and summoned two of her adult daughters for assistance. The daughters responded quickly, arriving at the family home with their husbands. In the ensuing discussion, Robert—after bragging about his sexual prowess—made advances toward his daughters. He had to be subdued by their husbands. (Adapted from Kleinmuntz, 1980, p. 309)

Although not rare, bipolar disorder is much less common than unipolar depression. Bipolar disorder affects about 1–2.5 percent of the population (Dubovsky et al., 2003). Unlike depressive disorder, bipolar disorder is seen equally often in men and women (Bauer, 2003). As Figure 15.11 shows, the onset of bipolar disorders is age related, with the peak of vulnerability occurring between the ages of 20 and 29 (Goodwin & Jamison, 1990).

Etiology of Mood Disorders

We know quite a bit about the etiology of mood disorders, although the puzzle hasn't been assembled completely. There appear to be a number of routes into these disorders, involving intricate interactions between psychological and biological factors.

Genetic Vulnerability

The evidence strongly suggests that genetic factors influence the likelihood of developing major depression or a bipolar mood disorder (Kalidindi & McGuffin, 2003; Sullivan, Neale, & Kendler, 2000). In studies that assess the impact of heredity on psychological disorders, investigators look at *concordance rates*. **A *concordance rate* indicates the percentage of twin pairs or other pairs of relatives that exhibit the same disorder.** If relatives who share more genetic similarity show higher concordance rates than relatives who share less genetic overlap, this finding supports the genetic hypothesis. Twin studies, which compare identical and fraternal twins (see Chapter 2), suggest that genetic factors *are* involved in mood disorders (Knowles, Kaufmann, & Rieder, 1999). Concordance rates average around 65–72 percent for identical twins but only 14–19 percent for fraternal twins, who share less genetic similarity. Thus, evidence suggests that heredity can create a *predisposition* to mood disorders. Environmental factors probably determine whether this predisposition is converted into an actual disorder. Research suggests that genetic vulnerability may play a larger role in women's depression than in men's (Bierut et al., 1999). The influence of genetic factors

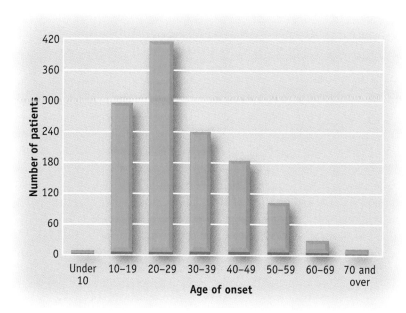

● **FIGURE 15.11**

Age of onset for bipolar mood disorder. The onset of bipolar disorder typically occurs in adolescence or early adulthood. The data graphed here, which were combined from ten studies, show the distribution of age of onset for 1304 bipolar patients. As you can see, bipolar disorder emerges most frequently during the 20s decade.

From Goodwin, F. K., & Jamison, K. R. (1990). *Manic-depressive illness.* New York: Oxford University Press. Copyright © 1990 Oxford University Press, Inc. Used by permission of Oxford University Press, Inc.

also appears to be stronger for bipolar disorder than for depression (Knowles et al., 1999).

Neurochemical Factors

Heredity may influence susceptibility to mood disorders by creating a predisposition toward certain types of neurochemical activity in the brain. Correlations have been found between mood disorders and the levels of two neurotransmitters in the brain—norepinephrine and serotonin—although other neurotransmitter disturbances may also contribute (Sher & Mann, 2003; Thase, Jindal, & Howland, 2002). The details remain elusive, but it seems clear that a neurochemical basis exists for at least some mood disorders. A variety of drug therapies are fairly effective in the treatment of severe mood disorders. Most of these drugs are known to affect the availability (in the brain) of the neurotransmitters that have been related to mood disorders (Garlow, Musselman, & Nemeroff, 1999). Because this effect is unlikely to be a coincidence, it bolsters the plausibility of the idea that neurochemical changes produce mood disturbances.

If alterations in neurotransmitter activity are the basis for many mood disorders, what causes the alterations in neurotransmitter activity? These changes probably depend on the individual's reactions to environmental events. Thus, a number of psychological factors have been implicated in the etiology of mood disorders. Here we focus on three such factors: patterns of thinking, interpersonal style, and stress.

Cognitive Factors

A variety of theories emphasize how cognitive factors contribute to depressive disorders (Abramson et al., 2002). We will discuss Aaron Beck's (1976, 1987) influential cognitive theory of depression in Chapter 16, where his approach to therapy is described. In this section, we examine Martin Seligman's *learned helplessness model* of depression (see Chapter 4) and its most recent descendant, *hopelessness theory.* Based largely on animal research, Seligman (1974) proposed that depression is caused by *learned helplessness*—passive "giving up" behavior produced by exposure to unavoidable aversive events (such as uncontrollable shock in the laboratory). He originally considered learned helplessness to be a product of conditioning but eventually revised his theory, giving it a cognitive slant. The reformulated theory of learned helplessness postulated that the roots of depression lie in how people explain the setbacks and other negative events that they experience (Abramson, Seligman, & Teasdale, 1978). According to Seligman (1990), people who exhibit a *pessimistic explanatory style* are especially vulnerable to depression (see Chapter 5). These people tend to attribute their setbacks to their personal flaws instead of situational factors, and

they tend to draw global, far-reaching conclusions about their personal inadequacies based on these setbacks.

Hopelessness theory builds on these insights by postulating a sense of hopelessness as the "final pathway" leading to depression and by incorporating additional factors that may interact with explanatory style to foster this sense of hopelessness (Abramson, Alloy, & Metalsky, 1995). According to hopelessness theory, a pessimistic explanatory style is just one of several or more factors—along with high stress, low self-esteem, and so forth—that may contribute to hopelessness, and thus depression. Although hopelessness theory casts a wider net than the learned helplessness model, it continues to emphasize the importance of people's *cognitive reactions* to the events in their lives.

In accord with this line of thinking, Susan Nolen-Hoeksema (1991, 2000) has found that people who *ruminate* about their problems and setbacks have elevated rates of depression and tend to remain depressed longer than those who do not ruminate. People who tend to ruminate repetitively focus their attention on their depressing feelings, thinking constantly about how sad, lethargic, and unmotivated they are. According to Nolen-Hoeksema (1995), excessive rumination tends to extend and amplify episodes of depression. She believes that women are more likely to ruminate than men and that this disparity may be a major reason why depression is more prevalent in women.

In sum, cognitive models of depression maintain that negative thinking is what leads to depression in many people. The principal problem with cognitive theories is their difficulty in separating cause from effect (Rehm, Wagner, & Ivens-Tyndal, 2001). Does negative thinking cause depression? Or does depression cause negative thinking (see Figure 15.12)? A *clear* demonstration of a causal link between negative thinking and depression is not possible because it would require manipulating people's explanatory style (which is not easy to change) in sufficient degree to produce full-fledged depressive disorders (which would not be ethical). However, recent research has provided impressive evidence consistent with a causal link between negative thinking and vulnerability to depression. Lauren Alloy and her colleagues (1999) assessed the explanatory style of a sample of first-year college students who were not depressed at the outset of the study. The students were characterized as being at high risk or low risk for depression based on whether they exhibited a negative cognitive style. The follow-up data over the ensuing 2.5 years on students who had no prior history of depression showed dramatic differences between the two groups in vulnerability to depression. During this relatively brief period, a major depressive disorder emerged in 17 percent of the high-risk students in comparison to only 1 percent of the

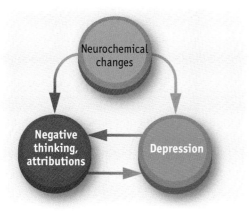

● FIGURE 15.12

Interpreting the correlation between negative thinking and depression. Cognitive theories of depression assert that consistent patterns of negative thinking cause depression. Although these theories are highly plausible, depression could cause negative thoughts, or both could be caused by a third factor, such as neurochemical changes in the brain.

low-risk students. These high-risk subjects also displayed a much greater incidence of minor depressive episodes (39 percent versus 6 percent). These findings and other data from the study (see Figure 15.13) suggest that negative thinking makes people more vulnerable to depression.

Interpersonal Roots

Some theorists suggest that inadequate social skills put people on the road to depressive disorders (Coyne, 1999; Lewinsohn & Gotlib, 1995). According to this notion, depression-prone people lack the social finesse needed to acquire many important kinds of reinforcers, such as good friends, top jobs, and desirable spouses. This paucity of reinforcers could understandably lead to negative emotions and depression (see Figure 15.14). Consistent with this theory, researchers

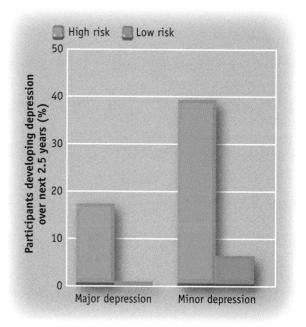

● FIGURE 15.13

Negative thinking and prediction of depression. Alloy and colleagues (1999) measured the explanatory style of first-year college students and characterized them as being high risk or low risk for depression. This graph shows the percentage of these students who experienced major or minor episodes of depression over the next 2.5 years. As you can see, the high risk students, who exhibited a negative thinking style, proved to be much more vulnerable to depression. (Data from Alloy et al., 1999)

have found correlations between poor social skills and depression (Ingram, Scott, & Siegle, 1999).

Another interpersonal consideration is that depressed people tend to be depressing (Joiner & Katz, 1999). Individuals suffering from depression are often irritable and pessimistic. They complain a lot, and they aren't very enjoyable companions. As a consequence, depressed people inadvertently court rejection from those around them (Joiner & Metalsky, 1995). In turn,

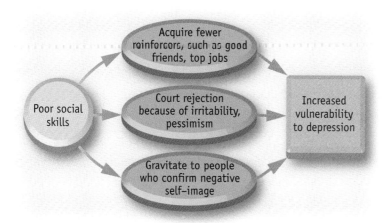

● FIGURE 15.14

Interpersonal factors in depression. Interpersonal theories about the etiology of depression emphasize how inadequate social skills may contribute to the development of the disorder.

rejection and lack of social support may aggravate and deepen a person's depression (Potthoff, Holahan, & Joiner, 1995). To compound these problems, evidence indicates that depressed people may gravitate to partners who view them unfavorably and hence reinforce their negative views of themselves (Joiner, 2002).

Precipitating Stress

Mood disorders sometimes appear mysteriously "out of the blue" in people who are leading benign, nonstressful lives. For this reason, experts used to believe that mood disorders are relatively uninfluenced by stress. However, recent advances in the measurement of personal stress have altered this picture. The evidence available today suggests a moderately strong link between stress and the onset of mood disorders (Kendler, Kuhn, & Prescott, 2004; Kessler, 1997). Stress also appears to affect how people with mood disorders respond to treatment and whether they experience a relapse of their disorder (Monroe & Hadjiyannakis, 2002).

Of course, many people endure great stress without getting depressed. The impact of stress varies in part because different people have different degrees of *vulnerability* to mood disorders (Lewinsohn, Joiner, & Rohde, 2001). Variations in vulnerability appear to depend primarily on biological makeup. Similar interactions between stress and vulnerability probably influence the development of many kinds of disorders, including those that are next on our agenda: the schizophrenic disorders.

Schizophrenic Disorders

LEARNING OBJECTIVES

- Describe the prevalence and general symptoms of schizophrenia.
- Describe four schizophrenic subtypes.
- Distinguish between positive and negative symptoms in schizophrenia.
- Identify factors related to the prognosis for schizophrenic patients.

- Summarize how genetic vulnerability and neurochemical factors may contribute to the etiology of schizophrenia.
- Discuss the evidence relating schizophrenia to structural abnormalities in the brain and neurodevelopmental insults to the brain.
- Summarize how expressed emotion and stress may contribute to schizophrenia.

Literally, *schizophrenia* means "split mind." However, when Eugen Bleuler coined the term in 1911, he was referring to the fragmenting of thought processes seen in the disorder—not to a "split personality." Unfortunately, writers in the popular media often assume that the split-mind notion refers to the syndrome in which a person manifests two or more personalities. As you have already learned, this syndrome is actually called *dissociative identity disorder*. Schizophrenia is a much more common, and altogether different, type of disorder.

Schizophrenic disorders are a class of disorders marked by disturbances in thought that spill over to affect perceptual, social, and emotional processes. How common is schizophrenia? Prevalence estimates suggest that about 1 percent of the population may suffer from schizophrenic disorders (Jablensky, 1999). That may not sound like much, but it means that in the United States alone there may be several million people troubled by schizophrenic disturbances. Moreover, schizophrenia is an extremely costly disorder for society, because it is a severe, debilitating illness that tends to have an early onset and often requires lengthy hospital care (Buchanan & Carpenter, 2000).

General Symptoms

Although there are a number of distinct schizophrenic syndromes, they share some general characteristics that we need to examine before looking at the subtypes. Many of these characteristics are apparent in the following case history (adapted from Sheehan, 1982).

Sylvia was first diagnosed as schizophrenic at age 15. She has been in and out of many types of psychiatric facilities since then. She has never been able to hold a job for any length of time. During severe flare-ups of her disorder, her personal hygiene deteriorates. She rarely washes, wears clothes that neither fit nor match, smears makeup on heavily but randomly, and slops food all over herself. Sylvia occasionally hears voices talking to her. Sylvia tends to be argumentative, aggressive, and emotionally volatile. Over the years, she has been involved in innumerable fights with fellow patients, psychiatric staff members, and strangers. Her thoughts can be highly irrational, as is apparent from the following quotation:

"Mick Jagger wants to marry me. If I have Mick Jagger, I don't have to covet Geraldo Rivera. Mick Jagger is St. Nicholas and the Maharishi is Santa Claus. I want to form a gospel rock group called the Thorn Oil, but Geraldo wants me to be the music critic on Eyewitness News, so what can I do? Got to listen to my boyfriend. Teddy Kennedy cured me of my ugliness. I'm pregnant with the son of God. I'm going to marry David Berkowitz and get it over with. Creedmoor is the headquarters of the American Nazi Party. They're eating the patients here. Archie

Bunker wants me to play his niece on his TV show. I work for Epic Records. I'm Joan of Arc. I'm Florence Nightingale. The door between the ward and the porch is the dividing line between New York and California. Divorce isn't a piece of paper, it's a feeling. Forget about Zip Codes. I need shock treatment." (Sheehan, 1982, pp.104–105)

Sylvia's case clearly shows that schizophrenic thinking can be bizarre and that schizophrenia is a brutally serious, psychologically disfiguring disorder. Although no single symptom is inevitably present, the following symptoms are commonly seen in schizophrenia (Cancro & Lehmann, 2000; Ho, Black, & Andreasen, 2003).

Irrational thought.   Disturbed, irrational thought processes are the central feature of schizophrenic disorders. Various kinds of delusions are common. ***Delusions are false beliefs that are maintained even though they clearly are out of touch with reality.*** For example, one patient's delusion that he is a tiger (with a deformed body) persisted for 15 years (Kulick, Pope, & Keck, 1990). More typically, affected persons believe that their private thoughts are being broadcast to other people, that thoughts are being injected into their mind against their will, or that their thoughts are being controlled by some external force (Maher, 2001). In *delusions of grandeur,* people maintain that they are extremely famous or important. Sylvia expressed an endless array of grandiose delusions, such as thinking that Mick Jagger wanted to marry her, that she dictated the hobbit stories to Tolkien, and that she was going to win the Nobel Prize for medicine. In addition to delusions, the schizophrenic person's train of thought deteriorates. Thinking becomes chaotic rather than logical and linear. There is a "loosening of associations" as the schizophrenic shifts topics in disjointed ways. The quotation from Sylvia illustrates this symptom dramatically. The entire passage involves a wild "flight of ideas," but at one point (beginning with the sentence "Creedmoor is the headquarters . . .") she rattles off ten consecutive sentences that have no apparent connection to the preceding sentence.

Deterioration of adaptive behavior.   Schizophrenia involves a noticeable deterioration in the quality of one's routine functioning in work, social relations, and personal care. Friends will often make remarks such as "Hal just isn't himself anymore." This deterioration is readily apparent in Sylvia's inability to get along with others or function in the work world. It's also apparent in her neglect of personal hygiene.

Distorted perception.   A variety of perceptual distortions may occur in schizophrenia, with the most common being auditory hallucinations. ***Hallucinations are sensory perceptions that occur in the absence of a real external stimulus or that represent gross distortions of perceptual input.*** Schizophrenics frequently report that they hear voices of nonexistent or absent people talking to them. Sylvia, for instance, heard messages from former Beatle Paul McCartney. These voices often provide an insulting running commentary on the person's behavior ("You're an idiot for shaking his hand"). The voices may be argumentative ("You don't need a bath"), and they may issue commands ("Prepare your home for visitors from outer space").

Disturbed emotion.   Normal emotional tone can be disrupted in schizophrenia in a variety of ways. Although it may not be an accurate indicator of their underlying emotional experience (Kring, 1999), some victims show little emotional responsiveness, a symptom referred to as "blunted or flat affect." Others show inappropriate emotional responses that don't jell with the situation or with what they are saying. People with schizophrenia may also become emotionally volatile. This pattern was displayed by Sylvia, who often overreacted emotionally in erratic, unpredictable ways.

Subtypes

Four subtypes of schizophrenic disorders are recognized, including a category for people who don't fit neatly into any of the first three categories (Ho et al., 2003).

Paranoid Type
As its name implies, ***paranoid schizophrenia is dominated by delusions of persecution, along with delusions of grandeur.*** In this common form of schizophrenia, people come to believe that they have many enemies who want to harass and oppress them. They may become suspicious of friends and relatives, or they may attribute the persecution to mysterious, unknown persons. They are convinced that they are being watched and manipulated in malicious ways. To make sense of this persecution, they often develop delusions of grandeur. They believe that they must be enormously important people, often seeing themselves as great inventors or as great religious or political leaders. For example, in the case described at the beginning of the chapter, Ed's belief that he was president of the United States was a delusion of grandeur.

Catatonic Type
Catatonic schizophrenia is marked by striking motor disturbances, ranging from muscular rigidity to random motor activity. Some catatonics go into an extreme form of withdrawal known as a catatonic stupor. They may remain virtually motionless and seem

oblivious to the environment around them for long periods of time. Others go into a state of catatonic excitement. They become hyperactive and incoherent. Some alternate between these dramatic extremes. The catatonic subtype is not particularly common, and its prevalence seems to be declining.

Disorganized Type

In *disorganized schizophrenia,* a particularly severe deterioration of adaptive behavior is seen. Prominent symptoms include emotional indifference, frequent incoherence, and virtually complete social withdrawal. Aimless babbling and giggling are common. Delusions often center on bodily functions ("My brain is melting out my ears").

Undifferentiated Type

People who are clearly schizophrenic but who cannot be placed into any of the three previous categories are said to have *undifferentiated schizophrenia,* which is marked by idiosyncratic mixtures of schizophrenic symptoms. The undifferentiated subtype is fairly common.

Positive Versus Negative Symptoms

Many theorists have raised doubts about the value of dividing schizophrenic disorders into these four subtypes (Sanislow & Carson, 2001). Critics note that the catatonic subtype is disappearing and that undifferentiated cases aren't a subtype so much as a hodgepodge of "leftovers." Critics also point out that the classic schizophrenic subtypes do not differ meaningfully in etiology, prognosis, or response to treatment. The absence of such differences casts doubt on the value of the current classification scheme.

Because of such problems, Nancy Andreasen (1990) and others (Carpenter, 1992; McGlashan & Fenton, 1992) have proposed an alternative approach to subtyping. This new scheme divides schizophrenic disor-

ders into just two categories based on the predominance of negative versus positive symptoms (see Figure 15.15). *Negative symptoms* involve behavioral deficits, such as flattened emotions, social withdrawal, apathy, impaired attention, and poverty of speech. *Positive symptoms* involve behavioral excesses or peculiarities, such as hallucinations, delusions, bizarre behavior, and wild flights of ideas.

Courtesy, Nancy Andreasen

Nancy Andreasen

Theorists advocating this scheme hoped to find consistent differences between the two subtypes in etiology, prognosis, and response to treatment, and some progress along these lines *has* been made. For example, a predominance of positive symptoms is associated with better adjustment prior to the onset of schizophrenia and greater responsiveness to treatment (Cuesta, Peralta, & DeLeon, 1994; Fenton & McGlashan, 1994). However, the assumption that patients can be placed into discrete categories based on this scheme now seems untenable. Most patients exhibit both types of symptoms and vary only in the degree to which positive or negative symptoms dominate (Black & Andreasen, 1994). Moreover, there is some debate about which symptoms should be classified as positive and which as negative, and some theorists have proposed a third category of symptoms reflecting *disorganization* of behavior (Toomey et al., 1997). Although it seems fair to say that the distinction between positive and negative symptoms is enhancing our understanding of schizophrenia, it has not yielded a classification scheme that can replace the traditional subtypes of schizophrenia.

Course and Outcome

Schizophrenic disorders usually emerge during adolescence or early adulthood and only infrequently after

---

● FIGURE 15.15

Examples of positive and negative symptoms in schizophrenia. Some theorists believe that schizophrenic disorders should be classified into just two types, depending on whether patients exhibit mostly positive symptoms (behavioral excesses) or negative symptoms (behavioral deficits). The percentages shown here, based on a sample of 111 schizophrenic patients studied by Andreasen (1987), provide an indication of how common each specific symptom is.

Positive and Negative Symptoms in Schizophrenia

Negative symptoms	Percent of patients	Positive symptoms	Percent of patients
Few friendship relationships	96	Delusions of persecution	81
Few recreational interests	95	Auditory hallucinations	75
Lack of persistence at work or school	95	Delusions of being controlled	46
Impaired grooming or hygiene	87	Derailment of thought	45
Paucity of expressive gestures	81	Delusions of grandeur	39
Social inattentiveness	78	Bizarre social, sexual behavior	33
Emotional nonresponsiveness	64	Delusions of thought insertion	31
Inappropriate emotion	63	Aggressive, agitated behavior	27
Poverty of speech	53	Incoherent thought	23

age 45 (Howard et al., 1993). The emergence of schizophrenia may be either sudden or gradual. Once it clearly emerges, the course of schizophrenia is variable, but patients tend to fall into three broad groups. Some patients, presumably those with milder disorders, are treated successfully and enjoy a full recovery. Other patients experience a partial recovery so that they can return to independent living for a time. However, they experience regular relapses and are in and out of treatment facilities for much of the remainder of their lives. Finally, a third group of patients endure chronic illness that sometimes results in permanent hospitalization. Estimates of the percentage of patients falling in each category vary. Overall, it appears that about 15–20 percent of schizophrenic patients enjoy a full recovery, although some long-term studies have yielded higher estimates (Modestin et al., 2003; Robinson et al., 2004).

A number of factors are related to the likelihood of recovery from schizophrenic disorders (Cancro & Lehmann, 2000; Liberman et al., 2002). A patient has a relatively *favorable prognosis* when (1) the onset of the disorder has been sudden rather than gradual, (2) the onset has occurred at a later age, (3) the patient's social and work adjustment were relatively good prior to the onset of the disorder, (4) the proportion of negative symptoms is relatively low, (5) the patient's cognitive functioning is relatively preserved, (6) the patient shows good adherence to treatment interventions, and (7) the patient has a relatively healthy, supportive family situation to return to. Many of these predictors are concerned with the etiology of schizophrenic illness, which is the matter we turn to next.

Etiology of Schizophrenia

Most of us can identify, at least to some extent, with people who suffer from mood disorders, somatoform disorders, and anxiety disorders. You can probably imagine events that might leave you struggling with depression, grappling with anxiety, or worrying about your physical health. But what could possibly have led Ed to believe that he had been fighting space wars and vampires? What could account for Sylvia thinking that she was Joan of Arc, or that she had dictated the hob-

bit novels to Tolkien? As mystifying as these delusions may seem, you'll see that the etiology of schizophrenic disorders is not all that different from the etiology of other disorders.

Genetic Vulnerability

Evidence is plentiful that hereditary factors play a role in the development of schizophrenic disorders (Tsuang, Glatt, & Faraone, 2003). For instance, in twin studies, concordance rates average around 48 percent for identical twins, in comparison to about 17 percent for fraternal twins (Gottesman, 1991, 2001). Studies also indicate that a child born to two schizophrenic parents has about a 46 percent probability of developing a schizophrenic disorder (as compared to the probability of about 1 percent for the population as a whole). These and other findings that demonstrate the genetic roots of schizophrenia are summarized in Figure 15.16 on the next page. Overall, the picture is similar to that seen for mood disorders. Several converging lines of evidence indicate that people inherit a genetically transmitted *vulnerability* to schizophrenia (Schneider & Deldin, 2001). Although genetic factors may account for more than two-thirds of the variability in susceptibility to schizophrenia, genetic mapping studies have made little progress in identifying the genes responsible (Levinson et al., 1998; Owen & O'Donovan, 2003).

Neurochemical Factors

Like mood disorders, schizophrenic disorders appear to be accompanied by changes in the activity of one or more neurotransmitters in the brain. Excess *dopamine* activity has been implicated as a likely cause of schizophrenia (Abi-Dargham et al., 1998). This hypothesis makes sense because most of the drugs that are useful in the treatment of schizophrenia are known to dampen dopamine activity in the brain (Tamminga & Carlsson, 2003). However, the evidence linking schizophrenia to high dopamine levels is riddled with inconsistencies, complexities, and interpretive problems (Egan & Hyde, 2000). Researchers are currently exploring how interactions between the dopamine, serotonin, and other neurotransmitter systems may contribute to schizophrenia (Patel, Pinals, & Breier, 2003). Thus, investigators are gradually making progress in their search for the neurochemical bases of schizophrenia.

Structural Abnormalities in the Brain

For decades, studies have suggested that individuals with schizophrenia exhibit a variety of deficits in attention, perception, and information processing (Bellack, Gearon, & Blanchard, 2000). Impairments in working (short-term) memory are especially prominent (Silver et al., 2003). These cognitive deficits suggest that schizophrenic disorders may be caused by neurological defects. Until recent decades, however, this theory was based more on speculation than on actual research. However, advances in brain-imaging technology have yielded mountains of intriguing data since the mid-1980s. The most reliable finding is that CT scans and MRI scans suggest an association between enlarged brain ventricles (the hollow, fluid-filled cavities in the brain depicted in Figure 15.17) and schizophrenic disturbance (Egan & Hyde, 2000). Enlarged ventricles are assumed to reflect either the degeneration or failure to develop of nearby brain tissue. The significance of enlarged ventricles is hotly debated, however. Structural deterioration in the brain could be a contributing *cause* or a *consequence* of schizophrenia.

Brain-imaging studies have also uncovered structural and metabolic abnormalities in the frontal lobes of individuals with schizophrenia. Although the research results are not entirely consistent, schizophrenia appears to be associated with smaller size and reduced metabolic activity in areas of the prefrontal cortex (Fowles, 2003). Scientists are also intrigued by the fact that a major dopamine pathway runs through the area in the prefrontal cortex where metabolic abnormalities have been found. A connection may exist between the abnormal dopamine activity implicated in schizophrenia and the dysfunctional metabolic activity seen in this area of the prefrontal cortex (Conklin & Iacono, 2002). Although the research on the prefrontal cortex is intriguing, Ho, Black, and Andreasen (2003) caution that the neural correlates of schizophrenia are complex and that the disease is not likely to be caused by "a single abnormality in a single region of the brain" (p. 408).

The Neurodevelopmental Hypothesis

In recent years, several new lines of evidence have led to the emergence of the *neurodevelopmental hypothesis* of schizophrenia, which posits that schizophrenia is caused in part by various disruptions in the normal maturational processes of the brain before or at birth (Brown, 1999). According to this hypothesis, insults to the brain during sensitive phases of prenatal development or during birth can cause subtle neurological damage that elevates individuals' vulnerability to schizophrenia years later in adolescence and early adulthood (see Figure 15.18). What are the sources of these early insults to the brain? Thus far, research has focused on viral infections or malnutrition during prenatal development and obstetrical complications during the birth process.

The evidence on viral infections has been building since Sarnoff Mednick and his colleagues (1988) discovered an elevated incidence of schizophrenia among individuals who were in their second trimester of prenatal development during a 1957 influenza epidemic in Finland. Several subsequent studies in other locations have also found a link between exposure to influenza during pregnancy and increased prevalence of schizophrenia (Brown et al., 2004). Another study, which investigated the possible impact of prenatal malnutrition, found an elevated incidence of schizophrenia in a cohort of people who were prenatally exposed to a severe famine in 1944–45 because of a Nazi blockade of food deliveries in the Netherlands during World War II (Susser et al., 1996). A follow-up study of some schizophrenic patients exposed to this famine found increased brain abnormalities among the patients, as the neurodevelopmental hypothesis would predict (Hulshoff et al., 2000). Other research has

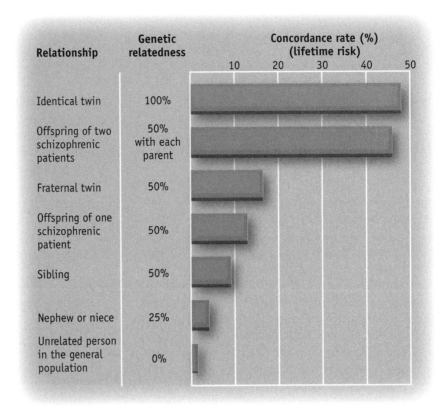

● FIGURE 15.16

Genetic vulnerability to schizophrenic disorders. Relatives of schizophrenic patients have an elevated risk for schizophrenia. This risk is greater among closer relatives. Although environment also plays a role in the etiology of schizophrenia, the concordance rates shown here suggest that there must be a genetic vulnerability to the disorder. These concordance estimates are based on pooled data from 40 studies conducted between 1920 and 1987.

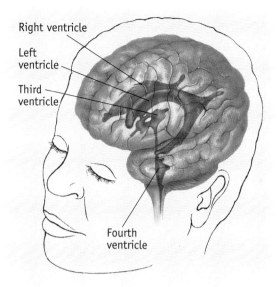

Right ventricle

Left ventricle

Third ventricle

Fourth ventricle

Cover image reprinted by permission of HarperCollins Publishers, Inc.

● **FIGURE 15.17**

Schizophrenia and the ventricles of the brain. Cerebrospinal fluid (CSF) circulates around the brain and spinal cord. The hollow cavities in the brain filled with CSF are called *ventricles*. The four ventricles in the human brain are depicted here. Studies with modern brain-imaging techniques suggest that an association exists between enlarged ventricles in the brain and the occurrence of schizophrenic disturbance.

shown that schizophrenic patients are more likely than control subjects to have a history of obstetrical complications (Geddes & Lawrie, 1995; Rosso et al., 2000). Finally, research suggests that minor physical anomalies (slight anatomical defects of the head, hands, feet, and face) that would be consistent with prenatal neurological damage are more common among people with schizophrenia than in other people (McNeil, Cantor-Graae, & Ismail, 2000; Schiffman et al., 2002). Collectively, these diverse studies argue for a relationship between early neurological trauma and a predisposition to schizophrenia (Mednick et al., 1998).

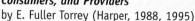

RECOMMENDED READING

Surviving Schizophrenia: A Manual for Families, Consumers, and Providers
by E. Fuller Torrey (Harper, 1988, 1995)

E. Fuller Torrey, a prominent psychiatrist who specializes in the study and treatment of schizophrenia, has written a practical book intended for the lay public. Torrey points out that many myths surrounding schizophrenia have added to the anguish of families who have been victimized by this illness. He explains that schizophrenia is *not* caused by childhood trauma, domineering mothers, or passive fathers. He discusses how genetic vulnerability, flawed brain chemistry, and other factors contribute to the development of schizophrenic disorders. Torrey discusses the treatment of schizophrenia at great length. He also explains the various ways in which the disease can evolve. Some of the best material is found in chapters on what the patient needs and what the family needs.

Throughout the book, Torrey writes with clarity, eloquence, and conviction. He is not reluctant to express strong opinions. For instance, in an appendix he lists the ten worst readings on schizophrenia (along with the ten best), and his evaluations are brutal. He characterizes one book as "absurd drivel" and dismisses another by saying, "If a prize were to be given to the book which has produced the most confusion about schizophrenia over the past twenty years, this book would win going away." Scientists and academicians are usually reluctant to express such strong opinions, so Torrey's candor is remarkably refreshing. Another excellent, down-to-earth book on schizophrenic disorders is *Understanding Schizophrenia: A Guide to the New Research on Causes and Treatment* by Richard S. E. Keefe and Philip D. Harvey (The Free Press, 1994).

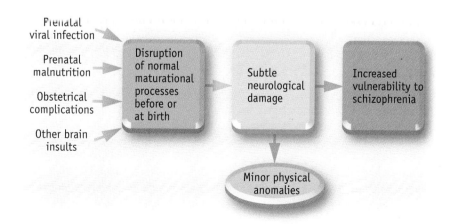

● **FIGURE 15.18**

The neurodevelopmental hypothesis of schizophrenia. Research suggests that insults to the brain sustained during prenatal development or at birth may disrupt crucial maturational processes in the brain, resulting in subtle neurological damage that gradually becomes apparent as youngsters develop. This neurological damage is believed to increase both vulnerability to schizophrenia and the incidence of minor physical anomalies.

Expressed Emotion

Studies of expressed emotion have primarily focused on how this element of family dynamics influences the *course* of schizophrenic illness after the onset of the disorder (Leff & Vaughn, 1985). *Expressed emotion (EE)* reflects the degree to which a relative of a schizophrenic patient displays highly critical or emotionally overinvolved attitudes toward the patient. Audiotaped interviews are used to assess relatives' expressed emotion. The interviews are carefully evaluated for critical comments, resentment toward the patient, and excessive emotional involvement (overprotective, overconcerned attitudes).

Studies show that a family's expressed emotion is a good predictor of the course of a schizophrenic patient's illness (Hooley & Candela, 1999; Kavanaugh, 1992). After release from a hospital, schizophrenic patients who return to a family high in expressed emotion show relapse rates three or four times those of patients who return to a family low in expressed emotion. Part of the problem for patients returning to

homes high in expressed emotion is that their families are probably sources of more stress than of social support (Cutting & Docherty, 2000). However, Rosenfarb et al. (1995) caution against placing all the blame on the families high in expressed emotion. They found that patients returning to high-EE homes exhibited more odd and disruptive behavior than patients returning to low-EE homes. Thus, the more critical, negative attitudes experienced by patients in high-EE homes may be caused in part by their own behavior.

Precipitating Stress

Many theories of schizophrenia assume that stress plays a role in triggering schizophrenic disorders (Walker, Baum, & Diforio, 1998). According to this notion, various biological and psychological factors influence individuals' *vulnerability* to schizophrenia. High stress may then serve to precipitate a schizophrenic disorder in someone who is vulnerable (McGlashan & Hoffman, 2000).

Psychological Disorders and the Law

LEARNING OBJECTIVES

- *Explain the reasoning underlying the insanity defense, and discuss how often it is used.*
- *Discuss the legal grounds for involuntary commitment.*

Societies use the law to enforce their norms of conformity. Given this function, the law has something to say about many issues related to abnormal behavior. In this section we briefly examine the legal issues of insanity and involuntary commitment.

Insanity

Insanity is *not* a diagnosis; it's purely a legal concept. **Insanity is a legal status indicating that a person cannot be held responsible for his or her actions because of mental illness.** Why is this an issue in the courtroom? Because criminal acts must be intentional. The law reasons that people who are "out of their mind" may not be able to appreciate the significance of what they're doing. The insanity defense is used in criminal trials by defendants who admit that they committed the crime but claim that they lacked intent.

No simple relationship exists between specific diagnoses of mental disorders and court findings of insanity. Most people with diagnosed psychological disorders would *not* qualify as insane. The people most likely to qualify are those troubled by severe schizophrenic disturbances. The courts apply several rules in making judgments about a defendant's sanity, depend-

ing on the jurisdiction. According to the most widely used rule, called the M'naghten rule, *insanity exists when a mental disorder makes a person unable to distinguish right from wrong.* As you can imagine, evaluating insanity as defined in the M'naghten rule can be difficult for judges and jurors, not to mention the psychologists and psychiatrists who are called into court as expert witnesses. Although highly publicized and controversial, the insanity defense is actually used less frequently and less successfully than widely believed (Phillips, Wolf, & Coons, 1988). One study found that the general public estimates that the insanity defense is used in 37 percent of felony cases, when in fact it is used in less than 1 percent (Silver, Cirincione, & Steadman, 1994). Another study of over 60,000 indictments in Baltimore found that only 190 defendants (0.31 percent) pleaded insanity, and of these, only 8 were successful (Janofsky et al., 1996).

Involuntary Commitment

The issue of insanity surfaces only in *criminal* proceedings. Far more people are affected by civil proceedings relating to involuntary commitment. **In *involuntary commitment* people are hospitalized in psychiatric fa-**

cilities against their will. What are the grounds for such a dramatic action? They vary some from state to state. Generally, people are subject to involuntary commitment when mental health professionals and legal authorities believe that a mental disorder makes them (1) dangerous to themselves (usually suicidal), (2) dangerous to others (potentially violent), or (3) in need of treatment (applied in cases of severe disorientation). In emergency situations psychologists and psychiatrists can authorize *temporary* commitment, usually for 24 to 72 hours. Orders for long-term involuntary commitment are usually set up for renewable six-month periods and can be issued by a court only after a formal hearing. Mental health professionals provide extensive input in these hearings, but the courts make the final decisions (Simon, 2003).

Most involuntary commitments occur because people appear to be *dangerous* to themselves or others. The difficulty, however, is in predicting dangerousness. Studies suggest that clinicians' short-term predictions about which patients are likely to become violent are only moderately accurate and that their long-term predictions of violent behavior are largely inaccurate (Simon, 2003; Stone, 1999). This inaccuracy in predicting dangerousness is unfortunate, because involuntary commitment involves the *detention* of people for what they *might* do in the future. Such detention goes against the grain of the American legal principle that people are *innocent until proven guilty.* The inherent difficulty in predicting dangerousness makes involuntary commitment a complex and controversial issue.

APPLICATION

Understanding Eating Disorders

LEARNING OBJECTIVES

- Describe the symptoms and medical complications of anorexia nervosa and bulimia nervosa.
- Discuss the history, prevalence, and gender distribution of eating disorders.
- Explain how genetic factors, personality, and culture may contribute to eating disorders.
- Explain how family dynamics and disturbed thinking may contribute to eating disorders.

Answer the following "true" or "false."

____ **1.** Although they have attracted attention only in recent years, eating disorders have a long history and have always been fairly common.

____ **2.** Eating disorders are universal problems found in virtually all cultures.

____ **3.** People with anorexia nervosa are much more likely to recognize their eating behavior as pathological than people suffering from bulimia nervosa.

____ **4.** The prevalence of eating disorders is twice as high in women as it is in men.

____ **5.** The binge-and-purge syndrome seen in bulimia nervosa is not common in anorexia nervosa.

____ **6.** Normal dieting is not a risk factor for eating disorders.

All six of these statements are false, as you will see in this Application. The psychological disorders that we discussed in the main body of the chapter have largely been recognized for centuries and generally are found in one form or another in all cultures and societies.

Eating disorders, however, present a sharp contrast to this picture: They have only been recognized in recent decades, and initially they were largely confined to affluent, Westernized cultures (Russell, 1995; Szmukler & Patton, 1995). In spite of these fascinating differences, eating disorders have much in common with traditional forms of pathology.

***Eating disorders* are severe disturbances in eating behavior characterized by preoccupation with weight and unhealthy efforts to control weight.** The vast majority of cases consist of two sometimes overlapping

WEB LINK 15.7

The Alliance for Eating Disorders Awareness
This site offers a great deal of information on eating disorders. Visitors can find statistics, suggested readings, information on symptoms and treatments, self-tests, success stories from people who have overcome their eating disorders, and links to other worthwhile websites.

syndromes: *anorexia nervosa* and *bulimia nervosa*. Although most people don't seem to take eating disorders as seriously as other types of psychological disorders, you will see that they can be dangerous and debilitating (Striegel-Moore & Smolak, 2001).

Anorexia Nervosa

Anorexia nervosa involves intense fear of gaining weight, disturbed body image, refusal to maintain normal weight, and dangerous measures to lose weight. Two subtypes have been distinguished (Herzog & Delinsky, 2001). In *restricting type anorexia nervosa,* people drastically reduce their intake of food, sometimes literally starving themselves. In *binge-eating/purging type anorexia nervosa,* victims attempt to lose weight by forcing themselves to vomit after meals, by misusing laxatives and diuretics, and by engaging in excessive exercise.

Both types entail a disturbed body image. No matter how frail and emaciated the victims become, they insist that they are too fat. Their morbid fear of obesity means that they are never satisfied with their weight. If they gain a pound or two, they panic. The only thing that makes them happy is to lose more weight. The common result is a relentless decline in body weight—in fact, patients entering treatment for anorexia nervosa are typically 25–30 percent below their normal weight (Hsu, 1990). Because of their disturbed body image, people suffering from anorexia generally do *not* appreciate the maladaptive quality of their behavior and rarely seek treatment on their own. They are typically coaxed or coerced into treatment by friends or family members who are alarmed by their appearance.

Anorexia nervosa eventually leads to a cascade of medical problems, including *amenorrhea* (a loss of menstrual cycles in women), gastrointestinal problems, low blood pressure, *osteoporosis* (a loss of bone density), and metabolic disturbances that can lead to cardiac arrest or circulatory collapse (Herzog & Becker, 1999; Pomeroy & Mitchell, 2002). Anorexia is a debilitating illness that leads to death in 5–10 percent of patients (Steinhausen, 2002).

Bulimia Nervosa

Bulimia nervosa involves habitually engaging in out-of-control overeating followed by unhealthy compensatory efforts, such as self-induced vomiting, fasting, abuse of laxatives and diuretics, and excessive exercise. The eating binges are usually carried out in secret and are followed by intense guilt and concern about gaining weight. These feelings motivate ill-advised strategies to undo the effects of the overeating. However, vomiting prevents the absorption of only about half of recently consumed food, and laxatives and diuretics have negligible impact on caloric intake, so people suffering from bulimia nervosa typically maintain a reasonably normal weight (Beumont, 2002; Kaye et al., 1993).

Medical problems associated with bulimia nervosa include cardiac arrythmias, dental problems, metabolic deficiencies and gastrointestinal problems (Halmi, 2002, 2003). Bulimia often coexists with other psychological disturbances, including depression, anxiety disorders, and substance abuse (P. Cooper, 1995; Wilson, 1993).

Obviously, bulimia nervosa shares many features with anorexia nervosa, such as a morbid fear of becoming obese, preoccupation with food, and rigid, maladaptive approaches to controlling weight that are grounded in naive all-or-none thinking. However, the syndromes also differ in crucial ways. First and foremost, bulimia is a less life-threatening condition. Second, although their weight and appearance usually is more "normal" than that seen in anorexia, people with bulimia are much more likely to recognize that their eating behavior is pathological and are more prone to cooperate with treatment (Striegel-Moore, Silberstein, & Rodin, 1993).

History and Prevalence

Historians have been able to track down descriptions of anorexia nervosa that date back centuries, so the disorder is not entirely new, but anorexia nervosa did not become a *common* affliction until the middle of the 20th century (Russell, 1995). Although binging and purging have a long history in some cultures, they were not part of a pathological effort to control weight, and bulimia nervosa appears to be an entirely new syndrome that emerged gradually in the middle of the 20th century and was first recognized in the 1970s (Parry-Jones & Parry-Jones, 1995; Russell, 1997).

Both disorders are a product of modern, affluent Western culture, where food is generally plentiful and the desirability of being thin is widely endorsed. Until recently, these problems were not seen outside of Western cultures (Hoek, 2002). However, in recent years, advances in communication have exported Western culture to farflung corners of the globe, and eating disorders have started showing up in many non-Western societies, especially affluent Asian countries (Lee & Katzman, 2002).

A huge gender gap exists in the likelihood of developing eating disorders. About 90–95 percent of individuals with anorexia nervosa and bulimia nervosa are female (Hoek, 2002). This staggering discrepancy appears to be a result of cultural pressures rather than biological factors (Smolak & Murnen, 2001). Western standards of attractiveness emphasize being slender more for females than for males, and women generally experience heavier pressure to be physically attractive than men do (Sobal, 1995). The prevalence of eating disorders is also elevated in certain groups that place an undue emphasis on thinness, such as fashion models, dancers, actresses, and athletes. Eating disorders mostly afflict *young* women. The typical age of onset for anorexia is 14–18, and for bulimia it is 15–21 (see Figure 15.19).

How common are eating disorders in Western societies? The prevalence of these disorders has increased dramatically in recent decades, although this escalation may be leveling off (Steiger & Seguin, 1999). Studies of young women suggest that about 1.0–1.5 percent develop anorexia nervosa (Walters & Kendler, 1995), and about 2–3 percent develop bulimia nervosa (Romano & Quinn, 2001). Although these figures may seem small, they mean that millions of young women are wrestling with serious eating problems.

Etiology of Eating Disorders

Like other types of psychological disorders, eating disorders are caused by multiple determinants that work interactively. Figure 15.20 on the next page provides an overview of the factors that contribute to the emergence of anorexia nervosa and bulimia nervosa.

Genetic Vulnerability

The scientific evidence is not nearly as strong or complete for eating disorders as it is for many other types of psychopathology (such as anxiety, mood, and schizophrenic disorders), but some people may inherit a genetic vulnerability to these problems. Studies show that relatives of patients with eating disorders have elevated rates of anorexia nervosa and bulimia nervosa (Bulik, 2004). And studies of female twins report higher concordance rates for identical twins than fraternal twins, suggesting that a genetic predisposition may be at work (Steiger, Bruce, & Israël, 2003).

Personality Factors

Strober (1995) has suggested that genetic factors may exert their influence indirectly by fostering certain personality traits that make people more vulnerable to eating disorders. Although there are innumerable exceptions, victims of anorexia nervosa tend to be obsessive, rigid, neurotic, and emotionally restrained, whereas victims of bulimia nervosa tend to be impulsive, overly sensitive, and low in self-esteem (Wonderlich, 2002). Recent research also suggests that perfectionism is a risk factor for anorexia (Halmi et al.,

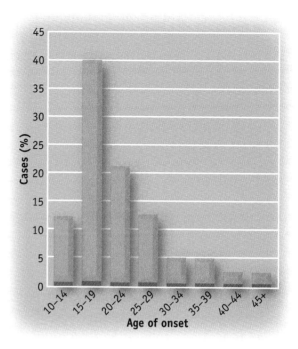

● FIGURE 15.19

Age of onset for anorexia nervosa. Eating disorders emerge primarily during adolescence, as these data for anorexia nervosa show. This graph shows how age of onset was distributed in a sample of 166 female patients from Minnesota. As you can see, over half experienced the onset of their illness before the age of 20, with vulnerability clearly peaking between the ages of 15 and 19. (Data from Lucas, et al., 1991)

2000). Most of these personality traits *are* influenced by genetics, making Strober's hypothesis plausible. Nonetheless, personality-based explanations of eating disorders remain speculative.

Cultural Values

The contribution of cultural values to the increased prevalence of eating disorders can hardly be overestimated (Anderson-Fye & Becker, 2004; Stice, 2001). In Western society, young women are socialized to believe that they must be attractive, and to be attractive, they must be as thin as the actresses and fashion models that dominate the media (Levine & Harrison, 2004). As Figure 15.21 on page 513 shows, the increased premium on being thin is reflected in statistics on Miss America contestants and *Playboy* centerfolds, whose average weight declined gradually between 1959 and 1988 (Garner et al., 1980; Wiseman et al., 1992). Thanks to this cultural milieu, many young women are dissatisfied with their weight because the societal ideals promoted by the media are unattainable for most of them (Thompson & Stice, 2001). Unfortunately, in a small portion of these women, the pressure to be thin,

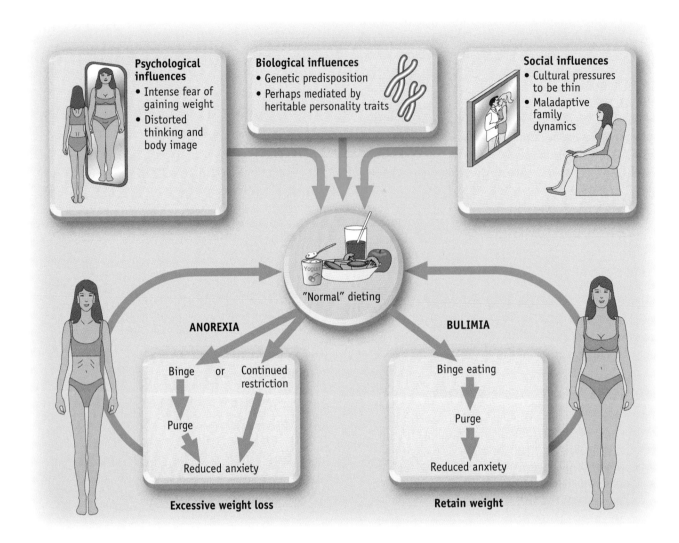

● **FIGURE 15.20**

The etiology of eating disorders. The causes of eating disorders are complex and multifaceted. Psychological, biological, and social factors often lead people into "normal" dieting, which sometimes spins out of control. Maladaptive weight control efforts temporarily relieve individuals' pathological fear of gaining weight, but this reduced anxiety has a tremendous cost, as anorexia nervosa and bulimia nervosa are dangerous illnesses.

Graphic adapted from Barlow. D. H., & Durand, V. M. (1999). *Abnormal psychology: An integrative approach*. Belmont, CA: Wadsworth. Copyright © 1999 Wadsworth Publishing. Reprinted by permission.

in combination with genetic vulnerability, family pathology, and other factors, leads to unhealthy efforts to control weight.

The Role of the Family

Many theorists emphasize how family dynamics can contribute to the development of anorexia nervosa and bulimia nervosa in young women (Haworth-Hoeppner, 2000). Some theorists suggest that parents who are overly involved in their children's lives turn the normal adolescent push for independence into an unhealthy struggle (Minuchin, Rosman, & Baker, 1978). Needing to assert their autonomy, some adolescent

girls seek extreme control over their bodies, leading to pathological patterns of eating (Bruch, 1978). Other theorists argue that parents of adolescents with eating disorders tend to define their children's needs for them instead of allowing them to define their own needs, thus making the youngsters insensitive to their internal needs (Bruch, 1973; Steiner et al., 1991). In contrast, Pike and Rodin (1991) maintain that some mothers contribute to eating disorders simply by endorsing society's message that "you can never be too thin" and by modeling unhealthy dieting behaviors of their own. Although the hypotheses about the role of family dynamics in eating pathology are speculative, it

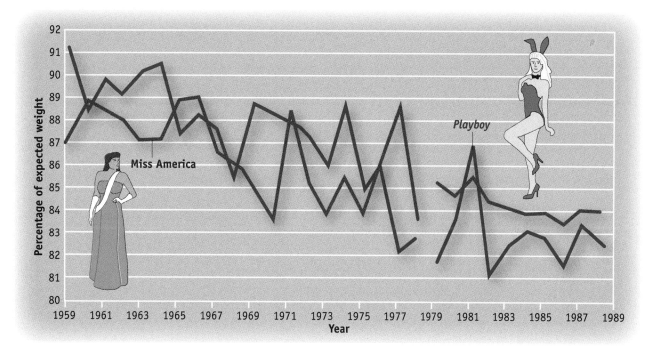

● FIGURE 15.21

Weight trends among *Playboy* centerfolds and Miss America contestants. This graph charts how the average weight of *Playboy* centerfolds and Miss America contestants changed over the course of 30 years (from 1959 to 1989). To control for age and height, each woman's weight was compared to the average weight for a woman of that age and height and expressed as a percentage of the expected weight. Given the small samples, the figures are a little erratic, but overall, the data show a clear downward trend. (Data from Garner et al., 1980; Wiseman et al., 1992)

Graphic adapted from Barlow. D. H., & Durand, V. M. (1999). *Abnormal psychology: An integrative approach.* Belmont, CA: Wadsworth. Copyright © 1999 Wadsworth Publishing. Reprinted by permission.

does appear that families can contribute to eating disorders in a variety of ways.

Cognitive Factors

Many theorists emphasize the role of disturbed thinking in the etiology of eating disorders (Williamson et al., 2001). For example, anorexic patients' typical belief that they are fat when they are really wasting away is a dramatic illustration of how thinking goes awry. Patients with eating disorders display rigid, all-or-none thinking and many maladaptive beliefs, such as "I must be thin to be accepted," "If I am not in complete control, I will lose all control," and "If I gain one pound, I'll go on to gain enormous weight." Additional research is needed to determine whether distorted thinking is a *cause* or merely a *symptom* of eating disorders.

Course and Outcome

Virtually all of the psychotherapies that we will discuss in the next chapter—such as insight therapy, group therapy, behavior therapy, and drug therapy—have been used in the treatment of eating disorders (Halmi, 2000). How successful are these therapeutic interventions? The picture is mixed. About 40–50 percent of patients experience a full recovery, while treatment is largely a failure for about 20–25 percent of patients (Steinhausen, 2002). The remaining patients fall somewhere in between, experiencing modest improvement along with continued struggles. The prognosis is somewhat better for bulimia nervosa than for anorexia; bulimia has a recovery rate of about 70 percent (Sullivan, 2002).

KEY IDEAS

Abnormal Behavior: Myths and Realities

■ The medical model assumes that it is useful to view abnormal behavior as a disease. There are serious problems with the medical model, but the disease analogy is useful if you keep in mind that it is only an analogy. Three criteria are used in deciding whether people suffer from psychological disorders: deviance, personal distress, and maladaptive behavior. Often, it is difficult to draw a clear line between normality and abnormality.

■ DSM-IV is the official psychodiagnostic classification system in the United States. This system asks for information about patients on five axes. Psychological disorders are more common than widely believed, with a lifetime prevalence of roughly 44 percent.

Anxiety Disorders

■ The anxiety disorders include generalized anxiety disorder, phobic disorder, panic disorder, and obsessive-compulsive disorder (OCD). These disorders have been linked to genetic predisposition, temperament, anxiety sensitivity, and neurochemical abnormalities in the brain.

■ Many anxiety responses, especially phobias, may be caused by classical conditioning and maintained by operant conditioning. Cognitive theorists maintain that some people are vulnerable to anxiety disorders because they see threat everywhere. Stress may also contribute to the onset of these disorders.

Somatoform Disorders

■ Somatoform disorders include somatization disorder, conversion disorder, and hypochondriasis. These disorders often emerge in people with highly suggestible, histrionic personalities, who think irrationally about their health. Somatoform disorders may be learned avoidance strategies reinforced by attention and sympathy.

Dissociative Disorders

■ Dissociative disorders include dissociative amnesia, dissociative fugue, and dissociative identity disorder (DID). These disorders appear to be uncommon, although there is some controversy about the prevalence of DID. Stress and childhood trauma may contribute to DID, but overall, the causes of dissociative disorders are not well understood.

Mood Disorders

■ The principal mood disorders are major depressive disorder and bipolar disorder. People vary in their genetic vulnerability to mood disorders, which are accompanied by changes in neurochemical activity in the brain.

■ Cognitive models posit that a pessimistic explanatory style, rumination, and other types of negative thinking contribute to depression. Depression is often rooted in interpersonal inadequacies, as people who lack social finesse often have difficulty acquiring life's reinforcers. Mood disorders are sometimes stress related.

Schizophrenic Disorders

■ Schizophrenic disorders are characterized by deterioration of adaptive behavior, irrational thought, distorted perception, and disturbed mood. Schizophrenic disorders are classified as paranoid, catatonic, disorganized, or undifferentiated. The distinction between positive and negative symptoms has proven useful, but it has not yielded an effective new classification scheme.

■ Research has linked schizophrenia to genetic vulnerability, changes in neurotransmitter activity, and enlarged ventricles in the brain. The neurodevelopmental hypothesis attributes schiz-

ophrenia to disruptions of normal maturational processes in the brain before or at birth. Patients who return to homes high in expressed emotion tend to have elevated relapse rates. Precipitating stress may also contribute to the emergence of schizophrenia.

Psychological Disorders and the Law

■ Insanity is a legal concept applied to people who cannot be held responsible for their actions because of mental illness. When people appear to be dangerous to themselves or others, courts may rule that they are subject to involuntary commitment in a hospital.

Application: Understanding Eating Disorders

■ The principal eating disorders are anorexia nervosa and bulimia nervosa. Both reflect a morbid fear of gaining weight. Anorexia and bulimia are both associated with other psychopathology, and both lead to a cascade of medical problems. Eating disorders appear to be a product of modern, affluent, Westernized culture.

■ Females account for 90–95 percent of eating disorders. The typical age of onset is roughly 15 to 20. There appears to be a genetic vulnerability to eating disorders, which may be mediated by heritable personality traits. Cultural pressures on young women to be thin clearly help foster eating disorders. Some theorists emphasize how family dynamics and disturbed thinking can contribute to the development of eating disorders.

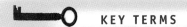

KEY TERMS

Agoraphobia   p. 488
Anorexia nervosa   p. 510
Anxiety disorders   p. 487
Bipolar disorder   p. 498
Bulimia nervosa   p. 510
Catatonic schizophrenia
   p. 503
Concordance rate   p. 499
Conversion disorder   p. 492
Delusions   p. 503
Diagnosis   p. 483
Disorganized schizophrenia
   p. 504
Dissociative amnesia   p. 494
Dissociative disorders
   p. 494
Dissociative fugue   p. 494
Dissociative identity disorder
   (DID)   p. 494
Eating disorders   p. 509
Epidemiology   p. 485
Etiology   p. 483
Generalized anxiety disorder
   pp. 487–488
Hallucinations   p. 503
Hypochondriasis   p. 493
Insanity   p. 508

Involuntary commitment
   pp. 508–509
Major depressive disorder
   p. 497
Manic-depressive disorder
   p. 498
Medical model   p. 482
Mood disorders   p. 497
Multiple-personality disorder
   p. 494
Neurotransmitters   p. 490
Obsessive-compulsive
   disorder (OCD)   p. 489
Panic disorder   p. 488
Paranoid schizophrenia
   p. 503
Phobic disorder   p. 488
Prevalence   p. 465
Prognosis   p. 483
Schizophrenic disorders
   p. 502
Somatization disorder
   p. 492
Somatoform disorders
   p. 491
Undifferentiated
   schizophrenia   p. 504

KEY PEOPLE

Nancy Andreasen   p. 504
Susan Nolen-Hoeksema
   pp. 498, 500

David Rosenhan
   pp. 484–485
Martin Seligman   p. 500
Thomas Szasz   p. 482

PRACTICE TEST

1. Sergio has just entered treatment for bipolar disorder and he is informed that most patients respond to drug treatment within a month. This information represents:
   a. a prognosis.
   c. a histology.
   b. an etiology.
   d. a concordance.

2. Although Sue always feels high levels of dread, worry, and anxiety, she still meets her daily responsibilities. Sue's behavior:
   a. should not be considered abnormal, since her adaptive functioning is not impaired.
   b. should not be considered abnormal, since everyone sometimes experiences worry and anxiety.
   c. can still be considered abnormal, since she feels great personal distress.
   d. both a and b.

3. Recent epidemiological studies have found that the most common types of psychological disorders are:
   a. mood disorders and anxiety disorders.
   b. anxiety disorders and schizophrenic disorders.
   c. substance-use disorders and anxiety disorders.
   d. substance-use disorders and somatoform disorders.

4. People who repeatedly perform senseless rituals to overcome their anxiety are said to have a(n):
   a. generalized anxiety disorder.
   b. manic disorder.
   c. obsessive-compulsive disorder.
   d. phobic disorder.

5. If a person has a paralyzed arm for which no organic basis can be found, she probably has:
   a. a conversion disorder.
   b. paralytic hypochondriasis.
   c. a dissociative disorder.
   d. a schizophrenic disorder.

6. After several months during which he was always gloomy and dejected, Mario has suddenly perked up. He feels elated and energetic and works around the clock on a writing project. He has also started to bet heavily on sporting events over the Internet, which he never did previously. Mario's behavior is consistent with:
   a. schizophrenia.
   b. obsessive-compulsive disorder.
   c. bipolar disorder.
   d. dissociative identity disorder.

7. A concordance rate indicates:
   a. the percentage of twin pairs or other relatives that exhibit the same disorder.
   b. the percentage of people with a given disorder that are currently receiving treatment.
   c. the prevalence of a given disorder in the general population.
   d. the rate of cure for a given disorder.

8. Which of the following would be a negative symptom of schizophrenia?
   a. Auditory hallucinations
   b. Delusions of persecution
   c. Having virtually no friendships
   d. Delusions of grandeur

9. Kyle, who works as a projectionist at the local theater, is convinced that everyone is out to get him. He is sure that his phone is tapped by ruthless enemies. He thinks that most of the people in the theater each night are there to spy on him. Worse yet, he is sure people follow him home from work every night. Kyle is probably suffering from:
   a. paranoid schizophrenia.
   b. catatonic schizophrenia.
   c. bipolar disorder.
   d. dissociative fugue.

10. About _____ percent of patients with eating disorders are female.
    a. 40
    c. 75
    b. 50–60
    d. 90–95

Book Companion Website

Visit the Book Companion Website at **http://psychology.wadsworth.com/weiten_lloyd8e,** where you will find tutorial quizzes, flashcards, and weblinks for every chapter, a final exam, and more! You can also link to the Thomson Wadsworth Psychology Resource Center (accessible directly at **http://psychology.wadsworth.com**) for a range of psychology-related resources.

Personal Explorations Workbook

The following exercises in your *Personal Explorations Workbook* may enhance your self-understanding in relation to issues raised in this chapter. **Questionnaire 15.1:** Manifest Anxiety Scale. **Personal Probe 15.1:** What Are Your Attitudes on Mental Illness? **Personal Probe 15.2:** Do You Think That We Are All Candidates for a Disorder?

ANSWERS

1. a Page 483
2. c Page 483
3. c Pages 485, 487
4. c Pages 489–490
5. a Page 492
6. c Pages 498–499
7. a Page 499
8. c Page 504
9. a Page 503
10. d Pages 510–511

Psychotherapy

What do you picture when you hear the term *psychotherapy*? If you're like most people, you probably envision a troubled patient lying on a couch in a therapist's office, with the therapist asking penetrating questions and providing sage advice. Typically, people believe that psychotherapy is only for those who are "sick" and that therapists have special powers that allow them to "see through" their clients. It is also widely believed that therapy requires years of deep probing into a client's innermost secrets. Many people further assume that therapists routinely tell their patients how to lead their lives. Like most stereotypes, this picture of psychotherapy is a mixture of fact and fiction, as you'll see in the upcoming pages.

In this chapter, we take a down-to-earth look at the process of *psychotherapy,* using the term in its broadest sense to refer to all the diverse approaches to the treatment of psychological problems. We start by discussing some general questions about the provision of treatment. Who seeks therapy? What kinds of professionals provide treatment? How many types of therapy are there? After considering these general issues, we examine some of the more widely used approaches to treating psychological maladies, analyzing their goals, techniques, and effectiveness. The Application at the end of the chapter focuses on practical issues involved in finding a therapist, in case you ever have to advise someone about seeking help.

The Elements of the Treatment Process

LEARNING OBJECTIVES

- *Identify the three major categories of therapy.*
- *Discuss why people do or do not seek psychotherapy.*
- *Describe the various types of mental health professionals involved in the provision of therapy.*

Today people have a bewildering array of psychotherapy approaches to choose from. In fact, the immense diversity of therapeutic treatments makes defining the concept of *psychotherapy* difficult. After organizing a landmark conference that brought together many of the world's leading authorities on psychotherapy, Jeffrey Zeig (1987) commented, "I do not believe there is any capsule definition of psychotherapy on which the 26 presenters could agree" (p. xix). In lieu of a definition, we can identify a few basic elements that the various approaches to treatment have in common. All psychotherapies involve a helping relationship (the treatment) between a professional with special training (the therapist) and another person in need of help (the client). As we look at each of these three elements, you'll see the diverse nature of modern psychotherapy.

Treatments: How Many Types Are There?

In their efforts to help people, mental health professionals use many methods of treatment, including discussion, emotional support, persuasion, conditioning procedures, relaxation training, role playing, drug therapy, biofeedback, and group therapy. Some therapists also use a variety of less conventional procedures, such as rebirthing, poetry therapy, and primal therapy. No one knows exactly how many approaches to treatment there are. One expert (Kazdin, 1994) estimates that there may be over 400 distinct types of psychotherapy! Fortunately, we can impose some order on this chaos. As varied as therapists' procedures are, approaches to treatment can be classified into three major categories:

1. *Insight therapies.* Insight therapy is "talk therapy" in the tradition of Freud's psychoanalysis. This is probably the approach to treatment that you envision when you think of psychotherapy. In insight therapies, clients engage in complex verbal interactions with their therapists. The goal in these discussions is to pursue increased insight regarding the nature of the client's difficulties and to sort through possible solutions. Insight therapy can be conducted with an individual or with a group.

2. *Behavior therapies.* Behavior therapies are based on the principles of learning and conditioning, which were introduced in Chapter 2. Instead of emphasizing personal insights, behavior therapists make direct efforts to alter problematic responses (phobic behaviors, for instance) and maladaptive habits (drug use, for instance). Behavior therapists work on changing clients' overt behaviors. They use different procedures for different kinds of problems.

3. *Biomedical therapies.* Biomedical approaches to therapy involve interventions into a person's physiological functioning. The most widely used procedures are drug therapy and electroconvulsive therapy. As the name bio*medical* therapies suggests, these treatments have traditionally been provided only by physicians with a medical degree (usually psychiatrists). This situation may change, however, as psychologists have begun to campaign for prescription privileges (Gutierrez & Silk, 1998; Sammons et al., 2000). They have made some progress toward this goal, even though many psychologists have argued against pursuing the right to prescribe medication (Albee, 1998; Dobson & Dozois, 2001).

In this chapter we examine approaches to therapy that fall into each of these three categories. Although different methods are used in each, the three major classes of treatment are not entirely incompatible. For example, a client being seen in insight therapy may also be given medication.

Clients: Who Seeks Therapy?

In the therapeutic triad (therapists, treatments, clients), the greatest diversity is seen among the clients. According to the 1999 U.S. Surgeon General's report on mental health (U.S. Department of Health and Human Services, 1999), about 15 percent of the U.S. population uses mental health services in a given year. These people bring to therapy the full range of human problems: anxiety, depression, unsatisfactory interpersonal relations, troublesome habits, poor self-control, low self-esteem, marital conflicts, self-doubt, a sense of emptiness, and feelings of personal stagnation. The two most common presenting problems are excessive

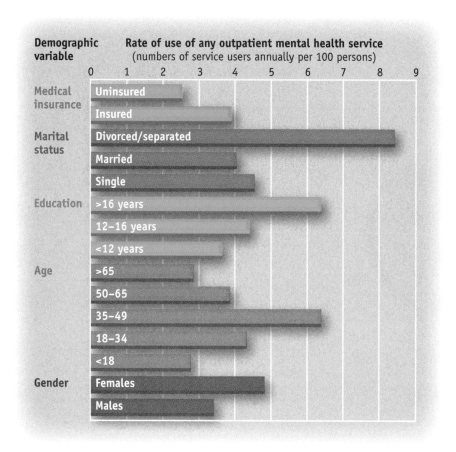

Demographic variable | **Rate of use of any outpatient mental health service** (numbers of service users annually per 100 persons)

- Medical insurance: Uninsured, Insured
- Marital status: Divorced/separated, Married, Single
- Education: >16 years, 12–16 years, <12 years
- Age: >65, 50–65, 35–49, 18–34, <18
- Gender: Females, Males

● FIGURE 16.1

Therapy utilization rates. Olfson and Pincus (1996) gathered data on the use of nonhospital outpatient mental health services in the United States in relation to various demographic variables. As you can see, people are more likely to enter therapy if they have medical insurance than if they do not. In regard to marital status, utilization rates are particularly high among those who are divorced or separated. The use of therapy is greater among those who have more education and, in terms of age, utilization peaks in the 35–49 age bracket. Finally, females are more likely to pursue therapy than males. (Data from Olfson & Pincus, 1996)

anxiety and depression (Narrow et al., 1993). Interestingly, people often hold off for many years before finally seeking treatment for their psychological problems (Kessler, Olfson, & Berglund, 1998).

A client in treatment does *not* necessarily have an identifiable psychological disorder. Some people seek professional help for everyday problems (career decisions, for instance) or vague feelings of discontent (Strupp, 1996). One surprising finding in the Surgeon General's report was that almost half of the people who use mental health services in a given year do not have a specific disorder.

People vary considerably in their willingness to seek psychotherapy. As you can see in Figure 16.1, women are more likely than men to receive therapy. Treatment is also more likely when people have medical insurance and when they have more education (Olfson & Pincus, 1996). *Unfortunately, it appears that*

many people who need therapy don't receive it (Kessler et al., 1999). As Figure 16.2 on the next page shows, only a portion of the people who need treatment receive it. People who could benefit from therapy do not seek it for a variety of reasons. Lack of health insurance and cost concerns appear to be major barriers to obtaining needed care for many people (Druss & Rosenheck, 1998). According to the Surgeon General's report, the biggest roadblock is the "stigma surrounding the receipt of mental health treatment." Unfortunately, many people equate seeking therapy with admitting personal weakness.

Therapists: Who Provides Professional Treatment?

Friends and relatives may provide excellent advice about personal problems, but their assistance does not

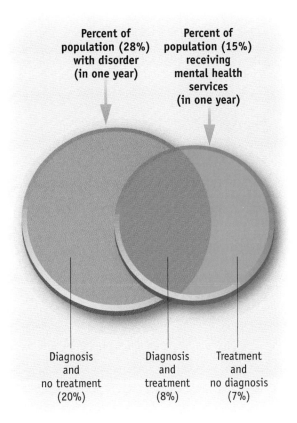

Percent of population (28%) with disorder (in one year)

Percent of population (15%) receiving mental health services (in one year)

Diagnosis and no treatment (20%)

Diagnosis and treatment (8%)

Treatment and no diagnosis (7%)

● FIGURE 16.2

Psychological disorders and professional treatment. Not everyone who has a psychological disorder receives professional treatment, and not everyone who seeks treatment has a clear disorder. This graph, from the 1999 Surgeon General's report on mental health, shows that 15 percent of the adult population receives mental health treatment each year. Almost half of these people (7 percent) did not receive a psychiatric diagnosis, although some of them probably have milder disorders that are not assessed in epidemiological research. This graph also shows that over two-thirds of the people who *do* have disorders do *not* receive professional treatment. (Data from *Mental Health: A Report from the Surgeon General,* U.S. Department of Health and Human Services, 1999)

Other mental health specialists 28.3%

Psychologists 35.5%

Psychiatrists 26.9%

General medical professionals 9.3%

● FIGURE 16.3

Who people see for therapy. Based on a national survey, Olfson and Pincus (1994) estimated that in 1987 Americans made 79.5 million outpatient psychotherapy visits. Information on the therapist's profession was missing for 11 percent of these visits. The pie chart shows how the remaining visits were distributed among psychologists, psychiatrists, other mental health professionals (social workers, counselors, and such), and general medical professionals (typically physicians specializing in family practice, internal medicine, or pediatrics). As you can see, psychologists and psychiatrists account for about 62 percent of outpatient treatment. (Data from Olfson & Pincus, 1994)

qualify as therapy. Psychotherapy refers to *professional treatment by someone with special training*. However, a common source of confusion about psychotherapy is the variety of "helping professions" available to offer assistance. Psychology and psychiatry are the principal professions involved in psychotherapy, providing the lion's share of mental health care (see Figure 16.3). However, therapy is also provided by social workers, psychiatric nurses, and counselors, as outlined in Figure 16.4.

Psychologists

Two types of psychologists may provide therapy, although the distinction between them is more theoretical than real. *Clinical psychologists* and *counseling psychologists* specialize in the diagnosis and treatment of psychological disorders and everyday behavioral problems. In theory, the training of clinical psychologists emphasizes treatment of full-fledged disorders, whereas the training of counseling psychologists is slanted toward treatment of everyday adjustment problems in normal people. In practice, however, there is great overlap between clinical and counseling psychologists in training, in skills, and in the clientele they serve.

Both types of psychologists must earn a doctoral degree (Ph.D., Psy.D., or Ed.D.). A doctorate in psy-

WEB LINK 16.1

Online Dictionary of Mental Health
This thematically arranged "dictionary" comprises diverse links involving many forms of psychotherapy, the treatment of psychological disorders, and general issues of mental health. It is sponsored by the Centre for Psychotherapeutic Studies at the University of Sheffield's Medical School in the UK.

Types of Therapists

Title	Degree	Years beyond bachelor's degree	Typical roles and activities
Clinical or counseling psychologist	Ph.D. Psy.D. Ed.D.	5–7	Diagnosis, psychological testing, insight and behavior therapy
Psychiatrist	M.D.	8	Diagnosis; insight, behavior, and biomedical therapy
Social worker	M.S.W.	2	Insight and behavior therapy, family therapy, helping patients return to the community
Psychiatric nurse	B.S., B.A., M.A.	0–2	Inpatient care, insight and behavior therapy
Counselor	M.A., M.S.	2	Insight and behavior therapy, working primarily with everyday adjustment and marital and career issues

● FIGURE 16.4

The principal mental health professions. Psychotherapists come from a variety of professional backgrounds. This chart provides an overview of various types of therapists' education and typical professional activities.

chology requires five to seven years of training beyond a bachelor's degree. The process of gaining admission to a Ph.D. program in clinical psychology is highly competitive (about as competitive as for medical school). Psychologists receive most of their training on university campuses, although they also serve a one- to two-year internship in a clinical setting, such as a hospital.

In providing therapy, psychologists use either insight or behavioral approaches. In comparison to psychiatrists, they are more likely to use behavioral techniques and less likely to use psychoanalytic methods. Clinical and counseling psychologists do psychological testing as well as psychotherapy, and many also conduct research.

Psychiatrists

Psychiatrists are physicians who specialize in the treatment of psychological disorders. Many psychiatrists also treat everyday behavioral problems. However, in comparison to psychologists, psychiatrists devote more time to relatively severe disorders (schizophrenia, mood disorders) and less time to everyday marital, family, job, and school problems. Psychiatrists have an M.D. degree. Their graduate training requires four years of course work in medical school and a four-year apprenticeship in a residency at an approved hospital. Their psychotherapy training occurs during their residency, since the required course work in medical school is essentially the

same for all students, whether they are going into surgery, pediatrics, or psychiatry.

In their provision of therapy, psychiatrists increasingly emphasize drug therapies (Olfson, Marcus, & Pincus, 1999), which the other, nonmedical helping professions cannot provide. In comparison to psychologists, psychiatrists are more likely to use psychoanalysis and less likely to use group therapies or behavior therapies.

Other Mental Health Professionals

Several other mental health professions provide psychotherapy services. In hospitals and other institutions, *psychiatric social workers* and *psychiatric nurses* often work as part of a treatment team with a psychologist or psychiatrist. Psychiatric nurses, who may have a bachelor's or master's degree in their field, play a large role in hospital inpatient treatment. Psychiatric social workers generally have a master's degree and typically work with patients and their families to ease the patient's integration back into the community. Although social workers have traditionally worked in hospitals and social service agencies, many are licensed as independent, private practitioners who provide a wide range of therapeutic services.

Many kinds of *counselors* also provide therapeutic services. Counselors are usually found working in schools, colleges, and human service agencies (youth centers, geriatric centers, family planning centers, and so forth). Counselors typically have a master's degree.

They often specialize in particular types of problems, such as vocational counseling, marital counseling, rehabilitation counseling, and drug counseling.

Although clear differences exist among the helping professions in education and training, their roles in the treatment process overlap considerably. In this chapter, we refer to psychologists or psychiatrists as needed, but otherwise we use the terms *clinician, therapist,* and *mental health professional* to refer to psychotherapists of all kinds, regardless of their professional degree.

Now that we have discussed the basic elements in psychotherapy, we can examine specific approaches to treatment in terms of their goals, procedures, and effectiveness. We begin with a few representative insight therapies.

Insight Therapies

LEARNING OBJECTIVES

- Explain the logic of psychoanalysis and describe the techniques used to probe the unconscious.
- Discuss interpretation, resistance, and transference in psychoanalysis.
- Explain the logic of client-centered therapy.
- Describe therapeutic climate and process in client-centered therapy.

- Discuss the logic, goals, and techniques of cognitive therapy.
- Describe how group therapy is generally conducted.
- Identify some advantages of group therapy.
- Summarize evidence on the efficacy of insight therapies.
- Summarize both sides of the recovered memories controversy.

Many schools of thought exist as to how to do insight therapy. Therapists with different theoretical orientations use different methods to pursue different kinds of insights. What these varied approaches have in common is that *insight therapies* **involve verbal interactions intended to enhance clients' self-knowledge and thus promote healthful changes in personality and behavior.** Although there may be hundreds of insight therapies, the leading eight or ten approaches appear to account for the lion's share of treatment. In this section, we delve into psychoanalysis, client-centered therapy, and cognitive therapy. We also discuss how insight therapy can be done with groups as well as individuals.

Psychoanalysis

Sigmund Freud worked as a psychotherapist for almost 50 years in Vienna. Through a painstaking process of trial and error, he developed innovative techniques for the treatment of psychological disorders and distress. His system of *psychoanalysis* came to dominate psychiatry for many decades. Although the dominance of psychoanalysis has eroded in recent decades, a diverse array of psychoanalytic approaches to therapy continue to evolve and to remain influential today (McWilliams & Weinberger, 2003; Ursano & Silberman, 2003).

Psychoanalysis is an insight therapy that emphasizes the recovery of unconscious conflicts, motives, and defenses through techniques such as free association, dream analysis, and transference. To appreciate the logic of psychoanalysis, we have to look at

Sigmund Freud

National Library of Medicine

Freud's thinking about the roots of mental disorders. Freud treated mostly anxiety-dominated disturbances, such as phobic, panic, obsessive-compulsive, and conversion disorders, which were then called *neuroses.* He believed that neurotic problems are caused by unconscious conflicts left over from early childhood. As explained in Chapter 2, he thought that these inner conflicts involve battles among the id, ego, and superego, usually over sexual and aggressive impulses. Freud theorized that people depend on defense mechanisms to avoid confronting these conflicts, which remain hidden in the depths of the unconscious. However, he noted that defensive maneuvers often lead to self-defeating behavior. Furthermore, he asserted that defenses tend to be only partially successful in alleviating anxiety, guilt, and other distressing emotions. With this model in mind, let's take a look at the therapeutic procedures used in psychoanalysis.

Probing the Unconscious

Given Freud's assumptions, we can see that the logic of psychoanalysis is very simple. The analyst attempts to probe the murky depths of the unconscious to discover the unresolved conflicts causing the client's neurotic behavior. In a sense, the analyst functions as a psychological detective. In this effort to explore the unconscious, he or she relies on two techniques: free association and dream analysis.

In *free association,* **clients spontaneously express their thoughts and feelings exactly as they occur, with as little censorship as possible.** Clients lie on a couch so they will be better able to let their minds drift freely. In free associating, clients expound on anything that comes to mind, regardless of how trivial, silly, or embarrassing it might be. Gradually, most clients begin to

In psychoanalysis, the therapist encourages the client to reveal thoughts, feelings, dreams, and memories that can then be interpreted in relation to the client's current problems.

let everything pour out without conscious censorship. The analyst studies these free associations for clues about what is going on in the unconscious.

In *dream analysis,* the therapist interprets the symbolic meaning of the client's dreams. For Freud, dreams were the "royal road to the unconscious," the most direct means of access to patients' innermost conflicts, wishes, and impulses. Clients are encouraged and trained to remember their dreams, which they describe in therapy. The therapist then analyzes the symbolism in these dreams to interpret their meaning.

To better illustrate these matters, let's look at an actual case treated through psychoanalysis (adapted from Greenson, 1967, pp. 40–41). Mr. N was troubled by an unsatisfactory marriage. He claimed to love his wife, but he preferred sexual relations with prostitutes. Mr. N reported that his parents also endured lifelong marital difficulties. His childhood conflicts about their relationship appeared to be related to his problems. Both dream analysis and free association can be seen in the following description of a session in Mr. N's treatment:

Mr. N reports a fragment of a dream. All that he can remember is that he is waiting for a red traffic light to change when he feels that someone has bumped into him from behind. . . . The associations led to Mr. N's love of cars, especially sports cars. He loved the sensation, in particular, of whizzing by those fat, old, expensive cars. . . . His father always hinted that he had been a great athlete, but he never substantiated it. . . . Mr. N doubted whether his father could really perform. His father would flirt with a waitress in a cafe or make sexual remarks about women passing by, but he seemed to be showing off. If he were really sexual, he wouldn't resort to that.

As is characteristic of free association, Mr. N's train of thought meanders about with little direction. Nonetheless, clues about his unconscious conflicts are apparent. What did Mr. N's therapist extract from this session? The therapist saw sexual overtones in the dream fragment, where Mr. N was bumped from behind. The therapist also inferred that Mr. N had a competitive orientation toward his father, based on the free association about whizzing by fat, old, expensive cars. As you can see, analysts must *interpret* their clients' dreams and free associations. This is a critical process throughout psychoanalysis.

Interpretation

Interpretation involves the therapist's attempts to explain the inner significance of the client's thoughts, feelings, memories, and behaviors. Contrary to popular belief, analysts do not interpret everything, and they generally don't try to dazzle clients with startling revelations. Instead, analysts move forward inch by inch, offering interpretations that should be just out of the client's own reach. Mr. N's therapist eventually offered the following interpretations to his client:

I said to Mr. N near the end of the hour that I felt he was struggling with his feelings about his father's sexual life. He seemed to be saying that his father was sexually not a very potent man. . . . He also recalls that he once found a packet of condoms under his father's pillow when he was an adolescent and he thought "My father must be going to prostitutes." I then intervened and pointed out that the condoms under his father's pillow seemed to indicate more obviously that his father used the condoms with his mother, who slept in the same bed. However, Mr. N wanted to believe his wish-fulfilling fantasy: mother doesn't want sex with father and father is not very potent. The patient was silent and the hour ended.

As you may already have guessed, the therapist has concluded that Mr. N's difficulties are rooted in an Oedipal complex (see Chapter 2). Mr. N has unresolved sexual feelings toward his mother and hostile feelings about his father. These unconscious conflicts, which are rooted in his childhood, are distorting his intimate relations as an adult.

WEB LINK 16.2

The American Psychoanalytic Association
The site for this professional organization provides a great deal of useful information about psychoanalytic approaches to treatment. The resources include news releases, background information on psychoanalysis, an engine for literature searches, and a bookstore.

Resistance

How would you expect Mr. N to respond to his therapist's suggestion that he was in competition with his father for the sexual attention of his mother? Obviously, most clients would have great difficulty accepting such an interpretation. Freud fully expected clients to display some resistance to therapeutic efforts. **Resistance involves largely unconscious defensive maneuvers intended to hinder the progress of therapy.** Why do clients try to resist the helping process? Because they don't want to face up to the painful, disturbing conflicts that they have buried in their unconscious. Although they have sought help, they are reluctant to confront their real problems.

Resistance may take many forms. Patients may show up late for their sessions, merely pretend to engage in free association, or express hostility toward the therapist. For instance, Mr. N's therapist noted that after the session just described, "The next day he began by telling me that he was furious with me." Analysts use a variety of strategies to deal with their clients' resistance. Often, a key consideration is the handling of *transference,* which we consider next.

Transference

Transference **occurs when clients start relating to their therapists in ways that mimic critical relationships in their lives.** Thus, a client might start relating to a therapist as if the therapist were an overprotective mother, rejecting brother, or passive spouse. In a sense, the client *transfers* conflicting feelings about important people onto the therapist. For instance, in his treatment, Mr. N transferred some of the competitive hostility he felt toward his father onto his analyst.

Psychoanalysts often encourage transference such that clients begin to reenact relations with crucial people in the context of therapy. These reenactments can help bring repressed feelings and conflicts to the surface, allowing the client to work through them. The therapist's handling of transference is complicated and difficult because transference may arouse confusing, highly charged emotions in the client.

Undergoing psychoanalysis is not easy. It can be a slow, painful process of self-examination that routinely requires three to five years of hard work. Ultimately, if resistance and transference can be handled effectively, the therapist's interpretations should lead the client to profound insights. For instance, Mr. N eventually admitted, "The old boy is probably right, it does tickle me to imagine that my mother preferred me and I could beat out my father. Later, I wondered whether this had something to do with my own screwed-up sex life with my wife." According to Freud, once clients recognize the unconscious sources of their conflicts, they can resolve these conflicts and discard their neurotic defenses.

Although still available, classical psychoanalysis as done by Freud is not widely practiced anymore (Kay & Kay, 2003). Freud's psychoanalytic method was geared to a particular kind of clientele that he was seeing in Vienna many years ago. As his followers fanned out across Europe and America, many found that it was necessary to adapt psychoanalysis to different cultures, changing times, and new kinds of patients. Thus, many variations on Freud's original approach to psychoanalysis have developed over the years. These descendants of psychoanalysis are collectively known as *psychodynamic approaches* to therapy.

Client-Centered Therapy

Courtesy, Carl Rogers Memorial Library

Carl Rogers

You may have heard of people going into therapy to "find themselves" or to "get in touch with their real feelings." These now-popular phrases emerged out of the human potential movement, which was stimulated in part by the work of Carl Rogers (1951, 1986). Taking a humanistic perspective, Rogers devised *client-centered therapy* (also known as *person-centered therapy*) in the 1940s and 1950s.

Client-centered therapy **is an insight therapy that emphasizes providing a supportive emotional climate for clients, who play a major role in determining the pace and direction of their therapy.** You may wonder why the troubled, untrained client is put in charge of the pace and direction of the therapy. Rogers (1961) provides a compelling justification:

It is the client who knows what hurts, what directions to go, what problems are crucial, what experiences have been deeply buried. It began to occur to me that unless I had a need to demonstrate my own cleverness and learning, I would do better to rely upon the client for the direction of movement in the process. (pp. 11–12)

Rogers's theory about the principal causes of neurotic anxieties is quite different from the Freudian explanation. As discussed in Chapter 2, Rogers maintained that most personal distress is due to inconsistency, or "incongruence," between a person's self-concept and reality (see Figure 16.5). According to his theory, incongruence makes people prone to feel threatened by realistic feedback about themselves from others. For example, if you inaccurately viewed yourself as a hardworking, dependable person, you would feel threatened by contradictory feedback from friends or co-workers. According to Rogers, anxiety about such feedback often leads to reliance on defense mechanisms, distortions of

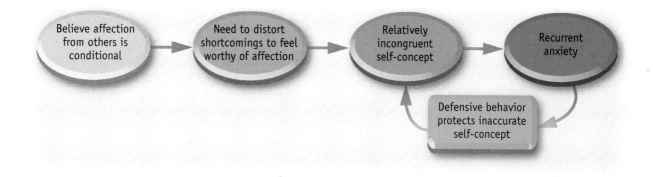

Rogers's view of the roots of disorders. Carl Rogers's theory posits that anxiety and self-defeating behavior are rooted in an incongruent self-concept that makes one prone to recurrent anxiety, which triggers defensive behavior, which fuels more incongruence.

reality, and stifled personal growth. Excessive incongruence is thought to be rooted in clients' overdependence on others for approval and acceptance.

Given Rogers's theory, client-centered therapists seek insights that are quite different from the repressed conflicts that psychoanalysts try to track down. Client-centered therapists help clients to realize that they do not have to worry constantly about pleasing others and winning acceptance. They encourage clients to respect their own feelings and values. They help people restructure their self-concept to correspond better to reality. Ultimately, they try to foster self-acceptance and personal growth.

Therapeutic Climate

In client-centered therapy, the *process* of therapy is not as important as the emotional *climate* in which the therapy takes place. According to Rogers, it is critical for the therapist to provide a warm, supportive, accepting climate in which clients can confront their shortcomings without feeling threatened. The lack of threat should reduce clients' defensive tendencies and thus help them to open up. To create this atmosphere of emotional support, Rogers believed that client-centered therapists must provide three conditions.

1. *Genuineness.* The therapist must be genuine with the client, communicating in an honest and spontaneous manner. The therapist should not be phony or defensive.

2. *Unconditional positive regard.* The therapist must also show complete, nonjudgmental acceptance of the client as a person. The therapist should provide warmth and caring for the client with no strings attached. This mandate does not mean that the therapist has to approve of everything that the client says or does.

A therapist can disapprove of a particular behavior while continuing to value the client as a human being.

3. *Empathy.* Finally, the therapist must provide accurate empathy for the client. This means that the therapist must understand the client's world from the client's point of view. Furthermore, the therapist must be articulate enough to communicate this understanding to the client.

Rogers firmly believed that a supportive emotional climate was the major force promoting healthy changes in therapy. However, some client-centered therapists have begun to place more emphasis on therapeutic process (Rice & Greenberg, 1992).

Therapeutic Process

In client-centered therapy, the client and therapist work together almost as equals. The therapist provides relatively little guidance and keeps interpretation and advice to a minimum. So, just what does the client-centered therapist do, besides creating a supportive climate? Primarily, the therapist provides feedback to help clients sort out their feelings. The therapist's key task is *clarification*. Client-centered therapists try to function like a human mirror, reflecting statements back to their clients, but with enhanced clarity. They help clients become more aware of their true feelings by highlighting themes that may be obscure in the clients' rambling discourse.

By working with clients to clarify their feelings, client-centered therapists hope to gradually build toward more far-reaching insights. In particular, they try to help clients become more aware of and comfortable about their genuine selves. Obviously, these are ambitious goals. Client-centered therapy resembles psychoanalysis in that both seek to achieve a major reconstruction of a client's personality. More limited and specific goals are found in cognitive therapy, which we consider next.

Cognitive Therapy

In Chapter 3 we saw that people's cognitive interpretations of events make all the difference in the world in how well they handle stress. In Chapter 15 we learned that cognitive factors play a key role in the development of depressive disorders. Citing the importance of findings such as these, two former psychoanalysts—Aaron Beck (1976, 1987) and Albert Ellis (1973, 1989)—independently devised cognitive-oriented therapies that became highly influential (Arnkoff & Glass, 1992). Since we covered the main ideas underlying Ellis's *rational-emotive behavior therapy* in our discussion of coping strategies in Chapter 4, we focus on Beck's system of *cognitive therapy* here. **Cognitive therapy is a treatment that emphasizes recognizing and changing negative thoughts and maladaptive beliefs.**

In recent years cognitive therapy has been applied fruitfully to a wide range of disorders (Beck, 1991; Rush & Beck, 2000), but it was originally devised as a treatment for depression. According to Beck, depression is caused by "errors" in thinking (see Figure 16.6). He asserts that depression-prone people tend to (1) blame their setbacks on personal inadequacies without considering circumstantial explanations, (2) focus selectively on negative events while ignoring positive ones,

Courtesy, Aaron T. Beck
Aaron Beck

(3) make unduly pessimistic projections about the future, and (4) draw negative conclusions about their worth as persons based on insignificant events. For instance, imagine that you earned a poor score on a minor quiz in a class. If you made the four kinds of errors in thinking just described, you might blame the score on your woeful stupidity, dismiss comments from a classmate that it was an unfair test, hysterically predict that you will surely flunk the course, and conclude that you are not genuine college material.

Goals and Techniques

The goal of cognitive therapy is to change the way clients think. To begin, clients are taught to detect their automatic negative thoughts. These are self-defeating statements that people are prone to make when analyzing problems. Examples might include "I'm just not smart enough," "No one really likes me," and "It's all my fault." Clients are then trained to subject these automatic thoughts to reality testing. The therapist helps them see how unrealistically negative the thoughts are.

The therapist's goal is not to promote unwarranted optimism but rather to help the client use more reasonable standards of evaluation. For example, a cognitive therapist might point out that a client's failure to get a desired promotion at work may be attributable to many factors and that this setback doesn't mean that the client is incompetent. Gradually, the therapist digs deeper, looking for the unrealistic assumptions that underlie clients' constant negative thinking. These, too, have to be changed.

Unlike client-centered therapists, cognitive therapists are actively involved in determining the pace and direction of treatment. They usually talk extensively in

---

● FIGURE 16.6

Beck's cognitive theory of depression. According to Aaron Beck (1976, 1987), depression is caused by certain patterns of negative thinking. This chart lists some of the particularly damaging cognitive errors that can foster depression.

Adapted from Beck, A. T. (1976). *Cognitive therapy and the emotional disorders.* New York: International Universities Press. Copyright © 1976 by International Universities Press, Inc. Adapted by permission of the publisher.

Cognitive Errors That Promote Depression

Cognitive error	Description
Overgeneralizing	If it is true in one case, it applies to any case that is even slightly similar.
Selective abstraction	The only events that matter are failures, deprivation, and so on. I should measure myself by errors, weaknesses, etc.
Excessive responsibility (assuming personal causality)	I am responsible for all bad things, failures, and so on.
Assuming temporal causality (predicting without sufficient evidence)	If it has been true in the past, then it is always going to be true.
Self-references	I am the center of everyone's attention, especially when it comes to bad performances or personal attributes.
"Catastrophizing"	Always think of the worst. It is most likely to happen to you.
Dichotomous thinking	Everything is either one extreme or another (black or white; good or bad).

the therapy sessions. They may argue openly with
clients as they try to persuade them to alter their patterns of thinking.

Kinship with Behavior Therapy

Cognitive therapy overlaps considerably with behavioral approaches to treatment, which we will discuss
shortly. Specifically, cognitive therapists often use
"homework assignments" that focus on changing
clients' overt behaviors (Wright, Beck, & Thase, 2003).
Clients may be instructed to engage in overt responses
on their own, outside of the clinician's office. For example, one shy, insecure young man in cognitive therapy was told to go to a singles bar and engage three different women in conversations for up to five minutes
each (Rush, 1984). He was instructed to record his
thoughts before and after each of the conversations.
This assignment elicited various maladaptive patterns
of thought that gave the young man and his therapist
plenty to talk about in subsequent sessions. As this example illustrates, cognitive therapy is a creative blend
of "talk therapy" and behavior therapy.

Cognitive therapy was originally designed as a
treatment for individuals. However, it has been adapted
for use with groups (Rose, 1999). Since most types of
insight therapy can be conducted on either an individual or a group basis (Kaplan & Sadock, 1993), let's take
a look at the dynamics of group therapy.

Group Therapy

Although it dates back to the early part of the 20th century, group therapy came of age during World War II
and its aftermath in the 1950s (Rosenbaum, Lakin, &
Roback, 1992). During this period, the expanding demand for therapeutic services forced clinicians to use
group techniques (Scheidlinger, 1993). *Group therapy*
**is the simultaneous treatment of several or more cli-
ents in a group.** Most major insight therapies have
been adapted for use with groups. In fact, the ideas underlying Rogers's client-centered therapy spawned the
much-publicized encounter group movement. Although group therapy can be conducted in a variety of

ways, we can provide a general overview of the process
as it usually unfolds (see Alonso, Alonso, & Piper, 2003;
Stone, 2003; Vinogradov, Cox, & Yalom, 2003).

Participants' Roles

A therapy group typically consists of about five to ten
participants. The therapist usually screens the participants, excluding anyone who seems likely to be disruptive. Some theorists maintain that judicious selection
of participants is crucial to effective group treatment
(Salvendy, 1993). There is some debate about whether
it is best to have a homogeneous group (people who
are similar in age, gender, and presenting problem).
Practical necessities usually dictate that groups be at
least somewhat diversified.

In group treatment, the therapist's responsibilities
include selecting participants, setting goals for the
group, initiating and maintaining the therapeutic
process, and protecting clients from harm (Weiner,
1993). The therapist often plays a relatively subtle role
in group therapy, staying in the background and focusing mainly on promoting group cohesiveness. The
therapist always retains a special status, but the therapist and clients are on much more equal footing in
group therapy than in individual therapy. The leader
in group therapy expresses emotions, shares feelings,
and copes with challenges from group members. In
other words, group therapists participate in the group's
exchanges and "bare their own souls" to some extent.

In group therapy, participants essentially function
as therapists for one another. Group members describe
their problems, trade viewpoints, share experiences,
and discuss coping strategies. Most important, they
provide acceptance and emotional support for each
other. In this supportive atmosphere, group members
work at peeling away the social masks that cover their
insecurities. Once their problems are exposed, members work at correcting them. As members come to
value one another's opinions, they work hard to display healthy changes to win the group's approval.

Advantages of the Group Experience

Group therapies obviously save time and money,
which can be critical in understaffed mental hospitals
and other institutional settings. Therapists in private
practice usually charge less for group than individual
therapy, making therapy affordable for more people.
However, group therapy is *not* just a less costly substitute for individual therapy. For many types of patients
and problems, group therapy can be just as effective as
individual treatment (Piper, 1993). Moreover, group
therapy has unique strengths of its own. Irwin Yalom
(1995), who has studied group therapy extensively, has
described some of these advantages:

Group therapies have proven particularly helpful when members share similar problems, such as alcoholism, overeating, or depression.

1. *In group therapy, participants often come to realize that their misery is not unique.* Clients often enter therapy feeling sorry for themselves. They think that they alone have a burdensome cross to bear. In the group situation, they quickly see that they are not unique. They are reassured to learn that many other people have similar or even worse problems.

2. *Group therapy provides an opportunity for participants to work on their social skills in a safe environment.* Many personal problems essentially involve difficulties in relating effectively to people. Group therapy can provide a workshop for improving interpersonal skills that cannot be matched by individual therapy.

3. *Certain kinds of problems are especially well suited to group treatment.* Specific types of problems and clients respond especially well to the social support that group therapy can provide. Peer self-help groups illustrate this advantage. In peer self-help groups, people who have a problem in common get together regularly to help one another out. The original peer self-help group was Alcoholics Anonymous. Today, similar groups are made up of former psychiatric patients, single parents, drug addicts, and so forth.

Whether treatment is conducted on a group or an individual basis, clients usually invest considerable time, effort, and money in insight therapies. Are they worth the investment?

Evaluating Insight Therapies

Evaluating the effectiveness of any approach to treatment is a complex challenge (Howard, Krasner, & Saunders, 2000; Nathan, Stuart, & Dolan, 2000). This is especially true for insight therapies. If you were to undergo insight therapy, how would you judge its effectiveness? By how you felt? By looking at your behavior? By asking your therapist? By consulting your friends and family? What would you be looking for? Various schools of thought pursue entirely different goals. And clients' ratings of their progress are likely to be slanted toward a favorable evaluation because they want to justify their effort, their heartache, their expense, and their time. Another problem that crops up in studies of the relative efficacy of different treatments is the *allegiance effect*—**researchers comparing different therapies tend to obtain results that favor the therapeutic approach they champion** (Luborsky, Singer, & Luborsky, 1999). Allegiance effects are probably due in part to the normal human tendency to see what one wants to see when making subjective evaluations. In any event, allegiance effects further complicate the daunting task of assessing the effectiveness of various insight therapies. In sum, evaluations of thera-

WEB LINK 16.4

The Effectiveness of Psychotherapy: The *Consumer Reports* Study
In 1995, *Consumer Reports* concluded that, indeed, psychotherapy is effective in the treatment of psychological problems and disorders. Martin Seligman, an important psychotherapy researcher, reviews the study's methods and compares its approach to other ways of judging psychotherapy's effects.

peutic outcomes tend to be subjective, with little consensus about the best way to assess clients' progress (Lambert & Hill, 1994).

In spite of these difficulties, hundreds of therapy outcome studies have been conducted over the past 50 years. These studies have examined a broad range of specific clinical problems and have used diverse methods to assess therapeutic outcomes, including scores on psychological tests and ratings by family members, as well as therapists' and clients' ratings. Collectively, these studies consistently indicate that insight therapy is superior to no treatment or to placebo treatment and that the effects of therapy are reasonably durable (Barlow, 1996b; Kopta et al., 1999; Lambert & Bergin, 1994). In one widely discussed study that focused on patients' self-reports, the vast majority of the respondents subjectively felt that they had derived considerable benefit from their therapy (Seligman, 1995).

Although there is considerable evidence that insight therapy tends to produce positive effects for a sizable majority of clients, there is vigorous debate about the *mechanisms of action* underlying these positive effects. The advocates of various therapies tend to attribute the benefits of therapy to the particular methods and procedures employed by each specific approach to therapy (Chambless & Hollon, 1998). In essence, they argue that different therapies achieve similar benefits through different processes. An alternative view espoused by many theorists is that the diverse approaches to therapy share certain common factors and that it is these common factors that account for much of the improvement experienced by clients (Frank & Frank, 1991). Evidence supporting the common factors view has mounted in recent years (Ahn & Wampold, 2001; Lambert & Barley, 2001).

What are the common denominators that lie at the core of diverse approaches to therapy? Although the models proposed to answer to this question vary considerably, there is some consensus. The most widely cited common factors include (1) the development of a therapeutic alliance with a professional helper, (2) the provision of emotional support and empathic understanding by the therapist, (3) the cultivation of hope and positive expectations in the client, (4) the provision of a rationale for the client's problems and a plausible method for ameliorating them, and (5) the opportunity to express feelings, confront problems, gain new insights, and learn new patterns of behavior (Grencavage & Norcross, 1990; Weinberger, 1995). How important are these common factors in therapy? Some theorists argue that common factors account for virtually *all* of the progress that clients make in therapy (Wampold, 2001). It seems more likely that the benefits of therapy represent the combined effects of common factors and specific procedures (Beutler & Harwood, 2002). Either way, it is clear that common factors play a significant role in insight therapy.

Therapy and the Recovered Memories Controversy

While debate about the efficacy of insight therapy has simmered for four decades, the 1990s brought an entirely new controversy to rock the psychotherapy profession like never before. The subject of this emotionally charged debate is the spate of reports of people recovering repressed memories of sexual abuse and other childhood trauma through therapy—often using methods that some critics characterize as questionable. You've no doubt read or seen media stories about people—including some celebrities—who have recovered long-lost recollections of sexual abuse, typically with the help of their therapists. For example, in 1991 TV star Roseanne suddenly recalled years of abuse by her parents, and a former Miss America remembered having been sexually assaulted by her father (Wielawski, 1991). These recovered memories have led to a rash of lawsuits in which adult plaintiffs have sued their parents, teachers, neighbors, pastors, and so forth for alleged child abuse 20 or 30 years earlier (even the Archbishop of Chicago was sued, although the suit was soon dropped). For the most part, these parents, teachers, and neighbors have denied the allegations. Many of them have seemed genuinely baffled by the accusations, which have torn some previously happy families apart

(Loftus & Ketcham, 1994; Wylie, 1998). In an effort to make sense of the charges, many accused parents have argued that their children's recollections are false memories created inadvertently by well-intentioned therapists through the power of suggestion.

The crux of the debate is that child abuse usually takes place behind closed doors, and in the absence of corroborative evidence, there isn't any way to reliably distinguish genuine recovered memories from those that are false. A handful of recovered memories have been substantiated by independent witnesses or belated admissions of guilt from the accused (Bull, 1999; Reisner, 1998; Schooler, 1999). But in the vast majority of cases, the allegations of abuse have been vehemently denied, and independent corroboration has not been available. Recovered recollections of sexual abuse have become so common, a support group has been formed for accused people who feel that they have been victimized by "false memory syndrome."

Psychologists are sharply divided on the issue of recovered memories, leaving the public understandably confused. Many psychologists, especially therapists in clinical practice, accept most recovered memories at face value (Banyard & Williams, 1999; Briere & Conte, 1993; Gleaves & Smith, 2004; Herman, 1994; Whitfield, 1995). They assert that it is common for patients to bury traumatic incidents in their unconscious (Del Monte, 2000; Wilsnack et al., 2002). Citing evidence that sexual abuse in childhood is far more widespread than most people realize (MacMillan et al., 1997), they argue that most repressed memories of abuse are probably genuine. They attribute the recent upsurge in reports of recovered memories to therapists' and clients' increased sensitivity to an issue that people used to be reluctant to discuss.

In contrast, many other psychologists, especially memory researchers, have expressed skepticism about the recent flood of recovered memories (Kihlstrom, 2004; Lindsay & Poole, 1995; Loftus, 1993, 1998; Lynn & Nash, 1994; McNally, 2004). These psychologists do not argue that people are lying about their repressed memories. Rather, they maintain that some suggestible, confused people struggling to understand profound personal problems have been convinced by persuasive therapists that their emotional problems must be the result of abuse that occurred years ago. Critics blame a small minority of therapists who presumably have good intentions but operate under the dubious assumption that virtually all psychological problems are attributable to childhood sexual abuse (Lindsay & Read, 1994; Spanos, 1994). Using hypnosis, dream interpretation, and leading questions, they supposedly prod and probe patients until they inadvertently create the memories of abuse that they are searching for. Consistent with this view, Yapko (1994) reviewed evidence that some therapists are (1) overly prone to see signs of abuse where

none has occurred, (2) unsophisticated about the extent to which memories can be distorted, and (3) naive about how much their expectations and beliefs can influence their patients' efforts to achieve self-understanding.

Psychologists who doubt the authenticity of repressed memories support their analysis by pointing to discredited cases of recovered memories (Brown, Goldstein, & Bjorklund, 2000). For example, with the help of a church counselor, one woman recovered memories of how her minister father repeatedly raped her, got her pregnant, and then aborted the pregnancy with a coathanger. However, subsequent evidence revealed that the woman was still a virgin and that her father had had a vasectomy years before (Loftus, 1997; Testa, 1996). The skeptics also point to published case histories that clearly involved suggestive questioning and to cases in which patients have recanted recovered memories of sexual abuse (see Figure 16.7) after realizing that these memories were implanted by their therapists (Goldstein & Farmer, 1993; Loftus, 1994). Those who question recovered memories also point to several lines of carefully controlled laboratory research that demonstrate that it is not all that difficult to create "memories" of events that never happened (Hyman & Kleinnecht, 1999; Lindsay et al., 2004; Roediger & McDermott, 1995, 2000). For example, studies have shown that subtle suggestions made to hypnotized subjects can be con-

Tom Rutherford (shown here with his wife, Joyce) received a $1 million settlement in a suit against a church therapist and a Springfield, Missouri, church in a false memory case. Under the church counselor's guidance, the Rutherfords' daughter, Beth, had "recalled" childhood memories of having been raped repeatedly by her minister father, gotten pregnant, and undergone a painful coat-hanger abortion. Her father lost his job and was ostracized. After he later revealed he'd had a vasectomy when Beth was age 4, and a physical exam revealed that at age 23 she was still a virgin, the memories were shown to be false.

A Case History of Recovered Memories Recanted

Suffering from a prolonged bout of depression and desperate for help, Melody Gavigan, 39, a computer specialist from Long Beach, California, checked herself into a local psychiatric hospital. As Gavigan recalls the experience, her problems were just beginning. During five weeks of treatment there, a family and marriage counselor repeatedly suggested that her depression stemmed from incest during her childhood. While at first Gavigan had no recollection of any abuse, the therapist kept prodding. "I was so distressed and needed help so desperately, I latched on to what he was offering me," she says. "I accepted his answers."

When asked for details, she wrote page after page of what she believed were emerging repressed memories. She told about running into the yard after being raped in the bathroom. She incorporated into another lurid rape scene an actual girlhood incident, in which she had dislocated a shoulder. She went on to recall being molested by her father when she was only a year old—as her diapers were being changed—and sodomized by him at five. Following what she says was the therapist's advice, Gavigan confronted her father with her accusations, severed her relationship with him, moved away, and formed an incest survivors' group.

But she remained uneasy. Signing up for a college psychology course, she examined her newfound memories more carefully and concluded that they were false. Now Gavigan has begged her father's forgiveness and filed a lawsuit against the psychiatric hospital for the pain that she and her family suffered.

● FIGURE 16.7

A case of recovered memories recanted. Recovered memories of sexual abuse are viewed with skepticism in some quarters. One reason is that some people who have recovered previously repressed recollections of childhood abuse have subsequently realized that their "memories" were the product of suggestion. A number of case histories, such as the one summarized here (from Jaroff, 1993), have demonstrated that therapists who relentlessly search for memories of abuse in their patients sometimes create the memories they are seeking.

From Jaroff, L. (1999, November 29). Lies of the mind. *Time,* pp. 52-59. Copyright © 1993 Time Inc. Reprinted by permission.

verted into "memories" of things they never saw (Sheehan, Green, & Truesdale, 1992).

Of course, psychologists who believe in recovered memories have mounted rebuttals to these arguments. For example, Kluft (1999) argues that a recantation of a recovered memory of abuse does not prove that the memory was false. Gleaves (1994) points out that individuals with a history of sexual abuse often vacillate between denying and accepting that the abuse occurred. Harvey (1999) argues that laboratory demonstrations showing how easy it is to create false memories have involved trivial memory distortions that are a far cry from the vivid, emotionally wrenching recollections of sexual abuse that have generated the recovered memories

controversy. Olio (1994) concludes, "The possibility of implanting entire multiple scenarios of horror that differ markedly from the individual's experience, such as memories of childhood abuse in an individual who does not have a trauma history, remains an unsubstantiated hypothesis" (p. 442). Moreover, even if one accepts the assertion that therapists *can* create false memories of abuse in their patients, some critics have noted that there is virtually no direct evidence on how often this occurs and no empirical basis for the claim that there has been an *epidemic* of such cases (Berliner & Briere, 1999; Calof, 1998; Leavitt, 2001).

So, what can we conclude about the recovered memories controversy? It seems pretty clear that therapists can unknowingly create false memories in their patients

and that a significant portion of recovered memories of abuse are the product of suggestion. But it also seems likely that some cases of recovered memories are authentic (Brown, Scheflin, Whitfield, 1999). At this point, we don't have adequate data to estimate what proportion of recovered memories of abuse fall in each category (Brown, Scheflin, & Hammond, 1998; Gow, 1999). Thus, the matter needs to be addressed with great caution. On the one hand, people should be extremely careful about accepting recovered memories of abuse in the absence of convincing corroboration. On the other hand, recovered memories of abuse cannot be summarily dismissed, and it would be tragic if the repressed memories controversy made people overly skeptical about the all-too-real problem of childhood sexual abuse.

Behavior Therapies

LEARNING OBJECTIVES

- Summarize the general approach and principles of behavior therapies.
- Describe the three steps in systematic desensitization and the logic underlying the treatment.
- Describe the use of aversion therapy and social skills training.
- Summarize evidence on the efficacy of behavior therapies.

Behavior therapy is different from insight therapy in that behavior therapists make no attempt to help clients achieve grand insights about themselves. Why not? Because behavior therapists believe that such insights aren't necessary in order to produce constructive change. Consider a client troubled by compulsive gambling. The behavior therapist doesn't care whether this behavior is rooted in unconscious conflicts or parental rejection. What the client needs is to get rid of the maladaptive behavior. Consequently, the therapist simply designs a program to eliminate the compulsive gambling. Actually, behavior therapists may work with clients to attain some limited insights about how en-

vironmental factors evoke troublesome behaviors (Franks & Barbrack, 1983). This information can be helpful in designing a behavioral therapy program.

The crux of the difference between insight therapy and behavior therapy lies in how each views symptoms. Insight therapists treat pathological symptoms as signs of an underlying problem. In contrast, behavior therapists think that the symptoms *are* the problem. Thus, **behavior therapies involve the application of the principles of learning to direct efforts to change clients' maladaptive behaviors.**

Behaviorism has been an influential school of thought in psychology since the 1920s. But behaviorists devoted little attention to clinical issues until the 1950s, when behavior therapy emerged out of three independent lines of research fostered by B. F. Skinner (1953) and his colleagues in the United States, Hans Eysenck (1959) and his colleagues in Britain, and Joseph Wolpe (1958) and his colleagues in South Africa (Glass & Arnkoff, 1992). Since then, there has been an explosion of interest in behavioral approaches to psychotherapy.

General Principles

Behavior therapies are based on certain assumptions (Agras & Berkowitz, 1999). *First, it is assumed that behavior is a product of learning.* No matter how self-defeating or pathological a client's behavior might be,

© 1999 by Sidney Harris

the behaviorist believes that it is the result of past conditioning. *Second, it is assumed that what has been learned can be unlearned.* The same learning principles that explain how the maladaptive behavior was acquired can be used to get rid of it. Thus, behavior therapists attempt to change clients' behavior by applying the principles of classical conditioning, operant conditioning, and observational learning.

Behavior therapies are close cousins of the self-modification procedures described in the Chapter 4 Application. Both use the same principles of learning to alter behavior directly. In discussing *self-modification,* we examined some relatively simple procedures that people can apply to themselves to improve everyday self-control. In our discussion of *behavior therapy,* we examine more complex procedures used by mental health professionals in the treatment of more severe problems.

Like self-modification, behavior therapy requires that clients' vague complaints ("My life is filled with frustration") be translated into specific, concrete behavioral goals ("I need to increase my use of assertive responses in dealing with colleagues"). Once the troublesome behaviors have been targeted, the therapist designs a program to alter these behaviors. The nature of the therapeutic program depends on the types of problems identified. Specific procedures are designed for specific types of problems, as you'll see in our discussion of systematic desensitization.

Systematic Desensitization

Devised by Joseph Wolpe (1958, 1987), systematic desensitization revolutionized psychotherapy by giving therapists their first useful alternative to traditional "talk therapy" (Fishman & Franks, 1992). *Systematic desensitization is a behavior therapy used to reduce clients' anxiety responses through counterconditioning.* The treatment assumes that most anxiety responses are acquired through classical conditioning (as we discussed in Chapter 15). According to this model, a harmless stimulus (for instance, a bridge) may be paired with a frightening event (lightning striking it), so it becomes a conditioned stimulus eliciting anxiety. The goal of systematic desensitization is to weaken the association between the conditioned stimulus (the bridge) and the conditioned response of anxiety (see Figure 16.8). Systematic desensitization involves three steps.

First, the therapist helps the client build an anxiety hierarchy. The hierarchy is a list of anxiety-arousing stimuli centering on the specific source of anxiety, such as flying, academic tests, or snakes. The client ranks

Joseph Wolpe

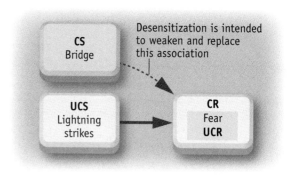

● FIGURE 16.8

The logic underlying systematic desensitization. Behaviorists argue that many phobic responses are acquired through classical conditioning, as in the example diagrammed here. Systematic desensitization targets the conditioned associations between phobic stimuli and fear responses.

the stimuli from the least anxiety arousing to the most anxiety arousing. This ordered list of related, anxiety-provoking stimuli constitutes the anxiety hierarchy. An example of an anxiety hierarchy for one woman's fear of heights is shown in Figure 16.9 on the next page.

The second step involves training the client in deep muscle relaxation. This second phase may begin during early sessions while the therapist and client are still constructing the anxiety hierarchy. Different therapists use different relaxation training procedures. Whatever procedures are used, the client must learn to engage in deep and thorough relaxation on command from the therapist.

In the third step, the client tries to work through the hierarchy, learning to remain relaxed while imagining each stimulus. Starting with the least anxiety-arousing stimulus, the client imagines the situation as vividly as possible while relaxing. If the client experiences strong anxiety, he or she drops the imaginary scene and concentrates on relaxation. The client keeps repeating this process until he or she can imagine a scene with little or no anxiety. Once a particular scene is conquered, the client moves on to the next stimulus situation in the anxiety hierarchy. Gradually, over a number of therapy sessions, the client progresses through the hierarchy, unlearning troublesome anxiety responses.

As clients conquer *imagined* phobic stimuli, they may be encouraged to confront the *real* stimuli. Although desensitization to imagined stimuli *can* be effective by itself, contemporary behavior therapists usually follow it up with direct exposures to the real anxiety-arousing stimuli (Emmelkamp & Scholing, 1990). Indeed, behavioral interventions emphasizing direct exposures to anxiety-arousing situations have become behavior therapists' treatment of choice for phobic and other anxiety disorders (Goldfried,

An Anxiety Hierarchy for Systematic Desensitization

Degree of fear

5	I'm standing on the balcony of the top floor of an apartment tower.
10	I'm standing on a stepladder in the kitchen to change a light bulb.
15	I'm walking on a ridge. The edge is hidden by shrubs and treetops.
20	I'm sitting on the slope of a mountain, looking out over the horizon.
25	I'm crossing a bridge 6 feet above a creek. The bridge consists of an 18-inch-wide board with a handrail on one side.
30	I'm riding a ski lift 8 feet above the ground.
35	I'm crossing a shallow, wide creek on an 18-inch-wide board, 3 feet above water level.
40	I'm climbing a ladder outside the house to reach a second-story window.
45	I'm pulling myself up a 30-degree wet, slippery slope on a steel cable.
50	I'm scrambling up a rock, 8 feet high.
55	I'm walking 10 feet on a resilient, 18-inch-wide board, which spans an 8-foot-deep gulch.
60	I'm walking on a wide plateau, 2 feet from the edge of a cliff.
65	I'm skiing an intermediate hill. The snow is packed.
70	I'm walking over a railway trestle.
75	I'm walking on the side of an embankment. The path slopes to the outside.
80	I'm riding a chair lift 15 feet above the ground.
85	I'm walking up a long, steep slope.
90	I'm walking up (or down) a 15-degree slope on a 3-foot-wide trail. On one side of the trail the terrain drops down sharply; on the other side is a steep upward slope.
95	I'm walking on a 3-foot-wide ridge. The slopes on both sides are long and more than 25 degrees steep.
100	I'm walking on a 3-foot-wide ridge. The trail slopes on one side. The drop on either side of the trail is more than 25 degrees.

● **FIGURE 16.9**

Example of an anxiety hierarchy. Systematic desensitization requires the construction of an anxiety hierarchy like the one shown here, which was developed for a woman with a fear of heights who had a penchant for hiking in the mountains.

Greenberg, & Marmar, 1990). Usually, these real-life confrontations prove harmless, and individuals' anxiety responses decline.

According to Wolpe (1958, 1990), the principle at work in systematic desensitization is simple. Anxiety and relaxation are incompatible responses. The trick is to recondition people so that the conditioned stimulus elicits relaxation instead of anxiety. This is *counterconditioning*—an attempt to reverse the process of classical conditioning by associating the crucial stimulus with a new conditioned response. Although Wolpe's explanation of how systematic desensitization works has been questioned, the technique's effectiveness in eliminating specific anxieties has been well documented (Spiegler & Guevremont, 1998).

Aversion Therapy

Aversion therapy is far and away the most controversial of the behavior therapies. It's not something that you would sign up for unless you were pretty desperate. Psychologists usually suggest it only as a treatment of last resort, after other interventions have failed. What's so terrible about aversion therapy? The client has to endure decidedly unpleasant stimuli, such as shocks or drug-induced nausea.

Aversion therapy **is a behavior therapy in which an aversive stimulus is paired with a stimulus that elicits an undesirable response.** For example, alcoholics have had drug-induced nausea paired with their favorite drinks during therapy sessions (Landabaso et al., 1999). By pairing an *emetic drug* (one that causes vomiting) with alcohol, the therapist hopes to create a conditioned aversion to alcohol (see Figure 16.10).

Aversion therapy takes advantage of the automatic nature of responses produced through classical conditioning. Admittedly, alcoholics treated with aversion therapy know that they won't be given an emetic outside of their therapy sessions. However, their reflex response to the stimulus of alcohol may be changed so that they respond to it with nausea and distaste. Obviously, this response should make it much easier to resist the urge to drink.

Troublesome behaviors treated successfully with aversion therapy include drug abuse, sexual deviance,

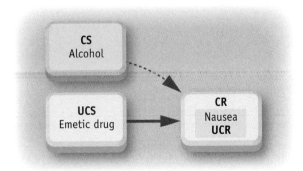

● **FIGURE 16.10**

Aversion therapy. Aversion therapy uses classical conditioning to create an aversion to a stimulus that has elicited problematic behavior. For example, in the treatment of drinking problems, alcohol may be paired with a nausea-inducing drug to create a conditioned aversion to alcohol.

How Do Clinicians Treat Posttraumatic Stress Disorder?

As discussed in Chapters 3 and 15, *posttraumatic stress disorder (PTSD)* involves enduring psychological disturbance following the experience of a major traumatic event. Given the apparent association between terrorist attacks and PTSD (see Chapter 15), interest has increased in clinical treatments for PTSD. Unfortunately, the research on the etiology and symptoms of PTSD has outstripped the research on its treatment, which remains in its infancy. This situation probably reflects the fact that PTSD wasn't widely recognized as an independent disorder until the 1980s. Nonetheless, PTSD has proven treatable (Livanou, 2001). As is the case with most other disorders, there is no consensus on a single, ideal approach to treating PTSD and the probability of successful treatment depends on the severity of a particular person's disorder.

Recovery from PTSD tends to be a gradual process, and clients need to be realistic about their goals. Once individuals have been severely traumatized, they are likely to always have some emotional pain lurking beneath the surface. However, therapy for PTSD can lead to fewer and less intense emotional reactions and to enhanced coping skills that help clients manage their emotions more effectively (Ruzek, 2001). According to the National Center for PTSD, treatment generally includes the following four components:

- Educating trauma survivors and their families about how persons get PTSD, how PTSD affects survivors and their loved ones, and other problems that commonly come along with PTSD symptoms.

- Exposing survivors to the event via imagery that allows them to reexperience it in a safe, controlled environment, while also carefully examining their reactions and beliefs in relation to that event.

- Examining and resolving strong feelings, such as anger, shame, or guilt, that are common among survivors of trauma.

- Teaching the survivor to cope with posttraumatic memories, reminders, reactions, and feelings without becoming overwhelmed or emotionally numb.

Given these elements in the treatment process, a variety of specific approaches to treatment are used (M. J. Friedman, 1996). *Cognitive therapy* with a strong behavioral slant is often employed. The cognitive part of this approach focuses on changing clients' thoughts that trigger emotional reactions, while the behavioral component usually involves some form of guided exposure to the trauma-arousing event, similar to systematic desensitization. Brief *psychodynamic therapy* is also used with PTSD patients. Psychodynamic therapists usually help clients confront their traumatic memories and intense emotions. *Group therapy* is another common approach. Trauma survivors seem to benefit from the peer-to-peer sharing that takes place in group treatment. *Drug therapies* are frequently used as an adjunct to other approaches. Antianxiety and antidepressant medications can reduce many of the symptoms associated with PTSD. Among the various approaches to treating PTSD, cognitive-behavioral approaches have the greatest empirical support for their efficacy (Hembree & Foa, 2000).

gambling, shoplifting, stuttering, cigarette smoking, and overeating (Sandler, 1975; Smith, Frawley, & Polissar, 1997; Wolpe, 1990). Typically, aversion therapy is only one element in a larger treatment program. Of course, this procedure should only be used with willing clients when other options have failed (Rimm & Cunningham, 1985).

Social Skills Training

Many psychological problems grow out of interpersonal difficulties. Behavior therapists point out that humans are not born with social finesse. People acquire their social skills through learning. Unfortunately, some people have not learned how to be friendly, how to make conversation, how to express anger appropriately, and so forth. Social ineptitude can contribute to anxiety, feelings of inferiority, and various kinds of disorders. In light of these findings, therapists are increasingly using social skills training in efforts to improve clients' social abilities. This approach to therapy has yielded promising results in the treatment of social anxiety (Shear & Beidel, 1998), autism (Gonzalez-Lopez & Kamps, 1997), and schizophrenia (Wallace, 1998).

Social skills training is a behavior therapy designed to improve interpersonal skills that emphasizes

shaping, modeling, and behavioral rehearsal. This type of behavior therapy can be conducted with individual clients or in groups. Social skills training depends on the principles of operant conditioning and observational learning. The therapist makes use of *modeling* by encouraging clients to watch socially skilled friends and colleagues, so that the clients can acquire responses (eye contact, active listening, and so on) through observation.

In *behavioral rehearsal*, the client tries to practice social techniques in structured role-playing exercises. The therapist provides corrective feedback and uses approval to reinforce progress. Eventually, clients try their newly acquired skills in real-world interactions. Usually, they are given specific homework assignments. *Shaping* is used in that clients are gradually asked to handle more complicated and delicate social situations. For example, a nonassertive client may begin by working on making requests of friends. Only much later will the client be asked to tackle standing up to his or her boss.

Evaluating Behavior Therapies

Behavior therapists have historically placed more emphasis than insight therapists on the importance of measuring therapeutic outcomes. As a result, there is ample research on the effectiveness of behavior therapy (Jacob & Pelham, 2000). How does the effectiveness of behavior therapy compare to that of insight therapy? In direct comparisons, the differences between the therapies are usually small. However, these modest differences tend to favor behavioral approaches for certain types of disorders (Lambert & Bergin, 1992). Of course, behavior therapies are not well suited to the treatment of some types of problems (vague feelings of discontent, for instance). Furthermore, it's misleading to make global statements about the effectiveness of behavior therapies, because they include many different procedures designed for different purposes. For example, the value of systematic desensitization for phobias has no bearing on the value of aversion therapy for sexual deviance.

For our purposes, it is sufficient to note that there is favorable evidence on the efficacy of most of the widely used behavioral interventions. Behavior therapies can make significant contributions to the treatment of anxiety problems, phobias, obsessive-compulsive disorders, sexual dysfunction, schizophrenia, drug-related problems, eating disorders, hyperactivity, autism, and mental retardation (Berkowitz, 2003; Emmelkamp, 1994).

Biomedical Therapies

LEARNING OBJECTIVES

- *Describe the principal drug therapies used in the treatment of psychological disorders and summarize evidence regarding their efficacy.*
- *Discuss some of the problems associated with drug therapies and their overall value.*
- *Describe ECT and discuss its efficacy and risks.*

In the 1950s, a French surgeon was looking for a drug that would reduce patients' autonomic response to surgical stress. The surgeon noticed that chlorpromazine produced a mild sedation. Based on this observation, Delay and Deniker (1952) decided to give chlorpromazine to hospitalized schizophrenic patients to see whether it would have a calming effect on them. Their experiment was a dramatic success. Chlorpromazine became the first effective antipsychotic drug—and a revolution in psychiatry was begun. Hundreds of thousands of severely disturbed patients—patients who had appeared doomed to lead the remainder of their lives in mental hospitals—were gradually sent home thanks to the therapeutic effects of antipsychotic drugs (see Figure 16.11). Today, biomedical therapies, such as drug treatment, lie at the core of psychiatric practice.

Biomedical therapies **are physiological interventions intended to reduce symptoms associated with psychological disorders.** These therapies assume that psychological disorders are caused, at least in part, by biological malfunctions. As we discussed in the previous chapter, this assumption clearly has merit for many disorders, especially the more severe ones. We will discuss two biomedical approaches to psychotherapy: drug therapy and electroconvulsive therapy.

Treatment with Drugs

Psychopharmacotherapy **is the treatment of mental disorders with medication.** We will refer to this kind of treatment more simply as *drug therapy*. Therapeutic drugs for psychological problems fall into four major groups: antianxiety drugs, antipsychotic drugs, antidepressant drugs, and mood stabilizers. Of these drugs, the antidepressant drugs have surpassed the antianxiety agents as the most widely prescribed psychiatric drugs (Pincus et al., 1998).

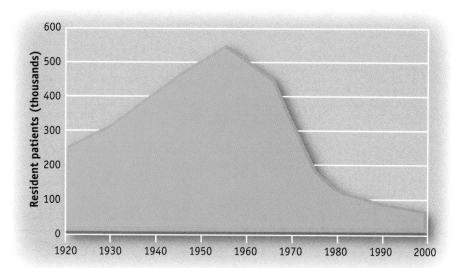

The declining inpatient population in mental hospitals. The number of inpatients in public mental hospitals has declined dramatically since the late 1950s. In part, this drop has been due to "deinstitutionalization"—a philosophy that emphasizes outpatient care whenever possible. However, above all else, this decline was made possible by the development of effective antipsychotic medications.

Antianxiety Drugs

Most of us know someone who pops pills to relieve anxiety. The drugs involved in this common coping strategy are *antianxiety drugs,* **which relieve tension, apprehension, and nervousness.** The most popular of these drugs are Valium and Xanax, which are the trade names (the proprietary names that pharmaceutical companies use in marketing drugs) for diazepam and alprazolam, respectively.

Valium, Xanax, and other drugs in the benzodiazepine family are often called *tranquilizers.* These drugs are routinely prescribed for people with anxiety disorders. They are also given to millions of people who simply suffer from chronic nervous tension. In the mid-1970s, pharmacists in the United States were filling nearly *100 million* prescriptions each year for Valium and similar antianxiety drugs. Many critics characterized this level of use as excessive (Lickey & Gordon, 1991).

Antianxiety drugs exert their effects almost immediately. They can be fairly effective in alleviating feelings of anxiety (Ballenger, 2000). However, their effects are measured in hours, so their impact is relatively short-lived. Common side effects of antianxiety drugs include drowsiness, depression, nausea, and confusion. These drugs also have some potential for abuse, dependency, and overdose problems (Ballenger, 2000). Another drawback is that patients who have been on antianxiety drugs for a while often experience withdrawal symptoms when their drug treatment is stopped (Danton & Antonuccio, 1997). Although some psychiatrists argue that the problems associated with the benzodiazepine drugs have been exaggerated, physicians have reduced their prescription of these drugs since the 1970s (Silberman, 1998).

A newer antianxiety drug called Buspar (buspirone), which does not belong to the benzodiazepine family, appears useful in the treatment of generalized anxiety disorder (Brawman-Mintzer, Lydiard, & Ballenger, 2000). Unlike Valium, Buspar is slow acting, exerting its effects in one to three weeks, but with fewer sedative side effects.

Antipsychotic Drugs

Antipsychotic drugs are used primarily in the treatment of schizophrenia. They are also given to people with severe mood disorders who become delusional. The trade names (and generic names) of some prominent drugs in this category are Thorazine (chlorpromazine), Mellaril (thioridazine), and Haldol (haloperidol). *Antipsychotic drugs* **are used to gradually reduce psychotic symptoms, including hyperactivity, mental confusion, hallucinations, and delusions.**

Studies suggest that antipsychotics reduce psychotic symptoms in about 70 percent of patients, albeit in varied degrees (Marder, 2000). When antipsychotic drugs are effective, they work their magic gradually, as shown in Figure 16.12 on the next page. Patients usually begin to respond within two days to a week. Further improvement may occur for several months. Many schizophrenic patients are placed on antipsychotics indefinitely because these drugs can reduce the likelihood of a relapse into an active schizophrenic episode (Marder & van Kammen, 2000).

Antipsychotic drugs undeniably make a major contribution to the treatment of severe mental disorders, but they are not without problems. They have many unpleasant side effects (Cohen, 1997). Drowsiness, constipation, and cotton mouth are common. Patients may also experience tremors, muscular rigidity, and impaired coordination. After being released from a hospital, many schizophrenic patients, supposedly placed on antipsychotics indefinitely, discontinue their drug regimen because of the disagreeable side effects. Unfortunately, a relapse eventually occurs in most patients after they stop taking antipsychotic medication

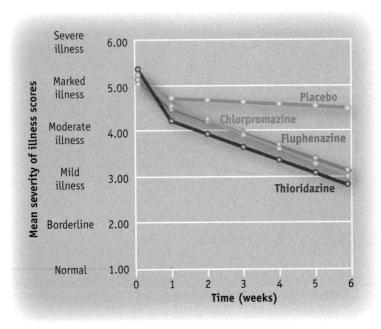

● FIGURE 16.12

The time course of antipsychotic drug effects. Antipsychotic drugs reduce psychotic symptoms gradually, over a span of weeks, as graphed here. In contrast, patients given placebo pills show little improvement.

From Cole, J. O., Goldberg, S. C., & Davis, J. M. (1966). Drugs in the treatment of psychosis. In P. Solomon (Ed.), *Psychiatric drugs.* New York: Grune & Stratton. From data in the NIMH-PSC Collaborative Study I. Reprinted by permission of J. M. Davis.

(Gitlin et al., 2001). In addition to minor side effects, antipsychotics may cause a severe and lasting problem called *tardive dyskinesia,* which is seen in about 20 percent of patients who receive long-term treatment with traditional antipsychotics (Miyamoto et al., 2003). **Tardive dyskinesia is a neurological disorder marked by chronic tremors and involuntary spastic movements.** Once this debilitating syndrome emerges, there is no cure, although spontaneous remission sometimes occurs after the discontinuation of antipsychotic medication (Pi & Simpson, 2000).

Psychiatrists are currently enthusiastic about a new class of antipsychotic agents called *atypical antipsychotic drugs* (such as clozapine, olanzapine, and quetiapine). These drugs are roughly as effective as traditional antipsychotics (Fleischhacker, 2002) and can help some patients who do not respond to conventional antipsychotic medications (Volavka et al., 2002).

WEB LINK 16.5

Psychopharmacology Tips by Dr. Bob
University of Chicago physician and pharmacology specialist Robert Hsiang provides both broad and specific references about the interface of drugs and the human mind, including a searchable archive of professional information and tips about the field.

Moreover, the atypical antipsychotics produce fewer unpleasant side effects and carry less risk for tardive dyskinesia (Correll, Leucht, & Kane, 2004; Lieberman et al., 2003). Of course, like all powerful drugs, they are not without their risks, as they appear to increase patients' vulnerability to diabetes and cardiovascular problems (Meltzer et al., 2002).

Antidepressant Drugs
As their name suggests, *antidepressant drugs* gradually elevate mood and help bring people out of a depression. Prior to 1987, there were two principal classes of antidepressants: *tricyclics* (such as Elavil) and *MAO inhibitors* (such as Nardil). These two sets of drugs affect neurochemical activity in different ways and tend to work with different patients. Overall, they are beneficial for about two-thirds of depressed patients (Gitlin, 2002), although only about one-third of treated patients experience a *complete resolution* of their symptoms (Shulman, 2001). The tricyclics have fewer problems with side effects and complications than the MAO inhibitors (Rush, 2000). Like antipsychotic drugs, antidepressants exert their effects gradually over a period of weeks.

Today, psychiatrists are more likely to prescribe a newer class of antidepressants, called *selective serotonin reuptake inhibitors (SSRIs),* which slow the reuptake process at serotonin synapses. The drugs in this class, which include Prozac (fluoxetine), Paxil (paroxetine), and Zoloft (sertraline), yield therapeutic gains similar to the tricyclics in the treatment of depression (Boland & Keller, 2003) while producing fewer unpleasant or dangerous side effects (Marangell et al., 2003). SSRIs have also proven valuable in the treatment of obsessive-compulsive disorders, panic disorders, and other anxiety disorders (Rivas-Vazquez, 2001). However, Prozac and the other SSRIs are not "miracle drugs," as suggested by some popular magazines. Like all drugs for psychological disorders, the SSRIs have side effects, such as weight gain, sleep problems, and sexual dysfunctions, that must be carefully weighed against their benefits (Baldessarini, 2001; Ferguson, 2001).

A major concern in recent years has been evidence from a number of studies that SSRIs may increase the risk for suicide (Healy & Whitaker, 2003; Holden, 2004). The challenge of collecting definitive data on this issue is much more daunting than one might guess, in part because suicide rates are already elevated among people who exhibit the disorders for which SSRIs are prescribed (Rihmer, 2003; Wessely & Kerwin, 2004). Some researchers have collected data that

"I think the dosage needs adjusting. I'm not nearly as happy as the people in the ads."

suggest that suicide rates have *declined* slightly because of widespread prescription of SSRIs (Olfson et al., 2003) and others have found no association between SSRIs and suicide (Lapiere, 2003; Tardiff, Marzuk, & Leon, 2002). At present, the data are too fragmentary and inconsistent to permit a firm, confident conclusion. That said, the issue should be taken seriously, and patients on SSRIs should be carefully monitored by their physicians and families (Culpepper et al., 2004). Elevated suicide risk appears to mainly be a problem among a small minority of children and adolescents in the first month after starting antidepressants, especially the first nine days (Jick, Kaye, & Jick, 2004).

Mood Stabilizers

Mood stabilizers **are drugs used to control mood swings in patients with bipolar mood disorders.** For many years, lithium was the only effective drug in this category. Lithium has proven valuable in preventing *future* episodes of both mania and depression in patients with bipolar illness (Geddes et al., 2004), and it can also be used in efforts to bring patients with bipolar illness out of *current* manic or depressive episodes. However, antipsychotics and antidepressants are more frequently used for these purposes. On the negative side of the ledger, lithium does have some dangerous side effects if its use isn't managed skillfully (Jefferson & Greist, 2000). Lithium levels in the patient's blood must be monitored carefully, because high concentrations can be toxic and even fatal. Kidney and thyroid gland complications are the other major problems associated with lithium therapy.

In recent years a number of alternatives to lithium have been developed. The most popular of these newer mood stabilizers is an anticonvulsant agent called *val-*

proate, which has become about as widely used as lithium in the treatment of bipolar disorders (Blanco et al., 2002). Valproate appears to be roughly as effective as lithium in efforts to treat current manic episodes and to prevent future affective disturbances (Moseman et al., 2003). The advantage provided by valproate is that it is better tolerated by patients.

Evaluating Drug Therapies

Drug therapies can produce clear therapeutic gains for many kinds of patients. What's especially impressive is that they can be effective in severe disorders that otherwise defy therapeutic endeavors. Nonetheless, drug therapies are controversial. Critics of drug therapy have raised a number of issues (Cohen & McCubbin, 1990; Greenberg & Fisher, 1997; Healy, 2004; Whitaker, 2002). First, some critics argue that drug therapies often produce superficial curative effects. For example, Valium does not really solve problems with anxiety—it merely provides temporary relief from an unpleasant symptom. Moreover, this temporary relief may lull patients into complacency about their problem and prevent them from working toward a more lasting solution. Second, critics charge that many drugs are overprescribed and many patients overmedicated. According to these critics, many physicians habitually hand out prescriptions without giving adequate consideration to more complicated and difficult interventions. Critics also argue that there is a tendency in some institutions to overmedicate patients to minimize disruptive behavior. Third, some critics charge that the side effects of therapeutic drugs are worse than the illnesses the drugs are supposed to cure. Citing problems such as tardive dyskinesia, lithium toxicity, and addiction to antianxiety agents, these critics argue that the risks of therapeutic drugs aren't worth the benefits.

Critics maintain that the negative effects of psychiatric drugs are not fully appreciated because the pharmaceutical industry has managed to gain undue influence over the research enterprise as it relates to drug testing (Angell, 2000, 2004; Healy, 2004). Today, most researchers who investigate the benefits and risks of medications and write treatment guidelines have lucrative financial arrangements with the pharmaceutical industry (Bodenheimer, 2000; Choudhry, Stelfox, & Detsky, 2002). Their studies are funded by drug companies and they often receive substantial consulting fees. Unfortunately, these financial ties appear to undermine the objectivity required in scientific research, as studies funded by pharmaceutical and other biomedical companies are far less likely to report unfavorable results than nonprofit-funded studies (Bekelman, Li, & Gross, 2003; Rennie & Luft, 2000). Industry-financed drug trials also tend to be much too brief to detect the long-term risks associated with new drugs (O'Brien, 1996), and when unfavorable results emerge, the data are often withheld from publication (Antonuccio, Danton, &

McClanahan, 2003). Also, research designs are often slanted in a multitude of ways so as to exaggerate the positive effects and minimize the negative effects of the drugs under scrutiny (Carpenter, 2002; Moncrieff, 2001; Rennie, 1999). The conflicts of interest that appear to be pervasive in contemporary drug research raise grave concerns that require attention from researchers, universities, and federal agencies.

Obviously, drug therapies have stirred up some debate. However, this controversy pales in comparison to the furious debates inspired by electroconvulsive (shock) therapy (ECT). ECT is so controversial that the residents of Berkeley, California, voted to outlaw ECT in their city. However, in subsequent lawsuits the courts ruled that scientific questions cannot be settled through a vote, and they overturned the law. What makes ECT so controversial? You'll see in the next section.

Electroconvulsive Therapy (ECT)

In the 1930s, a Hungarian psychiatrist named Ladislas Meduna speculated that epilepsy and schizophrenia could not coexist in the same body. On the basis of this observation, which turned out to be inaccurate, Meduna theorized that it might be useful to induce epileptic-like seizures in schizophrenic patients. Initially, a drug was used to trigger these seizures. However, by 1938, a pair of Italian psychiatrists (Cerletti & Bini, 1938) demonstrated that it was safer to elicit the seizures with electric shock. Thus, modern electroconvulsive therapy was born.

Electroconvulsive therapy (ECT) **is a biomedical treatment in which electric shock is used to produce a cortical seizure accompanied by convulsions.** In ECT, electrodes are attached to the skull over one or both temporal lobes of the brain (see the photo above). A light anesthesia is induced, and the patient is given a variety of drugs to minimize the likelihood of complications, such as spinal fractures. An electric current is then applied for about a second. The current should trigger a brief (5–20 seconds) convulsive seizure, during which the patient usually loses consciousness. Patients normally awaken in an hour or two. People typically receive between 6 and 12 treatments over a period of about a month (Glass, 2001).

The clinical use of ECT peaked in the 1940s and 1950s, before effective drug therapies were widely available. ECT has long been controversial, and its use did decline in the 1960s and 1970s. Nonetheless, there has been a resurgence in the use of ECT, and it is *not* a rare form of therapy. Although only about 8 percent of psychiatrists administer ECT (Hermann et al., 1998), estimates suggest that about 100,000 people receive ECT treatments each year in the United States (Hermann et al., 1995). Some critics argue that ECT is overused because it is a lucrative procedure that boosts psychiatrists' income while consuming relatively little

This patient is being prepared for electroconvulsive therapy. The mouthpiece keeps the patient from biting her tongue during the electrically induced seizures.

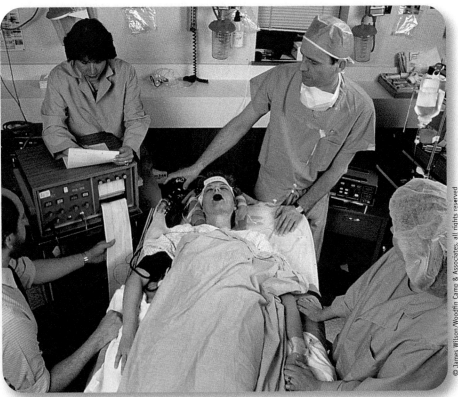

of their time in comparison to insight therapy (Frank, 1990). Conversely, some advocates argue that ECT is underutilized because the public harbors many misconceptions about its risks and side effects (Farah, 1997). Although ECT was once considered appropriate for a wide range of disorders, in recent decades it has primarily been recommended for the treatment of depression.

Controversy about ECT is also fueled by patients' reports that the treatment is painful, dehumanizing, and terrifying. Substantial improvements in the administration of ECT have made it less disagreeable than it once was (Bernstein et al., 1998). Nonetheless, some patients continue to report that they find the treatment extremely aversive (Johnstone, 1999).

Effectiveness of ECT

The evidence on the therapeutic efficacy of ECT is open to varied interpretations. Proponents of ECT maintain that it is a remarkably effective treatment for major depression (Prudic & Sackeim, 1999; Rudorfer, Henry, & Sackeim, 2003). Moreover, they note that many patients who do not benefit from antidepressant medication improve in response to ECT (Isenberg & Zorumski, 2000). However, opponents of ECT argue that the available studies are flawed and inconclusive and that ECT is probably no more effective than a placebo (Breggin, 1991; Friedberg, 1983). Overall, enough favorable evidence seems to exist to justify *conservative* use of ECT in treating severe mood disorders in patients who have not responded to medication (Carney & Geddes, 2003;

Metzger, 1999). Unfortunately, relapse rates after ECT are distressingly high. Over 50 percent of patients relapse within 6 to 12 months, although relapse rates can be reduced by giving ECT patients antidepressant drugs (Sackeim et al., 2001).

The debate about whether ECT works does *not* make ECT unique among approaches to the treatment of psychological disorders. Controversies exist regarding the effectiveness of most therapies. However, this controversy is especially problematic because ECT carries some risks.

Risks Associated with ECT

Even ECT proponents acknowledge that memory losses, impaired attention, and other cognitive deficits are common short-term side effects of electroconvulsive therapy (Isenberg & Zorumski, 2000; Lisanby et al., 2000). However, ECT proponents assert that these deficits are mild and usually disappear within a month or two (Glass, 2001). An American Psychiatric Association (2001) task force concluded that there is no objective evidence that ECT causes structural damage in the brain or that it has any lasting negative effects on the ability to learn and remember information. In contrast, ECT critics maintain that ECT-induced cognitive deficits are often significant and sometimes permanent (Breggin, 1991; Frank, 1990; Rose et al., 2003), although their evidence seems to be largely anecdotal. Given the concerns about the risks of ECT and the doubts about its efficacy, it appears that the use of ECT will remain controversial for some time to come.

Current Trends and Issues in Treatment

LEARNING OBJECTIVES

- *Discuss how managed care has affected the provision of therapy.*
- *Discuss the merits of blending approaches to therapy.*
- *Explain why therapy is underutilized by ethnic minorities.*

The controversy about ECT is only one of many contentious issues and shifting trends in the world of mental health care. In this section, we discuss the impact of managed care on psychotherapy, the continuing trend toward blending various approaches to therapy, and efforts to respond more effectively to increasing cultural diversity in Western societies.

Grappling with the Constraints of Managed Care

The 1990s brought a dramatic shift in how people in the United States pay for their health care. Alarmed by

skyrocketing health care costs, huge numbers of employers and individuals moved from traditional fee-for-service arrangements to managed care health plans (Kiesler, 2000). In the *fee-for-service* system, hospitals, physicians, psychologists, and other providers charged fees for whatever health care services were needed, and most of these fees were reimbursed by private insurance or the government (through Medicaid, Medicare, and other programs). In *managed care systems* people enroll in prepaid plans with small co-payments for services, typically run by health maintenance organizations (HMOs), which agree to provide ongoing health care for a specific sum of money. Managed care usually involves a tradeoff: Consumers pay lower prices for their care, but they give up much of their freedom to choose their providers and to obtain whatever treatments they believe necessary. If an HMO's treatment expenses become excessive, it won't turn a profit, so HMOs have powerful financial incentives to hold treatment costs down.

The HMOs originally promised individuals and employers that they would be able to hold costs down without having a negative impact on the quality of care, by negotiating lower fees from providers, reducing inefficiency, and cracking down on medically unnecessary services. However, critics charge that managed care systems have squeezed all the savings they can out of the "fat" that existed in the old system and that they have responded to continued inflation in their costs by rationing care and limiting access to medically *necessary* services (Duckworth & Borus, 1999; Giles & Marafiote, 1998; Sanchez & Turner, 2003).

The possibility that managed care is having a negative effect on the quality of care is a source of concern throughout the health care professions, but the issue is especially sensitive in the domain of mental health care (Bursztajn & Brodsky, 2002; Campbell, 2000). Critics maintain that mental health care has suffered particularly severe cuts in services because the question of what is "medically necessary" can be more subjective than in other treatment specialties (such as internal medicine or ophthalmology) and because patients who are denied psychotherapy services are relatively unlikely to complain (Duckworth & Borus, 1999). For example, a business executive who is trying to hide his depression or cocaine addiction from his employer will be reluctant to complain to his employer if therapeutic services are denied.

According to critics, the restriction of mental health services sometimes involves outright denial of treatment, but it often takes more subtle forms, such as underdiagnosing conditions, failing to make needed referrals to mental health specialists, and arbitrarily limiting the length of treatment (Bursztajn & Brodsky, 2002; Miller, 1996). Long-term therapy is becoming a thing of the past unless patients can pay for it out of pocket, and the goal of treatment has been reduced to reestablishing a reasonable level of functioning (Zatzick, 1999). Many managed care systems hold down costs by erecting *barriers to access,* such as requiring referrals from primary care physicians who don't have appointments available for weeks or months or authorizing only a few sessions of therapy at a time (Sanchez & Turner, 2003). Another cost-cutting strategy is the rerouting of patients from highly trained providers, such as psychiatrists and doctoral-level psychologists, to less-well-trained providers, such as masters-level counselors, who may not be adequately prepared to handle serious psychological disorders (Seligman &

Levant, 1998). Cost containment is also achieved by requiring physicians to prescribe older antidepressant and antipsychotic drugs instead of the newer and much more expensive SSRIs and atypical antipsychotics (Docherty, 1999).

The extensive utilization review procedures required by managed care have also raised concerns about providers' autonomy and clients' confidentiality (Plante, 1999a). Clinicians who have to "sell" their treatment plans to managed care bureaucrats who may know little about mental health care feel that they have lost control over their professional practice. They also worry that the need to divulge the details of clients' problems to justify treatment may breach the confidentiality of the therapist-client relationship.

Unfortunately, there are no simple solutions to these problems on the horizon. Restraining the burgeoning cost of health care without compromising the quality of care, consumers' freedom of choice, and providers' autonomy is an enormously complex and daunting challenge. At this juncture, it is difficult to predict what the future holds. However, it is clear that economic realities have ushered in an era of transition for the treatment of psychological disorders and problems.

Blending Approaches to Treatment

In this chapter we have reviewed many approaches to treatment, which are summarized and compared in Figure 16.13. However, there is no rule that a client must be treated with just one approach. Often, a clinician will use several techniques in working with a client. For example, a depressed person might receive cognitive therapy (an insight therapy), social skills training (a behavior therapy), and antidepressant medication (a biomedical therapy). Multiple approaches are particularly likely when a treatment *team* provides therapy. Studies suggest that combining approaches to treatment has merit (Glass, 2004; Klerman et al., 1994).

The value of multiple approaches may explain why a significant trend seems to have crept into the field of psychotherapy: a movement away from strong loyalty to individual schools of thought and a corresponding move toward integrating various approaches to therapy (Castonguay et al., 2003; Smith, 1999). Most clinicians used to depend exclusively on one system of therapy while rejecting the utility of all others. This era of fragmentation may be drawing to a close. In recent surveys of psychologists' theoretical orientations, researchers have been surprised to find that the greatest proportion of respondents described themselves as eclectic in approach (Garfield & Bergin, 1994). *Eclecticism* in the practice of therapy involves drawing ideas from two or more systems of therapy, instead of committing to just one system.

Major Approaches to Psychotherapy

Type of psychotherapy	Primary founders	Origin of disorder	Therapeutic goals	Therapeutic techniques
Psychoanalysis	Freud	Unconscious conflicts resulting from fixations in earlier development	Insights regarding unconscious conflicts and motives; personality reconstruction	Free association, dream analysis, interpretation, catharsis, transference
Client-centered therapy	Rogers	Incongruence between self-concept and actual experience; dependence on acceptance from others	Congruence between self-concept and experience; acceptance of genuine self; self-determination, personal growth	Genuineness, empathy, unconditional positive regard, clarification, reflecting back to client
Cognitive therapy	Beck Ellis	Irrational assumptions and negative, self-defeating thinking about events related to self	Detection of negative thinking; substitution of more realistic thinking	Thought stopping, recording automatic thoughts, refuting negative thinking, reattribution, homework assignments
Behavior therapies	Wolpe Skinner Eysenck	Maladaptive patterns of behavior acquired through learning	Elimination of symptomatic, maladaptive behaviors; acquisition of more adaptive responses	Classical and operant conditioning, reinforcement, punishment, extinction, shaping, aversive conditioning, systematic desensitization, social skills training
Biomedical therapies		Physiological malfunction, primarily abnormal neurotransmitter activity	Elimination of symptoms; prevention of relapse	Antipsychotic, antianxiety, antidepressant, and mood stabilizer drugs; electroconvulsive therapy (ECT)

● FIGURE 16.13

Comparison of psychotherapy approaches. This chart compares behavior therapies, biomedical therapies, and three leading approaches to insight therapy.

Increasing Multicultural Sensitivity in Treatment

Research on how cultural factors influence the process and outcome of psychotherapy has burgeoned in recent years, motivated in part by the need to improve mental health services for ethnic minority groups in American society (Lee & Ramirez, 2000). The data are ambiguous for a couple of ethnic groups, but studies suggest that American minority groups generally underutilize therapeutic services (Mays & Albee, 1992; Vega et al., 1999; Wells et al., 2001). Why? A variety of barriers appear to contribute to this problem, including the following (Sue, Zane, & Young, 1994; Takeuchi, Uehara, & Maramba, 1999; U.S. Department of Health and Human Services, 1999):

1. *Cultural barriers.* In times of psychological distress, some cultural groups are reluctant to turn to formal, professional sources of assistance. Given their socialization, they prefer to rely on informal assistance from family members, the clergy, respected elders,

Cultural barriers have emerged in the psychotherapy process. A number of minority groups in the United States shy away from using professional services in this field. Those who do try it also tend to quickly terminate treatment more often than white Americans.

herbalists, acupuncturists, and so forth, who share their cultural heritage. Many members of minority groups have a history of frustrating interactions with American bureaucracies and are distrustful of large, intimidating, foreign institutions, such as hospitals and community mental health centers (Pierce, 1992).

2. *Language barriers.* Effective communication is crucial to the provision of psychotherapy, yet most hospitals and mental health agencies are not adequately staffed with therapists who speak the languages used by minority groups in their service areas. The resulting communication problems make it awkward and difficult for many minority group members to explain their problems and obtain the type of help they need.

3. *Institutional barriers.* Stanley Sue and Nolan Zane (1987) argue that the "single most important explanation for the problems in service delivery involves the inability of therapists to provide culturally responsive forms of treatment" (p. 37). The vast majority of therapists have been trained almost exclusively in the treatment of middle-class white Americans and are not familiar with the cultural backgrounds and unique characteristics of various ethnic groups. This culture gap often leads to misunderstandings and ill-advised treatment strategies (Hughes, 1993). Unfortunately, there is a grievous shortage of ethnic therapists

to meet the needs of various ethnic groups (Mays & Albee, 1992).

What can be done to improve mental health services for American minority groups? Researchers in this area have offered a variety of suggestions (Homma-True et al., 1993; Hong, Garcia, & Soriano, 2000; Pedersen, 1994; Sue & Zane, 1987; Yamamoto et al., 1993). Discussions of possible solutions usually begin with the need to recruit and train more ethnic minority therapists. Studies show that ethnic minorities are more likely to go to mental health facilities that are staffed by a higher proportion of people who share their ethnic background (Snowden & Hu, 1996; Sue et al., 1994). Furthermore, clients' satisfaction with therapy tends to be greater when they are treated by therapists from their own culture. Therapists can also be given special training to work more effectively with people from different cultural backgrounds. For example, Wade and Bernstein (1991) found that a cultural sensitivity training program for white therapists working with an African American clientele resulted in improved client satisfaction. Finally, most authorities urge further investigation of how traditional approaches to therapy can be modified and tailored to be more compatible with specific cultural groups' attitudes, values, norms, and traditions.

APPLICATION

Looking for a Therapist

LEARNING OBJECTIVES

- *Discuss when and where to seek therapy.*
- *Evaluate the potential importance of a therapist's gender and professional background.*

- *Summarize the evidence on whether therapists' theoretical approaches influence their effectiveness.*
- *Discuss what one should expect from therapy.*

Answer the following "true" or "false."

____ **1.** Psychotherapy is an art as well as a science.

____ **2.** The type of professional degree that a therapist holds is relatively unimportant.

____ **3.** Psychotherapy can be harmful or damaging to a client.

____ **4.** Psychotherapy does not have to be expensive.

____ **5.** It is a good idea to shop around when choosing a therapist.

All of these statements are true. Do any of them surprise you? If so, you're in good company. Many people

know relatively little about the practicalities of selecting a therapist.

The task of finding an appropriate therapist is no less complex than shopping for any other major service. Should you see a psychologist or a psychiatrist? Should you opt for individual therapy or group therapy? Should you see a client-centered therapist or a behavior therapist? The unfortunate part of this decision process is that people seeking psychotherapy often feel overwhelmed by personal problems. The last thing they need is to be confronted by yet another complex problem.

Finding the right therapist is no easy task. You need to take into account the therapist's training and orientation, fees charged, and personality. An initial visit should give you a good idea of what a particular therapist is like.

Nonetheless, the importance of finding a good therapist cannot be overestimated. Therapy can sometimes have harmful rather than helpful effects. We have already discussed how drug therapies and ECT can sometimes be damaging, but problems are not limited to these interventions. Talking about your problems with a therapist may sound pretty harmless, but studies indicate that insight therapies can also backfire (Lambert & Bergin, 1994; McGlashan et al., 1990). Although a great many talented therapists are available, psychotherapy, like any other profession, has incompetent practitioners as well. Therefore, you should shop for a skilled therapist, just as you would for a good attorney or a good mechanic.

In this Application, we present some information that should be helpful if you ever have to look for a therapist for yourself or for a friend or family member (based on Amada, 1985; Bruckner-Gordon, Gangi, & Wallman, 1988; Ehrenberg & Ehrenberg, 1994; Pittman, 1994).

When Should You Seek Professional Treatment?

There is no simple answer to the question of when to seek treatment. Obviously, people *consider* the possibility of professional treatment when they are psychologically distressed. However, they have other options besides psychotherapy. There is much to be said for seeking advice from family, friends, the clergy, and so forth. Insights about personal problems do not belong exclusively to people with professional degrees.

So, when should you turn to professionals for help? You should begin to think seriously about therapy when (1) you have no one to lean on, (2) the peo-ple you lean on indicate that they're getting tired of it, (3) you feel helpless and overwhelmed, or (4) your life is seriously disrupted by your problems. Of course, you do not have to be falling apart to justify therapy. You may want to seek professional advice simply because you want to get more out of life.

Where Do You Find Therapeutic Services?

Psychotherapy can be found in a variety of settings. Contrary to general belief, most therapists are not in private practice. Many work in institutional settings such as community mental health centers, hospitals, and human service agencies. The principal sources of therapeutic services are described in Figure 16.14 on the next page. The exact configuration of therapeutic services available will vary from one community to another. To find out what your community has to offer, it is a good idea to consult your friends, your local phone book, or your local community mental health center.

Is the Therapist's Profession Important?

Psychotherapists may be trained in psychology, psychiatry, social work, counseling, psychiatric nursing, or marriage and family therapy. Researchers have *not* found any reliable associations between therapists' professional background and therapeutic efficacy (Beutler, Machado, & Neufeldt, 1994), probably because many talented therapists can be found in all of these professions. Thus, the kind of degree that a therapist holds doesn't need to be a crucial consideration in your selection process. It *is* true that in most states

FRANK & ERNEST reprinted by permission of Newspaper Enterprise Association, Inc.

only a physician can prescribe drugs for disorders that warrant drug therapy. However, some critics argue that many psychiatrists are too quick to use drugs to solve problems (Breggin, 1991). In any case, other types of therapists can refer you to a psychiatrist if they think that drug therapy would be helpful. If you have a health insurance policy that covers psychotherapy, you may want to check to see whether it carries any restrictions about the therapist's profession.

Is the Therapist's Gender Important?

If *you* feel that the therapist's gender is important, then for you it is. The therapeutic relationship must be characterized by trust and rapport. Feeling uncomfortable with a therapist of one gender or the other could inhibit the therapeutic process. Hence, you should feel free to look for a male or female therapist if you prefer to do so. This point is probably most relevant to female clients whose troubles may be related to the extensive sexism in our society (A. G. Kaplan, 1985). It is entirely reasonable for women to seek a therapist with a feminist perspective if that would make them feel more comfortable.

You should also be aware that sexual exploitation is an occasional problem in the context of therapy. Studies indicate that a small minority of therapists take advantage of their clients sexually (Pope, Keith-Spiegel, & Tabachnick, 1986). These incidents almost always involve a male therapist making advances to a female client. The available evidence indicates that these sexual liaisons are usually harmful to clients

Principal Sources of Therapeutic Services

Source	Comments
Private practitioners	Self-employed therapists are listed in the Yellow Pages under their professional category, such as psychologists or psychiatrists. Private practitioners tend to be relatively expensive, but they also tend to be highly experienced therapists.
Community mental health centers	Community mental health centers have salaried psychologists, psychiatrists, and social workers on staff. The centers provide a variety of services and often have staff available on weekends and at night to deal with emergencies.
Hospitals	Several kinds of hospitals provide therapeutic services. There are both public and private mental hospitals that specialize in the care of people with psychological disorders. Many general hospitals have a psychiatric ward, and those that do not will usually have psychiatrists and psychologists on staff and on call. Although hospitals tend to concentrate on inpatient treatment, many provide outpatient therapy as well.
Human service agencies	Various social service agencies employ therapists to provide short-term counseling. Depending on your community, you may find agencies that deal with family problems, juvenile problems, drug problems, and so forth.
Schools and workplaces	Most high schools and colleges have counseling centers where students can get help with personal problems. Similarly, some large businesses offer in-house counseling to their employees.

● FIGURE 16.14

Sources of therapeutic services. Therapists work in a variety of organizational settings. Foremost among them are the five described here.

(Williams, 1992). There are absolutely no situations in which therapist-client sexual relations are an ethical therapeutic practice. If a therapist makes sexual advances, the client should terminate treatment.

Is Therapy Always Expensive?

Psychotherapy does not have to be prohibitively expensive. Private practitioners tend to be the most expensive, charging between $25 and $140 per (50-minute) hour. These fees may seem high, but they are in line with those of similar professionals, such as dentists and attorneys. Community mental health centers and social service agencies are usually supported by tax dollars. Hence, they can charge lower fees than most therapists in private practice. Many of these organizations use a sliding scale, so that clients are charged according to how much they can afford to pay. Thus, most communities have inexpensive opportunities for psychotherapy. Moreover, many health insurance plans provide at least partial reimbursement for the cost of treatment.

Is the Therapist's Theoretical Approach Important?

Logically, you might expect that the diverse approaches to therapy vary in effectiveness. For the most part, that is *not* what researchers find, however. After reviewing the evidence, Jerome Frank (1961) and Lester Luborsky and his colleagues (1975) both quote the dodo bird who has just judged a race in *Alice in Wonderland:* "Everybody has won, and *all* must have prizes." Improvement rates for various theoretical orientations usually come out pretty close in most studies (Lambert & Bergin, 1994; Luborsky et al., 2002; Wampold, 2001). In their landmark review of outcome studies, Smith and Glass (1977) estimated the effectiveness of many major approaches to therapy. As Figure 16.15 shows, the estimates cluster together closely.

However, these findings are a little misleading, as they have been averaged across many types of patients and many types of problems. Most experts seem to think that *for certain types of problems, some approaches to therapy are more effective than others* (Beutler, 2002; Crits-Christoph, 1997; Norcross, 1995). For example, Martin Seligman (1995) asserts that panic disorders respond best to cognitive therapy, that specific phobias are most amenable to treatment with systematic desensitization, and that obsessive-compulsive disorders are best treated with behavior therapy or medication. Thus, for a specific type of problem, a therapist's theoretical approach *may* make a difference.

It is also important to point out that the finding that various approaches to therapy are roughly equal in overall efficacy does not mean that all *therapists* are cre-

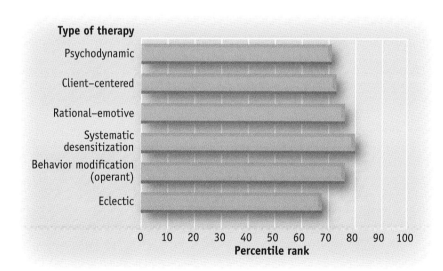

● **FIGURE 16.15**

Efficacy of different approaches to therapy. Smith and Glass (1977) reviewed nearly 400 studies in which clients who were treated with a specific type of therapy were compared with a control group made up of people with similar problems who went untreated. The bars indicate the percentile rank (on outcome measures) attained by the average client treated with each type of therapy when compared to control subjects. The higher the percentile, the more effective the therapy was. As you can see, the different approaches were fairly close in their apparent effectiveness.

Adapted from Smith, M. L., & Glass, G. V. (1977). Meta-analysis of psychotherapy outcome series. *American Psychologist, 32,* 752–760. Copyright © 1977 by the American Psychological Association. Adapted by permission of the author.

ated equal. Some therapists unquestionably are more effective than others. However, these variations in effectiveness appear to depend on individual therapists' personal skills rather than on their theoretical orientation (Beutler et al., 1994). Good, bad, and mediocre therapists are found within each school of thought.

The key point is that effective therapy requires skill and creativity. Arnold Lazarus (1989), who devised an approach to treatment called multimodal therapy, emphasizes that therapists "straddle the fence between science and art." Therapy is scientific in that interventions are based on extensive theory and empirical research (Forsyth & Strong, 1986). Ultimately, though, each client is a unique human being, and the therapist has to creatively fashion a treatment program that will help that individual.

What If There Isn't Any Progress?

If you feel that your therapy isn't going anywhere, you should probably discuss these feelings with your therapist. Don't be surprised, however, if the therapist suggests that it may be your own fault. Freud's concept of resistance has some validity. Some clients *do* have difficulty facing up to their problems. Thus, if your therapy isn't progressing, you may need to consider whether your resistance may be slowing progress. This self-examination isn't easy, as you are not an unbiased

Therapy is both a science and an art. It is scientific in that practitioners are guided in their work by a huge body of empirical research. It is an art in that therapists often have to be creative in adapting their treatment procedures to individual patients and their idiosyncrasies.

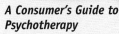
A Consumer's Guide to Psychotherapy
by Larry E. Beutler, Bruce Bongar, and Joel N. Shurkin
(Oxford University Press, 2001)

A CONSUMER'S GUIDE TO
PSYCHOTHERAPY
A Complete Guide to
Choosing the Therapist
and Treatment That's
Right for You

LARRY E. BEUTLER, BRUCE BONGAR,
AND JOEL N. SHURKIN

WITH A FOREWORD BY JOHN GRAY,
author of Men Are From Mars,
Women's Are From Venus

This book is a serious, sophisticated work that may be more thoroughly grounded in scientific research than any of its competitors. The character of the book is consistent with the fact that Larry Beutler is one of the leading researchers on the efficacy of psychotherapy. That is *not* to say that this is a research treatise. It is a pragmatic, readable discussion of everyday issues, such as what to look for in choosing a therapist, what questions to ask when you have doubts about your therapy, what role you play in the success of your treatment, how to recognize and deal with unprofessional or unethical behavior on the part of a therapist, and how to recognize when therapy is not working. The greatest strength of the book is its analysis of what research says about the effectiveness of specific therapies for particular problems. The authors carefully summarize the findings on what works best with what problems.

Cover image used by permission of Oxford University Press, Inc.

Signs of Resistance in Therapy

If you're dissatisfied with your progress in therapy, resistance may be the problem when:

1. You have nothing specific or concrete to complain about.
2. Your attitude about therapy changes suddenly just as you reach the truly sensitive issues.
3. You've had the same problem with other therapists in the past.
4. Your conflicts with the therapist resemble those that you have with other people.
5. You start hiding things from your therapist.

● **FIGURE 16.16**

Signs of resistance. Resistance in therapy may be subtle, but Ehrenberg and Ehrenberg (1994) have identified some telltale signs to look for.

observer. Some common signs of resistance identified by Ehrenberg and Ehrenberg (1994) are listed in Figure 16.16.

Given the very real possibility that poor progress may be due to resistance, you should not be too quick to leave therapy when dissatisfied. However, it *is* possible that your therapist isn't sufficiently skilled or that the two of you are incompatible. Thus, after careful and deliberate consideration, you should feel free to terminate your therapy.

What Is Therapy Like?

It is important to have realistic expectations about therapy, or you may be unnecessarily disappointed. Some people expect miracles. They expect to turn their life around quickly with little effort. Others expect their therapist to run their lives for them. These are unrealistic expectations.

Therapy is usually a slow process. Your problems are not likely to melt away quickly. Moreover, therapy is hard work, and your therapist is only a facilitator. Ultimately, *you* have to confront the challenge of changing your behavior, your feelings, or your personality. This process may not be pleasant. You may have to face up to some painful truths about yourself. As Ehrenberg and Ehrenberg (1994) point out, psychotherapy takes time, effort, and courage.

KEY IDEAS

The Elements of the Treatment Process

■ Psychotherapy involves three elements: treatments, clients, and therapists. Approaches to treatment are diverse, but they can be grouped into three categories: insight therapies, behavior therapies, and biomedical therapies. People vary considerably in their willingness to seek psychotherapy, and many people who need therapy do not receive it.

■ Therapists come from a variety of professional backgrounds. Clinical and counseling psychologists, psychiatrists, social workers, psychiatric nurses, and counselors are the principal providers of therapeutic services.

Insight Therapies

■ Insight therapies involve verbal interactions intended to enhance self-knowledge. In psychoanalysis, free association and dream analysis are used to explore the unconscious. When an analyst's probing hits sensitive areas, resistance can be expected. The transference relationship may be used to overcome this resistance. Classical psychoanalysis is not widely practiced anymore, but Freud's legacy lives on in a rich diversity of modern psychodynamic therapies.

■ The client-centered therapist tries to provide a supportive climate in which clients can restructure their self-concepts. The process of therapy emphasizes clarification of the client's feelings and self-acceptance. Cognitive therapy concentrates on changing the way clients think about events in their lives. Most theoretical approaches to insight therapy have been adapted for use with groups. Group therapy has unique advantages in comparison to individual therapy.

■ The weight of the evidence suggests that insight therapies can be effective. The benefits of insight therapies may be due in part to common factors. Repressed memories of childhood sexual abuse recovered through therapy are a new source of controversy in the mental health field. Although many recovered memories of abuse may be the product of suggestion, some probably are authentic.

Behavior Therapies

■ Behavior therapies use the principles of learning in direct efforts to change specific aspects of behavior. Systematic desensitization is a treatment for phobias. It involves the construction of an anxiety hierarchy, relaxation training, and step-by-step movement through the hierarchy.

■ In aversion therapy, a stimulus associated with an unwanted response is paired with an unpleasant stimulus in an effort to eliminate the maladaptive response. Social skills training can improve clients' interpersonal skills through shaping, modeling, and behavioral rehearsal. Ample evidence shows that behavior therapies are effective.

Biomedical Therapies

■ Biomedical therapies involve physiological interventions for psychological problems. Two examples of biomedical treatments are drug therapy and electroconvulsive therapy. A great variety of disorders are treated with drugs. The principal types of therapeutic drugs are antianxiety drugs, antipsychotic drugs, antidepressant drugs, and mood stabilizers.

■ Drug therapies can be effective, but they have their pitfalls. Many drugs produce problematic side effects, and some are overprescribed. Critics are also concerned that the pharmaceutical industry has gained too much influence over drug testing research.

■ Electroconvulsive therapy (ECT) is used to trigger a cortical seizure that is believed to have therapeutic value for depression. There is contradictory evidence and heated debate about the effectiveness of ECT and about possible risks associated with its use.

Current Trends and Issues in Treatment

■ Many clinicians and their clients believe that managed care has restricted access to mental health care and undermined its quality. Managed care has also raised concerns about providers' autonomy and clients' confidentiality.

■ Combinations of insight, behavioral, and biomedical therapies are often used fruitfully in the treatment of psychological disorders. Many modern therapists are eclectic, using ideas and techniques gleaned from a number of theoretical approaches.

■ Because of cultural, language, and access barriers, therapeutic services are underutilized by ethnic minorities in America. However, the crux of the problem is the failure of institutions to provide culturally sensitive forms of treatment for ethnic minorities.

Application: Looking for a Therapist

■ Therapeutic services are available in many settings, and such services do not have to be expensive. Excellent and mediocre therapists can be found in all of the mental health professions, using the full range of therapeutic approaches. Thus, therapists' personal skills are more important than their professional degree or their theoretical orientation.

■ In selecting a therapist, it is reasonable to insist on a therapist of one gender or the other. If progress is slow, your own resistance may be the problem. Therapy requires time, hard work, and the courage to confront your problems.

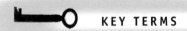

KEY TERMS

Allegiance effect p. 528	Free association p. 522
Antianxiety drugs p. 537	Group therapy p. 527
Antidepressant drugs p. 538	Insight therapies p. 522
Antipsychotic drugs p. 537	Interpretation p. 523
Aversion therapy p. 534	Mood stabilizers p. 539
Behavior therapies p. 532	Psychiatrists p. 521
Biomedical therapies p. 536	Psychoanalysis p. 522
Client-centered therapy p. 524	Psychopharmacotherapy p. 536
Clinical psychologists p. 520	Resistance p. 524
Cognitive therapy p. 526	Social skills training pp. 535–536
Counseling psychologists p. 520	Systematic desensitization p. 533
Dream analysis p. 523	Tardive dyskinesia p. 535
Electroconvulsive therapy (ECT) p. 540	Transference p. 524

KEY PEOPLE

Aaron Beck pp. 526–527	Carl Rogers pp. 524–525
Sigmund Freud pp. 522–524	Joseph Wolpe pp. 533–534

PRACTICE TEST

1. Which of the following approaches to psychotherapy is based on the theories of Sigmund Freud and his followers?
   a. Behavior therapies
   b. Client-centered therapy
   c. Biomedical therapies
   d. Psychoanalytic therapy

2. Miriam is seeing a therapist who encourages her to let her mind ramble and say whatever comes up, regardless of how trivial or irrelevant it may seem. The therapist explains that she is interested in probing the depths of Miriam's unconscious mind. This therapist appears to practice _____ and the technique in use is _____.
   a. psychoanalysis; transference
   b. psychoanalysis; free association
   c. cognitive therapy; free association
   d. client-centered therapy; clarification

3. Because Suzanne has an unconscious sexual attraction to her father, she behaves seductively toward her therapist. Suzanne's behavior is most likely a form of:
   a. resistance.   c. misinterpretation.
   b. transference.   d. spontaneous remission.

4. Client-centered therapy emphasizes:
   a. interpretation.   c. clarification.
   b. probing the unconscious. d. all of the above.

5. With regard to studies of the efficacy of various treatments, the allegiance effect refers to:
   a. a recovery that occurs without formal treatment.
   b. the tendency to obtain results that favor one's own approach to treatment.
   c. the failure to obtain results that favor one's own approach to treatment.
   d. the finding that treatment benefits are due to common factors.

6. According to behavior therapists, pathological behaviors:
   a. are signs of an underlying emotional or cognitive problem.
   b. should be viewed as the expression of an unconscious sexual or aggressive conflict.
   c. can be modified directly through the application of established principles of conditioning.
   d. both a and b.

7. A stimulus that elicits an undesirable response is paired with a noxious stimulus in:
   a. systematic desensitization.
   b. cognitive therapy.
   c. aversion therapy.
   d. psychoanalysis.

8. Bryce's psychiatrist has prescribed both Prozac and lithium for him. Bryce's diagnosis is probably:
   a. schizophrenia.
   b. obsessive-compulsive disorder.
   c. bipolar disorder.
   d. dissociative disorder.

9. Drug therapies have been criticized on the grounds that:
   a. they are ineffective in most patients.
   b. they temporarily relieve symptoms without addressing the real problem.
   c. many drugs are overprescribed and many patients are overmedicated.
   d. both b and c.

10. A therapist's theoretical approach is not nearly as important as his or her:
    a. age.
    b. appearance.
    c. personal characteristics and skills.
    d. type of professional training.

Book Companion Website

Visit the Book Companion Website at **http://psychology.wadsworth.com/weiten_lloyd8e,** where you will find tutorial quizzes, flashcards, and weblinks for every chapter, a final exam, and more! You can also link to the Thomson Wadsworth Psychology Resource Center (accessible directly at **http://psychology.wadsworth.com**) for a range of psychology-related resources.

Personal Explorations Workbook

The following exercises in your *Personal Explorations Workbook* may enhance your self-understanding in relation to issues raised in this chapter. **Questionnaire 16.1:** Attitudes Toward Seeking Professional Psychological Help. **Personal Probe 16.1:** What Are Your Feelings about Therapy? **Personal Probe 16.2:** Thinking About Therapy.

ANSWERS

1. d Page 522
2. b Pages 522–523
3. b Page 524
4. c Pages 524–525
5. b Page 528
6. c Pages 532–533
7. c Pages 534–535
8. c Pages 538–539
9. d Pages 539–540
10. c Pages 547–548

Glossary

acquired immune deficiency syndrome (AIDS) A disorder in which the immune system is gradually weakened and eventually disabled by the human immunodeficiency virus (HIV).

actor-observer effect The tendency to attribute one's own behavior to situational factors and others' behavior to personal factors.

acute stressors Threatening events that have a relatively short duration and a clear end point.

adjustment The psychological processes through which people manage or cope with the demands and challenges of everyday life.

aggression Any behavior intended to hurt someone, either physically or verbally.

agoraphobia A fear of going out to public places.

alcohol dependence *See* alcoholism

alcoholism A chronic, progressive disorder marked by a growing compulsion to drink and impaired control over drinking that eventually interfere with health and social behavior.

allegiance effect The idea that researchers comparing different therapies tend to obtain results that favor the therapeutic approach they champion.

ambient stress Chronic environmental conditions that, although not urgent, are negatively valued and place adaptive demands on people.

anal intercourse The insertion of the penis into a partner's anus and rectum.

androcentrism The belief that the male is the norm.

androgens The principal class of male sex hormones.

androgyny The coexistence of both masculine and feminine personality traits in an individual.

anorexia nervosa An eating disorder characterized by intense fear of gaining weight, disturbed body image, refusal to maintain normal weight, and dangerous methods to lose weight.

antecedents In behavior modification, events that typically precede a target response.

antianxiety drugs Drugs that relieve tension, apprehension, and nervousness.

antidepressant drugs Drugs that gradually elevate mood and help to bring people out of a depression.

antipsychotic drugs Drugs used to gradually reduce psychotic symptoms, including hyperactivity, mental confusion, hallucinations, and delusions.

anxiety disorders A class of psychological disorders marked by feelings of excessive apprehension and anxiety.

approach-approach conflict A conflict in which a choice must be made between two attractive goals.

approach-avoidance conflict A conflict in which a choice must be made about whether to pursue a single goal that has both attractive and unattractive aspects.

archetypes Emotionally charged images and thought forms that have universal meaning.

assertiveness Acting in one's own best interest by expressing one's feelings and thoughts honestly and directly.

atherosclerosis A disease characterized by gradual narrowing of the coronary arteries.

attachment styles Typical ways of interacting in close relationships.

attitudes Beliefs and feelings about people, objects, and ideas.

attributions Inferences that people draw about the causes of events, others' behavior, and their own behavior.

autonomic nervous system (ANS) That portion of the peripheral nervous system made up of the nerves that connect to the heart, blood vessels, smooth muscles, and glands.

aversion therapy A behavior therapy in which an aversive stimulus is paired with a stimulus that elicits an undesirable response.

avoidance-avoidance conflict A conflict in which a choice must be made between two unattractive goals.

basking in reflected glory The tendency to enhance one's image by publicly announcing one's association with those who are successful.

behavior Any overt (observable) response or activity by an organism.

behavior modification A systematic approach to changing behavior through the application of the principles of conditioning.

behavior therapies The application of the principles of learning to direct efforts to change clients' maladaptive behaviors.

behavioral contract A written agreement outlining a promise to adhere to the contingencies of a behavior modification program.

behaviorism A theoretical orientation based on the premise that scientific psychology should study observable behavior.

bereavement The painful loss of a loved one through death.

biomedical therapies Physiological interventions intended to reduce symptoms associated with psychological disorders.

biopsychosocial model The idea that physical illness is caused by a complex interaction of biological, psychological, and sociocultural factors.

bipolar disorders Psychological disorders marked by the experience of both depressed and manic periods.

bisexuals People who seek emotional-sexual relationships with members of both genders.

body mass index (BMI) Weight (in kilograms) divided by height (in meters) squared (kg/m2).

brainstorming Generating as many ideas as possible while withholding criticism and evaluation.

bulimia nervosa An eating disorder characterized by habitual out-of-control overeating followed by unhealthy compensatory efforts, such as self-induced vomiting, fasting, abuse of laxatives and diuretics, and excessive exercise.

burnout Physical, mental, and emotional exhaustion that is attributable to work-related stress.

bystander effect The social phenomenon in which individuals are less likely to provide needed help when others are present than when they are alone.

cancer Malignant cell growth, which may occur in many organ systems in the body.

cannabis The hemp plant from which marijuana, hashish, and THC are derived.

case study An in-depth investigation of an individual subject.

catastrophic thinking Unrealistic appraisals of stress that exaggerate the magnitude of one's problems.

catatonic schizophrenia A type of schizophrenia marked by striking motor disturbances, ranging from muscular rigidity to random motor activity.

catharsis The release of emotional tension.

cerebral hemispheres The right and left halves of the cerebrum, which is the convoluted outer layer of the brain.

channel The medium through which a message reaches the receiver.

chronic stressors Threatening events that have a relatively long duration and no readily apparent time limit.

classical conditioning A type of learning in which a neutral stimulus acquires the capacity to evoke a response that was originally evoked by another stimulus.

client-centered therapy An insight therapy that emphasizes providing a supportive emotional climate for clients, who play a major role in determining the pace and direction of their therapy.

clinical psychologists Psychologists who specialize in the diagnosis and treatment of psychological disorders and everyday behavioral problems.

clinical psychology The branch of psychology concerned with the diagnosis and treatment of psychological problems and disorders.

close relationships Relatively long-lasting relationships in which frequent interactions occur in a variety of settings and in which the impact of the interactions is strong.

cognitive therapy An insight therapy that emphasizes recognizing and changing negative thoughts and maladaptive beliefs.

cohabitation Living together in a sexually intimate relationship without the legal bonds of marriage.

coitus The insertion of the penis into the vagina and (typically) pelvic thrusting.

collective unconscious According to Jung, a storehouse of latent memory traces inherited from people's ancestral past that is shared with the entire human race.

collectivism Putting group goals ahead of personal goals and defining one's identity in terms of the groups to which one belongs.

commitment The decision and intent to maintain a relationship in spite of the difficulties and costs that may arise.

communication apprehension The anxiety caused by having to talk with others.

comparison level One's standard of what constitutes an acceptable balance of rewards and costs in a relationship.

comparison level for alternatives One's estimation of the available outcomes from alternative relationships.

compensation A defense mechanism characterized by efforts to overcome imagined or real inferiorities by developing one's abilities.

compliance Yielding to social pressure in one's public behavior, even though one's private beliefs have not changed.

concordance rate A statistic indicating the percentage of twin pairs or other pairs of relatives that exhibit the same disorder.

conditioned response (CR) A learned reaction to a conditioned stimulus that occurs because of previous conditioning.

conditioned stimulus (CS) A previously neutral stimulus that has, through conditioning, acquired the capacity to evoke a conditioned response.

confirmation bias The tendency to behave toward others in ways that confirm your expectations about them.

conflict The struggle that occurs when two or more incompatible motivations or behavioral impulses compete for expression.

conformity Yielding to real or imagined social pressure.

conscious According to Freud, whatever one is aware of at a particular point in time.

constructive coping Efforts to deal with stressful events that are judged to be relatively healthful.

context The environment in which communication takes place.

control group Subjects in an experiment who do not receive the special treatment given to the experimental group.

conversion disorder Psychological disorder characterized by a significant loss of physical function or by other physical symptoms (with no apparent organic basis), usually in a single organ system.

coping Active efforts to master, reduce, or tolerate the demands created by stress.

coronary heart disease A chronic disease characterized by a reduction in blood flow from the coronary arteries, which supply the heart with blood.

correlation The extent to which two variables are related to each other.

correlation coefficient A numerical index of the degree of relationship that exists between two variables.

counseling psychologists Psychologists who specialize in the treatment of everyday behavioral problems.

cunnilingus The oral stimulation of the female genitals.

date rape Forced and unwanted intercourse with someone in the context of dating.

death anxiety Fear and apprehension about one's own death.

death system The collection of rituals and procedures used by a culture to handle death.

defense mechanisms Largely unconscious reactions that protect a person from unpleasant emotions such as anxiety and guilt.

defensive attribution The tendency to blame victims for their misfortune, so that one feels less likely to be victimized in a similar way.

delusions False beliefs that are maintained even though they clearly are out of touch with reality.

dementia An abnormal condition marked by multiple cognitive defects that include memory impairment.

dependent variable In an experiment, the variable that is thought to be affected by manipulations of the independent variable.

diagnosis Distinguishing one illness from another.

discrimination Behaving differently, usually unfairly, toward members of a group.

disorganized schizophrenia A type of schizophrenia characterized by a particularly severe deterioration of adaptive behavior.

displaced workers Individuals who are unemployed because their jobs have disappeared.

displacement Diverting emotional feelings (usually anger) from their original source to a substitute target.

display rules Norms that govern the appropriate display of emotions.

dissociative amnesia A sudden loss of memory for important personal information that is too extensive to be due to normal forgetting.

dissociative disorders A class of psychological disorders characterized by loss of contact with portions of one's consciousness or memory, resulting in disruptions in one's sense of identity.

dissociative fugue A loss of memory for one's entire past life, along with one's sense of personal identity.

dissociative identity disorder Dissociative disorder involving the coexistence in one person of two or more largely complete, and usually very different, personalities. Also called multiple-personality disorder.

door-in-the-face technique Making a very large request that is likely to be turned down to increase the chance that people will agree to a smaller request later.

downward social comparison The defensive tendency to compare oneself with someone whose troubles are more serious than one's own.

dream analysis A psychotherapeutic technique in which the therapist interprets the symbolic meaning of the client's dreams.

dual-earner households Households in which both partners are employed.

eating disorders Severe disturbances in eating behavior characterized by preoccupation with weight and unhealthy efforts to control weight.

ego According to Freud, the decision-making component of personality that operates according to the reality principle.

elaboration likelihood model The idea that an individual's thoughts about a persuasive message (rather than the message itself) determine whether attitude change will occur.

electroconvulsive therapy (ECT) A biomedical treatment in which electric shock is used to produce a cortical seizure accompanied by convulsions.

emotional intelligence The ability to monitor, assess, express, or regulate one's emotions; the capacity to identify, interpret, and understand others' emotions; and the ability to use this information to guide one's thinking and actions.

emotions Powerful, largely uncontrollable feelings, accompanied by physiological changes.

empathy Adopting another's frame of reference to understand his or her point of view.

empiricism The premise that knowledge should be acquired through observation.

endocrine system Glands that secrete chemicals called hormones into the bloodstream.

endogamy The tendency of people to marry within their own social group.

epidemiology The study of the distribution of mental or physical disorders in a population.

erectile difficulties The male sexual dysfunction characterized by the persistent inability to achieve or maintain an erection adequate for intercourse.

erogenous zones Areas of the body that are sexually sensitive or responsive.

estrogens The principal class of female sex hormones.

etiology The apparent causation and developmental history of an illness.

evolutionary psychology A field of psychology that examines behavioral processes in terms of their adaptive value for members of a species over the course of many generations.

experiment A research method in which the investigator manipulates an (independent) variable under carefully controlled conditions and observes whether there are changes in a second (dependent) variable as a result.

experimental group The subjects in an experiment who receive some special treatment in regard to the independent variable.

explanatory style The tendency to use similar causal attributions for a wide variety of events in one's life.

expressiveness A style of communication characterized by the ability to express tender emotions easily and to be sensitive to the feelings of others.

external attributions Ascribing the causes of behavior to situational demands and environmental constraints.

extinction The gradual weakening and disappearance of a conditioned response tendency.

family life cycle An orderly sequence of developmental stages that families tend to progress through.

fellatio The oral stimulation of the penis.

fight-or-flight response A physiological reaction to threat that mobilizes an organism for attacking (fight) or fleeing (flight) an enemy.

fixation In Freud's theory, a failure to move forward from one stage to another as expected.

foot-in-the-door technique Getting people to agree to a small request to increase the chances that they will agree to a larger request later.

free association A psychotherapeutic technique in which clients spontaneously express their thoughts and feelings exactly as they occur, with as little censorship as possible.

frustration The feelings that occur in any situation in which the pursuit of some goal is thwarted.

fundamental attribution error The tendency to explain others' behavior as a result of personal rather than situational factors.

games Manipulative interactions progressing toward a predictable outcome, in which people conceal their real motivations.

gender The state of being male or female.

gender identity The ability to correctly classify oneself as male or female.

gender-role identity A person's identification with the traits regarded as masculine or feminine.

gender-role transcendence perspective The idea that to be fully human, people need to move beyond gender roles as a way of organizing the world and of perceiving themselves and others.

gender roles Cultural expectations about what is appropriate behavior for each gender.

gender schemas Cognitive structures that guide the processing of gender-relevant information.

gender stereotypes Widely shared beliefs about males' and females' abilities, personality traits, and social behavior.

general adaptation syndrome A model of the body's stress response, consisting of three stages: alarm, resistance, and exhaustion.

generalized anxiety disorder A psychological disorder marked by a chronic high level of anxiety that is not tied to any specific threat.

glass ceiling An invisible barrier that prevents most women and ethnic minorities from advancing to the highest levels of an occupation.

gonads The sex glands.

group therapy The simultaneous treatment of several or more clients in a group.

hallucinations Sensory perceptions that occur in the absence of a real external stimulus or that represent gross distortions of perceptual input.

hallucinogens A diverse group of drugs that have powerful effects on mental and emotional functioning, marked most prominently by distortions in sensory and perceptual experience.

hardiness A personality syndrome marked by commitment, challenge, and control that is purportedly associated with strong stress resistance.

health psychology The subfield of psychology concerned with the relation of psychosocial factors to the promotion and maintenance of health, and with the causation, prevention, and treatment of illness.

hedonic adaptation The phenomenon that occurs when the mental scale that people use to judge the pleasantness and unpleasantness of their experiences shifts so that their neutral point, or baseline for comparison, is changed.

heritability ratio An estimate of the proportion of trait variability in a population that is determined by variations in genetic inheritance.

heterosexism The assumption that all individuals and relationships are heterosexual.

heterosexuals People whose sexual desires and erotic behaviors are directed toward the other gender.

hierarchy of needs A systematic arrangement of needs, according to priority, in which basic needs must be met before less basic needs are aroused.

homogamy The tendency of people to marry others who have similar personal characteristics.

homophobia The intense fear and intolerance of homosexuality.

homosexuals People who seek emotional-sexual relationships with members of the same gender.

hormones Chemical substances released into the bloodstream by the endocrine glands.

humanism A theoretical orientation that emphasizes the unique qualities of humans, especially their free will and their potential for personal growth.

hypoactive sexual desire Lack of interest in sexual activity.

hypochondriasis (hypochondria) Excessive preoccupation with health concerns and incessant worry about developing physical illnesses.

id In Freud's theory, the primitive, instinctive component of personality that operates according to the pleasure principle.

identification Bolstering self-esteem by forming an imaginary or real alliance with some person or group.

identity A relatively clear and stable sense of who one is and what one stands for.

immune response The body's defensive reaction to invasion by bacteria, viral agents, or other foreign substances.

impression management Usually conscious efforts to influence the way others think of one.

incongruence The disparity between one's self-concept and one's actual experience.

independent variable In an experiment, a condition or event that an experimenter varies in order to see its impact on another variable.

individualism Putting personal goals ahead of group goals and defining one's identity in terms of personal attributes rather than group memberships.

industrial/organizational (I/O) psychology The study of human behavior in the workplace.

infant attachment The strong emotional bond that infants usually develop with their caregivers during the first year of their lives.

informational influence Pressure to conform that operates when people look to others for how to behave in ambiguous situations.

ingratiation Efforts to make oneself likable to others.

insanity A legal status indicating that a person cannot be held responsible for his or her actions because of mental illness.

insight therapies A group of psychotherapies in which verbal interactions are intended to enhance clients' self-knowledge and thus promote healthful changes in personality and behavior.

instrumentality A style of communication that focuses on reaching practical goals and finding solutions to problems.

interference Forgetting information because of competition from other learned material.

internal attributions Ascribing the causes of behavior to personal dispositions, traits, abilities, and feelings rather than to external events.

Internet addiction Spending an inordinate amount of time on the Internet and inability to control online use.

interpersonal communication An interactional process whereby one person sends a message to another.

interpersonal conflict Disagreement among two or more people.

interpretation A therapist's attempts to explain the inner significance of the client's thoughts, feelings, memories, and behaviors.

intimacy Warmth, closeness, and sharing in a relationship.

intimate violence Aggression toward those who are in close relationships to the aggressor.

investments Things that people contribute to a relationship that they can't get back if the relationship ends.

involuntary commitment Hospitalizing people in psychiatric facilities against their will.

kinesics The study of communication through body movements.

labor force All people who are employed as well as those who are currently unemployed but are looking for work.

learned helplessness Passive behavior produced by exposure to unavoidable aversive events.

leisure Unpaid activities one chooses to engage in because they are personally meaningful.

life changes Any noticeable alterations in one's living circumstances that require readjustment.

loneliness The emotional state that occurs when a person has fewer interpersonal relationships than desired or when these relationships are not as satisfying as desired.

lowball technique Getting people to commit themselves to an attractive proposition before its hidden costs are revealed.

major depressive disorder Psychological disorder characterized by persistent feelings of sadness and despair and a loss of interest in previous sources of pleasure.

manic-depressive disorder *See* bipolar disorder.

marriage The legally and socially sanctioned union of sexually intimate adults.

matching hypothesis The idea that people of similar levels of physical attractiveness gravitate toward each other.

medical model The idea that it is useful to think of abnormal behavior as a disease.

meditation A family of mental exercises in which a conscious attempt is made to focus attention in a nonanalytical way.

menarche The first occurrence of menstruation.

menopause The cessation of menstruation.

mere exposure effect An increase in positive feelings toward a novel stimulus (such as a person) based on frequent exposure to it.

message The information or meaning that is transmitted from one person to another.

meta-analysis A statistical technique that evaluates the results of many studies on the same question.

midlife crisis A turbulent period of doubts and reappraisals of one's life.

mnemonic devices Strategies for enhancing memory.

mood disorders A class of disorders marked by emotional disturbances that may spill over to disrupt physical, perceptual, social, and thought processes.

mood stabilizers Drugs used to control mood swings in patients with bipolar mood disorders.

mourning Formal practices of an individual and a community in response to a death.

multiple-personality disorder *See* dissociative identity disorder

narcissism The tendency to regard oneself as grandiosely self-important.

narcotics (opiates) Drugs derived from opium that are capable of relieving pain.

naturalistic observation An approach to research in which the researcher engages in careful observation of behavior without intervening directly with the subjects.

need for self-actualization The need to fulfill one's potential; the highest need in Maslow's motivational hierarchy.

negative reinforcement The strengthening of a response because it is followed by the removal of a (presumably) unpleasant stimulus.

neurons Individual cells that receive, integrate, and transmit information.

neuroticism A broad personality trait associated with chronic anxiety, insecurity, and self-consciousness.

neurotransmitters Chemicals that carry signals from one neuron to another.

noise Any stimulus that interferes with accurately expressing or understanding a message.

nonverbal communication The transmission of meaning from one person to another through means or symbols other than words.

normative influence Pressure to conform that operates when people conform to social norms for fear of negative social consequences.

nutrition A collection of processes (mainly food consumption) through which an organism uses the materials (nutrients) required for survival and growth.

obedience A form of compliance that occurs when people follow direct commands, usually from someone in a position of authority.

observational learning Learning that occurs when an organism's responding is influenced by observing others, who are called models.

obsessive-compulsive disorder (OCD) A psychological disorder marked by persistent uncontrollable intrusions of unwanted thoughts (obsessions) and by urges to engage in senseless rituals (compulsions).

occupational interest inventories Tests that measure one's interests as they relate to various jobs or careers.

Oedipal complex According to Freud, a child's erotically tinged desires for the other-sex parent, accompanied by feelings of hostility toward the same-sex parent.

operant conditioning A form of learning in which voluntary responses come to be controlled by their consequences.

optimism A general tendency to expect good outcomes.

orgasm The release that occurs when sexual arousal reaches its peak intensity and is discharged in a series of muscular contractions that pulsate through the pelvic area.

orgasmic difficulties Sexual disorders characterized by an ability to experience sexual arousal but persistent problems in achieving orgasm.

overcompensation Making up for frustration in one area by seeking overgratification in another area.

overdose An excessive dose of a drug that can seriously threaten one's life.

panic disorder Recurrent attacks of overwhelming anxiety that usually occur suddenly and unexpectedly.

paralanguage All vocal cues other than the content of the verbal message itself.

paranoid schizophrenia A type of schizophrenia dominated by delusions of persecution, along with delusions of grandeur.

passion The intense feelings (both positive and negative) experienced in love relationships, including sexual desire.

person perception The process of forming impressions of others.

personal space A zone of space surrounding a person that is felt to "belong" to that person.

personality An individual's unique constellation of consistent behavioral traits.

personality trait A durable disposition to behave in a particular way in a variety of situations.

persuasion The communication of arguments and information intended to change another person's attitudes.

phobic disorders Anxiety disorders marked by a persistent and irrational fear of an object or situation that presents no realistic danger.

physical dependence The need to continue to take a drug to avoid withdrawal illness.

polygraph A device that records fluctuations in physiological arousal as a person answers questions.

positive reinforcement The strengthening of a response because it is followed by the arrival of a (presumably) pleasant stimulus.

possible selves One's conceptions about the kind of person one might become in the future.

posttraumatic stress disorder (PTSD) Disturbed behavior that emerges sometime after a major stressful event is over.

preconscious According to Freud, material just beneath the surface of awareness that can be easily retrieved.

prejudice A negative attitude toward members of a group.

premature ejaculation Impaired sexual relations because a man consistently reaches orgasm too quickly.

pressure Expectations or demands that one behave in a certain way.

prevalence The percentage of a population that exhibits a disorder during a specified time period.

primacy effect The fact that initial information tends to carry more weight than subsequent information.

primary appraisal An initial evaluation of whether an event is (1) irrelevant to one, (2) relevant, but not threatening, or (3) stressful.

primary sex characteristics The structures necessary for reproduction.

procrastination The tendency to delay tackling tasks until the last minute.

prognosis A forecast about the probable course of an illness.

projection Attributing one's own thoughts, feelings, or motives to another person.

projective tests Personality tests that ask subjects to respond to vague, ambiguous stimuli in ways that may reveal the subjects' needs, feelings, and personality traits.

proxemics The study of people's use of interpersonal space.

proximity Geographic, residential, and other forms of spatial closeness.

psychiatrists Physicians who specialize in the treatment of psychological disorders.

psychoanalysis An insight therapy that emphasizes the recovery of unconscious conflicts, motives, and defenses through techniques such as free association, dream analysis, and transference.

psychodynamic theories All the diverse theories descended from the work of Sigmund Freud that focus on unconscious mental forces.

psychological dependence The need to continue to take a drug to satisfy intense mental and emotional craving for it.

psychological test A standardized measure of a sample of a person's behavior.

psychology The science that studies behavior and the physiological and mental processes that underlie it and the profession that applies the accumulated knowledge of this science to practical problems.

psychopharmacotherapy The treatment of mental disorders with medication.

psychosexual stages In Freud's theory, developmental periods with a characteristic sexual focus that leave their mark on adult personality.

psychosomatic diseases Genuine physical ailments caused in part by psychological factors, especially emotional distress.

puberty The stage during which sexual functions reach maturity and that marks the beginning of adolescence.

pubescence The two-year span preceding puberty during which the changes leading to physical and sexual maturity take place.

punishment The weakening (decrease in frequency) of a response because it is followed by the arrival of a (presumably) unpleasant stimulus.

rational-emotive therapy An approach to therapy that focuses on altering clients' patterns of irrational thinking to reduce maladaptive emotions and behavior.

rationalization Creating false but plausible excuses to justify unacceptable behavior.

reaction formation Behaving in a way that is exactly the opposite of one's true feelings.

receiver The person to whom a message is targeted.

reciprocal liking Liking those who show they like you.

reciprocity principle The rule that one should pay back in kind what one receives from others.

reference group A set of people against whom one compares oneself.

refractory period A time after orgasm during which males are unable to experience another orgasm.

regression A reversion to immature patterns of behavior.

relationship maintenance The actions and activities used to sustain the desired quality of a relationship.

reliability The measurement consistency of a test.

repression Keeping distressing thoughts and feelings buried in the unconscious.

resistance Largely unconscious defensive maneuvers intended to hinder the progress of therapy.

schizophrenic disorders A class of disorders marked by disturbances in thought that spill over to affect perceptual, social, and emotional processes.

secondary appraisal An evaluation of one's coping resources and options for dealing with stress.

secondary sex characteristics The physical features that distinguish one gender from the other but are not essential for reproduction.

sedatives Sleep-inducing drugs that tend to decrease central nervous system and behavioral activity.

self-actualization *See* need for self-actualization.

self-attributions Inferences that people draw about the causes of their own behavior.

self-concept A collection of beliefs about one's basic nature, unique qualities, and typical behavior.

self-defeating behaviors Seemingly intentional acts that thwart a person's self-interest.

self-disclosure The voluntary act of verbally communicating private information about oneself to another person.

self-discrepancy The mismatching of self-perceptions.

self-efficacy One's belief about one's ability to perform behaviors that should lead to expected outcomes.

self-enhancement The tendency to maintain positive views of oneself.

self-esteem One's overall assessment of one's worth as a person; the evaluative component of the self-concept.

self-fulfilling prophecy The process whereby expectations about a person cause the person to behave in ways that confirm the expectations.

self-handicapping The tendency to sabotage one's performance to provide an excuse for possible failure.

self-monitoring The degree to which people attend to and control the impressions they make on others.

self-regulation Directing and controlling one's behavior.

self-report inventories Personality scales that ask individuals to answer a series of questions about their characteristic behavior.

self-serving bias The tendency to attribute one's successes to personal factors and one's failures to situational factors.

self-verification theory The idea that people prefer to receive feedback from others that is consistent with their own self-views.

sensate focus A sex-therapy exercise in which partners take turns pleasuring each other with guided verbal feedback while certain kinds of stimulation are temporarily forbidden.

set-point theory The idea that there is a natural point of stability in body weight, thought to involve the monitoring of fat cell levels.

settling-point theory The idea that weight tends to drift around the level at which the constellation of factors that determine food consumption and energy expenditure achieve an equilibrium.

sex therapy The professional treatment of sexual dysfunctions.

sexism Discrimination against people on the basis of their sex.

sexual dysfunctions Impairments in sexual functioning that cause subjective distress.

sexual harassment The subjection of individuals to unwelcome sexually oriented behavior.

sexual identity The complex of personal qualities, self-perceptions, attitudes, values, and preferences that guide one's sexual behavior.

sexual orientation A person's preference for emotional and sexual relationships with individuals of the same gender, the other gender, or either gender.

sexually transmitted disease (STD) An illness that is transmitted primarily through sexual contact.

shaping Modifying behavior by reinforcing closer and closer approximations of a desired response.

shyness Discomfort, inhibition, and excessive caution in interpersonal relations.

social clock A person's notion of a developmental schedule that specifies what the person should have accomplished by certain points in life.

social comparison theory The idea that people need to compare themselves with others in order to gain insight into their own behavior.

social constructionism The assertion that individuals construct their own reality based on societal expectations, conditioning, and selfsocialization.

social exchange theory The idea that interpersonal relationships are governed by perceptions of the rewards and costs exchanged in interactions.

social role theory The assertion that minor gender differences are exaggerated by the different social roles that males and females occupy.

social skills training A behavior therapy designed to improve interpersonal skills that emphasizes shaping, modeling, and behavioral rehearsal.

social support Aid and succor provided by members of one's social networks.

socialization The process by which individuals acquire the norms and roles expected of people in a particular society.

somatization disorder A psychological disorder marked by a history of diverse physical complaints that appear to be psychological in origin.

somatoform disorders A class of psychological disorders involving physical ailments that have no authentic organic basis but are due solely to psychological factors.

source The person who initiates, or sends, a message.

spermarche An adolescent male's first ejaculation.

SQ3R A study system designed to promote effective reading that includes five steps: survey, question, read, recite, and review.

standardization The uniform procedures used to administer and score a test.

stereotypes Widely held beliefs that people have certain characteristics simply because of their membership in a particular group.

stimulants Drugs that tend to increase central nervous system and behavioral activity.

stress Any circumstances that threaten or are perceived to threaten one's well-being and thereby tax one's coping abilities.

subjective well-being Individuals' personal assessments of their overall happiness or life satisfaction.

superego According to Freud, the moral component of personality that incorporates social standards about what represents right and wrong.

superordinate goals Requiring two groups to work together to achieve a mutual goal.

surveys Structured questionnaires designed to solicit information about specific aspects of subjects' behavior.

systematic desensitization A behavior therapy used to reduce clients' anxiety responses through counterconditioning.

tardive dyskinesia A neurological disorder marked by chronic tremors and involuntary spastic movements.

test norms Statistics that provide information about where a score on a psychological test ranks in relation to other scores on that test.

token A symbol of all the members of a group.

token economy A system for doling out symbolic reinforcers that are exchanged later for a variety of genuine reinforcers.

tolerance A progressive decrease in responsiveness to a drug with continued use.

transference A phenomenon that occurs when clients start relating to their therapist in ways that mimic critical relationships in their lives.

Type A personality A personality style marked by a competitive orientation, impatience and urgency, and anger and hostility.

Type B personality A personality style marked by relatively relaxed, patient, easygoing, amicable behavior.

unconditioned response (UCR) An unlearned reaction to an unconditioned stimulus that occurs without previous conditioning.

unconditioned stimulus (UCS) A stimulus that evokes an unconditioned response without previous conditioning.

unconscious According to Freud, thoughts, memories, and desires that are well below the surface of conscious awareness but that nonetheless exert great influence on our behavior.

underemployment Settling for a job that does not make full use of one's skills, abilities, and training.

undifferentiated schizophrenia A type of schizophrenia marked by idiosyncratic mixtures of schizophrenic symptoms.

validity The ability of a test to measure what it was designed to measure.

variables *See* dependent variable; independent variable.

vasocongestion Engorgement of blood vessels.

work An activity that produces something of value for others.

work-family conflict The feeling of being pulled in multiple directions by competing demands from job and family.

References

AAUW Educational Foundation (1992). *How schools shortchange girls.* Washington, DC: AAUW.

Abbey, A., Clinton-Sherrod, A. M., McAuslan, P., Zawacki, T., & Buck, P. O. (2003). The relationship between the quantity of alcohol consumed and the severity of sexual assaults committed by college men. *Journal of Interpersonal Violence, 18*(7), 813–833.

Abbey, A., McAuslan, P., Zawacki, T. , Clinton, A. M., & Buck, P. O. (2001). Attitudinal, experimental, and situational predictors of sexual assault perpetration. *Journal of Interpersonal Violence, 16*(8), 784–807.

Abbey, A., Zawacki, T., Buck, P. O., Clinton, A. M., & McAuslan, P. (2001). Alcohol and sexual assault. *Alcohol Research and Health, 25*(1), 43–51.

Abbey, A., Zawacki, T., Buck, P. O., Clinton, A. M., & McAuslan, P. (2004). Sexual assault and alcohol consumption: What do we know about their relationship and what types of research are still needed? *Aggression and Violent Behavior, 9*(3), 271–303.

Abel, M. H. (1998). Interaction of humor and gender in moderating relationships between stress and outcomes. *Journal of Psychology, 132,* 267–276.

Abel, M. H. (2002). Humor, stress, and coping strategies. *Humor: International Journal of Humor Research, 15*(4), 365–381.

Aber, J. L., Brown, J. L., & Jones, S. M. (2003). Developmental trajectories toward violence in middle childhood: Course, demographic differences, and response to school-based intervention. *Developmental Psychology, 39*(2), 324–348.

Abi-Dargham, A., Gil, R., Krystal, J., Baldwin, R. M., Seibyl, J. P., Bowers, M., van Dyck, C. H., Charney, D. S., Innis, R. B., & Laruelle, M. (1998). Increased striatal dopamine transmission in schizophrenia: Confirmation in a second cohort. *American Journal of Psychiatry, 155,* 761–767.

Aboud, F. E., & Mendelson, M. J. (1996). Determinants of friendship selection and quality: Developmental perspectives. In W. M. Bukowski, A. F. Newcomb, & W. W. Hartup (Eds.), *The company they keep: Friendship in childhood and adolescence* (pp. 87–112). Cambridge, UK: Cambridge University Press.

Abramson, L. Y., Alloy, L. B., Hankin, B. L., Haeffel, G. J., MacCoon, D. G., & Gibb, B. E. (2002). Cognitive vulnerability-stress models of depression in a self-regulatory and psychobiological context. In I. H. Gotlib & C. L. Hammen (Eds.), *Handbook of depression.* New York: Guilford.

Abramson, L. Y., Alloy, L. B., & Metalsky, J. I. (1995). Hopelessness depression. In J. N. Buchanan & M. E. P. Seligman (Eds.), *Explanatory style* (pp. 113–134). Hillsdale, NJ: Erlbaum.

Abramson, L. Y., Seligman, M. E. P., & Teasdale, J. D. (1978). Learned helplessness in humans: Critique and reformulation. *Journal of Abnormal Psychology, 87,* 49–74.

Ackerman, S., Zuroff, D. C., & Moskowitz, D. S. (2000). Generativity in midlife and young adults: Links to agency, communion, and subjective well-being. *International Journal of Aging and Human Development, 50*(1), 17–41.

Acock, A. C., & Demo, D. H. (1994). *Family diversity and well-being.* Thousand Oaks, CA: Sage.

ACSF investigators (1992, December). AIDS and sexual behaviour in France. *Nature, 360,* 407–409.

Adams, G., Anderson, S. L., & Adonu, J. K. (2004). The cultural grounding of closeness and intimacy. In D. J. Mashek & A. Aron (Eds.), *Handbook of closeness and intimacy.* Mahwah, NJ: Erlbaum.

Adams, H. E., Wright, L. W., Jr., & Lohr, B. A. (1996). Is homophobia associated with homosexual arousal? *Journal of Abnormal Psychology, 105,* 440–445.

Adams, K. A. (1980). Who has the final word? Sex, race, and dominance behavior. *Journal of Personality and Social Psychology, 38,* 1–8.

Adams, K. A. (1983). Aspects of social context as determinants of black women's resistance to challenges. *Journal of Social Issues, 39,* 69–78.

Adcock, C. J. (1965). Thematic Apperception Test. In O. K. Buros (Ed.), *Sixth Mental Measurements Yearbook.* Highland Park, NY: Gryphon Press.

Addis, M. E., & Mahalik, J. R. (2003). Men, masculinity, and the contexts of help seeking. *American Psychologist, 58*(1), 5-14.

Ader, R. (2001). Psychoneuroimmunology. *Current Directions in Psychological Science, 10*(3), 94–98.

Adler, A. (1917). *Study of organ inferiority and its psychical compensation.* New York: Nervous and Mental Diseases Publishing.

Adler, A. (1927). *Practice and theory of individual psychology.* New York: Harcourt, Brace & World.

Adler, N. E., & Snibbe, A. C. (2003). The role of psychological processes in explaining the gradient between socioeconomic status and health. *Current Directions in Psychological Science, 12*(4), 119–123.

Adorno, T. W., Frenkel-Brunswik, E., Levinson, D. J., & Sanford, R. W. (1950). *The authoritarian personality.* New York: Harper & Row.

Agras, W. S., & Berkowitz, R. I. (1999). Behavior therapies. In R. E. Hales, S. C. Yudofsky, & J. A. Talbott (Eds.), *American Psychiatric Press textbook of psychiatry.* Washington, DC: American Psychiatric Press.

Ahn, H., & Wampold, B. E. (2001). Where oh where are the specific ingredients? A meta–analysis of component studies in counseling and psychotherapy. *Journal of Counseling Psychology, 48,* 251–257.

Ahrons, C. R. (1999). Divorce: An unscheduled family transition. In B. Carter & M. McGoldrick (Eds.), *The expanded family life cycle: Individual, family, and social perspectives* (3rd ed., pp. 381–398). Boston: Allyn & Bacon.

Ainsworth, M. D. S., Blehar, M. C., Waters, E., & Wall, S. (1978). *Patterns of attachment: A psychological study of the strange situation.* Hillsdale, NJ: Erlbaum.

Akgun, S., & Ciarrochi, J. (2003). Learned resourcefulness moderates the relationship between academic stress and academic performance. *Educational Psychology, 23*(3), 287-294.

Akimoto, S. A., & Sanbonmatsu, D. M. (1999). Differences in self-effacing behavior between European and Japanese Americans: Effect on competence evaluations. *Journal of Cross-Cultural Psychology, 30,* 159–177.

Akiskal, H. S. (2000). Mood disorders: Clinical features. In B. J. Sadock & V. A. Sadock (Eds.), *Kaplan and Sadock's comprehensive textbook of psychiatry* (7th ed., Vol. 1, pp. 1338–1376). Philadelphia: Lippincott/Williams & Wilkins.

Albee, G. W. (1998). Fifty years of clinical psychology: Selling our soul to the devil. *Applied and Preventive Psychology, 7*(3), 189–194.

Albert, C. M., Ma, J., Rifai, N., Stampfer, M. J., & Ridker, P. M. (2002). Prospective study of C-reactive protein, homocysteine, and plasma lipid levels as predictors of sudden cardiac death. *Circulation, 105,* 2595–2599.

Alberti, R. E., & Emmons, M. L. (2001). *Your perfect right.* San Luis Obispo, CA: Impact Publishers.

Alexander, C. N., Davies, J. L., Dixon, C. A., Dillbeck, M. C., Druker, S. M., Oetzel, R. M., Muehlman, J. M., & Orme-Johnson, D. W. (1990). Growth of higher states of consciousness: The Vedic psychology of human development. In C. N. Alexander & E. J. Langer (Eds.), *Higher stages of human development: Perspectives on adult growth.* New York: Oxford University Press.

Alexander, C. N., Robinson, P., Orme-Johnson, D. W., Schneider, R. H., et al. (1994). The effects of transcendental meditation compared with other methods of relaxation and meditation in reducing risk factors, morbidity, and mortality. *Homeostasis in Health & Disease, 35,* 243–263.

Alicke, M. D. (1985). Global self-evaluation as determined by the desirability and controllability of trait adjectives. *Journal of Personality and Social Psychology, 49*(6), 1621–1630.

Alicke, M. D., Smith, R. H., & Klotz, J. L. (1986). Judgments of personal attractiveness: The role of faces and bodies. *Personality and Social Psychology Bulletin, 12,* 381–389.

Allegro, J. T., & Veerman, T. J. (1998). Sickness absence. In P. J. D. Drenth, H. Thierry, & C. J. de Wolff (Eds.), *Handbook of work and organizational psychology.* East Sussex, UK: Psychology Press.

Allen, K., Blascovich, J., & Mendes, W. B. (2002). Cardiovascular reactivity in the presence of pets, friends, and spouses: The truth about cats and dogs. *Psychosomatic Medicine, 64*(5), 727–739.

Allen, K. R., & Demo, D. H. (1995). The families of lesbians and gay men: A new frontier in family research. *Journal of Marriage and the Family, 57,* 111–127.

Allison, D. B., Fontaine, K. R., Manson, J. E., Stevens, J., & VanItallie, T. B. (1999). Annual deaths attributable to obesity in the United States. *Journal of the American Medical Association, 282*(16), 1530–1538.

Allison, D. B., Heshka, S., Neale, M. C., Lykken, D. T., & Heymsfield, S. B. (1994). A genetic analysis of relative weight among 4,020 twin pairs, with an emphasis on sex effects. *Health Psychology, 13,* 362–365.

Alloy, L. B., & Abramson, L. Y. (1988). Depressive realism: Four theoretical perspectives. In L. B. Alloy (Ed.), *Cognitive processes in depression.* New York: Guilford Press.

Alloy, L. B., Abramson, L. Y., Whitehouse, W. G., Hogan, M. E., Tashman, N. A., Steinberg, D. L., Rose, D. T., & Donovan, P. (1999). Depressogenic cognitive styles: Predictive validity, information processing and personality characteristics, and developmental origins. *Behavioral Research and Therapy, 37,* 503–531.

Allport, G. W. (1937). *Personality: A psychological interpretation.* New York: Holt.

Allport, G. W. (1961). *Pattern and growth in personality.* New York: Holt, Rinehart & Winston.

Alonso, A., Alonso, S., & Piper, W. (2003). Group psychotherapy. In G. Stricker, & T. A. Widiger (Eds.), *Handbook of psychology: Vol. 8. Clinical psychology.* New York: Wiley.

Altemeyer, B. (1988a). *Enemies of freedom: Understanding right-wing authoritarianism.* San Francisco: Jossey-Bass.

Altemeyer, B. (1988b). The good soldier, marching in step: A psychological explanation of state terror. *Sciences, March/April,* 30–38.

Altemeyer, B. (1996). *The authoritarian specter.* Cambridge, MA: Harvard University Press.

Altemeyer, B. (1998). The other "authoritarian personality." *Advances in Experimental Social Psychology, 30,* 47–92.

Altman, I., Vinsel, A., & Brown, B. A. (1981). Dialectic conceptions in social psychology: An application to social penetration and privacy regulation. In L. Berkowitz (Ed.), *Advances in experimental social psychology* (Vol. 14). New York: Academic Press.

Amada, G. (1985). *A guide to psychotherapy.* Lanham, MD: Madison Books.

Amato, P. R. (1996). Explaining the intergenerational transmission of divorce. *Journal of Marriage and the Family, 58,* 628–640.

Amato, P. R. (1999). Children of divorced parents as young adults. In E. M. Hetherington (Ed.), *Coping with divorce, single parenting, and remarriage: A risk and resiliency perspective.* Mahwah, NJ: Erlbaum.

Amato, P. R. (2001). The consequences of divorce for adults and children. In R. M. Milardo (Ed.), *Understanding families into the new millennium: A decade in review* (pp. 488–506). Minneapolis, MN: National Council on Family Relations.

Amato, P. R. (2003). Reconciling divergent perspectives: Judith Wallerstein, quantitative family research, and children of divorce. *Family Relations: Interdisciplinary Journal of Applied Family Studies, 52*(4), 332–339.

Amato, P. R. (2004a). Divorce in social and historical context: Changing scientific perspectives on children and marital dissolution. In M. Coleman & L. H. Ganong (Eds.), *Handbook of contemporary families: Considering the past, contemplating the future.* Thousand Oaks, CA: Sage.

Amato, P. R. (2004b). Tension between institutional and individual views of marriage. *Journal of Marriage and Family, 66,* 959–965.

Amato, P. R., & DeBoer, D. D. (2001). The transmission of marital instability across generations: Relationship skills or commitment to marriage? *Journal of Marriage and Family, 63,* 1038–1051.

Amato, P. R., Johnson, D. R., Booth, A., & Rogers, S. J. (2003). Continuity and change in marital quality between 1980 and 2000. *Journal of Marriage and Family, 65,* 1–22.

Amato, P. R., & Previti, D. (2003). People's reasons for divorcing: Gender, social class, the life course, and adjustment. *Journal of Family Issues, 24*(5), 602–626.

Amato, P. R., & Rogers, S. J. (1997). A longitudinal study of marital problems and subsequent divorce. *Journal of Marriage and the Family, 59,* 612–624.

Ambady, N., LaPlante, D., Nguyen, T., Rosenthal, R., Chaumeton, N., & Levinson W. (2002). Surgeon's tone of voice: A clue to malpractice history. *Surgery, 132,* 5–9.

American Association of University Women. (1994). *Shortchanging girls, shortchanging America.* Washington, DC: Author.

American Council on Education. (1997). Many college graduates participate in training courses to improve their job skills. *Higher Education and National Affairs, 46*(19), 3.

American Psychiatric Association. (1994). *Diagnostic and statistical manual of mental disorders* (4th ed.). Washington, DC: Author.

American Psychiatric Association Task Force on Electroconvulsive Therapy. (2001). *The practice of electroconvulsive therapy: Recommendations for treatment* (2nd ed.). Washington, DC: American Psychiatric Association.

Ames, S. C., Jones, G. N., Howe, J. T., & Brantley, P. J. (2001). A prospective study of the impact of stress on quality of life: An investigation of low-income individuals with hypertension. *Annals of Behavioral Medicine, 23*(2), 112–119.

Andersen, B. L., Golden-Kreutz, D. M., & DiLillo, V. (2001). Cancer. In A. Baum, T. A. Revenson, & J. E. Singer (Eds.), *Handbook of health psychology* (pp. 709–726). Mahwah, NJ: Erlbaum.

Andersen, B. L., Kiecolt-Glaser, J. K., & Glaser, R. (1994). A biobehavioral model of cancer stress and disease course. *American Psychologist, 49,* 389–404.

Anderson, C., John, O. P., Keltner, D., & Kring, A. M. (2001). Who attains social status? Effects of personality and physical attractiveness in social groups. *Journal of Personality and Social Psychology, 81*(1), 116–132.

Anderson, C. A., Berkowitz, L., Donnerstein, E., Huesmann, L. R., Johnson, J. D., Linz, D., Malamuth, N. M., & Wartella, E. (2003). The influence of media violence on youth. *Psychological Science in the Public Interest, 4*(3), 81–110.

Anderson, C. A., & Huesmann, L. R. (2003). Human aggression: A social-cognitive view. In M. A. Hogg & J. Cooper (Eds.), *The Sage handbook of social psychology.* Thousand Oaks, CA: Sage Publications.

Anderson, C. A., Miller, R. S., Riger, A. L., Dill, J. C., & Sedikides, C. (1994). Behavioral and characterological attributional styles as predictors of depression and loneliness: Review, refinement, and test. *Journal of Personality and Social Psychology, 66,* 549–558.

Anderson, J. R. (1980). *Cognitive psychology and its implications.* New York: Freeman.

Anderson, K. J. (1990). Arousal and the inverted-U hypothesis: A critique of Neiss's "reconceptualizing arousal." *Psychological Bulletin, 107,* 96–100.

Anderson, K. J., & Leaper, C. (1998). Meta-analyses of gender effects on conversational interruption: Who, what, when, where, and how. *Sex Roles, 39*(3/4), 225–252.

Anderson, P. A. (1999). *Nonverbal communication: Forms and functions.* Mountain View, CA: Mayfield.

Anderson, S. E., Dallal, G. E., & Must, A. (2003). Relative weight and race influence average age at menarche: Results from two nationally representative surveys of U.S. girls studied 25 years apart. *Pediatrics, 111,* 844–850.

Anderson, V. L., Levinson, E. M., Barker, W., & Kiewra, K. R. (1999). The effects of meditation on teacher-perceived occupational stress, state and trait anxiety and burnout. *School Psychology Quarterly, 14,* 3–25.

Anderson-Fye, E. P., & Becker, A. E. (2004). Sociocultural aspects of eating disorders. In J. K. Thompson (Ed.), *Handbook of eating disorders and obesity.* New York: Wiley.

Andreasen, N. C. (1987). The diagnosis of schizophrenia. *Schizophrenia Bulletin, 13,* 9–22.

Andreasen, N. C. (1990). Positive and negative symptoms: Historical and conceptual aspects. In N. C. Andreasen (Ed.), *Modern problems of pharmacopsychiatry: Positive and negative symptoms and syndromes.* Basel: Karger.

Andresen, J. (2000). Meditation meets behavioural medicine: The story of experimental research on meditation. *Journal of Consciousness Studies, 7*(11–12), 17–73.

Angell, M. (2000). Is academic medicine for sale? *New England Journal of Medicine, 342,* 1516–1518.

Angell, M. (2004). *The truth about the drug companies: How they decieve us and what to do about it.* New York: Random House.

Ankey, C. D. (1992). Sex differences in relative brain size: The mismeasure of woman, too? *Intelligence, 16,* 329–336.

Antonucci, T., & Akiyama, H. (1997). Concern with others at midlife: Care, comfort, or compromise? In M. E. Lachman & J. B. James (Eds.), *Multiple paths of midlife development* (pp. 145–169). Chicago: University of Chicago Press.

Antonuccio, D. O., Danton, W. G., & McClanahan, T. M. (2003). Psychology in the presciption era: Building a firewall between marketing and science. *American Psychologist, 58*(12), 1028–1043.

Antony, M. M., & McCabe, R. E. (2003). Anxiety disorders: Social and specific phobias. In A. Tasman, J. Kay, & J. A. Lieberman (Eds.), *Psychiatry.* New York: Wiley.

Apperloo, M. J. A., Van Der Stege, J. G., Hoek, A., & Weijmar Schultz, W. C. M. (2003). In the mood for sex: The value of androgens. *Journal of Sex and Marital Therapy, 29*(2), 87–102.

Aquilino, W. S. (1997). From adolescent to young adult: A prospective study of parent-child relations during the transition to adulthood. *Journal of Marriage and the Family, 59,* 670–686.

Arbona, C. (2005). Promoting the career development and academic achievement of at-risk youth: College access programs. In S. D. Brown & R. W. Lent (Eds.), *Career development and counseling: Putting theory and research to work.* New York: Wiley.

Archer, J. (1996). Sex differences in social behavior: Are the social role and evolutionary explanations compatible? *American Psychologist, 51,* 909–917.

Archer, J. (2005). Are women or men the more aggressive sex? In S. Fein, G. R. Goethals, & M. J. Sandstrom (Eds.), *Gender and aggression: Interdisciplinary perspectives.* Mahwah, NJ: Erlbaum.

Arendell, T. (2000). Conceiving and investigating motherhood: The decade's scholarship. *Journal of Marriage and the Family, 62*(4), 1192–1207.

Argyle, M. (1987). *The psychology of happiness.* London: Metheun.

Argyle, M. (1999). Causes and correlates of happiness. In D. Kahneman, E. Diener, & N. Schwarz (Eds.), *Well-being: The foundations of hedonic psychology* (pp. 353–373). New York: Sage.

Argyle, M. (2001). *The psychology of happiness* (2nd ed.). New York: Routledge.

Argyle, M., & Henderson, M. (1984). The rules of friendship. *Journal of Social and Personal Relationships, 1,* 211–237.

Ariely, D., & Wertenbroch, K. (2002). Procrastination, deadlines, and performance: Self-control by precommitment. *Psychological Science, 13*(3), 219–224.

Aries, E. (1998). Gender differences in interaction: A reexamination. In D. J. Canary & K. Dindia (Eds.), *Sex differences and similarities in communication: Critical essays and empirical investigations of sex and gender in interaction* (pp. 65–81). Mahwah, NJ: Erlbaum.

Armbruster, B. B. (2000). Taking notes from lectures. In R. F. Flippo & D. C. Caverly (Eds.), *Handbook of college reading and study strategy research.* Mahwah, NJ: Erlbaum.

Armour, S. (2004, May 4). Some moms quit as offices scrap family-friendliness. *USA Today,* pp. 1A–2A.

Arndt, J., Goldenberg, J. L., Greenberg, J., Pyszczynski, T., & Solomon, S. (2000). Death can be hazardous to your health: Adaptive and ironic consequences of defenses against the terror of death. In P. R. Duberstein & J. M. Masling (Eds.), *Psychodynamic perspectives on sickness and health.* Washington, DC: American Psychological Association.

Arnett, J. J. (1999). Adolescent storm and stress, reconsidered. *American Psychologist, 54*(5), 317–326.

Arnkoff, D. B., & Glass, C. R. (1992). Cognitive therapy and psychotherapy. In D. K. Freedheim (Ed.), *History of psycho-therapy: A century of change.* Washington, DC: American Psychological Association.

Arnold, K. D. (1995). *Lives of promise: What becomes of high school valedictorians.* San Francisco: Jossey-Bass.

Arnold, L. M. (2000). Psychocutaneous disorders. In B. J. Sadock & V. A. Sadock (Eds.), *Kaplan and Sadock's comprehensive textbook of psychiatry* (7th ed., pp. 1818–1827). Philadelphia: Lippincott/Williams & Wilkins.

Aron, A. (1988). The matching hypothesis reconsidered again: Comment on Kalick and Hamilton. *Journal of Personality and Social Psychology, 54,* 441–446.

Aron, A., Norman, C. C., Aron, E. N., McKenna, C., & Heyman, R. E. (2000). Couples' shared participation in novel and arousing activities and experienced relationship quality. *Journal of Personality and Social Psychology, 78,* 273–284.

Aron, A., & Westbay, L. (1996). Dimensions of the prototype of love. *Journal of Personality and Social Psychology, 70,* 535–551.

Aron, E. N., & Aron, A. (1997). Sensory-processing sensitivity and its relation to introversion and emotionality. *Journal of Personality and Social Psychology, 73*(2), 345–368.

Aronson, E., & Patnoe, S. (1997). *Cooperation in the classroom: The jigsaw method.* New York: Longman.

Arrigo, J. M., & Pezdek, K. (1997). Lessons from the study of psychogenic amnesia. *Current Directions in Psychological Science, 6,* 148–152.

Asch, S. E. (1955). Opinions and social pressures. *Scientific American, 193*(5), 31–35.

Asch, S. E. (1956). Studies of independence and conformity: A minority of one against a unanimous majority. *Psychological Monographs, 70* (9, Whole No. 416).

Asher, S., & Paquette, J. A. (2003). Loneliness and peer relations in childhood. *Current Directions in Psychological Science, 12*(3), 75–78.

Ashmore, R. D. (1990). Sex, gender, and the individual. In L. A. Pervin (Ed.), *Handbook of personality* (pp. 486–526). New York: Guilford Press.

Ashton, M. C., Lee, K., Perugini, M. , Szarota, P., de Vries, R. E., Di Blas, L., Boies, K., & De Raad, B. (2004). A six-factor structure of personality-descriptive adjectives: Solutions from psycholexical studies in seven languages. *Journal of Personality and Social Psychology, 86*(2), 356–366.

Aspinwall, L. G., Richter, L., & Hoffman R. R., III. (2001). Understanding how optimism works: An examination of optimists' adaptive moderation of belief and behavior. In E. C. Chang (Ed.), *Optimism and pessimism: Implications for theory, research, and practice* (pp. 217–238). Washington, DC: American Psychological Association.

Aspinwall, L. G., & Staudinger, U. M. (2003). A psychology of human strengths: Some central issues of an emerging field. In L. G. Aspinwall & U. M. Staudinger (Eds.), *A psychology of human strengths: Fundamental questions and future directions for a positive psychology.* Washington, DC: American Psychological Association.

Athenstaedt, U., Haas, E., & Schwab, S. (2004). Gender role self-concept and gender-typed communication behavior in mixed-sex and same-sex dyads. *Sex Roles, 50*(1/2), 37–52.

Atwood, J., & Seifer, M. (1997). Extramarital affairs and constructed meanings: A social constructionist therapeutic approach. *American Journal of Family Therapy, 25,* 55–75.

Atwood, J. D., & Gagnon, J. H. (1987). Masturbatory behavior in college youth. *Journal of Sex Education and Therapy, 13*(2), 35–42.

Aubé, J., & Koestner, R. (1995). Gender characteristics and relationship adjustment: Another look at similarity-complementarity hypotheses. *Journal of Personality, 63,* 879–904.

Aubin, S., & Heiman, J. R. (2004). Sexual dysfunction from a relationship perspective. In J. H. Harvey , A. Wenzel & S. Sprecher (Eds.), *The handbook of sexuality in close relationships.* Mahwah, NJ: Lawrence Erlbaum.

Auerbach, S. M., & Gramling, S. E. (1998). *Stress management psychological foundations.* Upper Saddle River, NJ: Prentice-Hall.

Ayanian, J. Z., & Cleary, P. D. (1999). Perceived risks of heart disease and cancer among cigarette smokers. *Journal of the American Medical Association, 281*(11), 1019–1021.

Ayres, J. J. B. (1998). Fear conditioning and avoidance. In W. O'Donohue (Ed.), *Learning and behavior therapy* . Boston, MA: Allyn and Bacon.

Babcock, J. C., Green, C. E., & Robie, C. (2004). Does batterers' treatment work? A meta-analytic review of domestic violence treatment. *Clinical Psychology Review, 23*(8), 1023–1053.

Bacon, J. B. (1996). Support groups for bereaved children. In C. A. Corr & D. M. Corr (Eds.), *Handbook of childhood death and bereavement.* New York: Springer-Verlag.

Badgett, M. V. L. (2003). Employment and sexual orientation: Disclosure and discrimination in the workplace. In L. D. Garnets & D. C. Kimmel (Eds.), *Psychological perspectives on lesbian, gay, and bisexual experiences* (2nd ed,). New York: Columbia University Press.

Bagley, C. (1995). *Child sexual abuse and mental health in adolescents and adults.* Aldershot, UK: Ashgate.

Bailey, J. M. (2003). Biological perspectives on sexual orientation. In L. D. Garnets & D. C. Kimmel (Eds.), *Psychological perspectives on lesbian, gay, and bisexual experiences* (2nd ed.). New York: Columbia University Press.

Bailey, J. M., & Dawood, K. (1998). Behavior genetics, sexual orientation, and the family. In C. J. Patterson & A. R. D'Augelli (Eds.), *Lesbian, gay and bisexual identities in families: Psychological perspectives.* New York: Oxford University Press.

Bailey, J. M., Dunne, M. P., & Martin, N. G. (2000). Genetic and environmental influences on sexual orientation and its correlates in an Australian twin sample. *Journal of Personality and Social Psychology, 78*(3), 524–536.

Bailey, J. M., Kim, P. Y., Hills, A. , & Linsenmeier, J. A. W. (1997). Butch, femme, or straight acting? Partner preferences of gay men and lesbians. *Journal of Personality and Social Psychology, 73*(5), 960–973.

Bailey, J. M., & Pillard, R. C. (1991). A genetic study of male sexual orientation. *Archives of General Psychiatry, 48,* 1089–1096.

Bailey, J. M., Pillard, R. C., Neale, M. C., & Agyei, Y. (1993). Heritable factors influence sexual orientation in women. *Archives of General Psychiatry, 50,* 217–223.

Bailey, J. M., Willerman, L., & Parks, C. (1991). A test of maternal stress theory of human male homosexuality. *Archives of Sexual Behavior, 20,* 277–294.

Bailey, J. M., & Zucker, K. J. (1995). Childhood sex-typed behavior and sexual orientation: A conceptual analysis and quantitative review. *Developmental Psychology, 31,* 43–55.

Baker, F., Ainsworth, S. R., Dye, J. T., Crammer, C., Thun, M. J., Hoffmann, D., Repace, J. L., Henningfield, J. E., Slade, J., Pinney, J., Shanks, T., Burns, D. M., Connolly, G. N., & Shopland, D. R. (2000). Health risks associated with cigar smoking. *Journal of the American Medical Association, 284,* 735–740.

Baker, O. (1996). Managing diversity: Implications for white managers. In B. P. Bowser & R. G. Hunt (Eds.), *Impacts of racism on white Americans.* Newbury Park, CA: Sage.

Baldessarini, R. J. (2001). Drugs and the treatment of psychiatric disorders: Depression and the anxiety disorders. In J. G. Hardman & L. E. Limbird (Eds.), *Goodman & Gilman's The pharmacological basis of therapeutics.* New York: McGraw-Hill.

Baldwin, M., & Fehr, B. (1995). On the instability of attachment style ratings. *Personal Relationships, 2,* 247–261.

Ballenger, J. C. (2000). Benzodiazepine receptor agonists and antagonists. In B. J. Sadock & V. A. Sadock (Eds.), *Kaplan and Sadock's comprehensive textbook of psychiatry.* Philadelphia: Lippincott/Williams & Wilkins.

Bancroft, J. (2002a). Biological factors in human sexuality. *The Journal of Sex Research, 39*(1), 15–21.

Bancroft, J. (2002b). The medicalization of female sexual dysfunction: The need for caution. *Archives of Sexual Behavior, 31*(5), 451–455.

Bandura, A. (1973). *Aggression: A social learning analysis.* Englewood Cliffs, NJ: Prentice-Hall.

Bandura, A. (1977). *Social learning theory.* Englewood Cliffs, NJ: Prentice-Hall.

Bandura, A. (1986). *Social foundations of thought and action: A social-cognitive theory.* Englewood Cliffs, NJ: Prentice-Hall.

Bandura, A. (1990a). Perceived self-efficacy in the exercise of personal agency. *Journal of Applied Sport Psychology, 2,* 128–163.

Bandura, A. (1990b). Self-regulation of motivation through goal systems. In R. A. Dienstbier (Ed.), *Nebraska symposium on motivation* (Vol. 38). Lincoln: University of Nebraska Press.

Bandura, A. (1993). Perceived self-efficacy in cognitive development and functioning. *Educational Psychologist, 28,* 117–148.

Bandura, A. (1997). *Self-efficacy: The exercise of control.* New York: W. H. Freeman.

Bandura, A. (1999a). A sociocognitive analysis of substance abuse: An agentic perspective. *Psychological Science, 10*(3), 214–217.

Bandura, A. (1999b). Social cognitive theory of personality. In L. A. Pervin & O. P. John (Eds.), *Handbook of personality: Theory and research* (2nd ed., pp. 154–196). New York: Guilford Press.

Bandura, A. (2000). Social cognitive theory: An agentic perspective. *Annual Review of Psychology, 52,* 1–26.

Bank, B. J., & Hansford, S. L. (2000). Gender and friendship: Why are men's best same-sex friendships less intimate and supportive? *Personal Relationships, 7*(1), 63–78.

Banks, A., & Gartrell, N. K. (1995). Hormones and sexual orientation: A questionable link. *Journal of Homosexuality, 28,* 247–268.

Banse, R., & Scherer, K. R. (1996). Acoustic profiles in vocal emotion expression. *Journal of Personality and Social Psychology, 70*(3), 614636.

Banyard, V. L., & Williams, L. M. (1999). Memories for child sexual abuse and mental health functioning: Findings on a sample of women and implications for future research. In L. M. Williams & V. L. Banyard (Eds.), *Trauma & memory.* Thousand Oaks, CA: Sage.

Barber, B. K. (1994). Cultural, family, and personal contexts of parent-adolescent conflict. *Journal of Marriage and the Family, 56,* 375–386.

Bargh, J. A. (1997). The automaticity of everyday life. In R. S. Wyer Jr.(Ed.), *Advances in social cognition* (Vol. 10). Mahwah, NJ: Erlbaum.

Bargh, J. A. (1999). The cognitive monster: The case against the controllability of automatic stereotype effects. In S. Chaiken & Y. Trope (Eds.), *Dual process theories in social psychology.* New York: Guilford.

Bargh, J. A., & McKenna, K. Y. A. (2004). The Internet and social life. *Annual Review of Psychology, 55,* 573–590.

Bargh, J. A., McKenna, K. Y. A., & Fitzsimons, G. M. (2002). Can you see the real me? Activation and expression of the "true self" on the Internet. *Journal of Social Issues, 58*(1), 33–48.

Barlett, D. L., & Steele, J. B. (1979). *Empire: The life, legend and madness of Howard Hughes.* New York: Norton.

Barlow, D. H. (1996a). Health care policy, psychotherapy research, and the future of psychotherapy. *American Psychologist, 50,* 1050–1058.

Barlow, D. H. (1996b). The effectiveness of psychotherapy: Science and policy. *Clinical Psychology: Science & Practice, 3*(3), 236–240.

Barlow, D. H., & Durand, V. M. (1999). *Abnormal psychology: An Investigative approach.* Belmont, CA: Wadsworth.

Barlow, D. H., Pincus, D. B., Heinrichs, N., & Choate, M. L. (2003). Anxiety disorders. In G. Stricker & T. A. Widiger (Eds.), *Handbook of psychology: Vol. 8. Clinical psychology.* New York: Wiley.

Barnes, M. L., & Buss, D. M. (1985). Sex differences in the interpersonal behavior of married couples. *Journal of Personality and Social Psychology, 48,* 654–661.

Barnes, V. A., Treiber, F., & Davis, H. (2001). The Impact of Transcendental Meditation on cardiovascular function at rest and during acute stress in adolescents with high norspeed in old age. *Current Directions in Psychological Science, 6,* 163–169.

Barnett, D, Ganiban, J., & Cicchetti, D. (1999). Maltreatment, negative expressivity, and the development of Type D attachments from 12 to 24 months of age. *Monographs of the Society for Research in Child Development, 64*(3, Serial No. 258).

Barnett, H. L., Keel, P. K., & Conoscenti, L. M. (2001). Body type preferences in Asian and Caucasian college students. *Sex Roles, 45* (11–12), 867–878.

Barnett, O. W., & LaViolette, A. D. (1993). *It could happen to anyone: Why battered women stay.* Thousand Oaks, CA: Sage.

Barnett, R. C., & Hyde, J. S. (2001). Women, men, work, and family: An expansionist theory. *American Psychologist, 56*(10), 781–796.

Baron, R. A., & Byrne, D. (1997). *Social psychology.* Boston: Allyn & Bacon.

Baron, R. A., Neuman, J. H., & Geddes, D. (1999). Social and personal determinants of workplace aggression: Evidence for the impact of perceived injustice and the Type A behavior pattern. *Aggressive Behavior, 25*(4), 261–296.

Baron, R. S. (2000). Arousal, capacity, and intense indoctrination. *Personality and Social Psychology Review, 4*(3), 238–254.

Barrick, C. B. (1999). Sad, glad, or mad hearts? Epidemiological evidence for a causal relationship between mood disorders and coronary artery disease. *Journal of Affective Disorders, 53*(2), 193–201.

Barsky, A. J. (1988). The paradox of health. *New England Journal of Medicine, 318*, 414–418.

Barsky, A. J. (2001). Somatosensory amplification and hypochondriasis. In V. Starcevic & D. R. Lipsitt (Eds.), *Hypochondriasis: Modern perspectives on an ancient malady.* New York: Oxford University Press.

Barsky, A. J., Coeytaux, R. R., Sarnie, M. K., & Cleary, P. D. (1993). Hypochondriacal patients' beliefs about good health. *American Journal of Psychiatry, 150*, 1085–1090.

Bartholomew, K. (1990). Avoidance of intimacy: An attachment perspective. *Journal of Social and Personal Relationships, 7*, 47–178.

Bartholomew, K., & Horowitz, L. M. (1991). Attachment styles among young adults: A test of a four-category model. *Journal of Personality and Social Psychology, 61*, 226–244.

Bartlett, M. S., Hager, J. C., Ekman, P., & Sejnowski, T. J. (1999). Measuring facial expressions by computer image analysis. *Psychophysiology, 36*, 253–263.

Baruch, G. K. (1984). The psychological well-being of women in the middle years. In G. K. Baruch & J. Brooks-Gunn (Eds.), *Women in midlife.* New York: Plenum.

Basow, S. A. (1992). *Gender stereotypes and roles* (3rd ed.). Pacific Grove, CA: Brooks/Cole.

Basow, S. A., & Rubenfeld, K. (2003). "Troubles Talk": Effects of gender and gender-typing. *Sex Roles, 48*(3/4), 183–187.

Bauer, M. S. (2003). Mood disorders: Bipolar (manic-depressive) disorders. In A. Tasman, J. Kay, & J. A. Lieberman (Eds.), *Psychiatry.* New York: Wiley.

Baumeister, R. F. (1984). Choking under pressure: Self-consciousness and paradoxical effects of incentives on skillful performance. *Journal of Personality and Social Psychology, 46*, 610–620.

Baumeister, R. F. (1989). The optimal margin of illusion. *Journal of Social and Clinical Psychology, 8*, 176–189.

Baumeister, R. F. (1995). Disputing the effects of championship pressures and home audiences. *Journal of Personality and Social Psychology, 68*, 644–648.

Baumeister, R. F. (1997). Esteem threat, self-regulatory breakdown, and emotional distress as factors in self defeating behavior. *Review of General Psychology, 1*, 145–174.

Baumeister, R. F. (1998). The self. In D. T. Gilbert, S. T. Fiske, & G. Lindzey (Eds.), *The handbook of social psychology.* Boston: Mcgraw-Hill.

Baumeister, R. F. (1999). The nature and structure of the self: An overview. In R. F. Baumeister (Ed.), *The self in social psychology* (pp. 1–20). Ann Arbor, MI: Edwards Bros.

Baumeister, R. F. (2000). Gender differences in erotic plasticity: The female sex drive as socially flexible and responsive. *Psychological Bulletin, 126*(3), 347–374.

Baumeister, R. F., & Bratslavsky, E. (1999). Passion, intimacy, and time: Passionate love as a function of change in intimacy. *Personality and Social Psychology Review, 3*(1), 49–67.

Baumeister, R. F., Bratslavsky, E., Muraven, M., & Tice, D. M. (1998). Ego depletion: Is the active self

a limited resource? *Journal of Personality and Social Psychology, 74*(5), 1252–1265.

Baumeister, R. F., Bushman, B. J., & Campbell, W. K. (2000). Self-esteem, narcissism, and aggression: Does violence result from low self-esteem or from threatened egotism? *Current Directions in Psychological Science, 9*(1), 26–29.

Baumeister, R. F., Campbell, J. D., Krueger, J. I., & Vohs, K. D. (2003). Does high self-esteem cause better performance, interpersonal success, happiness, or healthier lifestyles? *Psychological Science in the Public Interest, 4*(1), 1–44.

Baumeister, R. F., & Leary, M. R. (1995). The need to belong: Desire for interpersonal attachments as a fundamental human motivation. *Psychological Bulletin, 117*(3), 497–529.

Baumeister, R. F., Muraven, M., & Tice, D. M. (2000). Ego depletion: A resource model of volition, self regulation, and controlled processing. *Social Cognition, 18*(2), 130–150.

Baumeister, R. F., & Scher, S. J. (1988). Self-defeating behavior patterns among normal individuals: Review and analysis of common self-destructive tendencies. *Psychological Bulletin, 104*(1), 3–22.

Baumeister, R. F., Smart, L., & Boden, J. M. (1996). Relation of threatened egotism to violence and aggression: The dark side of high self-esteem. *Psychological Review, 103*, 5–33.

Baumeister, R. F., & Sommer, K. L. (1997). What do men want? Gender differences and two spheres of belongingness: Comment on Cross and Madson (1997). *Psychological Bulletin, 122*(1), 38–44.

Baumeister, R. F., & Steinhilber, A. (1984). Paradoxical effects of supportive audiences on performance under pressure: The home field disadvantage in sports championships. *Journal of Personality and Social Psychology, 47*, 85–93.

Baumeister, R. F., & Twenge, J. M. (2003). The social self. In T. Millon & M. J. Lerner (Eds.) *Handbook of psychology: Vol. 5. Personality and social psychology.* New York: Wiley.

Baumeister, R. F., & Vohs, K. D. (2003). Self regulation and the executive function of the self. In M.R. Leary & J. P. Tangney (Eds.), *Handbook of Self and Identity.* New York: Guilford.

Baumrind, D. (1964). Some thoughts on the ethics of reading Milgram's "Behavioral study of obedience." *American Psychologist, 19*, 421–423.

Baumrind, D. (1967). Child care practices anteceding three patterns of preschool behavior. *Genetic Psychology Monographs, 75*, 43–88.

Baumrind, D. (1971). Current patterns of parental authority. *Developmental Psychology Monographs, 4* (1, Part 2).

Baumrind, D. (1978). Parental disciplinary patterns and social competence in children. *Youth and Society, 9*, 239–276.

Baumrind, D. (1991). The influence of parenting style on adolescent competence and sustance abuse. *Journal of Early Adolescence, 11*(1), 56–95.

Baumrind, D., Larzelere, R. E., & Cowan, P. A. (2002). Ordinary physical punishment: Is it harmful? Comment on Gershoff (2002). *Psychological Bulletin, 128*(4), 580–589.

Bavelas, J. B., Coates, L., & Johnson, T. (2002). Listener responses as a collaborative process: The role of gaze. *Journal of Communication, 52*(3), 566–580.

Baxter, L. A. (1988). A dialectical perspective on communication strategies in relationship development. In S. Duck (Ed.), *Handbook of personal relationships.* New York: Wiley.

Bay-Cheng, L. Y., Zucker, A. N., Stewart, A. J., & Pomerleau, C. S. (2002). Linking femininity, weight concern, and mental health among Latina, black, and white women. *Psychology of Women Quarterly, 26*(1), 36–45.

Beck, A. T. (1976). *Cognitive therapy and the emotional disorders.* New York: International Universities Press.

Beck, A. T. (1987). Cognitive therapy. In J. K. Zeig (Ed.), *The evolution of psychotherapy.* New York: Brunner/Mazel.

Beck, A. T. (1991). Cognitive therapy: A 30-year retrospective. *American Psychologist, 46*, 368–375.

Beck, A. T. (1997). Cognitive therapy: Reflections. In J. K. Zeig (Ed.), *The evolution of psychotherapy: The third conference .* New York: Brunner/Mazel.

Becker, B. J. (1986). Influence again: Another look at gender differences in social influence. In J. S. Hyde & M. C. Linn (Eds.), *The psychology of gender: Advances through meta-analysis.* Baltimore: Johns Hopkins University Press.

Beer, J. M., Arnold, R. D., & Loehlin, J. C. (1998). Genetic and environmental influences on MMPI factor scale: Joint model fitting to twin and adoption data. *Journal of Personality and Social Psychology, 74*, 818–827.

Behar, R. (1991, May 6). The thriving cult of greed and power. *Time,* pp. 50–77.

Beisecker, A. E. (1990). Patient power in doctor-patient communication: What do we know? *Health Communication, 2,* 105–122.

Bekelman, J. E., Li, Y., & Gross, C. P. (2003). Scope and impact of financial conflicts of interests in biomedical research. *Journal of the American Medical Association, 289,* 454–465.

Bell, A. P., & Weinberg, M. S. (1978). *Homosexualities: A study of diversity among men and women.* New York: Simon & Schuster.

Bell, A. P., Weinberg, M. S., & Hammersmith, K. S. (1981). *Sexual preference—Its development in men and women.* Bloomington: Indiana University Press.

Bell, R. A. (1991). Gender, friendship network density, and loneliness. *Journal of Social Behavior and Personality, 6,* 45–56.

Bellack, A. S., Gearon, J. S., & Blanchard, J. J. (2000). Schizophrenia: Psychopathology. In M. Hersen & A. S. Bellack (Eds.), *Psychopathology in adulthood.* Boston: Allyn & Bacon.

Beller, M., & Gafni, N. (1996). The 1991 international assessment of educational progress in mathematics and sciences: The gender differences perspective. *Journal of Educational Psychology, 88,* 365–377.

Belluck, P. (2000, April 21). States declare war on divorce rates before any I do's. *New York Times,* p. A1.

Belmore, S. M. (1987). Determinants of attention during impression formation. *Journal of Experimental Psychology: Learning, Memory, and Cognition, 13,* 480–489.

Belsky, J. (1992). Consequences of child care for children's development: A deconstructionist view. In A. Booth (Ed.), *Child care in the 1990s.* Hillsdale, NJ: Erlbaum.

Belsky, J., & Kelly, J. (1994). *The transition to parenthood.* New York: Dell.

Bem, D. J. (2000). Exotic becomes erotic: Interpreting the biological correlates of sexual orientation. *Archives of Sexual Behavior, 29*(6), 531–548.

Bem, S. L. (1975, September). Androgyny vs. the tight little lives of fluffy women and chesty men. *Psychology Today,* pp. 58–62.

Bem, S. L. (1983). Gender schema theory and its implications for child development: Raising gender-aschematic children in a gender-schematic society. *Signs, 8,* 598–616.

Bem, S. L. (1985). Androgyny and gender schema theory: A conceptual and empirical integration. In T. B. Sonderegger (Ed.), *Nebraska symposium on motivation 1984: Psychology and gender* (Vol. 32). Lincoln: University of Nebraska Press.

Bem, S. L. (1993). The lenses of gender: *Transforming the debate on sexual inequality.* New Haven, CT: Yale University Press.

Benbow, C. P. (1988). Sex differences in mathematical reasoning ability in intellectually talented preadolescents: Their nature, effects, and possible causes. *Behavioral and Brain Sciences, 11,* 169–232.

Bender, R., Jockel, K. H., Trautner, C., Spraul, M., & Berger, M. (1999). Effect of age on excess mortality in obesity. *Journal of the American Medical Association, 281,* 1498–1504.

Bendis, D. (1997, May). A dose of moral adrenaline from Dr. Laura. *The Christian Century,* 476–478.

Benet, V., & Waller, N. G. (1995). The big seven factor model of personality description: Evidence for its cross-cultural generality in a Spanish sample. *Journal of Personality and Social Psychology, 69,* 701–718.

Benjamin, L. T., Jr., Cavell, T. A., & Shallenberger, W. R., III. (1984). Staying with initial answers on objective tests: Is it a myth? *Teaching of Psychology, 11,* 133–141.

Benson, H. (1975). *The relaxation response* (1st ed.). New York: Morrow.

Benson, H. (1984). *Beyond the relaxation response.* Times Books.

Benson, H., & Klipper, M. Z. (1988). *The relaxation response* (2nd ed.). New York: Avon.

Berenbaum, S. A., & Snyder, E. (1995). Early hormonal influences on childhood sex-typed activity and playmate preferences: Implications for the development of sexual orientation. *Developmental Psychology, 31,* 31–42.

Bergen, D. J., & Williams, J. E. (1991). Sex stereotypes in the United States revisited: 1972–1988. *Sex Roles, 24,* 413–423.

Berkman, C. S., & Gurland, B. J. (1998). The relationship between ethnoracial group and functional level in older persons. *Ethnicity and Health, 3*(3), 175–188.

Berkowitz, L. (1989). Frustration-aggression hypothesis: Examination and reformulation. *Psychological Bulletin, 106,* 59–73.

Berkowitz, L. (1993). *Aggression: Its causes, consequences, and control.* New York: McGraw-Hill.

Berkowitz, L. (1999). Evil is more than banal: Situationism and the concept of evil. *Personality and Social Psychology Review, 3*(3), 246–253.

Berkowitz, R. I. (2003). Behavior therapies. In R. E. Hales & S. C. Yudofsky (Eds.), *Textbook of clinical psychiatry.* Washington, DC: American Psychiatric Publishing.

Berliner, K., Jacob, D., & Schwartzberg, N. (1999). The single adult and the family life cycle. In B. Carter & M. McGoldrick (Eds.), *The expanded family life cycle: Individual, family, and social perspectives* (3rd ed., pp. 362–372). Boston: Allyn & Bacon.

Berliner, L., & Briere, J. (1999). Trauma, memory, and clinical practice. In L. M. Williams & V. L. Banyard (Eds.), *Trauma & memory.* Thousand Oaks, CA: Sage.

Berman, J. J., Murphy-Berman, V., & Pachauri, A. (1988). Sex differences in friendship patterns in India and in the United States. *Basic and Applied Social Psychology, 9,* 61–71.

Bernard, L. C., & Krupat, E. (1994). *Health psychology: Biopsychosocial factors in health and illness.* Fort Worth, TX: Harcourt Brace.

Berne, E. (1964). *Games people play.* New York: Grove Press.

Berne, P. H., & Savary, L. M. (1993). *Building self-esteem in children.* New York: Continuum.

Bernstein, H. J., Beale, M. D., Burns, C., & Kellner, C. H. (1998). Patient attitudes about ECT after treatment. *Psychiatric Annals, 28,* 524–527.

Berrington, A., & Diamond, I. (1999). Marital dissolution among the 1958 British birth cohort: The role of cohabitation. *Population Studies, 53,* 19–38.

Berry, D. S., Pennebaker, J. W., Mueller, J. S., & Hiller, W. S. (1997). Linguistic bases of social perception. *Personality and Social Psychology Bulletin, 23*(5), 526–537.

Berry, J. W., & Ataca, B. (2000). Cultural factors. In G. Fink (Ed.), *Encyclopedia of stress* (Vol. 1, pp. 604–610). San Diego: Academic Press.

Berscheid, E., & Reis, H. T. (1998). Attraction and close relationships. In D. T. Gilbert, S. T. Fiske, & G. Lindzey (Eds.), *The handbook of social psychology* (Vol. 2). Boston: McGraw-Hill.

Berscheid, E., Snyder, M., & Omoto, A. M. (1989). The relationship closeness inventory: Assessing the closeness of interpersonal relationships. *Journal of Personality and Social Psychology, 57,* 792–807.

Berscheid, E., & Walster, E. (1978). *Interpersonal attraction.* Reading, MA: Addison-Wesley.

Bertakis, K. D., Azari, R., Helms, J. L., Callahan, E. J., & Robbins, J. A. (2000). Gender differences in the utilization of health care services. *Journal of Family Practice, 49*(2), 147–152.

Berzon, B. (2004). *Permanent partners: Building gay and lesbian relationships that last.* New York: The Penguin Group.

Berzonsky, M. D., & Kuk, L. S. (2000). Identity status, identity processing style, and the transition to university. *Journal of Adolescent Research, 15*(1), 81–98.

Bettencourt, B. A., & Miller, N. (1996). Gender differences in aggression as a function of provocation: A meta-analysis. *Psychological Bulletin, 119,* 422–447.

Betz, N. E. (1993). Women's career development. In F. L. Denmark & M. A. Paludi (Eds.), *Psychology of women: A handbook of issues and theories.* Westport, CT: Greenwood Press.

Betz, N. E. (2005). Women's career development. In S. D. Brown & R. W. Lent (Eds.), *Career development and counseling: Putting theory and research to work.* New York: Wiley.

Betz, N. E., & Klein, K. L. (1996). Relationships among measures of career self-efficacy, generalized self-efficacy, and global self-esteem. *Journal of Career Assessment, 4*(3), 285–298.

Beumont, P. J. V. (2002). Clinical presentation of anorexia nervosa and bulimia nervosa. In C. G. Fairburn & K. D. Brownell (Eds.), *Eating disorders and obesity: A comprehensive handbook.* New York: Guilford.

Beutler, L. E. (2000). David and Goliath: When empirical and clinical standards of practice meet. *American Psychologist, 55*(9), 997–1007.

Beutler, L. E. (2002). The dodo bird is extinct. *Clinical Psychology: Science & Practice, 9*(1), 30–34.

Beutler, L. E., Bongar, B., & Shurkin, J. N. (1998). *Am I crazy, or is it my shrink?* New York: Oxford University Press.

Beutler, L. E., Bongar, B., & Shurkin, J. N. (2001). *A consumers guide to psychotherapy.* New York: Oxford University Press.

Beutler, L. E., & Harwood, T. M. (2002). What is and can be attributed to the therapeutic relationship? *Journal of Contemporary Psychotherapy, 32*(1), 25–33.

Beutler, L. E., Machado, P. P. P., & Neufeldt, S. A. (1994). Therapist variables. In A. E. Bergin & S. L. Garfield (Eds.), *Handbook of psychotherapy and behavior change* (4th ed.). New York: Wiley.

Bhattachary, S., & Powell, J. H. (2001). Recreational use of 3,4-methylenedioxymethamphetamine (MDMA) or "ecstasy": Evidence for cognitive impairment. *Psychological Medicine, 31*(4), 647–658.

Bianchi, S. (2000). Maternal employment and time with children: Dramatic change or surprising continuity? *Demography, 37,* 401–414.

Bianchi, S., Milkie, M. A., Sayer, L. C., & Robinson, J. P. (2000). Is anyone doing the housework? Trends in the gender division of household labor. *Social Forces, 79*(1), 191–228.

Bianchi, S. M., & Casper, L. M. (2000). American families. *Population Bulletin* (Vol. 55, Chap. 4). Washington, DC: Population Reference Bureau.

Bianchi, S. M., Subaiya, L., & Kahn, J. R. (1999). The gender gap in the economic well-being of nonresident fathers and custodial mothers. *Demography, 36,* 195–203.

Bierly, M. M. (1985). Prejudice toward contemporary outgroups as a generalized attitude. *Journal of Applied Social Psychology, 15,* 189–199.

Biernat, M., & Billings, L. S. (2001). Standards, expectancies and social comparison. In A. Tesser & N. Schwarz (Eds.), *Blackwell handbook of social psychology: Intraindividual processes.* Malden, MA: Blackwell.

Biernat, M., & Kobrynowicz, D. (1997). Gender- and race-based standards of competence: Lower minimum standards but higher ability standards for devalued groups. *Journal of Personality and Social Psychology, 72*(3), 544–557.

Bierut, L. J., Heath, A. C., Bucholz, K. K., Dinwiddie, S. H., Madden, P. A. F., Statham, D. J., Dunne, M. P., & Martin, N. G. (1999). Major depressive disorder in a community-based twin sample. *Archives of General Psychiatry, 56,* 557–563.

Bishop, S. R. (2002). What do we really know about mindfulness-based stress reduction? *Psychosomatic Medicine, 64*(1), 71–83.

Bitter, R. G. (1986). Late marriage and marital instability: The effects of heterogeneity and inflexibility. *Journal of Marriage and the Family, 48,* 631–640.

Björntorp, P. (2002). Definition and classification of obesity. In C. G. Fairburn & K. D. Brownell (Eds.), *Eating disorders and obesity: A comprehensive handbook.* New York: Guilford.

Black, D. W., & Andreasen, N. C. (1994). Schizophrenia, schizophreniform disorder, and delusional (paranoid) disorder. In R. E. Hales, S. C. Yudofsky, & J. A. Talbott (Eds.), *The American Psychiatric Press textbook of psychiatry* (2nd ed.). Washington, DC: American Psychiatric Press.

Blacker, D., & Tsuang, M. T. (1999). Classification and DSM-IV. In A. M. Nicholi (Ed.), *The Harvard guide to psychiatry* (pp. 65–83). Cambridge, MA: Harvard University Press.

Blacker, L. (1999). The launching phase of the life cycle. In B. Carter & M. McGoldrick (Eds.), *The expanded family life cycle: Individual, family, and social perspectives* (3rd ed., pp. 287–306). Boston: Allyn & Bacon.

Blair, S. N., Cheng, Y., & Holder, J. S. (2001). Is physical activity or physical fitness more important in defining health benefits? *Medicine and Science in Sports and Exercise, 33,* S379–S399.

Blakemore, J. E. O. (2003). Children's beliefs about violating gender norms: Boys shouldn't look like girls, and girls shouldn't act like boys. *Sex Roles, 48*(9/10), 411–419.

Blanchard, E. B., & Keefer, L. (2003). Irritable bowel syndrome. In A. M. Nezu, C. M. Nezu, & P. A. Geller (Eds.), *Handbook of psychology: Vol. 9. Health psychology.* New York: Wiley.

Blanco, C., Laje, G., Olfson, M., Marcus, S. C., & Pincus, H. A. (2002). Trends in the treatment of bipolar disorder by outpatient psychiatrists. *American Journal of Psychiatry, 159,* 1005–1010.

Blass, T. (1999). The Milgram paradigm after 35 years: Some things we now know about obedience to authority. *Journal of Applied Social Psychology, 29*(5), 955–978.

Blazer, D. G. (2000). Mood disorders: Epidemiology. In B. J. Sadock & V. A. Sadock (Eds.), *Kaplan and Sadock's Comprehensive textbook of psychiatry* (7th ed., Vol. 1). Philadelphia: Lippincott/Williams & Wilkins.

Bleier, R. (1984). *Science and gender: A critique of biology and its theories on women.* New York: Pergamon Press.

Block, J. H. (1973). Conceptions of sex role: Some cross-cultural and longitudinal perspectives. *American Psychologist, 28,* 512–526.

Bloodworth, R. C. (1987). Major problems associated with marijuana abuse. *Psychiatric Medicine, 3,* 173–184.

Bloomfield, H. (2000). *Making peace with your past: The six essential steps to enjoying a great future.* New York: HarperCollins.

Bloomfield, H. H., & Kory, R. B. (1976). *Happiness: The TM program, psychiatry, and enlightenment*. New York: Simon & Schuster.

Blumenthal, J. A., Jiang, W., Babyak, M. A., Krantz, D. S., Frid, D. J., Coleman, R. E., Waugh, R., Hanson, M., Applebaum, M., O'Connor, C., & Morris, J. J. (1997). Stress management and exercise training in cardiac patients with myocardial ischemia: Effects on prognosis and evaluation of mechanisms. *Archives of Internal Medicine, 157*, 2213–2223.

Blumstein, P., & Schwartz, P. (1983). *American couples: Money, work, sex*. New York: Morrow.

Blustein, D. L., Prezioso, M. S., & Schultheiss, D. P. (1995). Current status and future directions. *The Counseling Psychologist, 23*, 416–432.

Bobek, B. L., & Robbins, S. B. (2005). Counseling for career transition: Career pathing, job loss, and reentry. In S. D. Brown & R. W. Lent (Eds.), *Career development and counseling: Putting theory and research to work*. New York: Wiley.

Boden, J. M., & Baumeister, R. F. (1997). Repressive coping: Distraction using pleasant thoughts and memories. *Journal of Personality and Social Psychology, 73*(1), 45–62.

Bodenhausen, G. V. (1988). Stereotypic biases in social decision making and memory: Testing process models of stereotype use. *Journal of Personality and Social Psychology, 55*, 726–737.

Bodenhausen. G. V., Macrae, C. N., & Hugenberg, K. (2003). Social cognition. In T. Millon, & M. J. Lerner (Eds.) *Handbook of psychology: Vol. 5. Personality and social psychology*. New York: Wiley.

Bodenheimer, T. (2000). Uneasy alliance: Clinical investigators and the pharmaceutical industry. *New England Journal of Medicine, 342*,1539–1544.

Boen, F., Vanbeselaere, N., & Feys, J. (2002). Behavioral consequenes of fluctuating group success: An Internet study of soccer-team fans. *Journal of Social Psychology, 142*(6), 769–781.

Boeringer, S. B. (1994). Pornography and sexual aggression: Associations of violent and nonviolent depictions with rape and rape proclivity. *Deviant Behavior, 15*(3), 289–304.

Boland, R. J., & Keller, M. B. (2003). Antidepressants. In A. Tasman, J. Kay, & J. A. Lieberman (Eds.), *Psychiatry*. New York: Wiley.

Bolger, N. (1990). Coping as a personality process: A prospective study. *Journal of Personality and Social Psychology, 59*, 525–537.

Bolles, R. N. (2005). *What color is your parachute? A practical manual for job-hunters and career-changers*. Berkeley, CA: Ten Speed Press.

Bonanno, G. A. (1998). The concept of "working through" loss: A critical evaluation of the cultural, historical, and empirical evidence. In A. Maercker, M. Schuetzwohl, & Z. Solomon (Eds.), *Posttraumatic stress disorder: Vulnerability and resilience in the life-span* (pp. 221–247). Göttingen, Germany: Hogrefe and Huber.

Bonanno, G. A., & Kaltman, S. (1999). Toward an integrative perspective on bereavement. *Psychological Bulletin, 125*(6), 760–776.

Bonanno, G. A., & Keltner, D. (1997). Facial expressions of emotion and the course of bereavement. *Journal of Abnormal Psychology, 106*, 126–137.

Bonanno, G. A., Wortman, C. B., Lehman, D. R., Tweed, R. G., Haring, M., Sonnega, J., Carr, D., & Nesse, R. M. (2002). Resilience to loss and chronic grief: A prospective study from preloss to 18-months postloss. *Journal of Personality and Social Psychology, 83*(5), 1150–1164.

Bond, J. T., Thompson, C., Galinsky, E., & Prottas, D. (2003). *The 2002 national study of the changing workforce*. New York: Families and Work Institute.

Bond, R., & Smith, P. B. (1996). Culture and conformity: A meta-analysis of studies using Asch's (1952b, 1956) line judgment task. *Psychological Bulletin, 119*(1), 111–137.

Bonebright, C. A., Clay, D. L., & Ankenmann, R. D. (2000). The relationship of workaholism with

work-life conflict, life satisfaction, and purpose in life. *Journal of Counseling Psychology, 47*, 469–477.

Booth, A., & Amato, P. R. (1994). Parental gender role nontraditionalism and offspring outcomes. *Journal of Marriage and the Family, 56*, 865–877.

Booth, A., & Amato, P. R. (2001). Parental predivorce relations and offspring postdivorce well-being. *Journal of Marriage and Family, 63*, 197–212.

Borman, W. C., Klimoski, R. J., & Ilgen, D. R. (2003). Stability and change in industrial and organizational psychology. In W. C. Borman, D. R. Ilgen, & R. J. Klimoski (Eds.), *Handbook of psychology: Vol. 12. Industrial and organizational psychology*. New York: Wiley.

Borys, S., & Perlman, D. (1985). Gender differences in loneliness. *Personality and Social Psychology Bulletin, 11*, 63–74.

Bossé, R., Spiro, A., & Kressin, N. R. (1996). The psychology of retirement. In R. T. Woods (Ed.), *Handbook of the clinical psychology of aging*. Chicester, UK: Wiley.

Bost, K. K., Cox, M. J., Burchinal, M. R., & Payne, C. (2002). Structural and supporting changes in couples' family and friendships networks across the transition to parenthood. *Journal of Marriage and the Family, 64*, 517–31.

Bouchard, C. (2002). Genetic influences on body weight. In C. G. Fairburn & K. D. Brownell (Eds.), *Eating disorders and obesity: A comprehensive handbook* (pp. 16–21). New York: Guilford.

Bouchard, G., Lussier, Y., & Sabourin, S. (1999). Personality and marital adjustment: Utility of the five-factor model of personality. *Journal of Marriage and the Family, 61*, 651–660.

Bouchard, T. J., Jr., Lykken, D. T., McGue, M., Segal, N. L., & Tellegen, A. (1990). Sources of human psychological differences: The Minnesota study of twins reared apart. *Science, 250*, 223–228.

Boudreaux, E., Carmack, C. L., Scarinci, I. C., & Brantley, P. J. (1998). Predicting smoking stage of change among a sample of low socioeconomic status, primary care outpatients: Replication and extension using decisional balance and self-efficacy theories. *International Journal of Behavioral Medicine, 5*(2), 148–165.

Bouman, T. K., Eifert, G. H., & Lejeuz, C. W. (1999). Somatoform disorders. In T. Millon, P. H. Blaney, & R. D. Davis (Eds.), *Oxford textbook of psychopathology* (pp. 444–465). New York: Oxford University Press.

Bower, G. H. (1970). Organizational factors in memory. *Cognitive Psychology, 1*, 18–46.

Bower, G. H., & Clark, M. C. (1969). Narrative stories as mediators of serial learning. *Psychonomic Science, 14*, 181–182.

Bower, S. A., & Bower, G. H. (1991). *Asserting yourself: A practical guide for positive change* (2nd ed.). Reading, MA: Addison-Wesley.

Bower, S. A., & Bower, G. H. (2004). *Asserting yourself: A practical guide for positive change* (updated ed.). Cambridge, MA: Da Capo Press/Perseus.

Bowers, J. W., Metts, S. M., & Duncanson, W. T. (1985). Emotion and interpersonal communication. In M. L. Knapp & G. R. Miller (Eds.), *Handbook of interpersonal communication*. Newbury Park, CA: Sage.

Bowes-Sperry, L., & Tata, J. (1999). A multiperspective framework of sexual harassment. In G. N. Powell (Ed.), *Handbook of gender and work*. Thousand Oaks, CA: Sage.

Bowins, B. (2004). Psychological defense mechanisms: A new perspective. *American Journal of Psychoanalysis, 64*(1), 1–26.

Bowlby, J. (1980). *Attachment and loss: Vol. 3. Loss: Sadness and depression*. New York: Basic Books.

Bozett, F. W. (1987). Children of gay fathers. In F. W. Bozett (Ed.), *Gay and lesbian parents*. New York: Praeger.

Bradbury, T. N., Campbell, S. M., & Fincham, F. D. (1995). Longitudinal and behavioral analysis of masculinity and femininity in marriage. *Journal of Personality and Social Psychology, 68*(2), 328–341.

Bradbury, T. N., & Fincham, F. D. (1990). Attributions in marriage: Review and critique. *Psychological Bulletin, 107*, 3–33.

Bradford, J., & Ryan, C. (1987). *National lesbian health care survey: Mental health implications*. Washington, DC: National Lesbian and Gay Health Foundation.

Bramlett, M. D., & Mosher, W. D. (2001). *First marriage dissolution, divorce, and remarriage: United States. Advance data from vital and health statistics, No. 323*. Hyattsville, MD: National Center for Health Statistics.

Brannon, L. (2005). *Gender: Psychological perspectives*. Boston: Allyn & Bacon.

Brannon, R. (1976). The male sex role: Our culture's blueprint of manhood, and what it's done for us lately. In D. David & R. Brannon (Eds.), *The forty-nine percent majority*. Reading, MA: Addison-Wesley.

Branscombe, N. R., Wann, D. L., Noel, J. G., & Coleman, J. (1993). In-group or out-group extremity: Importance of the threatened social identity. *Personality and Social Psychology Bulletin, 19*, 381–388.

Brawman-Mintzer, O., Lydiard, R. B., & Ballenger, J. C. (2000). Buspirone. In B. J. Sadock & V. A. Sadock (Eds.), *Kaplan and Sadock's comprehensive textbook of psychiatry* (7th ed., Vol. 1, pp. 2329–2333). Philadelphia: Lippincott/Williams & Wilkins.

Brehm, J. W. (1966). *A theory of psychological reactance*. New York: Academic Press.

Brehm, S. S. (1992). *Intimate relationships* (2nd ed.). New York: McGraw-Hill.

Brehm, S. S., & Brehm, J. W. (1981). *Psychological reactance*. New York: Academic Press.

Brehm, S. S., & Kassin, S. M. (1993). *Social psychology* (2nd ed.). Boston: Houghton Mifflin.

Brehm, S. S., Kassin, S. M., & Fein, S. (2002). *Social psychology*. Boston: Houghton Mifflin.

Brehm, S. S., Miller, R. S., Perlman, D., & Campbell, S. (2002). *Intimate relationships* (3rd ed.). Boston: McGraw-Hill.

Brende, J. O. (2000). Stress effects of floods. In G. Fink (Ed.), *Encyclopedia of stress* (Vol. 2, pp. 153–157). San Diego: Academic Press.

Brennan, K. A., Clark, C. L., & Shaver, P. R. (1998). Self-report measurement of adult attachment: An integrative overview. In J. A. Simpson & W. S. Rholes (Eds.), *Attachment theory and close relationships* (pp. 46–76). New York: Guilford Press.

Brett, J. M. (1980). The effect of job transfer on employees and their families. In C. L. Cooper & R. Payne (Eds.), *Current concerns in occupational stress*. New York: Wiley.

Brettle, R. P., & Leen, L. S. (1991). The natural history of HIV and AIDS in women. *AIDS, 5*, 1283–1292.

Brewer, M. B. (1999). The psychology of prejudice: Ingroup love or outgroup hate? *Journal of Social Issues, 55*(3), 429–444.

Brewer, M. B., & Brown, R. J. (1998). Inter-group relations. In D. T. Gilbert, S. T. Fiske, & G. Lindzey (Eds.), *The handbook of social psychology* (4th ed., Vol. 2, pp. 554–594). New York: McGraw-Hill.

Brewin, C. R., Andrews, B., & Valentine, J. D. (2000). Meta-analysis of risk factors for posttraumatic stress disorder in trauma-exposed adults. *Journal of Consulting and Clinical Psychology, 68*(5), 748–766.

Brewster, K. L., & Padavic, I. (2000). Change in gender-ideology, 1977–1996: The contributions of intracohort change and population turn-over. *Journal of Marriage and the Family, 62*(2), 477–487.

Brewster, M. P. (2002). Domestic violence, theories, research, and practice implications. In A. R. Roberts (Ed.), *Handbook of domestic violence intervention strategies: Policies, programs, and legal remedies*. New York: Oxford University Press.

Brickman, P., Coates, D., & Janoff-Bulman, R. (1978). Lottery winners and accident victims: Is happiness relative? *Journal of Personality and Social Psychology, 36*(8), 917–927.

Bridges, K. R., & Roig, M. (1997). Academic procrastination and irrational thinking: A re-examination with context controlled. *Personality & Individual Differences, 22*, 941–944.

Briere, J., & Conte, J. R. (1993). Self-reported amnesia for abuse in adults molested as children. *Journal of Traumatic Stress, 6*, 21–31.

Brissette, I., Scheier, M. F., & Carver, C. S. (2002). The role of optimism in social network development, coping, and psychological adjustment during a life transition. *Journal of Personality and Social Psychology, 82*(1), 102–111.

Brod, C. (1988). *Technostress: Human cost of the computer revolution.* Reading, MA: Addison-Wesley.

Brody, J. E. (1997, November 4). Girls and puberty: The crisis years. *The New York Times,* p. C9.

Brody, L. R. (2000). The socialization of gender differences in emotional expression: Display rules, infant temperament, and differentiation. In A. H. Fischer (Ed.), *Gender and emotion: Social psychological perspectives* (pp. 24–47). Cambridge, UK: Cambridge University Press.

Brody, L. R., & Hall, J. A. (1993). Gender and emotion. In M. Lewis & J. M. Haviland (Eds.), *Handbook of emotions* (pp. 447–460). New York: Guilford Press.

Brody, N., & Crowley, M. J. (1995). Environmental (and genetic) influences on personality and intelligence. In D. H. Saklofske & M. Zeidner (Eds.), *International handbook of personality and intelligence.* New York: Plenum Press.

Broidy, L. M., Nagin, D. S., Tremblay, R. E., Bates, J. E., Brame, B., Dodge, K. A., Fergusson, D., Horwood, J. L., Loeber, R., Laird, R., Lynam, D. R., Moffitt, T. E., Pettit, G. S., & Vitaro, F. (2003). Developmental trajectories of childhood disruptive behaviors and adolescent delinquency: A six-site, cross-national study. *Developmental Psychology, 39*(2), 222–245.

Bromage, B. K., & Mayer, R. E. (1986). Quantitative and qualitative effects of repetition on learning from technical text. *Journal of Educational Psychology, 78*, 271–278.

Bromley, M., & Blieszner, R. (1997). Planning for long-term care: Filial behavior and relationship quality of adult children with independent parents. *Family Relations,* 155–162.

Brooks-Gunn, J. (1991). Maturational timing variations in adolescent girls, antecedents of. In R. M. Lerner, A. C. Petersen, & J. Brooks-Gunn (Eds.), *Encyclopedia of adolescence.* New York: Garland.

Broomhall, H. S., & Winefield, A. H. (1990). A comparison of the affective well-being of young and middle-aged unemployed men matched for length of employment. *British Journal of Medical Psychology, 63*, 43–52.

Brown, A. S. (1999). New perspectives on the neurodevelopmental hypothesis of schizophrenia. *Psychiatric Annals, 29*(3), 128–130.

Brown, A. S., Begg, M. D., Gravenstein, S., Schaefer, C. A., Wyatt, R. J., Bresnahan, M., Babulas, V. P., & Susser, E. S. (2004). Serologic evidence of prenatal influenza in the etiology of schizophrenia. *Archives of General Psychiatry, 61*(8), 774–780.

Brown, D., Scheflin, A. W., & Hammond, D. C. (1998). *Memory, trauma treatment, and the law.* New York: W. W. Norton.

Brown, D., Scheflin, A. W., & Whitfield, C. L. (1999). Recovered memories: The current weight of the evidence in science and in the courts. *Journal of Psychiatry & Law, 27*, 5–156.

Brown, E. (1994). Affairs: The hidden meanings have major impact on therapeutic approach. *Behavior Today,* 3–4.

Brown, E. J., Juster, H. R., Heimberg, R. G., & Winning, C. D. (1998). Stressful life events and personality styles: Relation to impairment and treatment outcome in patients with social phobia. *Journal of Anxiety Disorders, 12*(3), 233–251.

Brown, J. D., & McGill, K. L. (1989). The cost of good fortune: When positive life events produce negative health consequences. *Journal of Personality and Social Psychology, 57*, 1103–1110.

Brown, R., Maras, P., Masser, B., Vivian J., & Hewstone, M. (2001). Life on the ocean wave: Testing some intergroup hypotheses in a naturalistic setting. *Group Processes and Intergroup Relations, 4*(2), 81–97.

Brown, R. D., Goldstein, E., & Bjorklund, D. F. (2000). The history and zeitgeist of the repressed–false memory debate: Scientific and sociological perspectives on suggestibility and childhood memory. In D. F. Bjorklund (Ed.), *False-memory creation in children and adults* (pp. 1–30). Mahwah, NJ: Erlbaum.

Brown, S., & Booth, A. (1996). Cohabitation versus marriage: A comparison of relationship quality. *Journal of Marriage and the Family,* 668–678.

Brown, S. L., Nesse, R. M., Vinokur, A. D., & Smith, D. M. (2003). Providing social support may be more beneficial than receiving it: Results from a prospective study of mortality. *Psychological Science, 14*(4), 320–327.

Brown, T. A. (2001). Generalized anxiety disorder and obsessive-compulsive disorder. In T. Millon, P. H. Blaney, & R. D. Davis (Eds.), *Oxford textbook of psychopathology* (pp. 114–143). New York: Oxford University Press.

Browne, A. (1993a). Family violence and homelessness: The relevance of trauma histories in the lives of homeless women. *American Journal of Orthopsychiatry, 63*, 370–384.

Browne, A. (1993b). Violence against women by male partners: Prevalence, outcomes, and policy implications. *American Psychologist, 48*, 1077–1087.

Brownell, K. D. (1989, June). When and how to diet. *Psychology Today,* pp. 40–46.

Brownell, K. D. (1995). Exercise in the treatment of obesity. In K. D. Brownell & C. G. Fairburn (Eds.), *Eating disorders and obesity: A comprehensive handbook.* New York: Guilford Press.

Brownell, K. D., & Wadden, T. A. (2000). Obesity. In B. J. Sadock, & V. A. Sadock (Eds.), *Kaplan and Sadock's comprehensive textbook of psychiatry* (7th ed., pp. 1787–1796). Philadelphia: Lippincott/ Williams & Wilkins.

Brubaker, T. (1990). Families in later life: A burgeoning research area. *Journal of Marriage and the Family, 52*, 959–982.

Bruch, H. (1973). *Eating disorders: Obesity, anorexia nervosa and the person within.* New York: Basic Books.

Bruch, H. (1978). *The golden cage: The enigma of anorexia nervosa.* Cambridge, MA: Harvard University Press.

Bruckner-Gordon, F., Gangi, B. K., & Wallman, G. U. (1988). *Making therapy work: Your guide to choosing, using, and ending therapy.* New York: HarperCollins.

Brummett, B. H., Barefoot, J. C., Siegler, I. C., Clapp-Channing, N. E., Lytle, B. L., Bosworth, H. B., Williams, R. B., & Mark, D. B. (2001). Characteristics of socially isolated patients with coronary artery disease who are at elevated risk for mortality. *Psychosomatic Medicine, 63*(2), 267–272.

Bryan, A. D., Aiken, L. S., & West, S. G. (1999). The impact of males proposing condom use on perceptions of an initial sexual encounter. *Personality and Social Psychology Bulletin, 25*(3), 275–286.

Bryant, J., & Rockwell, S. C. (1994). Effects of massive exposure to sexually oriented prime-time television programming on adolescents' moral judgment. In D. Zillman, J. Bryant, & A. C. Houston (Eds.), *Media, children, and the family: Social, scientific, psychodynamic, and clinical perspectives.* Hillsdale, NJ: Erlbaum.

Bryant, S., & Rakowski, W. (1992). Predictors of mortality among elderly African-Americans. *Research on Aging, 14*, 50–67.

Bryant, S. S., & Demian. (1994). Relationship characteristics of American gay and lesbian couples: Findings from a national survey. *Journal of Gay and Lesbian Social Services, 1*, 101–117.

Bryden, M. P. (1988). An overview of the dichotic listening procedure and its relation to cerebral organization. In K. Hugdahl (Ed.), *Handbook of dichotic listening.* Chichester, England: Wiley.

Bryer, K. B. (1979). The Amish way of death: A study of family support systems. *American Psychologist, 34*, 255–261.

Buchanan, R. W., & Carpenter, W. T. (2000). Schizophrenia: Introduction and overview. In B. J. Sadock & V. A. Sadock (Eds.), *Kaplan and Sadock's comprehensive textbook of psychiatry* (7th ed., Vol. 1). Philadelphia: Lippincott/Williams & Wilkins.

Buck, E. B., Newton, B. J., & Muramatsu, Y. (1984). Independence and obedience in the U.S. and Japan. *International Journal of Intercultural Relations, 8*, 279–300.

Buckingham, J. T., & Alicke, M. D. (2002). The influence of individual versus aggregate social comparison and the presence of others on self–evaluations. *Journal of Personality and Social Psychology, 83*(5), 1117–1130.

Buckman, R. (2002). Communications and emotions: Skills and effort are key. *British Medical Journal, 325*, 672.

Buehlman, K. T., Gottman, J. M., & Katz, L. F. (1992). How a couple views their past predicts their future: Predicting divorce from an oral history interview. *Journal of Family Psychology, 5*, 295–318.

Buelens, M., & Poelmans, S. A. Y. (2004). Enriching the Spence and Robbins' typology of workaholism: Demographic, motivational and organizational correlates. *Journal of Organizational Change Management, 17*(5), 440–458.

Bulcroft, R., & Teachman, J. (2004). Ambiguous constructions: Development of a childless or child-free life course. In M. Coleman, & L. H. Ganong (Eds.), *Handbook of contemporary families: Considering the past, contemplating the future.* Thousand Oaks, CA: Sage.

Bulik, C. M. (2004). Genetic and biological risk factors. In J. K. Thompson (Ed.), *Handbook of eating disorders and obesity.* New York: Wiley.

Bull, D. L. (1999). A verified case of recovered memories of sexual abuse. *American Journal of Psychotherapy, 53*, 221–224.

Bullock, W. A., & Gilliland, K. (1993). Eysenck's arousal theory of introversion-extraversion: A converging measures investigation. *Journal of Personality and Social Psychology, 64*, 113–123.

Bumpass, L. L., & Lu, H. H. (2000). Trends in cohabitation and implications for children's family contexts in the United States. *Population Studies, 54*, 29–41.

Bumpass, L. L., Raley, R. K., & Sweet, J. (1995). The changing character of stepfamilies: Implications of cohabitation and nonmarital childbearing. *Demography, 32*, 425–436.

Bumpass, L. L., Sweet, J. A., & Martin, T. C. (1990). Changing patterns of remarriage. *Journal of Marriage and the Family, 52*, 747–756.

Burger, J. M. (1999). The foot-in-the-door compliance procedure: A multiple-process analysis and review. *Personality and Social Psychology Review, 3*(4), 303–325.

Burger, J. M. (2000). *Personality* (5th ed.). Belmont, CA: Wadsworth.

Burger, J. M., & Caldwell, D. F. (2003). The effects of monetary incentives and labelling on the foot-in-the-door effect: Evidence for a self-perception process. *Basic and Applied Social Psychology, 25*(3), 235–241.

Burger, J. M., & Cornelius, T. (2003). Raising the price of agreement: Public commitment and the lowball compliance procedure. *Journal of Applied Social Psychology, 33*(5), 923–934.

Burger, J. M., & Guadagno, R. E. (2003). Self-concept clarity and the foot-in-the-door procedure. *Basic and Applied Social Psychology, 25*(1), 79–86.

Burgess, C., O'Donohoe, A., & Gill, M. (2000). Agony and ecstasy: A review of MDMA effects and toxicity. *European Psychiatry, 15*(5), 287–294.

Burgess, E. O. (2004). Sexuality in midlife and later life couples. In J. H. Harvey & S. Sprecher (Eds.), *The handbook of sexuality in close relationships*. Mahwah, NJ: Lawrence Erlbaum.

Burgoon, J. K. (1994). Nonverbal signals. In M. L. Knapp & G. R. Miller (Eds.), *Handbook of interpersonal communication* (2nd ed.). Thousand Oaks, CA: Sage.

Burhans, K. K., & Dweck, C. S. (1995). Helplessness in early childhood: The role of contingent worth. *Child Development, 66*, 1719–1738.

Burke, R. J. (2000). Workaholism in organizations: Psychological and physical well-being. *Stress Medicine, 16*(1), 11–16.

Burke, R. J. (2001). Workaholism in organizations: The role of organizational values. *Personnel Review, 30*(6), 637–645.

Burleson, B. R., & Denton, W. H. (1997). The relationship between communication skill and marital satisfaction: Some moderating effects. *Journal of Marriage and the Family, 59*, 884–902.

Bursztajn, H. J., & Brodsky, A. (2002). Managed healthcare complications, liability risk, and clinical remedies. *Primary Psychiatry, 9*(4), 37–41.

Buscaglia, L. (1982). *Living, loving and learning*. Thorofare, NJ: Charles B. Slack.

Bushman, B. J. (2002). Does venting anger feed or extinguish the flame? Catharsis, rumination, distraction, anger, and aggressive responding. *Personality and Social Psychology Bulletin, 28*(6), 724–731.

Bushman, B. J., & Baumeister, R. F. (1998). Threatened egotism, narcissism, self-esteem, and direct and displaced aggression: Does self-love or self-hate lead to violence? *Journal of Personality and Social Psychology, 75*(1), 219–229.

Bushman, B. J., & Baumeister, R. F. (2002). Does self-love or self-hate lead to violence? *Journal of Research in Personality, 36*(6), 543–545.

Bushman, B. J., Baumeister, R. F., & Stack, A. D. (1999). Catharsis, aggression, and persuasive influence: Self-fulfilling or self-defeating prophecies? *Journal of Personality and Social Psychology, 76*, 367–376.

Buss, D. M. (1985). Human mate selection. *American Scientist, 73*, 47–51.

Buss, D. M. (1988). The evolution of human intrasexual competition: Tactics of mate attraction. *Journal of Personality and Social Psychology, 54*, 616–628.

Buss, D. M. (1989). Sex differences in human mate preferences: Evolutionary hypotheses tested in 37 cultures. *Behavioral and Brain Sciences, 12*, 1–14.

Buss, D. M. (1991). Evolutionary personality psychology. *Annual Review of Psychology, 42*, 459–491.

Buss, D. M. (1994). Mate preferences in 37 cultures. In W. J. Lonner & R. S. Malpass (Eds.), *Psychology and culture*. Boston: Allyn & Bacon.

Buss, D. M. (1995). Evolutionary psychology: A new paradigm for psychological science. *Psychological Inquiry, 6*, 1–30.

Buss, D. M. (1996). The evolutionary psychology of human social strategies. In E. T. Higgins & A. W. Kruglanski (Eds.), *Social psychology: Handbook of basic principles*. New York: Guilford Press.

Buss, D. M. (1997). Evolutionary foundation of personality. In R. Hogan, J. Johnson, & S. Briggs (Eds.), *Handbook of personality psychology*. San Diego: Academic Press.

Buss, D. M. (1998). The psychology of human mate selection: Exploring the complexity of the strategic repertoire. In C. Crawford & D. L. Krebs (Eds.), *Handbook of evolutionary psychology: Ideas, issues, and applications*. Mahwah, NJ: Erlbaum.

Buss, D. M., & Kenrick, D. T. (1998). Evolutionary social psychology. In D. T. Gilbert, S. T. Fiske, &

G. Lindzey (Eds.), *The handbook of social psychology* (pp. 982–1026). New York: McGraw-Hill.

Buss, D. M., Shackelford, T. K., Kirkpatrick, L. A., & Larsen, R. J. (2001). A half century of mate preferences: The cultural evolution of values. *Journal of Marriage and Family, 63*, 491–503.

Bussey, K., & Bandura, A. (1984). Influence of gender constancy and social power on sex-linked modeling. *Journal of Personality and Social Psychology, 47*, 1292–1302.

Bussey, K., & Bandura, A. (1999). Social cognitive theory of gender development and differentiation. *Psychological Review, 106*(4), 676–713.

Butler, E. A., Egloff, B., Wlhelm, F. H., Smith, N. C., Erickson, E. A., & Gross, J. J. (2003). The social consequences of expressive suppression. *Emotion, 3*(1), 48–67.

Butler, J. L., & Baumeister, R. F. (1998). The trouble with friendly faces: Skilled performance with a supportive audience. *Journal of Personality and Social Psychology, 75*(5), 1213–1230.

Butler, R., & Lewis, M. (1982). *Aging and mental health* (3rd ed.). St. Louis: Mosby.

Buunk, B. P., de Jonge, J., Ybema, J. F., & de Wolff, C. J. (1998). Psychosocial aspects of occupational stress. In P. J. D. Drenth, H. Thierry, & C. J. de Wolff (Eds.), *Handbook of work and organizational psychology*. East Sussex, UK: Psychology Press.

Buxton, M. N., Arkel, Y., Lagos, J., Deposito, F., Lowenthal, H., & Simring, S. (1981). Stress and platelet aggregation in hemophiliac children and their family members. *Research Communications in Psychology, Psychiatry and Behavior, 6*, 21–48.

Byrne, D. (1971). *The attraction paradigm*. New York: Academic Press.

Byrne, D., & Clore, G. L. (1970). A reinforcement model of evaluative responses. *Personality: An International Journal, 1*(2), 103–128.

Byrne, D., Clore, G. L., & Smeaton, G. (1986). The attraction hypothesis: Do similar attitudes affect anything? *Journal of Personality and Social Psychology, 51*, 1167–1170.

Byrnes, J. P. (2001). *Cognitive development and learning in instructional contexts* (2nd ed.). Needham Heights, MA: Allyn & Bacon.

Byrnes, J. P., Miller, D. C., & Schafer, W. D. (1999). Gender differences in risk-taking: A meta-analysis. *Psychological Bulletin, 125*(3), 367–383.

Caldwell, B. M. (1993). Impact of day care on the child. *Pediatrics, 91*, 225–228.

Caldwell, L. L., Smith, E. A., & Weissinger, E. (1992). The relationship of leisure activities and perceived health of college students. *Society and Leisure, 15*, 545–556.

Calhoun, L. G., & Tedeschi, R. G. (2001). Posttraumatic growth: The positive lessons of loss. In R. A. Neimeyer (Ed.), *Meaning reconstruction and the experience of loss* (pp. 157–172). Washington, DC: American Psychological Association.

Call, V., Sprecher, S., & Schwartz, P. (1995). The incidence and frequency of marital sex in a national sample. *Journal of Marriage and the Family, 57*, 639–650.

Calof, D. (1998). Facing the truth about false memory. In R. A. Baker (Ed.), *Child sexual abuse and false memory syndrome*. Amherst, NY: Prometheus Books.

Camara, W. J., & Schneider, D. L. (1994). Integrity tests: Facts and unresolved issues. *American Psychologist, 49*(2), 112–119.

Cameron, L., Leventhal, E. A., & Leventhal, H. (1993). Symptom representations and affect as determinants of care seeking in a community-dwelling, adult sample population. *Health Psychology, 12*, 171–179.

Cameron, N. (1963). *Personality development and psychopathology*. Boston: Houghton Mifflin.

Campbell, E. Q., & Pettigrew, T. F. (1959). Racial and moral crisis: The role of Little Rock ministers. *American Journal of Sociology, 64*, 509–516.

Campbell, J. C. (2002). Health consequences of intimate partner violence. *Lancet, 359*, 1331–1336.

Campbell, J. D. (1990). Self-esteem and clarity of the self-concept. *Journal of Personality and Social Psychology, 59*, 538–549.

Campbell, J. D., & Lavallee, L. F. (1993). Who am I? The role of self-concept confusion in understanding the behavior of people with low self-esteem. In R. Baumeister (Ed.), *Self-esteem: The puzzle of low self-regard*. New York: Plenum.

Campbell, J. D., Assanand, S., & DiPaula, A. (2000). Structural features of the self-concept and adjustment. In A. Tesser, R. B. Felson, & J. M. Suls (Eds.), *Psychological perspectives on self and identity* (pp. 67–87). Washington, DC: American Psychological Association.

Campbell, L. F., & Smith, T. P. (2003). Integrating self-help books into psychotherapy. *Journal of Clinical Psychology, 59*(2), 177–186.

Campbell, R. J. (2000). Managed care. In B. J. Sadock & V. A. Sadock (Eds.), *Kaplan and Sadock's comprehensive textbook of psychiatry* (7th ed., Vol. 2). Philadelphia: Lippincott/Williams & Wilkins.

Campbell, W. K., & Sedikides, C. (1999). Self-threat magnifies the self-serving bias: A meta-analytic integration. *Review of General Psychology, 3*(1), 23–43.

Campbell, W. K., Sedikides, C., Reeder, G. D., & Elliot A. J. (2000). Among friends? An examination of friendship and the self-serving bias. *British Journal of Social Psychology, 39*(2), 229–239.

Canary, D. J., & Stafford, L. (1994). Maintaining relationships through strategic and routine interaction. In D. J. Canary & L. Stafford (Eds.), *Communication and relationship maintenance* (pp. 3–22). San Diego: Academic Press.

Canary, D. J., & Stafford, L. (2001). Equity in the preservation of personal relationships. In J. H. Harvey & A. E. Wenzel (Eds.), *Close romantic relationships: Maintenance and enhancement*. Mahwah, NJ: Erlbaum.

Cancro, R., & Lehmann, H. E. (2000). Schizophrenia: Clinical features. In B. J. Sadock, & V. A. Sadock (Eds.), *Kaplan and Sadock's comprehensive textbook of psychiatry* (7th ed., Vol. 1, pp. 1169–1198). Philadelphia: Lippincott/Williams & Wilkins.

Canetto, S. S., & Sakinofsky, I. (1998). The gender paradox in suicide. *Suicide and Life-Threatening Behavior, 28*, 1–23.

Cannon, W. B. (1932). *The wisdom of the body*. New York: Norton.

Cantor, N. (1990). Social psychology and sociobiology: What can we leave to evolution? *Motivation and Emotion, 14*, 245–254.

Carducci, B. J. (1999). *The pocket guide to making successful small talk*. New Albany, IN: Pocket Guide Publications.

Carey, M. P., & Vanable, P. A. (2003). AIDS/HIV. In A. M. Nezu, C. M. Nezu, & P. A. Geller (Eds.), *Handbook of psychology: Vol. 9. Health psychology*. New York: Wiley.

Carli, L. J. (1990). Gender, language, and influence. *Journal of Personality and Social Psychology, 59*, 941–951.

Carli, L. L., & Bukatko, D. (2000). Gender, communication, and social influence: A developmental perspective. In T. Eckes & H. M. Trautner (Eds.), *The developmental social psychology of gender*. Mahwah, NJ: Erlbaum.

Carlson, E. A. (1998). A prospective longitudinal study of attachment disorganization/disorientation. *Child Development, 69*, 1107–1128.

Carlson, R. (1997). *Don't sweat the small stuff . . . and it's all small stuff: Simple ways to keep the little things from taking over your life*. New York: Hyperion.

Carney, S., & Geddes, J. (2003). Electroconvulsive therapy. *British Medical Journal, 326*, 1343–1344.

Carpenter, W. T. (1992). The negative symptom challenge. *Archives of General Psychiatry, 49*, 236–237.

Carpenter, W. T. (2002). From clinical trial to prescription. *Archives of General Psychology, 59,* 282–285.

Carr, V. J. (2000). Stress effects of earthquakes. In G. Fink (Ed.), *Encyclopedia of stress* (Vol. 2, pp. 1–3). San Diego: Academic Press.

Carrington, P. (1987). Managing meditation in clinical practice. In M. A. West (Ed.), *The psychology of meditation.* Oxford: Clarendon Press.

Carrington, P. (1993). Modern forms of meditation. In P. M. Lehrer & R. L. Woolfolk (Eds.), *Principles and practice of stress management* (2nd ed.). New York: Guilford Press.

Carroll, J. L., Volk, K. D., & Hyde, J. S. (1985). Differences between males and females in motives for engaging in sexual intercourse. *Archives of Sexual Behavior, 14,* 131–139.

Carstensen, L. L. (1995). Evidence for a life-span theory of socioemotional selectivity. *Current Directions in Psychological Science, 4*(5), 151–156.

Carter, B. (1999). Becoming parents: The family with young children. In B. Carter & M. McGoldrick (Eds.), *The expanded family life cycle: Individual, family, and social perspectives* (3rd ed., pp. 249–273). Boston: Allyn & Bacon.

Carter, B., & McGoldrick, M. (1999). Overview: The expanded family life cycle: Individual, family, and social perspectives. In B. Carter & M. McGoldrick (Eds.), *The expanded family life cycle: Individual, family, and social perspectives* (3rd ed., pp. 1–26). Boston: Allyn & Bacon.

Carter, E. A., & McGoldrick, M. (1988). Overview: The changing family life cycle—A framework for family therapy. In E. A. Carter & M. McGoldrick (Eds.), *The changing family life cycle: A framework for family therapy* (2nd ed.). New York: Gardner Press.

Carter, M. J. (1999). Moving beyond the Surgeon General's report: An HPERD challenge? *Journal of Physical Education, Recreation and Dance, 70*(2).

Carver, C. S., & Scheier, M. F. (1994). Situational coping and coping dispositions in a stressful transaction. *Journal of Personality and Social Psychology, 66,* 184–195.

Carver, C. S., & Scheier, M. F. (1999). Optimism. In C. R. Snyder (Ed.), *Coping: The psychology of what works* (pp. 182–204). New York: Oxford University Press.

Carver, C. S., & Scheier, M. F. (2002). Optimism. In C. R. Snyder & S. J. Lopez (Eds.), *Handbook of positive psychology.* New York: Oxford University Press.

Carver, C. S., Pozo, C., Harris, S. D., Noriega, V., Scheier, M. F., Robinson, D. S., Ketcham, A. S., Moffat, F. L., Jr., & Clark, K. C. (1993). How coping mediates the effect of optimism on distress: A study of women with early-stage breast cancer. *Journal of Personality and Social Psychology, 65,* 375–390.

Carver, C. S., Scheier, M. F., & Weintraub, J. K. (1989). Assessing coping strategies: A theoretically based approach. *Journal of Personality and Social Psychology, 56,* 267–283.

Caspi, A., & Herbener, E. S. (1990). Continuity and change. Assortative marriage and the consistency of personality in adulthood. *Journal of Personality and Social Psychology, 58,* 250–258.

Cassel, R. N. (2000). Third force psychology and person-centered theory: From ego-status to ego-ideal. *Psychology: A Journal of Human Behavior, 37*(3), 44–48.

Castonguay, L. G., Reid Jr., J. J., Halperin, G. S., & Goldfried, M. R. (2003). Psychotherapy integration. In G. Stricker, & T. A. Widiger (Eds.), *Handbook of psychology: Vol. 8. Clinical psychology.* New York: Wiley.

Catania, J. A., Binson, D., Dolcini, M. M., Moskowitz, J. T., & van der Straten, A. (2001). In A. Baum, T. A. Revenson, & J. E. Singer (Eds.), *Handbook of health psychology.* Mahwah, NJ: Erlbaum.

Cate, R. M., & Lloyd, S. A. (1988). Courtship. In S. Duck (Ed.), *Handbook of personal relationships.* New York: Wiley.

Cate, R. M., & Lloyd, S. A. (1992). *Courtship.* Newbury Park, CA: Sage.

Cates, Jr. W. (2004). Reproductive tract infections. In R. A. Hatcher, J. Trussell, F. H. Stewart, A. L. Nelson, W. Cates Jr., F. Guest, & D. Kowal (Eds.), *Contraceptive technology.* New York: Ardent Media.

Cattell, R. B. (1950). *Personality: A systematic, theoretical and factual study.* New York: McGraw-Hill.

Cattell, R. B. (1966). *The scientific analysis of personality.* Chicago: Aldine.

Cattell, R. B., Eber, H. W., & Tatsuoka, M. M. (1970). *Handbook of the Sixteen Personality Factor Questionnaire (16PF).* Champaign, IL: Institute for Personality and Ability Testing.

Catz, S. L., & Kelly, J. A. (2001). Living with HIV disease. In A. Baum, T. A. Revenson, & J. E. Singer (Eds.), *Handbook of health psychology* (pp. 841–850). Mahwah, NJ: Erlbaum.

Cavanaugh, J. C. (1993). *Adult development and aging* (2nd ed.). Pacific Grove, CA: Brooks/Cole.

Cavanaugh, J. C. (2000). Metamemory from a social-cognitive perspective. In D. Park & N. Schwarz (Eds.), *Cognitive aging: A primer.* Philadelphia: Psychology Press.

Cavanaugh, J. C., Feldman, J. M., & Hertzog, C. (1998). Meta-memory as social cognition: A reconceptualization of what memory questionnaires assess. *Review of General Psychology, 2,* 48–65.

Caverly, D. C., Orlando, V. P., & Mullen, J. L. (2000). Textbook study reading. In R. F. Flippo & D. C. Caverly (Eds.), *Handbook of college reading and study strategy research.* Mahwah, NJ: Erlbaum.

Cegala, D. J., & Sillars, A. L. (1989). Further examination of nonverbal manifestations of interaction involvement. *Communication Reports, 2,* 39–47.

Center for Communication and Social Policy. (1998). *National Television Violence Study.* Newbury Park, CA: Sage.

Centers for Disease Control. (2000). Adoption of protective behavior among persons with recent HIV infection and diagnosis—Alabama, New Jersey, and Tennessee, 1997–1998. *Morbidity and Mortality Weekly Report, 49,* 512–515.

Centers for Disease Control. (2002a). *HIV/AIDS among U.S. women: Minority and young women at continuing risk.* Fact Sheet of the U.S. Centers for Disease Control and Prevention, National Center for HIV, STD, and TB Prevention. Atlanta: Centers for Disease Control.

Centers for Disease Control. (2002b). Trends in sexual risk behavior among high school students—United States, 1991–2001. *Morbidity and Mortality Weekly, 51*(38), 856–859.

Centers for Disease Control. (2003). Advancing HIV prevention: New strategies for a changing epidemic—United States, 2003. *Morbidity and Mortality Weekly Report, 52,* 329–332.

Cerletti, U., & Bini, L. (1938). Un nuevo metodo di shockterapie "L'eletro-shock." Boll. Acad. Med. *Roma, 64, 136* 130.

Chaiken, S. (1979). Communicator's physical attractiveness and persuasion. *Journal of Personality and Social Psychology, 37,* 1387–1397.

Chambless, D. L., & Hollon, S. D. (1998). Defining empirically supported therapies. *Journal of Consulting & Clinical Psychology, 66*(1), 7–18.

Chambless, D. L., & Ollendick, T. H. (2001). Empirically supported psychological interventions: Controversies and evidence. *Annual Review of Psychology, 52,* 685–716.

Chan, R. W., Brooks, R. C., Raboy, B., & Patterson, C. J. (1998). Division of labor among lesbian and heterosexual parents: Associations with children's adjustment. *Journal of Family Psychology, 12,* 402–419.

Chang, E. C. (1996). Cultural differences in optimism, pessimism, and coping: Predictors of subsequent adjustment in Asian American and Caucasian American college students. *Journal of Counseling Psychology, 43,* 113–123.

Chang, E. C., & Sanna, L. J. (2003). Experience of life hassles and psychological adjustment among adolescents: Does it make a difference if one is optimistic or pessimistic? *Personality and Individual Differences, 34*(5), 857–879.

Chang, R. Y., & Kelly, P. K. (1993). *Step-by-step problem solving: A practical guide to ensure problems get (and stay) solved.* Irvine, CA: Richard Chang Associates.

Chaplin, W. F., Phillips, J. B., Brown, J. D., Clanton, N. R., & Stein, J. L. (2000). Handshaking, gender, personality, and first impressions. *Journal of Personality and Social Psychology, 79*(1), 110–117.

Chappell, K. D., & Davis, K. E. (1998). Attachment, partner choice, and perception of romantic partners: An experimental test of the attachment-security hypothesis. *Personal Relationships, 5*(3), 327–342.

Charlesworth, W. R., & Dzur, C. (1987). Gender comparisons of preschoolers' behavior and resource utilization in group problem-solving. *Child Development, 58,* 191–200.

Chartrand, T., Pinckert, S., & Burger, J. M. (1999). When manipulation backfires: The effects of time delay and requester on the foot-in-the-door technique. *Journal of Applied Social Psychology, 29*(1), 211–221.

Chemers, M. M., Hu, L., & Garcia, B. F. (2001). Academic self-efficacy and first-year college student performance and adjustment. *Journal of Educational Psychology, 93*(1), 55–64.

Cheng, C. (2001). Assessing coping flexibility in real-life and laboratory settings: A multimethod approach. *Journal of Personality and Social Psychology, 80*(5), 814–833.

Cherlin, A. J. (1999). Going to extremes: Family structure, children's well-being, and social science. *Demography, 36,* 421–428.

Cherlin, A. J. (2004). The deinstitutionalization of American marriage. *Journal of Marriage and Family, 66,* 848–861.

Chia, R. C., Moore, J. L., Lam, K. N., Chuang, C. J., & Cheng, B. S. (1994). Cultural differences in gender role attitudes between Chinese and American students. *Sex Roles, 31,* 23–29.

Chiappelli, F., & Hodgson, D. (2000). Immune suppression. In G. Fink (Ed.), *Encyclopedia of stress* (Vol. 2, pp. 531–535). San Diego: Academic Press.

Chiappelli, F., & Liu, Q. N. (2000). Immunity. In G. Fink (Ed.), *Encyclopedia of stress* (pp. 541–546). San Diego: Academic Press.

Chick, J. (1998). Alcohol, health, and the heart: Implications for clinicians. *Alcohol and Alcoholism, 33*(6), 576–591.

Chiriboga, D. A. (1987). Personality in later life. In P. Silverman (Ed.), *The elderly as modern pioneers.* Bloomington: Indiana University Press.

Chiriboga, D. A. (1989). Mental health at the midpoint: Crisis, challenge, or relief? In S. Hunter & M. Sundel (Eds.), *Mid-life myths: Issues, findings, and practical implications.* Thousand Oaks, CA: Sage.

Choi, I., Dalal, R., Kim-Prieto, C., & Park, H. (2003). Culture and judgment of causal relevance. *Journal of Personality and Social Psychology, 84*(1), 46-59.

Choi, I., Nisbett, R. E., & Norenzayan, A. (1999). Causal attribution across cultures: Variation and universality. *Psychological Bulletin, 125*(1), 47–63.

Choice, P., & Lamke, L. K. (1997). A conceptual approach to understanding abused women's stay/leave decisions. *Journal of Family Issues, 18,* 290–314.

Chopra, D. (1993). *Ageless body, timeless mind.* New York: Crown.

Choudhry, N. K., Stelfox, H. T., & Detsky, A. S. (2002). Relationships between authors of clinical practice guidelines and the pharmaceutical industry. *Journal of the American Medical Association, 287*(5), 612–617.

Christensen, A., & Heavey, C. L. (1990). Gender and social structure in the demand/withdraw pattern of marital conflict. *Journal of Personality and Social Psychology, 59,* 73–81.

Christensen, A., & Jacobson, N. S. (2000). *Reconcilable differences.* New York: Guilford Press.

Christensen, A. J., & Johnson, J. A. (2002). Patient adherence with medical treatment regimens: An interactive approach. *Current Directions in Psychological Science, 11*(3), 94–97.

Christensen, P., & Kashy, D. (1998). Perceptions of and by lonely people in initial social interaction. *Personality and Social Psychology Bulletin, 24*(3), 322–329.

Christoph, R. T., Schoenfeld, G. A., & Tansky, J. W. (1998). Overcoming barriers to training utilizing technology: The influence of self-efficacy factors on multimedia-based training receptiveness. *Human Resource Development Quarterly, 9*(1), 25–38.

Christophe, V., & Rime, B. (1997). Exposure to the social sharing of emotion: Emotional impact, listener responses and secondary social sharing. *European Journal of Social Psychology, 27,* 37–54.

Christopher, F. S., & Sprecher, S. (2000). Sexuality in marriage, dating, and other relationships: A decade review. *Journal of Marriage and the Family, 62,* 999–1017.

Church, A. T. (1994). Relating to Tellegen and five-factor models of personality structure. *Journal of Personality and Social Psychology, 67,* 898–909.

Church, A. T., & Burke, P. J. (1994). Exploratory and confirmatory tests of the Big Five and Tellegen's three- and four-dimensional models. *Journal of Personality and Social Psychology, 66,* 93–114.

Cialdini, R. B. (2001). *Influence: Science and practice* (4th ed.). Boston: Allyn & Bacon.

Cialdini, R. B., & Goldstein, N. J. (2004). Social Influence: Compliance and comformity. *Annual Review of Psychology, 55,* 591–621.

Cialdini, R. B., Borden, R. J., Thorne, A., Walker, M. R., Freeman, S., & Sloan, L. R. (1976). Basking in reflected glory: Three (football) field studies. *Journal of Personality and Social Psychology, 34,* 366–375.

Ciarrochi, J., Dean, F. P., & Anderson, S. (2002). Emotional intelligence moderates the relationship between stress and mental health. *Personality & Individual Differences, 32,* 197–209.

Cicirelli, V. G. (1996). Sibling relationships in middle and old age. In G. H. Brody (Ed.), *Sibling relationships: Their causes and consequences.* Norwood, NJ: Ablex.

Cicirelli, V. G. (1999). Personality and demographic factors in older adults' fear of death. *Gerontologist, 39*(5), 569–579.

Cicirelli, V. G. (2002). *Older adults' views on death.* New York: Springer.

Claar, R. L., & Blumenthal, J. A. (2003). The value of stress-management interventions in life-threatening medical conditions. *Current Directions in Psychological Science, 12*(4), 133–137.

Clark, D. A., Beck, A. T., & Beck, J. S. (1994). Symptom differences in major depression, dysthymia, panic disorder, and generalized anxiety disorder. *American Journal of Psychiatry, 151,* 205–209.

Clark, M. S., & Bennett, M. E. (1992). Research on relationships: Implications for mental health. In D. N. Ruble, P. R. Costanzo & M. E. Oliveri (Eds.), *The social psychology of mental health.* New York: Guilford Press.

Clark, M. S., & Grote, N. K. (2003). Close relationships. In T. Millon & M. J. Lerner (Eds.) *Handbook of psychology: Vol. 5. Personality and social psychology.* New York: Wiley.

Clark, M. S., & Mills, J. (1993). The difference between communal and exchange relationships: What it is and is not. *Journal of Personality and Social Psychology Bulletin, 19,* 684–691.

Clark, R., Anderson, N. B., Clark, V. R., & Williams, D. R. (1999). Racism as a stressor for African Americans. *American Psychologist, 54*(10), 805–816.

Clarke-Stewart, K. A., & Bailey, B. L. (1989). Adjusting to divorce: Why do men have it easier? *Journal of Divorce, 13,* 75–94.

Cleek, M. G., & Pearson, T. A. (1985). Perceived causes of divorce: An analysis of interrelationships. *Journal of Marriage and the Family, 47,* 179–183.

Clement, U. (1990). Surveys of heterosexual behavior. *Annual Review of Sex Research, 1,* 45–74.

Clements, M. L., Stanley, S. M., & Markman, H. J. (2004). Before they said "I do": Discriminating among marital outcomes over 13 years. *Journal of Marriage and Family, 66,* 613–626.

Cloitre, M., Morin, N. A., & Linares, O. (2004, January-February). Children's resilience in the face of trauma. *The New York University Child Study Letter.*

Clow, A. (2001). The physiology of stress. In F. Jones & J. Bright (Eds.), *Stress: Myth, theory and research.* Harlow, England: Pearson Education.

Coates, T. J., & Collins, C. (1998). Preventing HIV infection. *Scientific American, 279*(1), 96–97.

Coats, E. J., & Feldman, R. S. (1996). Gender differences in nonverbal correlates of social status. *Personality and Social Psychology Bulletin, 22*(10), 1014–1022.

Cochran, S. D. (2001). Emerging issues in research on lesbians' and gay men's mental health: Does sexual orientation really matter? *American Psychologist, 56,* 931–947.

Cohan, C. L., & Kleinbaum, S. (2002). Toward a greater understanding of the cohabitation effect: Premarital cohabitation and marital communication. *Journal of Marriage and Family, 64,* 180–192.

Cohen, C. E. (1981). Person categories and social perception: Testing some boundaries of the processing effects of prior knowledge. *Journal of Personality and Social Psychology, 40,* 441–452.

Cohen, D. (1997). A critique of the use of neuroleptic drugs in psychiatry. In S. Fisher & R. P. Greenberg (Eds.), *From placebo to panacea: Putting psychiatric drugs to the test.* New York: Wiley.

Cohen, D., & McCubbin, M. (1990). The political economy of tardive dyskinesia: Asymmetries in power and responsibility. *The Journal of Mind and Behavior, 11,* 465–488.

Cohen, D. B. (1999). *Stranger in the nest: Do parents really shape their child's personality, intelligence, or character?* New York: Wiley.

Cohen, F. (1979). Personality, stress and the development of physical illness. In G. C. Stone, F. Cohen, N. E. Adler, & associates (Eds.), *Health psychology—A handbook.* San Francisco: Jossey-Bass.

Cohen, F., Solomon, S., Maxfield, M. , Pyszczynski, T., & Greenberg, J. (2004). Fatal attraction: The effects of mortality salience on evaluations of charismatic, task-oriented, and relationship-oriented leaders. *Psychological Science, 15,* 846–851.

Cohen, M. J. M., Kunkel, E. S., & Levenson, J. L. (1998). Associations between psychosocial stress and malignancy. In J. R. Hubbard & E. A. Workman (Eds.), *Handbook of stress medicine: An organ system approach.* Boca Raton: CRC Press.

Cohen, S., Doyle, W. J., Turner, R., Alper, C. M., & Skoner, D. P. (2003). Sociability and susceptibility to the common cold. *Psychological Science, 14*(5), 389–395.

Cohen, S., Evans, G. W., Krantz, D. S., & Stokols, D. (1980). Physiological, motivational, and cognitive effects of aircraft noise on children: Moving from the laboratory to the field. *American Psychologist, 35,* 231–243.

Cohen, S., Hamrick, N., Rodriguez, M. S., Feldman, P. J., Rabin, B. S., & Manuck, S. B. (2002). Reactivity and vulnerability to stress-associated risk for upper respiratory illness. *Psychosomatic Illness, 64,* 302–310.

Cohen, S., Kessler, R. C., & Gordon, L. U. (1995). Strategies for measuring stress in studies of psy-

chiatric and physical disorders. In S. Cohen, R. C. Kessler, & L. U. Gordon (Eds.), *Measuring stress: A guide for health and social scientists* (pp. 3–28). New York: Oxford University Press.

Cohen, S., Lichtenstein, E., Prochaska, J. O., Rossi, J. S., Gritz, E. R., Carr, C. R., Orleans, C. T., Schoenbach, V. J., Biener, L., Abrams, D., DiClemente, C., Curry, S., Marlatt, G. A., Cummings, K. M., Emont, S. L., Giovino, A., & Ossip-Klein, D. (1989). Debunking myths about self-quitting: Evidence from 10 prospective studies of persons who attempt to quit smoking by themselves. *American Psychologist, 44,* 1355–1365.

Cohen, S., Tyrrell, D. A., & Smith, A. P. (1993). Negative life events, perceived stress, negative affect, and susceptibility to the common cold. *Journal of Personality and Social Psychology, 64,* 131–140.

Cohn, E., Cohn, S., & Bradley, J. (1995). Notetaking, working memory, and learning principles of economics. *Journal of Economics Education, 26,* 291–307.

Cohn, L. D., & Adler, N. E. (1992). Female and male perceptions of ideal body shapes: Distorted views among Caucasian college students. *Psychology of Women Quarterly, 16*(1), 69–79.

Coie, J. D., & Dodge, K. A. (1997). Aggression and antisocial behavior. In W. Damon & N. Eisenberg (Eds.), *Handbook of child psychology* (Vol. 3). New York: Wiley.

Coker, A. L., Davis, K. E., Arias, I., Desai, S., Sanderson, M., Brandt, H. M., & Smith, P. H. (2002). Physical and mental health effects of intimate partner violence for men and women. *American Journal of Preventive Medicine, 23*(4), 260–268.

Colder, C. R. (2001). Life stress, physiological and subjective indexes of negative emotionality and coping reasons for drinking: Is there evidence for a self-medication model of alcohol use? *Psychology of Addictive Behaviors, 15*(3), 237–245.

Cole, J. O., Goldberg, S. C., & Davis, J. M. (1966). Drugs in the treatment of psychosis. In P. Solomon (Ed.), *Psychiatric drugs.* New York: Grune & Stratton.

Cole, S. W., Kemeny, M. E., Taylor, S. E., & Visscher, B. R. (1996). Elevated physical health risk among gay men who conceal their homosexual identity. *Health Psychology, 15,* 243–251.

Coleman, M., Ganong, L., & Fine, M. (2001). Reinvestigating remarriage: Another decade of progress. In R. M. Milardo (Ed.), *Understanding families into the new millennium: A decade in review* (pp. 507–526). Minneapolis: National Council on Family Relations.

Collaer, M. L., & Hines, M. (1995). Human behavioral sex differences: A role for gonadal hormones during early development? *Psychological Bulletin, 118,* 55–107.

Colley, A., & Todd, Z. (2002). Gender-linked differences in the style and content of e-mails to friends. *Journal of Language and Social Psychology, 21*(4), 380–392.

Collins, N. L., & Feeney, B. C. (2004). An attachment theory perspective on closeness and intimacy. In D. J. Mashek & A. Aron (Eds.), *Handbook of closeness and intimacy.* Mahwah, NJ: Erlbaum.

Collins, N. L., & Miller, L. C. (1994). Self-disclosure and liking: A meta-analytic review. *Psychological Bulletin, 116,* 457–475.

Collins, N. L., & Read, S. J. (1990). Adult attachment, working models, and relationship quality in dating couples. *Journal of Personality and Social Psychology, 58,* 644–663.

Collins, R. L. (1996). For better or worse: The impact of upward social comparison on self-evaluations. *Psychological Bulletin, 119*(1), 51–69.

Collins, W. A., Maccoby, E. E., Steinberg, L., Hetherington, E. M., & Bornstein, M. H. (2000). Contemporary research in parenting: The case for nature and nurture. *American Psychologist, 55,* 218–232.

Coltrane, S. (2001). Marketing the marriage "solution": Misplaced simplicity in the politics of fatherhood. *Sociological Perspectives, 44*(4), 387–418.

Coltrane, S., & Adams, M. (2003). The social construction of the divorce "problem": Morality, child victims, and the politics of gender. *Family Relations: Interdisciplinary Journal of Applied Family Studies, 52*(4), 363–372.

Colvin, C. R., & Block, J. (1994). Do positive illusions foster mental health? An examination of the Taylor and Brown formulation. *Psychological Bulletin, 116*, 3–20.

Colvin, C. R., Block, J., & Funder, D. C. (1995). Overly positive self-evaluations and personality: Negative implications for mental health. *Journal of Personality and Social Psychology, 68*, 1152–1162.

Comas-Diaz, L. (1987). Feminist therapy with mainland Puerto Rican women. *Psychology of Women Quarterly, 11*, 461–474.

Comas-Diaz, L. (1991). Feminism and diversity in psychology: The case of women of color. *Psychology of Women Quarterly, 15*, 597–609.

Condoms—extra protection. (2005, February). *Consumer Reports*, pp. 34–38.

Condon, J. W., & Crano, W. D. (1988). Inferred evaluation and the relation between attitude similarity and interpersonal attraction. *Journal of Personality and Social Psychology, 54*(5), 789–797.

Conklin, H. M., & Iacono, W. G. (2002). Schizophrenia: A neurodevelopmental perspective. *Current Directions in Psychological Science, 11*, 33–37.

Connell, C. M., & Janevic, M. R. (2003). Health and human development. In R. M. Lerner, M. A. Easterbrooks, & J. Mistry (Eds.), *Handbook of psychology: Vol. 6. Developmental psychology*. New York: Wiley.

Connidis, I. A., & McMullin, J. A. (1999). Permanent childlessness: Perceived advantages and disadvantages among older persons. *Canadian Journal on Aging, 18*, 447–465.

Contrada, R. J., Ashmore, R. D., Gary, M. L., Coups, E., Egeth, J. D., Sewell, A., Ewell, K., Goyal, T. M., & Chasse, V. (2000). Ethnicity-related sources of stress and their effects on well-being. *Current Directions in Psychological Science, 9*(4), 136–139.

Coontz, S. (1997, November 17). Divorcing reality. *The Nation*, pp. 21–24.

Coontz, S. (2000). *The way we never were: American families and the nostalgia trap*. New York: Basic Books.

Cooper, A. (2002). *Sex and the Internet*. Philadelphia: Brunner-Routledge.

Cooper A., Boies, S., Maheu, M., & Greenfield, D. (2000). Sexuality and the Internet: The next sexual revolution. In L. T. Szuchman & F. Muscarella (Eds.), *Psychological perspectives on human sexuality*. New York: Wiley.

Cooper, A., & Griffin-Shelley, E. (2002). A quick tour of online sexuality: Part 1. *Annals of the American Psychotherapy Association, 5*(6), 11–13.

Cooper, A., Morahan-Martin, J., Mathy, R. M., & Maheu, M. (2002). Toward an increased understanding of user demographics in online sexual activities. *Journal of Sex and Marital Therapy, 28*, 105–129.

Cooper, A., Scherer, C. R., Boies, S. C., & Gordon, B. L. (1999). Sexuality on the Internet: From sexual exploration to pathological expression. *Professional Psychology: Research and Practice, 30*(2), 154–164.

Cooper, A., & Sportolari, L. (1997). Romance in cyberspace: Understanding online attraction. *Journal of Sex Education and Therapy, 22*, 7–14.

Cooper, C. L., & Dewe, P. (2004). *Stress: A brief history*. Malden, MA: Blackwell Publishing.

Cooper, L., & Bright. J. (2001). Individual differences in reactions to stress. In F. Jones & J. Bright (Eds.), *Stress: Myth, theory and research*. Harlow, England: Pearson Education.

Cooper, M. L., Albino, A. W., Orcutt, H. K., & Williams, N. (2004). Attachment styles and intrapersonal adjustment: A longitudinal study from adolescence into young adulthood. In W. S. Rholes & J. A. Simpson (Eds.), *Adult attachment: Theory,*

research, and clinical implications. New York: Guilford.

Cooper, P. J. (1995). Eating disorders and their relationship to mood and anxiety disorders. In K. D. Brownell & C. G. Fairburn (Eds.), *Eating disorders and obesity: A comprehensive handbook*. New York: Guilford Press.

Cope, M. B., Fernández, J. R., & Allilson, D. B. (2004). Genetic and biological risk factors. In J. K. Thompson (Ed.), *Handbook of eating disorders and obesity*. New York: Wiley.

Corr, C. A. (1993). Coping with dying: Lessons that we should and should not learn from the work of Elisabeth Kübler-Ross. *Death Studies, 17*(1), 69–83.

Correll, C. U., Leucht, S., & Kane, J. M. (2004). Lower risk for tardive dyskinesia associated with second-generation antipsychotics: A systematic review of 1-year studies. *American Journal of Psychiatry, 161*, 414–425.

Corsica, J. A., & Perri, M. G. (2003). Obesity. In A. M. Nezu, C. M. Nezu, & P. A. Geller (Eds.), *Handbook of psychology: Vol. 9. Health psychology*. New York: Wiley.

Costa, P. T., Jr., & McCrae, R. R. (1985). *NEO Personality Inventory*. Odessa, FL: Psychological Assessment Resources.

Costa, P. T., Jr., & McCrae, R. R. (1988). Personality in adulthood: A six-year longitudinal study of self-reports and spouse ratings on the NEO Personality Inventory. *Journal of Personality and Social Psychology, 54*, 853–863.

Costa, P. T., Jr., & McCrae, R. R. (1992). *Revised NEO Personality Inventory: NEO PI and NEO Five-Factor Inventory (Professional Manual)*. Odessa, FL: Psychological Assessment Resources.

Costa, P. T., Jr., & McCrae, R. R. (1994). Set like plaster? Evidence for the stability of adult personality. In T. F. Heatherton & J. L. Weinberger (Eds.), *Can personality change?* Washington, DC: American Psychological Association.

Costa, P. T., Jr., & McCrae, R. R. (1997). Longitudinal stability of adult personality. In R. Hogan, J. Johnson, & S. Briggs (Eds.), *Handbook of personality psychology* (pp. 269–290). San Diego: Academic Press.

Couch, K. A. (1998). Late-life job displacement. *The Gerontologist, 38*, 7–17.

Courtenay, W. H. (2000). Behavioral factors associated with disease, injury, and death among men: Evidence and implications for prevention. *Journal of Men's Studies, 9*(1), 81–142.

Cowan, C. P., & Cowan, P. A. (1997). Working with couples during stressful transitions. In S. Dreman (Ed.), *The family on the threshold of the 21st century* (pp. 17–47). Mahwah, NJ: Erlbaum.

Cowan, C. P., & Cowan, P. A. (2000). *When partners become parents*. Mahwah, NJ: Erlbaum.

Cowley, G., & Murr, A. (2004, December 6). The new face of AIDS. *Newsweek*, pp. 76–78.

Cox, M. J., Paley, B., Burchinal, M., & Payne, C. C. (1999). Marital perceptions and interactions across the transition to parenthood. *Journal of Marriage and the Family, 61*, 611–625.

Coyne, J. C. (1999). Thinking interactionally about depression: A radical restatement. In T. E. Joiner & J. C. Coyne (Eds.), *Interpersonal processes in depression* (pp. 369–392). Washington, DC: American Psychological Association.

Craik, F. I. M., & Tulving, E. (1975). Depth of processing and the retention of words in episodic memory. *Journal of Experimental Psychology. General, 104*, 268–294.

Cramer, P. (2000). Defense mechanisms in psychology today: Further processes for adaptation. *American Psychologist, 55*(6), 637–646.

Cramer, P. (2002). Defense mechanisms, behavior, and affect in young adulthood. *Journal of Personality, 70*(1), 103–126.

Creed, F. (1989). Appendectomy. In G. W. Brown & T. O. Harris (Eds.), *Life events and illness*. New York: Guilford Press.

Crepaz, N., Hart, T. A., & Marks, G. (2004). Highly active antiretroviral therapy and sexual risk behavior. *Journal of the American Medical Association, 292*(2), 224–236.

Crick, N. R., Casas, J. F., & Nelson, D. A. (2002). Toward a more comprehensive understanding of peer maltreatment: Studies of relational victimization. *Current Directions in Psychological Science, 11*(3), 98–101.

Crick, N. R., & Rose, A. J. (2000). Toward a gender-balanced approach to the study of social-emotional development: A look at relational aggression. In R. G. Geen & E. Donnerstein (Eds.), *Human aggression: Theories, research, and implications for social policy* (pp. 153–168). San Diego: Academic Press.

Crimmins, E. M., & Ingegneri, D. G. (1990). Interaction and living arrangements of older parents and their children. *Research on Aging, 12*, 3–35.

Critelli, J. W., & Ee, J. S. (1996). Stress and physical illness: Development of an integrative model. In T. W. Miller (Ed.), *Theory and assessment of stressful life events*. Madison, CT: International Universities Press.

Crits-Christoph, P. (1997). Limitations of the dodo bird verdict and the role of clinical trials in psychotherapy research: Comment on Wampold, et al. (1997). *Psychological Bulletin, 122*, 216–220.

Crocker, J., & Luhtanen, R. (1990). Collective self-esteem and ingroup bias. *Journal of Personality and Social Psychology, 58*, 60–67.

Crocker, J., & McGraw, K. M. (1984). What's good for the goose is not good for the gander: Solo status as an obstacle to occupational achievement for males and females. *American Behavioral Scientist, 27*, 357–370.

Crockett, L. J. (1990). Sex role and sex typing in adolescence. In R. M. Lerner, A. C. Petersen, & J. Brooks-Gunn (Eds.), *The encyclopedia of adolescence* (Vol. 2). New York: Garland.

Crohan, S. E. (1992). Marital happiness and spousal consensus on beliefs about marital conflict: A longitudinal investigation. *Journal of Social and Personal Relationships, 9*, 89–102.

Crook, R. H., Healy, C. C., & O'Shay, D. W. (1984). The linkage of work achievement to self-esteem, career maturity, and college achievement. *Journal of Vocational Behavior, 25*, 70–79.

Crooks, R., & Baur, K. (2005). *Our sexuality*. Belmont, CA: Wadsworth.

Cross, C. K., & Hirschfeld, R. M. A. (1986). Epidemiology of disorders in adulthood: Suicide. In G. L. Klerman, M. M. Weissman, P. S. Appelbaum, & L. H. Roth (Eds.), *Psychiatry: Vol. 5. Social, epidemiologic, and legal psychiatry*. New York: Basic Books.

Cross, P. (1977). Not can but will college teaching be improved? *New Directions for Higher Education, 17*, 1–15.

Cross, S., & Markus, H. (1991). Possible selves across the life span. *Human Development, 34*(4), 230–255.

Cross, S. E., & Gore, J. S. (2003). Cultural models of the self, In M. R. Leary & J. P. Tangney (Eds.), *Handbook of self and identity*. New York: Guilford.

Cross, S. E., & Madson, L. (1997). Models of the self: Self-construal and gender. *Psychological Bulletin, 122*(1), 5–37.

Cross, S. E., & Markus, H. R. (1999). The cultural constitution of personality. In L. A. Pervin & O. P. John (Eds.), *Handbook of personality: Theory and research* (2nd ed., pp. 378–396). New York: Guilford Press.

Cross, S. E., Bacon, P. L., & Morris, M. L. (2000). The relational-interdependent self-construal and relationships. *Journal of Personality and Social Psychology, 78*(4), 791–808.

Crouter, A. C., & Bumpus, M. F. (2001). Linking parents' work stress to children's and adolescents' psychological adjustment. *Current Directions in Psychological Science, 10*(5), 156–159.

Crouter, A. C., Bumpus, M. F., Maguire, M. C., & McHale, S. M. (1999). Linking parents' work pressure and adolescents' well-being: Insights into dynamics in dual-earner families. *Developmental Psychology, 35,* 1453–1461.

Crovitz, H. F. (1971). The capacity of memory loci in artificial memory. *Psychonomic Science, 24,* 187–188.

Crowell, J. A., Treboux, D., & Waters, E. (2002). Stability of attachment representations: The transition to marriage. *Developmental Psychology, 38,* 467–479.

Crowley, A. E., & Hoyer, W. D. (1994). An integrative framework for understanding two-sided persuasion. *Journal of Consumer Research, 20,* 561–574.

Crowley, B. J., Hayslip, B. Jr., & Hobdy, J. (2003). Psychological hardiness and adjustment to life events in adulthood. *Journal of Adult Development, 10*(4), 237–248.

Cudney, M. R., & Hardy, R. E. (1991). *Self-defeating behaviors.* New York: Harper.

Cuesta, M. J., Peralta, B., & DeLeon, J. (1994). Schizophrenic syndromes associated with treatment response. *Progress in Neurology, Psychopharmacology, and Biological Psychiatry, 18,* 87–99.

Culpepper, L., Davidson, J. R. T., Dietrich, A. J., Goodman, W. K., Kroenke, K., & Schwenk, T. L. (2004). Suicidality as a possible effect of antidepressant treatment. *Journal of Clinical Psychiatry, 65*(6), 742–749.

Cummings, E. M., Braungart-Rieker, J. M., & du Rocher-Schudlich, T. (2003). Emotion and personality development in childhood. In R. M. Lerner, M. A. Easterbrooks, & J. Mistry (Eds.), *Handbook of psychology: Vol. 6. Developmental psychology.* New York: Wiley.

Cunningham, C. O., & Selwyn, P. A. (2005). HIV-related medical complications and treatment. In J. H. Lowinson, P. Ruiz, R. B. Millman, & J. G. Langrod (Eds.), *Substance abuse: A comprehensive textbook.* Philadelphia: Lippincott/Williams & Wilkins.

Cunningham, M. (2001). The influence of parental attitudes and behaviors on children's attitudes toward gender and household labor in early adulthood. *Journal of Marriage and the Family, 63*(1), 111–122.

Cunningham, M. R., Barbee, A. P., & Pike, C. L. (1990). What do women want? Facialmetric assessment of multiple motives in the perception of male facial physical attractiveness. *Journal of Personality and Social Psychology, 59,* 61–72.

Cunningham, M. R., Druen, P. B., & Barbee, A. P. (1997). Angels, mentors, and friends: Trade-offs among evolutionary, social, and individual variables in physical appearance. In J. A. Simpson & D. T. Kenrick (Eds.), *Evolutionary Social Psychology* (pp. 109–140). Mahwah, NJ: Erlbaum.

Cunningham, M. R., Roberts, A. R., Barbee, A. P., Druen, P. B., & Wu, C., (1995). "Their ideas of beauty are, on the whole, the same as ours": Consistency and variability in the cross-cultural perception of female physical attractiveness. *Journal of Personality and Social Psychology, 68,* 261–279.

Curtis, R. C., & Miller, K. (1986). Believing another likes or dislikes you: Behaviors making the beliefs come true. *Journal of Personality and Social Psychology, 51,* 284–290.

Cutrona, C. E. (1982). Transition to college: Loneliness and the process of social adjustment. In L. A. Peplau & D. Perlman (Eds.), *Loneliness: A sourcebook of current theory, research, and therapy.* New York: Wiley.

Cutting, L. P., & Docherty, N. M. (2000). Schizophrenia outpatients' perceptions of their parents: Is expressed emotion a factor? *Journal of Abnormal Psychology, 109*(2), 266–272.

Dabbs, J. M., with Dabbs, M. G. (2000). *Heroes, rogues, and lovers: Testosterone and behavior.* New York: McGraw-Hill.

Dainton, M. (2000). Maintenance behaviors, expectations for maintenance, and satisfaction: Linking comparison levels to relational maintenance strategies. *Journal of Social and Personal Relationships, 17*(6), 827–842.

Dainton, M., & Aylor, B. (2002). Routine and strategic maintenance efforts: Behavioral patterns, variations associated with relational length, and the prediction of relational characteristics. *Communication Monographs, 69*(1), 52–66.

Dallman, M. F., Bhatnagar, S., & Viau, V. (2000). Hypothalamo-pituitary-adrenal axis. In G. Fink (Ed.), *Encyclopedia of stress* (Vol. 2, pp. 468–476). San Diego: Academic Press.

D'Amico, M. L. (1998). Internet has become a necessity, U.S. poll shows. *CNNinteractive [Internet Magazine],*1.

D'Andrade, R. G. (1966). Sex differences and cultural institutions. In E. Maccoby (Ed.), *The development of sex differences.* Stanford, CA: Stanford University Press.

Danieli, Y., Engdahl, B., & Schlenger, W. E. (2004). The psychological aftermath of terrorism. In F. M. Moghaddam & A. J. Marsella (Eds.), *Understanding terrorism: Psychological roots, consequences, and interventions.* Washington, D.C.: American Psychological Association.

Danton, W. G., & Antonuccio, D. O. (1997). A focused empirical analysis of treatments for panic and anxiety. In S. Fisher & R.P. Greenberg (Eds.), *From placebo to panacea: Putting psychiatric drugs to the test.* New York: Wiley.

Dantzer, R., & Mormede, P. (1995). Psychoneuroimmunology of stress. In B. E. Leonard & K. Miller (Eds.), *Stress, the immune system and psychiatry.* New York: Wiley.

Darley, J. M., & Gilbert, D. T. (1985). Social psychological aspects of environmental psychology. In G. Lindzey & E. Aronson (Eds.), *Handbook of social psychology* (3rd ed., Vol. 2). New York: Random House.

Darling, C. A., Davidson, J. K., & Conway-Welch, C. (1990). Female ejaculation: Perceived origins, the Grafenberg spot/area, and sexual responsiveness. *Archives of Sexual Behavior, 19,* 29–47.

Darling, C. A., Davidson, J. K., & Cox, R. P. (1991). Female sexual response and the timing of partner orgasm. *Journal of Sex and Marital Therapy, 17,* 3–21.

Das, E. H. H. J., de Wit, J. B. F., & Stroebe, W. (2003). Fear appeals motivate acceptance of action recommendations: Evidence for a positive bias in the processing of persuasive messages. *Personality and Social Psychology Bulletin, 29*(5), 650–664.

D'Augelli, A. R., & Hershberger, S. L. (1993). Lesbian, gay, and bisexual youth in community settings: Personal challenges and mental health problems. *American Journal of Community Psychology, 21,* 421–448.

Davidson, J. K., & Moore, N. B. (1994). Masturbation and premarital sexual intercourse among college women: Making choices for sexual fulfillment. *Journal of Sex and Marital Therapy, 20,* 178–199.

Davidson, M. J., & Fielden, S. (1999). Stress and the working woman. In G. N. Powell (Ed.), *Handbook of gender and work* (pp. 413–426). Thousand Oaks, CA: Sage.

Davies, L. (1995). A closer look at gender and distress among the never married. *Women and Health, 23,* 13–30.

Davis, J. A., & Smith, T. (1991). *General social surveys, 1972–1991.* Storrs, CT: University of Connecticut, Roper Center for Public Opinion Research.

Davis, J. L., & Rusbult, C. E. (2001). Attitude alignment in close relationships. *Journal of Personality and Social Psychology, 81*(1), 65–84.

Davis, K. L., Mohs, R. C., Marin, D., Purohit, D. P., Perl, D. P., Lantz, M., Austin, G., & Haroutunian, V. (1999). Cholinergic markers in elderly patients with early signs of Alzheimer's disease. *Journal of the American Medical Association, 281,* 1401–1406.

Davis, M. H., Morris, M. M., & Kraus, L. A. (1998). Relationship-specific and global perceptions of social support: Associations with well-being and attachment. *Journal of Personality and Social Psychology, 74,* 468–481.

Davis, P., & Lay-Yee, R. (1999). Early sex and its behavioral consequences in New Zealand. *Journal of Sex Research, 36,* 135–144.

Davis, R. A. (2001). A cognitive-behavioral model of pathological Internet use. *Computers in Human Behavior, 17*(2), 187–195.

Dawod, N. (1995). Stressors encountered by junior high school students and their relation to grade point average, sex and grade. *Dirasat, 22A(Supplement),* 3671–3706.

Day, S. X., & Rounds, J. (1998). Universality of vocational interest structure among racial and ethnic minorities. *American Psychologist, 53*(7), 728–736.

Day, S. X., Rounds, J., & Swaney, K. (1998). The structure of vocational interests for diverse racial-ethnic groups. *Psychological Science, 9*(1), 40–44.

DeAngelis, T. (2001, December). Are men emotional mummies? *Monitor on Psychology,* pp. 40–41.

DeAngelis, T. (2002). New data on lesbian, gay, and bisexual mental health. *Monitor on Psychology, 33*(2), 46–47.

Deaux, K., & Hanna, R. (1984). Courtship in the personals column: The influence of gender and sexual orientation. *Sex Roles, 11,* 363–375.

Deaux, K., & La France, M. (1998). Gender. In D. T. Gilbert, S. T. Fiske, & G. Lindzey (Eds.), *The handbook of social psychology.* Boston: McGraw-Hill.

Deaux, K., & Lewis, L. L. (1983). Components of gender stereotypes. *Psychological Documents, 13,* Ms. No. 2583.

Deaux, K., & Lewis, L. L. (1984). Structure of gender stereotypes: Interrelationships among components and gender label. *Journal of Personality and Social Psychology, 46,* 991–1004.

De Beni, R., Mo, A., & Cornoldi, C. (1997). Learning from texts or lectures: Loci mnemonics can interfere with reading but not with listening. *European Journal of Cognitive Psychology, 9,* 401–415.

DeCarvalho, R. J. (1991). *The founders of humanistic psychology.* New York: Praeger.

De Cock, K. M., & Janssen, R. S. (2002). An unequal epidemic in an unequal world. *Journal of the American Medical Association, 288*(2), 236–238.

DeFrain, J., & Olson, D. H. (1999). Contemporary family patterns and relationships. In M. B. Sussman, S. K. Steinmetz, & G. W. Peterson (Eds.), *Handbook of marriage and the family* (pp. 309–326). New York: Plenum Press.

Deikman, A. J. (1990). *The wrong way home: Uncovering the patterns of cult behavior in American society.* Boston: Beacon Press.

de Jong, P. J., & Merckelbach, H. (2000). Phobia-relevant illusory correlations: The role of phobic responsivity. *Journal of Abnormal Psychology, 109,* 597–601.

deJong-Gierveld, J. (1986). Loneliness and the degree of intimacy in interpersonal relationships. In R. Gilmour & S. Duck (Eds.), *The emerging field of personal relationships* (pp. 241–249). Hillsdale, NJ: Erlbaum.

Delahanty, D. L., & Baum, A. (2001). Stress and breast cancer. In A. Baum, T. A. Revenson, & J. E. Singer (Eds.), *Handbook of health psychology* (pp. 747–756). Mahwah, NJ: Erlbaum.

Delay, J., & Deniker, P. (1952). *Trente-huit cas de psychoses traitees par la cure prolongee et continue de 4560 RP.* Paris: Masson et Cie.

DelMonte, M. M. (2000). Retrieved memories of childhood sexual abuse. *British Journal of Medical Psychology, 73,* 1–13.

DeLongis, A., Folkman, S., & Lazarus, R. S. (1988). The impact of daily stress on health and mood: Psychological and social resources as mediators. *Journal of Personality and Social Psychology, 54,* 486–495.

DeMaris, A., Benson, M. L., Fox, G. L., Hill, T., & Van Wyk, J. (2003). Distal and proximal factors in domestic violence: A test of an integrated model. *Journal of Marriage and Family, 65,* 652–667.

DeMaris, A., & Swinford, S. (1996). Female victims of spousal violence: Factors influencing their level of fearfulness. *Family Relations, 45*(1), 98–106.

Demo, D. H. (1992). Parent-child relations: Assessing recent changes. *Journal of Marriage and the Family, 54,* 104–117.

Dempsey, C. (1994). Health and social issues of gay, lesbian, and bisexual adolescents. *Families in Society: The Journal of Contemporary Human Services,* 160–167.

Dempster, F. N. (1996). Distributing and managing the conditions of encoding and practice. In E. L. Bjork & R. A. Bjork (Eds.), *Memory.* San Diego: Academic Press.

Denisoff, E., & Endler, N. S. (2000). Life experiences, coping, and weight preoccupation in young adult women. *Canadian Journal of Behavioural Science, 32*(2), 97–103.

Dennerstein, L., Dudley, E., & Guthrie, J. (2002). Empty nest or revolving door? A prospective study of women's quality of life in midlife during the phase of children leaving and re-entering the home. *Psychological Medicine, 32*(3), 545–550.

Dennis, W. (1966). Creative productivity between the ages of 20 and 80 years. *Journal of Gerontology, 21,* 1–8.

DePaulo, B. M. (1992). Nonverbal behavior and self-presentation. *Psychological Bulletin, 111,* 203–243.

DePaulo, B. M. (1994). Spotting lies: Can humans learn to do better? *Current Directions in Psychological Science, 3*(3), 83–86.

DePaulo, B. M., Charlton, K., Cooper, H., Lindsay, J. J., & Muhlenbruck, L. (1997). The accuracy-confidence correlation in the detection of deception. *Personality and Social Psychology Review, 1*(4), 346–357.

DePaulo, B. M., & Friedman, H. (1998). Nonverbal communication. In D. T. Gilbert, S. T. Fiske, & G. Lindzey (Eds.), *The handbook of social psychology* (Vol. 2). Boston: McGraw-Hill.

DePaulo, B. M., LeMay, C. S., & Epstein, J. A. (1991). Effects of importance of success and expectations for success on effectiveness at deceiving. *Personality and Social Psychology Bulletin, 17,* 14–24.

DePaulo, B. M., Lindsay, J. J., Malone, B. E., Muhlenbruck, L., Charlton, K., & Cooper, H. (2003). Cues to deception. *Psychological Bulletin, 129*(1), 74–118.

DePaulo, B. M., Stone, J., & Lassiter, G. D. (1985). Deceiving and detecting deceit. In B. R. Schlenker (Ed.), *The self and social life.* New York: McGraw-Hill.

Derlega, V. J., Winstead, B. A., Wong, P. T. P., & Hunter, S. (1985). Gender effects in an initial encounter: A case where men exceed women in disclosure. *Journal of Social and Personal Relationships, 2,* 25–44.

Derogatis, L. R. (1982). Self-report measures of stress. In L. Goldberger & S. Breznitz (Eds.), *Handbook of stress: Theoretical and clinical aspects.* New York: Free Press.

Derogatis, L. R., & Coons, H. L. (1993). Self-report measures of stress. In L. Goldberger & S. Breznitz (Eds.), *Handbook of stress: Theoretical and clinical aspects* (2nd ed.). New York: Free Press.

DeRoma, V., Saylor, C., Swickert, R. , Sinsi, C., Marable, T. B., & Vickery, P. (2003). College students' PTSD symptoms, coping, and perceived benefits following media exposure to 9/11. *Journal of College Student Psychotherapy, 18*(1), 49–64.

Des Jarlais, D. C., Hagan, H., & Friedman, S. R. (2005). Epidemiology and emerging public heath perspectives. In J. H. Lowinson, P. Ruiz, R. B. Millman, & J. G. Langrod (Eds.), *Substance abuse: A comprehensive textbook.* Philadelphia: Lippincott/Williams & Wilkins.

DeSpelder, L. A., & Strickland, A. L. (1983). *The last dance: Encountering death and dying.* Palo Alto, CA: Mayfield.

Dessler, W. A. (2000). Indigenous societies. In G. Fink (Ed.), *Encyclopedia of stress* (Vol. 1, pp. 558–564). San Diego: Academic Press.

Deutsch, M., & Gerard, H. B. (1955). A study of normative and informational social influences upon individual judgment. *Journal of Abnormal and Social Psychology, 51,* 629–636.

Deveny, K. (2003, June 30). We're not in the mood. *Newsweek,* pp. 41–46.

Devine, P. G. (1989). Stereotypes and prejudice: Their automatic and controlled components. *Journal of Personality and Social Psychology, 56,* 5–18.

Devlin, M. J., Yanovski, S. Z., & Wilson, G. T. (2000). Obesity: What mental health professionals need to know. *American Journal of Psychiatry, 157*(6), 854–866.

de Vries, B. (1996). The understanding of friendship: An adult life course perspective. In C. Magai & S. H. McFadden (Eds), *Handbook of emotion, adult development, and aging.* San Diego, CA: Academic Press.

Dew, M. A., Bromet, E. J., & Switzer, G. E. (2000). Epidemiology. In M. Hersen & A. S. Bellack (Eds.), *Psychopathology in adulthood.* Boston: Allyn & Bacon.

de Wilde, E. J., Kienhorst, I. C. W. M., Diekstra, R. F. W., & Wolters, W. H. G. (1992). The relationship between adolescent suicidal behavior and life events in childhood and adolescence. *American Journal of Psychiatry, 149,* 45–51.

DeWolff, M. S., & van Ijzendoorn, M. H. (1997). Sensitivity and attachment: A meta-analysis on parental antecedents of infant attachment. *Child Development, 68,* 571–591.

Di Chiara, G. (1999). Drug addiction as dopamine-dependent associative learning disorder. *European Journal of Pharmacology, 375,* 13–30.

DiClemente, C. C., Fairhurst, S. K., & Piotrowski, N. A. (1995). Self-efficacy and addictive behaviors. In J. E. Maddux (Ed.), *Self-efficacy, adaptation, and adjustment: Theory, research and application.* New York: Plenum Press.

DiClemente, R. J., Hansen, W. B., & Ponton, L. E. (1995). *Handbook of adolescent health risk behavior.* New York: Plenum Press.

Diekman, A. B., & Eagly, A. H. (2000). Stereotypes as dynamic constructs: Women and men of the past, present, and future. *Personality and Social Psychology Bulletin, 26*(10), 1171–1188.

Diekman, A. B., & Murnen, S. K. (2004). Learning to be little women and little men: The inequitable gender equality of nonsexist children's literature. *Sex Roles, 50*(5/6), 373–385.

Diener, E. (1984). Subjective well-being. *Psychological Bulletin, 93,* 542–575.

Diener, E., & Diener, C. (1996). Most people are happy. *Psychological Science, 7,* 181–185.

Diener, E., Gohm, C. L., Suh, E., & Oishi, S. (2000). Similarity of the relations between marital status and subjective well being across cultures. *Journal of Cross-Cultural Psychology, 31,* 419–436.

Diener, E., & Lucas, R. E. (1999). Personality and subjective well-being. In D. Kahneman, E. Diener, & N. Schwarz (Eds.), *Well-being: The foundations of hedonic psychology* (pp. 213–229). New York: Sage.

Diener, E., Sandvik, E., Seidlitz, L., & Diener, M. (1993). The relationship between income and subjective well-being: Relative or absolute? *Social Indicators Research, 28,* 195–223.

Diener, E., & Seligman, M. E. P. (2002). Very happy people. *Psychological Science, 13,* 80–83.

Diener, E., & Seligman, M. E. P. (2004). Beyond money: Toward an economy of well-being. *Psychological Science in the Public Interest, 5*(1), 1–31.

Diener, E., Suh, E. M., Lucas, R. E. , & Smith, H. L. (1999). Subjective well-being: Three decades of progress. *Psychological Bulletin, 125*(2), 276–302.

Diener, E., Wolsic, B., & Fujita, F. (1995). Physical attractiveness and subjective well-being. *Journal of Personality and Social Psychology, 69,* 120–129.

Dilsaver, S. C., Chen, Y. R., Shoaib, A. M., & Swann, A. C. (1999). Phenomenology of mania: Evidence for distinct depressed, dysphoric, and euphoric presentations. *American Journal of Psychiatry, 156,* 426–430.

DiMatteo, M. R. (1991). *The psychology of health, illness, and medical care: An individual perspective.* Pacific Grove, CA: Brooks/Cole.

DiMatteo, M. R. (1997). Health behaviors and care decisions: An overview of professional-patient communication. In D. S. Gochman (Ed.), *Handbook of health behavior research II: Provider determinants.* New York: Plenum Press.

DiMatteo, M. R. (2004a). Social support and patient adherence to medical treatment: A meta-analysis. *Health Psychology, 23*(2), 207–218.

DiMatteo, M. R. (2004b). Variations in patients' adherence to medical recommendations: A quantitative review of 50 years of research. *Medical Care, 42*(3), 200–209.

DiMatteo, M. R., Giordani, P. J., Lepper, H. S., & Croghan, T. W. (2002). Patient adherence and medial treatment outcomes: A meta-analysis. *Medical Care, 40*(9), 794–811.

Dimsdale, J. E. (1988). A perspective on Type A behavior and coronary disease. *New England Journal of Medicine, 318,* 110–112.

Din, J. N., Newby, D. E., & Flapan, A. D. (2004). Omega 3 fatty acids and cardiovascular disease—fishing for a natural treatment. *British Medical Journal, 328,* 30–35.

Dinan, T. G. (2001). Stress, depression and cardiovascular disease. *Stress and Health: Journal of the International Society for the Investigation of Stress, 17*(2), 65–66.

Dindia, K. (2000). Sex differences in self-disclosure, reciprocity of self-disclosure, and self-disclosure and liking: Three meta-analyses reviewed. In S. Petronio (Ed.), *Balancing the secrets of private disclosures.* Mahwah, NJ: Erlbaum.

Dindia, K., & Allen, M. (1992). Sex differences in self-disclosure: A meta-analysis. *Psychological Bulletin, 112,* 106–124.

Dion, K. K., & Dion, K. L. (1993). Individualistic and collectivistic perspectives on gender and the cultural context of love and intimacy. *Journal of Social Issues, 49,* 53–69.

Dion, K. K., Berscheid, E., & Walster, E. (1972). What is beautiful is good. *Journal of Personality and Social Psychology, 24,* 285–290.

Dion, K. L. (2003). Prejudice, racism and discrimination. In T. Millon & M. J. Lerner (Eds.), *Handbook of psychology: Vol. 5. Personality and social psychology.* New York: Wiley.

Dion, K. L., & Dion, K. K. (1988). Romantic love: Individual and cultural perspectives. In R. J. Sternberg & M. L. Barnes (Eds.), *The psychology of love.* New Haven, CT: Yale University Press.

Dipboye, R. L. (1992). *Selection interviews: Process perspectives.* Cincinnati: South-Western.

Dishotsky, N. I., Loughman, W. D., Mogar, R. E., & Lipscomb, W. R. (1971). LSD and genetic damage: Is LSD chromosome damaging, carcinogenic, mutagenic, or teratogenic? *Science, 172,* 431–440.

DiTommaso, E., Brannen-McNulty, C., Ross, L., & Burgess, M. (2003). Attachment styles, social skills and loneliness in young adults. *Personality and Individual Differences, 35*(2), 303–312.

Dixon, L., & Browne, K. (2003). The heterogeneity of spouse abuse: A review. *Aggression and Violent Behavior, 8*(1), 107–130.

Dixon, R. A., & Cohen, A. (2003). Cognitive development in adulthood. In R. M. Lerner, M. A. Easterbrooks, & J. Mistry (Eds.), *Handbook of psychology: Vol. 6. Developmental psychology.* New York: Wiley.

Dobson, K. S., & Dozois, D. J. A. (2001). Professional psychology and the prescription debate: Still not ready to go to the altar. *Canadian Psychology, 42*(2), 131–135.

Docherty, J. P. (1999). Cost of treating mental illness from a managed care perspective. *Journal of Clinical Psychiatry, 60*, 49–53.

Dohrenwend, B. P., Raphael, K. G., Schwartz, S., Stueve, A., & Skodol, A. (1993). The structured event probe and narrative rating method for measuring stressful life events. In L. Goldberger & S. Breznitz (Eds.), *Handbook of stress: Theoretical and clinical aspects* (2nd ed.). New York: Free Press.

Dolgin, K. L. (2001). Men's friendships: Mismeasured, demeaned, and misunderstood? In T. F. Cohen (Ed.), *Men and masculinity*. New York: Wadsworth.

Dollard, J., Doob, L. W., Miller, N. E., Mowrer, O. H., & Sears, R. R. (1939). *Frustration and aggression*. New Haven, CT: Yale University Press.

Domar, A. D., & Dreher, H. (2000). *Self-nurture: Learning to care for yourself as effectively as you care for everyone else*. New York: Viking.

Donahue, E. M., Robins, R. W., Roberts, B. W., & John, O. P. (1993). The divided self: Concurrent and longitudinal effects of psychological adjustment and social roles on self-concept differentiation. *Journal of Personality and Social Psychology, 64*, 834–846.

Donnerstein, E., & Malamuth, N. (1997). Pornography: Its consequences on the observer. In L. B. Schlesinger & E. Revitch (Eds.), *Sexual dynamics of anti-social behavior* (2nd ed., pp. 30–49). Springfield, IL: Charles C. Thomas.

Donovan, P. (1997). Confronting a hidden epidemic: The Institute of Medicine's report on sexually transmitted diseases. *Family Planning Perspectives, 29*, 87–89.

Donovan, R. L., & Jackson, B. L. (1990). Deciding to divorce: A process guided by social exchange, attachment and cognitive dissonance theories. *Journal of Divorce, 13*, 23–35.

Dougall, A. L., & Baum, A. (2000). Three Mile Island, stress effects of. In G. Fink (Ed.), *Encyclopedia of stress* (Vol. 3, pp. 595–597). San Diego: Academic Press.

Dougall, A. L., & Baum, A. (2001). Stress, health, and illness. In A. Baum, T. A. Revenson, & J. E. Singer (Eds.), *Handbook of health psychology* (pp. 321–338). Mahwah, NJ: Erlbaum.

Dougherty, T. W., Turban, D. B., & Callender, J. C. (1994). Confirming first impressions in the employment interview: A field study of interview behavior. *Journal of Applied Psychology, 79*(5), 659–665.

Douglass, M. E., & Douglass, D. N. (1993). *Manage your time, your work, yourself*. New York: American Management Association.

Dovidio, J. F., Ellyson, S. L., Keating, C. F., Heltman, K., & Brown, C. E. (1988). The relationship of social power to visual display of dominance between men and women. *Journal of Personality and Social Psychology, 54*, 233–242.

Dovidio, J. F., & Gaertner, S. L. (1996). Affirmative action, unintentional racial biases, and intergroup relations. *Journal of Social Issues, 52*, 51–75.

Dovidio, J. F., & Gaertner, S. L. (1999). Reducing prejudice: Combating intergroup biases. *Current Directions in Psychological Science, 8*, 101–105.

Dovidio, J. F., Gaertner, S. L., Esses, V. M., & Brewer, M. B. (2003). Social conflict, harmony, and integration. In T. Millon & M. J. Lerner (Eds.), *Handbook of psychology: Vol. 5. Personality and social psychology*. New York: Wiley.

Doyle, J. A. (1989). *The male experience*. Dubuque, IA: William C. Brown.

Draijer, N., & Langeland, W. (1999). Childhood trauma and perceived parental dysfunction in the etiology of dissociative symptoms in psychiatric inpatients. *American Journal of Psychiatry, 156*, 379–385.

Drigotas, S. M., Rusbult, C. E., Wieselquist, J., & Whitton, S. W. (1999). Close partner as sculptor of the ideal self: Behavioral affirmation and the Michelangelo phenomenon. *Journal of Personality and Social Psychology, 77*(2), 293–323.

Driskell, J. E., Willis, R. P., & Copper, C. (1992). Effect of overlearning on retention. *Journal of Applied Psychology, 77*, 615–622.

Driver, J., Tabares, A., Shapiro, A. , Nahm, E. Y., & Gottman, J. M. (2003). Interactional patterns in marital success and failure: Gottman laboratory studies. In F. Walsh (Ed.), *Normal family processes: Growing diversity and complexity*. New York: Guilford.

Druss, B. G., & Rosenheck, R. A. (1998). Mental disorders and access to medical care in the United States. *American Journal of Psychiatry, 155*, 1775–1777.

Dryer, D. C., & Horowitz, L. M. (1997). When do opposites attract? Interpersonal complementarity versus similarity. *Journal of Personality and Social Psychology, 72*(3), 592–603.

Dubbert, P. M., King, A. C., Marcus, B. H., & Sallis, J. F. (2004). Promotion of physical activity through the life span. In J. M. Raczynski & L. C. Leviton (Eds.), *Handbook of clinical health psychology: Vol. 2. Disorders of behavior and health*. Washington, DC: American Psychological Association.

Dubovsky, S. L., Davies, R., & Dubovsky, A. N. (2003). Mood disorders. In R. E. Hales & S. C. Yudofsky (Eds.), *Textbook of clinical psychiatry*. Washington, DC: American Psychiatric Publishing.

Duck, S. (1994). *Meaningful relationships: Talking, sense, and relating*. Thousand Oaks, CA: Sage.

Duck, S., Pond, K., & Leatham, G. (1995). Loneliness and the evaluation of relational events. *Journal of Social and Personal Relationships, 11*, 253–276.

Duckworth, K., & Borus, J. F. (1999). Population-based psychiatry in the public sector and managed care. In A. M. Nicholi, Jr. (Ed.), *The Harvard guide to psychiatry*. Cambridge, MA: Harvard University Press.

Duffy, S. M., & Rusbult, C. E. (1986). Satisfaction and commitment in homosexual and heterosexual relationships. *Journal of Homosexuality, 12*, 1–23.

DuFrene, D. D., & Lehman, C. M. (2002). Persuasive appeal for clean language. *Business Communication Quarterly, 65*(1), 48–56.

Duggan, E. S., & Brennan, K. A. (1994). Social avoidance and its relation to Bartholomew's adult attachment typology. *Journal of Social and Personal Relationships, 11*, 147–153.

Dunbar-Jacob, J., & Schlenk, E. (2001). Patient adherence to treatment regimen. In A. Baum, T. A. Revenson, & J. E. Singer (Eds.), *Handbook of health psychology* (pp. 571–580). Mahwah, NJ: Erlbaum.

Dunkel-Schetter, C., Gurung, R. A. R., Lobel, M., & Wadhwa, P. D. (2001). Stress processes in pregnancy and birth: Psychological, biological, and sociocultural influences. In A. Baum, T. A. Revenson, & J. E. Singer (Eds.), *Handbook of health psychology* (pp. 495–518). Mahwah, NJ: Erlbaum.

Dunn, A. L., Trivedi, M. H., & O'Neal, H. A. (2001). Physical activity dose-response effects on outomes of depression and anxiety. *Medicine and Science in Sports and Exercise, 33*, S587–S597.

Dunning, D., & Sherman, D. A. (1997). Stereotypes and tacit inference. *Journal of Personality and Social Psychology, 73*(3), 459–471.

Dupuis, S. L., & Smale, B. J. A. (1995). An examination of the relationship between psychological well-being and depression and leisure activity participation among older adults. *Society and Leisure, 18*, 67–92.

Dweck, C. S., Higgins, E. T., & Grant-Pillow, H. (2003). Self-systems give unique meaning to self variables. In M. R. Leary & J. P. Tangney (Eds.), *Handbook of self and identity*. New York: Guilford.

Dwoskin, H., & Levenson, L. (2002). *Happiness is free: And it's easier than you think!* Sedona, AZ: Sedona Press.

Dyer, J. (2000). Evolving abuse of GHB in California: Bodybuilding drug to date-rape drug. *Journal of Toxicology, 38*, 184.

Dyer, W. W. (1976). *Your erroneous zones*. New York: Crowell.

Dyk, P. H., & Adams, G. R. (1990). Identity and intimacy: An initial investigation of three theoretical models using cross-lag panel correlations. *Journal of Youth and Adolescence, 19*, 91–110.

Eagly, A. H. (1987). *Sex differences in social behavior: A social-role interpretation*. Hillsdale, NJ: Erlbaum.

Eagly, A. H., Ashmore, R. D., Makhijani, M. G., & Longo, L. C. (1991). What is beautiful is good, but . . . : A meta-analytic review of research on the physical attractiveness stereotype. *Psychology Bulletin, 110*, 107–128.

Eagly, A. H., & Carli, L. L. (1981). Sex of researchers and sex-typed communications as determinants of sex differences in influenceability: A meta-analysis of social influence studies. *Psychological Bulletin, 90*, 1–20.

Eagly, A. H., & Karau, S. J. (2002). Role congruity theory of prejudice toward female leaders. *Psychological Review, 109*(3), 573–598.

Eagly, A. H., & Wood, W. (1999). The origins of sex differences in human behavior: Evolved dispositions versus social roles. *American Psychologist, 54*(6), 408–423.

Eagly, A. H., Wood, W., & Diekman, A. B. (2000). Social role theory of sex differences and similarities: A current appraisal. In T. Eckes & H. M. Trautner (Eds.), *The developmental social psychology of gender*. Mahwah, NJ: Erlbaum.

Eaker, E. D., Sullivan, L. M., Kelly-Hayes, M., D'Agostino, R. B., & Benjamin, E. J. (2004). Anger and hostility predict the development of atrial fibrillation in men in the Framingham Offspring Study. *Circulation, 109*(10), 1267–1271.

Eals, M., & Silverman, I. (1994). The hunter-gatherer theory of spatial sex differences: Proximate factors mediating the female advantage in recall of object arrays. *Ethology and Sociobiology, 15*, 95–115.

Easterbrook, G. (2003). *The progress paradox: How life gets better while people feel worse*. New York: Random House.

Easterlin, B. L., & Cardena, E. (1999). Cognitive and emotional differences between short- and long-term Vipassana meditators. *Imagination, Cognition and Personality, 18*(1), 68–81.

Eaton, W. W., Dryman, A., & Weissman, M. M. (1991). Panic and phobia. In L. N. Robins & D. A. Regier (Eds.), *Psychiatric disorders in America: The epidemiologic catchment area study*. New York: Free Press.

Ebbinghaus, H. (1885/1964). *Memory: A contribution to experimental psychology*. (H. A. Ruger & E. R. Bussemius, Trans.). New York: Dover. (Original work published 1885)

Eccles, J. S. (2001). Achievement. In J. Worrell (Ed.), *Encyclopedia of women and gender*. San Diego: Academic Press.

Eccles, J. S., Early, D., Frasier, K., Belansky, E., & McCarthy, K. (1997). The relation of connection, regulation, and support for autonomy to adolescents' functioning. *Journal of Adolescent Research, 12*, 263–286.

Eccles, J. S., Wigfield, A., & Byrnes, J. (2003). Cognitive development in adolescence. In R. M. Lerner, M.A. Easterbrooks, & J. Mistry (Eds.), *Handbook of psychology: Vol. 6. Developmental psychology*. New York: Wiley.

Eckert, P., & McConnell-Ginet, S. (2003). *Language and gender*. Cambridge, UK: Cambridge University Press.

Edlin, G., & Golanty, E. (1992). *Health and wellness: A holistic approach*. Boston: Jones and Bartlett.

Edwards, K., & Smith, E. E. (1996). A disconfirmation bias in the evaluation of arguments. *Journal of Personality and Social Psychology, 71*, 5–24.

Edwards, R., & Hamilton, M. A. (2004). You need to understand my gender role: An empirical test of Tannen's model of gender and communication. *Sex Roles, 50*(7/8), 491–504.

Egan, M. F., & Hyde, T. M. (2000). Schizophrenia: Neurobiology. In B. J. Sadock & V. A. Sadock (Eds.), *Kaplan and Sadock's comprehensive textbook of psychiatry* (7th ed., Vol. 1, pp. 1129–1146). Philadelphia: Lippincott/Williams & Wilkins.

Egan, T. (2000, October 23). Technology sent Wall Street into market for pornography. *New York Times*, pp. 1–20.

Egeland, B., & Hiester, M. (1995). The long-term consequences of infant day-care and mother-infant attachment. *Child Development, 66*, 474–485.

Ehrenberg, O., & Ehrenberg, M. (1994). *The psychotherapy maze: A consumer's guide to getting in and out of therapy*. Northvale, NJ: Jason Aronson.

Ehrenreich, H., Rinn, T., Kunert, H. J., Moeller, M. R., Poser, W., Schilling, L., Gigerenzer, G., & Hoehe, M. R. (1999). Specific attentional dysfunction in adults following early start of cannabis use. *Psychopharmacology, 142*, 295–301.

Eich, E., Macaulay, D., Loewenstein, R. J., & Dihle, P. H. (1997). Memory, amnesia, and dissociative identity disorder. *Psychological Science, 8*, 417–422.

Eisler, R. M., & Ragsdale, K. (1992). Masculine gender role and midlife transition in men. In V. B. Van Hasselt & M. Hersen (Eds.), *Handbook of social development: A lifespan perspective*. New York: Plenum.

Ekman, P. (1972). Universals and cultural differences in facial expressions of emotion. In J. Cole (Ed.), *Nebraska symposium on motivation, 1971*. Lincoln, NE: University of Nebraska Press.

Ekman, P. (1975, September). The universal smile: Face muscles talk every language. *Psychology Today*, pp. 35–39.

Ekman, P. (1994). Strong evidence for universals in facial expressions: A reply to Russell's mistaken critique. *Psychological Bulletin, 115*, 268–287.

Ekman, P., & Friesen, W. V. (1974). Detecting deception from the body or face. *Journal of Personality and Social Psychology, 29*(3), 288–298.

Ekman, P., & Friesen, W. V. (1984). *Unmasking the face*. Palo Alto, CA: Consulting Psychologists Press.

Ekman, P., & O'Sullivan, M. (1991). Who can catch a liar? *American Psychologist, 44*(9), 913–920.

Ekman, P., O'Sullivan, M., & Frank, M. G. (1999). A few can catch a liar. *Psychological Science, 10*(3), 263–266.

Elfenbein, H. A., & Ambady, N. (2002). On the universality and cultural specificity of emotion recognition: A meta-analysis. *Psychological Bulletin, 128*(2), 203–235.

Elias, M. F., Elias, J. W., & Elias, P. K. (1990). Biological and health influences on behavior. In J. E. Birren & K. W. Schaie (Eds.), *Handbook of the psychology of aging*. San Diego: Academic Press.

Eliot, R. S., & Breo, D. L. (1989). *Is it worth dying for?* New York: Bantam Books.

Ellington, L., & Wiebe, D. J. (1999). Neuroticism, symptom presentation, and medical decision making. *Health Psychology, 18*(6), 634–643.

Elliot, L., & Brantley, C. (1997). *Sex on campus*. New York: Random House.

Ellis, A. (1973). *Humanistic psychotherapy: The rational-emotive approach*. New York: Julian Press.

Ellis, A. (1977). *Reason and emotion in psychotherapy*. Seacaucus, NJ: Lyle Stuart.

Ellis, A. (1985). *How to live with and without anger*. New York: Citadel Press.

Ellis, A. (1987). The evolution of rational-emotive therapy (RET) and cognitive behavior therapy (CBT). In J. K. Zeig (Ed.), *The evolution of psychotherapy*. New York: Brunner/Mazel.

Ellis, A. (1989). Rational-emotive therapy. In R. J. Corsini & D. Wedding (Eds.), *Current Psychotherapies*. Itasca, IL: Peacock.

Ellis, A. (1993). The advantages and disadvantages of self-help therapy materials. *Professional Psychology: Research and Practice, 24*, 335–339.

Ellis, A. (1994). *Reason and emotion in psychotherapy*. Seacaucus, NJ: Birch Lane Press.

Ellis, A. (1995). Thinking processes involved in irrational beliefs and their disturbed consequences. *Journal of Cognitive Psychotherapy, 9*, 105–116.

Ellis, A. (1996). How I learned to help clients feel better and get better. *Psychotherapy, 33*, 149–151.

Ellis, A. (1999). *How to make yourself happy and remarkably less disturbable*. Atascadero, CA: Impact Publishers.

Ellis, A. (2001a). *Feeling better, getting better, staying better: Profound self-help therapy for your emotions*. Atascadero, CA: Impact Publishers.

Ellis, A. (2001b). *Overcoming destructive beliefs, feelings, and behaviors: New directions for Rational Emotive Behavior Therapy*. Amherst, NY: Prometheus Books.

Ellis, A. (2003). *Ask Albert Ellis: Straight answers and sound advice from America's best-known psychologist*. Atascadero, CA: Impact Publishers.

Ellis, L., & Ebertz, L. (1997). The ascendency of biology: At long last! In L. Ellis & L. Ebertz (Eds.), *Sexual orientation: Toward biological understanding*. Westport, CT: Praeger.

Elms, A., & Milgram, S. (1966). Personality characteristics associated with obedience and defiance toward authoritative command. *Journal of Experimental Research in Personality, 1*, 282–289.

Emanuel, H. M. (1987). Put time on your side. In A. D. Timpe (Ed.), *The management of time*. New York: Facts On File.

Emavardhana, T., & Tori, C. D. (1997). Changes in self-concept, ego defense mechanisms, and religiosity following seven-day Vipassana meditation retreats. *Journal for the Scientific Study of Religion, 36*, 194–206.

Emmelkamp, P. M. G. (1994). Behavior therapy with adults. In A. E. Bergin & S. L. Garfield (Eds.), *Handbook of psychotherapy and behavior change* (4th ed.). New York: Wiley.

Emmelkamp, P. M. G., & Scholing, A. (1990). Behavioral treatment for simple and social phobias. In R. Noyes, Jr., M. Roth, & G. D. Burrows (Eds.), *Handbook of anxiety: The treatment of anxiety* (Vol. 4). Amsterdam: Elsevier.

Employers bemoan workers' writing skills. (2004, September 15). *The Statesboro Herald*, p. 9.

Epstein, R. (2001). Physiologist Laura. *Psychology Today, 34*(4), 5.

Epstein, S. P. (1990). Cognitive-experiential self-theory. In L. A. Pervin (Ed.), *Handbook of personality: Theory and research*. New York: Guilford Press.

Epstein, S. P., & Katz, L. (1992). Coping ability, stress, productive load, and symptoms. *Journal of Personality and Social Psychology, 62*, 813–825.

Epstein, S. P., & Meier, P. (1989). Constructive thinking: A broad coping variable with specific components. *Journal of Personality and Social Psychology, 57*, 332–350.

Erdelyi, M. H. (2001). Defense processes can be conscious or unconscious. *American Psychologist, 56*(9), 761–762.

Erikson, E. H. (1963). *Childhood and society*. New York: Norton.

Erikson, E. H. (1968). *Identity: Youth and crisis*. New York: Norton.

Ernst, C., & Angst, J. (1983). Birth order: Its influence on personality. *Behavioral and Brain Sciences, 10*(1), 55.

Espiritu, D. A. V., Rashid, H., Mast, B. T., Fitzgerald, J., Steinberg, J., & Lichtenberg, P. A. (2001). Depression, cognitive impairment and function in Alzheimer's disease. *International Journal of Geriatric Psychiatry, 16*(11), 1098–1103.

Esterling, B. A., Kiecolt-Glaser, J. K., Bodnar, J. D., & Glaser, R. (1994). Chronic stress, social support, and persistent alterations in the natural killer cell response to cytokines in older adults. *Health Psychology, 13*, 291–298.

Esterson, A. (1993). *Seductive mirage: An exploration of the work of Sigmund Freud*. Chicago: Open Court.

Etaugh, C. (1993). Maternal employment: Effects on children. In J. Frankel (Ed.), *The employed mother and the family context*. New York: Springer.

Evans, G. W. (2001). Environmental stress and health. In A. Baum, T. A. Revenson, & J. E. Singer (Eds.), *Handbook of health psychology* (pp. 365–386). Mahwah, NJ: Erlbaum.

Evans, G. W., Hygge, S., & Bullinger, M. (1995). Chronic noise and psychological stress. *Psychological Science, 6*, 333–338.

Evans, G. W., Lepore, S. J., & Schroeder, A. (1996). The role of interior design elements in human responses to crowding. *Journal of Personality and Social Psychology, 70*, 41–46.

Evans, G. W., & Stecker, R. (2004). Motivational consequences of environmental stress. *Journal of Environmental Psychology, 24*(2), 143–165.

Evans, R. G., & Dinning, W. D. (1982). MMPI correlates of the Bem Sex Role Inventory and Extended Personal Attributes Questionnaire in a male psychiatric sample. *Journal of Clinical Psychology, 38*, 811–815.

Everly, G. S., Jr., & Mitchell, J. T. (2001). America under attack: The "10 commandments" of responding to mass terrorist attacks. *International Journal of Emergency Mental Health, 3*, 133–135.

Everson, S. A., Kauhanen, J., Kaplan, G. A., Goldberg, D. E., Julkunen, J., Tuomilehto, J., & Salonen, J. T. (1997). Hostility and increased risk of mortality and acute myocardial infarction: The mediating role of behavioral risk factors. *American Journal of Epidemiology, 146*(2), 142–152.

Ewart, C. K., & Suchday, S. (2002). Discovering how urban poverty and violence affect health: Development and validation of a neighborhood stress index. *Health Psychology, 21*(3), 254–262.

Eysenck, H. J. (1959). Learning theory and behaviour therapy. *Journal of Mental Science, 195*, 61–75.

Eysenck, H. J. (1967). *The biological basis of personality*. Springfield, IL: Charles C Thomas.

Eysenck, H. J. (1982). *Personality, genetics and behavior: Selected papers*. New York: Praeger.

Eysenck, H. J. (1988, December). Health's character. *Psychology Today*, pp. 28–35.

Eysenck, H. J. (1990). Biological dimensions of personality. In L. A. Pervin (Ed.), *Handbook of personality: Theory and research*. New York: Guilford Press.

Eysenck, H. J. (1991). Dimensions of personality: 16, 5, or 3?—Criteria for a taxonomic paradigm. *Personality and Individual Differences, 12*, 773–790.

Eysenck, H. J. (1992). Four ways five factors are not basic. *Personality and Individual Differences, 13*, 667–673.

Eysenck, H. J. (1993a). Forty years on: The outcome problem in psychotherapy revisited. In T. R. Giles (Ed.), *Handbook of effective psychotherapy*. New York: Plenum.

Eysenck, H. J. (1993b). Prediction of cancer and coronary heart disease: Mortality by means of a personality inventory: Results of a 15-year follow-up study. *Psychological Reports, 72*, 499–516.

Eysenck, M. W., Mogg, K., May, J., Richards, A., & Mathews, A. (1991). Bias in interpretation of ambiguous sentences related to threat in anxiety. *Journal of Abnormal Psychology, 100*, 144–150.

Fagot, B. I., & Hagan, R. (1991). Observations of parent reactions to sex-stereotyped behaviors: Age and sex effects. *Child Development, 62*, 617–628.

Fagot, B. I., Hagan, R., Leinbach, M. D., & Kronsberg, S. (1985). Differential reactions to assertive and communicative acts of toddler boys and girls. *Child Development, 56*, 1499–1505.

Fairbank, J. A. (1998). Health status, somatization, and severity of posttraumatic stress disorder in Vietnam combat veterans with posttraumatic stress disorder. *American Journal of Psychiatry, 155*, 1565–1569.

Fairbank, J. A., Ebert, L., & Caddell, J. M. (2001). Posttraumatic stress disorder. In P. B. Sunker & H. E. Adams (Eds.), *Comprehensive handbook of psychopathology* (3rd ed., pp. 183–210). New York: Kluwer Academic/Plenum Publishers.

Fairbrother, K., & Warn, J. (2003). Workplace dimensions, stress, and job satisfaction. *Journal of Managerial Psychology, 18*(1), 8–21.

Falk, P. (1994). The gap between psychological assumptions and empirical research in lesbian-mother child custody cases. In A. E. Gottfried & A. W. Gottfried (Eds.), *Redefining families: Implications for children's development*. New York: Plenum.

Falsetti, S. A., & Ballenger, J. C. (1998). Stress and anxiety disorders. In J. R. Hubbard & E. A. Workman (Eds.), *Handbook of stress medicine: An organ system approach*. New York: CRC Press.

Families and Work Institute. (2004). *Generation and gender in the workplace*. New York: Families and Work Institute.

Fancher, R. E. (1979). *Pioneers of psychology*. New York: Norton.

Farah, A. (1997). An overview of ECT. *Primary Psychiatry, 4*, 58–62.

Faravelli, C., & Pallanti, S. (1989). Recent life events and panic disorders. *American Journal of Psychiatry, 146*, 622–626.

Farina, A., Burns, G. L., Austad, C., Bugglin, C., & Fischer, E. H. (1986). The role of physical attractiveness in the readjustment of discharged psychiatric patients. *Journal of Abnormal Psychology, 95*, 139–143.

Farnsworth, L. (2002, August 25). Why courtesy counts. *Parade Magazine*, pp. 8–9.

Farrington, D. P., & Loeber, R. (2000). Epidemiology of juvenile violence. *Juvenile Violence, 9*, 733–748.

Fassler, D. (2001). *Talking to children about war and terrorism: 20 tips for parents*. Retrieved November 20, 2001 from American Psychiatric Association Web site: http://www.psych.org/disaster/20tipsparents11801.cfm.

Faust, K. A., & McKibben, J. N. (1999). Marital dissolution: Divorce, separation, annulment, and widowhood. In M. B. Sussman, S. K. Steinmetz, & G. W. Peterson (Eds.), *Handbook of marriage and the family* (pp. 475–502). New York: Plenum Press.

Fausto-Sterling, A. (1992). *Myths of gender: Biological theories about women and men* (2nd ed.). New York: Basic Books.

Federal Bureau of Investigation (1995). *Uniform crime reports: Crime in the United States*. Washington, DC: U.S. Government Printing Office.

Federal Interagency Forum on Aging-Related Statistics. (2004). *Older Americans 2004: Key indicators of well-being*. Washington, DC: Government Printing Office.

Feeney, J. A. (1994). Attachment style, communication patterns, and satisfaction across the life cycle of marriage. *Personal Relationships,1*, 333–348.

Feeney, J. A. (1999). Adult attachment, emotional control, and marital satisfaction. *Personal Relationships, 6*, 169–185.

Feeney, J. A. (2004). Adult attachment and relationship functioning under stressful conditions: Understanding partners' responses to conflict and challenge. In W. S. Rholes & J. A. Simpson (Eds.), *Adult attachment: Theory, research, and clinical implications*. New York: Guilford.

Feeney, J. A., & Noller, P. (1990). Attachment style as a predictor of adult romantic relationships. *Journal of Personality and Social Psychology, 58*, 281–291.

Fehr, B. (1996). *Friendship processes*. Thousand Oaks, CA: Sage.

Fehr, B. (2000). The life cycle of friendship. In C. Hendrick & S. S. Hendrick (Eds.), *Close relationships: A sourcebook* (pp. 71–82). Thousand Oaks, CA: Sage.

Fehr, B. (2004). Intimacy expectations in same-sex friendships: A prototype interaction-pattern model. *Journal of Personality and Social Psychology, 86*(2), 265–284.

Fein, S. (1996). Effects of suspicion on attributional thinking and the correspondence bias. *Journal of Personality and Social Psychology, 70*, 1164–1184.

Feingold, A. (1988). Matching for attractiveness in romantic partners and same-sex friends: A meta-analysis and theoretical critique. *Psychological Bulletin, 104*, 226–235.

Feingold, A. (1990). Gender differences in effects of physical attractiveness on romantic attraction: A comparison across five research paradigms. *Journal of Personality and Social Psychology, 59*, 981–993.

Feingold, A. (1992a). Gender differences in mate selection preferences: A test of the parental investment model. *Psychological Bulletin, 112*, 125–139.

Feingold, A. (1992b). Good-looking people are not what we think. *Psychological Bulletin, 111*, 304–341.

Feiring, C., & Lewis, M. (1987). The child's social network: Sex differences from three to six years. *Sex Roles, 17*, 621–636.

Feldman, P. J., Cohen, S., Doyle, W. J., Skoner, D. P., & Gwaltney, J. M., Jr. (1999). The impact of personality on the reporting of unfounded symptoms and illness. *Journal of Personality and Social Psychology, 77*(2), 370–378.

Feldman-Barrett, L., & Swim, J. K. (1998). Appraisals of prejudice and discrimination. In J. K. Swim & C. Stangor (Eds.), *Prejudice: The target's perspective* (pp. 11–36). New York: Academic Press.

Felker, B., & Hubbard, J. R. (1998). Influence of mental stress on the endocrine system. In J. R. Hubbard & E. A. Workman (Eds.), *Handbook of stress medicine: An organ system approach*. New York: CRC Press.

Felmlee, D. H. (1995). Causes and consequences of women's employment discontinuity, 1967–1973. *Work and Occupation, 22*, 167–187.

Felmlee, D., Sprecher, S., & Bassin, E. (1990). The dissolution of intimate relationships: A hazard model. *Social Psychology Quarterly*, 513–30.

Felson, R. B. (1989). Parents and the reflected appraisal process: A longitudinal analysis. *Journal of Personality and Social Psychology, 56*, 965–971.

Felson, R. B. (1992). Coming to see ourselves: Social sources of self-appraisals. *Advances in Group Processes, 9*, 185–205.

Felsten, G. (1996). Hostility, stress, and symptoms of depression. *Personality and Individual Differences, 21*(4), 461–467.

Fenton, W. S., & McGlashan, T. H. (1994). Antecedents, symptom progression, and long-term outcome of the deficit syndrome in schizophrenia. *American Journal of Psychiatry, 151*, 351–356.

Fenwick, P. (1987). Meditation and the EEG. In M. A. West (Ed.), *The psychology of meditation*. Oxford: Clarendon Press.

Ferguson, J. M. (2001). SSRI antidepressant medications: Adverse effects and tolerability. *Primary Care Companion Journal of Clinical Psychiatry, 3*, 22–27.

Ferguson, T. (1993). Working with your doctor. In D. Goleman & J. Gurin (Eds.), *Mind-body medicine: How to use your mind for better health*. Yonkers, NY: Consumer Reports Books.

Feroli, K., & Burstein, G. (2003). Adolescent sexually transmitted diseases. *American Journal of Maternal/Child Nursing, 28*, 113–118.

Ferrari, J. R. (1992). Psychometric validation of two adult measures of procrastination: Arousal and avoidance measures. *Journal of Psychopathology & Behavioral Assessment, 14*, 97–100.

Ferrari, J. R. (2001). Getting things done on time: Conquering procrastination. In C. R. Snyder (Ed.), *Coping with stress: Effective people and processes*. New York: Oxford University Press.

Ferrari, J. R., Johnson, J. L., & McCown, W. G. (1995). *Procrastination and task avoidance: Theory research and treatment*. New York: Plenum Press.

Ferriss, A. L. (2002). Religion and the quality of life. *Journal of Happiness Studies, 3*, 199–215.

Festinger, L. (1954). A theory of social comparison processes. *Human Relations, 7*, 117–140.

Festinger, L., Schachter, S., & Back, K. (1950). *Social pressures in informal groups: A study of human factors in housing*. Stanford, CA: Stanford University Press.

Fields, R. (2001, August 20). Seven states still classify cohabitation as illegal. *Los Angeles Times*, p. 3.

Fiese, B. H., & Skillman, G. (2000). Gender differences in family stories: Moderating influence of parent gender role and child gender. *Sex Roles, 43*(5–6), 267–283.

Fincham, F. D. (2003). Marital conflict: Correlates, structure, and context. *Current Directions in Psychological Science, 12*(1), 23–27.

Fine, R. (1990). *The history of psychoanalysis*. New York: Continuum.

Finkelhor, D., Mitchell, K., & Wolak, J. (2000). *Online victimization: A report on the nation's youth*. Washington, DC: National Center for Missing and Exploited Children.

Finkenauer, C., & Hazam, H. (2000). Disclosure and secrecy in marriage: Do both contribute to marital satisfaction? *Journal of Social and Personal Relationships, 17*(2), 245–263.

First, M. B. (2003). Psychiatric classification. In A. Tasman, J. Kay, & J. A. Lieberman (Eds.), *Psychiatry*. New York: Wiley.

Fisher, E. B., Brownson, R. C., Heath, A. C., Luke, D. A., & Sumner II, W. (2004). Cigarette smoking. In J. M. Raczynski & L. C. Leviton (Eds.), *Handbook of clinical health psychology: Vol. 2. Disorders of behavior and health*. Washington, DC: American Psychological Association.

Fisher, S., & Greenberg, R. P. (1996). *Freud scientifically reappraised: Testing the theories and therapy*. New York: Wiley.

Fishman, D. B., & Franks, C. M. (1992). Evolution and differentiation within behavior therapy: A theoretical epistemological review. In D. K. Freedheim (Ed.), *History of psychotherapy: A century of change*. Washington, DC: American Psychological Association.

Fiske, S. T. (1993). Social cognition and social perception. *Annual Review of Psychology, 44*, 155–194.

Fiske, S. T. (1998). Stereotyping, prejudice, and discrimination. In D. T. Gilbert, S. T. Fiske, & G. Lindzey (Eds.), *The handbook of social psychology*. New York: McGraw-Hill.

Fiske, S. T. (2002). What we know now about bias and intergroup conflict, the problem of the century. *Current Directions in Psychological Science, 11*(4), 123–128.

Fiske, S. T., & Ruscher, J. B. (1993). Negative interdependence and prejudice: Whence the affect? In D. M. Mackie & D. L. Hamilton (Eds.), *Affect, cognition, and stereotyping: Interactive processes in group perception*. New York: Academic.

Fiske, S. T., & Taylor, S. E. (1991). *Social cognition*. New York: McGraw-Hill.

Fitch, S. A., & Adams, G. R. (1983). Ego identity and intimacy status: Replication and extension. *Developmental Psychology, 19*, 839–845.

Fitness, J., Fletcher, G., & Overall, N. (2003). Interpersonal attraction and intimate relationships. In M. A. Hogg & J. Cooper (Eds.), *The Sage handbook of social psychology*. Thousand Oaks, CA: Sage Publications.

Fitzgerald, H. E., Mann, T., Cabrera, N., & Wong, M. M. (2003). Diversity in caregiving contexts. In R. M. Lerner, M.A. Easterbrooks, & J. Mistry (Eds.), *Handbook of psychology: Vol. 6. Developmental psychology*. New York: Wiley.

Flaks, D. K., Ficher, I., Masterpasqua, M., & Joseph, G. (1995). Lesbians choosing motherhood: A comparative study of lesbians and heterosexual parents and their children. *Developmental Psychology, 31*, 105–114.

Flannagan, D., & Perese, S. (1998). Emotional references in mother-daughter and mother-son dyads' conversations about school. *Sex Roles, 39*(5–6), 353–367.

Flannery, R. B., Jr. (1999). Psychological trauma and posttraumatic stress disorder: A review. *International Journal of Mental Health, 1*(2), 135–140.

Flavin, C., & Dunn, S. (1999). Reinventing the energy system. In L. R. Brown, C. Flavin, H. French, J. Abramovitz, S. Dunn, G. Gardner, A. Mattoon, A. P. McGinn, M. O'Meara, M. Renner, D. Roodman, P. Sampat, L. Starke, & J. Tuxill (Eds.), *State of the world 1999* (pp. 22–40). New York: Norton.

Fleeson, W., Malanos, A. B., & Achille, N. M. (2002). An intraindividual process approach to the relationship between extraversion and positive affect: Is acting extraverted as "good" as being extraverted? *Journal of Personality and Social Psychology, 83*(6), 1409–1422.

Flegal, K. M., Carroll, M. D., Ogden, C. L., & Johnson, C. L. (2002). Prevalence and trends in obesity among U.S. adults, 1999–2000. *Journal of the American Medical Association, 288,* 1723–1727.

Fleischhacker, W. W. (2002). Second-generation antipsychotics. *Psychopharmacology, 162*(1), 90–91.

Fletcher, G. J. O., & Thomas, G. (2000). Behavior and on-line cognition in marital interaction. *Personal Relationships, 7*(1), 111–130.

Fletcher, G. J. O., & Ward, C. (1988). Attribution theory and processes: A cross-cultural perspective. In M. H. Bond (Ed.), *The cross-cultural challenge to social psychology.* Newbury Park, CA: Sage.

Flett, G. L., Hewitt, P. L., & Martin, T. R. (1995). Dimensions of perfectionism and procrastination. In J. R. Ferrari, J. L. Johnson, & W. G. McCown (Eds.), *Procrastination and task avoidance: Theory, research, and treatment.* New York: Plenum Press.

Flippen, C., & Tienda, M. (2000). Pathways to retirement: Patterns of labor force participation and labor market exit among pre-retirement population by race, Hispanic orgin, and sex . *Journals of Gerontology: Series B: Psychological Sciences and Social Sciences, 55B*(1), S14–S27.

Floyd, M. (2003). Bibliotherapy as an adjunct to psychotherapy for depression in older adults. *Journal of Clinical Psychology, 59*(2), 187–195.

Foa, E. B. (1998). Rape and posttraumatic stress disorder. In E. A. Blechman & K. D. Brownell (Eds.), *Behavioral medicine and women: A comprehensive handbook* (pp. 742–746). New York: Guilford Press.

Foa, E. B., Hembree, E. A., Riggs, D., Rauch, S., & Franklin, M. (2001). *Common reactions to trauma.* Retrieved November 21, 2001 from U.S. Department of Veterans Affairs National Cen-ter for PTSD Web site: http:www.ncptsd.org/facts/disasters/fs_foa_handout.html.

Folkman, S. (1997). Positive psychological states and coping with severe stress. *Social Science and Medicine, 45,* 1207–1221.

Folkman, S., & Moskowitz, J. T. (2000). Positive affect and the other side of coping. *American Psychologist, 55*(6), 647–654.

Folkman, S., Moskowitz, J. T., Ozer, E. M., & Park, C. L. (1997). Positive meaningful events and coping in the context of HIV/AIDS. In B. H. Gottlieb (Ed.), *Coping with chronic stress* (pp. 293–314). New York: Plenum.

Forbes, G. B., Adams-Curtis, L. E., & White, K. B. (2004). First- and second-generation measures of sexism, rape, myths and related beliefs, and hostility toward women: Their interrelationships and associations with college students' experience with dating aggression and sexual coercion. *Violence Against Women, 10*(3), 236–261.

Formicelli, L. (2001, March/April). Baby blues. *Psychology Today,* p. 24.

Forrest, J. A., & Feldman, R. S. (2000). Detecting deception and judge's involvement: Lower task involvement leads to better lie detection. *Personality and Social Psychology Bulletin, 26*(1), 118–125.

Forsyth, D. R., & Strong, S. R. (1986). The scientific study of counseling and psychotherapy: A

unificationist view. *American Psychologist, 41,* 113–119.

Forsythe, S., Drake, M. F., & Cox, C. E. (1985). Influence of applicant's dress on interviewer's selection decisions. *Journal of Applied Psychology, 70,* 374–378.

Fouts, G., & Burggraf, K. (1999). Television situation comedies: Female body images and verbal reinforcements. *Sex Roles, 40*(5/6), 473–481.

Fouts, G., & Vaughan, K. (2002). Television situation comedies: Male weight, negative references, and audience reactions. *Sex Roles, 46*(11/12), 439–442.

Fowers, B. J. (2000). *Beyond the myth of marital happiness: How embracing the virtues of loyalty, generosity, justice, and courage can strengthen your relationship.* San Francisco: Jossey-Bass.

Fowers, B. J., Applegate, B., Olson, D. H., & Pomerantz, B. (1994). Marital conventionalization as a measure of marital satisfaction: A confirmatory factor analysis. *Journal of Family Psychology, 8,* 98–103.

Fowers, B. J., Lyons, E., Montel, K. H., & Shaked, N. (2001). Positive illusions about marriage among married and single individuals. *Journal of Family Psychology, 15*(1), 95–109.

Fowles, D. C. (2003). Schizophrenia spectrum disorders. In G. Stricker & T. A. Widiger (Eds.), *Handbook of psychology: Vol. 8. Clinical psychology.* New York: Wiley.

Fox, G. L., Bruce, C., & Combs-Orme, T. (2000). Parenting expectations and concerns of fathers and mothers of newborn infants. *Family Relations, 49*(2), 123–131.

Fox, G. L., & Chancey, D. (1998). Sources of economic distress: Individual and family outcomes. *Journal of Family Issues, 19,* 725–749.

Fox, R. (1996). Bisexuality in perspective: A review of theory and research. In B. Firestein (Ed.), *Bisexuality: The psychology and politics of an invisible minority.* Thousand Oaks, CA: Sage.

Fraley, R. C. (2002). Attachment stability from infancy to adulthood: Meta-analysis and dynamic modeling of developmental mechanisms. *Personality and Social Psychology Review, 6*(2), 123–151.

Fraley, R. C., & Brumbaugh, C. C. (2004). A dynamical systems approach to conceptualizing and studying stability and change in attachment security. In W. S. Rholes & J. A. Simpson (Eds.), *Adult attachment: Theory, research, and clinical implications.* New York: The Guilford.

Frank, E., Anderson, C., & Rubinstein, D. (1978). Frequency of sexual dysfunction in "normal" couples. *New England Journal of Medicine, 299,* 111–115.

Frank, J. D. (1961). *Persuasion and healing.* Baltimore: John Hopkins University Press.

Frank, J. D., & Frank, J. B. (1991). *Persuasion and healing: A comparison study of psychotherapy.* Baltimore: Johns Hopkins University Press.

Frank, L. R. (1990). Electroshock: Death, brain damage, memory loss, and brainwashing. *The Journal of Mind and Behavior, 11,* 489–512.

Frank, M. G., & Ekman, P. (1997). The ability to detect deceit generalizes different types of high-stake lies. *Journal of Personality and Social Psychology, 72*(6), 1429–1439.

Frank, R. H. (1999). *Luxury fever: Why money fails to satisfy in an era of excess.* New York: Free Press.

Frankel, F. H. (1993). Adult reconstruction of childhood events in the multiple personality literature. *American Journal of Psychiatry, 150,* 954–958.

Franks, C. M., & Barbrack, C. R. (1983). Behavior therapy with adults: An integrative perspective. In M. Hersen, A. E. Kazdin, & A. S. Bellack (Eds.), *The clinical psychology handbook.* New York: Pergamon.

Franzoi, S. L., & Herzog, M. E. (1987). Judging personal attractiveness: What body aspects do we use? *Personality and Social Psychology Bulletin, 13,* 19–33.

Frazier, P. A., Byer, A. L., Fischer, A. R., Wright, D. M., & DeBord, K. A. (1996). Adult attachment style and partner choice: Correlational and experimental findings. *Personal Relationships, 3,* 117–136.

Frederick, S., & Loewenstein, G. (1999). Hedonic adaptation. In D. Kahneman, E. Diener, & N. Schwarz (Eds.), *Well-being: The foundations of hedonic psychology* (pp. 302–329). New York: Sage.

Fredrickson, B. L. (1998). What good are positive emotions? *Review of General Psychology, 2,* 300–319.

Fredrickson, B. L. (2001). The role of positive emotions in positive psychology: The broaden-and-build theory of positive emotions. *American Psychologist, 56,* 218–226.

Fredrickson, B. L., Tugade, M. M., Waugh, C. E., & Larkin, G. R. (2003). What good are positive emotions in crises? A prospective study of resilience and emotions following the terrorist attacks on the United States on September 11th, 2001. *Journal of Personality and Social Psychology, 84*(2), 365–376.

Freedberg, K., Losina, E., Weinstein, M., Paltiel, A., Cohen, C., Seage, G., Craven, D., Zhang, H., Kimmel, A., & Goldie, S. (2001). The cost effectiveness of combination antiretroviral therapy for HIV disease. *New England Journal of Medicine,* 824–831.

Freedman, J. L., & Fraser, S. C. (1966). Compliance without pressure: The foot-in-the-door technique. *Journal of Personality and Social Psychology, 4,* 195–202.

Freeman, E., Bloom, D., & McGuire, E. (2001). A brief history of testosterone. *Journal of Urology, 165,* 371–373.

Freese, J., Powell, B., & Steelman, L. C. (1999). Rebel without a cause or effect: Birth order and social attitudes. *American Sociological Review, 64,* 207–231.

French, S. A., Harnack, L., & Jeffrey, R. W. (2000). Fast food restaurant use among women in the Pound of Prevention study: Dietary, behavioral and demographic correlates. *International Journal of Obesity, 24,* 1353–1359.

Freud, S. (1901/1960). *The psychopathology of everyday life* (Standard ed., Vol. 6.) London: Hogarth. (Original work published 1901)

Freud, S. (1920/1924). *A general introduction to psychoanalysis.* New York: Boni and Liveright. (Original work published 1920)

Freud, S. (1923). *The ego and the id* (Standard ed., Vol. 19.) London: Hogarth.

Frey, B. S., & Stutzer, A. (2002). What can economists learn from happiness research? *Journal of Economic Literature, 40,* 402–435.

Fried, S. B., & Schultis, G. A. (1995). *The best self-help and self-awareness books: A topic-by-topic guide to quality information.* Chicago: American Library Association.

Friedan, B. (1964). *The feminine mystique.* New York: Dell.

Friedberg, J. M. (1983). Shock treatment II: Resistance in the 1970s. In R. F. Morgan (Ed.), *The iatrogenics handbook: A critical look at research and practice in the helping professions.* Fair Oaks, CA: Morgan Foundation Publishers.

Friedman, H. S. (1991). *The self-healing personality: Why some people achieve health and others succumb to illness.* New York: Holt.

Friedman, J. (1989). The impact of homophobia on male sexual development. *Siecus Report, 17,* 8–9.

Friedman, M. (1996). *Type A behavior: Its diagnosis and treatment.* New York: Plenum Press.

Friedman, M., & Rosenman, R. F. (1974). *Type A behavior and your heart.* New York: Knopf.

Friedman, M. J. (1996). PTSD diagnosis and treatment for mental health clinicians. *Community Mental Health Journal, 32*(2), 173–189.

Friedrich, M. J. (2004). To "E" or not to "E," vitamin E's role in health and disease is the question. *Journal of the American Medical Association, 292*(6), 671–673.

Fromm, E. (1963). *Escape from freedom.* New York: Holt.

Fromm, E. (1981). *Sane society.* New York: Fawcett.

Fullerton, H. N., Jr. (1997). Labor force 2006: Slowing down and changing composition. *Monthly Labor Review, 120,* 23–38.

Funder, D. C. (2001). Personality. *Annual Review of Psychology, 52,* 197–221.

Furman, E. (1984). Children's patterns in mourning the death of a loved one. In H. Wass & C. A. Corr (Eds.), *Childhood and death.* Washington, DC: Hemisphere.

Furnham, A., & Cheng, H. (2000). Perceived parental behavior, self-esteem and happiness. *Social Psychiatry and Psychiatric Epidemiology, 35*(10), 463–470.

Furnham, A., & Mak, T. (1999). Sex-role stereotyping in television commercials: A review and comparison of fourteen studies done on five continents over 25 years. *Sex Roles, 41,* 413–437.

Furnham, A., & Procter, E. (1989). Belief in a just world: Review and critique of the individual difference literature. *British Journal of Social Psychology, 28*(4), 365–384.

Furstenberg, F. F., Jr. (2001). The sociology of adolescence and youth in the 1990s: A critical commentary. In R. M. Milardo (Ed.), *Understanding families into the new millennium: A decade in review* (pp. 115–129). Minneapolis, MN: National Council on Family Relations.

Furstenberg, F. F., Jr. & Kiernan, K. E. (2001). Delayed parental divorce: How much do children benefit? *Journal of Marriage and Family, 63,* 446–457.

Fyer, A. J. (2000). Anxiety disorders: Genetics. In B. J. Sadock & V. A. Sadock (Eds.), *Kaplan and Sadock's comprehensive textbook of psychiatry* (7th ed., Vol. 1, pp. 1457–1463). Philadelphia: Lippincott/Williams & Wilkins.

Gabrel, C. S. (2000). *Advance data from Vital and Health Statistics of the Centers for Disease Control and Prevention.* Washington, DC: U.S. Department of Health and Human Services.

Gabriel, S., & Gardner, W. L. (1999). Are there "his" and "hers" types of interdependence? The implications of gender differences in collective versus relational interdependence for affect, behavior, and cognition. *Journal of Personality and Social Psychology, 77*(3), 642–655.

Gaertner, S. L., & Dovidio, J. F. (1986). The aversive form of racism. In J. F. Dovidio & S. L. Gaertner (Eds.), *Prejudice, discrimination, and racism: Theory and research.* Orlando, FL: Academic Press.

Gall, T. L., Evans, D. R., & Howard, J. (1997). The retirement adjustment process: Changes in the well-being of male retirees across time. *Journal of Gerontology: Psychological Sciences, 52,* 110–117.

Gallagher, R., & Chase, A. (2002). *Building resilience in children in the face of fear and tragedy.* Retrieved January 11, 2005 From the New York University Child Study Center Website: Http://www.Aboutourkids.Org/Aboutour/Articles/Crisis_Resilience.html.

Gambone, J. C., Reiter, R. C., & DiMatteo, M. R. (1994). *The PREPARED provider: A guide for improved patient communication.* Beaverton, OR: Mosybl Great Performance.

Gangestad, S. W. (1993). Sexual selection and physical attractiveness: Implications for mating dynamics. *Human Nature, 4,* 205–235.

Gangestad, S. W., & Snyder, M. (2000). Self-monitoring appraisal and reappraisal. *Psychological Bulletin, 126*(4), 530–555.

Gantt, W. H. (1975, April 25). Unpublished lecture, Ohio State University. Cited in D. Hothersall (1984), *History of psychology.* New York: Random House.

Gao, G. (2001). Intimacy, passion and commitment in Chinese and U.S. American romantic relationships. *International Journal of Intercultural Relations, 25*(3), 329–342.

Garb, H. N., Florio, C. M., & Grove, W. M. (1998). The validity of the Rorschach and the Minnesota Multiphasic Personality Inventory: Results from meta-analysis. *Psychological Science, 9,* 402–404.

Garfield, S. L., & Bergin, A. E. (1994). Introduction and historical overview. In A. E. Bergin & S. L. Garfield (Eds.), *Handbook of psychotherapy and behavior change* (4th ed.). New York: Wiley.

Garfinkel, P. E. (1995). Classification and diagnosis of eating disorders. In K. D. Brownell & C. G. Fairburn (Eds.), *Eating disorders and obesity: A comprehensive handbook.* New York: Guilford Press.

Garland, A. F., & Zigler, E. (1993). Adolescent suicide prevention: Current research and social policy implications. *American Psychologist, 48,* 169–182.

Garlow, S. J., Musselman, D. L., & Nemeroff, C. B. (1999). The neurochemistry of mood disorders: Clinical studies. In D. S. Charney, E. J. Nestler, & B. S. Bunney (Eds.), *Neurobiology of mental illness* (pp. 348–364). New York: Oxford University Press.

Garner, D. M., Garfinkel, P. E., Schwartz, D., & Thompson, M. (1980). Cultural expectations of thinness in women. *Psychological Reports, 47,* 483–491.

Garnets, L., & Kimmel, D. (1991). Lesbian and gay male dimensions in the psychological study of human diversity. In J. D. Goodchilds (Ed.), *Psychological perspectives on human diversity in America.* Washington, DC: American Psychological Association.

Garnets, L. D., & Kimmel, D. C. (2003a). Identity development and stigma management. In L. D. Garnets & D. C. Kimmel (Eds.), *Psychological perspectives on lesbian, gay, and bisexual experiences.* New York: Columbia University Press.

Garnets, L. D., & Kimmel, D. C. (2003b). Lesbian, gay male, and bisexual dimensions in the psychological study of human diversity. In L. D. Garnets & D. C. Kimmel (Eds.), *Psychological perspectives on lesbian, gay and bisexual experiences.* New York: Columbia University Press.

Garnets, L. D., & Kimmel, D. C. (2003c). Mental health. In L. D. Garnets & D. C. Kimmel (Eds.), *Psychological perspectives on lesbian, gay, and bisexual experiences.* New York: Columbia University Press.

Gartrell, N., Banks, A., Hamilton, J., Reed, N., Bishop, H., & Rodas, C. (1999). The national lesbian family study: Interviews with mothers of toddlers. *American Journal of Orthopsychiatry, 69,* 362–369.

Gatz, M., & Smyer, M. A. (2001). Mental health and aging at the outset of the twenty-first century. In J. E. Birren & K. W. Schaie (Eds.), *Handbook of the psychology of aging.* San Diego, CA: Academic Press.

Gavin, L. E., Black, M. M., Minor, S., Abel, Y., & Bentley, M. E. (2002). Young, disadvantaged fathers' involvement with their infants: An ecological perspective. *Journal of Adolescent Health, 31,* 266–276.

Ge X., G., Conger, R. D., & Elder, G. H. Jr. (2001). The relation between puberty and psychological distress in adolescent boys. *Journal of Research on Adolescence, 11*(1), 49–70.

Ge, X., Conger, R. D., & Elder, G. H. Jr. (1996). Coming of age too early: Pubertal influences on girls' vulnerability to psychological distress. *Child Development, 67,* 3386–3400.

Gecas, V., & Schwalbe, M. L. (1986). Parental behavior and adolescent self-esteem. *Journal of Marriage and the Family, 48,* 37–46.

Gecas, V., & Seff, M. A. (1990). Families and adolescents: A review of the 1980s. *Journal of Marriage and the Family, 52,* 941–958.

Geddes, J. R., Burgess, S., Hawton, K., Jamison, K., & Goodwin, G. M. (2004). Long-term lithium therapy for bipolar disorder: Systematic review and meta-analysis of randomized controlled trials. *American Journal of Psychiatry, 161,* 217–222.

Geddes, J. R., & Lawrie, S. M. (1995). Obstetrical complications and schizophrenia: A meta-analysis. *British Journal of Psychiatry, 167,* 786–793.

Geen, R. G. (1997). Psychophysiological approaches to personality. In R. Hogan, J. Johnson, & S. Briggs (Eds.), *Handbook of personality psychology* (pp. 387–408). San Diego, CA: Academic Press.

Geen, R. G. (1998). Aggression and antisocial behavior. In D. T. Gilbert, S. T. Fiske, & G. Lindzey (Eds.), *The handbook of social psychology* (4th ed., Vol. 2, pp. 317–356). Boston: McGraw-Hill.

Geller, A. (2003, October 23). Employers looking for places to trim worker flexibility programs. *Statesboro Herald.*

Gelles, R. J. (1996). *The book of David: How preserving families can cost children's lives.* New York: Basic Books.

Gelles, R. J. (1997). *Intimate violence in families* (3rd ed.). Thousand Oaks, CA: Sage.

Genuis, S., & Genuis, S. (1995). Adolescent sexual involvement: Time for primary prevention. *The Lancet, 345,* 240–241.

George, S. A. (2002). The menopause experience: A woman's perspective. *Journal of Obstetric, Gynecologic, and Neonatal Nursing, 31,* 71–85.

Gerbner, G., Gross, L., Morgan, M., & Signorielli, N. (1986). Living with television: The dynamics of the cultivation process. In J. Bryant & D. Zillmann (Eds.), *Perspectives on media effects* (pp. 17–40). Hillsdale, NJ: Erlbaum.

Gershoff, E. T. (2002). Corporal punishment by parents and associated child behaviors and experiences: A meta-analytic and theoretical review. *Psychological Bulletin, 128*(4), 539–579.

Ghosh, T. B., & Victor, B. S. (1994). Suicide. In R. E. Hales, S. C. Yudofsky, & J. A. Talbott (Eds.), *The American Psychiatric Press textbook of psychiatry* (2nd ed.). Washington, DC: American Psychiatric Press.

Gibbons, J. L. (2000). Gender development in cross-cultural perspective. In T. Eckes & H. M. Trautner (Eds.), *The developmental social psychology of gender.* Mahwah, NJ: Erlbaum.

Gibson, B., & Sachau, D. (2000). Sandbagging as a self-presentational strategy: Claiming to be less than you are. *Personality and Social Psychology Bulletin, 26,* 56-70.

Giddens, A. (2001). The global revolution in family and personal life. In A. S. Skolnick, & J. H. Skolnick (Eds.), *Families in Transition.* Boston: Allyn & Bacon.

Gilbert, D. T., & Malone, P. S. (1995). The correspondence bias. *Psychological Bulletin, 117,* 21–38.

Gilder, G. F. (1992). *Men and marriage.* New York: Pelican.

Giles, T. R., & Marafiote, R. A. (1998). Managed care and the practitioner: A call for unity. *Clinical Psychology: Science & Practice, 5,* 41–50.

Gilham, J. E., Shatté, A. J., Reivich, K. J., & Seligman, M. E. P. (2001). Optimism, pessimism, and explanatory style. In E. C. Chang (Ed.), *Optimism & pessimism: Implications for theory, research, and practice* (pp. 53–76). Washington, DC: American Psychological Association.

Gilovich, T., & Savitsky, K. (1999). The spotlight effect and the illusion of transparency: Egocentric assessments of how we are seen by others. *Psychological Science, 8*(6), 165–168.

Gitlin, M. (2002). Pharmacological treatment of depression. In I. H. Gotlib & C. L. Hammen (Eds.), *Handbook of depression.* New York: Guilford.

Gitlin, M., Nuechterlein, K., Subotnik, K. L., Ventura, J., Mintz, J., Fogelson, D. L., Bartzokis, G., & Aravagiri, M. (2001). Clinical outcome following neuroleptic discontinuation in patients with remitted recent-onset schizophrenia. *American Journal of Psychiatry, 158,* 1835–1842.

Glascock, J. (2001). Gender roles on prime-time network television: Demograhics and behaviors. *Journal of Broadcasting and Electronic Media, 45*(4), 656–669.

Glass, C. R., & Arnkoff, D. B. (1992). Behavior therapy. In D. K. Freedheim (Ed.), *History of psychotherapy: A century of change*. Washington, DC: American Psychological Association.

Glass, R. M. (2001). Electroconvulsive therapy. *Journal of the American Medical Association, 285*(10), 1346–1348.

Glass, R. M. (2004). Treatment of adolescents with major depression: Contributions of a major trial. *Journal of the American Medical Association, 292*(7), 861–863.

Glassman, A., Shapiro, P. A., Ford, D. E., Culpepper, L., Finkel, M. S., Swenson, J. R., Bigger, J. T., Rollman, B. L., & Wise, T. N. (2003). Cardiovascular health and depression. *Journal of Psychiatric Practice, 9*(6), 409–421.

Glazer, M. P., & Glazer, P. M. (1990). *The whistleblowers: Exposing corruption in government and industry*. New York: Basic Books.

Gleason, J. B., & Ely, R. (2002). Gender differences in language development. In A. McGillicuddy-DeLisi & R. DeLisi (Eds.), *Biology, society, and behavior: The development of sex differences in cognition. Advances in applied developmental psychology, 21*. Westport, CT: Ablex.

Gleaves, D. H. (1994). On "the reality of repressed memories." *American Psychologist, 49*, 440–441.

Gleaves, D. H., May, M. C., & Cardena, E. (2001). An examination of the diagnostic validity of dissociative identity disorders. *Clinical Psychology Review, 21*, 577–608.

Gleaves, D. H., Miller, K. J., Williams, T. J., & Summers, S. A. (2000). Eating disorders: An overview. In K. J. Miller & J. S. Mizes (Eds.), *Comparative treatments for eating disorders*. New York: Springer.

Gleaves D. H., & Smith. S. M. (2004). False and recovered memories in the laboratory and clinic: A review of experimental and clinical evidence. *Clinical Psychology: Science and Practice, 11*(1), 2–28.

Glei, D. A. (1999). Measuring contraceptive use patterns among teenage and adult women. *Family Planning Perspectives, 31*(2), 73–80.

Glenberg, A. M. (1992). Disturbed practice effects. In L. R. Squire (Ed.), *Encyclopedia of learning and memory*. New York: Macmillan.

Glenn, N. D. (1998). The course of marital success and failure in five American 10-year marriage cohorts. *Journal of Marriage and the Family, 60*, 569–576.

Goeders, N. E. (2004). Stress, motivation, and drug addiction. *Current Directions in Psychological Science, 13*(1), 33–35.

Goetting, A. (1986). Parental satisfaction: A review of research. *Journal of Family Issues, 7*, 83–109.

Gold, D. T. (1990). Late-life sibling relationships: Does race affect typological distribution? *The Gerontologist, 30*, 741–748.

Gold, M. S., & Jacobs, W. S. (2005). Cocaine and crack: Clinical aspects. In J. H. Lowinson, P. Ruiz, R. B. Millman, & J. G. Langrod (Eds.), *Substance abuse: A comprehensive textbook*. Philadelphia: Lippincott/Williams & Wilkins.

Gold, M. S., Miller, N. S., & Jonas, J. M. (1992). Cocaine (and crack): Neurobiology. In J. H. Lowinson, P. Ruiz, & R. B. Millman (Eds.), *Substance abuse: A comprehensive textbook* (2nd ed.). Baltimore: Williams & Wilkins.

Goldberg, C., & Zhang, L. (2004). Simple and joint effects of gender and self-esteem on responses to same-sex sexual harrassment. *Sex Roles, 50*(11/12), 823–833.

Goldberg, M. (1985). Remarriage: Repetition versus new beginnings. In D. C. Goldberg (Ed.), *Contemporary marriage: Special issues in couples therapy*. Homewood, IL: Dorsey Press.

Goldberger, L. (1993). Sensory deprivation and overload. In L. Goldberger & S. Breznitz (Eds.), *Handbook of stress: Theoretical and clinical aspects* (2nd ed.). New York: Free Press.

Goldenberg, J. L., Pyszczynski, T., McCoy, S. K., Greenberg, J., & Solomon, S. (1999). Death, sex, love and neuroticism: Why is sex such a problem? *Journal of Personality and Social Psychology, 77*(6), 1173–1187.

Goldfried, M. R. (2001). Integrating gay, lesbian, and bisexual issues into mainstream psychology. *American Psychologist, 56*(11), 977–988.

Goldfried, M. R., Greenberg, L. S., & Marmar, C. (1990). Individual psychotherapy: Process and outcome. *Annual Review of Psychology, 41*, 659–688.

Golding, J. M. (1996). Sexual assault history and women's reproductive and sexual health. *Psychology of Women Quarterly, 20*, 101–121.

Goldscheider, F. K., & Goldscheider, C. (1998). The effects of childhood family structure on leaving and returning home. *Journal of Marriage and the Family, 60*, 745–756.

Goldstein, E., & Farmer, K. (Eds.). (1993). *True stories of false memories*. Boca Raton, FL: Sirs Publishing.

Goldstein, J. R. (1999). The leveling of divorce in the United States. *Demography, 36*, 409–414.

Golombok, S., Perry, B., Burnston, A., Murray, C., Money-Somers, J., Stevens, M., & Golding, J. (2003). Children with lesbian parents: A community study. *Developmental Psychology, 39*, 20–33.

Gonsiorek, J. (1991). The empirical basis for the demise of the illness model of homosexuality. In J. Gonsiorek & J. Weinrich (Eds.), *Homosexuality: Research implications for public policy*. Newbury Park, CA: Sage.

Gonsiorek, J. C., & Weinrich, J. D. (1991). The definition and scope of sexual orientation. In J. C. Gonsiorek & J. D. Weinrich (Eds.), *Homosexuality: Research implications for public policy*. Newbury Park, CA: Sage.

Gonzales, M. H., & Meyers, S. A. (1993). "Your mother would like me": Self-presentation in the personals ads of heterosexual and homosexual men and women. *Personality and Social Psychology Bulletin, 19*, 131–142.

Gonzalez-Lopez, A., & Kamps, D. M. (1997). Social skills training to increase social interactions between children with autism and their typical peers. *Focus on Autism & Other Developmental Disabilities, 12*, 2–14.

Goodall, K. (1972, November). Field report: Shapers at work. *Psychology Today*, pp. 53–63, 132–138.

Gooden, A. M., & Gooden, M. A. (2001). Gender representation in notable children's picture books: 1995–1999. *Sex Roles, 45*(1/2), 89–101.

Goodrick, G. K., Pendleton, V. R., Kimball, K. T., Poston, W. S., Carlos, R., Rebecca, S., & Foreyt, J. P. (1999). Binge eating severity, self-concept, dieting self-efficacy and social support during treatment of binge eating disorder. *International Journal of Eating Disorders, 26*(3), 295–300.

Goodwin, F. K., & Jamison, K. R. (1990). *Manic-depressive illness*. New York: Oxford University Press.

Gordon, R. A. (1996). Impact of ingratiation on judgments and evaluations: A meta-analytic investigation. *Journal of Personality and Social Psychology, 71*(1), 54–70.

Gottdiener, J. S., Krantz, D. S., & Howell, R. H., Hecht, G. M., Klein, J., Falconer, J. J., & Rozanski, A. (1994). Induction of silent myocardial ischemia with mental stress testing: Relationship to the triggers of ischemia during daily life activities and to ischemic functional severity. *Journal of the American College of Cardiology, 24*, 1645–1651.

Gottesman, I. I. (1991). *Schizophrenia genesis: The origins of madness*. New York: Freeman.

Gottesman, I. I. (2001). Psychopathology through a life span–genetic prism. *American Psychologist, 56*, 867–878.

Gottman, J. M. (1993). The roles of conflict engagement, escalation, and avoidance in marital interaction: A longitudinal view of five types of couples. *Journal of Consulting and Clinical Psychology, 61*(1), 6–15.

Gottman, J. M., Coan, J., Carrere, S., & Swanson, C. (1998). Predicting marital happiness and stability from newlywed interactions. *Journal of Marriage and the Family, 60*, 5–22.

Gottman, J. M. (with DeClaire, J.). (2001). *The relationship cure: A five-step guide for building better connections with family, friends, and lovers*. New York: Crown.

Gottman, J. M., Ryan, K. D., Carrére, S., & Erley, A. M. (2002). Toward a scientifically based marital therapy. In H. Liddle & D. Santisteban (Eds.), *Family psychology: Science-based interventions*. Washington, DC: American Psychological Association.

Gottman, J. M. (with Silver, N.). (1994). *Why marriages succeed or fail . . . And how you can make yours last*. New York: Simon & Schuster.

Gottman, J. M. (with Silver, N.). (1999). *The seven principles for making marriage work*. New York: Three Rivers Press.

Gould, R. L. (1978). *Transformations: Growth and change in adult life*. New York: Simon & Schuster.

Gourevitch, M. N., & Arnsten, J. H. (2005). Medical complications of drug use. In J. H. Lowinson, P. Ruiz, R. B. Millman, & J. G. Langrod (Eds.), *Substance abuse: A comprehensive textbook*. Philadelphia: Lippincott/Williams & Wilkins.

Gouzoulis-Mayfrank, E., Daumann, J., Tuchtenhagen, F., Pelz, S., Becker, S., Kunert, H.-J., Fimm, B., & Sass, H. (2000). Impaired cognitive performance in drug-free users of recreational ecstasy (MDMA). *Journal of Neurology, Neurosurgery, and Psychiatry, 68*(6), 719–725.

Gow, K. M. (1999). Recovered memories of abuse: Real, fabricated, or both? *Australian Journal of Clinical & Experimental Hypnosis, 27*(2), 81–97.

Graber, J. A., Lewinsohn, P. M., Seeley, J. R., & Brooks-Gunn, J. (1997). Is psychopathology associated with the timing of pubertal development? *Journal of the American Academy of Child and Adolescent Psychiatry, 36*, 1768–1776.

Graber, J. A., Petersen, A. C., & Brooks-Gunn, J. (1996). Pubertal processes: Methods, measures, and models. In J. A. Graber, J. Brooks-Gunn, & A. C. Petersen (Eds.), *Transitions through adolescence* (pp. 23–53). Mahwah, NJ: Erlbaum.

Graber, J. A., Seeley, J. R., Brooks-Gunn, J., & Lewinsohn, P. M. (2004). Is pubertal timing associated with psychopathology in young adulthood? *Journal of American Academy of Child and Adolescent Psychiatry, 43*(6), 718–726.

Graig, E. (1993). Stress as a consequence of the urban physical environment. In L. Goldberger & S. Breznitz (Eds.), *Handbook of stress: Theoretical and clinical aspects* (2nd ed.). New York: Free Press.

Grant, I., McDonald, W. I., Patterson, T., & Trimble, M. R. (1989). Multiple sclerosis. In G. W. Brown & T. O. Harris (Eds.), *Life events and illness*. New York: Guilford Press.

Gray, J. (1992). *Men are from Mars, women are from Venus: A practical guide for improving communication and getting what you want in your relationship*. New York: HarperCollins.

Gray-Little, B., & Hafdahl, A. R. (2000). Factors influencing racial comparisons of self-esteem: A quantitative review. *Psychological Bulletin, 126*, 26–54.

Graziano, W. G., & Eisenberg, N. H. (1997). Agreeableness: A dimension of personality. In R. Hogan, J. Johnson, & S. Briggs (Eds), *Handbook of personality psychology*. San Diego, CA: Academic Press.

Green, L. R., Richardson, D. S., Lago, T., & Schatten-Jones, E. C. (2001). Network correlates of social and emotional loneliness in young and older adults. *Personality and Social Psychology Bulletin, 27*(3), 281–288.

Green, S. K., Buchanan, D. R., & Heuer, S. K. (1984). Winners, losers, and choosers: A field investigation of dating initiation. *Personality and Social Psychology Bulletin, 10*, 502–511.

Greenberg, J. S. (2002). *Comprehensive stress management: Health and human performance.* New York: McGraw-Hill.

Greenberg, J., Solomon, S., & Pyszczynski, T. (1997). Terror management theory of self-esteem and cultural worldviews: Empirical assessments and conceptual refinements. *Advances in Experimental Social Psychology, 29,* 61–139.

Greenberg, R. P., & Fisher, S. (1997). Mood-mending medicines: Probing drug, psychotherapy and placebo solutions. In S. Fisher & R. P. Greenberg (Eds.), *From placebo to panacea: Putting psychiatric drugs to the test.* New York: Wiley.

Greene, R. L. (1992). *Human memory: Paradigms and paradoxes.* Hillsdale, NJ: Erlbaum.

Greenfield, D. N. (1999). Psychological characteristics of compulsive Internet use: A preliminary analysis. *CyberPsychology and Behavior, 2*(5), 403–412.

Greenhaus, J. H. (2003). Career dynamics. In W. C. Borman, D. R. Ilgen, & R. J. Klimoski (Eds.), *Handbook of psychology: Vol. 12. Industrial and organizational psychology.* New York: Wiley.

Greenland, P., Knoll, M. D., Stamler, J., Neaton, J. D., Dyer, A. R., Garside, D. B., & Wilson, P. W. (2003). Major risk factors as antecedents of fatal and nonfatal coronary heart disease events. *Journal of the American Medical Association, 290,* 891–897.

Greenson, R. R. (1967). *The technique and practice of psychoanalysis* (Vol. 1). New York: International Universities Press.

Greenwald, A. G., & Banaji, M. R. (1995). Implicit social cognition: Attitudes, self-esteem, and stereotypes. *Psychological Review, 102*(1), 4–27.

Greenwood, G. L., Relf, M. V., Huang, B., Pollack, L. M., Canchola, J. A., & Catania, J. A. (2002). Battering victimization among a probability-based sample of men who have sex with men. *American Journal of Public Health, 92*(12), 1964–1969.

Gregersen, E. (1982). *Sexual practices.* New York: Franklin Watts.

Gregory, R. J., Schwer Canning, S., Lee, T. W., & Wise, J. C. (2004). Cognitive bibliotherapy for depression: A meta-analysis. *Professional Psychology: Research and Practice, 35*(3), 275–280.

Grencavage, L. M., & Norcross, J. C. (1990). Where are the commonalities among the therapeutic factors? *Professional Psychology: Research and Practice, 21,* 372–378.

Griffith, K. H., & Hebl, M. R. (2002). The disclosure dilemma for gay men and lesbians: "Coming out" at work. *Journal of Applied Psychology, 87*(6), 1191–1199.

Griffiths, M. (1999). Internet addiction: Fact or fiction? *Psychologist, 12*(5), 246–250.

Grinspoon, L., & Bakalar, J. B. (1997). Marihuana. In J. H. Lowinson, P. Ruiz, R. H. Millman, & J. G. Langrod (Eds.), *Substance abuse: A comprehensive textbook* (3rd ed.). Baltimore: Williams & Wilkins.

Grinspoon, L., Bakalar, J. B., & Russo, E. (2005). Marihuana: Clinical aspects. In J. H. Lowinson, P. Ruiz, R. B. Millman, & J. G. Langrod (Eds.), *Substance abuse: A comprehensive textbook.* Philadelphia: Lippincott/Williams & Wilkins.

Groat, H. T., Giordano, P. C., Cernkovich, S. A., Pugh, M. D., & Swinford, S. P. (1997). Attitudes toward childbearing among young parents. *Journal of Marriage and the Family, 59,* 568–581.

Grob, C. S., & Poland, R. E. (1997). MDMA. In J. H. Lowinson, P. Ruiz, R. B. Millman, & J. G. Langrod (Eds.), *Substance abuse: A comprehensive textbook* (3rd ed.). Baltimore: Williams & Wilkins.

Grob, C. S., & Poland, R. E. (2005). MDMA. In J. H. Lowinson, P. Ruiz, R. B. Millman, & J. G. Langrod (Eds.), *Substance abuse: A comprehensive textbook.* Philadelphia: Lippincott/Williams & Wilkins.

Grob, G. N. (1983). Disease and environment in American history. In D. Mechanic (Ed.), *Handbook of health, health care, and the health professions.* New York: Free Press.

Grolnick, W. S., & Ryan, R. M. (1989). Parent styles associated with children's self-regulation and competence in school. *Journal of Educational Psychology, 81,* 143–154.

Gross, J. J. (2001). Emotion regulation in adulthood: Timing is everything. *Current Directions in Psychological Science, 10,* 214–219.

Gross, M. (2003). The second wave will drown us. *American Journal of Public Health, 93*(6), 872–881.

Grossbaum, M. F., & Bates, G. W. (2002). Correlates of psychological well-being at midlife: The role of generativity, agency and communion, and narrative themes. *International Journal of Behavioral Development, 26*(2), 120–127.

Gruber, J. E. (1990). Methodological problems and policy implication in sexual harassment research. *Population Research and Policy Review, 9,* 235–254.

Gruenberg, A. M., & Goldstein, R. D. (2003). Mood disorders: Depression. In A. Tasman, J. Kay, & J. A. Lieberman (Eds.), *Psychiatry.* New York: Wiley.

Grunberg, N. E., Faraday, M. M., & Rahman, M. A. (2001). The psychobiology of nicotine self-administration. In A. Baum, T. A. Revenson, & J. E. Singer (Eds.), *Handbook of health psychology* (pp. 249–262). Mahwah, NJ: Erlbaum.

Guest, F. (2004). HIV/AIDS and reproductive health. In R. A. Hatcher, J. Trussell, F. H. Stewart, A. L. Nelson, W. Cates Jr., F. Guest, & D. Kowal (Eds.), *Contraceptive technology.* New York: Ardent Media.

Guggenheim, F. G. (2000). Somatoform disorders. In B. J. Sadock & V. A. Sadock (Eds.), *Kaplan and Sadock's comprehensive textbook of psychiatry* (7th ed., Vol. 1, pp. 1504–1532). Philadelphia: Lippincott/Williams & Wilkins.

Gullette, E. C. D., Blumenthal, J. A., Babyak, M., Jiang, W., Waugh, R. A., Frid, D. J., O'Connor, C. M., Morris, J. J., & Krantz, D. S. (1997). Effects of mental stress on myocardial ischema during daily life. *Journal of the American Medical Association, 277,* 1521–1526.

Gupta, G. R. (1992). Love, arranged marriage, and the Indian social structure. In J. J. Macionis & N. V. Benokraitis (Eds.), *Seeing ourselves: Classic, contemporary and cross-cultural reading in sociology.* Englewood Cliffs, NJ: Prentice-Hall.

Gupta, U., & Singh, P. (1982). Exploratory study of love and liking type of marriages. Indian *Journal of Applied Psychology, 19,* 92–97.

Gureje, O., Simon, G. E., Ustun, T. B., & Goldberg, D. P. (1997). Somatization in cross-cultural perspective: A world health organization study in primary care. *American Journal of Psychiatry, 154,* 989–995.

Gurland, B. J., Wilder, D. E., Lantigua, R., Stern, Y., Chen, J., Killeffer, E. H., & Mayeux, R. (1999). Rates of dementia in three ethnoracial groups. *International Journal of Geriatric Psychiatry, 14,* 481–493.

Gutek, B. A. (1989). Relocation, family, and the bottom line: Results from the Division 35 survey. *Psychology of Women Quarterly, 16,* 5–7.

Gutek, B. A. (1993). Responses to sexual harassment. In S. Oskamp & M. Costanzo (Eds.), *Gender issues in contemporary society.* Newbury Park, CA: Sage.

Gutierrez, P. M., & Silk, K. R. (1998). Prescription privileges for psychologists: A review of the psychological literature. *Professional Psychology: Research and Practice, 29*(3), 213–222.

Haan, N., Millsap, R., & Hartka, E. (1986). As time goes by: Change and stability in personality over 50 years. *Psychology of Aging, 1,* 220–232.

Haas, A., & Haas, K. (1993). *Understanding sexuality.* St. Louis: Times Mirror/Mosby.

Haas, L. (1999). Families and work. In M. B. Sussman, S. K. Steinmetz, & G. W. Peterson *Handbook of marriage and the family* (pp. 571–612). New York: Plenum Press.

Hackam, D. G., & Anand, S. S. (2003). Emerging risk factors for atherosclerotic vascular disease: A critical review of the evidence. *Journal of the American Medical Association, 290*(7), 932–940.

Hackett, G., & Watkins, C. E., Jr. (1995). Research in career assessment: Abilities, interests, decision making, and career development. In W. B. Walsh, & S. H. Osipow (Eds.), *Handbook of vocational psychology* (2nd ed., pp. 181–216). Mahwah, NJ: Erlbaum.

Hackstaff, K. B. (1999). *Marriage in a culture of divorce.* Philadelphia: Temple University Press.

Hafen, B. Q., & Hoeger, W. W. K. (1998). *Wellness: Guidelines for a healthy lifestyle.* Englewood, CO: Morton Publishing.

Hafer, C. L. (2000). Do innocent victims threaten the belief in a just world? Evidence from a modified Stroop task. *Journal of Personality and Social Psychology, 79*(2), 165–173.

Hagerty, M. R. (2000). Social comparisons of income in one's community: Evidence from national surveys of income and happiness. *Journal of Personality and Social Psychology, 78,* 746–771.

Hall, D. R. (1996). Marriage as a pure relationship: Exploring the link between premarital cohabitation and divorce in Canada. *Journal of Comparative Family Studies, 27,* 1–12.

Hall, E. T. (1966) *The hidden dimension.* Garden City, NY: Doubleday.

Hall, G. S. (1904). *Adolescence.* New York: Appleton.

Hall, J. A. (1984). *Nonverbal sex differences: Communication accuracy and expressive style.* Baltimore: Johns Hopkins University Press.

Hall, J. A. (1990). *Nonverbal sex differences: Communication accuracy and expressive style* (2nd ed.). Baltimore: Johns Hopkins University Press.

Hall, J. A. (1998). How big are nonverbal sex differences? The case of smiling and sensitivity to nonverbal cues. In D. J. Canary & K. Dindia (Eds.), *Sex differences and similarities in communication: Critical essays and empirical investigations of sex and gender in interaction* (pp. 155–177). Mahwah, NJ: Erlbaum.

Hall, J. A., Carter, J. D., & Horgan, T. G. (2000). Gender differences in the nonverbal communication of emotion. In A. Fischer (Ed.), *Gender and emotion.* Cambridge, UK: Cambridge University Press.

Hall, J. A., & Friedman, G. B. (1999). Status, gender, and nonverbal behavior: A study of structured interactions between employees of a company. *Personality and Social Psychology Bulletin, 25*(9), 1082–1091.

Hall, J. A., & Matsumoto, D. (2004). Gender differences in judgments of multiple emotions from facial expressions. *Emotion, 4*(2), 201–206.

Hall, J. A., & Veccia, E. M. (1990). More "touching" observations: New insights on men, women, and interpersonal touch. *Journal of Personality and Social Psychology, 59,* 1155–1162.

Hall, J. A., & Veccia, E. M. (1991). Touch asymmetry between the sexes. In C. L. Ridgeway (Ed.), *Gender, interaction, and inequality.* New York: Springer-Verlag.

Hall, R. M., & Sandler, B. R. (1982). *The classroom climate: A chilly one for women?* Washington, DC: Association of American Colleges.

Hall, S. A. (2002). Teaching and doing gender in African American families. *Sex Roles, 47*(11–12), 493–506.

Hall, W., Solowij, N., & Lemon, J. (1994). *The health and psychological consequences of cannabis use.* Canberra, Australia: Australian Government Publishing Service.

Halmi, K. A. (1999). Eating disorders: Anorexia nervosa, bulimia nervosa, and obesity. In R. E. Hales, S. C. Yudofsky, & J. A. Talbott (Eds.), *American Psychiatric Press Textbook of Psychiatry* (pp. 983–1002). Washington, DC: American Psychiatric Press.

Halmi, K. A. (2000). Eating disorders. In B. J. Sadock & V. A. Sadock (Eds.), *Kaplan and Sadock's* comprehensive textbook of psychiatry (7th ed., Vol. 1, pp. 1663–1676). Philadelphia: Lippincott/Williams & Wilkins.

Halmi, K. A. (2002). Physiology of anorexia nervosa and bulimia nervosa. In C. G. Fairburn & K. D. Brownell (Eds.), Eating disorders and obesity: A comprehensive handbook. New York: Guilford.

Halmi, K. A. (2003). Eating disorders: Anorexia nervosa, bulimia nervosa, and obesity. In R. E. Hales & S. C. Yudofsky (Eds.), Textbook of clinical psychiatry. Washington, DC: American Psychiatric Publishing.

Halmi, K. A., Sunday, S. R., Strober, M., Kaplan, A., Woodside, D. B., Fichter, M., Treasure, J., Berrettini, W. H., & Kaye, W. H. (2000). Perfectionism in anorexia nervosa: Variation by clinical subtype, obsessionality, and pathological eating behavior. American Journal of Psychiatry, 157, 1799–1805.

Halpern, C. T., Udry, J. R., Campbell, B., & Suchindran, C. (1999). Effects of body fat on weight concerns, dating, and sexual activity: A longitudinal analysis of black and white adolescent girls. Developmental Psychology, 35(3), 721–736.

Halpern, D. F. (1997). Sex differences in intelligence: Implications for education. American Psychologist, 52, 1091–1102.

Halpern, D. F. (2000). Sex differences in cognitive abilities (3rd ed.). Mahwah, NJ: Erlbaum.

Halpern, D. F. (2004). A cognitive-process taxonomy for sex differences in cognitive abilities. Current Directions in Psychological Science, 13(4), 135–139.

Halverson, A. M., Hallahan, M., Hart, A. J., & Rosenthal, R. (1997). Reducing the biasing effects of judges' nonverbal behavior with simplified jury instruction. Journal of Applied Social Psychology, 82(4), 590–598.

Hamilton, A. (1999). You've got mail! Time, 83.

Hamilton, J. C., Deemer, H. N., & Janata, J. W. (2003). Feeling sad but looking good: Sick role features that lead to favorable interpersonal judgments. Journal of Social & Clinical Psychology, 22(3), 253–274.

Hammen, C. (2003). Mood disorders. In G. Stricker & T. A. Widiger (Eds.), Handbook of psychology: Vol. 8. Clinical psychology. New York: Wiley.

Hammersley, R., Ditton, J., Smith, I., & Short, E. (1999). Patterns of ecstasy use by drug users. British Journal of Criminology, 39(4), 625–647.

Han, S., & Moen, P. (1999). Work and family over time: A life course approach. Annals of the American Academy of Political and Social Science, 562, 98–110.

Han, W., Waldfogel, J., & Brooks-Gunn, J. (2001). The effects of early maternal employment on later cognitive and behavioral outcomes. Journal of Marriage and the Family, 63, 336–354.

Hancock, D. R. (2001). Effects of test anxiety and evaluative threat on students' achievement and motivation. Journal of Educational Research, 94(5), 284–290.

Handy, B. (1998a, May 4). The Viagra craze. Time, 50–57.

Handy, B. (1998b, August 31). How we really feel about fidelity. Time, 52–54.

Hankin, B. L. (2002). Gender differences in depression from childhood through adulthood: A review of course, causes and treatment. Primary Psychiatry, 9(10), 32–36.

Hanna, S. L. (2003). Person to person: Positive relationships don't just happen. Upper Saddle River, NJ: Prentice Hall.

Hansen, C. H., & Hansen, R. D. (1988). How rock music videos can change what is seen when boy meets girl: Priming stereotypic appraisal of social interactions. Sex Roles, 19, 287–316.

Hansen, J. C. (2005). Assessment of interests. In S. D. Brown & R. W. Lent (Eds.), Career development and counseling: Putting theory and research to work. New York: Wiley.

Happonen, P., Voutilainen, S., & Salonen, J. T. (2004). Coffee drinking is dose dependently related to the risk of acute coronary events in middle-aged men. Journal of Nutrition, 134(9), 2381–2386.

Haring, M., Hewitt, P. L., & Flett, G. L. (2003). Perfectionism, coping, and quality of intimate relationships. Journal of Marriage & Family, 65(1), 143–158.

Harmsen, P., Rosengren, A., Tsipogianni, A., & Wilhelmsen, L. (1990). Risk factors for stroke in middle-aged men in Goteborg, Sweden. Stroke, 21, 23–29.

Harpaz, I., & Snir, R. (2003). Workaholism: Its definition and nature. Human Relations, 56(3), 291–319.

Harrigan, J. A., Lucic, K. S., Kay, D., McLaney, A., & Rosenthal, R. (1991). Effect of expresser role and type of self-touching on observers' perceptions. Journal of Applied Psychology, 21, 585–609.

Harris, J. R. (1995). Where is the child's environment? A group socialization theory of development. Psychological Review, 102, 458–189.

Harris, J. R. (1998). The nurture assumption: Why children turn out the way they do. New York: Free Press.

Harris, J. R. (2000). Context-specific learning, personality, and birth order. Current Directions in Psychological Science, 9(5), 174–177.

Harris, M. B. (1996). Aggressive experiences and aggressiveness: Relationship to ethnicity, gender, and age. Journal of Applied Social Psychology, 26(10), 843–870.

Harris, M. J., & Perkins, R. (1995). Effects of distraction on interpersonal expectancy effects: A social interaction test of the cognitive busyness hypothesis. Social Cognition, 13, 163–182.

Harris, T. (1967). I'm OK—You're OK. New York: HarperCollins.

Harrison, J. A., & Wells, R. B. (1991). Bystander effects on male helping behavior: Social comparison and diffusion of responsibility. Representative Research in Social Psychology, 19(1), 53–63.

Harrison, K. (2003). Television viewers' ideal body proportions: The case of the curvaceously thin woman. Sex Roles, 48(5/6), 255–264.

Harrison, K., & Cantor, J. (1997). The relationship between media consumption and eating disorders. Journal of Communication, 47(1), 40–67.

Harry, J. (1983). Gay male and lesbian relationships. In E. D. Macklin & R. H. Rubin (Eds.), Contemporary families and alternative lifestyles: Handbook on research and theory. Newbury Park, CA: Sage.

Hart, K. E. (1999). Cynical hostility and deficiencies in functional support: The moderating role of gender in psychosocial vulnerability to disease. Personality and Individual Differences, 27(1), 69–83.

Harter, S. (1998). The development of self-representations. In N. Eisenberg (Ed.), Handbook of child psychology: Vol. 3. Social, emotional, and personality development. New York: Wiley.

Harter, S. (2003). The development of self representations during childhood and adolescence. In M. R. Leary & J. P. Tangney (Eds.), Handbook of self and identity. New York: Guilford.

Hartley, A. A., & McKenzie, C. R. M. (1991). Attentional and perceptual contributions to the identification of extrafoveal stimuli: Adult age comparisons. Journal of Gerontology, 46, P202–P206.

Hartup, W. W., & Stevens, N. (1999). Friendships and adaptation across the life span. Current Directions in Psychological Science, 8(3), 76–79.

Harvey, E. (1999). Short-term and long-term effects of parental employment on children of the National Longitudinal Survey of Youth. Developmental Psychology, 35, 445–459.

Harvey, J. H., & Omarzu, J. (1997). Minding the close relationship. Personality and Social Psychology Review, 1(3), 224–240.

Harvey, M. H. (1999). Memory research and clinical practice: A critique of three paradigms and a framework for psychotherapy with trauma survivors. In L. M. Williams, & V. L. Banyard (Eds.), Trauma & memory. Thousand Oaks, CA: Sage.

Hass, D. M., & Stafford, L. (1998). An initial examination of maintenance behaviors in gay and lesbian relationships. Journal of Social and Personal Relationships, 15(6), 846–855.

Hatala, M. N., & Prehodka, J. (1996). A content analysis of gay male and lesbian personal advertisements. Psychological Reports, 78, 371–374.

Hatcher, R. A., Trussell, J., Stewart, F. H., Nelson, A. L., Cates, W. Jr., Guest, F., & Kowal, D. (2004). Contraceptive Technology. New York: Ardent Media.

Hatfield, E. (1988). Passionate and companionate love. In R. J. Sternberg & M. L. Barnes (Eds.), The psychology of love. New Haven, CT: Yale University Press.

Hatfield, E., & Rapson, R. L. (1993). Love, sex, and intimacy: Their psychology, biology, and history. New York: HarperCollins.

Hatfield, E., & Rapson, R. L. (1996). Love and sex: Cross-cultural perspectives. Boston: Allyn & Bacon.

Hattery, A. (2001). Women, work, and family: Balancing and weaving. Thousand Oaks, CA: Sage.

Hawkins, A. J., Nock, S. L., Wilson, J. C., Sanchez, L., & Wright, J. D. (2002). Attitudes about covenant marriage and divorce: Policy implications from a three state comparison. Family Relations, 51, 166–75.

Hawkley, L. C., & Cicioppo, J. T. (2003). Loneliness and pathways to disease. Brain, Behavior and Immunity, 17(1), S98–S105.

Haworth-Hoeppner, S. (2000). The critical shapes of body image: The role of culture and family in the production of eating disorders. Journal of Marriage and the Family, 62, 212–227.

Haycock, L. A., McCarthy, P., & Skay, C. L. (1998). Procrastination in college students: The role of self-efficacy and anxiety. Journal of Counseling & Development, 76, 317–324.

Hays, K. F. (1999). Working it out: Using exercise in psychotherapy. Washington, DC: American Psychological Association.

Hazan, C., & Shaver, P. (1986). Parental caregiving style questionnaire. Unpublished questionnaire.

Hazan, C., & Shaver, P. (1987). Romantic love conceptualized as an attachment process. Journal of Personality and Social Psychology, 52, 511–524.

Hazan, C., & Shaver, P. R. (1990). Love and work: An attachment-theoretical perspective. Journal of Personality and Social Psychology, 59, 270–280.

Healy, D. (2004). Let them eat Prozac: The unhealthy relationship between the pharmaceutical industry and depression. New York: NYU Press.

Healy, D., & Whitaker, C. (2003). Antidepressants and suicide: Risk-benefit conundrums. Journal of Psychiatry & Neuroscience, 28(5), 340–347.

Heaton, T. B. (2002). Factors contributing to increasing marital stability in the United States. Journal of Family Issues, 23, 392–409.

Heaton, T. B., Jacobson, C. K. & Holland, K. (1999). Persistence and change in decisions to remain childless. Journal of Marriage and the Family, 61, 531–539.

Heavey, C. L., Christensen, A., & Malamuth, N. M. (1995). The longitudinal impact of demand and withdrawal during marital conflict. Journal of Consulting and Clinical Psychology, 63(5), 797–801.

Hebl, M. R., & Mannix, L. M. (2003). The weight of obesity in evaluating others: A mere proximity effect. Personality and Social Psychology, 29(1), 28–38.

Hecker, D. E. (2001). Employment outlook: 2000–10. Monthly Labor Review, 124(11), 57–84.

Heckert, D. A., Nowak, T. C., & Snyder, K. A. (1998). The impact of husbands' and wives' relative earnings on marital disruption. Journal of Marriage and the Family, 60, 690–703.

Hedges, L. V., & Nowell, A. (1995). Sex differences in mental test scores, variability, and numbers of high-scoring individuals. *Science, 269,* 41–45.

Heejung, K., & Markus, H. R. (1999). Deviance or uniqueness, harmony or conformity? A cultural analysis. *Journal of Personality and Social Psychology, 77*(4), 785.

Heider, F. (1958). *The psychology of interpersonal relations.* New York: Wiley.

Heilman, M. E., McCullough, W. F., & Gilbert, D. (1996). The other side of affirmative action: Reactions of nonbeneficiaries to sex-based preferential selection. *Journal of Applied Psychology, 81,* 346–357.

Heiman, J. R., & Meston, C. M. (1997). Empirically validated treatment for sexual dysfunction. *Annual Review of Sex Research, 8,* 148–194.

Heine, S. J., & Renshaw, K. (2002). Interjudge agreement, self-enhancement, and liking: Cross-cultural divergences. *Personality and Social Psychology Bulletin, 28*(5), 578–587.

Heine, S. J., Kitayama, S., Lehman, D. R., Takata, T., Ide, E., Leung, C., & Matsumoto, H. (2001). Divergent consequences of success and failure in Japan and North America: An investigation of self-improving motivations and malleable selves. *Journal of Personality and Social Psychology, 81,* 599–615.

Helgeson, V. S. (1994). Relation of agency and communion to well-being: Evidence and potential explanations. *Psychological Bulletin, 116,* 412–428.

Helgeson, V. S., Shaver, O., & Dyer, M. (1987). Prototypes of intimacy and distance in same-sex and opposite-sex relationships. *Journal of Social and Personal Relationships, 4,* 195–233.

Hellström, A., & Tekle, J. (1994). Person perception through facial photographs: Effects of glasses, hair, and beard on judgments of occupation and personal qualities. *European Journal of Social Psychology, 24*(6), 693–705.

Helson, R., Mitchell, V., & Moane, G. (1984). Personality and patterns of adherence and nonadherence to the social clock. *Journal of Personality and Social Psychology, 46,* 1079–1096.

Helson, R., & Moane, G. (1987). Personality change in women from college to midlife. *Journal of Personality and Social Psychology, 53,* 176–186.

Helson, R., & Stewart, A. (1994). Personality change in adulthood. In T. F. Heatherton & J. L. Weinberger (Eds.), *Can personality change?* Washington, DC: American Psychological Association.

Helweg-Larsen, M., & Shepperd, J. A. (2001). Do moderators of the optimistic bias affect personal or target risk estimates? A review of the literature. *Personality & Social Psychology Review, 5*(1), 74–95.

Hembree, E. A., & Foa, E. (2000). Posttraumatic stress disorder: Psychological factors and psychosocial interventions. *Journal of Clinical Psychiatry, 61*(7), 33–39.

Hemenover, S. H. (2003). The good, the bad, and the healthy: Impacts of emotional disclosure of trauma on resilient self-concept and psychological distress. *Personality and Social Psychology Bulletin, 29*(10), 1236–1244.

Henderson, K. E., & Brownell, K. D. (2004). The toxic environment and obesity: Contribution and cure. In J. K. Thompson (Ed.), *Handbook of eating disorders and obesity.* New York: Wiley.

Hendrick, C., & Hendrick, S. S. (1989). Research on love: Does it measure up? *Journal of Personality and Social Psychology, 56,* 784–794.

Hendrick, S. S., & Hendrick, C. (1992). *Liking, loving, and relating* (2nd ed.). Pacific Grove, CA: Brooks/Cole.

Hendrick, S. S., & Hendrick, C. (2000). Romantic love. In C. Hendrick & S. S. Hendrick (Eds.), *Close relationships: A sourcebook* (pp. 203–215). Thousand Oaks, CA: Sage.

Hendrick, S. S., Hendrick, C., & Adler, N. L. (1988). Romantic relationships: Love, satisfaction, and staying together. *Journal of Personality and Social Psychology, 54,* 980–988.

Henley, N. M. (1977). *Body politics: Power, sex and nonverbal communication.* Englewood Cliffs, NJ: Prentice-Hall.

Henley, N. M. (1986). *Body politics: Power, sex, and nonverbal communication* (2nd ed.). New York: Simon & Schuster.

Henley, N. M., & Freeman, J. (1995). The sexual politics of interpersonal behavior. In J. Freeman (Ed.), *Women: A feminist perspective* (5th ed., pp. 79–91). Mountain View, CA: Mayfield.

Hennessy, D. A., & Wiesenthal, D. L. (1999). Traffic congestion, driver stress, and driver aggression. *Aggressive Behavior, 25*(6), 409–423.

Henshaw, S. K. (1997). Teenage abortion and pregnancy statistics by state. *Family Planning Perspectives, 29,* 115–122.

Heppner, P. P., & Lee, D. (2002). Problem-solving appraisal and psychological adjustment. In C. R. Snyder & S. J. Lopez (Eds.), *Handbook of positive psychology.* New York: Oxford University Press.

Herbert, T. B., & Cohen, S. (1993). Stress and immunity in humans: A meta-analytic review. *Psychosomatic Medicine, 5,* 364–379.

Herek, G. M. (1996). Heterosexism and homophobia. In R. P. Cabaj & T. S. Stein (Eds.), *Textbook of homosexuality and mental health* (pp. 101–114). Washington, DC: American Psychiatric Press.

Herek, G. M. (2000). The psychology of sexual prejudice. *Current Directions in Psychological Science, 9,* 19–22.

Herek, G. M. (2002). Gender gaps in public opinion about lesbians and gay men. *Public Opinion Quarterly, 66*(2), 40–66.

Herek, G. M. (2003). The psychology of sexual prejudice. In L. D. Garnets & D. C. Kimmel (Eds.), *Psychological perspectives on lesbian, gay, and bisexual experiences.* New York: Columbia University Press.

Herek, G. M., & Capitanio, J. (1996). "Some of my best friends": Intergroup contact concealable stigma, and heterosexuals' attitudes toward gay men and lesbians. *Personality and Social Psychology Bulletin, 22,* 412–424.

Herek, G. M., Cogan, J. C., & Gillis, J. R. (2002). Victim experiences in hate crimes based on sexual orientation. *Journal of Social Issues, 58*(2), 319–339.

Herek, G. M., Gillis, J. R., & Cogan, J. C. (1999). Psychological sequelae of hate-crime victimization among lesbian, gay, and bisexual adults. *Journal of Consulting and Clinical Psychology, 67*(6), 945–951.

Herman, J. L. (1994). Presuming to know the truth. *Nieman Reports, 48,* 43–45.

Hermann, R. C., Dorwart, R. A., Hoover, C. W., & Brody, J. (1995). Variation in ECT use in the United States. *American Journal of Psychiatry, 152,* 869–875.

Hermann, R. C., Ettner, S. L., Dorwart, R. A., Hoover, C. W., & Yeung, E. (1998). Characteristics of psychiatrists who perform ECT. *American Journal of Psychiatry, 155,* 889–894.

Herrett-Skjellum, J., & Allen, M. (1996). Television programming and sex stereotyping: A meta-analysis. In B. Burleson (Ed.), *Communication Yearbook 1995.* Thousand Oaks, CA: Sage.

Hershsberger, S. L., & D'Augelli, A. R. (2000). Issues in counseling lesbian, gay, and bisexual adolescents. In R. M. Perez, K. A. DeBord, & K. J. Bieschke (Eds.), *Handbook of counseling and psychotherapy with lesbian, gay, and bisexual clients* (pp. 225–247). Washington, DC: American Psychological Association.

Herzog, D. B., & Becker, A. E. (1999). Eating disorders. In A. M. Nicholi (Ed.), *The Harvard guide to psychiatry* (pp. 400–683). Cambridge, MA: Harvard University Press.

Herzog, D. B., & Delinski, S. S. (2001). Classification of eating disorders. In R. H. Striegel-Moore & L. Smolak (Eds.), *Eating disorders* (pp. 31–50). Washington, DC: American Psychological Association.

Herzog, T. A., Abrams, D. B., Emmons, K. M., Linnan, L. A., & Shadel, W. G. (1999). Do processes of change predict smoking stage movements? A prospective analysis of the transtheoretical model. *Health Psychology, 18*(4), 369–375.

Heszen-Niejodek, I. (1997). Coping style and its role in coping with stressful encounters. *European Psychologist, 2,* 342–351.

Hetherington, E. M. (1993). An overview of the Virginia longitudinal study of divorce and remarriage with a focus on early adolescence. *Journal of Family Psychology, 7,* 1–18.

Hetherington, E. M. (1999). Should we stay together for the sake of the children? In E. M. Hetherington (Ed.), *Coping with divorce, single parenting, and remarriage: A risk and resiliency perspective* (pp. 93–116). Mahwah, NJ: Erlbaum.

Hetherington, E. M. (2003). Intimate pathways: Changing patterns in close personal relationships across time. *Family Relations: Interdisciplinary Journal of Applied Family Studies, 52*(4), 318–331.

Hetherington, E. M., Reiss, D., & Plomin, R. (1994). *Separate social worlds of siblings: The impact of nonshared environment on development.* Hillsdale, NJ: Erlbaum.

Hettema, J. M., Neale, M. C., & Kendler, K. S. (2001). A review and meta-analysis of the genetic epidemiology of anxiety disorders. *American Journal of Psychiatry, 158,* 1568–1578.

Hewstone, M. (1990). The ultimate attribution error? A review of the literature on intergroup causal attribution. *European Journal of Social Psychology, 20,* 311–335.

Heymann, J., Earle, A., Simmons, S., Breslow, S., & Kuehnhoff, A. (2004). *The work, family, and equity index: Where does the United States stand globally?* Boston: Harvard School of Public Health.

Hiedemann, B., Suhomlinova, O., & O'Rand, A. M. (1998). Economic independence, economic status, and empty nest in midlife marital disruption. *Journal of Marriage and the Family, 60,* 219–231.

Higgins, E. T. (1987). Self-discrepancy: A theory relating self and affect. *Psychological Review, 94*(3), 319–340.

Higgins, E. T. (1999). When do self-descrepancies have specific relations to emotions? The second-generation question of Tangney, Niedenthal, Covert, and Barlow (1998). *Journal of Personality and Social Psychology, 77*(6), 1313–1317.

Higgins, E. T., Shah, J., & Friedman, R. (1997). Emotional responses to goal attainment: Strength of regulatory focus as a moderator. *Journal of Personality and Social Psychology, 72*(3), 515–525.

Hilgard, E. R. (1987). *Psychology in America: A historical survey.* San Diego: Harcourt Brace Jovanovich.

Hill, A. J. (2002). Prevalence and demographics of dieting. In C. G. Fairburn & K. D. Brownell (Eds.), *Eating disorders and obesity: A comprehensive handbook.* New York: Guilford.

Hill, C. A. (1997). The distinctiveness of sexual motives in relation to sexual desire and desirable partner attributes. *Journal of Sex Research, 34,* 139–153.

Hill, C. A., & Preston, L. K. (1996). Individual differences in the experience of sexual motivation: Theory and measurement of dispositional sexual motives. *Journal of Sex Research, 33,* 27–45.

Hill, C. T., Rubin, Z., & Peplau, L. A. (1976). Breakups before marriage: The end of 103 affairs. *Journal of Social Issues, 32,* 147–168.

Hilton, J. L., & Darley, J. M. (1985). Constructing other persons: A limit on the effect. *Journal of Experimental Social Psychology, 21,* 1–18.

Hines, A. M. (1997). Divorce-related transitions, adolescent development, and the role of the parent-child relationship: A review of the literature. *Journal of Marriage and the Family, 59,* 375–388.

Hines, M. (1982). Prenatal gonadal hormones and sex differences in human behavior. *Psychological Bulletin, 92,* 56–80.

Hines, M. (1990). Gonadal hormones and human cognitive development. In J. Balthazart (Ed.), *Hormones, brain and behavior in vertebrates: 1. Sexual differentiation, neuroanatomical aspects, neurotransmitters and neuropeptides.* Basel: Karger.

Hiroto, D. S., & Seligman, M. E. P. (1975). Generality of learned helplessness in man. *Journal of Personality and Social Psychology, 31,* 311–327.

Hirschl, T. A., Altobelli, J., & Rank, M. R. (2003). Does marriage increase the odds of affluence? Exploring the life course probabilities. *Journal of Marriage and Family, 65,* 927–938.

Ho, B., Black, D. W., & Andreasen, N. C. (2003). Schizophrenia and other psychotic disorders. In R. E. Hales & S. C. Yudofsky (Eds.), *Textbook of clinical psychiatry.* Washington, DC: American Psychiatric Publishing.

Hobfoll, S. E., & Vaux, A. (1993). Social support: Resources and context. In L. Goldberger & S. Breznitz (Eds.), *Handbook of stress: Theoretical and clinical aspects* (2nd ed.). New York: Free Press.

Hobson, C. J., & Delunas, L. (2001). National norms and life-event frequencies for the revised Social Readjustment Rating Scale. *International Journal of Stress Management, 8*(4), 299–314.

Hochschild, A. R. (1997). *The time bind: When work becomes home and home becomes work.* New York: Holt.

Hochschild, A. R. (2001). *The time bind.* New York: Owl Books.

Hodge, B. (2002, March). PCs and the healthy office. *Smart Computing,* pp. 64–67.

Hoek, H. W. (2002). Distribution of eating disorders. In C. G. Fairburn & K. D. Brownell (Eds.), *Eating disorders and obesity: A comprehensive handbook.* New York: Guilford.

Hoek, H. W., Bartelds, A. I. M., Bosveld, J. J. F., van der Graaf, Y., Limpens, V. E. L., Maiwald, M., & Spaaij, C. J. K. (1995). Impact of urbanization on detection rates of eating disorders. *American Journal of Psychiatry, 152,* 1272–1278.

Hoffman, E. (1994). *The drive for self: Alfred Adler and the founding of individual psychology.* Reading, MA: Addison-Wesley.

Hoffnung, M. (2004). Wanting it all: Career, marriage, and motherhood during college-educated women's 20s. *Sex Roles, 50*(9/10), 711–723.

Hofstede, G. (1980). *Culture's consequences: International differences in work-related values.* Newbury Park, CA: Sage.

Hofstede, G. (1983). Dimensions of national cultures in fifty countries and three regions. In J. Deregowski, S. Dziurawiec, & R. Annis (Eds.), *Explications in cross-cultural psychology.* Lisse: Swets and Zeitlinger.

Hogan, J., & Ones, D. S. (1997). Conscientiousness and integrity at work. In R. Hogan, J. Johnson, & S. Briggs (Eds), *Handbook of personality psychology.* San Diego: Academic Press.

Holahan, C. J., & Moos, R. H. (1985). Life stress and health: Personality, coping, and family support in stress resistance. *Journal of Personality and Social Psychology, 49,* 739–747.

Holahan, C. J., & Moos, R. H. (1990). Life stressors, resistance factors, and improved psychological functioning: An extension of the stress resistance paradigm. *Journal of Personality and Social Psychology, 58,* 909–917.

Holahan, C. J., & Moos, R. H. (1994). Life stressors and mental health: Advances in conceptualizing stress resistance. In W. R. Avison & I. H. Gotlib (Eds.), *Stress and mental health: Contemporary issues and prospects for the future.* New York: Plenum.

Holden, C. (2004). FDA weighs suicide risk in children on antidepressants. *Science, 303,* 745.

Holen, A. (2000). Posttraumatic stress disorder, delayed. In G. Fink (Ed.), *Encyclopedia of stress* (Vol. 3, pp. 179–180). San Diego: Academic Press.

Holland, J. C., & Lewis, S. (1993). Emotions and cancer: What do we really know? In D. Goleman & J. Gurin (Eds.), *Mind/body medicine: How to use your mind for better health.* Yonkers, NY: Consumer Reports Books.

Holland, J. L. (1985). *Making vocational choices: A theory of vocational personalities and work environments.* Englewood Cliffs, NJ: Prentice-Hall.

Holland, J. L. (1996). Exploring careers with a typology: What we have learned and some new directions. *American Psychologist, 51,* 397–406.

Hollander, E., & Simeon, D. (2003). Anxiety disorders. In R. E. Hales & S. C. Yudofsky (Eds.), *Textbook of clinical psychiatry.* Washington, DC: American Psychiatric Publishing.

Hollister, L. E. (1988). Marijuana and immunity. *Journal of Psychoactive Drugs, 20,* 3–7.

Hollister, L. E. (1998). Health aspects of cannabis: Revisited. *International Journal of Neuropsychopharmacology, 1*(1), 71–80.

Holmes, T. H., & Rahe, R. H. (1967). The Social Readjustment Rating Scale. *Journal of Psychosomatic Research, 11,* 213–218.

Homma-True, R., Greene, B., Lopez, S. R., & Trimble, J. E. (1993). Ethnocultural diversity in clinical psychology. *The Clinical Psychologist, 46*(2), 50–63.

Hong, G. K., Garcia, M., & Soriano, M. (2000). Responding to the challenge: Preparing mental health professionals for the new millennium. In I. Cuellar & F. A. Paniagua (Eds.), *Handbook of multicultural mental health: Assessment and treatment of diverse populations.* San Diego: Academic Press.

Hood, K. E., Draper, P., Crockett, L. J., & Petersen, A. C. (1987). The ontogeny and phylogeny of sexual differences in development: A biopsychosocial synthesis. In B. Carter (Ed.), *Current conceptions of sex roles and sex typing: Theory and research.* New York: Praeger.

Hooker, E. (1957). The adjustment of the male overt homosexual. *Journal of Projective Techniques, 21,* 18–31.

Hooley, J. M., & Candela, S. F. (1999). Interpersonal functioning in schizophrenia. In T. Millon, P. H. Blaney, & R. D. Davis (Eds.), *Oxford textbook of psychopathology* (pp. 311–338). New York: Oxford University Press.

Hopper, J. (2001). The symbolic origins of conflict in divorce. *Journal of Marriage and Family, 63,* 430–445.

Horwath, E., & Weissman, M. M. (2000). Anxiety disorders: Epidemiology. In B. J. Sadock & V. A. Sadock (Eds.), *Kaplan and Sadock's comprehensive textbook of psychiatry* (7th ed., Vol. 1, pp. 1441–1449). Philadelphia: Lippincott/Williams & Wilkins.

Houts, A. C. (2002). Discovery, invention, and the expansion of the modern *Diagnostic and Statistical Manuals of Mental Disorders.* In L. E. Beutler & M. L. Malik (Eds.), *Rethinking the DSM.* Washington, DC: American Psychological Association.

Howard, G. S. (2000). Adapting human lifestyles for the 21st century. *American Psychologist, 55*(5), 509–515.

Howard, K. I., Krasner, R. F., & Saunders, S. M. (2000). Evaluation of psychotherapy. In D. J. Sadock & V. A. Sadock (Eds.), *Kaplan and Sadock's comprehensive textbook of psychiatry* (7th ed., Vol. 1, pp. 2217–2224). Philadelphia: Lippincott/Williams & Wilkins.

Howard, K. I., Moras, K., Brill, P. L., Martinovich, Z., & Lutz, W. (1996). Evaluation of psychotherapy: Efficacy, effectiveness, and patient progress. *American Psychologist, 51,* 1059–1064.

Howard, M., & McCabe, J. B. (1990). Helping teenagers postpone sexual involvement. *Family Planning Perspectives, 22,* 21–26.

Howard, R., Castle, D., Wessely, S., & Murray, R. (1993). A comparative study of 470 cases of early-onset and late-onset schizophrenia. *British Journal of Psychiatry, 163,* 352–357.

Hsu, L. K. G. (1990). *Eating disorders.* New York: Guilford Press.

Hu, F. B., & Willett, W. C. (2002). Optimal diets for prevention of coronary heart disease. *Journal of the American Medical Association, 288*(20), 2569–2578.

Hubbard, J. A., & Coie, J. D. (1994). Emotional correlates of social competence in children's peer relationships. *Merrill-Palmer Quarterly, 40,* 1–20.

Hubbard, J. R., & Workman, E. A. (1998). *Handbook of stress medicine: An organ system approach.* New York: CRC Press.

Hubbard, L. R. (1989). *Scientology: The fundamentals of thought.* Los Angeles: Bridge.

Huesmann, L. R., & Moise J. (1998). The stability and continuity of aggression from early childhood to young adulthood. In D.J. Flannery & C.R. Huff (Eds.), *Youth violence: Prevention, intervention, and social policy.* Washington, DC: American Psychiatric Press.

Hughes, C. C. (1993). Culture in clinical psychiatry. In A. C. Gaw (Ed.), *Culture, ethnicity, and mental illness* (pp. 3–41). Washington, DC: American Psychiatric Press.

Hughes, D. (2001 May). Falling "in like" online. *USA Weekend,* p. 9.

Hull, J. G., & Young, R. D. (1983). Self-consciousness, self-esteem, and success-failure as determinants of alcohol consumption in male social drinkers. *Journal of Personality and Social Psychology, 44,* 1097–1109.

Hull, J. G., Young, R. D. & Jouriles, E. (1986). Applications of the self-awareness model of alcohol consumption: Predicting patterns of use and abuse. *Journal of Personality and Social Psychology, 51,* 790–796.

Hulshoff, H. E., Hoek, H. W., Susser, E., Brown, A. S., Dingemans, A., Schnack, H. G., van Haren, N. E. M., Ramos, L. M. P., Gispen-de Wied, C. C., & Kahn, R. S. (2000). Prenatal exposure to famine and brain morphology in schizophrenia. *American Journal of Psychiatry, 157,* 1170–1172.

Hunsley, J., Lee, C. M., & Wood, J. M. (2003). Controversial and questionable assessment techniques. In S. O. Lilienfeld, S. J. Lynn, & J. M. Lohr (Eds.), *Science and pseudoscience in clinical psychology.* New York: Guilford.

Hunt, C., & Andrews, G. (1995). Comorbidity in the anxiety disorders: The use of a life-chart approach. *Journal of Psychiatric Research, 29*(6), 467–480.

Hunt, M. (1974). *Sexual behavior in the 1970s.* Chicago: Playboy Press.

Huston, A. C., & Wright, J. C. (1998). Mass media and children's development. In W. Damon (Series Ed.), *Handbook of child psychology* (Vol. 4). New York: Wiley.

Huston, A. C., Donnerstein, E., Fairchild, H., Feshbach, N. D., Katz, P. A., Murray, J. P., Rubinstein, E. A., Wilcox, B. L., & Zuckerman, D. (1992). *Big world, small screen: The role of television in American society.* Lincoln: University of Nebraska Press.

Huston, A. C., Wright, J. C., Rice, M. L., Kerkman, D., & St. Peters, M. (1990). Development of television viewing patterns in early childhood: A longitudinal investigation. *Developmental Psychology, 26,* 409–420.

Huston, T. L., & Melz, H. (2004). The case for (promoting). *Journal of Marriage and Family, 66,* 943–958.

Huston, T. L., Niehuis, S., & Smith, S. E. (2001). The early marital roots of conjugal distress and divorce. *Current Directions in Psychological Science, 10*(4), 116–119.

Hyde, J. S. (1994a). *Understanding human sexuality* (5th ed.). New York: McGraw-Hill.

Hyde, J. S. (1994b). Can meta-analysis make feminist transformations in psychology? *Psychology of Women Quarterly, 18,* 451–462.

Hyde, J. S. (1996). Where are the gender differences? Where are the gender similarities? In D.M. Buss & N. M. Malamuth (Eds.), *Sex, power, conflict: Evolutionary and feminist perspectives.* New York: Oxford University Press.

Hyde, J. S. (2004). *Half the human experience: The psychology of women.* Boston: Houghton Mifflin.

Hyde, J. S., & DeLamater, J. D. (2003). *Understanding human sexuality.* New York: McGraw-Hill.

Hyde, J. S., Fennema, E., & Lamon, S. J. (1990). Gender differences in mathematics performance: A meta-analysis. *Psychological Bulletin, 107,* 139–155.

Hyde, J. S., & Frost, L. A. (1993). Meta-analysis in the psychology of women. In F. L. Denmark & M. A. Paludi (Eds.), *Psychology of women: A handbook of issue and theories.* Westport, CT: Greenwood Press.

Hyde, J. S., & Kling, K. C. (2001). Women, motivation, and achievement. *Psychology of Women Quarterly, 25,* 364–378.

Hyde, J. S., & Linn, M. C. (1988). Gender differences in verbal ability: A meta-analysis. *Psychological Bulletin, 104,* 53–69.

Hyde, J. S., & Oliver, M. B. (2000). Gender differences in sexuality: Results from meta-analysis. In C. B. Travis & J. W. White (Eds.), *Sexuality, society, and feminism.* Washington, DC: American Psychological Association.

Hygge, S., Evans, G. W., & Bullinger, M. (2002). A prospective study of some effects of aircraft noise on cognitive performance in school children. *Psychological Science, 13*(5), 469–474.

Hyman, I. E., & Kleinknecht, E. E. (1999). False childhood memories: Research, theory, and applications. In L. M. Williams & V. L. Banyard (Eds.), *Trauma & memory.* Thousand Oaks, CA: Sage.

Iaccino, J. F. (1996). A further examination of the bizarre imagery mnemonic: Its effectiveness with mixed context and delayed testing. *Perceptual & Motor Skills, 83,* 881–882.

Iacono, W. G., & Lykken, D. T. (1997). The validity of the lie detector: Two surveys of scientific opinion. *Journal of Applied Psychology, 82*(3), 426–433.

Iacono, W. G., & Patrick, C. J. (1999). Polygraph ("lie detector") testing: The state of the art. In A. K. Hess & I. B. Weiner (Eds.), *The handbook of forensic psychology.* New York: Wiley.

Ickes, W. (1993). Traditional gender roles: Do they make and then break our relationships? *Journal of Social Issues, 3,* 71–85.

Ickes, W. J., Patterson, M. L., Rajecki, D. W., & Tanford, S. (1982). Behavioral and cognitive consequences of reciprocal versus compensatory responses to preinteraction expectancies. *Social Cognition, 1,* 160–190.

Ickovics, J. R., Thayaparan, B., & Ethier, K. A. (2001). Women and AIDS: A contextual analysis. In A. Baum, T. A. Revenson, & J. E. Singer (Eds.), *Handbook of health psychology* (pp. 817–840). Mahwah, NJ: Erlbaum.

Iezzi, T., Duckworth, M. P., & Adams, H. E. (2001). Somatoform and factitious disorders. In P. B. Sutker & H. E. Adams (Eds.), *Comprehensive handbook of psychopathology* (3rd ed., pp. 211–258). New York: Kluwer Academic/Plenum Publishers.

Ilgen, D. R. (1990). Health issues at work: Opportunities for industrial/organization psychology. *American Psychologist, 45,* 252–261.

Infante, J. R., Torres-Avisbal, M., Pinel, P., Vallejo, J. A., Peran, F., Gonzalez, F., Contreras, P., Pacheco, C., Roldan, A., & Latre, J. M. (2001). Catecholamine levels in practitioners of the transcendental meditation technique. *Physiology & Behavior, 72*(1-2), 141–146.

Inglehart, R. (1990). *Culture shift in advanced industrial society.* Princeton, NJ: Princeton University Press.

Ingoldsby, B. B. (1995). Mate selection and marriage. In B. B. Ingoldsby & S. Smith (Eds.), *Families in multicultural perspective* (pp. 143–160). New York: Guilford Press.

Ingram, R. E., Scott, W., & Siegle, G. (1999). Depression: Social and cognitive aspects. In T. Millon, P. H. Blaney, & R. D. Davis (Eds.), *Oxford*

textbook of psychopathology* (pp. 203–226). New York: Oxford University Press.

Innocenti, G. M. (1994). Some new trends in the study of the corpus callosum. *Behavioral and Brain Research, 64,* 1–8.

Insko, C. A., Smith, R. H., Alicke, M. D., Wade, J., & Taylor, S. (1985). Conformity and group size: The concern with being right and the concern with being liked. *Personality and Social Psychology Bulletin, 11,* 41–50.

International Labour Office. (2002). *Key indicators of the labour market, 2001–2002.* Geneva: United Nations International Labour Office.

Iribarren, C., Sidney, S., Bild, D. E., Liu, K., Markovitz, J. H., Roseman, J. M., & Matthews, K. (2000). Association of hostility with coronary artery calcification in young adults: The CARDIA study. *Journal of the American Medical Association, 283*(19), 2546–2551.

Ironson, G., Wynings, C., Sschneiderman, N., Baum, A., Rodriguez, M., Greenwood, D., Benight, C., Antoni, M., LaPerriere, A., Huang, H. S., Klimas, N., & Fletcher, M. A. (1997). Post-traumatic stress symptoms, intrusive thoughts, loss, and immune function after Hurricane Andrew. *Psychosomatic Medicine, 59,* 128–141.

Isenberg, K. E., & Zorumski, C. F. (2000). Electroconvulsive therapy. In B. J. Sadock & V. A. Sadock (Eds.), *Kaplan and Sadock's Comprehensive textbook of psychiatry* (7th ed., Vol. 1, pp. 2503–2515). Philadelphia: Lippincott/Williams & Wilkins.

Ivancevich, J. M., Matteson, M. T., Freedman, S. M., & Phillips, J. S. (1990). Worksite stress management interventions. *American Psychologist, 45,* 252–261.

Iwao, S. (1993). *The Japanese woman: Traditional image and changing reality.* New York: Free Press.

Izard, C., Fine, S., Schultz, D., Mostow, A., Ackerman, B., & Youngstrom, E. (2001). Emotion knowledge as a predictor of social behavior and academic competence in children at risk. *Psychological Science, 12*(1), 18–23.

Jablensky, A. (1999). The 100-year epidemiology of schizophrenia. *Schizophrenia Research, 28,* 111–125.

Jaccard, J., Dittus, P., & Gordon, V. (2000). Parent-teen communication about premarital sex. *Journal of Adolescent Research, 15,* 187–208.

Jackicic, J., & Gallagher, K. I. (2002). Physical activity considerations for management of body weight. In D. H. Bessesen, & R. Kushner (Eds.), *Evaluation & Management of Obesity.* Philadelphia: Hanley & Belfus.

Jackson, L. A., & McGill, O. D. (1996). Body type preferences and body characteristics associated with attractive and unattractive bodies by African Americans and Anglo Americans. *Sex Roles, 35*(5–6), 295–307.

Jackson, T., Fritch, A., Nagasaka, T., & Gunderson, J. (2002). Towards explaining the association between shyness and loneliness: A path analysis with American college students. *Social Behavior and Personality, 30*(3), 263–270.

Jacob, R. G., & Pelham, W. H. (2000). Behavior therapy. In B. J. Sadock, & V. A. Sadock (Eds.), *Kaplan and Sadock's comprehensive textbook of psychiatry* (7th ed., Vol. 1, pp. 2080–2127). Philadelphia: Lippincott/Williams & Wilkins.

Jacobs, C., & Wolf, E. (1995). School sexuality education and adolescent risk-taking behavior. *Journal of School Health, 65,* 91–95.

Jacobs, H. S. (2001). Idea of male menopause is not useful. *Medical Crossfire, 3,* 52–55.

Jacobs, J. A. (1999). The sex segregation of occupations. In G. N. Powell (Ed.), *Handbook of gender and work* (pp. 125–144). Thousand Oaks, CA: Sage.

Jacobson, E. (1938). *Progressive relaxation.* Chicago: University of Chicago Press.

Jacques, R. (1997). The unbearable whiteness of being: Reflections of a pale, stale male. In P. Prasad,

A. Mills, M. Elmes, & A. Prasad (Eds.), *Managing the organizational melting pot: Dilemmas of workplace diversity.* Thousand Oaks, CA: Sage.

Jahoda, M. (1958). *Current concepts of positive mental health.* New York: Basic Books.

Jakupcak, M., Salters, K., Gratz, K. L., & Roemer, L. (2003). Masculinity and emotionality: An investigation of men's primary and secondary emotional responding. *Sex Roles, 49*(3/4), 111–120.

James, D., & Drakich, J. (1993). Understanding gender differences in amount of talk: A critical review of research. In D. Tannen (Ed.), *Gender and conversational interaction* (pp. 281–312). New York: Oxford University Press.

James, J. E. (2004). Critical review of dietary caffeine and blood pressure: A relationship that should be taken more seriously. *Psychosomatic Medicine, 66*(1), 63–71.

Janis, I. L. (1958). *Psychological stress.* New York: Wiley.

Janis, I. L. (1993). Decision making under stress. In L. Goldberger & S. Breznitz (Eds.), *Handbook of stress: Theoretical and clinical aspects* (2nd ed.). New York: Free Press.

Jankowiak, W. R., & Fischer, E. F. (1992). A cross-cultural perspective on romantic love. *Ethnology, 31,* 149–155.

Janofsky, J. S., Dunn, M. H., Roskes, E. J., Briskin, J. K., & Rudolph, M. S. L. (1996). Insanity defense pleas in Baltimore city: An analysis of outcome. *American Journal of Psychiatry, 153,* 1464–1468.

Jansz, J. (2000). Masculine identity and restrictive emotionality. In A. H. Fischer (Ed.), *Gender and emotion: Social psychological perspectives* (pp. 166–186). Cambridge, UK: Cambridge University Press.

Jaroff, L. (1993, November 29). Lies of the mind. *Time,* pp. 52–59.

Jaskiewicz, J. A., & McAnarney, E. R. (1994). Pregnancy during adolescence. *Pediatrics in Review, 15,* 32–38.

Jay, K., & Young, A. (1979). *The gay report.* New York: Summit Books.

Jefferson, J. W., & Greist, J. H. (2000). Lithium. In B. J. Sadock & V. A. Sadock (Eds.), *Kaplan and Sadock's comprehensive textbook of psychiatry* (7th ed., Vol. 1, pp. 2377–2389). Philadelphia: Lippincott/Williams & Wilkins.

Jeffery, R. W. (2001). Public health strategies for obesity treatment and prevention. *American Journal of Health Behavior, 25*(3), 252–259.

Jeffery, R. W., Epstein, L. H., Wilson, G. T., Drewnowski, A., Stunkard, A. J., Wing, R. R., & Hill, D. R. (2000). Long-term maintenance of weight loss: Current status. *Health Psychology, 19*(1), 5–16.

Jemmott, J. B., III, & Magloire, K. (1988). Academic stress, social support, and secretory Immunoglobin A. *Journal of Personality and Social Psychology, 55,* 803–810.

Jepsen, L. K., & Jepsen, C. A. (2002). An empirical analysis of the matching patterns of same-sex and opposite-sex couples. *Demography, 39,* 435–453.

Jex, S. M., Bliese, P. D., Buzzell, S., & Primeau, J. (2001). The impact of self-efficacy on stressor-strain relations: Coping style as an explanatory mechanism. *Journal of Applied Psychology, 86,* 401–409.

Jick, H., Kaye, J. A., & Jick, S. S. (2004). Antidepressants and the risk of suicidal behaviors. *Journal of the American Medical Association, 292*(3), 338–343.

John, O. P., & Srivastava, S. (1999). The big five trait taxonomy: History, measurement, and theoretical perspectives. In L. A. Pervin & O. P. John (Eds.), *Handbook of personality: Theory and research* (2nd ed., pp. 102–138). New York: Guilford Press.

Johnson, A. M., Wadsworth, J., Wellings, K., Bradshaw, S., & Field, J. (1992). Sexual lifestyles and HIV risk. *Nature, 360,* 410–412.

Johnson, B. A., & Ait-Dauod, N. (2005). Alcohol: Clinical aspects. In J. H. Lowinson, P. Ruiz, R. B.

Millman, & J. G. Langrod (Eds.), *Substance abuse: A comprehensive textbook*. Philadelphia: Lippincott/Williams & Wilkins.

Johnson, D. W., & Johnson, F. P. (1999). *Joining together. Group theory and group skills* (7th ed.). Boston: Allyn & Bacon.

Johnson, I. M., Crowley, J., & Sigler, R. T. (1992). Agency response to domestic violence: Services provided to battered women. In E. C. Viano (Ed.), *Intimate violence: Interdisciplinary perspectives*. Washington, DC: Hemisphere.

Johnson, M. P. (2000). Conflict and control: Images of symmetry and asymmetry in domestic violence. In A. Booth, A. C. Crouter, & M. Clements (Eds.), *Couples in conflict*. Hillsdale, NJ: Erlbaum.

Johnson, M. P., & Ferraro, K. J. (2001). Research on domestic violence in the 1990's: Making distinctions. In R. M. Milardo (Ed.), *Understanding families into the new millennium: A decade in review* (pp. 167–182). Minneapolis, MN: National Council on Family Relations.

Johnson, S. B., & Carlson, D. N. (2004). Medical regimen adherence: Concepts, assessment, and interventions. In J. M. Raczynski, & L. C. Leviton (Eds.), *Handbook of clinical health psychology: Vol. 2. Disorders of behavior and health*. Washington, DC: American Psychological Association.

Johnson, T. W., & Colucci, P. (1999). Lesbians, gay men, and the family life cycle. In B. Carter & M. McGoldrick (Eds.), *The expanded family life cycle: Individual, family, and social perspectives* (3rd ed., pp. 346–361). Boston: Allyn & Bacon.

Johnstone, L. (1999). Adverse psychological effects of ECT. *Journal of Mental Health, 8,* 69–85.

Joiner, T. E. (2002). Depression in its interpersonal context. In I. H. Gotlib & C. L. Hammen (Eds.), *Handbook of depression*. New York: Guilford.

Joiner, T. E., & Katz, J. (1999). Contagion of depressive symptoms and mood: Meta-analytic review and explanations from cognitive, behavioral, and interpersonal viewpoints. *Clinical Psychology: Science and Practice, 6,* 149–164.

Joiner, T. E., Jr., & Metalsky, G. I. (1995). A prospective test of an integrative interpersonal theory of depression: A naturalistic study of college students. *Journal of Personality and Social Psychology, 69,* 778–788.

Jones, D. (1995). Sexual selection, physical attractiveness, and facial neotony: Cross-cultural evidence and implications. *Current Anthropology, 36,* 723–748.

Jones, E. E. (1990). *Interpersonal perception*. New York: Freeman.

Jones, E. E., & Davis, K. (1965). From acts to dispositions: The attribution process in person perception. In L. Berkowitz (Ed.), *Advances in experimental social psychology* (Vol. 2). New York: Academic Press.

Jones, F., & Kinman, G. (2001). Approaches to studying stress. In F. Jones & J. Bright (Eds.), *Stress: Myth, theory and research* . Harlow, England: Pearson Education.

Jones, M. (1993, July 5). Getting away from the "R" word. *Publishers Weekly,* pp. 42–45.

Jones, R. A., & Brehm, J. W. (1970). Persuasiveness of one- and two-sided communications as a function of awareness there are two sides. *Journal of Experimental Social Psychology, 6,* 47–56.

Jorgensen, R. S., Johnson, B. T., Kolodziej, M. E., & Schreer, G. E. (1996). Elevated blood pressure and personality: A meta-analytic review. *Psychological Bulletin, 120,* 293–320.

Joung, I. M. A., Stronks, K., Van De Mheen, H., Van Poppel, F. W. A., Van Der Meer, J. B. W., & Mackenbach, J. P. (1997). The contribution of intermediary factors to marital status differences in self-reported health. *Journal of Marriage and the Family, 59,* 476–490.

Jourard, S. M., & Landsman, T. (1980). *Healthy personality: An approach from the viewpoint of humanistic psychology.* New York: Macmillan.

Joyner, T. (1999, November 14). All-work is American way: Atlanta poll finds 21 percent work 50-plus hours a week. *The Atlanta Journal-Constitution,* pp. R1, R5.

Joyner, T. (2001, May 27). Why can't we enjoy a vacation? Americans getting tired, and it shows at work. *The Atlanta Journal-Constitution,* pp. D1, D3.

Judge, T. A., & Bono, J. E. (2000). Five-factor model of personality and transformational leadership. *Journal of Applied Psychology, 85,* 751–765.

Julien, R. M. (2001). *A primer of drug action.* New York: Freeman.

Jung, C. G. (1921). Psychological types. In *Collected Works* (Vol. 6). Princeton, NJ: Princeton University Press.

Jung, C. G. (1933). *Modern man in search of a soul.* New York: Harcourt, Brace & World.

Kagan, J. (1998). Biology and the child. In W. Damon (Ed.), *Handbook of child psychology (Vol. 3): Social, emotional, and personality development.* New York: Wiley.

Kagan, J., Snidman, N., & Arcus, D. M. (1992). Initial reactions to unfamiliarity. *Current Directions in Psychological Science, 1,* 171–174.

Kahn, A. S., & Andreoli Mathie, V. (1999). Sexuality, society, and feminism: Psychological perspectives on women. In C. B. Travis & J. W. White (Eds.), *Sexuality, society, and feminism: Psychological perspectives on women.* Washington, DC: American Psychological Association.

Kahneman, D. (1999). Objective happiness. In D. Kahneman, E. Diener, & N. Schwarz (Eds.), *Well-being: The foundations of hedonic psychology* (pp. 3–25). New York: Sage.

Kaiser, C. R., Vick, B. S., & Major, B. (2004). A prospective investigation of the relationship between just-world beliefs and the desire for revenge after September 11, 2001. *Psychological Science, 15*(7), 503–506.

Kaiser Family Foundation. (2004). *Sex education in America: Principals' survey.* Menlo Park, CA: Henry J. Kaiser Family Foundation.

Kaiser Family Foundation, Holt, T., Greene, L., & Davis, J. (2003). *National Survey of adolescents and young adults: Sexual health knowledge, attitudes, and experiences.* Menlo Park, CA: Henry J. Kaiser Family Foundation.

Kalant, H., & Kalant, O. J. (1979). Death in amphetamine users: Causes and rates. In D. E. Smith (Ed.), *Amphetamine use, misuse and abuse.* Boston: G. K. Hall.

Kalichman, S. C. (1995). *Understanding AIDS: A guide for mental health professionals.* Washington, DC: American Psychological Association.

Kalichman, S. C., Roffman, R. A., Picciano, J. F., & Bolan, M. (1998). Risk for HIV infection among bisexual men seeking HIV-prevention services and risks posed to their female partners. *Health Psychology, 17*(4), 320–327.

Kalick, S. M., & Hamilton, T. E., III. (1986). The matching hypothesis reexamined. *Journal of Personality and Social Psychology, 51,* 673–602.

Kalidindi, S., & McGuffin, P. (2003). The genetics of affective disorders: Present and future. In R. Plomin, J. C. Defries, I. W. Craig, & P. McGuffin (Eds.), *Behavioral genetics in the postgenomic era.* Washington, DC: American Psychological Association.

Kalmijn, M. (1998). Intermarriage and homogamy: Causes, patterns, trends. *Annual Review of Sociology, 24,* 395–421.

Kalwarf, H. J., Khoury, J. C., & Lanphear, B. P. (2003). Milk intake during childhood and adolescence, adult bone density, and osteoporotic fractures in US women. *American Journal of Clinical Nutrition, 77,* 257–265.

Kamp Dush, C. M., Cohan, C. L., & Amato, P. R. (2003). The relationship between cohabitation and marital quality and stability: Change across co-

horts? *Journal of Marriage and Family, 65,* 539–549.

Kanagawa, C., Cross, S. E., & Markus, H. R. (2001). "Who am I?" The cultural psychology of the conceptual self. *Personality and Social Psychology Bulletin, 27*(1), 90–103.

Kandell, J. J. (1998). Internet addiction on campus: The vulnerability of college students. *CyberPsychology and Behavior, 1*(1), 11–17.

Kane, E. W. (2000). Racial and ethnic variations in gender-related attitudes. *Annual review of sociology, 26,* 419–439.

Kane, J. (1991). *Be sick well: A healthy approach to chronic illness.* Oakland, CA: New Harbinger.

Kane, T. D., Marks, M. A., Zaccaro, S. J., & Blair, V. (1996). Self-efficacy, personal goals, and wrestlers' self-regulation. *Journal of Sport & Exercise Psychology, 18*(1), 36–48.

Kanner, A. D., Coyne, J. C., Schaefer, C., & Lazarus, R. S. (1981). Comparison of two modes of stress measurement: Daily hassles and uplifts versus major life events. *Journal of Behavioral Medicine, 4,* 1–39.

Kanner, A. D., & Soule, R. G. (2004). Globalization, corporate culture, and freedom. In T. Kasser & A. D. Kanner (Eds.), *Psychology and consumer culture: The struggle for a good life in a materialistic world.* Washington, DC: American Psychological Association.

Kant, A. K., Schatzkin, A., Graubard, B. I., & Schairer, C. (2000). A prospective study of diet quality and mortality in women. *Journal of the American Medical Association, 283,* 2109–02115.

Kaplan, A. G. (1985). Female or male therapists for women patients: New formulations. *Psychiatry, 48,* 111–121.

Kaplan, H. I. (1989). History of psychosomatic medicine. In H. I. Kaplan & B. J. Sadock (Eds.), *Comprehensive textbook of psychiatry/V* (Vol. 2) (5th ed.). Baltimore: Williams & Wilkins.

Kaplan, H. I., & Sadock, B. J. (Eds.). (1993). *Comprehensive group psychotherapy.* Baltimore: Williams & Wilkins.

Kaplan, H. S. (1979). *Disorders of sexual desire.* New York: Simon & Schuster.

Karasek, R. A., Jr. (1979). Job demands, job decision latitude, and mental strain: Implications for job redesign. *Administrative Science Quarterly, 24,* 285–308.

Karasek, R. A., Jr., Baker, D., Marxer, F., Ahlbom, A., & Theorell, T. (1981). Job decision latitude, job demands, and cardiovascular disease: A prospective study of Swedish men. *American Journal of Public Health, 71,* 694–705.

Karasek, R. A., Jr., & Theorell, T. (1990). *Healthy work: Stress, productivity, and the reconstruction of working life.* New York: Basic Books.

Karney, B. R., & Bradbury, T. N. (2000). Attributions in marriage: State or trait? A growth curve analysis. *Journal of Personality and Social Psychology, 78*(2), 295–309.

Karp, D. A. (2001). *The burden of sympathy: How families cope with mental illness.* New York: Oxford University Press.

Kasper, H. T. (2002). The changing role of community college. *Occupational Outlook Quarterly,* 14–21.

Kassel, J. D., Stroud, L. R., & Paronis, C. A. (2003). Smoking, stress, and negative affect: Correlation, causation, and context across stages of smoking. *Psychological Bulletin, 129*(2), 270–304.

Kasser, T. (2002). *The high prices of materialism.* Cambridge, MA: MIT Press.

Kasser, T., Ryan, R. M., Couchman, C. E., & Sheldon, K. M. (2004). Materialistic values: Their causes and consequences. In T. Kasser & A. D. Kanner (Eds.), *Psychology and consumer culture: The struggle for a good life in a materialistic world.* Washington, DC: American Psychological Association.

Kastenbaum, R. (1999). Dying and bereavement. In J. C. Cavanaugh & S. K. Whitbourne (Eds.),

Gerontology: An interdisciplinary perspective . New York: Oxford University Press.

Kastenbaum, R. J. (2001). *Death, society, and human experience* (7th ed.). Boston: Allyn & Bacon.

Kausler, D. H. (1994). *Learning and memory in normal aging.* San Diego: Academic Press.

Kavanagh, D. J. (1992). Recent developments in expressed emotion in schizophrenia. *British Journal of Psychiatry, 160,* 601–620.

Kavesh, L., & Lavin, C. (1988). *Tales from the front.* New York: Doubleday.

Kay, J., & Kay, R. L. (2003). Individual psychoanalytic psychotherapy. In A. Tasman, J. Kay, & J. A. Lieberman (Eds.), *Psychiatry.* New York: Wiley.

Kaye, W. H., Weltzin, T. E., Hsu, L. K. G., McConaha, C. W., & Bolton, B. (1993). Amount of calories retained after binge eating and vomiting. *American Journal of Psychiatry, 150,* 969–971.

Kazdin, A. E. (1982). History of behavior modification. In A. S. Bellack, M. Hersen, & A. E. Kazdin (Eds.), *International handbook of behavior modification and behavior therapy.* New York: Plenum.

Kazdin, A. E. (1994). Methodology, design, and evaluation in psychotherapy research. In A. E. Bergin & S. L. Garfield (Eds.), *Handbook of psychotherapy and behavior change* (4th ed.). New York: Wiley.

Kazdin, A. E. (2001). *Behavior modification in applied settings.* Belmont, CA: Wadsworth.

Kazdin, A. E., & Benjet, C. (2003). Spanking children: Evidence and issues. *Current Directions in Psychological Science,* 99–103.

Keefe, F. J., Smith, S. J., Buffington, A. L. H., Gibson, J., Studts, J. L., & Caldwell, D. S. (2002). Recent advances and future directions in the biopsychosocial assessment and treatment of arthritis. *Journal of Consulting & Clinical Psychology, 70*(3), 640–655.

Keefe, S. E. (1984). Real and ideal extended familism among Mexican Americans and Anglo Americans: On the meaning of "close" family ties. *Human Organization, 43,* 65–70.

Keesey, R. E. (1993). Physiological regulation of body energy: Implications for obesity. In A. J. Stunkard & T. A. Wadden (Eds.), *Obesity: Theory and therapy.* New York: Raven Press.

Keesey, R. E. (1995). A set-point model of body weight regulation. In K. D. Brownell & C. G. Fairburn (Eds.), *Eating disorders and obesity: A comprehensive handbook.* New York: Guilford Press.

Kegan, R. (1994). *In over our heads: The mental demands of modern life.* Cambridge, MA: Harvard University Press.

Keinan, G. (1987). Decision making under stress: Scanning of alternatives under controllable and uncontrollable threats. *Journal of Personality and Social Psychology, 52,* 639–644.

Keita, G. P., & Hurrell, J. J., Jr. (1994). *Job stress in a changing workforce.* Washington, DC: American Psychological Association.

Keller, S. N., & Brown, J. D. Media interventions to promote responsible sexual behavior. *The Journal of Sex Research, 39*(1), 67–72.

Kelley, H. H. (1950). The warm-cold dimension in first impressions of persons. *Journal of Personality, 18,* 431–439.

Kelley, H. H. (1967). Attribution theory in social psychology. In D. Levine (Ed.), *Nebraska Symposium on Motivation* (Vol. 15). Lincoln: University of Nebraska Press.

Kelley, H. H., & Thibaut, J. W. (1978). *Interpersonal relations: A theory of interdependence.* New York: Wiley-Interscience.

Kellogg, J. S., Hopko, D. R., & Ashcraft, M. H. (1999). The effects of time pressure on arithmetic performance. *Journal of Anxiety Disorders, 13*(6), 591–600.

Kelly, J. B., & Emery, R. E. (2003). Children's adjustment following divorce: Risk and resilience perspectives. *Family Relations: Interdisciplinary Journal of Applied Family Studies, 52*(4), 352–362.

Kelly, K. M., & Schramke, C. J. (2000). Epilepsy. In G. Fink (Ed.), *Encyclopedia of stress* (pp. 66–70). San Diego: Academic Press.

Kelly, K. R., & Cobb, S. J. (1991). A profile of the career development characteristics of young gifted adolescents: Examining gender and multicultural differences. *Roeper Review, 13,* 202–206.

Kelman, H. C., & Hamilton, V. L. (1989). *Crimes of obedience: Toward a social psychology of authority and responsibility.* New Haven, CT: Yale University Press.

Kemeny, M. E. (2003). The psychobiology of stress. *Current Directions in Psychological Science, 12*(4), 124–129.

Kemeny, M. E., Weiner, H., Duran, R., Taylor, S. E., Visscher, B., & Fahey, J. L. (1995). Immune system changes after the death of a partner in HIV-positive gay men. *Psychosomatic Medicine, 57,* 547–554.

Kendler, K. S. (2000). Schizophrenia: Genetics. In B. J. Sadock & V. A. Sadock (Eds.), *Kaplan and Sadock's comprehensive textbook of psychiatry* (7th ed., Vol. 1, pp. 1147–1158). Philadelphia: Lippincott/Williams & Wilkins.

Kendler, K. S., & Gardner, C. O., Jr. (1998). Boundaries of major depression: An evaluation of DSM-IV criteria. *American Journal of Psychiatry, 155,* 172–177.

Kendler, K. S., Kuhn, J., & Prescott, C. A. (2004). The interrelationship of neuroticism, sex, and stressful life events in the prediction of episodes of major depression. *American Journal of Psychiatry, 161,* 631–636.

Kendler, K. S., Thornton, L. M., Gilman, S. E., & Kessler, R. C. (2000). Sexual orientation in a U.S. national sample of twin and nontwin sibling pairs. *American Journal of Psychiatry, 157*(11), 1843–1846.

Kenny, D. A. (1994). Using the social relations model to understand relationships. In R. Erber & R. Gilmour (Eds.), *Theoretical frameworks for personal relationships.* Hillsdale, NJ: Erlbaum.

Kenrick, D. T., Sadalla, E. K., Groth, G., & Trost, M. R. (1990). Evolution, traits, and the stages of human courtship: Qualifying the parental investment model. *Journal of Personality, 58,* 97–116.

Kenrick, D. T., & Trost, M. R. (1993). The evolutionary perspective. In A. E. Beall & R. J. Sternberg (Eds.), *The psychology of gender.* New York: Guilford Press.

Keogh, E., Bond, F. W., French, C. C., Richards, A., & Davis, R. E. (2004). Test anxiety, susceptibility to distraction and examination performance. *Anxiety, Stress and Coping: An International Journal, 17*(3), 241–252.

Kernis, M. H. (2003a). Optimal self-esteem and authenticity: Separating fantasy from reality. *Psychological Inquiry, 14*(1), 83–89.

Kernis, M. H. (2003b). Toward a conceptualization of optimal self-esteem. *Psychological Inquiry, 14*(1), 1–26.

Kernis, M. H., & Goldman, B. M. (2003). Stability and variability in self-concept and self-esteem. In M. R. Leary and J. P. Tangney (Eds.), *Handbook of self and identity.* New York: Guilford.

Kessler, R. C. (1997). The effects of stressful life events on depression. *Annual Review of Psychology, 48,* 191–214.

Kessler, R. C. (2002). Epidemiology of depression. In I. H. Gotlib & C. L. Hammen (Eds.), *Handbook of depression.* New York: Guilford.

Kessler, R. C., Berglund, P., Demler, O., Jin, R., Koretz, D., Merikangas, K. R., Rush, A. J., Walters, E. E., & Wang, P. S. (2003). The epidemiology of major depressive disorder: Results from the national comorbidity survey replication (NCS-R). *The Journal of the American Medical Association, 289*(23), 3095–3105.

Kessler, R. C., Olfson, M., & Berglund, P. A. (1998). Patterns and predictors of treatment contact after first onset of psychiatric disorders. *American Journal of Psychiatry, 155,* 62–69.

Kessler, R. C., & Zhao, S. (1999). The prevalence of mental illness. In A. V. Horvitz & T. L. Scheid (Eds.), *A handbook for the study of mental health: Social contexts, theories, and systems.* New York: Cambridge University Press.

Kessler, R. C., Zhao, S., Katz, S. J., Kouzis, A. C., Frank, R. G., Edlund, M., & Leaf, P. (1999). Past-year use of outpatient services for psychiatric problems in the National Comorbidity Survey. *American Journal of Psychiatry, 156,* 115–123.

Keyes, R. (1991). *Timelock: How life got so hectic and what you can do about it.* New York: Harper-Collins.

Khot, U. N., Khot, M. B., Bajzer, C. T., Sapp, S. K., Ohman, E. M., Brener, S. J., Ellis, S. G., Lincoff, M. A., & Topol, E. J. (2003). Prevalence of conventional risk factors in patients with coronary heart disease. *Journal of the American Medical Association, 290,* 898–904.

Kiecolt-Glaser, J. K., & Glaser, R. (1995). Measurement of immune response. In S. Cohen, R. C. Kessler, & L. U. Gordon (Eds.), *Measuring stress: A guide for health and social scientists.* New York: Oxford University Press.

Kiecolt-Glaser, J. K., & Glaser, R. (2001). Stress and immunity: Age enhances the risks. *Current Directions in Psychological Science, 10*(1), 18–21.

Kiecolt-Glaser, J. K., Garner, W., Speicher, C., Penn, G. M., Holliday, J., & Glaser, R. (1984). Psychosocial modifiers of immunocompetence in medical students. *Psychosomatic Medicine, 46,* 7–14.

Kiecolt-Glaser, J. K., Glaser, R., Cacioppo, J. T., MacCallum, R. C., Snydersmith, M., Kim, C., & Malarkey, W. B. (1997). Marital conflict in older adults: Endocrinological and immunological correlates. *Psychosomatic Medicine, 59,* 339–349.

Kiecolt-Glaser, J. K., Kennedy, S., Malkoff, S., Fisher, L., Speicher, C. E., & Glaser, R. (1988). Marital discord and immunity in males. *Psychosomatic Medicine, 50,* 213–229.

Kierein, N. M., & Gold, M. A. (2000). Pygmalion in work organizations: A meta-analysis. *Journal of Organizational Behavior, 21*(8), 913–928.

Kiernan, K. (2004). Redrawing the boundaries of marriage. *Journal of Marriage and Family, 66,* 980–987.

Kiesler, C. A. (2000). The next wave of change for psychology and mental health services in the health care revolution. *American Psychologist, 55*(5), 481–487.

Kiesler, D. J. (1999). *Beyond the disease model of mental disorders.* New York: Praeger.

Kihlstrom, J. F. (1998). Exhumed memory. In S. J. Lynn & K. M. McConkey (Eds.), *Truth in memory.* New York: Guilford Press.

Kihlstrom, J. F. (2001). Dissociative disorders. In P. B. Sutker & H. E. Adams (Eds.), *Comprehensive handbook of psychopathology* (3rd ed., pp. 259–276). New York: Kluwer Academic/Plenum Publishers.

Kihlstrom, J. F. (2004). An unbalanced balancing act: Blocked, recovered, and false memories in the laboratory and clinic. *Clinical Psychology: Science & Practice, 11*(1), 34–41.

Kihlstrom, J. F., Glisky, M. L., & Angiulo, M. J. (1994). Dissociative tendencies and dissociative disorders. *Journal of Abnormal Psychology, 103,* 117–124.

Kilby, R. W. (1993). *The study of human values.* Lanham, MD: University Press of America.

Kilmartin, C. (2000). *The masculine self* (2nd ed.). Boston: McGraw-Hill.

Kim, H., & Markus, H. R. (1999). Deviance or uniqueness, harmony or conformity? A cultural analysis. *Journal of Personality and Social Psychology, 77*(4), 785–800.

Kimura, D., & Hampson, E. (1993). Neural and hormonal mechanisms mediating sex differences in cognition. In P. A. Vernon (Ed.), *Biological approaches to the study of human intelligence.* Norwood, NJ: Ablex.

Kindlon, D., & Thompson, M. (with Barker, T.). (1999). *Raising Cain: Protecting the emotional life of boys.* New York: Ballantine.

King, B. M. (2005). *Human sexuality today.* Upper Saddle River, NJ: Pearson Prentice Hall.

King, C. A. (1997). Suicidal behavior in adolescence. In R. W. Maris, M. M. Silverman, & S. S. Canetto (Eds.), *Review of suicidology* (pp. 61–95). New York: Guilford Press.

King, G. R., & Ellinwood Jr., E. H. (2005). Amphetamines and other stimulants. In J. H. Lowinson, P. Ruiz, R. B. Millman, & J. G. Langrod (Eds.), *Substance abuse: A comprehensive textbook.* Philadelphia: Lippincott/Williams & Wilkins.

King, J. L. (2004). *On the down low: A journey into the lives of "straight" black men who sleep with men.* New York: Broadway Books.

King, L. A., & Emmons, R. A. (1990). Conflict over emotional expression: Psychological and physical correlates. *Journal of Personality and Social Psychology, 58,* 864–877.

King, L. A., & Emmons, R. A. (1991). Psychological, physical, and interpersonal correlates of emotional expressiveness, conflict and control. *European Journal of Personality, 5,* 131–150.

King, L. A., King, D. W., Fairbank, J. A., Keane, T. M., & Adams, G. A. (1998). Resilience-recovery factors in post-traumatic stress disorder among female and male Vietnam veterans: Hardiness, postwar social support, and additional stressful life events. *Journal of Personality and Social Psychology, 74,* 420–434.

King, N. J., Eleonora, G., & Ollendick, T. H. (1998). Etiology of childhood phobias: Current status of Rachman's three pathways theory. *Behaviour Research and Therapy, 36,* 297–309.

Kinsey, A. C., Pomeroy, W. B., & Martin, C. E. (1948). *Sexual behavior in the human male.* Philadelphia: Saunders.

Kinsey, A. C., Pomeroy, W. B., Martin, C. E., & Gebhard, P. H. (1953). *Sexual behavior in the human female.* Philadelphia: Saunders.

Kinsman, R. A., Dirks, J. F., & Jones, N. F. (1982). Psychomaintenance of chronic physical illness: Clinical assessment of personal styles affecting medical management. In T. Millon, C. Green, & R. Meagher (Eds.), *Handbook of clinical health psychology.* New York: Plenum.

Kirby, D. (2000). Making condoms available in schools. *Western Journal of Medicine, 172,* 149–151.

Kirkpatrick, L. A. (1998). God as a substitute attachment figure: A longitudinal study of adult attachment style and religious change in college students. *Personality and Social Psychology Bulletin, 24*(9), 961–973.

Kirkpatrick, L. A., & Davis, K. E. (1994). Attachment style, gender, and relationship stability: A longitudinal analysis. *Journal of Personality and Social Psychology, 66,* 502–512.

Kirkpatrick, L. A., & Hazan, C. (1994). Attachment styles and close relationships: A four-year prospective study. *Personal Relationships, 1,* 123–142.

Kirmayer, L. J., Robbins, J. M., & Paris, J. (1994). Somatoform disorders: Personality and the social matrix of somatic distress. *Journal of Abnormal Psychology, 103,* 125–136.

Kite, M. E., & Whitley, B. E., Jr. (1996). Sex differences in attitudes toward homosexual persons, behaviors, and civil rights: A meta-analysis. *Personality and Social Psychology Bulletin, 22,* 336–353.

Kitson, G. C. (1992). *Portrait of divorce: Adjustment to marital breakdown.* New York: Guilford Press.

Klag, S., & Bradley, G. (2004). The role of hardiness in stress and illness: An exploration of the effect of negative affectivity and gender. *British Journal of Health Psychology, 9*(2), 137–161.

Klass, D. (1996). The deceased child in the psychic and social worlds of bereaved parents during the resolution of grief. In D. Klass, P. R. Silverman, & S. L. Nickman (Eds.), *Continuing bonds: New understandings of grief* (pp. 199–215). Washington, DC: Taylor and Francis.

Klassen, M. (1987). How to get the most out of your time. In A. D. Timpe (Ed.), *The management of time.* New York: Facts on File.

Kleiman, C. (2003, September 7). Web job boards fall short. *Atlanta Journal-Constitution,* p. R3.

Klein, D. N., & Rubovits, D. R. (1987). The reliability of subjects' reports of life events inventories: A longitudinal study. *Journal of Behavioral Medicine, 10,* 501–512.

Klein, F., Sepekoff, B., & Wolf, T. J. (1985). Sexual orientation: A multivariable dynamic process. *Journal of Homosexuality, 11,* 35–49.

Klein, K. J., & Hodges, S. D. (2001). Gender differences, motivation, and empathic accuracy: When it pays to understand. *Personality and Social Psychology Bulletin, 27*(6), 720–730.

Kleinginna, P. R., & Kleinginna, A. M. (1988). Current trends toward convergence of the behavioristic, functional, and cognitive perspectives in experimental psychology. *The Psychological Record, 38,* 369–392.

Kleinke, C. L. (1986). Gaze and eye contact: A research review. *Psychological Bulletin, 100,* 78–100.

Kleinke, C. L., Meeker, F. B., & Staneski, R. A. (1986). Preference for opening lines: Comparing ratings by men and women. *Sex Roles, 15,* 585–600.

Kleinmuntz, B. (1980). *Essentials of abnormal psychology.* San Francisco: Harper & Row.

Klerman, G. L., Weissman, M. M., Markowitz, J. C., Glick, I., Wilner, P. J., Mason. B., & Shear, M. K. (1994). Medication and psychotherapy. In A. E. Bergin & S. L. Garfield (Eds.), *Handbook of psychotherapy and behavior change* (4th ed.). New York: Wiley.

Kline, D. W., Kline, T. J. B., Fozard, J. L., Kosnik, W., Schieber, F., & Sekuler, R. (1992). Vision, aging, and driving: The problems of older drivers. *Journal of Gerontology, 42,* P27–P34.

Kline, P. (1995). A critical review of the measurement of personality and intelligence. In D. H. Saklofske & M. Zeidner (Eds.), *International handbook of personality and intelligence.* New York: Plenum Press.

Kling, K. C., Hyde, J. S., Showers, C. J., & Buswell, B. N. (1999). Gender differences in self-esteem: A meta-analysis. *Psychological Bulletin, 125*(4), 470–500.

Klonoff, E. A., & Landrine, H. (1999). Cross-validation of the schedule of racist events. *Journal of Black Psychology, 25*(2), 231–254.

Kluft, R. P. (1996). Dissociative identity disorder. In L. K. Michelson & W. J. Ray (Eds.), *Handbook of dissociation: Theoretical, empirical, and clinical perspectives.* New York: Plenum.

Kluft, R. P. (1999). True lies, false truths, and naturalistic raw data: Applying clinical research findings to the false memory debate. In L. M. Williams & V. L. Banyard (Eds.), *Trauma & memory.* Thousand Oaks, CA: Sage.

Kluger, J. (2002 June 10). Pumping up your past. *Time,* p. 45.

Kluwer, E. S., Heesink, J. A. M., & Van de Vliert, E. (1996). Marital conflict about the division of household labor and paid work. *Journal of Marriage and the Family, 58,* 958–969.

Knapp, C. M., Ciraulo, D. A., & Jaffe, J. (2005). Opiates: Clinical aspects. In J. H. Lowinson, P. Ruiz, R. B. Millman, & J. G. Langrod (Eds.), *Substance abuse: A comprehensive textbook.* Philadelphia: Lippincott/Williams & Wilkins.

Knapp, D. E., Faley, R. H., Ekeberg, W. C., & Dubois, C. L. Z. (1997). Determinants of target responses to sexual harassment: A conceptual framework. *Academy of Management Review, 22*(3), 687–729.

Knaus, W. (2000). Procrastination, blame, and change. *Journal of Social Behavior and Personality, 15,* 153–166.

Knickmeyer, N., Sexton, K., & Nishimura, N. (2002). The impact of same-sex friendships on the well-being of women: A review of the literature. *Women and Therapy, 25*(1), 37–59.

Knowles, J. A., Kaufmann, C. A., & Rieder, R. O. (1999). Genetics. In R. E. Hales, S. C. Yudofsky, & J. A. Talbott (Eds.), *American Psychiatric Press textbook of psychiatry* (pp. 35–82). Washington, DC: American Psychiatric Press.

Knowles, R. B., Wyart, C., Buldyrev, S. V., Cruz, L., Urbanc, B., Hasselmo, M. E., Stanley, H. E., & Hyman, B. T. (1999). Plaque-induced neurite abnormalities: Implications of disruption of neuronal networks in Alzheimer's disease. *Proceedings of the National Academy of Sciences, 96,* 5274–5279.

Knox, D. (2000). *The divorced dad's survival book: How to stay connected to your kids.* New York: Perseus.

Kobasa, S. C. (1979). Stressful life events, personality, and health: An inquiry into hardiness. *Journal of Personality and Social Psychology, 37,* 1–11.

Kobasa, S. C. (1984, September). How much stress can you survive? *American Health,* pp. 64–77.

Konrad, A. M. (2003). Family demands and job attribute preferences: A 4-year longitudinal study of women and men. *Sex Roles, 49*(1–2), 35–46.

Koopman, C., Classen, C., & Spiegel, D. (1994). Predictors of posttraumatic stress symptoms among survivors of the Oakland/Berkeley, Calif., firestorm. *American Journal of Psychiatry, 151,* 888–894.

Kop, W. J., Gottdiener, J. S., & Krantz, D. S. (2001). Stress and silent ischemia. In A. Baum, T. A. Revenson, & J. E. Singer (Eds.), *Handbook of health psychology* (pp. 669–682). Mahwah, NJ: Erlbaum.

Kopta, S. M., Lueger, R. J., Saunders, S. M., & Howard, K. I. (1999). Individual psychotherapy outcome and process research: Challenges leading to greater turmoil or a positive transition? *Annual Review of Psychology, 50,* 441–469.

Koren, D., Arnon, I., & Klein, E. (1999). Acute stress response and posttraumatic stress disorder in traffic accident victims: A one-year prospective, follow-up study. *American Journal of Psychiatry, 156*(3), 367–373.

Koren, P., Carlton, K., & Shaw, D. (1980). Marital conflict: Relations among behaviors, outcomes, and distress. *Journal of Consulting and Clinical Psychology, 48,* 460–468.

Koss, M. P., & Cook, S. I. (1993). Facing the facts: Date and acquaintance rape are significant problems for women. In R. J. Gelles, & D. R. Losede (Eds.), *Current controversies on family violence* (pp. 104–119). Thousand Oaks, CA: Sage.

Koss, M. P., Gidycz, C. A., & Wisniewski, N. (1988). The scope of rape: Incidence and prevalence of sexual aggression and victimization in a national sample of higher education students. *Journal of Consulting and Clinical Psychology, 55,* 162–170.

Koss, M. P., Goodman, L. A., Browne, A., Fitzgerald, L. F., Keita, G. P., & Russo, N. F. (1994). *No safe haven: Male violence against women at home, at work, and in the community.* Washington, DC: American Psychological Association.

Kowalski, R. M. (1993). Inferring sexual interest from behavioral cues: Effects of gender and sexually relevant attitudes. *Sex Roles, 29,* 13–36.

Kozlowski, S. W. J., & Bell, B. S. (2003). Work groups and teams in organizations. In W. C. Borman, D. R. Ilgen, & R. J. Klimoski (Eds.), *Handbook of psychology: Vol. 12. Industrial and organizational psychology.* New York: Wiley.

Kramer, H. (1994). *Liberating the adult within.* New York: Simon & Schuster.

Krantz, D. S., Sheps, D. S., Carney, R. M., & Natelson, B. H. (2000). Effects of mental stress in patients with coronary artery disease. *Journal of* the American Medical Association, 283(14), 1800–1802.

Kraut, R., Patterson, M., Lundmark, V., Kiesler, S., Mukopadhyay, T., & Scherlis, W. (1998). Internet paradox: A social technology that reduces social involvement and psychological well-being? American Psychologist, 53, 1017–1031.

Kreinin, T., Rodriquez, M., & Edwards, M. (December 2000/January 2001). Adolescents would prefer parents as primary sexuality educators. Siecus Report Supplement, 1.

Kring, A. M. (1999). Emotion in schizophrenia: Old mystery, new understanding. Current Directions in Psychological Science, 8, 160–163.

Kring, A. M., & Gordon, A. H. (1998). Sex differences in emotion: Expression, experience, and physiology. Journal of Personality and Social Psychology, 74(3), 686–703.

Kroger, J. (1997). Gender and identity: The intersection of structure, content, and context. Sex Roles, 36(11/12), 747–770.

Krueger, W. C. F. (1929). The effect of overlearning on retention. Journal of Experimental Psychology, 12, 71–78.

Kübler-Ross, E. (1969). On death and dying. New York: Macmillan.

Kübler-Ross, E. (1970). The dying patient's point of view. In O. G. Brim, Jr., H. E. Freeman, S. Levine, & N. A. Scotch (Eds.), The dying patient. New York: Sage.

Kulick, A. R., Pope, H. G., & Keck, P. E. (1990). Lycanthropy and self-identification. Journal of Nervous and Mental Disease, 178, 134–137.

Kulik, L. (2000). Jobless men and women: A comparative analysis of job search intensity, attitudes toward unemployment and related responses. Journal of Occupational and Behavioral Psychology, 73(4), 487–500.

Kurdek, L. A. (1991). Sexuality in homosexual and heterosexual couples. In K. McKinney & S. Sprecher (Eds.), Sexuality in close relationships. Hillside, NJ: Erlbaum.

Kurdek, L. A. (1993a). Predicting marital dissolution: A five-year prospective longitudinal study of newlywed couples. Journal of Personality and Social Psychology, 64(2), 221–242.

Kurdek, L. A. (1993b). The allocation of household labor in gay, lesbian, and heterosexual married couples. Journal of Social Issues, 49(3), 127–139.

Kurdek, L. A. (1994). The nature and correlates of relationship quality in gay, lesbian, and heterosexual cohabiting couples. In B. Greene & G. M. Herek (Eds.), Lesbian and gay psychology. Thousand Oaks, CA: Sage.

Kurdek, L. A. (1998). Relationship outcomes and their predictors: Longitudinal evidence from heterosexual married, gay cohabiting, and lesbian cohabiting couples. Journal of Marriage and the Family, 30, 553–568.

Kurdek, L. A. (2004). Gay men and lesbians: The family context. In M. Coleman & L. H. Ganong (Eds.), Handbook of contemporary families: Considering the past, contemplating the future. Thousand Oaks, CA: Sage.

Kurdek, L. A., & Schmitt, J. P. (1986a). Early development of relationship quality in heterosexual married, heterosexual cohabiting, gay, and lesbian couples. Developmental Psychology, 22, 305–309.

Kurdek, L. A., & Schmitt, J. P. (1986b). Interaction of sex role self-concept with relationship quality and relationship beliefs in married, heterosexual cohabiting, gay, and lesbian couples. Journal of Personality and Social Psychology, 51, 365–370.

Kutchins, H., & Kirk, S. A. (1997). Making us crazy: DSM—The psychiatric Bible and the creation of mental disorders. New York: Free Press.

Lachman, M. E. (2004). Development in midlife. Annual Review of Psychology, 55, 305–331.

Lachman, M. E., & Bertrand, R. M. (2001). Personality and the self in midlife. In M. E. Lachman (Ed.), Handbook of midlife development. New York: Wiley.

LaFrance, M. (2001). Gender and social interaction. In R. K. Unger (Ed.), Handbook of the psychology of women and gender. New York: Wiley.

La Greca, A. M. (2000). Posttraumatic stress disorder in children. In G. Fink (Ed.), Encyclopedia of stress (Vol. 3, pp. 181–185). San Diego: Academic Press.

Laitinen, J., Ek, E., & Sovio, U. (2002). Stress-related eating and drinking behavior and body mass index and predictors of this behavior. Preventive Medicine: An International Journal Devoted to Practice & Theory, 34, 29–39

Lakein, A. (1996). How to get control of your time and your life. New York: New American Library.

Lam, L. T., & Kirby, S. L. (2002). Is emotional intelligence an advantage? An exploration of the impact of emotional and general intelligence on individual performance. Journal of Social Psychology, 142, 133–143.

Lamb, M. E., Sternberg, K. J., & Prodromidis, M. (1992). Nonmaternal care and the security of infant-mother attachment: A reanalysis of the data. Infant Behavior and Development, 15, 71–83.

Lambert, M. J., & Barley, D. E. (2001). Research summary on the therapeutic relationship and psychotherapy outcome. Psychotherapy: Theory, Research, Practice, Training, 38, 357–361.

Lambert, M. J., & Bergin, A. E. (1992). Achievements and limitations of psychotherapy research. In D. K. Freedheim (Ed.), History of psychotherapy: A century of change. Washington, DC: American Psychological Association.

Lambert, M. J., & Bergin, A. E. (1994). The effectiveness of psychotherapy. In A. E. Bergin & S. L. Garfield (Eds.), Handbook of psychotherapy and behavior change (4th ed.). New York: Wiley.

Lambert, M. J., & Hill, C. E. (1994). Assessing psychotherapy outcomes and processes. In A. E. Bergin & S. L. Garfield (Eds.), Handbook of psychotherapy and behavior change (4th ed.). New York: Wiley.

Lamborn, S. D., Mounts, N. S., Steinberg, L., & Dornbusch, S. M. (1991). Patterns of competence and adjustment among adolescents from authoritative, authoritarian, indulgent, and neglectful families. Child Development, 62, 1049–1065.

Lammers, C., Ireland, M., Resnick, M., & Blum, R. (2000). Influences on adolescents' decisions to postpone onset of sexual intercourse: A survival analysis of virginity among youths ages 13 to 18 years. Journal of Adolescent Health, 26, 42–48.

Lampe, A., Soellner, W., Krismer, M., Rumpold, G., Kantner-Rumplmair, W., Ogon, M., & Rathner, G. (1998). The impact of stressful life events on exacerbation of chronic low-back pain. Journal of Psychosomatic Research, 44(5), 555–563.

Landabaso, M. A., Iraurgi, I., Sanz, J., Calle, R., Ruiz de Apodaka, J., Jimenez-Lerma, J. M., & Gutierrez-Fraile, M. (1999). Naltrexone in the treatment of alcoholism. Two-year follow up results. European Journal of Psychiatry, 13, 97–105.

Landau, E. (1988). Teenagers talk about school. Englewood Cliffs, NJ: Julian Messner.

Landel-Graham, J., Yount, S. E., & Rudnicki, S. R. (2003). Diabetes mellitus. In A. M. Nezu, C. M. Nezu, & P. A. Geller (Eds.), Handbook of psychology: Vol. 9. Health psychology. New York: Wiley.

Langer, E. (1989). Mindfulness. New York: Addison-Wesley.

Langer, E. J. (1975). The illusion of control. Journal of Personality and Social Psychology, 32(2), 311–328.

Langer, E., Bashner, R., & Chanowitz, B. (1985). Decreasing prejudice by increasing discrimination. Journal of Personality and Social Psychology, 49, 113–120.

Langlois, J. H., Kalakanis, L., Rubenstein, A. J., Larson, A., Hallam, M., & Smoot, M. (2000). Maxims or myths of beauty? A meta-analytic and theoretical review. Psychological Bulletin, 126(3), 390–423.

Lansford, J. E., Sherman, A. M., & Antonucci, T. C. (1998). Satisfaction with social networks: An examination of socioemotional selectivity theory across cohorts. Psychology and Aging, 13(4), 544–552.

Lanyon, R. I., & Goodstein, L. D. (1997). Personality assessment. New York: Wiley.

Lanza, S. T., & Collins, L. M. (2002). Pubertal timing and the onset of substance use in females during early adolescence. Prevention Science, 3(1), 69–82.

Lapierre, Y. D. (2003). Suicidality with selective serotonin reuptake inhibitors: Valid claim? Journal of Psychiatry & Neuroscience, 28(5), 340–347.

LaPoire, B. A., Burgoon, J. K., & Parrott, R. (1992). Status and privacy restoring communication in the workplace. Journal of Applied Communication Research, 4, 419–436.

Larose, S., & Bernier, A. (2001). Social support processes: Mediators of attachment state of mind and adjustment in late adolescence. Attachment and Human Development, 3(1), 96–120.

Larson, K. (2004, July 11). N. J. begins recognizing same-sex marriages. Statesboro Herald, p. 8A.

Larson, R., & Pleck, J. (1998). Hidden feelings: Emotionality in boys and men. In Gender and motivation (Vol. 45, pp. 25–74). Lincoln, NE: University of Nebraska Press.

Larson, R., & Richards, M. H. (1994). Divergent realities: The emotional lives of mothers, fathers, and adolescents. New York: Basic Books.

Larzelere, R. E. (2000). Child outcomes of nonabusive and customary physical punishment by parents: An updated literature review. Clinical Child and Family Psychology Review, 3(4), 199–221.

Laskoff, M. B. (2004). Landing on the right side of your ass: A survival guide for the recently unemployed. New York: Three Rivers Press.

Latané, B., & Nida, S. A. (1981). Ten years of research on group size and helping. Psychological Bulletin, 89, 308–324.

Lating, J. M., Sherman, M. F., Everly, G. S., Lowry, J. L., & Peragine, T. F. (2004). PTSD reactions and functioning of American Airlines flight attendants in the wake of September 11. Journal of Nervous & Mental Disease, 192(6), 435–441.

Lauer, J., & Lauer, R. (1985, June). Marriages made to last. Psychology Today, pp. 22–26.

Laughlin, H. (1967). The neuroses. Washington, DC: Butterworth.

Laughlin, H. (1979). The ego and its defenses. New York: Aronson.

Laumann, E. O., Gagnon, J. H., Michael, R. T., & Michaels, S. (1994). The social organization of sexuality: Sexual practices in the United States. Chicago: University of Chicago Press.

Laurenceau, J. P., Barrett, L. F., & Pietromonaco, P. R. (1998). Intimacy as an interpersonal process: The importance of self-disclosure, partner disclosure, and perceived partner responsiveness in interpersonal exchanges. Journal of Personality and Social Psychology, 74(5), 1238–1251.

Laursen, B., Coy, K. C., & Collins, W. A. (1998). Reconsidering changes in parent-child conflict across adolescence: A meta-analysis. Child Development, 69, 817–832.

Lauzen, M. M., & Dozier, D. M. (2002). You look mahvelous: An examination of gender and appearance comments in the 1999–2000 prime-time season. Sex Roles, 46(11/12), 429–437.

Lavine, H., Sweeney, D., & Wagner, S. H. (1999). Depicting women as sex objects in television advertising: Effects on body dissatisfaction. Personality and Social Psychology Bulletin, 25(8), 1049–1058.

Lay, C. H. (1992). Trait procrastination and the perception of person-task characteristics. Journal of Social Behavior and Personality, 7, 483–494.

Lay, C. H. (1995). Trait procrastination, agitation, dejection, and self-discrepancy. In J. R. Ferrari, J. L. Johnson, & W. G. McCown (Eds.), Procrastination and task avoidance: Theory, research, and treatment. New York: Plenum.

Lay, C. H., Edwards, J. M., Parker, J. D. A., & Endler, N. S. (1989). An assessment of appraisal anxiety, coping, and procrastination during an examination period. *European Journal of Personality, 3,* 195–208.

Lazarus, A. A. (1989). Multimodal therapy. In R. J. Corsini & D. Wedding (Eds.), *Current psychotherapies.* Itasca, IL: F. E. Peacock.

Lazarus, R. S. (1991). *Emotion and adaptation.* New York: Oxford.

Lazarus, R. S. (1993). Why we should think of stress as a subset of emotion. In L. Goldberger & S. Breznitz (Eds.), *Handbook of stress: Theoretical and clinical aspects* (2nd ed.). New York: Free Press.

Lazarus, R. S., & Folkman, S. (1984). *Stress, appraisal and coping.* New York: Springer.

Le, B., & Agnew, C. R. (2003). Commitment and its theorized determinants: A meta-analysis of the investment model. *Personal Relationships, 10*(1), 37–57.

Leadbeater, B., & Way, N. (1995). *Urban adolescent girls: Resisting stereotypes.* New York: University Press.

Leahy, J. M. (1993). A comparison of depression in women bereaved of a spouse, a child, or a parent. *Omega, 26,* 207–217.

Leana, C. R., & Feldman, D. C. (1991). Gender differences in responses to unemployment. *Journal of Vocational Behavior, 38,* 65–77.

Leary, M. R. (2004). The function of self-esteem in terror management theory and sociometer theory: Comment on Pyszczynski et al. (2004). *Psychological Bulletin, 130*(3), 478–482.

Leary, M. R., & Baumeister, R. F. (2000). The nature and function of self-esteem: Sociometer theory. In M. P. Zanna (Ed.), *Advances in experimental social psychology* (Vol. 32). San Diego, CA: Academic Press.

Leary, M. R., Tambor, E. S., Terdal, S. K., & Downs, D. L. (1995). Self-esteem as an interpersonal monitor: The sociometer hypothesis. *Journal of Personality and Social Psychology, 68*(3), 519–530.

Leary, M. R., Tchividjian, L. R., & Kraxberger, B. E. (1994). Self-presentation can be hazardous to your health: Impression management and health risk. *Health Psychology, 13,* 461–470.

Leavitt, F. (1995). *Drugs and behavior* (3rd ed.). Thousand Oaks, CA: Sage.

Leavitt, F. (2001). Iatrogenic recovered memories: Examining the empirical evidence. *American Journal of Forensic Psychology, 19*(2), 21–32.

LeBlanc, M. M., & Barling, J. (2004). Workplace aggression. *Current Directions in Psychological Science, 13*(1), 9–12.

LeBoeuf, M. (1980, February). Managing time means managing yourself. *Business Horizons,* pp. 41–46.

Le Bourdais, C. E., & Lapierre-Adamcyk, E. (2004). Changes in conjugal life in Canada: Is cohabitation progressively replacing marriage? *Journal of Marriage and Family, 66,* 929–942.

Leckman, J. F., Grice, D. E., Boardman, J., Zhang, H., Vitale, A., Bondi, C., Alsobrook, J., Peterson, B. S., Cohen, D. J., Rasmussen, S. A., Goodman, W. K., McDougle, C. J., & Pauls, D. L. (1997). Symptoms of obsessive-compulsive disorder. *American Journal of Psychiatry, 154,* 911–917.

Ledray, L. E. (1994). *Recovering from rape* (2nd ed.). New York: Henry Holt.

Lee, G. R. (1988). Marital satisfaction in later life: The effects of nonmarital roles. *Journal of Marriage and the Family, 50,* 775–783.

Lee, G. R., Willetts, M. C., & Seccombe, K. (1998). Widowhood and depression. *Research on Aging, 20,* 611–630.

Lee, I.-M., Rexrode, K. M., Cook, N. R., Manson, J. E., & Buring, J. E. (2001). Physical activity and coronary heart disease in women: Is "no pain, no

gain" passé? *Journal of the American Medical Association, 285,* 1447–1454.

Lee, I.-M., & Skerrett, P. J. (2001). Physical activity and all-cause mortality. What is the dose-response relation? *Medicine and Science in Sports and Exercise, 33,* S459–S471.

Lee, R. M., & Ramirez, M. (2000).The history, current status, and future of multicultural psychotherapy. In I. Cuellar & F. A. Paniagua (Eds.), *Handbook of multicultural mental health: Assessment and treatment of diverse populations.* San Diego: Academic Press.

Lee, S., & Katzman, M. A. (2002). Cross-cultural perspectives on eating disorders. In C. G. Fairburn & K. D. Brownell (Eds.), *Eating disorders and obesity: A comprehensive handbook.* New York: Guilford.

Lee, Y. T., & Seligman, M. E. P. (1997). Are Americans more optimistic than the Chinese? *Personality and Social Psychology Bulletin, 23,* 32–40.

Lefcourt, H. M. (2001). The humor solution. In C. R. Snyder (Ed.), *Coping with stress: Effective people and processes* (pp. 68–92). New York: Oxford University Press.

Lefcourt, H. M., Davidson, K., Shepherd, R., Phillips, M., Prkachin, K., & Mills, D. (1995). Perspective-taking humor: Accounting for stress moderation. *Journal of Social and Clinical Psychology, 14,* 373–391.

Leff, J., & Vaughn, C. (1985). *Expressed emotion in families.* New York: Guilford Press.

Lehrer, P. M., & Woolfolk, R. L. (1984). Are stress reduction techniques interchangeable, or do they have specific effects? A review of the comparative empirical literature. In R. L. Woolfolk & P. M. Lehrer (Eds.), *Principles and practice of stress management.* New York: Guilford Press.

Lehrer, P. M., & Woolfolk, R. L. (1993). Specific effects of stress management techniques. In P. M. Lehrer & R. L. Woolfolk (Eds.), *Principles and practice of stress management* (2nd ed.). New York: Guilford Press.

Lehrer, P., Feldman, J., Giardino, N., Song, H., & Schmaling, K. (2002). Psychological aspects of asthma. *Journal of Consulting & Clinical Psychology, 70*(3), 691–711.

Leigh, G. K., Holman, T. B., & Burr, W. R. (1984). An empirical test of sequence in Murstein's SVR Theory of mate selection. *Family Relations, 33* 225–231.

Leigh, G. K., Holman, T. B., & Burr, W. R. (1987). Some confusions and exclusions of the SVR theory of dyadic pairing: A response to Murstein. *Journal of Marriage and the Family, 49,* 933–937.

Leitenberg, H., Detzer, M. J., & Srebnik, D. (1993). Gender differences in masturbation and the relation of masturbation experience in preadolescence and/or early adolescence to sexual behavior and sexual adjustment in young adulthood. *Archives of Sexual Behavior, 22,* 87–98.

Leitenberg, H., & Henning, K. (1995). Sexual fantasy. *Psychological Bulletin, 117,* 469–496.

Leiter, M. P., & Maslach, C. (2001). Burnout and health. In A. Baum, T. A. Revenson, & J. E. Singer (Eds.), *Handbook of health psychology* (pp. 415–426). Mahwah, NJ: Erlbaum.

Lemack, G. E., Uzzo, R. G., & Poppas, D. P. (1998). Effects of stress on male reproductive function. In J. R. Hubbard & E. A. Workman (Eds.), *Handbook of stress medicine: An organ system approach.* New York: CRC Press.

Lemieux, R., & Hale, J. L. (2002). Cross-sectional analysis of intimacy, passion, and commitment: Testing the assumption of the triangular theory of love. *Psychological Reports, 90* (3, Pt. 1), 1009–1014.

Lemme, B. H. (1999). *Development in adulthood.* Boston: Allyn & Bacon.

Leo, J. (1987, January 12). Exploring the traits of twins. *Time,* p. 63.

Lerman, H. (1986). *A mote in Freud's eye: From psychoanalysis to the psychology of women.* New York: Springer.

Lerner, M. J. (1980). *The belief in a just world: A fundamental decision.* New York: Plenum.

Lerner, M. J. (1998). The two forms of belief in a just world: Some thoughts on why and how people care about justice. In L. Montada & M. J. Lerner (Eds.), *Responses to victimizations and belief in a just world: Critical issues in social justice.* New York: Plenum Press.

Lesage, A. D., Boyer, R., Grunberg, F., Vanier, C., Morissette, R., Menard-Buteau, C., & Loyer, M. (1994). Suicide and mental disorders: A case-control study of young men. *American Journal of Psychiatry, 151,* 1063–1068.

Letherby, G., & Williams, C. (1999). Non-motherhood: Ambivalent autobiographies. *Feminist Studies, 25,* 719–728.

Lett, H. S., Blumenthal, J. A., Babyak, M. A., Sherwood, A., Strauman, T., Robins, C., & Newman, M. F. (2004). Depression as a risk factor for coronary artery disease: Evidence, mechanisms, and treatment. *Psychosomatic Medicine, 66*(3), 305–315.

Levant, R. F. (1996). The new psychology of men. *Professional Psychology: Research and Practice, 27,* 259–265.

Levant, R. F. (2003, Fall). Why study boys and men? *Nova Southeastern University Center for Psychological Studies Newsletter,* pp. 12–13.

Levant, R. F., Barbanel, L., & DeLeon, P. H. (2004). Psychology's response to terrorism. In F. M. Moghaddam & A. J. Marsella (Eds.), *Understanding terrorism: Psychological roots, consequences, and interventions.* Washington, DC: American Psychological Association.

LeVay, S. (1996). *Queer science: The use and abuse of research into homosexuality.* Cambridge, MA: The MIT Press.

Levenson, J. L., McDaniel, J. S., Moran, M. G., & Stoudemire, A. (1999). Psychological factors affecting medical conditions. In R. E. Hales, S. C. Yudofsky, & J. A. Talbott (Eds.), *Textbook of psychiatry* (3rd ed., pp. 635–662). Washington, DC: American Psychiatric Press, Inc.

Levenstein, S. (2002). Psychosocial factors in peptic ulcer and inflammatory bowel disease. *Journal of Consulting & Clinical Psychology, 70*(3), 739–750.

Lever, J. (1994, August 24). Sexual revelations. *The Advocate,* 17–24.

Levin, S., van Laar, C., & Sidanius, J. (2003). The effects of ingroup and outgroup friendship on ethnic attitudes in college: A longitudinal study. *Group Processes and Intergroup Relations, 6*(1), 76–92.

Levine, M. P., & Harrison, K. (2004). Media's role in the perpetuation and prevention of negative body image and disordered eating. In J. K. Thompson (Ed.), *Handbook of eating disorders and obesity.* New York: Wiley.

Levine, R. V., Martinez, T. S., Brase, G., & Sorenson, K. (1994). Helping in 36 U.S. cities. *Journal of Personality and Social Psychology, 67*(1), 69–82.

Levine, R. V., Sato, S., Hashimoto, T., & Verma, J. (1995). Love and marriage in eleven cultures. *Journal of Cross-Cultural Psychology, 26*(5), 554–571.

Levine, S. B. (2003). Erectile dysfunction: Why drug therapy isn't always enough. *Cleveland Clinic Journal of Medicine, 70*(3), 241–246.

Levinson, D. F., Mahtani, M. M., Nancarrow, D. J., Brown, D. M., Kruglyak, L., Kirby, A., Hayward, N. K., Crowe, R. R., Andreasen, N. C., Black, D. W., Silverman, J. M., Endicott, J., Sharpe, L., Mohs, R. C., Siever, L. J., Walters, M. K., lennon, D. P., Jones, H. L., Nurs, B., Nertney, D. A., Daly, M. J., Gladis, M., & Mowry, B. J. (1998). Genome scan of schizophrenia. *American Journal of Psychiatry, 155,* 741–750.

Levinson, D. J., Darrow, C. M., Klein, E. G., Levinson, M. H., & McKee, B. (1978). *The seasons of a man's life.* New York: Knopf.

Levinthal, C. E. (2002). *Drugs, behavior, and modern society* . Boston: Allyn & Bacon.

Levis, D. J. (1989). The case for a return to a two-factor theory of avoidance: The failure of non-fear interpretations. In S. B. Klein & R. R. Bowrer (Eds.), *Contemporary learning theories: Pavlovian conditioning and the status of traditional learning theory*. Hillsdale, NJ: Erlbaum.

Levy, B., & Langer, E. (1994). Aging free from negative stereotypes: Successful memory in China and among the American deaf. *Journal of Personality and Social Psychology, 66*, 989–997.

Levy, S. M., Herberman, R. B., Simons, A., Whiteside, T., Lee, J., McDonald, R., & Beadle, M. (1989). Persistently low natural killer cell activity in normal adults: Immunological, hormonal and mood correlates. *Natural Immune Cell Growth Regulation, 8*, 173–186.

Levy, S. R., Stroessner, S. J., & Dweck, C. S. (1998). Stereotype formation and endorsement: The role of implicit theories. *Journal of Personality and Social Psychology, 74*(6), 1421–1436.

Lewin, E. (2004). Does marriage have a future? *Journal of Marriage and Family, 66*, 1000–1006.

Lewin, K. (1935). *A dynamic theory of personality*. New York: McGraw-Hill.

Lewinsohn, P. M., & Gotlib, I. H. (1995). Behavioral theory and treatment of depression. In E. E. Beckham & W. R. Leber (Eds.), *Handbook of depression* (2nd ed.). New York: Guilford Press.

Lewinsohn, P. M., Joiner, T. E. Jr., & Rohde, P. (2001). Evaluation of cognitive diathesis-stress models in predicting major depressive disorder in adolescents. *Journal of Abnormal Psychology, 110*(2), 203–215.

Lewis, B. P., & Linder, D. E. (1997). Thinking about choking? Attentional processes and paradoxical performance. *Personality and Social Psychology Bulletin, 23*, 937–944.

Lewis, D. O., Yeager, C. A., Swica, Y., Pincus, J. H., & Lewis, M. (1997). Objective documentation of child abuse and dissociation in 12 murderers with dissociative identity disorder. *American Journal of Psychiatry, 154*, 1703–1710.

Lewis, R. A., & Lin, L.-W. (1996). Adults and their midlife parents. In N. Vanzetti & S. Duck (Eds.), *A lifetime of relationships* (pp. 364–382). Pacific Grove, CA: Brooks/Cole.

Ley, P. (1997). Compliance among patients. In A. Baum, S. Newman, J. Weiman, R. West, & C. McManus (Eds.), *Cambridge handbook of psychology, health, and medicine* (pp. 281–284). Cambridge, UK: Cambridge University Press.

Libby, P., Ridker, P. M., & Maseri, A. (2002). Inflammation and atherosclerosis. *Circulation, 105*, 1135–1143.

Liberman, R. P., Kopelowicz, A., Ventura, J., & Gutkind, D. (2002). Operational criteria and factors related to recovery from schizophrenia. *International Review of Psychiatry, 14*(4), 256–272.

Licata, N. (2002). Should premarital counseling be mandatory as a requisite to obtaining a marriage license? *Family Court Review, 40*, 518–532.

Lichter, D. T., Batson, C. D., & Brown, J. B. (2004). Welfare reform and marriage promotion: The marital expectations and desires of single and cohabiting mothers. *Social Service Review, 78*(1), 2–25.

Lickey, M. E., & Gordon, B. (1991). *Medicine and mental illness: The use of drugs in psychiatry*. New York: Freeman.

Lieberman, J. A., Tollefson, G., Tohen, M., Green, A. I., Gur, R. E., Kahn, R., McEvoy, J., Perkins, D., Sharma, T., Zipursky, R., Wei, H., Hamer, R. M., & HGDH Study Group. (2003). Comparative efficacy and safety of atypical and conventional antipsychotic drugs in first-episode psychosis: A randomized double-blind trial of olanzapine versus haloperidol. *American Journal of Psychiatry, 160*, 1396–1404.

Lieberman, M. A. (1993). Bereavement self-help groups: A review of conceptual and methodological issues. In M. S. Stroebe, W. Stroebe, & R. O. Hansson (Eds.), *Handbook of bereavement*. New York: Cambridge University Press.

Lieberman, M. D., Gaunt, R., Gilbert, D. T., & Trope, Y. (2004). Reflection and reflexion: A social cognitive neuroscience approach to attributional inference. In M. P. Zanna (Ed.), *Advances in experimental social psychology* (Vol. 34). San Diego, CA: Academic Press.

Liebert, R. M., & Liebert, L. L. (1998). *Liebert & Spiegler's personality strategies and issues*. Pacific Grove: Brooks/Cole.

Liebert, R. M., & Sprafkin, J. N. (1988). *The early window: Effects of television on children and youth*. New York: Pergamon.

Lilenfeld, S. O., Lynn, S. J., Kirsch, I., Chaves, J. F., Sarbin, T. R., Ganaway, G. K., & Powell, R. A. (1999). Dissociative identity disorder and the sociocognitive model: Recalling the lessons of the past. *Psychological Bulletin, 125*(5), 507–523.

Lilienfeld, S. O., Wood, J. M., & Garb, H. N. (2000). The scientific status of projective tests. *Psychological Science in the Public Interest, 1*(2), 27–66.

Lim, G. Y., & Roloff, M. E. (1999). Attributing sexual consent. *Journal of Applied Communication Research, 27*(1), 1–23.

Linden, W. (1993). The autogenic training method of J. H. Schultz. In P. M. Lehrer & R. L. Woolfolk (Eds.), *Principles and practice of stress management* (2nd ed.). New York: Guilford Press.

Lindgren, H. C. (1969). *The psychology of college success: A dynamic approach*. New York: Wiley.

Lindsay D. S., Hagen, L., Read, J. D., Wade, K. A., & Garry, M. (2004). True photographs and false memories. *Psychological Science, 15*(3), 149–154.

Lindsay, D. S., & Poole, D. A. (1995). Remembering childhood sexual abuse in therapy: Psychotherapists' self-reported beliefs, practices, and experiences. *Journal of Psychiatry & Law, 23*, 461–476.

Lindsay, D. S., & Read, J. D. (1994). Psychotherapy and memories of childhood sexual abuse: A cognitive perspective. *Applied Cognitive Psychology, 8*, 281–338.

Lipkus, I. M., Dalbert, C., & Siegler, I. C. (1996). The importance of distinguishing the belief in a just world for self versus for others: Implications for psychological well-being. *Personality and Social Psychology Bulletin, 22*, 666–677.

Lippa, R. A. (1994). *Introduction to social psychology*. Pacific Grove, CA: Brooks/Cole.

Lips, H. M. (2005). *Sex and gender*. New York: McGraw-Hill.

Lisanby, S. H., Maddox, J. H., Prudic, J., Devanand, D. P., & Sackeim, H. A. (2000). The effects of electroconvulsive therapy on memory of autobiographical and public events. *General Psychiatry, 57*, 581–590.

Livanou, M. (2001). Psychological treatments for post-traumatic stress disorder: An overview. *International Review of Psychiatry, 13*(3), 181–188.

Lock, R. D. (2000). *Taking charge of your career direction: Career planning guide, book 1*. Belmont, CA: Wadsworth.

Lock, R. D. (2005a). *Taking charge of your career direction: Career planning guide, Book 1*. Belmont, CA: Wadsworth.

Lock, R. D. (2005b). *Job Search: Career Planning Guide, Book 2*. Belmont, CA: Wadsworth.

Loehlin, J. C. (1992). *Genes and environment in personality development*. Newbury Park, CA: Sage.

Loewenstein, R. J. (1996). Dissociative amnesia and dissociative fugue. In L. K. Michelson & W. J. Ray (Eds.), *Handbook of dissociation: Theoretical, empirical, and clinical perspectives*. New York: Plenum Press.

Loftus, E. F. (1993). The reality of repressed memories. *American Psychologist, 48*, 518–537.

Loftus, E. F. (1994). The repressed memory controversy. *American Psychologist, 49*, 443–445.

Loftus, E. F. (1997). Creating false memories. *Scientific American*, 71–75.

Loftus, E. F. (1998). Remembering dangerously. In R. A. Baker (Ed.), *Child sexual abuse and false memory syndrome*. Amherst, NY: Prometheus Books.

Loftus, E. F., & Ketcham, K. (1994). *The myth of repressed memory: False memories and allegations of sexual abuse*. New York: St. Martin's Press.

Longman, D. G., & Atkinson, R. H. (2002). *College learning and study skills*. Belmont, CA: Wadsworth.

Lopes, P. N., Brackett, M. A., Nezlek, J. B., Schutz, A., Sellin, I., & Salovey, P. (2004). Emotional intelligence and social interaction. *Personality and Social Psychology Bulletin, 30*(8), 1018–1034.

Lopez, F. G., & Gormley, B. (2002). Stability and change in adult attachment style over the first-year college transition: Relations to self-confidence, coping, and distress patterns. *Journal of Counseling Psychology, 49*(3), 355.

Lowinson, J. H., Ruiz, P., Millman, R. B., & Langrod, J. G. (2005). *Substance abuse: A comprehensive textbook*. Philadelphia: Lippincott/Williams & Wilkins.

Lowman, R. L. (1991). *The clinical practice of career assessment: Interests, abilities, and personality*. Washington, DC: American Psychological Association.

Lubkin, I. M. (1990). Illness roles. In I. M. Lubkin (Ed.), *Chronic illness: Impact and interventions* (2nd ed.). Boston: Jones and Bartlett.

Luborsky, L., Diguer, L., Seligman, D. A., Rosenthal, R., Krause, E. D., Johnson, S., Halperin, G., Bishop, M., Berman, J. S., & Schweizer, E. (1999). The researcher's own therapy allegiance: A "wild card" in comparisons of treatment efficacy. *Clinical Psychology: Science & Practice, 6*(1), 95–106.

Luborsky, L., Rosenthal, R., Diguer, L., Andrusyna, T. P., Berman, J. S., Levitt, J. T., Seligman, D. A., & Krause, E. D. (2002). The dodo bird verdict is alive and well—mostly. *Clinical Psychology: Science & Practice, 9*, 2–12.

Luborsky, L., Singer, B., & Luborsky, L. (1975). Comparative studies of psychotherapies: Is it true that everyone has won and all must have prizes? *Archives of General Psychiatry, 32*, 995–1008.

Lucas, A. R., Beard, C. M., O'Fallon, W. M., & Kurland, L. T. (1991). 50-year trends in the incidence of anorexia nervosa in Rochester, Minn.: A population-based study. *American Journal of Psychiatry, 148*, 917–922.

Lucas, R. E., Clark, A. E., Georgellis, Y., & Diener, E. (2003). Reexamining adaptation and set point model of happiness: Reactions to changes in marital status. *Journal of Personality and Social Psychology, 84*(3), 527–539.

Lucas, R. E., Clark, A. E., Georgellis, Y., & Diener, E. (2004). Unemployment alters the set point for life satisfaction. *Psychological Science, 15*(1), 8–13.

Lucas, R. E., Diener, E., & Suh, E. (1996). Discriminant validity of well-being measures. *Journal of Personality and Social Psychology, 71*, 616–628.

Ludwig, D. S., Pereira, M. A., Kroenke, C. H., Hilner, J. E., Van Horn, L., Slattery, M. L., & Jacobs, D. R. Jr. (1999). Dietary fiber, weight gain, and cardiovascular disease risk factors in young adults. *Journal of the American Medical Association, 282*(16), 1539–1546.

Luecke-Aleska, D., Anderson, D. R., Collins, P. A., & Schmitt, K. L. (1995). Gender constancy and television viewing. *Developmental Psychology, 31*, 773–780.

Luhtanen, R., & Crocker, J. (1992). A collective self-esteem scale: Self-evaluation of one's social identity. *Personality and Social Psychology Bulletin, 18*, 302–318.

Lulofs, R. S. (1994). *Conflict: From theory to action*. Scottsdale, AZ: Gorsuch Scarisbuck Publishers.

Lulofs, R. S., & Cahn, D. D. (2000). *Conflict: From theory to action* (2nd ed.). Boston: Allyn & Bacon.

Lundberg, U. (2000). Catecholamines. In G. Fink (Ed.), *Encyclopedia of stress* (Vol. 1, pp. 408–413). San Diego: Academic Press.

Lundeburg, K., Stith, S. M., Penn, C. E., & Ward, D. B. (2004). A comparison of nonviolent, psychologically violent, and physically violent male college daters. *Journal of Interpersonal Violence,* *19*(10), 1191–1200.

Lutz, C. J., & Ross, S. R. (2003). Elaboration versus fragmentation: Distinguishing between self-complexity and self-concept differentiation. *Journal of Social and Clinical Psychology, 22*(5), 537–559.

Lye, D. N., & Biblarz, T. J. (1993). The effects of attitudes toward family life and gender roles on marital satisfaction. *Journal of Family Issues, 14,* 157–188.

Lye, D., & Waldron, I. (1997). Attitudes toward cohabitation, family, and gender roles: Relationships to values and political ideology. *Sociological Perspectives, 40,* 199–225.

Lykken, D. T. (1998). *A tremor in the blood: Uses and abuses of the lie detector.* New York: Plenum Press.

Lykken, D. T., McGue, M., Tellegen, A., & Bouchard, T. J., Jr. (1992). Emergenesis: Genetic traits that may not run in families. *American Psychologist, 47*(12), 1565–1577.

Lykken, D., & Tellegen, A. (1996). Happiness is a stochastic phenomenon. *Psychological Science, 7,* 186–189.

Lynn, D. J., & Vaillant, G. E. (1998). Anonymity, neutrality, and confidentiality in the actual methods of Sigmund Freud: A review of 43 cases, 1907–1939. *American Journal of Psychiatry, 155,* 163–171.

Lynn, M., & Mynier, K. (1993). Effects of server posture on restaurant tipping. *Journal of Applied Social Psychology, 23,* 678–685.

Lynn, M., & Shurgot, B. A. (1984). Responses to lonely hearts advertisements: Effects of reported physical attractiveness, physique, and coloration. *Personality and Social Psychology Bulletin, 10,* 349–357.

Lynn, S. J., & Nash, M. (1994). Truth in memory: Ramifications for psychotherapy and hypnotherapy. *American Journal of Clinical Hypnosis, 36,* 194–208.

Lytton, H., & Romney, D. M. (1991). Parents' differential socialization of boys and girls: A meta-analysis. *Psychological Bulletin, 109,* 267–296.

Maccoby, E. E. (1990). Gender and relationships: A developmental account. *American Psychologist, 45,* 513–520.

Maccoby, E. E. (1998). *The two sexes: Growing up apart, coming together.* Cambridge, MA: Belknap Press.

Maccoby, E. E. (2000). Parenting and its effects on children: On reading and misreading behavior genetics. *Annual Review of Psychology, 51,* 1–27.

Maccoby, E. E. (2002). Gender and group processes: A developmental perspective. *Current Direction in Psychological Science, 11*(2), 54–58.

Maccoby, E. E., & Martin, J. A. (1983). Socialization in the context of the family: Parent-child interaction. In P. H. Mussen (Series Ed.) & E. M. Hetherington (Vol. Ed.), *Handbook of child psychology: Vol. 4. Socialization, personality, and social development.* New York: Wiley.

MacDonald, G., Saltzman, J. L., & Leary, M. R. (2003). Social approval and trait self-esteem. *Journal of Research in Personality, 37*(2), 23–40.

MacDonald, T. K., Zanna, M. P., & Fong, G. T. (1996). Why common sense goes out the window: Effects of alcohol on intentions to use condoms. *Personality and Social Psychology Bulletin, 22*(8), 763–775.

MacGeorge, E. L., Graves, A. R., Feng, B., Gillihan, S. J., & Burleson, B. R. (2004). The myth of gender cultures: Similarities outweigh differences in men's and women's provision of and responses to supportive communication. *Sex Roles, 50*(3/4), 143–175.

Macionis, J. J. (1997). *Sociology* (6th ed.). Upper Saddle River, NJ: Prentice Hall.

Mack, A. H., Franklin Jr., J. E., & Frances, R. J. (2003). Substance use disorders. In R. E. Hales & S. C. Yudofsky (Eds.), *Textbook of clinical psychiatry.* Washington, DC: American Psychiatric Publishing.

MacKenzie, R. A. (1997). *The time trap.* New York: AMACOM.

Mackie, D. M., Worth, L. T., & Asuncion, A. G. (1990). Processing of persuasive in-group messages. *Journal of Personality and Social Psychology, 58,* 812–822.

MacMillan, H. L., Fleming, J. E., Streiner, D. L., Lin, E., Boyle, M. H., Jamieson, E., Duku, E. K., Walsh, C. A., Wong, M. Y. Y., & Beardslee, W. R. (2001). Childhood abuse and lifetime psychopathology in a community sample. *American Journal of Psychiatry, 158,* 1878–1883.

MacMillian, H. L., Fleming, J. E., Trocme, N., Boyle, M. H., Wong, M., Racine, Y. A., Beardslee, W. R., & Offord, D. R. (1997). Prevalence of child physical and sexual abuse in the community: Results from the Ontario health supplement. *Journal of the American Medical Association, 278,* 131–135.

Macmillan, M. (1991). *Freud evaluated: The completed arc.* Amsterdam: North-Holland.

Maddi, S. R. (1989). *Personality theories: A comparative analysis.* Chicago, IL: Dorsey Press.

Maddi, S. R. (1999). Comments on trends in hardiness: Research and theorizing. *Consulting Psychology Journal: Practice and Research, 51*(2), 67–71.

Maddi, S. R. (2002). The story of hardiness: Twenty years of theorizing, research, and practice. *Consulting Psychology Journal: Practice and Research, 54*(3), 175–185.

Maddi, S. R., & Hightower, M. (1999). Hardiness and optimism as expressed in coping patterns. *Consulting Psychology Journal: Practice and Research, 51*(2), 95–105.

Maddox, G. L. (2001). Housing and living arrangements. In R. H. Binstock & L. K. George (Eds.), *Handbook of aging and the social sciences.* San Diego: Academic Press.

Maddux, J. E., & Gosselin, J. T. (2003). Self-efficacy. In M. R. Leary & J. P. Tangney (Eds.), *Handbook of self and identity.* New York: Guilford.

Maher, B. A. (2001). Delusions. In P. B. Sutker & H. E. Adams (Eds.), *Comprehensive handbook of psychopathology* (3rd ed., pp. 309–370). New York: Kluwer Academic/Plenum Publishers.

Maheu, M., & Subotnik, R. (2001). *Infidelity and the Internet: Virtual relationships and real betrayal.* New York: Sourcebooks.

Mahoney, M. J. (1979). *Self-change: Strategies for solving personal problems.* New York: Norton.

Main, M., & Solomon, J. (1990). Procedures for identifying infants as disorganized/disoriented during the Ainsworth Strange Situation. In M. T. Greenberg, D. Cicchetti, & E. M. Cummings (Eds.), *Attachment in the preschool years: Theory, research, and intervention.* Chicago: University of Chicago Press.

Maisey, D. S., Vale, E. L. E., Cornelissen, P. L., & Tovee, M. J. (1999). Characteristics of male attractiveness for women. *Lancet, 353,* 1500.

Major, B., Barr, L., Zubeck, J., & Babey, S. H. (1999). Gender and self-esteem: A meta-analysis. In W. B. Swann, Jr., J. H. Langlois, & L. A. Gilbert (Eds.), *Sexism and stereotypes in modern society: The gender science of Janet Taylor Spence* (pp. 223–254). Washington, DC: American Psychological Association.

Major, B., Schmidlin, A. M., & Williams, L. (1990). Gender patterns in social touch: The impact of setting and age. *Journal of Personality and Social Psychology, 58,* 634–643.

Maldonado, J. R., & Spiegel, D. (2003). Dissociative disorders. In R. E. Hales & S. C. Yudofsky (Eds.), *Textbook of clinical psychiatry.* Washington, DC: American Psychiatric Publishing.

Malefo, V. (2000). Psycho-social factors and academic performance among African women students at a predominantly white university in South Africa. *South African Journal of Psychology, 30*(4), 40–45.

Malina, R. M. (1990). Physical growth and performance during the transitional years (9–16). In G. R. Adams & T. P. Gullota (Eds.), *From childhood to adolescence: A transitional period?* Newbury Park, CA: Sage.

Malle, B. F., & Knobe, J. (1997). Which behaviors do people explain? A basic actor-observer asymmetry. *Journal of Personality and Social Psychology, 72,* 288–304.

Mallen, M. J., Day, S. X., & Green, M. A. (2003). Online versus face-to-face conversations: An examination of relational and discourse variable. *Psychotherapy: Theory, Research, Practice, Training, 40*(1–2), 155–163.

Mallory, M. (2001, June 24). Make style work. *The Atlanta Journal-Constitution,* p. R1.

Maltz, D. N., & Borker, R. A. (1983). A cultural approach to male-female miscommunication. In J. A. Gumperz (Ed.), *Language and social identity.* New York: Cambridge University Press.

Mandler, G. (1993). Thought, memory, and learning: Effects of emotional stress. In L. Goldberger & S. Breznitz (Eds.), *Handbook of stress: Theoretical and clinical aspects* (2nd ed.). New York: Free Press.

Manian, N., Strauman, T. J., & Denney, N. (1998). Temperament, recalled parenting styles, and self-regulation: Testing the developmental postulates of self-discrepancy theory. *Journal of Personality and Social Psychology, 75*(5), 1321–1332.

Mann, J., Tarantola, D. J. M., & Netter, T. W. (1992). *A global report: AIDS in the world.* New York: Oxford University Press.

Manning, W. D. (2004). Children and the stability of cohabiting couples. *Journal of Mariage and Family, 66,* 674–689.

Manson, J. E., Skerrett, P. J., & Willett, W. C. (2002). Epidemiology of health risks associated with obesity. In C. G. Fairburn & K. D. Brownell (Eds.), *Eating disorders and obesity: A comprehensive handbook* (pp. 422–428). New York: Guilford.

Marangell, L. B., Silver, J. M., Goff, D. C., & Yudofsky, S. C. (2003). Psychopharmacology and electroconvulsive therapy. In R. E. Hales & S. C. Yudofsky (Eds.), *Textbook of clinical psychiatry.* Washington, DC: American Psychiatric Publishing.

Marcenes, W. G., & Sheiham, A. (1992). The relationship between work stress and oral health status. *Social Science and Medicine, 35,* 1511.

Marchand, J. F., & Hock, E. (2000). Avoidance and attacking conflict-resolution strategies among married couples: Relations to depressive symptoms and marital satisfaction. *Family Relations, 49*(2), 201–206.

Marcia, J. E. (1980). Identity in adolescence. In J. Adelson (Ed.), *Handbook of adolescent psychology.* New York: Wiley.

Marcia, J. E. (1991). Identity and self-development. In R. M. Lerner, A. C. Petersen, & J. Brooks-Gunn (Eds.), *Encyclopedia of adolescence* (Vol. 1). New York: Garland.

Marcus-Newhall, A., Pedersen, W. C., Carlson, M., & Miller, N. (2000). Displaced aggression is alive and well: A meta-analytic review. *Journal of Personality and Social Psychology, 78*(4), 670–689.

Marder, S. R. (2000). Schizophrenia: Somatic treatment. In B. J. Sadock & V. A. Sadock (Eds.), *Kaplan and Sadock's comprehensive textbook of psychiatry* (7th ed., Vol. 1, pp. 1199–1209). Philadelphia: Lippincott/Williams & Wilkins.

Marder, S. R., & van Kammen, D. P. (2000). Dopamine receptor antagonists (typical antipsychotics). In B. J. Sadock & V. A. Sadock (Eds.), *Kaplan and Sadock's comprehensive textbook of psychiatry* (7th ed., Vol. 1, pp. 2356–2376). Philadelphia: Lippincott/Williams & Wilkins.

Maracek, J. (2001). Disorderly constructs: Feminist frameworks for clinical psychology. In R. K. Unger (Ed.), *Handbook of women and gender.* New York: Wiley.

Mariani, M. (2001, Summer). Distance learning in post-secondary education. *Occupational Outlook Quarterly,* pp. 2–10.

Maris, R. W., Berman, A. L., & Silverman, M. M. (2000). *Comprehensive textbook of suicidology*. New York: Guilford.

Marker, N. F. (1996). Flying solo at midlife: Gender, marital status, and psychological well-being. *Journal of Marriage and the Family, 58,* 917–932.

Markey, P. M. (2000). Bystander intervention in computer-mediated communication. *Computers in Human Behavior, 16*(2), 183–188.

Markides, K. S., & Krause, N. (1985). Intergenerational solidarity and psychological well-being among older Mexican Americans: A three-generations study. *Journal of Gerontology, 40,* 390–392.

Marks, I. M. (1969). *Fears and phobias.* New York: Academic Press.

Marks, N. F., Lambert, J. D., & Choi, H. (2002). Transitions to caregiving, gender, and psychological well-being: A prospective U. S. national study. *Journal of Marriage and Family, 64,* 657–667.

Markus, H., & Kitayama, S. (1991). Culture and the self: Implications for cognition, emotion, and motivation. *Psychological Review, 98,* 224–253.

Markus, H., & Nurius, P. (1986). Possible selves. *American Psychologist, 41,* 954–969.

Markus, H., & Wurf, E. (1987). The dynamic self-concept: A social psychological perspective. *Annual Review of Psychology, 38,* 299–337.

Marsella, A. J. (2004). Reflections on international terrorism: Issues, concepts, and directions. In F. M. Moghaddam & A. J. Marsella (Eds.), *Understanding terrorism: Psychological roots, consequences, and interventions.* Washington, DC: American Psychological Association.

Marsh, H. W., & Hau, K. (2003). Big-fish-little-pond effect on academic self-concept: A cross-cultural (26-country) test of the negative effects of academically selective schools. *American Psychologist, 58*(5), 364–376.

Marsh, H. W., & Parker, J. W. (1984). Determinants of student self-concept: Is it better to be a relatively large fish in a small pond even if you don't learn to swim well? *Journal of Personality and Social Psychology, 47,* 213–231.

Marsh, P. (Ed). (1988). *Eye to eye: How people interact.* Topsfield, MA: Salem House.

Martin, C. L., & Ruble, D. (2004). Children's search for gender cues: Cognitive perspectives on gender development. *Current Direction in Psychological Science, 13*(2), 67–70.

Martin, C. L., Ruble, D. N., & Szkrybalo, J. (2002). Cognitive theories of early gender development. *Psychological Bulletin, 128*(6), 903–933.

Martin, R., & Hewstone, M. (2003). Social-influence prcoesses of control and change: Comformity, obedience to authority, and innovation. In M. A. Hogg & J. Cooper (Eds.), *The Sage handbook of social psychology.* Thousand Oaks, CA: Sage Publications.

Martin, R., & Leventhal, H. (2004). Symptom perception and health care–seeking behavior. In J. M. Raczynski & L. C. Leviton (Eds.), *Handbook of clinical health psychology: Vol. 2. Disorders of behavior and health.* Washington, DC: American Psychological Association.

Martin, R., Rothrock, N., Leventhal, H., & Leventhal, E. (2003). Common sense models of illness: Implications for symptom perception and health-related behaviors. In J. Suls & K. A. Wallston (Eds.), *Social psychological foundations of health and illness.* Malden, MA: Blackwell Publishing.

Martin, R. A. (1996). The situational humor response questionnaire (SHRQ) and coping humor scale (CHS): A decade of research findings. *Humor: International Journal of Humor Research, 9,* 251–272.

Martin, R. A. (2001). Humor, laughter, and physical health: Methodological issues and research findings. *Psychological Bulletin, 127*(4), 504–519.

Martin, R. A. (2002). Is laughter the best medicine? Humor, laughter, and physical health. *Current Directions in Psychological Science, 11*(6), 216–220.

Martin, R. A., & Lefcourt, H. M. (1983). Sense of humor as a moderator of the relation between stressors and moods. *Journal of Personality and Social Psychology, 45,* 1313–1324.

Martin, T. C., & Bumpass, L. L. (1989). Recent trends in marital disruption. *Demography, 26,* 37–51.

Martin-Krumm, C. P., Sarrazin, P. G., Peterson, C., & Famose, J. (2003). Explanatory style and resilience after sports failure. *Personality and Individual Differences, 35*(7), 1685–1695.

Masheter, C. (1997). Healthy and unhealthy friendship and hostility between ex-spouses. *Journal of Marriage and the Family, 59,* 463–475.

Masi, L., & Bilezikian, J. P. (1997). Osteoporosis: New hope for the future. *International Journal of Fertility and Women's Medicine, 42,* 245–254.

Maslach, C. (2003). Job burnout: New directions in research and intervention. *Current Directions in Psychological Science, 12*(5), 189–192.

Maslach, C., & Goldberg, J. (1998). Prevention of burnout: New perspectives. *Applied and Preventive Psychology, 7,* 63–74.

Maslach, C., & Leiter, M. P. (1997). *The truth about burnout.* San Francisco: Jossey-Bass.

Maslach, C., & Leiter, M. P. (2000). Burnout. In G. Fink (Ed.), *Encyclopedia of stress* (Vol. 1, pp. 358–362). San Diego: Academic Press.

Maslow, A. (1968). *Toward a psychology of being.* New York: Van Nostrand.

Maslow, A. (1970). *Motivation and personality.* New York: Harper & Row.

Mason, M. A. (1998). The modern American stepfamily: Problems and possibilities. In M. A. Mason, A. Skolnick & S. D. Sugarman (Eds.), *All our families: New policies for a new century.* New York: Oxford University Press.

Masten, A. S. (2001). Ordinary magic: Resilience processes in development. *American Psychologist, 56*(3), 227–238.

Masters, W. H., & Johnson, V. E. (1966). *Human sexual response.* Boston: Little, Brown.

Masters, W. H., & Johnson, V. E. (1970). *Human sexual inadequacy.* Boston: Little, Brown.

Masters, W. H., Johnson, V. E., & Kolodny, R. C. (1988). *Human sexuality.* Glenview, IL: Scott, Foresman.

Mathew, R., Wilson, W., Blazer, D., & George, L. (1993). Psychiatric disorders in adult children of alcoholics: Data from the epidemiologic catchment area project. *American Journal of Psychiatry, 150,* 793–796.

Mathews, C. A., & Reus, V. I. (2001). Assortative mating in the affective disorders: A systematic review and meta-analysis. *Comprehensive Psychiatry, 42*(4), 257–262.

Matlin, M. W. (2000). *The psychology of women* (4th ed.). New York: Harcourt Brace.

Matlin, M. W. (2004). *The psychology of women* (5th ed.). Belmont, CA: Wadsworth.

Matsumoto, D. (1994). *People: Psychology from a cultural perspective.* Pacific Grove, CA: Brooks/Cole.

Matthews, K. A. (1992). Myths and realities of menopause. *Psychosomatic Medicine, 54,* 1–9.

Maume, D. J., Jr. (1999). Glass ceilings and glass escalators: Occupational segregation and race and sex differences in managerial promotions. *Work and Occupations, 26*(4), 483–509.

Maurer, L. (1999). Transgressing sex and gender: Deconstruction zone ahead? *SIECUS Report, 27,* 14–21.

Mayer, J. D., Perkins, D. M., Caruso, D. R., & Salovey, P. (2001). Emotional intelligence and giftedness. *Roeper Review, 23,* 131–137.

Mayer, J. D., Salovey, P., & Caruso, D. R. (2002). *Mayer-Salovey-Caruso Emotional Intelligence Test (MSCEIT): User's manual.* Toronto, Canada: Multi-Health Systems.

Mays, V. M., & Albee, G. W. (1992). Psychotherapy and ethnic minorities. In D. K. Freedheim (Ed.), *History of psychotherapy: A century of change* (pp. 552–570). Washington, DC: American Psychological Association.

Mazzuca, J. (2003, March 25). *Open dialogue: Parents talk to teens about sex.* Retrieved January 25, 2005 from http://www.Gallup.Com/Poll/Content/?Ci=8047.

McAdams, D. P. (1988). *Power, intimacy, and the life story.* New York: Guilford Press.

McAdams, D. P., de St. Aubin, E., & Logan, R. (1993). Generativity in young, midlife, and older adults. *Psychology and Aging, 8,* 221–230.

McAllister, W. R., & McAllister, D. E. (1995). Two-factor fear theory: Implications from understanding anxiety-based clinical phenomena. In W. O'Donohue & L. Krasner (Eds.), *Theories of behavior change: Exploring behavior change.* Washington, DC: American Psychological Association.

McCarthy, B. W., Bodnar, L. E., & Handal, M. (2004). Integrating sex therapy and couple therapy. In J. H. Harvey, A. Wenzel, & S. Sprecher (Eds.), *The handbook of sexuality in close relationships.* Mahwah, NJ: Lawrence Erlbaum.

McCarty, R., & Pacak, K. (2000). Alarm phase and general adaptation syndrome. In G. Fink (Ed.), *Encyclopedia of stress* (Vol. 1, pp. 126–130). San Diego: Academic Press.

McCrae, R. R. (1984). Situational determinants of coping responses: Loss, threat and challenge. *Journal of Personality and Social Psychology, 46,* 919–928.

McCrae, R. R. (1996). Social consequences of experimental openness. *Psychological Bulletin, 120,* 323–337.

McCrae, R. R., & Costa, P. T., Jr. (1984). *Emerging lives, enduring dispositions: Personality in adulthood.* Boston: Little, Brown.

McCrae, R. R., & Costa, P. T., Jr. (1987). Validation of the five-factor model of personality across instruments and observers. *Journal of Personality and Social Psychology, 52,* 81–90.

McCrae, R. R., & Costa, P. T., Jr. (1990). *Personality in adulthood.* New York: Guilford Press.

McCrae, R. R., & Costa, P. T., Jr. (1997). Personality trait structure as a human universal. *American Psychologist, 52,* 509–516.

McCrae, R. R., & Costa, P. T., Jr. (1999). A five-factor theory of personality. In L. A. Pervin, & O. P. John (Eds.), *Handbook of personality: Theory and research* (2nd ed., pp. 139–153). New York: The Guilford Press.

McCullough, M. E. (2001). Forgiving. In C. R. Snyder (Ed.), *Coping with stress: Effective people and processes* (pp. 93–113). New York: Oxford University Press.

McCullough, M. E., Bellah, C. G., Kilpatrick, S. D., & Johnson, J. L. (2001). Vengefulness: Relationships with forgiveness, rumination, well-being, and the Big Five. *Personality and Social Psychology Bulletin, 27*(5), 601–610.

McCullough, M. E., & Witvliet, C. V. (2002). The psychology of forgiveness. In C. R. Synder & S. J. Lopez (Eds.), *Handbook of positive psychology.* New York: Oxford University Press.

McDaniel, M. A., Waddill, P. J., & Shakesby, P. S. (1996). Study strategies, interest, and learning from text: The application of material appropriate processing. In D. J. Herrmann, C. McEvoy, C. Hertzog, P. Hertel, & M. K. Johnson (Eds.), *Basic and applied memory research: Theory in context* (Vol. 1). Mahwah, NJ: Erlbaum.

McDougle, L. G. (1987). Time management: Making every minute count. In A. D. Timpe (Ed.), *The management of time.* New York: Facts on File.

McEwen, B. S. (2000). Stress, definitions and concepts of. In G. Fink (Ed.), *Encyclopedia of stress* (Vol. 3, pp. 508–509). San Diego: Academic Press.

McEwen, B. S., & Lasley, E. N. (2002). *The end of stress as we know it.* Washington, DC: Joseph Henry Press.

McFarland, S. G., Ageyev, V. S., & Abalakina-Paap, M. A. (1992). Authoritarianism in the former

Soviet Union. *Journal of Personality and Social Psychology, 63*(6), 1004–1010.

McFarland, S. G., Ageyev, V. S., & Djintcharadze, N. (1996). Russian authoritarianism two years after communism. *Personality and Social Psychology Bulletin, 22*(2), 210–217.

McFarlane, M., Bull, S. S., & Rietmeijer, C. A. (2000). The Internet as a newly emerging risk environment for sexually transmitted diseases. *Journal of the American Medical Association, 284,* 443–446.

McGee-Cooper, A., & Trammell, D. (1994). *Time management for unmanageable people.* New York: Bantam Books.

McGlashan, T. H., & Fenton, W. S. (1992). The positive-negative distinction in schizophrenia: Review of natural history validators. *Archives of General Psychiatry, 49,* 63–72.

McGlashan, T. H., & Hoffman, R. E. (2000). Schizophrenia: Psychodynamic to neurodynamic theories. In B. J. Sadock & V. A. Sadock (Eds.), *Kaplan and Sadock's comprehensive textbook of psychiatry* (7th ed., Vol. 1, pp. 1159–1168). Philadelphia: Lippincott/Williams & Wilkins.

McGlashan, T. H., Mohr, D. C., Beutler, L. E., Engle, D., Shoham-Salomon, V., Bergan, J., Kaszniak, A. W., & Yost, E. B. (1990). Identification of patients at risk for nonresponse and negative outcome in psychotherapy. *Journal of Consulting and Clinical Psychology, 58,* 622–628.

McGoldrick, M. (1999). Becoming a couple. In B. Carter & M. McGoldrick (Eds.), *The expanded family life cycle: Individual, family, and social perspectives* (3rd ed., pp. 231–248). Boston: Allyn & Bacon.

McGraw, L. A., & Walker, A. J. (2004). The more things change, the more they stay the same. In M. Coleman & L. H. Ganong (Eds.), *Handbook of contemporary families: Considering the past, contemplating the future.* Thousand Oaks, CA: Sage.

McGraw, P. C. (1999). *Life strategies: Doing what works, doing what matters.* New York: Hyperion Press.

McGregor, H. A., Lieberman, J. D., Greenberg, J., Solomon, S., Arndt, J., Simon, L., & Pyszczynski, T. (1998). Terror management and aggression: Evidence that mortality salience motivates aggression against worldview-threatening others. *Journal of Personality and Social Psychology, 74*(3), 590–605.

McGuigan, F. J. (1993). Progressive relaxation: Origins, principles, and clinical applications. In P. M. Lehrer & R. L. Woolfolk (Eds.), *Principles and practice of stress management* (2nd ed.). New York: Guilford Press.

McGuire, P. A. (1999, May). Worker stress, health reaching critical point. *APA Monitor, 30*(5), 1, 27.

McHugh, P. R. (1995). Dissociative identity disorder as a socially constructed artifact. *Journal of Practical Psychiatry and Behavioral Health, 1,* 158–166.

McKay, A., & Holoway, P. (1997). Sexual health education: A study of adolescents' opinions, self-perceived needs, and current and preferred sources of information. *Canadian Journal of Human Sexuality, 6,* 29–38.

McKay, M., Davis, M., & Fanning, P. (1995). *Messages: The communication skills book.* Oakland, CA: New Harbinger.

McKay, M., & Fanning, P. (2000). *Self-esteem* (3rd ed.). Oakland, CA: New Harbinger.

McKeever, V. M., & Huff, M. E. (2003). A diathesis-stress model of posttraumatic stress disorder: Ecological, biological and residual stress pathways. *Review of General Psychology, 7*(3), 237–250.

McKenna, K. Y. A., & Bargh, J. A. (2000). Plan 9 from cyberspace: The implications of the Internet for personality and social psychology. *Personality and Social Psychology Review, 4*(1), 57–75.

McKenna, K. Y. A., Green, A., & Gleason, M. (2002). Relationship formation on the Internet: What's the big attraction? *Journal of Social Issues, 58,* 9–31.

McKenna, M. C., Zevon, M. A., Corn, B., & Rounds, J. (1999). Psychosocial factors and the development of breast cancer: A meta-analysis. *Health Psychology, 18*(5), 520–531.

McLean, D. E., & Link, B. G. (1994). Unraveling complexity: Strategies to refine concepts, measures, and research designs in the study of life events and mental health. In W. R. Avison & I. H. Gotlib (Eds.), *Stress and mental health: Contemporary issues and prospects for the future.* New York: Plenum Press.

McManus, P. A., & DiPrete, T. (2001). Losers and winners: Financial consequences of separation and divorce for men. *American Sociological Review, 66,* 246–268.

McNally, R. J. (1994). Cognitive bias in panic disorder. *Current Directions in Psychological Science, 3,* 129–132.

McNally, R. J. (1996). *Panic disorder: A critical analysis.* New York: Guilford Press.

McNally, R. J. (2004). Is traumatic amnesia nothing but psychiatric folklore? *Cognitive Behaviour Therapy, 33*(2), 97–101.

McNeil, T. F., Cantor-Graae, E., & Ismail, B. (2000). Obstetrics complications and congenital malformation in schizophrenia. *Brain Research Reviews, 31,* 166–178.

McWhirter, B. T. (1990). Loneliness: A review of current literature, with implications for counseling and research. *Journal of Counseling and Development, 68,* 417–422.

McWilliams, N., & Weinberger, J. (2003). Psychodynamic psychotherapy. In G. Stricker & T. A. Widiger (Eds.), *Handbook of psychology: Vol. 8. Clinical psychology.* New York: Wiley.

Mead, M. (1950). *Sex and temperament in three primitive societies.* New York: Mentor Books.

Mechanic, D. (1999). Mental health and mental illness. In A. V. Horvitz & T. L. Scheid (Eds.), *A handbook for the study of mental health: Social contexts, theories, and systems.* New York: Cambridge University Press.

Mednick, S. A., Machon, R. A., Huttunen, M. O., & Bonett, D. (1988). Adult schizophrenia following prenatal exposure to an influenza epidemic. *Archives of General Psychiatry, 45,* 189–192.

Mednick, S. A., Watson, J. B., Huttunen, M., Cannon, T. D., Katila, H., Machon, R., Mednick, B., Hollister, M., Parnas, J., Schulsinger, F., Sajaniemi, N., Voldsgaard, P., Pyhala, R., Gutkind, D., & Wang, X. (1998). A two-hit working model of the etiology of schizophrenia. In M. F. Lenzenweger & R. H. Dworkin (Eds.), *Origins and development of schizophrenia: Advances in experimental psychopathology.* Washington DC: American Psychological Association.

Medora, N. P., Larson, J. H., Hortacsu, N., & Dave, P. (2002). Perceived attitudes towards romanticism: A cross-cultural study of American, Asian-Indian, and Turkish young adults. *Journal of Comparative Family Studies, 33*(2), 155–178.

Meehan, P. J., Lamb, J. A., Saltzman, L. E., & O'Carroll, P. W. (1992). Attempted suicide among young adults: Progress toward a meaningful estimate of prevalence. *American Journal of Psychiatry, 149,* 41–44.

Meeks, B. S., Hendrick, S. S., & Hendrick, C. (1998). Communication, love and relationship satisfaction. *Journal of Social and Personal Relationships, 15*(6), 755–773.

Meeus, W. (1996). Studies on identity development in adolescence: An overview of research and some new data. *Journal of Youth and Adolescence, 25*(5), 569–598.

Meichenbaum, D. (1993). Stress inoculation training: A 20-year update. In P. M. Lehrer & R. L. Woolfolk (Eds.), *Principles and practice of stress management* (2nd ed.). New York: Guilford Press.

Mellers, B. A., Richards, V., & Birnbaum, M. H. (1992). Distributional theories of impression formation. *Organizational Behavior and Human Decision Processes, 51,* 313–343.

Meltzer, H. Y., Davidson, M., Glassman, A. H., & Vieweg, V. R. (2002). Assessing cardiovascular risks versus clinical benefits of atypical antipsychotic drug treatment. *Journal of Clinical Psychiatry, 63*(9), 25–29.

Merton, R. (1948). The self-fulfilling prophecy. *Antioch Review, 8,* 193–210.

Meschke, L., Bartholomae, S., & Zentall, S. (2000). Adolescent sexuality and parent-adolescent processes: Promoting healthy teen choices. *Family Relations, 49,* 143–154.

Metz, M. E., & Pryor, J. L. (2000). Premature ejaculation: A psychological approach for assessment and management. *Journal of Sex and Marital Therapy, 26,* 293–320.

Metzger, E. D. (1999). Electroconvulsive therapy. In A. M. Nicholi (Ed.), *The Harvard guide to psychiatry.* Cambridge, MA: Harvard University Press.

Meyer, I. H. (2003). Minority stress and mental health in gay men. In L. D. Garnets & D. C. Kimmel (Eds.), *Psychological perspectives on lesbian, gay, and bisexual experiences.* New York: Columbia University Press.

Michael, R. T., Gagnon, J. H., Laumann, E. O., & Kolata, G. (1994). *Sex in America.* Boston: Little, Brown.

Michaels, S. (1996). The prevalence of homosexuality in the United States. In R. P. Cabaj & T. S. Stein (Eds.), *Textbook of homosexuality and mental health* (pp. 43–64). Washington, DC: American Psychiatric Press.

Michaud, S. L., & Warner, R. M. (1997). Gender differences in self-reported response to troubles talk. *Sex Roles, 37*(7–8), 527–540.

Mickelson, K. D., Kessler, R. C., & Shaver, P. R. (1997). Adult attachment in a nationally representative sample. *Journal of Personality and Social Psychology, 73,* 1092–1106.

Mikulincer, M., Florian, V., & Tolmacz, R. (1990). Attachment styles and fear of personal death: A case study of affect regulation. *Journal of Personality and Social Psychology, 58,* 273–280.

Mikulincer, M., & Shaver, P. R. (2003). The attachment behavioral system in adulthood: Activation, psychodynamics, and interpersonal processes. In Mark P. Zanna (Ed.), *Advances in Experimental Social Psychology* (Vol. 35). San Diego: Academic Press.

Milgram, N., Marshevsky, S., & Sadeh, C. (1995). Correlates of academic procrastination: Discomfort, task aversiveness, and task capability. *Journal of Psychology, 129,* 145–155.

Milgram, S. (1963). Behavioral study of obedience. *Journal of Abnormal and Social Psychology, 67,* 371–378.

Milgram, S. (1974). *Obedience to authority.* New York: Harper & Row.

Milkie, M. A., & Peltola, P. (1999). Playing all the roles: Gender and the work-family balancing act. *Journal of Marriage and the Family, 61,* 476–490.

Miller, D. T., & Ross, M. (1975). Self-serving biases in the attribution of causality: Fact or fiction? *Psychological Bulletin, 82,* 213–225.

Miller, G. P. (1978). *Life choices: How to make the critical decisions—about your education, career, marriage, family, life style.* New York: Thomas Y. Crowell.

Miller, I. J. (1996). Managed care is harmful to outpatient mental health services: A call for accountability. *Professional Psychology: Research and Practice, 27,* 349–363.

Miller, J. G. (1984). Culture and the development of everyday social explanation. *Journal of Personality and Social Psychology, 46,* 961–978.

Miller, L. C., Berg, J. H., & Archer, R. L. (1983). Openers: Individuals who elicit intimate self-disclosure. *Journal of Personality and Social Psychology, 44,* 1234–1244.

Miller, M. L., & Thayer, J. F. (1988). On the nature of self-monitoring: Relationships with adjustment and identity. *Personality and Social Psychology Bulletin, 14,* 544–553.

Miller, N. E. (1944). Experimental studies of conflict. In J. McV. Hunt (Ed.), *Personality and the behavior disorders* (Vol. 1). New York: Ronald.

Miller, N. E. (1959). Liberalization of basic S-R concepts: Extension to conflict behavior, motivation, and social learning. In S. Koch (Ed.), *Psychology: A study of a science*. (Vol. 2). New York: McGraw-Hill.

Miller, R. S. (1991). On decorum in close relationships: Why aren't we polite to those we love? *Contemporary Social Psychology, 15*, 63–65.

Miller, T. (2000). Diagnostic evaluation of erectile dysfunction. *American Family Physician, 61*, 95–104.

Millett, K. (1970). *Sexual politics*. Garden City, NY: Doubleday.

Millman, R. B., & Beeder, A. B. (1994). The new psychedelic culture: LSD, ecstasy, "rave" parties and the Grateful Dead. *Psychiatric Annals, 24*(3), 148–150.

Mino, I., Profit, W. E., & Pierce, C. M. (2000). Minorities and stress. In G. Fink (Ed.), *Encyclopedia of stress* (Vol. 1, pp. 771–776). San Diego: Academic Press.

Minuchin, S., Rosman, B. L., & Baker, L. (1978). *Psychosomatic families: Anorexia nervosa in context*. Cambridge, MA: Harvard University Press.

Mischel, W. (1973). Toward a cognitive social learning conceptualization of personality. *Psychological Review, 80*, 252–283.

Mischel, W. (1990). Personality dispositions revisited and revised: A view after three decades. In L. A. Pervin (Ed.), *Handbook of personality: Theory and research*. New York: Guilford Press.

Mischel, W., & Mischel, H. N. (1976). A cognitive social learning approach to morality and self-regulation. In T. Lickona (Ed.), *Moral development and behavior: Theory, research and social issues*. New York: Holt, Rinehart & Winston.

Mischel, W., & Morf, C. C. (2003). The self as a psycho-social dynamic processing system: A meta-perspective on a century of the self in psychology. In M. R. Leary & J. P. Tangney (Eds.), *Handbook of self and identity*. New York: Guilford.

Mischel, W., Shoda, Y., & Peake, P. K. (1988). The nature of adolescent competencies predicted by preschool delay of gratification. *Journal of Personality and Social Psychology, 54*, 687–696.

Mishel, L., Bernstein, J., & Schmitt, J. (2001). *The state of working America 2000–2001*. Ithaca, NY: Cornell University Press.

Mitchell, V. F. (1987). Rx for improving staff effectiveness. In A. D. Timpe (Ed.), *The management of time*. New York: Facts on File.

Mittlehauser, M. (1998). The outlook for college graduates, 1996–2006: Prepare yourself. *Occupational Outlook Quarterly, 42*(2), 2–9.

Miyamoto, S., Lieberman, J. A., Fleischhacker, W. W., Aoba, A., & Marder, S. R. (2003). Antipsychotic drugs. In A. Tasman, J. Kay, & J. A. Lieberman (Eds.), *Psychiatry*. New York: Wiley.

Miyamoto, Y., & Kitayama, S. (2002). Cultural variation in correspondence bias: The critical role of attitude diagnosticity of socially constrained behavior. *Journal of Personality and Social Psychology, 83*(5), 1239–1248.

Moak, D. H., & Anton, R. F. (1999). Alcohol. In B. S. McCrady & E. E. Epstein (Eds.), *Addictions: A comprehensive guidebook* (pp. 75–94). New York: Oxford University Press.

Modestin, J. (1992). Multiple personality disorder in Switzerland. *American Journal of Psychiatry, 149*, 88–92.

Modestin, J., Huber, A., Satirli, E., Malti, T., & Hell, D. (2003). Long-term course of schizophrenic illness: Bleuler's study reconsidered. *American Journal of Psychiatry, 160*, 2202–2208.

Moen, P., Fields, V., Quick, H. E., & Hofmeister, H. (2000). A life course approach to retirement and social integration. In K. Pillemer & P. Moen (Eds.), *Social integration in the second half of life*. Baltimore: John Hopkins University Press.

Mohren, D. C. L., Swaen, G. M. H., Borm, P. J. A., Bast, A., & Galama, J. M. D. (2001). Psychological job demands as a a risk factor for common cold in a Dutch working population. *Journal of Psychomatic Research, 50*(1), 21–27.

Mokdad, A. H., Marks, J. S., Stroup, D. F., & Gerberding, J. L. (2004). Actual causes of death in the United States, 2000. *Journal of the American Medical Association, 291*, 1238–1245.

Möller, J., Hallqvist, J., Diderichsen, F., Theorell, T., Reuterwall, C., & Ahlbom, A. (1999). Do episodes of anger trigger myocardial infarction? A case-crossover analysis in the Stockholm heart epidemiology program (SHEEP). *Psychosomatic Medicine, 61*, 842–849.

Moncrieff, J. (2001). Are antidepressants overrated? A review of methodological problems in antidepressant trials. *Journal of Nervous and Mental Disorders, 189*, 288–295.

Monroe, S. M., & Hadjiyannakis, K. (2002). The social environment and depression: Focusing on severe life stress. In I. H. Gotlib & C. L. Hammen (Eds.), *Handbook of depression*. New York: Guilford.

Monroe, S. M., & Kelley, J. M. (1995). Measurement of stress appraisal. In S. Cohen, R. C. Kessler, & L. U. Gordon (Eds.), *Measuring stress: A guide for health and social scientists*. New York: Oxford University Press.

Monroe, S. M., & McQuaid, J. R. (1994). Measuring life stress and assessing its impact on mental health. In W. R. Avison & I. H. Gotlib (Eds.), *Stress and mental health: Contemporary issues and prospects for the future*. New York: Plenum.

Montepare, J. M., & Lachman, M. (1989). "You're only as old as you feel": Self-perceptions of age, fears of aging, and life satisfaction from adolescence to old age. *Psychology and Aging, 4*(1), 73–78.

Moore, D. W. (2001, August 31). Most American workers satisfied with their job: One-third would be happier in another job. [On-line]. The Gallup Organization. Available: www.gallup.com/poll/releases/pr010831.asp. Retrieved 1/19/2002.

Moore, D. W. (2003, January 3). *Family, health most important aspects of life*. Retrieved January 20, 2005, from http://www.Gallup.Com/Poll/Content/?Ci=7504.

Moore, D. W. (2004, May 20). *Modest rebound in public acceptance of homosexuals*. Retrieved January 31, 2005 from http://www.Gallup.Com/Poll/Content/?Ci=11755.

Moore, M. K. (1992). An empirical investigation of the relationship between religiosity and death concern. *Dissertation Abstracts International, 53*, 527.

Moore, N. B., & Davidson, J. K. (1997). Guilt about first intercourse: An antecedent of sexual dissatisfaction among college women. *Journal of Sex and Marital Therapy, 23*, 29–46.

Moos, R. H., & Billings, A. G. (1982). Conceptualizing and measuring coping resources and processes. In L. Goldberger & S. Breznitz (Eds.), *Handbook of stress: Theoretical and clinical aspects*. New York: Free Press.

Moos, R. H., & Schaefer, J. A. (1993). Coping resources and processes: Current concepts and measures. In L. Goldberger & S. Breznitz (Eds.), *Handbook of stress: Theoretical and clinical aspects* (2nd ed.). New York: Free Press.

Morahan-Martin, J., & Schumacher, P. (2000). Incidence and correlates of pathological Internet use among college students. *Computers in Human Behavior, 16*(1), 13–29.

Morahan-Martin, J., & Schumacher, P. (2003). Loneliness and social uses of the Internet. *Computers in Human Behavior, 19*(6), 659–671.

Moray, N. (1959). Attention in dichotic listening: Affective cues and the influence of instructions. *Quarterly Journal of Experimental Psychology, 11*, 56–60.

Morell, C. (2000). Saying no: Women's experiences with reproductive refusal. *Feminism & Psychology, 10*, 313–322.

Moretti, M. M., & Higgins, E. T. (1990). Relating self-discrepancy to self-esteem: The contribution of discrepancy beyond actual-self ratings. *Journal of Experimental Social Psychology, 26*, 108–123.

Morgan, H. J., & Janoff-Bulman, R. (1994). Victims' responses to traumatic life events: An unjust world or an uncaring world? *Social Justice Research, 7*, 47–68.

Morgan, M. J. (2000). Ecstasy (MDMA): A review of its possible persistent psychological effects. *Psychopharmacology, 152*(3), 230–248.

Morgenstern, J. (2000). *Time management from the inside out*. New York: Holt.

Morley, J. E. (2001). Male menopause is underdiagnosed and undertreated. *Medical Crossfire, 3*(1), 46–47, 51.

Morley, J. E., & Perry H. M. (2003). Androgens and women at the menopause and beyond. *The Journal of Gerontology, 58*(5), 409–416.

Morris, M. W., & Peng, K. (1994). Culture and cause: American and Chinese attributions for social and physical events. *Journal of Personality and Social Psychology, 67*, 949–971.

Morrison, D. R., & Cherlin, A. J. (1995). The divorce process and young children's well-being: A prospective analysis. *Journal of Marriage and the Family, 57*, 800–812.

Morrison, D. R., & Coiro, M. J. (1999). Parental conflict and marital disruption: Do children benefit when high-conflict marriages are dissolved? *Journal of Marriage and the Family, 61*, 626–637.

Morrison, T. G., Morrison, M. A., & Hopkins, C. (2003). Striving for bodily perfection? An exploration of the drive for masculinity in Canadian men. *Psychology of Men and Masculinity, 4*(2), 111–120.

Morse, S., & Gergen, K. J. (1970). Social comparison, self-consistency, and the concept of self. *Journal of Personality and Social Psychology, 16*, 148–156.

Moseman, S. E., Freeman, M. P., Misiaszek, J., & Gelenberg, A. J. (2003). Mood stabilizers. In A. Tasman, J. Kay, & J. A. Lieberman (Eds.), *Psychiatry*. New York: Wiley.

Mosher, D. L. (1991). Macho men, machismo, and sexuality. *Annual Review of Sex Research, 2*, 199–248.

Mowrer, O. H. (1947). On the dual nature of learning—A reinterpretaton of "conditioning" and "problem-solving." *Harvard Educational Review, 17*, 102–150.

Moynihan, J. A., & Ader, R. (1996). Psychoneuroimmunology: Animal models of disease. *Psychosomatic Medicine, 58*, 546–558.

Muehlenhard, C. L., & McCoy, M. L. (1991). Double standard/double bind: The sexual double standard and women's communication about sex. *Psychology of Women Quarterly, 15*, 447–461.

Mukamal, K. J., Conigrave, K. M., Mittleman, M. A., Camargo, C. A., Stampfer, M. J., Willet, W. C., & Rimm, E. B. (2003). Roles of drinking pattern and type of alcohol consumed in coronary heart disease in men. *New England Journal of Medicine, 348*(2), 109–118.

Mullin, C. R., & Linz, D. (1995). Desensitization and resensitization to violence against women: Effects of exposure to sexually violent films on judgments of domestic violence victims. *Journal of Personality and Social Psychology, 69*(3), 449–459.

Munck, A. (2000). Corticosteroids and stress. In G. Fink (Ed.), *Encyclopedia of stress* (Vol. 1, pp. 570–577). San Diego: Academic Press.

Muris, P. (2002). Relationships between self-efficacy and symptoms of anxiety disorders and depression in a normal adolescent sample. *Personality and Individual Differences, 32*, 337–348.

Murphy, M., Glaser, K., & Grundy, E. (1997). Marital status and long-term illness in Great Britain. *Journal of Marriage and the Family, 59*, 156–164.

Murphy, S. P., Rose, D., Hudes, M., & Viteri, F. E. (1992). Demographic and economic factors associated with dietary quality for adults in the 1987–88 nationwide food consumption theory. *Journal of the American Diet Association, 92*, 1352–1357.

Murray, C. (2001). *Family formation.* Washington, DC: American Enterprise Institute.

Murrell, A. J., Dietz-Uhler, B. L., Dovidio, J. F., Gaertner, S. L., & Drout, E. (1994). Aversive racism and resistance to affirmative action: Perceptions of justice are not necessarily color blind. *Basic and Applied Social Psychology, 17*(1–2), 71–86.

Murrell, A. J., & James, E. H. (2001). Gender and diversity in organizations: Past, present, and future directions. *Sex Roles, 45*(5/6), 243–257.

Murry, V. M. (1996). An ecological analysis of coital timing among middle-class African American adolescent females. *Journal of Adolescent Research, 11*(2), 261–279.

Murstein, B. I. (1976). *Who will marry whom? Theories and research in marital choice.* New York: Springer.

Murstein, B. I. (1986). *Paths to marriage.* Newbury Park, CA: Sage.

Mutchler, J. E., Burr, J. A., Pienta, A. M., & Massagli, M. P. (1997). Pathways to labor force exit: Work transitions and work instability. *Journal of Gerontology, 52,* 4–12.

Myers, D. G. (1980). *Inflated self: Human illusions and the biblical call to hope.* New York: Seabury Press.

Myers, D. G. (1992). *The pursuit of happiness: Who is happy—and why.* New York: Morrow.

Myers, D. G. (1999). Close relationships and quality of life. In D. Kahneman, E. Diener, & N. Schwarz (Eds.), *Well-being: The foundations of hedonic psychology* (pp. 374–391). New York: Sage.

Myers, D. G. (2000). *The American paradox: Spiritual hunger in an age of plenty.* New Haven, CT: Yale University Press.

Myers, D. G. (2001, December). Do we fear the right things? *American Psychological Society Observer, 14*(10), 3.

Myers, D. G., & Diener, E. (1995). Who is happy? *Psychological Science, 6,* 10–19.

Myers, D. G., & Diener, E. (1997). The pursuit of happiness. *Scientific American, Special Issue 7,* 40–43.

Nabi, R. L., & Sullivan, J. L. (2001). Does television viewing relate to engagement in protective action against crime? A cultivation analysis from a theory of reasoned action perpective. *Communication Research, 28*(6), 802–825.

Nader, K. O. (1997). Treating traumatic grief in systems. In C. R. Figley, B. E. Bride, & N. Mazza (Eds.), *Death and trauma: The traumatology of grieving* (pp. 159–192). Washington, DC: Taylor and Francis.

Naisbitt, J., & Aburdene, P. (1991). *Megatrends 2000.* New York: Morrow.

Nalwa, K., & Anand, A. P. (2003). Internet addiction in students: A cause of concern. *CyberPsychology and Behavior, 6*(6), 653–656.

Narrow, W. E., Regier, D. A., Rae, D. S., Manderscheid, R. W., & Locke, B. Z. (1993). Use of services by persons with mental and addictive disorders: Findings from the National Institute of Mental Health Epidemiologic Catchment Area Program. *Archives of General Psychiatry, 50,* 95–107.

Nash, M. (1997). Gift of love. *Time,* 80–82.

Nathan, P. E., & Langenbucher, J. (2003). Diagnosis and classification. In G. Stricker & T. A. Widiger (Eds.), *Handbook of psychology: Vol. 8. Clinical psychology.* New York: Wiley.

Nathan, P. E., Stuart, S. P., & Dolan, S. L. (2000). Research on psychotherapy efficacy and effectiveness: Between Scylla and Charybdis? *Psychological Bulletin, 126*(6), 964–981.

Nathanson, A. I. (1999). Identifying and explaining the relationship between parental mediation and children's aggression. *Communication Research, 26*(2), 124–143.

National Institute of Mental Health. (2001). *Helping children and adolescents cope with violence and disasters.* Bethesda, MD: National Institute of Mental Health.

Naveh-Benjamin, M., Lavi, H., McKeachie, W. J., & Lin, Y. (1997). Individual differences in students' retention of knowledge and conceptual structures learned in university and high school courses: The case of test anxiety. *Applied Cognitive Psychology, 11,* 507–526.

Naylor, T. H., Willimon, W. H., & Naylor, M. R. (1994). *The search for meaning.* Nashville: Abingdon Press.

Neese, R. M., & Young, E. A. (2000). Evolutionary origins and functions of the stress response. In G. Fink (Ed.), *Encyclopedia of stress* (Vol. 2, pp. 79–83). San Diego: Academic Press.

Neimeyer, R. A., & Van Brunt, D. (1995). Death anxiety. In H. Wass & R. A. Neimeyer (Eds.), *Dying: Facing the facts* (3rd ed.). Washington, DC: Taylor & Francis.

Neiss, R. (1988). Reconceptualizing arousal: Psychobiological states in motor performance. *Psychological Bulletin, 103,* 345–366.

Neiss, R. (1990). Ending arousal's reign of error: A reply to Anderson. *Psychological Bulletin, 107,* 101–105.

Nemeth, C., & Chiles, C. (1988). Modelling courage: The role of dissent in fostering independence. *European Journal of Social Psychology, 18,* 275–280.

Nemiah, J. C. (1985). Somatoform disorders. In H. I. Kaplan & B. J. Sadock (Eds.), *Comprehensive textbook of psychiatry/IV.* Baltimore: Williams & Wilkins.

Newberg, A., Alavi, A., Baime, M., Pourdehnad, M., Santanna, J., & D'Aquili. E. (2001). The measurement of regional cerebral blood flow tions on nocturnal dream content. *Journal of Personality and Social Psychology, 75,* 242–255.

Newcomb, M. D. (1990). Social support and personal characteristics: A developmental and interactional perspective. *Journal of Social and Clinical Psychology, 9,* 54–68.

Newell, G. R. (1991, May). Stress and cancer. *Primary Care and Cancer,* 29–30.

Newman, L. S., Duff, K. J., & Baumeister, R. F. (1997). A new look at defensive projection: Thought suppression, accessibility, and biased person perception. *Journal of Personality and Social Psychology, 72*(5), 980–1001.

Newman, M., & Berkowitz, B. (1976). *How to be awake and alive.* Westminster, MD: Ballantine.

Nezu, A. M., Nezu, C. M., Felgoise, S. H., & Zwick, M. L. (2003). Psychosocial oncology. In A. M. Nezu, C. M. Nezu, & P. A. Geller (Eds.), *Handbook of psychology: Vol. 9. Health psychology.* New York: Wiley.

Niaura, R., & Abrams, D. B. (2002). Smoking cessation: Progress, priorities, and prospectus. *Journal of Consulting & Clinical Psychology, 70*(3), 494–509.

Niaura, R., Todaro, J. F., Stroud, L., Spiro, A., Ward, K. D., & Weiss, S. (2002). Hostility, the metabolic syndrome, and incident coronary heart disease. *Health Psychology, 21*(16), 588–593.

NICHD Early Child Care Research Network. (1997). The effects of infant child care on infant-mother attachment security: Results of the NICHD Study of Early Child Care. *Child Development, 68,* 860–879.

Nickerson, C., Schwarz, N., Diener, E., & Kahneman, D. (2003). Zeroing in on the dark side of the American dream: A closer look at the negative consequences of the goal for financial success. *Psychological Science , 14*(6), 531–536.

Nie N. H., & Erbring, L. (2000). *Internet and society: A preliminary report.* Stanford, CA: Stanford Institutional Qualitative Study Society.

Nielsen, J. M. (1990). *Sex and gender in society: Perspective on stratification* (2nd ed.). Prospect Heights, IL: Waveland.

Niemann, Y. F., Jennings, L., Rozelle, R. M., Baxter, J. C., & Sullivan, E. (1994). Use of free responses and cluster analysis to determine stereotypes of eight groups. *Personality and Social Psychology Bulletin, 20,* 379–390.

Nisbett, R. E., Peng, K., Choi, I., & Norenzayan, A. (2001). Culture and systems of thought: Holistic versus analytic cognition. *Psychological Review, 108*(2), 291–310.

Nock, S. L. (1995). A comparison of marriages and cohabitating relationships. *Journal of Family Issues, 13,* 53–76.

Noel, J. G., Wann, D. L., & Branscombe, N. R. (1995). Peripheral ingroup membership status and public negativity toward outgroups. *Journal of Personality and Social Psychology, 68,* 127–137.

Nolen-Hoeksema, S. (1991). Responses to depression and their effects on the duration of depressive episodes. *Journal of Abnormal Psychology, 100,* 569–582.

Nolen-Hoeksema, S. (1995). Gender differences in coping with depression across the lifespan. *Depression, 3,* 81–90.

Nolen-Hoeksema, S. (2000). The role of rumination in depressive disorders and mixed anxiety/depressive symptoms. *Journal of Abnormal Psychology, 109*(3), 504–511.

Nolen-Hoeksema, S. (2001). Gender differences in depression. *Current Directions in Psychological Science, 10,*173–176.

Nolen-Hoeksema, S. (2002). Gender differences in depression. In I. H. Gotlib & C. L. Hammen (Eds.), *Handbook of depression.* New York: Guilford.

Nolen-Hoeksema, S., & Keita, G. P. (2003). Women and depression: An introduction. *Psychology of Women Quarterly, 27,* 89–90.

Noller, P. (1985). Negative communications in marriage. *Journal of Social and Personal Relationships, 2,* 289–301.

Noller, P. (1987). Nonverbal communication in marriage. In D. Perlman & S. Duck (Eds.), *Intimate relationships: Development, dynamics, and deterioration.* Newbury Park, CA: Sage.

Noller, P., Feeney, J. A., Bonnell, D., & Callan, V. (1994). A longitudinal study of conflict in early marriage. *Journal of Social and Personal Relationships, 11,* 233–252.

Noller, P., & Fitzpatrick, M. A. (1990). Marital communication in the eighties. *Journal of Marriage and the Family, 52,* 832–843.

Noller, P., & Gallois, C. (1988). Understanding and misunderstanding in marriage: Sex and marital adjustment differences in structured and free interaction. In P. Noller & M. A. Fitzpatrick (Eds.), *Perspectives on marital interaction.* Clevedon, England: Multilingual Matters.

Nomaguchi, K. M., & Milkie, M. A. (2003). Costs and rewards of children: The effects of becoming a parent on adults' lives. *Journal of Marriage and Family, 65,* 356–374.

Norcross, J. C. (1995). Dispelling the dodo bird verdict and the exclusivity myth in psychotherapy. *Psychotherapy, 32,* 500–504.

Norcross, J. C., Santrock, J. W., Campbell, L. F., Smith, T. P., Sommer, R., & Zuckerman, E. L. (2003). *Authoritative guide to self-help resources in mental health.* New York: Guilford.

Norris, F. H., & Kaniasty, K. (1996). Received and perceived social support in times of stress: A test of the social support deterioration deterrence model. *Journal of Personality and Social Psychology, 71*(3), 498–511.

Norton, P. G. W. (2004, February 1). Low-fat foods helped fuel obesity epidemic. *Family Practice News,* p. 22.

Norton, S. (2002). Women exposed: Sexual harassment and female vulnerability. In L. Diamant & J. Lee (Eds.), *The psychology of sex, gender, and jobs.* Westport, CT: Praeger.

Nowell, A., & Hedges, L. V. (1998). Trends in gender differences in academic achievement from 1960–1994: An analysis of differences in mean, variance, and extreme scores. *Sex Roles, 39*(1/2), 21–43.

Nurminen, E., Malmivaara, A., Ilmarinen, J., Ylöstalo, P., Mutanen, P., Ahonen, G., & Aro, T. (2002). Effectiveness of a worksite exercise program with respect to perceived work ability and sick leaves among women with physical work. *Scandinavian Journal of Work, Environment and Health, 28*(2), 85–93.

Nurnberger, J. I., & Zimmerman, J. (1970). Applied analysis of human behavior: An alternative to conventional motivational inferences and unconscious determination in therapeutic programming. *Behavior Therapy, 1*, 59–69.

Oakes, P. (2001). The root of all evil in intergroup relations? Unearthing the categorization process. In R. Brown & S. L. Gaertner (Eds.), *Blackwell handbook of social psychology: Intergroup processes.* London: Blackwell.

O'Brien, B. (1996). Economic evaluation of pharmaceuticals. *Medical Care, 34*, 99–108.

O'Callahan, M., Andrews, A. M., & Krantz, D. S. (2003). Coronary heart disease and hypertension. In A. M. Nezu, C. M. Nezu, & P. A. Geller (Eds.), *Handbook of psychology: Vol. 9. Health psychology.* New York: Wiley.

O'Connor, N. (1994). *How to grow up when you're grown up: Achieving balance in adulthood.* Tucson, AZ: La Mariposa Press.

O'Donnell, A., & Dansereau, D. F. (1993). Learning from lectures: Effects of cooperative review. *Journal of Experimental Education, 61*, 116–125.

O'Donohue, W., & Crouch, J. L. (1996). Marital therapy and gender-linked factors in communication. *Journal of Marital and Family Therapy, 22*, 87–101.

Oesterman, K., Bjoerkqvist, K., Lagerspetz, K. M. J., Kaukiainen, A., Landau, S. F., Fraczek, A., & Caprara, G. V. (1998). Cross-cultural evidence of female indirect aggression. *Aggressive Behavior, 24*(1), 1–80.

Oettingen, G., & Gollwitzer, P. M. (2001). Goal setting and goal striving. In A. Tesser & N. Schwarz. (Eds.), *Blackwell handbook of social psychology: Intraindividual processes.* Malden, MA: Blackwell.

O'Halloran, C. M., & Altmaier, E. M. (1996). Awareness of death among children: Does a life-threatening illness alter the process of discovery? *Journal of Counseling and Development, 74*, 259–262.

Ohman, A., & Mineka, S. (2003). The malicious serpent: Snakes as a prototypical stimulus for an evolved module of fear. *Current Directions in Psychological Science, 12*, 5–9.

O'Keefe, D. J., & Hale, S. L. (2001). An odds-ratio based meta-analysis of research on the door-in-the-face influence strategy. *Communication Reports, 14*(1), 31–38.

Olfson, M., Marcus, S. C., & Pincus, H. A. (1999). Trends in office-based psychiatric practice. *American Journal of Psychiatry, 156*, 451–457.

Olfson, M., & Pincus, H. A. (1996). Outpatient mental health care in nonhospital settings: Distribution of patients across provider groups. *American Journal of Psychiatry, 153*, 1353–1356.

Olfson, M., Shaffer, D., Marcus, S. C., & Greenberg, T. (2003). Relationship between antidepressant medication treatment and suicide in adolescents. *Archives of General Psychiatry, 60*(10), 978–982.

Olio, K. (1994). Truth in memory. *American Psychologist, 49*, 442–443.

Olivardia, R., Pope, H. G., & Phillips, K. A. (2000). *The Adonis complex: The secret crisis of male body obsession.* New York: Free Press.

Oliver, M. B., & Hyde, J. S. (1993). Gender differences in sexuality: A meta-analysis. *Psychological Bulletin, 114*, 29–51.

O'Neil, J. M., & Egan, J. (1992). Men's and women's gender role journeys: A metaphor for healing, transition, and transformation. In B. Wainrib (Ed.), *Gender issues across the life cycle* (pp. 107–123). New York: Springer.

O'Neill, N., & O'Neill, G. (1972). *Open marriage.* New York: Evans.

Ono, H. (1998). Husbands' and wives' resources and marital dissolution. *Journal of Marriage and the Family, 60*, 674–689.

Orenstein, P. (1994). *School girls: Young women, self-esteem, and the confidence gap.* New York: Doubleday.

Organista, P. B., & Miranda, J. (1991). Psychosomatic symptoms in medical outpatients: An investigation of self-handicapping theory. *Health Psychology, 10*, 427–431.

Orlofsky, J. L., Marcia, J. E., & Lesser, I. M. (1973). Ego identity status and the intimacy versus isolation crisis of young adulthood. *Journal of Personality and Social Psychology, 27*, 211–219.

Orth-Gomer, K., Wamala, S. P., Horsten, M., Schenck-Gustafsson, K., Schneiderman, N., & Mittleman, M. A. (2000). Marital stress worsens prognosis in women with coronary heart disease: The Stockholm female coronary risk study. *Journal of the American Medical Association, 284*(23), 3008–3014.

Oskamp, S. (2000). A sustainable future for humanity? How psychology can help. *American Psychologist, 55*(5), 496–508.

Osman, S. L. (2003). Predicting men's rape perceptions based on the belief that "no" really means "yes." *Journal of Applied Social Psychology, 33*(4), 683–692.

Otto, M. W., Pollack, M. H., Jenike, M. A., & Rosenbaum, J. F. (1999). Anxiety disorders and their treatment. In A. M. Nicholi (Ed.), *The Harvard guide to psychiatry* (3rd ed., pp. 220–239). Cambridge, MA: Harvard University Press.

Ouellette, S. C. (1993). Inquiries into hardiness. In L. Goldberger & S. Breznitz (Eds.), *Handbook of stress: Theoretical and clinical aspects* (2nd ed.). New York: Free Press.

Ouellette, S. C., & DiPlacido, J. (2001). Personality's role in the protection and enhancement of health: Where the research has been, where it is stuck, how it might move . In A. Baum, T. A. Revenson, & J. E. Singer *Handbook of health psychology* (pp. 175–194). Mahwah, NJ: Erlbaum.

Owen, M. J., & O'Donovan, M. C. (2003). Schizophrenia and genetics. In R. Plomin, J. C. Defries, I. W. Craig & P. McGuffin (Eds.), *Behavioral genetics in the postgenomic era.* Washington, DC: American Psychological Association.

Ozer, D. J., & Reise, S. P. (1994). Personality assessment. *Annual Review of Psychology, 45*, 357–388.

Ozer, E. J., Best, S. R., Lipsey, T. L., & Weiss, D. S. (2003). Predictors of posttraumatic stress disorder and symptoms in adults: A meta-analysis. *Psychological Bulletin, 129*(1), 52–73.

Ozer, E. J., & Weiss, D. S. (2004). Who develops posttraumatic stress disorder? *Current Directions in Psychological Science, 13*, 169–172.

Ozer, E. M., & Bandura, A. (1990). Mechanisms governing empowerment effects: A self-efficacy analysis. *Journal of Personality and Social Psychology, 58*, 472–486.

Padgett, D. A., & Sheridan, J. F. (2000). Herpesviruses. In G. Fink (Ed.), *Encyclopedia of stress* (pp. 357–363). San Diego: Academic Press.

Paivio, A. (1986). *Mental representations: A dual coding approach.* New York: Oxford University Press.

Papalia, D. E., & Olds, C. W. (1995). *Human Development* (6th ed.). New York: McGraw-Hill.

Papp, L. M., Cummings, E. M., & Schermerhorn, A. C. (2004). Pathways among marital distress, parental symptomatology, and child adjustment. *Journal of Marriage and Family, 66*, 368–384.

Pardun, C. J., & McKee, K. B. (1995). Strange bedfellows: Images of religion and sexuality on MTV. *Youth and Society, 26*, 438–449.

Park, C. L., & Fenster, J. R. (2004). Stress-related growth: Predictors of occurrence and correlates with psychological adjustment. *Journal of Social and Clinical Psychology, 23*(2), 195–215.

Park, C. W., & Young, S. M. (1986). Consumer response to television commercials: The impact of involvement and background music on brand attitude formation. *Journal of Marketing Research, 23* 11–24.

Parks, M. R., & Floyd, K. (1996). Making friends in cyberspace. *Journal of Communication, 46*, 80–97.

Parrott, A. C. (2000). Human research on MDMA (3,4-Methylenedioxymethamphetamine) neurotoxicity: Cognitive and behavioural indices of change. *Neuropsychobiology, 42*(1), 17–24.

Parry-Jones, B., & Parry-Jones, W. L. (1995). History of bulimia and bulimia nervosa. In K. D. Brownell & C. G. Fairburn (Eds.), *Eating disorders and obesity: A comprehensive handbook.* New York: Guilford Press.

Parsons, T., & Bales, R. F. (1995). *Family, socialization, and interaction process.* Glencoe, IL: Free Press.

Pasley, K., & Moorefield, B. S. (2004). Stepfamilies: Changes and challenges. In M. Coleman, & L. H. Ganong (Eds.), *Handbook of contemporary families: Considering the past, contemplating the future.* Thousand Oaks, CA: Sage.

Patel, J. K., Pinals, D. A., & Breier, A. (2003). Schizophrenia and other psychoses. In A. Tasman, J. Kay, & J. A. Lieberman (Eds.), *Psychiatry.* New York: Wiley.

Pato, M. T., Eisen, J. L., & Phillips, K. A. (2003). Obsessive-compulsive disorder. In A. Tasman, J. Kay, & J. A. Lieberman (Eds.), *Psychiatry.* New York: Wiley.

Patterson, C. J. (2001). Family relationships of lesbians and gay men. In R. M. Milardo (Ed.), *Understanding families into the new millennium: A decade in review* (pp. 271–288). Minneapolis: National Council on Family Relations.

Patterson, C. J. (2003). Children of lesbian and gay parents. In L. D. Garnets & D. C. Kimmel (Eds.), *Psychological perspectives on lesbian, gay, and bisexual experiences.* New York: Columbia University Press.

Patterson, C. J., & Redding, R. E. (1996). Lesbian and gay families with children: Implications of social science research for policy. *Journal of Social Issues, 52*(3), 29–50.

Patterson, G. R., DeBaryshe, B. D., & Ramsey, E. (1989). A developmental perspective on antisocial behavior. *American Psychologist, 44*(2), 329–335.

Patterson, M. L. (1988). Functions of nonverbal behavior in close relationships. In S. Duck (Ed.), *Handbook of personal relationships: Theory, research, and interventions.* New York: Wiley.

Paul, A. M. (2001). Self-help: Shattering the myths. *Psychology Today, 34*(2), 60.

Paul, E. L., McManus, B., & Hayes, A. (2000). "Hookups": Characteristics and correlates of college students' spontaneous and anonymous sexual experiences. *Journal of Sex Research, 37*(1), 76–88.

Paulhus, D. L. (1991). Measurement and control of response bias. In J. P. Robinson, P. Shaver, & L. S. Wrightsman (Eds.), *Measures of personality and social psychological attitudes.* San Diego: Academic Press.

Paulhus, D. L., Fridhandler, B., & Hayes, S. (1997). Psychological defense: Contemporary theory and research. In R. Hogan, J. Johnson, & S. Briggs (Eds), *Handbook of personality psychology.* San Diego: Academic Press.

Paulhus, D. L., Trapnell, P. D., & Chen, D. (1999). Birth order effects on personality and achievement within families. *Psychological Science, 10*, 482–488.

Paunonen, S. (1998). Hierarchical organization of personality and prediction of behavior. *Journal of Personality and Social Psychology, 74*(2), 538–556.

Pavlov, I. P. (1906). The scientific investigation of psychical faculties or processes in the higher animals. *Science, 24*, 613–619.

Payne, D. G., & Wenger, M. J. (1996). Practice effects in memory: Data, theory, and unanswered questions. In D. J. Herrmann, C. McEvoy, C. Hertzog, P. Hertel, & M. K. Johnson (Eds.), *Basic and applied memory research: Practical applications* (Vol. 2). Mahwah, NJ: Erlbaum.

Pearce, L. (1974). Duck! It's the new journalism. *New Times, 2*, 40–41.

Pearson, P. (1998). *When she was bad: Violent women and the myth of innocence.* New York: Viking.

Pearson, Q. M. (1998). Job satisfaction, leisure satisfaction, and psychological health. *Career Development Quarterly, 46*(4), 416–426.

Pechacek, T. F., & Babb, S. (2004). Commentary: How acute and reversible are the cardiovascular risks of secondhand smoke? *British Medical Journal, 328,* 980–983.

Pechnick, R. N., & Ungerleider, J. T. (1997). Hallucinogens. In J. H. Lowinson, P. Ruiz, R. B. Millman, & J. G. Langrod (Eds.), *Substance abuse: A comprehensive textbook* (3rd ed.). Baltimore: Williams & Wilkins.

Pechnick, R. N., & Ungerleider, T. J. (2005). Hallucinogens. In J. H. Lowinson, P. Ruiz, R. B. Millman, & J. G. Langrod (Eds.), *Substance abuse: A comprehensive textbook.* Philadelphia: Lippincott/Williams & Wilkins.

Pedersen, P. (1994). A culture-centered approach to counseling. In W. J. Lonner & R. Malpass (Eds.), *Psychology and culture* (pp. 291–295). Boston: Allyn & Bacon.

Pedersen, W., & Skrondal, A. (1999). Ecstasy and new patterns of drug use: A normal population study. *Addiction, 94*(11), 1695–1706.

Pederson, D. R., & Moran, G. (1996). Expressions of the attachment relationship outside of the strange situation. *Child Development, 67,* 915–927.

Peirce, R. S., Frone, M. R., Russell, M., & Cooper, M. L. (1996). Financial stress, social support, and alcohol involvement: A longitudinal test of the buffering hypothesis in a general population survey. *Health Psychology, 15,* 38–47.

Pennebaker, J. W. (1997). *Opening up: The healing power of expressing emotions.* New York: Guilford.

Pennebaker, J. W., Colder, M., & Sharp, L. K. (1990). Accelerating the coping process. *Journal of Personality and Social Psychology, 58,* 528–537.

Peplau, L. A. (1988). Research on homosexual couples: An overview. In J. P. De Cecco (Ed.), *Gay relationships.* New York: Harrington Park Press.

Peplau, L. A. (1991). Lesbian and gay relationships. In J. C. Gonsiorek & J. D. Weinrich (Eds.), *Homosexuality: Research implications for public policy.* Newbury Park, CA: Sage.

Peplau, L. A. (2003). Human sexuality: How do men and women differ? *Current Directions in Psychological Science, 12*(2), 37–40.

Peplau, L. A., & Cochran, S. D. (1990). A relational perspective on homosexuality. In D. P. McWhirter, S. A. Sanders, & J. M. Reinisch (Eds.), *Homosexuality/heterosexuality: Concepts of sexual orientation.* New York: Oxford University Press.

Peplau, L. A., Cochran, S. D., & Mays, V. M. (1997). A national survey of the intimate relationships of African-American lesbians and gay men: A look at commitment, satisfaction, sexual behavior, and HIV disease. In B. Greene (Ed.), *Ethnic and cultural diversity among lesbians and gay men.* Thousand Oaks, CA: Sage.

Peplau, L. A., Fingerhut, A., & Beals, K. P. (2004). Sexuality in the relationships of lesbians and gay men. In J. H. Harvey, A. Wenzel, & S. Sprecher (Eds.), *The handbook of sexuality in close relationships.* Mahwah, NJ: Lawrence Erlbaum.

Peplau, L. A., & Garnets, L. D. (2000). A new paradigm for understanding women's sexuality and sexual orientation. *Journal of Social Issues, 56*(2), 329–350.

Peplau, L. A., & Gordon, S. L. (1985). Women and men in love: Gender differences in close heterosexual relationships. In V. E. O'Leary, R. K. Unger, & B. S. Wallston (Eds.), *Women, gender, and social psychology* (pp. 257–291). Hillsdale, NJ: Erlbaum.

Peplau, L. A., Hill, C. T., & Rubin, Z. (1993). Sex role attitudes in dating and marriage: A 15-year follow-up of the Boston couples study. *Journal of Social Issues, 49,* 31–52.

Peplau, L. A., & Spalding, L. R. (2000). The close relationships of lesbians, gay men, and bisexuals. In C. Hendrick & S. S. Hendrick (Eds.), *Close relationships: A sourcebook* (pp. 111–123). Thousand Oaks, CA: Sage.

Peplau, L. A., & Spalding, L. R. (2003). The close relationships of lesbians, gay men, and bisexuals. In L. D. Garnets & D. C. Kimmel (Eds.), *Psychological perspectives on lesbian, gay, and bisexual experiences.* New York: Columbia University Press.

Peretti, P. O., & Abplanalp, R. R., Jr. (2004). Chemistry in the college dating process: Structure and function. *Social Behavior and Personality, 32*(2), 147–154.

Perkins, D. F., & Borden, L. M. (2003). Positive behaviors, problem behaviors, and resiliency in adolescence. In R. M. Lerner, M.A. Easterbrooks, & J. Mistry (Eds.), *Handbook of psychology: Vol. 6. Developmental psychology.* New York: Wiley.

Perloff, R. M. (1993). *The dynamics of persuasion.* Hillsdale, NJ: Erlbaum.

Perreault, S., & Bourhis, R. Y. (1999). Ethnocentrism, social identification, and discrimination. *Personality and Social Psychology Bulletin, 25*(1), 92–103.

Perrett, D. I., Lee, K. J., Penton-Voak, I., Rowland, D., Yoshikawa, S., Burt, D. M., Henzi, S. P., Castles, D. L., & Akamatsu, S. (1998). Effects of sexual dimorphism on facial attractiveness. *Nature, 394,* 884–887.

Perri, M. G., Anton, S. D., Durning, P. E., Ketterson, T. U., Sydeman, S. J., Berlant, N. E., Kanasky Jr., W. F., Newton Jr., R. L., Llimacher, M. C., & Martin, A. D. (2002). Adherence to exercise prescriptions: Effects of prescribing moderate versus higher levels of intensity and frequency. *Health Psychology, 21*(5), 452–458.

Perry-Jenkins, M., & Turner, E. (2004). Jobs, marriage, and parenting: Working it out in dual-earner families. In M. Coleman, & L. H. Ganong (Eds.), *Handbook of contemporary families: Considering the past, contemplating the future.* Thousand Oaks, CA: Sage.

Perry-Jenkins, M., Repetti, R. L., & Crouter, A. C. (2001). Work and family in the 1990s. In R. M. Milardo (Ed.), *Understanding families into the new millennium: A decade in review* (pp. 200–217). Minneapolis, MN: National Council on Family Relations.

Person, E. S. (1990). The influence of values in psychoanalysis: The case of female psychology. In C. Zanardi (Ed.), *Essential papers in psychoanalysis* (pp. 305–325). New York: New York University Press.

Pervin, L. A. (1994). Personality stability, personality change, and the question of process. In T. F. Heatherton & J. L. Weinberger (Eds.), *Can personality change?* Washington, DC: American Psychological Association.

Petersen, A. C. (1987, September). Those gangly years. *Psychology Today,* pp. 28–34.

Petersen, A. C. (1988). Adolescent development. *Annual Review of Psychology, 39,* 583–607.

Peterson, B. E., & Lane, M. D. (2001). Implications of authoritarianism for young adulthood: Longitudinal analysis of college experiences and future goals. *Personality and Social Psychology Bulletin, 27*(6), 678–690.

Peterson, C., & Bossio, L. M. (2001). Optimism and physical well-being. In E. C. Chang (Ed.), *Optimism and pessimism: Implications for theory, research, and practice* (pp. 127–146). Washington, DC: American Psychological Association.

Peterson, C., Maier, S. F., & Seligman, M. E. P. (1993). *Learned helplessness: A theory for the age of personal control.* New York: Oxford University Press.

Peterson, C., & Seligman, M. E. P. (2004). *Character strengths and virtues: A handbook and classification.* Washington, DC: American Psychological Association/New York: Oxford University Press.

Peterson, C., Seligman, M. E. P., & Vaillant, G. E. (1988). Pessimistic explanatory style is a risk factor for physical illness: A thirty-five-year longitudinal study. *Journal of Personality and Social Psychology, 55,* 23–27.

Peterson, C., Seligman, M. E. P., Yurko, K. H., Martin, L. R., & Friedman, H. S. (1998). Catastrophizing and untimely death. *Psychological Science, 9,* 127–130.

Peterson, N., & González, R. (2005). *The role of work in people's lives: Applied career counseling and vocational psychology.* Belmont, CA: Wadsworth.

Petras, R., & Petras, K. (1993). *The 776 stupidest things ever said.* New York: Doubleday.

Petrocelli, W., & Repa, B. K. (1998). *Sexual harassment on the job: What it is and how to stop it* (3rd ed.). Berkeley, CA: Nolo Press.

Petticrew, M., Fraser, J. M., & Regan, M. F. (1999). Adverse life-events and risk of breast cancer: A meta-analysis. *British Journal of Health Psychology, 4,* 1–17.

Pettigrew, T. F., & Meertens, R. W. (1995). Subtle and blatant prejudice in Western Europe. *European Journal of Social Psychology, 25,* 57–75.

Pettigrew, T. F., & Tropp, L. R. (2000). Does intergroup contact reduce prejudice: Recent meta-analytic findings. In S. Oskamp (Ed.), *Reducing prejudice and discrimination.* Mahwah, NJ: Erlbaum.

Petty, R. E., & Cacioppo, J. T. (1986). The elaboration likelihood model of persuasion. In L. Berkowitz (Ed.), *Advances in experimental social psychology* (Vol. 19). Orlando, FL: Academic Press.

Petty, R. E., & Cacioppo, J. T. (1990). Involvement and persuasion: Tradition versus integration. *Psychological Bulletin, 107,* 367–374.

Petty, R. E., & Wegener, D. T. (1998). Attitude change: Multiple roles for persuasion variables. In D. T. Gilbert, S. T. Fiske, & G. Lindzey (Eds.), *The handbook of social psychology* (4th ed., Vol. 1, pp. 323–390). New York: McGraw-Hill.

Petty, R. E., Fleming, M. A., Priester, J. R., & Feinstein, A. H. (2001). Individual versus group interest violation: Surprise as a determinant of argument scrutiny and persuasion. *Social Cognition, 19*(4), 418–442.

Petty, R. E., Priester, J. R., & Wegener, D. T. (1994). Cognitive processes in attitude change. In R. S. Wyer & T. K. Srull (Eds.), *Handbook of social cognition* (Vol. 2). Hillsdale, NJ: Erlbaum.

Petty, R. E., Wegener, D. T., & Fabrigar, L. R. (1997). Attitudes and attitude change. *Annual Review of Psychology, 48,* 609–647.

Petty, R. E., Wegener, D. T., & White, P. (1998). Flexible correction processes in persuasion. *Social Cognition, 16,* 93–113.

Petty, R. E., Wheeler, S. C., & Tormala, Z. L. (2003). Persuasion and attitude change. In T. Millon, & M.J. Lerner (Eds.), *Handbook of psychology: Vol. 5. Personality and social psychology.* New York: Wiley.

Phelps, S., & Austin, N. (1997). *The assertive woman.* San Luis Obispo, CA: Impact.

Phelps, S., & Austin, N. (2002). *The assertive woman.* San Luis Obispo, CA: Impact Publishers.

Phillips, M. R., Wolf, A. S., & Coons, D. J. (1988). Psychiatry and the criminal justice system: Testing the myths. *American Journal of Psychiatry, 145,* 605–610.

Phillips, W. T., Kiernan, M., & King, A. C. (2001). The effects of physical activity on physical and psychological health. In A. Baum, T. A. Revenson, & J. E. Singer (Eds.), *Handbook of health psychology* (pp. 627–660). Mahwah, NJ: Erlbaum.

Pi, E. H., & Simpson, G. M. (2001). Medication-induced movement disorders. In B. J. Sadock & V. A. Sadock (Eds.), *Kaplan and Sadock's comprehensive textbook of psychiatry* (7th ed., Vol. 2). Philadelphia: Lippincott/ Williams & Wilkins.

Pierce, C. M. (1992). Contemporary psychiatry: Racial perspectives on the past and future. In A. Kales, C. M. Pierce, & M. Greenblatt (Eds.), *The mosaic of contemporary psychiatry in perspective.* New York: Springer-Verlag.

Pietromonaco, P. R., Greenwood, D., & Barrett, L. F. (2004). Conflict in adult close relationships: An attachment perspective. In W. S. Rholes & J. A. Simpson (Eds.), *Adult attachment: Theory, research, and clinical implications.* New York: Guilford.

Pike, A., Manke, B., Reiss, D., & Plomin, R. (2000). A genetic analysis of differential experiences of adolescent siblings across three years. *Social Development, 9,* 96–114.

Pike, K. M., & Rodin, J. (1991). Mothers, daughters, and disordered eating. *Journal of Abnormal Psychology, 100,* 198–294.

Pillow, D. R., Zautra, A. J., & Sandler, I. (1996). Major life events and minor stressors: Identifying mediational links in the stress process. *Journal of Personality and Social Psychology, 70,* 381–394.

Pilowsky, I. (1993). Aspects of abnormal illness behaviour. *Psychotherapy and Psychosomatics, 60,* 62–74.

Pincus, H. A., Tanielian, T. L., Marcus, S. C., Olfson, M., Zarin, D. A., Thompson, J., & Zito, J. M. (1998). Prescribing trends in psychotropic medications: Primary care, psychiatry, and other medical specialties. *Journal of the American Medical Association, 279,* 526–531.

Pine, D. S. (2000). Anxiety disorders: Clinical features. In B. J. Sadock & V. A. Sadock (Eds.), *Kaplan and Sadock's comprehensive textbook of psychiatry* (7th ed., Vol. 1, pp. 1476–1489). Philadelphia: Lippincott/Williams & Wilkins.

Pinel, J. P. J., Assanand, S., & Lehman, D. R. (2000). Hunger, eating, and ill health. *American Psychologist, 55,* 1105–1116.

Pines, A. M. (1993). Burnout. In L. Goldberger & S. Breznitz (Eds.), *Handbook of stress: Theoretical and clinical aspects* (2nd ed.). New York: Free Press.

Pingitore, R., Dugoni, B. L., Tindale, R. S., & Spring, B. (1994). Bias against overweight job applicants in a simulated employment interview. *Journal of Applied and Social Psychology, 79,* 909–917.

Pink, D. H. (2001). *Free agent nation: The future of working for yourself.* New York: Warner Business Books.

Piotrkowski, C. S., & Brannen, S. J. (2002). Exposure, threat appraisal, and lost confidence as predictors of PTSD symptoms following September 11, 2001. *American Journal of Orthopsychiatry, 72*(4), 476–485.

Piper, W. E. (1993). Group psychotherapy research. In H. I. Kaplan & B. J. Sadock (Eds.), *Comprehensive group psychotherapy.* Baltimore: Williams & Wilkins.

Pipher, M. (1994). *Reviving Ophelia: Saving the selves of adolescent girls.* New York: Ballantine.

Pi-Sunyer, F. X. (2002). Medical complications of obesity in adults. In C. G. Fairburn & K. D. Brownell (Eds.), *Eating disorders and obesity: A comprehensive handbook* (pp. 467–472). New York: Guilford.

Pittman, F., III. (1994, January/February). A buyer's guide to psychotherapy. *Psychology Today,* pp. 50–53, 74–81.

Pittman, J. F., & Lloyd, S. A. (1988). Quality of family life, social support, and stress. *Journal of Marriage and the Family, 50,* 53–67.

Piver, S. (2000). *The hard questions: 100 questions to ask before you say "I do."* New York: Jeremy P. Tarcher/Putnam.

Plante, T. G., Caputo, D., & Chizmar, L. (2000). Perceived fitness and responses to laboratory induced stress. *International Journal of Stress Management, 7*(1), 61–73.

Pleck, J. H. (1981). *The myth of masculinity.* Cambridge, MA: MIT Press.

Pleck, J. H. (1995). The gender role strain paradigm: An update. In R. F. Levant & W. S. Pollack (Eds.), *A new psychology of men.* New York: Basic Books.

Plomin, R. (1994). Nature, nurture, and development. In R. J. Sternberg (Ed.), *Encyclopedia of human intelligence* (pp. 754–764). New York: Macmillan.

Plomin, R., & Caspi, A. (1999). Behavioral genetics and personality. In L. A. Pervin & O. P. John (Eds.), *Handbook of personality: Theory and research* (2nd ed., pp. 251–276). New York: Guilford Press.

Plous, S. L., & Zimbardo, P. G. (2004, September 10). How social science can reduce terrorism. *The Chronicle of Higher Education,* pp. B9–B10.

Polivy, J., & Herman, C. P. (2002). Causes of eating disorder. *Annual Review of Psychology, 53,* 187–213.

Pollack, W. (1998). *Real boys: Rescuing our sons from the myths of boyhood.* New York: Random House.

Polonsky, D. (2000). Premature ejaculation. In S. Leiblum & R. Rosen (Eds.), *Principles and practice of sex therapy.* New York: Guilford.

Pomeroy, C., & Mitchell, J. E. (2002). Medical complications of anorexia nervosa and bulimia nervosa. In C. G. Fairburn & K. D. Brownell (Eds.), *Eating disorders and obesity: A comprehensive handbook.* New York: Guilford.

Pope, E., & Shouldice, M. (2001). Drugs and sexual assault: A review. *Trauma Violence and Abuse, 2*(1), 51–55.

Pope, H., Phillips, K., & Olivardia, R. (2000). *The Adonis complex: The secret crisis of male body obsession.* New York: Free Press.

Pope, H. G., Gruber, A. J., Hudson, J. I., Huestis, M. A., & Yurgelun-Todd, D. (2001). Neuropsychological performance in long-term cannabis users. *Archives of General Psychiatry, 58,* 909–915.

Pope, H. G., Gruber, A. J., & Yurgelun-Todd, D. (2001). Residual neuropsychologic effects of cannabis. *Current Psychiatry Report, 3,* 507–512.

Pope, H. G., Oliva, P. S., Hudson, J. I., Bodkin, J. A., & Gruber, A. J. (1999). Attitudes toward DSM-IV dissociative disorders diagnoses among board-certified American psychiatrists. *American Journal of Psychiatry, 156*(2), 321–323.

Pope, K. S., Keith-Spiegel, P., & Tabachnick, B. G. (1986). Sexual attraction to clients. *American Psychologist, 41,* 147–158.

Popenoe, D. (1993). American family decline, 1960–1990: A review and appraisal. *Journal of Marriage and the Family, 55,* 527–555.

Popenoe, D. (1999). *Life without father: Compelling new evidence that fatherhood and marriage are indispensable for the good of children and society.* Cambridge, MA: Harvard University Press.

Porter, G. (1996). Organizational impact of workaholism: Suggestions for researching the negative outcomes of excessive work. *Journal of Occupational Health Psychology, 1,* 70–84.

Potthoff, J. G., Holahan, C. J., & Joiner, T. E., Jr. (1995). Reassurance-seeking, stress generation, and depressive symptoms: An integrative model. *Journal of Personality and Social Psychology, 68,* 664–670.

Powell, J. L., & Drucker, A. D. (1997). The role of peer conformity in the decision to ride with an intoxicated driver. *Journal of Alcohol and Drug Education, 43*(1), 1–7.

Powell, R. A., & Gee, T. L. (1999). The effects of hypnosis on dissociative identity disorder: A re-examination of the evidence. *Canadian Journal of Psychiatry, 44,* 914–916.

Pratkanis, A. R., & Aronson, E. (2000). *Age of propaganda: The everyday use and abuse of persuasion.* New York: Freeman.

Pratt, L. A., Ford, D. E., Crum, R. M., Armenian, H. K., Gallo, J. J., & Eaton, W. W. (1996). Depression, psychotropic medication, and risk of myocardial infarction: Prospective data from the Baltimore ECA follow-up. *Archives of Internal Medicine, 94,* 3123–3129.

Presser, H. B. (2000). Nonstandard work schedules and marital instability. *Journal of Marriage and the Family, 62,* 93–110.

Pressman, S. (1993). *Outrageous betrayal: The real story of Werner Erhard, EST and the Forum.* New York: St. Martin's Press.

Preto, N. G. (1999). Transformation of the family system during adolescence. In B. Carter & M. McGoldrick (Eds.), *The expanded family life cycle: Individual, family, and social perspectives* (3rd ed., pp. 274–286). Boston: Allyn & Bacon.

Prochaska, J. O. (1994). Strong and weak principles for progressing from precontemplation to action on the basis of twelve problem behaviors. *Health Psychology, 13*(1), 47–51.

Pruchno, R., & Rosenbaum, J. (2003). Social relationships in adulthood and old age. In R. M. Lerner, M. A. Easterbrooks, & J. Mistry (Eds.), *Handbook of psychology: Vol. 6. Developmental psychology.* New York: Wiley.

Prudic, J., & Sackeim, H. A. (1999). Electroconvulsive therapy and suicide risk. *Journal of Clinical Psychiatry, 60,* 104–110.

Pryor, F. L., & Schaffer, D. (1997, July). Wages and the university educated: A paradox resolved. *Monthly Labor Review,* 3–14.

Pryor, J. B., Giedd, J. L., & Williams, K. B. (1995). A social psychological model for predicting sexual harassment. *Journal of Social Issues, 51,* 69–84.

Putnam, R. D. (1996). The strange disappearance of civic America. *The American Prospect, 24,* 34–46.

Putney, N. M., & Bengtson, V. L. (2001). Families, intergenerational relationships, and kinkeeping in midlife. In M. E. Lachman (Ed.), *Handbook of midlife development.* New York: Wiley.

Pyszczynski, T., Greenberg, J., & Goldenberg, J. L. (2003). Freedom versus fear: On the defense, growth, and expansion of the self. In M. R. Leary & J. P. Tangney (Eds.), *Handbook of self and identity.* New York: Guilford.

Pyszczynski, T., Greenberg, J., & Solomon, S. (1999). A dual-process model of defense against conscious and unconscious death-related thoughts: An extension of terror management theory. *Psychological Review, 106*(4), 835–845.

Pyszczynski, T., Greenberg, J., Solomon, S., Arndt, J., & Schimel, J. (2004). Why do people need self-esteem? A theoretical and empirical review. *Psychological Bulletin, 130*(3), 435–468.

Pyszczynski, T., Solomon, S., & Greenberg, J. (2003). *In the wake of 9/11: The psychology of terror.* Washington, DC: American Psychological Association.

Quinn, K. A., Macrae, C. N., & Bodenhausen, G. V. (2003). Stereotyping and impression formation: How categorical thinking shapes person perception. In M. A. Hogg & J. Cooper (Eds.), *The Sage handbook of social psychology.* Thousand Oaks, CA: Sage Publications.

Rabbitt, P., & McGinnis, L. (1988). Do clever old people have earlier and richer first memories? *Psychology and Aging, 3,* 338–341.

Rabinowitz, F. E., & Cochran, S. V. (1994). *Man alive: A primer of men's issues.* Pacific Grove, CA: Brooks/Cole.

Rabkin, J. G. (1993). Stress and psychiatric disorders. In L. Goldberger & S. Breznitz (Eds.), *Handbook of stress: Theoretical and clinical aspects* (2nd ed.). New York: Free Press.

Rachman, S. J. (1990). *Fear and courage.* New York: Freeman.

Rachman, S. J. (1992). Behavior therapy. In L. R. Squire (Ed.), *Encyclopedia of learning and memory.* New York: Macmillan.

Ragheb, M. G. (1993). Leisure and perceived wellness: A field investigation. *Leisure Sciences, 12,* 13–24.

Ragland, D. R., & Brand, R. J. (1988). Type A behavior and mortality from coronary heart disease. *The New England Journal of Medicine, 318,* 65–69.

Rahe, R. H., & Arthur, R. H. (1978). Life change and illness studies. *Journal of Human Stress, 4,* 3–15.

Rahe, R. H., Veach, T. L., Tolles, R. L., & Murakami, K. (2000). The stress and coping inventory: An educational and research instrument. *Stress Medicine, 16,* 199–208.

Rahim, M. A., & Magner, N. R. (1995). Confirmatory factor analysis of the styles of handling interpersonal conflict: First-order factor model and its invariance across groups. *Journal of Applied Psychology, 80,* 122–132.

Ramadan, N. M. (2000). Migraine. In G. Fink (Ed.), *Encyclopedia of stress* (pp. 757–770). San Diego: Academic Press.

Ramaekers, J. G., Robbe, H. W. J., & O'Hanlon, J. F. (2000). Marijuana, alcohol and actual driving performance. *Human Psychopharmacology Clinical & Experimental, 15(7),* 551–558.

Randhawa, B. S., & Hunter, D. M. (2001). Validity of performance assessment in mathematics for early adolescents. *Canadian Journal of Behavioral Science, 33,* 14–24.

Rank, M. R. (2004). The disturbing paradox of poverty in American families: What we have learned over the past four decades. In M. Coleman & L. H. Ganong (Eds.), *Handbook of contemporary families: Considering the past, contemplating the future.* Thousand Oaks, CA: Sage.

Rapee, R. M., & Barlow, D. H. (2001). Generalized anxiety disorders, panic disorders, and phobias. In P. B. Sutker & H. E. Adams (Eds.), *Comprehensive handbook of psychopathology* (3rd ed., pp. 131–154). New York: Kluwer Academic/Plenum Publishers.

Raphael, B., & Dobson, M. (2000). Effects of public disasters. In G. Fink (Ed.), *Encyclopedia of stress* (Vol. 1, pp. 699–705). San Diego: Academic Press.

Raskin, P. M. (1986). The relationship between identity and intimacy in early adulthood. *Journal of Genetic Psychology, 147,* 167–181.

Rasmussen, C., Knapp, T. J., & Garner, L. (2000). Driving-induced stress in urban college students. *Perceptual & Motor Skills, 90(2),* 437–443.

Ray, G. E., Cohen, R., Secrist, M. E., & Duncan, M. K. (1997). Relating aggressive and victimization behaviors to children's sociometric status and friendships. *Journal of Social and Personal Relationships, 14(1),* 95–108.

Read, C. R. (1991). Achievement and career choices: Comparisons of males and females. *Roeper Review, 13* 188–193.

Reddy, B. S. (1999). Role of dietary fiber in colon cancer: An overview. *American Journal of Medicine, 106(1A),* 16S–19S.

Reed, G. M., Kemeny, M. E., Taylor, S. E., & Visscher, B. R. (1999). Negative HIV-specific expectancies and AIDS-related bereavement as predictors of symptom onset in asymptomatic HIV-positive gay men. *Health Psychology, 18,* 354–363.

Regan, P. C. (1996). Sexual outcasts: The perceived impact of body weight and gender on sexuality. *Journal of Applied Social Psychology, 26,* 1803–1815.

Regan, P. C. (2003). *The mating game: A primer on love, sex, and marriage.* Thousand Oaks, CA: Sage Publications.

Regan, P. C., & Berscheid, E. (1997). Gender differences in characteristics desired in potential sexual and marriage partners. *Journal of Psychology and Human Sexuality, 9(1),* 25–37.

Reggin, P. R. (1991). *Toxic psychiatry.* New York: St. Martin's Press.

Regier, D. A., Boyd, J. H., Burke, J. D., Rea, D. S., Myers, J. K., Kramer, M., Robins, L. N., George, L. K., Karno, M., & Locke, B. Z. (1988). One-month prevalance of mental disorders in the United States. *Archives of General Psychiatry, 45,* 977–986.

Regier, D. A., & Burke, J. D. (2000). Epidemiology. In B. J. Sadock & V. A. Sadock (Eds.), *Kaplan and Sadock's comprehensive textbook of psychiatry.* Philadelphia: Lippincott/Williams & Wilkins.

Regier, D. A., & Kaelber, C. T. (1995). The epidemiologic catchment area (ECA) program: Studying the prevalence and incidence of psychopathology. In M. T. Tsuang, M. Tohen, & G. E. P. Zahner (Eds.), *Textbook in psychiatric epidemiology.* New York: Wiley.

Rehm, L. P., Wagner, A., & Ivens-Tyndal, Co. (2001). Mood disorders: Unipolar and bipolar. In P. B. Sutker & H. E. Adams (Eds.), *Comprehensive handbook of psychopathology* (3rd ed., pp. 277–308). New York: Kluwer Academic/Plenum.

Reibel, D. K., Greeson, J. M., Brainard, G. C., & Rosenzweig, S. (2001). Mindfulness-based stress reduction and health-related quality of life in a heterogeneous patient population. *General Hospital Psychiatry, 23(4),* 183–192.

Reid, P. T., & Paludi, M. A. (1993). Developmental psychology of women: Conception to adolescence. In F. L. Denmark & M. A. Paludi (Eds.), *Psychology of women: A handbook of issues and theories.* Westport, CT: Greenwood Press.

Reifman, A., Klein, J. G., & Murphy, S. T. (1989). Self-monitoring and age. *Psychology and Aging, 4,* 245–246.

Reimann, R. (1997). Does biology matter?: Lesbian couples' transition to parenthood and their division of labor. *Qualitative Sociology, 20(2),* 153–185.

Reinisch, J. M. (1990). *The Kinsey Institute new report on sex: What you must know to be sexually literate.* New York: St. Martin's.

Reis, H. T. (1998). Gender differences in intimacy and related behaviors: Context and processes. In D. Canary & K. Dindia (Eds.), *Sex and gender in communication: Similarities and differences.* Mahwah, NJ: Erlbaum.

Reis, H. T., & Patrick. B. C. (1996). Attachment and intimacy: Component processes. In E. T. Higgins & A. Kruglanski (Eds.), *Social psychology: Handbook of basic principles.* New York: Guilford.

Reis, H. T., & Shaver, P. (1988). Intimacy as an interpersonal process. In S. W. Duck (Ed.), *Handbook of personal relationships.* New York: Wiley.

Reis, H. T., & Wheeler, L. (1991). Studying social interaction with the Rochester Interaction Record. *Advances in Experimental Social Psychology, 24,* 269–318.

Reis, T. J., Gerrard, M., & Gibbons, F. X. (1993). Social comparison and the pill: Reactions to upward and downward comparison of contraceptive behavior. *Personality and Social Psychology Bulletin, 19,* 13–21.

Reisner, A. D. (1998). Repressed memories: True and false. In R. A. Baker (Ed.), *Child sexual abuse and false memory syndrome.* Amherst, NY: Prometheus Books.

Reiss, I. L. (1986). *Journey into sexuality: An exploratory voyage.* Englewood Cliffs, NJ: Prentice-Hall.

Reiss, S. (1991). Expectancy model of fear, anxiety and panic. *Clinical Psychology Review, 11,* 141–154.

Reissman, C., Aron, A., & Bergen, M. R. (1993). Shared activities and marital satisfaction: Causal direction and self-expansion versus boredom. *Journal of Social and Personal Relationships, 10,* 243–254.

Remland, M. S., Jones, T. S., & Brinkman, H. (1995). Interpersonal distance, body orientation, and touch: Effects of culture, gender, and age. *Journal of Social Psychology, 135(3),* 281–297.

Renaud, C. A., & Byers, E. S. (2001). Positive and negative sexual cognitions: Subjective experience and relationships to sexual adjustment. *Journal of Sex Research, 38(3),* 252–262.

Rennie, D. (1999). Fair conduct and fair reporting of clinical trials. *Journal of the American Medical Association, 282,* 1766–1768.

Rennie, D., & Luft, H. S. (2000). Making them transparent, making them credible. *Journal of the American Medical Association, 283,* 2516–2521.

Rennison, C. M., & Welchans, S. (2000). *Intimate partner violence.* Washington, DC: U.S. Department of Justice, Office of Justice Programs, Bureau of Justice Statistics.

Renzetti, C. (1995). Violence in gay and lesbian relationships. In R. J. Gelles (Ed.), *Vision 2010: Families and violence, abuse and neglect.* Minneapolis: National Council on Family Relations.

Repetti, R. L., & Wood, J. (1997). Effects of daily stress at work on mothers' interactions with preschoolers. *Journal of Family Psychology, 11,* 90–108.

Repetto, M., & Gold, M. S. (2005). Cocaine and crack: Neurobiology. In J. H. Lowinson, P. Ruiz, R. B. Millman, & J. G. Langrod (Eds.), *Substance abuse: A comprehensive textbook.* Philadelphia: Lippincott/Williams & Wilkins.

Rhodewalt, F., Sanbonmatsu, D. M., Tschanz, B., Feick, D. L., & Waller, A. (1995). Self-handicapping and interpersonal trade-offs: The effects of claimed self-handicaps on observers' performance evaluations and feedback. *Personality and Social Psychology Bulletin, 21,* 1042–1050

Rice, L. N., & Greenberg, L. S. (1992). Humanistic approaches to psychotherapy. In D. K. Freedheim (Ed.), *History of psychotherapy: A century of change.* Washington, DC: American Psychological Association.

Richardson, C. R., Kriska, A. M., Lantz, P. M., & Hayword, R. A. (2004). Physical activity and mortality across cardiovascular disease risk groups. *Medicine and Science in Sports and Exercise, 36(11),* 1923–1929.

Richardson, J. G., & Simpson, C. H. (1982). Children, gender and social structure: An analysis of the contents of letters to Santa Claus. *Child Development, 53* 429–436.

Richmond, V. P., & McCroskey, J. C. (1995). *Communication: Apprehension, avoidance, and effectiveness* (5th ed.). Boston: Allyn & Bacon.

Ridge, S. R., & Feeney, J. A. (1998). Relationship history and relationship attitudes in gay males and lesbians: Attachment style and gender differences. *Australian and New Zealand Journal of Psychiatry, 32(6),* 848–859.

Ridker, P. M. (2001). High-sensitivity C-reactive protein: Potential adjunct for global risk assessment in the primary prevention of cardiovascular disease. *Circulation, 103,* 1813–1818.

Riemann, R., Angleitner, A., & Strelau, J. (1997). Genetic and environmental influences on personality: A study of twins reared together using the self- and peer report NEO-FFI scales. *Journal of Personality, 65,* 449–476.

Rierdan, J., & Koff, E. (1991). Depressive symptomatology among very early maturing girls. *Journal of Youth and Adolescence, 20,* 415–425.

Rifkin, J. (1989). *Time wars: The primary conflict in human history.* New York: Simon & Schuster.

Riggio, R. E., & Throckmorton, B. (1988). The relative effect of verbal and nonverbal behavior, appearance, and social skills on valuations made in hiring interviews. *Journal of Applied Social Psychology, 18,* 331–348.

Rigotti, N. A., Lee, J. E., & Wechsler, H. (2000). U.S. college students' use of tobacco products: Results of a national survey. *Journal of the American Medical Association, 284,* 699–705.

Rihmer, Z. (2003). Do SSRI's increase the risk of suicide among depressives even if they are only taking placebo? *Psychotherapy & Psychosomatics, 72(6),* 357–358.

Rimal R. N. (2001). Longitudinal influences of knowledge and self-efficacy on exercise behavior:

Tests of a mutual reinforcement model. *Journal of Health Psychology, 6,* 31–46.

Rimm, D. C., & Cunningham, H. M. (1985). Behavior therapies. In S. J. Lynn & J. P. Garske (Eds.), *Contemporary psychotherapies: Models and methods.* Columbus, OH: Merrill.

Rindfuss, R. R. (1991). The young adult years: Diversity, structural change, and fertility. *Demography, 28,* 493–512.

Riso, L. P., du Toit, P. L., Blandino, J. A., Penna, S., Dacey, S., Duin, J. S., Pacoe, E. M., Grant, M. M., & Ulmer, C. S. (2003). Cognitive aspects of chronic depression. *Journal of Abnormal Psychology, 112*(1), 72–80.

Ritz, T., Steptoe, A., DeWilde, S., & Costa, M. (2000). Emotions and stress increase respiratory resistance in asthma. *Psychosomatic Medicine, 62*(3), 401–412.

Rivas-Vazquez, R. A. (2001). Antidepressants as first-line agents in the current pharmacotherapy of anxiety disorders. *Professional Psychology: Research & Practice, 32*(1), 101–104.

Road rage plagues drivers. (1997, November/December). *AAA Going Places,* 41–42.

Robbins, A., & Wilner, A. (2001). *Quarterlife crisis: The unique challenges of life in your twenties.* New York: Putnam.

Roberts, A. R. (2002). Myths, facts, and realities regarding battered women and their children: An overview. In A. R. Roberts (Ed.), *Handbook of domestic violence intervention strategies: Policies, programs, and legal remedies.* New York: Oxford University Press.

Roberts, B. W., & DelVecchio. W. F. (2000). The rank-order consistency of personality traits from childhood to old age: A quantitative review of the longitudinal studies. *Psychological Bulletin, 126,* 3–25.

Roberts, D. F., Foehr, U. G., Rideout, V. J., & Vrodie, M. (1999). Kids and media @ the new millennium. Menlo Park, CA: Kaiser Family Foundation.

Roberts, L. J. (2000). Fire and ice in marital communication: Hostile and distancing behaviors as predictors of marital distress. *Journal of Marriage and the Family, 62,* 693–707.

Roberts, L. J., & Krokoff, L. J. (1990). A time series analysis of withdrawal, hostility, and displeasure in satisfied and dissatisfied marriages. *Journal of Marriage and the Family, 52,* 95–105.

Roberts, P., & Newton, P. M. (1987). Levinsonian studies of women's adult development. *Psychology and Aging, 2,* 154–163.

Robins, L. N., Locke, B. Z., & Regier, D. A. (1991). An overview of psychiatric disorders in America. In L. N. Robins & D. A. Regier (Eds.), *Psychiatric disorders in America: The epidemiologic catchment area study.* New York: Free Press.

Robins, R. W., Norem, J. K., & Cheek, J. M. (1999). Naturalizing the self. In L. A. Pervin & O. P. Johns (Eds.), *Handbook of personality: Theory and research* (2nd ed., pp. 443–477). New York : Guilford Press.

Robinson, B. E. (1998). The workaholic family: A clinical perspective. *American Journal of Family Therapy, 26*(1), 65–75.

Robinson, D. G., Woerner, M. G., McMeniman, M., Mendelowitz, A., & Bilder, R. M. (2004). Symptomatic and functional recovery from a first episode of schizophrenia or schizoaffective disorder. *American Journal of Psychiatry, 161,* 473–479.

Robinson, F. P. (1970). *Effective study* (4th ed.). New York: HarperCollins.

Robinson, J. P., & Godbey, G. (1997). *Time for life: The surprising ways Americans use their time.* University Park, PA: Pennsylvania State University Press.

Rodin, J., Schank, D., & Striegel-Moore, R. H. (1989). Psychological features of obesity. *Medical Clinics of North America, 73* 47–66.

Roediger, H. L., III, & McDermott, K. B. (1995). Creating false memories: Remembering words not presented in lists. *Journal of Experimental Psychology: Learning, Memory, and Cognition, 21,* 803–814.

Roediger, H. L., III, & McDermott, K. B. (2000). Tricks of memory. *Current Directions in Psychological Science, 9,* 123–127.

Rogers, C. R. (1951). *Client-centered therapy: Its current practice, implications, and theory.* Boston: Houghton Mifflin.

Rogers, C. R. (1961). *On becoming a person: A therapist's view of psychotherapy.* Boston: Houghton Mifflin.

Rogers, C. R. (1977). *Carl Rogers on personal power.* New York: Delacorte.

Rogers, C. R. (1980). *A way of being.* Boston: Houghton Mifflin.

Rogers, C. R. (1986). Client-centered therapy. In I. L. Kutash & A. Wolf (Eds.), *Psychotherapist's casebook.* San Francisco: Jossey-Bass.

Rogers, M. P., Fricchione, G., & Reich, P. (1999). Psychosomatic medicine and consultation-liaison psychiatry. In A. M. Nicholi (Ed.), *The Harvard guide to psychiatry* (3rd ed., pp. 362–389). Cambridge, MA: Harvard University Press.

Rogers, R. W., & Prentice-Dunn, S. (1997). Protection motivation theory. In D. Gochman (Ed.), *Handbook of health behavior research* (Vol. 1, pp. 113–132). New York: Plenum.

Rogers, S. J., & White, L. K. (1998). Satisfaction with parenting: The role of marital happiness, family structure, and parents' gender. *Journal of Marriage and the Family, 60,* 293–308.

Roggman, L. A., Langlois, J. H., Hubbs-Tait, L., & Rieser-Danner, L. A. (1994). Infant day-care, attachment, and the "file drawer problem." *Child Development, 65,* 1429–1443.

Rohner, R. P., & Veneziano, R. A. (2001). The importance of father love: History and contemporary evidence. *Review of General Psychology, 5*(4), 382–405.

Rojewski, J. W. (2005). Occupational aspirations: Constructs, meanings, and application. In S. D. Brown & R. W. Lent (Eds.), *Career development and counseling: Putting theory and research to work.* New York: Wiley.

Romano, S. J., & Quinn, L. (2001). Evaluation and treatment of bulimia nervosa. *Primary Psychiatry, 8*(2), 57–62.

Rook, K. S. (1998). Investigating the positive and negative sides of personal relationships: Through a lens darkly? In B. H. Spitzberg & W. R. Cupach (Eds.), *The dark side of close relationships.* Mahwah, NJ: Lawrence Erlbaum.

Rose, D., Wykes, T., Leese, M., Bindman, J., & Fleischmann, P. (2003). Patient's perspectives on electroconvulsive therapy: Systematic review. *British Medical Journal, 326,* 1363–1365.

Rose, D. P. (1997). Dietary fatty acids and cancer. *American Journal of Clinical Nutrition, 66*(4), 998S–1003S.

Rose, S. D. (1999). Group therapy: A cognitive-behavioral approach. In J. R. Price & D. R. Hescheles (Eds.), *A guide to starting psychotherapy groups.* San Diego, CA: Academic Press.

Rosen, D. H. (1974). *Lesbianism: A study of female homosexuality.* Springfield, IL: Charles C Thomas.

Rosen, G. M. (1987). Self-help treatment books and the commercialization of psychotherapy. *American Psychologist, 42,* 46–51.

Rosen, R. (2000). Medical and psychological interventions for erectile dysfunction. In S. Leiblum & R. Rosen (Eds.), *Principles and practice of sex therapy.* New York: Guilford.

Rosen, R. D. (1977). *Psychobabble.* New York: Atheneum.

Rosenbaum, M., Lakin, M., & Roback, H. B. (1992). Psychotherapy in groups. In D. K. Freedheim (Ed.), *History of psychotherapy: A century of change.* Washington, DC: American Psychological Association.

Rosenberg, E. L., & Ekman, P. (1994). Coherence between expressive systems in emotion. *Cognition and Emotion, 8,* 201–229.

Rosenblatt, A., Greenberg, J., Solomon, S., Pyszczynski, T., & Lyon, D. (1989). Evidence for terror management theory: I. The effects of mortality salience on reactions to those who violate or uphold cultural values. *Journal of Personality and Social Psychology, 57*(4), 681–690.

Rosenbluth, S. C. (1997). Is sexual orientation a matter of choice? *Psychology of Women Quarterly, 21,* 595–610.

Rosenfarb, I. S., Goldstein, M. J., Mintz, J., & Nuechterlein, K. H. (1995). Expressed emotion and subclinical psychopathology observable within the transactions between schizophrenic patients and their family members. *Journal of Abnormal Psychology, 104,* 259–267.

Rosenfeld, L. B., Stewart, S. C., Stinnett, H. J., & Jackson, L. A. (1999). Preferences for body type and body characteristics associated with attractive and unattractive bodies: Jackson and McGill revisited. *Perceptual and Motor Skills, 89*(2), 459–470.

Rosenfield, S. (1999). Splitting the difference: Gender, the self and mental health. In C. S. Aneshensel & J. C. Phelan (Eds.), *Handbook of the sociology of mental health.* New York: Kluwer Academic.

Rosenhan, D. L. (1973). On being sane in insane places. *Science, 179,* 250–258.

Rosenman, R. H. (1993). Relationships of the Type A behavior pattern with coronary heart disease. In L. Goldberger & S. Breznitz (Eds.), *Handbook of stress: Theoretical and clinical aspects* (2nd ed.). New York: Free Press.

Rosenthal, R. (1985). From unconscious experimenter bias to teacher expectancy effects. In J. B. Dusek, V. C. Hall, & W. J. Meyer (Eds.), *Teacher expectancies.* Hillsdale, NJ: Erlbaum.

Rosenthal, R. (2003). Covert communication in laboratories, classrooms, and the truly real world. *Current Directions in Psychological Science, 12*(5), 151–154.

Ross, C. A. (1999). Dissociative disorders. In T. Millon, P. H. Blaney, & R. D. Davis (Eds.), *Oxford textbook of psychopathology* (pp. 466–484). New York: Oxford University Press.

Ross, C. E., & Drentea, P. (1998). Consequences of retirement activities for distress and the sense of personal control. *Journal of Health and Social Behavior, 39*(4), 317–334.

Ross, C. E., & Van Willigen, M. (1997). Education and the subjective quality of life. *Journal of Health & Social Behavior, 38,* 275–297.

Ross, L. D. (1977). The intuitive psychologist and his shortcomings: Distortions in the attribution process. In L. Berkowitz (Ed.), *Advances in experimental social psychology* (Vol. 10). New York: Academic Press.

Ross, M., & Conway, M. (1986). Remembering one's own past: The construction of personal histories. In R. M. Sorrentino & E. T. Higgins (Eds.), *Handbook of motivation and cognition: Foundations of social behavior.* New York: Guilford Press.

Ross, M., McFarland, C., & Fletcher, G. J. O. (1981). The effect of attitude on the recall of personal histories. *Journal of Personality and Social Psychology, 10,* 627–634.

Rosso, I. M., Cannon, T. D., Huttunen, T., Huttunen, M. O., Lönnqvist, J., & Gasperoni, T. L. (2000). Obstetric risk factors for early-onset schizophrenia in a Finnish birth cohort. *American Journal of Psychiatry, 157,* 801–807.

Roter, D. L., Hall, J. A., Merisca, R., Nordstrom, B., Cretin, D., & Svarstad, B. (1998). Effectiveness of interventions to promote patient compliance. *Medical Care, 36,* 1138–1161.

Rotter, J. B. (1982). *The development and application of social learning theory.* New York: Praeger.

Roughton, B. (2001, May 27). In Europe, workers time off adds up. *The Atlanta Journal-Constitution,* pp. D1–D2.

Rousseau, D. M. (1997). Organizational behavior in the new organizational era. In J. T. Spence, J. M. Darley, & D. J. Foss (Eds.), *Annual review of psychology* (pp. 515–533). Palo Alto, CA: Annual Reviews, Inc.

Rowe, D. (1994). *The limits of family influence: Genes, experience, and behavior.* New York: Guilford.

Rowe, D. C. (1997). Genetics, temperament, and personality. In R. Hogan, J. Johnson, & S. Briggs (Eds), *Handbook of personality psychology.* San Diego: Academic Press.

Rowe, D. C. (1999). Heredity. In V. J. Derlega, B. A. Winstead, & W. H. Jones (Eds.), *Personality: Contemporary theory and research* (2nd ed., pp. 66–100). Chicago: Nelson-Hall.

Rozanski, A., Blumenthal, J. A., & Kaplan, J. (1999). Impact of psychological factors on the pathogenesis of cardiovascular disease and implications for therapy. *Circulation, 99*(16), 2192–2197.

Rozee, P. D., Bateman, P., & Gilmore, T. (1991). The personal perspective of acquaintance rape prevention: A three-tier approach. In A. Parrot & L. Bechhofer (Eds.), *Acquaintance rape: The hidden crime.* New York: Wiley.

Rubenstein, C. M., & Shaver, P. (1982). The experience of loneliness. In L. A. Peplau & D. Perlman (Eds.), *Loneliness: A sourcebook of current theory, research and therapy.* New York: Wiley.

Rubin, Z., Peplau, L. A., & Hill, C. T. (1981). Loving and leaving: Sex differences in romantic attachments. *Sex Roles, 7,* 821–835.

Ruble, T. L. (1983). Sex stereotypes: Issues of change in the 1970s. *Sex Roles, 9,* 397–402.

Rudisch, B., & Nemeroff, C. B. (2003). Epidemiology of comorbid coronary artery disease and depression. *Biological Psychiatry, 54*(3), 227–240.

Rudorfer, M. V., Henry, M. E., & Sackeim, H. A. (2003). Electroconvulsive therapy. In A. Tasman, J. Kay, & J. A. Lieberman (Eds.), *Psychiatry.* New York: Wiley.

Rusbult, C. E., Drigotas, S. M., & Verette, J. (1994). The investment model: An interdependence analysis of commitment processes and relationship maintenance phenomena. In D. J. Canary & L. Stafford (Eds.), *Communication and relational maintenance.* San Diego: Academic Press.

Rush, A. J. (1984). Cognitive therapy. In T. B. Karasu (Ed.), *The psychiatric therapies.* Washington, DC: American Psychiatric Association.

Rush, A. J. (2000). Mood disorders: Treatment of depression. In B. J. Sadock & V. A. Sadock (Eds.), *Kaplan and Sadock's comprehensive textbook of psychiatry* (7th ed., Vol. 1, pp. 1377–1384). Philadelphia: Lippincott/Williams and Wilkins.

Rush, A. J., & Beck, A. T. (2000). Cognitive therapy. In B. J. Sadock & V. A. Sadock (Eds.), *Kaplan and Sadock's comprehensive textbook of psychiatry* (7th ed., Vol. 1, pp. 2167–2177). Philadelphia: Lippincott/Williams & Wilkins.

Russell, G. F. M. (1995). Anorexia nervosa through time. In G. Szmukler, C. Dare, & J. Treasure (Eds.), *Handbook of eating disorders: Theory, treatment, and research.* New York: Wiley.

Russell, G. F. M. (1997). The history of bulimia nervosa. In D. M. Garner & P. E. Garfinkel (Eds.), *Handbook of treatment for eating disorders* (2nd ed.). New York: Guilford Press.

Russo, N. F. (1979). Overview: Sex roles, fertility, and the motherhood mandate. *Psychology of Women Quarterly, 4,* 7–15.

Ruzek, J. (2001). *Coping with PTSD and recommended lifestyle changes for PTSD patients.* Retrieved November 28, 2001 from U.S. Department of Veterans Affairs National Center for PTSD Website: http://www.ncptsd.org/facts/treatment/fs_coping.html.

Ryan, C., & Futterman, D. (1997). Lesbian and gay youth: Care and counseling. *Adolescent Medicine, 8,* 221.

Ryan, R. M., & Deci, E. L. (2001). On happiness and human potentials: A review of research on hedonic and eudaimonic well–being. *Annual Review of Psychology, 52,* 141–166.

Rynes, S., & Rosen, B. (1995). A field study of factors affecting the adoption and perceived success of diversity training. *Personnel Psychology, 48*(2), 247–270.

Saad, L. (1996, December). Americans growing more tolerant of gays. *The Gallup Poll Monthly,* 12–14.

Saad, L. (1999, September 3). *American workers generally satisfied, but indicate their jobs leave much to be desired.* Princeton, NJ: Gallup News Service.

Sabatelli, R. M., & Ripoll, K. (2004). Variations in marriage over time: An ecological/exchange perspective. In M. Coleman & L. H. Ganong (Eds.), *Handbook of contemporary families: Considering the past, contemplating the future.* Thousand Oaks, CA: Sage.

Sackeim, H. A., Haskett, R. F., Mulsant, B. H., Thase, M. E., Mann, J. J., Pettinati, H. M., Greenberg, R. M., Crowe, R. R., Cooper, T. B., & Prudic, J. (2001). Continuation pharmacotherapy in the prevention of relapse following electroconvulsive therapy: A randomized controlled trial. *Journal of the American Medical Association, 285*(10), 1299–1307.

Sadker, M., & Sadker, D. (1994). *Failing at fairness: How America's schools cheat girls.* New York: Scribners.

Saghir, M. T., & Robins, E. R. (1973). *Male and female homosexuality: A comprehensive investigation.* Baltimore: Williams & Wilkins.

Sagrestano, L. M. (2004). Health implications of workplace diversity. In M. S. Stockdale & F. J. Crosby (Eds.), *The psychology and management of workplace diversity.* UK: Blackwell.

Salkovskis, P. M., & Warwick, H. M. C. (2001). Meaning, misinterpretations, and medicine: A cognitive-behavioral approach to understanding health anxiety and hypochondriasis. In V. Starcevic & D. R. Lipsitt (Eds.), *Hypochondriasis: Modern perspectives on an ancient malady.* New York: Oxford University Press.

Salovey, P., & Mayer, J. D. (1990). Emotional intelligence. *Imagination, Cognition, and Personality, 9,* 185–211.

Salovey, P., Mayer, J. D., & Caruso, D. (2002). The positive psychology of emotional intelligence. In C. R. Synder & S. J. Lopez (Eds.), *Handbook of positive psychology.* New York: Oxford University Press.

Salovey, P., Rothman, A. J., Detweiler, J. B., & Steward, W. T. (2000). Emotional states and physical health. *American Psychologist, 55*(1), 110–121.

Salthouse, T. A. (2000). Steps toward the explanation of adult age differences in cognition. In T. Perfect & E. Maylor (Eds.), *Theoretical debate in cognitive aging.* Oxford, UK: Oxford University Press.

Salthouse, T. A. (2004). What and when of cognitive aging. *Current Directions in Psychological Science, 13*(4), 140–144.

Salvendy, J. T. (1993). Selection and preparation of patients and organization of the group. In H. I. Kaplan & B. J. Sadock (Eds.), *Comprehensive group psychotherapy.* Baltimore: Williams & Wilkins.

Samet, J. M. (1992). The health benefits of smoking cessation. *Medical Clinics of North America, 76,* 399–414.

Sammons, M. T., Gorny, S. W., Zinner, E. S., & Allen, R. P. (2000). Prescriptive authority for psychologists: A consensus of support. *Professsional Psychology: Research and Practice, 31*(6), 604–609.

Samovar, L. A., & Porter, R. E. (2004). *Communication between cultures.* Belmont, CA: Wadsworth.

Samovar, L. A., Porter, R. E., & Stefani, L. A. (1998). *Communication between cultures* (2nd ed.). Belmont, CA: Wadsworth.

Sanchez, L. M., & Turner, S. M. (2003). Practicing psychology in the era of managed care: Implications for practice and training. *American Psychologist, 58*(2), 116–129.

Sande, M. A., & Ronald, A. (2004). Treatment of HIV/AIDS: Do the dilemmas only increase? *Journal of the American Medical Association, 292*(2), 224–236.

Sanders, G. (2000). Men together: Working with gay couples in contemporary times. In P. Papp (Ed.), *Couples on the fault line.* New York: Guilford Press.

Sanderson, W. C., & Barlow, D. H. (1990). A description of patients diagnosed with DSM-III-R generalized anxiety disorder. *Journal of Nervous and Mental Disease, 178,* 588–591.

Sandler, J. (1975). Aversion methods. In F. H. Kanfer & A. P. Goldstein (Eds.), *Helping people change: A textbook of methods.* New York: Pergamon.

Sandnabba, N. K., & Ahlberg, C. (1999). Parents' attitudes and expectations about children's cross-gender behavior. *Sex Roles, 40*(3–4), 249–263.

Sanislow, C. A., & Carson, R. C. (2001). Schizophrenia: A critical examination. In P. B. Sutker & H. E. Adams (Eds.), *Comprehensive handbook of psychopathology* (3rd ed., pp. 403–444). New York: Kluwer Academic/Plenum.

Santrock, J. W., Minnett, A. M., & Campbell, B. D. (1994). *The authoritative guide to self-help books.* New York: Guilford Press.

Sanz de Acedo, M. L., & Garcia Ganuza, J. M. (2003). Improvement of mental rotation in girls and boys. *Sex Roles, 49*(5–6), 277–286.

Sarason, I. G., Johnson, J. H., & Siegel, J. M. (1978). Assessing the impact of life changes: Development of the Life Experiences Survey. *Journal of Consulting and Clinical Psychology, 46,* 932–946.

Sarason, I. G., Pierce, G. R., & Sarason, B. R. (1994). General and specific perceptions of social support. In W. R. Avison & I. H. Gotlib (Eds.), *Stress and mental health: Contemporary issues and prospects for the future.* New York: Plenum.

Sarwer, D. B., Foster, G. D., & Wadden, T. A. (2004). Treatment of obesity I: Adult obesity. In J. K. Thompson (Ed.), *Handbook of eating disorders and obesity.* New York: Wiley.

Saxe, G. N., van der Kolk, B. A., Berkowitz, R., Chinman, G., Hall, K., Lieberg, G., & Schwartz, J. (1993). Dissociative disorders in psychiatric inpatients. *American Journal of Psychiatry, 150,* 1037–1042.

Saxe, L., & Ben-Shakhar, G. (1999). Admissibility of polygraph tests: The application of scientific standards post-Daubert. *Psychology, Public Policy, and Law, 5*(1), 203–223.

Sayers, S. L. (2004). Depression and heart disease: The interrelationship between these two common disorders is complex and requires careful diagnostic and treatment methods. *Psychiatric Annals, 34*(4), 282–288.

Scanzoni, J. (2004). Household diversity: The starting point for healthy families in the new century. In M. Coleman & L. H. Ganong (Eds.), *Handbook of contemporary families: Considering the past, contemplating the future.* Thousand Oaks, CA: Sage.

Schachter, S. (1959). *The psychology of affiliation.* Stanford, CA: Stanford University Press.

Schaefer, J., & Moos, R. (1992). Life crises and personal growth. In B. Carpenter (Ed.), *Personal coping: Theory, research, and application.* Westport, CT: Praeger.

Schaffer, D. R. (1989). *Developmental psychology: Childhood and adolescence.* Pacific Grove, CA: Brooks/Cole.

Schaie, K. W. (1990). Intellectual development in adulthood. In J. E. Birren & K. W. Schaie (Eds.), *Handbook of the psychology of aging* (3rd ed.). San Diego: Academic Press.

Schaie, K. W. (1994). The course of adult development. *American Psychologist, 49*(4), 304–313.

Schaninger, C. M., & Buss, W. C. (1986). A longitudinal comparison of consumption and finance handling between happily married and divorced couples. *Journal of Marriage and the Family, 48,* 129–136.

Scheidlinger, S. (1993). History of group psychotherapy. In H. I. Kaplan & B. J. Sadock (Eds.), *Comprehensive group psychotherapy.* Baltimore: Williams & Wilkins.

Scheier, M. F., & Carver, C. S. (1985). Optimism, coping, and health: Assessment and implications of generalized outcome expectancies. *Health Psychology, 4,* 219–247.

Scheier, M. F., Carver, C. S., & Bridges, M. W. (2001). Optimism, pessimism, and psychological well-being. In E. C. Chang (Ed.), *Optimism and pessimism: Implications for theory, research, and practice* (pp. 189–216). Washington, DC: American Psychological Association.

Scheier, M. F., Matthews, K. A., Owens, J. F., Magovern, G. J., Sr., Lefebvre, R. C., Abbott, R. A., & Carver, C. S. (1989). Dispositional optimism and recovery from coronary artery bypass surgery: The beneficial effects on physical and psychological well-being. *Journal of Personality and Social Psychology, 57,* 1024–1040.

Schiffman, J., Ekstrom, M., LaBrie, J., Schulsinger, F., Sorenson, H., & Mednick, S. (2002). Minor physical anomalies and schizophrenia spectrum disorders: A prospective investigation. *American Journal of Psychiatry, 159,* 238–243.

Schilit, W. K. (1987). Thinking about managing your time. In A. D. Timpe (Ed.), *The management of time.* New York: Facts On File.

Schimel, J., Simon, L., Greenberg, J., Pyszczynski, T., Solomon, S., Waxmonsky, J., & Arndt, J. (1999). Stereotypes and terror management: Evidence that mortality salience enhances stereotypic thinking and preferences. *Journal of Personality and Social Psychology, 77*(5), 905–926.

Schirmer, L. L., & Lopez, F. G. (2001). Probing the social support and work strain relationship among adult workers: Contributions of adult attachment orientations. *Journal of Vocational Behavior, 59*(1), 17–33.

Schlegel, A., & Barry, H., III. (1991). *Adolescence: An anthropological inquiry.* New York: Free Press.

Schlenger, W. E., Kulka, R. A., Fairbank, J. A., Hough, R. L., et al. (1992). The prevalence of posttraumatic stress disorder in the Vietnam generation: A multimethod, multisource assessment of psychiatric disorder. *Journal of Traumatic Stress, 5,* 333–363.

Schlenker, B. R. (2003). Self-presentation. In M.R. Leary & J. P. Tangney (Eds.), *Handbook of self and identity.* New York: Guilford.

Schlenker, B. R., & Pontari, B. A. (2000). The strategic control of information: Impression management and self-presentation in daily life. In A. Tesser, R. B. Felson, & J. M. Suls (Eds.), *Psychological perspectives on self and identity* (pp. 199–232). Washington, DC: American Psychological Association.

Schmitz, J. M., & DeLaune, K. A. (2005). Nicotine. In J. H. Lowinson, P. Ruiz, R. B. Millman, & J. G. Langrod (Eds.), *Substance abuse: A comprehensive textbook.* Philadelphia: Lippincott/Williams & Wilkins.

Schneer, J. A., & Reitman, F. (1993). Effects of alternative family structures on managerial career paths. *Academy of Management Journal, 36,* 830–843.

Schneider, B. H., Atkinson, L., & Tardif, C. (2001). Child-parent attachment and children's peer relations: A quantitative review. *Developmental Psychology, 37*(1), 86–100.

Schneider, F., & Deldin, P. J. (2001). Genetics and schizophrenia. In P. B. Sutker & H. E. Adams (Eds.), *Comprehensive handbook of psychopathology* (3rd ed., pp. 371–402). New York: Kluwer Academic/Plenum.

Schneider, J. P. (2003). The impact of compulsive cybersex behaviors on the family. *Sexual and Relationship Therapy, 18*(3), 329–354.

Schofield, P. E., Pattison, P. E., Hill, D. J., & Borland, R. (2001). The influence of group identifi-

cation on the adoption of peer group smoking norms. *Psychology and Health, 16*(1), 1–16.

Schooler, D., Ward, L. M., Merriwether, A., & Caruthers, A. (2004). Who's that girl: Television's role in the body image development of young white and black women. *Psychology of Women Quarterly, 28,* 38–47.

Schooler, J. W. (1999). Seeking the core: The issues and evidence surrounding recovered accounts of sexual trauma. In L. M. Williams & V. L. Banyard (Eds.), *Trauma & memory.* Thousand Oaks, CA: Sage.

Schoon, I., & Parsons, S. (2002). Teenage aspirations for future careers and occupational outcomes. *Journal of Vocational Behavior, 60*(2), 262–288.

Schor, J. (1991). *The overworked American.* New York: Basic Books.

Schreiber, F. R. (1973). *Sybil.* New York: Warner.

Schroeder, D. H., & Costa, P. T., Jr. (1984). Influence of life events stress on physical illness: Substantive effects or methodological flaws? *Journal of Personality and Social Psychology, 46,* 853–863.

Schuckit, M. A. (2000). Alcohol-related disorders. In B. J. Sadock & V. A. Sadock (Eds.), *Kaplan and Sadock's comprehensive textbook of psychiatry* (7th ed., pp. 953–970). Philadelphia: Lippincott/Williams & Wilkins.

Schultz, J. H., & Luthe, W. (1969). *Autogenic therapy: Vol. 1. Autogenic methods.* New York: Grune & Stratton.

Schunk, D. H. (2003). Self-efficacy for reading and writing: Influence of modeling, goal setting, and self-evaluation. *Reading and Writing Quarterly: Overcoming Learning Difficulties, 19*(2), 159–172.

Schwartz, B. (2004). *The paradox of choice: Why more is less.* New York: Ecco.

Schwartz, J. E., Neale, J., Marco, C., Shiffman, S. S., & Stone, A. A. (1999). Does trait coping exist? A momentary assessment approach to the evaluation of traits. *Journal of Personality and Social Psychology, 77*(2), 360–369.

Schwartz, L., Slater, M. A., & Birchler, G. R. (1994). Interpersonal stress and pain behaviors in patients with chronic pain. *Journal of Consulting and Clinical Psychology, 62,* 861–864.

Schwarz, N., & Strack, F. (1999). Reports of subjective well-being: Judgmental processes and their methodological implications. In D. Kahneman, E. Diener, & N. Schwarz (Eds.), *Well-being: The foundations of hedonic psychology* (pp. 61–84). New York: Russell Sage Foundation.

Schwarzer, R., & Schulz, U. (2003). Stressful life events. In A. M. Nezu, C. M. Nezu, & P. A. Geller (Eds.), *Handbook of psychology: Vol. 9. Health psychology.* New York: Wiley.

Scroppo, J. C., Drob, S. L., Weinberger, J. L., & Eagle, P. (1998). Identifying dissociative identity disorder: A self-report and projective study. *Journal of Abnormal Psychology, 107,* 272–284.

Scully, J. A., Tosi, H., & Banning, K. (2000). Life event checklists: Revisiting the social readjustment rating scale after 30 years. *Educational & Psychological Measurement, 60*(6), 864–876.

Scarle, A., & Bennett, P. (2001). Psychological factors and inflammatory bowel disease: A review of a decade of literature. *Psychology, Health and Medicine, 6*(2), 121–135.

Seccombe, K. (1987). Children: Their impact on the elderly in declining health. *Research on Aging, 9,* 312–326.

Seccombe, K. (2001). Families in poverty in the 1990s: Trends, causes, consequences, and lessons learned. In R. M. Milardo (Ed.), *Understanding families into the new millennium: A decade in review* (pp. 313–332). Minneapolis: National Council on Family Relations.

Sedikides, C. (1993). Assessment, enhancement, and verification determinants of the self-evaluation process. *Journal of Personality and Social Psychology, 65*(2), 317–338.

Sedikides, C., Gaertner, L., & Toguchi, Y. (2003). Pancultural self-enhancement. *Journal of Personality and Social Psychology, 84*(1), 60–79.

Sedikides, C., & Strube, M. J. (1997). Self-evaluation: To thine own self be good, to thine own self be sure, to thine own self be true, and to thine own self be better. In M. P. Zanna (Ed.), *Advances in experimental social psychology* (Vol. 29). New York: Academic Press.

Segal, M. W. (1974). Alphabet and attraction: An unobtrusive measure of the effect of propinquity in a field setting. *Journal of Personality and Social Psychology, 30,* 654–657.

Segall, A. (1997). Sick role concepts and health behavior. In D. S. Gochman (Ed.), *Handbook of health behavior research I: Personal and social determinants.* New York : Plenum Press.

Segerstrom, S. C., & Miller, G. E. (2004). Psychological stress and the human immune system: A meta-analytic study of 30 years of inquiry. *Psychological Bulletin, 130*(4), 601–630.

Segerstrom, S. C., Taylor, S. E., Kemeny, M. E., & Fahey, J. L. (1998). Optimism is associated with mood, coping and immune change in response to stress. *Journal of Personality and Social Psychology, 74,* 1646–1655.

Seidlitz, L., & Diener, E. (1993). Memory for positive versus negative life events: Theories for the differences between happy and unhappy persons. *Journal of Personality and Social Psychology, 64,* 654–664.

Self, D. W. (1998). Neural substrates of drug craving and relapse in drug addiction. *Annals of Medicine, 30,* 379–389.

Seligman, M. E. P. (1971). Phobias and preparedness. *Behavior Therapy, 2,* 307–321.

Seligman, M. E. P. (1974). Depression and learned helplessness. In R. J. Friedman & M. M. Katz (Eds.), *The psychology of depression: Contemporary theory and research.* New York: Wiley.

Seligman, M. E. P. (1990). *Learned optimism: How to change your mind and your life.* New York: Pocket Books.

Seligman, M. E. P. (1991). *Learned optimism.* New York: Alfred A. Knopf.

Seligman, M. E. P. (1992). *Helplessness: On depression, development, and death.* New York: Freeman.

Seligman, M. E. P. (1994). *What you can change and what you can't.* New York: Knopf.

Seligman, M. E. P. (1995). The effectiveness of psychotherapy. *American Psychologist, 50,* 965–974.

Seligman, M. E. P. (2003). The past and future of positive psychology. In C. L. M. Keyes & J. Haidt (Eds.), *Flourishing: Positive psychology and the life well-lived.* Washington, DC: American Psychological Association.

Seligman, M. E. P., & Csikszentmihalyi, M. (2000). Positive psychology: An introduction. *American Psychologist, 55*(1), 5–14.

Seligman, M. E. P., & Isaacowitz, D. M. (2000). Learned helplessness. In G. Fink (Ed.), *Encyclopedia of stress* (Vol. 2, pp. 599–602). San Diego: Academic Press.

Seligman, M. E. P., & Levant, R. F. (1998). Managed care policies rely on inadequate science. *Professional Psychology: Research and Practice, 29,* 211–212.

Seligman, M. E. P., Schulman, P., DeRubeis, R. J., & Hollon, S. D. (1999). The prevention of depression and anxiety. *Prevention and Treatment,* http://journals.apa.org/prevention/volume2/pre00 20008a.html

Seltzer, J. A. (2001). Families formed outside of marriage. In R. M. Milardo (Ed.), *Understanding families into the new millennium: A decade in review* (pp. 466–487). Minneapolis: National Council on Family Relations.

Seltzer, J. A. (2004). Cohabitation and family change. In M. Coleman & L. H. Ganong (Eds.), *Handbook of contemporary families: Considering the past, contemplating the future.* Thousand Oaks, CA: Sage.

Selye, H. (1936). A syndrome produced by diverse nocuous agents. *Nature, 138,* 32.

Selye, H. (1956). *The stress of life.* New York: McGraw-Hill.

Selye, H. (1974). *Stress without distress.* New York: Lippincott.

Selye, H. (1982). History and present status of the stress concept. In L. Goldberger & S. Breznitz (Eds.), *Handbook of stress: Theoretical and clinical aspects.* New York: Free Press.

Semans, J. H. (1956). Premature ejaculation: A new approach. *Journal of Southern Medicine, 79,* 353–361.

Senecal, C., Lavoie, K., & Koestner, R. (1997). Trait and situational factors in procrastination: An interactional model. *Journal of Social Behavior and Personality, 12,* 889–903.

Servan-Schreiber, D., Kolb, R., & Tabas, G. (1999). The somatizing patient. *Primary Care, 26*(2), 225–242.

Sesso, H. D., Buring, J. E., Rifai, N., Blake, G. J., Gaziano, J. M., & Ridker, P. M. (2003). C-reactive protein and the risk of developing hypertension. *Journal of the American Medical Association, 290*(22), 2945–2951.

Seta, J. J., Seta, C. E., & McElroy, T. (2002). Strategies for reducing the stress of negative life experiences: An averaging/summation analysis. *Personality and Social Psychology Bulletin, 28*(11), 1574–1585.

Seto, M. C., Maric, A., & Barbaree, H. E. (2002). The role of pornography in the etiology of sexual aggression. *Journal of Sexual Aggression, 8*(3), 4–42.

Shaffer, D. R. (1989). *Developmental psychology: Childhood and adolescence.* Pacific Grove, CA: Brooks/Cole.

Shalev, A. Y. (2001). Posttraumatic stress disorder. *Primary Psychiatry, 8*(10), 41–46.

Shapiro, A. F., Gottman, J. M., & Carrère, S. (2000). The baby and marriage: Identifying factors that buffer against decline in marital satisfaction after the first baby arrives. *Journal of Family Psychology, 14*(1), 59–70.

Shapiro, D. H., Jr. (1984). Overview: Clinical and physiological comparison of meditation with other self-control strategies. In D. H. Shapiro, Jr. & R. N. Walsh (Eds.), *Meditation: Classic and contemporary perspectives.* New York: Aldine.

Shapiro, D. H., Jr. (1987). Implications of psychotherapy research for the study of meditation. In M. A. West (Ed.), *The psychology of meditation.* Oxford: Clarendon Press.

Shapiro, S. L., Schwartz, G. E. R., & Santerre, C. (2002). Meditation and positive psychology. In C. R. Snyder & S. J. Lopez (Eds.), *Handbook of positive psychology.* New York: Oxford University Press.

Shavelson, R. J., Hubner, J. J., & Stanton, G. C. (1976). Self-concept: Validation of construct interpretations. *Review of Educational Research, 46,* 407–411.

Shaver, P. R., & Brennan, K. A. (1992). Attachment styles and the "Big Five" personality traits. Their connections with each other and with romantic relationship outcomes. *Personality and Social Psychology Bulletin, 18,* 536–545.

Shaver, P. R., & Hazan, C. (1992). Adult romantic attachment: Theory and evidence. In D. Perlman & W. Jones (Eds.), *Advances in personal relationships* (Vol. 4). Bristol, PA: Taylor & Francis.

Shaver, P. R., & Hazan, C. (1993). Adult attachment: Theory and research. In W. Jones & D. Perlman (Eds.), *Advances in personal relationships* (Vol. 4). London: Jessica Kingsley.

Shaver, P. R., Wu, S., & Schwartz, J. C. (1991). Cross-cultural similarities and differences in emotion and its representation: A prototype approach. In M. S. Clark (Ed.), *Review of personality and social psychology* (Vol. 13). Newbury Park, CA: Sage.

Shaw, L. H., & Gant, L. M. (2002). In defense of the Internet: The relationship between Internet communication and depression, loneliness, self-esteem, and perceived social support. *CyberPsychology, 5*(2), 157–171.

Shear, M. K., & Beidel, D. C. (1998). Psychotherapy in the overall management strategy for social anxiety disorder. *Journal of Clinical Psychiatry, 59,* 39–46.

Sheehan, P. W., Green, V., & Truesdale, P. (1992). Influence of rapport on hypnotically induced pseudomemory. *Journal of Abnormal Psychology, 101,* 690–700.

Sheehan, S. (1982). *Is there no place on earth for me?* Boston: Houghton Mifflin.

Sheldon, K. M., & Kasser, T. (2001a). Getting older, getting better? Personal strivings and psychological maturity across the life span. *Developmental Psychology, 37*(4), 491–501.

Sheldon, K. M., & Kasser, T. (2001b). Goals, congruence, and positive well-being: New empirical support for humanistic theories. *Journal of Humanistic Psychology, 41*(1), 30–50.

Shephard, R. J. (1986). Passive smoking: Attitudes, health, and performance. In T. Ney & A. Gale (Eds.), *Smoking and human behavior.* Chichester: Wiley.

Shepperd, J. A., & McNulty, J. K. (2002). The affective consequences of expected and unexpected outcomes. *Psychological Science, 13,* 85–88.

Sher, L. (2003). Daily hassles, cortisol, and depression. *Australian and New Zealand Journal of Psychiatry, 37*(3), 383–384.

Sher, L., & Mann, J. J. (2003). Psychiatric pathophysiology: Mood disorders. In A. Tasman, J. Kay, & J. A. Lieberman (Eds.), *Psychiatry.* New York: Wiley.

Sher, T. G., & Baucom, D. H. (1993). Marital communication: Differences among maritally distressed, depressed, and nondistressed-nondepressed couples. *Journal of Family Psychology, 7,* 148–153.

Sherer, M., Maddox, J. E., Mercandante, B., Prentice-Dunn, S., Jacobs, B., & Rogers, R. W. (1982). The self-efficacy scale: Construction and validation. *Psychological Reports, 51,* 663–671.

Sherif, M. (1936). *The psychology of social norms.* New York: Harper.

Sherif, M., Harvey, L. J., White, B. J., Hood, W. R., & Sherif, C. W. (1988). *The robbers cave experiment: Intergroup conflict and cooperation.* Middletown, CT: Wesleyan University Press.

Sherif, M., & Hovland, C. I. (1961). *Social judgment: Assimilation and contrast effects in communication and attitude change.* New Haven, CT: Yale University Press.

Sherman, A. M., de Vries, B., & Lansford, J. E. (2000). Friendship in childhood and adulthood: Lessons across the life span. *International Journal of Aging and Human Development, 51*(1), 31–51.

Shike, M. (1999). Diet and lifestyle in the prevention of colorectal cancer: An overview. *American Journal of Medicine, 106*(1A), 11S–15S, 50S–51S.

Shiono, P. H., Klebanoff, M. A., Nugent, R. P., Cotch, M. F., Wilkins, D. G., Rollins, D. E., Carey, J. C., & Behrman, R. E. (1995). The impact of cocaine and marijuana use on low birth weight and preterm birth: A multicenter study. *American Journal of Obstetrics and Gynecology, 172,* 19–27.

Shoda, Y., Mischel, W., & Peake, P. K. (1990). Predicting adolescent cognitive and self-regulatory competencies from preschool delay of gratification: Identifying diagnostic conditions. *Developmental Psychology, 26,* 978–986.

Shors, T. J. (2004). Learning during stressful times. *Learning and Memory, 11*(2), 137–144.

Shotland, R. L., & Hunter, B. A. (1995). Women's "token resistant" and compliant sexual behaviors are related to uncertain sexual intentions and rape. *Personality and Social Psychology Bulletin, 21,* 226–236.

Shuchter, S. R., & Zisook, S. (1993). The course of normal grief. In M. S. Stroebe, W. Stroebe, & R. O.

Hansson (Eds.), *Handbook of bereavement: Theory, research, and intervention* (pp. 23–43). Cambridge, England: Cambridge University Press.

Shulman, R. B. (2001). Response versus remission in the treatment of depression: Understanding residual symptoms. *Primary Psychiatry, 8*(5), 28–30, 34.

Shuval, J. T. (1993). Migration and stress. In L. Goldberger & S. Breznitz (Eds.), *Handbook of stress: Theoretical and clinical aspects* (2nd ed.). New York: Free Press.

Siebert, A. (1995). *Student success: How to succeed in college and still have time for your friends.* Fort Worth, TX: Harcourt Brace.

SIECUS. (2004, Fall). SIECUS Fact Sheet: Public support for comprehensive sexuality education. Retrieved January 25, 2005 from http://63.73. 227.69/Pubs/Fact/Fact0017.html.

Siegel, O. (1982). Personality development in adolescence. In B. B. Wolman (Ed.), *Handbook of developmental psychology.* Englewood Cliffs, NJ: Prentice-Hall.

Siegler, I. C., Bosworth, H. B., & Poon, L. W. (2003). Disease, health and aging. In R. M. Lerner, M.A. Easterbrooks, & J. Mistry (Eds.), *Handbook of psychology: Vol. 6. Developmental psychology.* New York: Wiley.

Siegler, I. C., & Brummett, B. H. (2000). Associations among NEO personality assessments and well-being at mid-life: Facet-level analyses. *Psychology & Aging, 15,* 710–714.

Siegler, I. C., Peterson, B. L., Barefoot, J. C., & Williams, R. B. (1992). Hostility during late adolescence predicts coronary risk factors at mid-life. *American Journal of Epidemiology, 136*(2), 146–154.

Siegman, A. W., Townsend, S. T., Civelek, A. C., & Blumenthal, R. S. (2000). Antagonistic behavior, dominance, hostility, and coronary heart disease. *Psychosomatic Medicine, 62*(2), 248–257.

Signorielli, N., & Bacue, A. (1999). Recognition and respect: A content analysis of prime-time television characters. *Sex Roles, 40*(7/8), 527–544.

Silberman, E. K. (1998). Psychiatrists' and internists' beliefs. *Primary Psychiatry, 5,* 65–71.

Silke, A. (2003). *Terrorists, victims, and society: Psychological perspectives on terrrorism and its consequences.* New York: Wiley.

Silver, E., Cirincion, C., & Steadman, H. J. (1994). Demythologizing inaccurate perceptions of the insanity defense. *Law & Human Behavior, 18*(1), 63–70.

Silver, H., Feldman, P., Bilker, W., & Gur, R. C. (2003). Working memory deficit as a core neuropsychological dysfunction in schizophrenia. *American Journal of Psychiatry, 160,* 1809–1816.

Silver, M. (2002, June 10). What they're seeing. *U.S. News & World Report,* p. 41.

Silverman, P. R., & Worden, J. M. (1992). Children's reactions in the early months after the death of a parent. *American Journal of Orthopsychiatry, 62,* 93–104.

Simon, R. I. (2003). The law and psychiatry. In R. E. Hales & S. C. Yudofsky (Eds.), *Textbook of clinical psychiatry.* Washington, DC: American Psychiatric Publishing.

Simonton, D. K. (1997). Creative productivity: A predictive and explanatory model of career trajectories and landmarks. *Psychological Review, 104*(1), 66–89.

Sinclair, R. C., Mark, M. M., & Clore, G. L. (1994). Mood-related persuasion depends on (mis)attributions. *Social Cognition, 12,* 309–326.

Singh, D. (1993). Adaptive significance of female physical attractiveness: Role of waist-to-hip ratio. *Journal of Personality and Social Psychology, 65,* 293–307.

Singh, D. (1995). Female judgment of male attractiveness and desirability for relationships: Role of waist-to-hip ratio and financial status. *Journal of Personality and Social Psychology, 69,* 1089–1101.

Sinnott, J. D. (1989). A model for solution of ill-structured problems: Implications for everyday and abstract problem solving. In J. D. Sinnott (Ed.), *Everyday problem solving: Theory and application*. New York: Praeger.

Sirois, F. M., Melia-Gordon, M. L., & Pychyl, T. A. (2003). "I'll look after my health, later": An investigation of procrastination and health. *Personality and Individual Differences, 35*(5), 1167–1184.

Skinner, B. F. (1953). *Science and human behavior*. New York: Macmillan.

Skinner, B. F. (1974). *About behaviorism*. New York: Knopf.

Skinner, B. F. (1987). Whatever happened to psychology as the science of behavior? *American Psychologist, 42*, 780–786.

Skinner, B. F. (1990). Can psychology be a science of mind? *American Psychologist, 45*, 1206–1210.

Skinner, P. H., & Shelton, R. L. (1985). *Speech, language, and hearing: Normal processes and disorders* (2nd ed.). New York: Wiley.

Skolnick, P. (2003). Psychiatric pathophysiology: Anxiety disorders. In A. Tasman, J. Kay, & J. A. Lieberman (Eds.), *Psychiatry*. New York: Wiley.

Slashinki, M. J., Coker, A. L., & Davis, K. E. (2003). Physical aggression, forced sex, and stalking victimization by a dating partner: An analysis of the National Violence Against Women Survey. *Violence & Victims, 18*(6), 595–617.

Slaski, M., & Cartwright, S. (2003). Emotional intelligence training and its implications for stress, health and performance. *Stress and Health: Journal of the International Society for the Investigation of Stress, 19*(4), 233–239.

Slavney, P. R. (1990). *Perspectives on hysteria*. Baltimore: John Hopkins University Press.

Sloan, D. M., & Marx, B. P. (2004). A closer examination of the structured written disclosure procedure. *Journal of Consulting and Clinical Psychology, 72*(2), 165–175.

Slovic, P., Fischhoff, B., & Lichtenstein, S. (1982). Facts versus fears: Understanding perceived risk. In D. Kahneman, P. Slovic, & A. Tversky (Eds.), *Judgment under uncertainty: Heuristics and biases*. Cambridge, England: Cambridge University Press.

Smiler, A. P. (2004). Thirty years after the discovery of gender: Psychological concepts and measures of masculinity. *Sex Roles, 50*(1–2), 15–26.

Smith, A., Jussim, L., & Eccles, J. (1999). Do self-fulfilling prophecies accumulate, dissipate, or remain stable over time? *Journal of Personality and Social Psychology, 77*, 548–565.

Smith, A. K. (2000, November 6). Charting your own course. *U.S. News & World Report*, 56–60, 62, 64–65.

Smith, A. L., & Weissman, M. M. (1992). Epidemiology. In E. S. Paykel (Ed.), *Handbook of affective disorders* (2nd ed.). New York: Guilford.

Smith, C. A., & Lazarus, R. S. (1993). Appraisal components, core relational themes, and the emotions. *Cognition and Emotion, 7*, 233–269.

Smith, D. A. (1999). The end of theoretical orientations? *Applied & Preventative Psychology, 8*, 269–280.

Smith, D. M., & Gates, G. J. (2001) *Gay and lesbian families in the United States: Same-sex unmarried partner households: Preliminary analysis of 2000 U.S. census data, a human rights campaign report* [Web Page]. URL www.hrc.org.

Smith, E. R., & Mackie, D. M. (1995). *Social psychology*. New York: Worth.

Smith, G. S., Branas, C. C., & Miller, T. R. (1999). Fatal nontraffic injuries involving alcohol: A meta-analysis. *Annals of Emergency Medicine, 33*(6), 659–668.

Smith, J. C. (1975). Meditation and psychotherapy: A review of the literature. *Psychological Bulletin, 32*, 553–564.

Smith, J. W., Frawley, P. J., & Polissar, N. L. (1997). Six- and twelve-month abstinence rates in inpatient alcoholics treated with either faradic aversion or chemical aversion compared with matched inpatients from a treatment registry. *Journal of Addictive Diseases, 16*, 5–24.

Smith, M., & Pazder, L. (1980). *Michelle remembers*. New York: Pocket Books.

Smith, M. L., & Glass, G. V. (1977). Meta-analysis of psychotherapy outcome studies. *American Psychologist, 32*, 752–760.

Smith, P. B., & Bond, M. H. (1994). *Social psychology across cultures*. Boston: Allyn & Bacon.

Smith, P. B., & Bond, M. H. (1999). *Social psychology across cultures*. Boston: Allyn & Bacon.

Smith, R. E. (1989). Effects of coping skills training on generalized self-efficacy and locus of control. *Journal of Personality and Social Psychology, 56*, 228–233.

Smith, T. W. (1999). *The emerging 21st century American family*. University of Chicago: National Opinion Research Center.

Smith, T. W., & Gallo, L. C. (1999). Hostility and cardiovascular reactivity during marital interaction. *Psychosomatic Medicine, 61*, 436–445.

Smith, T. W., & Gallo, L. C. (2001). Personality traits as risk factors for physical illness. In A. Baum, T. A. Revenson, & J. E. Singer (Eds.), *Handbook of health psychology* (pp. 139–174). Mahwah, NJ: Erlbaum.

Smith, T. W., Pope, M. K., Sanders, J. D., Allred, K. D., & O'Keefe, J. L. (1988). Cynical hostility at home and work: Psychosocial vulnerability across domains. *Journal of Research in Personality, 22*, 525–548.

Smith, W. P., Compton, W. C., & West, W. B. (1995). Meditation as an adjunct to a happiness enhancement program. *Journal of Clinical Psychology, 51*, 269–273.

Smock, P. J. (2000). Cohabitation in the United States: An appraisal of research themes, findings, and implications. *Annual Review of Sociology, 26*, 1–20.

Smock, P. J., Manning, W. D., & Gupta, S. (1999). The effect of marriage and divorce on women's economic well-being. *American Sociological Review, 64*, 794–812.

Smolak, L., & Murnen, S. K. (2001). Gender and eating problems. In R. H. Striegel-Moore & L. Smolak (Eds.), *Eating disorders: Innovative directions in research and practice* (pp. 91–10). Washington, DC: American Psychological Association.

Smoll, F. L., & Schutz, R. W. (1990). Quantifying gender differences in physical performance: A developmental perspective. *Developmental Psychology, 26*, 360–369.

Smyth, J., Litcher, L., Hurewitz, A., & Stone, A. (2001). Relaxation training and cortisol secretion in adult asthmatics. *Journal of Health Psychology, 6*(2), 217–227.

Smyth, J. M. (1998). Written emotional expression: Effect sizes, outcome types, and moderating variables. *Journal of Consulting and Clinical Psychology, 66*, 174–184.

Smyth, J. M., & Pennebaker, J. W. (1999). Sharing one's story: Translating emotional experiences into words as a coping tool. In C. R. Snyder (Ed.), *Coping: The psychology of what works* (pp. 70–89). New York: Oxford University Press.

Smyth, J. M., & Pennebaker, J. W. (2001). What are the health effects of disclosure? In A. Baum, T. A. Revenson, & J. E. Singer (Eds.), *Handbook of health psychology* (pp. 339–348). Mahwah, NJ: Erlbaum.

Snodgrass, S. F. (1985). Women's intuition: The effect of subordinate role on interpersonal sensitivity. *Journal of Personality and Social Psychology, 49*, 146–155.

Snodgrass, S. E. (1992). Further effects of role versus gender on interpersonal sensitivity. *Journal of Personality and Social Psychology, 62*, 154–158.

Snodgrass, S. E., Hecht, M. A., & Ploutz-Snyder, R. (1998). Interpersonal sensitivity: Expressivity or perceptivity? *Journal of Personality and Social Psychology, 74*(1), 238–249.

Snowden, L. R., & Hu, T. W. (1996). Outpatient service use in minority-serving mental health programs. *Administration and Policy in Mental Health, 24*, 149–159.

Snowdon, D. (2001). *Aging with grace: What the nun study teaches us about leading longer, healthier, and more meaningful lives*. New York: Bantam Books.

Snyder, M. (1979). Self-monitoring processes. In L. Berkowitz (Ed.), *Advances in experimental social psychology* (Vol. 12). New York: Academic Press.

Snyder, M. (1986). *Public appearances/Private realities: The psychology of self-monitoring*. New York: Freeman.

Snyder, M., & Swann, W. B., Jr. (1978). Hypothesis-testing processes in social interaction. *Journal of Personality and Social Psychology, 36*(11), 1202–1212.

Sobal, J. (1995). Social influences on body weight. In K. D. Brownell & C. G. Fairburn (Eds.), *Eating disorders and obesity: A comprehensive handbook*. New York: Guilford Press.

Solberg, E. C., Diener, E., & Robinson, M. (2004). Why are materialists less satisfied? In T. Kasser & A. D. Kanner (Eds.). *Psychology and consumer culture: The struggle for a good life in a materialistic world*. Washington, DC: American Psychological Association.

Solberg, E. C., Diener, E., Wirtz, D., Lucas, R. E., & Oishi, S. (2002). Wanting, having, and satisfaction: Examining the role of desire discrepancies in satisfaction with income. *Journal of Personality and Social Psychology, 83*(3), 725–734.

Solomon, D. A., Keller, M. B., Leon, A. C., Mueller, T. I., Shea, M. T., Warshaw, M., Maser, J. D., Coryell, W., & Endicott, J. (1997). Recovery from major depression: A 10-year prospective follow-up across multiple episodes. *Archives of General Psychiatry, 54*, 1001–1006.

Solomon, S. E., Rothblum, E. D., & Balsam, K. F. (2004). Pioneers in partnership: Lesbian and gay male couples in civil unions compared with those not in civil unions and married heterosexual siblings. *Journal of Family Psychology, 18*(2), 275–286.

Solomon, S., Greenberg, J., & Pyszczynski, T. (1991). A terror management theory of social behavior: The psychological functions of self-esteem and cultural worldviews. In M. Zanna (Ed.), *Advances in experimental social psychology* (Vol. 24). Orlando, FL: Academic Press.

Solomon, S., Greenberg, J. L., & Pyszczynski, T. A. (2004). Lethal consumption: Death-denying materialism. In T. Kasser & A. D. Kanner (Eds.), *Psychology and consumer culture: The struggle for a good life in a materialistic world*. Washington, DC: American Psychological Association.

Solowij, N., Stephens, R. S., Roffman, R. A., Babor, T., Kadden, R., Miller, M., Christiansen. K., McRee, B., & Vendetti, J. (2002). Cognitive functioning of long-term heavy cannabis users seeking treatment. *Journal of the American Medical Association, 287*, 1123–1131.

Sommers-Flanagan, R., Sommers-Flanagan, J., & Davis, B. (1993). What's happening on music television? A gender-role content analysis. *Sex Roles, 28*, 745–753.

Sonnentag, S., & Frese, M. (2003). Stress in organizations. In W. C. Borman , D. R. Ilgen, & R. J. Klimoski (Eds.), *Handbook of psychology: Vol. 12. Industrial and organizational psychology*. New York: Wiley.

Sonstroem, R. J. (1997). Physical activity and self-esteem. In W. P. Morgan (Ed.), *Physical activity and mental health*. Washington, DC: Taylor & Francis.

Sorensen, J. L., Haug, N. A., & Batki, S. L. (2005). Psychosocial issues of HIV/AIDS among drug users in treatment. In J. H. Lowinson, P. Ruiz, R. B. Millman, & J. G. Langrod (Eds.), *Substance abuse: A comprehensive textbook*. Philadelphia: Lippincott/Williams & Wilkins.

Sotiriou, P. E. (2002). *Integrating college study skills: Reasoning in reading, listening, and writing.* Belmont, CA: Wadsworth.

South, S. J. (1991). Sociodemographic differentials in mate selection preferences. *Journal of Marriage and the Family, 53* 928–940.

South, S. J. (1993). Racial and ethnic differences in the desire to marry. *Journal of Marriage and the Family, 55,* 357–370.

South, S. J., Bose, S., & Trent, K. (2004). Anticipating divorce: Spousal agreement, predictive accuracy, and effects on labor supply and fertility. *Journal of Divorce and Remarriage, 40*(3–4), 1–22.

South, S. J., & Lloyd, K. M. (1995). Spousal alternatives and marital dissolution. *American Sociological Review, 60,* 21–35.

Sowell, T. (1994). *Race and culture: A world view.* New York: Basic Books.

Spanos, N. P. (1994). Multiple identity enactments and multiple personality disorder: A sociocognitive perspective. *Psychological Bulletin, 116,* 143–165.

Spanos, N. P. (1996). *Multiple identities and false memories.* Washington, DC: American Psychological Association.

Spector, I., & Carey, M. (1990). Incidence and prevalence of the sexual dysfunctions: A critical review of the empirical literature. *Archives of Sexual Behavior, 19,* 389–408.

Spence, J. T. (1983). Comment on Lubinski, Tellegen, and Butcher's "Masculinity, femininity, and androgyny viewed and assessed as distinct concepts." *Journal of Personality and Social Psychology, 44,* 440–446.

Spence, J. T., & Buckner, C. E. (2000). Instrumental and expressive traits, trait stereotypes, and sexist attitudes. *Psychology of Women Quarterly, 24,* 44–62.

Spence, J. T., & Robbins, A. S. (1992). Workaholism: Definition, measurement, and preliminary results. *Journal of Personality Assessment, 58,* 160–178.

Sperry, R. W. (1982). Some effects of disconnecting the cerebral hemispheres. *Science, 217,* 1223–1226, 1250.

Spiegel, D., Bloom, J. R., Kraemer, H. C., & Gottheil, E. (1989). Psychological support for cancer patients. *Lancet, 2,* 1447.

Spiegler, M. D., & Guevremont, D. C. (1998). *Contemporary behavior therapy.* Pacific Grove, CA: Brooks/Cole.

Spitzberg, B. H. (1999). An analysis of empirical estimates of sexual aggression victimization and perpetration. *Violence and Victims, 14*(3), 241–260.

Spokane, A. R., & Cruza-Guet, M. C. (2005). Holland's theory of vocational personalities in work environments. In S. D. Brown & R. W. Lent (Eds.), *Career development and counseling: Putting theory and research to work.* New York: Wiley.

Sprecher, S. (1994). Two sides to the breakup of dating relationships. *Personal Relationships, 1,* 199–222.

Sprecher, S. (2002). Sexual satisfaction in premarital relationships: Associations with satisfaction, love, commitment, and stability. *The Journal of Sex Research, 39*(3), 190–196.

Sprecher, S., & Cate, R. M. (2004). Sexual satisfaction and sexual expression as predictors of relationship satisfaction and stability. In J. H. Harvey, A. Wenzel, & S. Sprecher (Eds.), *The handbook of sexuality and close relationships.* Mahwah, NJ: Lawrence Erlbaum.

Sprecher, S., & Duck, S. (1994). Sweet talk: The importance of perceived communication for romantic and friendship attraction experienced during a get-acquainted date. *Personality and Social Psychology Bulletin, 20*(4), 391–400.

Sprecher, S., & Regan, P. C. (1998). Passionate and companionate love in courting and young married couples. *Sociological Inquiry, 68*(2), 163–185.

Sprecher, S., Sullivan, Q., & Hatfield, E. (1994). Mate selection preferences: Gender differences examined in a national sample. *Journal of Personality and Social Psychology, 66,* 1074–1080.

Springen, K. (2004, November 1). Under the knife. *Newsweek,* pp. 59–60.

Springer, S. P., & Deutsch, G. (1998). *Left brain, right brain.* New York: Freeman.

Stack, S. (1998). Marriage, family and loneliness: A cross-national study. *Sociological Perspectives, 41,* 415–432.

Stack, S., & Eshleman, J. R. (1998). Marital status and happiness: A 17-nation study. *Journal of Marriage and the Family, 60,* 527–536.

Stafford, L., & Canary, D. J. (1991). Maintenance strategies and romantic relationship type, gender and relational characteristics. *Journal of Social and Personal Relationships, 8,* 217–242.

Stajkovic, A. D., & Luthans, F. (1998). Self-efficacy and work-related performance: A meta-analysis. *Psychological Bulletin, 124*(2), 240–261.

Stamler, J., Daviglus, M. L., Garside, D. B., Dyer, A. R., Greenland, P., & Neaton, J. D. (2000). Relationship of baseline serum cholesterol levels in 3 large cohorts of younger men to long-term coronary, cardiovascular, and all-cause mortality and to longevity. *Journal of the American Medical Association, 284,* 311–318.

Stanford, E. P., Happersett, C. J., Morton, D. J., Molgaard, C. A., & Peddecord, K. M. (1991). Early retirement and functional impairment from a multi-ethnic perspective. *Research on Aging, 13,* 5–38.

Stanton, A. L., Lobel, M., Sears, S. , & DeLuca, R. S. (2002). Psychosocial aspects of selected issues in women's reproductive health: Current status and future directions. *Journal of Consulting & Clinical Psychology, 70*(3), 751–770.

Starcevic, V. (2001). Clinical features and diagnosis of hypochondriasis. In V. Starcevic & D. R. Lipsitt (Eds.), *Hypochondriasis: Modern perspectives on an ancient malady.* New York: Oxford University Press.

Starker, S. (1990). Self-help books: Ubiquitous agents of health care. *Medical Psychotherapy: An International Journal, 3* 187–194.

Starker, S. (1992). Characteristics of self-help book readers among VA medical outpatients. *Medical Psychotherapy: An International Journal, 5,* 89–93.

Starrels, M. E., Ingersoll-Dayton, B., Dowler, D. W., & Neal, M. B. (1997). The stress of caring for a parent: Effects of the elder's impairment on an employed adult child. *Journal of Marriage and the Family, 59,* 860–872.

Statt, D. A. (1994). *Psychology and the world of work.* New York: New York University Press.

Stattin, H., & Magnusson, D. (1990). *Pubertal maturation in female development.* Hillsdale, NJ: Erlbaum.

Steele, C. M. (1997). A threat in the air: How stereotypes shape intellectual identity and performance. *American Psychologist, 52,* 613–629.

Steiger, H., Bruce, K. R., & Israël, M. (2003). Eating disorders. In G. Stricker & T. A. Widiger (Eds.), *Handbook of psychology: Vol. 8. Clinical psychology.* New York: Wiley.

Steiger, H., & Seguin, J. R. (1999). Eating disorders: Anorexia nervosa and bulimia nervosa. In T. Millon, P. H. Blaney, & R. D. Davis (Eds.), *Oxford textbook of psychopathology* (pp. 365–389). New York: Oxford University Press.

Stein, M. B., Forde, D. R., Anderson, G., & Walker, J. R. (1997a). Obsessive-compulsive disorder in the community: An epidemiologic survey with clinical reappraisal. *American Journal of Psychiatry, 154,* 1120–1126.

Stein, M. B., Walker, J. R., Hazen, A. L., & Forde, D. R. (1997b). Full and partial posttraumatic stress disorder: Findings from a community survey. *American Journal of Psychiatry, 154,* 1114–1119.

Stein, N., Marshall, N. L., & Tropp, L. R. (1993). *Secrets in public: Sexual harassment in our schools.* Wellesley, MA: Center for Research on Women at Wellesley College and the NOW Legal Defense and Education Fund.

Stein, P. J. (1975). Singlehood: An alternative to marriage. *Family Coordinator, 24,* 489–503.

Stein, P. J. (1976). *Single.* Englewood Cliffs, NJ: Prentice-Hall.

Stein, R. J., O'Byrne, K. K., Suminski, R. R., & Haddock, C. K. (1999). Etiology and treatment of obesity in adults and children: Implications for the addiction model. *Drugs and Society, 15*(1–2), 103–121.

Steinberg, L. (2001). We know some things: Parent-adolescent relationships in retrospect and prospect. *Journal of Research on Adolescence, 11*(1), 1–19.

Steinberg, L. (2004). *The ten basic principles of good parenting.* New York: Simon & Schuster.

Steinberg, L., & Levine, A. (1997). *You and your adolescent: A parents' guide for ages 10 to 20.* New York: Harper Perennial.

Steiner, H., Smith, C., Rosenkranz, R. T., & Litt, I. (1991). The early care and feeding of anorexics. *Child Psychiatry and Human Development, 21,* 163–167.

Steiner-Pappalardo, N. L., & Gurung, R. A. R. (2002). The femininity effect: Relationship quality, sex, gender, attachment, and significant-other concepts. *Personal Relationships, 9*(3), 313–325.

Steinhausen, H. (2002). The outcome of anorexia nervosa in the 20th century. *American Journal of Psychiatry, 159,* 1284–1293.

Steinmetz, H., Staiger, J. F., Schluag, G., Huang, Y., & Jancke, L. (1995). Corpus callosum and brain volume in women and men. *Neuroreport, 3,* 1002–1004.

Stephens, R. S. (1999). Cannabis and hallucinogens. In B. S. McCrady, & E. E. Epstein (Eds.), *Addictions: A comprehensive guidebook.* New York: Oxford University Press.

Sternberg, R. J. (1986). A triangular theory of love. *Psychological Review, 93* 119–135.

Sternberg, R. J. (1988). Triangulating love. In R. J. Sternberg & M. L. Barnes (Eds.), *The psychology of love.* New Haven, CT: Yale University Press.

Stevens, G., Owens, D., & Schaefer, E. C. (1990). Education and attractiveness in marriage choices. *Social Psychology Quarterly, 53* 62–70.

Stewart, A. J., & Ostrove, J. M. (1998). Women's personality in middle age: Gender, history, and midcourse corrections. *American Psychologist, 53,* 1185–1194.

Stewart, A., Ostrove, J. M., & Helson, R. (2001). Middle aging in women: Patterns of personality change from the 30's to the 50's. *Journal of Adult Development, 8*(1), 23–37.

Stewart, F. H., Ellertson, C., & Cates, W. Jr. (2004). Abortion. In R. A. Hatcher, J. Trussell, F. H. Stewart, A. L. Nelson, W. Cates Jr., F. Guest, & D. Kowal (Eds.), *Contraceptive technology* (18th rev. ed.). New York: Ardent Media.

Stice, E. (2001). Risk factors for eating pathology: Recent advances and future directions. In R. H. Striegel-Moore & L. Smolak (Eds.), *Eating disorders: Innovative directions in research and practice* (pp. 51–74). Washington, DC: American Psychological Association.

Stillion, J. M. (1995). Death in the lives of adults: Responding to the tolling of the bell. in H. Wass & R. A. Neimeyer (Eds.), *Dying: Facing the facts.* New York: Taylor & Francis.

Stith, S. M., Rosen, K. H., Middleton, K. A., Busch, A. L., Lundeberg, K., & Carlton, R. P. (2000). The intergenerational transmission of spouse abuse: A meta-analysis. *Journal of Marriage and the Family, 62,* 640–654.

Stith, S. M., Smith, D. B., Penn, C. E., Ward, D. B., & Tritt, D. (2004). Intimate partner physical abuse perpetration and victimization risk factors: A meta-analytic review. *Aggression and Violent Behavior, 10,* 65–98.

Stoffer, G. R., Davis, K. E., & Brown, J. B., Jr. (1977). The consequences of changing initial answers on objective tests: A stable effect and a stable misconception. *Journal of Educational Research, 70,* 272–277.

Stone, A. A. (1999). Psychiatry and the law. In A. M. Nicholi (Ed.), *The Harvard guide to psychiatry.* Cambridge, MA: Harvard University Press.

Stone, L. (1977). *The family, sex and marriage in England 1500–1800.* New York: Harper & Row.

Stone, W. N. (2003). Group psychotherapy. In A. Tasman, J. Kay, & J. A. Lieberman (Eds.), *Psychiatry.* New York: Wiley.

Stoney, C. M. (2003). Gender and cardiovascular disease: A psychobiological and integrative approach. *Current Directions in Psychological Science, 12*(4), 129–133.

Stoolmiller, M. (1999). Implications of the restricted range of family environments for estimates of heritability and nonshared environment in behavior-genetic adoption studies. *Psychological Bulletin, 125,* 392–409.

Strauman, T. J., Vookles, J., Berenstein, V., Chaiken, S., & Higgins, E. T. (1991). Self-discrepancies and vulnerability to body dissatisfaction and disordered eating. *Journal of Personality and Social Psychology, 61,* 946–956.

Strickland, C. J. (1997). Suicide among American Indian, Alaskan Native, and Canadian Aboriginal youth: Advancing the research agenda. *International Journal of Mental Health, 25,* 11–32.

Striegel-Moore, R. H., McMahon, R. P., Biro, F. M., Schreiber, G., Crawford, P. B., & Voorhees, C. (2001). Exploring the relationship between timing of menarche and eating disorder symptoms in black and white adolescent girls. *International Journal of Eating Disorders, 30*(4), 421–433.

Striegel-Moore, R. H., Silberstein, L. R., & Rodin, J. (1993). The social self in bulimia nervosa: Public self-consciousness, social anxiety, and perceived fraudulence. *Journal of Abnormal Psychology, 102,* 297–303.

Striegel-Moore, R. H., & Smolak, L. (2001). Introduction. In R. H. Striegel-Moore & L. Smolak (Eds.), *Eating disorders: Innovative directions in research and practice* (pp. 3–8). Washington, DC: American Psychological Association.

Strober, M. (1995). Family-genetic perspectives on anorexia nervosa and bulimia nervosa. In K. D. Brownell & C. G. Fairburn (Eds.), *Eating disorders and obesity: A comprehensive handbook.* New York: Guilford Press.

Stroebe, W., Stroebe, M., Abakoumkin, G., & Schut, H. (1996). The role of loneliness and social support in adjustment to loss: A test of attachment versus stress theory. *Journal of Personality and Social Psychology, 70*(6), 1241–1249.

Stroh, L. K., Brett, J. M., & Reilly, A. H. (1996). Family structure, glass ceiling, and traditional explanations for the differential rate of turnover of female and male managers. *Journal of Vocational Behavior, 49,* 99–118.

Strupp, H. H. (1996). The tripartite model and the *Consumer Reports* study. *American Psychologist, 51,* 1017–1024.

Stuart, P. (1992). Murder on the job. *Personnel Journal, 71,* 72–84.

Stunkard, A. J., Harris, J. R., Pederson, N. L., & McClearn, G. E. (1990). The body-mass index of twins who have been reared apart. *New England Journal of Medicine, 322,* 1483–1487.

Stunkard, A. J., Sorensen, T., Hanis, C., Teasdale, T. W., Chakraborty, R., Schull, W. J., & Schulsinger, F. (1986). An adoption study of human obesity. *New England Journal of Medicine, 314,* 193–198.

Suarez, E. C. (2004). C-reactive protein is associated with psychological risk factors of cardiovascular disease in apparently healthy adults. *Psychosomatic Medicine, 66*(5), 684–691.

Suarez, E. C., Kuhn, C. M., Schanberg, S. M., Williams, R. B., Jr., & Zimmermann, E. A. (1998). Neuroendocrine, cardiovascular, and emotional responses of hostile men: The role of interpersonal challenge. *Psychosomatic Medicine, 60*(1), 78–88.

Suarez-Orozco, C., & Suarez-Orozco, M. M. (1995). *Transformation: Immigration, family life, and achievement motivation among Latino adolescents.* Stanford, CA: Stanford University Press.

Sue, D. (1979). Erotic fantasies of college students during coitus. *Journal of Sex Research, 15,* 299–305.

Sue, S., & Zane, N. (1987). The role of culture and cultural techniques in psychotherapy: A critique and reformulation. *American Psychologist, 42,* 37–45.

Sue, S., Zane, N., & Young, K. (1994). Research on psychotherapy with culturally diverse populations. In A. E. Bergin & S. L. Garfield (Eds.), *Handbook of psychotherapy and behavior change* (4th ed., pp. 783–817). New York: John Wiley.

Suinn, R. M. (1984). *Fundamentals of abnormal psychology.* Chicago: Nelson-Hall.

Sullivan, A. (2004, July 26). If at first you don't succeed . . . *Time,* p. 78.

Sullivan, G. M., & Coplan, J. D. (2000). Anxiety disorders: Biochemical aspects. In B. J. Sadock & V. A. Sadock (Eds.), *Kaplan and Sadock's comprehensive textbook of psychiatry,* (7th ed., Vol. 1). Philadelphia: Lippincott/Williams & Wilkins.

Sullivan, P. F. (2002). Course and outcome of anorexia nervosa and bulimia nervosa. In C. G. Fairburn & K. D. Brownell (Eds.), *Eating disorders and obesity: A comprehensive handbook.* New York: Guilford.

Sullivan, P. F., Neale, M. C., & Kendler, K. S. (2000). Genetic epidemiology of major depression: Review and meta-analysis. *American Journal of Psychiatry, 157,* 1552–1562.

Sulloway, F. J. (1991). Reassessing Freud's case histories: The social construction of psychoanalysis. *ISIS, 82,* 245–275.

Sulloway, F. J. (1995). Birth order and evolutionary psychology: A meta-analytic overview. *Psychological Inquiry, 6,* 75–80.

Sulloway, F. J. (1996). *Born to rebel: Birth order, family dynamics, and creative lives.* New York: Pantheon Books.

Suls, J., & Rothman, A. (2004). Evolution of the biopsychosocial model: Prospects and challenges for health psychology. *Health Psychology, 23*(2), 119–125.

Super, D. E. (1957). *The psychology of careers.* New York: HarperCollins.

Super, D. E. (1985). Career and life development. In D. Brown & L. Brooks (Eds.), *Career choice and development.* San Francisco: Jossey-Bass.

Super, D. E. (1988). Vocational adjustment: Implementing a self-concept. *The Career Development Quarterly, 36,* 351–357.

Surra, C. A. (1990). Research and theory on mate selection and premarital relationships in the 1980s. *Journal of Marriage and the Family, 52,* 844–865.

Susman, E. J., Dorn, L. D., & Schiefelbein, V. L. (2003). Puberty, sexuality, and health. In R. M. Lerner, M.A. Easterbrooks, & J. Mistry (Eds.), *Handbook of psychology: Vol. 6. Developmental psychology.* New York: Wiley.

Susser, E., Neugebauer, R., Hoek, H. W., Brown, A. S., Lin, S., Labovitz, D., & Gorman, J. M. (1996). Schizophrenia after prenatal famine: Further evidence. *Archives of General Psychiatry, 53,* 25–31.

Sutherland, V. J. (2000). Understimulation/boredom. In G. Fink (Ed.), *Encyclopedia of stress* (Vol. 3, pp. 634–636). San Diego: Academic Press.

Swain, S. (1989). Covert intimacy: Closeness in men's friendships. In B. J. Risman & P. Schwartz (Eds.), *Gender in intimate relationships* (pp. 71–86). Belmont, CA: Wadsworth.

Swan, G. E., Hudmon, K. S., & Khroyan, T. V. (2003). Tobacco dependence. In A. M. Nezu, C. M. Nezu , & P. A. Geller (Eds.), *Handbook of psychology: Vol. 9. Health psychology.* New York: Wiley.

Swann, W. B., Rentfrow, P. J., & Guinn, J. S. (2003). Self-verification: The search for coherence.

In M. R. Leary & J. P. Tangney (Eds.), *Handbook of self and identity.* New York: Guilford.

Swann, W. B., Stein-Seroussi, A., & Giesler, R. B. (1992). Why people self-verify. *Journal of Personality and Social Psychology, 62,* 392–401.

Swann, W. B., Jr., & Ely, R. J. (1984). A battle of wills: Self-verification versus behavioral confirmation. *Journal of Personality and Social Psychology, 46,* 1287–1302.

Swann, W. B., Jr., Stein-Seroussi, A., & McNulty, S. E. (1992). Outcasts in a white-lie society: The enigmatic worlds of people with negative self-conceptions. *Journal of Personality and Social Psychology, 62,* 618–624.

Swanson, J. L., & D'Achiardi, C. (2005). Beyond interests, needs/values, and abilities: Assessing other important career constructs over the life span. In S. D. Brown & R. W. Lent (Eds.), *Career development and counseling: Putting theory and research to work.* New York: Wiley.

Swap, W. C. (1977). Interpersonal attraction and repeated exposure to rewarders and punishers. *Personality and Social Psychology Bulletin, 3,* 248–251.

Swim, J. K., Aikin, K. J., Hall, W. S., & Hunter, B. A. (1995). Sexism and racism: Old-fashioned and modern prejudices. *Journal of Personality and Social Psychology, 68,* 199–214.

Swoboda, F. (1995, November 25). Law, education failing to break glass ceiling. *Washington Post,* C1, C2.

Sygnatur, E. F., & Toscano, G. A. (2000, Spring). Work-related homicides: The facts. *Compensation and Working Conditions,* 3–8.

Szasz, T. S. (1974). *The myth of mental illness.* New York: HarperCollins.

Szasz, T. S. (1993). *A lexicon of lunacy: Metaphoric malady, moral responsibility, and psychiatry.* New Brunswick, NJ: Transaction.

Szmukler, G. I., & Patton, G. (1995). Sociocultural models of eating disorders. In G. Szmukler, C. Dare, & J. Treasure (Eds.), *Handbook of eating disorders: Theory, treatment and research.* New York: Wiley.

Tajfel, H. (1982). *Social identity and intergroup relations.* London: Cambridge University Press.

Takanishi, R. (1993). The opportunities of adolescence—Research, interventions, and policy. *American Psychologist, 48,* 85–87.

Takeuchi, D. T., Uehara, E., & Maramba, G. (1999). Cultural diversity and mental health treatment. In A. V. Horwitz & T. L. Scheid (Eds.), *A handbook for the study of mental health.* New York: Cambridge University Press.

Tamminga, C. A. (1999). Principles of the pharmacotherapy of schizophrenia. In D. S. Charney, E. J. Nestler & B. S. Bunney (Eds.), *Neurobiology of mental illness* (pp. 272–290). New York: Oxford University Press.

Tamminga, C. A., & Carlsson, A. (2003). Psychiatric pathophysiology: Schizophrenia. In A. Tasman, J. Kay, & J. A. Lieberman (Eds.), *Psychiatry.* New York: Wiley.

Tang, M. (2002). A comparison of Asian American, Caucasian American, and Chinese college students: An initial report. *Journal of Multicultural Counseling and Development, 30*(2), 124–134.

Tannen, D. (1990). *You just don't understand: Women and men in conversation.* New York: Ballantine.

Tannen, D. (1998). *The argument culture: Moving from debate to dialogue.* New York: Random House.

Tanner, J. M. (1990). *Fetus into man: Physical growth from conception to maturity.* Cambridge, MA: Harvard University Press.

Tardiff, K., Marzuk, P. M., & Leon, A. C. (2002). Role of anitdepressants in murder and suicide. *American Journal of Psychiatry, 159,* 1248–1249.

Tavris, C. (1982). *Anger: The misunderstood emotion.* New York: Simon & Schuster.

Tavris, C. (1989). *Anger: The misunderstood emotion* (2nd ed.). New York: Simon & Schuster.

Tavris, C., & Sadd, S. (1977). *The Redbook report on female sexuality.* New York: Delacorte.

Taylor, D. A., & Altman, I. (1987). Communication in interpersonal relationships: Social penetration processes. In M. E. Roloff & G. R. Miller (Eds.), *Interpersonal processes: New directions in communication research.* Newbury Park, CA: Sage.

Taylor, E. (2001). Positive psychology and humanistic psychology: A reply to Seligman. *Journal of Humanistic Psychology, 41*(1), 13–29.

Taylor, R. J., Chatters, L. M., Tucker, M. B., & Lewis, E. (1990). Developments in research on black families: A decade review. *Journal of Marriage and the Family, 52,* 993–1014.

Taylor, S. E. (1981a). A categorization approach to stereotyping. In D. H. Hamilton (Ed.), *Cognitive processes in stereotyping and intergroup relations* (pp. 418–429). Hillsdale, NJ: Erlbaum.

Taylor, S. E. (1981b). The interface of cognitive and social psychology. In J. Harvey (Ed.), *Cognition, social behavior, and the environment* (pp. 189–211). Hillsdale, NJ: Erlbaum.

Taylor, S. E., & Brown, J. D. (1988). Illusion and well-being: A social psychological perspective on mental health. *Psychological Bulletin, 103,* 193–210.

Taylor, S. E., & Brown, J. D. (1994). Positive illusions and well-being revisited: Separating fact from fiction. *Psychological Bulletin, 116,* 21–27.

Taylor, S. E., Klein, L. C., Lewis, B. P., Gruenewald, T. L., Gurung, R. A. R., & Updegraff, J. A. (2000). Biobehavioral responses to stress in females: Tend-and-befriend, not fight-or-flight. *Psychological Review, 107*(3), 411–429.

Taylor, S. E., Lerner, J. S., Sherman, D. K., Sage, R. M., & McDowell, N. K. (2003). Are self-enhancing cognitions associated with healthy or unhealthy biological profiles? *Journal of Personality and Social Psychology, 85*(4), 605–615.

Teachman, J. (2003). Premarital sex, premarital cohabitation, and the risk of subsequent marital dissolution among women. *Journal of Marriage and Family, 65,* 444–445.

Teachman, J. D., Polonko, K. A., & Scanzoni, J. (1999). Demography and families. In M. B. Sussman, S. K. Steinmetz & G. W. Peterson (Eds.), *Handbook of marriage and the family* (pp. 39–76). New York: Plenum.

Teachman, J. D., Tedrow, L. M., & Crowder, K. D. (2001). The changing demography of America's families. In R. M. Milardo (Ed.), *Understanding families into the new millennium: A decade in review* (pp. 453–465). Minneapolis: National Council on Family Relations.

Tedeschi, R. G., Park, C. L., & Calhoun, L. G. (1998). Posttraumatic growth: Conceptual issues. In R. G. Tedeschi, C. L. Park, & L. G. Calhoun (Eds.), *Posttraumatic growth: Positive changes in the aftermath of crisis* (pp. 1–22). Mahwah, NJ: Erlbaum.

Tellegen, A., Lykken, D. T., Bouchard, T. J., Jr., Wilcox, K. J., Segal, N. L., & Rich, S. (1988). Personality similarity in twins reared apart and together. *Journal of Personality and Social Psychology, 54,* 1031–1039.

Temoshok, L. (1987). Personality, coping style, emotion and cancer: Towards an integrative model. *Cancer Surveys, 6,* 545–567.

Tennen, H., & Affleck, G. (1999). Finding benefits in adversity. In C. R. Snyder (Ed.), *Coping: The psychology of what works* (pp. 279–304). New York: Oxford University Press.

Tennen, H., & Affleck, G. (2002). Benefit-finding and benefit-reminding. In C. R. Synder & S. J. Lopez (Eds.), *Handbook of positive psychology.* New York: Oxford University Press.

Tesch, S. A., & Whitbourne, S. K. (1982). Intimacy and identity status in young adults. *Journal of Personality and Social Psychology, 43,* 1041–1051.

Tesser, A. (2001). Self-esteem. In A. Tesser & N. Schwarz (Eds.), *Blackwell handbook of social psychology: Intraindividual processes.* Malden, MA: Blackwell.

Testa, K. (1996). Church to pay $1 million in false-memory case. *San Jose Mercury News,* 8A.

Thase, M. E., Jindal, R., & Howland, R. H. (2002). Biological aspects of depression. In I. H. Gotlib & C. L. Hammen (Eds.), *Handbook of depression.* New York: Guilford.

Theisen, T. (2002, March 17). Too many are lying to get the job. *Atlanta Journal-Constitution,* p. R5.

Thibaut, J. W., & Kelley, H. H. (1959). *The social psychology of groups.* New York: Wiley.

Thomas, A. J., Kalaria, R. N., & O'Brien, J. T. (2004). Depression and vascular disease: What is the relationship? *Journal of Affective Disorders, 79*(1–3), 81–95.

Thomas, K. M. (2005). *Diversity dynamics in the workplace.* Belmont, CA: Wadsworth.

Thomas, M. (2000). Abstinence-based programs for prevention of adolescent pregnancies. *Journal of Adolescents Health, 26,* 5–17.

Thompson, J. K., & Stice, E. (2001). Thin-ideal internalization: Mounting evidence for a new risk factor for body-image disturbance and eating pathology. *Current Directions in Psychological Science, 10*(5), 181–183.

Thompson, T. L., & Zerbinos, E. (1995). Gender roles in animated cartoons: Has the picture changed in 20 years? *Sex Roles, 32,* 651–673.

Thorndyke, P. W., & Hayes-Roth, B. (1979). The use of schemata in the acquisition and transfer of knowledge. *Cognitive Psychology, 11,* 83–106.

Thornton, A., & Young-DeMarco, L. (2001). Four decades of trends in attitudes toward family issues in the United States: The 1960s through the 1990s. *Journal of Marriage and Family, 63,* 1009–1037.

Thorson, J. A., & Powell, F. C. (2000). Death anxiety in younger and older adults. In A. Tomer (Ed.), *Death attitudes and the older adult: Theories, concepts, and applications.* Philadelphia: Brunner-Routledge.

Thune, I., & Furberg, A. (2001). Physical activity and cancer risk: Dose-response and cancer, all sites and site specific. *Medicine and Science in Sports and Exercise, 33*(6), S530–S550.

Tice, D. M. (1991). Esteem protection or enhancement? Self-handicapping motives and attributions differ by trait self-esteem. *Journal of Personality and Social Psychology, 5,* 711–725.

Tice, D. M., & Baumeister, R. F. (1997). Longitudinal study of procrastination, performance, stress, and health: The cost and benefits of dawdling. *Psychological Science, 8,* 454–458.

Tice, D. M., Bratslavsky, E., & Baumeister, R. F. (2001). Emotional distress regulation takes precedence over impulse control: If you feel bad, do it! *Journal of Personality and Social Psychology, 80*(1), 53–67.

Tice, D. M., Butler, J. L., Muraven M. B., & Stillwell A. M. (1995). When modesty prevails: Differential favorability of self-presentation to friends and strangers. *Journal of Personality and Social Psychology, 69,* 1120–1138.

Tice, D. M., & Wallace, H. M. (2003). The reflected self: Creating yourself as (you think) others see you. In M. R. Leary & J. P. Tangney (Eds.), *Handbook of self and identity.* New York: Guilford.

Tigner, R. B. (1999). Putting memory research to good use: Hints from cognitive psychology. *College Teaching, 47*(4), 149–151.

Ting-Toomey, S. (2000). Managing intercultural conflicts effectively. In L. A. Samovar & R. E. Porter (Eds.), *Intercultural communications: A reader* (9th ed., pp. 388–399). Belmont, CA: Wadsworth.

Tjaden, P., & Thoennes, N. (2000). Prevalence and consequences of male-to-female and female-to-male intimate partner violence as measured by the National Violence Against Women Survey. *Violence Against Women, 6,* 142–161.

Tobin-Richards, M. H., Boxer, A. M., & Petersen, A. C. (1983). The psychological significance of pubertal change: Sex differences in perceptions of self during early adolescence. In J. Brooks-Gunn & A. C. Petersen (Eds.), *Girls at puberty: Biological and psychosocial perspectives.* New York: Plenum.

Toffler, A. (1970). *Future shock.* New York: Random House.

Toffler, A. (1980). *The third wave.* New York: Bantam Books.

Tolman, D. L. (2002). *Dilemmas of desire: Teenage girls talk about sexuality.* Cambridge, MA: Harvard University Press.

Toomey, R., Kremen, W. S., Simpson, J. C., Samson, J. A., Seidman, L. J., Lyons, M. J., Faraone, S. V., & Tsuang, M. T. (1997). Revisiting the factor structure for positive and negative symptoms: Evidence for a large heterogeneous group of psychiatric patients. *American Journal of Psychology, 154,* 371–377.

Torrey, E. F. (1992). *Freudian fraud: The malignant effect of Freud's theory on American thought and culture.* New York: Harper Perennial.

Torrey, E. F., Bowler, A. E., Taylor, E. H., & Gottesman, I. I. (1994). *Schizophrenia and manic-depressive disorder.* New York: Basic Books.

Townsend, J. (1995). Sex without emotional involvement: An evolutionary interpretation of sex differences. *Archives of Sexual Behavior, 24,* 173–182.

Trachtenberg, J. D., & Sande, M. A. (2002). Emerging resistance to nonnucleoside reverse transcriptase inhibitors: A warning and a challenge. *Journal of the American Medical Association, 288*(2), 239–241.

Travis, C. B., & Meginnis-Payne, K. L. (2001). Beauty politics and patriarchy: The impact on women's lives. In J. Worrell (Ed.), *Encyclopedia of women and gender.* San Diego: Academic Press.

Travis, F. (2001). Autonomic and EEG patterns distinguish transcending from other experiences during Transcendental Meditation practice. *International Journal of Psychophysiology, 42,* 1–9.

Travis, L. A., Bliwise, N. G., Binder, J. L., & Horne-Moyer, H. L. (2001). Changes in clients' attachment style over the course of time-limited dynamic psychotherapy. *Psychotherapy: Theory, Research, Practice, Training, 38*(2), 149–159.

Treas, J., & Giesen, D. (2000). Sexual infidelity among married and cohabiting Americans. *Journal of Marriage and the Family, 62,* 48–60.

Treas, J., & Lawton, L. (1999). Family relations in adulthood. In M. B. Sussman, S. K. Steinmetz, & G. W. Peterson (Eds.), *Handbook of marriage and the family* (pp. 425–438). New York: Plenum Press.

Triandis, H. C. (1989). Self and social behavior in differing cultural contexts. *Psychological Review, 96,* 269–289.

Triandis, H. C. (1994). *Culture and social behavior.* New York: McGraw-Hill.

Triandis, H. C. (2001). Individualism-collectivism and personality. *Journal of Personality, 69*(6), 907–924.

Trope, Y. (1983). Self-assessment in achievement behavior. In J. Suls & A. Greenwald (Eds.), *Psychological perspectives* (Vol. 2, pp. 93–121). Hillsdale, NJ: Erlbaum.

Trope, Y. (1986). Self-enhancement and self-assessment in achievement behavior. In R. Sorrentino & E. T. Higgins (Eds.), *Handbook of motivation and cognition* (Vol. 2, pp. 350–378). New York: Guilford Press.

Trope, Y., & Gaunt, R. (2003). Attribution and person perception. In M. A. Hogg & J. Cooper (Eds.), *The Sage handbook of social psychology.* Thousand Oaks, CA: Sage Publications.

Trussell, J. (2004). Contraceptive efficacy. In R. A. Hatcher, J. Trussell, F. H. Stewart, A. L. Nelson, W. Cates Jr., F. Guest, & D. Kowal *Contraceptive technology.* New York: Ardent Media.

Trussell, J., Brown, S., & Hogue, C. (2004). Adolescent sexual behavior, pregnancy, and childbearing. In R. A. Hatcher, J. Trussell, F. H. Stewart, A. L. Nelson, W. Cates Jr., F. Guest, & D. Kowal (Eds.), *Contraceptive technology*. New York: Ardent Media.

Trzesniewski, K. H., Donnellan, M. B., & Robins, R. W. (2003). Stability of self-esteem across the life span. *Journal of Personality and Social Psychology, 84*(1), 205–220.

Tsai, M., & Uemera, A. (1988). Asian Americans: The struggles, the conflicts, and the successes. In P. Bronstein & K. Quina (Eds.), *Teaching a psychology of people*. Washington, DC: American Psychological Association.

Tsuang, M. T., Glatt, S. J., & Faraone, S. V. (2003). Genetics and genomics in schizophrenia. *Primary Psychiatry, 10*(3), 37–40, 50.

Tucker, V., & Cho, C. (1991). AIDS and adolescents. *Postgraduate Medicine, 89*, 49–53.

Tugade, M. M., & Fredrickson, B. L. (2004). Resilient individuals use positive emotions to bounce back from negative emotional experiences. *Journal of Personality and Social Psychology, 86*(2), 320–333.

Turkheimer, E., & Waldron, M. (2000). Nonshared environment: A theoretical, methodological, and quantitative review. *Psychological Bulletin, 126*, 78–108.

Turner, J. C. (1987). *Rediscovering the social group: A self-categorization theory*. Oxford, England: Basil Blackwell.

Turner, J. R., & Wheaton, B. (1995). Checklist measurement of stressful life events. In S. Cohen, R. C. Kessler, & L. U. Gordon (Eds.), *Measuring stress: A guide for health and social scientists*. New York: Oxford University Press.

Turner, S. M., Beidel, D. C., Stanley, M. A., & Heiser, N. (2001). Obsessive-compulsive disorder. In P. B. Sutker & H. E. Adams (Eds.), *Comprehensive textbook of psychiatry* (3rd ed., pp. 155–182). New York: Kluwer Academic/Plenum.

Twenge, J. M. (2000). The age of anxiety? Birth cohort change in anxiety and neuroticism, 1952–1993. *Journal of Personality and Social Psychology, 79*(6), 1007–1021.

Twenge, J. M., & Campbell W. K. (2003). Isn't it fun to get the respect that we're going to deserve? Narcissism, social rejection, and aggression. *Personality and Social Psychology, 29*(2), 261–272.

Twenge, J. M., Campbell, W. K., & Foster, C. A. (2003). Parenthood and marital satisfaction: A meta-analytic review. *Journal of Marriage and Family, 65*, 574–83.

Twenge, J. M., & Crocker, J. (2002). Race and self-esteem: Meta-analyses comparing whites, blacks, Hispanics, Asians, and American Indians and comment on Gray-Little and Hafdahl (2000). *Psychological Bulletin, 128*(3), 371–408.

Uchino, B. N., Cacioppo, J. T., & Kiecolt-Glaser, J. K. (1996). The relationship between social support and physiological processes: A review with emphasis on underlying mechanisms and implications for health. *Psychological Bulletin, 119*, 488–531.

Uleman, J. S., Hon, A., Roman, R. J., & Moskowitz, G. B. (1996). Online evidence for spontaneous trait inferences at encoding. *Personality and Psychology Bulletin, 22*(4), 377–394.

Ullman, S. E. (2004). Sexual assault victimization and suicidal behavior in women: A review of the literature. *Aggression and Violent Behavior, 9*(4), 331–351.

Ulrich, M., & Weatherall, A. (2000). Motherhood and infertility: Viewing motherhood through the lens of infertility. *Feminism & Psychology, 10*, 323–336.

Umberson, D., Wortman, C. B., & Kessler, R. C. (1992). Widowhood and depression: Explaining long-term gender differences in vulnerability. *Journal of Health and Social Behavior, 33*, 10–24.

Ursano, R. J., Fullerton, C. S., Vance, K., & Kao, T. C. (1999). Posttraumatic stress disorder and identification in disaster workers. *American Journal of Psychiatry, 156*, 353–359.

Ursano, R. J., & Silberman, E. K. (2003). Psychoanalysis, psychoanalytic psychotherapy, and supportive psychotherapy. In R. E. Hales & S. C. Yudofsky (Eds.), *Textbook of clinical psychiatry*. Washington, DC: American Psychiatric Publishing.

U.S. Bureau of Labor Statistics. (1998). *Occupational outlook handbook: 1998–1999*. Washington, DC: U.S. Government Printing Office.

U.S. Bureau of Labor Statistics. (2003). Highlight of women's earnings in 2002. Retrieved December 12, 2004 from http://www.bls.gov/cps/cpswom2002.pdf.

U.S. Bureau of Labor Statistics. (2004). *Occupational outlook handbook: 2004–2005*. Washington, DC: U.S. Government Printing Office.

U.S. Bureau of the Census. (2000). *Statistical abstract of the United States: 2000*. Washington, DC: U.S. Government Printing Office.

U.S. Bureau of the Census. (2003). *Statistical abstract of the United States: 2003*. Washington, DC: U.S. Government Printing Office.

U.S. Bureau of the Census. (2004a). *Statistical abstract of the United States: 2004–2005*. Washington, DC: U.S. Government Printing Office.

U.S. Bureau of the Census. (2004b). *America's families and living arrangements: 2003*. Washington, DC: U.S. Government Printing Office.

U. S. Department of Health and Human Services. (1990). *The health benefits of smoking cessation: A report of the surgeon general*. Washington, DC: U.S. Government Printing Office.

U. S. Department of Health and Human Services. (1999). *Mental health: A report of the Surgeon General*. Washington, DC: U.S. Government Printing Office.

U. S. Department of Health and Human Services. (2002, June 10). Preventing teenage pregnancy. Retrieved January 30, 2005 From http://www.Hhs.Gov/News/Press/2002pres/Teenpreg.html.

U. S. Department of Health and Human Services. (2003). *Profile of older Americans: 2003*. Washington, DC: U.S. Government Printing Office.

U.S. Department of Justice. (2003). *Crime in the United States— 2003: Uniform crime reports*. Washington, DC: U.S. Government Printing Office.

U. S. Department of Labor. (1992). *Pipelines of progress: An update on the glass ceiling initiative*. Washington, DC: U.S. Government Printing Office.

U. S. Department of Labor. (2000, Summer). Futurework: Trends and challenges for work in the 21st century. *Occupational Outlook Quarterly*, pp. 31–36.

U. S. Department of Labor. (2003). *Facts on women workers*. Washington, DC: U.S. Government Printing Office.

Vaillant, G. E. (2000). Adaptive mental mechanisms: Their role in a positive psychology. *American Psychologist, 55*(1), 89–98.

Valent, P. (2000). Disaster syndrome. In G. Fink (Ed.), *Encyclopedia of stress* (Vol. 1, pp. 706–708). San Diego: Academic Press.

Valian, V. (1998). *Why so slow?: The advancement of women*. Cambridge, MA: MIT Press.

Valleroy, L. A., MacKellar, D. A., Karon, J. M., Rosen, D. H., McFarland, W., Shehan, D. A., Stoyanoff, S. R., LaLota, M., Celentano, D. D., Koblin, B. A., Thiede, H., Katz, M. H., Torian, L. V., & Janssen, R. S. (2000). HIV prevalence and associated risks in young men who have sex with men. *Journal of the American Medical Association, 284*, 198–204.

Vandenberg, S. G. (1987). Sex differences in mental retardation and their implications for sex differences in ability. In J. M. Reinisch, L. A. Rosenblum, & S. A. Sanders (Eds.), *Masculinity/Femininity: Basic perspectives*. New York: Oxford University Press.

Vartanian, L. R., Giant, C. L., & Passino, R. M. (2001). "Ally McBeal vs. Arnold Schwarzenegger":

Comparing mass media, interpersonal feedback and gender as predictors of satisfaction with body thinness and masculinity. *Social Behavior and Personality, 29*(7), 711–723.

Vaughn, B. E., & Bost, K. K. (1999). Attachment and temperament: Redundant, independent, or interacting influences on interpersonal adaptation and personality development? In J. Cassidy & P. R. Shaver (Eds.), *Handbook of attachment: Theory, research, and clinical applications*. New York: Guilford.

Vazire, S., & Gosling, S. D. (2004). e-Perceptions: Personality impressions based on personal websites. *Journal of Personality and Social Psychology, 87*(1), 123–132.

Veenhoven, R. (1993). *Happiness in nations*. Rotterdam, Netherlands: Risbo.

Veevers, J. E., Gee, E. M., & Wister, A. V. (1996). Homeleaving age norms: Conflict or consensus? *International Journal of Aging and Human Development, 43*(4), 277–295.

Vega, W. A., Kolody, B., Aguilar-Gaxiola, S., & Catalano, R. (1999). Gaps in service utilization by Mexican Americans with mental health problems. *American Journal of Psychiatry, 156*, 928–934.

Verderber, K. S., & Verderber, R. F. (2001). *Interact: Interpersonal communication, concepts, skills, and contexts* (9th ed.). Belmont, CA: Wadsworth.

Verderber, R. F., & Verderber, K. S. (2004). *InterAct: Interpersonal communication concepts, skills, and contexts*. New York: Oxford University Press.

Verderber, R. F., & Verderber, K. S. (2005). *Communicate*. Belmont, CA: Wadsworth.

Vernberg, E. M., La Greca, A. M., Silverman, W. K., & Prinstein, M. J. (1996). Prediction of posttraumatic stress symptoms in children after Hurricane Andrew. *Journal of Abnormal Psychology, 105*, 237–248.

Vgontzas, A. N., Bixler, E. O., & Kales, A. K. (2000). Sleep, sleep disorders, and stress. In G. Fink (Ed.), *Encyclopedia of stress* (Vol. 3, p. 449–457). San Diego: Academic Press.

Vinogradov, S., Cox, P. D., & Yalom, I. D. (2003). Group therapy. In R. E. Hales & S. C. Yudofsky (Eds.), *Textbook of clinical psychiatry*. Washington, DC: American Psychiatric Publishing.

Vinokur, A. D., Price, R. H., & Caplan, R. D. (1996). Hard times and hurtful partners: How financial strain affects depression and relationship satisfaction of unemployed persons and their spouses. *Journal of Personality and Social Psychology, 71*, 166–179.

Vittengl, J. R., & Holt, C. S. (2000). Getting acquainted: The relationship of self-disclosure and social attraction to positive affect. *Journal of Social and Personal Relationships, 17*(1), 53–56.

Volavka, J., Czobor, P., Sheitman, B., Lindenmayer, J. P., Citrome, L., McEvoy, J. P., Cooper, T. B., Chakos, M., & Lieberman, J. A. (2002). Clozapine, olanzapine, risperidone, haloperidol in the treatment of patients with chronic schizophrenia and schizoaffective disorder. *American Journal of Psychiatry, 159*, 255–262.

Vollmer, W. M., Sacks, F. M., Ard, J., Appel, L. J., Bray, G. A., Simons-Morton, D. G., & et al. (2001). Effects of diet and sodium intake on blood pressure: Subgroup analysis of the DASH-sodium trial. *Annals of Internal Medicine, 18*, 1019–1028.

Von Baeyer, C. L., Sherk, D. L., & Zanna, M. P. (1981). Impression management in the job interview: When the female applicant meets the male (chauvinist) interviewer. *Personality and Social Psychology Bulletin, 7*, 45–51.

Vorauer, J. D., Cameron, J. J., Holmes, J. G., & Pearce, D. G. (2003). Invisible overtures: Fears of rejection and the signal amplification bias. *Journal of Personality and Social Psychology, 84*(4), 793–812.

Voydanoff, P., & Donnelly, B. W. (1999). Multiple roles and psychological distress: The intersection of the paid worker, spouse, and parent roles with the role of the adult child. *Journal of Marriage and the Family, 61*, 725–738.

Voyer, D., Voyer, S., & Bryden, M. P. (1995). Magnitude of sex differences in spatial abilities: A meta-analysis and consideration of critical variables. *Psychological Bulletin, 117,* 250–270.

Vrugt, A., & Luyerink, M. (2000). The contribution of bodily posture to gender stereotypical impressions. *Social Behavior and Personality, 28*(1), 91–103.

Wachtel, P. L. (1989). *The poverty of affluence: A psychological portrait of the American way of life.* Philadelphia: New Society.

Wade, C., & Tavris, C. (1990). *Learning to think critically: A handbook to accompany psychology.* New York: HarperCollins.

Wade, P., & Bernstein, B. (1991). Culture sensitivity training and counselor's race: Effects on black female clients' perceptions and attrition. *Journal of Counseling Psychology, 38,* 9–15.

Wagner, D. M. (1998, Feb 1). Divorce reform: New directions. *Current,* pp. 7–10.

Waite, L. (2000). Trends in men's and women's well-being in marriage. In L. J. Waite (Ed.), *The ties that bind.* New York: Aldine de Gruyter.

Waite, L., & Gallagher, M. (2000). *The case for marriage: Why married people are happier, healthier, and better off financially.* New York: Doubleday.

Waite, L. J. (1995). Does marriage matter? *Demography, 32,* 483–507.

Wakefield, J. C. (1999). The measurement of mental disorder. In A. V. Horvitz & T. L. Scheid (Eds.), *A handbook for the study of mental health: Social contexts, theories, and systems.* New York: Cambridge University Press.

Waldfogel, J. (1997). The effect of children on women's wages. *American Sociological Review, 62*(2), 209–217.

Waldrop, D., Lightsey, O. R., Ethington, C. A., Woemmel, C. A., & Coke, A. L. (2001). Self-efficacy, optimism, health competence, and recovery from orthopedic surgery. *Journal of Counseling Psychology, 48,* 233–238.

Walker, E. F., Baum, K. M., & Diforio, D. (1998). Developmental changes in behavioral expression and vulnerability for schizophrenia. In M. F. Lenzenweger & R. H. Dworkin (Eds.), *Origins and development of schizophrenia: Advances in experimental psychopathology.* Washington DC: American Psychological Association.

Walker, K. (1994). Men, women, and friendship: What they say, what they do. *Gender & Society, 8,* 246–265.

Walker, L. (1984) *The battered woman.* New York: Springer Publishing.

Walker, L. S., Claar, R. L., & Garber, J. (2002). Social consequences of children's pain: When do they encourage symptoms of maintenance? *Journal of Pediatric Psychology, 27*(8), 689–698.

Wallace, C. J. (1998). Social skills training in psychiatric rehabilitation: Recent findings. *International Review of Psychiatry, 10,* 9–10.

Wallace-Broscious, A., Serafica, F. C., & Osipow, S. H. (1994). Adolescent career development: Relationships to self-concept and identity status. *Journal of Research on Adolescence, 4,* 127–149.

Wallerstein, J. S., & Blakeslee, S. (1989). *Second chances: Men, women, and children a decade after divorce.* Boston: Houghton Mifflin.

Wallerstein, J. S., & Kelly, J. B. (1980). *Surviving the breakup: How children and parents cope with divorce.* New York: Basic Books.

Wallerstein, J. S., Lewis, J. M., & Blakeslee, S. (2000). *The unexpected legacy of divorce: A 25-year landmark study.* New York: Hyperion.

Wallis, C. (2003, December 15). Does kindergarten need cops? *Time,* pp. 52–53.

Wallis, C. (2004, March 22). The case for staying home. *Time,* pp. 51–59.

Walsh, F. (1999). Families in later life: Challenges and opportunities. In B. Carter & M. McGoldrick (Eds.), *The expanded family life cycle: Individual,* *family, and social perspectives* (3rd ed., pp. 307–326). Boston: Allyn & Bacon.

Walster, E., Aronson, E., Abrahams, D., & Rottman, L. (1966). Importance of physical attractiveness in dating behavior. *Journal of Personality and Social Psychology, 4,* 508–516.

Walter, C. A. (2000). The psychosocial meaning of menopause: Women's experiences. *Journal of Women and Aging, 12*(3–4), 117–131.

Walters, E. E., & Kendler, K. S. (1995). Anorexia nervosa and anorexic-like syndromes in a population-based female twin sample. *American Journal of Psychiatry, 152,* 64–71.

Wampold, B. E. (2001). *The great psychotherapy debate.* Mahwah, NJ: Erlbaum.

Wang, H., & Amato, P. R. (2000). Predictors of divorce adjustment: Stressors, resources, and definitions. *Journal of Marriage and the Family, 62,* 655–668.

Warner, L., Hatcher, R. A., & Steiner, M. J. (2004). Male condoms. In R. A. Hatcher, J. Trussell, F. H. Stewart, A. L. Nelson, W. Cates Jr., F. Guest, & D. Kowal (Eds.), *Contraceptive technology* (18th rev. ed.). New York: Ardent Media.

Warr, P. (1999). Well-being and the workplace. In D. Kahneman, E. Diener, & N. Schwarz (Eds.), *Well-being: The foundations of hedonic psychology* (pp. 392–412). New York: Sage.

Waters, E., Merrick, S., Treboux, D., Crowell, J., & Albersheim, L. (2000). Attachment security in infancy and early adulthood: A twenty-year longitudinal study. *Child Development, 71*(3), 684–689.

Watkins, C. E., Campbell, V. L., Nieberding, R., & Hallmark, R. (1995). Contemporary practice of psychological assessment by clinical psychologists. *Professional Psychology: Research and Practice, 26,* 54–60.

Watson, D. C. (2001). Procrastination and the five-factor model: A facet-level analysis. *Personality and Individual Differences, 30*(1), 149–158.

Watson, D., & Clark, L. A. (1997). Extraversion and its positive emotional core. In R. Hogan, J. Johnson, & S. Briggs (Eds), *Handbook of personality psychology.* San Diego: Academic Press.

Watson, D., David, J. P., & Suls, J. (1999). Personality, affectivity, and coping. In C. R. Snyder (Ed.), *Coping: The psychology of what works* (pp. 119–140). New York: Oxford University Press.

Watson, D., & Pennebaker, J. W. (1989). Health complaints, stress, and distress: Exploring the central role of negative affectivity. *Psychological Review, 96,* 234–254.

Watson, D., Suls, J., & Haig, J. (2002). Global self-esteem in relation to structural models of personality and affectivity. *Journal of Personality and Social Psychology, 83,* 185–197.

Watson, D. L., & Tharp, R. G. (2002). *Self-directed behavior: Self-modification for personal adjustment.* Belmont, CA: Wadsworth.

Watson, J. B. (1913). Psychology as the behaviorist views it. *Psychological Review, 20,* 158–177.

Weaver, M. F., & Schnoll, S. H. (1999). Stimulants: Amphetamines and cocaine. In B. S. McCrady & E. E. Epstein (Eds.), *Addictions: A comprehensive guidebook.* New York: Oxford University Press.

Webster, D. M. (1993). Motivated augmentation and reduction of the overattribution bias. *Journal of Personality and Social Psychology, 65,* 261–271.

Webster, D. M., Richter, L., & Kruglanski, A. W. (1996). On leaping to conclusions when feeling tired: Mental fatigue effects on impressional primacy. *Journal of Experimental Social Psychology, 32,* 181–195.

Wechsler, H., Lee, J. E., Kuo, M., Seibring, M., Nelson, T. F., & Lee, H. (2002). Trends in college binge drinking during a period of increased prevention efforts. *Journal of American College Health, 50*(5), 203–217.

Weems, C. F., Hayward, C., Killen, J., & Taylor, C. B. (2002). A longitudinal investigation of anxiety sensitivity in adolescence. *Journal of Abnormal Psychology, 111,* 471–477.

Weil, M. M., & Rosen, L. D. (1997). *TechnoStress: Coping with technology @ home @ work @ play.* New York: Wiley.

Weimer, B. L., Kerns, K. A., & Oldenburg, C. M. (2004). Adolescents' interactions with a best friend: Associations with attachment style. *Journal of Experimental Child Psychology, 88*(1), 102–120.

Weinberg, C. (1979). *Self creation.* New York: Avon.

Weinberger, D. A. (1990). The construct validity of the repressive coping style. In J. L. Singer (Ed.), *Repression and dissociation.* Chicago: University of Chicago Press.

Weinberger, D. A., & Davidson, M. A. (1994). Styles of inhibiting emotional expression: Distinguishing repressive coping from impression management. *Journal of Personality, 62,* 589–611.

Weinberger, J. (1995). Common factors aren't so common: The common factors dilemma. *Clinical Psychology: Science and Practice, 2,* 45–69, 1915–1933.

Weiner, B. (1986). *An attribution theory of emotion and motivation.* New York: Springer-Verlag.

Weiner, B. (1994). Integrating social and personal theories of achievement striving. *Review of Educational Research, 64,* 557–573.

Weiner, B. (Ed.). (1974). *Achievement motivation and attribution theory.* Morristown, NJ: General Learning Press.

Weiner, H. (1992). *Perturbing the organism: The biology of stressful experience.* Chicago: University of Chicago Press.

Weiner, M. F. (1993). Role of the leader in group psychotherapy. In H. I. Kaplan & B.J. Sadock (Eds.), *Comprehensive group psychotherapy.* Baltimore: Williams &Wilkins.

Weinfield, N., Sroufe, L. A., & Egeland, B. (2000). Attachment from early infancy to early adulthood in a high-risk sample: Continuity, discontinuity, and their correlates. *Child Development, 71*(3), 695–702.

Weinstein, N. D. (1980). Unrealistic optimism about future life events. *Journal of Personality and Social Psychology, 39,* 806–820.

Weinstein, N. D. (2003). Exploring the links between risk perceptions and preventive behavior. In J. Suls & K. A. Wallston (Eds.), *Social psychological foundations of health and illness.* Malden, MA: Blackwell Publishing.

Weinstein, N. D., & Klein, W. M. (1996). Unrealistic optimism: Present and future. *Journal of Social and Clinical Psychology, 15*(1), 1–8.

Weisaeth, L. (1993). Disasters: Psychological and psychiatric aspects. In L. Goldberger & S. Breznitz (Eds.), *Handbook of stress: Theoretical and clinical aspects* (2nd ed.). New York: Free Press.

Weiss, R. (1973). *Loneliness: The experience of emotional and social isolation.* Cambridge, MA: MIT Press.

Weiss, R. S. (1975). *Marital separation.* New York: Basic Books.

Weisz, J. R., Rothbaum, F. M., & Blackburn, T. C. (1984). Standing out and standing in: The psychology of control in America and Japan. *American Psychologist, 39,* 955–969.

Weiten, W. (1988). Pressure as a form of stress and its relationship to psychological symptomatology. *Journal of Social and Clinical Psychology, 6,* 127–139.

Weiten, W. (1998). Pressure, major life events, and psychological symptoms. *Journal of Social Behavior and Personality, 13,* 51–68.

Weiten, W., Guadagno, R. E., & Beck, C. A. (1996). Students' perceptions of textbook pedagogical aids. *Teaching of Psychology, 23,* 105–107.

Weitzman, L. (1996). The economic consequences of divorce are still unequal: Comment on Peterson. *American Sociological Review, 61,* 537–538.

Wells, K., Klap, R., Koike, A., & Sherbourne, C. (2001). Ethnic disparities in unmet need for alcoholism, drug abuse, and mental health care. *American Journal of Psychiatry, 158,* 2027–2032.

Wessely, S., & Kerwin, R. (2004). Suicide risk and the SSRI's. *Journal of the American Medical Association, 292*(3), 379–381.

Wesson, D. R., Smith, D. E., Ling, W., & Seymour, R. B. (2005). Sedatives–hypnotics. In J. H. Lowinson, P. Ruiz, R. B. Millman, & J. G. Langrod (Eds.), *Substance abuse: A comprehensive textbook*. Philadelphia: Lippincott/Williams & Wilkins.

West, D. S., Harvey-Berino, J., & Raczynski, J. M. (2004). Behavioral aspects of obesity, dietary intake, and chronic disease. In J. M. Raczynski & L. C. Leviton (Eds.), *Handbook of clinical health psychology: Vol. 2. Disorders of behavior and health*. Washington, DC: American Psychological Association.

Westefeld, J. S., Maples, M. R., Buford, B., & Taylor, S. (2001). Gay, lesbian, and bisexual college students: The relationship between sexual orientation and depression, loneliness and suicide. *Journal of College Student Psychotherapy, 15*(3), 71–82.

Westen, D. (1998). The scientific legacy of Sigmund Freud: Toward a psychodynamically informed psychological science. *Psychological Bulletin, 124*(3), 333–371.

Westen, D., & Gabbard, G. O. (1999). Psychoanalytic approaches to personality. In L. A. Pervin & O. P. John (Eds.), *Handbook of personality: Theory and research* (2nd ed., pp. 57–101). New York: Guilford Press.

Wethington, E. (2000). Life events scale. In G. Fink (Ed.), *Encyclopedia of stress* (Vol. 1, pp. 618–622). San Diego: Academic Press.

Wethington, E., Kessler, R., & Pixley, J. (2004). Turning points in adulthood. In O. G. Brim, C. D. Ryff, & R. Kessler (Eds.), *How healthy are we: A national study of well-being in midlife*. Chicago: University of Chicago Press.

Wheaton, B. (1994). Sampling the stress universe. In W. R. Avison & I. H. Gotlib (Eds.), *Stress and mental health: Contemporary issues and prospects for the future*. New York: Plenum Press.

Wheeler, L., & Kim, Y. (1997). What is beautiful is culturally good: The physical attractiveness stereotype has different content in collectivistic cultures. *Personality and Social Psychology Bulletin, 23*(8), 795–800.

Wheeler, L., Reis, H. T., & Bond, M. H. (1989). Collectivism-individualism in everyday social life: The middle kingdom and the melting pot. *Journal of Personality and Social Psychology, 57*, 79–86.

When you fear someone (n.d.). Retrieved January 10, 2005 from http://www.afsp.org/about/whattodo.htm.

Whiston, S. C., & Keller, B. K. (2004). The influences of the family of origin on career development: A review and analysis. *Counseling Psychologist, 32*(4), 493–568.

Whitaker, D., Miller, K., May, D., & Levin, M. (1999). Teenage partners' communication about sexual risk and condom use: The importance of parent-teenagers discussions. *Family Planning Perspectives, 31*, 117–121.

Whitaker, R. (2002). *Mad in America: Bad science, bad medicine, and the enduring mistreatment of the mentally ill*. New York: Perseus Publishing.

Whitbourne, S. K. (1996). *The aging individual: Physical and psychological perspectives*. New York: Springer.

Whitbourne, S. K. (2001). The physical aging process in midlife: Interactions with psychological and sociocultural factors. In M. E. Lachman (Ed.), *Handbook of midlife development*. New York: Wiley.

Whitbourne, S. K., & Tesch, S. A. (1985). A comparison of identity and intimacy statuses in college students and alumni. *Developmental Psychology, 21*, 1039–1044.

Whitbourne, S. K., Zuschlag, M. K., Elliot, L. B., & Waterman, A. S. (1992). Psychosocial development in adulthood: A 22-year sequential study. *Journal of Personality and Social Psychology, 63*, 260–271.

White, L. (2001). Sibling relationships over the life course: A panel analysis. *Journal of Marriage and the Family, 63*(2), 555–568.

White, L. K., & Edwards, J. N. (1990). Emptying the nest and parental well-being: An analysis of national panel data. *American Sociological Review, 55*(2), 235–242.

White, L. K., & Rogers, S. J. (1997). Strong support but uneasy relationships: Coresident and adult children's relationships with their parents. *Journal of Marriage and the Family, 59*, 62–76.

White, L. K., & Rogers, S. J. (1997). Strong support but uneasy relationships: Coresidence and adult children's relationships with their parents. *Journal of Marriage and the Family, 59*(1), 62–76.

White, L. K., & Rogers, S. J. (2001). Economic circumstances and family outcomes: A review of the 1990s. In R. M. Milardo (Ed.), *Understanding families into the new millennium: A decade in review* (pp. 254–270). Minneapolis: National Council on Family Relations.

Whitehead, B. D., & Popenoe, D. (2001). *The state of our unions: The social health of marriage in America, 2001*. Piscataway, NJ: The National Marriage Project.

Whiteman, S. D., McHale, S. M., & Crouter, A. C. (2003). What parents learn from experience: The first child as a first draft? *Journal of Marriage and Family, 65*, 608–621.

Whitfield, C. L. (1995). *Memory and abuse: Remembering and healing the effects of trauma*. Deerfield Beach, FL: Health Communications.

Whitley, B. E. (1983). Sex role orientation and self-esteem: A critical meta-analytic review. *Journal of Personality and Social Psychology, 44*, 765–778.

Whitley, B. E. (1999). Right-wing authoritarianism, social dominance orientation, and prejudice. *Journal of Personality and Social Psychology, 77*(1), 126–134.

Wickrama, K. A. S., Lorenz, F. O., Conger, R. D., & Elder, G. H. (1997). Marital quality and physical illness: A latent growth curve analysis. *Journal of Marriage and Family, 59*, 143–155.

Widiger, T. A. (2001). Official classification systems. In W. J. Livesley (Ed.), *Handbook of personality disorders: Theory, research, and treatment*. New York: Guilford.

Widiger, T. A., & Sankis, L. M. (2000). Adult psychopathology: Issues and controversies. *Annual Review of Psychology, 51*, 377–404.

Wiederman, M. W. (1993). Evolved gender differences in mate preferences: Evidence from personal advertisements. *Ethology and Sociobiology, 14*, 331–352.

Wiederman, M. W. (1997). Extramarital sex: Prevalence and correlates in a national survey. *Journal of Sex Research, 34*, 167–174.

Wiederman, M. W. (2004). Methodological issues in studying sexuality in close relationships. In J. H. Harvey, A. Wenzel, & S. Sprecher (Eds.), *The handbook of sexuality in close relationships*. Mahwah, NJ: Lawrence Erlbaum.

Wiclawski, I. (1991, October 3). *Unlocking the secrets of memory*. Los Angeles Times, p. 1.

Wiggins, J. S., & Trapnell, P. D. (1997). Personality structure: The return of the big five. In R. Hogan, J. Johnson, & S. Briggs (Eds), *Handbook of personality psychology*. San Diego: Academic Press.

Wilgosh, L. (2001). Enhancing gifts and talents of women and girls. *High Ability Studies, 12*(1), 45–59.

Willets, M. C., Sprecher, S., & Beck, F. D. (2004). Overview of sexual practices and attitudes within relationship contexts. In J. H. Harvey, A. Wenzel, & S. Sprecher (Eds.), *The handbook of sexuality in close relationships*. Mahwah, NJ: Lawrence Erlbaum.

Willett, W. C. (2001). *Eat, drink, and be healthy: The Harvard Medical School guide to healthy eating*. New York: Free Press.

Willett, W. C., & Stampfer, W. J. (2003). Rebuilding the food pyramid. *Scientific American, 288*(1), 64–71.

Williams, C. G., Gagne, M., Ryan, R. M., & Deci, E. L. (2002). Facilitating autonomous motivation for smoking cessation. *Health Psychology, 21*, 40–50.

Williams, C. L. (1998). The glass escalator: Hidden advantages for men in the female professions. In M. S. Kimmel & M. A. Messner (Eds.), *Men's lives* (pp. 285–299). Boston: Allyn & Bacon.

Williams, J. B. W. (1999). Psychiatric Classification. In R. E. Hales, S. C. Yudofsky, & J. A. Talbott (Eds.), *American Psychiatric Press textbook of psychiatry* (pp. 227–252). Washington, DC: American Psychiatry Press.

Williams, J. E., & Best, D. L. (1982). *Measuring sex stereotypes: A thirty-nation study*. Newbury Park, CA: Sage.

Williams, J. E., & Best, D. L. (1990). *Measuring sex stereotypes: A multination study* (Rev. ed.). Newbury Park, CA: Sage Publications.

Williams, J. E., Paton, C. C., Siegler, I. C., Eigenbrodt, M. L., Neito, F. J., & Tyroler, H. A. (2000). Anger proneness predicts coronary heart disease risk. *Circulation, 101*, 2034–2039.

Williams, J. E., Satterwhite, R. C., & Best, D. L. (1999). Pancultural gender stereotypes revisited: The five-factor model. *Sex Roles, 40*, 513–526.

Williams, J. M. G., Watts, F. N., MacLeod, C., & Mathews, A. (1997). *Cognitive psychology and emotional disorders* (2nd ed.). Chichester, UK: Wiley.

Williams, K. B., Radefeld, P. S., Binning, J. F., & Sudak, J. R. (1993). When job candidates are "hard-" versus "easy-to-get": Effects of candidate availability on employment decisions. *Journal of Applied Social Psychology, 23*(3), 169–198.

Williams, K. E., & Bond, M. J. (2002). The roles of self-efficacy, outcome expectancies and social support in the self-care behaviors of diabetics. *Psychology, Health & Medicine, 7*(2), 127–141.

Williams, M. H. (1992). Exploitation and inference: Mapping the damage from therapist-patient sexual involvement. *American Psychologist, 47*, 412–421.

Williams, N. A., & Deffenbacher, J. L. (1983). Life stress and chronic yeast infections. *Journal of Human Stress, 9*, 26–31.

Williams, R. B. (2001). Hostility (and other psychosocial risk factors): Effects on health and the potential for successful behavioral approaches to prevention and treatment. In A. Baum, T. A. Revenson, & J. E. Singer (Eds.), *Handbook of health psychology* (pp. 661–668). Mahwah, NJ: Erlbaum.

Williams, R. B., & Williams, V. P. (1993). *Anger kills: Seventeen strategies for controlling the hostility that can harm your health*. New York: Times Books/Random House.

Williams, R. B., & Williams, V. P. (2001). Managing hostile thoughts, feelings, and actions: The lifeskills approach. In C. R. Snyder (Ed.), *Coping with stress: Effective people and processes* (pp. 137–153). New York: Oxford University Press.

Williams, S. L. (1995). Self-efficacy, anxiety, and phobic disorders. In J. E. Maddux (Ed.), *Self-efficacy, adaptation, and adjustment: Theory, research, and application*. New York: Plenum Press.

Williamson, D. A., Zucker, N. L., Martin, C. K., & Smeets, M. A. M. (2001). Etiology and management of eating disorders. In P. B. Sutker & H. E. Adams (Eds.), *Comprehensive handbook of psychopathology* (3rd ed., pp. 641–670). New York: Kluwer Academic/Plenum.

Wills, T. A., & Fegan, M. (2001). Social networks and social support. In A. Baum, T. A. Revenson, & J. E. Singer (Eds.), *Handbook of health psychology* (pp. 209–234). Mahwah, NJ: Erlbaum.

Wills, T. A., & Sandy, J. M. (2001). Comparing favorably: A cognitive approach to coping through comparison with other persons. In C. R. Snyder

(Ed.), *Coping with stress: Effective people and processes* (pp. 154–177). New York: Oxford University Press.

Wilpert, B. (1995). Organizational behavior. *Annual review of psychology, 46,* 59–90

Wilsnack, S. C., Wonderlich, S. A., Kristjanson, A. F., Vogeltanz-Holm, N. D., & Wilsnack, R. W. (2002). Self-reports of forgetting and remembering childhood sexual abuse in a nationally representative sample of U.S. women. *Child Abuse and Neglect, 26*(2), 139–147.

Wilson, G. T. (1993). Binge eating and addictive disorders. In C. G. Fairburn, & G. T. Wilson (Eds.), *Binge eating: Nature, assessment, and treatment.* New York: Guilford Press.

Wilson, R. S., & Bennett, D. A. (2003). Cognitive activity and the risk of Alzheimer's disease. *Current Directions in Psychological Science, 12*(3), 87–91.

Wing, R. R., & Polley, B. A. (2001). Obesity. In A. Baum, T. A. Revenson, & J. E. Singer (Eds.), *Handbook of health psychology* (pp. 263–279). Mahwah, NJ: Erlbaum.

Wingert, P., & Kantrowitz, B. (2000, March 20). Two kids and two moms. *Newsweek,* pp. 50–53.

Winick, C., & Norman, R. L. (2005). Epidemiology. In J. H. Lowinson, P. Ruiz, R. B. Millman, & J. G. Langrod (Eds.), *Substance abuse: A comprehensive textbook.* Philadelphia: Lippincott/ Williams & Wilkins.

Winter, D. D. N. (2004). Shopping for sustainability: Psychological solutions to overconsumption. In T. Kasser & A. D. Kanner (Eds.), *Psychology and consumer culture: The struggle for a good life in a materialistic world.* Washington, DC: American Psychological Association.

Winzelberg, A. J., & Luskin, F. M. (1999). The effect of a meditation training in stress levels in secondary school teachers. *Stress Medicine, 15,* 69–77.

Wiseman, C. V., Gray, J. J., Mosimann, J. E., & Ahrens, A. H. (1992). Cultural expectations of thinness in women: An update. *International Journal of Eating Disorders, 11,* 85–89.

Witmer, D. F., & Katzman, S. L. (1997). Online smiles: Does gender make a difference in the use of graphic accents? *Journal of Computer-Mediated Communication, 2*(4), np.

Wittenberg, M. T., & Reis, H. T. (1986). Loneliness, social skills, and social perception. *Personality and Social Psychology Bulletin, 12,* 121–130.

Witvliet, C., Ludwig, T. E., & Vander Laan, K. L. (2001). Granting forgiveness or harboring grudges: Implications for emotion, physiology, and health. *Psychological Science, 121*(2), 117–123.

Wolinsky, F. D. (1988). Sick role legitimation. In D. S. Gochman (Ed.), *Health behavior: Emerging research perspectives.* New York: Plenum Press.

Wolk, A., Manson, J. E., Stampfer, M. J., Colditz, G. A., Hu, F. B., Speizer, F. E., Hennekens, C. H., & Willett, W. C. (1999). Long-term intake of dietary fiber and decreased risk of coronary heart disease among women. *Journal of the American Medical Association, 281*(21), 1998–2004.

Woloshin, S., Schwartz, L. M., & Welch, H. G. (2002). Risk charts: Putting cancer in context. *Journal of the National Cancer Institute, 94,* 799–804.

Wolpe, J. (1958). *Psychotherapy by reciprocal inhibition.* Stanford, CA: Stanford University Press.

Wolpe, J. (1987). The promotion of scientific therapy: A long voyage. In J. K. Zeig (Ed.), *The evolution of psychotherapy.* New York: Brunner/Mazel.

Wolpe, J. (1990). *The practice of behavior therapy.* Elmsford, NY: Pergamon.

Women clerics find sexual harassment. (1990, December 1). *Washington Post, C12.*

Wonderlich, S. A. (2002). Personality and eating disorders. In C. G. Fairburn & K. D. Brownell

(Eds.), *Eating disorders and obesity: A comprehensive handbook.* New York: Guilford.

Wood, E., Desmarais, S., & Gugula, S. (2002). The impact of parenting experience on gender stereotyped toy play of children. *Sex Roles, 47*(1–2), 39–49.

Wood, J. V. (1989). Theory and research concerning social comparisons of personal attributes. *Psychological Bulletin, 106,* 231–248.

Wood, J. V., & Wilson, A. E. (2003). How important is social comparison? In M. R. Leary , & J. P. Tangney (Eds.), *Handbook of self and identity.* New York: Guilford.

Wood, M. D., Vinson, D. C., & Sher, K. J. (2001). Alcohol use and misuse. In A. Baum, T. A. Revenson, & J. E. Singer (Eds.), *Handbook of health psychology* (pp. 280–320). Mahwah, NJ: Erlbaum.

Wood, N., & Cowan, N. (1995). The cocktail party phenomenon revisited: How frequent are attention shifts to one's name in an irrelevant auditory channel? *Journal of Experimental Psychology: Learning, Memory, and Cognition, 21,* 255–260.

Wood, W. (2000). Attitude change: Persuasion and social influence. *Annual Review of Psychology, 51,* 539–570.

Wood, W., & Eagly, A. H. (2002). A cross-cultural analysis of the behavior of women and men: Implications for the origins of sex differences. *Psychological Bulletin, 128*(5), 699–727.

Wood, W., & Kallgren, C. A. (1988). Communicator attributes and persuasion: Recipients' access to attitude-relevant information in memory. *Personality and Social Psychology Bulletin, 14,* 172–182.

Wood, W., & Quinn, J. M. (2003). Forewarned and forearmed? Two meta-analytic syntheses of forewarnings of influence appeals. *Psychological Bulletin, 129*(1), 119–138.

Woodard, E. H., & Gridina. (2000). *Media in the home 2000: The fifth annual survey of parents and children (Survey Series No. 7).* Philadelphia: Annenberg Public Policy Center of the University of Pennsylvania.

Woolis, R. (1992). *When someone you love has a mental illness: A handbook for family, friends, and caregivers.* New York: Jeremy P. Tarcher/Putnam.

Worthen, J. B. (1997). Resiliency of bizarreness effects under varying conditions of verbal and imaginal elaboration and list composition. *Journal of Mental Imagery, 21,* 167–194.

Worthington, E. L. Jr., & Scherer, M. (2004). Forgiveness is an emotion-focused coping strategy that can reduce health risks and promote health resilience: Theory, review, and hypotheses. *Psychology and Health, 19*(3), 385–405.

Worthington, R. L., Flores, L. Y., & Navarro, R. L. (2005). Career development in context: Research with people of color. In S. D. Brown & R. W. Lent (Eds.), *Career development and counseling: Putting theory and research to work.* New York: Wiley.

Wortman, C. B., & Silver, R. C. (1990). Successful mastery of bereavement and widowhood: A life-course perspective. In P. B. Baltes & M. M. Baltes (Eds.), *Successful aging.* Cambridge, MA: Cambridge University Press.

Wortman, C. B., Wolff, K., & Bonanno, G. A. (2004). Loss of an intimate partner through death. In D. J. Mashek & A. Aron (Eds.), *Handbook of closeness and intimacy.* Mahwah, NJ: Erlbaum.

Wright, J. H., Beck, A. T., & Thase, M. E. (2003). Cognitive therapy. In R. E. Hales & S. C. Yudofsky (Eds.), *Textbook of clinical psychiatry.* Washington, DC: American Psychiatric Publishing.

Wright, R. A., & Contrada, R. J. (1986). Dating selectivity and interpersonal attraction: Toward a better understanding of the "elusive phenomenon." *Journal of Social and Personal Relationships, 3,* 131–148.

Wright, S. C., & Taylor, D. M. (2003). The social psychology of cultural diversity: Social stereotyping, prejudice, and discrimination. In M. A. Hogg

& J. Cooper (Eds.), *The Sage handbook of social psychology.* Thousand Oaks, CA: Sage Publications.

Wu, Z., & Hart, R. (2002). The effects of marital and nonmarital union transition on health. *Journal of Marriage and Family, 64,* 430–432.

Wylie, M. S. (1998). The shadow of a doubt. In R. A. Baker (Ed.), *Child sexual abuse and false memory syndrome.* Amherst, NY: Prometheus Books.

Wynder, E. L., Cohen, L. A., Muscat, J. E., Winters, B., Dwyer, J. T., & Blackburn, G. (1997). Breast cancer: Weighing the evidence for a promoting role of dietary fat. *Journal of the National Cancer Institute, 89*(11), 766–775.

Xiaohe, X., & Whyte, M. K. (1990). Love matches and arranged marriages: A Chinese replication. *Journal of Marriage and the Family, 52,* 709–722.

Yalom, I. D. (1995). *The theory and practice of group psychotherapy* (4th ed.). New York: Basic Books.

Yamamoto, J., Silva, J. A., Justice, L. R., Chang, C. Y., & Leong, G. B. (1993). Cross-cultural psychotherapy. In A. C. Gaw (Ed.), *Culture, ethnicity, and mental illness* (pp. 101–124). Washington, DC: American Psychological Press.

Yang, A. S. (1997). The polls—Trends: Attitudes toward homosexuality. *Public Opinion Quarterly, 61,* 477–507.

Yang, H., Liu, T., & Zang, D. (2000). A study of stressful life events before the onset of hypothyroidism. *Chinese Mental Health Journal, 14*(3), 201–202.

Yapko, M. D. (1994). *Suggestions of abuse: True and false memories of childhood sexual trauma.* New York: Simon & Schuster.

Yi, H., Stinson, F. S., Williams, G. D., & Dufour, M. C. (1999). *Surveillance report #53: Trends in alcohol-related fatal traffic crashes, United States, 1977–1998.* Rockville, MD: National Institute on Alcohol Abuse and Alcoholism.

Yoder, J. D. (2001). Military women. In J. Worrel (Ed.), *Encyclopedia of women and gender.* San Diego: Academic Press.

Yoder, J. D., & Kahn, A. S. (2003). Making gender comparisons more meaningful: A call for more attention to social context. *Psychology of Women Quarterly, 27,* 281–290.

Young, J. E. (1982). Loneliness, depression and cognitive therapy: Theory and application. In L. A. Peplau & D. Perlman (Eds.), *Loneliness: A sourcebook of current theory, research and therapy.* New York: Wiley.

Young, K. S. (1998). *Caught in the net: How to recognize the signs of Internet addiction—and a winning strategy for recovery.* New York: Wiley.

Young, K. S., Pistner, M., O'Mara, J., & Buchanan, J. (1999). Cyber disorders: The mental health concern for the new millennium. *CyberPsychology and Behavior, 2*(5), 475–479.

Young, K. S., & Rogers, R. C. (1998). The relationship between depression and Internet addiction. *CyberPsychology and Behavior, 1*(1), 25–28.

Younkin, S. L., & Betz, N. E. (1996). Psychological hardiness: A reconceptualization and measurement. In T. W. Miller (Ed.), *Theory and assessment of stressful life events.* Madison, CT: International Universities Press.

Yutzy, S. H. (2003). Somatoform disorders. In R. E. Hales & S. C. Yudofsky (Eds.), *Textbook of clinical psychiatry.* Washington, DC: American Psychiatric Publishing.

Zajonc, R. B. (1968). Attitudinal effects of mere exposure. *Journal of Personality and Social Psychology, 9,* 1–27.

Zakzanis, K. K., & Young, D. A. (2001). Memory impairment in abstinent MDMA ("Ecstasy") users: A longitudinal investigation. *Neurology, 56,* 966–969.

Zammichieli, M. E., Gilroy, F. D., & Sherman, M. F. (1988). Relation between sex-role orientation and marital satisfaction. *Personality and Social Psychology Bulletin, 14,* 747–754.

Zatzick, D. F. (1999). Managed care and psychiatry. In R. E. Hales, S. C. Yudofsky, & J. A. Talbott (Eds.), *American Psychiatric Press textbook of psychiatry.* Washington, DC: American Psychiatric Press.

Zautra, A. J., & Smith, B. W. (2001). Depression and reactivity to stress in older women with rheumatoid arthritis and osteoarthritis. *Psychosomatic Medicine, 63*(4), 687–696.

Zebrowitz, L. A., & Montepare, J. M. (2000). "Too young, too old": Stigmatizing adolescents and elders. In T. F. Heatheron et al. (Eds.), *The social psychology of stigma.* New York: Guilford.

Zechmeister, E. B., & Nyberg, S. E. (1982). *Human memory: An introduction to research and theory.* Pacific Grove, CA: Brooks/Cole.

Zeig, J. K. (1987). Introduction: The evolution of psychotherapy—Fundamental issues. In J. K. Zeig (Ed.), *The evolution of psychotherapy.* New York: Brunner/Mazel.

Zellman, G. L., & Goodchilds, J. D. (1983). Becoming sexual in adolescence. In E. R. Allgeier & N. B. McCormick (Eds.), *Changing boundaries.* Palo Alto, CA: Mayfield.

Zemishlany, Z., Aizenberg, D., & Weizman, A. (2001). Subjective effects of MDMA ("Ecstasy") on human sexual function. *European Psychiatry, 16*(2), 127–130.

Zilbergeld, B., & Evans, M. (1980, August). The inadequacy of Masters and Johnson. *Psychology Today,* pp. 28–34, 37–43.

Zimbardo, P. G. (1977). *Shyness: What it is, what to do about it.* Reading, MA: Addison-Wesley.

Zimbardo, P. G. (1990). *Shyness.* Reading, MA: Addison-Wesley.

Zimbardo, P. G. (1992). Cults in everyday life: Dependency and power. *Contemporary Psychology, 37,* 1187–1189.

Zimmerman, B. J. (1995). Self-efficacy and educational development. In A. Bandura (Ed.), *Self-efficacy in changing societies.* New York: Cambridge University Press.

Zittleman, K., & Sadker, D. (2002). Gender bias in teacher education texts: New (and old) lessons. *Journal of Teacher Education, 53*(2), 168–180.

Zuckerman, M. (1979). *Sensation seeking: Beyond the optimal level of arousal.* Hillsdale, NJ: Erlbaum.

Zuckerman, M. (1995). Good and bad humors: Biochemical bases of personality and its disorders. *Psychological Science, 6,* 325–332.

Zuckerman, M., Kieffer, S. C., & Knee, C. R. (1998). Consequences of self-handicapping: Effects of coping, academic performance, and adjustment. *Journal of Personality and Social Psychology, 74*(6), 1619–1628.

Zuo, J., & Tang, S. (2000). Breadwinner status and gender ideologies of men and women regarding family roles. *Sociological Perspectives, 43*(1), 29–43.

Zvonkovic, A. N., Greaves, K. M., Schmiege, C. J., & Hall, L. D. (1996). The marital construction of gender through work and family decisions: A qualitative analysis. *Journal of Marriage and the Family, 58,* 1, 91–100.

Credits

This page constitutes an extension of the copyright page. We have made every effort to trace the ownership of all copyrighted material and to secure permission from copyright holders. In the event of any question arising as to the use of any material, we will be pleased to make the necessary corrections in future printings. Thanks are due to the following authors, publishers, and agents for permission to use the material indicated.

Photo Credits

Chapter 1
3: © AP/Wide World Photos 4: © Randy Faris/Corbis 5: bottom right, © Blake Little/Corbis Sygma 5: bottom left, © Christopher J. Morris/Corbis 7: © David Young-Wolff/Photo Edit 18: © David Young-Wolff/Photo Edit 22: © Stuart Hughes/Corbis 23: top left, © Charles Gupton/Corbis 23: bottom right, © Rolf Bruderer/Masterfile 26: © Esbin-Anderson/The Image Works

Chapter 2
35: National Library of Medicine 36: © Peter Aprahamian/Corbis 41: right, © Bettmann/Corbis 41: top, © Michael Newman/Photo Edit 42: © Bettmann/Corbis 45: © Bettmann/Corbis 47: Courtesy of B. F. Skinner 48: © J. Clarke/Taxi/Getty Images 49: Courtesy, Albert Bandura 51: Carl Rogers Memorial Library 53: Courtesy, Abraham Maslow 56: center, Courtesy, Hans Eysenck, photo by Mark Gerson 56: top, © Michael Nichols/Magnum Photos 62: right, © Andy Sacks/Stone/Getty Images 62: left, © Cheryl Maeder/Corbis 67: © Laura Dwight/Photo Edit

Chapter 3
72: Courtesy, Richard Lazarus 74: left, © AP/Wide World Photos 74: right, © Richard Lord/PhotoEdit 76: Courtesy, Neal Miller 80: left, © Allen Birnbach/Masterfile 80: right, © Kelvin Murray/Stone/Getty Images 84: Courtesy, Susan Folkman 86: right, © Bettmann/Corbis 92: © Kim Kyung-Hoon/Reuters/Corbis 95: right, Courtesy, Suzanne C. Ouellette 95: top, © Ghislain & Marie David de Lossy/The Image Bank/Getty Images 97: Courtesy, Eleanor Holmes Williams

Chapter 4
107: Courtesy, Dr. Martin Seligman 108: © Paul Thomas/The Image Bank/Getty Images 109: top right, © Rachel Epstein/The Images Works 113: Courtesy, Shelley Taylor 115: Courtesy, Albert Ellis Institute 122: © Bruce Ayres/Stone/Getty Images 127: left, © Bill Ling/Taxi/Getty Images 127: right, © Stephanie Maze/Corbis 128: © Acey Harper/Time Life Pictures/Getty Images

Chapter 5
140: center, Stanford University News Service, photo by L. A. Cicero 143: © Spencer Grant/Photo Edit 144: top, Brooks/Cole Collection 144: bottom, Brooks/Cole Collection 145: © David Young-Wolff/Photo Edit 147: Courtesy, Roy Baumeister 151: © Robert W. Ginn/Photo Edit 156: © GDT/Stone/Getty Images 159: top, Courtesy, Albert Bandura 159: bottom, © Mary Kate Denny/Photo Edit 161: © Marc Vaughn/Masterfile 162: © 2004 AP/Wide World Photos 164: Courtesy, Mark Synder 166: right, © Evan Agostini/Getty Images 166: left, © Pascal Le Segretain/Getty Images

Chapter 6
172: © RNT Productions/Corbis 173: Courtesy, Susan Fiske 178: © Andrew Holbrooke/The Image Works 187: right, AFP/AFP/Getty Images 187: left, © 2004 AP/Wide World Photos 188: center right, Courtesy, John T. Cacioppo 188: top, Courtesy, Richard E. Petty 189: © Scott Olson/Getty Images 192: top left, © Soctt Barbour/Getty Images 192: right, © 1981 Eric Kroll, courtesy of Alexandra Milgram 193: inset, Photos copyright 1965 by Stanley Milgram. From the film Obedience, distributed by The Pennsylvania State University. Obedience, distributed by The Pennsylvania State University. Reprinted by permission of Alexandra Milgram 195: Courtesy, Robert Cialdini 197: bottom, © Tony Freeman/Photo Edit

Chapter 7
204: © Martin Parr/Magnum Photos 206: © 2004 AP/Wide World Photos 208: top, Photos from Unmasking the Face, © 1975 by Paul Ekman, photographs courtesy of Paul Ekman 208: bottom, © 2004 AP/Wide World Photos 209: right, © Tony Freeman/Photo Edit 209: left, © Walter Hodges/Corbis 210: © Bob Daemmrich/The Image Works 212: Courtesy, Bella DePaulo 213: © Bob Daemmrich/The Image Works 217: © Mary Kate Denny/PhotoEdit 218: © Dana Hursey/Masterfile 219: © Michael Newman/Photo Edit 222: © Eric K.K. Yu/Corbis 225: top right, Photo by Sara Barrett, courtesy of Random House 225: bottom right, © Jose Luis Pelaez/Corbis

Chapter 8
236: left, © Earl & Nazima Kowalt/Corbis 236: right, © Michael Newman/Photo Edit 238: © Mary Kate Denny/Photo Edit 242: © Ephraim Ben-Shimon/Corbis 244: © Paul Hawthorne/Getty Images 250: © 2004 AP/Wide World Photos 252: top left, Michael Marsland/Yale University 252: top right, Photo by Bill Warren/Ithaca Journal 252: center right, Photo provided by Philip Shaver 259: © Ronnie Kaufman/

Corbis 260: © Michael Newman/Photo Edit 261: © AP/Wide World Photos

Chapter 9
271: Photo by NBC Studios/Getty Images 273: © Trujillo-Paumier/Stone/Getty Images 277: © Thinkstock/Getty Images 283: center right, Photo by Sharon M. Fentiman 286: © Matthew McVay/Corbis Saba 289: top, Courtesy, E. Mavis Hetherington 289: right, © Michelle D. Bridewell/Photo Edit 292: © Ron Chapple/Thinkstock/Alamy 297: © AP/Wide World Photos

Chapter 10
303: Courtesy, Janet Shibley Hyde 310: top right, Courtesy, Alice Eagly 312: Wadsworth Collection 314: © Ken Fisher/Stone/Getty Images 315: left, © Laura Dwight/Photo Edit 315: right, © Stephen Marks/Taxi/Getty Images 316: © Michelle D. Bridwell/Photo Edit 319: Photo © Reichel Jean-Noel- FPG /Getty Images. 326: © Jim Zukerman/Corbis 328: Courtesy, Sandra Bem 330: bottom, Photo by Sara Barrett, courtesy of Random House

Chapter 11
339: © David Young Wolff/Stone/Getty Images 342: © Ted Streshinsky/Corbis 344: © Nancy Richmond/The Image Works 346: © Arlene Collins/The Image Works 349: © Jutta Klee/Stone/Getty Images 351: © Spencer Grant/Photo Edit 352: Courtesy, Susan Whitbourne 356: right, © AP/Wide World Photos 356: left, © Syracuse Newspaper, photo by Randi Anglin/The Image Works 359: © Roos/Gamma Liaison-Getty Images 360: © Spencer Grant/Photo Edit 362: © Arko Datta/Reuters/Corbis 364: Courtesy, Diana Baumrind 365: © David Young-Wolff/Photo Edit 368: top, Courtesy, Laurence Steinberg 368: bottom, © Jonathan Nourok/Photo Edit

Chapter 12
375: © B. Busco/The Image Bank/Getty Images 379: top, Columbia University Archives-Columbiana Library 382: © Mark Richards/Photo Edit 385: © Michael Newman/PhotoEdit 388: © Bill Stormont/Corbis 403: © Martin Leissl/Visum/The Image Works

Chapter 13
411: Courtesy, Letitia Anne Peplau 413: right, © AP/Wide World Photos 413: top, © Michael Newman/Photo Edit 415: © Justin Sullivan/Getty Images 416: center right, Courtesy, Douglas C Kimmel 416: top right, Courtesy, Linda Doris Garnets 416: bottom, © 2004 AP/Wide World Photos 426: © Paul Wright/Masterfile 428: © NBC photo by Paul Drinkwater/Getty Images 435: © Marc Romanelli/The Image

Bank/Getty Images **438:** © Bettmann/
Corbis

Chapter 14
447: © Annabella Bluesky/Photo Researchers, Inc. **451:** Courtesy, Janice Kiecott-Glaser **457:** © Paul A. Souders/Corbis **467:** © Jim Cummings/Taxi/Getty Images **470:** Courtesy, Robin DiMatteo **471:** © A. Ramey/PhotoEdit **472:** © image100/Alamy Images

Chapter 15
482: top, Courtesy, Thomas Szasz **483:** © 2003 AP/Wide World Photos **484:** center, Courtesy, David Rosenhan **489:** top right, © Jeffrey MacMillan/U.S. News & World Report **496:** right, © 2004 AP/Wide World Photos **496:** center, © Graeme Robertson/Getty Images **496:** left, © Katy Winn/Corbis **498:** Courtesy, Susan Nolen-Hoeksema **504:** Courtesy, Nancy Andreasen

Chapter 16
522: National Library of Medicine **523:** © Bruce Ayres/Stone/Getty Images **524:** Courtesy, Carl Rogers Memorial Library **526:** center, Courtesy, Aaron T. Beck **528:** © Michael Newman/Photo Edit **530:** © AP/Wide World Photos **533:** Courtesy, Joseph Wolpe **540:** © James Wilson/Woodfin Camp & Associates, all rights reserved **543:** © Rhoda Sidney/PhotoEdit **545:** Tom McCarthey/SKA **547:** © Tom Stewart/Corbis

Text Credits

Chapter 1
6: top right, Cartoon: Copyright © 2000. Used by permission. tomtomorrow@ix.netcom.com **7:** DOONESBURY© 1978 G. B. Trudeau. Reprinted with permission of UNIVERSAL PRESS SYNDICATE. All rights reserved. **8:** Entire hardcover Book cover of The Paradox of Choice: Why More is Less, by Barry Schwartz. Copyright © 2004 by Barry Schwartz. Reprinted by permission of HarperCollins Publishers, Inc. **9:** CALVIN AND HOBBES © 1993 Watterson. Reprinted with permission of UNIVERSAL PRESS SYNDICATE. All rights reserved. **10:** Cover of What You Can Change & What You Can't by Martin E. P. Seligman. Copyright © 1994 Alfred A. Knopf, Inc. Reprinted by permission. **11:** Figure 1.1: From Wade, Carol; Tavris, Carole, Learning to Think Critically, 2nd Edition. Copyright © 1989. Reprinted by permission of Pearson Education, Inc., Upper Saddle River, N. J.. Used by permission. **21:** Cover: The Pursuit of Happiness by David G. Myers. Copyright © 1992 by the David G. and Carol P. Myers Charitable Foundation. Reprinted by permission of HarperCollins Publishers, Inc. **22:** Figure 1.10: Adapted from D. G. Myers, "Close Relationships and Quality of Life," 1999, Figure 19.1. In Well-Being: The Handbook of Hedonic Psychology by

Daniel Kahneman, Edward Diener and Norbert Schwarz, (Eds.) 1999. Copyright © 1999 Russell Sage Foundation, 112 East 64th Street, New York, NY 10021. Reprinted with permission. **28:** DOONESBURY© G. B. Trudeau. Reprinted with permission of UNIVERSAL PRESS SYNDICATE. All rights reserved. **29:** Figure 1.14: Adapted from G. H. Bower and M. C. Clark, "Narrative Stories as Mediators of Serial Learning," Psychonomic Science, 14, 181–182. Copyright © 1969 by the Psychonomic Society. Adapted by permission of the Psychonomic Society and the author. **29:** Figure 1.14: Adapted from G. H. Bower, "Analysis of a Mnemonic Device," 1970, American Scientist (September-October), 58, 496–499. Copyright © 1970 by American Scientist. Reprinted by permission of the publisher and the author.

Chapter 2
37: 38: top left, Cartoon © 1999 by Sidney Harris **50:** Figure 2.13: Reproduced with permission of authors and publisher from Sherer, M., Maddox, J. E., Mercandante, B., Prentice-Dunn, S., Jacobs, B., and Rogers, R. W., "The Self-efficacy Scale: Construction and Validation." Psychological Reports, 1982, 51, 663–671. © Psychological Reports 1982. **52:** Cover: Three Psychologists: Perspectives from Freud, Skinner, and Rogers, by Robert D. Nye, © 2000, Wadsworth Group **55:** PEANUTS reprinted by permission of United Feature Syndicate, Inc. **57:** Figure 2.18: From H. J. Eysenck, The Biological Basis of Personality (1st Edition), p. 36, 1967. Courtesy of Charles C. Thomas, Publisher, Springfield, IL. **58:** Figure 2.19: Based on R. Plomin and A. Caspi, "Behavioral Genetics and Personality," 1999 . In L. A. Pervin, & O. P. John (Eds.), Handbook of Personality: Theory and Research. The Guilford Press. **66:** Figure 2.23: Reprinted by permission of Daniel S. Kirschenbaum from page 101 of Adjustment and Competence: Concepts and Applications, by A. F. Grasha & D. S. Kirschenbaum, © 1986. West Publishing Company. **67:** Figure 2.24: From R. B. Cattell, "Personality pinned down," in Psychology Today, July 1973, 40–46. Reprinted with permission from Psychology Today Magazine. Copyright © 1973 (Sussex Publishers, Inc.).

Chapter 3
73: Figure 3.2: Adapted from G. W. Evans, S. Hygge, and M. Bullinger, "Chronic Noise and Psychological Stress" Psychological Science, Vol. 6, p. 333–338, figure 3.2. Copyright © 1995 Blackwell Publishers. Adapted by permission. **75:** top right, Cover: The End of Stress As We Know It by Bruce McEwen, Elizabeth Norton Lasley, Elizabeth Lasley. cover © 2002 Joseph Henry Press. Reprinted by permission National Academies Press. **77:** top, BLONDIE © 2001. Reprinted with special permission of King Features Syndicate.

79: Figure 3.5: Reprinted from Journal of Psychosomatic Research, 11 by T. H. Holmes and R. H. Rahe in "The Social Readjustment Rating Scale," 213–218, Copyright © 1967, with permission from Elsevier . **86:** Cartoon: DILBERT reprinted by permission of United Features Syndicate, Inc. **93:** Cover: Why Zebras Don't Get Ulcers: An Updated Guide to Stress-Related Diseases, and Coping, by Robert M. Sapolsky; cover © 1998 Scientific American Library. Reprinted by permission W. H. Freeman and Company Publishers. **96:** CALVIN AND HOBBES © Watterson. Reprinted with permission of Universal Press Syndicate. All rights reserved. **96:** Figure 3.17: Adapted from M.F. Scheier and C. S. Carver, "Optimism, Coping, and Health: Assessment and Implications of Generalized Outcome Expectancies," Health Psychology, 4, 219–247. Copyright © 1985 Lawrence Erlbaum & Associates. Adapted by permission and author. **99:** Figure 3.19: From I. G. Sarason, J. H. Johnson, and J. M. Siegel, "Assessing the Impact of Life Changes," 1978, Journal of Consulting and Clinical Psychology, 46, 932–946. Copyright © 1978 by the American Psychological Association. Reprinted by permission of the author. **100:** Figure 3.20: From I. G. Sarason, J. H. Johnson, and J. M. Siegel, "Assessing the Impact of Life Changes," 1978, Journal of Consulting and Clinical Psychology, 46, 932–946. Copyright © 1978 by the American Psychological Association. Reprinted by permission of the author.

Chapter 4
106: Figure 4.1: From C. S. Carver, M. F. Scheier, and J. K. Weintraub, "Assessing Coping Strategies: A Theoretically Based Approach," 1989, Journal of Personality and Social Psychology, 56(2), 267–283. Copyright © 1989 America Psychological Association. Reprinted by permission of the author. **108:** Cover: Anger: The Misunderstood Emotion, by Carol Tavris. Book cover, Copyright © 1989 by Simon & Schuster, Inc. Reproduction by permission of the publisher. All rights reserved. **109:** bottom, CATHY © Cathy Guisewite Reprinted with permission of UNIVERSAL PRESS SYNDICATE. All rights reserved. **110:** Figure 4.2: From K. S. Young, Caught in the Net: How to Recognize the Signs of Internet Addiction—and a Winning Strategy for Recovery, copyright ©1998 John Wiley & Sons, Inc. Reprinted with permission of John Wiley & Sons, Inc. **111:** Figure 4.3: Adapted from R. C. Carson, J. N. Butcher & C. C. Coleman, Abnormal Psychology and Modern Life (8/e), pp. 64–65. Copyright © 1988 by Scott, Foresman and Company. Adapted by permission. **112:** CALVIN AND HOBBES © Watterson. Reprinted with permission of UNIVERSAL PRESS SYNDICATE. All rights reserved. **114:** Car-

toon: Sally Forth Copyright © 1984 News Group Chicago, reprinted by permission of North America Syndicate. **116:** Cover: How to Stubbornly Refuse to Make Yourself Miserable About Anything—Yes, Anything! by Albert Ellis. Copyright © 1988 Carol Publishing Group. Reprinted by permission. **117:** Figure 4.6: Adapted from R. A. Martin and H. M. Lefcourt, "Sense of Humor as a Moderator of the Relation Between Stressors and Moods," 1983, Journal of Personality and Social Psychology, 45 (6), 1313–1324. Copyright © 1983 by the American Psychological Association. Adapted by permission of the author. **121:** Figure 4.8: From M LeBoeuf, "Managing Time Means Managing Yourself," Questionnaire, p. 45. Reprinted from Business Horizons Magazine, February 1980. Copyright by the Foundation for the School of Business at Indiana University. Used with permission. **124:** Cover: Time Management From the Inside Out by Julie Morgenstern; cover, © 2000 by Henry Holt and Co. Reprinted by permission of Henry Holt & Co., LLC. **126:** Cover: Emotional Intelligence: Why It Can Matter More Than IQ by Daniel Goleman, Copyright © 1995, Bantam Books. Reprinted by permission of Bantam Books. **127:** Figure 4.12: Excerpt from "Sharing One's Story," [J. M. Smyth and J. W. Pennebaker,] pg.84 from Coping: The Psychology of What Works, edited by C. R. Snyder, copyright © 1999 by Oxford University Press. Inc.. Used by permission of Oxford University Press, Inc. **129:** Figure 4.13: Adapted from illustration on p. 86 by Lorelle Marie Raboni in Scientific American, 226, 85–90, February 1972) "The Psychology of Meditation," by R. K. Wallace & H. Bensen. Copyright © 1972 by Scientific American, Inc. All rights reserved. Adapted by permission of the artist. **130:** Figure 4.14: (from) Page 114–115 from The Relaxation Response by Herbert Benson, M.D. with Miriam Z. Klipper. Copyright © 1975 by William Morrow & Company, Inc. Reprinted by permission of HarperCollins Publishers, Inc. **133:** Figure 4.17: From D. L. Watson & R. L. Tharp, Self-Directed Behavior: Self-Modification for Personal Adjustment, Fourth Edition, , p. 213–214. Copyright © 1972, 1977, 1981, 1985, 1993 by Brooks/Cole Publishing Company.

Chapter 5
142: Figure 5.3: From J. G. Hull and R. D. Young, "Self-Consciousness, Self-Esteem, and Success-Failure as Determinants of Alcohol Consumption in Male Social Drinkers," 1983, Journal of Personality and Social Psychology, 44 (6), 1097–1109. Copyright © 1983 American Psychological Association. Reprinted by permission of the author. **146:** Figure 5.5: Adapted from H. R. Markus and Shinobu Kitayama, "Culture and the Self: Implications for Cognition, Emotion, and Motivation",

1991, Psychological Review, 98 (2) 224–253. Copyright © 1991 American Psychological Association. Reprinted by permission of the author. **148:** Figure 5.7: Adapted from Sharon S. Brehm and Saul M. Kassin, Social Psychology, 2nd Edition. Copyright © 1993 Houghton-Mifflin Company. Adapted by permission. **153:** Figure 5.10: From B. Weiner, I. Frieze, A. Kukla, L. Reed, & R. M. Rosenbaum," Perceiving the Causes of Success and Failure." In E. E. Jones, D. E. Kanuouse, H. H. Kelly, R. E. Nisbett, S. Valins, & B. Weiner (Eds.), Perceiving Causes of Behavior, 1972, General Learning Press. Reprinted by permission of the author. **157:** PEANUTS reprinted by permission of United Feature Syndicate, Inc. **161:** Entire Book cover from Self-Defeating Behaviors, by Milton R. Cudney and Robert E. Hardy. Copyright © 1975 by Lifegiving Enterprises, Inc. Copyright © 1991 by Milton R. Cudney and Robert E. Hardy. Reprinted by permission of HarperCollins Publishers, Inc. **166:** Cover: Self-Esteem, by Matthew McKay and Patrick Fanning. Copyright © 2000 New Harbinger Publications. Reprinted by permission. **167:** FRANK & ERNEST reprinted by permission of Newspaper Enterprise Association, Inc.

Chapter 6
173: Figure 6.1: Adapted from Sharon S. Brehm and Saul M. Kassin, Social Psychology, Second Edition. Copyright © 1993 by Houghton Mifflin Company. Adapted with permission **174:** Cartoon: DILBERT Reprinted by permission of United Feature Syndicate, Inc. **175:** Figure 6.2: Adapted from E. R. Smith and D. M. Mackie, Social Psychology, p. 103. Copyright © 1995 Worth Publishing. Reprinted by permission. **177:** Figure 6.3: Data from 1999, September 15: Americans Agree That Being Attractive is a Plus in American Society. Taken from 2001, June 10, from http://gallup.com/poll/releases/pr990915. **182:** Figure 6.7: Statements from J. K. Swim, K. J. Aikin, W. S. Hall, & B. A. Hunter, "Sexism and Racism: Old-Fashioned and Modern Prejudices," Journal of Personality and Social Psychology, 68 (2), 199–214. Copyright © 1995 American Psychological Association. Reprinted by permission of the author. **184:** Figure 6.8: Adapted from Sharon S. Brehm and Saul M. Kassin, Social Psychology, Second Edition. Copyright © 1993 by Houghton Mifflin Company. Adapted with permission. **186:** Cover: Age of Propaganda: The Everyday Use and Abuse of Persuasion, by Anthony R. Pratkanis and Elliot Aronson. Copyright © 2001. Reprinted by permission of Henry Holt & Co., LLC. **189:** Cover of Robert B. Cialdini, Influence: Science and Practice. Published by Allyn and Bacon, Boston, MA. Copyright © 2001 by Pearson Education. Reprinted by permission of the publisher. **190:** Figure 6.11: Adapted from illustration by Sarah Love

on p. 35, Scientific American, November 1955, from "Opinion and Social Pressure," by Solomon Asch. Copyright © 1955 by Scientific American, Inc. All rights reserved. **191:** Figure 6.12: Adapted from illustration by Sarah Love on p. 32, Scientific American, November 1955, from "Opinion and Social Pressure," by Solomon Asch. Copyright © 1955 by Scientific American, Inc. All rights reserved. **197:** CALVIN AND HOBBES © Watterson. Reprinted with permission of UNIVERSAL PRESS SYNDICATE. All rights reserved.

Chapter 7
203: Cover: Multicultural Manners: New Rules of Etiquette for a Changing Society, by Norine Dresser. Copyright © 1996 by John Wiley & Sons. The material is used by permission of John Wiley & Sons, Inc. **211:** Figure 7.6: "Where friends touch each other," page 89, [adapted] from Eye to Eye: How People Interact, by Peter Marsh. Copyright © 1988 by Andromeda Oxford Ltd. Reprinted by permission of HarperCollins, Publishers, Inc. and Andromeda Oxford Ltd. **214:** Cover: Messages: The Communication Skills Book, by Matthew McKay, Martha Davis, and Patrick Fanning. Copyright © 2000 New Harbinger Publications. Cover design by Shelby Design & Associates. Reprinted by permission. **216:** Cartoon DAVE © 1993 Dave Miller. Reprinted with permission of the artist. All rights reserved. **225:** "Cover", copyright © 1997 by Random House, Inc. of The Argument Culture by Deborah Tannen. Used by permission of Random House, Inc. **226:** Figure 7.12: From "Road Rage Plagues Drivers," 1997, AAA Going Places, November-December, 1997, 41–42. Copyright © 1997 by American Automobile Association. **228:** Cartoon by Marlette: KUDZU © Tribune Media Services, Inc. All Rights Reserved. Reprinted with permission. **228, 229:** Excerpts from Asserting Yourself: A Practical Guide for Positive Change by Sharon Anthony Bower and Gordon H. Bower, pp 8,9,11. Copyright © 1991 by Sharon Anthony Bower and Gordon H. Bower. Reprinted by permission of Perseus Books Publishers, a member of Perseus Books, L.L.C. **229:** Cover: Asserting Yourself: A Practical Guide for Positive Change by Sharon Anthony Bower and Gordon H. Bower. Copyright © 1991 by Sharon Anthony Bower and Gordon H. Bower. Reprinted by permission of Perseus Books Publishers, a member of Perseus Books, L.L.C. **230:** Figure 7.13: From Asserting Yourself: A Practical Guide for Positive Change by Sharon Anthony Bower and Gordon H. Bower. Da Capo Press. Copyright © 1991 by Sharon Anthony Bower and Gordon H. Bower. Reprinted by permission of Perseus Books Publishers, a member of Perseus Books, L.L.C. **231:** Figure 7.13: From Asserting Yourself: A Practical Guide for Positive Change by Sharon

Anthony Bower and Gordon H. Bower. Da Capo Press. Copyright © 1991 by Sharon Anthony Bower and Gordon H. Bower. Reprinted by permission of Perseus Books Publishers, a member of Perseus Books, L.L.C.

Chapter 8

237: Figure 8.1: Adapted from R. Levine, S. Sato, T. Hashimoto, J. Verma, " Love and Marriage in Eleven Cultures", 1995, Journal of Cross-Cultural Psychology 26(5), 561, 564. Copyright © 1995 by Sage Publications, Inc. Adapted by permission of Sage Publications. **239:** CATHY © 1993 by Cathy Guisewite. Reprinted with permission of UNIVERSAL PRESS SYNDICATE. All rights reserved. **241:** Figure 8.2: From D. M. Buss, "Sex Differences in Human Mate Preferences: Evolutionary Hypotheses Tested in 37 Cultures," 1989, Behavioral and Brain Sciences, 12, 1–14. Copyright © 1989 by Cambridge University Press. Reprinted with the permission of Cambridge University Press. **242:** Figure 8.3: Adapted from D. M. Buss, "The Evolution of Human Intrasexual Competition: Tactics of Mate Attraction,", 1988, Journal of Personality and Social Psychology, 54(4), 616–628. Copyright © 1988 by the American Psychological Association. Adapted by permission of the author. **245:** Figure 8.6: Adapted from M. H. Gonzales, J. M. Davis, G. L. Loeny, C. K. Lukens, & C. H. Junghans, "Interactional Approach to Interpersonal Attraction," 1983, Journal of Personality and Social Psychology, 44, 1191–1197. Copyright © 1983 by the American Psychological Association. Adapted by permission of the author. **246:** Figure 8.7: Based on Regan, P.C. & Berscheid, E. "Gender differences in characteristics desired in a potential sexual marriage partner," 1997, Journal of Psychology and Human Sexuality, 9, Table 1, p.32. Haworth Press, Inc. **247:** Figure 8.9: From Sharon S. Brehm and Saul M. Kassin, Social Psychology, Second Edition. Copyright © 1993 by Houghton Mifflin Company. Reprinted with permission. **248:** Cover art by Jan Yager, Ph.D. from her original photograph Copyright © 1999 by Jan Yager, Ph.D. All rights reserved. Non-exclusive permission granted to Wadsworth for reproduction of the book jacket of Friendshifts® published by Hannacroix Creek Books, Inc. in Psychology Applied to Modern Life, 8th edition. Book jacket and original photograph copyright © 1999 by Jan Yager, Ph.D. All rights reserved. (Any requests for further reproduction or printing of this cover art should be directed to the publisher: hannacroix@aol.com. **251:** Figure 8.11: From R. J. Sternberg, "A Triangular Theory of Love," 1986, Psychological Review, 93, 119–135. Copyright © 1986 by the American Psychological Association. Reprinted by permission of the author.

256: Cover: The Mating Game: a Primer on Love, Sex, and Marriage, by Pamela C. Regan, 2003. Copyright © 2003 by Sage Publications. Reproduced by permission of Sage Publications, Inc. **257:** Figure 8.15: Adapted from C. T. Hill, Z. Rubin, & L. A. Peplau, "Breakups Before Marriage: The End of 103 Affairs," 1976, Journal of Social Issues, 32, 147–168. Basic Books Publishing Co., Inc. Adapted by permission of the author. All rights reserved. **258:** For Better or For Worse® cartoon © Lynn Johnston Productions, Inc./Distributed by Universal Press Syndicate. Reprinted with permission. All rights reserved. **262:** Cover: P. Zimbardo, Shyness, © 1977 Philip Zimbardo Inc. Cover illustration © 1989 by Bart Goldman. Reprinted by permission of Addison-Wesley Publishing Company, Inc. and Bart Goldman. **263:** Figure 8.17: From Shyness: What Is It, What To Do About It, by Philip Zimbardo. Copyright © 1977 by Philip Zimbardo, Inc. Reprinted by permission of Perseus Books Publishers, a member of Perseus Books, L.L.C. **264:** Figure 8.18: From a paper presented at the annual convention of the American Psychological Association, 9/2/79. An expanded version of this paper apperars in New Directions in Cognitive Therapy, edited by Emery, Hollan, and Bedrosian, Guilford Press, 1981 and in Lonliness: A Sourcebook of Current Theory, Research and Therapy, by L. A. Peplau and D. Perlman (Eds.). Copyright © 1982 by John Wiley & Sons, Inc., and Jeffrey Young. **265:** Figure 8.19 based on P. Shaver, & C. Rubenstein, 1980, "Childhood attachment experience ans adult loneliness." In L. Wheeler (Ed.), Review of personality and social psychology, Vol. 1, pp. 42–73. Thousand Oaks, CA: Sage Publications.

Chapter 9

273: Figure 9.3: Adapted from Peter J. Stein, "Singlehood: An Alternative to Marriage," The Family Coordinator, 24(4), 500. Copyrighted © 1975 by the National Council on Family Relations, 3989 Central Ave. N. E., Suite 550, Minneapolis, MN 55421. Reprinted by permission. **279:** CATHY © 1994 Cathy Guisewite. Reprinted with permission of UNIVERSAL PRESS SYNDICATE. All rights reserved. **280:** Cartoon: SALLY FORTH Reprinted with special permission of King Features Syndicate. **282:** Cover: Reconcilable Differences, by Andrew Christiansen and Neil S. Jacobson, 2000, The Guilford Press, jacket design by Paul Gordon. Reproduced by permission of Guilford Publications. **284:** CATHY © Cathy Guisewite. Reprinted with permission of UNIVERSAL PRESS SYNDICATE. All rights reserved. **284:** Cover: Why Marriages Succeed or Fail . . . and How You Can Make Yours Last, by John Gottman Ph.D. with Nan Silver. Book cover, Copyright © 1994 by

Simon & Schuster, Inc. Reproduced by permission of the publisher. All rights reserved. **288:** Cartoon © 1992 The New Yorker Collection 1992 Michael Maslin from cartoonbank.com. All rights reserved. **294:** Figure 9.14: From L. A. Peplau, "What Homosexuals Want," March 1981, Psychology Today, 3, 28–38. Reprinted with permission from Psychology Today Magazine. Copyright © 1981 (Sussex Publishers, Inc.). **299:** Figure 9.17: From I. M. Johnson, J. Crowley, and R. T. Sigler, "Agency Response to Domestic Violence: Services Provided to Battered Women," 1992. In E. C. Viano (Ed.), Intimate Violence: Interdisciplinary Perspectives, pp 191–202 (Table on p. 199). Copyright © 1992 Hemisphere Publishing. Reprinted with permission of Taylor & Francis, Inc.

Chapter 10

304: CATHY © Cathy Guisewite. Reprinted with permission of UNIVERSAL PRESS SYNDICATE. All rights reserved. **305:** Figure 10.2: Adapted from T. L. Ruble, "Sex Stereotypes: Issues of Change in the 70s," 1983, Sex Roles, 9, 397–402. Copyright © 1983 Plenum Publishing Co. Adapted by permission of Springer Science and Business Media and the author. **307:** Figure 10.4: Adapted from R. N. Shepard and J. N. Metzler, "Mental Rotation of Three-Dimensionl Objects," Science, 171, 701–703. Copyright © 1971 by American Association for the Advancement of Science. Adapted by permission of the publisher and author. **309:** Figure 10.6: Adapted from A. M. Kring and A. H. Gordon, "Sex Differences in Emotions: Expression, Experience and Physiology," 1998, Journal of Personality and Social Psychology, 74 (3), 686–703. Copyright © 1998 by American Psychological Association. Adapted by permission of the author. **316:** Figure 10.8: Adapted from J. G. Richardson & C. H. Simpson, "Children, Gender and Social Structure: An Analysis of the Contents of Letters to Santa Claus," 1982, Child Development, 53, 429–436. Copyright © 1982 by the Society for Research in Child Development, Inc. Adapted by permission. **317:** Figure 10.9: Adapted from Robert M. Liebert & Joyce Sprafkin, The Early Window: Effects of Television on Children and Youth, 3/e. Published by Allyn and Bacon, Boston, Ma. Copyright © 1988 by Pearson Education. Adapted by permission of the publisher. **318:** Cartoon © The New Yorker Collection 2001 Barbara Smaller from cartoonbank.com. All rights reserved. **321:** DOONSBURY © 1975 G. B. Trudeau. Reprinted with permission of UNIVERSAL PRESS SYNDICATE. All rights reserved. **323:** The Mismeasure of Woman, by Carol Tavris. Book cover, Copyright © 1992 by Simon & Schuster, Inc. Reproduction by permission of the publisher. All rights reserved. **325:** Figure

Chapter 16

519: Figure 16.1: Data from M. Oflson and H. A. Pincus, "Outpatient Mental Health Care in Nonhospital Settings: Distribution of Patients Across Provider Groups," 1996, American Journal of Psychiatry, 153, 1353–1356 **526:** Figure 16.6: Adapted from A. T. Beck, Cognitive Therapy and the Emotional Disorders, 1976, International Universities Press. Copyright © 1976 by International Universities Press, Inc. Adapted by permission of the publisher. **529:** Cover: The Psychotherapy Maze, by O. Ehrenberg and M. Ehrenberg. Copyright © 1986 Aronson. Reprinted by permission. **531:** DOONESBURY © 1994 G. B. Trudeau. Reprinted with permission of UNIVERSAL PRESS SYNDICATE. All rights reserved. **531:** Figure 16.7: From "Lies of the Mind" Time , 11/29/93. Copyright © 1993 Time Inc. Reprinted by permission. **532:** Cartoon: © 1999 by Sidney Harris **538:** Figure 16.12: From data in NIMH-PSC Collaborative Study I and reported in "Drugs in the Treament of Psychosis," by J.O. Cole, S. C. Goldberg, and J. M. Davis, 1966. In P. Solomon (Ed.) Psychiatric Drugs, Grune & Stratton. Additional data added from J. M. Davis, 1985. By permission of the author. **539:** Cartoon © The New Yorker Collection 2001 Barbara Smaller from cartoonbank. com. All rights reserved. **546:** Cartoon: FRANK & ERNEST reprinted by permission of Newspaper Enterprise Association, Inc. **548:** Cartoon: Inside Woody Allen by Stuart Hample. Reprinted by permission. © King Features Syndicate, Inc., 1977. World rights reserved. **548:** Figure 16.15: Adapted from M. L. Smith & G. V. Glass, "Meta Analysis of Psychotherapy Outcome Series," 1977, American Psychologist, 32 (September), 752–760. Copyright © 1977 by the American Psychological Association. Adapted by permission of the author. **549:** Cover: A Consumer's Guide to Psychotherapy, by Larry E. Beutler, Bruce Bongar & Joel Shurkin. copyright © 2001 by Larry E. Beutler, Bruce Bongar & Joel Shurkin. Used by permission of Oxford University Press, Inc.

Name Index

A

Abalakina-Paap, M. A., 182
Abbey, A., 296, 297
Abel, M. H., 117
Aber, J. L., 226
Abi-Dargham, A., 505
Aboud, F. E., 240
Abplanalp, R. R., Jr., 240
Abrams, D. B., 455
Abramson, L. Y., 108, 500
Aburdene, P., 378
Achille, N. M., 22
Ackerman, S., 348
Acock, A. C., 290
Acton, G. S., 55., 311
Adams, G., 237
Adams, G. R., 347
Adams, H. E., 493
Adams, K. A., 308
Adams, M., 288
Adams-Curtis, L. E., 297
Adcock, c. J., 67
Addis, M. E., M. E., 320
Ader, R., 451
Adler, A., 41, 42–43
Adler, L. 252
Adler, N. E., 241., 291, 322
Adonu, J. K., 236
Adorno, R., 182
Affleck, G., 93, 118
Ageyev, V. S., 182
Agnew, C. R., 248
Agras, W. S., 532
Ahlberg, C., 314
Ahn, H., 529
Ahrons, C. R., 286
Aiken, L. S., 429
Ainsworth, M. D. S., 252, 363
Ait-Daoud, N., 457, 459
Akgun, S., 92
Akimoto, S. A., 156
Akishkal, H. S., 497
Akiyama, H., 345
Albee, G. W., 518, 543, 544
Albert, C. M., 445
Alberti, R. E., 224, 227, 228, 231
Alexander, C. N., 128, 129
Alicke, M. D., 155., 240
Allegro, J. T., 388
Allen, K., 95
Allen, K. R., 295
Allen, M., 251, 318
Allison, D. B., 460, 461
Alloy, L. B., 500, 501
Allport, G., 34
Alonso, A., 527
Alonso, S., 527
Altemeyer, B., 182, 415
Altman, I., 215, 217
Altnaier, E. M., 359
Altobelli, J., 291
Amada, G., 545
Amato, P. R., 270, 271, 272, 274, 285, 286,
    287, 288, 289, 292
Ambady, N., 175, 208
Ames, S. C., 98
Anand, A. P., 264

Anand, S. S., 445
Anderson, B. L., 450
Anderson, C., 3, 435
Anderson, C. A., 226
Anderson, J. R., 28
Anderson, K. J., 84
Anderson, P. A., 210
Anderson, S., 126
Anderson, S. E., 339
Anderson, S. L., 236
Anderson, V. L., 129
Anderson-Fye, E. P., 511
Andreasen, N. C., 503, 504, 506
Andresen, J., 128
Andrews, A. M., 451
Andrews, B., 495
Andrews, G., 487
Andrioli, M., 296
Angell, M., 539
Angiulo, M. J., 495
Angleitner, A., 57
Angst, J., 42
Ankenmann, R. D., 395
Anton, R. F., 458
Antonucci, T. C., 345, 351
Antonuccio, D. O., 537, 539
Antony, M. M., 490
Apperloo, M. J. A., 409
Aqilino, W. S., 278
Arbona, C., 375
Archer, J., 273, 308, 311
Archer, R. L., 331
Arendell, T., 321
Argyle, M., 20, 21, 22, 248, 249
Ariely, D., 122
Aries, E., 309
Armbruster, B. B., 26
Armour, S., 396
Arndt, J., 60
Arnett, J. J., 343, 349
Arnkoff, D. B., 527, 532
Arnold, K., 321
Arnold, K. D., 381
Arnold, L. M., 451
Arnold, R. D., 58
Arnon, L., 91
Arnsten, J. H., 475
Aron, A., 242, 252, 259
Aronson, E., 185, 186
Arrigo, J. M, 494
Arthur, R. H., 78
Asch, S. E., 180, 190–191
Ashcraft, M. H., 89
Asher, S., 262
Ashmore, R. D., 309
Ashton, M. C., 35
Aspinwall, L. G., 93, 97
Assanand, S., 140, 460
Asuncion, A. G., 187
Ataca, B., 74
Athenstadt, U., 309
Atkinson, L., 363
Atkinson, R. H., 27
Atwood, J. H., 423, 427
Aubé, J., 245
Aubin, S., 437, 438, 439
Auerbach, S. M., 393

Ayanian, J. Z., 454
Aylor, B., 246
Ayres, J. J. B., 46

B

Babcock, J. C., 299
Back, K., 239
Bacon, J. B., 362
Bacue, A., 317, 318
Bader, K. O., 361
Badgett, M. V. L., 385, 388
Bailey, B. L., 288
Bailey, J. M., 240, 295, 414, 415
Bailey, M., 414
Bakalar, J. B., 476, 477
Baker, F., 454
Baker, L., 512
Baker, O., 387
Baldessarini, R. J., 538
Baldwin, D., 91
Baldwin, M., 256
Bales, R. F., 305
Ballenger, J. C., 92, 537
Balsam, K. F., 294
Banaji, M. R., 177
Bancroft, J., 313, 422, 437
Bandura, A., 49–50, 158–159, 314
Bank, B. J., 249
Banks, A., 414
Banning, K., 79
Banse, R., 211
Banyard, V. L., 530
Barbanel, L., 3
Barbaree, H. E., 297
Barbee, A. P., 240, 241
Barber, B. K., 278
Barbrack, C. R., 532
Bargh, J. A., 152, 177, 204, 216, 237, 238, 264
Barlett, D. L., 489
Barley, D. E., 529
Barling, J., 393
Barlow, D. H., 488, 491, 529
Barnes, M. L., 331
Barnes, V. A., 129
Barnett, D., 363
Barnett, H. L., 322
Barnett, O. W., 299
Barnett, R. C., 282, 396
Baron, R. A., 393
Baron, R. S., 5
Barrett, L. F., 216
Barrett, S., 8
Barry, H., III, 338
Barsky, A. J., 469, 493
Bartholomae, S., 410
Bartholomew, K., 254, 262
Bartlett, M. S., 212
Baruch, G. K., 350
Bashner, R., 184
Basow, S. A., 313, 330
Bassin, E., 258
Bates, G. W., 348
Batki, S. L., 468
Batson, C. D., 292
Baucom, D. H., 283
Bauer, M. S., 499
Baum, A., 73, 75, 92, 450

Brown, R., 183
Brown, R. D., 530
Brown, R. J., 176, 185
Brown, S., 289, 292, 424
Brown, S. L., 95
Browne, A., 299
Browne, K., 298
Brownell, K. D., 459, 460, 461, 462
Brubaker, T., 279
Bruce, K. R., 511
Bruch, H., 512
Bruckner-Gordon, F., 545
Brumbaugh, C. C., 256
Brummett, B. H., 35, 448
Bryan, A. D., 429
Bryant, J., 411
Bryant, S., 352
Bryant, S. S., 294
Bryden, M. P., 307, 312
Bryer, K. B., 359
Buchanan, D. R., 242
Buchanan, R. W., 502
Buck, E. B., 194
Buckingham, J. T., 155
Buckman, R., 470
Buckner, C. E., 305
Buehlman, K. T., 283
Buelens, M., 395
Bukatko, D., 309
Bulcroft, R., 271, 277, 348
Bulik, C. M., 511
Bull, D. L., 530
Bull, S. S., 412
Bullinger, M., 73
Bumpass, L. L., 275, 285, 291, 292
Bumpus, M. F., 281
Burger, J. M., 55, 196
Burgess, C., 477
Burgess, E. O., 427
Burggraf, K., 318
Burgoon, J. K., 210, 211
Burhans, K. K., 144
Burke, J. D., 485, 487
Burke, P. J., 35, 395
Burleson, B. R., 285
Burr, W. R., 274
Burstein, G., 431
Bursztajn, H. J., 542
Buscaglia, L., 6
Bushman, B. J., 109, 149
Buss, D. M., 58–59, 240, 241, 242, 243, 257, 273, 311, 331, 418
Buss, W. C., 283
Bussey, K., 49, 314
Butcher, J. N., 111
Butler, E. A., 126
Butler, J. L., 89
Butler, R., 360
Buunk, B. P., 388
Buxton, M. N., 451
Byers, E. S., 436
Byrne, D., 245
Byrnes, J., 340, 341

C

Cacioppo, J. T., 95, 188, 255, 264
Caddell, M., 91
Caldwell, B. M., 363
Caldwell, D. F., 196
Caldwell, L. L., 398
Calhoun, L. G., 93

Call, B., 257
Call, V., 427
Callander, J. C., 174
Calof, D., 532
Camara, W. J., 212
Cameron, L., 469
Cameron, N., 492
Campbell, E. Q., 191
Campbell, J. C., 298
Campbell, J. D., 140, 146
Campbell, L. F., 7
Campbell, R. J., 542
Campbell, S. M., 328
Campbell, W. K., 148, 149, 156, 277
Canary, D. J., 246
Cancro, R., 503, 505
Candela, S. F., 508
Canetto, S. S., 344
Cannon, W., 85
Cantor, J., 322
Cantor-Graae, E., 507
Capitanio, J., 248, 415
Caplan, R. D., 393
Caputo, D., 466
Cardena, E., 129, 496
Carducci, B., 215
Carey, M., 421, 467, 468
Carli, L. L., 308, 309
Carlson, D. N., 470, 471
Carlson, E. A., 363
Carlsson, A., 505
Carlton, K., 259
Carney, S., 541
Carpenter, W. T., 502, 504, 540
Carr, V. J., 73
Carrere, 277
Carrington, P., 129
Carroll, J. L., 418
Carson, R. C., 111, 504
Carstensen, L. L., 351
Carter, B., 275, 276, 277
Carter, E. A., 288
Carter, J. D., 208, 309
Cartwright, S., 125
Caruso, D. R., 125
Carver, C. S., 96, 97, 106, 108, 248
Casas, J. F., 308
Casper, L. M., 270, 271, 287
Caspi, A., 58, 245
Cassel, R. N., 51
Castronguay, L. G., 542
Catania, J. A., 468
Cate, R. M., 274, 419, 426
Cates, W., Jr., 431
Cattell, R. B., 34, 65, 67
Catz, S. L., 468
Cavanaugh, J. C., 353, 357
Cavell, T. A., 17
Caverly, D. C., 25, 26
Cegala, D. J., 209
Cerletti, U., 540
Chaiken, S., 187
Chambless, D. L., 529
Chan, R. W., 295
Chancey, D., 283
Chang, E. C., 72, 97
Chang, R. Y., 118
Chanowitz, B., 184
Chaplin, W. F., 403
Chappell, K. D., 255

Charlesworth, W. R., 330
Chartrand, T., 196
Chase, A., 366
Chemers, M. M., 50
Chen, D., 43
Cheng, C., 106
Cheng, H., 149
Cheng, Y., 466
Cherlin, A. J., 270, 286, 288
Chia, R. C., 315
Chiappelli, F., 88, 451
Chick, J., 458
Chiles, C., 190
Chiriboga, D. A., 345, 350
Chizmar, L., 466
Cho, C., 429
Choi, H., 278
Choi, I., 178
Choi, L., 177
Choice, P., 299
Chopra, D., 6
Chouldhry, N. K., 539
Christensen, A., 259, 282, 283
Christensen, A. J., 471, 472
Christensen, P., 263
Christoph, R. T., 50
Christophe, B., 216
Christopher, F. S., 18, 424
Church, A. T., 35
Cialdini, R. B., 157, 189, 191, 195, 196, 197
Ciarrochi, J., 92, 126
Cicchetti, D., 363
Cicirelli, V. G., 351, 359
Ciraulo, D. A., 474
Cirincione, C., 508
Claar, R. L., 448, 470
Clark, C. L., 254
Clark, D., 417
Clark, L. A., 34
Clark, M. C., 28, 29
Clark, M. S., 222, 248
Clark, R., 75
Clarke-Stewart, K. A., 288
Classen, C., 91
Clay, D. L., 395
Cleary, P. D., 454
Cleek, M. G., 283
Clements, M. L., 275
Cloitre, M., 366
Clore, G. L., 188, 245
Clow, A., 87
Coate, D., 22
Coates, L., 209
Coates, T. J., 468
Coats, E. J., 309
Cobb, S. J., 323
Cochran, S. B., 303
Cochran, S. D., 245, 294, 417
Cogan, J. C., 293, 416
Cohan, C. L., 292, 298
Cohen, A., 356, 357
Cohen, C. E., 174
Cohen, D. B., 58
Cohen, D., 537, 539
Cohen, F., 60, 97
Cohen, L. D., 241
Cohen, M. J. M., 450
Cohen, S., 73, 95, 255, 451, 452, 455
Cohn, E., 26
Cohn, L. D., 322
Cohn, S., 26

Coie, J. D., 213
Coiro, M. J., 289
Coker, A. L., 296
Colder, C. R., 109
Colder, M., 127
Cole, S. W., 126
Coleman, J. C., 111
Coleman, M., 289
Collaer, M. L., 313
Colley, A., 249
Collins, C., 468
Collins, L. M., 340
Collins, N. L., 215, 254, 255
Collins, R. L., 155
Collins, W. A., 343
Colluci, P., 295
Coltrane, S., 280, 281, 287, 288
Colvin, C. R., 113
Comas-Diaz, L., 315
Compton, W. C., 129
Condon, J. W., 245
Conger, R. D., 340
Conklin, H. M., 506
Connell, C. M., 355
Connidis, I. A., 277
Conoscenti, L. M., 322
Conrad, C. C., 467
Conte, J. R., 530
Contrada, R. J., 244, 75
Conway, M., 154
Conway-Welch, C., 421
Cook, S. I., 296
Coons, D. J., 508
Coons, H. L., 79
Coontz, S., 271, 287
Cooper, A., 17, 18, 411, 412, 428
Cooper, C. L., 72, 73, 86
Cooper, M. L., 254
Cooper, P. J., 92, 510
Cope, M. B., 461
Coplan, J. D., 490
Copper, C., 27
Corhan, S. E., 283
Cornelius, T., 196
Cornoldi, C., 29
Corr, C. A., 359
Correll, C. U., 538
Corsica, J. A., 460, 466
Costa, P. T., Jr., 34, 35, 66, 97, 350, 358
Couch, K. A., 393
Courtenay, W. H., 322
Cowan, C. P., 277, 348
Cowan, N., 152
Cowan, P. A., 277, 348, 368
Cowley, J., 431
Cox, M. J., 277
Cox, P. D., 527
Coy, K. C., 343
Coyne, J. C., 501
Craik, F. I. M., 28
Cramer, P., 111, 113
Crano, W. D., 245
Creed, F., 451
Crepaz, N., 468
Crick, N. R., 308
Crimmins, E. M., 351
Critelli, J. W., 92, 98
Crits-Christoph, P., 547
Crocker, J., 151, 176, 184, 307, 308
Crooks, R. H., 381, 422, 425, 434, 439
Cross, C. K., 344

Cross, P., 155
Cross, S. E., 141, 145, 146, 155
Crouter, A. C., 278, 281, 348
Crovitz, H. F., 29
Crowder, K. D., 290
Crowell, J. A., 275
Crowley, A. E., 187
Crowley, B. J., 95
Crowley, J., 299
Crowley, M. J., 59
Cruza-Guet, M. C., 379
Csikszentmihalyi, M., 93
Cudney, M. R., 161
Cuesta, M. J., 504
Culpepper, L., 539
Cummings, E. M., 289, 365
Cunningham, C. O., 467
Cunningham, H. M., 535
Cunningham, M. R., 240, 241, 315
Curtis, R. C., 244
Cutrona, C. E., 261, 262
Cutting, L. P., 508

D
Dabbs, J. M., 313
D'Achiardi, C., 375
Dainton, M., 246
Dalbert, C., 178
Dallal, G. E., 339
Dallman, M. F., 87
D'Amico, M. L., 238
D'Andrade, R. G., 331
Danieli, Y., 3, 82
Dansereau, D. F., 26
Danton, W. G., 537, 539
Dantzer, R., 88
Darley, J. M., 176, 207
Darling, C. A., 421
Das, E. H. H., 187
D'Augelli, A. R., 344, 417
David, J. P., 73, 98
Davidson, J. K., 421
Davidson, M. J., 388, 391, 392
Davies, L., 291
Davies, R., 498
Davis, B., 317
Davis, H., 129
Davis, J. L., 245
Davis, K., 173
Davis, K. E., 255, 257, 296
Davis, K. F., 16
Davis, K. L., 353
Davis, M., 210, 214
Davis, M. N., 95
Davis, P., 426
Davis, R. A., 110
Dawood, K., 295
Day, S. X., 238, 379
Dean, F. P., 126
DeAngelis, T., 309, 417
Deaux, K., 240, 242, 305, 310
DeBaryshe, B. D., 364
De Beni, R., 29
DeBoer, D. D., 274
DeCarvalho, R. J., 51
Deci, E. L., 20
De Cock, K. M., 467
Deemer, H. N., 470
Deffenbacher, J. L., 451
DeFrain, J., 276, 291
Deikman, A. J., 5

de Jong, P. J., 491
DeJong-Gierveld, J., 261
Del Monte, M. M., 530
Delahanty, D. L., 450
DeLamater, J. D., 323, 415, 432, 434, 425
Delaune, K. A., 454, 456
Delay, J., 536
Deldin, P. G., 505
DeLeon, J., 504
DeLeon, P. H., 3
DeLillo, V., 450
Delinsky, S. S., 510
Delongis, A., 72
Delunas, L., 79, 98
DelVecchio, W. F., 358
DeMaris, A., 298, 299
Demian, 294
Demo, D. H., 277, 290, 295, 349
Dempster, F. N., 27
Deniker, P., 536
Denisoff, E., 98
Dennerstein, L., 279, 349
Denney, N., 142
Dennis, W., 356, 357
Denton, W. H., 285
DePaulo, B. M., 206, 211, 212
Derlega, V. J., 217
Derogotis, L. R., 79, 97
DeRoma, V., 495
Des Jarlais, D. C., 475
Desmarais, S., 315
DeSpelder, L. A., 359
Dessler, W. A., 74
de St. Aubin, E., 348
Detsky, A. S., 539
Detzer, M. J., 423
Deutsch, G., 312
Deutsch, M., 191
Devine, P. G., 177, 184
Devlin, M. J., 461
de Vries, B., 249, 351
Dew, M. A., 487
Dewe, P., 72, 86
De Wilde, E. J., 344
DeWit, J. B. F., 187
DeWolff, M. S., 363
DiClemente, C. C., 159
DiClemente, R. J., 341
Diekman, A. B., 305, 317
Diener, C., 19, 20
Diener, E., 2, 3, 19, 20, 21, 22, 73, 255
Diforio, D., 508
Dikel, M. F., 376
Dilsaver, S. C., 499
DiMatteo, R. M., 470, 471
Din, J. N., 463
Dindia, K., 217, 251
Dinning, W. D., 327
Dion, K. K., 176, 237, 251, 182, 237, 251
DiPaula, A., 140
Dipboye, R. L., 403
DiPlacido, J., 96
DiPrete, T., 288
Dirks, J. F., 470
Dishotsky, N. L., 476
DiTommaso, E., 262
Dittus, P., 410
Dixon, L., 298
Dixon, R. A., 356
Djintcharadze, N., 182
Dobson, K. S., 518

Gordon, S. L., 251
Gordon, V., 410
Gore, J. S., 145, 146
Gormley, B., 256
Gosling, S. D., 180
Gosselin, J. T., 159
Gotlib, D. A., 437
Gotlib, I. H., 501
Gottdiener, J. S., 448
Gottesman, I. I., 505, 506
Gottman, J. M., 259, 277, 283, 284, 285
Gould, R., 349–350
Gourevitch, M. N., 475
Gouzoulis-Mayfrank, E., 477
Gow, K. M., 532
Graber, J. A., 339, 340
Graig, E., 76
Gramling, S. E., 393
Grant, I., 451
Grant-Pillow, H., 142
Gray, J., 6
Gray-Little, B., 151
Graziano, W. G., 35
Green, A., 238
Green, C. E., 299
Green, L. R., 261
Green, M. A., 238
Green, S. K., 242
Greenberg, J., 150, 179
Greenberg, J. L., 59–60, 61, 62
Greenberg, J. S., 466
Greenberg, L. S., 525, 534
Greenberg, R. P., 43, 539
Greene, R. L., 27
Greenfield, D. N., 110
Greenhaus, J. H., 381
Greenland, P., 445
Greenson, R. R., 523
Greenwald, A. G., 177
Greenwood, D., 254, 298
Gregerson, E. 416
Gregory, R. J., 7
Grencavage, L. M., 529
Griest, J. H., 539
Griffin-Shelley, E., 428
Griffith, K. H., 386
Griffiths, M., 110
Grinspoon, L., 476, 477
Grob, C. S., 477
Grob, G. N., 443
Grohol, J., 484
Gross, C. P., 539
Gross, J. J., 126, 431
Grossbaum, M. F., 348
Grote, N. K., 222, 248
Grove, W. M., 67
Gruber, A. J., 477
Gruber, J. E., 391
Gruenberg, A. M., 498
Grunberg, N. E., 455
Grundy, E., 291
Guadagno, R. E., 196
Guest, F., 423
Guevremont, D. C., 534
Guggenheim, F. G., 492
Gugula, S., 315
Guinn, I. S., 155
Gullette, E. C. D., 448
Gupta, G. R., 236
Gupta, S., 288
Gupta, U., 237

Gureje, O., 492
Gurland, B. J., 353, 354
Gurung, R. A. R., 255
Gutek, B. A., 391
Guthrie, J., 279, 349
Gutierrez, P. M., 518

H
Haan, N., 358
Haas, D. M., 246
Haas, E., 309
Haas, L., 280, 281, 282
Hackam, D. G., 445
Hackett, G., 377
Hackstaff, K. B., 287
Hadjiyannakis, K., 502
Hafdahl, A. R., 151
Hafer, C. L., 178
Hagan, H., 475
Hagan, R., 314
Hagerty, M. R., 22
Haig, J., 35
Hale, J. L., 256
Hale, S. L., 197
Hall, D. R., 292
Hall, E. T., 207
Hall, G. S., 343
Hall, J. A., 207, 208, 210, 213, 309, 331
Hall, R. M., 303
Hall, W., 476
Halmi, K, A., 510, 511, 513
Halpern, C. T., 241
Halpern, D. F., 306, 307, 310, 311
Halverson, A. M., 175
Hamilton, A., 238
Hamilton, J. C., 470
Hamilton, M. A., 330
Hamilton, T. E., III, 242
Hamilton, V. L., 194
Hammen, C., 497
Hammersley, R., 477
Hammersmith, K. S., 414
Hammond, D. C., 532
Hampson, E., 312
Hamsen, P., 451
Han, S., 381
Han, W., 282
Hancock, D. R., 84
Handal, M., 438
Handy, B., 428, 438
Hanna, R., 240, 242
Hanna, S. L., 218
Hansen, C. H., 317
Hansen, J. C., 377
Hansen, R. D., 317
Hansen, W. B., 341
Hansford, S. L., 249
Happonen, P., 463
Hardy, R. E., 161
Haring, M., 275
Harnack, L., 461
Harpaz, I., 395
Harrigan, J. A., 210
Harris, J. R., 43, 58
Harris, M. B., 308
Harris, M. J., 175
Harris, T., 6
Harrison, J. A., 192
Harrison, K., 322, 511
Harry, J., 413
Hart, K. E., 448

Hart, R., 291
Hart, T. A., 468
Harter, S., 144, 149, 150
Hartka, E., 358
Hartley, A. A., 356
Hartup, W. W., 248
Harvey, J. H., 246
Harvey, M. H., 282, 531
Harvey, P. D., 507
Harwood, T. M., 529
Hatala, M. N., 240
Hatcher, R. A., 430, 431, 433
Hatfield, E., 236, 243, 245, 257, 408, 411, 419
Hattery, A., 381
Hau, K., 151
Haug, N. A., 468
Hawkins, A. J., 287
Hawkley, L. C., 264
Haworth-Hoeppner, S., 512
Haycock, L. A., 122
Hayes, A., 426
Hayes, S., 39
Hayes-Roth, B., 28
Hays, K. F., 466
Hayskip, B., Jr., 95
Hazam, H., 217
Hazan, C., 252–256, 262
Healy, C. C., 381
Healy, D., 538, 539
Heaton, T. B., 272, 277
Heavey, C. L., 259, 283
Hebi, M. R., 241, 386
Hecht, M. A., 213
Hedges, L. V., 306, 307
Heider, F., 152
Heiman, J. R., 437, 438, 439
Heine, S. J., 156
Helgeson, V. S., 249, 327
Hellstrom, A., 172
Helson, R., 345, 348, 358
Helweg-Larsen, M., 155
Hembree, E. A., 535
Hemenover, S. H., 127
Henderson, K. E., 461
Henderson, L., 263
Henderson, M., 248, 249
Hendrick, C., 204, 245, 252, 257
Hendrick, S. S., 204, 245, 252, 257, 258
Henley, N. M., 207, 209., 210, 213
Hennessy, D. A., 76
Henning, K., 422, 436
Henry, M. E., 541
Heppner, P. P., 118
Herbener, E. S., 245
Herek, G. M., 248, 293, 320, 415, 416
Herman, C. P., 241, 322
Herman, J. L., 530
Hermann, R. C., 540
Herrett-Skjellum, J., 318
Hershberger, S. L., 344, 417
Hertzog, C., 357
Herzog, D. B., 510
Herzog, M. E., 241
Herzog, T. A., 456
Heszen-Niejodek, I., 106
Hetherington, E. M., 58, 288, 289
Hettema, J. M., 490
Heuer, S. K., 242
Hewitt, P. L., 122, 275
Hewstone, M., 183, 191
Heymann, J., 387

Hiedelmann, B., 286
Hiester, M., 363
Higgins, E. T., 141, 142
Hightower, M., 95
Hilgard, E. R., 63
Hill, A. J., 315, 316, 461
Hill, C. A., 418
Hill, C. E., 529
Hill, C. T., 251, 257
Hilton, J. L., 176
Hines, A. M., 289
Hines, M., 312, 313
Hiroto, D. S., 107
Hirschfeld, R. M. A., 344
Hirschl, T. A., 291
Ho, B., 503, 506
Hobdy, J., 95
Hobfoll, S. E., 95
Hobson, C. J., 79, 98
Hochschild, A. R., 281, 396
Hodge, B., 387
Hodges, S. D., 213
Hodgson, D., 88, 451
Hoek, J. W., 510
Hoffman, E., 42
Hoffman, R. E., 92, 508
Hoffman, R. R., III, 97
Hoffnung, M., 323
Hofstede, G., 145
Hogan, J., 35
Hogue., C. 424
Holahan, C. J., 94, 112, 502
Holden, C., 538
Holder, J. S., 466
Holen, A., 91
Holland, J. C., 451
Holland, J. L., 378–379
Holland, K., 277
Hollander, E., 489
Hollister, L. E., 476
Hollon, S. D., 529
Holman, T. B., 274
Holmes, T. H., 78–79, 95, 97
Holoway, P., 410
Holt, C. S., 215
Homma-True, R., 544
Hong, G. K., 544
Hood, K. E., 312
Hooker, E., 417
Hooley, J. M., 508
Hopkins, C., 322
Hopko, D. R., 89
Hopper, J., 289
Horgan, T. G., 208, 309
Horowitz, L. M., 245, 254
Horwath, E., 489
Houts, A. C., 485
Howard, G. S., 4
Howard, J., 351
Howard, K. I., 528
Howard, M., 410
Howard, R., 505
Howland, R. H., 500
Hoyer, W. D., 187
Hsiang, R., 538
Hsu, L. K. G., 510
Hu, F. B., 462
Hu, L., 50
Hu, T. W., 544
Hubbard, J. A., 213
Hubbard, J. R., 87, 92

Hubner, J. J., 147
Hudman, K. S., 455
Huesmann, L. R., 226
Huff, M. E., 91
Hugenberg, K., 177
Hughes, C. C., 544
Hull, J. G., 142
Hulshoff, H. E., 506
Hunsley, J., 67
Hunt, C., 487
Hunt, M., 18
Hunter, B. A., 297
Hunter, D. M., 306
Hurrell, J., 388
Huston, A. C., 226, 227, 317
Huston, T. L., 285, 287
Hyde, J. S., 282, 303, 306, 307, 308, 310, 323,
    324, 328, 339, 396, 411, 413, 415, 418, 425,
    432, 434
Hyde, T. M., 505, 506
Hygge, S., 73
Hyman, I. E., 530

I
Iaccino, J. F., 29
Iacono, W. G., 212, 506
Iawao, S., 236
Ickes, W., 183, 327
Ickovics, J. R., 468
Iezzi, T., 493
Ilgen, D. R., 373, 391
Infante, J. R., 129
Ingegneri, D. G., 351
Inglehart, R., 20
Ingoldsby, B. B., 272
Ingram, R. E., 7, 501
Innocenti, G. M., 312
Insko, C. A., 191
Irabarren, C., 447
Ironson, G., 451
Isaacowitz, D. M., 108
Isenberg, K. E., 541
Ismail, B., 507
Israël, M., 511
Ivancevich, J. M., 389
Ivens-Tyndal, C., 92, 498, 500
Izard, C., 213

J
Jablensky, A., 502
Jaccard, J., 410
Jackson, B. L., 286
Jackson, L. A., 241
Jackson, T., 263
Jacob, D., 290
Jacob, R. G., 536
Jacobs, H. S., 354
Jacobs, J. A., 386
Jacobs, W. S., 475, 476
Jacobson, C. K., 277
Jacobson, E., 129
Jacobson, N. S., 282
Jacques, R., 387
Jaffe, J., 474
Jahoda, M., 113
Jakicici, J., 466
Jakupcak, M., 320
James, E. H., 386
James, J. E., 463
Jamison, K. R., 498, 499
Janata, J. W., 470
Janevic, M. R., 355

Janis, I. L., 73, 84
Jankowiak, W. R., 236
Janoff-Bulman, R., 22, 141
Janofsky, J. S., 508
Janssen, R. S., 467
Jansz, J., 318, 320
Jaroff, L., 531
Jay, K., 424
Jefferson, J. W., 539
Jeffrey, R. W., 461, 462
Jemmott, J. B., III, 94, 255
Jepsen, C. A., 272C
Jepsen, L. K., 272
Jex, S. M., 50
Jick, H., 539
Jick, S. S., 539
Jindal, K., 500
John, O. P., 35
Johnson, A. M., 413
Johnson, B. A., 457, 459
Johnson, D. W., 224
Johnson, F. P, 224
Johnson, I. M., 299
Johnson, J. A., 471, 472
Johnson, J. H., 99, 100
Johnson, J. L., 122
Johnson, M. P., 298, 299
Johnson, S. B., 470, 471
Johnson, T., 209
Johnson, T. W., 295
Johnson, V. E., 419, 420–421, 438, 439
Johnstone, L., 541
Joiner, T. E., 501, 502
Jonas, J. M., 475
Jones, D., 240
Jones, E. E., 152, 163, 173, 174
Jones, F., 79
Jones, N. F., 470
Jones, R. A., 187
Jones, S. M., 226
Jones, T. S., 207
Jorgensen, R. S., 126
Joung, I. M. A., 291
Jourard, S. M., 113
Jouriles, E., 142
Joyner, T., 395, 397
Judge, T. A., 35
Julien, R. M., 473, 474
Jung, C. G., 41–42
Jussim, L., 175

K
Kaelber, C. T., 309, 485
Kagan, J., 490
Kahn, A. S., 310
Kahn, J. R., 288
Kahneman, D., 23
Kaiser, C. R., 179
Kalant, H., 476
Kalant, O. J., 476
Kales, A. K., 92
Kalichman, S. C., 468, 469
Kalick, S. M., 242
Kalidindi, S., 499
Kalkwarf, H. J., 463
Kallgren, C. A., 186
Kalmijn, M., 272
Kaltman, S., 360
Kamp Dush, C. M., 292
Kamps, D. M., 535
Kanagawa, C., 155

Moos, R. H., 89, 94, 109, 112, 114
Morahan-Martin, J., 110, 264
Moran, G., 363
Moray, N., 152
Morell, C., 277
Moretti, M. M., 141
Morgan, H. J., 141
Morgan, M. J., 477
Morgenstern, J., 123, 124
Morley, J. E., 354, 409
Mormede, P., 88
Morris, M. M., 95
Morris, M. W., 178
Morrison, D. R., 286, 289
Morrison, M. A., 322
Morrison, T. G., 322
Morse, S., 143
Moseman, S. E., 539
Mosher, D. L., 327
Mosher, W. D., 274, 285, 289
Moskowitz, D. S., 348
Moskowitz, J., 83–84, 93
Mowrer, O. H., 490
Moynihan, J. A., 451
Muehlenhard, C. L., 297
Mukamal, K. J., 458
Mullen, J. L., 25, 26
Mullin, C. R., 296
Munck, A., 88
Muramatsu, V., 194
Muraven, M., 158
Muris, P., 50
Murnen, S. K., 317, 510
Murphy, M., 291
Murphy, S. P., 463
Murphy, S. T., 164
Murphy-Berman, V., 250
Murr, A., 431
Murray, C., 287
Murrell, A. H., 386
Murrell, A. J., 182
Murry, V. M., 426
Murstein, B., 274
Musselman, D. L., 500
Must, A., 339
Mutchler, J. E., 351
Myers, D. G., 2, 19, 20, 21, 22, 120, 143
Mynier, K., 209

N
Nabi, R. L., 226
Naisbitt, J., 378
Nalwa, K., 264
Narrow, W. E., 519
Nash, M., 353, 530
Nathan, P. E., 485, 528
Nathanson, A. I., 226
Navarro, R. L., 377
Naveh-Benjamin, M., 84
Naylor, M. R., 4
Naylor, T. H., 4
Neale, M. C., 490, 499
Necomb, M. D., 119
Neese, R. M., 86
Neimeyer, R. A., 359
Neiss, R., 85
Nelson, D. A., 308
Nemeroff, C. B., 449, 500
Nemeth, C., 190
Nemiah, J. C., 493
Neufeldt, S. A., 545

Neuman, J. H., 393
Nevid, J., 425
Newberg, A., 129
Newby, D. E., 463
Newell, G. R., 450
Newman, M., 6
Newport, F., 177
Newton, B. J., 194
Newton, P. M., 350
Nezu, A. M., 450
Niaura, R., 447, 455
Nickerson, C., 20
Nida, S. A., 192
Nie, N. H., 238
Niehuis, S., 285
Nielsen, J. M., 326
Niemann, Y. F., 305
Nisbett, R. E., 177, 178
Nishimura, N., 248
Nock, S. L., 292
Nolen-Hoeksema, S., 309, 498, 500
Noller, P., 222., 254, 283, 331
Nomaguchi, K. M., 277
Norcross, J. C., 7, 529, 547
Norenzayan, A., 177
Norman, R. L., 472, 474
Norns, F. H., 255
Norton, P. G. W., 464
Norton, S., 392
Nowell, A., 306, 307
Nurius, P., 141
Nurminen, E., 390
Nurnberger, J. L., 134
Nyberg, S. E., 27
Nye, R. D., 52

O
Oakes, P., 176
O'Brien, B., 539
O'Callahan, M., 451
O'Conner, N., 347
O'Donnell, A., 26
O'Donohoe, A., 477
O'Donovan, M. C., 505
Oesterman, K., 308
Oettingen, G., 154
O'Halloran, C. M., 359
O'Hanlon, J. F., 476
Ohman, A P., 491
O'Keefe, D. J., 197
Oldenburg, C. M., 255
Olds, C. W., 349
Olfson, M., 519, 520, 521, 539
Olio, K., 532
Olivardia, R., 322., 408
Oliver, M. B., 308
Ollendick, T. H., 490
Olsman, S. L., 297
Olson, D. H., 276, 291
Olver, M. B., 411
Omarzu, J., 246
Omoto, A. M., 236
O'Neil, J., 329
O'Neill, G., 427
O'Neill, N., 427
Ones, D. S., 35
Ono, H., 283
O'Rand, A. M., 286
Orenstein, P., 151, 307
Organista, P. B., 493
Orlando, V. P., 25, 26

Orlofsky, J., 346
Orth-Gomer, K., 451
O'Shay, D. W., 381
Osipow, S. H., 381
Oskamp, S., 4
Ostrove, J. M., 345, 348
O'Sullivan, M., 208, 211
Otto, M. W., 490
Oulette, S., 95, 96
Overall, N., 244
Owen, M. J., 505
Owens, D., 240
Ozer, D. J., 35
Ozer, E. J., 90, 91, 495
Ozer, E. M., 159

P
Pacak, K., 87
Pachauri, A., 250
Padavic, I., 270
Padgett, D. A., 451
Paivio, A., 29
Pallanti, S P., 491
Paludi, M. A., 316
Papalia, D. E., 349
Papp, L. M., 289
Paquette, J. A., 262
Pardun, C. J., 411
Paris, J., 493
Park, C. L., 93
Park, C. W., 188
Park, J., 251
Parker, J. W., 151
Parks, M. R., 238
Paronis, C. A., 109
Parrott, A. C., 477
Parrott, R., 210
Parry-Jones, B., 510
Parry-Jones, W. L., 510
Parsons, S., 375
Parsons, T., 305
Pasley, K., 289
Passino, R. M., 322
Patel, J. K., 505
Patnoe, S., 185
Pato, M. T., 489
Patrick, B. C., 217, 258
Patrick, C. J., 212
Patterson, C. J., 295, 396, 414, 417
Patterson, G. R., 364
Patterson, M. L., 209
Patton, G., 509
Paul, A. M., 6, 8
Paul, E. L., 426
Paulhus, D. L., 39, 43, 66
Pavlov, I., 45, 50
Payne, D. G., 27
Pazder, L., 496
Peake, P. K., 158
Pearce, L., 481
Pearson, P., 298, 398
Pearson, T. A., 283
Pechnick, R. N., 476
Pedersen, P., 544
Pederson, D. R., 363
Pederson, W., 477
Peirce, R. S., 95
Pelham, W. H., 536
Peltola, P., 281
Peng, K., 178
Pennebaker, J. W., 126–127, 216, 451

Peplau, L. A., 239, 245, 248, 251, 257, 294, 308, 347, 348, 411, 413, 414, 417, 418, 422, 427, 428
Peralta, B., 504
Perese, S., 316
Peretti, P. O., 240
Perkins, D. F., 343
Perkins, R., 175
Perloff, R. M., 187
Perreault, S., 184
Perrett, D. L., 241
Perri, M. G., 460, 466
Perry, B., 364
Perry, H. M., 409
Perry-Jenkins, M., 281, 282, 348
Person, E. S., 43
Pervin, L., 358
Petersen, A. C., 339, 341, 343, 344
Peterson, B. E., 182
Peterson, C., 93, 96–97, 154
Peterson, N., 347
Petras, K., 203
Petras, R., 203
Petrocelli, W., 391
Petticrew, M., 450
Pettigrew, T. F., 181, 185, 191
Petty, R. E., 186, 187, 188, 189
Pezedek, K., 494
Phillips, K. A., 322, 408, 489
Phillips, M. R., 508
Phillips, W. T., 466
Pi, E. H., 538
Pierce, C. M., 74, 544
Pierce, G. R., 95
Pietromonaco, P. R., 216, 254
Pike, A., 58
Pike, C. L., 241
Pike, K. M., 512
Pillard, R. C., 414, 415
Pillow, D. R., 72
Pilowsky, I., 493
Pinals, D. A., 505
Pinckert, S., 196
Pincus, H. A., 519, 520, 521, 536
Pine, D. S., 489
Pinel, J. P. J., 460, 461
Pines, A. M., 90
Pingitore, R., 403
Pink, D. H., 383
Piotrkowski, C. S., 495
Piotrowski, N. A., 159
Piper, W., 527
Pipher, M., 151
Pi-Sunyer, F. X., 460
Pittman, F., III, 545
Pittman, J. F., 283
Piver, S., 259
Pixley, J., 350
Plante, G. G., 466
Pleck, J. H., 318, 319, 327, 331
Plomin, R., 57, 58
Plous, S. L., 173, 179
Ploutz-Snyder, R., 213
Poelmans, S. A. Y., 395
Poland, R. E., 477
Polissar, N. L., 535
Polivy, J., 241, 322
Pollack, W., 319
Polley, B. A., 461, 462
Polonko, K. A., 347
Polonsky, D., 439

Pomeroy, C., 510
Pond, K., 263
Pontari, B. A., 154
Ponton, L. E., 341
Poole, D. A., 530
Poon, L. W., 353
Pope, E., 296
Pope, H. G., 322, 477, 496, 503
Pope, H., 408
Pope, K. S., 546
Popenoe, D., 271, 285, 287
Poppas, D. P., 92
Porter, G., 395
Porter, R. E., 206, 209, 210, 223, 227
Potthoff, J. G., 502
Powell, B., 43
Powell, F. C., 359
Powell, J. A., 194
Powell, J. H., 477
Powell, R. A., 494
Pratkanis, A. R., 185, 186
Pratt, L. A., 449
Prehodka, J., 240
Prentice-Dunn, S., 187
Prescott, C. A., 502
Presser, H. B., 282
Pressman, S., 5
Preston, L. K., 418
Preto, N. G., 278
Previti, D., 286
Prezioso, M. S., 374
Price, R. H., 393
Priester, J. R., 189
Prochaska, J. O., 456
Procter, E., 179
Prodromidis, M., 363
Profit, W. E., 74
Pruchno, R., 351
Prudic, J., 541
Pryor, F. L., 384
Pryor, J. B., 392
Pryor, J. L., 437
Putnam, R. D., 262
Putney, N. M., 349
Pychyl, T. A., 122
Pyszczynski, T. A., 59–60, 61, 62, 150, 179

Q
Quinn, J. M., 188
Quinn, K. A., 177
Quinn, L., 511

R
Rabbitt, P., 358
Rabinowitz, F. E., 303
Rabkin, J. G., 97
Rachman, S. J., 131, 491
Radel, J., 219
Ragheb, M. G., 397
Ragland, D. R., 446
Ragsdale, K., 350
Rahe, R. H., 78–79, 95, 97, 98
Rahim, M. A., 223
Rahman, M. A., 455
Rakowski, W., 352
Raley, R. K., 285
Ramaden, N. M., 451
Ramaekers, J. G., 476
Ramirez, M., 543
Ramsey, E., 364
Randhawa, B. S., 306

Rank, M. R., 282, 291
Rapee, R. M., 488, 491
Raphael, B., 72
Rapson, R. L., 236, 245, 246, 408, 411, 419
Raskin, P. M., 347
Rasmussen, C., 76
Rathus, S., 425
Ray, G. E., 262
Read, C. R., 317
Read, J. D., 530
Read, S. J., 255
Redding, R. E., 417
Reddy, B. S., 463
Reed, G. M., 113
Regan, M. F., 450
Regan, P. C., 241, 245, 246, 256, 257
Regier, D. A., 309, 485, 487
Rehm, L. P., 92
Reibel, D. K., 129
Reich, P., 92
Reid, P. T., 316
Reifman, A., 164
Reilly, A. H., 386
Reimann, R., 294
Reinisch, J. M., 418, 429, 432
Reis, H. T., 216, 217, 240, 245, 249, 250, 257, 258, 263
Reis, T. J., 155
Reise, S. P., 35
Reisner, A. D., 530
Reiss, D., 58
Reiss, S., 490
Reissman, C., 259
Reiter, R. C., 470
Reitman, F., 381
Reitmeijer, C. A., 412
Remland, M. S., 207
Renaud, C. A., 436
Rennie, D., 539, 540
Rennison, C. M., 298
Renshaw, K., 156
Rentfrow, P. J., 155
Renzetti, C., 298
Repa, B. K., 391
Repetti, R. L., 281, 348
Repetto, M., 475
Rhem, L. P., 498, 500
Rhodes, K., 195
Rhodewalt, F., 157
Rice, L. N., 525
Richards, M. H., 343
Richards, V., 180
Richardson, C. R., 465
Richardson, J. G., 316
Richmond, V. P., 219, 220
Richter, L., 97, 180
Ridge, S. R., 254
Ridker, P. M., 445, 446
Rieder, R. O., 499
Riemann, R., 57
Rierdan, J., 340
Rifkin, J., 2
Riggio, R. E., 403
Rigotti, N. A., 454
Rihmer, Z., 538
Rimal, R. N., 50
Rime, B., 216
Rimm, D. C., 535
Rindfuss, R. R., 346
Ripoll, K., 286
Riso, L. P., 152

Ritz, T., 450
Rivas-Vazquez, R. A., 538
Roback, H. B., 490, 527
Robbe, H. W., 476
Robbins, A., 350
Robbins, A. S., 395
Robbins, E. R., 426
Robbins, J. M., 493
Robbins, S. B., 393, 394
Roberts, A. R., 298, 299
Roberts, B. W., 358
Roberts, D. F., 317
Roberts, L. J., 259, 283
Roberts, P., 350
Robie, C., 299
Robins, L. N., 485
Robins, R. W., 147
Robinson, B. E., 395
Robinson, D. G., 505
Robinson, F. P., 25–26
Robinson, J. P., 2
Robinson, M., 2
Rockwell, S. C., 411
Rodin, J., 460, 510, 512
Rodriguez, M., 409
Roediger, H. L., III, 530
Rogers, C. R., 51–53, 63, 165, 524–526
Rogers, M. P., 92
Rogers, R. W., 187
Rogers, S. J., 277, 278, 283, 286, 349
Roggman, L. A., 363
Rohde, P., 502
Rohner, R. P., 320
Roig, M., 122
Rojewski, J. W., 375
Roloff, M. E., 297
Romano, S. J., 511
Romney, D. M., 314, 315
Ronald, A., 468
Rook, K. S., 263
Rose, A. J., 308
Rose, C. A., 527
Rose, D., 541
Rose, D. P., 463
Rosen, B., 387
Rosen, D. H., 417
Rosen, G. M., 8
Rosen, L. D., 2
Rosen, R., 438
Rosen, R. D., 8
Rosenbaum, J., 351
Rosenbaum, M., 490, 527
Rosenblatt, A., 60
Rosenbluth, S. C., 294
Rosenfarb, I. S., 508
Rosenfeld, L. B., 241
Rosenfield, S., 310
Rosenhan, D. L., 484–485
Rosenheck, R. A., 519
Rosenman, R. H., 445–446
Rosenthal, R., 175
Rosman, B. L., 512
Ross, C. A., 494
Ross, C. E., 20, 381
Ross, L., 177
Ross, M., 154, 155, 156
Ross, S. R., 162
Rosso, I. M., 507
Roter, D. L., 472
Rothbaum, F. M., 178
Rothblum, E. D., 294

Rothman, A., 444
Rotter, J., 49
Roughton, B., 397
Rounds, J., 379
Rousseau, D. M., 383
Rowe, D. C., 57, 58
Rozanski, A., 446, 448
Rozee, P. D., 298
Rubenfeld, K., 330
Rubenstein, C. M., 261, 263, 264, 265
Rubenstein, D., 435
Rubin, Z., 251, 257
Ruble, D. N., 314, 315
Ruble, T. L., 305
Rubovits, D. R., 98
Rudisch, B., 449
Rudorfer, M. V., 541
Rusbult, C. E., 245, 248
Ruscher, J. B., 183
Rush, A. J., 527, 538
Russell, G. F. M., 509, 510
Russo, E., 476
Russo, N. F., 320
Ruzek, J., 535
Ryan, C., 416
Ryan, R. M., 20
Rynes, S., 387

S

Saad, L., 376
Sabatelli, R. M., 286
Sabourin, S., 275
Sachau, D., 157
Sackeim, H. A., 541
Sadker, D., 317
Sadker, M., 317
Sadock, B. J., 527
Saghir, M. T., 426
Sagrestano, L. M., 387
Sakinofsky, I., 344
Salkovskis, P. M., 493
Salonen, J. T., 463
Salovey, P., 84, 125
Salthouse, T. A., 356
Saltzman, J. L., 150
Salvendy, J. T., 527
Sammons, M. T., 518
Samovar, L. A., 206, 209, 210, 223, 227
San de Acedo, M. L., 307
Sanbonmatsu, D. M., 156
Sanchez, L. M., 542
Sande, M. A., 468
Sanders, G., 427
Sanderson, W. C., 488
Sandler, B. R., 303
Sandler, I., 72
Sandler, J., 535
Sandnabba, N. K., 314
Sandy, J. M., 118
Sanislaw, C. A., 504
Sankis, L. M., 483
Sanna, L. J., 72
Santerre, C., 129
Sapolsky, R. M., 93
Sarason, B. R., 95, 498
Sarason, I. G., 95, 98, 99, 100, 498
Sarwer, D. B., 460, 462
Satterwhite, R. C., 305
Saunders, S. M., 528
Savary, L. M., 144
Savitsky, K., 162

Saxe, G. N., 494
Saxe, L., 212
Sayers, S. L., 449
Scanzoni, J., 287, 347
Schachter, S., 13, 14, 15, 239
Schaefer, E. C., 240
Schaefer, J. B., 89
Schafer, W. D., 341
Schaffer, D., 384
Schaie, K. W., 355, 356
Schaninger, C. M., 283
Schank, D., 460
Scheflin, A. W., 532
Scheidlinger, S., 527
Scheier, M. F., 96, 97, 106, 248
Scher, S. J., 160
Scherer, K. R., 211
Scherer, M., 128
Schermerhorn, A. C., 289
Schiefelbein, V. L., 338
Schiffman, J., 507
Schilit, W. K., 124
Schimel, J., 60, 150
Schirmer, L. L., 255
Schlegel, A., 338
Schlenger, W. E., 3, 82
Schlenk, E., 471
Schlenker, B. R., 154, 162, 163
Schmidlin, A. M., 210
Schmitt, J. P., 248, 328, 397
Schmitz, J. M., 454, 456
Schneer, J. A., 381
Schneider, B. H., 363
Schneider, D. L., 212
Schneider, F., 505
Schneider, J. P., 412
Schnoll, S. H., 475
Schoenfeld, G. A., 50
Schofield, P. E., 191
Scholing, A., 533
Schooler, D., 322
Schooler, J. W., 530
Schoon, L., 375
Schor, J., 2
Schramke, C. J., 451
Schreiber, F. R., 496
Schroeder, A., 73
Schroeder, D. H., 97
Schuchter, S. R., 360
Schuckit, M.. A., 458
Schultheiss, D. P., 374
Schultis, G. A., 7
Schultz, J. H., 129
Schulz, U., 452
Schumacher, P., 110, 264
Schunk, D. H., 159
Schutz, R. W., 340
Schwab, S., 309
Schwartz, B., 2, 8
Schwartz, G. E. R., 129
Schwartz, J. C., 237
Schwartz, J. E., 106
Schwartz, L., 493
Schwartz, L. M., 454
Schwartz, P., 257, 275, 279, 413, 427, 428
Schwartzberg, N., 290
Schwarz, N., 22
Schwarzer, R., 452
Scott, W., 7, 501
Scroppo, J. C., 496
Scully, J. A., 79

Searle, A., 451
Seccombe, K., 351
Sedikides, C., 154, 155, 156
Seecombe, K., 283
Seff, M. A., 278
Segal, M. W., 240
Segall, A., 470
Segerstrom, S. C., 88, 96, 451
Seguin, J. R., 511
Seidlitz, L., 73
Seifer, M., 427
Self, D. W., 473
Seligman, M. E. P., 3, 10, 20, 21, 93, 96, 107, 108, 153, 154, 156, 491, 500, 528, 542, 547
Seltzer, J. A., 291, 292
Selwyn, P. A., 467
Selye, H., 86–87
Semans, J. H., 439
Senecal, C., 122
Sepekoff, B., 413
Serafica, F. C., 381
Servan-Schreiber, D., 492
Sesso, H. D., 445
Seta, C. E., 72
Seta, J. J., 72
Seto, M. C., 297
Sexton, K., 248
Shakesby, P. S., 28
Shalev, A. Y., 91
Shallenberger, W. R., III, 17
Shapiro, A. F., 277, 278
Shapiro, D. H., Jr., 129
Sharp, L. K., 127
Shavelson, R. J., 147
Shaver, O., 249
Shaver, P. R., 237, 252–256, 256, 216, 261, 262, 264, 265
Shaw, D., 259
Shaw, J., 141, 142
Shaw, L. H., 264
Shear, M. K., 535
Sheehan, P. W., 531
Sheehan, S., 503
Sheiham, A., 450, 451
Sheldon, K., 350
Shelton, R. L., 306
Shepperd, J. A., 23, 155
Sher, K. J., 457
Sher, L., 72, 500
Sher, T. G., 283
Sherer, M., 50
Sheridan, J. F., 451
Sherif, M., 183, 191
Sherk, D. L., 162
Sherman, A. M., 351
Sherman, D. A., 177
Shike, M., 463
Shoda, Y., 158
Shotland, R. L., 297
Shouldice, M., 296
Shulman, R. B., 538
Shurgot, B. A., 241
Shurkin, J. N., 549
Shuval, J. T., 80
Sidanius, J., 248
Siebert, A., 24
Siegel, J. M., 99, 100
Siegel, O., 340
Siegle, G., 7, 501
Siegler, I. C., 35, 178, 353, 448
Sigler, R. T., 299

Signoreielli, N., 317, 318
Silberman, E. K., 522, 537
Silberstein, L. R., 510
Silk, K. R., 518
Silke, A., 179
Sillars, A. L., 209
Silver, E., 508
Silver, H., 505
Silver, M., 411
Silver, R. C., 361
Silverman, I., 311
Silverman, M. M., 309, 344
Silverman, P. R., 361
Sime, W., 83
Simeon, D., 489
Simon, R. I., 509
Simonton, D. T., 356
Simpson, C. H., 316
Simpson, G. M., 538
Sinclair, R. C., 188
Singer, B., 528
Singh, D., 241
Singh, P., 237
Sinnott, J. D., 356
Sirois, F. M., 122
Skay, C. L., 122
Skerrett, P. J., 460
Skillman, G., 316
Skinner, B. F., 47–48, 50, 63, 532
Skinner, P. H., 306
Skolnick, P., 490
Skrondal, A., 477
Slashinski, M. J., 296
Slaski, M., 125
Slater, M. A., 493
Slavney, P. R., 493
Sloan, D. M., 216
Slovic, P., 120
Smale, B. J. A., 398
Smart, L., 149
Smeaton, G., 245
Smiler, A. P., 319
Smith, A., 175
Smith, A. K., 378, 382
Smith, A. L., 487
Smith, A. P., 451
Smith, B. W., 450
Smith, C. A., 82
Smith, D. M., 293
Smith, E. A., 398
Smith, E. E., 188
Smith, E. R., 174, 175
Smith, G. S., 458
Smith, J. C., 129
Smith, J. W., 535
Smith, M. L., 547, 548
Smith, M., 496
Smith, P. B., 156., 190, 194, 217
Smith, R. E., 159
Smith, R. H., 240
Smith, S. E., 285
Smith, S. M., 530
Smith, T. P., 7
Smith, T. W., 277, 446, 447, 448, 451, 542
Smith, W. P., 129
Smock, P. J., 270, 288, 292
Smolak, L., 510
Smoll, F. L., 340
Smyer, M. A., 353
Smyth, J. M., 127, 129
Snibbe, A. C., 291

Snir, R., 395
Snodgrass, S. E., 213
Snowdon, D., 353, 354
Snowdon, L. R., 544
Snyder, E., 414
Snyder, M., 164, 174, 208, 236
Sobal, J., 511
Solberg, E. C., 2, 20
Solomon, D. A., 498
Solomon, J., 363
Solomon, S., 59–60, 61, 62, 150, 179, 294
Solowij, N., 476, 477
Sommer, K. L., 146
Sommers-Flanagan, J., 317
Sommers-Flanagan, R., 317
Sonnenberg, S., 388, 389
Sonstroem, R. J., 466
Sorenson, J. L., 468
Soriano, M., 544
Sotiriou, P. E., 27
Soule, R. G., 2
South, S. J., 258, 272, 283, 286, 291
Sovio, U., 109
Sowell, T., 387
Spalding, L. R., 347, 348
Spanos, N., 495–496, 530
Spaulding, L. R., 239, 248, 251, 413, 417
Spector, L., 421
Spence, J. T., 305, 328, 395
Sperry, R. W., 312
Spiegel, D., 91, 255, 494
Spiegler, M. D., 534
Spiro, A., 351
Spitzberg, B. H., 296
Spokane, A. R., 379
Sportolari, L., 412
Sprafkin, J. N., 317
Sprecher, S., 18
Sprecher, S., 240, 243, 256, 257, 258, 419, 423, 424, 426, 427
Springen, K., 241, 322, 408
Springer, S. P., 312
Srebnik, D., 423
Sroufe, L. A., 256
Stack, A. D., 109
Stack, S., 261, 291
Stafford, L., 246
Stajkovic, A. D., 50, 159
Stamler, J., 462, 463
Stampfer, W. J., 464
Staneski, R. A., 215
Stanley, S. M., 275
Stanton, A. L., 451
Stanton, G. C., 147
Starcevic, V., 493
Starker, S., 7
Starrels, M. E., 278
Stattin, H., 340
Staudinger, U. M., 93
Steadman, H. J., 508
Stecker, R., 107
Steele, C. M., 75
Steele, J. B., 489
Steelman, L. C., 43
Steiger, H., 511
Stein, M. B., 91, 490
Stein, N., 325
Stein, P. J., 272, 273
Steinberg, L., 278, 349, 365, 367, 368, 369
Steiner, J., 512
Steiner, M. J., 431

Subject Index

anxiety sensitivity, 490
appeals, emotional, 187
appearance. *See* physical appearance
appearance pressure, 322
appraisal, of stress, 72–73, 81, 82, 98
appraisal-focused coping, 114, 115–118
approach-approach conflict, 76–77
approach-avoidance conflict, 77–78
approval, self-esteem and, 150
aptitudes, 374
Arapesh, 314
archetypes, 41–42
argument culture, 225–227
Argument Culture, The (Tannen), 225
arguments, two-sided, 187
arousal
    emotional, 84–85
    optimal level of, 84–85
    as response to traumatic events, 82
arthritis, 450
Asian Americans
    elder care among, 355
    self-esteem in, 151
    in workforce, 385
    See also minority groups
assault, sexual, 297
Asserting Yourself (Bower & Bower), 229
assertiveness, 224, 227–231
assertiveness training, 228–231
assumptions, irrational, 116, 117
asthma, 450
atherosclerosis, 445
attachment, love as, 252–256
attachment styles, 363
    adult, 252–256
    infant, 252–253, 363
    loneliness and, 262
attention
    aging and, 356
    arousal and, 84
    marijuana use and, 477
    to nonverbal cues, 216, 218–219
    selective, 152, 220
    stress and, 89
attitudes
    changing, 185, 189, 194
    sexual, 419, 437, 439
    similarity in, 245
attraction
    factors in, 239–245
    stimulus value and, 274
    tactics of, 241, 242
attractiveness, 240–244
    advantages of, 176
    aging and, 348–349, 352
    of communication sources, 187
    culture and, 176–177
    eating disorders and, 511
    factors in, 240–241
    gender stereotypes and, 322
    happiness and, 20
    psychiatric patients' adjustment and, 17
    stereotypes about, 176–177
attribution process, 177–178
attributions
    controllable vs. uncontrollable, 153
    defensive, 178, 179, 183
    defined, 173
    errors in, 177–178, 183
    internal vs. external, 152, 153, 173–174
    loneliness and, 264, 265
    in romantic relationships, 258–259
    self, 152-153, 264

stable vs. unstable, 153
authoritarian parenting, 149, 364, 365, 367
authoritarianism, 182. 193
authoritative parenting, 149, 364, 365, 367
authority, obedience to, 192–194
autoeroticism, 423
autogenic training, 129
automatic processing, 152, 184
autonomic nervous system (ANS), 85, 87–88
availability heuristic, 120
aversive stimuli, 48
avoidance, 48, 392
    of conflict, 221, 223
    as response to traumatic events, 82
avoidance-avoidance conflict, 77
awareness, levels of, 36–37

B

baby boom generation, 354, 381, 396
baldness, 352
barbiturates, 475
bargaining, as stage of dying, 359
baseline data, 131
basking in reflected glory (BIRG), 156–157
battering, 297–299
beauty, 240
behavior, defined, 11
behavior modification, 25, 131–135,
    230–231, 455, 462, 533, 548
behavior therapies, 518, 529–536, 543
    aversion therapy, 534–535
    effectiveness of, 536
    general principles of, 532–533
    social skills training, 535–536
    systematic desensitization, 533–534
behavioral confirmation, 175
behavioral contract, 135
behavioral disengagement, 108
behavioral genetics, 57–58
behavioral perspectives, on personality,
    44–51
behavioral rehearsal, 536
behaviorism, 44
belief in a just world (BJW), 179
beliefs, 186
belligerence, 285
benefit finding, 118
benzodiazepines, 475, 537
bereavement, 360
bereavement overload, 361
better-than-average effect, 155
biases, pointing out, 189
Big Five personality traits, 34–35
    birth order and, 42–43
    evolutionary perspective on, 58–59
    heredity and, 57, 58
    marital success and, 275
binge eating/purging, 510
biological perspectives, on personality,
    55–59
biomedical therapies, 518, 536–540, 543
    antianxiety drugs, 537
    antidepressant drugs, 538–539
    antipsychotic drugs, 537–538
    effectiveness of, 539–540, 541
    electroconvulsive therapy (ECT), 540–541
    mood stabilizers, 539
biopsychosocial model, 444
bipolar disorder, 497, 498–499
    treatment for, 539
BIRG (basking in reflected glory), 156–157
birth control, 429–431
birth control pills, 430–431

birth order, 42–43, 58
bisexuals, 250, 293, 408, 413
BJW (belief in a just world), 179
blaming oneself, 111
blaming the victim, 178, 179, 183
blood pressure, 460, 463
    ambient stress and, 73
    heart disease and, 445
BMI, 459, 460
body image, 322, 408
    disturbed, 510
body language, 210
body mass index (BMI), 459, 460
body weight. *See* weight
bonding, infant, 256
boomerang generation, 278
boredom, 93
Boston Couples Study, 257
brain
    aging and, 353
    gender differences in, 312
    schizophrenia and, 505–506, 507
brain-imaging studies, 506
brainstorming, 119
breakups, of relationships, 257
breast cancer, 255
Brockovich, Erin, 194
brontophobia, 488
Bryant, Kobe, 187, 297
bulimia nervosa, 510–514
Burden of Sympathy, The (Karp), 484
burnout, 90, 389, 395
Bush, George W., 206
Buspar, 537
bystander effect, 193

C

caffeine, 463, 475
Campbell Interest and Skill Survey (CISS),
    377
cancer, 444
    alcohol and, 458
    diet and, 463
    oral contraceptives and, 431
    physical fitness and, 466
    smoking and, 454
    stress and, 449–450
cannabis, 473, 474, 476–477
car accidents, 352
    alcohol and, 458
    mortality rate for, 453
carbohydrates, 464
cardiovascular disease. *See* heart disease
career advancement, barriers to, 386
career choice, models of, 378–381
career counseling, gender bias in, 317
career development, 379–381
career information, 376
career patterns, 349
career planning, 374–378, 399–403
careers
    gender and, 323, 377
    interest inventories for, 377
    See also occupations
caregivers, stress for, 83
caregiving, of elderly parents, 278
Carter, Jimmy, 356
Carter, Rosalyn, 356
case studies, 17, 350
catastrophic thinking, 111, 115–117, 493
catatonic schizophrenia, 503–504
catecholamines, 88
categorization, social, 176, 182–183

catharsis, 109
cause-effect relationships, 14, 18–19, 22–23
cell phones, 203, 205
cerebral hemispheres, 312
cervical cap, 430
change, as source of stress, 78–80
channels
	communication, 186
	sensory, 202–203
chat rooms, 238
cheating, on partner, 428
child abuse, repressed memories of, 529–530
child care, 323, 348, 390
childlessness, 271, 277, 347–348
childrearing, 58, 349, 362–369
	culture and, 145
	dimensions of, 363–364
	See also parenting
children
	adult, 349
	of alcoholics, 459
	arrival of, 277
	day care for, 363, 383
	effect of divorce on, 288–289
	effect of remarriage on, 289–290
	exposure to aggression, 226
	gender-role socialization of, 314–318
	grief in, 361
	of homosexual parents, 417
	marital violence and, 298
	maternal employment and, 282
	media influence on, 226, 317–318
	overweight, 460
	personality development of, 39–41, 44, 47,
		48, 52, 53, 58
	psychosocial stages of, 39–41
	resilience in, 366–367
	sex information for, 409, 410
	traumatic events and, 366–367
China, 203, 236, 237
chlamydia, 433
chlorpromazine, 536, 537, 538
choices
	overabundance of, 2–3
	as source of conflict, 76–77
choking under pressure, 89
cholesterol, 462, 463, 464
	heart disease and, 445, 446
chronic diseases, 355, 443–444
	See also cancer; heart disease
Cialis, 438
City Stress Index, 74
clarifying, 218, 525
class attendance, academic success and, 26,
	27
classical conditioning, 45–47
	of anxiety disorders, 490
	in behavior therapies, 533, 534
	observational learning and, 49
claustrophobia, 488
client-centered therapy, 524–526, 543, 548
clinical psychologists, 520–521
clinical psychology, 12
Clinton, Bill, 391
clitoris, 421, 437
close relationships. *See* relationships
clozapine, 538
clutter, dealing with, 121–122
Coca-Cola, 203
cocaine, 475
cocktail party effect, 152
cognitive abilities, gender differences in,
	306–307

cognitive appraisal, of stress, 81, 82
cognitive behavioral therapy, 154
cognitive distortions, 176–178, 182–183
cognitive misers, 152, 173, 177
cognitive therapy, 265, 526–527, 535
cohabitation, 270, 291–292, 295, 428
coitus, 424
collaborating, 224
collective unconscious, 41–42
collectivism, 145, 151
collectivist cultures
	attractiveness in, 177
	attributions in, 178
	interpersonal conflict in, 221
	marriage in, 236–237
	self-disclosure in, 217
	self-effacing bias in, 156
	self-enhancement in, 155
college education
	occupation and, 376–377, 384
	underemployment and, 384
college students
	alcohol use of, 456, 458
	loneliness and, 261
Coming Out to Parents (Borhek), 417
commercials, TV, 317
commitment
	in romantic relationships, 252, 256, 257
	to career, 380
commitment, to mental hospital, 508–509
communal relationships, 248
communication
	adjustment and, 204
	aggressive, 228, 229
	assertive, 227–231
	barriers to effective, 220–221
	computer-mediated, 204
	conversation skills, 214-215
	defined, 202
	effective, 213–219
	in emergencies, 205
	gender differences in, 309
	with health providers, 470–471
	improving, 333
	via Internet, 237–238
	interpersonal, 202–204, 237–238, 329–333
	marital satisfaction and, 283–285
	persuasive, 185–189
	problems in, 219–221, 331–333
	public, 225-227
	self-disclosure in, 215-217
	about sex, 410, 418–419, 434–435
	submissive, 227–228
	technology and, 203–204, 205
	See also nonverbal communication
communication apprehension, 219–220
communication channels, 186
communication styles, gender differences in,
	329–333
community mental health centers, 546, 547
companies, researching, 401–402
comparison level, 247
compensation, 42
competing, in interpersonal conflict, 223
competition
	between groups, 183
	self-esteem and, 151
compliance, 192
compromising, 223–224
compulsions, 489
computer literacy, 385
computers, effects on workplace, 382, 388
concordance rates, 415, 499, 505, 506

conditionability, 56
conditioned fears, 490, 491
conditioned reflex, 45
conditioned response (CR), 45–46
conditioned stimulus (CS), 45–46, 490
conditioning
	classical, 45–47, 490, 533, 534
	of maladaptive behavior, 533
	operant, 47–49, 314, 490, 533
	for self-control, 131–135
condoms, 429, 430, 431, 468
confidentiality, of clients, 542
confirmation bias, 174–175, 177, 180, 403
conflict(s)
	avoidance of, 221, 223
	between groups, 183, 185
	ego-based, 223
	intergenerational, 365
	internal, 37–38, 76, 522
	interpersonal, 221–224
	managing, 223–224, 257–258, 259
	marital, 283–285, 348
	among motives, 76–77
	parent-adolescent, 278, 343, 349
	in relationships, 254, 257–258, 331
	types of, 76–77, 222
	work-family, 395
conform, pressure to, 80, 192, 193
conformity, 190–192
	Asch's study of, 190–191
	compliance vs., 191
	culture and, 194
	gender differences in, 308
	resisting, 191–192
confrontations, 221, 222
congenital adrenal hyperplasia, 313
congruence, in personality, 52, 53
conscientiousness, 35, 58, 59
conscious, Freud's view of, 36–37
consistency
	as aspect of personality, 34
	in person perception, 180
constructive coping, 113–114
	appraisal-focused, 114, 115–118
	emotion-focused, 114, 125–130
	problem-focused, 114, 118–125
Consumer's Guide to Psychotherapy, A
	(Beutler et al.), 549
contagious diseases. 443-444
contempt, 285
context, for communication, 203
continuing education, 382
contraception, 429–431
contract work, 383
control
	illusions of, 155
	parental, 149, 364
control group, 14
controlled processing, 152, 184
conversation skllls, 214-215
conversion disorder, 492
coping, 88–89
	defensive, 111–113
	defined, 106
	with loss, 360–362
	self-esteem and, 148
	styles of, 106–107
	with unemployment, 392–394
coping strategies, 106
	constructive, 113–130
	counterproductive, 107–113
coronary heart disease, 445–449
corpus callosum, 312

eating disorders and, 511
environment, 59, 63
homosexuality and, 414, 415
mood disorders and, 499
obesity and, 460
personality and, 56, 57–58
schizophrenia and, 505
See also genetic predisposition
heritability ratios, 57
heroes, need for, 61
heroin, 474–475
herpes, 433
heterosexism, 250
heterosexuals, 250, 408, 413
hexagonal model, of career choice, 378
hidden agenda, 214, 221
hierarchy of needs, 53–54
High Price of Materialism (Kasser), 2
highly active antiretroviral therapy, 468
Hill, Anita, 391
Hispanic Americans
elder care among, 355
family relationships of, 351
gender-role socialization and, 315, 316
gender stereotypes and, 305
in workforce, 385
self-esteem in, 151
stress and, 75
histrionic personality, 493
HIV infection, 424, 431, 432, 468
hobbies, 397
holistic mentality, 178
home, working at, 383
homogamy, 272–273
homophobia, 320, 415–416
homosexual relationships, 239, 241, 248, 259–251, 292–295, 348
homosexuality
attitudes toward, 415–416
concealing, 126
disclosing, 416
origins of, 414–415
prevalence of, 293
homosexuals, 408, 413
adjustment of, 417
adolescent, 344
AIDS and, 468
heterosexual activity of, 426
as parents, 295, 417
percent of population, 413
romantic relationships of, 250–251
sexual behavior in, 422, 423, 424, 427
honesty, 214
"hooking up," 426
hopelessness theory, 500
hormone-based contraceptives, 430–431
hormones, 312–313, 87–88
aging and, 354
homosexuality and, 414
puberty and, 338
sexuality and, 408–409
hospitals, mental health services of, 546
hostility, 40, 225
between groups, 183. 185
heart disease and, 445–448
managing, 127–128
household chores, 323, 348
gender and, 315–316
in marriage, 280–281
How to Grow Up When You're Grown Up, 347
*How to Stubbornly Refuse to Make Yourself
Miserable About Anything* (Ellis), 116
Hughes, Howard, 489, 493

human immunodeficiency virus. *See* HIV
human nature, 51, 55
human potential movement, 51
human service agencies, 546
Human Sexuality Today (King), 425
humanism, 51
humanistic perspectives, 51–55
evaluation of, 55
Maslow's self-actualization theory, 53–54
Rogers's person-centered theory, 51–53
humor, as stress reducer, 117–118
hunting-and-gathering societies, 311, 326
Hurried Child, The (Elkind), 341
hydrophobia, 488
hypertension, 460, 463
hypnosis, memory and, 530
hypoactive sexual desire, 437–438, 439
hypochondriasis, 492–493
hypothalamus, 87

I
id, 36, 37
identical twins, 55–56, 57
identification
as defense mechanism, 39
group, 192
identity
career choice and, 374
gender-role, 327
search for, 342-343
sexual, 408, 409–411
social, 184
identity crisis, 342, 346
identity statuses, 342-343, 347
career maturity and, 381
illness
biopsychosocial model of, 444
life changes and, 79
reactions to, 469–472
stress and, 87, 92–93
See also disease(s); health-impairing habits
illusions
of control, 155
defense mechanisms as, 112-113
imitation, 49, 314
immune functioning
marijuana and, 476
stress and, 88, 95, 96, 450–451
impatience, 446
impotence, 437
impression formation, 172–180
impression management, 162–164, 208
in job interviews, 403
impressions, first, 172, 174, 180, 403
income
children and, 283
education and, 384
happiness and, 20
job identity and, 374
incongruence, in personality, 52, 524–525
independent variable, 14
independent view of self, 145–146
India, 236, 237
individual differences, 310
individual psychology, 42–43
individualism, 145
self-esteem and, 151
individualistic cultures
adversarial approach in, 225
attributions in, 178
interpersonal conflict in, 221
love in, 237
self-disclosure in, 217

self-enhancement in, 155
self-serving bias in, 156
industrial/organizational (I/O) psychology, 373
infant attachment, 252–253, 363
infectious diseases, 443–444
inferiority complex, 42
infidelity, 427–429
inflammation, heart disease and, 445, 446
influence, normative vs. informational, 191
Influence: Science and Practice (Cialdini), 189, 195
influenza, schizophrenia and, 506
information, memorizing, 27–29
information processing, 152
aging and, 356
ingratiation, 163
ingroup favoritism, 184
ingroups, 176, 182–183
inhibitions, 126–127, 263
conditioned, 56
inkblot test, 67
insanity, 508
insight therapies, 518, 522–529, 543
client-centered, 522–524
cognitive, 526–527
effectiveness of, 528–529, 548
group, 527–528
psychoanalytic, 522–524
instrumental style, 331
instrumentality, 305
integrity vs. despair, 350
intellectualization, 111
intelligence
aging and, 355
constructive coping and, 115
emotional, 125–126
gender differences in, 306
happiness and, 20
occupation and, 374
intercourse, sexual, 421
interdependence theory, 247–248
interdependent view of self, 145–146
interest inventories, 377
interests, occupation and, 374–375, 377
interference, in learning, 27–28
Internet
infidelity and, 428
interpersonal communication and, 203–204
job boards on, 402
for overcoming loneliness, 264
relationships via, 237–238
sexual activities and, 17–18, 412
as source of news, 205
as source of sex information, 411
surfing, 397
Internet addiction, 109–110, 264
Internet sex addiction, 412
interpersonal climate, 214
interpersonal communication, 202–204
See also communication
interpretation, in psychoanalysis, 523
interviews, job, 402–403
In the Wake of 9/11 (Pyszczynski, Solomon, & Greenberg), 61
intimacy, 245–246
in friendships, 249–250
love and, 251–252, 256, 257
sex and, 308, 320, 411
intimacy statuses, 346–347
intimacy vs. isolation, 346–347
intimidation, 163

mental health services and, 543
prejudice against, 181–182
self-esteem of, 151
stereotypes of, 176, 183
stress and, 75
in workforce, 385, 386
See also ethnic groups; specific minorities
Mismeasure of Woman, The (Tavris), 323
M'Naghten rule, 508
mnemonic devices, 28–29
models (modeling), 49, 160
for gender roles, 314
for social skills, 536
modernization, 74
money
happiness and, 20
marriage and, 282–283
monogamy, 271
mood disorders, 486, 487, 496–502
bipolar disorder, 498–499
cognitive factors in, 500–501
etiology of, 499–502
genetic vulnerability to, 499–500
interpersonal roots of, 501–502
major depressive disorder, 497–498
neurochemical factors in, 500
prevalence of, 498
stress and, 502
mood stabilizers, 539
morphine, 474
mortality rates
exercise and, 466
from health-impairing behavior, 453
for major diseases, 444
mortality salience, 60, 61
motherhood mandate, 320–321
mother-infant bonding, 256
motivation
persuasion and, 189
reinforcement and, 47
motives
Maslow's hierarchy of, 53–54
for self-understanding, 154–155
sexual, 418
mourning, 360
Multicultural Manners: New Rules of Etiquette for a Changing Society (Dresser), 203
multimodal therapy, 548
multiple personality disorder, 494–496
Mundugumor, 314
music videos, 317, 411
myocardial infarction, 445
myocardial ischemia, 445, 448
mythopoetic movement, 319

N

narcissism, 148–149
narcotics, 173, 474–475
Nardil, 538
narrative methods, 28, 29
National Business Employment Weekly, 402
National Television Violence Study, 226
Native Americans, 354
natural selection, 58, 243, 311
naturalistic observation, 16–17
nature vs. nurture, 63
in gender differences, 311
in personality, 57–58
need for self-actualization, 53–54
needs, hierarchy of, 53–54
negative correlation, 16–17
negative emotionality, 35
negative reinforcement, 47–48, 369

negative self-talk, 111, 115, 167, 264
negative thinking, 500–501, 526
neglectful parents, 149, 364, 365, 367
NEO Personality Inventory, 66
neurodevelopmental hypothesis, of schizophrenia, 506–507
neurons, 353
neuroses, 522
neuroticism, 34–35, 58, 59, 60, 493
marital adjustment and, 275
stress and, 98
neurotransmitters, 490, 500, 505
news programs, 205
newsgroups, 238
nicotine, 475
nicotine substitutes, 456
no, saying, 121
noise
in communication, 203
in environment, 73
nonverbal communication, 202, 205–213
assertive, 229
culture and, 206
deception and, 211–212
elements of, 206–211
gender differences in, 309, 331
impression formation and, 172
in job interviews, 403
self-disclosure and, 216
significance of, 213
norepinephrine, 73, 500
normality, criteria of, 483–485
norms, social, 37, 38, 413
note taking, in lectures, 26–27
novelty, in relationships, 259
nuclear family, 271
Nun study, 353, 354
nursing homes, 354
nurturing role, 310
nutrients, essential, 464
nutrition, 462–465
nutritional deficiencies, 463

O

obedience, 192–194
obesity, 241, 459–461
fear of, 510
observation
naturalistic, 16-17
person perception and, 172
observational learning, 49
of gender roles, 314
obsessions, 489
obsessive-compulsive disorder, 489–490
occupation
choosing, 347, 374–378
marriage and, 281–282
occupational choice
Holland's model of, 378–379
Super's model of, 379–381
occupational interest inventories, 377
Occupational Outlook Handbook, 376, 401
occupations
high-growth, 383–384
high-stress, 388, 389
information about, 376–377
personal characteristics and, 374–375
for women, 324
Oedipal complex, 40–41, 414
olanzapine, 538
omega 3 fatty acids, 462–463
opening lines, 215
openness to experience, 35, 58, 59
operant conditioning, 47–49

of anxiety disorders, 490
in behavior therapies, 533
observational learning and, 49
socialization and, 314
opiates, 474
opinions, expressing, 214
optimal level of arousal, 84–85
optimism, 113, 96–97
happiness and, 22
unrealistic, 155
optimistic explanatory style, 96–97, 153–154
oral contraceptives, 430–431
oral presentations, 220
oral sex, 423
oral stage, 40
organic mental disorders, 486
orgasmic difficulties, 437, 439
orgasmic phase, of sexual response cycle, 421
orgasms
age and, 427
faking, 422
gender differences in, 421–422
osteoporosis, 354, 355, 463, 510
outgroup derogation, 184
outgroup homogeneity effect, 176
outgroups, 176, 182–183
outlining, 28
outsourcing, 383
overcommunication, 220
overcompensation, 42, 111, 113
overdose, 474
alcohol, 457
cocaine, 476
heroin, 474
sedative, 475
overeating, 134, 160, 459–461
overlearning, 27
overweight, 459
See also obesity; weight
Oxycontin, 474

P

panic disorder, 488–489
Paradox of Choice, The (Schwarz), 8
paralanguage, 210–211
paralysis, 492
paranoid schizophrenia, 503
paraphrasing, 218
parasympathetic division, 85
parent, death of, 361
parental control, 364
parental investment theory, 243
parenthood, 277–278, 348
happiness and, 20
parenting, 226–227, 349, 362–369
child's self-esteem and, 149
effective, 367
parenting styles, 149–151, 364–365, 367
career choice and, 375
infant attachment and, 252–253
parents
of adolescents, 278
aging, 278, 351
conflict with adolescents, 343
discipline by, 48
feedback from, 144
homosexual, 295, 417
role in gender-role socialization, 315–316
role in personality development, 58
as source of sex information, 409, 410
paroxetine, 538
partner abuse, 297–299
passion, 252, 256
passive aggression, 228

treatment of, 517–549
See also specific disorders
psychological tests, 64–67
  for career decisions, 377
psychologists, 520–521
psychology
  defined, 11
  health, 444
  positive, 55, 93
  as profession, 12
  research methods in, 13–19
  as science, 11–12
  theoretical diversity of, 62–63
psychopathology, 482
psychopharmacotherapy, 536
psychosexual stages, 39–41
psychosocial development, stages of, 342, 346–347, 348, 350
psychosomatic diseases, 92
Psychotherapy Maze, The (Ehrenberg & Ehrenberg), 529
psychotherapy
  barriers to seeking, 519
  behavioral approaches to, 518, 529–536, 543
  benefits of, 529
  biomedical approaches to, 518, 536–540, 543
  blending approaches to, 542
  client-centered approach to, 524–526
  clients for, 518–519
  cognitive approach to, 526–527
  cost of, 547
  cultural barriers to, 543–544
  definition of, 517, 518
  eclecticism in, 542, 548
  effectiveness of, 528–529, 536, 547, 548
  elements of, 518–522
  group, 527–528
  multimodal, 548
  outcome of, 529
  process of, 549
  psychoanalytic approach to, 522–524
  recovered memory controversy and, 529–532
  sources of, 545, 546
  types of, 518
  utilization rates for, 519
  See also therapists
puberty, 338–340, 409
pubescence, 338, 339, 340
pubic lice, 433
public communication, 225–227
public speaking, 219–220
pulmonary diseases, 454, 476
punishment
  in operant conditioning, 48, 134
  of gender-inappropriate behavior, 314
  parental, 368–369
Pursuit of Happiness: Who Is Happy—And Why (Myers), 21
put-downs, 231
puzzles, 398
Pygmalion effect, 175

Q

questions, diagnostic, 175
quetiapine, 538

R

race, eye contact and, 209
racial profiling, 183
racial stereotypes, 75, 183

racism, 75, 388
  modern, 181, 182
radio
  advice on, 5–6
  news programming on, 205
Raelian UFO cult, 5
rage, as response to stress, 83
Raising Cain (Kindlon & Thompson), 319
rap music, 411
rape, 295–297, 458
rational outness, 416
rational-emotive behavior therapy, 115, 526, 548
rationalization, 39
raves, 477
reactance, 197
reaction formation, 39
reading
  improving, 25–26
  leisure, 397
Real Boys (Pollack), 319
reality, denial of, 111
reality principle, 36
reasoning skills, 341
receiver, of message, 186, 188, 202
reciprocal liking, 244
reciprocity principle, 196–197
Reconcilable Differences (Christensen & Jacobson), 282
recreation, 397–398
recreational drugs, 472–477
reference groups, 143, 151
reflex, conditioned, 45–46
refractory period, following orgasm, 421, 427
regression, 39
rehearsal, 27
reinforcement, 47–48, 132, 314, 369
reinforcement contingencies, 132-133
reinforcers, personal, 132, 134
reinterpretation, of events, 118
rejection, 167
  poor social skills and, 501
rejection anxiety, 263-264
relationship maintenance, 246–247
relationships, 236–238
  abusive, 299
  building, 244–245
  cohabiting, 270, 291–292
  communicating in, 434–435
  communicating about sex in, 418–419
  culture and, 236-237
  exchange theory of, 247–248
  failure of, 257–258
  Internet and, 237–238
  maintaining, 245–248
  minding, 246
  priorities in, 294
  self-disclosure in, 216–217
  sex in, 426–427
  See also friendship; homosexual relationships; marriage; romantic relationships
relaxation procedures, 129–130
relaxation training, 533
reliability, of psychological tests, 65
religion, happiness and, 21
remarriage, 289–290
repressed memories, recovery of, 529–532
repression, 39
reproductive fitness, 58, 311
research methods, 13–19
resilience, 83–84
  in children, 366–367

resistance, in psychoanalysis, 524, 548–549
resolution phase, of sexual response cycle, 420
response tendencies, 44
responsibility, delegating, 121
résumé, 400–401
retention, improving, 27–29
retirement, 381
  adjusting to, 350–351
revenge, 179
rewards, in relationships, 247
rhymes, for memorization, 28
rhythm method, 430
right-wing authoritarianism (RWA), 182
risk taking, in adolescence, 341, 343
risks, underestimating, 453
ritual kind, 351–352
rituals, surrounding death, 360
road rage, 108, 209, 226
rock music, 411
rohypnol, 296
role changes, in early adulthood, 346
role conflicts, 281–282
role expectations
  for females, 320–324
  for males, 318–320
  in marriage, 279–281
role models, 141, 314
role overload, 396
roles
  marital, 280
  multiple, 323
romantic love, 250–259
  as attachment, 252–256
  course of, 256–259
  culture and, 236–237
  theories of, 251–256
  triangular theory of, 251-252
romantic relationships
  ending of, 257–258
  happiness and, 21
  initial attraction in, 239–245
  maintaining, 258–259
  See also relationships
Rorschach test, 67
rumination, 498, 500
Rutherford, Tom, 530

S

sadness, as response to stress, 83
safe sex, 432
salaries, 377, 384, 403
  gender gap in, 324, 325
sales techniques, 195–197
salivation response, 45
salt intake, 463, 464
sandbagging, 157
sandwich generation, 278
scarcity principle, 197
scheduling, 24, 25, 124
schizophrenia, 486, 487, 502–508
  brain abnormalities and, 505–506, 507
  course and outcome of, 504–505
  drug treatment for, 537–538
  emergence of, 505
  etiology of, 505–508
  family dynamics and, 508
  genetic vulnerability to, 505
  neurochemical factors in, 505
  neurodevelopmental hypothesis of, 506–507
  positive vs. negative symptoms in, 504
  prevalence of, 502

social activity, happiness and, 21
social categorization, 176, 182–183
social change, fear of, 182
social class, gender-role socialization and , 316
social clock, 345, 350
social cognitive theory, 49–50, 314
social comparison, 166
    downward, 155–156
social comparison theory, 143
social constructionism, 310
social desirability bias, 66
social exchange theory, 247–248, 274
social identity theory, 184
social influence
    to comply, 192–194
    to conform, 190–192
    culture and, 194
    normative vs. informational, 191
    tactics of, 195–197
social isolation, 345, 346
social learning theory. See social cognitive theory
social norms, 37, 38, 413
social phobia, 488, 491
social pressure, 190–194
Social Readjustment Rating Scale (SRRS), 78–80
    problems with, 97–98
social role theory, 310, 314
social skills
    group therapy for, 528
    loneliness and, 262, 263–264, 265
    occupation and, 374
    poor, 501
social skills training, 265, 535–536
social support, 249
    adherence to medical advice and, 471
    coronary risk and, 448
    job loss and, 393
    lack of, 502
    loneliness and, 261
    for older adults, 351–352
    posttraumatic stress disorder and, 495
    stress and, 94–95, 119
    in traumatic events, 255
social workers, 521
socialization, 217, 313–314
    gender-role, 314-318
    sexual, 411, 413
socioeconomic status
    occupation and, 375
    self-esteem and, 307
sociometer theory, 148
sodomy, 424
somatization disorder, 492
somatoform disorders, 486, 491–493
    etiology of, 493
    types of, 492–493
source, of message, 186–187
spanking, 368
spatial abilities, gender differences in, 307, 311
speaking, public, 219-220
spectatoring, 435
speech, functions of, 330
speech patterns, 211
spermarche, 339
spermicides, 430
sponge, contraceptive, 430
sports, 398, 467
spotlight effect, 162
spouse, loss of, 360–361
SQ3R, 25–26

stage of exhaustion, 87
stage of resistance, 87
stages
    of dying, 359
    Erikson's psychosocial, 342, 346–347, 348, 350
    Freud's psychosocial, 346–347
    of family life cycle, 275–279
    of occupational life cycle, 380–381
standardization, of tests, 64
status
    Big Five traits and, 35
    eye contact and, 209
    mate selection and, 243–244
    personal distance and, 207
    posture and, 210
    touch and, 210
stepfamilies, 289–290
stereotype confirmation, 75
stereotypes, 176–177, 183, 304
    of elderly, 357
    gender, 304–306
    overriding, 184
    racial, 75
Stiller, Ben, 496
stimulants, 473, 474, 475–476
stimulus, aversive, 48
stimulus-value-role (S-V-R) theory, 274
Sting, 496
stonewalling, 285
Stop Smoking Workbook, The (Stevic-Rust & Maximin), 456
stress
    ambient, 73–74
    anxiety disorders and, 491
    appraisal of, 72–73, 81, 82, 98
    behavioral responses to, 88–89
    brain-body pathways in, 87–88
    cancer and, 449–450
    chronic, 92
    defined, 71
    disease and, 444
    divorce and, 288
    effects of, 89–93
    emotional responses to, 81–85
    environmental, 73–74, 76, 107
    as everyday event, 71
    exercise and, 466
    heart disease and, 448
    humor as moderator of, 117–118
    immune functioning and, 450–451
    influence of culture on, 74–75
    job, 387–391
    managing, 105–106, 113–130
    moderator variables in, 94–97
    monitoring, 97–101
    mood disorders and, 502
    overview of, 94
    physiological responses to, 85–88
    positive effects of, 93
    prolonged, 87, 92, 389
    from retirement, 351
    schizophrenia and, 508
    as self-imposed, 74
    Selye's view of, 86–87
    social support and, 255
    tolerance for, 93, 94–97
    types of, 75–81
    work-related, 90
stress management, 105–106, 113–130, 389–390, 448
stress resistance, self-efficacy and, 50
stressors
    acute, 75

chronic, 75–76
minor, 71
stroke, 444, 446
Strong Interest Inventory (SII), 377
study skills, 24–25
subjective well-being, 19, 350
submissive communication, 227–228
substance-related disorders, 486, 487
sugar, in diet, 464
suicide
    adolescent, 344–345
    job loss and, 393
    SRRI use and, 538–539
superego, 36, 37
superiority, striving for, 42
superordinate goals, 185
supplication, 163
support groups, 362
surveys, 17–18
Surviving Schizophrenia (Torrey), 507
swinging, 427
Sybil (Schreiber), 496
symbols, archetypal, 42
sympathetic division, 85, 87–88
syphilis, 433
systematic desensitization, 533–534, 548

T
tardive dyskinesia, 538
task performance
    arousal and, 84–85
    procrastination and, 122
    stress and, 89
Tchambuili, 314
teachers
    role in gender-role socialization, 317
    sexual harassment by, 326
technology
    interpersonal communication and, 203–204, 205
    progress and, 2
    in workplace, 382, 388
technostress, 387
teenage pregnancy, 424
television
    body image and, 322
    commercials on, 187
    news programming on, 205
    role in gender-role socialization, 317–318
    sexual content of, 411
    time taken by, 2
    viewing, 398
    violence on, 226
temperament, anxiety disorders and, 490
Ten Principles of Good Parenting, The (Steinberg), 369
"tend and befriend" response, 85–86
terror management theory, 59–62, 150, 359
terrorism, 3
    emotional reactions to, 82
    posttraumatic stress disorder and, 495
    psychological impact of, 61
    self-esteem and, 150
    thinking rationally about, 120
    as vengeful aggression, 179
test anxiety, 84, 112, 159
test norms, 64
testosterone, 313, 409
tests
    aptitude, 377
    changing answers on, 16–17
    personality, 64–67
    projective, 66–67
    mental ability, 64

CONTENTS

INTRODUCTION

In your textbook, *Psychology Applied to Modern Life* the value of developing an accurate self-concept is emphasized repeatedly. A little self-deception may occasionally be adaptive, (see Chapter 4 in your text), but most theories of psychological health endorse the importance of forming a realistic picture of one's personal qualities and capabilities. The *Personal Explorations Workbook* designed to accompany your text contains three types of exercises intended to help you achieve this goal. They are (1) a series of Personal Probes intended to help you systematically analyze various aspects of your life, and (2) a series of Questionnaires or self-scoring psychological scales intended to help you gain insight into your attitudes and personality traits, and (3) exercises applying concepts in the chapter which bring further personal insight.

How you use these personal exploration exercises will depend, in large part, on your instructor. Many Instructors will formally assign some of these exercises and then collect them, either for individual scrutiny or class discussion. That is why the pages of this book are perforated—to make it convenient for those instructors who like to assign the exercises as homework. Other instructors may simply encourage students to complete the exercises that they find intriguing. Furthermore, it is possible to vary from the use of the perforated pages and assign students to respond to questions using a Word processor. We believe that even if the exercises are not assigned, you will find many of them to be very interesting, and we encourage you to complete them on your own. Let's briefly take a closer look at these exercises.

QUESTIONNAIRES

The Questionnaires are a collection of attitude scales and personality tests that psychologists have used in their research. At least one Questionnaire has been selected for each chapter in your text. Instructions are provided so that you can administer these scales to yourself and then compute your score. Each Questionnaire also includes an explanation of what the scale measures, followed by a brief review of the research on the scale. These reviews discuss the evidence on the reliability, validity, and behavioral correlates of each scale. The final section of each Questionnaire provides information to allow you to interpret the meaning of your score. Test norms are supplied to indicate what represents a high, intermediate, or low score on the scale. We

hope you may gain some useful insights about yourself by responding to these scales.

However, you should be careful about attributing too much significance to your scores. As explained in the Application for Chapter 2 in your text, the results of psychological tests can be misleading, and caution is always in order when interpreting test scores. It is probably best to view your scores as interesting "food for thought', rather than as definitive statements about your personal traits or abilities.

Most of the scales included in this book are self-report inventories. Your scores on such tests are only as accurate as the information that you provide in your responses. Hence, we hasten to emphasize that these Questionnaires will only be as valuable as you make them, by striving to respond honestly. Usually, people taking a scale do not know what the scale measures. The conventional approach is to put some sort of vague or misleading title, such as "Biographical Inventory," at the top of the scale. We have not adhered to this practice because you could easily find out what any scale measures simply by reading ahead a little. Thus, you will be taking each scale with some idea (based on the title) of what the scale measures. Bear in mind, however, that these scales are intended to satisfy your curiosity. There is no reason to try to impress or mislead anyone—including yourself. Your test scores will be accurate and meaningful only if you try very hard to respond in a candid manner.

PERSONAL PROBES

The Personal Probes consist of sets of questions designed to make you think about yourself and your personal experiences in relation to specific issues and topics raised in your text. They involve systematic inquiries into how you behave in certain situations, how your behavior has been shaped by past events, how you feel about certain issues, how you might improve yourself in some areas, how you anticipate behaving under certain circumstances in the future, and so forth. There are at least 2 Personal Probes for each of the 16 chapters in your textbook. The aspects of life probed by these inquiries are, of course, tied to the content of the chapters in your text. You will probably derive the most benefit from them if you read the corresponding text chapter before completing the Personal Probe.

Wayne Weiten
John Pulver

ABOUT THE AUTHORS

John Pulver M.S., is a Professor of Human Behavior at the Community College of Southern Nevada where he teaches courses in sociology and psychology, both online and in the classroom. He has used the *Psychology Applied to Modern Life* textbook since 1994 and is presently developing an online course which will also utilize this text. John uses interactive modules, writing assignments, as well as group work in his teaching and believes in the value of students and professors learning *from each other*. His research interests include curriculum development, mate selection, communication, gerontology, media effects, longevity in relationships, counseling theory, and social change. Mr. Pulver is also a Licensed Marriage and Family Therapist and a Licensed Substance Abuse Counselor. He is married to Pamela and is the father of 5 sons and currently practicing grand-parenting with 3 grandchildren.

Wayne Weiten is a graduate of Bradley University and received his Ph.D. in social psychology from the University of Illinois, Chicago in 1981. He currently teaches at the University of Nevada, Las Vegas. He has received distinguished teaching awards from Division Two of the American Psychological Association (APA) and from the College of DuPage, where he taught until 1991. He is a Fellow of Divisions One and Two of the American Psychological Association. In 1991, he helped chair the APA National Conference on Enhancing the Quality of Undergraduate Education in Psychology and in 1996–1997 he served as President of the Society for the Teaching of Psychology. Weiten has conducted research on a wide range of topics, including educational measurement, jury decision-making, attribution theory, stress, and cerebral specialization. His recent interests have included pressure as a form of stress and the technology of textbooks. He is also the author of *Psychology: Themes & Variations* (Wadsworth, 2004) and the creator of an educational CD-ROM titled *PsykTrek: A Multimedia Introduction to Psychology*.

ACKNOWLEDGEMENTS

Thanks to William and Joyce Pulver for their love and encouragement over the years, to my wife and children for their patience with Dad during this project, to Wayne Weiten for his contributions to this workbook and his confidence in me, to Jennifer Keever, Assistant Editor for Psychology, for her gentle nudging and assistance, and finally, to all my students and former clients who I continue to receive enrichment from as I process the things they have taught me.

John Pulver

Testwiseness Scale

INSTRUCTIONS

Below you will find a series of 24 history questions for which you are not expected to know the answer based on your knowledge of history. However, you should be able to make a good guess on each of the questions if you can spot the flaws that exist in them. Each question is flawed in some way so as to permit solution by testwise examinees. Record your choice for each question by circling the letter for the correct alternative.

THE SCALE

1. The Locarno Pact
   a. is an international agreement for the maintenance of peace through the guarantee of national boundaries of France, Germany, Italy, Belgium, and other countries of Western Europe.
   b. allowed France to occupy the Ruhr Valley.
   c. provided for the dismemberment of Austria-Hungary.
   d. provided for the protection of Red Cross bases during wartime.

2. The disputed Hayes-Tilden election of 1876 was settled by an
   a. resolution of the House of Representatives.
   b. decision of the United States Supreme Court.
   c. Electoral Commission.
   d. joint resolution of Congress.

3. The Factory Act of 1833 made new provisions for the inspection of the mills. This new arrangement was important because
   a. the inspectors were not local men and therefore they had no local ties that might affect the carrying-out of their job; they were responsible to the national govern-ment rather than to the local authorities; and they were encouraged to develop a professional skill in handling their work.
   b. the inspectorate was recruited from the factory workers.
   c. the inspectors were asked to recommend new legislation.
   d. the establishment of the factory inspectorate gave employment to large numbers of the educated middle class.

4. The Ostend Manifesto aimed to
   a. discourage Southern expansionism.
   b. prevent expansion in the South.
   c. aid Southern expansionism.
   d. all of the above

5. The august character of the work of Pericles in Athens frequently causes his work to be likened to that in Rome of
   a. Augustus.
   b. Sulla.
   c. Pompey.
   d. Claudius.

6. The Webster-Ashburton Treaty settled a long-standing dispute between Great Britain and the United States over
   a. the Maine boundary.
   b. numerous contested claims to property as well as many other sources of ill will.
   c. damages growing out of the War of 1812 and subsequent events.
   d. fishing rights on the Great Lakes and in international waters.

7. Men who opposed the "Ten Hour Movement" in British factory history
   a. was a leader in the dominant political party.
   b. is convinced that shorter hours of work are bad for the morals of the laboring classes.
   c. is primarily motivated by concern for his own profits.
   d. were convinced that intervention would endanger the economic welfare of Britain.

8. The career of Marius (157-86 B.C.), the opponent of Sulla, is significant in Roman history because
   a. he gave many outstanding dinners and entertainments for royalty.
   b. he succeeded in arming the gladiators.
   c. he showed that the civil authority could be thrust aside by the military.
   d. he made it possible for the popular party to conduct party rallies outside the city of Rome.

9. The Locarno Pact
   a. was an agreement between Greece and Turkey.
   b. gave the Tyrol to Italy.
   c. was a conspiracy to blow up the League of Nations building at Locarno.
   d. guaranteed the boundary arrangements in Western Europe.

10. The first presidential election dispute in the United States to be settled by an appointed Electoral Commission was
    a. the Hayes-Tilden election.
    b. the Jefferson-Madison election.
    c. the John Quincy Adams-Henry Clay election.
    d. the Garfield-McKinley election.

11. The first of the alliances against the "Central Powers" that ended in World War I is to be found in
    a. the defensive treaty between China and Japan.
    b. the dual alliance of Mexico and the United States.
    c. the dual alliance of France and Russia.
    d. India's resentment against South Africa's attitude toward the Boer War, and her ensuing alliance with Japan.

12. The Proclamation of 1763
    a. forbade colonists to settle territory acquired in the French and Indian wars.
    b. encouraged colonists to settle territory acquired in the French and Indian wars.
    c. provided financial incentives for settlement of territory acquired in the French and Indian wars.
    d. all of the above

13. About what fraction of the 1920 population of the United States was foreign-born?
    a. less than 5%
    b. between 14% and 28%
    c. 25%
    d. between 30% and 50%

14. The Alabama claims were
    a. all settled completely and satisfactorily.
    b. claims against Jefferson Davis for seizure of all of the property in the state during wartime.
    c. claims of the United States against Great Britain.
    d. claims of every citizen of Alabama against every citizen of Georgia.

15. During the Italian Renaissance
    a. the papacy gained political power.
    b. there were frequent changes in government.
    c. the papacy became more important in Italian political affairs.
    d. all of the above

16. The 12th century was distinguished by a "real European patriotism" that expressed itself in
    a. the flowering of lyrical and epical poetry in the vernacular.
    b. great patriotic loyalty to the undivided unit of European Christendom.
    c. recurring attempts to form a world with a centralized administration.
    d. proposals to remove the custom barriers between the different countries of the time.

17. The dispute between Great Britain and the United States over the boundary of Maine was settled by
    a. the Treaty of Quebec.
    b. the Treaty of Niagara.
    c. the Webster-Ashburton Treaty.
    d. the Pendleton-Scott Treaty.

18. In the *Dartmouth College* case the United States Supreme Court held
    a. that the courts had no right under any circumstances ever to nullify an Act of Congress.
    b. that a state could not impair a contract.
    c. that all contracts must be agreeable to the state legislature.
    d. that all contracts must inevitably be certified.

19. The accession of Henry VII marked the close of the
    a. Crusades
    b. War of the Roses, between rival factions of the English nobility.
    c. Hundred Years' War.
    d. Peasants' Revolt.

20. The Magna Carta was signed
    a. before the Norman invasion.
    b. in 1215.
    c. after the opening of the 17th century.
    d. about the middle of the 14th century.

21. The Progressive Party in 1912
    a. favored complete protective tariffs.
    b. favored an appointed Congress.
    c. favored the creation of a nonpartisan tariff commission.
    d. favored restriction of the ballot to certain influential persons.

22. The first systematic attempt to establish the Alexandrian synthesis between Christian religious belief and Greek civilization was undertaken at
    a. Rome.
    b. Alexandria.
    c. Athens.
    d. Jerusalem.

23. The Bland-Allison Act
    a. made all forms of money redeemable in silver.
    b. standardized all gold dollars in terms of silver and cop-per.
    c. made none of the paper money redeemable in silver.
    d. directed the Treasury Department to purchase a certain amount of silver bullion each month.

24. The famed Bayeaux Tapestry is a
    a. enormous re-creation of the Magna Carta scene.
    b. extremely large impression of the Edict of Nantes.
    c. immense picture of the Battle of Tours.
    d. large representation of the Norman Conquest of England.

SCORING THE SCALE

There are eight item-writing flaws that appear on the Testwiseness Scale three times each. They are described below.

Flaw #1: The incorrect options are highly implausible.

Flaw #2: Equivalence and/or contradictions among options allow one to eliminate the incorrect options.

Flaw #3: Content information in other items provides the answer.

Flaw #4: The correct option is more detailed and/or specific than all the other options.

Flaw #5: The correct option is longer than all of the other options.

Flaw #6: There is grammatical inconsistency between the stem and the incorrect options but not the correct option.

Flaw #7: The incorrect options include certain key words that tend to appear in false statements (such as *always, must, never,* and so on).

Flaw #8: There is a resemblance between the stem and the correct option but not the incorrect options.

The scoring key is reproduced in the space below. For each item it tells you the correct answer and indicates which flaw (as numbered above) you should have spotted to arrive at the answer. Circle those items that you got correct. Add up the number of correct items, and that is your score on the Testwiseness Scale. Record your score below.

1. .A (5)	**7.** D (6)	**13.** C (4)	**19.** B (5)
2. C (6)	**8.** C (1)	**14.** C (7)	**20.** B (4)
3. A (5)	**9.** D (3)	**15.** D (2)	**21.** C (1)
4. C (2)	**10.** A (3)	**16.** B (8)	**22.** B (8)
5. A (8)	**11.** C (1)	**17.** C (3)	**23.** D (7)
6. A (4)	**12.** A (2)	**18.** B (7)	**24.** D (6)

MY SCORE_____

WHAT THE SCALE MEASURES

As its title indicates, this scale simply measures your ability to reason your way to answers on multiple-choice exams. The Testwiseness Scale (TWS) assesses test-taking skills. The scale you have just completed is an abbreviated version of a scale developed by Wayne Weiten (Weiten, Clery, & Bowbin, 1980). The full scale is a 40-item test with five items for each kind of flaw.

The TWS is built on some pioneering work by Gibb (1964). Through a series of revisions, reliability and validity have gradually been improved. The full-length version yields internal reliability coefficients in the .70s and .80s. Two lines of evidence currently provide support for the scale's validity. First, scores on the scale are very much affected (positively) by training in the principles of testwiseness. Second, as one would expect, the scale correlates positively (.40s) with classroom performance on multiple-choice tests. More important, this correlation between the TWS and classroom performance remains significant even when the influence of intelligence on both variables is factored out statistically.

INTERPRETING YOUR SCORE

Our norms are based on the performance of 76 undergraduates who took the most recent revision of the scale. These norms are for people who have not had any testwiseness training.

NORMS

High score:	17–24
Intermediate score:	9–16
Low score:	0–8

What Are Your Study Habits Like?

Do you usually complete your class assignments on time?   YES   NO

Do you usually find time to prepare adequately for your exams?   YES   NO

Do you frequently delay schoolwork until the last minute?   YES   NO

When do you usually study (mornings, evenings, weekends, etc.)?

Do you write out and follow a study schedule?   YES   NO

Are your study times planned for when you're likely to be alert?   YES   NO

Do you allow time for brief study breaks?   YES   NO

Where do you usually study (library, kitchen, bedroom, etc.)?

Do you have a special place set up for studying and nothing else?   YES   NO

What types of auditory, visual, and social distractions are present in your study areas?

Can you suggest any changes to reduce distractions in your study areas?

What Factors Affect Your Current Adjustment In Life?

1. Have scientific and technological advances really improved the quality of our lives? Are the payoffs worth the costs and problems?

2. Do you sometimes feel that the range of choices available to us has gotten out of hand? How does this range of choice affect our adjustment to life?

3. What conditions need to be present in order for you to achieve happiness, in your estimation?

4. Research on behavior is undertaken in psychology so that objective, tested statements can be made about relationships and behavior. Recall a time when a friend or family member made a comment about another person's behavior and said something like this: "Well, we all know why so-and-so does_____(what behavior they described). It is because of _____(usually just one cause is stated as the sole reason why the behavior occurs). Write the statement below and then with your critical thinking skills and information learned in this chapter, identify other factors which might influence the behavior occurring.

5. What do you see as the advantages and disadvantages of living in a culture which is individualistic versus collectivist?

Individualistic:

Advantages:

Disadvantages:

Collectivist:

Advantages

Disadvantages:

Desirability of Control Scale

INSTRUCTIONS

Below you will find a series of statements. Please read each statement carefully and respond to it by expressing the extent to which you believe the statement applies to you. For all items, a response from 1 to 7 is required. Use the number that best reflects your belief when the scale is defined as follows:

1 = The statement does not apply to me at all
2 = The statement usually does not apply to me
3 = Most often, the statement does not apply
4 = I am unsure about whether or not the statement applies to me, or it applies to me about half the time
5 = The statement applies more often than not
6 = The statement usually applies to me
7 = The statement always applies to me

THE SCALE

_____ 1. I prefer a job where I have a lot of control over what I do and when I do it.

_____ 2. I enjoy political participation because I want to have as much of a say in running government as possible.

_____ 3. I try to avoid situations where someone else tells me what to do.

_____ 4. I would prefer to be a leader than a follower.

_____ 5. I enjoy being able to influence the actions of others.

_____ 6. I am careful to check everything on an automobile before I leave for a long trip.

_____ 7. Others usually know what is best for me.

_____ 8. I enjoy making my own decisions.

_____ 9. I enjoy having control over my own destiny.

_____ 10. I would rather someone else take over the leadership role when I'm involved in a group project.

_____ 11. I consider myself to be generally more capable of handling situations than others are.

_____ 12. I'd rather run my own business and make my own mistakes than listen to someone else's orders.

_____ 13. I like to get a good idea of what a job is all about before I begin.

_____ 14. When I see a problem, I prefer to do something about it rather than sit by and let it continue.

_____ 15. When it comes to orders, I would rather give them than receive them.

_____ 16. I wish I could push many of life's daily decisions off on someone else.

_____ 17 When driving, I try to avoid putting myself in a situation where I could be hurt by another person's mistake.

_____ 18. I prefer to avoid situations where someone else has to tell me what it is I should be doing.

_____ 19. There are many situations in which I would prefer only one choice rather than having to make a decision.

_____ 20. I like to wait and see if someone else is going to solve a problem so that I don't have to be bothered with it.

SCORING THE SCALE

To score this scale, you must reverse the numbers you entered for five of the items. The responses to be reversed are those for items 7, 10, 16, 19, and 20. For each of these items, make the following conversions: If you entered 1, change it to 7. If you entered 2, change it to 6. If you entered 3, change it to 5. If you entered 4, leave it unchanged. If you entered 5, change it to 3. If you entered 6, change it to 2. If you entered 7, change it to 1.

Now add up the numbers for all 20 items, using the new numbers for the reversed items. This sum is your score on the Desirability of Control Scale. Enter it below.

MY SCORE _____

Source: Burger & Cooper, 1979

WHAT THE SCALE MEASURES

Devised by Jerry Burger and Harris Cooper (1979), the Desirability of Control (DC) Scale measures the degree to which people are motivated to see themselves in control of the events that take place in their lives. In other words, the DC scale basically taps your *need for control.* Burger views the desire for control as a general personality trait, and he has conducted extensive research relating this trait to many aspects of behavior, including social interaction, achievement strivings, gambling, and reactions to stress. Some of the more interesting findings on desire for control, summarized in a recent book (Burger, 1990), include the following. In comparison to those who score low in the desire for control, people who have a high desire for control make more efforts to influence others. According to Burger, it's not that high DC people want to run others' lives; rather they work to influence others in order to exert more control over their own outcomes. Indeed, they appear to be very reluctant to surrender any control over their own lives, and they react more negatively than low DC people when others try to influence them.

In regard to achievement issues, people high in the desire for control tend to set high standards for themselves, and they work extra hard on challenging tasks to demonstrate their personal mastery and control. How does the desire for control affect gambling habits? The relations between DC and *how much* people gamble are complex, but desire for control does have a fairly consistent effect on which games of chance people prefer to play. High DC people prefer games that offer some perception—perhaps illusory—that one exerts some control over outcomes (blackjack versus roulette, for instance). Who handles stress more effectively? The answer appears to be complex. On the one hand, high DC people seem to do a better job of structuring their lives to avoid stressful, uncontrollable situations. On the other hand, when they are confronted with an uncontrollable situation, high DC people tend to get more upset than those who are low in the desire for control.

INTERPRETING YOUR SCORE

Among older subjects, males tend to score a little higher in desire for control than do females, but gender differences in DC scores are minimal among college students, so we will use a unified set of norms, which are shown below.

NORMS

High score:	**111–140**
Intermediate score:	**90–110**
Low score:	**20–89**

Who Are You?

1. Below you will find 75 personality-trait words taken from the list assembled by Anderson (1968). Try to select the 20 traits (20 only!) that describe you best. Check them.

sincere	headstrong	friendly	tactful
pessimistic	naive	gracious	loyal
open-minded	sloppy	shy	reliable
suspicious	grouchy	short-tempered	outgoing
patient	ethical	compulsive	dependable
tense	persuasive	sarcastic	persistent
cooperative	nervous	respectful	orderly
neat	clumsy	imaginative	energetic
logical	rebellious	impolite	modest
vain	studious	diligent	smart
sociable	understanding	prideful	kind
scornful	truthful	optimistic	good-humored
cheerful	mature	considerate	unselfish
honest	skeptical	courteous	cordial
reasonable	efficient	candid	wholesome
forgetful	resourceful	idealistic	generous
crafty	perceptive	warm	boastful
methodical	punctual	versatile	daring
sly	prejudiced	courageous	

2. Review the 20 traits that you chose. Overall, is it a favorable or unfavorable picture that you have sketched?

3. Considering Carl Rogers' point that we often distort reality and construct an overly favorable self-concept, do you feel that you were objective?

4. What characteristics make you unique?

5. What are your greatest strengths?

6. What are your greatest weaknesses?

How You See Personality

1. How changeable do you believe your personality to be? Elaborate in a few sentences.

2. Do you believe it is possible to "learn" traits one at a time, and thus change your personality over time? Identify traits you believe you have changed.

3. Which personality theorist makes the most sense to you and why.

4. How do you think significant others in your life describe your personality?

5. How different is that description from the one which you would make of your personality?

Sensation-Seeking Scale

INSTRUCTIONS

Each of the items below contains two choices, A and B. Please indicate in the spaces provided on the left which of the choices most describes your likes or the way you feel. It is important that you respond to all items with only one choice, A or B. In some cases you may find that both choices describe your likes or the way you feel. Please choose the one that better describes your likes or feelings. In some cases you may not like either choice. In these cases mark the choice you dislike least. We are interested only in your likes or feelings, not in how others feel about these things or how one is supposed to feel. There are no right or wrong answers. Be frank and give your honest appraisal of yourself.

THE SCALE

_____ 1. A. I would like a job which would require a lot of traveling.
       B. I would prefer a job in one location.

_____ 2. A. I am invigorated by a brisk, cold day.
       B. I can't wait to get indoors on a cold day.

_____ 3. A. I find a certain pleasure in routine kinds of work
       B. Although it is sometimes necessary, I usually dislike routine kinds of work.

_____ 4. A. I often wish I could be a mountain climber.
       B. I can't understand people who risk their necks climbing mountains.

_____ 5. A. I dislike all body odors.
       B. I like some of the earthy body smells.

_____ 6. A. I get bored seeing the same old faces.
       B. I like the comfortable familiarity of everyday friends.

_____ 7. A. I like to explore a strange city or section of town by myself, even if it means getting lost.
       B. I prefer a guide when I am in a place I don't know well.

_____ 8. A. I find the quickest and easiest route to a place and stick to it.
       B. I sometimes take different routes to a place I often go, just for variety's sake.

_____ 9. A. I would not like to try any drug that might produce strange and dangerous effects on me.
       B. I would like to try some of the new drugs that produce hallucinations.

_____ 10. A. I would prefer living in an ideal society where everyone is safe, secure, and happy.
       B. I would have preferred living in the unsettled days of our history.

_____ 11. A. I sometimes like to do things that are a little frightening.
       B. A sensible person avoids activities that are dangerous.

_____ 12. A. I order dishes with which I am familiar, so as to avoid disappointment and unpleasantness.
       B. I like to try new foods that I have never tasted before.

_____ 13. A. I can't stand riding with a person who likes to speed.
       B. I sometimes like to drive very fast because I find it exciting.

_____ 14. A. If I were a salesperson, I would prefer a straight salary rather than the risk of making little or nothing on a commission basis.
       B. If I were a salesperson, I would prefer working on a commission if I had a chance to make more money than I could on a salary.

_____ 15. A. I would like to take up the sport of water skiing.
       B. I would not like to take up the sport of water skiing.

_____ 16. A. I don't like to argue with people whose beliefs are sharply divergent from mine, since such arguments are never resolved.
       B. I find people who disagree with my beliefs more stimulating than people who agree with me.

_____ 17. A. When I go on a trip, I like to plan my route and timetable fairly carefully.
       B. I would like to take off on a trip with no pre-planned or definite routes or timetables.

_____ 18. A. I enjoy the thrills of watching car races.
       B. I find car races unpleasant.

_____ 19. A. Most people spend entirely too much money on life insurance.
       B. Life insurance is something that no one can afford to be without.

_____ 20. A. I would like to learn to fly an airplane.
       B. I would not like to learn to fly an airplane.

_____ 21. A. I would not like to be hypnotized.
       B. I would like to have the experience of being hypnotized.

_____ 22. A. The most important goal of life is to live it to the fullest and experience as much of it as you can.
B. The most important goal of life is to find peace and happiness.

_____ 23. A. I would like to try parachute jumping.
B. I would never want to try jumping out of a plane, with or without a parachute.

_____ 24. A. I enter cold water gradually, giving myself time to get used to it.
B. I like to dive or jump right into the ocean or a cold pool.

_____ 25. A. I do not like the irregularity and discord of most modern music.
B. I like to listen to new and unusual kinds of music.

_____ 26. A. I prefer friends who are excitingly unpredictable.
B. I prefer friends who are reliable and predictable.

_____ 27. A. When I go on a vacation, I prefer the comfort of a good room and bed.
B. When I go on a vacation, I would prefer the change of camping out.

_____ 28. A. The essence of good art is in its clarity, symmetry of form, and harmony of colors.
B. I often find beauty in the "clashing" colors and irregular forms of modern paintings.

_____ 29. A. The worst social sin is to be rude.
B. The worst social sin is to be a bore.

_____ 30. A. I look forward to a good night of rest after a long day.
B. I wish I didn't have to waste so much of a day sleeping.

_____ 31. A. I prefer people who are emotionally expressive even if they are a bit unstable.
B. I prefer people who are calm and even-tempered.

_____ 32. A. A good painting should shock or jolt the senses.
B. A good painting should give one a feeling of peace and security.

_____ 33. A. When I feel discouraged, I recover by relaxing and having some soothing diversion.
B. When I feel discouraged, I recover by going out and doing something new and exciting.

_____ 34. A. People who ride motorcycles must have some kind of an unconscious need to hurt them-selves.
B. I would like to drive or ride on a motorcycle.

SCORING THE SCALE

The scoring key is reproduced below. You should circle your response of A or B each time it corresponds to the keyed response below. Add up the number of responses you circle. This total is your score on the Sensation-Seeking Scale. Record your score below.

1. A	8. B	15. A	22. A	29. B
2. A	9. B	16. B	23. A	30. B
3. B	10. B	17. B	24. B	31. A
4. A	11. A	18. A	25. B	32. A
5. B	12. B	19. A	26. A	33. B
6. A	13. B	20. A	27. B	34. B
7. A	14. B	21. B	28. B	

MY SCORE _____

WHAT THE SCALE MEASURES

As its name implies, the Sensation-Seeking Scale (SSS) measures one's need for a high level of stimulation. Sensation seeking involves the active pursuit of experiences that many people would find very stressful. Marvin Zuckerman (1979) believes that this thirst for sensation is a general personality trait that leads people to seek thrills, adventures, and new experiences.

The scale you have just responded to is the second version of the SSS. Test-retest reliabilities are quite respectable and there is ample evidence to support the scale's validity. For example, studies show that high sensation seekers appraise hypothetical situations as less risky than low sensation seekers and are more willing to volunteer for an experiment in which they will be hypnotized. The scale also shows robust positive correlations with measures of change seeking, novelty seeking, extraversion, and impulsiveness. Interestingly, SSS scores tend to decline with age.

INTERPRETING YOUR SCORE

Our norms are based on percentiles reported by Zuckerman and colleagues for a sample of 62 undergraduates. Although males generally tend to score a bit higher than females on the SSS, the differences are small enough to report one set of (averaged) norms. Remember, sensation-seeking scores tend to decline with age. So, if you're not in the modal college student age range (17-23), these norms may be a bit high.

NORMS

High score:	21–34
Intermediate score:	11–20
Low score:	0–10

Source: Zuckerman, 1979

Where's the Stress In Your Life?

As you learned in Chapter 3, it's a good idea to be aware of the stress in your life. For this exercise you should keep a stress awareness record for one week. Construct a record sheet like that shown below. About twice a day, fill in the information on any stressful events that have occurred. Under "Type of Stress" indicate whether the event involves frustration, conflict, pressure, change, or some combination.

Day	Time	Stressful Event	Type of Stress	Your Reaction

At the end of the week, answer the following questions.

1. Is there a particular type of stress that is most frequent in your life?

2. Is there a particular locale or set of responsibilities that produces a great deal of stress for you?

3. Are there certain reactions to stressful events that you display consistently?

4. Is there anything reasonable that you could do to reduce the amount of stress in your life?

Stress—How Do You Control It?

1. Do modern lifestyles create more stress than in the past? How so?

2. How do YOU create stress in your own life?

3. How could you change the nature of our society to make it less stressful?

4. It could be said that some of our stress comes from leading "out-of-balance" lives. What can we do to "keep it simple"? Furthermore, in what ways can we control the amount of stressors we will encounter beforehand?

5. How could you change the way in which you interact with your school demands or your work demands to change the amount of stress that you feel?

Working Through and Assessing the Impact of a Stressful Event

Identify an event, circumstance, or experience which you found or find to be stressful. Answer the following questions to assist you in looking at the process of how you manage(d) it and the resulting growth for your life. Use this page over again to analyze other experiences.

1. Describe the event, circumstance, or experience that you found to be stressful.

2. How often does this event, circumstance or experience happen in your life?

3. If it has happened more than once, describe briefly how you historically have responded to it.

4. Is this event currently going on in your life or are you still currently reacting to it?

5. Rate the tension that you feel during the experience on a scale of 0 to 10 (0 being no tension, 10 being extreme tension). How long does the tension last?

6. Did you or did you not seek help or assistance in dealing with this situation?

7. From what type of sources did you seek help? (Examples may include, but are not limited to the following: family members you live with, significant other you live with, family member you don't live with, significant other you don't live with, acquaintance, organized support group, school or church help agents, hot line, drop-in center, crisis service, professional help or public agencies including counseling services.)

8. Would you describe the source listed in number 7 gave as more emotionally sustaining or more action-oriented help or both?

9. Describe your satisfaction with the help you received (examples might include "I got much less help than I needed or wanted," "I got about as much as I needed," or "I got much more help than I needed or wanted").

10. How would you rate the "helpfulness" of the strategy you listed in number 7 with this event or circumstance? In the future, would you choose the same approach, modify it, or try something else?

11. How would you evaluate the impact of this experience, event or circumstance upon your growth as an individual and your capability of handling similar things in the future?

Adapted by John Pulver from the College Student Life Events Scale by Murray Levine and David V. Perkins, 1979.

Barnes-Vulcano Rationality Test

INSTRUCTIONS

For each of the following statements, please indicate the degree to which you tend to either agree or disagree with the statement according to the following five-point scale:

1	2	3	4	5
Agree Strongly	Agree	Neither Agree nor Disagree	Disagree	Disagree Strongly

THE SCALE

_____ 1. I do not need to feel that everyone I meet likes me.

_____ 2. I frequently worry about things over which I have no control.

_____ 3. I find it easy to overcome irrational fears.

_____ 4. I can usually shut off thoughts that are causing me to feel anxious.

_____ 5. Life is a ceaseless battle against irrational worries.

_____ 6. I frequently worry about death.

_____ 7. Crowds make me nervous.

_____ 8. I frequently worry about the state of my health.

_____ 9. I tend to worry about things before they actually happen.

_____ 10. If I were told that someone had a criminal record I would not hire him or her to work for me.

_____ 11. When I make a mistake I feel worthless and inadequate.

_____ 12. When someone is wrong I sure let them know.

_____ 13. When I am frustrated the first thing I do is ask myself whether there is anything I can do to change it now.

_____ 14. Whenever something goes wrong I ask myself, "Why did this have to happen to me?"

_____ 15. Whenever things go wrong I say to myself, "I don't like this, I can't stand it."

_____ 16. I usually find a cure for my own depression when it occurs.

_____ 17. Once I am depressed it takes me a long while to recover.

_____ 18. I feel that when I become depressed or unhappy it is caused by other people or the events that happen.

_____ 19. People have little or no ability to control their sorrows or rid themselves of their negative feelings.

_____ 20. When I become angry I usually control my anger.

_____ 21. I can usually control my appetite for food and alcohol.

_____ 22. The value of a human being is directly proportionate to her/his accomplishments; if s/he is not thoroughly competent and adequate in achieving s/he might as well curl up and die.

_____ 23. The important part of playing the game is that you succeed.

_____ 24. I feel badly when my achievement level is lower than others'.

_____ 25. I feel that I must succeed at everything I undertake.

_____ 26. When I feel doubts about potential success I avoid participating and risking the chance of failure.

_____ 27. When I set out to accomplish a task I stick with it to the end.

_____ 28. If I find difficulties in life I discipline myself to face them.

_____ 29. If I try to do something and encounter problems I give up easily.

_____ 30. I find it difficult to work at tasks that have a long-range payoff.

_____ 31. I usually like to face my problems head on.

_____ 32. A person never learns from his/her mistakes.

_____ 33. Life is what you make of it.

_____ 34. Unhappy childhoods inevitably lead to problems in adult life.

_____ 35. I try not to brood over past mistakes.

_____ 36. People who are selfish make me mad because they really should not be that way.

_____ 37. If I had to nag someone to get what I wanted I would not think it was worth the trouble.

_____ 38. I frequently find that life is boring.

_____ 39. I often wish that something new and exciting would happen.

_____ 40. I experience life as just the same old thing from day to day.

_____ 41. I often wish life were more stimulating.

_____42. I often feel that everything is tiresome and dull.

_____43. I wish I could change places with someone who lives an exciting life.

_____44. I often wish life were different than it is.

Source: Barnes & Vulcano, 1982

SCORING THE SCALE

To score this scale, you must reverse the numbers you entered for 12 of the items. The responses to be reversed are those for items 1, 3, 4, 13, 16, 20, 21, 27, 28, 31, 33, and 35. For each of these items, make the following conversions: If you circled 1, change it to 5. If you circled 2, change it to 4. If you circled 3, leave it unchanged. If you circled 4, change it to 2. If you circled 5, change it to 1.

Now add up the numbers for all 44 items, using the new numbers for the reversed items. This sum, which should fall somewhere between 44 and 220, is your score on the Barnes–Vulcano Rationality Test. Enter it below.

MY SCORE _____

WHAT THE SCALE MEASURES

Devised by Gordon Barnes and Brent Vulcano (1982), the Barnes–Vulcano Rationality Test (BVRT) measures the degree to which people do or do not subscribe to the irrational assumptions described by Albert Ellis (1962, 1973). As Chapter 4 in your text explains, Ellis believes that troublesome emotions and overreactions to stress are caused by negative self-talk or catastrophic thinking. This catastrophic thinking is thought to be derived from irrational assumptions that people hold. The items on the BVRT are based on 10 of the irrational assumptions described by Ellis, such as the idea that one must receive love and affection from certain people, or the idea that one must be thoroughly competent in all endeavors. The scale is set up so that high scores indicate that one tends to think relatively rationally, whereas low scores indicate that one is prone to the irrational thinking described by Ellis. The BVRT has excellent reliability, and the authors took steps to minimize contamination from social desirability bias. Evidence regarding the test's validity can be gleaned from various correlational analyses. For example, high scores on the BVRT have been found to correlate negatively with measures of neuroticism (-.50), depression (-.55), and fear (-.31), indicating that respondents who score high on the test tend to be less neurotic, depressed, or fearful than others.

INTERPRETING YOUR SCORE

Our norms, which are shown below, are based on combined data from two sets of adults studied by Barnes and Vulcano (1982). The first sample consisted of 172 subjects (with a mean age of 22), and the second included 177 subjects (with a mean age of 27).

NORMS

High score:	166-220
Intermediate score:	136-165
Low score:	44-135

Can You Detect Your Irrational Thinking?

You should begin this exercise by reviewing the theories of Albert Ellis. To briefly recapitulate, Ellis believes that unpleasant emotional reactions are caused not by events themselves, but by catastrophic interpretations of events derived from irrational assumptions. It is therefore important to detect and dispute these catastrophic modes of thinking. Over a period of a week or so, see if you can spot two examples of irrational thinking on your part. Describe these examples as requested below.

EXAMPLE NO. 1
Activating event:

Irrational self-talk:

Consequent emotional reaction:

Irrational assumption producing irrational thought:

More rational, alternative view:

EXAMPLE NO. 2
Activating event:

Irrational self-talk:

Consequent emotional reaction:

Irrational assumption producing irrational thought:

More rational, alternative view:

Analyzing Coping Strategies

1. You just generally feel "lousy" but are unsure as to what might be causing it. How would you go about figuring out what is wrong? What questions would you ask yourself to ensure that you come to an accurate conclusion?

2. What are some of the phrases that a person might use who is operating in the mode of "learned helplessness"? How could you help an individual tell the difference between something they have control over and something they do not?

3. Rationalization is a mechanism that is fraught with consequences. List some negative consequences of rationalization in the following areas: school, work, home, and in relationships.

4. Discuss the issue of deadlines as they apply to any area of your life. How do you react to deadline pressures? What are some positive and negative coping strategies you have used in dealing with deadlines?

5. How do you explain negative events that occur in your life? What is your explanatory style?

Recognizing Coping Tactics

For each coping strategy below, write an example from a real life situation. See page 106 of your text for general examples that should clarify the meaning of each strategy.

Active Coping:

Planning:

Suppression of competing activities:

Restraint coping:

Seeking social support for instrumental reasons:

Seeking social support for emotional reasons:

Positive reinterpretation and growth:

Acceptance:

Turning to religion:

Focus on and venting of emotions:

Denial:

Behavioral disengagement:

Mental disengagement:

Alcohol-drug disengagement:

Self-Monitoring Scale

INSTRUCTIONS

The statements below concern your personal reactions to a number of situations. No two statements are exactly alike, so consider each statement carefully before answering. If a statement is true or mostly true as applied to you, mark T as your answer. If a statement is false or not usually true as applied to you, mark F as your answer. It is important that you answer as frankly and as honestly as you can. Record your responses in the spaces provided on the left.

THE SCALE

_____1.   I find it hard to imitate the behavior of other people.

_____2.   My behavior is usually an expression of my true inner feelings, attitudes, and beliefs.

_____3.   At parties and social gatherings, I do not attempt to do or say things that others will like.

_____4.   I can only argue for ideas I already believe.

_____5.   I can make impromptu speeches even on topics about which I have almost no information.

_____6.   I guess I put on a show to impress or entertain people.

_____7.   When I am uncertain how to act in a social situation, I look to the behavior of others for cues.

_____8.   I would probably make a good actor.

_____9.   I rarely need the advice of my friends to choose movies, books, or music.

_____10.   I sometimes appear to others to be experiencing deeper emotions than I actually am.

_____11.   I laugh more when I watch a comedy with others than when alone.

_____12.   In a group of people I am rarely the center of attention.

_____13.   In different situations and with different people, I often act like very different persons.

_____14.   I am not particularly good at making other people like me.

_____15.   Even if I am not enjoying myself, I often pretend to be having a good time.

_____16.   I'm not always the person I appear to be.

_____17.   I would not change my opinions (or the way I do things) in order to please someone else or win their favor.

_____18.   I have considered being an entertainer.

_____19.   In order to get along and be liked, I tend to be what people expect me to be rather than anything else.

_____20.   I have never been good at games like charades or improvisational acting.

_____21.   I have trouble changing my behavior to suit different people and different situations.

_____22.   At a party, I let others keep the jokes and stories going.

_____23.   I feel a bit awkward in company and do not show up quite so well as I should.

_____24.   I can look anyone in the eye and tell a lie with a straight face (if for a right end).

_____25.   I may deceive people by being friendly when I really dislike them.

SCORING THE SCALE

The scoring key is reproduced below. You should circle your response of true or false each time it corresponds to the keyed response below. Add up the number of responses you circle. This total is your score on the Self-Monitoring Scale. Record your score below.

1. False   2. False   3. False   4. False   5. True   6. True   7. True   8. True   9. False   10. True

11. True   12. False   13. True   14. False   15. True   16. True   17. False   18. True   19. True   20. False

21. False   22. False   23. False   24. True   25. True

MY SCORE _____

Source: Snyder, 1974

WHAT THE SCALE MEASURES

Developed by Mark Snyder (1974), the Self-Monitoring (SM) Scale measures the extent to which you consciously employ impression management strategies in social interactions. Basically, the scale assesses the degree to which you manipulate the nonverbal signals that you send to others and the degree to which you adjust your behavior to situational demands. Research shows that some people work harder at managing their public images than do others.

In his original study, Snyder (1974) reported very reasonable test-retest reliability (.83 for one month) and, for an initial study, provided ample evidence regarding the scale's validity. In assessing the validity of the scale, he found that in comparison to low SM subjects, high SM subjects were rated by peers as being better at emotional self-control and better at figuring out how to behave appropriately in new social situations. Furthermore, Snyder found that stage actors tended to score higher on the scale than undergraduates, as one would expect. Additionally, Ickes and Barnes (1977) summarize evidence that high SM people are (1) very sensitive to situational cues, (2) particularly skilled at detecting deception on the part of others, and (3) especially insightful about how to influence the emotions of others.

INTERPRETING YOUR SCORE

Our norms are based on guidelines provided by Ickes and Barnes (1977). The divisions are based on data from 207 undergraduate subjects.

NORMS

High score:	15-22
Intermediate score:	9-14
Low score:	0-8

How Does Your Self-Concept Compare to Your Self-Ideal?

Below you will find a list of 15 traits, each portrayed on a 9-point continuum. Mark with an X where you think you fall on each trait. Try to be candid and accurate; these marks will collectively describe a portion of your self-concept. When you are finished, go back and circle where you wish you could be on each dimension. These marks describe your self-ideal. Finally, in the spaces on the right, indicate the size of the discrepancy between self-concept and self-ideal for each trait.

1. Decisive   Indecisive_____

    9   8   7   6   5   4   3   2   1

2. Anxious   Relaxed_____

    9   8   7   6   5   4   3   2   1

3. Easily influenced   Independent thinker _____

    9   8   7   6   5   4   3   2   1

4. Very intelligent   Less intelligent _____

    9   8   7   6   5   4   3   2   1

5. In good physical shape   In poor physical shape _____

    9   8   7   6   5   4   3   2   1

6. Undependable   Dependable _____

    9   8   7   6   5   4   3   2   1

7. Deceitful   Honest _____

    9   8   7   6   5   4   3   2   1

8. A leader   A follower _____

    9   8   7   6   5   4   3   2   1

9. Unambitious   Ambitious _____

    9   8   7   6   5   4   3   2   1

10. Self-confident   Insecure _____

    9   8   7   6   5   4   3   2   1

11. Conservative   Adventurous _____

    9   8   7   6   5   4   3   2   1

12. Extraverted   Introverted _____

    9   8   7   6   5   4   3   2   1

13. Physically attractive   Physically unattractive _____

    9   8   7   6   5   4   3   2   1

14. Lazy   Hardworking _____

    9   8   7   6   5   4   3   2   1

15. Funny   Little sense of humor _____

    9   8   7   6   5   4   3   2   1

Overall, how would you describe the discrepancy between your self-concept and your self-ideal (large, moderate, small, large on a few dimensions)?

How do sizable gaps on any of the traits affect your self-esteem?

Do you feel that any of the gaps exist because you have had others' ideals imposed on you or because you have thoughtlessly accepted others' ideals?

Examining Your Self Evaluation

1. How would you characterize yourself at this time if you were to use adjectives to describe yourself? Perhaps to do this, you could fill in the blank, "I am a person who_____" or "Others would describe me as_____". What experiences have you had in your life that have promoted these characteristics within you?

2. What do you see as your strengths and weaknesses as an individual at this time and what experiences have contributed to these?

3. What are your values; that is, what is valuable to you? What has contributed to the emergence of these values in your life?

4. List and explain five experiences in your life that you feel have been the most growth provoking in developing you into the person that you are today.

Analyzing Your Emerging Self

1. Where do you feel your self-esteem is coming from? What are the underpinnings or foundations that you rely upon for your self-esteem?

2. As you look at your "possible selves", are they mostly feared possible selves or hoped-for possible selves? How do these selves affect your daily life?

3. It has been said that "No one can make you feel inferior without your permission." Since we all are vulnerable to the feedback of others as we develop a sense of self, what needs to happen inside us so that we have more control over our self-assessments?

4. Give some examples of how identifying your identity as either the gender male or female influences how you evaluate your behavior.

5. Do you think you operate in your life with a pessimistic attributional style or an optimistic attributional style? Has it depended at all on the situation(s) you were in? (This is not a popular question, since no one likely wants to realize or think that they approach life with a pessimistic style. However, this analysis is a useful one to do.)

Argumentativeness Scale

INSTRUCTIONS

This questionnaire contains statements about arguing controversial issues. Indicate how often each statement is true for you personally by placing the appropriate number in the blank to the left of the statement:

1	2	3	4	5
Almost never true	Rarely true	Occasionally true	Often true	Almost always true

THE SCALE

_____ 1. While in an argument, I worry that the person I am arguing with will form a negative impression of me.

_____ 2. Arguing over controversial issues improves my intelligence.

_____ 3. I enjoy avoiding arguments.

_____ 4. I am energetic and enthusiastic when I argue.

_____ 5. Once I finish an argument I promise myself that I will not get into another.

_____ 6. Arguing with a person creates more problems for me than it solves.

_____ 7. I have a pleasant, good feeling when I win a point in an argument.

_____ 8. When I finish arguing with someone I feel nervous and upset.

_____ 9. I enjoy a good argument over a controversial issue.

_____ 10. I get an unpleasant feeling when I realize I am about to get into an argument.

_____ 11. I enjoy defending my point of view on an issue.

_____ 12. I am happy when I keep an argument from happening.

_____ 13. I do not like to miss the opportunity to argue a controversial issue.

_____ 14. I prefer being with people who rarely disagree with me.

_____ 15. I consider an argument an exciting intellectual challenge.

_____ 16. I find myself unable to think of effective points during an argument.

_____ 17. I feel refreshed and satisfied after an argument on a controversial issue.

_____ 18. I have the ability to do well in an argument.

_____ 19. I try to avoid getting into arguments.

_____ 20. I feel excitement when I expect that a conversation I am in is leading to an argument.

SCORING THE SCALE

Add up the numbers that you have recorded for items 1, 3, 5, 6, 8, 10, 12, 14, 16, and 19. This total reflects your tendency to avoid getting into arguments. Next, add up the numbers that you have recorded for items 2, 4, 7, 9, 11, 13, 15, 17, 18, and 20. This total reflects your tendency to approach argumentative situations. Record these subtotals in the spaces below. Subtract your avoidance score from your approach score to arrive at your overall score.

_____   -   _____   =   _____

Approach score   Avoidance score   Total score

Source: Infante & Rancer, 1982

WHAT THE SCALE MEASURES

This questionnaire measures an aspect of your social influence behavior. Specifically, it assesses your tendency to argue with others in persuasive efforts. Persons who score high on this scale are not bashful about tackling controversial issues, are willing to attack others verbally to make their points, and are less compliant than the average person. Developed by Infante and Rancer (1982), this scale has high test-retest reliability (.91 for a period of one week). Examinations of the scale's validity show that it correlates well with other measures of communication tendencies and with friends' ratings of subjects' argumentativeness.

INTERPRETING YOUR SCORE

Our norms are based on the responses of over 800 undergraduate subjects studied by Infante and Rancer (1982).

NORMS

High score:	16 and above
Intermediate score:	-6 to 15
Low score:	-7 and below

Can You Identify Your Prejudicial Stereotypes?

1.   List and briefly describe examples of three prejudicial stereotypes that you hold or have held at one time.

Example 1:

Example 2:

Example 3:

2. Try to identify the sources (family, friends, media, etc.) of each of these stereotypes.

Example 1:

Example 2:

Example 3:

3. For each stereotype, how much actual interaction have you had with the stereotyped group, and has this interaction affected your views?

Example 1:

Example 2:

Example 3:

4. Can you think of any ways in which the fundamental attribution error or defensive attribution has contributed to these stereotypes?

Fundamental attribution error:

Defensive attribution:

How Do You Operate In a Group?

1. Give an example of a time in which you committed the "fundamental attribution error" in which you attributed a characteristic to an individual based upon a behavior you observed, and later found out that the behavior was more the result of the situation.

2. Describe a recent incident where you conformed to group norms. Was this a difficult experience for you?

3. Identify a group that you have belonged to and list some of the behavioral norms of the group and describe what you believe your role in the group has been.

4. Identify an experience or two that you might have had that tells you that you were treated the way you were either because of the color of your skin, your status, or your perceived status in other's eyes.

5. Have you ever been in a situation where you were a member of a group or crowd and saw a situation that was in need of attention and found yourself hesitant to assist? What was that situation?

Opener Scale

INSTRUCTIONS

For each statement, indicate your degree of agreement or disagreement, using the scale shown below. Record your responses in the spaces on the left.

4 = I strongly agree
3 = I slightly agree
2 = I am certain
1 = I slightly disagree
0 = I strongly disagree

THE SCALE

_____ 1. People frequently tell me about themselves.

_____ 2. I've been told that I'm a good listener.

_____ 3. I'm very accepting of others.

_____ 4. People trust me with their secrets.

_____ 5. I easily get people to "open up."

_____ 6. People feel relaxed around me.

_____ 7. I enjoy listening to people.

_____ 8. I'm sympathetic to people's problems.

_____ 9. I encourage people to tell me how they are feeling.

_____ 10. I can keep people talking about themselves.

SCORING THE SCALE

This scale is easy to score! Simply add up the numbers that you have recorded in the spaces on the left. This total is your score on the Opener Scale.

MY SCORE _____

Source: Miller, Berg, & Archer, 1983

WHAT THE SCALE MEASURES

Devised by Lynn Miller, John Berg, and Richard Archer (1983), the Opener Scale is intended to measure your perception of your ability to get others to "open up" around you. In other words, the scale assesses your tendency to elicit intimate self-disclosure from people. The items assess your perceptions of (a) others' reactions to you ("People feel relaxed around me"), (b) your interest in listening ("I enjoy listening to people"), and (c) your interpersonal skills ("I can keep people talking about themselves").

In spite of its brevity, the scale has reasonable test-retest reliability (.69 over a period of six weeks). Correlations with other personality measures were modest, but in the expected directions. For instance, scores on the Opener Scale correlate positively with a measure of empathy and negatively with a measure of shyness. Further evidence for the validity of the scale was obtained in a laboratory study of interactions between same-sex strangers. Subjects who scored high on the scale compared to those who scored low elicited more self-disclosure from people who weren't prone to engage in much disclosure.

INTERPRETING YOUR SCORE

Our norms are based on the original sample of 740 undergraduates studied by Miller, Berg, and Archer (1983). They found a small but statistically significant difference between males and females. Begin by finishing the incomplete sentences below (adapted from Egan, 1977). Go through the sentences fairly quickly; do not ponder your responses too long. There are no right or wrong answers.

NORMS

	Females	Males
High score:	35–40	33–40
Intermediate score:	26–34	23–32
Low score:	0–25	0–22

How Do You Feel About Self-Disclosure?

This exercise is intended to make you think about your self-disclosure behavior. Begin by finishing the incomplete sentences below (adapted from Egan, 1977). Go through the sentences fairly quickly; do not ponder your responses too long. There are no right or wrong answers.

1. I dislike people who . . .

2. Those who really know me . . .

3. When I let someone know something I don't like about myself . . .

4. When I'm in a group of strangers . . .

5. I envy . . .

6. I get hurt when . . .

7. I daydream about . . .

8. Few people know that I . . .

9. One thing I really dislike about myself is . . .

10. When I share my values with someone . . .

Source: Adapted from Egan, 1977

Based on your responses to the incomplete sentences, do you feel you engage in the right amount of self-disclosure? Too little? Too much?

In general, what prevents you from engaging in self-disclosure?

Are there particular topics on which you find it difficult to be self-disclosing?

Are you the recipient of much self-disclosure from others, or do people have difficulty opening up to you?

Reflections on Your Communication Style and Feelings About Conflict

1. What topics and areas in life do you like to talk about? What areas do you dislike or find more difficult? Are you willing to try to become more comfortable about discussing these?

2. Which of your parents is your current communication pattern most like and how do you think this has affected your relationships?

3. How do you FEEL about conflict?

4. At this point in your life, how do you usually act during a conflict? What do you expect of the person you are having the conflict with when you are behaving in this manner?

5. In your family growing up, how did your parents handle disagreements? How does this affect how you manage conflict?

Social Avoidance and Distress Scale

INSTRUCTIONS

The statements below inquire about your personal reactions to a variety of situations. Consider each statement carefully. Then indicate whether the statement is true or false in regard to your typical behavior. Record your responses (true or false) in the space provided on the left.

THE SCALE

_____ 1. I feel relaxed even in unfamiliar social situations.

_____ 2. I try to avoid situations which force me to be very sociable.

_____ 3. It is easy for me to relax when I am with strangers.

_____ 4. I have no particular desire to avoid people.

_____ 5. I often find social occasions upsetting.

_____ 6. I usually feel calm and comfortable at social occasions.

_____ 7. I am usually at ease when talking to someone of the opposite sex.

_____ 8. I try to avoid talking to people unless I know them well.

_____ 9. If the chance comes to meet new people, I often take it.

_____ 10. I often feel nervous or tense in casual get-togethers in which both sexes are present.

_____ 11. I am usually nervous with people unless I know them well.

_____ 12. I usually feel relaxed when I am with a group of people.

_____ 13. I often want to get away from people.

_____ 14. I usually feel uncomfortable when I am in a group of people I don't know.

_____ 15. I usually feel relaxed when I meet someone for the first time.

_____ 16. Being introduced to people makes me tense and nervous.

_____ 17. Even though a room is full of strangers, I may enter it anyway.

_____ 18. I would avoid walking up and joining a large group of people.

_____ 19. When my superiors want to talk with me, I talk willingly.

_____ 20. I often feel on edge when I am with a group of people.

_____ 21. I tend to withdraw from people.

_____ 22. I don't mind talking to people at parties or social gatherings.

_____ 23. I am seldom at ease in a large group of people.

_____ 24. I often think up excuses in order to avoid social engagements.

_____ 25. I sometimes take the responsibility for introducing people to each other.

_____ 26. I try to avoid formal social occasions.

_____ 27. I usually go to whatever social engagements I have.

_____ 28. I find it easy to relax with other people.

Source: Watson & Friend, 1969

SCORING THE SCALE

The scoring key is reproduced below. You should circle your true or false response each time it corresponds to the keyed response below. Add up the number of responses you circle, and this total is your score on the Social Avoidance and Distress (SAD) Scale. Record your score below.

1. False	8. True	15. False	22. False
2. True	9. False	16. True	23. True
3. False	10. True	17. False	24. True
4. False	11. True	18. True	25. False
5. True	12. False	19. False	26. True
6. False	13. True	20. True	27. False
7. False	14. True	21. True	28. False

MY SCORE _____

WHAT THE SCALE MEASURES

As its name implies, this scale measures avoidance and distress in social interactions. David Watson and Ronald Friend (1969) developed the scale to assess the extent to which individuals experience discomfort, fear, and anxiety in social situations and the extent to which they therefore try to evade many kinds of social encounters. To check the validity of the scale, they used it to predict subjects' social behavior in experimentally contrived situations. As projected, they found that people who scored high on the SAD Scale were less willing than low scorers to participate in a group discussion. The high scorers also reported anticipating more anxiety about their participation in the discussion than the low scorers. Additionally, Watson and Friend found a strong negative correlation (-.76) between the SAD and a measure of affiliation drive (the need to seek the company of others).

INTERPRETING YOUR SCORE

Our norms are based on data collected by Watson and Friend (1969) on over 200 university students.

NORMS

High score:	16-28
Intermediate score:	6-15
Low score:	0-5

How Do You Relate to Friends?

The following questions (adapted from Egan, 1977) are designed to help you think about how you deal with friendships.

1. Do you have many friends or very few?

2. Whether many or few, do you usually spend a lot of time with your friends?

3. What do you like in other people—that is, what makes you choose them as friends?

4. Are the people you go around with like you or different from you? Or are they in some ways like you and in other ways different? How?

5. Do you like to control others, to get them to do things your way? Do you let others control you? Do you give in to others much of the time?

6. Are there ways in which your friendships are one-sided?

Source: Adapted from Egan, 1977

Analyzing Your Views of Social Connectedness

1. In your own experience, do attractive people seem to differ in personality from unattractive people? Does the "attractiveness stereotype" seem to have any validity?

2. Do you think attachment style is "fixed" early in life by the quality of care in childhood, or is it malleable in adulthood? What kinds of experiences would people with insecure attachment histories need in order to experience the quality of adult relationships available to the securely attached person?

3. Write an autobiographical sketch addressing one of the following statements: " When I was in love," "What it is like to be in love," "Why my love will last," "Why my love didn't last," or "My personal experiences with being in love and what I have learned." If you have never been in love write on "My concepts of love."

4. How much time during a month/week or year do you picture yourself spending with friends you have prior to the beginning of a marital partnership?

5. What's the best way you've been able to deal with loneliness?

Self-Report Jealousy Scale

INSTRUCTIONS

The following scale lists some situations in which you may have been involved, or in which you could be involved. Rate them with regard to how you would feel if you were confronted with the situation by circling a number that corresponds to one of the reactions shown on the right. Do not omit any items.

0	1	2	3	4
Pleased	Mildly upset	Upset	Very upset	Extremely upset

THE SCALE

_____1. Your partner expresses the desire that you both develop other romantic relationships.

_____2. Your partner spends increasingly more time at work with a co-employee you feel could be sexually attractive to your partner.

_____3. Your partner suddenly shows an interest in going to a party when he or she finds out that someone will be there with whom he or she has been romantically involved with previously.

_____4. At a party, your partner hugs someone other than you.

_____5. You notice your partner repeatedly looking at another.

_____6. Your partner spends increasingly more time in outside activities and hobbies in which you are not included.

_____7. At a party, your partner kisses someone you do not know.

_____8. Your boss, with whom you have had a good working relationship in the past, now seems to be more interested in the work of a co-worker.

_____9. Your partner goes to a bar several evenings without you.

_____10. Your partner recently received a promotion, and the new position requires a great deal of travel, business dinners, and parties, most of which you are not invited to attend.

_____11. At a party, your partner dances with someone you do not know.

_____12. You and a co-worker worked very hard on an extremely important project. However, your boss gave your co-worker full credit for it.

_____13. Someone flirts with your partner.

_____14. At a party, _your_ partner repeatedly kisses someone you do not know.

_____15. Your partner has sexual relations with someone else.

_____16. Your brother or sister is given more freedom, such as staying up later, or driving the car.

_____17. Your partner comments to you on how attractive another person is.

_____18. While at a social gathering of a group of friends, your partner spends little time talking to you, but engages the others in animated conversation.

_____19. Grandparents visit your family, and they seem to devote most of their attention to a brother or sister instead of you.

_____20. Your partner flirts with someone else.

_____21. Your brother or sister seems to be receiving more affection and/or attention from your parents.

_____22. You have just discovered your partner is having an affair with someone at work.

_____23. The person who has been your assistant for a number of years at work decides to take a similar position with someone else.

_____24. The group to which you belong appears to be leaving you out of plans, activities, etc.

_____25. Your best friend suddenly shows interest in doing things with someone else.

Source: Bringle et at., 1979

SCORING THE SCALE

Give yourself 4 points for every item where your response was "extremely upset," 3 points for every item where your response was "very upset," 2 points for every item where your response was "upset," 1 point for every item where your response was "mildly upset," and 0 for every item where *your* response was "pleased." In other words, add up the numbers you recorded. This total is your score on the Self-Report Jealousy Scale.

MY SCORE _____

WHAT THE SCALE MEASURES

As its name indicates, this scale measures your tendency to get jealous in a variety of situations. It does not measure romantic jealousy exclusively, as ten of the items relate to nonromantic jealousy. Hence, it assesses jealousy in a general way, with a heavy emphasis on romantic relationships.

This scale, which was developed by Bringle, Roach, Andle, and Evenbeck (1979), has adequate test-retest reliability. Correlations with other personality traits have been examined in efforts to demonstrate its validity. People who score high on the scale tend to have low self-esteem, to be anxious, to see the world in negative terms, and to feel they have little control over their lives. These are interesting preliminary findings, although more research is needed to better validate this instrument.

INTERPRETING YOUR SCORE

Our norms are based on the sample of 162 college students studied by Bringle et al. (1979). They may be inappropriate for older, nontraditional college students.

NORMS

High score:	83-100
Intermediate score:	59-82
Low score:	0-58

How Do You Behave In Intimate Relationships?

The following questions (adapted from Corey & Corey, 1986, 1997) are intended to make you think about how you act in intimate relationships. They are designed for people in "couple-type" relationships, but if you are not currently involved in one, you can apply them to whatever relationship is most significant in your life (for instance, with your parents, children, or best friend).

1. What are some sources of conflict in your relationship? Check any of the following items that apply to you, and list any other areas of conflict in the space provided.

_____Spending money

_____ Use of free time

_____ What to do about boredom

_____ Investment of energy in work

_____ Interest in others of the opposite sex

_____ Outside friendships

_____ Wanting children

_____ How to deal with children

_____ Differences in basic values

_____ In-laws

_____ Sexual needs and satisfaction

_____ Expression of caring and loving

_____ Power struggles

_____ Role conflicts

_____ Others (list below)

2. How do you generally cope with these conflicts in your relationship? Check the items that most apply to you.

_____ By open dialogue

_____ By avoidance

_____ By fighting and arguing

_____ By compromising

_____ By getting involved with other people or in projects

List other ways in which you deal with conflicts in your relationships.

Source: Adapted from Corey & Corey, 1986, 1997

3. List some ways in which you've changed during the period of your relationship. How have your changes affected the relationship?

4. How much do you need (and depend upon) the other person? Imagine that he or she is no longer in *your* life, and write down how your life might be different.

Thinking About Your Attitudes About Marriage and Cohabitation

1. Regardless of your current marital status, what are your ideal criteria for selecting a mate?

2. How do you know if you are really ready for marriage?

3. What areas of self-awareness or knowledge of self do you feel you need to be settled in before you would make a long-term commitment to a relationship?

4. In what ways is cohabitation a realistic preparation for marriage and in what ways is it not?

Personal Attributes Questionnaire

INSTRUCTIONS

The items below inquire about what kind of a person you think you are. Each item consists of a pair of characteristics, with the letters A–E in between. For example:

Not At All Artistic   A   B   C   D   E   Very Artistic

Each pair describes contradictory characteristics—that is, you cannot be both at the same time, such as very artistic and not at all artistic.

The letters form a scale between the two extremes. You are to enter a letter that describes where you fall on the scale. For example, if you think you have no artistic ability, you would enter A. If you think you are pretty good, you might enter D. If you are only medium, you might enter C, and so forth.

THE SCALE

_____1.	Not at all aggressive	A	B	C	D	E	Very aggressive
_____2.	Not at all independent	A	B	C	D	E	Very independent
_____3.	Not at all emotional	A	B	C	D	E	Very emotional
_____4.	Very submissive	A	B	C	D	E	Very dominant
_____5.	Not at all excitable in a major crisis	A	B	C	D	E	Very excitable in a major crisis
_____6.	Very passive	A	B	C	D	E	Very active
_____7.	Not at all able to devote self completely to others	A	B	C	D	E	Able to devote self completely to others
_____8.	Very rough	A	B	C	D	E	Very gentle
_____9.	Not at all helpful to others	A	B	C	D	E	Very helpful to others
_____10.	Not at all competitive	A	B	C	D	E	Very competitive
_____11.	Very home oriented	A	B	C	D	E	Very worldly
_____12.	Not at all kind	A	B	C	D	E	Very kind
_____13.	Indifferent to others' approval	A	B	C	D	E	Highly needful of others' approval
_____14.	Feelings not easily hurt	A	B	C	D	E	Feelings easily hurt
_____15.	Not at all aware of feelings of others	A	B	C	D	E	Very aware of feelings of others
_____16.	Can make decisions easily	A	B	C	D	E	Has difficulty making decisions
_____17.	Gives up very easily	A	B	C	D	E	Never gives up easily
_____18.	Never cries	A	B	C	D	E	Cries very easily
_____19.	Not at all self-confident	A	B	C	D	E	Very self-confident
_____20.	Feels very inferior	A	B	C	D	E	Feels very superior
_____21.	Not at all understanding of others	A	B	C	D	E	Very understanding of others
_____22.	Very cold in relations with others	A	B	C	D	E	Very warm in relations with others
_____23.	Very little need for security	A	B	C	D	E	Very strong need for security
_____24.	Goes to pieces under pressure	A	B	C	D	E	Stands up well under pressure

Source: Spence & Helmreich, 1978

SCORING THE SCALE

The Personal Attributes Questionnaire (PAQ) is made up of three 8-item subscales, but we are only going to compute scores for two of these subscales, so the first step is to eliminate the 8 items from the unused subscale. Put an X in the spaces to the left of the items for the following items: 1, 4, 5, 11, 13, 14, 18, and 23. These items belong to the subscale that we won't be using, and they can be ignored. Of the remaining items, one (item 16) is reverse-scored as follows. If you circled A, enter 4 in the space to the left of item 5; if you circled B, enter 3; if you circled C, enter 2; if you circled D, enter 1; and if you circled E, enter 0. All the rest of the items are scored in the following manner: A = 0, B = 1, C = 2, D = 3, and E = 4. Based on the responses you circled, enter the appropriate numbers for the remaining items in the spaces to the left of the items.

The next step is to compute your scores on the femininity and masculinity subscales of the PAQ. To compute your score on the *femininity* subscale, add up the numbers next to items 3, 7, 8, 9, 12, 15, 21, and 22, and enter your score in the space below. To compute *your* score on the *masculinity* subscale, add up the numbers next to items 2, 6, 10, 16, 17, 19, 20, and 24, and enter your score in the space below.

MY SCORE ON THE FEMININITY SUBSCALE _____

MY SCORE ON THE MASCULINITY SUBSCALE _____

WHAT THE SCALE MEASURES

Devised by Janet Spence and Robert Helmreich (1978), the PAQ assesses masculinity and femininity in terms of respondents' self-perceived possession of various personality traits that are stereotypically believed to differentiate the sexes. The authors emphasize that the PAQ taps only limited aspects of sex roles: certain self-assertive/instrumental traits traditionally associated with masculinity and certain interpersonal/expressive traits traditionally associated with femininity. Although the PAQ should not be viewed as a global measure of mas-culinity and femininity, it has been widely used in research to provide a rough classification of subjects in terms of their gender-role identity. As explained in your text, people who score high in both masculinity and femininity are said to be androgynous. People who score high in femininity and low in masculinity are said to be feminine sex-typed. Those who score high in masculinity and low in femininity are characterized as masculine sex-typed, and those who score low on both dimensions are said to be sex-role undifferentiated.

INTERPRETING YOUR SCORE

You can use the chart shown below to classify yourself in terms of gender-role identity. Our norms are based on a sample of 715 college students studied by Spence and Helmreich (1978). The cutoffs for "high" scores on the masculinity and femininity subscales are the medians for each scale. Obviously, these are very arbitrary cutoffs, and results may be misleading for people who score very close to the median on either scale, as a difference of a point or two could change their classification. Hence, if either of your scores is within a couple of points of the median, you should view your gender-role classification as very tentative.

MY CLASSIFICATION _____

What percentage of subjects falls into each of the four gender-role categories? The exact breakdown will vary depending on the nature of the sample, but Spence and Helmreich (1978) reported the following distribution for their sample of 715 college students.

CATEGORY	Males	Females
Androgynous	25%	35%
Feminine	8%	32%
Masculine	44%	14%
Undifferentiated	23%	18%

How Do You Feel About Gender Roles?

1. Can you recall any experiences that were particularly influential in shaping your attitudes about gender roles? If yes, give a couple of examples.

2. Have you ever engaged in cross-sex-typed behavior? Can you think of a couple of examples? How did people react?

3. Do you ever feel restricted by gender roles? If so, in what ways?

4. Have you ever been a victim of sex discrimination (sexism)? If so, describe the circumstances.

5. How do you think the transition in gender roles has affected you personally?

Reflecting on the Power of Gender Roles

1. In what general ways do you think men and women differ?

2. Might someone else consider your views stereotypes? Why or why not?

3. In the effort to achieve civil rights, some gay activist groups have compared themselves to other minority groups such as African Americans and women. There is a broad range of opinion about the appropriateness of such comparisons, both within the minority groups and among majority group members. Do you think the comparison is valid? Do you think it will be useful politically?

4. Where do you think gender roles are heading in the next 15 to 30 years? Will we retain some of the aspects of traditional roles in some way—reverse them, throw them out, or modify them? What do you think?

Death Anxiety Scale

INSTRUCTIONS
If a statement is true or mostly true as applied to you, circle T. If a statement is false or mostly false as applied to you, circle F.

THE SCALE

T   F   1.   I am very much afraid to die.

T   F   2.   The thought of death seldom enters my mind.

T   F   3.   It doesn't make me nervous when people talk about death.

T   F   4.   I dread to think about having to have an operation.

T   F   5.   I am not at all afraid to die.

T   F   6.   I am not particularly afraid of getting cancer.

T   F   7.   The thought of death never bothers me.

T   F   8.   I am often distressed by the way time flies so very rapidly.

T   F   9.   I fear dying a painful death.

T   F   10.   The subject of life after death troubles me greatly.

T   F   11.   I am really scared of having a heart attack.

T   F   12.   I often think about how short life really is.

T   F   13.   I shudder when I hear people talking about a World War III.

T   F   14.   The sight of a dead body is horrifying to me.

T   F   15.   I feel that the future holds nothing for me to fear.

SCORING THE SCALE
The scoring key is reproduced below. You should circle your response each time it corresponds to the keyed response below. Add up the number of responses that you circle. This total is your score on the Death Anxiety Scale.

1. True	6. False	11. True
2. False	7. False	12. True
3. False	8. True	13. True
4. True	9. True	14. True
5. False	10. True	15. False

MY SCORE_____

Source: Lonetto & Templer, 1983

WHAT THE SCALE MEASURES
Virtually no one looks forward to death, but some of us fear death more than others. Some people are reasonably comfortable with their mortality, and others have difficulty confronting the idea that someday they will die. This scale measures the strength of your anxiety about death. When investigators do research on how age, sex, religion, health, and other variables are related to death anxiety, they use scales such as this one. Developed by Lonetto and Templer (1983), the Death Anxiety Scale has excellent reliability. Demonstrating the validity of a scale that measures death anxiety is complex, but the scale does correlate with other measures of death anxiety. Scores also correlate positively with clinical judgments of subjects' death anxiety.

INTERPRETING YOUR SCORE
Our norms are based on a sample of 1271 adults (parents of adolescents) cited by Lonetto and Templer (1983). Although females tend to score a little higher than males on this scale, we have reported combined norms.

Norms

High score:	9-15
Intermediate score:	4-8
Low score:	0-3

How Do You Feel About Age Roles?

1. Discuss how your behavior has been restricted by age roles. (For example, has anyone ever told you to "act your age"?)

2. Have you ever been a victim of ageism? If so, describe.

3. Give an example of how a social clock has influenced your behavior.

4. List seven adjectives that you associate with being elderly.

5. Given the information reviewed in the chapter, do you feel that the adjectives you chose are accurate descriptions of the elderly? To what degree do they reflect stereotypes of the elderly?

How Flexible Is Development?

1. Recall your family of origin when you were an adolescent. How did you and your parents deal with establishing new family boundaries and with issues of autonomy and independence?

2. What was the process of "launching" into the adult world like for you? Has it been completed? If you continue to live at home, what difficulties has it caused your parents? Yourself?

3. As you look at the stages Erikson proposes, where are you in the life cycle? What is the psychological task that Erikson says you need to accomplish? Is it an important issue for you? How are you resolving it?

4. We have all seen examples of people who do not seem to "have their act together" at some point in their lives. What do you see as the primary cause of this? How much do you agree that it could be as a result of some unresolved process that should have been taken care of at some earlier stage of their lives?

5. How do stereotypes hold us back in our development? What are some of the stereotypes about getting older that we will likely have to eliminate as more and more individuals reach old age?

Assertive Job-Hunting Survey

INSTRUCTIONS

This inventory is designed to provide information about the way in which you look for a job. Picture yourself in each of these job-hunting situations and indicate how likely it is that you would respond in the described manner. If you have never job-hunted before, answer according to how you would try to find a job. Please record your responses in the spaces to the left of the items. Use the following key for your responses:

1	2	3	4	5	6
Very unlikely	Somewhat unlikely	Slightly unlikely	Slightly likely	Somewhat likely	Very likely

THE SCALE

_____1. When asked to indicate my experiences for a position, I would mention only my paid work experience.

_____2. If I heard someone talking about an interesting job opening, I'd be reluctant to ask for more information unless I knew the person.

_____3. I would ask an employer who did not have an opening if he knew of other employers who might have job openings.

_____4. I downplay my qualifications so that an employer won't think I'm more qualified than I really am.

_____5. I would rather use an employment agency to find a job than apply to employers directly.

_____6. Before an interview, I would contact an employee of the organization to learn more about that organization.

_____7. I hesitate to ask questions when I'm being interviewed for a job.

_____8. I avoid contacting potential employers by phone or in person because I feel they are too busy to talk with me.

_____9. If an interviewer were very late for my interview, I would leave or arrange for another appointment.

_____10. I believe an experienced employment counselor would have a better idea of what jobs I should apply for than I would have.

_____11. If a secretary told me that a potential employer was too busy to see me, I would stop trying to contact that employer.

_____12. Getting the job I want is largely a matter of luck.

_____13. I'd directly contact the person for whom I would be working, rather than the personnel department of an organization.

_____14. I am reluctant to ask professors or supervisors to write letters of recommendation for me.

_____15. I would not apply for a job unless I had all the qualifications listed on the published job description.

_____16. I would ask an employer for a second interview if I felt the first one went poorly.

_____17. I am reluctant to contact an organization about employment unless I know there is a job opening.

_____18. If I didn't get a job, I would call the employer and ask how I could improve my chances for a similar position.

_____19. I feel uncomfortable asking friends for job leads.

_____20. With the job market as tight as it is, I had better take whatever job I can get.

_____21. If the personnel office refused to refer me for an interview, I would directly contact the person I wanted to work for, if I felt qualified for the position.

_____22. I would rather interview with recruiters who come to the college campus than contact employers directly.

_____23. If an interviewer says "I'll contact you if there are any openings," I figure there's nothing else I can do.

_____24. I'd check out available job openings before deciding what kind of job I'd like to have.

_____25. I am reluctant to contact someone I don't know for information about career fields in which I am interested.

SCORING THE SCALE

To score this scale, you have to begin by reversing your responses on 18 of the items. On these items, convert the response you entered as follows: 1 = 6, 2 = 5, 3 = 4, 4 = 3, 5 = 2, and 6 = 1. The items to be reversed are 1, 2, 4, 5, 7, 8, 10, 11, 12, 14, 15, 17, 19, 20, 22, 23, 24, and 25. After making your reversals, add up the numbers that you have recorded for the 25 items on the scale. This total is your score on the Assertive Job-Hunting Survey.

MY SCORE _____

Source: Becker et al., 1980

WHAT THE SCALE MEASURES

Developed by Heather Becker, Susan Brown, Pat LaFitte, Mary Jo Magruder, Bob Murff, and Bill Phillips, this scale measures your job-seeking style (Becker, 1980). Some people conduct a job search in a relatively passive way—waiting for jobs to come to them. Others tend to seek jobs in a more vigorous, assertive manner. They act on their environment to procure needed information, obtain helpful contacts, and get their foot in the door at attractive companies. This scale measures your tendency to pursue jobs assertively.

Test-retest reliability for this scale is reasonable (.77 for an interval of two weeks). The scale's validity has been supported by demonstrations that subjects' scores increase as a result of training programs designed to enhance their job-hunting assertiveness. Also, those who have job-hunted before tend to score higher than those who have never job-hunted.

INTERPRETING YOUR SCORE

Our norms are based on a sample of college students who had applied to a university counseling center for career-planning assistance.

NORMS

High score:	117–150
Intermediate score:	95–116
Low score:	0–94

What Do You Know About the Career That Interests You?

Important vocational decisions require information. Your assignment in this exercise is to pick a vocation and research it. You should begin by reading some occupational literature. Then you should interview someone in the field. Use the outline below to summarize your findings.

1. ***The nature of the work.*** What are the duties and responsibilities on a day-to-day basis?

2. ***Working conditions.*** Is the working environment pleasant or unpleasant, low-key or high-pressure?

3. ***Job entry requirements.*** What kind of education and training are required to break into this occupational area?

4. ***Potential earnings.*** What are entry-level salaries, and how much can you hope to earn if you're exceptionally successful?

5. ***Opportunities for advancement.*** How do you "move up" in this field? Are there adequate opportunities for promotion and advancement?

6. ***Intrinsic job satisfactions.*** What can you derive in the way of personal satisfaction from this job?

7. ***Future outlook.*** How is supply and demand projected to shape up in the future for this occupational area?

How Will Your Job or Career Fit With Your Life Needs?

1. Many jobs or careers start with the choice of a college major or schooling requirements. Considering your current choice of a college major, list the external/environmental pressures and the internal/self-directed issues that have influenced your choice. If you do not have a current college major, what are three questions you will need to ask in order to make that decision?

2. The following are atmospheric elements that may be present in a work experience: Being the boss or your own boss, having a quiet environment, having less or more responsibility, supervising others, having clear deadlines, having flexible hours, having consistent hours, setting you own hours, inside vs. outside work, vacation periods, level of daily supervision, amount of say in the direction of the work you are involved in, amount of creative license, time of day or night you are working, amount and type of feedback on your work you are comfortable with, and the size of organization you are comfortable with.

   What are the atmospheric elements that go into a successful work experience for you? What do you need to have in that experience?

3. In a marriage and family setting, how do you feel about each partner having a job or career? Will one of the partner's careers take priority over the other?

4. What means and strategies will you use to plan for retirement?

Sexuality Scale

INSTRUCTIONS

For the 30 items that follow, indicate the extent of your agreement or disagreement with each statement, using the key shown below. Record your responses in the spaces to the left of the items.

+2	+1	0	-1	-2
Agree	Slightly agree	Neither agree nor disagree	Slightly agree	Disagree

THE SCALE

_____1.   I am a good sexual partner.

_____2.   I am depressed about the sexual aspects of my life.

_____3.   I think about sex all the time.

_____4.   I would rate my sexual skill quite highly.

_____5.   I feel good about my sexuality.

_____6.   I think about sex more than anything else.

_____7.   I am better at sex than most other people.

_____8.   I am disappointed about the quality of my sex life.

_____9.   I don't daydream about sexual situations.

_____10. I sometimes have doubts about my sexual competence.

_____11. Thinking about sex makes me happy.

_____12. I tend to be preoccupied with sex.

_____13. I am not very confident in sexual encounters.

_____14. I derive pleasure and enjoyment from sex.

_____15. I'm constantly thinking about having sex.

_____16. I think of myself as a very good sexual partner.

_____17. I feel down about my sex life.

_____18. I think about sex a great deal of the time.

_____19. I would rate myself low as a sexual partner.

_____20. I feel unhappy about my sexual relationships.

_____21. I seldom think about sex.

_____22. I am confident about myself as a sexual partner.

_____23. I feel pleased with my sex life.

_____24. I hardly ever fantasize about having sex.

_____25. I am not very confident about myself as a sexual partner.

_____26. I feel sad when I think about my sexual experiences.

_____27. I probably think about sex less often than most people.

_____28. I sometimes doubt my sexual competence.

_____29. I am not discouraged about sex.

_____30. I don't think about sex very often.

SCORING THE SCALE

To arrive at your scores on the three subscales of this questionnaire, transfer your responses into the spaces provided below. If an item number has an R next to it, this item is reverse-scored, so you should change the + or – sign in front of the number you recorded. After recording your responses, add up the numbers in each column, taking into account the algebraic sign in front of each number. The totals for each column are your scores on the three subscales of the Sexuality Scale. Record your scores at the bottom of each column.

Sexual Esteem	Sexual Depression	Sexual Preoccupation
1. _____	2. _____	3. _____
4. _____	5.R _____	6. _____
7. _____	8. _____	9.R _____
10.R _____	11.R _____	12. _____
13.R _____	14.R _____	15. _____
16. _____	17. _____	18. _____
19.R _____	20. _____	21.R _____
22. _____	23.R _____	24. _____
25.R _____	26. _____	27.R _____
28.R _____	29.R _____	30.R _____
_____	_____	_____

Source: Snell & Papini, 1989

WHAT THE SCALE MEASURES

Developed by William Snell and Dennis Papini (1989), the Sexuality Scale measures three aspects of your sexual identity. The Sexual Esteem subscale measures your tendency to evaluate yourself in a positive way in terms of your capacity to relate sexually to others. The Sexual Depression subscale measures your tendency to feel saddened and discouraged by your ability to relate sexually to others. The Sexual Preoccupation subscale measures your tendency to become absorbed in thoughts about sex on a persistent basis.

Internal reliability is excellent. Thus far, the scale's validity has been examined through factor analysis, which can be used to evaluate the extent of overlap among the subscales. The factor analysis showed that the three sub-scales do measure independent aspects of one's sexuality.

INTERPRETING YOUR SCORES

Our norms are based on Snell and Papini's (1989) sample of 296 college students drawn from a small university in the Midwest. Significant gender differences were found only on the Sexual Preoccupation subscale, so we report separate norms for males and females only for this subscale.

NORMS

	Sexual Esteem	Sexual Depression	Sexual Preoccupation	
	Both Sexes	Both Sexes	Males	Females
High Score	+14 to +20	+1 to +20	+8 to +20	-1 to +20
Intermediate Score	0 to +13	-12 to 0	-2 to +7	-10 to -2
Low Score	-20 to -1	-20 to -13	-20 to -3	-20 to -11

How Did You Acquire Your Attitudes About Sex?

1. Whom do you feel was most important in shaping your attitudes regarding sexual behavior (parents, teachers, peers, early girlfriend or boyfriend, and so forth)?

2. What was the nature of their influence?

3. If the answer to the first question was not your parents, what kind of information did you get at home? Were your parents comfortable talking about sex?

4. In childhood, were you ever made to feel shameful, guilty, or fearful about sex? How?

5. Were your parents open or secretive about their own sex lives?

6. Do you feel comfortable with your sexuality today?

Reflecting on the Place of Sexuality Throughout Your Life

1. What conditions, feelings, timings or commitments need to be present in order for you to have sexual intercourse for the first time?

2. How would you handle the situation of finding out that your partner has had a sexual relationship with another person? What is your feeling about sexual access to each other in a relationship? In relation to this sexual access to each other, during what times do see yourselves NOT being sexual with one another?

3. How skilled are you at this time in discussing your sexual needs and desires openly? Are there sexual activities that you consider distasteful and would prefer not to engage in? (Do not list) If there are such activities, how would you handle this if these activities are NOT distasteful to your partner?

4. How would you expect to deal with either your own or your partner's sexual dysfunction if that occurred?

5. What do you agree to do in order to maintain satisfaction in your sexual relationship over the long-term commitment of a relationship? Be specific in addressing the different cycles of life and how enhancement can be accomplished during those times. (Use other side of this page if necessary.)

Chronic Self-Destructiveness Scale

INSTRUCTIONS

For each of the following statements, indicate the degree to which the statement describes you. Record your responses in the spaces provided by writing in a letter from A to E, using the following scale: **A** expresses *strongest* agreement; **B** expresses moderate *agreement;* **C** indicates that you're *unsure or undecided,* or that it's a toss-up; **D** expresses moderate *disagreement;* **E** expresses *strongest disagreement.*

_____ 1. I like to listen to music with the volume turned up as loud as possible.

_____ 2. Life can be pretty boring.

_____ 3. When I was a kid, I was suspended from school.

_____ 4. I usually eat breakfast.

_____ 5. I do not stay late at school functions when I must get up early.

_____ 6. I use or have used street drugs.

_____ 7. I like to spend my free time 'messing around.'

_____ 8. As a rule, I do not put off doing chores.

_____ 9. Riding fast in a car is thrilling.

_____ 10. I tend to defy people in authority.

_____ 11. I have a complete physical examination once a year.

_____ 12. I have done dangerous things just for the thrill of it.

_____ 13. I am the kind of person who would stand up on a roller coaster.

_____ 14. I do not believe in gambling.

_____ 15. I find it necessary to plan my finances and keep a budget.

_____ 16. I let people take advantage of me.

_____ 17. I hate any kind of schedule or routine.

_____ 18. I usually meet deadlines with no trouble.

_____ 19. I am familiar with basic first-aid practices.

_____ 20. Even when I have to get up early, I like to stay up late.

_____ 21. I insist on traveling safely rather than quickly.

_____ 22. I have my car serviced regularly.

_____ 23. People tell me I am disorganized.

_____ 24. It is important to get revenge when someone does you wrong.

_____ 25. Sometimes I don't seem to care what happens to me.

_____ 26. I like to play poker for high stakes.

_____ 27. I smoke over a pack of cigarettes a day.

_____ 28. I have frequently fallen in love with the wrong person.

Source: Kelley et al., 1985

_____ 29. I just don't know where my money goes.

_____ 30. Wearing a helmet ruins the fun of a motorcycle ride.

_____ 31. I take care to eat a balanced diet.

_____ 32. Lots of laws seem made to be broken.

_____ 33. I am almost always on time.

_____ 34. I like jobs with an element of danger.

_____ 35. I often walk out in the middle of an argument.

_____ 36. Often I don't take very good care of myself.

_____ 37. I rarely put things off.

_____ 38. I speak my mind even when it's not in my best interest.

_____ 39. I usually follow through on projects.

_____ 40. I've made positive contributions to my community.

_____ 41. I make promises that I don't keep.

_____ 42. An occasional fight makes a guy more of a man.

_____ 43. I always do what my doctor or dentist recommends.

_____ 44. I know the various warning signs of cancer.

_____ 45. I usually call a doctor when I'm sure I'm becoming ill.

_____ 46. I maintain an up-to-date address/phone book.

_____ 47. I sometimes forget important appointments I wanted to keep.

_____ 48. I drink two or fewer cups of coffee a day.

_____ 49. It's easy to get a raw deal from life.

_____ 50. I eat too much.

_____ 51. I often skip meals.

_____ 52. I don't usually lock my house or apartment door.

_____ 53. I know who to call in an emergency.

_____ 54. I can drink more alcohol than most of my friends.

_____ 55. The dangers from using contraceptives are greater than the dangers from not using them.

_____ 56. I seem to keep making the same mistakes.

_____ 57. I have my eyes examined at least once a year.

_____ 58. I lose often when I gamble for money.

_____ 59. I leave on an outdoor light when I know I'll be coming home late.

_____ 60. Using contraceptives is too much trouble.

_____ 61. I often use nonprescription medicines (aspirin, laxatives, etc.).

_____ 62. I do things I know will turn out badly.

_____ 63. When I was in high school, I was considered a good student.

_____ 64. I have trouble keeping up with bills and paper-work.

_____ 65. I rarely misplace even small sums of money.

_____ 66. I am frequently late for important things.

_____ 67. I frequently don't do boring things I'm supposed to do.

_____ 68. I feel really good when I'm drinking alcohol.

_____ 69. Sometimes when I don't have anything to drink, I think about how good some booze would taste.

_____ 70. It's really satisfying to inhale a cigarette.

_____ 71. I like to smoke.

_____ 72. I believe that saving money gives a person a real sense of accomplishment.

_____ 73. I like to exercise.

SCORING THE SCALE

The scoring instructions are different for males and females. The 73 items you just responded to actually represent two overlapping 52-item scales for each sex.

Females: Convert your letter responses to numbers from 1 to 5 (A=1,B=2,C=3,D=4,E=5) for items 5, 8, 11, 15, 18, 19, 21, 22, 31, 33, 37, 39, 40, 43, 44, 45, 46, 53, and 63. Convert your responses in the opposite way (A = 5, B = 4, C = 3, D = 2, E = I) for items 1, 2, 6, 7, 9, 10, 12, 16, 17, 20, 23, 24, 25, 26, 28, 29, 30, 32, 36, 38, 41, 47, 49, 54, 56, 58, 60, 61, 62, 64, 66, 67, and 69. You should now have 52 items for which you have a number recorded instead of a letter. Add up these numbers, and the total is your score on the Chronic Self-Destructiveness Scale (CSDS).

Males: Convert your letter responses to numbers from 1 to 5 (A = 1, B = 2, C = 3, D = 4, E = 5) for items 4, 14, 18, 21, 22, 39, 40, 45, 48, 53, 57, 59, 63, 65, 72, and 73. Convert *your* responses in the opposite way (A = 5, B = 4, C = 3, D = 2, E = I) for items 2, 3, 10, 12, 13, 17, 25, 26, 27, 28, 29, 30, 32, 34, 35, 36, 41, 42, 47, 49, 50, 51, 52, 54, 55, 56, 58, 60, 62, 64, 66, 67, 68, 69, 70, and 71. You should now have 52 items for which you have a number recorded instead of a letter. Add up these numbers, and the total is your score on the Chronic Self-Destructiveness Scale (CSDS).

MY SCORE_ _____

WHAT THE SCALE MEASURES

Developed by Kathryn Kelley and associates (Kelley et al., 1985), this scale measures your tendency to behave in a self-destructive manner. Kelley et al. (1985) define chronic self-destructiveness as a generalized tendency to engage in acts that increase the likelihood of future negative consequences and/or decrease the likelihood of future positive consequences. In other words, chronic self-destructiveness involves behavior that probably will be detrimental to one's well-being in the long run. This self-destructive quality is viewed as an aspect of personality that may underlie a diverse array of counterproductive, often health-impairing habits.

In their initial series of studies, Kelley et al. (1985) administered their scale to 12 groups of undergraduates, a group of businesswomen, and a group of hospital patients. In comparison to people with low scores, high scorers on the CSDS were more likely to (a) report having cheated in classes, (b) have violated traffic laws, (c) indulge in drug or alcohol abuse meriting treatment, (d) recall a rebellious stage in adolescence, and (e) postpone important medical tests.

INTERPRETING YOUR SCORE

Our norms are based on 234 female and 168 male undergraduates studied by Kelley et al. (1985). In light of the age trends mentioned above, these norms may not be appropriate for older students.

NORMS

	Females	Males
High score	157-260	158-260
Intermediate score	105-156	97-157
Low score	52-104	52-96

How Do Your Health Habits Rate?

	Almost Always	Sometimes	Almost Never
EATING HABITS			
1. I eat a variety of foods each day, such as fruits and vegetables, whole-grain breads and cereals, lean meats, dairy products, dry peas and beans, and nuts and seeds.	4	1	0
2. I limit the amount of fat, saturated fat, and cholesterol I eat (including fat on meats, eggs, butter, cream, shortenings, and organ meats such as liver).	2	1	0
3. I limit the amount of salt I eat by cooking with only small amounts, not adding salt at the table, and avoiding salty snacks.	2	1	0
4. I avoid eating too much sugar (especially frequent snacks of sticky candy or soft drinks).	2	1	0

EATING HABITS SCORE:_____

	Almost Always	Sometimes	Almost Never
EXERCISE/FITNESS			
1. I maintain a desired weight, avoiding overweight and underweight.	3	1	0
2. I do vigorous exercises for 15 to 30 minutes at least three times a week (examples include running, swimming, and brisk walking).	3	1	0
3. I do exercises that enhance my muscle tone for 15 to 30 minutes at least three times a week (examples include yoga and calisthenics).	2	1	0
4. I use part of my leisure time participating in individual, family, or team activities that increase my level of fitness (such as gardening, bowling, golf, and baseball).	2	1	0

EXERCISE/FITNESS SCORE: _____

	Almost Always	Sometimes	Almost Never
ALCOHOL AND DRUGS			
1. I avoid drinking alcoholic beverages or I drink no more than one or two drinks a day.	4	1	0
2. I avoid using alcohol or other drugs (especially illegal drugs) as a way of handling stressful situations or the problems in my life.	2	1	0
3. I am careful not to drink alcohol when taking certain medicines (for example, medicine for sleeping, pain, colds, and allergies).	2	1	0
4. I read and follow the label directions when using prescribed and over-the-counter drugs.	2	1	0

ALCOHOL AND DRUGS SCORE:_____

WHAT YOUR SCORES MEAN:

9-10	Excellent
6-8	Good
3-5	Mediocre
0-2	Poor

Do any of your scores surprise you? Why?

Source: Adapted from the Department of Health and Human Services, 1981

Examining Specific Health Habits

1. Have you had a situation where you were attempting to change a habit or behavior and found a void in your life as you let go of that habit or behavior? What did you do with the void that was created?

2. Examine the extent to which you use legal, over-the-counter type drugs to manage your life. Taken to its natural course, where do you see this leading you?

3. List below what you consider to be your healthy and unhealthy habits that may be affecting your psychological and/or physical health.

   Healthy: Unhealthy:

4. For most people, the use of substances performs some type of function for them such as feeling, avoiding, or managing their emotions, relaxation, distraction, numbing, a sense of connection with others, and so forth. Identify what function you think any substances you use play in your life.

5. What types of exercise do you enjoy? How could (or do) you make this a part of your life?

Manifest Anxiety Scale

INSTRUCTIONS

The statements below inquire about your behavior and emotions. Consider each statement carefully. Then indicate whether the statement is generally true or false for you. Record your responses (true or false) in the spaces provided.

THE SCALE

_____1. I do not tire quickly.

_____2. I believe I am no more nervous than most others.

_____3. I have very few headaches.

_____4. I work under a great deal of tension.

_____5. I frequently notice my hand shakes when I try to do something.

_____6. I blush no more often than others.

_____7. I have diarrhea once a month or more.

_____8. I worry quite a bit over possible misfortunes.

_____9. I practically never blush.

_____10. I am often afraid that I am going to blush.

_____11. My hands and feet are usually warm enough.

_____12. I sweat very easily even on cool days.

_____13. Sometimes when embarrassed, I break out in a sweat that annoys me greatly.

_____14. I hardly ever notice my heart pounding, and I am seldom short of breath.

_____15. I feel hungry almost all the time.

_____16. I am very seldom troubled by constipation.

_____17. I have a great deal of stomach trouble.

_____18. I have had periods in which I lost sleep over worry.

_____19. I am easily embarrassed.

_____20. I am more sensitive than most other people.

_____21. I frequently find myself worrying about something.

_____22. I wish I could be as happy as others seem to be.

_____23. I am usually calm and not easily upset.

_____24. I feel anxiety about something or someone almost all the time.

_____25. I am happy most of the time.

_____26. It makes me nervous to have to wait.

_____27. Sometimes I become so excited that I find it hard to get to sleep.

_____28. I have sometimes felt that difficulties were piling up so high that I could not overcome them.

_____29. I must admit that I have at times been worried beyond reason over something that really did not matter.

_____30. I have very few fears compared to my friends.

_____31. I certainly feel useless at times.

_____32. I find it hard to keep my mind on a task or job.

_____33. I am unusually self-conscious.

_____34. I am inclined to take things hard.

_____35. At times I think I am no good at all.

_____36. I am certainly lacking in self-confidence.

_____37. I sometimes feel that I am about to go to pieces.

_____38. I am entirely self-confident.

Source: Taylor, 1953

SCORING THE SCALE

The scoring key is reproduced below. You should circle each of your true or false responses that correspond to the keyed responses. Add up the number of responses you circle, and this total is your score on the Manifest Anxiety Scale.

1.False	2.False	3.False	4.True
5.True	6.False	7.True	8.True
9.False	10.True	11.False	12.True
13.True	14.False	15.True	16.False
17.True	18.True	19.True	20.True
21.True	22.True	23.False	24.True
25.False	26.True	27.True	28.True
29.True	30.False	31.True	32.True
33.True	34.True	35.True	36.True
37.True	38.False		

MY SCORE _____

WHAT THE SCALE MEASURES

You just took a form of the Taylor Manifest Anxiety Scale (1953), as revised by Richard Suinn (1968). Suinn took the original 50-item scale and identified all items for which there was a social desirability bias (11) or a response set (1). He eliminated these 12 items and found that the scale's reliability and validity were not appreciably decreased. Essentially, the scale measures trait anxiety—that is, the tendency to experience anxiety in a wide variety of situations.

RESEARCH ON THE SCALE

Hundreds of studies have been done on the various versions of the Taylor Manifest Anxiety Scale. The validity of the scale has been supported by demonstrations that various groups of psychiatric patients score higher than unselected groups of "normals" and by demonstrations that the scale correlates well with other measures of anxiety. Although the Manifest Anxiety Scale is no longer a "state of the art" measure of anxiety, it is an old classic that is relatively easy to score.

INTERPRETING YOUR SCORE

Our norms are based on data collected by Suinn (1968) on 89 undergraduates who responded to the scale anonymously.

NORMS

High score:	16-38
Intermediate score:	6-15
Low score:	0-5

What Are Your Attitudes on Mental Illness?

1. List seven adjectives that you associate with people who are diagnosed as mentally ill.

2. If you meet someone who was once diagnosed as mentally ill, what are your immediate reactions?

3. List some comments about people with psychological disorders that you heard when you were a child.

4. Have you had any actual interactions with 'mentally ill' people that have supported or contradicted your expectations?

5. Do you agree with the idea that psychological disorders should be viewed as an illness or disease? Defend your position.

Do You Think We Are All Candidates for a Disorder?

1. What effect do you think psychiatric labels have upon an individual's functioning in a work and home setting?

2. How do you feel about the tendency in today's society to push pharmacological solutions on people for just about every ailment or condition?

3. If you had a friend or family member who was exhibiting symptoms which you found disturbing, how would you go about discussing what you are seeing with that individual?

4. What do you think about the idea of "extreme makeovers" (including various plastic surgeries) in helping an individual deal with low self esteem or to enhance their job prospects?

Attitudes Toward Seeking Professional Psychological Help

INSTRUCTIONS

Read each statement carefully and indicate your agreement or disagreement, using the scale below. Please express your frank opinion in responding to each statement, answering as you honestly feel or believe.

0 = Disagreement
1 = Probable disagreement
2 = Probable agreement
3 = Agreement

THE SCALE

_____1. Although there are clinics for people with mental troubles, I would not have much faith in them.

_____2. If a good friend asked my advice about a mental health problem, I might recommend that he see a psychiatrist.

_____3. I would feel uneasy going to a psychiatrist because of what some people would think.

_____4. A person with a strong character can get over mental conflicts by himself, and would have little need of a psychiatrist.

_____5. There are times when I have felt completely lost and would have welcomed professional advice for a personal or emotional problem.

_____6. Considering the time and expense involved in psychotherapy, it would have doubtful value for a person like me.

_____7. I would willingly confide intimate matters to an appropriate person if I thought it might help me or a member of my family.

_____8. I would rather live with certain mental conflicts than go through the ordeal of getting psychiatric treatment.

_____9. Emotional difficulties, like many things, tend to work out by themselves.

_____10. There are certain problems that should not be discussed outside of one's immediate family.

_____11. A person with a serious emotional disturbance would probably feel most secure in a good mental hospital.

_____12. If I believed I was having a mental breakdown, my first inclination would be to get professional attention.

_____13. Keeping one's mind on a job is a good solution for avoiding personal worries and concerns.

_____14. Having been a psychiatric patient is a blot on a person's life.

_____15. I would rather be advised by a close friend than by a psychologist, even for an emotional problem.

_____16. A person with an emotional problem is not likely to solve it alone; he or she is likely to solve it with professional help.

_____17. I resent a person—professionally trained or not who wants to know about my personal difficulties.

_____18. I would want to get psychiatric attention if I was worried or upset for a long period of time.

_____19. The idea of talking about problems with a psychologist strikes me as a poor way to get rid of emotional conflicts.

_____20. Having been mentally ill carries with it a burden of shame.

_____21. There are experiences in my life I would not discuss with anyone.

_____22. It is probably best not to know everything about oneself.

_____23. If I were experiencing a serious emotional crisis at this point in my life, I would be confident that I could find relief in psychotherapy.

_____24. There is something admirable in the attitude of a person who is willing to cope with his conflicts and fears without resorting to professional help.

_____25. At some future time I might want to have psychological counseling.

_____26. A person should work out his own problems; getting psychological counseling would be a last resort.

_____27. Had I received treatment in a mental hospital, I would not feel that it had to be 'covered up.'

_____28. If I thought I needed psychiatric help, I would get it no matter who knew about it.

_____29. It is difficult to talk about personal affairs with highly educated people such as doctors, teachers, and clergymen.

SCORING THE SCALE

Begin by reversing your response (0 = 3, 1 = 2, 2 = 1, 3 = 0) for items 1, 3, 4, 6, 8, 9, 10, 13, 14, 15, 17, 19, 20, 21, 22, 24, 26, and 29. Then add up the numbers for all 29 items on the scale. This total is your score. Record your score below.

MY SCORE _____

WHAT THE SCALE MEASURES

The scale assesses the degree to which you have favorable attitudes toward professional psychotherapy (Fischer & Turner, 1970). The higher your score, the more positive your attitudes about therapy. As discussed in your text, there are many negative stereotypes about therapy, and many people are very reluctant to pursue therapy. This is unfortunate, because negative attitudes often prevent people from seeking therapy that could be beneficial to them.

NORMS

High score:	64–87
Medium score:	50–63
Low score:	0–49

What Are Your Feelings About Therapy?

The following questions are intended to help you examine your attitudes regarding professional psychotherapy.

1. If you have had any experience with mental health professionals, describe what it was like.

2. Based on your experience, would you recommend professional counseling to a friend?

3. List any considerations that might prevent you from seeking some form of therapy even if you felt a need or desire to do so.

4. If you were looking for a therapist, what criteria would you employ in making your choice?

5. Briefly describe what you would expect to get out of professional therapy or counseling.

Thinking About Therapy

1. What type of therapeutic approach do you think you would respond best to if you were seeing a therapist? In looking at this question, consider not only approaches, but whether you want to experience a therapist who emphasizes cognition over emotion, the present over the past, short-term behavioral change over more extensive analysis, male versus female, individual therapy versus group therapy, and so on.

2. Do you have a sense of what your family beliefs are about psychotherapy and its use? If you had to articulate it in a few sentences, what would you say?

3. Before you read Ch. 16, what did you picture in your mind as happening in a therapy session? How accurate was that picture?

4. Have you ever read a self-help book? In what ways did it help you, if any?

5. Statistics show that more women seek psychotherapy than men. Why do you think this is so?

REFERENCES

Anderson, N. H. (1968). Likableness ratings of 555 personality trait words. *Journal of Personality and* Social *Psychology, 9,* 272-279.

Barnes, G. E., & Vukano, B. A. (1982). Measuring rationality independent of social desirability. *Personality and Individual Differences, 3,* 303-309.

Becker, H. A. (1980). The Assertive Job-Hunting Survey. *Measurement and Evaluation in Guidance, 13,* 43-48.

Bringle, R., Roach, S., Andler, C., & Evenbeck, S. (1979). Measuring the intensity of jealous reactions. *Catalogue of Selected* Documents *in Psychology, 9,* 23-24.

Burger, J. M. (1992). *Desire for control: Personality, social, and dinical perspectives.* New York: Plenum.

Burger, J. M., & Cooper, H. M. (1979). The desirability of control. *Motivation and Emotion, 3,* 381-393.
Corcoran, Kevin and Fischer, Joel (2000) Measures for Clinical Practice: A Sourcebook, Volumes 1 and 2   New York: N.Y. The Free Press

Corey, G., & Corey, M. S. (1986, 1997). *I never knew I had a choice* (3rd & 6th eds.). Pacific Grove, CA: Brooks/Cole

Egan, G. (1977). *You and me: The skills of communicating and relating* to others. Pacific Grove, CA: Brooks/Cole.

Ellis, A. (1962). Reason *and emotion in psychotherapy.* Seacaucus, NJ: Lyle Stuart.

Fischer, E. H., & Turner, J. L. (1970). Orientations to seeking professional help: Development and research utility of an attitude scale. *Journal of Consulting and Clinical Psychology, 35,* 82-83.

Glbb, B. (1964). *Test-wiseness* as secondary cue response. Unpublished doctoral dissertation, Stanford University, California.

Ickes, W., &. Barnes, R. D. (1977). The role of sex and self-monitoring in unstructured dyadic interactions. *Journal of Personality and* Social *Psychology, 35,* 315-330.

Infante, D. A., & Rancer, A. S. (1982). A conceptualization and measure of argumentativeness. *Journal of Personality* Assessment, 46, 72-80.

Kelley, K., Byrne, D., Przybyla, D. P. J., Eberly, C., Eberly, B., Greendlinger, V., Wan, C. K., & Gorsky, J. (1985). Chronic self-destructiveness: Conceptualization, measurement and initial validation of the construct. *Motivation and Emotion, 9,* 135-151.

Levine, Murray and Perkins, David V. (1979) College Student Life Events Scale   ETS Test Collection 016671 Educational Testing Service, Princeton, NJ 08541

Lonetto, R., &. Templer, D. I. (1983). The nature of death anxiety. In C. D. Spielberger & J. N. Butcher (Eds.), Advances *in personality* assessment (Vol. 3). Hillsdale, NJ: Erlbaum.

Miller, L. C., Berg, J. H., & Archer, R. L (1983). Openers: Individuals who elicit intimate self-disclosure. *Journal of Personality and Social Psychology, 44,* 1234-1244.

Snell, W. E., Jr., & Papini, D. R. (1989). The sexuality scale: An instrument to measure sexual-esteem, sexual-depression, and sexual-preoccupation. *Journal of* Sex *Research, 26,* 256-263.

Snyder, M. (1974). Self-monitoring of expressive behavior. *Journal of Personality and Social Psychology, 30,* 526-537.

Spence, J. T., & Helmreich, R. L. (1978). *Masculinity and femininity: Their psychological dimensions, correlates, and* antecedents. Austin, TX: University of Texas Press.

Suinn, R. M. (1968). Removal of social desirability and response set items from the Manifest Anxiety Scale. *Educational and Psychological* Measurement, 28, 1189-1192.

Taylor, J. A. (1953). A personality scale of manifest anxiety. *Journal of Abnormal and* Social *Psychology, 48,* 285-290.

Watson, D. L., & Friend, R. (1969). Measurement of social-evaluative anxiety. *Journal of Consulting and Clinical Psychology, 33,* 448-57.

Welten, W., Clery, J., & Bowlin, G. (1900, September). *Test-wiseness: Its composition and significance in educational measurement* Paper presented at the meeting of the American Psychological Association, Montreal, Quebec.

Zuckerman, M. (1979). *Sensation seeking: Beyond the optimal level of arousal.* Hillsdale, NJ: Erlbaum.